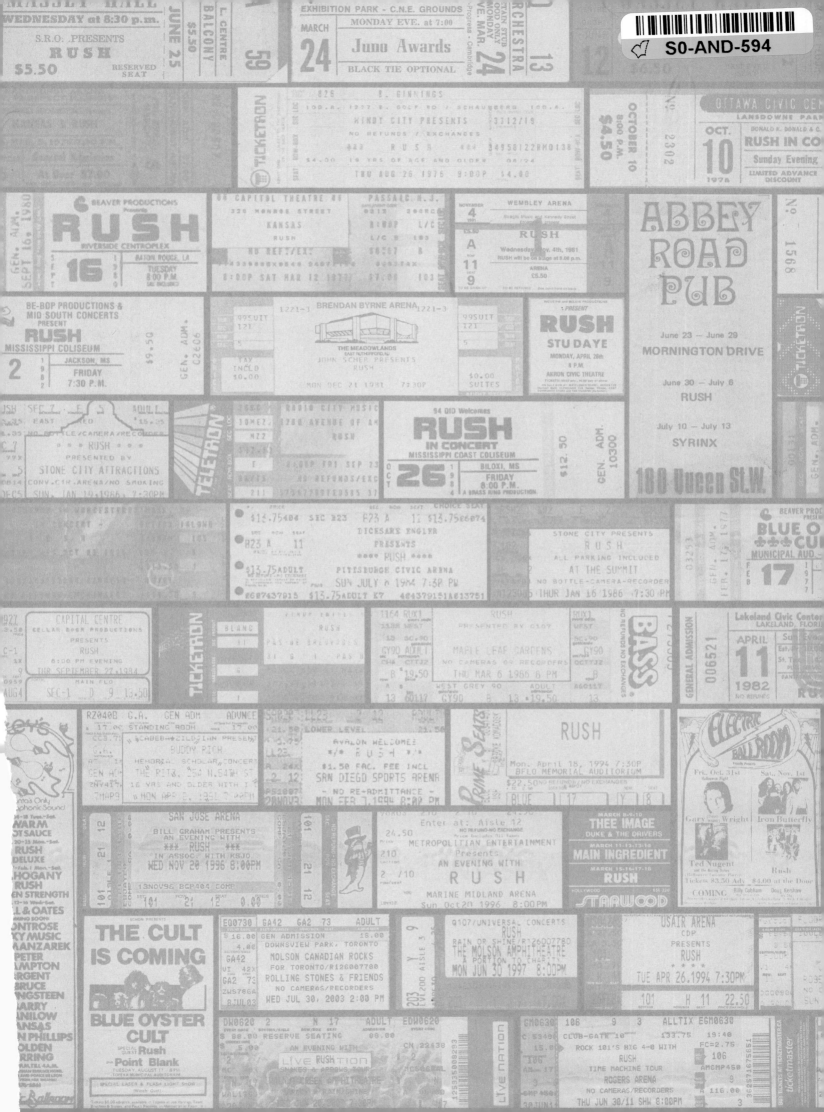

WANDERING THE FACE OF THE EARTH

WANDERING THE FACE OF THE EARTH
THE OFFICIAL TOURING HISTORY

SKIP DALY AND ERIC HANSEN

FOREWORD BY **LES CLAYPOOL**

INTRODUCTION BY **HOWARD UNGERLEIDER**

AFTERWORD BY **STEWART COPELAND**

INSIGHT
EDITIONS

San Rafael · Los Angeles · London

CONTENTS

LES CLAYPOOL

I was fourteen years old when some friends and I loaded ourselves into Dan Maloney's van to head from the semirural suburb of El Sobrante, California, to the Cow Palace in San Francisco. Dan was the older brother of my twin pals Joe and Mike Maloney, and he was not only known as the guy who built cool guitars out of exotic hunks of wood, but he was also appreciated for being able to buy beer for us at a local place called Nick's Delicatessen. Nick was from Italy and he reckoned it was silly that in America you had to be twenty-one to buy beer, so he'd turn a blind eye to underage purchases as long as you were at least eighteen. The unfortunate thing about Nick's beer was that it was in an open cooler and would usually be just below room temperature, making it not very palatable to newbie beer drinkers such as myself. The beer of choice that evening was Löwenbräu, and by the time we got over the Bay Bridge, I was choking down my third bottle, which at that point was quite warm. Upon our arrival to the Cow Palace parking lot, the van door was flung open, we piled out, and I immediately evacuated the warm, foamy contents of my stomach on the asphalt. After a bit of comradely ribbing, my pals and I moved gleefully on. I was about to see my first real rock concert, and to top it off, it was my favorite band—Rush.

I'm often asked in discussion groups with fans what my first concert was, and folks always gasp in envy and amazement when I proudly say Rush's "Tour of the Hemispheres." For months prior to that night, I had spent many hours staring at and studying the album cover and sleeve of their live record, *All the World's a Stage*. I had received that wondrous double disc from the RCA Record Club as part of my six-records-for-ten-cents introductory package. I was mesmerized by the music as well as by the cover photos from Massey Hall in Toronto that depicted not only the three fellows in all their bell-bottomed and platform-shoed splendor, but also the gear and elaborate stage setup. As a young musician, I geeked out over that. So, that evening at the Cow Palace, there I was, standing front and center, wide-eyed and eager, gazing at the instruments and amps that I had studied so

often in photos. Midstage was Neil's big mahogany Tama Superstar drum kit that seemed to go on forever as well as Alex's stacks with his Roland Space Echo units sitting on top and glowing. But most important to me was Geddy's black Rickenbacker 4001, poised majestically on a stand just a few yards from my face. I marveled at the sleek upper horn that curved up just a little higher than most basses of the time as well as the sparkled triangle inlays on the fingerboard that made the instrument look like something the Cat in the Hat might play. It was glorious to behold and I was just shy of salivating when I heard, "Mine looks just like that." It was Bill Peterson boasting from over my left shoulder. Bill was another bass player from my school, and he tended to have some money now and again—hence some pretty amazing gear. Me, I had no funds to speak of so I played a

Memphis P-Bass copy with old flatwound strings through a borrowed suitcase guitar amp with one twelve-inch speaker. When I played through it, it sounded more like syncopated farts than bass guitar. "Someday I'm going to have a Rickenbacker just like that," I thought to myself with a combination of disdain and envy for Bill. After a few more minutes of my dreamy-eyed ogling, the house lights abruptly came down, the crowd roared, and my life changed forever. Afterward, fully exhilarated by what I had just witnessed, I bought a T-shirt in the parking lot to commemorate my first show. I wore it every day for a week.

I would make it my mission, if not my obsession, to see Rush every time they came through the Bay Area after that initial *Hemispheres* show. Back in the general admission days, I'd work my way as close to the front as possible, waiting to watch the Rocinante glide through the black hole of Cygnus X-1 on the big screen while Geddy rumbled out the sparse and taunting intro. Sometimes the crowd would be pulsing and pressing forward in hot, swampy perspiration toward the barrier, so it was a welcome treat when Alex would start "Xanadu" and the dry ice vapor would drift from the stage over us like a cool fog. For the throngs of intrepid air drummers, it was always an anticipated highlight to experience Neil's melodic drum solo, which has yet to be challenged as a consistent piece of pure percussive magic. The glide down the highway in "Red Barchetta," the face-melting riffs of "YYZ" (which Geddy recently showed me in person, confirming I've been playing it wrong all these years), "La Villa Strangiato," the battle of "By-Tor and the Snow Dog," and of course "2112 Overture." These are just slivers of the glory that I was able to experience live back in my youth, and Rush always presented them with a precision and consistency that I'd never seen from any other live band of that era.

PAGE 2: Toronto; *Beetle* Magazine photo shoot, "Off to Work We Go!"

PAGE 4: Geddy on the *R40* tour.

TOP: Geddy with some of the crew on the *Hemispheres* tour.

"Who wants to go sturgeon fishing tomorrow?" I announced to the room. Ler LaLonde and I had been fixing up an old twenty-four-foot Sea Ray, and being that we had a day off between gigs, we were planning on hitting the bay. It was a little over a decade after that first Rush concert, and my band Primus was in the beginning of a tour supporting those three fellows from Toronto. It was amazing to be playing nightly with Geddy, Alex, and Neil; even more so, it was surreal that we had, in a relatively short amount of time, become friends with guys who had been superheroes to us in our high school days. "I'll go," said Geddy. Had he seen the 1976 Sea Ray prior to showing up at the launch ramp, he may not have been quite as enthusiastic, but there she was the next day in all her glory with *El Bastardo* splayed across her stern in raised wooden letters. Ler and I had put in fresh indoor-outdoor carpet, enclosed her in green Sunbrella canvas, and repowered her with a new 351 crate motor, so it was much to our surprise when we heard a loud *ZZZZPPPHHFFFTTTINGGG* come from the engine compartment while motoring at full cruise across the bay. We'd thrown a fan belt, leaving us powerless halfway between the Berkeley Marina and the channel markers of San Quentin. I dropped anchor just off the northwest side of Red Rock, a small island in the south shadow of the Richmond–San Rafael Bridge. How many Rush-ites would crawl over

broken glass in their underwear to take Geddy Lee out fishing in the middle of San Pablo Bay? I've often thought, Well, Ler and I did it . . . and got stranded to boot. Geddy was a good sport about the whole thing, actually videotaping me as I radioed the Coast Guard for the help that would never come. We killed the hours by catching a slew of small leopard sharks, but as the sun sank lower on the horizon, Geddy was beginning to get a bit twitchy. Here he was with a couple Rush-geek musicians in their early twenties that he'd just met a few days earlier, stuck in the middle of San Pablo Bay in the winter with no one responding to our radioed pleas for assistance. Eventually a fellow fisherman took pity and towed us, to the opposite shore, just in time for Geddy to hop in a cab and get to the dinner engagement in San Francisco that he had been nervously reminding us of. Ler and I then taxied to the auto parts store to get the belt needed to motor back across the bay, in pitch black, with Ler holding a flashlight and freezing his ass off on the bow. The next day as I'm walking through the hallway backstage of the Oakland Arena, I hear the familiar voice of Alex, goading me with the theme song from *Gilligan's Island*.

We would go on to do three different tours with Rush, including a rare run through Europe. In the early nineties, a Rush fan was not necessarily the "hippest" thing to be, and in fact, we got quite a bit of flack from the press, especially overseas, for supporting those shows. We didn't give a shit. Being a Rush fan was never about being "hip." Besides, we were privy to the behind-the-scenes world of one of the most influential groups of rock musicians of the seventies and eighties. In my high school days, Rush were the musical barometer by which we young, eager fledglings set our standard, so to jam face-to-face with Geddy while Alex played guitar using a tortilla chip as a pick and Neil banged his sticks on the metal doors during one of our many locker-room backstage jams was pretty sweet. Crouching behind Neil's throne as he blistered away at his legendary drum solo in an arena full of punters; getting drunk in an outdoor café in Berlin and convincing the fellows to start playing "Cygnus X-1" live again; watching Alex put a bowl on Ler's head and cut his hair—the stories go on and on. Had I been able to look into a crystal ball when I was sixteen years old and see that bit of my future, I would have surely soiled myself. So, when my manager emailed and said I had been asked to write the foreword to the new Rush book, I grew teary-eyed with a sense of honor.

Rush fans don't need me to remind them of the spectacular live shows of their glorious heroes, but I'm happy to let them all know that Geddy, Alex, and Neil are three of the most genuine, fun-loving, and kind fellows I've met in all my years in the music industry. They are also laced with just the right amount of eccentricity to make them incredibly interesting, so any documentation of said fellows should be thoroughly studied, absorbed, and relished.

I remember one day during that first Rush-Primus tour, I dug out my old Rush *Hemispheres* T-shirt that I purchased at that infamous first concert. It was a bit snug by then, but I squeezed into it and proudly paraded through the corridors of the arena we were playing that evening, anxiously seeking out one of the three so I could impress them with my sacred piece of Rush memorabilia. I stumbled across Alex. "Hey, hey . . . whattaya think?" I said, pointing at the image of him, Geddy, and Neil on my puffed-out chest. He gazed at it for a moment, then, with a cynical laugh, he pointed and shouted to his mates, "It's a fucking bootleg!"

Enjoy the glorious pages that follow.

HOWARD UNGERLEIDER

I was working for a talent agency in New York called American Talent International (ATI), run by Jeff Franklin, Sal Sapien, and Ira Blacker, when Rush signed with us. Ira Blacker, in particular, was keen on Rush and wanted to make sure that he placed somebody on the band's new management team that they would like. He asked me to go to Toronto and educate them to the ways of touring. Prior to that, in the early days of ATI, I had worked as a junior agent with many different acts (Savoy Brown, Deep Purple, Fleetwood Mac, Rod Stewart, Atomic Rooster, and Blue Oyster Cult, to name a few); I used to travel with the bands and make sure the contracts were adhered to. If there were problems getting a band paid, I would have to straighten it out. Lighting design and special effects were also longtime hobbies of mine. In short, I had lots of experience with what goes into the organizing and producing of tour travel and shows.

So there I was—on a train from the United States to Canada to teach this bar band how to do it professionally—but no one from their team knew I was coming. I walked into the management office and went up to Sheila Posner, SRO Management's accountant and office manager, and said, "Hi, I'm Howard Ungerleider from ATI, New York. I'm here to work with Rush and need $10,000 flowed to me immediately." My job, as I knew it, was to organize the band, touring schedule, travel schedule, everything. They were so accommodating, I couldn't tell at the time that they were all freaking out behind the scenes. They didn't have the money! Ray Danniels and Vic Wilson of SRO/Anthem were wondering, Who is this guy and what does he want? We better be nice to him, we just signed the deal with ATI . . .

Whatever they did, it worked out, and I eventually got to meet the guys in Rush. They didn't know me from a hole in the wall. For touring staff, the band had Liam Birt and Ian Grandy. Liam was the guitar tech for Alex and did a lot of other things for the shows; Ian did the sound and helped as well. They drove around in a truck up front of the band's van, those two. Later on, they had Jimmy Johnson in there; lots of people came and went over the years. That was the beginning of my time with Rush—and it was a good time.

It was quite interesting: I was an experienced tour manager, and they were new to the pros. They had certain things in their heads about what should happen on the road, and I would tell them how it really was. Of course, I was coming from the States into Canada for the first time, which often made me the novice.

In one memorable example, we had to drive up to Cochrane, Ontario, for my first tour stop with Rush. Cochrane is a long drive—north of Toronto, on the way to Thunder Bay. It can take eight or ten hours. Driving the rental car with

OPPOSITE TOP: Liam Birt and Neil.
OPPOSITE BOTTOM: Geddy and Alex.

11

the band, I had my jean jacket, jeans, and running shoes on. Halfway into the journey, Alex and Ged said to me, "Um, do you have any warm clothes?" "Yeah, I'm wearing them." They said, "No, this is a jean jacket you have on. Do you realize that if anything happened with the car and you had to go outside, you would probably die?" Being from New York, I said, "That's bullshit. I know what I can handle." Ged and Al looked at each other, and then said, "Okay! Pull the car over. We want to see you get out of the car and take a deep breath and let us know what you think." "Sure, no problem." I pulled the car over to the side of the road and got out. Stepping out into the fresh Northern Canada air, I took a deep breath (they told me to!), and it felt like someone took two knives and sliced my nostrils off. All of sudden, it had gotten so freaking cold (-30°F!). I'd never experienced that. When I went to grab the door handle to open it up, my hand stuck to it like when you put your tongue to a fire hydrant— and I realized they'd locked me out and were all laughing in the car. Finally, they opened the doors and said, "Well, what do you think?" "Okay, you're right." I immediately went and bought true cold-weather gear. That was my introduction to Canada, and my icebreaker with Rush.

I came across good crew guys in this business while I was working for other bands and in the early days of Rush's touring. So I started

handpicking guys I wanted on our crew—guys that worked hard and showed up every night. Rush played the Palace in Detroit and I met Skip Gildersleeve, whom I liked immediately and brought into the fold. Then Tony Geranios, aka "Jack Secret," who worked for Blue Oyster Cult at the time. Larry Allen was a friend of Neil's from before Neil auditioned for Rush. We needed a drum tech during the transition period from John Rutsey through auditions to whoever would replace John, and though Neil wasn't keen on the idea of hiring friends, I thought Larry would be an excellent drum tech for him; he was a genuinely good guy. I am big on old-school loyalty. My dad, who was a drill sergeant, brought me up and was very strict. He taught me that loyalty and honor really work in business. The qualities that were instilled in me, I look for in other people. So when we went on tour, we had a nucleus of good, sharp people and we were hitting two hundred cities a year— we were young!

I was in my early twenties and the guys were a little bit younger than that, and it worked well. We were driving every night, five hundred miles sometimes. Though the band members all had their alone time, in the beginning we were all very tight. We had a room rotation list, and people were sharing rooms to cut costs. No one wanted to share with me because my phone was constantly ringing, so I got my own room all the time. For the rest of the crew and band, depending on what day of the week it was, they would room with someone else. It was kind of funny, but also helped in that us-against-the-world way. I did a lot of the driving—probably most of the driving—but there was a driving rotation as well. I remember Alex bartering: "You know, if you don't want to drive, I'll drive—pay me $50 and I'll take your shift." I was like, "Sure, sure. Here's $50." I wanted to sleep!

It was crazy, but we just kept doing it and with every tour, the band was jamming and coming up with the next songs—a lot of their great material—*during the tour*, sometimes while playing upward of two hundred cities in a stretch. Back then, record labels demanded that you have albums coming out to support your touring. And the success of Rush was based on their grassroots audience because they were playing every city and building that audience, show by show. I mean, we played Ochoco Lake, Ohio—who plays there?

Everywhere that existed that we could do a show, we did. So songwriting had to happen on the road alongside everything else.

Of course, we didn't always juggle sleep, navigation, and album production perfectly, yours truly included. We were in Chicago and everybody was in the car to head to Cleveland, Ohio. The band was putting together the tracks for *Fly by Night* then. We were kind of distracted, and I started driving—thinking that I was driving toward Cleveland. I was actually driving south, toward Memphis. Eventually someone said, "Hey, we are not going to make it to Cleveland in time." What could we do? So I said let's find the nearest airport and get a plane. We didn't have cells phones back then, so we had to go somewhere to find a pay phone and try to book a flight from Indiana to Cleveland. So I got on the phone and figured out what it was going to cost, flight time, etc. I booked this flight (victory!), and we made a beeline toward Evansville Regional. Of course, we got stuck in this ridiculous downpour of rain—a storm came in from the Midwest, tornadoes, sideways rain, and stuff. It was really bad, flooding everywhere.

We didn't make it.

We actually pulled into the Evansville airport to see our flight airborne. So, we continued driving to Ohio. We eventually arrived in the middle of the night. I think we

ended up canceling the date—but snags like this built a bond between us. Sometimes someone screwed up, sometimes nature got in our way. We'd always move on to the next city. We were like a traveling family, like brothers. The bond we had working together day after day was amazing. And that energy and unity all centered on the band.

I was pretty jaded by the time I first heard Rush—I'd toured with lots of big rock acts, loved bands like the Who, listened to the radio all the time, went to the Fillmore East. So the electricity and cohesiveness of this band really struck me. You just knew they were going to be successful, just by listening to them play. I saw Led Zeppelin with Woody Herman and His Orchestra in 1969 at the Fillmore, I had seen my favorite band, the Who, killing it live—and seeing Rush gave me that same familiar feeling of *gelling*, of a band firing on all cylinders with no assistance. No background tapes, no added musicians behind the curtain. Just pure, unadulterated talent exploding onstage. Once I heard them, I knew this was special. We had to deliver a show that was as special as the music, and I had to surround them and myself with talented, reliable people. I'm telling you—that road crew that we had for the first twenty years was amazing. We could count on everyone, no matter what the situation was. We would adapt

OPPOSITE: Neil in the studio.
TOP: Geddy and Neil.

to that situation, as ugly as it may have been or as great as it was. We would be there and we would deliver shows—a lot of times under the duress of the headliner. Rush were so powerful, the headliners were afraid.

It's no secret we opened for one megastar band on a lengthy seventy-night tour, and every night, the sound system was turned down on us. I'm not sure the headlining band knew what was happening—maybe their tour managers were told to do it, maybe they took it upon themselves. All I know is you couldn't hear Rush well at all, and the main act sounded great. Our soundman did his best, but we couldn't even hold sound checks ahead of shows. Further, our contract rider for what we got in the dressing room was cut to nothing, we couldn't have Canadian beer for the guys ("When you are touring in the United States with this band, you'll drink American beer and like it!"), and we weren't allowed to have dinner until all of the main act's crew were finished.

It wasn't a very good experience, but it was a sign that something was working. That was a competitive time, and Rush were a contender.

Although, not all bands were worried about us. Because Rush were constantly on the road in the early days, they were, on occasion, strange bedfellows with other touring acts. Case in point: Sha Na Na as the headliners, in 1974 Baltimore, Maryland. Rush got booed off the stage. They say tragedy begets comedy . . . and it was hilarious.

Now, the complete opposite of these experiences was when we toured with Kiss in 1974 and 1975. They embraced the band, and so did their audience. We all got along like we had been together forever. Those guys are some of the best guys we've ever toured with, and they were fun to be around before and after shows. By now, I think our fans know the story of "the Bag"—Alex's fun persona, made from a

dry-cleaning bag, lots of imagination, and perhaps a few substances—and how stuff like that bonded the two bands. The guys in Rush really appreciated learning the ins and outs of the road on those tour dates, I think.

Later on, as the band became more established, better gigs continued to come our way. A standout was the Pinkpop Festival in Holland in 1979. The Police, Peter Tosh with Mick Jagger, Elvis Costello, Dire Straits, and Average White Band were among the acts. We all stood on the side of the stage, watching these incredible musicians. It kind of freaked us all out—we were a part of this, and it was huge.

That's not to say that the antics stopped. We ran into Van Halen at a Holiday Inn, in Sheffield, England, of all places. We were passing through on our way to a show the following day. We got in very late and went to the bar, paying a good sum to keep the place open so we could relax and have some fun before we turned in. Suddenly, in came Van Halen, who were also leaving Sheffield the next day. Things got a bit crazy. If memory serves, some of our road crew took poorly to something some of their road crew said or did. Tom Whitaker, our driver at the time, decided to make a point and put out his cigarette in Eddie Van Halen's beer. The beer was spilled on a tape recorder that Geddy was listening to with Eddie at the time. Luckily, Eddie is really the sweetest guy in the world.

Geddy was my creative partner on production design—our two-man brain trust. Before every tour, we'd sit in Ged's living room, and he'd share these ideas of what he wanted. There will be a good rabbit and a bad rabbit. On the back line, let's have chickens roasting onstage, let's have washing machines, and let's have appliances! At these brainstorming sessions, we brought in different animators and film people from Toronto to meet with Ged and myself. Some of these folks were developers of software like Houdini, After Effects, Bonafide—people that really were cutting-edge at the time. We'd try to put storyboards together after talking about the songs and what Geddy wanted to see visually. I was concerned with how it would all work—making sure it was all formatted correctly, ensuring the animation colors blended in with the show, things like that.

We experimented with styles and techniques over the years. We used different animators with different feels for different songs. One might have a Monty Python style, and another would be a serious documentarian doing animation for educational series. Eventually, Geddy's little brother, Allan Weinrib, grew up and became an animation producer, so we expanded the brain trust to include him and video director Dale Heslip. I threw a lot of curveballs at them. New technology opened up creative opportunities like moving video screens, and I wanted to put that to use. Sometimes they thought I was crazy, but once they learned something new, they were able to do more and more with it. For example, for "The Garden" on the final tour, I wanted to combine small screens and big screens to lend a sense of dimension. The team hated the little screens initially. They had no idea where to set the animation lines so they could blend. But they ended up making it magical. It wasn't all camaraderie and fun. It was often a learning experience. But the end result was always spectacular.

One of the most insane times we had was when we tried to do surround sound with speakers all over the arena. Everyone always went out and saw Pink Floyd because they sounded amazing—they had these sound effects go around the audience via all these speakers. Rush tried to do music through the same setup and discovered it just didn't work with the harder rock style they played—because the sound would come back to the stage with a delay and just mess their timing up completely. They had really created a problem for themselves. We eventually learned to limit what came through and keep the sounds manageable.

As time had gone on, Geddy had stepped back from production design and as Neil took care of the creative with the actual albums, working with Hugh Syme, neither he nor Alex was much interested in the production of the live shows either. Actually, they had no idea what was going on. At one point, Geddy saw the Talking Heads by himself, and he goes, "You know, I saw Talking Heads the other night and they had this amazing effect." I asked, "What was it?" "Well, they had these lampposts on stage and David Byrne was standing under them and they projected this solid color that went to almost looking like strobe effects." I said, "We use those!" We had each taken on separate jobs, and even though we didn't always know what the others were doing, we trusted each other. We made the perfect team.

When Rush started filming and editing show film later on, they used to let outside people do a lot of the work. Ged was more concerned with the sound than with the visuals, so he never really sat in the editing suite. He spent more time in the sound studio listening to the tracks. He would see rough footage, but he never really had time to watch the show. Eventually, on the last four tours, he started to watch more because his brother was involved and he wanted to make sure it was perfect. Alex and Neil started to look at things a little more at this point too. For the first time in their careers, they saw what I did! One day, Alex came up to me and said, "Listen—don't tell the other guys I said this, but the fucking show was amazing! I never realized all this was happening." I said, "Well, thank you. Now you know what I do." He just said, "Wow!"

My job was a bit . . . multifaceted. I loved the production design, but I also handled the money.

And being the guy who handles the money means you might someday have a plastic bag of cash in your hand and three guns to your head.

When Rush would play arenas and big clubs, they sometimes had occasion to do filler dates. The guys wanted to do five, sometimes even six shows a week. There were some weeks where we did ten shows in a row! So it would happen, you are passing through such and such city with such and such 1,500-seat club. Can you play there, our management would ask. Sure, we will stop and play, sight unseen. Some of these clubs were not conducive to the equipment we were carrying. There was one place we went into where our drum riser was the size of the stage of the club! You could probably get three thousand people in there, just the same.

You always came into situations like this in your travels. You're young and you hang out with radio guys that are taking you to their places. The guys at KISS-FM, a radio station in San Antonio, had their own restaurant and bar. After the show was over, they would take the band there, getting hammered and enjoying themselves. Meanwhile, I'm stuck back at the venue with a gun to my head, needing to settle the show with three unreasonable gentlemen. They had oversold the show, printing the tickets and then taking the real tickets and locking them in a safe. Luckily (or unluckily, in retrospect), I caught them and confiscated all the money. I put it in a big plastic bag and went up to the office to count it out. That's when they came up; next thing I know, there are guns pointed at my head. The radio station had commandeered the band and took them away while I'm in there sweating my brains out.

I got out of that place with the money, looking behind me. Luckily, one of the other guys there on behalf of the promoter reasoned with them.

San Antonio, Texas, is usually full of police, but not that night. I had this huge plastic bag of cash, and these guys knew I had it, and I was freaked out, so I purposely sped at one hundred miles an hour hoping a cop would see me, but there was not a cop in sight. I got to the hotel, hid the money, and went on to find the band partying at the restaurant. That was the night of the pineapple wine—long before they were wine connoisseurs. They had no idea that drinking pineapple wine is the worst. We loved it.

You get the good, you get the bad. You get bands that have egos and the audiences that boo you and the venues that try to screw you, and you also get the crowds that love you and the career doing what you love. Somehow you get through it all.

The guys in Rush are, simply put, really good guys. Alex and I still hang out together to this day. I just had Thanksgiving with him! Geddy, as well. They're very, very intelligent and down to earth. They have bad days like everyone else; they might have skipped a public appearance or snubbed a fan because someone else just tried to pull jewelry off their neck. But there have been so many people that the band have embraced.

To many, Rush were just another heavy metal band. Some ignored them, some criticized them,

many misunderstood them. Over time they made huge strides with success on the radio, despite the fact that they stayed away from the media for a full *decade* because they were tired of being slammed for who they were. But while every band has critics, not every band lasts for fifty years. Rush had that electricity, that magical electricity, and the people who get it have shown up and stuck around for decades.

We didn't know how long it would take, but we knew they'd get there. I remember one night when we were touring in Canada. Coming back home, I was the one to collect all the money at each stop. Geddy wanted to go home and visit his mom, so we went over to his mom's house and I had to count all this money, get it organized, and get it into the office. Geddy's mom came down and was looking at all this money and she asked, "Is this all for my son?" And I said yes. She then asked me, "Tell me Howard, do you think my son is going to be famous?" I said, "He's hired me, of course he's going to be famous. I wouldn't be here if he wasn't going to be famous!" She laughed and laughed.

The hard-core fans that loved Rush and supported their every move—they kept the machine rolling along. But in the last four, maybe five years of touring, Rush were more accepted. We saw the audience change—more women in the audience, more people attending shows, and more people listening to their music and loving it. It was a change, and it was incredible and it was passionate.

I can't pretend a stranger is a long-awaited friend.

A lot of the lyrics Neil has written are so appropriate. They played "Losing It" on the last tour—really sums it all up, you know. If you're a great sports star, eventually you wear down and you cannot perform like you used to. Same goes for performers. At some point, you have to make

a choice—to go out at the top of your game, knowing you can't do what the fans expect and you'll probably sound miserable. That's the choice. You have to respect that. When you recognize your abilities are not 100 percent anymore, it's not worth it for the band or the fans.

The legacy of Rush will take time to grow, just as their career took time. But I think it is an amazing legacy. Because they stuck to their guns and did what they thought was best. They didn't listen to their labels—they were shit-disturbers of the highest order. But they did it with the highest integrity. How rock and roll is that?

I don't think they will ever be forgotten, but we're all immortal for a limited time. I was there for forty-two years of their career, from '74, in between drummers, until the LA Forum at the end. I've been lucky to call them friends, live life on the road with them, and make memories that will last forever.

Chapter 1

ORIGINS . . .

Over the course of their more than forty-year recording and touring career, Rush have sold millions of records and played on the largest stages, to capacity audiences, throughout the world. But the band's early history has remained relatively undocumented. Before their first official tour in 1974, Rush had been gigging around Toronto and southern Ontario for six years. Initially, the band performed primarily at drop-in centers and high school dances. When Ontario lowered the drinking age in 1971, Rush began playing in bars, and that was, by all accounts, when things became much more serious. By mid-1972 and throughout 1973, the guys—Geddy Lee, Alex Lifeson, and drummer John Rutsey—performed five to six nights per week. Meanwhile, Neil Peart was busy drumming in a wide array of bands prior to joining forces with Geddy and Alex in 1974. While Rush were not on tour, per se, during this period in the early '70s, they were working hard to build the foundation of the band.

By this time, Alex and Geddy had already known one another for years. The two—Alex (né Aleksandar Živojinovic), a first-generation Canadian and the son of Serbian refugees, and Geddy (né Gary Lee Weinrib), whose parents were Polish Jews that had survived the Holocaust—first met in 1966 in the neighborhood of Willowdale in Toronto, Ontario, when they were just thirteen years old.

"We were aliens in a class of conformity, and we became best friends," recalled Alex. "It was at junior high, in that 'getting to know you'

RIGHT: Willowdale, Toronto; St. Theodore of Canterbury Anglican Church. The Coff-In was in the basement.

OPPOSITE: Toronto, Ontario; Alex at the Gasworks.

stage, that Geddy and I got heavily into music. For a long time we were in different bands, but we always jammed together. We loved to learn all those great Cream songs, play along to the record player, and play [songs] better and better and better. It was really a lot of fun. It was just the two of us—no drummer. The good old days!"

Geddy added, "We understood where each other came from, culturally. We were sons of Eastern European immigrants who had left Europe after the Second World War to start a new life in Canada. So we were, both of us, a little bit different . . ."

Meanwhile, John, one year older, was already playing drums in his first band, the Guilde. In 1967, John left the Guilde and formed a new outfit, the Lost Cause (soon renamed the Projection), which included his friend Alex on guitar. By the following summer, John and Alex had started another new band

with a local bassist named Jeff Jones. "I don't remember how we met him," John recalled. "I guess we met him at a party or Alex knew him. We did a couple of practices together and got this job playing at a drop-in center for kids in a church basement."

With some help from John's older brother, Bill, the three eventually settled on a band name.

"They were all banging away down in the basement at our house, and you could hear that they were trying to figure out what to call the band," said Bill Rutsey. "I can't remember any of the silly names that they were coming up with, but I was sitting upstairs and I just finally had heard enough and so I shouted downstairs: 'Just call the band Rush!' And they said, 'Rush? What's that?' And I said, 'You know, like drugs! . . . Rush!' So that's exactly how that happened."

The newly christened Rush's first paying gig came on September 6, 1968, at the Coff-In, a venue in the basement of the St. Theodore of Canterbury Anglican Church in Toronto. There were approximately thirty people in attendance. The band had a second show scheduled there one week later, on September 13, but on the afternoon of the gig, Jeff Jones abruptly quit the band.

"We were set to play the Coff-In every Friday night, and the second week Jeff phoned up and said that he wasn't going to play because he was going to a party," recounted John Rutsey. "So we sort of said, 'Okay, you go to the party and we'll see ya later!' We were stuck that night. Then Alex said, 'I know a guy in my class, Ged, who plays bass and sings.' I said, 'Great, get him down here,' and he came down. We told him that he had to sing, and he wasn't too thrilled about that because he thought it was just going to be kind of a jam—which it was. We basically knew a few songs between us and we went up and really kind of jammed. I can't really even remember what

kind of a PA system we had. It would have been some ridiculous little thing for a PA, but it didn't really matter at that place. That was our first job. We got twenty-five dollars for playing there, which we thought was great."

As the new Rush lineup evolved through fall 1968, their repertoire came to include songs by the Who, the Rolling Stones, the Jeff Beck Group, Blue Cheer, and Elvis Presley. The band continued to perform weekly gigs at the Coff-In (adding in the local YMCA as well), eventually picking up a fourth member, keyboardist Lindy Young, as well as their first roadie, Ian Grandy. The set list expanded to include covers of songs by the Allman Brothers Band, Traffic, the Grateful Dead, John Mayall, Cream, and more. The next batch of changes included picking up a manger, Ray Danniels . . . and getting rid of Geddy Lee.

Said Lee, "This is how Ray came into the band. . . . He approached the guys about management, and he didn't really talk to me much. And then suddenly I was told the band was dissolving. Apparently, they had decided

SPECIAL STEIN 25¢
NOON to 8 p.m.

GASWORKS EVENING ENTERTAINMENT LIST

September 24-29	Wednesday
October 1-6	Tommy Graham
October 8-13	Abraham
October 15-20	Rush
October 22-27	Orleans
October 29 – November 3	Flag
November 5-10	Outlaw Music
November 12-17	The British are Here

OPPOSITE: Ontario; Alex and John onstage in the early days.

LEFT TOP: Hadrian. From left to right: Joe Perna, Alex Lifeson, John Rutsey, and Lindy Young.

LEFT BOTTOM: Advertisement for gigs at the Gasworks.

that I wasn't suitable to be in the band—this was a lot at Ray's urging. So anyway, I get tossed from the band, and they started another band. That was my first introduction to Ray Danniels. He had to live that down for a really long time."

In recent years, Ray defended his decision, saying, "In those days, he wouldn't have been an obvious front man, no."

Alex, John, and Lindy (now on vocals in addition to keys), formed a new band, Hadrian, with a bassist named Joe Perna. Taking the high road, Geddy skipped the last Toronto-area performance by the Jimi Hendrix Experience in order to attend the first Hadrian gig on May 3, 1969, and help Lindy out with some of the words. He also joined a band named Ogilvie (later Judd), which included Lindy following his departure from Hadrian.

By September 1969, however, Rush were back together.

"John ended up calling Ged back and saying, 'Listen, I'm sorry that things went the way they did, everything got real crazy. So, eventually . . . not right away, but eventually, Ged came back.'"

Throughout 1969 and 1970, the reformed Rush played various high schools throughout the Ontario region—the band members being too young to perform in bars. The influence of Led Zeppelin became more apparent during this time: Geddy developed the higher end of his vocal range, and the band performed some Zeppelin tunes in their set, including "Whole Lotta Love" and "Heartbreaker." At this point, Rush were also focused on writing and improving their original material. Known song titles from the era included "Losing Again," "Child Reborn," "Number 1," "Keep in Line," "Run Willie Run," "Mike's Idea," "Tale," "Sing Guitar," "Morning Star," "Marguerite," "Feel So Good," "Love Light," "Garden Road," "Fancy Dancer," "Slaughterhouse," "The Swan," and "You Can't Fight It."

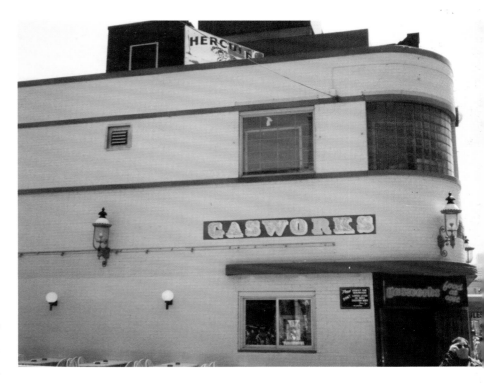

In July 1971, the Ontario drinking age was lowered from twenty-one to eighteen, opening a world of new gig possibilities for the young band. "Finally we could get into bars to play, so then we played bars forever," Geddy said. Rush's first bar gig is believed to have been at Toronto's the Gasworks, in August 1971. "We were scared to death," John recalled. "We played really low. I was sort of scared that people would yell 'shut up,' 'turn down,' and start throwing beer bottles at us and that sort of thing. It was our first gig in a bar. You've got to remember who we were. None of us had really even gone out to that many bars drinking. We were kind of suburban kids."

There were other growing pains still to be had. For a brief period in fall 1971 into early 1972, Rush once again expanded to a four-piece with the addition of Mitch Bossi on second guitar. Eventually, he was let go. "It really wasn't happening with Mitch the way we'd all hoped," Alex recalled. "He played guitar and he made an effort as much as he could, but I don't think his heart was really into the music. He was more into the 'being in a band' kind of thing."

Once again a trio (and with an additional roadie, Liam Birt), Rush gigged incessantly

OPPOSITE TOP: Ontario; Geddy onstage.
OPPOSITE BOTTOM: Ontario; John onstage.
TOP: Toronto; the Gasworks.

throughout Ontario in 1972 and 1973, playing numerous, often consecutive-night gigs at Toronto clubs like Abbey Road Pub, the Gasworks, the Piccadilly Tube, and the Colonial Tavern. "Anywhere there was a gig, we would do it," Geddy said. In mid-April 1973, they entered Toronto Sound Studios to record their debut album, with David Stock producing. Additionally, they cut their first singles, a cover of Buddy Holly's "Not Fade Away," and a Rush original titled "You Can't Fight It."

"They'd finish their last set in the bars at 1:00 a.m., then at 1:30 a.m., they'd go into the studio until nine or ten the next morning," said Ray. "The only way that we could afford to go into a studio was to take it when no one else would want it. They did that for about a week and a half and came up with what became the first album, with no record company."

However, the endless nights of performing (with some partying) began bringing John's health problems—he had been diagnosed with diabetes as a child—to the fore, so much so that a drummer named Stan reportedly had to fill in for a couple gigs. By fall 1973, John's departure seemed imminent, and Geddy and Alex began rehearsing with another local drummer, Gerry Fielding. In October, however, John returned to the band, playing a spate of dates that included two shows at Toronto's Victory Burlesque Theatre on October 27 opening for the New York Dolls. Two days later, Rush commenced a grueling run of seventeen consecutive shows at the Thunder Bay Motor Hotel in Thunder Bay, Ontario.

The day after the last show, November 15, they entered Toronto Sound Studios to rework their debut album, now with Terry Brown (Donovan, Manfred Mann, the Who) producing.

"'Finding My Way,' 'Need Some Love,' and, I think, 'Here Again' were the songs that we rerecorded for the record," said Geddy. "So we dropped 'Not Fade Away,' 'You Can't Fight It,'

and there may have been another one. 'In the Mood' was probably at least two years old, if not three, when we recorded the first record."

All the while, about seventy miles away from where the members of Rush were struggling to make a name for themselves—in St. Catharines, Ontario, specifically—young drummer Neil Peart was engaged in his own struggles to break into the music business. His path would be the antithesis of Geddy and Alex's early years, in that he would perform in a surprising number of bands—outfits with names like the Royal Bakers (his first, in 1966), the Eternal Triangle, Mumblin' Sumpthin', Wayne and the Younger Generation, the Majority, David, and JR Flood—in this formative period.

After that last band, JR Flood, failed to land a record deal, Neil made the dramatic decision to pack his drums in a crate and move to London, intent on finding fame and fortune overseas, just as some of his idols like the Jimi Hendrix Experience had done. But his bands there—English Rose and the rather unimaginatively named Music among them—stalled out as well, and Neil eventually returned to St. Catharines, beginning work in the parts department of his father's farm equipment dealership.

He eventually worked his way up to manager, deciding that he would perform music as a hobby and not rely on it for income. But Neil's hunger to play was relentless, and every time he found a new group, his ambition seemed to prevent him from approaching a band with anything less than 100 percent intensity. Sometime in 1973, he joined the band Hush, which featured Brian Collins on guitar, Bob Luciani on bass, Paul Lauzon on guitar, and JR Flood alumnus Gary Luciani on vocals. The group played all cover tunes, including all four sides of the Who's *Quadrophenia*. Recalled Brian Collins, "Neil was playing drums in 1974 for what turned out to be the last incarnation of Hush when the phone

call came: Would Neil be interested in auditioning for Rush, whose drummer had just quit? Neil actually had to think it over. He was working full-time at his dad's business and had recently returned disappointed after trying to 'make it' as a drummer in England. At the time, Hush members saw Rush as merely a Led Zeppelin clone band. 'You're making a big mistake, Neil,' one of us sagely opined at a band meeting."

Neil, of course, saw things differently. And the rest, as they say is history.

"I spent an important part of my youth, around 19, 20, 21 years old, in London, struggling for fame and fortune," Neil later recalled. "I didn't know it was in Toronto!"

ABOVE: Ontario; Alex, John, and Geddy onstage.
LEFT: Geddy onstage.

OPPOSITE: Early shot of Alex, John, and Geddy.
TOP LEFT: John, Alex, Ian Grandy, and Liam Birt.
TOP RIGHT: Geddy.
BOTTOM LEFT: Geddy and John in a dressing room.
BOTTOM RIGHT: Alex.

TOP: Alex.
ABOVE: Geddy.
OPPOSITE: Early biography.

RUSH is a three piece generator of energized rock.

Alex Lifeson, lead guitar and background vocals;
Geddy Lee, bass and lead singer; and John Rutsy
drums; are the talented musicians that give you
a RUSH.

Hailing from the same suburb that brought you
David Clayton Thomas of Blood, Sweat and Tears
fame, they formed their group about five years
ago. At that time, they were all in School
and like many other kids in 1968 they formed a
Rock Band. John and Alex had lived across
the street from each other since diaper days
and kiddingly refer to themselves as Child-
hood Sweethearts. Although none of the members have recieved any hard core formal
training, they have through long hours of practice and emulation developed their talents and
a very distinctive style.

One of the outstanding characteristics of the
band is Geddy's voice. It cannot be described
but some who have tried have said, 'Like a
Martian'; 'Sort of like Mickey Mouse' ; 'An
LP on 45 RPM' etc. Regardless, of how you describe his voice and its unique quality it
is obvious that it compliments his own bass

THIS PAGE: Geddy and John performing at the Gasworks.
OPPOSITE: Geddy performing at the Gasworks.

TOUR HISTORY

1965 TO FEBRUARY 1974

DISCLAIMER: *Few official records have lasted from this time period, and there are no existing records from 1965 to September 1968. That means there were likely many more showings than what is listed here. This list has been pieced together from what newspaper ads could be found, as well as other verifiable sources.*

SEPTEMBER 6, 1968
TORONTO, ONTARIO
ST. THEODORE OF CANTERBURY ANGLICAN CHURCH, THE COFF-IN,
111 Cactus Avenue
Founded in 1961.
ATTENDANCE: 30 (approximate)
RUSH'S GROSS: $25.00 CAD
NOTES: First paying gig as "Rush." Alex Lifeson (guitar), John Rutsey (drums), Jeff Jones (bass and vocals).
ALEX: "We played at a church basement called the Coff-In, with Jeff on bass. And we worked out a deal with the people there, where we would play for twenty-five bucks on Friday nights. Rush was a local band from North Toronto, and there weren't too many local groups around. A few people came, and I guess that there were twenty-five or thirty people on that first night."[1]
JEFF: "We played songs like 'Purple Haze,' 'Sunshine of Your Love,' and 'Spoonful.' We played at least one church basement."[2]

SEPTEMBER 13, 1968
TORONTO, ONTARIO
ST. THEODORE OF CANTERBURY ANGLICAN CHURCH, THE COFF-IN,
111 Cactus Avenue
RUSH'S GROSS: $25.00 CAD
NOTES: Jeff Jones quit the band during the afternoon, so Geddy filled in, making his Rush debut. As Alex recalls, "We did Jimi Hendrix's 'Foxy Lady,' Cream's 'Spoonful' and 'Crossroads,' the Yardbirds' 'Shapes of Things,' and maybe a few others." The show was deemed a success, and the trio split their $25 earnings, celebrating afterward with chips at Moe Pancer's Deli.

SEPTEMBER 20, 27; OCTOBER 4, 11, 18, 25; NOVEMBER 1, 8, 15, 22, 29; DECEMBER 6, 13, 20, 1968
TORONTO, ONTARIO
ST. THEODORE OF CANTERBURY ANGLICAN CHURCH, THE COFF-IN,
111 Cactus Avenue
RUSH'S GROSS: $25.00 CAD per show
NOTES: As the band evolved into the fall of 1968, Rush's repertoire expanded to include songs by the Who, the Rolling Stones, the Jeff Beck Group, Blue Cheer, and Elvis Presley.

JANUARY 3, 1969
TORONTO, ONTARIO
ST. THEODORE OF CANTERBURY ANGLICAN CHURCH, THE COFF-IN,
111 Cactus Avenue
SET LIST: During the set, Rush covered songs by John Mayall, Willie Dixon, Ten Years After, Cream, and Traffic. They closed the evening with Willie Dixon's classic "Spoonful," though their version more closely resembled Cream's take on the song.
NOTES: Although Lindy Young had jammed with them a few times previously, this was the official debut of the four-person Rush, with Lindy on keyboards.
LINDY: "We closed with 'Spoonful,' complete with electric piano."[3]

JANUARY 10, 1969
TORONTO, ONTARIO
ST. THEODORE OF CANTERBURY ANGLICAN CHURCH, THE COFF-IN,
111 Cactus Avenue
NOTES: Ian Grandy's first date working with the band.

JANUARY–APRIL 1969
TORONTO, ONTARIO
ST. THEODORE OF CANTERBURY ANGLICAN CHURCH, THE COFF-IN,
111 Cactus Avenue
NOTES: Rush is the main band at the Coff-In, with shows on Friday nights.

FEBRUARY 1969
TORONTO, ONTARIO
WILLOWDALE YMCA
NOTES: In addition to appearing regularly on Friday nights at the Coff-In, Rush started performing every couple of weeks at the Willowdale YMCA. The addition of Lindy Young enabled the band to widen their scope musically, and they began playing more complicated arrangements by the Allman Brothers (Lindy provided lead vocals on "You Don't Love Me"), Traffic, the Grateful Dead, and John Mayall & the Bluesbreakers. Another song Rush played with Lindy was a tune by Buddy Knox called "The Girl with the Golden Hair."

MARCH 1969
TORONTO, ONTARIO
WILLOWDALE YMCA

APRIL 1969
TORONTO, ONTARIO
WILLOWDALE YMCA

APRIL 1969
Ray Danniels begins managing Rush, and Geddy is kicked out of the band.

MAY 3, 1969 (HADRIAN)
TORONTO, ONTARIO
WILLOWDALE UNITED CHURCH,
349 Kenneth Avenue
Built in 1954.
NOTES: First Hadrian show. Alex Lifeson (guitar), Lindy Young (keyboards and vocals), John Rutsey (drums), and Joe

Perna (bass). Taking the high road, Geddy skipped the last Toronto-area performance by the Jimi Hendrix Experience to attend the Hadrian gig in order to help Lindy out with some of the words. Earlier in the day, Hendrix was arrested for illegal possession of narcotics while going through customs at the Toronto airport (airport code YYZ, namesake of Rush's 1981 song).

JUNE 1969 (HADRIAN)
TORONTO, ONTARIO
NORTHMINSTER UNITED CHURCH,
255 Finch

NOTES: Hadrian show. Lindy Young quit just before this gig, and the band got a friend named Bob Vopni to fill in.

IAN GRANDY RECALLS BOB VOPNI: "Tall, curly hair, and a smiling face . . . a decent guitar player."

LINDY: "This show was either the first or second Saturday of June 1969. I bailed out of that gig—the first and only time I have ever done that to a band. The group was in a very bad state at that time, and I just couldn't face playing another gig with them. I quit that day and was definitely in Alex and John's bad books for quite a while. They hired a friend of the band to fill in."[4]

IAN: "I introduced them as 'Just back from their tour of Yugoslavia: Hadrian!' Joe [Perna] was a good guy, but a terrible bass player. There's a song by the Jeff Beck Group called 'Let Me Love You' that has a very simple eight-note run right before the ending chords, and he practiced it again and again, but he still totally fucked it up. I remember John looking at me and giving an exasperated shake of the head like he wanted to kill Joe. So, the Hadrian shows were a debacle. Joe Perna could not play even the most basic bass riffs, and the shows were embarrassing. I remember Alex apologizing to the crowd after they were done."[5]

LATE JUNE 1969 (HADRIAN)
TORONTO, ONTARIO
CANADIAN LEGION,
948 Sheppard Avenue West

ATTENDANCE: Fewer than 40 (approximate)

NOTES: Final Hadrian show. With Lindy's departure, Hadrian floundered because there wasn't anyone to sing lead vocals.

IAN: "I can still picture them at the Legion, playing 'Respect,' with John coming off of his kit and dancing in front of the stage . . . for the twelve people in the audience."[6]

JUNE–JULY 1969 (OGILVIE)
GEDDY PERFORMS LOCAL SHOWS AS PART OF OGILVIE.

NOTES: The lineup included Geddy on bass and lead vocals, Lindy Young on keyboards, Sammy Rohr (Geddy's cousin) on drums, and Xavier "Sam" Dangle on guitar. With Geddy on bass and lead vocals, they had a jazz-blues feel, performing originals and covers by bands like Ten Years After.

AUGUST 1969 (JUDD)
HAMILTON, ONTARIO
OGILVIE IS RENAMED JUDD.

NOTES: Geddy's band continued gigging, maintaining a reasonable performance schedule, including an August show in Hamilton, Ontario. They call it quits at the end of the summer, however.

SEPTEMBER 1969
RUSH REFORMS.

EARLY FALL 1969
TORONTO, ONTARIO
ST. GABRIEL'S SCHOOL AUDITORIUM,
Sheppard Avenue

NOTES: This "battle of the bands," produced and promoted by Ray Danniels, featured the infamous "Wild Woodpecker Revue" performance.

IAN: "You never hear about this, but a couple of times we (the band, me, and a couple of other clowns) appeared as the 'Wild Woodpecker Revue' with us totally slicked up and doing R&B songs (not very well). The first time was in the fall of 1969. It was while Rush's 'reformation' was going on, after the short-lived Hadrian—I can't even tell you whether Rush had actually played any gigs again as of yet. Ray Danniels put on a kind of battle of the bands. We practiced once and went on last (which was twelfth). I was one of the 'singers' and John Rutsey was the other. Along with Geddy and Alex, we had Sammy Rohr on drums and Steve "Stove" Moffat on guitar. We were introduced as 'strutting out of the R&B world' and did 'In the Midnight Hour,' 'Last Kiss' and a few others. John

and I totally lost our voices and even though we did it as a joke some people thought we were pretty good. I can still recall singing 'In the Midnight Hour.' Al Dunikowski was supposed to take pictures, but he'd done some acid and was afraid of us when the curtain opened up, so, no photos. I remember washing my hair about fifty times, and I still couldn't get the Vaseline out of it. Then we did it at a high school a couple of years later, after Rush had finished their show. . . . We had a fucking riot doing it, but twice was certainly enough."[7]

1969–1970
ONTARIO
VARIOUS HIGH SCHOOL PERFORMANCES THROUGHOUT THE REGION:
Sudbury, North Bay, Cochrane, Kirkland Lake, London, Deep River, Windsor, and Midland

NOTES: In late 1969, the influence of Led Zeppelin became more apparent. Geddy developed the higher end of his vocal range, and Rush began performing Zeppelin in their set. Geddy would later recall performing "Livin' Lovin' Maid (She's Just a Woman)" in their "high school band days," but adds that he "[doesn't] know if they ever played Zeppelin in the bars." As the band members were too young at this point to perform in bars, 1969 and 1970 were spent performing at drop-in centers and high school dances.

1970 (ESTIMATED)
TORONTO, ONTARIO
EARL HAIG SECONDARY SCHOOL,
100 Princess Avenue.
Opened in 1930.

NOTES: Date and year unconfirmed. Alex and Geddy both recall playing at the school several times in the early days.

ALEX: "Earl Haig high school, where Geddy and I had played I don't know how many times in the early days."

IAN: "I don't recall playing at Earl Haig even once."[8]

FEBRUARY 1970
NORTH BAY, ONTARIO

FEBRUARY 1970
DEEP RIVER, ONTARIO
MACKENZIE HIGH SCHOOL GYM,
2 Brockhouse Way. Venue built in the 1950s.

ALEX: "I have a tape from when we were playing high schools . . . from Deep River, Ontario, at this little high school that we played. I remember the gig too. It's a tape of the whole set with all of the old songs in it and whatever else we played at the time. It was usually just us playing, with no other groups, and back then a high school show was three forty-minute sets or two sixty-minute sets. It was like a concert in an auditorium or a gym, wherever they happen to have a stage set up. It wasn't until later that we did really well in high schools. In the earlier days, in a place like Deep River for instance, maybe eighty or one hundred kids would show up, and that was pretty good for back then."[9]

JUNE 21, 1970
TORONTO, ONTARIO
HART HOUSE, UNIVERSITY OF
TORONTO, 7 Hart House Circle
WITH: Atlantis, Bittersweet, Boogie Dick, Sun, Global Village Sublimes, and Guerrilla Theatre
NOTES: Free outdoor show. After this gig, John began acting as the band's front man.
IAN: "At Hart House, Geddy spoke to the crowd about how cool it was to be there and various other embarrassing things. That doesn't sound so bad, but the other guys started finding something to do with their equipment because they didn't want to look at the crowd. Certainly John did all the talking after that."

SEPTEMBER 1970
STAYNER, ONTARIO
STAYNER COLLEGIATE INSTITUTE (SCI)
GYMNASIUM, 7578 Highway 26.
School founded in the fall of 1961.
ATTENDANCE: 350[10]
RUSH'S FEE: $250 CAD

JEFF PARTON (SCI STUDENT COUNCIL PRESIDENT): "There was a lot of yelling. The place just went wild. They did predominantly covers. The Rolling Stones, some heavier stuff. I think they did some Grand Funk Railroad. I can't remember exactly what tunes because I was doing a bunch of running around making sure the night was running smoothly. People loved it."[11]

DECEMBER 21, 1970
TORONTO, ONTARIO
A. Y. JACKSON SECONDARY SCHOOL,
50 Francine Drive. Founded in 1970.
NOTES: In between gigs, Alex attended classes at this high school.

1970 (ESTIMATED)
WARKWORTH, ONTARIO
PERCY CENTENNIAL PUBLIC SCHOOL,
129 Church Street. Erected in 1967.
NOTES: Venue unconfirmed.
HAL GREENSON: "'Run Willie Run' was indeed Alex's venture into country music. We had played a high school in Warkworth, Ontario, where Warkworth prison is. It's a penitentiary town. We're talking major 'country'—this is not a town where a band playing heavy music should be playing. They wanted to hear country music. That was the first night that 'Run Willie Run' was ever played. He pretty much made it up on the spot, and I think they had to play it four or five times that night."[12]

EARLY 1971
TORONTO, ONTARIO
R. H. KING COLLEGIATE INSTITUTE,
3800 St. Clair Avenue East.
Founded in 1922.
NOTES: Show and date unconfirmed.

APRIL 1971
STAYNER, ONTARIO
STAYNER COLLEGIATE INSTITUTE (SCI)
GYMNASIUM, 7578 Highway 26
RUSH'S FEE: $600 CAD
JEFF PARTON (SCI STUDENT COUNCIL PRESIDENT): "We paid $600 for them in April because they were just getting more popular. The neat thing was I thought—because of the long hair—they were much older, but they were my age."[13]

1971 (ESTIMATED)
TORONTO, ONTARIO
PROVINCIAL LUNATIC ASYLUM,
1001 Queen Street West. Opened on January 26, 1850.
NOTES: Date and year unconfirmed. Alex recalls it as "probably 1970–1971." Venue aka 999 Queen Street.
IAN: "Rush at 999 Queen Street. I don't believe it's there anymore, but for years 999 Queen Street was an insane asylum. The guys belonged to the musician's union, and there was an older guard of people who ran the union and its elections. I was never there, but John used to keep me updated. Anyway, there was a big to-do because the guys who held the key to the ballot box and counted the votes were also the guys running for office, which kind of stunk. There were a couple of loud meetings that ended up as the 'rock guys' against those 'older guys.' As punishment for John speaking up, Rush was obligated to do a 'trust fund' gig (for the one and only time) at this insane asylum. The union could assign you a gig for which you were only paid scale, which I think was around $125 for three musicians. So, we drive to the hospital and report in at the desk. I remember sitting there, and a patient goes stalking by like a big bird, out the front door he goes, and we were like, 'Is anybody going to stop this guy!' Anyway, they take us by these ten-foot-high barricaded doors, and you're thinking, 'Who the heck is kept in there?' We get to a padded and locked door, knock on it, and a slot opens so they can eyeball us before opening it. As they open it, a guy who looked like half of his head has been melted tries to get out, and they tackle him to the ground. OK, so we get to this room, and then I make the mistake of asking where we should set up. Four different guys came up, and all of them point to a different spot. So we made our own decision. The band gets there, and the 'crowd' is led in—maybe sixty people, including one who thought he was Elvis. The most pathetic were about seven old ladies who they put right in front of the PA speakers, and they sat there unblinking and almost catatonic and seemed totally unaware. I couldn't help but think that they were somebody's mother, and what a sad way to end up. Anyway, the band plays, and some of

these folks dance. At the time, Rush was doing a version of the old Wilbert Harrison song 'Kansas City.' They get to the line, 'They got some crazy little women there, and I'm gonna get me one,' and the five of us (band and crew) are trying not to laugh too much as Geddy skips over the word *crazy*. It wasn't that big a deal, but any time the subject of 'weird gigs' came up, we held the trump card with 999 Queen. No one in Toronto could ever top that one."[14]

ALEX: "I remember it because my mom would always say, 'One day you're going to drive me to 999.' We got there, and some of the patients helped with the gear, and it was like a scene from *One Flew Over the Cuckoo's Nest*, except with guitars, and amps, and drums. We set up and started playing, and they stood about thirty feet away from us. Eventually, they started to dance, and it was the most bizarre thing I've ever seen. Afterward, we had to go to the bathroom, and most of the crowd was in the bathroom [*laughs*]. And that was really interesting, just the dialogue and the singing in the bathroom."

SUMMER 1971
MIDLAND, ONTARIO
OPENED FOR: Mashmakhan
NOTES: This date (and the timeframe for it) is unconfirmed but likely, based on Ian Grandy's recollection. Named after a form of hashish, Mashmakhan was a Canadian rock fusion band from L'Île-Perrot, Quebec, established in 1969. The group is best known for the song "As the Years Go By," which topped the Canadian charts in 1970. In September of 1970, Mashmakhan had coheadlined the Brock Festival, which included an extensive list of bands—including JR Flood, with Neil Peart on drums.
IAN: "We played with Mashmakhan in Midland, Ontario. They got $2,500. The promoter and crowd hated them. We blew them away and got $500. They were from Montreal and had a couple of radio semi-hits. This was so early it was pre-Liam."[15]

AUGUST 1971
TORONTO, ONTARIO
THE GASWORKS, 585 Yonge Street West. Venue opened in 1968.
CAPACITY: 300 downstairs, 250 upstairs (approximate)

NOTES: While no hard evidence has been found to prove or disprove this gig, Ian's recollection is that the first bar performance took place before Alex turned eighteen, while John recalled the band's first bar show was at the Gasworks.

1971 (ESTIMATED)
GEORGIAN BAY, ONTARIO
HONEY HARBOUR
NOTES: Year unconfirmed.
HAL GREENSON: "There was a gig we played on an island in Georgian Bay, at Honey Harbour. We got to the loading dock, and we had to move all the equipment onto a boat so that we could get it out to an island where the schoolhouse was. It was in the middle of nowhere, and we went there two or three times. A couple of the guys' girlfriends showed up at the gig on this island, and we were all just like, 'How the hell did you get here?'"[16]

FALL 1971
TORONTO, ONTARIO
THE PIPE ROOM, York Glendon College (campus of York University), 2275 Bayview Avenue. Founded in 1961.
NOTES: Date and venue unconfirmed. Based on Mitch Bossi's recollections, this was probably his first gig with the band.
MITCH BOSSI: "I don't know if it was a coffee shop kind of thing they had there in the dorm or what it was, something like that. I'm pretty sure that was my first gig with the band. Rush did a fair bit of covers. For a time, we opened up playing an old blues tune that the Yardbirds and then Led Zeppelin covered called 'Train Kept a-Rollin.' I remember it was one of the ones where there wasn't much in the way of lyrics—there was a lot of soloing, and I even did a little bit, because typically I didn't, as I wasn't nearly as accomplished a guitar player as Alex. He must have had the patience of Job to allow me to actually do a couple of little runs, and I might have actually hit a few notes that were in the correct key!"[17]

NOVEMBER 19–20, 1971
TORONTO, ONTARIO
ABBEY ROAD PUB, 180 Queen Street
NOTES: At time of publication, this is Rush's first *substantiated* bar gig, though Ian and John's recollections of their first bar gig predate this by several months.

IAN: "My first date with Nancy (my ex) was in 1971, and she came with me to the Abbey Road. When people would ask her about me being a roadie she would answer, 'Our first date was a gig, and I helped them load out.' She knew what she was getting into."[18]

DOC COOPER: "John and I used to go to the bank and put in some money every Monday, after the weekend's bar gigs."

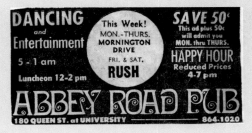

LATE 1971
LONDON, ONTARIO
LONDON GARDENS, 4380 Wellington Road South. Venue opened in September 1964.
OPENED FOR: Fludd
CAPACITY: 5,075
NOTES: This was a festival performance. Mitch Bossi was interviewed backstage before the show for local radio.
MITCH BOSSI: "Probably the largest audience I ever played to."
HAL GREENSON: "One of the local radio stations was doing an interview backstage with Mitch. He'd been with the band for like, a nanosecond, and Ian and I had been there forever. It was like family, like you worked with your brothers. Ian and I knew what our roles were with the gig and the band. Well, Mitch was back doing the interview, and he kicked Ian and me out of the dressing room! Big fucking mistake. Bear in mind that I did the sound for the band back then. So when Mitch went up to do background harmonies, his mic didn't work. Ian was on the stage . . . and Mitch's guitar came unplugged, so nothing was coming out and he couldn't hear himself. Well, Ian didn't plug him back in. After the show, Ian and I were just laughing our heads off."[19]

LATE 1971
WINDSOR, ONTARIO
ST. CLAIR COLLEGE, 2000 Talbot Road West. Founded in 1966.
NOTES: This was Liam Birt's first show working for Rush. Liam had seen Rush play, but only at their high school gigs

because he was only seventeen at the time and underage for the bar scene. With Hal's departure, Ian took over the task of running live sound for the band.

IAN: "Liam Birt's first gig with Rush. On a Wednesday evening, we find out we're playing Windsor (240 miles down Highway 401, beside Detroit). So, it's me and the new kid, and I'm driving the truck. Hal didn't drive, so I'm thinking, 'I'm hungover and this guy can drive.' Well, Liam is seventeen, and I don't know what the fuck he's ever driven . . . so within ten minutes he's gone off the pavement, scuffing up the gravel on one lane and then on the other side. Scared the heck out of me. So we switched, and I drove. He got to be a good driver (after he wrecked our first van . . . that's another story). The infamous 'underwear photo' was taken that night at the Madrid Motor Inn. We stayed there when we played St. Clair. Liam must have wondered what the fuck he was getting into! Hard to forget taking that picture."[20]

DECEMBER 1971
TORONTO, ONTARIO
EAST YORK
NOTES: Anyone bringing a toy for the Christmas Fund got a reduced admission.

JANUARY 7, 1972
ST. MARYS, ONTARIO
ST. MARYS DCVI HIGH SCHOOL,
338 Elizabeth Street. Opened in 1954.
NOTES: Venue unconfirmed.

IAN: "On my twenty-first birthday, we were on our way to a gig in St. Marys, Ontario. It was me, my girlfriend Nancy, and Liam. We skidded into a drift and had to get a tow. Neither Liam nor I had any money. Nancy had twenty bucks and lent it to us to get towed. Never traveled without a 'float' again."[21]

JANUARY 21–22, 1972
TORONTO, ONTARIO
ABBEY ROAD PUB, 180 Queen Street

EARLY 1972
TORONTO, ONTARIO
MINKLER AUDITORIUM, Seneca College campus, 1750 Finch Avenue East. Venue opened in July 1970.
OPENED FOR: Crowbar, King Biscuit Boy
TICKETS: $3.00 (advance) / $3.50 (at the door)

CAPACITY: 1,111
NOTES: With Mitch Bossi on guitar.
IAN: "First time I mixed sound on another board . . . nervous!"[22]
MITCH BOSSI: "I'm 100 percent sure that Minkler was dead of winter, probably January or February. It was cold and quite a lot of snow. That was one of the bigger gigs that I played with Rush. I have a picture of me at that gig doing a copycat Pete Townshend windmill thing with my Les Paul."[23]
ROLY GREENWAY (CROWBAR BASSIST): "We opened for bands, and then we became the headliner and tons of bands opened for us. Rush opened for us at one point. They're superstars, and we got on the same stage as them. They were just coming up the ladder."[24]

EARLY 1972
CARNARVON, ONTARIO
MITCH BOSSI: "I remember playing in Carnarvon at a really divey kind of hamburger joint. I think the owner wanted to get some more kids coming in. I was driving my parents' 1970 white Oldsmobile Cutlass. I remember driving was a little hairy at times; there was a lot of snow out."

EARLY 1972
TORONTO, ONTARIO
SENECA COLLEGE (YORK CAMPUS), 70 The Pond Road. Established in 1967.
MITCH BOSSI: "We played a second time at Seneca, but it was not in Minkler Auditorium. It was in a room that was more like a cafeteria. I remember that because it was the only time that my parents came and saw me play. I don't know if that was the first time, or the second time—I am not sure of the chronology of it."

EARLY 1972
LAFONTAINE, ONTARIO
NOTES: With Mitch Bossi on guitar.

FEBRUARY 25, 1972
GRAVENHURST, ONTARIO
GRAVENHURST HIGH SCHOOL, 325 Mary Street. Founded in 1896.
TICKETS: $1.75 / $3.00 per couple
NOTES: School dance, 9:00 p.m. to 11:30 p.m.

FEBRUARY 28–29; MARCH 1–4, 1972
OSHAWA, ONTARIO
HARRY'S HIDEAWAY, GENOSHA HOTEL, 70 King Street East
NOTES: It might have been during this run of dates that a small fire broke out in the Genosha Hotel.

MARCH 20–23, 1972
TORONTO, ONTARIO
ABBEY ROAD PUB, 180 Queen Street

EARLY 1972
NIAGARA FALLS, ONTARIO
NOTES: Unconfirmed.

MARCH 1972 (ESTIMATED)
MITCH BOSSI LEAVES THE BAND.
ALEX: Mitch was going to university during the day and gigging at night, so his priorities were different. Unfortunately, he was just starting to get into it before he left. He was starting to get into the music, really making an effort and starting to enjoy it."[25]
MITCH BOSSI: "For years I told people that I had left the band, or I would tell people that it was a mutual decision, because frankly I felt a little ashamed and embarrassed, but the truth is I was let go. I was called into Ray Danniels's office, and I guess they felt that I 'wasn't contributing,' for lack of a better way to describe it. I had a difficult time with it, to be honest. I remember the next morning waking up and being upset, and I remember crying about it. I was very upset. I internalized it and had a lot of self-blame for it happening, and for many years I really kind of beat myself up for it—especially as they started to become more and more famous, I thought 'Oh my God, I had such an opportunity and I blew it, I wasn't good enough, I didn't work hard enough, I didn't practice enough.' But ultimately I was kind of redundant, as they never

had another guitar player, so clearly they didn't need a second guitar. . . . Anyway, I became an elementary school teacher for the Toronto District School Board. I retired at age fifty-four, but I still do some occasional teaching. I still enjoy it, and it feeds my addictive habit of golfing. Alex and I have that in common."[26]

APRIL 7, 1972
MISSISSAUGA, ONTARIO
THOMAS L. KENNEDY SECONDARY SCHOOL, 3100 Hurontario Street. Founded in 1953.
CONCERT GROSS: $800 CAD, $350 CAD paid to Rush

MAY 26–27, 1972
TORONTO, ONTARIO
ABBEY ROAD PUB, 180 Queen Street

JUNE 16–17, 1972
TORONTO, ONTARIO
PENTHOUSE MOTOR INN, 1625 Military Trail

1972 (ESTIMATED)
ETOBICOKE, ONTARIO
WARRENDALE CENTRE FOR CHILDREN, Warrendale Court, off of Kendleton Drive. Opened in December 1965.
NOTES: Date and year unconfirmed, and Ian does not recall this gig at all.
ALEX: "The union set up another gig for us at Warrendale, which was for kids that were mentally disturbed, that would kill people and burn houses down. There was something about the union; they didn't like us very much."

JUNE 30; JULY 1–6, 1972
TORONTO, ONTARIO
ABBEY ROAD PUB, 180 Queen Street

AUGUST 12, 19, 1972
REGENCY HOTEL

AUGUST 21–26, 28–31; SEPTEMBER 1–2, 1972
TORONTO, ONTARIO
THE GASWORKS, 585 Yonge Street West. Venue opened in 1968.
CAPACITY: 300 downstairs, 250 upstairs (approximate)
NOTES: The Gasworks included two bars (upstairs and downstairs), where different bands would perform simultaneously.

SEPTEMBER 18–23, 1972
TORONTO, ONTARIO
THE PICCADILLY TUBE, 316 Yonge Street at Dundas
NOTES: Only the September 23 date is confirmed.

SEPTEMBER 1972
BURLINGTON, ONTARIO
LORD ELGIN HIGH SCHOOL, 5151 New Street. Founded in 1970.

OCTOBER 14, 1972
NOTES: Location and venue unknown.

NOVEMBER 25, 1972
BROCK HOUSE
NOTES: Location of show unconfirmed.

DECEMBER 1, 1972
TORONTO, ONTARIO
BOND ACADEMY, 720 Midland Avenue. Founded in 1962.
RUSH'S FEE: $450 CAD
NOTES: School dance. Three forty-minute sets.

DECEMBER 15, 1972
TORONTO, ONTARIO
LEWIS S. BEATTIE SECONDARY SCHOOL, 110 Drewry Avenue. Founded in 1965.
TICKETS: $2.25 (with ID card) / $3.00 CAD

DECEMBER 26–30, 1972
TORONTO, ONTARIO
THE GASWORKS, 585 Yonge Street West
CAPACITY: 300 downstairs, 250 upstairs (approximate)

1973
OAKVILLE, ONTARIO
GENERAL WOLFE HIGH SCHOOL, 1330 Montclair Drive. Founded in 1965.
NOTES: Date unknown.

1973 (ESTIMATED)
SMITHS FALLS, ONTARIO
RUSSELL HOTEL, 2 Beckwith Street
NOTES: Dates and year unconfirmed. A one-week run of shows.
ALEX: "There was a bar that we played in a hotel in Smiths Falls, and they really, really hated us there. I remember we finished the first song, and there wasn't a sound. And after the second song it was like, 'Fuck off! Get out of here!' And it stayed like that through the whole night. They never really warmed up to us [laughs]. And we were sharing rooms, and they were really awful. The doors were all cracked with holes in them, and they didn't close properly."
IAN: "Smiths Falls was the Russell Hotel. One week of gigs, and only one time. Maybe 1973? When you're staying right at the gig, there's more chance for romance. Somehow we all had our own room."[27]

FEBRUARY 17, 1973
NOTES: Location and venue unknown.

FEBRUARY 19–24, 1973
OSHAWA, ONTARIO
HARRY'S HIDEAWAY, GENOSHA HOTEL, 70 King Street East

MARCH 5–10, 1973
WINDSOR, ONTARIO
EMBASSY HOTEL, 2998 Tecumseh Road East

MARCH 26–31; APRIL 2–7, 1973
TORONTO, ONTARIO
THE PICCADILLY TUBE, 316 Yonge Street at Dundas
NOTES: The March 26–30, 1973, dates are unconfirmed.

MAY 7–12, 1973
TORONTO, ONTARIO
THE MEET MARKET AT THE COLONIAL TAVERN, 201–203 Yonge Street. Venue rebuilt in 1961 after a fire gutted the original 1890s building.
NOTES: The Colonial was one of the first clubs in Toronto to be granted a liquor license after World War II. The downstairs rock room was known as the "Meet Market."
ALEX: "The Meet Market was notorious because it was a really, really rough downtown crowd, and every time we played there, there were at least one or two fights during the week that we played there."

MAY 28–31; JUNE 1–2, 4–9, 1973
TORONTO, ONTARIO
ABBEY ROAD PUB, 180 Queen Street
JUNE 23, 1973
TORONTO, ONTARIO
GSU PUB (UNIVERSITY OF TORONTO),
16 Bancroft Avenue. Founded in 1919.
The name of the event was "the Guerilla
Birthday."
WITH: Peter Matheson, Killaloe
Mountain Band, Horn, Noflies, Doug
Austen, Midnight Otto, Process Version,
Stoneage Sound.

JULY 2–7, 1973
TORONTO, ONTARIO
**THE MEET MARKET AT THE COLONIAL
TAVERN**, 201–203 Yonge Street
NOTES: The June 2–6, 1973, dates are
unconfirmed, but possible, due to a July
7 date listed in the Canadian Musicians'
Pension Fund archives. The July 3,
1973, edition of the *Toronto Star* includes
a Colonial ad which only mentions Muddy
Waters as performing this week, but the
Meet Market often wasn't advertised.

JULY 7, 1973
TORONTO, ONTARIO
**THE MEET MARKET AT THE COLONIAL
TAVERN**, 201–203 Yonge Street

JULY 9–14, 1973
TORONTO, ONTARIO
ABBEY ROAD PUB, 180 Queen Street

JULY 19–21, 1973
OTTAWA, ONTARIO
THE PUB, Carleton University Unicentre,
1125 Colonel By Drive
TICKETS: $0.50
NOTES: The band performed two gigs on
July 19—a free outdoor concert at 2:00
p.m., and then a 9:00 p.m. show at the
Pub. On July 21, Alex's Echoplex was
stolen, but the culprit was caught and
the pedal later recovered by Ian.
IAN: "It was like when the Beatles played
for weeks at a time in Germany. So much
time to fill, so songs would come and go,
and you're playing them over and over. We
were a big band on that circuit and filled
the bars, leading you to think that you
could actually make a living doing this. In
the summer of 1973, we played Toronto
bars (not just the Gasworks) every week
but one, and that week we went to Ottawa
and played in a bar there. Steve Barringer

was a good guy and a friend of Alex's. It
was the last day of the stand, and
suddenly Alex's Echoplex is gone. Steve
happens to be there and says that he saw
some guy walk out with it. So, while the
band plays, Steve and I walk around
downtown Ottawa looking for him. Just as
I'm ready to give up, Steve points across
the street and says, 'That's him.' He goes
to find a cop, and I confront this guy who's
sitting in a booth with three ladies. I have
a hammer in my hand, and I say, 'Where's
my Echoplex?' and he stupidly says, 'I've
already sold it.' He then tells me he
doesn't know what an Echoplex is. His
girlfriend asks, 'What's an Echoplex?' and
he proceeds to explain to her exactly what
it was. By now the cop is there listening,
and then he arrests him. I had to fly
[back] up to Ottawa to retrieve the pedal."

JULY 26, 1973
AJAX, ONTARIO
**ANNANDALE GOLF AND CURLING
CLUB**, 221 Church Street South.
Founded in 1963.
OPENED FOR: A Foot in Coldwater
TICKETS: $2.75 CAD

JULY 28, 1973
TORONTO, ONTARIO
THE PICCADILLY TUBE, 316 Yonge
Street at Dundas
NOTES: Even though Geddy recalled this
gig as being on his birthday, the bars
were closed on Sunday nights, so his
recollection almost certainly comes from
it being after midnight during the
Saturday night (July 28) show.
GEDDY: "It was my birthday, and we
were playing a club in Toronto called
Piccadilly Tube, and I was a little tipsy,
and I fell off the stage . . . forward, into
the crowd, and they pushed me back
onto the stage."[28]

AUGUST 4, 1973
TORONTO, ONTARIO
PENTHOUSE MOTOR INN, 1625
Military Trail
NOTES: The endless nights of performing
(and some partying) were making John's
health problems a larger issue, so much
so that a drummer named Stan (from the
SRO Productions band Fear) had to fill in
for a couple gigs. This may not be the
exact date when it happened, but Ian
recalls the substitution occurring at the

Penthouse Motor Inn in the summer of
1973.
AUGUST 18, 1973
NOTES: Location and venue unknown.

AUGUST 25, 1973
TORONTO, ONTARIO
THE PICCADILLY TUBE, 316 Yonge
Street at Dundas
NOTES: Party hosted by SRO / Music
Shoppe.

SEPTEMBER 3–8, 1973
TORONTO, ONTARIO
ABBEY ROAD PUB, 180 Queen Street
West

SEPTEMBER 24–29, 1973
TORONTO, ONTARIO
**THE MEET MARKET AT THE COLONIAL
TAVERN**, 201–203 Yonge Street
NOTES: The September 24–26 and
28–29 dates are unconfirmed.

FALL 1973
TORONTO, ONTARIO
LEASIDE HIGH SCHOOL, 200 Hanna
Road. Founded in 1945.

OCTOBER 12, 1973
WATERLOO, ONTARIO
**QUADRANGLE AT WATERLOO
LUTHERAN UNIVERSITY (WLU)**, 75
University Ave West. Origins date back
to 1911.
WITH: Orleans
TICKETS: Free show
RUSH'S FEE: $300 CAD
NOTES: This noon to 4:00 p.m. outdoor
gig was part of WLU's Sixtieth Anniversary
Homecoming celebration. In case of
rain, the event was to be moved to the
ballroom. Rush performed two sixty-
minute sets. The school was renamed
Wilfrid Laurier University on November
1, 1973.

OCTOBER 15–20, 1973
TORONTO, ONTARIO
THE GASWORKS, 585 Yonge Street
West
CAPACITY: 300 downstairs, 250
upstairs (approximate)
NOTES: The Musicians' Pension Fund
records indicate the October 20 date as
being Abbey Road Pub, but the Gasworks
dates are corroborated by a flier in
Geddy's personal collection. It is

possible, based on the timing of announcements in *RPM Weekly* and the rehearsals with Gerry Fielding, that this series of Gasworks dates was not actually performed.

OCTOBER 27, 1973
TORONTO, ONTARIO
VICTORY BURLESQUE THEATRE, 287 Spadina Avenue. Venue opened on August 18, 1921.
OPENED FOR: The New York Dolls
TICKETS: $4.00 CAD
ATTENDANCE: 1,200
NOTES: Two shows, at 8:00 p.m. and 11:00 p.m.
ALEX: "It was an old burlesque theater, pretty run-down and crappy, but to us it might as well have been Wembley. That crowd was excited to see the New York Dolls—not so much a local heavy metal band. But it was exciting being around the Dolls. Watching them backstage, it was all what you would expect. They were all drunk before they got onstage. They had girls back there. It was a whole rock 'n' roll scene. We were typically Canadian and shy and stayed out of their way. I do recall, though, after that gig I was hitchhiking home with a friend of mine. I had my guitar with me. This couple picked me up, and we were chatting, and they said they'd been to the Dolls show at the Victory, and they said, "Yeah, they were great, but the opening act, God, they sucked." They were chuckling, and the guy's girlfriend turned back and saw the guitar and saw me, and her face just kind of froze. It was silent in the car, and I felt so crestfallen. I said, 'We'll get out at the next block, please.' I got out of the car and I wanted to throw my guitar away. That was the first really bad review that we got [*laughs*]."[29]
IAN: "By the second show, the Dolls were so drunk they literally were lying on the stage, flailing at their guitars. By the end, there were about 50 people (out of the original 1,200) still enduring them."[30]
CHEAP THRILLS MAGAZINE: "Rush came out and shredded every ear in sight by whipping out number after number in true heavy metal tradition."
TORONTO STAR: "The opening group, a hard rock trio called Rush, had been bad enough, but the Dolls only seemed worse because they had promised so much more."

BUSTER POINDEXTER (DAVID JOHANSEN'S ALTER EGO): "Geddy Lee awesome ay."[31]

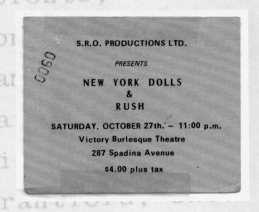

S.R.O. PRODUCTIONS LTD.

PRESENTS

NEW YORK DOLLS
&
RUSH

SATURDAY, OCTOBER 27th. – 11:00 p.m.

Victory Burlesque Theatre
287 Spadina Avenue

$4.00 plus tax

OCTOBER 29–31;
NOVEMBER 1–11, 1973
THUNDER BAY, ONTARIO
THUNDER BAY MOTOR HOTEL, 761 Kingsway Street. Built in 1958, renamed in 1973.
NOTES: Two weeks of dates. These were most likely the gigs that Gerry Fielding had been preparing to play before John returned to the band.
IAN: "After the Victory, our next gig was at the Thunder Bay Motor Hotel, 900 miles away—two days later for two weeks at a biker bar. And the bikers would unplug our speakers on stage left. Two miserable weeks. And the train ran so many times a day about forty yards from our rooms. Our first two weeks away from home, and there was a ton of snow. It was a frozen fifty-six degrees in our rooms, and you slept with your hair dryer in the bed, so you could turn it on and let the hot air warm you up."[32]
ALEX: "We played at the Thunder Bay Motor Inn, and we did two weeks there. This was in late October, so it was cold. The owner put us in the very end of the motel, where the rooms were probably forty-two degrees Fahrenheit. And everywhere else in the place was empty, and he stuck us down there. And we would play, and he would come down and say, 'Hey boys, you want some drinks?' And we'd be like, 'Yeah that would be awesome. He's such a great guy, let's have some drinks.' 'Do you want something to eat?' And we had these meals. So, at the end of two weeks we went to get paid, and he gave us the list of everything we drank and

ate, and we left there with about forty dollars for two weeks."[33]

NOVEMBER 12–14, 1973
TORONTO, ONTARIO
LARRY'S HIDEAWAY, 121 Carlton Street
CAPACITY: 350 (approximate)

EARLY 1974
TORONTO, ONTARIO
SIR OLIVER MOWAT COLLEGIATE INSTITUTE, 5400 Lawrence Avenue East Built in 1969.
NOTES: Unconfirmed date, but strongly corroborated by fan account.

FEBRUARY 4–7, 1974
TORONTO, ONTARIO
LARRY'S HIDEAWAY, 121 Carlton Street
CAPACITY: 350 (approximate)
NOTES: The band's bar room performances were looser, edgier, and imbued with more frivolity than their later arena tours. The set lists varied and contained new originals as well as old favorites.

FEBRUARY 18, 1974
KINGSTON, ONTARIO
LA SALLE SECONDARY SCHOOL, 773 Route 15. Opened on September 6, 1966.
SUPPORT ACTS: Curtis Lee, Abraham
TICKETS: $3.00 / $3.50

1. Bill Banasiewicz. Interview with Alex Lifeson, December 1981.
2. Skip Daly. Interview with Jeff Jones, March 3, 2011.
3. Skip Daly. Interview with Lindy Young, June 29, 2012.
4. Bill Banasiewicz. Interview with Lindy Young, 1987.
5. Skip Daly. Interview with Ian Grandy, 2009.
6. Ian Grandy, May 1, 2014.
7. Skip Daly. Interview with Ian Grandy, 2012.
8. Skip Daly. Interview with Ian Grandy, November 15, 2016.
9. Bill Banasiewicz. Interview with Alex Lifeson, March 1985.
10. "'Rush' on stage in Stayner," Simcoe.com, March 17, 2011.
11. "'Rush' on stage in Stayner," Simcoe.com, March 17, 2011.
12. Interview with Hal Greenson, December 6, 2012.
13. "'Rush' on stage in Stayner," Simcoe.com, March 17, 2011.
14. Skip Daly. Interview with Ian Grandy, 2012.
15. Ian Grandy, Facebook.com, September 2015.
16. Skip Daly. Interview with Hal Greenson, December 6, 2012.
17. Skip Daly. Interview with Mike Bossi, February 12, 2015.
18. Skip Daly. Interview with Ian Grandy, May 19, 2016.
19. Skip Daly. Interview with Hal Greenson, December 6, 2012.
20. Ian Grandy, Facebook.com, April 27, 2017.
21. Skip Daly. Interview with Ian Grandy, May 19, 2016.
22. Skip Daly. Interview with Ian Grandy, May 5, 2016.
23. Skip Daly. Interview with Mike Bossi, February 12, 2015.
24. Interview with Roly Greenway, Jack Cool Radio, January 13, 2015.
25. Bill Banasiewicz. Interview with Alex Lifeson, March 1985.
26. Skip Daly. Interview with Mitch Bossi, December 10, 2012.
27. Skip Daly. Interview with Ian Grandy, November 15, 2016.
28. Interview with Geddy Lee, RollingStone.com, November 16, 2015.
29. Interview with Alex Lifeson, Teamrock.com, May 15, 2015.
30. Ian Grandy, Facebook.com, September 2, 2015.
31. Skip Daly. Interview with David Johansen, May 1, 2014.
32. Skip Daly. Interview with Ian Grandy, 2012.
33. Dave Bidini. Interview with Alex Lifeson, March 7, 2016.

Chapter 2

THE RUSH TOUR

In many ways, 1974 could be considered the birth of Rush. It was the year they landed a US-based booking at American Talent International, the year they signed a major-label recording contract with Mercury Records, and the year they released their self-titled debut album.

Most significantly, it was also the year that they solidified their long-term lineup, with John Rutsey exiting the band amicably and Neil Peart entering their world. Recalled Geddy about the auditions to replace John, "Neil was the third guy to come in, and I felt for the fourth guy having to follow Neil. Who'd want to be that guy? I felt so bad for him because he had written charts of the first album and he was sitting there playing while reading the charts and he was very polite and we had just experienced this whirlwind that was Neil."

Neil, amusingly, was less enamored of his own performance that day: "I could have played better and should have played better, but . . . they picked me."

Neil officially joined the band on July 29, 1974, and roughly two weeks later, on August 10, *Rush* was released on Mercury Records (it had been issued earlier that year on Canadian label Moon Records). Soon after, life as they knew it changed for the band, as they embarked on endless months of touring, usually as the support act for well-known artists like Blue Oyster Cult, Mountain, and Hawkwind. Thanks to Mercury, they also had plenty of new gear to take along on the ride, including a silver Slingerland drum kit for Neil and a black Rickenbacker 4001 bass for Geddy.

"We got an advance and went out and did some shopping at Long & McQuade," Alex recalled. "We went crazy saying, 'I'll take that guitar and those amps. He'll take those drums.' It's something you dream about for years and

RIGHT TOP: Marquee at the Whisky a Go Go.

RIGHT: Geddy's stage pass for the *Don Kirshner's Rock Concert* filming.

OPPOSITE: North Lansing, MI; Advertisement for Rush's first-ever United States appearance.

NORTHSIDE Concert

Dr. John
Liverpool
Skyhook · Rush
Cosmic Beam Experience
Max Bone
The British Are Here
I See The
Light Show

May 18·74

kosmic kowboy   **Northside Drive·In US 27, North Lansing, Mich.** 517·482·7409

years, and we actually got to do it. I bought a Marshall 50-watt amp and a '74 Les Paul Deluxe."

Beginning in September, Rush embarked on a slew of dates opening for Kiss. In October, they recorded segments for ABC's *In Concert* and *Don Kirshner's Rock Concert*, performing three songs—"Finding My Way," "In the Mood," and "Best I Can"—on the latter. "Over the past couple of months, everything has sort of exploded," Geddy said in a 1974 interview with the *Hamilton Spectator*. "The band's been around for about five years and nothing much happened. Now everything's happening at once."

The set list on this tour varied quite a bit, as the amount of performance time differed based on the circumstances of each show, and the band's material and personnel were in a state of transition. Once Neil joined, "Finding My Way" was typically the opening song, with

"In the Mood," "Working Man," "Need Some Love," and "What You're Doing" frequently featured. Headlining performances sometimes included the older songs "Fancy Dancer" and "Garden Road"—true rarities that never appeared on an album—in addition to the upbeat cover of "Bad Boy." As the trek progressed into the fall, the fruit of the trio's new writing partnership began to see stage time with the premiere of "Anthem" and "Fly by Night," as Rush began working on material for their second album—and first with Neil—focusing on expanding their sound.

Geddy, commenting on the band's sound, said, "A lot of bands with three men just look at it as, we're three men—there's only so much we can do. But you can't look at it like that. You've got three instruments, and there are a lot of notes on each instrument, and there are a lot of things that can be done."

TOP LEFT: Postcard from the band to their old friend Doc Cooper.

LEFT: Cleveland, OH; Geddy, Alex, and Neil in front of a mural advertisement.

ABOVE: Promotional photo for Gerry Fielding's band Yukon. Gerry is pictured on the far left.

OPPOSITE TOP LEFT: Neil.

OPPOSITE TOP RIGHT: Geddy.

OPPOSITE BOTTOM: Cleveland, OH; Doc Cooper's car in front of a mural advertisement as the band arrives for their second United States performance.

TOUR HISTORY

RUSH

MARCH 18–23, 1974
TORONTO, ONTARIO
THE PICCADILLY TUBE, 316 Yonge
Street at Dundas
NOTES: This series of dates marked the
release of the debut album on Moon
Records.
ATTENDANCE: Sold out
DOC COOPER: "Piccadilly Tube was
right across the street from Sam the
Record Man. When the first album came
out in March of 1974, we played there
for a week, and that's where they intro-
duced the record."[1]
TORONTO STAR: "Rush broke the all-
time attendance record at the Piccadilly
Tube in Toronto, March 18–23."

MARCH 24, 1974
ARKONA, ONTARIO
TAXANDRIA CO-OP, off Arkona Road

APRIL 5, 1974
TORONTO, ONTARIO
**GEORGES VANIER SECONDARY
SCHOOL**, 3000 Don Mills Road.
Founded in 1968.
NOTES: Alex and Geddy attended this
high school.

APRIL 6, 1974
ST. THOMAS, ONTARIO
PARKSIDE COLLEGIATE INSTITUTE, 241
Sunset Drive
OPENED FOR: Bearfoot
**TERRY DANKO (BEARFOOT SINGER,
GUITARIST):** "We did a few shows with
Rush along the way. They would do their
show and stand backstage to watch us,
and then disappear before we were off. I
never got to know them very well, how-
ever they did mention how they would
sneak into the Nickelodeon on Yonge
Street to watch us play and thanked us
for the inspiration. I always thought that
was cool. Great band."[2]

APRIL 8–11, 1974
NIAGARA FALLS, ONTARIO
SUNDOWNER MOTOR HOTEL, 8870
Lundy's Lane
CAPACITY: 500 (approximate)
NOTES: Over the years, the Sundowner
has become a legendary strip club.
IAN: "We had a riot in Niagara Falls
because you stayed in a funky apartment
right over the bar. . . . We were fairly big
on the bar circuit back then."

APRIL 12, 1974
TORONTO, ONTARIO
VICTORY BURLESQUE THEATRE,
287 Spadina Avenue.
OPENED FOR: Bloodrock
TICKETS: $3.85 CAD
NOTES: Two shows, at 7:00 p.m. and
10:00 p.m. This date is in SRO records
as "Niagara Falls," which could indicate
a last-minute change in the band's itinerary or a misprint in the documentation.
The venue was originally known as the
Standard Theatre, but in 1941 the name
was changed to the Victory Theatre in
anticipation of the Nazis' defeat.

**STEVIE HILL (BLOODROCK KEYBOARD-
IST):** "Not including festivals, we played
one show with Rush. The theater was
small, and I remember publicity photos
on our dressing room walls of burlesque
dancers. Rush played before us. I
watched the show from the wings. Their
band sounded very strong. I remember
Geddy Lee wearing a pink boa."

APRIL 13, 1974
NIAGARA FALLS, ONTARIO
SUNDOWNER MOTOR HOTEL, 8870
Lundy's Lane
CAPACITY: 500 (approximate)

APRIL 15–20, 1974
CORNWALL, ONTARIO
THE AARDVARK, 33 First Street East.
Venue opened April 15, 1974. First built
circa 1820.
TICKETS: $1.00 CAD
ATTENDANCE: 250 per show; sold out
RUSH'S FEE: $175 CAD per show
NOTES: SRO data indicates this run of
dates was at "Lafayette Hotel," however
the name was changed from Lafayette
Tavern to the Aardvark right before Rush
opened up the brand-new club owned by
Peter Gatien.
PETER GATIEN (CLUB OWNER): "I
bought a run-down country-and-western
tavern in Cornwall, transformed it into a
rock club over a weekend, with Rush as
my opening act. Cornwall was just a
small town, and this was a rare opportunity for folks there to see a powerful
band that was rising fast in an intimate
setting. I'll never forget the first show; it
was sold out, and Rush had all of this
gear, and at the end of their first song,
there was five seconds of complete
silence. The crowd was in utter awe. It
was magic! . . . Rush would have gone on
at nine and played at least two, probably
three sets a night. There were seventeen

rooms above the tavern where the band stayed, and everybody partied all week long. They got paid $1,000 for six nights (Monday through Saturday), which in those days was a lot of money, so they were on the upper echelon as far as salaries went. I remember Alex used to paint his fingernails in those days. They were really nice guys."[3]

ALEX: "In the past, if you were in the mood for a fight you went there [Lafayette Hotel]. But now the place is completely different. The two guys who run it and the kids that go there are just incredible. They really know how to appreciate a band. Cornwall is a hard rock town for sure."[4]

APRIL 21, 1974
TORONTO, ONTARIO
DON MILLS COLLEGIATE INSTITUTE, 15 The Donway East. Founded in 1959.

APRIL 22, 1974
TORONTO, ONTARIO
SIR OLIVER MOWAT COLLEGIATE INSTITUTE, 5400 Lawrence Avenue East. Built in 1969.

SPRING 1974
ST. CATHARINES, ONTARIO
LAURA SECORD SECONDARY SCHOOL, 349 Niagara Street. Founded in September 1966.
NOTES: This performance was filmed for the *Canadian Bandstand* program, broadcast on CKCO-TV. It is unknown whether the footage, released in 2014 as part of the *R40* set, represents the band's entire performance, but it is fascinating in that it contains two unreleased Rush originals from the early days and also reveals John Rutsey acting as front man. Although Alex remembers a song title as "The Loser," it is possible that this is actually the song "Losing Again," which was the first original Rush had ever composed (circa 1969–1970).
SET LIST (PARTIAL): "Need Some Love," "Before and After," "Best I Can," "I've Been Running," "Bad Boy," "The Loser," "Working Man," "In the Mood."
JOHN (ONSTAGE): "This is another tune of ours from our album. We're gonna do this one for everyone out there today. It's very nice to be here in St. Catharines. It's our first time here, and we hope to see you back many more times. This is a number of ours we're gonna do called 'Working Man.'"

RON ECKSTEIN (RUSH FAN): "I was there, and I think it was the springtime. Classes were cut short that day for the show to be produced. I remember the removal of some of the bolted-down theater seating to allow for the large TV cameras of the day. We had no idea the fame Rush would achieve. Beyond that my memory is foggy about the event other than the singer of Rush was unlike anyone I'd ever heard before."

MAY 3–4, 1974
TORONTO, ONTARIO
THE COLONIAL TAVERN, 201–203 Yonge Street

MAY 10, 1974
GRAVENHURST, ONTARIO
GRAVENHURST HIGH SCHOOL, 325 Mary Street. Founded in 1896. Gymnasium built in 1973.

MAY 11, 1974
NORTH BAY, ONTARIO
CHIPPEWA SECONDARY SCHOOL, 539 Chippewa Street West. Founded in 1958.

MAY 15, 1974
ALLISTON, ONTARIO
BANTING MEMORIAL HIGH SCHOOL, 203 Victoria Street East. Opened in 1951.

MAY 17, 1974
NORTH BAY, ONTARIO
MEMORIAL GARDENS, 100 Chippewa Street West. Venue opened on November 15, 1955.
CAPACITY: 4,025 for general admission concerts
NOTES: Recent renovations have increased the capacity.

MAY 18, 1974
EAST LANSING, MICHIGAN
NORTHSIDE DRIVE-IN, US Route 27. Opened on August 29, 1952.
WITH: The New York Dolls (last-minute replacement for Dr. John, who canceled), Liverpool, Skyhook, Cosmic Beam Experience, Max Bone, the British Are Here, I See the Light Show
TICKETS: $7.00
ATTENDANCE: Fewer than 3,000
NOTES: This was Rush's first performance in the United States. The local (Michigan State University) cable station filmed the show, which ran from noon until midnight. The taping was intended to produce a "Super Spectacular Rock Movie," but that never came to fruition. The drive-in featured three screens and a capacity for 800 cars. Over the course of the day, four youths were taken to local Sparrow Hospital for drug overdoses (mostly PCP). Nighttime temperatures dipped to fifty degrees, causing fans to ignite small fires throughout the grounds.
LANSING STATE JOURNAL: "Controversial Rock Concert Not Even Mini-Woodstock: The speakers and amplifiers on stage were stacked like skyscrapers, and out of them poured 12 solid hours of car-shattering rock music. The nine bands writhed and wailed in appropriate doses, to the freaked-out ecstasy of some and the obvious boredom of others."

DOC COOPER: "We drove all the way down from Toronto. I remember we got sick drinking that lousy American beer. I almost got fired from my job for taking all that time off. But it was fun."[5]

MARK MONDOL (VIDEOGRAPHER): "Dr. John did not show up (making for a rather ugly crowd at times), and the New York Dolls were the replacement act—not exactly an act the Lansing crowd 'got.'" [6]

MAY 19, 1974
PORT DOVER, ONTARIO
SUMMER GARDEN DANCE HALL, Walker Street at the Beach. Carousel-shaped venue, built in 1929.
WITH: Curtis Lee
TICKETS: $2.25 CAD
CAPACITY: 500 to 700
NOTES: Venue run by Mike McLoughlin, who frequently booked the band and eventually went on to manage their merchandising company, Showtech, with Mike's son Patrick running Showtech to this day.

PAT TOMPKINS (RUSH FAN): "We'd bring up a box of beer and suntan during the day, then go to see Rush at night. It was a small venue with no seating, and packed full at around 300 people. We knew they had talent but never imagined they'd get this big."[7]

MAY 20–25, 1974
TORONTO, ONTARIO
ABBEY ROAD PUB, 180 Queen Street West

MAY 27–31; JUNE 1, 1974
CORNWALL, ONTARIO
THE AARDVARK, 33 First Street East
TICKETS: $1.00 CAD
ATTENDANCE: 250 per show; sold out
RUSH'S FEE: $175 CAD per show
PETER GATIEN (CLUB OWNER): "About a month later we had Rush back for another week of shows, which was entirely sold out. Some of the magic from the first time had been lost, because the crowd was now used to big national acts playing in Cornwall."[8]
NOTES: Later in the '70s, club owner Peter Gatien opened a chain of successful disco clubs in America and England called Limelight.

JUNE 3–6, 1974
TORONTO, ONTARIO
LARRY'S HIDEAWAY, 121 Carlton Street
CAPACITY: 350 (approximate)
NOTES: SRO has this date as "Lafayette Hotel," but the Musicians' Pension Fund records indicate it as "Larry's Hideaway," and an advertisement corroborates this.

JUNE 7, 1974
PETROLIA, ONTARIO
PETROLIA ARENA, 4065 Dufferin Avenue. Venue opened in 1961.
CAPACITY: 1,100 (for ice hockey)

JUNE 8, 1974
MISSISSAUGA, ONTARIO
PORT CREDIT SECONDARY SCHOOL AUDITORIUM, 70 Mineola Road East. Founded in 1919. Moved to current location on May 13, 1963.
SUPPORT ACT: Max Webster
NOTES: This performance was professionally filmed.
COLIN TYLER (PROMOTER): "The concert was videotaped, but to no practical use, unfortunately. The band was aware of

the recording and wanted a copy afterward, all on the basis that its use would be noncommercial—only for our show. The Port Credit Secondary School Auditorium was darkened, the opening act Max Webster started to play, and then the special effects lighting crew lit up the stage with an array of brilliant lighting . . . all to the detriment of the basic cable cameras of the day! The video levels were up and down and, really, for the most part, very annoying to watch on our black-and-white monitors. I can't even remember if we were even able to use any of the video on the show the next Friday. Any old videotapes we had of our old show were apparently stored on planks in the rafters above the studio floor. Heat rose daily about them, they were not tape repacked, and I'm sure that the adjacent layer migration of magnetic particles all led to the demise of our recordings. When the cable TV studio moved somewhere along the line, word was they were all thrown out as useless!"[9]

JUNE 12, 1974
CANNINGTON, ONTARIO
BROCK DISTRICT HIGH SCHOOL, C1590, Regional Road 12. Founded in 1953.

JUNE 13, 1974
TORONTO, ONTARIO
GEORGE S. HENRY SECONDARY SCHOOL, 200 Graydon Hall Drive. Opened on December 6, 1965.

JUNE 14, 1974
ELLIOT LAKE, ONTARIO

JUNE 17–22, 1974
HAMILTON, ONTARIO
THE ROCKPILE AT DUFFY'S TAVERN, 59 King Street East. Structure built in 1870. Venue opened in 1940.
NOTES: "Dance to Rush." "Delicious Buffet 11:30 a.m. to 2:30 p.m." The Rockpile was a small bar in the basement of Duffy's Tavern.
IAN: "A fine place to get killed by one of the guys or laid by one of the girls—in that order."
ALEX: "I remember the dressing room was under the stairwell behind the coat rack, and there was that stupid support pole on the stage. I have very fond memories of those times, nineteen years old and having a riot."[10]

JUNE 24, 1974
TORONTO, ONTARIO
LARRY'S HIDEAWAY, 121 Carlton Street
CAPACITY: 350 (approximate)
NOTES: "Appearing One Day Only, Moon recording artists Rush."

JUNE 28, 1974
CLEVELAND, OHIO
ALLEN THEATRE, 1407 Euclid Avenue. Venue opened on April 1, 1921.
OPENED FOR: ZZ Top; Locomotiv GT opened the show.
TICKETS: $5.00 (advance) / $6.00 (day of)
ATTENDANCE: 3,003; sold out
NOTES: This was Rush's second US performance, their first in Cleveland, and it was booked based on airplay the band was getting on WMMS-FM. ZZ Top's crew ordered the lights turned up before Rush could return for an encore.
DONNA HALPER (WMMS-FM): "I showed the band around when they first arrived in Cleveland—just from Geddy's picture on the import album cover, people were calling out his name as he walked down the street. And when the band performed their first gig in Cleveland, people knew several of the songs and sang along. They were very nervous and very stiff on stage—who wouldn't have been—but Vic [Wilson] (who came with them on their first trip) and I stood at the back of the hall and Vic said to me, 'Don't worry, we won't let you down.' And they never have, to this day."[11]
***TELEGRAPH JOURNAL,* GEDDY:** "We opened for ZZ Top and were scheduled to play about forty minutes. Well, we played for one hour, and the kids were standing on the chairs and screaming. We earned an encore, but ZZ wouldn't let us back on."[12]
IAN: "The problem was the opening act, Locomotiv GT. They were supposed to play thirty minutes. They were finally kicked off the stage after forty-five minutes. The middle of three acts always gets screwed in a situation like that. Rush did very well and deserved an encore, but with the show running late, there was no way an encore was gonna happen. I understood what was going on and was not pissed about it. The story's grown over the years that ZZ fucked us over, but that is not true."[13]
JOHN: "One thing really surprised me. We were doing the gig with ZZ Top in

Cleveland, and a radio station down there picked up on the album and was playing it. We went to Cleveland and I'd introduce a song, and the crowd knew what the song was, and they'd start clapping and reacting before we even played, which was an unbelievable shock. Although it was a nice feeling, it was quite a surprise!"[14]

DOC COOPER: "I have a picture in front of a record store from the first time Rush played Cleveland, opening for ZZ Top, with my car (a '74 Nova SS—they called it the 'Coop mobile'), and the debut album cover painted on the whole wall."[15]

LIAM: "It was a big deal. In retrospect, it wasn't that big a gig. It was not a really big hall, but it was a big thrill. It was a whole new experience from the crew's point of view, because it was the first time we had encountered working with union stage hands, and Cleveland being one of the more strict cities as far as that went. It was an eye-opening experience."[16]

***CLEVELAND SCENE* MAGAZINE:** "The only bad thing about them was their vocals. The bass player did most of the singing, which he forced out in a shrill, girlish sounding voice."

JULY 1, 1974
TORONTO, ONTARIO
MINKLER AUDITORIUM, Seneca College campus, 1750 Finch Avenue East. Venue opened in July 1970.
OPENED FOR: Nazareth
TICKETS: $4.40 / $5.50 CAD
CAPACITY: 1,111
CHUM-FM: "Rush did a fine job starting things off. They've gotten exceptionally tight, and I was impressed by the lead work from Alex Lifeson. I imagine in six months to a year we'll probably see them in the Gardens."

Colonial Tavern (203 Yonge; 363-6168), July 1-6: Rush — a band that's very heavy with myopic 14-year-olds who fantasize about their big brothers wearing funny clothes. Is the Colonial wooing the wee-wee-boppers? Goo only knows.

JULY 2–6, 1974
TORONTO, ONTARIO
THE COLONIAL TAVERN, 201–203 Yonge Street

JULY 12, 1974
ST. CATHARINES, ONTARIO
GARDEN CITY ARENA, 8 Gale Crescent Street. Venue opened on December 20, 1938.
OPENED FOR: Mahogany Rush; Bullrush opened the show.
TICKETS: $3.25 (advance) / $3.75 (at the door) CAD
ATTENDANCE: Fewer than 1,000
CAPACITY: 3,046, for ice hockey
NOTES: Bullrush was a hard rock band from St. Catharines that includes former JR Flood members Paul Dickinson on guitar and Bob Morrison on keyboards. Rounding out the group are Brian Gagnon on bass and vocals and Glen Gratto on drums. Neil would later recall seeing advertisements for this concert with his former JR Flood bandmates, though he did not attend.
***ST. CATHARINES STANDARD*:** "According to those who listened, Rush fell short of grabbing anyone's attention for long. Pre-concert publicity billed their style of rock, heavy and loud but 'very tight.' The audience obviously didn't think so."

JULY 13, 1974
SARNIA, ONTARIO
SARNIA ARENA, 134 Brock Street South. Venue opened in 1948.
OPENED FOR: Mahogany Rush; Bullrush opened the show.
TICKETS: $3.25 (advance) / $3.75 (at the door) CAD
CAPACITY: 2,302

JULY 15, 1974
BRAMALEA, ONTARIO
LESTER B. PEARSON THEATRE, BRAMALEA CIVIC CENTRE, 150 Central Park Drive. Venue opened in 1972.
OPENED FOR: Mahogany Rush; Bullrush opened the show.
TICKETS: $3.25 (advance) / $3.75 (at the door) CAD
CAPACITY: 462
NOTES: A few years later, Mahogany Rush changed their name to Frank Marino and Mahogany Rush to avoid any confusion with the other Canadian hard-rock trio, Rush. According to Frank Marino, "The confusion was usually to the disadvantage of Mahogany Rush."[17]

JULY 18, 1974
HAMILTON, ONTARIO
HAMILTON FORUM, Barton Street between Sanford Avenue and Wentworth Streets. Venue opened on October 1, 1953.
OPENED FOR: Mahogany Rush; Bullrush opened the show.
TICKETS: $3.25 (advance) / $3.75 (at the door) CAD

HABB PRODUCTIONS PRESENTS
IN CONCERT
Mahogany Rush
CANADA'S HEAVIEST ROCK SHOW
WITH **Rush** AND **Bull Rush**
THURS. JULY 18 7 P.M.
HAMILTON FORUM
Tickets $3.25 in advance $3.75 at the door. Tickets available at Connaught Ticket Agency

---

JULY 19, 1974
CORNWALL, ONTARIO
CORNWALL COMMUNITY ARENA, 229 Water Street East. Venue opened in 1936.
OPENED FOR: Mahogany Rush; Bullrush opened the show.
TICKETS: $3.25 (advance) / $3.75 (at the door) CAD
CAPACITY: 1,500
NOTES: Aka Water Street Arena
GLEN GRATTO
(DRUMMER FOR BULLRUSH):
"The last gig on that tour was Cornwall Arena. We finished that show and both bands—Bullrush and Rush—went to a hotel that we both played at on the circuit. So the bar owner knew both bands. There was a band playing there by the name Mara Loves. It was like a show band, and they had two female front singers. One girl had a ring in her nose, which was very controversial back then. Well, the bar owner at this place kept sending over trays of tequila to our table. This got really messy. John Rutsey, God rest his soul, had a crush on the one female singer. OK, now we're consuming a lot of tequila—it's the wind-down from the tour, so we're relaxing. Rutsey is just hammered. Now he wants to approach this girl on the break. So we're saying,

'You know what, man, you can barely walk, I wouldn't go over there,' because we thought he might fall down. John gets up from the table and she was sitting behind the PA stack. And John goes over to introduce himself, and he threw up all over her feet! So he made a great impression! John was a great guy."[18]

JULY 20, 1974
OTTAWA, ONTARIO

OTTAWA CIVIC CENTRE, Lansdowne Park, 1015 Bank Street. Venue opened on December 29, 1967.
OPENED FOR: Mahogany Rush; Bullrush opened the show.
TICKETS: $3.25 (advance) / $3.75 (at the door) CAD
CAPACITY: 9,349
NOTES: This date is in SRO's records (albeit with no attendance data), and advertisements for the concert were published in the July 18 and 19 *Ottawa Citizen*, but a poster for the gig states that it was canceled, with Glen Gratto corroborating the cancellation.

JULY 21, 1974
PORT DOVER, ONTARIO

SUMMER GARDEN, Walker Street at the Beach
CAPACITY: 500 to 700

JULY 22–23, 1974
PAIN COURT, ONTARIO

DOVER HOTEL, on Winterline Road
CAPACITY: 350 (approximate)
NOTES: Rush performed at a strip club adjacent to the hotel. July 23 was their final headline show with John on drums.

JULY 25, 1974
LONDON, ONTARIO

CENTENNIAL HALL, 550 Wellington Street. Venue opened on June 21, 1967.
OPENED FOR: Kiss
TICKETS: $3.50 (advance) / $4.50 (at the door) CAD
CAPACITY: 1,637
NOTES: This gig marked the first time that Kiss and Rush shared a bill and was John Rutsey's last performance with Rush. At some point after parting ways with Alex and Geddy, John would go on to rehearse with a band called Stinger[19], but it's uncertain how long this went on or whether this new project even made it to the stage.

MICK CAMPISE (KISS ROAD CREW): "It was this one-off gig that had to be done for some reason. We blew out the PA during the first song. The whole show was a disaster."

PETER ORECKINTO (KISS ROAD CREW): "They had these old A4 Altec-Lansing speakers that were designed to show movies. What a piece-of-shit sound system; you couldn't hear anything."[20]

NICK PANASEIKO (PROMOTER): "Ronny Legg, the MC of the show, was a DJ from CJOM-FM in Windsor, Ontario. And he helped discover Kiss and put them on the map in Detroit. As promoter, I brought Kiss into Canada for one of their first major concerts. Rush impressed Kiss so much at this concert that they went on to tour as the opener, giving them their first major break in many US cities."[21]

JULY 26, 1974
ACTON, ONTARIO

M. Z. BENNETT PUBLIC SCHOOL, 69 Acton Boulevard. Built in 1954.
TICKETS: $2.00 CAD
NOTES: This summer dance performance would have marked John Rutsey's final date with Rush, but, based on Ian's recollections (and despite a poster and an advertisement for the show), it was canceled.

JULY 28, 1974
AJAX, ONTARIO

NOTES: Geddy and Alex audition drummers.
GEDDY: "We tried to poach Max Webster's drummer and he'd said yes, and then a few days later he said no. So that's why we had the auditions."[22]

IAN: "We were set up at a rehearsal place. The first guy was nowhere. The second guy was Gerry Fielding. They liked him, but I think all of us knew he wasn't good enough. Then this guy Neil shows up. Geddy looks at me and says, 'He's a greaseball,' because Neil had what came to be called his 'submariner' hair style. . . . Neil had this small funky gray drum kit and set it up himself. They proceeded to jam for about forty minutes, and I recorded it as best I could with three microphones. After that, Geddy asked me, 'Was this guy as good as we think he is?' And I couldn't do anything but agree because I don't think I had ever seen or heard anyone play like he did."[23]

DOC COOPER: "When he came in he looked like . . . a skinny geek. And then he just started pounding the drums. He always talked to me. He was always very nice to me, considering I was someone he never knew from the earlier years."[24]

AUGUST 14, 1974
PITTSBURGH, PENNSYLVANIA

CIVIC ARENA, 300 Auditorium Place. Venue opened on September 17, 1961.
OPENED FOR: Uriah Heep, Manfred Mann's Earth Band
TICKETS: $4.50 / $5.50 / $6.50
ATTENDANCE: 11,642
NOTES: Neil Peart's first performance with Rush. It was also Howard Ungerleider's first date with the band as tour manager. Geddy took a ceremonial shot of Southern Comfort before going onstage and it went "straight to his head." After the long, droning, "A Clockwork Orange" intro tape, the MC's voice shouted out, "From Toronto, Canada . . . Mercury recording artists . . . Let's have a warm welcome for Rush!" Alex would later recall that Howard left the band's pay from this gig on the roof of the car: "We were at a red light and somebody said, 'Hey, you have something on your roof.' He got out. It was in like one of those money bags. Fortunately, it didn't blow away. Otherwise we wouldn't have been able to stay at the crappy Holiday Inn we were staying at, all in the same room."
SET LIST: "Finding My Way," "In the Mood," "Bad Boy," "Working Man" (with drum solo).

VALLEY NEWS DISPATCH: "A Canadian trio, Rush, rocked in the preliminary. Manfred Mann gave an inspired set. So good was it, in fact, they could have been the featured attraction and satisfied the near-capacity audience. Flashing holiday lights accentuated a blue curtain backdrop on which Uriah Heep's name and 'Wonderworld,' were emblazoned. Heep came on, and the first three rows of the floor's center section stood for practically the entire performance. This necessitated thousands of patrons behind those rows to stand to be able to see. Next time the joker in front of you blocks your view, remind him that $6 is a lot of money to pay for standing-room-only."

PITTSBURGH PRESS: "Pittsburgh likes heavy, slam-bang rock. That's all that

Rush, a promising Canadian trio, offered ('Working Man' was its best song). What it plays is loud, crashing rock and boogie, nothing subtle, nothing cutesy, a lot of racket for just three men."

GEDDY: "We were very bubbly, but very nervous as the people were filing in. We'd never been in a big hall before. The equipment didn't have cases. We just pulled in and set up. It was such a short set—I think we played twenty-six minutes—I don't think we noticed what was going on. It was a pretty awesome experience for a young Canadian musician. It was a panic set. We were just trying to remember all the parts. We just played our songs, and bang, we were off. It was all finished, and we were pleased with ourselves that we could put the set together in two weeks. It was good to have the first one under our belt. We all had aspirations and dreams of being successful and making a lot of records. At that point, it was so unreal I don't think we could see past the tour. It was really just for the moment."[25]

NEIL: "I would never forget standing on the floor beside stage left while Uriah Heep played 'Stealin.' The big dark building, colored lights on the heroic figures up on the stage, the roaring audience, the sheer electricity in that place. Halfway through their show, the retractable dome of the Civic Arena had peeled back, open to the summer night."[26]

AUGUST 15, 1974
CLEVELAND, OHIO
PUBLIC HALL, 500 Lakeside Avenue. Historic venue opened on April 15, 1922.
OPENED FOR: Uriah Heep, Manfred Mann's Earth Band
TICKETS: $5.50 (advance) / $6.50 (day of)
CAPACITY: 7,200

AUGUST 16, 1974
CINCINNATI, OHIO
CINCINNATI GARDENS, 2250 Seymour Avenue. Venue opened on February 22, 1949.
OPENED FOR: Uriah Heep, Manfred Mann's Earth Band
TICKETS: $5.00 (advance) / $6.00 (day of), general admission
CAPACITY: 11,438
CINCINNATI ENQUIRER, **GEDDY:** "This is the fourth day of our first American

tour, so we're still sort of settling into things. Mercury has sort of swept us off our feet lately. It's strange hearing the album they've released. We did it almost two years ago, and although I'm pleased with it, it's sort of old to me. I see it from a different standpoint."

AUGUST 17, 1974
CHARLESTON, WEST VIRGINIA
CHARLESTON CIVIC CENTER ARENA, Reynolds Street. Venue dedicated on January 25, 1959.
OPENED FOR: Uriah Heep, Manfred Mann's Earth Band
TICKETS: $6.00
CAPACITY: 8,400
NOTES: Prior to Rush's first US tour, this date was originally scheduled for Bowmanville, Ontario, with Max Webster at Four Corners (complete with Fireworks). After pop success in his namesake's band during the British invasion of the '60s, Manfred Mann formed a progressive hard rock unit called Manfred Mann's Earth Band. At this point in 1974, they were touring in support of their fifth album, *The Good Earth*, with a lineup that included Manfred Mann on keyboards and vocals, Mick Rogers on guitar and vocals, Chris Slade on drums, and Colin Pattenden on bass. Their set list featured prog interpretations of Bob Dylan's "Father of Day, Father of Night" and "Quinn the Eskimo (The Mighty Quinn)." The latter was a top ten single in 1968 by the band Manfred Mann.

AUGUST 19, 1974
WASHINGTON, DC
WDCA-TV (CHANNEL 20) STUDIOS, River Road. *Barry Richards Rock and Soul* television taping.
NOTES: This was supposed to be a "live" television performance, but Neil refused to air drum, so it ended up being just a short interview. This was a precursor of things to come—the band would never compromise their musical integrity for anything or anyone. During the 2010 Winter Olympics in Vancouver, it was rumored that Rush would perform at the closing ceremonies, which had to be lip-synched for worldwide broadcast. In the end, the band chose not to take part.
IAN: "I remember driving five hundred miles to DC, and we did not play that day. We guested on some local show,

and Neil flat out refused to air drum. They wanted the band to lip-synch and Neil to fake the drumming, and he just came up to me and said, 'Ian, don't set up my kit,' and that was that. He was just not going to do it. So the ultracool host asked Geddy one question: 'Hey, what's it been like playing with Uriah Heep?' to which Geddy replied, 'It's been great'—and that was the whole thing. Neil was always open and honest with those of us inside his 'inner circle.' I think he just got burned too many times, especially at the beginning, by promoters and management putting him in promotional situations he felt extremely uncomfortable in. His eventual reaction was to withdraw from these things."[27]

AUGUST 20, 1974
PITTSBURGH, PENNSYLVANIA
STANLEY THEATRE, 719 Liberty Avenue. Venue opened on February 27, 1928.
OPENED FOR: Blue Oyster Cult, Climax Blues Band
TICKETS: $6.50
ATTENDANCE: 3,400+
CAPACITY: 3,800
NOTES: Dave Scace's first gig as a roadie for Rush. The venue air-conditioning was on the blink, resulting in a sweltering building, with hot, anxious fans forced to endure long waits in between bands.
SET LIST: "Finding My Way," "Working Man."
LIAM: "We did one show in Pittsburgh where I think the band played four songs, and that was their set. It was very limiting. There wasn't any time at shows for them to try anything out. We were lucky if we got a sound check. Most of the time we wouldn't. We'd be low man on the pole, so Rush was only allotted a few minutes. Even as the doors were opening we'd still be setting our gear up, maybe even just getting it onstage."[28]
VALLEY NEWS DISPATCH: "A last minute warmup act, Rush was added to the bill. The between-set delays that resulted were inevitable. Musically, it was a fine show. Rush, which was in town only last week with Uriah Heep, are good rockers, though their set was limited to twenty minutes."
PITTSBURGH TIMES: "Someone from their label told me 'I've got a new band from Toronto, and I need you to put them on your show,'" longtime concert

promoter Rich Engler said. "But I was like, 'Aw, man, I already have a good support act.' But he was like, 'Please, please put them on your show, I only want a half hour, and they'll be really happy.'" Engler reluctantly agreed and increasingly regretted that decision as the minutes ticked away, and Rush still hadn't shown up to the venue. "Finally, at like 7:15 for a 7:30 p.m. show, this kid comes running up to me out of breath and says, 'Hey, I'm Geddy Lee, of Rush, and we're here to play.' He said their van had broken down," Engler recalled. "I told him, 'I don't know, it's pretty late,' but Geddy said, 'Yes, but we're just a three-piece band, and we can set up fast.'" Engler said OK, but they could play just one song. Lee successfully lobbied for two. The band ended up playing two-and-a-half, "and they were so grateful that they got to play them. I brought them back two or three more times to the Stanley, and by then people were loving them."

AUGUST 21, 1974
ST. LOUIS, MISSOURI
KHORASSAN BALLROOM, CHASE PARK PLAZA HOTEL, 212–232 North King Highway Boulevard. Historic venue built in 1929.
CAPACITY: 2,500
NOTES: Rush's first headlining gig with Neil on drums. Before the show, the band met Mercury's radio promotion rep Cliff Burnstein for the first time, as he picked Geddy up to do an on-air interview at KSHE-FM (while Alex, Neil, and the crew listened from the hotel). Band and crew enjoyed a riotous party after the concert.

AUGUST 23, 1974
ST. LOUIS, MISSOURI
AMBASSADOR THEATRE, 411 North Seventh Street. Venue opened in 1926.
OPENED FOR: Climax Blues Band, Premiata Forneria Marconi (PFM)
CAPACITY: 3,000
NOTES: PFM was a progressive rock band from Italy. Alex, Geddy, and Neil wrote "Making Memories" in their rental car the next day (August 24), while Howard was unknowingly driving in the wrong direction, away from the next gig in Cleveland.

AUGUST 24, 1974
BALA, ONTARIO
KEE TO BALA, 1012 Bala Falls Road. Venue opened summer, 1942.
OPENED FOR: Crowbar and Greaseball Boogie Band
TICKETS: $3.25 CAD
CAPACITY: 700
NOTES: "Dancing 9–1." Though an ad exists for this show, Rush's appearance was almost certainly canceled in order to remain focused on the US dates (and avoid significant travel time from the previous night's gig in St. Louis).

AUGUST 26, 1974
CLEVELAND, OHIO
THE AGORA BALLROOM, 1730 East 24th Street
SUPPORT ACT: Reign
TICKETS: $3.00 (advance) / $3.50 (at the door)
ATTENDANCE: 700; sold out
NOTES: Recorded and broadcast as part of the WMMS *Live from the Agora* concert series. Performances were recorded on a Monday night and were broadcast on that Wednesday.
SET LIST: "Finding My Way," "Best I Can," "Need Some Love," "In the End," "Fancy Dancer," "In the Mood," "Bad Boy," "Here Again," "Working Man" (with drum solo), "What You're Doing," and "Garden Road."
GEDDY: "The album just went—whoosh—up to number one in Cleveland. And the last time we went there, we played a huge club, and it was incredible; we sold out in just a couple of days."[29]
IAN: "We finally got our first (bright yellow) flight cases. We packed them for the first time in the Agora's parking lot, at 2:00 a.m. The next morning, we had a 7:00 a.m. flight to Minneapolis, and we were onstage there by 1:00 p.m."[30]
***CLEVELAND SCENE* MAGAZINE:** "As for the rest of the Canadian trio, I was most impressed with drummer John Rutsey [Ed.: Neil Peart]. Though not an especially inventive drummer (they never are in this type of band), he did keep a strong undercurrent going, and was able to insert a few nice fills here and there."

AUGUST 27, 1974
NORTH ST. PAUL, MINNESOTA
MINNESOTA STATE FAIR, 1265 Snelling Avenue North. Young America Youth Expo '74.
OPENED FOR: Freddie King, Renaissance, and Isis
TICKETS: $1.00 for access to Youth Expo '74, after paying $1.50 (including parking) to gain access to the state fairgrounds
ATTENDANCE: 108,551 (entire state fair on this date, general admission)
NOTES: Alex's twenty-first birthday, with Rush performing at 1:30 p.m. The Minnesota State Fair included Youth Expo '74, a place where teenagers "can go and do their thing away from everyone else," according to one official. This was a separate area inside the fairgrounds, where teens paid $1.00 for weekday rock concerts by up-and-coming bands. No beer permitted. Renaissance was originally formed by ex-Yardbirds Keith Relf and Jim McCarty in 1969. The group went through a number of sonic and personnel changes before settling on a symphonic-progressive sound led by Annie Haslam on lead vocals.

AUGUST 28, 1974
NORTH ST. PAUL, MINNESOTA
MINNESOTA STATE FAIR, 1265 Snelling Avenue North. Young America Youth Expo '74.
OPENED FOR: Freddie King, Isis, and Heartsfield
TICKETS: $1.00 for access to Youth Expo '74, after paying $1.50 (including parking) to gain access to the state fairgrounds
ATTENDANCE: 113,969 (entire state fair on this date, general admission)
NOTES: Neil was in his element, as it was Farm Equipment Day at the fair. Rush performed at 1:30 p.m. Blues legend Freddie King, known as one of the three kings of electric blues guitar, along with Albert King and B. B. King, also performed. His unique hybrid of Texas and Chicago blues was a major influence on the fretwork of Eric Clapton, Jeff Beck, and Stevie Ray Vaughan among others. In Minnesota, Freddie King was touring in support of his fourteenth album, *Burglar*, which features guest appearances by Eric Clapton and Brian Auger.

AUGUST 29, 1974
ASBURY PARK, NEW JERSEY
CASINO ARENA, 700 Ocean Avenue.
Venue built in 1930.
OPENED FOR: Mountain
TICKETS: $5.00 (advance) / $6.00 (at the door)
ATTENDANCE: 4,500; sold out
NOTES: During the summer of '74, the Casino Arena reopened for the first time since fire gutted the building eight years before. The first show at the rehabilitated venue was by King Crimson, who recorded their *USA* live album, which included a new song titled "Asbury Park."
ROADSHOW NEIL: "My only experience of the Jersey Shore was a 1974 show at a waterfront ballroom in Asbury Park, opening for the band Mountain—aptly named after their massive guitarist, Leslie West. During their set, Howard assembled the contents of our deli tray into one giant sandwich and left it in Mountain's dressing room."
CORKY LAING
(DRUMMER FOR MOUNTAIN):
"That gig was right on the boardwalk in an old casino building. It wasn't a pretty place, which is why they had rock concerts there. That concert was during Mountain's last tour, which was a good era for the band, and it was a sold-out show. It seemed as though Neil was having a good time playing that night, and Rush was a great live band, even back then. Rush has done a great job over the years, and you've got to hand it to them. That's the Canadian in them coming out. There's a chemistry that's more prevalent in Canada, where you stick together, no matter what. Rush is a real Canadian band, which is more like a family."[31]

AUGUST 30, 1974
PARSIPPANY, NEW JERSEY
JOINT IN THE WOODS, 400 Smith Road
OPENED FOR: Hudson Ford
CAPACITY: 1,500
NOTES: Two shows: 10:00 p.m. and 11:30 p.m. The "Joint" was literally in the woods, down a dirt road, on the former Mazdabrook Farm off of Smith Road. Richard Hudson and John Ford left the UK prog band Strawbs in 1973. Here, they were touring in support of their second A&M release, *Free Spirit*.

NEW YORK DAILY NEWS: "Rush are an energetic trio in the heavy metal genre, which means smashing your musical points home at full volume. They were pleased to be playing Parsippany, feeling it's another step in the right direction."
BILLBOARD: "If fault is to be found with Rush, it is with its failure to compensate for the inherent limitations of the basic three-man lineup, but their sheer brazenness and ability to do what they are doing well, without compromise proved to be their calling card, a commendable quality which should not be overlooked."
CASH BOX: "Alex Lifeson is very fast and clean and might just be able to trade some riffs with Jimmy Page. The drummer, John Rutsey [Ed.: Neil Peart] is a driving musician, and together this talented trio of hard-driving rock and rollers make some direct straightforward music. The set was highlighted by their soon-to-be-released single 'Finding My Way.'"

AUGUST 31, 1974
BALA, ONTARIO
KEE TO BALA, 1012 Bala Falls Road. Venue opened summer, 1942.
TICKETS: $3.00 CAD
CAPACITY: 700
NOTES: Based on a dated photo, Rush did a daytime taping in Toronto for the new television show *Boogie* before performing this nearby gig. Alex, Geddy, and Neil were interviewed by CHUM-FM DJ Brian Master. The program aired the following month on CITY-TV in Canada.

SEPTEMBER 1, 1974
MINDEN, ONTARIO
MINDEN ARENA, 55 Parkside Crescent. Venue opened in 1972.
CAPACITY: 700 (floor)

SEPTEMBER 2, 1974
CHESTERLAND, OHIO
PINEWAY TRAILS PARK FESTIVAL IN MUNSON TOWNSHIP, Wilson Mills Road, east of Route 306
OPENED FOR: Rainbow Canyon, East Wind, and Sweetleaf
TICKETS: $7.50 (advance) / $8.50 (day of)
ATTENDANCE: 2,200
NOTES: Rare Earth had been scheduled to perform, but they missed a connecting flight in Los Angeles and arrived too late to take the stage. *The Scene* magazine held a

promotion where the first twenty-five callers got a copy of Rush's debut album.
THE PLAIN DEALER: "Rush singer Geddy Lee, with the long, stringy hair and flimsy blouse, sang his heart out for the crowd."

SEPTEMBER 6, 1974
DETROIT, MICHIGAN
MICHIGAN PALACE, 238 Bagley Street. Building opened on August 23, 1926.
OPENED FOR: Hawkwind
TICKETS: $4.50 (advance) / $5.00 (at the door)
ATTENDANCE: 4,651+

SEPTEMBER 11, 1974
TORONTO, ONTARIO
MINKLER AUDITORIUM, Seneca College campus, 1750 Finch Avenue East
CAPACITY: 1,111
NOTES: Venue unconfirmed. This performance is recorded for the *King Biscuit Flower Hour*.

SEPTEMBER 13, 1974
CATONSVILLE, MARYLAND
UNIVERSITY OF MARYLAND, BALTIMORE COUNTY, GYM II, 1000 Hilltop Circle. Venue built in 1972.
OPENED FOR: Sha Na Na
TICKETS: $6.00
CAPACITY: 1,200 (approximate)
NOTES: Rush was booed off of the stage. Ironically, the guys in Sha Na Na (who took their name from the doo-wop introduction to the 1957 hit "Get a Job" by the Silhouettes) have vast experience in odd musical pairings, having opened for the Grateful Dead and Frank Zappa among others. Sha Na Na's eighth gig as a band saw them preceding Jimi Hendrix at Woodstock. "We went to cash the $350 check from Woodstock," says drummer John 'Jocko' Marcellino, "and it bounced! Back in those days, if there was an audience, you played the gig."
IAN: "The truck got a flat on the New York State Thruway, and then we got lost in downtown (scary) Baltimore. I think there were two campuses for the college, and we went to the downtown one, not knowing any better. It turned out the correct campus was on some sort of beltway. Anyway, Rush was roundly booed by a drunk college crowd dressed up as greasers—this was the only time I ever saw the band booed off stage. What promoter thought Rush and Sha Na Na was

a good match? Bowzer from Sha Na Na watched the boys play and came to the dressing room and told them that, although it obviously wasn't our audience, he thought they were a damned good band. The agent that booked that should have been shot!"[32]

HOWARD: "The agents in New York just packaged things up based on availability. They don't care about genres of music. It didn't work very well. The Sha Na Na audience didn't tolerate Rush. They were booing and throwing things. It was ugly."[33]

ALEX: "Just before the show we came out to sort of peek around to look at the audience before the doors opened, and we saw that the girls were dressed in little white socks and long skirts and all the guys had greaser hairdos. It turned out to be one of these '50s sock hop things. We went on and were wearing satin pants and big high boots. And we started with 'Finding My Way' from the first record. They just sort of stood there and stared at us. Then by the second song they started to rumble. By the fourth song it was 'BOOOOO. Get out of here! Get off!' So of course we turned everything up a little bit and continued to play. Then finally the promoter said, 'Thanks guys. You're done.' But they were nasty. They were really pissed off. I'm sure if we would have kept going they would have thrown their greasy combs at us."[34]

NEIL: "I always thought that Rush opening for Sha Na Na was one of the worst matchups in history—until five years later, when Blondie opened for us [*laughs*]. Bad choice."[35]

SCREAMIN' SCOTT SIMON (SHA NA NA KEYBOARDIST): "We were a ten-man group probably performing at a 90-decibel sound level, and here's this trio of Canadians playing at about 120 decibels. Our audiences weren't that interested in loud instrumental music with a super-loud lead vocal, rather preferring the almost a cappella, vocally oriented music that we did. Rush certainly had plenty of attitude, and they kept true to their music, but it just wasn't what an audience paying to see us expected or welcomed. Glad they went on to find their audience. . . . I blame the promoter who paired us for their lukewarm reception."[36]

JOHN "JOCKO" MARCELLINO (SHA NA NA DRUMMER): "Even though it didn't

really work out that night for Rush, it was a good opportunity for them to get their music in front of an audience. If the tables were turned, we would be booed off of the stage. Maybe someday we can open for Rush?"[37]

UNIVERSITY OF MARYLAND NEWSPAPER: "(Sha Na Na) saxophonist Lennie Baker interrupted his concert preparations to wander backstage. A few minutes later, his 250 or so pounds waddled back into the dressing room. 'What's the name of that group?' 'Rush—they're from Canada.' 'Well they oughta go back there. Christ, Grand Funk isn't that loud.'"

SEPTEMBER 15, 1974
LOCK HAVEN, PENNSYLVANIA
LOCK HAVEN UNIVERSITY, Thomas Fieldhouse, 401 North Fairview Street. Venue built in 1935.
OPENED FOR: Blue Oyster Cult, Kiss
TICKETS: $5.50 (students with ID) / $6.00 (guests) / $6.00 (all tickets at the door), general admission
ATTENDANCE: 2,000
CAPACITY: 2,500
NOTES: Officially formed in New York City during January 1973, Kiss put on their makeup and set out to conquer the world. At this point, Gene Simmons, Paul Stanley, Ace Frehley, and Peter Criss were touring in support of their self-titled debut album, with a set list that featured "Deuce," "Strutter," "Black Diamond," and "Firehouse." "Gene Simmons's concoction of blood underwent a few changes until it was perfected," according to the Kiss Vault. "The original blend of flour, water, and red dye plugged up Gene's throat and forced Paul to cover Gene's songs for the rest of the concert in Toronto. His second attempt, using bacon grease and corn syrup, looked so disgusting that the other members began vomiting onstage (which Lock Haven fans assumed was part of the act). His third attempt, using red-dyed flour, eggs, baking soda, vegetable oil, and milk, has worked well ever since."[38]

SEPTEMBER 16, 1974
WILKES-BARRE, PENNSYLVANIA
PARAMOUNT THEATRE, 71 Public Square. Historic venue opened on August 18, 1938.
OPENED FOR: Blue Oyster Cult, Kiss
TICKETS: $6.00 (advance) / $6.50 (at the door)
ATTENDANCE: 2,000; sold out

SEPTEMBER 18, 1974
ATLANTA, GEORGIA
ALEX COOLEY'S ELECTRIC BALLROOM, corner of Peachtree Street Northeast and Ponce de Leon Avenue. Venue opened on March 13, 1974.
OPENED FOR: Kiss, Fat Chance
ATTENDANCE: 1,100
NOTES: Alex Cooley held concerts in the Electric Ballroom from March 1974 until 1976, when he moved on to larger venues. The ballroom was located in the Ponce building at Atlanta's busiest intersection. Although the official capacity of the ballroom was 1,100, that would swell to as many as 2,000 "depending on who was watching,"[39] laughs the famed promoter.

SEPTEMBER 19–20, 1974
ATLANTA, GEORGIA
ALEX COOLEY'S ELECTRIC BALLROOM, corner of Peachtree Street Northeast and Ponce de Leon Avenue
OPENED FOR: Kiss, Fat Chance
ATTENDANCE: 1,100 per show

SEPTEMBER 21, 1974
ST. PETERSBURG, FLORIDA
PAPA'S DREAM, Central Avenue and 19th Street. Venue opened on September 20, 1974.
WITH: The Papa's Dream Band
TICKETS: $3.50

SEPTEMBER 22, 1974
ORLANDO, FLORIDA
ORLANDO MUNICIPAL AUDITORIUM, 401 West Livingston Street. Venue opened on February 21, 1927.
OPENED FOR: The Marshall Tucker Band, Elvin Bishop Group
TICKETS: $5.00 (advance) / $6.00 (at the door)
CAPACITY: 3,250
SET LIST: "Finding My Way," "In the Mood," "Bad Boy," "Best I Can," "Working Man" (with drum solo).
ORLANDO SENTINEL: "The 'Southern Music' evening will also introduce Rush, a new group."

SEPTEMBER 23, 1974
GAINESVILLE, FLORIDA
GREAT SOUTHERN MUSIC HALL, 233 West University Avenue. Venue opened on March 29, 1974.
AN EVENING WITH RUSH

CAPACITY: 800
NOTES: Two shows, 8:30 p.m. and 11:00 p.m. Venue originally opened as the Florida Theater on September 10, 1928.

SEPTEMBER 24, 1974
NORTHAMPTON, PENNSYLVANIA
ROXY THEATER, 2004 Main Street. Venue first opened on February 1, 1921.
OPENED FOR: Elf
TICKETS: $2.50
CAPACITY: 650
NOTES: Elf was a hard rock band from Cortland, New York, led by Ronnie James Dio on lead vocals. During the day, the band and the crew flew to New York City and then drove to Northampton. The band was late to arrive, delaying the show.
IAN: "Dave Scace and I were by ourselves. By the time we paid cash to rent a truck in New York and paid our freight charges, we had no money left. It was a one-dollar toll to get across the bridge, and we didn't have it. Scace found a pack of cigarettes in the truck, sold them for a buck on the street, and got the money for the toll. We were told there was a twenty-five-cent toll on the way to the gig. We stopped and got gas, and the guy was kind enough to let us put twenty-five cents on the credit card with the gas. We had no money for food, and so we did not eat."[40]

SEPTEMBER 25, 1974
COLUMBUS, OHIO
AGORA BALLROOM, 1722 North High Street. Venue opened in 1970.
SUPPORT ACT: Law
CAPACITY: 1,700
IAN: "On the way to the gig, I was driving the truck and was stopped at a light when a Columbus city bus pulled away from the curb and—with me stopped—whacked into my passenger-side mirror, breaking it and his mirror too. The cop comes along and charges me. He said, 'I know you weren't moving, but the bus driver's a city employee, and so am I, so you're taking the charge.' Vic Wilson tried to dock my pay for it, and the band put their foot down and told him no. The club that night had a house PA, and I'm wondering where the heck the soundboard was. It turned out to be in a room

upstairs—you have to look out a window to see the band, and you really couldn't hear the mix, so I had to keep running down into the crowd to check it out."[41]

SEPTEMBER 27, 1974
WORCESTER, MASSACHUSETTS
MEMORIAL AUDITORIUM, Lincoln Square. Venue opened in 1933.
OPENED FOR: T. Rex; Albatross opened the show.
TICKETS: $5.50
CAPACITY: 3,508,

SEPTEMBER 28, 1974
JOHNSTOWN, PENNSYLVANIA
FUN CITY GRANDSTAND, Fun City Amusement Park, Ideal Park on Peterson Drive (Somerset Pike)
OPENED FOR: T. Rex
TICKETS: $4.00 (advance) / $5.00 (at gate)
NOTES: Outdoor concert from 2:00 p.m. to 5:00 p.m.

SEPTEMBER 29, 1974
EVANSVILLE, INDIANA
ROBERTS MUNICIPAL STADIUM, University of Evansville campus, 2600 Division Street. Venue dedicated on December 1, 1956.
OPENED FOR: Billy Preston, Kiss
TICKETS: $5.50 (advance) / $6.50 (day of)
CAPACITY: 12,732

OCTOBER 1, 1974
JACKSONVILLE, ALABAMA
LEONE COLE AUDITORIUM, Jacksonville State University, on Trustee Circle
OPENED FOR: Kiss
TICKETS: $3.00 (advance) / $4.00 (day of), general admission
ATTENDANCE: 1,000
CAPACITY: 5,000

OCTOBER 3, 1974
NASHVILLE, TENNESSEE
NASHVILLE WAR MEMORIAL AUDITORIUM, 301 Sixth Avenue North. Venue dedicated on September 21, 1925.
OPENED FOR: Hawkwind; Liquid Len and the Lensmen, and Andy Dunkley
TICKETS: $4.00 (advance) / $5.00 (day of)
CAPACITY: 2,044
NOTES: Canceled at the eleventh hour because of Hawkwind's financial troubles with the IRS, who had confiscated their equipment. Alex, Geddy, and Neil enjoy a day off in Houston, where they join the members of Kiss and jam with a young, local band in a furniture warehouse.
IAN: "We had only been on the road about two months, and we were in Houston on a day off. Guys were wandering in and out of the bar, putting things on a tab. I had two beers and left ten dollars to cover me. Neil came late, had one or two scotches, and found himself stuck with a two-hundred-dollar bar bill. That was about as mad as I ever saw Neil get. You did not offend Neil's sense of fairness."[42]
MICK CAMPISE (KISS ROAD CREW): "The thing that used to kill me about Kiss was that they couldn't play anyone else's music. Ace could do his Page-Yardbirds

thing, and Peter could play a bit. But Paul and Gene really couldn't do much; they couldn't jam. When we first played in Houston, they came and jammed with my younger brother's band in this old furniture warehouse. These kids were fifteen or sixteen years old, and they were floored; they could not believe it. Peter, Ace, and Paul, and Alex and Geddy all got together and were going to jam with them. But Paul couldn't play much of anything. I will never forget that my little brother's guitar player was playing, and Paul was wearing his guitar and leaning against the amps because he couldn't play."[43]

OCTOBER 4, 1974
HOUSTON, TEXAS
MUSIC HALL, 801 Bagby Street. Venue opened in April 1938.
OPENED FOR: Kiss; the New Cactus Band opened the show.
TICKETS: "Available at Evolution Tapes and Records"
CAPACITY: 3,024
NOTES: Final date of Kiss's tour, after which the members of Kiss flew back to New York for a short break. The band Cactus dissolved in 1972 when founding members Carmine Appice and Tim Bogert went on to form Beck, Bogert & Appice with guitarist Jeff Beck. The New Cactus Band, which included none of the original members, was fronted by Duane Hitchings on keyboards and Mike Pinera on guitar and was touring in support of their only release, *Son of Cactus.* Promoters would often still market the group as "Cactus."
HOUSTON CHRONICLE:
"Rush, a hard-hitting rock band performed its first concert in Houston. It was a dynamic flurry of lights and sound held together by a vague, but nonetheless discernible concept."

OCTOBER 6, 1974
OAKBROOK TERRACE, ILLINOIS
OAKBROOK TERRACE FORUM
OPENED FOR: Steppenwolf, Canned Heat

OCTOBER 11, 1974
HOLLYWOOD, CALIFORNIA
AQUARIUS THEATER, 6230 Sunset Boulevard. Historic venue opened in 1938 as the Earl Carroll Theatre, becoming the Aquarius Theater in late 1968.

WITH: Donovan, Sly and the Family Stone, Minnie Riperton
CAPACITY: 1,000
NOTES: *ABC in Concert* (television taping). Season 3, Episode 6 (show #49). Air date: December 6. Legendary producer Jorn Winther and acclaimed director Stanley Dorfman filmed Rush performing "Best I Can." Winther's long list of credits includes: the Beatles, *California Jam 2*, Sonny & Cher, *Shindig!*, and *20/20*, while Dorfman coproduced and directed Britain's *Top of the Pops*, where he filmed most of rock's royalty, including the Beatles, the Rolling Stones, the Who, and David Bowie among others.

OCTOBER 16, 1974
LONG BEACH, CALIFORNIA
LONG BEACH AUDITORIUM CONCERT HALL, 300 East Ocean Boulevard. Historic venue opened on March 6, 1932.
NOTES: *Don Kirshner's Rock Concert* (television taping). Many artists are shot in one day and then broadcast on different dates throughout the season. On this day, Focus, Billy Preston, and the Stampeders were filmed as well. An October 19, 1974, article in the *Hamilton Spectator* indicates that *Don Kirshner's Rock Concert* was filmed prior to *ABC in Concert*, but Ian recalls the Don Kirshner shoot as being on October 16. Doors opened at 4:00 p.m. Showtime: 4:30 p.m. The band performed "Finding My Way," "In the Mood," and "Best I Can," and it aired on March 29, 1975 (episode 26). Neil broke a bass drum head during "Best I Can," and filming paused in order to change the head. He ran into George Harrison backstage, who was there to support his friend Billy Preston. *Don Kirshner's Rock Concert* won acclaim because the musicians actually played live, as opposed to most other television shows at the time, where they were forced to lip-synch to recordings of their own music.

OCTOBER 17, 1974
DALLAS, TEXAS
TRAVIS STREET ELECTRIC COMPANY, 4527 Travis Street
TICKETS: $2.00
CAPACITY: 800

NOTES: Geddy, Alex, and Neil gave a short interview backstage with Don Moore for Dallas radio.
GEDDY: "Neil has just been in the band for about three months now. We got Neil a week before we came to the US. Since Neil's been in the band, we've started writing—the three of us together."[44]
DALLAS NEWSPAPER (UNKNOWN SOURCE): "Rush's performance was professional, complete with costume changes between sets and between encores, something few groups do. This is exemplary of the group's attention to detail. The sound was well balanced, and the lighting was executed in conjunction with what was being played. Rush's three-man group has a well-organized, tight approach—also difficult in view of the massive amount of music coming from the speakers."
TEXAS WESLEYAN UNIVERSITY NEWSPAPER, *THE RAMBLER:* "Neil Peart has the shortest tenure with them, but with his imaginative and hard driving sounds, he should be a definite asset to a band that has super success potential. All in all, the group's whole act was professionally tight, and thoroughly enjoyable."
ALEX: "I remember having such a great show in Dallas that night. We were playing a lot of our bar set—stuff we put together very quickly with Neil off the first show. We played 'Bad Boy,' the Beatles song. We were out with Uriah Heep, Rory Gallagher, Nazareth, relegated to twenty-minute, half-hour sets. So we would pick up these club dates where we would play for a couple of hours, and that was a really exciting night, because nobody knew who we were, and we won the crowd over that night. The place was just roaring by the end of it, and we all just thought, 'Texas is awesome!'"[45]
IAN: "I remember the Dallas gig. I'd been charged with 'careless driving' in Tampa the previous month. We did *Don Kirshner's Rock Concert* in LA on the sixteenth. I left early and caught a flight to Florida, settled the legal matter, and flew back to Dallas. The band, crew, and gear flew in from LA. We played the club in Dallas that night, then drove 550 miles to Kansas City and did a gig with Hawkwind the next night (October 18). So, in forty-eight hours I was in LA, Tampa, Dallas, and then KC. I fell asleep on the flight cases while Hawkwind played—now that is fucking tired."

OCTOBER 18, 1974
KANSAS CITY, KANSAS
SOLDIER AND SAILOR'S MEMORIAL HALL, 600 North Seventh Street. Venue cornerstone laid on May 26, 1924.
TICKETS: $5.00 (advance) / $6.00 (at the door), general admission
OPENED FOR: Hawkwind
CAPACITY: 3,500
NOTES: An ad for Rush supporting Kiss at the Parthenon Theatre in Hammond, Indiana, must have been printed prior to Rush signing on for this run of gigs with Hawkwind. The English space rockers' US tour began in September but came to an abrupt pause after a gig on September 21, also in Hammond, when Indiana State Police impounded their gear, with the IRS claiming they owed eight thousand dollars because of a new levy on visiting bands.[46] Hawkwind returned to Britain, and all postponed dates were rescheduled in the eleventh hour, hence this series of October concerts with Rush.

OCTOBER 19, 1974
LINCOLN, NEBRASKA
PERSHING MEMORIAL AUDITORIUM, 226 Centennial Mall South. Venue dedicated on March 10, 1957.
OPENED FOR: Hawkwind
TICKETS: $4.00 (advance) / $5.00 (at the door)
CAPACITY: 7,500
IAN: "There was [only] a tiny wee crowd for Hawkwind. I remember it because I heard Lemmy speak."[47]

OCTOBER 20, 1974
OKLAHOMA CITY, OKLAHOMA
CIVIC CENTER MUSIC HALL, 201 North Walker Avenue. Venue opened on October 4, 1937.
OPENED FOR: Hawkwind
CAPACITY: 2,447
NOTES: Venue unconfirmed.
GEDDY: "I'll never forget opening for Hawkwind. Lemmy rolled the biggest joint that Alex and I had ever seen in our lives. It was huge! And everyone spent the whole night trying to smoke this thing."[48]

OCTOBER 22, 1974
WICHITA, KANSAS
CENTURY II CONVENTION HALL, 225 West Douglas Avenue. Venue opened on January 11, 1969.

OPENED FOR: Hawkwind
TICKETS: $3.00 (advance) / $4.00 (day of)
CAPACITY: 5,022
NOTES: Dave Scace's final gig.

OCTOBER 23, 1974
LONDON, ONTARIO
WESTERN UNIVERSITY, 1151 Richmond Street. Founded on March 7, 1878.
OPENED FOR: Nazareth
IAN: "Two hundred miles to Kansas City, flying to Chicago, and catching another flight to Toronto (with the gear as well). We then drove 110 miles straight to London, Ontario, to support Nazareth that night on absolutely zero sleep."

OCTOBER 24, 1974
TORONTO, ONTARIO
MASSEY HALL, 178 Victoria Street. Historic venue opened June 14, 1894.
OPENED FOR: Nazareth
TICKETS: $4.50 / $5.50 / $6.60 CAD
CAPACITY: 2,765
GLOBE AND MAIL: "The band does have a couple things going for it besides pure volume. Bassist Lee's banshee vocals are immediately arresting and are bound to become the band's most distinguishing characteristic. It may not be new, but the group's knock-down power is appreciated."
CANADIAN COMPOSER: "The volume is incredible; thundering drum patterns, skittering and screaming guitar lines, Lee's shrieked vocals, high in the upper registers. Instinctively, you know why the critics hate it and the kids love it—the noise and the sheer flash of it all."

OCTOBER 25, 1974
WATERLOO, ONTARIO
LAURIER THEATRE AUDITORIUM, Sir Wilfrid Laurier University, 75 University Avenue West
OPENED FOR: Nazareth
TICKETS: $4.00 (students) / $4.50 (general admission) / $5.00 (at the door) CAD
ATTENDANCE: 1,200 (first show; sold out); 1,340 (second show; oversold)[49]
NOTES: Two shows (7:00 p.m. and 10:00 p.m.). The fire code mandated a maximum of 910 persons inside the venue, which was ignored.[50]
HAMILTON SPECTATOR, GEDDY: "Too many people, I think, have the idea that

a trio restricts a group's flexibility. They seem to think that a trio has to be restricted to playing Cream-like music. Well, that isn't the case."[51]

OCTOBER 26, 1974
HAMILTON, ONTARIO
HAMILTON FORUM, Barton Street between Sanford Avenue and Wentworth Streets. Venue opened on October 1, 1953.
OPENED FOR: Nazareth
CAPACITY: 2,800
NOTES: This was Jimmy Johnson's first gig as stage left technician with Rush, replacing Dave Scace. Jimmy had grown up in Niagara Falls and had worked as a roadie with Wayne and the Younger Generation back in 1967, when Neil was in the band, and then later on with Bullrush. In addition to his history with Neil, Jimmy (JJ) had casually known Liam, Ian, Geddy, and Alex from the Ontario music scene. It was through Neil that he heard Rush was looking for somebody to go on the road to look after Geddy's basses (and, eventually, Alex's guitars). At the time, JJ had a good job in the construction business and was reluctant to give it up, so he initially declined. A few days later, after a particularly bad day at work, he got another call from Howard, and this time he accepted.
HAMILTON SPECTATOR, GEDDY: "Over the past couple of months, everything has sort of exploded. The band's been around for about five years, and nothing much happened. Now everything's happening at once."[52]

OCTOBER 27, 1974
KINGSTON, ONTARIO
GRANT HALL, QUEEN'S UNIVERSITY, University Avenue, north of Bader Lane. Venue built in 1905.
OPENED FOR: Nazareth
TICKETS: $3.50 (all seats)
CAPACITY: 900
NOTES: Two shows, 7:00 p.m. and 9:30 p.m.
THE WHIG-STANDARD (KINGSTON): "The trio is a product of the Toronto suburbs, but their music has a high tension, inner city sound."

OCTOBER 28–29, 1974
ROSLYN, NEW YORK
MY FATHER'S PLACE, 19 Bryant Avenue.
Venue opened in 1971.
CAPACITY: 300
NOTES: These dates are not present in SRO's records. A venue ad in the October 24 edition of the *Village Voice* has no band listed at all for these dates. Perhaps Rush was a late addition, or perhaps contractual obligations with the Beacon concert (November 5) didn't permit advertising of another gig so close to that one.

OCTOBER 31, 1974
OTTAWA, ONTARIO
OTTAWA CIVIC CENTRE, Lansdowne Park, 1015 Bank Street
OPENED FOR: Nazareth, Hudson Ford
TICKETS: $3.50 (advance) / $4.50 CAD
CAPACITY: 9,349
NOTES: Rush's appearance ends up being canceled, despite them being on a day-of-show ad.

NOVEMBER 1, 1974
MONTREAL, QUEBEC
MONTREAL FORUM CONCERT BOWL, 2313 Saint Catherine Street West. Historic venue opened on November 29, 1924.
OPENED FOR: Rory Gallagher, Nazareth
TICKETS: $5.50 CAD
ATTENDANCE: 7,500; sold out
NOTES: Rory Gallagher didn't take the stage until around midnight, with the show ending about 1:30 a.m. The Forum played host to twenty-four Stanley Cup championships.

MONTREAL STAR: "The first act, Rush build themselves up as playing hard and simple, with no frills, just a band that can shake down the walls of any hall it plays. At the Forum they got their message across to pile-driver effect; I hope they make their million before they go deaf."

MONTREAL GAZETTE: "Three bands on a bill is a little much, especially when they're as worthless as Rush, a group that even had to cop their name from Montreal's Mahogany Rush."

POP ROCK: "Four hours of energetic rock with Rush, Nazareth, and Rory Gallagher: Rush, a group from Toronto who just made its mark across the border during a recent tour of the States, has demonstrated a fairly powerful rock style, but a little heavy for the ears. Rush has nevertheless managed to get its message and professionalism across among the admirers."

NOVEMBER 2, 1974
PETERBOROUGH, ONTARIO
PETERBOROUGH MEMORIAL CENTRE, 121 Lansdowne Street West. Venue opened on November 8, 1956.
CAPACITY: 3,908

NOVEMBER 3, 1974
PARSIPPANY, NEW JERSEY
JOINT IN THE WOODS, 400 Smith Road
OPENED FOR: Rory Gallagher
TICKETS: $3.00
CAPACITY: 1,500
NOTES: Special 2:00 p.m. show.

NOVEMBER 4, 1974
UPPER DARBY, PENNSYLVANIA
TOWER THEATER, 69th and Ludlow. Venue opened on October 1, 1928.
CAPACITY: 3,119
NOTES: Although this date is listed in early advertising, Geddy's recollections are that Rush did not perform, and there is no additional evidence of any such gig.

NOVEMBER 5, 1974
NEW YORK, NEW YORK
BEACON THEATER, 2124 Broadway. Historic venue opened on December 24, 1929.
OPENED FOR: Rory Gallagher, If
TICKETS: $5.00 / $5.50 / $6.50
CAPACITY: 2,894
CONCERT GROSS: $10,000
NOTES: Alison Steele acted as MC.

BILLBOARD: "Rush is an exciting Canadian trio, which appeared for the first time in New York. They are excellent musicians and play with unusual drive and determination. Their onstage appearance is tinged with a sense of the dramatic, and if they lower their volume a lot they may attract back some of the spectators who left the theater in droves after several of their numbers."

NOVEMBER 7, 1974
SCHAUMBURG, ILLINOIS
B'GINNINGS, 1227 East Golf Road. Venue opened in September 1974.
OPENED FOR: Rory Gallagher
CAPACITY: 936
NOTES: This date is not present in SRO's records and, despite an October 12, 1974, *Billboard* advertisement, almost certainly did not happen. The venue was owned by the drummer from the band Chicago, Danny Seraphine, and named after their hit song "Beginnings."

NOVEMBER 9, 1974
DETROIT, MICHIGAN
MICHIGAN PALACE, 238 Bagley Street. Building opened on August 23, 1926.
OPENED FOR: Tim Buckley, Rory Gallagher
TICKETS: $5.00 (all seats)
CAPACITY: 4,050
NOTES: The venue was located inside the thirteen-story Michigan Building, originally the site of Henry Ford's first garage.

NOVEMBER 10, 1974
ST. LOUIS, MISSOURI
AMBASSADOR THEATRE, 411 North Seventh Street. Venue opened in 1926.
OPENED FOR: Rory Gallagher
TICKETS: $4.00 / $5.00 / $6.00
CAPACITY: 3,000

NOVEMBER 11, 1974
LANSING, MICHIGAN
THE BREWERY, 3411 East Michigan Avenue. Venue opened in 1972.
SUPPORT ACT: Brother Bait
TICKETS: $2.50
CAPACITY: 690; sold out
MICHIGAN STATE NEWS: "The group is in the process of breaking in a new drummer, Neil Peare [sic], and it shows. His drum style did not fit the group comfortably Monday night, being too scattered and weak for a three-piece band. Time should

take care of that problem. Fast material was what Rush played best, hands down. Lee and Lifeson complimented [sic] each other very well, and Lee, in the position of having to sing and play bass simultaneously, does very well. Rush's slow material, however, just did not measure up. It appears the group feels the need to pace their set, which is commendable, but the quality of their compositions declined. Aside from Peare's [sic] drumming, and the slow material, Rush has few problems left to iron out. The three encores they received at the Brewery would indicate they indeed have potential."

NOVEMBER 12, 1974
MILWAUKEE, WISCONSIN
RIVERSIDE THEATER, 116 West Wisconsin. Historic venue opened on April 29, 1928.
OPENED FOR: Rory Gallagher, Wet Willie
TICKETS: $5.00 / $5.50 / $6.00
CAPACITY: 2,558
NOTES: Promoter Randy McElrath invited the band out to dinner at the Pfister Hotel. With a bottle of Château Margaux and Château Latour Bordeaux, he started Geddy and Alex on the path that would lead them to becoming serious wine connoisseurs.
MILWAUKEE SENTINEL: "The evening might have been better all-around if someone had cared to inform either group or Rush, the third ensemble, that they were performing in the cozy Riverside Theater and not the arena. The electronic amplification was ridiculous."
GEDDY: "It was the first time we'd had wine of that caliber. We both were stunned by the wine's texture, complexity, and flavors."[53]

NOVEMBER 13, 1974
TOLEDO, OHIO
SPORTS ARENA, 1 North Main Street. Venue opened on November 13, 1947.
OPENED FOR: Rory Gallagher, Carmen
TICKETS: $4.00 (advance) / $5.00 (day of)
CAPACITY: 7,000
DAVID CLARK ALLEN (FOUNDING CARMEN GUITARIST/VOCALIST): "I remember meeting and chatting with Rush. They were making crazy air raid siren sounds—vocally—in their dressing room, and I knocked and asked what was up. They told me they'd been on the road so long they were going loopy! They said

they owed so much money to their record company that they needed to constantly tour. They were funny and friendly, besides being awesomely tight as a performing band."[54]

NOVEMBER 14, 1974
COLUMBUS, OHIO
VETERAN'S MEMORIAL AUDITORIUM, 300 West Broad Street. Venue dedicated on November 11, 1955.
OPENED FOR: Rory Gallagher
TICKETS: $5.00 (advance) / $5.50 (at the door)
CAPACITY: 3,964
COLUMBUS DISPATCH: "Rush put on a dazzling display of heavy rock that had the crowd chomping at the bit for more, more, more."

NOVEMBER 15, 1974
CHICAGO, ILLINOIS
ARAGON BALLROOM, 1106 West Lawrence Avenue. Venue opened in July 1926.
OPENED FOR: Rory Gallagher, Wet Willie
TICKETS: $5.50
CAPACITY: 4,500
CHICAGO SUN-TIMES: "Rush appeared to be moving into the void left by Grand Funk Railroad and Black Sabbath with lead guitarist Alex Lifeson doing a credible Robert Plant–style screaming vocal."

NOVEMBER 16, 1974
WICHITA, KANSAS
ORPHEUM THEATRE, 200 North Broadway. Historic venue opened on September 4, 1922.
OPENED FOR: Rory Gallagher
TICKETS: $4.00 (at the door) / $3.00 (advance)
CAPACITY: 1,700
NOTES: Midnight show. This performance is not present in SRO's records, and Rush might not have been on the bill. An ad lists Lander Ballard as the support act, with no mention of Rush.
IAN: "Certainly not starting after midnight, and the date means we'd have driven from Wichita to Seattle, which I don't remember."[55]

NOVEMBER 1974
LINCOLN, NEBRASKA
PERSHING MEMORIAL AUDITORIUM, 226 Centennial Mall South

OPENED FOR: Rory Gallagher
ATTENDANCE: 150 (approximate)
NOTES: Ian Grandy recalls the performance, but this is an unconfirmed show, and extensive library research turned up no evidence of it.
IAN: "I do remember Lincoln, Nebraska, with Rory because there weren't even 150 people there."[56]

NOVEMBER 19, 1974
SEATTLE, WASHINGTON
PARAMOUNT NORTHWEST THEATRE, 901 Pine Street. Historic venue opened on March 1, 1928.
OPENED FOR: Rory Gallagher
ATTENDANCE: 1,000[57]
CAPACITY: 3,054
NOTES: Earliest known live performance of "Anthem." Neil worked on the lyrics for "Beneath, Between, and Behind."
SET LIST: "Finding My Way," "What You're Doing," "In the Mood," "Here Again," "Fancy Dancer," "Bad Boy," "Working Man" (with drum solo), "Anthem."
SEATTLE TIMES: "A band from Canada called Rush opened the show and came off sounding like another imitation Led Zeppelin, despite some nice guitar work by Alex Lifeson."

NOVEMBER 20, 1974
PORTLAND, OREGON
PARAMOUNT NORTHWEST THEATRE, 1037 Southwest Broadway. Venue opened on March 8, 1928.
OPENED FOR: Rory Gallagher
CAPACITY: 3,036

NOVEMBER 22, 1974
SAN DIEGO, CALIFORNIA
TUESDAY'S BALLROOM, 211 West G Street
OPENED FOR: Rory Gallagher, Earth Quake
TICKETS: $5.00 (advance) / $5.50 (at the door)

NOVEMBER 23, 1974
LOS ANGELES, CALIFORNIA
SHRINE AUDITORIUM, 665 West Jefferson Boulevard Historic venue opened on January 23, 1926.
OPENED FOR: Rory Gallagher, Wet Willie
TICKETS: $4.50 / $5.50 / $6.50
CAPACITY: 6,442

NOVEMBER 26, 1974
VENTURA, CALIFORNIA
VENTURA THEATER, 26 South Chestnut Street. Historic venue opened in 1928.
OPENED FOR: Rory Gallagher
CAPACITY: 1,150

NOVEMBER 27, 1974;
DECEMBER 1, 1974
WEST HOLLYWOOD, CALIFORNIA
WHISKY A GO GO, 8901 Sunset Boulevard. Venue opened on January 16, 1964.
WITH: The Butts Band
CAPACITY: 500
NOTES: The Butts Band featured Robby Krieger and John Densmore of the Doors.
LOS ANGELES TIMES: "Rush, which is currently at the Whisky, is one of those fledgling groups with an alarming disregard for originality. Rush's flagrantly derivative music was neither interesting nor listenable. It was amplified many decibels beyond what is considered comfortable for even the heartiest ears."
JOHN DENSMORE (DRUMMER FOR THE DOORS AND THE BUTTS BAND): "I don't remember much about those Rush gigs, except that they were very loud! Although I do really like Neil Peart's playing."[58]
IAN: "Each band played two alternating sets per night. So the crews had to really cooperate—back and forth four times a night! They had a roadie named Tex who'd worked for the likes of Paul Revere and the Raiders. He was a funny dude with a hundred stories, and I met the guys from

the Doors, which was cool with me. There was a giant dressing room and a tiny stage. A big tray of shots—whiskey, Jack, tequila—was delivered gratis to the dressing room every night. Being responsible, we tried to leave no waste. Tex told me on the sidewalk after loading out that they'd wondered if we'd be assholes, but that we were pros. That felt good."

DECEMBER 1974
LOS ANGELES, CALIFORNIA
NOTES: A scheduled appearance on *The Midnight Special* television show is called off at the eleventh hour.

DECEMBER 10, 1974
OTTAWA, ONTARIO
CIVIC CENTRE, Lansdowne Park, 1015 Bank Street
OPENED FOR: Manfred Mann's Earth Band, the Stampeders
TICKETS: $4.00 (limited advance) / $5.00 (remainder) CAD
CAPACITY: 9,349

DECEMBER 12, 1974
TORONTO, ONTARIO
CONVOCATION HALL, UNIVERSITY OF TORONTO, 31 King's College Circle. Venue opened in 1907.
OPENED FOR: Manfred Mann's Earth Band
TICKETS: $5.00
CAPACITY: 1,731 (seated)
SET LIST: "Finding My Way," "Best I Can," "In the Mood," "Anthem," "Here Again," "Bad Boy," "Working Man" (with drum solo).
MICK ROGERS (GUITARIST FOR MANFRED MANN'S EARTH BAND): "I can't remember much about Rush being on with us. I love the band, and Neil is a monster."[59]

DECEMBER 14, 1974
KALAMAZOO, MICHIGAN
HACKETT AUDITORIUM, John R. Hackett Catholic Prep High School, 1000 West Kilgore. Venue dedicated on October 4, 1964.
OPENED FOR: Foghat
TICKETS: $5.00 (advance) / $6.00 (at the door)
CAPACITY: 520
NOTES: Hackett Auditorium is a theater, with all seats reserved.

DECEMBER 16–17, 1974
CLEVELAND, OHIO
THE AGORA BALLROOM, 1730 East 24th Street. Venue opened on March 31, 1913.
SUPPORT ACT: Law
TICKETS: $3.00 (advance) / $3.50 (at the door), general admission
CAPACITY: 700
NOTES: Recorded and broadcast as part of the WMMS *Live from the Agora* concert series and featured the debut of the title track "Fly by Night."
SET LIST (DECEMBER 16): "Finding My Way," "Best I Can," "What You're Doing," "Fly by Night," "Here Again," "Anthem," "Bad Boy," "Working Man" (with drum solo).
NORTHEASTERN OHIO SCENE: "The next time Rush comes to town they ought to arm the audience with a few Marshalls and Stratocasters. Then they can battle it out, and whoever walks out of whatever is left of the building can say they've been to hell and back."[60]

DECEMBER 19, 1974
HAMILTON, ONTARIO
MOHAWK THEATRE, Mohawk College, Fennell Avenue West. Founded in 1966.
SUPPORT ACTS: Curtis Lee, Abraham
TICKETS: $3.50 (advance) / $4.00 (at the door) CAD

DECEMBER 20–21, 1974
DETROIT, MICHIGAN
MICHIGAN PALACE, 238 Bagley Street
OPENED FOR: Kiss; Fancy opened the show.
TICKETS: $5.00 (advance) / $5.50 (at the door)
ATTENDANCE: 4,050; sold out
NOTES (DEC. 20): The Michigan Palace hosted a birthday reception for Kiss's Peter Criss following the gig.
IAN: "We got along really great with the guys in Kiss. I used to help Mick, their drum roadie, as a counterweight when Peter's kit raised, and we would drive with the roadies on days off. It was so long ago that their crew had rental cars, not a bus, and Kiss flew a lot, whereas Rush drove and drove. Gene never indulged, but during a party at the Michigan Palace for the Christmas 1974 shows, they fed him some loaded cookies, and he was wrecked. He and I got into a food-throwing thing with their

roadies, and Gene was laughing and having a great time. I don't know if he ever figured out what happened."[61]

NEIL: "We still joke about the gay promoter at the Palace hitting on Alex, looking at him in the eyes and quoting the Olivia Newton-John song, 'Have you ever been mellow?'"[62]

fan, it was quite a thrill for me personally to be in that studio."[63]

DECEMBER 28, 1974
BOSTON, MASSACHUSETTS
ORPHEUM THEATRE, 1 Hamilton Place. Historic venue opened in 1852.
OPENED FOR: Blue Oyster Cult; American Tears opened the show.
TICKETS: $4.50 / $5.50 / $6.50
CAPACITY: 2,700
NOTES: Despite being listed in SRO's records and being corroborated by an ad, Rush did not appear on this bill nor the next night in Waterbury.

DECEMBER 29, 1974
WATERBURY, CONNECTICUT
PALACE THEATRE, 100 East Main Street. Historic venue opened in 1922.
OPENED FOR: Blue Oyster Cult
TICKETS: $6.50, general admission
CAPACITY: 2,543
IAN: "My recollection is that we were supposed to go [to Boston on December 28 and Waterbury on December 29], but instead the boys went into the studio. I have no recollection of those gigs."[64]

DECEMBER 22, 1974
NEW YORK, NEW YORK
ELECTRIC LADY STUDIOS, 52 West Eighth Street. World-famous recording studio built by Jimi Hendrix in 1970.
NOTES: An in-studio performance before a handful of folks, broadcast live over WQIV-FM. The radio station, which was only in existence from November 7, 1974, to August 25, 1975, broadcast in quadrophonic stereo sound.
SET LIST: "Finding My Way," "Best I Can," "In the Mood," "Anthem," "Need Some Love," "Fly by Night," "Here Again," "Bad Boy," "Working Man" (with drum solo).
IAN: "The engineer mixing it had the bass and guitar real low, and I practically had to punch him to get it fixed. He eventually threw up his hands and told me to handle the mix. As a huge Hendrix

1. Skip Daly. Interview with Doc Cooper, March 25, 2011.
2. Skip Daly. Interview with Terry Danko, May 1, 2014.
3. Bill Banasiewicz. Interview with Peter Gatien, December 17, 2015.
4. Interview with Alex Lifeson, *The Toronto Star*, April 1974.
5. Skip Daly. Interview with Doc Cooper, March 25, 2011.
6. Skip Daly. Interview with Mark Mondol, April 23, 2009.
7. CBC News.
8. Bill Banasiewicz. Interview with Peter Gatien, December 17, 2015.
9. Skip Daly. Interview with Colin Tyler, February 25, 2013.
10. *The Hamilton Spectator*, June 22, 2013.
11. Donna Halper. "In the Beginning: The Story of the Discovery of Rush." 2112.net, 1998.
12. Interview with Geddy Lee. *Telegraph Journal*, October 2, 1976.
13. Ian Grandy. Facebook.com, February 17, 2014.
14. Bill Banasiewicz. Interview with John Rutsey, August 12, 1984.
15. Skip Daly. Interview with Doc Cooper, March 25, 2011.
16. Bill Banasiewicz. Interview with Liam Birt, January 20, 1984.
17. *Albuquerque Journal*, September 11, 1977.
18. Paul Miil. "Origin of Neil Peart: St. Catharines Epock B4 Rush." Youtube. com, February 15, 2015.
19. *City Magazine*.
20. Curt Gooch and Jess Suhs. *Kiss Alive Forever: The Complete Touring History*. Billboard Books, 2002.
21. Skip Daly. Interview with Nick Panaseiko, January 2010.
22. *Classic Rock Magazine*, October 2015.
23. Skip Daly. Interview with Ian Grandy, 2012.
24. Skip Daly. Interview with Doc Cooper, March 25, 2011.
25. *Pittsburgh Press*, July 5, 1984.
26. Neil Peart. *Roadshow: Landscape with Drums: A Concert Tour by Motorcycle*. Rounder Books, 2006.
27. Skip Daly. Interview with Ian Grandy, 2012.
28. Bill Banasiewicz. Interview with Liam Birt, January 20, 1984.
29. Interview with Geddy Lee. *The Hamilton Spectator*, October 19, 1974.
30. Skip Daly. Interview with Ian Grandy, January 5, 2015.
31. Bill Banasiewicz. Interview with Corky Laing, June 11, 2014.
32. Skip Daly. Interview with Ian Grandy, 2012.

33. Eric Hansen. Interview with Howard Ungerleider, July 11, 2012.
34. Lawrence.com, February 13, 2004.
35. Martin Popoff. *Contents Under Pressure*. ECW Press, 2004.
36. Bill Banasiewicz. Interview with Scott Simon, February 2014.
37. Bill Banasiewicz. Interview with John "Jocko" Marcellino, February 2014.
38. Rich Hund. "Alternate Album Focus – 'HOTTER THAN HELL.'" kissasylum.com, 2000.
39. Bill Banasiewicz. Interview with Alex Cooley.
40. Skip Daly. Interview with Ian Grandy, May 12, 2014.
41. Skip Daly. Interview with Ian Grandy, 2012.
42. Skip Daly. Interview with Ian Grandy, 2012.
43. Curt Gooch and Jess Suhs. *Kiss Alive Forever: The Complete Touring History*. Billboard Books, 2002.
44. Don Moore. Interview with Geddy Lee. Travis Street Electric Co., October 17, 1974.
45. Interview with Alex Lifeson. *Dallas Morning News*, November 22, 2013.
46. Ian Abrahams. *Hawkwind: Sonic Assassins*. SAF Publishing Ltd, 2004.
47. Ian Grandy. Facebook.com, November 17, 2015.
48. Bill Banasiewicz. Interview with Geddy Lee, 1985.
49. *The Cord Weekly*.
50. *The Cord Weekly*.
51. Interview with Geddy Lee. *The Hamilton Spectator*, October 19, 1974.
52. Interview with Geddy Lee. *The Hamilton Spectator*, October 19, 1974.
53. *Guitar Aficionado*, 2011.
54. Bill Banasiewicz. Interview with David Clark Allen, September 21, 2015.
55. Ian Grandy. Facebook.com, November 17, 2015.
56. Ian Grandy. Facebook.com, November 17, 2015.
57. *Seattle Times*.
58. Bill Banasiewicz. Interview with John Densmore, May 2014.
59. Bill Banasiewicz. Interview with Mick Rogers, April 21, 2017.
60. Henry Keiluhn. *Northeastern Ohio Scene*, December 19, 1974.
61. Skip Daly. Interview with Ian Grandy, 2012.
62. Neil Peart. *Roadshow: Landscape with Drums: A Concert Tour by Motorcycle*. Rounder Books, 2006.
63. Skip Daly. Interview with Ian Grandy, 2012.
64. Skip Daly. Interview with Ian Grandy, October 5, 2014.

KISS キッス

Fan club mailing address: P.O. BOX 5272. Grand central station. New York. New York 10017

DEAR ALEX,

PLEASE SAY HELLO TO EVERYONE (TIME IS SHORT AND I CAN'T DO THREE LETTERS)———!!!

HOPE CANADA IS TREATING ITS HOME-GROWN HEROS IN GRAND STYLE——!!

WE HAVE A LIVE ONE COMING OUT IN AUGUST (DOUBLE!!)

OH YEAH, MIDNIGHT SPECIAL ON July 11TH 'IS US... WATCH IT! TELL THE BOYS, AS WELL...

MUST RUN, HOPE YOU DON'T MIND THIS SHORT ONE...

MY BEST—
GENE SIMMONS

Chapter 3

THE FLY BY NIGHT TOUR

A s 1975 got underway, Rush emerged from the studio with their second album, *Fly by Night*, released on February 15. It was, unquestionably, a definitive step forward in their development, exhibiting a chemistry between Geddy, Alex, and "the new guy," Neil Peart, that had been forged in the crucible of several months of hard touring.

There was plenty more hard touring ahead. The *Fly by Night* tour kicked off in Winnipeg and ran for six months, covering most of the United States. The set list still varied with the amount of stage time. "Finding My Way" was the opening song, and most of the new album was performed (save for "Making Memories" and "Rivendell"). Rush were still primarily a support act at this point, opening for the likes of Aerosmith and Ted Nugent, though they were picking up significant momentum in pockets of North America, particularly the Midwest.

In early March, they did a run of headline dates—six shows in six nights—at Alex Cooley's Electric Ballroom in Atlanta, bringing New York City punk goofballs the Dictators along as support. Unfortunately, the bill proved a tough sell to the average Rush fan, and the Dictators were fired after two performances. "We threw White Castle hamburgers at the audience once," recalled Dictators singer "Handsome Dick" Manitoba. "All of us loved White Castle hamburgers, so, naturally, we thought our audience would love 'em too. Unfortunately, we forgot that we were opening for Rush and this wasn't exactly our audience. There I was, this 210-pound guy with an afro and a wrestling

OPPOSITE: Letter from Gene Simmons to Alex.

ABOVE: Belleville, IL; Alex, Neil, and Geddy doing a sound check at Belleville College.

LEFT: Richmond, VA; Rush and Kiss backstage celebrating Kiss guitarist Ace Frehley's birthday.

outfit, throwing hamburgers at a crowd of Rush fans staring back at us in horrified shock."

The next week, Alex married his longtime girlfriend, Charlene, but kept up his busy tour schedule with Rush. Charlene later recalled having to go on their honeymoon alone, with

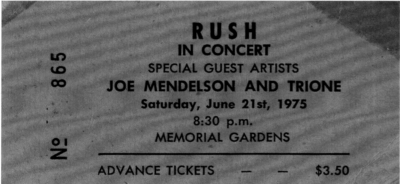

head with a couple of holes poked in it so he could see and breathe. [He] would go into this routine with the bag over his head while smoking a joint out of his eye. He put everyone into total hysterics."

Rush wrapped the *Fly by Night* tour with a series of triumphant headline shows in Ontario, including a sold-out date at Toronto's legendary Massey Hall. The gig demonstrated the strength of Rush's growing fan base, even if the critics weren't fully on board yet. Wrote a reviewer in the Toronto *Globe and Mail*, "The sell-out crowd greeted the returning hometown heroes by cramming the aisles and lighting sparklers. All this for Rush? I could see it for the Rolling Stones, but Rush?"

Alex joining her later, as "he had a couple of shows to do."

And the shows kept getting bigger. On April 13, Rush played the KSHE Kite Fly Festival in St. Louis, Missouri, in front of a reported seventy thousand fans. Then came another run of theaters and small arenas with Kiss, during which time some backstage high jinks ensued, among them Alex's debut as "the Bag."   "Alex used to do this hysterical routine with a large paper laundry bag," recalled Kiss guitarist Ace Frehley. "He'd draw a ridiculous giant face on the bag with a black marker and put it over his

TOP RIGHT: London, Ontario; Geddy, Alex, and Neil backstage with promoter Nick Panaseiko.
OPPOSITE: St. Louis, MO; Alex, Geddy, and Neil onstage at the KSHE Kite Festival.

TOUR HISTORY
FLY BY NIGHT

> **SET LIST:**
> **(Sample from June 25, 1975)**
> "Finding My Way"
> "Best I Can"
> "Anthem"
> "Beneath, Between, & Behind"
> "In The End"
>
> "Fly by Night"
> "By-Tor and the Snow Dog"
> "Working Man" (with drum solo)
> "In the Mood"
> "Need Some Love"
> "What You're Doing"

JANUARY 10, 1975
REXDALE, ONTARIO
UTM CAFETERIA AT ERINDALE COLLEGE, 3359 Mississauga Road North. Founded in 1965.
SUPPORT ACTS: Schroeder, Joe Mendelson
NOTES: 7:00 p.m. show; free with ID
IAN: "The college gig was right after the recording of *Fly by Night*, and I think before any mixing of the album. We pulled the gear straight out of the studio. It was a college pub night and don't forget that there's always the inclination for people to think, 'Oh they're from around here, so how good can they be?' The people there were way more interested in drinking than in watching the band. After a set or two, we all decided to get as drunk as the crowd. That's where the picture on *Fly by Night* of Liam, JJ, and I was taken, and we were all smashed. It was a memorable gig for pretty much all the wrong reasons. Maybe the worst I ever heard the band play."

JANUARY 15, 1975
WINNIPEG, MANITOBA
WINNIPEG CONVENTION CENTRE, 3rd Floor Exhibition Hall, 375 York Avenue. Venue opened on January 14, 1975.
SUPPORT ACTS: the Winnipeg Symphony Orchestra, Next
TICKETS: $6.50 CAD (all seats)
ATTENDANCE: 6,200
CAPACITY: 6,500
NOTES: "Celebrations '75." Rush headlined the very first public event at the new convention center after Rare Earth was forced to postpone their performance at the last moment because their keyboardist was ill. Alex later recalled that the band completed the mixing of *Fly by Night* in the early morning hours of

January 15, 1975, and then caught a 10:30 a.m. flight to Winnipeg for the show.
WINNIPEG FREE PRESS: "Rush was greeted by a standing ovation from a large segment of the crowd, a courtesy reserved for true stars. Alex Lifeson distinguished himself as an exciting young guitarist whose fast-fingered technique drew some well-deserved roars of approval from the crowd. Rush went down well with most of those in attendance, grinding out an hour's worth of hard-as-nails riff rockers in rapid-fire succession."
WINNIPEG TRIBUNE:
"Toronto band lively but loud: The trio executed a selection of old and new material with enthusiasm, but the music was too loud to make the lyrics audible. Musically, Rush is a tight, well-rehearsed band, even if its performance scope is narrow."

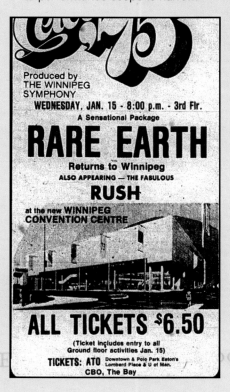

Produced by
THE WINNIPEG SYMPHONY
WEDNESDAY, JAN. 15 · 8:00 p.m. · 3rd Flr.
A Sensational Package
RARE EARTH
Returns to Winnipeg
ALSO APPEARING — THE FABULOUS
RUSH
at the new **WINNIPEG CONVENTION CENTRE**
ALL TICKETS $6.50
(Ticket includes entry to all Ground floor activities Jan. 15)
TICKETS: ATO Downtown & Polo Park Eaton's Lombard Place & U of Man.
CBO, The Bay

JANUARY 17, 1975
ETOBICOKE, ONTARIO
ETOBICOKE COLLEGIATE INSTITUTE, 86 Montgomery Road. Founded in 1928.

JANUARY 18, 1975
DELHI, ONTARIO
BELGIAN CLUB, 360 James Street North. Venue opened in 1948.
CAPACITY: 640
SUPPORT ACT: Max Webster
NOTES: This date is in SRO's records as January 19 (with Max Webster), but the venue has January 18. A January 9 newspaper ad corroborates the subsequent Hamilton date as being January 19, so it is likely that the venue has this correct.

JANUARY 19, 1975
HAMILTON, ONTARIO
MOHAWK THEATRE, Mohawk College, Fennell Avenue West. Founded in 1966.
SUPPORT ACT: Joe Mendelson
TICKETS: $3.50 (advance) / $4.00 (at the door)
NOTES: SRO lists this date as "Delhi, Ontario," but a January 9 newspaper ad corroborates Hamilton as being January nineteenth. It's *possible* that Hamilton was rescheduled to January 29 sometime after the ad went to print. (In which case, it's also possible that a second Delhi performance was added on the nineteenth).

JANUARY 20–25, 1975
ATLANTA, GEORGIA
ALEX COOLEY'S ELECTRIC BALLROOM, corner of Peachtree Street NE and Ponce de Leon Avenue. Built in 1913. Venue opened on March 13, 1974.
SUPPORT ACT: Deluxe
CAPACITY: 1,100

NOTES: It was possibly at some point during this run of dates in Atlanta that the band took time to film the promotional videos for "Anthem" and "Fly by Night" at a nearby school.

ALEX COOLEY: "Rush were always a real favorite here in Atlanta. They were like the house band at the Electric Ballroom [*laughs*]. They were really a great live band. People would stand up when they came onstage and stay on their feet for the entire performance."[1]

GEDDY: "It wasn't a church. It was a school in Georgia, actually. We were doing a gig that night, and we loaded in, and there was this castle setup in another auditorium. We just happened to have a guy with us who was a camera guy; I think he was working for the record company, and so we just did the song, and he just quickly shot it just for our own kind of use."[2]

IAN: "[It was either] 1974 or '75 at the Electric Ballroom in Atlanta, Georgia. Last set . . . Geddy and Alex donned cowboy hats and were introduced as 'from Southern Ontario . . . ZedZedRush!'"[3]

JANUARY 29, 1975
HAMILTON, ONTARIO
MOHAWK THEATRE, Mohawk College, Fennell Avenue West. Founded in 1966.
NOTES: SRO data includes this date. However, based on a January 9 ad, the "January 29" SRO entry is likely a typo for January 19, or (less likely) the January 19 Hamilton date was rescheduled to January 29 (in order to accommodate a second Delhi performance on the nineteenth).

JANUARY 31, 1975
ROSEVILLE, MICHIGAN
CIRCUS CIRCUS CONCERT HALL, at the Trading Place, 13½ Mile and Gratiot Avenue
TICKETS: $4.00 (advance) / $5.00 (at the door)
CAPACITY: 1,200 (approximate)
NOTES: Two shows, at 8:00 p.m. and 11:00 p.m. Venue owned by outspoken Tigers pitcher Denny McLain.

HOWARD: "Denny McLain was a famous baseball player, and he had a club in Detroit that held about 1,200 people. Rush sold it out in the early days, and we were supposed to play with the James Gang the next night in Evansville, Indiana. But Denny was so happy that we sold it out that he padlocked the doors and told us that we were going to stay and play another night. He didn't know we were already booked the next night, so I had a big argument with him, and the guy pulled a gun on me. He said, 'You're not going anywhere. You're playing here tomorrow night whether you like it or not.' I had to get on the phone and call New York and say, 'Listen, this guy is really serious. He's got a gun and he's not letting us leave.' After that, a phone

call was made, the padlocks came off, and we were on our way."[4]

PHOENIXMIKE (RUSH FAN): "I was big into collecting records back in the '70s, and my brother and I went to a local record show in Roseville. It was in January of 1975, and the small auditorium was set up for a band to play, so we sat down along with about thirty other people to watch the band. I didn't know it at the time, but it was Rush! I remember thinking how strange their music sounded, compared to the other bands at the time. We both remember the band strolling around the vendor area, looking at records."[5]

FEBRUARY 1, 1975
EVANSVILLE, INDIANA
SOLDIERS AND SAILORS MEMORIAL COLISEUM, 300 Court Street
OPENED FOR: James Gang
CAPACITY: 3,500
NOTES: This date is not in SRO's records. Based on Ian's recollection, it was canceled and likely rescheduled for March 16.

FEBRUARY 2, 1975
ROSEVILLE, MICHIGAN
CIRCUS CIRCUS CONCERT HALL, at the Trading Place, 13½ Mile and Gratiot Avenue
TICKETS: $4.00 (advance) / $5.00 (at the door)
CAPACITY: 1,200 (approximate)
NOTES: Two shows, at 8:00 p.m. and 11:00 p.m. This date is unconfirmed but is corroborated based on crew accounts.

IAN: "The crew had no problem loading out. It was Howard who had the problem with McLain. Something else happened at these gigs though. Some kid had also snuck behind our amp line and swiped a Les Paul. We were all pissed off as we made our way to Evansville, but the next night's gig blew up and had been canceled. We got drunk, and then the band did a radio interview (which was hilarious because we'd all been drinking, and all of a sudden, they got a call to come on down and do this interview). Then we went back to the Trading Post on Sunday and Alex's Les Paul was there. Apparently, the kid had brought it home and his dad asked him where the heck he had gotten it. The dad then returned it, 'no questions asked.'"[6]

FEBRUARY 8, 1975
COCHRANE, ONTARIO
ST. JOSEPH'S ELEMENTARY SCHOOL
GYMNASIUM, 207 6th Street. School
was established in 1912.
TICKETS: $4.00 (advance)
CAPACITY: 250
NOTES: Despite subdued applause at the
end of the show, the band was begged by
the promoter to perform an encore, and
they obliged.
IAN: "We knew from past visits that
there were only mom-and-pop motels in
Cochrane. Howard had not booked a
motel, saying, 'We'll pick one up.' It was
minus thirty-eight degrees Fahrenheit,
and the only hotel is (pardon the expression) a drunk Indian hotel where eight
rooms cost a total of seventy-two dollars
(i.e., nine bucks each). Someone had
drained our truck's gas tank, so us crew
had to run two miles to the hotel wearing
denim jackets. When we got there, there
was a fistfight going on in the lobby.
Needless to say, Howard was requested
to never do that again."[7]

FEBRUARY 13, 1975
BELLE RIVER, ONTARIO
COMMUNITY CENTRE ARENA, 304
Rourke Line Road. Venue built in 1973.
SUPPORT ACT: Rose
CAPACITY: 2,000 (1,000 in bleachers)

FEBRUARY 15, 1975
KINGSTON, ONTARIO
KINGSTON MEMORIAL CENTRE
ARENA, 303 York Street. Venue opened
in November 1951.
CAPACITY: 3,300

FEBRUARY 16, 1975
BARRIE, ONTARIO
BARRIE ARENA, 155 Dunlop Street
West. Venue opened in 1934.
CAPACITY: 3,000
NOTES: This date is not in SRO's
records, and the venue is unconfirmed.

FEBRUARY 17, 1975
LONDON, ONTARIO
LONDON ARENA, 65 Bathurst Street.
Venue opened in the mid 1920s.
WITH: Thundermug
CAPACITY: 5,000
NOTES: This date is not in SRO's
records.

FEBRUARY 20, 1975
INDIANAPOLIS, INDIANA
INDIANA CONVENTION CENTER, 100
South Capitol. Venue opened in 1972.
OPENED FOR: Rod Stewart and the
Faces, Montrose
TICKETS: $5.50 (advance) / $6.50 (at
the door)
CAPACITY: 10,000

FEBRUARY 21, 1975
MOUNT PLEASANT, MICHIGAN
FINCH FIELDHOUSE, Central Michigan
University, Franklin Street and East
Preston Street. Venue dedicated on
October 20, 1962.
OPENED FOR: ZZ Top
TICKETS: $4.00 (advance) / $4.50 (at
the door)
CAPACITY: 4,700
CENTRAL MICHIGAN LIFE: "The crowd
reaction to Rush didn't warrant an
encore, but they came back anyway with
their new hit single (get this down kid-
dies) 'Everybody's in the Mood.' My only
question was what mood was everybody
really in after being subjected to that?"

FEBRUARY 24–25, 1975
LANSING, MICHIGAN
THE BREWERY, 3411 East Michigan
Avenue. Venue opened in 1972.
SUPPORT ACT: Brother Bait
ATTENDANCE: 690 per show (approxi-
mate); sold out
NOTES: Rush performed three encores
to a capacity crowd on February 24. The
February 25 show was added just days
before due to popular demand. During
the band's time in Lansing, Neil worked
on the lyrics to "The Fountain" and "I
Think I'm Going Bald."
IAN: "The second time there they put up
a notice to the staff that Rush had hit
122 decibels the last time and to wear
your earplugs."[8]

FEBRUARY 27, 1975
DALLAS, TEXAS
TRAVIS STREET ELECTRIC COMPANY,
4527 Travis Street
SUPPORT ACT: Baked Bears
TICKETS: $3.00
CAPACITY: 800
NOTES: "Back by Popular Demand!"
Neil spent some time working on the lyr-
ics to "No One at the Bridge" and "The
Fountain."

FEBRUARY 28, 1975
LA PORTE, TEXAS
SYLVAN BEACH PAVILION, 1 Sylvan
Beach Drive, overlooking Galveston Bay.
Venue built in 1954.
SUPPORT ACT: Steve Long Group
TICKETS: $3.50 (advance) / $4.00 (at
the door)

MARCH 1, 1975
CORPUS CHRISTI, TEXAS
RITZ MUSIC HALL, 715 North Chaparral
Street. Venue opened on December 25,
1929.
CAPACITY: 1,300
NOTES: Neil worked on the lyrics for
"Panacea."

MARCH 3–4, 1975
ATLANTA, GEORGIA
ALEX COOLEY'S ELECTRIC BALLROOM,
corner of Peachtree Street NE and
Ponce de Leon Avenue
SUPPORT ACT: The Dictators
CAPACITY: 1,100
NOTES: Initially (as of February 13), this
run at the Electric Ballroom was slated to
be March 5 to 8 with Heavy Metal Kids
opening. The run was extended (on
February 27) with the Dictators as the
support.
**MANITOBA (THE DICTATORS LEAD
SINGER):** "We threw White Castle hamburgers at the audience once. All of us
loved White Castle hamburgers, so, naturally, we thought our audience would love
'em too. Unfortunately, we forgot that we
were opening for Rush and this wasn't
exactly our audience. There I was, this
210-pound guy with an afro and a wrestling outfit, throwing hamburgers at a
crowd of Rush fans staring back at us in
horrified shock. I don't think the world,
or that part of it at any rate, was ready
for us yet."[9]

MARCH 5–8, 1975
ATLANTA, GEORGIA
ALEX COOLEY'S ELECTRIC BALLROOM,
corner of Peachtree Street NE and
Ponce de Leon Avenue
SUPPORT ACT: Heavy Metal Kids
CAPACITY: 1,100
NOTES: The Dictators were slated to open
all the Atlanta concerts, but the audience
hated them and their sloppy, proto-punk
sets, so they were fired after only two gigs
and replaced by Heavy Metal Kids.

ANDY SHERNOFF (THE DICTATORS BASSIST): "This was like our first road trip together as a band. We all drove down from New York to open for Rush, and we weren't really getting along very well to begin with. And in those days, there wasn't a circuit of punk clubs for us to tour, so we were stuck on many inappropriate bills. You must remember this was before the Ramones, the Sex Pistols, or MTV, so we were from outer space as far as the audience in Atlanta was concerned. Here's this punkish band throwing White Castle hamburgers at them, just to cause a row, and it worked. After the second show, our road manager came back and told us to head back to NYC. We fired our drummer when we arrived back home. Auspicious timing, as our first album was released in April 1975."[10]

MARCH 10, 1975
NORTHAMPTON, PENNSYLVANIA
ROXY THEATER, 2004 Main Street. Venue first opened on February 1, 1921.
SUPPORT ACT: Man
TICKETS: $2.50
CAPACITY: 650
NOTES: Neil completed the lyrics to "Bacchus Plateau." This show was recorded and broadcast as part of the WSAN-AM concert series.

MARCH 11, 1975
NEWARK, DELAWARE
THE STONE BALLOON, 115 East Main Street. Venue opened on February 22, 1972.
TICKETS: $3.50
ATTENDANCE: 550
CAPACITY: 900
RUSH'S FEE: $2,000
NOTES: This date was added just a week before the gig.
BILL STEVENSON III (STONE BALLOON OWNER): "ATI did a lot of our bookings, and a week before the show I got a call that Rush was looking to fill in some dates. They wanted to book a gig on Sunday, March 9, but we only held concerts on Tuesday nights. Herman's Hermits had been booked and promoted to play on the eleventh, but I had a great relationship with them, and they agreed to reschedule their show in order to open up the date for Rush. We put them on

sale with little promotion, and right away we sold over three hundred tickets. But back then $3.50 was a lot of money for a college kid, so it didn't sell out. I loved Rush. When they arrived, they seemed to be a little tired, and in a bit of turmoil, but they were very professional. They played one set (about an hour) and left for Canada right after the gig. They put on a great show, and the crowd loved them."[11]

MARCH 13, 1975
BALA, ONTARIO
KEE TO BALA, 1012 Bala Falls Road. Venue opened during the summer of 1942.
CAPACITY: 700
NOTES: This date is not in SRO's records but is confirmed by Charlene Lifeson.

MARCH 14, 1975
ORILLIA, ONTARIO
THE PAVILION (AKA "THE PAV"), in Couchiching Park. Venue opened in 1942.
CAPACITY: 1,000
NOTES: This date is not in SRO's records.

MARCH 16, 1975
EVANSVILLE, INDIANA
SOLDIERS AND SAILORS MEMORIAL COLISEUM, 300 Court Street. Historic venue dedicated on April 18, 1917.
OPENED FOR: James Gang
TICKETS: $6.50
CAPACITY: 3,500
NOTES: This gig was most likely rescheduled from February 1, based on crew accounts.

MARCH 18, 1975
SOUTH BEND, INDIANA
MORRIS CIVIC AUDITORIUM, 211 North Michigan Street. Venue opened on November 2, 1922.
OPENED FOR: Aerosmith; Leo Sayer opened the show.
TICKETS: $5.50 (advance) / $6.50 (day of)
CAPACITY: 2,468
NOTES: Opening night of Aerosmith's *Toys in the Attic* Tour. Neil spent some time working on the lyrics to "Lakeside Park" and "No One at the Bridge."

MARCH 19, 1975
BATTLE CREEK, MICHIGAN
THE RAFTERS, 11300 East Michigan Avenue. Venue opened in December 1974.
TICKETS: $2.50

MARCH 20, 1975
TERRE HAUTE, INDIANA
HULMAN CIVIC UNIVERSITY CENTER, Indiana State University campus, 200 North 8th Street. Venue opened on December 14, 1973.
OPENED FOR: Aerosmith, Styx
TICKETS: $5.00 (advance) / $6.00 (day of), general admission
ATTENDANCE: 7,508
CAPACITY: 10,200
NOTES: This gig was originally scheduled for March 21. Neil spent some time working on the lyrics to "Lakeside Park."

MARCH 22, 1975
CINCINNATI, OHIO
SCHMIDT MEMORIAL FIELD HOUSE, Xavier University, 3900 Winding Way. Venue opened on March 7, 1928.
OPENED FOR: Aerosmith, Styx
TICKETS: $5.00 (advance) / $5.50 (day of)
CAPACITY: 3,000 seats
NOTES: Neil spent some time working on the lyrics to "Lakeside Park."
XAVIER UNIVERSITY NEWS: "The lead-off group, Rush, was worse than terrible. They were loud and terrible, producing a severe headache for the reviewer and little music of quality. Styx was not much better. The five-member group has the same fault on solos as Rush, instead of the other persons using less volume, the soloist is forced to be twice as loud. This is not easy on the eardrums of listeners."

MARCH 24, 1975
SAGINAW, MICHIGAN
WENDLER ARENA AT SAGINAW CIVIC CENTER, 303 Johnson Street. Venue opened on October 15, 1972.
OPENED FOR: Aerosmith
TICKETS: $5.00 (advance) / $5.50 (at the door), general admission
ATTENDANCE: 7,000; sold out
NOTES: Neil spent some time working on the lyrics to "I Think I'm Going Bald" and "Lakeside Park." Five people

attending the show were rushed to the emergency room for apparent drug overdoses. All were treated and released, with no arrests reported. "I thought the thing ran rather well," police sergeant Donald Wagner told the *Saginaw Times*. "But there were 7,000 kids there, and about half of them were smoking pot, and there is nothing you can do about it in a place like that. You would need a policeman for every kid to control it." The gig took place despite a 1973 moratorium on rock concerts, which had been eased of late.

MARCH 26, 1975
FORT WAYNE, INDIANA
ALLEN COUNTY WAR MEMORIAL COLISEUM, 4000 Parnell Avenue
OPENED FOR: Aerosmith, James Gang
TICKETS: $5.50 (advance) / $6.50 (day of)
CAPACITY: 10,000, general admission

MARCH 27, 1975
KENOSHA, WISCONSIN
KENOSHA ICE ARENA, 7727 60th Avenue. Venue built in 1970.
OPENED FOR: Kiss (Thin Lizzy was slated to open but canceled at the last minute.)

TICKETS: $5.50 (advance) / $6.50 (day of), general admission
ATTENDANCE: 4,500 (approximate)
NOTES: Despite online claims by promoter Rick Carr (Twin Productions) that the "Rush" on this bill was actually a local Kenosha band (whose name was later changed to HMS Hood), this date is listed in SRO's tour listing, and the concert fits with Rush's tour routing. It is doubtful that a local band would be billed above Thin Lizzy, and the print ad is in Geddy's personal collection (also included in the *Rush ReDISCovered* package released in 2014).

MARCH 28, 1975
CHICAGO, ILLINOIS
ARAGON BALLROOM, 1106 West Lawrence Avenue. Venue dedicated in July 1926.
OPENED FOR: Aerosmith; Pavlov's Dog opened the show.
TICKETS: $6.00
CAPACITY: 4,500
NOTES: Neil spent some time working on the lyrics to "The Fountain."

MARCH 30, 1975
SCHERERVILLE, INDIANA
OMNI 41 SPORTS CENTER ICE RINK, 221 US Route 41 (Wood Hollow Road). Venue built in 1973.
CAPACITY: 1,200 (approximate)

MARCH 31, 1975
LANSING, MICHIGAN
METRO ICE ARENA, 1475 Lake Lansing Road. Venue dedicated in late 1973.
OPENED FOR: Aerosmith, Ted Nugent
TICKETS: $5.50 (advance) / $6.00 (day of)
CAPACITY: 4,600
NOTES: Neil continued work on the lyrics to *Caress of Steel*. Although a review indicates the Amboy Dukes on the bill, more than likely it was Ted Nugent's newly formed solo band.
MICHIGAN STATE NEWS: "Thousands of hard-rock addicts assembled for a ritualistic appreciation of the electronic excesses of three bands."

APRIL 1, 1975
MOUNT PLEASANT, MICHIGAN
ALIBI EAST, 3965 East Broomfield
SUPPORT ACT: Wedsel's Edsels

TICKETS: $2.00 (advance) / $2.50 (at the door)
NOTES: This date is not in SRO's records, but it is corroborated by an advertisement. The Alibi East is a small college bar near the Carnegie Mellon University campus.

APRIL 2, 1975
COLUMBUS, OHIO
VETERANS MEMORIAL AUDITORIUM, 300 West Broad Street. Venue dedicated on November 11, 1955.
OPENED FOR: Aerosmith
CAPACITY: 3,964

APRIL 4, 1975
BUFFALO, NEW YORK
NEW CENTURY THEATRE, 511 Main Street. Venue opened on October 17, 1921.
OPENED FOR: Aerosmith, Les Variations
TICKETS: $4.00 / $5.00 / $6.00
CAPACITY: 3,076
NOTES: This date is not in SRO's records but is corroborated by an advertisement. Venue is aka the Century Theatre. The concert is billed as "New Year's Eve in April."

APRIL 5, 1975
YOUNGSTOWN, OHIO
YOUNGSTOWN STATE UNIVERSITY (YSU) BEEGHLY CENTER, 224 West Spring Street. Venue dedicated on December 2, 1972.
OPENED FOR: Aerosmith; REO Speedwagon was slated to open.
TICKETS: $4.00 (advance) / $5.00 (at the door)
CAPACITY: 6,000
NOTES: Canceled concert. Rush was slated to make its Youngstown debut, as part of a YSU show featuring Aerosmith and REO Speedwagon, but Aerosmith's Joe Perry injured himself by falling off the stage the previous night in Buffalo, necessitating a reschedule of the YSU show. (Rush was not on the bill for the April 13 rescheduled date, as they were performing at the KSHE Kite Festival in St. Louis on that date.) There is a slight chance that Rush *might* have performed at Youngstown's Tomorrow Club on April 5, after the cancellation of the YSU gig, but this is unknown.

APRIL 6, 1975
WASHINGTON, DC
LISNER AUDITORIUM, GEORGE WASHINGTON UNIVERSITY (GWU), 730 21st Street Northwest. Venue dedicated in 1943.
OPENED FOR: Kiss; Heavy Metal Kids opened the show.
TICKETS: $5.00
ATTENDANCE: 1,506; sold out
NOTES: Benefit concert for the Hillcrest Children's Medical Center at GWU.
WASHINGTON POST: "Rush, a three-member group, played next. Since every song was in the same key, and since the group employed a maximum of five chords in each, it rapidly became impossible to tell when one song ended, and another had begun. Besides, the singing bass player sounded like someone's grandma frantically berating an assailant who nonetheless continued to pound her toes with a hammer."

APRIL 7, 1975
CLEVELAND, OHIO
THE AGORA BALLROOM, 1730 East 24th Street. Venue opened on March 31, 1913.
SUPPORT ACT: Sky King
TICKETS: $3.00 (advance) / $3.50 (at the door)
CAPACITY: 700
NOTES: Recorded and broadcast by WMMS-FM on April 9 as part of the WMMS *Live from the Agora* concert series. Often mislabeled by bootleg traders as "May 15, 1975," this recording has long been the premiere bootleg from the *Fly by Night* tour.
SET LIST: "Finding My Way," "Best I Can," "What You're Doing," "Anthem," "Beneath, Between, and Behind," "In the End," "Fly by Night," "Working Man" (with drum solo), "In the Mood," "Need Some Love," "Bad Boy."

APRIL 8, 1975
AKRON, OHIO
AKRON CIVIC THEATRE, 182 South Main Street. Historic venue opened on April 21, 1929.
OPENED FOR: Kiss, Heavy Metal Kids
TICKETS: $5.00 (advance) / $6.00 (day of)
ATTENDANCE: 2,918; oversold
CAPACITY: 2,642

APRIL 9, 1975
ERIE, PENNSYLVANIA
ERIE COUNTY FIELDHOUSE, 5750 Wattsburg Road. Venue opened in early 1974.
OPENED FOR: Kiss; Vitale's Madmen opened the gig.
TICKETS: $4.50 (advance) / $5.50 (day of)
CAPACITY: 5,250 (3,750 permanent seats)
JOE VITALE (LEGENDARY DRUMMER): "I do remember that show because it was the first time I got to see Rush live and, of course, Neil Peart (one of my faves). Rush is one of those special bands that have managed to keep delivering great music and *not* break up. . . . Imagine that! That, I believe, is the primary reason for their longevity. Neil Peart has given a lifetime of inspiration to millions of drummers and musicians of all walks of life. It's sad that many of the best bands out there broke up due to silly grievances, petty bickering, egos, etc. . . . Bravo Rush!"[12]

APRIL 11, 1975
DETROIT, MICHIGAN
MICHIGAN PALACE, 238 Bagley Street. Building opened on August 23, 1926.
SUPPORT ACT: Status Quo
TICKETS: $5.00 (advance) / $5.50 (at the door)
ATTENDANCE: 4,050; sold out
NOTES: Rush's first headline concert at a medium-sized venue.
CIRCUS: "Detroit's Michigan Palace was full to the brim. Canada's premier metallic trio were onstage grinding out their rock 'n' roll in a close Grand Funk mold. The joint was jumping."
LIAM: "The promoter had gone a little heavy on the advertising and claimed something to the effect that we were bringing in three tons of equipment, and we had nothing near that. So, in order to keep up with what people were expecting, we had to go out and rent a lot of gear to fill the stage, a lot more bass and guitar cabinets which weren't being used at all. But the advertisement led people to believe it was going to be a ridiculous amount of equipment, which was very popular at the time, so we had to go ahead and rent a lot more gear. This was also the first gig where the white shag carpet was used, and Neil got a drum riser as well. Previously, he

had just been playing off of the floor with drum boards."[13]
HOWARD: "One of the first Rush shows at the Michigan Palace, I used to have five guys on one of those piano boards. There had to be about seventy different levers on it and they all locked in, so you'd have groups of people locking down switches and then throwing the big master. It took two people sometimes to do the cross-fades. It was amazing. It's incredible how far lighting has come and the board changes now—a far cry from there."[14]

APRIL 12, 1975
NORMAL, ILLINOIS
UNION AUDITORIUM, ILLINOIS STATE UNIVERSITY, 100 North University Street. Venue opened in September 1973.
OPENED FOR: Kiss
TICKETS: $5.00 (all seats reserved)
CAPACITY: 3,457

APRIL 13, 1975
ST. LOUIS, MISSOURI
KSHE KITE FESTIVAL, AVIATION FIELD, Forest Park, 5500 Clayton Avenue. Field dedicated on June 24, 1876.
OPENED FOR: The Charlie Daniels Band; Backdraft opened the concert.
TICKETS: Free
ATTENDANCE: 70,000+ (approximate)
NOTES: A photo from this gig appeared in the packaging for the *Beyond the Lighted Stage* documentary. The show ran from noon to 5:00 p.m., with Rush the second of three acts. Despite the large crowd, there were only four arrests for minor drug offenses and one injury reported.
CHARLIE DANIELS: "I have recollections of the show, but they do not involve Rush as I flew in and, due to a security snarl, took quite a while to get to the venue, making it in time to play but little else."[15]

APRIL 15, 1975
PITTSBURGH, PENNSYLVANIA
STANLEY THEATRE, 719 Liberty Avenue. Venue opened on February 27, 1928.
OPENED FOR: Kiss; Heavy Metal Kids opened the show.
ATTENDANCE: 3,700; sold out
NOTES: General admission concert. Neil spent some time working on the lyrics to "Bastille Day." The Kids were added to the bill during the last week of March.

PITTSBURGH PRESS: "Rock Bands Battle, Fans the Winner: It was a rowdy crowd that invaded the Stanley, guards at the front door filling carton after carton with bottles and cans of potent liquids. From Toronto came Rush, the trio which did so well opening for Uriah Heep last August. They continue the same good sounds, and you could hear them all—and they all deserve to be heard. Bassist Geddy Lee screams like Robert Plant; Neil Peart, a big man, beats the drums like the devil; guitarist Alex Lifeson was superb, especially on 'By-Tor and the Snow Dog' when he used a volume pedal to make his guitar sound like an organ."

NEIL: "I remember the rats in the back alley by the stage door."[16]

APRIL 17, 1975
BURLINGTON, IOWA
BURLINGTON MEMORIAL AUDITORIUM, 200 Front Street
OPENED FOR: Kiss; the Kids opened the show.
TICKETS: $5.00 (advance), general admission
CAPACITY: 2,530
NOTES: The Heavy Metal Kids shortened their name to the Kids for a brief period after the release of their second album in 1975.

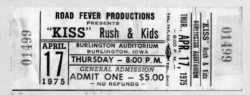

APRIL 18, 1975
BELLEVILLE, ILLINOIS
STUDENT ACTIVITIES BUILDING, Belleville Area College, 2500 Carlyle Avenue. College established in 1971.
SUPPORTING ACTS: Megan McDonough, Star (featuring J. Welch)
ADMISSION: Free
ATTENDANCE: "It wasn't packed."[17]
NOTES: In order to do the gig, the band rented half of Kiss's PA system. Members of the local band Star became angry at front man J. Welch for self-promotion, so the entire band quit on him just prior to this show, forcing Welch to do a solo set. Students had to take off their shoes upon entrance, so as not to ruin the floor of the new gym.[18]

APRIL 19, 1975
PALATINE, ILLINOIS
WILLIAM FREMD HIGH SCHOOL, Main Gym, 1000 South Quentin Road. School established in 1961.
OPENED FOR: Kiss
TICKETS: $4.50
CAPACITY: 3,000 (approximate)
NOTES: Remaining seats were $4.00 at the door.[19] The local band Rockandy was advertised as the opener, but they did not perform. Proceeds from the concert were used to pay for a special events sign at the school, which Ted Nugent attended. A *Billboard* blurb published on this date states that "Rush will tour Canada in mid-summer with Rory Gallagher," but this would not come to fruition.

APRIL 21, 1975
LOUISVILLE, KENTUCKY
MEMORIAL AUDITORIUM, 970 South 4th Street. Historic venue dedicated on May 30, 1929.
OPENED FOR: Kiss
TICKETS: $5.50 (advance) / $6.50 (at the door)
CAPACITY: 1,742 (1,429 main floor, 313 balcony)
NOTES: Neil spent some time working on the lyrics to "Bastille Day" and "The Fountain."

APRIL 22, 1975
INDIANAPOLIS, INDIANA
CONVENTION CENTER, 100 South Capitol
OPENED FOR: Kiss; Status Quo opened the concert.
TICKETS: $5.00 (advance) / $6.00 (day of)
CAPACITY: 10,000

APRIL 24, 1975
JOHNSON CITY, TENNESSEE
FREEDOM HALL CIVIC CENTER, 1320 Pactolas Road. Venue opened on July 5, 1974.
OPENED FOR: Kiss; the Kids opened the show.
ATTENDANCE: 3,000 (approximate)[20]
CAPACITY: 7,500
NOTES: General admission concert. Fourteen people were arrested, eleven of them for public drunkenness. The majority of the arrests occured outside the venue before the concert.[21]

APRIL 25, 1975
CHARLOTTE, NORTH CAROLINA
CHARLOTTE PARK CENTER, Central Piedmont Community College, 310 North Kings Highway Drive. Venue dedicated on July 16, 1956.
OPENED FOR: Kiss
TICKETS: $5.00 (advance) / $6.00 (at the door), general admission
ATTENDANCE: 3,000; sold out
NOTES: A Kiss fan en route to this concert is killed in a car accident. The tragedy provides the story line to the band's 1976 anthem "Detroit Rock City."

APRIL 26, 1975
FAYETTEVILLE, NORTH CAROLINA
CUMBERLAND COUNTY MEMORIAL ARENA, 1960 Coliseum Drive. Venue opened on January 23, 1968.
OPENED FOR: Kiss; Atlanta Rhythm Section opened the concert.
TICKETS: $5.00 (advance)
ATTENDANCE: 3,564
CAPACITY: 7,000

APRIL 27, 1975
RICHMOND, VIRGINIA
RICHMOND ARENA, Boulevard and Hermitage Road. Venue dedicated in 1908.
OPENED FOR: Kiss; Brian Auger's Oblivion Express and MS Funk opened the concert.
TICKETS: $5.00 (advance) / $6.00 (at the door), general admission
ATTENDANCE: 3,732
CAPACITY: 6,022
NOTES: Rush were "special guests" on the bill. MS Funk featured Tommy Shaw, just before he joined Styx. Brian Auger's Oblivion Express was a jazz-infused rock group that included many musicians who went on to make their name in other groups like the Average White Band and Return to Forever. For this Richmond performance, future Santana vocalist Alex Ligertwood was center stage. When he worked for ATI before joining Rush, Howard Ungerleider toured with Brian Auger's Oblivion Express.

MAY 2, 1975
ANGOLA, INDIANA
HERSHEY HALL FIELDHOUSE, Tri-State University campus, Park Street. School founded in 1884.
OPENED FOR: Kiss
CAPACITY: 4,500

NOTES: An early tour advertisement lists this date as "Johnstown, PA," but SRO's records indicate "Angola, Indiana," so it likely reflects a restructuring of the tour after the ad went to print.

MAY 3, 1975
BEDFORD, OHIO
ST. PETER CHANEL HIGH SCHOOL, 480 Northfield Road. School founded in 1957.
SUPPORT ACT: Sweetleaf
TICKETS: $3.50 (advance) / $4.00 (day of)
CY SULAK (SWEETLEAF GUITARIST): "I remember enjoying the concert because their music was fresh and unique for the time! Alex impressed me with the amount of sound and complexity he displayed being the main instrument in a three-piece band."[22]

MAY 6, 1975
MILWAUKEE, WISCONSIN
RIVERSIDE THEATER, 116 West Wisconsin. Venue opened on April 29, 1928.
OPENED FOR: Kiss
TICKETS: $4.00 / $5.00 / $6.00
CAPACITY: 2,558
NOTES: Following Rush's set, a stage announcement was made warning the audience of bad pills circulating at the concert.
IAN: "Alex asked his tech, Jim Johnson, to set up a small rig in an upper dressing room so he could test all the effects pedals of that era that he owned. Out of seven, there were three that did not function. Alex said to get rid of the three. JJ, Liam, and I took one each and flipped them out the window into the river. Ten seconds later, Alex returns and says 'No, I want to take those three pedals home.'"[23]

MAY 8, 1975
ROMEOVILLE, ILLINOIS
JOHN F. KENNEDY SPORTS CENTER GYMNASIUM, Lewis University campus, University Drive West. Gym built in the late 1960s; school founded in 1932.
OPENED FOR: Kiss
TICKETS: $3.00 (free for students with ID)
ATTENDANCE: 2,200; sold out
NOTES: This date is not in SRO's records but is corroborated by an ad from the day of the concert.

MAY 9, 1975
LITTLE ROCK, ARKANSAS / ADA, OHIO
NOTES: This date is not in SRO's records. Initially listed in an early tour ad as "Little Rock, Arkansas," the week of May 9–15 was most likely canceled due to Geddy having tonsillitis.[24] Although a later ad and ticket stub indicates Rush supporting Kiss and James Gang in Ada, Ohio, on this date, they are a late cancellation and are replaced by a jazz-rock band from Chicago called the Flock.

MAY 10, 1975
NEW ORLEANS, LOUISIANA
THE WAREHOUSE, 1820 Tchoupitoulas Street. Historic venue opened on January 30, 1970.
CAPACITY: 3,500
NOTES: This performance is not in SRO's records. Initially listed in an early tour ad, the week of May 9–15 was most likely canceled due to Geddy having tonsillitis.[25] Another advertisement lists Rush with Aerosmith in Harrisburg, Pennsylvania, on this date, but Rush's participation is questionable there as well.

MAY 11, 1975
DOTHAN, ALABAMA
CIVIC CENTER, 126 North Saint Andrews Street. Venue dedicated on January 25, 1975.
CAPACITY: 3,100
NOTES: This date is not in SRO's records. Initially listed in an early tour ad, the week of May 9–15 was most likely canceled due to Geddy having tonsillitis.[26]

MAY 16, 1975
PORT CHESTER, NEW YORK
CAPITOL THEATER, 149 Westchester Avenue. Venue opened on August 18, 1926.
OPENED FOR: Blue Oyster Cult
TICKETS: $5.50 (advance) / $6.00 (day of)
CAPACITY: 1,800

MAY 17, 1975
JOHNSTOWN, PENNSYLVANIA
CAMBRIA COUNTY WAR MEMORIAL ARENA, 326 Napoleon Street. Venue opened in October 16, 1950.
OPENED FOR: Kiss
TICKETS: $5.00 (advance) / $6.00 (day of)
CAPACITY: 5,500

MAY 18, 1975
MACOMB, ILLINOIS
CAMPUS GROUNDS, WESTERN ILLINOIS UNIVERSITY (WIU), 103 University Drive. Established in 1899.
OPENED FOR: Mason Proffit, Windfall, and Roger Cooper; the Wright Brothers Overland Stage Company opened the show.
ADMISSION: Free
NOTES: Free outdoor concert, part of WIU's "Hey Days of May" celebration. An early tour advertisement states this date as "Memphis, TN," but SRO's records indicate Macomb, Illinois, so it likely reflects a restructuring of the tour after the ad went to print.

MAY 19, 1975
ST. PAUL, MINNESOTA
ST. PAUL CIVIC CENTER THEATER, 143 West Fourth Street. Venue opened on January 1, 1973.
OPENED FOR: Kiss
NOTES: This date is not in SRO's tour listing, and it is unconfirmed. Library research in St. Paul failed to turn up any evidence of the concert in local papers. The book *Kiss Alive Forever* does list this gig, but with Hydra as the opening band. If the show occurred, it is doubtful that Rush was involved.

MAY 22, 1975
YAKIMA, WASHINGTON
SHERAR GYMNASIUM, Yakima Valley Community College campus, 1000 South 12th Avenue. Venue opened in 1957.
OPENED FOR: Kiss
TICKETS: $5.00 (advance) / $6.00 (day of)
CAPACITY: 1,500 (seats)
NOTES: According to fan accounts, the flames shooting out of Kiss's flash pots went so high that they bounced off the ceiling. The crowd could feel the heat every time they were ignited.

MAY 23, 1975
MEDFORD, OREGON
MEDFORD ARMORY, 1701 South Pacific Avenue. Venue dedicated on May 25, 1957.
OPENED FOR: Kiss
TICKETS: $5.00 (advance) / $6.00 (day of), general admission
CAPACITY: 3,000

MAY 24, 1975
PORTLAND, OREGON
PARAMOUNT NORTHWEST THEATRE, 1037 Southwest Broadway. Venue opened on March 8, 1928.
OPENED FOR: Kiss
TICKETS: $5.00 (advance) / $6.00 (day of), general admission
ATTENDANCE: 3,036; sold out

MAY 25, 1975
SEATTLE, WASHINGTON
PARAMOUNT NORTHWEST THEATRE, 901 Pine Street. Historic venue built March 1, 1928.
OPENED FOR: Kiss
TICKETS: $5.00 (advance) / $6.00 (day of), general admission
ATTENDANCE: 2,976 (*Walrus*)
CAPACITY: 3,054
WALRUS: "The crowd went crazy—They were on their feet when Rush got on the stage. They were berserk by the time Kiss left."

MAY 26, 1975
PORTLAND, OREGON
PARAMOUNT NORTHWEST THEATRE, 1037 Southwest Broadway
OPENED FOR: Kiss
TICKETS: $5.00 (advance) / $6.00 (day of), general admission
CAPACITY: 3,036

MAY 27, 1975
SPOKANE, WASHINGTON
SPOKANE COLISEUM, 1101 North Howard Street. Venue opened on December 3, 1954.
OPENED FOR: Kiss
TICKETS: $5.00 (advance) / $6.00 (day of)
ATTENDANCE: 4,000 (approximate)
CAPACITY: 8,500

MAY 29, 1975
LAS VEGAS, NEVADA
SPACE CENTER, SAHARA HOTEL, 32535 Las Vegas Boulevard South. Venue opened in the fall of 1968.
OPENED FOR: Kiss
TICKETS: $6.50
CAPACITY: 4,500; sold out
NOTES: 10:00 p.m. performance. These Sahara concerts were among the very first by a hard rock band in a casino hotel, so promoter Gary Naseef had to come up with a unique way of marketing Kiss. "I asked their agent if he had video on them, and he said he had a Beta [max tape], so I pulled all my advertising from the radio and put it onto Channel 5," Naseef remembers. "I must've run twenty commercials a day showing these guys with their pyrotechnics and their makeup and [Gene Simmons's] tongue and blood, and it worked. I only paid Kiss seven hundred dollars total for two shows that night—8:00 p.m. and 2:00 a.m.—and they sold out 4,500 seats at each show. And we also got an opening band, which was Rush. Everybody walked out of that show and said, 'That was outrageous.'"[27]

MAY 30, 1975
LAS VEGAS, NEVADA
SPACE CENTER, SAHARA HOTEL, 32535 Las Vegas Boulevard South. Venue opened in the fall of 1968.
OPENED FOR: Kiss
TICKETS: $7.50
CAPACITY: 4,500; sold out
TWO-SHOW CONCERT GROSS: $28,730
NOTES: This was a 2:00 a.m. performance. Load-out didn't finish until 7:00 a.m. Tickets to this 2:00 a.m. gig were one dollar more than the 10:00 p.m. concert so that the promoter could pay the obligatory ten stagehands overtime. These gigs were part of the Sahara Command Performance Concert Series. Gene Simmons (from Kiss) accidentally singed his hair during this show. An early tour ad lists a May 30, 1975, Sacramento date, but Ian indicates that there was no performance that night.
BILLBOARD: "Officially dubbed 'Glitter Night' on the Strip, Kiss unleashed controlled chaos. The four authors of Armageddon dazzled, delighted, and devastated hardcore rock fanatics in a tightly packaged electronic horror show. Canadian-born Rush opened both shows in forty-five-minute displays of hard rock musicianship. The trio set the mood from songs on their two released albums."

MAY 31, 1975
LOS ANGELES, CALIFORNIA
SHRINE AUDITORIUM, 665 West Jefferson Boulevard Historic venue opened on January 23, 1926.
OPENED FOR: Nazareth
CAPACITY: 6,442
NOTES: This date is not in SRO's records but is corroborated by an ad in the May 30 edition of the *Van Nuys Valley News* (which erroneously also lists Kiss on the bill). While many fan sites list Rush with Kiss and James Gang at Long Beach Arena on this date, a review of the Long Beach concert confirms that Rush was *not* on that bill.

JUNE 1, 1975
SAN FRANCISCO, CALIFORNIA
WINTERLAND BALLROOM, Post and Steiner Streets. Historic building opened on June 29, 1928.
OPENED FOR: Kiss, the Tubes
TICKETS: $5.00 (advance) / $6.00 (at the door)
ATTENDANCE: 2,200
CAPACITY: 5,400
NOTES: Bill Graham began promoting concerts at Winterland on September 23, 1966 with Jefferson Airplane and transformed it into a concert-only venue in 1971. This gig was filmed by Bill Graham Presents, but the film is rumored to have been destroyed in an early '80s fire, although the video from the Tubes performance has been released. A careless stagehand knocked over one of Alex's Marshall stacks, leading to Rush's crew butting heads with the Bill Graham Presents roadies, who denied having done anything. Howard Ungerleider tried to have the damages added to Rush's wage but was unsuccessful.
RICK MUNROE (KISS ROAD CREW): "When we got to Winterland, the opening act was already set up onstage rehearsing. We thought, 'What the hell is this? An opening act onstage before the headliner?' I remember us doing our New York thing, getting brash, vocal, and walking right out in the middle of

the stage, and all of us going, 'What the fuck is going on out here?' Just then, Bill Graham came out onstage and he let us have it: 'This is my house. This is my stage. This is my group. You are going to be doing what I tell you to do, when I tell you to do it. Now, get the hell off the stage!' We all looked at each other, 'Well that's never happened to us before.' The band was the Tubes. Bill Graham used the sold-out Kiss concert to showcase the Tubes. So we were stuck with them onstage, and we had to build around them, even though we were the headliner."[28]

IAN: "This guy somehow put his hand through the grill and wrecked a speaker. Howie and Alex were livid because, instead of owning up and paying $100, I ended up in a very small room surrounded by big guys and this guy. I was told, 'He says he didn't do it. Whatcha gonna do about it?' Not much I could do. At the next gig, Kiss roadies tell us this clown is their new stage manager and would I please not kill him. On an English tour a few years later the jerk shows up on the lighting crew. Howie asks me, 'Where do I know this guy from?' We figure it out, and guess who was off the tour? Revenge."[29]

JUNE 2–5, 1975
WEST HOLLYWOOD, CALIFORNIA
THE STARWOOD, 8151 Santa Monica Boulevard. Building opened in the 1960s.
SUPPORT ACT: Masters of the Airwaves
CAPACITY: 999
NOTES: June 2 was Ladies Night. Mercury records hosted a promotional party for the band. June 3 was Student Night. While this gig is in SRO's records, and is confirmed by ads and blurbs, an early tour advertisement indicates Rush was originally scheduled to perform in Long Beach, California, on this date. Masters of the Airwaves only performed on Monday (June 2) and Tuesday (June 3). Note that the ad lists them as "Masters of the Airways." The Starwood comprised three separate venues centered around a large bar area. The main concert room had a legal capacity of 498, but the capacity was 999 for the entire premises, thus allowing shows to far exceed the capacity deemed safe by the LA County fire marshal. During this

week in Los Angeles, Neil worked on lyrics to "The Necromancer." While this gig is in SRO's records, an early tour advertisement shows Rush originally scheduled to perform on June 5 in San Bernardino, California.

JUNE 6, 1975
FRESNO, CALIFORNIA
WARNORS THEATRE, 1400 Fulton Street. Historic venue opened on October 20, 1928.
OPENED FOR: Kiss
TICKETS: $5.00 (advance) / $6.00 (day of)
CAPACITY: 2,164
NOTES: General admission concert.

JUNE 7, 1975
SAN DIEGO, CALIFORNIA
CIVIC THEATRE, 1100 3rd Avenue at B Street. Venue opened on January 12, 1965.
OPENED FOR: Kiss
TICKETS: $6.50
ATTENDANCE: 1,600
CAPACITY: 2,902
NOTES: Final date of the Kiss tour. A whipped-cream-pie fight transpired onstage between Kiss and Rush. Ian spent the next two days cleaning off the drum kit, enlisting his father to help.
RICK MUNROE (KISS ROAD CREW): "It started with our crew wanting to get their crew. Then Kiss found out about it and said, 'Hell, we'll go out and cream the band.' It was a pretty well-organized sneak attack, to the point where the front-of-house people only saw the pies a split second before it hit them. We had people come out behind them to get them there. Rush retaliated by dancing around onstage during Kiss's set dressed up in Indian costumes and war paint."[30]
NEIL: "We were gonna dress up as them. Put on their makeup, and go out and do our set as them, but what finally happened was an onstage pie fight in front of 3,000 screaming kids. They caught us at the end of our set by surprise, and the whole stage was covered in shaving cream and whipped cream. Then it was our turn at the end of their set. All of their guitars and drums and machines were completely buried in shaving cream, so their encore sounded just great!"[31]

IAN: "The drum kit was totally covered in this sticky sweet crap. Having no time to clean it after the gig, it went straight into the cases, to the truck, and right to LAX for the flight back to Toronto. The customs guys made me open up all of the drum cases and laughed their asses off about what a mess they were. I spent two of my off days cleaning the gunk from them, and it wasn't easy."

JUNE 9, 1975
DUNDAS, ONTARIO
ARENA, 35 Market Street South. Venue opened December 12, 1950.
SUPPORT ACT: Joe Mendelson (unconfirmed)
CAPACITY: 940
NOTES: While SRO's records include this date, it was rescheduled for June 22, which is corroborated by an advertisement.

JUNE 13, 1975
WINDSOR, ONTARIO
CLEARY AUDITORIUM, 201 Riverside Drive. Venue opened in 1960.
SUPPORT ACT: Joe Mendelson
ATTENDANCE: 1,000[32]
WINDSOR STAR: "The lights spun a pink cocoon over the stage, with sprays of green and mauve hitting the musicians. Gold spots under Neil's drum kit threw an angelic glow through his floppy white shirt. A rear projector sent the snow owl from *Fly by Night* glowering on a transparent scrim behind the band, while a rotating mirror ball caught flecks of light and tossed them into the auditorium. Alex and Geddy danced on a white shag rug while sending their heavy-metal abrasions."

JUNE 14, 1975
WHITBY, ONTARIO
IROQUOIS PARK SPORTS CENTRE
ARENA 1, 500 Victoria Street West. Venue opened in 1974.
SUPPORT ACT: Joe Mendelson
CAPACITY: 2,500
NOTES: Joe Mendelson changed his name to Mendelson Joe sometime in 1975. In that same year, he frequently worked with Ben Mink, who would later become a member of FM and also collaborate with Geddy on "My Favorite Headache" and "Losing It."

JUNE 19, 1975
REGINA, SASKATCHEWAN
TRIANON BALLROOM, 2400 12th
Avenue
SUPPORT ACT: Cambridge
CAPACITY: 1,700 (approximate)
NOTES: Two shows. According to fans, it felt like a hundred degrees inside the venue. The members of Cambridge were only sixteen years old at the time of this performance. Rush was originally slated to perform at Winnipeg Convention Centre (with Joe Mendelson and Holy Hannah as support), but that date was canceled just two days prior to the gig because of poor ticket sales ("barely 700 tickets had been sold").[33]
THE LEADER-POST: "Rush worth encores: The Regina concert, two shows, was not everything it might have been. The band is a punishingly heavy power trio that plays at excruciatingly high volume levels. The sound was thick and undifferentiated, which it is not on the albums. Not a great concert, but still worth the price for those who got out for it. The word isn't out on Rush yet, but it soon will be."

JUNE 20, 1975
THUNDER BAY, ONTARIO
FORT WILLIAM GARDENS, 901 Miles Street. Venue opened on March 6, 1951.
SUPPORT ACT: Joe Mendelson
CAPACITY: 5,024
NOTES: Before the Canadian tour was finalized, Rush was slated to open for Kiss on this date at Convention Hall in Asbury Park, New Jersey. While the band flew in from Regina, the crew had an eight-hundred-mile drive. The concert ran late, with Rush not going onstage until around midnight, performing to a rambunctious audience. Opener Joe Mendelson was greeted with a barrage of glass bottles and chants of "We want Rush!" during his short set. There were no spotlights because the venue lacked a power supply. The slide show was also axed when the projector blew out, and the band's monitors were malfunctioning.
MUSICANADA: "Rush Concert Flops: When Rush finally came on, the juvenile audience charged the stage, leaving most of the seats empty. And get this: they sat and kneeled in the broken glass they'd hurled only minutes before. After a seventy-minute set plagued by the poor

acoustics of the Gardens, Rush did an encore. They shouldn't have. The audience didn't deserve it."

JUNE 22, 1975
SAULT STE. MARIE, ONTARIO
SAULT MEMORIAL GARDENS, 269 Queen Street. Venue opened on February 20, 1949.
SUPPORT ACTS: Joe Mendelson, Trione
TICKETS: $3.50 (advance) / $4.00 (day of) CAD
ATTENDANCE: 2,200[34]
CAPACITY: 3,990
NOTES: Originally slated for June 21, this date is rebooked at the eleventh hour because the band's equipment truck broke down en route from Thunder Bay. Existing tickets were honored. A previously scheduled concert at Dundas Arena on June 22 is promptly moved to June 24. "One of the biggest most sophisticated light shows to enter Canada. Don't Miss This One." Ticket numbers 756 to 774 and 800 to 1000 were not valid due to theft.
SAULT DAILY STAR: "Gardens rocked to heavy music, flashing lights."

JUNE 23, 1975
LAKEFIELD, ONTARIO
LAKEFIELD-SMITH COMMUNITY CENTER ARENA, 20 Concession Street. Venue opened in 1972.
SUPPORT ACT: Fludd
CAPACITY: 1,100
NOTES: The Lakefield concert is listed in a May 24 *RPM* magazine ad as June 30, but this gig is in SRO's records as June 23, and there is an ad in the June 20 *Peterborough Examiner* for June 23, so it may have ended up being rescheduled to this date.

JUNE 24, 1975
DUNDAS, ONTARIO
MARKET STREET ARENA, 35 Market Street South. Venue opened on December 12, 1950.
SUPPORT ACT: Max Webster
CAPACITY: 1,300
NOTES: This date was postponed at the last minute from June 22 to June 24 because the band's equipment truck broke down in Northern Ontario.
IAN: "Max's crew didn't pack although they could have, and I bitched them out when they held up our load-out."

JUNE 25, 1975
TORONTO, ONTARIO
MASSEY HALL, 178 Victoria Street. Historic venue opened on June 14, 1894.
SUPPORT ACT: Max Webster
TICKETS: $3.50 / $4.50 / $5.50 CAD
CAPACITY: 2,765; sold out
CONCERT GROSS: $11,936 CAD
NOTES: Rush's first headlining appearance at Massey Hall is sold out, with the band turning away many fans at the door. By this time, Neil had added four high concert toms to his kit (the copper drums were added sometime in the spring). Photos from this concert later appeared in the *Caress of Steel* liner notes. After the show Polydor Records held a small dinner in the band's honor, attended by the band, their friends, and a few select media personalities.
SET LIST: "Finding My Way," "Best I Can," "Anthem," "Beneath, Between, and Behind," "In the End," "Fly by Night," "By-Tor and the Snow Dog," "Working Man" (with drum solo), "In the Mood," "Need Some Love," "What You're Doing."
GEDDY (ONSTAGE): "Thank you! How's everybody doing? It's nice to be home. We've been away for a while. We seem to be getting a lot of flowers tonight. Thank you! Is it as hot out there as it is up here?"
RECORD WEEK: "Rush made what could only be termed a triumphant return to Toronto, filling Massey Hall to its absolute capacity. 2,765 souls, all of them screaming, and some of them flooding the foot of the stage and filling the center aisle."
CHUM-FM: "It could only be described as a triumphant homecoming for

Toronto's Rush. A good share of the audience spent the evening singing along to the hard rock coming off the stage. Rush has organized a few visuals for themselves, including a replica of their *Fly by Night* cover on a rear screen. The eyes light up a lot, glaring at the crowd. They use only four-dozen actual spots and flood lights, but they're used with economy and forethought."

IAN: "Massey Hall is an important, historic venue that we were thrilled to play. As far as a gig, it's kind of primitive—no room for the road cases backstage and a very basic dressing room. It's got great acoustics but very little room for a PA. My girl Nancy, brought my mom to the show. The lights go down and half of the place fires up a joint. My mom asks Nancy, 'What the heck is that smell?' Hey Mom—it's rock 'n' roll!"

GLOBE AND MAIL: "Rush ear-splitting band with no variety: The sell-out crowd greeted the returning hometown heroes by cramming the aisles and lighting sparklers. All this for Rush? I could see it for the Rolling Stones, but Rush? The young and fresh-faced crowd seemed to be completely content with Rush's totally unsophisticated approach to rock. Rush's only distinctive characteristic is Lee's voice. He sounds like the damned howling in Hades. Still, they must be doing something right judging by the number of young women who leapt on to the stage to give Lee roses and plant wet ones on his cheek."

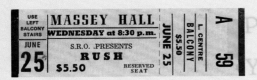

JUNE 26, 1975
WATERLOO, ONTARIO
LAURIER THEATRE AUDITORIUM, SIR WILFRID LAURIER UNIVERSITY, 75 University Avenue West. Venue opened in 1969.
SUPPORT ACT: Joe Mendelson
TICKETS: $4.50 (advance) / $5.00 (at the door) CAD
CAPACITY: 849
NOTES: The band performed a nine-song, hour-long set, culled mostly from *Fly by Night*.[35] In Canada, *Fly by Night* had sold more than thirty-five thousand

copies in two months and *Rush* had sold twenty thousand in a year.[36]
KITCHENER-WATERLOO RECORD: "Rush's frenzied loudness infectious: When Rush first appeared, there was a sudden surge forward toward the stage by the audience on the auditorium's floor level. They stood up throughout the first couple of numbers, finally sitting only after being asked three or four times by Geddy Lee. Peart, incidentally, contributes some outstanding work with a great deal of flourish in his handling of the sticks. A particular highlight was his solo addition to 'Working Man.'"

JUNE 27, 1975
LONDON, ONTARIO
CENTENNIAL HALL, 550 Wellington Street. Venue opened on June 21, 1967.
SUPPORT ACT: Symphonic Slam
TICKETS: $3.50 (advance) / $4.50 (at the door) CAD, general admission
ATTENDANCE: 1,100
CAPACITY: 1,637, seated
NOTES: Symphonic Slam was a classic progressive-rock band in the vein of Genesis and the Moody Blues.
LONDON FREE PRESS: "The somewhat glitter-influenced Rush contrasted in style with the formally-attired Slam. To Rush, nothing matters much beside their primitive-styled hard-rock sound."

JUNE 28, 1975
BALA, ONTARIO
KEE TO BALA, 1012 Bala Falls Road
TICKETS: $3.50 CAD
CAPACITY: 700

JUNE 29, 1975
PORT DOVER, ONTARIO
SUMMER GARDEN DANCE HALL, Walker Street at the beach. Venue built in 1929.
SUPPORT ACTS: Max Webster, Joe Mendelson
TICKETS: $4.00 (advance) CAD
CAPACITY: 500 to 700
NOTES: An ad two weeks before the show in the *Simcoe Reformer* lists advance tickets at four dollars, while an ad the week of the date indicates advance tickets as one dollar. So either the latter is a misprint, or the price was drastically reduced just before the gig.

1. Bill Banasiewicz. Interview with Alex Cooley.
2. *RockLine*, May 9, 2007.
3. Ian Grandy. Facebook.com, October 26, 2015.
4. Eric Hansen. Interview with Howard Ungerleider, July 11, 2012.
5. PhoenixMike. *The Rush Forum*, June 28, 2010.
6. Skip Daly. Interview with Ian Grandy, 2012.
7. Ian Grandy. Facebook.com, June 13, 2016.
8. Ian Grandy. Facebook.com, July 28, 2015.
9. Al Muzer. Interview with Manitoba, 1997.
10. Bill Banasiewicz. Interview with Andy Shernoff, June 2014.
11. Bill Banasiewicz. Interview with Bill Stevenson III, December 30, 2015.
12. Bill Banasiewicz. Interview with Joe Vitale, April 22, 2017.
13. Bill Banasiewicz. Interview with Liam Birt, January 20, 1984.
14. Brad Parmerter. Interview with Howard Ungerleider. Livejournal.com, July 22, 2013.
15. Bill Banasiewicz. Interview with Charlie Daniels, May 1, 2017.
16. Neil Peart. *Roadshow: Landscape with Drums: A Concert Tour by Motorcycle.* Rounder Books, 2006.
17. *The Belleville News-Democrat*, February 17, 2008.
18. *The Belleville News-Democrat*, February 17, 2008.
19. *Elk Grove Herald.*
20. *Kingston Times-News.*
21. *Kingston Times-News.*
22. Bill Banasiewicz. Interview with Cy Sulak, July 23, 2018.
23. Ian Grandy. Facebook.com, February 15, 2017.
24. *Record Week*, June 30, 1975.
25. *Record Week*, June 30, 1975.
26. *Record Week*, June 30, 1975.
27. *Las Vegas Sun*, April 26, 2007.
28. Curt Gooch and Jess Suhs. *Kiss Alive Forever: The Complete Touring History*. Billboard Books, 2002.
29. Skip Daly. Interview with Ian Grandy, July 13, 2016.
30. Curt Gooch and Jess Suhs. *Kiss Alive Forever: The Complete Touring History*. Billboard Books, 2002.
31. Interview with Neil Peart. *Circus.*
32. *Windsor Star.*
33. *Winnipeg Free Press.*
34. *The Sault Daily Star.*
35. *Kitchener-Waterloo Record.*
36. *The Toronto Star*, June 21, 1975.

Chapter 4

THE CARESS OF STEEL TOUR

T he *Caress of Steel* tour has long been seen as something of a black hole in Rush's touring history. The album itself was poorly received, and the resulting trek was nicknamed by band and crew the "Down the Tubes" tour. At one show, at the Rafters in Battle Creek, Michigan, on November 5, the band played to what Ian Grandy described as "maybe fifty 'fans.'"

With its heavier focus on longer, more progressive pieces (see: the almost twenty-minute "The Fountain of Lamneth," which ran the entire second side of the album), *Caress of Steel* proved a commercial failure. As a result, Alex, Geddy, and Neil were under intense pressure from their record label, agency, and management company, and this run of dates marked one of the most tenuous points in the band's existence.

RIGHT: Rush onstage.
OPPOSITE: Geddy onstage.

Despite playing alongside the likes of Ted Nugent, Nazareth, Kiss, REO Speedwagon, and Lynyrd Skynyrd, Rush remained a support act for much of the tour, often in secondary markets, with occasional headlining shows in clubs. Very little is known about the set list during this time, and only one recording from the tour is known to exist. The November 15, 1975, show—a support date—represents the only confirmed *Caress of Steel* tour set list; it featured "Bastille Day" as the opening song, along with performances of "Lakeside Park" and the complete version of "The Necromancer." Despite rumors to the contrary, there is no evidence that any part of "The Fountain of Lamneth" was ever performed live, and crew recollections support that it wasn't. Said Ian

Grandy, "I think that was left alone. They did play 'I Think I'm Going Bald' for a little while, but it never went over for shit and that's why it didn't last long."

Recalled Geddy of the *Caress of Steel* trek, "We were very low at that point. I remember we were traveling overnight to a gig in Atlanta, and we were so bluesed out that we thought, 'What's the point? Let's give up and go home.'"

"But we said, 'Before we make this decision, let's not see each other for three days and think about it.' So outside of the gig, we didn't see or talk to each other. Then we got back together and just said, 'Fuck these people! There's no reason for us to quit just because these people are bummed out. It doesn't change the reasons we're here.'"

OPPOSITE AND ABOVE: Alex onstage.

TOUR HISTORY
CARESS OF STEEL

> **SET LIST:**
> (Sample from November 15, 1975)
> "Bastille Day"
> "Anthem"
> "Lakeside Park"
>
> "The Necromancer"
> "By-Tor and the Snow Dog"
> "Working Man" (with drum solo)

JULY 25, 1975
PETERBOROUGH, ONTARIO
PETERBOROUGH MEMORIAL CENTRE,
151 Lansdowne Street West. Venue opened on November 8, 1956.
CAPACITY: 3,908
NOTES: Although *RPM* magazine published a list of tour dates indicating a handful of shows beforehand, the first confirmed *Caress of Steel* tour date in SRO's records is the August 24 Lansdowne Park band shell performance in Ottawa.

AUGUST 2, 1975
DELHI, ONTARIO
BELGIAN CLUB, 360 James Street. Building opened in June 1948.
CAPACITY: 640

AUGUST 15, 1975
ST. CATHARINES, ONTARIO
GARDEN CITY ARENA, 8 Gale Crescent Street. Venue opened on December 20, 1938.
CAPACITY: 3,046 (for ice hockey)

AUGUST 16, 1975
SIMCOE, ONTARIO
TALBOT GARDENS ARENA, 10 Talbot Street North. Venue opened in 1946.
CAPACITY: 1,200

AUGUST 24, 1975
OTTAWA, ONTARIO
CENTRAL CANADA EXHIBITION
BANDSTAND, Lansdowne Park, 1015 Bank Street
TICKETS: Free concert (with park admission)
NOTES: Two performances, at 7:30 and 9:30 p.m. Olivia Newton John performed at 5:30 and 8:30 p.m. in the nearby grandstand, though this was prior to her 1980 hit "Xanadu." The first annual Central Canada Exhibition opened on September 20, 1888.

IAN: "RCMP visited us in the afternoon regarding equipment we (road crew) had discretely smuggled home in our truck."[1]

AUGUST 27, 1975
MONTREAL, QUEBEC
PLACE DES NATIONS, Parc Jean-Drapeau on Isle Sainte Helene. Venue opened on April 27, 1967.
OPENED FOR: Nazareth
TICKETS: $5.00 CAD (all seats)
CAPACITY: 7,000
NOTES: Outdoor venue constructed for Expo '67. SRO records and an August *RPM* date listing both include an August 28 Montreal date, but that was an (unneeded) rain date for the twenty-seventh. (There was only a light rain shower in Montreal on the twenty-seventh, between 6:15 and 6:45 p.m.)
PETE AGNEW (NAZARETH BASSIST): "Some people back home don't realize that a group can do a whole tour of Canada without ever touching the US."[2]

AUGUST 30, 1975
MONCTON, NEW BRUNSWICK
MONCTON COLISEUM, 377 Killam Drive. Venue opened on April 19, 1973.
OPENED FOR: Nazareth
TICKETS: $5.00 (advance)
NOTES: This date is not in SRO's records, but it is corroborated by a Nazareth ticket stub and a fan account. Ironically, on this date Moncton's Riverview Youth Theatre is rehearsing *Tom Sawyer.*

AUGUST 31, 1975
HALIFAX, NOVA SCOTIA
HALIFAX FORUM, 2901 Windsor Street. Venue opened on December 26, 1927.
OPENED FOR: Nazareth
CAPACITY: 5,860

SEPTEMBER 15, 1975
COCHRANE, ONTARIO
TIM HORTON ARENA, 155 Third Avenue. Venue built in 1961.
SUPPORT ACT: Max Webster
TICKETS: $5.00 (advance) CAD
CAPACITY: 800 (no seats)
NOTES: Cochrane Community Arena was renamed Tim Horton Arena in September 1975.

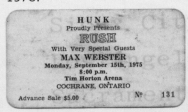

SEPTEMBER 17, 1975
WINNIPEG, MANITOBA
WINNIPEG ARENA, 1430 Maroons Road. Venue opened on October 18, 1955.
OPENED FOR: Nazareth
TICKETS: $4.00 / $5.00 / $6.00 CAD
ATTENDANCE: 7,000[3]
NOTES: Skip Gildersleeve's first gig as a Rush crew member. Alex, Geddy, and Neil played an energetic fifty-minute set before an appreciative crowd. Most of the material is culled from *Fly by Night*, with the title track performed as the encore.[4]
WINNIPEG FREE PRESS: "Rush appeared in the city last January. This time around the group's potential star quality is more apparent. What Rush still seems to lack is a sound sufficiently free from their acid rock forbears—a sound which they can clearly call their own."[5]

SEPTEMBER 19, 1975
SASKATOON, SASKATCHEWAN
SASKATOON ARENA, 19th Street at First Avenue. Venue opened on October 30, 1937.
OPENED FOR: Nazareth
TICKETS: $5.00 (advance) / $6.00 (at the door) CAD

ATTENDANCE: 4,800[6]
CAPACITY: 5,000
NOTES: The day before the gig, more than three thousand tickets had been sold, and the concert seemed to be "headed towards a Friday night sell-out of more than five thousand." To increase production value, the promoter brought in a power generator, three Super Trouper spotlights, and other assorted visuals from Calgary, along with dry ice from Regina.[7] By the recollection of one fan, Rush's performance was marred by an audience member throwing a sparkler that landed on Neil's drum kit during his solo. The show was stopped immediately, the house lights were brought up, and the crowd was warned that the performance would end if the behavior didn't stop.[8]

IAN: "Saskatoon had a little old arena back then that the rest of the crew hated, but I loved it because, after playing all the other arenas that sounded like echo chambers, this place had acoustical foam sprayed on the walls and ceiling, and it had an awesome tight sound."

SEPTEMBER 20, 1975
EDMONTON, ALBERTA
KIMSMEN FIELD HOUSE, 9100 Walterdale Hill. Venue opened on January 3, 1968.
OPENED FOR: Nazareth
ATTENDANCE: 5,000; sold out[9]
EDMONTON JOURNAL: "When Rush hits the bandstand nothing else can replace it."
THE GATEWAY
(UNIVERSITY OF ALBERTA): "If Rush's popularity continues to grow, they could very well be stars soon."

SEPTEMBER 21, 1975
CALGARY, ALBERTA
CLEARWATER BEACH, North Side of Highway 8 at 101st Street Southwest
OPENED FOR: Nazareth
TICKETS: $6.00 (advance) / $7.00 (gate) CAD
ATTENDANCE: 2,500 (approximate)
NOTES: 5:00 p.m. show time, outdoor gig. Champion wrestler Stu Hart owned Clearwater Beach, which was a 160-acre man-made sandbar just west of Calgary in the Elbow River. His brother Dean promoted concerts on the property. The shows were poorly managed, and riots at

this Nazareth-Rush gig cost Hart thousands of dollars, eventually forcing him to sell the property in the mid-'70s. Things got so bad that Nazareth stopped their set when someone lit a dog on fire. Coincidentally, or perhaps not, Nazareth was touring their *Hair of the Dog* album.

IAN: "Beautiful sunny day. I was packing the drums and there were a couple of big bikers leaning on the security fence. I pull my bass drum case—apparently, it's been supporting the fence, so they go ass over teakettle. Fortunately, they got up and laughed. Nazareth and us ate post show at three picnic tables. Good day all around."[10]

IAN MARK (PHOTOGRAPHER): "This concert was held in a farmer's field about fifteen minutes outside of Calgary on a hot Sunday afternoon. There were no seats—it was standing room only for everyone. This was a grassroots rock concert, with security provided by a motorcycle gang. After Rush finished their set, a fight broke out as people were leaving which was handled by the motorcycle gang using gang methods. The instigator was hurt but not killed. I remember that during the Nazareth set, another fight broke out in front of the stage. Their lead singer, Dan, stopped the concert, jumped off the stage and walked to the combatants and stopped the fight himself. This was no Altamont with the Stones playing. The stage was your basic stage with very little coverage overhead. I would say that there were around 2,500 at the concert. To be honest I didn't even know who Rush were. I remember asking someone in the line, waiting to get in, who they were. This guy said that he was at the concert not for Nazareth but for Rush. When they took the stage, I was taken aback by Geddy's high-pitched voice and their fashionable stage apparel. I took hundreds of shots of Alex because I loved watching his facial contortions. With every new note he had a different contortion. I never tired of watching a new one appear."

SEPTEMBER 26, 1975
VANCOUVER, BRITISH COLUMBIA
PACIFIC COLISEUM, Pacific National Exhibition Fairgrounds, 100 North Renfrew. Venue dedicated on January 8, 1968.
OPENED FOR: Nazareth

TICKETS: $6.00 CAD (advance, plus $0.25 service charge)
ATTENDANCE: 14,000 (approximate)
CAPACITY: 16,123
VANCOUVER SUN: "Rush has been hiding for some time in the East, but finally took the giant step and visited B.C. The band so impressed Nazareth that it invited Rush to participate in an English tour, but unfortunately schedules are in conflict."

SEPTEMBER 29, 1975
MELVILLE, SASKATCHEWAN
MELVILLE STADIUM, 123 2nd Avenue West. Venue built in late 1966.
SUPPORT ACT: Cambridge
CAPACITY: 3,366
NOTES: Cambridge got the attention of manager Gary Stratychuk. He booked the band to open for Rush at the Trianon Ballroom (June 19, 1975). Even though they were only sixteen and playing mostly cover material, a friendship grew with the members of Rush and their crew. On Rush's next tour of Saskatchewan, they asked if they would again be opening. It was to be a very memorable tour, and Cambridge really got to see what the road could be like at the next level up. There was to be no turning back after that. They liked what they saw. The members of Rush were very open with the boys and gave them fateful advice.[11]

SEPTEMBER 30, 1975
ESTEVAN, SASKATCHEWAN
CIVIC AUDITORIUM, Estevan Community Centre, 811 Souris Avenue. Venue built in 1957.
SUPPORT ACT: Cambridge
CAPACITY: 1,900
NOTES: A bitter letter from the promoter was given to the band on the day of show, summing up the financial situation: "We lost everything but hope . . . Thanx."

GEDDY: "We were playing in Estevan, Saskatchewan. We were scheduled to play at the arena in the evening, but when we arrived in the afternoon to do our sound check, we discovered that the local hockey team had refused to allow the ice to be covered. They had a big game coming up and thought that the concert might wreck the ice. So our gear was set up at one end of the rink, the mixing consoles were in the stands, and the lighting console was onstage with us. Just as we began sound check, the team started skating around the rink and practicing. It was very surreal. In the evening, the crowd was seated at the far end of the stands, and we were playing down at the other end because the ice remained uncovered."[12]

IAN: "That went down in Estevan. Just the lighting and sound platforms on the floor. No crowd or plywood on the floor. Froze my ass."[13]

OCTOBER 2, 1975
REGINA, SASKATCHEWAN
TRIANON BALLROOM, 2400 12th Avenue
SUPPORT ACT: Cambridge
TICKETS: $4.50 (advance) / $5.00 (at the door)
CAPACITY: 1,700 (approximate)
THE LEADER-POST: "The band premiered a couple of cuts from the new album, before a modest crowd. It's obvious that Rush is really beginning to stretch out. The featured number, 'Lakeside Park,' was a much more progressive effort than we've come to expect from Rush. Full of complex, convoluted melody changes and rich, waterfall guitar, the song was beautiful in the extreme. The concert Thursday night was admittedly better than the June show."

OCTOBER 4, 1975
COCHRANE, ONTARIO
TIM HORTON ARENA, 155 Third Avenue
SUPPORT ACT: Max Webster (unconfirmed)
CAPACITY: 800
NOTES: At this point, Max Webster had yet to record their 1976 self-titled debut.

OCTOBER 5, 1975
ST. CATHARINES, ONTARIO
UNIVERSITY GYM ONE, Physical Education Complex, Brock University Campus, 500 Glenridge Avenue. University established in 1964.
SUPPORT ACT: Max Webster; Fat Rabbit opened the show.
TICKETS: $5.25
ATTENDANCE: 1,500 (approximate)
ST. CATHARINES STANDARD: "Brock Concert, Unbearably Loud: There was something for nearly everyone: for heavy metal kids—Rush; for weird and decadent people with a warped sense of humor—Max Webster; for the

locals—Fat Rabbit. The audience rises to its feet to welcome Rush rocketing into new material from *Caress of Steel*. The spotlight focuses on lead guitarist, Alex Lifeson, 22, gleaming in a chrome jacket, his silky blonde hair shining. Knees bent, body stationary, with twitching contorted expressions, Alex concentrates all his energy in thrusting his fingers across the frets. Behind him on the drum riser, Neil Peart, 23, pounds out the beat between gulps of wine, while Geddy Lee, 22, thunders out the bass line that underscores the speeding surge of the lead like a jackhammer busting concrete. Rush's numbers are perhaps too long to hold the attention of their predominantly young audiences. Most obvious are the guitar and drum solos which seem to be dragged-out, scene-stealing, [sic] self-gratification. Underneath the band's volume is solid musicianship, and there's no denying that the intense, hypnotic numbness of Rush's roar has found a young audience. But whether Rush is a fly-by-night group or a viable force depends on their success with the American audiences."

OCTOBER 6, 1975
GUELPH, ONTARIO
WAR MEMORIAL HALL, University of Guelph campus, 390 Gordon Street. Venue built in June 1924.
SUPPORT ACT: Max Webster
TICKETS: $4.00 CAD
CAPACITY: 700
NOTES: Two shows: 7:00 p.m. and 9:30 p.m.

OCTOBER 11, 1975
FRANKLIN, INDIANA
FRANKLIN GYMNASIUM, Franklin College campus, Grizzly Drive. Gym opened in 1908.
SUPPORT ACT: Ginger
TICKETS: $4.00 (all seats); students free with ID
CAPACITY: 500 (basketball)
NOTES: This concert was a part of weekend homecoming activities presented by the Student Entertainment Board. The venue is nicknamed the Barn because of its shape.

OCTOBER 13, 1975
JOHNSON CITY, TENNESSEE
FREEDOM HALL CIVIC CENTER, 1320 Pactolas Road. Venue opened on July 5, 1974.
OPENED FOR: Aerosmith, Ted Nugent
TICKETS: $5.50 to $6.50
CAPACITY: 7,500
NOTES: Some sites list Kiss as the headliner, but Aerosmith and Ted Nugent were confirmed on this date by venue contracts. The confusion is probably because Aerosmith and Ted Nugent also performed at Freedom Hall on October 1, returning by popular demand on the thirteenth with Rush.

OCTOBER 14, 1975
JONESBORO, ARKANSAS
INDIAN FIELDHOUSE, ARKANSAS STATE UNIVERSITY. College founded in 1930.
OPENED FOR: Ted Nugent; Diamond Reo opened the show.
TICKETS: $4.00 (advance) / $5.00 (at the door)
CAPACITY: 5,000

OCTOBER 16, 1975
JOPLIN, MISSOURI
JOPLIN MEMORIAL HALL, 212 West 8th Street. Venue dedicated on October 28, 1925.
OPENED FOR: Ted Nugent
CAPACITY: 3,018

OCTOBER 17, 1975
LINCOLN, NEBRASKA
PERSHING MEMORIAL AUDITORIUM, 226 Centennial Mall South. Venue dedicated on March 10, 1957.
OPENED FOR: Ted Nugent; Head East opened the show.
TICKETS: $5.00 (advance) / $6.00 (at the door)
CAPACITY: 7,500

OCTOBER 18, 1975
KANSAS CITY, KANSAS
SOLDIER AND SAILOR'S MEMORIAL HALL, 600 North Seventh Street. Venue cornerstone laid on May 26, 1924.
OPENED FOR: Ted Nugent
CAPACITY: 3,500

OCTOBER 21, 1975
WICHITA, KANSAS
CENTURY II CONVENTION HALL, 225 West Douglas Avenue. Venue opened on January 11, 1969.
OPENED FOR: Head East, Ted Nugent
TICKETS: $5.00 / $6.00
ATTENDANCE: 5,022
CAPACITY: 7,500
WALRUS: "Head East good except for some sound problems; Ted Nugent as loud and explosive as ever; Rush nothing spectacular."

OCTOBER 24, 1975
TULSA, OKLAHOMA
TULSA ASSEMBLY CENTER, 100 Civic Center. Venue opened on March 8, 1964.
OPENED FOR: Ted Nugent; Head East opened the show.
TICKETS: $4.00 / $5.00 / $6.00
CAPACITY: 8,900

OCTOBER 25, 1975
AMARILLO, TEXAS
CIVIC CENTER COLISEUM, 401 South Buchanan Street. Venue opened on September 2, 1968.
OPENED FOR: Ted Nugent
CAPACITY: 7,200

OCTOBER 28, 1975
SAN ANTONIO, TEXAS
RANDY'S RODEO, 1534 Bandera Road. Venue originated in the 1960s.
SUPPORT ACT: Heyoka

TICKETS: $3.00 (advance) / $4.50 (at the door)
ATTENDANCE: 2,200; sold out
NOTES: Tour manager Howard Ungerleider was held at gunpoint by the club owners. Skip Gildersleeve was christened "Slider" (for his dance skills) at a postconcert party. Similar to WMMS in Cleveland, radio station KISS-FM in San Antonio received an import copy of the first Rush album (on the Moon label) and began playing it in heavy rotation. In advance of this gig, KISS-FM played twenty-four straight hours of *Rush*, *Fly by Night*, and *Caress of Steel*, firing up fans in the Alamo City.

MARK GIERTH (SON OF PROMOTER): "[Local radio personality] Lou Roney told my dad about a Canadian band that needed a place to play in San Antonio, so Lou and my dad copromoted Rush at Randy's Rodeo. So many people came out that there was a near riot outside, and the show went great. Afterwards, Lou Roney, my brother, my dad, and myself all went with Rush to a pizza place, ate, and played a few pinball and video games. My father and brother later kept in contact with them."[14]

NEIL: "The show was being promoted by a small local radio station, and as we arrived in town, we were amazed to hear them playing nothing but Rush songs (we only had three albums at the time, so there wasn't much variety) all day and all night."[15]

IAN: "There were about 2,500 people stuffed into the place. It took me ten minutes to get out to the soundboard. We had zero idea we were big in San Antonio, and the venue was described to me as 'a bowling alley.' It was an off day on a tour with Ted Nugent, and I think we 'borrowed' the sound crew from that tour."

HOWARD: "Basically it was a converted bowling alley where the lanes had been ripped out, and it had been turned into a country-and-western bar. The bar was the length of the bowling alley—it was huge, and the guys who ran it weren't real promoters, they were just club owners. We got there about three days early and realized there was no real stage. It was just a little country-and-western stage, and here we had Rush coming in to play, and we had to deal with it. I hired local production, and we went to this local high school and got their shop class to build a wooden stage for us—they prefabbed it and they did it for free, and we let them in the show. And then of course they oversold the show, because the greed factor kicked in when they realized they had a band that was drawing people. The place held maybe 2,700, and they must have sold 4,000 tickets. The whole front of the building was glass, and it's not a pretty picture when you have an angry crowd pressing up against glass. And of course there was this huge bar, so everybody's drunk, and that just adds fuel to the fire. Eventually, the band took the stage. I was trying to keep an eye on the door count, to make sure the money's going to be accounted for accurately—and I saw the ticket takers put money in their pockets and all sorts of stuff like that. I got really upset and grabbed a green plastic garbage bag and made everybody empty their pockets into it. I also confiscated all the cash from the box office, and I took it up to the office—all of this while the band was onstage playing. The lighting back then was pretty basic—I set it up and pretty much just left it on while they played, so I'm up in the office trying to sort out the money when both of the owners of the place come in with guns drawn and tell me to give them back their money! It was very ugly for many hours. It went on so long that Joe Anthony and Lou Roney took the band out to a restaurant for a party after the show, while I'm still sitting in this room with guns to my head. They just kept telling me that I'm not leaving with any money, and it was just brutal. Thankfully there was one guy there who worked for the club owners, who had some common sense, and he helped work it out, and I actually left with the band's share of the money. I hightailed it out of there, and then I couldn't find everyone because I didn't know where this restaurant was, so I went back to the hotel and stashed the money in the hotel room. Finally I found the band in this restaurant and they were all partying, drinking pineapple wine, and celebrating their wonderful show, not knowing that any of this had even gone on. We met a bunch of crazy people in San Antonio who were acquaintances for the next ten years, but the show went on."[16]

OCTOBER 29–30, 1975
AUSTIN, TEXAS
ARMADILLO WORLD HEADQUARTERS, 525½ Barton Springs Road. Venue opened on August 7, 1970.
OPENED FOR: Ted Nugent
CAPACITY: 1,500
NOTES: Aka the 'Dillo.

OCTOBER 31, 1975
CORPUS CHRISTI, TEXAS
RITZ MUSIC HALL, 715 North Chaparral Street. Venue opened on December 25, 1929.
SUPPORT ACT: Novae
ATTENDANCE: 1,400
CAPACITY: 1,500
CONCERT GROSS: $4,500
NOTES: Halloween show, complete with a Halloween costume contest.
IAN: "The Ritz Music Hall was an old funky theater that some guys had made into a rock 'n' roll theater. Corpus was kind of run-down in those days, but the crowd was rabid and fired up."

NOVEMBER 1, 1975
DALLAS, TEXAS
ELECTRIC BALLROOM, 1010 South Industrial Boulevard
OPENED FOR: Iron Butterfly
TICKETS: $3.50 (advance) / $4.00 (at the door)

NOVEMBER 4, 1975
LANSING, MICHIGAN
SILVER DOLLAR SALOON, 3411 East Michigan Avenue. The venue, a former indoor golf range, opened in late April 1972.
TICKETS: $3.50
ATTENDANCE: 690 (approximate); sold out
NOTES: The venue changed its name from the Brewery in April 1975.
UTE NEWS: "Several of the tunes performed Tuesday (all new ones, incidentally) dragged and plodded semi-melodically while vocalist Lee tried to keep up, screaming lyrics like: 'Panacea-passion pure/I can't resist your gentle lure.' But all this can't change the fact that within themselves the members of Rush form an exceptionally tight band. Guitarist Lifeson's huge Marshall amplifiers have to be heard live to be appreciated, and, even to those who find the band less than

desirable, bassist Lee's voice sounded unusually strong in the live context. Their performance Tuesday night drew a tremendous reaction from the capacity crown in the Silver Dollar."

NOVEMBER 5, 1975
BATTLE CREEK, MICHIGAN
THE RAFTERS, 11300 East Michigan Avenue. Venue opened in December 1974.
SUPPORT ACT: Star Trooper
TICKETS: $3.50
ATTENDANCE: 20 to 50 (approximate)[17]
GARY WEIMER (STAR TROOPER BASSIST): "Rush even gave us part of the deli tray. Nice guys . . . funny during sound check."[18]
LIAM: "You would find yourself in places like Battle Creek, Michigan, playing to twenty people, wondering why you were still continuing. Everybody thought that it was over. The audiences were becoming smaller and smaller, so we thought that the end was near."[19]
IAN: "Maybe fifty 'fans' . . . and maybe the lowest point."[20]

NOVEMBER 7, 1975
AKRON, OHIO
AKRON CIVIC THEATRE, 182 South Main Street. Historic venue opened on April 21, 1929.
WITH: Ted Nugent (cobill); Artful Dodger opened the concert.
TICKETS: $5.00 (advance) / $6.00 (day of)
CAPACITY: 2,642
NOTES: According to fan accounts, "The Necromancer" is performed.

NOVEMBER 8, 1975
CLEVELAND, OHIO
ALLEN THEATRE, 1407 Euclid Avenue. Venue opened on April 1, 1921.
OPENED FOR: Ted Nugent; Artful Dodger opened the show.
CAPACITY: 3,003
NOTES: Marking a change of venue from most of their previous Cleveland appearances, this performance was at the Allen Theatre rather than the Agora Ballroom—a shame given that the Agora was in the habit of recording most shows held in the venue. Had Rush played at the Agora on this run, it's very likely that a high-quality *Caress of Steel* performance would have been captured for posterity.

SCENE: "Vying with Blue Oyster Cult and Blue Cheer for the all-time decibel championship, Rush showed their uniqueness by not naming themselves Blue Rush. But they did give a good performance—when compared with their other performances—delighting their fans with material from their latest album, *Caress of Steel*. However, though initially an attention grabber, the monotony of Rush's material did tend to grate on the nerves. And that's a shame because there was some good musicianship going to waste up there on stage. A little more diversity in material, a little less on the volume, and Rush could have been quite interesting. As it was, they were pretty boring."

NOVEMBER 9, 1975
ST. LOUIS, MISSOURI
HENRY W. KIEL MUNICIPAL AUDITORIUM, 1401 Clark Street. Historic venue dedicated on April 14, 1934.
OPENED FOR: David Essex, Journey, and Grinderswitch
TICKETS: $3.95 (all seats)
CAPACITY: 9,300

NOVEMBER 10, 1975
WATERLOO, IOWA
MCELROY AUDITORIUM, 250 Ansborough Avenue. Venue opened on September 28, 1936.
OPENED FOR: Ted Nugent
CAPACITY: 8,735
NOTES: This date is not in SRO's records and is unconfirmed. At this time, the venue was referred to as the "new" Hippodrome. The original venue (the Hippodrome) opened on September 22, 1919, and had a capacity of about two thousand. In 1936 the building was completely rebuilt (using the existing side wall and roof), and the capacity increased to more than eight thousand.

NOVEMBER 11, 1975
ARLINGTON HEIGHTS, ILLINOIS
HERSEY GYMNASIUM, JOHN HERSEY HIGH SCHOOL, 1900 East Thomas Street. Venue opened in September 1968.
CAPACITY: 3,300
NOTES: This date is not in SRO's records and is unconfirmed.

NOVEMBER 14, 1975
FORT WAYNE, INDIANA
ALLEN COUNTY WAR MEMORIAL COLISEUM, 4000 Parnell Avenue. Venue dedicated on September 28, 1952.
OPENED FOR: Frank Zappa and the Mothers
TICKETS: $5.50 (advance) / $6.50 (at the door)
CAPACITY: 10,322
NOTES: Rush is not listed on any of the concert ads, including the day of the gig. Ian photographed Neil's drum setup before this gig, with the new blue platform he'd been forced to build after Air "No-Can-Do" (the band's nickname for Air Canada) lost his white platform the prior January. Frank and the Mothers were touring the *Bongo Fury* album with the new five-person Zappa combo, featuring Roy Estrada on bass, Napoleon Murphy Brock on tenor sax, André Lewis on keyboards, and Terry Bozzio on drums. In 2008, Bozzio took part in Neil's Buddy Rich memorial concert.

NOVEMBER 15, 1975
ROCKFORD, ILLINOIS
NATIONAL GUARD ARMORY, 605 Main Street. Historic venue dedicated in 1937.
OPENED FOR: Kiss
TICKETS: $6.50 (advance) / $7.00 (day of)
ATTENDANCE: 3,610; sold out
CONCERT GROSS: $23,465
SET LIST: "Bastille Day," "Anthem," "Lakeside Park," "The Necromancer," "By-Tor and the Snow Dog," "Working Man" (with drum solo).

GEDDY (ONSTAGE): "Thank you! How ya doing? We hope you're all in high spirits tonight! We'd like to do something else from our new album. This is a long song. It's a short story. It's called 'The Necromancer.'"

NOVEMBER 16, 1975
MADISON, WISCONSIN
DANE COUNTY VETERANS MEMORIAL COLISEUM, Dane County Expo Center Fairgrounds, 2200 Rimrock Road. Venue opened on March 16, 1967.
OPENED FOR: Aerosmith; Ted Nugent opened the show.
TICKETS: $5.50 (advance) / $6.00 (day of)
ATTENDANCE: 4,000 (approximate)
CAPACITY: 5,500
NOTES: Theater presentation. Although many sites list Rush opening for Kiss in Flint, Michigan, on this date, SRO records confirm that Rush was in Madison, while Mott opened for Kiss on November 16 in Flint.
WALRUS: "Rush was the definite highlight of the evening. Singer Geddy Lee powered Rush through their set, which included 'Anthem' and 'Finding My Way' as the high points. Rush is a very dynamic three-man band and should be watched closely."

NOVEMBER 17, 1975
FLINT, MICHIGAN
IMA AUDITORIUM, near the Flint River between Harrison Street and James P. Cole Boulevard. Venue opened in 1929.
OPENED FOR: Kiss
TICKETS: $6.00
ATTENDANCE: 5,300; sold out
NOTES: IMA stands for Industrial Mutual Association. Kiss is in the middle of their *Alive!* '75–'76 North American tour.

NOVEMBER 18, 1975
PORT HURON, MICHIGAN
MCMORRAN PLACE ARENA, 701 McMorran Boulevard. Venue opened on January 21, 1960.
OPENED FOR: Kiss
TICKETS: $5.00 (obstructed view) / $6.50 / $7.50
ATTENDANCE: 3,788; oversold
CONCERT GROSS: $25,077
NOTES: This gig sold out in three days, prompting the promoter to place about six hundred obstructed-view seats on sale for five dollars each. Total promoter costs: twenty thousand dollars.

CHRIS COLE (PROMOTER): "The reason we went with Kiss was because we were sure of a sellout. We weren't out to make money on their show, so we priced tickets so we would break even if we sold out.[21] . . . The crowd is so well behaved I can't believe it. Kiss loved it. Rush had a good time. It's just beautiful."[22]
TIMES HERALD: "3,700 teens jam arena: The concert's first act, Rush won generous applause with a straightforward set."
ERIE SQUARE GAZETTE: "The Concert Of The Year: "Kiss and Rush together on one bill! What more could anyone ask?! Rush stresses the music a little more than the glitter."

NOVEMBER 19, 1975
TRAVERSE CITY, MICHIGAN
GLACIER DOME, 1610 Barlow Street
OPENED FOR: Kiss; Styx opened the show.
ATTENDANCE: 6,000 (approximate)
CAPACITY: 4,154
NOTES: This date is not included in SRO's records, and although listed on many fan sites, Rush was *not* on the bill. Rush wasn't the only band that didn't perform at this gig—Kiss didn't either. While Styx was playing their final song, there was an electrical short, resulting in $12,000 damage to Kiss's amps, speakers, and lighting, thus abruptly ending the show. However, the issues affecting this gig were more serious, as the concert was dangerously oversold. The whole situation, plus police seizures of "$1,300 of illegal drugs and paraphernalia from the fans," begs the question of whether the "short" might have been seen as a convenient way out of a potentially dangerous situation.

NOVEMBER 21, 1975
TERRE HAUTE, INDIANA
HULMAN CIVIC UNIVERSITY CENTER, Indiana State University campus, 200 North 8th Street. Venue opened on December 14, 1973.
OPENED FOR: Kiss
TICKETS: $5.50 (advance) / $6.50 (day of), general admission
ATTENDANCE: 10,000; sold out
CONCERT GROSS: $60,000 (house record)
NOTES: First concert promoted by the newly formed Kiss Army fan club. The *Terre Haute Tribune* dated November 15 also lists Mott on the bill, but final records indicate that they were not.

NOVEMBER 22, 1975
CHICAGO, ILLINOIS
AUDITORIUM THEATRE, Roosevelt University, 50 East Congress Parkway. National Historic Landmark dedicated on December 9, 1889.
OPENED FOR: Ritchie Blackmore's Rainbow
CAPACITY: 3,875
NOTES: Rush's appearance was canceled at the last minute, when Blackmore's people refused to move the keyboard rig to allow Rush sufficient space on the seventy-five-foot stage. Geddy was reportedly given only about two square feet to move in. In actuality, the reasons for the cancellation were probably twofold, as Rush weren't given enough assurance that they would be paid. Alex, Geddy, Neil, and crew then headed over to the International Amphitheater to watch Kiss's show (where Mott and the Kids opened; Leslie West was scheduled but did not appear).
IAN: "We unloaded and waited our time. They told us their organ rig would *not* be moved, leaving us about two-thirds of the stage width-wise. It wasn't a very wide stage, and they were just being dicks as far as I was concerned. Two guys on their Showco crew later came and apologized to us. They were a little embarrassed. The band and Howie showed up and, when I explained it to them, they just shrugged and said, 'We are not playing.' Mercury Records took the band, Howie, and myself to supper, and then we went to see Kiss at the Amphitheater."

NOVEMBER 23, 1975
EVANSVILLE, INDIANA
ROBERTS MUNICIPAL STADIUM, University of Evansville campus, 2600 Division Street. Venue dedicated on December 1, 1956.
OPENED FOR: Kiss, Mott
TICKETS: $5.50 (advance) / $6.50 (day of)
ATTENDANCE: 11,200; sold out
CONCERT GROSS: $67,200 (house record)
NOTES: This gig broke the Doobie Brothers' previous attendance record and was actually oversold by two hundred tickets. The recently released Kiss single "Rock and Roll All Nite (Live)" is #44 in America, on its climb to #12.

NOVEMBER 24, 1975
GREEN BAY, WISCONSIN
BROWN COUNTY VETERANS MEMORIAL ARENA, 1901 South Oneida Street. Venue opened on November 11, 1957.
OPENED FOR: Black Oak Arkansas, Montrose (special guest)
TICKETS: $5.50 (advance) / $6.00 (day of)
CAPACITY: 7,500 (general admission) or 6,820 (seated concert, circa 1975)
GREEN BAY PRESS GAZETTE: "Rush is a trio of glittery boys who do loud things with guitar, drums, and bass."

NOVEMBER 26, 1975
HUNTINGTON, WEST VIRGINIA
VETERANS MEMORIAL FIELDHOUSE, 2590 Fifth Avenue. Venue opened in October 1950.
OPENED FOR: Kiss; Mott opened the show.
TICKETS: $5.50 (advance) / $6.50 (day of), general admission
ATTENDANCE: 8,500; sold out
NOTES: This concert broke the Doobie Brothers' previous attendance record. Following this performance, a depressed Rush contemplated their future.

NOVEMBER 27, 1975
ATLANTA, GEORGIA
ALEX COOLEY'S ELECTRIC BALLROOM, corner of Peachtree Street NE and Ponce de Leon Avenue. Building opened in 1913.
SUPPORT ACT: Artful Dodger
CAPACITY: 1,100
NOTES: Howard steps in to do an interview with the Dutch press on the band's behalf.

NOVEMBER 28–29, 1975
ATLANTA, GEORGIA
ALEX COOLEY'S ELECTRIC BALLROOM, corner of Peachtree Street NE and Ponce de Leon Avenue.

SUPPORT ACT: Artful Dodger
CAPACITY: 1,100
NOTES: Contrary to crew memories, at least one fan in attendance at the Atlanta gigs claimed "The Fountain of Lamneth" made a rare live appearance.
STEVE WHITE (ATLANTA FAN/PHOTOGRAPHER): "I went to both nights. The opening band played a set, then Rush played a set. Then the opening band came back on and played a set, and then Rush played another set which lasted way into the early hours of the morning. I stayed for both sets. In one of the sets they played 'Fountain of Lamneth' (minus 'Panacea'). Neil did a mini drum solo during 'Didacts and Narpets.' 'Bacchus Plateau' is my favorite part of 'Lamneth' and I remember it was just wonderful."

NOVEMBER 30, 1975
LARGO, MARYLAND
CAPITAL CENTRE, 1 Harry S. Truman Drive. Venue opened on December 2, 1973.
OPENED FOR: Kiss, with Styx and Mott
TICKETS: $5.50
CAPACITY: 21,000, general admission
CONCERT GROSS: $128,749
NOTES: Though listed on many fan sites, this date is not included in SRO's records and Rush was not on the bill. Between the three Electric Ballroom dates and the December 7 Morris Auditorium gig, there is some uncertainty as to what Rush was doing from November 30 through December 6. Some sources indicate that the band opened for Kiss in Maryland, Georgia, Alabama, and Florida, though the ads that have come to light do not support this, and SRO's records do not contain any of these dates, so this might have been a short break.

DECEMBER 5, 1975
ATLANTA, GEORGIA
THE OMNI, 100 Techwood Drive Northwest. Venue opened on October 14, 1972.
OPENED FOR: Kiss with special guest Leslie West; Styx opened the show.
TICKETS: $4.50 / $5.50 / $6.50
CAPACITY: 16,181
NOTES: Despite fan accounts to the contrary, Rush is not listed in a week-of-concert ad. This date is also not included in SRO data, so most likely they did not perform.

DECEMBER 7, 1975
SOUTH BEND, INDIANA
MORRIS CIVIC AUDITORIUM, 211
North Michigan Street. Venue opened
on November 2, 1922.
OPENED FOR: REO Speedwagon
TICKETS: $5.50 (advance) / $6.50
(day of)
CAPACITY: 2,468

___

DECEMBER 12, 1975
SYRACUSE, NEW YORK
ONONDAGA COUNTY WAR
MEMORIAL AUDITORIUM, 515
Montgomery Street. Venue opened on
September 1, 1951.
CAPACITY: 8,200
NOTES: Though listed on many fan sites,
this date is not included in SRO's records
and Rush was not on the bill. In reality,
this was a Black Sabbath show with Kiss
supporting.

___

DECEMBER 14, 1975
QUINCY, ILLINOIS
TURNER HALL, 926 Hampshire Street
SUPPORT ACT: Smokehouse
TICKETS: $4.00 (available at the door
only)
CAPACITY: 400

___

DECEMBER 15, 1975
TOLEDO, OHIO
SPORTS ARENA, 1 North Main Street.
Venue opened on November 13, 1947.
OPENED FOR: Lynyrd Skynyrd, the
Leslie West Band
TICKETS: $5.50 (advance) / $6.50
(day of)
CAPACITY: 7,000

___

DECEMBER 16, 1975
NILES, ILLINOIS
MILL RUN THEATRE, adjacent to Golf
Mill Shopping Center, Golf Road, and
Milwaukee Avenue. Venue opened on
July 2, 1965.
CAPACITY: 1,600
NOTES: This date is not included in SRO's
records and is unconfirmed. The listed
venue, which featured a rotating stage, is
likewise unconfirmed. Based on some fan
accounts, it is possible this performance
instead took place at Notre Dame High
School for Boys (7655 West Dempster
Street. Founded in June 1955). No Rush
concert is listed in school yearbooks

(1974-1976), but it's also possible that it
was not a school-sanctioned event.

___

DECEMBER 17, 1975
ELGIN, ILLINOIS
HEMMENS AUDITORIUM, at the
Hemmens Cultural Center, 45
Symphony Way. Venue opened in
October 1969.
CAPACITY: 1,225
NOTES: Venue unconfirmed.

___

DECEMBER 18, 1975
LANSING, MICHIGAN
SILVER DOLLAR SALOON, 3411 E.
Michigan Avenue
CAPACITY: 690
RICK BECKER (OWNER, SILVER DOLLAR
SALOON): "They'd be coming through
the doors after a minimum thirty-minute
wait in line. The scene was freshmen and
sophomores—hippies and druggies look-
ing to catch a buzz."[23]

___

DECEMBER 19, 1975
BINGHAMTON, NEW YORK
BROOME COUNTY WAR MEMORIAL
ARENA, 1 Stuart Street. Venue opened
on August 29, 1973.
OPENED FOR: Kiss, Styx
TICKETS: $5.50 (advance) / $6.50 (at
the door)
CAPACITY: 6,600
NOTES: General admission concert. This
date is not included in SRO's records, so
Rush may not have been on the bill. An ad
dated December 14 lists only Styx as sole
support, so if Rush was added, it was at
the eleventh hour. A December 20 review
in the Binghamton *Press and Sun-Bulletin*
fails to mention the openers.

___

DECEMBER 20, 1975
PITTSBURGH, PENNSYLVANIA
CIVIC ARENA, 300 Auditorium Place.
Venue opened on September 17, 1961.
OPENED FOR: Kiss, Mott
TICKETS: $5.50
ATTENDANCE: 15,432
CAPACITY: 17,000
NOTES: The *Valley News Dispatch*
(December 20, 1975) claims the atten-
dance was 15,165, just shy of the all-
time record at Pitt Civic Arena of 15,280
set by the Doobie Brothers. Fans endure
evening snow and icy roads to and from
the gig. It likely marked Rush's last per-
formance with Kiss.

BEAVER TIMES: "Rush opened the show
and was eagerly accepted by the crowd.
The great reception Rush received was
quite surprising, and if Rush had been
the headliners, the fans would probably
have felt completely satisfied. It's quite
unusual for an opening act on a bill of
three to receive an encore call, but Rush
did and easily pleased the fans with their
most popular number 'Fly by Night.'
Rush is one of the new hard rock groups
that kids really love. I'm sure it won't be
long before they play Pittsburgh as
headliners."

___

DECEMBER 21, 1975
YOUNGSTOWN, OHIO
TOMORROW CLUB, 213 Federal Plaza
West. Venue built in 1927 (as the State
Theater); the Tomorrow Club opened on
October 20, 1974.
SUPPORT ACT: Mojo
TICKETS: $2.00 (advance) / $3.00 (at
the door)
CAPACITY: 2,142
NOTES: Likely Mark Cherry's first date
working for Rush, as part of the Atlantis
Systems lighting crew.

___

DECEMBER 22, 1975
ALLENTOWN, PENNSYLVANIA
AGRICULTURAL HALL, Great Allentown
Fairgrounds, 1725 Chew Street. Venue
opened on September 16, 1957.
WITH: Styx (cobill); Mott opened the
show.
ATTENDANCE: "A good-sized crowd."[24]
CAPACITY: 4,100
NOTES: General admission concert.
"Plenty of good seats available at the
door."
MORNING CALL: "Rush contended with
the usual problem of poor [venue] acoustics and occasional feedback. Geddy Lee
managed to keep body and soul together
on stage, though, as he belted out 'I
Think I'm Going Bald' and 'Working
Man.' Lifeson and Peart also made an
admirable effort to perform despite the
distracting reverberations from bare steel
girders. It was a pretty good show, considering the acoustical handicap all three
groups had to battle."

DECEMBER 26, 1975
CHICAGO, ILLINOIS
ARAGON BALLROOM, 1106 West Lawrence Avenue. Venue dedicated in July 1926.
OPENED FOR: Blue Oyster Cult; Artful Dodger opened the show.
CAPACITY: 4,500
SET LIST: "Bastille Day," "Anthem," "Lakeside Park," "The Necromancer," "By-Tor and the Snow Dog," "Working Man" (with drum solo).[25]
STEVE COOPER (ARTFUL DODGER BASSIST): "We did indeed play two back-to-back nights at the Aragon Ballroom in late '75 as the opening act on a three-act show each night. Two other bands played each night, and three of them were Rush, BOC, and Iron Butterfly." (Ted Nugent was the other.) "What I do remember clearly is that we were soundly booed! Before we played a note! The crowd wanted no part of us. We artfully dodged quite a few projectiles. The next night the stagehands couldn't believe we came back for more abuse. They were laughing it up . . . and we got basically the same response."[26]
IAN: "I went to Christmas dinner with my family, drank and ate way too much, then went home, showered, and Howie picked me and the others up and we drove to Chicago overnight. The Aragon was about twelve degrees Fahrenheit. We had to go off the front of the stage with the gear, with security pushing back the crowd. I had to take the drum kit apart with kids all of two feet away. I remember telling one guy, 'If you touch the kit again . . .' He did, and I socked him before security took him away."[27]

DECEMBER 27, 1975
KALAMAZOO, MICHIGAN
WINGS STADIUM, 3600 Van Rick Drive. Venue opened on October 30, 1974.
OPENED FOR: REO Speedwagon
TICKETS: $6.50 (all seats)
CAPACITY: 8,596
NOTES: "A Holiday Rock Spectacular."

DECEMBER 28, 1975
INDIANAPOLIS, INDIANA
INDIANA CONVENTION CENTER, 100 South Capitol. Venue opened in 1972.
WITH: Blue Oyster Cult, Ted Nugent, Mott, the Outlaws, Peter Frampton, Black Sheep

TICKETS: $5.75 (advance) / $7.00 (at the door)
CAPACITY: 10,000
NOTES: Billed as a "Christmas concert."

DECEMBER 29, 1975
DETROIT, MICHIGAN
COBO HALL ARENA, 1 Washington Boulevard. Venue opened on October 17, 1960.
OPENED FOR: Ted Nugent
TICKETS: $4.00 / $5.00 / $6.00
CAPACITY: 11,400
HOWARD: "[When] we went to work with Ted it was really great. His brother, John Nugent, was tour managing at the time, and he was a nice guy, but on this one show in Detroit, all of a sudden, for some reason, this miserable guy from Aerosmith came in for this leg of the tour. John Nugent was still out there but, being Ted's brother, he was driving the rented Lincoln with Ted. So I had a friend that worked as a rigger for Cobo Hall and when I found out that this tour manager was going to be there, I knew Rush was not going to get any production, and it was a really important show. So I designed this little light show with a huge white scrim and a bunch of beam projectors, just all this special-effect lighting. I had my friend fly it to the ceiling, so it just looked like it was just part of the rigging hanging from the ceiling of the building. And he spaced it out for me so that when he brought it in it would cover all of Ted's production and you wouldn't see anything. So of course, that afternoon the tour manager came up to me and told me that I wasn't allowed to use anything but these three faders, just like I expected. And I said to him, 'Well, you know, I think I'd rather just use spotlights, I won't use anything.' And in order to pull this off my lighting board had to be buried under the stage where no one could see it, so I'd have to run the lights from the side of the stage. We didn't have a long enough cord to get it out further and we didn't want people knowing about it, so I just sort of snuck it in there. When Rush came up onstage, all the stuff dropped in, and it basically looked like a huge production. Everything was prefocused, and we just did the best we could. We rolled down our white carpet, and this scrim came in, and the band started playing, and about into the

second or third song I feel I'm being choked. I turn around and it's Ted—strangling me—like, 'Why are you doing this?' Pretty crazy, but it was all right [laughs]. He wasn't happy at the time, but after that he was all right."[28]

JANUARY 2, 1976
MUSKEGON, MICHIGAN
L. C. WALKER SPORTS ARENA, 955 Fourth Street. Venue opened on October 27, 1960.
OPENED FOR: REO Speedwagon
TICKETS: $4.50 (advance) / $5.50 (day of), general admission
CAPACITY: 6,316
NOTES: "A Holiday Rock Spectacular."

JANUARY 3, 1976
COLUMBUS, OHIO
VETERANS MEMORIAL AUDITORIUM, 300 West Broad Street. Venue dedicated on November 11, 1955.
SUPPORT ACT: Mott
TICKETS: $5.00 / $6.00
ATTENDANCE: 3,964 (another source lists 3,917); sold out
CONCERT GROSS: $22,676
NOTES: Rescheduled from December 30, 1975.
CASHBOX: "Rush, playing second on the bill at a recent Ohio date, sold out the auditorium before a headlining act was added to the bill. Hence they were elevated to the top spot."

WNCI and Sunshine Present

The 1st Annual Holiday Concert

RUSH

and Special Guest

MOTT

Formerly Mott the Hoople

Sat., Jan. 3 — 8:00 P.M.
Vets Memorial Auditorium

all seats reserved at $5 and $6

on sale now at Central Ticket office, all Sears stores, Buzzard's Nest Record Shops, Mershon Ticket office and all local and out of town CTO outlets.

JANUARY 4, 1976
LARGO, MARYLAND
CAPITAL CENTRE, 1 Harry S. Truman Drive
OPENED FOR: Blue Oyster Cult, Ted Nugent, REO Speedwagon, and Leslie West
TICKETS: $5.50 (advance) / $6.50 (at the door), general admission
ATTENDANCE: 16,000 (approximate)[29]
CAPACITY: 19,000
NOTES: Concert started at 5:00 p.m. "Holiday Spectacular! Six hours of Rock & Roll." Rush opens and Leslie West closes, despite the fact that Blue Oyster Cult is the headliner.

JANUARY 10, 1976
TORONTO, ONTARIO
MASSEY HALL, 178 Victoria Street. Historic venue opened on June 14, 1894.
SUPPORT ACT: Mainline
TICKETS: $4.50 CAD
CAPACITY: 2,752
TORONTO SUN: "Raw, riffy Rush in new season starter: Rush is better than most. This hometown concert was a triumph for them, crammed with fans who roared approval at the announcement of every selection and thundered them back for three separate encores after a solid hour and a half of music that was raw, riffy, and loud."

LEFT: Alex's lyric sheet: "Lessons."

1. Ian Grandy. Facebook.com, April 21, 2015.
2. Interview with Pete Agnew. Montreal Gazette, August 1975.
3. Winnipeg Free Press.
4. Winnipeg Free Press.
5. Winnipeg Free Press, September 18, 1975.
6. Saskatoon Star Phoenix.
7. Saskatoon Star-Phoenix, September 18, 1975.
8. Skip Daly. Interview with Richard Kolke, July 19, 2010.
9. Edmonton Journal.
10. Ian Grandy. Facebook.com, December 5, 2014.
11. queencitykids.com/story.html
12. Dave Bidini. For Those About To Rock: A Road Map for Being in a Band. Tundra Books, 2004.
13. Ian Grandy. Facebook.com, September 25, 2015.
14. randysrodeo.com.
15. Neil Peart. Roadshow: Landscape with Drums: A Concert Tour by Motorcycle. Rounder Books, 2006.
16. Eric Hansen. Interview with Howard Ungerleider, July 11, 2012.
17. Scot McFadyen and Sam Dunn, dir. Beyond The Lighted Stage, 2010.
18. Gary Weimer. Facebook.com, June 2017.
19. Scot McFadyen and Sam Dunn, dir. Beyond The Lighted Stage, 2010.
20. Ian Grandy. Facebook.com, November 5, 2015.
21. Interview with Chris Cole. The Erie Square Gazette, October 31, 1975.
22. The Times Herald, November 19, 1975.
23. Interview with Rick Becker. Lansing City Pulse, June 28, 2015.
24. The Morning Call.
25. Jim Bossier.
26. artfuldodgersite.com
27. Skip Daly. Interview with Ian Grandy, 2012.
28. Interview with Howard Ungerleider. A Show Of Fans no. 16, 1997.
29. The Washington Post.

UPCOMING EVENTS

Thursday, June 17 at 8 P.M.
at the Welland Arena

ROCK CONCERT

—featuring—

RUSH
John McLaughlin
"MAX WEBSTER"

Tickets Available At—
Sam's—St. Catharines—Niagara Falls—Hamilton
Central Music—252 Main Street East
Circle of Sound—Seaway Mall

ROSE FESTIVAL

Chapter 5

THE 2112 TOUR

Rush's fourth effort proved to be a turning point for the band. Following the commercial and critical failure of *Caress of Steel*, they opted to double down on their more progressive tendencies with another concept album, this one arguably even more ambitious in scope, with a twenty-minute-plus title track that took up all of the first side. The courageous move paid major dividends; *2112* resonated with rock fans on a grassroots level and ultimately bought Rush their creative freedom. As Geddy told *Creem* magazine, "We took a risk with *2112*. Individualism, concepts of thought, and morality are causes that we believe in. We all know that boogie is definitely the philosophy of the '70s. Everybody is out there for a fast buck. The Aerosmiths give birth to groups like Starz. It has become OK to say that you're only in rock 'n' roll for the money. We've tried to transcend that by having something for everyone. We don't ask that everyone believe in what we do. Let them take our stuff on any level they want."

On tour, the band began performing more cobills (with the likes of Kansas and Styx) and headline dates. The most significant event of the *2112* tour was the three-night stand at Massey Hall in June 1976, and the recording of these shows for Rush's first live album: *All the World's a Stage*. Most of the live album ended up being culled from the final night's performance, despite Neil having had various equipment difficulties. At the time, the three-night stand was the highest-grossing rock show in the history of the venue.

"Every time you play hometown, it's different from any other show," said Geddy. "It's hard to know what the objective, world view of Massey Hall is, but I would think that it's our version of the Royal Albert Hall. Massey Hall was the pinnacle, prestige gig to us. To me, this building represented musical success. It was the unattainable dream for every young player. Suddenly, there were all these live albums being made. Humble Pie had put out a double record and it was a huge success. So, we said, 'Let's do a live album.' So, we did three nights, and we tried to re-create the feeling of being at the Rush show. We'd never done a live album before, so we really did not know what we were doing. It was a crazy, crazy three nights. Really exciting, and totally nerve-racking. We were not to be dealt with— we were all completely anxious."

ABOVE: Hamilton, Ontario; CKOC's Nevin Grant and John Oliver, Polydor's Bob Ansell, and contest winner Charley Price (and friend) with Rush.

THESE PAGES: Toronto, Ontario; Rush onstage at Massey Hall during the three-night stand, which yielded the *All the World's a Stage* live album.

TOUR HISTORY
2112

FEBRUARY 6–7, 1976
LONDON, ONTARIO
CENTENNIAL HALL, 550 Wellington Street. Venue opened on June 21, 1967.
CAPACITY: 1,637 (seated)
NOTES: As with all of the early tours, it's difficult to draw a clear line of demarcation between the end of the *Caress of Steel* tour and the start of the *2112* tour. The album was recorded and mixed in January and February 1976, in the wake of the band's January 10 performance at Massey Hall, but SRO's records indicate some early February performances in Ontario—a month after Massey Hall, but still a full month before the release of *2112*. For our purposes, we're considering these February Ontario dates to be part of the *2112* tour.

FEBRUARY 9, 1976
HAMILTON, ONTARIO
GREAT HALL, HAMILTON PLACE, 10 Macnab Street South. Venue inaugurated on September 22, 1973.
SUPPORT ACT: Ian Thomas
TICKETS: $4.50 / $5.50 / $6.50 CAD
ATTENDANCE: 2,200; sold out (a week in advance)
NOTES: Ian Thomas is the younger brother of Dave Thomas, who portrayed Doug McKenzie on SCTV, and was featured on the song "Take Off" with Geddy Lee and Rick Moranis. Rush graphic designer and guest musician Hugh Syme was the keyboard player for the Ian Thomas Band. CKOC-FM sponsored a "dinner with Rush" contest. Winner Charley Price and a friend dined with the band and won front-row seats to the show and an autographed copy of *Caress of Steel*.
HAMILTON SPECTATOR: "Audience happy with NOISE: What attracted a sold-out house was a mind-numbing, sledgehammer kind of basic rhythm.

There was nothing pretentious about their expectations, just as there was nothing pretentious in Rush's work."
ALEX: "We've always had great concerts [in Hamilton]. We played Hamilton Place when it was new. I had the flu, and I had to run off stage, throw up into a bucket, run back on, and keep playing. A rough night."[1]

FEBRUARY 14, 1976
WATERLOO, ONTARIO
LAURIER THEATRE AUDITORIUM, Sir Wilfrid Laurier University, 75 University Avenue West. Venue opened in 1969.
SUPPORT ACT: Max Webster
TICKETS: $4.00 (students with IDs) / $5.00 (general admission) CAD
CAPACITY: 1,000 (per show)
NOTES: Two performances: 7 p.m. and 10 p.m. Balance paid to band: $2,041.95.
***THE CORD* (LAURIER UNIVERSITY):** "Rush indicted on vicious auditory assault: One number, 'The Necromancer,' featured ten minutes of Alex Lifeson running his guitar pick up and down the strings. Other gimmicks such as echo boxes and a background narrator, which sounded like the Friendly Giant, had the high school crowd pleading for more. Although they have recently found some success, their musical future seems limited to perhaps a greatest hits album and being relegated to playing local bars."

FEBRUARY 19, 1976
KINGSTON, ONTARIO
KINGSTON MEMORIAL CENTRE ARENA, 303 York Street. Venue opened in November 1951.
SUPPORT ACT: Thundermug
TICKETS: $4.50 (advance) / $5.00 (at the door) CAD
CAPACITY: 3,300

NOTES: GKLC-FM sponsored a "dinner with Rush" contest. The winner and a friend dined with the band and were also awarded front-row seats.

FEBRUARY 21, 1976
BRANTFORD, ONTARIO
BCI TRIPLE GYM, BRANTFORD COLLEGIATE INSTITUTE, 120 Brant Avenue. School founded in 1910.
SUPPORT ACT: Max Webster
TICKETS: $4.00 (advance) / $5.00 (at the door) CAD
ATTENDANCE: 2,000 (approximate)
RUSH'S FEE: $3,500[2]
NOTES: Based on a review (assuming it's accurate), the set list consisted of three songs from each of the first three albums, and the band was not yet performing any of the *2112* material live.
BCI NEWSPAPER, GEDDY: "We had a tour planned for Europe, but we canceled it at the last minute because we felt that we should still be concentrating on the US. Sweden is our second biggest market in the world right now [after America]. . . . The hall here tonight had a pretty bad sound, but the audience made up for it. If that had been a dull crowd, it would have been a write-off for us."
BCI NEWSPAPER: "Rush put on a fine show. The best high school concert I've seen."

FEBRUARY 26, 1976
LINCOLN, NEBRASKA
PERSHING MEMORIAL AUDITORIUM, 226 Centennial Mall South. Venue dedicated on March 10, 1957.
OPENED FOR: Kansas, Head East
TICKETS: $5.00 (advance) / $6.00 (day of)
CAPACITY: 7,500
NOTES: Not in SRO's records. Although ads fail to list Rush, two *Lincoln Journal* blurbs during the week of the concert (and on the day of the gig) do include them as the opener.

FEBRUARY 27, 1976
DAVENPORT, IOWA
RKO ORPHEUM THEATRE, 136 East Third Street. Historic venue opened on November 25, 1931.
OPENED FOR: Kansas; Head East opened the show.
CAPACITY: 2,700
NOTES: This date is not in SRO's records, and it is unconfirmed that Rush was on the bill. A February 21 blurb in the *Quad-City Times* lists only Kansas.

MARCH 2, 1976
OTTAWA, ONTARIO
OTTAWA CIVIC CENTRE, 1015 Bank Street. Venue opened on December 29, 1967.
OPENED FOR: Electric Light Orchestra
TICKETS: $5.50 (advance) / $6.50 (at the door) CAD
ATTENDANCE: 7,000
CAPACITY: 9,862
NOTES: Little Feat was originally on the bill, but Rush replaced them far enough in advance to be listed in the ad. Showtime was delayed an hour due to a massive ice storm that brought southern Ontario to a standstill.
IAN: "Rush supported ELO one time in Ottawa. There was a bit of a fight. They were way late . . . snotty and had no respect for us. Their monitor mixer walked away from the board. Skip Gildersleeve punched the guy and got into it with a big limey."[3]
OTTAWA CITIZEN: "The boisterous crowd gave substitute warm-up act Rush a surprisingly strong reception. Rush turned in a creditable but not especially exciting forty-five-minute set, coming across strangely muted for a supposedly high-energy trio."

MARCH 5, 1976
MOUNT PROSPECT, ILLINOIS
RANDHURST TWIN ICE ARENA, 350 East Kensington. Venue built in 1974.
WITH: Kansas (cobill); Starcastle opened the show.
TICKETS: $6.00 (advance) / $7.00 (at the door)
ATTENDANCE: 4,500; sold out
NOTES: This was just the third rock concert held in Mount Prospect despite a village ordinance against "hard rock." Security was increased to ten police officers after excessive partying took place during a January 30 concert by Blue

Oyster Cult and Bob Seger.[4] Longtime fan Jim Bossier attended this show and reports that "I Think I'm Going Bald" was performed and that a bootleg recording existed at one point but has since been lost.
SET LIST: "Bastille Day," "Anthem," "Lakeside Park," "Fly by Night," "I Think I'm Going Bald," "By-Tor and the Snow Dog," "Working Man" (with drum solo), "Finding My Way" (encore).[5]
IAN: "If I had to guess, I'd say they played 'Bald' maybe ten times. It never went over really well."[6]
WALRUS: "Musically speaking, Rush were OK. The audience liked them a lot in spite of the set's blandness."

MARCH 8, 1976
SIOUX CITY, IOWA
MUNICIPAL AUDITORIUM, 401 Gordan Drive. Historic venue dedicated on September 9, 1950.
OPENED FOR: Kansas; Head East opened the show.
CAPACITY: 4,620 (seated); 5,000 (festival)

MARCH 13, 1976
OVER ONE HUNDRED THOUSAND COPIES OF 2112 HAVE BEEN SOLD IN THE FIVE DAYS SINCE ITS RELEASE.
NEIL: "Polygram had written us off before *2112* had come out—we'd seen their financial predictions and we weren't even on it!"[7]

MARCH 15–18, 1976
WEST HOLLYWOOD, CALIFORNIA
THE STARWOOD, 8151 Santa Monica Boulevard. Building opened in the 1960s.
SUPPORT ACT: The Stars
CAPACITY: 999
LOS ANGELES TIMES: "Rush opened a four-nighter at the Starwood on Monday with a set of determined power rock that could enthrall only the numbest of boogie fanatics. The band's musical concepts are proportionately mundane, the bulk of its set consisting of riffs piling upon chords with little regard to tension, development or even to direct, uncluttered energy."

MARCH 21, 1976
SACRAMENTO, CALIFORNIA
MEMORIAL AUDITORIUM, 15th and J Street. Historic venue dedicated on February 22, 1927.
SUPPORT ACT: Sutherland Brothers and Quiver
ATTENDANCE: 633[8]
CAPACITY: 4,500
NOTES: Styx was a late cancellation due to the flu, with just twenty-one ticket holders accepting the offered refund. The crowd was small (filling in the first fifteen rows)[9] but very vocal, bringing Rush back for two encores.
SACRAMENTO UNION: "Rock concert cup full; house nearly empty: The volume level of Rush's whole set was enormously loud, but they moved well through seventy minutes of metal mashing and echo-effects—mostly promoting their new album. Peart, especially, is fantastic—one of the finest rock drummers in the business. His style fits in nicely with Rush's progressive-hard-rock sound."

MARCH 23, 1976
FRESNO, CALIFORNIA
WARNORS THEATRE, 1400 Fulton Street. Historic venue opened on October 20, 1928.
WITH: Styx (cobill); Sutherland Brothers and Quiver opened the show.
TICKETS: $5.00 (advance) / $6.50 (at the door)
CAPACITY: 2,164

MARCH 25, 1976
MEDFORD, OREGON
MEDFORD ARMORY, 1701 South Pacific Avenue. Venue dedicated on May 25, 1957.
WITH: Styx (cobill); Sutherland Brothers and Quiver opened the show.
TICKETS: $5.00 (advance) / $6.00 (at the door)
CAPACITY: 3,000

MARCH 26, 1976
SEATTLE, WASHINGTON
PARAMOUNT NORTHWEST THEATRE, 901 Pine Street. Historic venue opened on March 1, 1928.
WITH: Styx (cobill); Sutherland Brothers and Quiver opened the show.
CAPACITY: 3,054
NOTES: Rush's performance was allegedly recorded by KZOK-FM and was to be broadcast on April 20, 1976.[10]

STEVE SLATON (LONGTIME SEATTLE DJ): "Back in those days, it wasn't uncommon for a local station to record a concert and just broadcast it."[11]

MARCH 27, 1976
SPOKANE, WASHINGTON
JOHN F. KENNEDY PAVILION, Gonzaga University campus, 710 East Lower Kennedy Drive. Venue opened on December 3, 1965.
WITH: Styx (cobill); Sutherland Brothers and Quiver opened the show.
TICKETS: $5.00 (advance) / $6.00 (at the door)
CAPACITY: 4,000

MARCH 28, 1976
PORTLAND, OREGON
PARAMOUNT THEATRE, 1037 Southwest Broadway. Venue opened on March 8, 1928.
SUPPORT ACT: Sutherland Brothers and Quiver
TICKETS: $5.50 (advance) / $6.50 (at the door)
ATTENDANCE: 2,400
CAPACITY: 3,036
NOTES: Aka Paramount Northwest Theatre. Styx was scheduled to perform but canceled when their equipment truck broke down en route in Washington state.
THE OREGONIAN: "The drums were rather lyrical in a manner not usually found in hard rock. It was a tight trio that attacked its music with verve and showed Rush to be a good purveyor of heavy rock."

MARCH 29, 1976
TACOMA, WASHINGTON
TACOMA NATIONAL GUARD ARMORY, 715 South 11th Street. Historic venue opened on December 31, 1908.
WITH: Styx (cobill); Sutherland Brothers and Quiver opened the show (unconfirmed).
NOTES: This date is not present in SRO's records, so it may or may not have actually happened.

MARCH 30, 1976
YAKIMA, WASHINGTON
SHERAR GYMNASIUM, Yakima Valley Community College campus, 1000 South 12th Avenue. Venue opened in 1957.
SUPPORT ACT: Sutherland Brothers and Quiver (unconfirmed)

CAPACITY: 1,500 (seats)
NOTES: Venue unconfirmed.

APRIL 7, 1976
PITTSBURGH, PENNSYLVANIA
CIVIC ARENA, 300 Auditorium Place. Venue opened on September 17, 1961.
OPENED FOR: Bad Company
TICKETS: $4.50 / $5.50 / $6.50
CAPACITY: 17,000
PITTSBURGH PRESS: "Rush has gotten into 'theme' pieces and included excerpts from their latest, *2112*. The story line is coherent, and praise is due Rush for their willingness to experiment. When Rush headlines in such towns as St. Louis, a projectionist enhances *2112* with appropriate visual effects."

APRIL 9, 1976
INDIANAPOLIS, INDIANA
INDIANA STATE FAIRGROUNDS COLISEUM, 1202 East 38th Street. Historic venue opened in August 1939.
SUPPORT ACTS: Ted Nugent (special guest); Sutherland Brothers and Quiver opened the show.
TICKETS: $5.50 (advance) / $6.50 (at the door), general admission
ATTENDANCE: 5,531
CONCERT GROSS: $32,076
WALRUS: "Rush had the stage set, lighting, down perfect, but you can only take Geddy Lee for so long."

APRIL 10, 1976
SOUTH BEND, INDIANA
MORRIS CIVIC AUDITORIUM, 211 North Michigan Street. Venue opened on November 2, 1922.
SUPPORT ACTS: Starcastle; Sutherland Brothers and Quiver opened the show.
TICKETS: $5.50 (advance) / $6.50 (day of)
ATTENDANCE: 1,195
CAPACITY: 2,468
CONCERT GROSS: $6,689

APRIL 11, 1976
WAUKEGAN, ILLINOIS
WAUKEGAN ICE ARENA, 3340 Grand Avenue. Venue built in 1974.
SUPPORT ACTS: Starcastle; Pentwater opened the show.
TICKETS: $6.00 (advance) / $7.00 (at the door)
ATTENDANCE: 3,000

MIKE KONOPKA (PENTWATER MULTI-INSTRUMENTALIST): "When we played that show in Waukegan, we had never heard of Rush. I recall that Neil Peart was admiring our own drummer's rather large Slingerland kit. Neil was totally nice to us. However, Rush's surly crew tried to fine us $150 for using our fog machine (this was the '70s after all) during our opening set."[12]

APRIL 15, 1976
ST. LOUIS, MISSOURI
AMBASSADOR THEATRE, 411 North Seventh Street. Venue opened in 1926.
SUPPORT ACT: Heart
TICKETS: $3.00 / $4.00 / $5.00
ATTENDANCE: 3,400; sold out
NOTES: One thousand people were turned away at the door.
ALEX: "I remember we played with Heart once. This was very early, maybe 1975. There was so much talk about Heart and the Wilson sisters. We were really looking forward to meeting them. We were backstage, and Roger Fisher said to me, 'We're gonna blow you guys off the stage tonight, you just watch.' And I thought, wow, what a weird thing to say. But I think I played that much harder that night."[13]
RECORD WEEK: "It was Rush's fourth [sic] appearance in this Midwest city and, judging from the crowd, they have built up a strong following with local concert goers. The constant and grueling tour schedule that Rush keeps up throughout the year has given them a poise that only experience can nurture. If Rush's audience in St. Louis was any indication, it's a stoned crowd that is drawn to the band. The LA smog has nothing on the cloud of smoke that hung over the theater throughout the show as Rush ground out a set of dynamically structured rock compositions."

APRIL 17, 1976
PEKIN, ILLINOIS
PEKIN MEMORIAL ARENA, 250 Red Bud Drive. Venue opened in 1964.
SUPPORT ACTS: Thin Lizzy; Starcastle opened the show.
TICKETS: $5.50 (advance) / $6.50 (at the door)
CAPACITY: 1,500 (ice hockey)
NOTES: A couple hours after the gig, Thin Lizzy's Scott Gorham had a knock at his hotel door. "Loaded on booze and

weed, and busy entertaining two local girls," he cautiously opened the door and peered out. There stood Rush, dressed as characters from the late-'50s American sitcom *Leave It to Beaver*: Alex as dad Ward Cleaver, his long hair slicked back, wearing a smoking jacket; Geddy as mom June Cleaver, hair in pigtails, wearing a floral-print night dress; and Neil as son "Beaver" Cleaver, in school uniform. Gorham invited them into the room, where the trio proceeded to act out scenes from the TV show, to the bewilderment of the two girls sitting on the bed. By Gorham's reckoning, the act went on for forty-five minutes, by which time he was laughing so hard there were tears rolling down his face.[14]

SCOTT GORHAM (THIN LIZZY GUITARIST): "At first we were all totally confused. We were stoned, and this was just so bizarre. Talk about an icebreaker. I thought, *Oh, that's what they're really like*. The musicianship was incredible. All that musicality . . . all the intricacies . . . and all that power from just three guys. This wasn't like all the pansy shit you'd hear from some progressive bands—they really powered down on it. We respected the hell out of them."[15]

APRIL 21–23, 1976
ATLANTA, GEORGIA
ALEX COOLEY'S ELECTRIC BALLROOM, corner of Peachtree Street NE and Ponce de Leon Avenue. Building opened in 1913.
SUPPORT ACT: Kokomo
CAPACITY: 1,100

APRIL 26, 1976
AKRON, OHIO
AKRON CIVIC THEATRE, 182 South Main Street. Historic venue opened on April 21, 1929.
SUPPORT ACT: Stu Daye
TICKETS: $5.50 (advance) / $6.50 (at the door)
CAPACITY: 2,642

APRIL 27, 1976
CLEVELAND, OHIO
ALLEN THEATRE, 1407 Euclid Avenue. Venue opened on April 21, 1921.
SUPPORT ACT: Stu Daye
TICKETS: $5.50 (advance) / $6.50 (at the door)

CAPACITY: 3,003
PLAIN DEALER, **GEDDY:** "We're trying to put more emphasis on lyrics, on melody, more complex structures. We're expanding."

APRIL 28, 1976
FLINT, MICHIGAN
IMA SPORTS ARENA, 3501 Lapeer Road. Venue opened on October 19, 1969.
SUPPORT ACT: Journey
CAPACITY: 6,469, general admission
NOTES: Rare Earth was scheduled to headline but canceled, according to Ian (though a fan account claims they played and were booed offstage). IMA stands for Industrial Mutual Auditorium.
IAN: "Rare Earth was a no-show for this gig."[16]
FAN ACCOUNT: "Rush came on second and blew everyone away. Journey was pretty good as well."

APRIL 29, 1976
COLUMBUS, OHIO
VETERAN'S MEMORIAL AUDITORIUM, 300 West Broad Street. Venue dedicated on November 11, 1955.
SUPPORT ACTS: Thin Lizzy; Stu Daye opened the show.
TICKETS: $5.00 / $6.00 (all seats reserved)
ATTENDANCE: 3,203
CAPACITY: 3,964
CONCERT GROSS: $18,905

APRIL 30, 1976
WATERLOO, IOWA
MCELROY AUDITORIUM, 250 Ansborough Avenue. Venue opened on September 28, 1936.
OPENED FOR: Aerosmith; Angel opened the show.
TICKETS: $6.00 (advance) / $7.00 (at the door)
ATTENDANCE: 9,700; oversold[17]
NOTES: The gig was completely oversold, with about 5,000 people being turned away at the door, causing the mayor and promoter to debate the possibility of lowering the venue capacity to 7,500. Despite the overflow crowd, the audience was well-behaved, with only two arrests occurring, both of which were before the start of the show.[18]

MAY 1, 1976
ROLLA, MISSOURI
UNIVERSITY OF MISSOURI ROLLA, Multi-Purpose Building. University of Missouri campus, 705 West 10th Street. Venue opened on December 5, 1969.
CAPACITY: 4,524
NOTES: Venue unconfirmed.

MAY 2, 1976
KANSAS CITY, KANSAS
SOLDIER AND SAILOR'S MEMORIAL HALL, 600 North Seventh Street. Venue cornerstone laid on May 26, 1924.
OPENED FOR: Uriah Heep
TICKETS: $6.00
CAPACITY: 3,500

MAY 3, 1976
SIOUX FALLS, SOUTH DAKOTA
SIOUX FALLS ARENA, 1201 West Avenue North. Venue dedicated on December 10, 1961.
OPENED FOR: Uriah Heep; Flash Cadillac opened the show.
CAPACITY: 7,200

MAY 9, 1976
YOUNGSTOWN, OHIO
TOMORROW CLUB, 213 Federal Plaza West. Venue opened on October 20, 1974.
SUPPORT ACT: Paris
TICKETS: $3.00 (advance) / $4.00 (day of)
CAPACITY: 2,142

MAY 11, 1976
DETROIT, MICHIGAN
MASONIC AUDITORIUM, 500 Temple Street. Historic venue dedicated on November 25, 1926.
SUPPORT ACTS: Starcastle; Artful Dodger opened the show.
TICKETS: $5.50 (advance) / $6.50 (at the door)
CAPACITY: 4,404

MAY 13, 1976
BIG RAPIDS, MICHIGAN
STARR AUDITORIUM, STARR EDUCATIONAL CENTER, Ferris State College, 901 South State Street. Venue dedicated on February 22, 1962.
SUPPORT ACT: Pete Texas
TICKETS: $1.00 (general admission)
CAPACITY: 1,644 (seated)

MAY 21, 1976
SPRINGFIELD, MISSOURI
SHRINE MOSQUE, 601 St. Louis Street. Historic building dedicated November 3, 1923.
OPENED FOR: J. Geils Band
TICKETS: $5.50 (advance)
CAPACITY: 4,750
NOTES: This date is not included in SRO data.

MAY 22, 1976
DAVENPORT, IOWA
RKO ORPHEUM THEATRE, 136 East Third Street. Historic venue opened on November 25, 1931.
OPENED FOR: Blue Oyster Cult
TICKETS: $6.50 (advance) / $7.50 (day of)
CAPACITY: 2,700
NOTES: Neil's future drum tech, Larry Allen, tagged along and attended.
IAN: "Larry came with the band to Davenport as a friend. They asked him in the dressing room afterwards how it sounded, and he replied that it had taken me about a minute into the first song for the mix to be excellent. He wasn't working for us yet, but I think he joined fairly soon after that."[19]

MAY 23, 1976
DULUTH, MINNESOTA
DULUTH ARENA, 350 Harbor Drive. Venue opened on August 5, 1966.
WITH: Blue Oyster Cult (cobill); Ozone Crater and the Moon Rock Band opened the show.

TICKETS: $5.00 (advance) / $6.00 (at the door)
ATTENDANCE: 4,500 [20]
CAPACITY: 6,400
NOTES: In the afternoon Neil conducted a phone interview with *Sound* magazine (Canada). During their set, Geddy asked, "How many Canadians are here tonight?" and ". . . the Arena virtually erupted when the Northerners responded," according to the University of Minnesota Duluth (UMD) *Statesman*.
UMD *STATESMAN*: "Though lacking in media exposure, Rush came to Duluth carrying a reputation of being a damn fine group. They lived up to every word."
NEIL: "Instead of adding that extra man, we're going to try to expand on the possibilities open to the three of us. We're going to be looking for new textures and new sounds. We're going to be adding different instruments that will be good for our sound."[21]

MAY 24, 1976
LA CROSSE, WISCONSIN
MARY E. SAWYER AUDITORIUM, Sixth Street North and Vine Street. Historic venue opened on August 27, 1955.
OPENED FOR: Blue Oyster Cult; Sunblind Lion was sceduled to open.
TICKETS: $5.00 (advance) / $6.00 (at the door)
CAPACITY: 4,000
NOTES: Canceled because of an apparent lack of ticket sales; not present in SRO's records.

MAY 25, 1976
FORT WAYNE, INDIANA
ALLEN COUNTY WAR MEMORIAL COLISEUM, 4000 Parnell Avenue. Venue opened on September 28, 1952.
OPENED FOR: Aerosmith, Thin Lizzy (unconfirmed); Stu Daye opened the show.
ATTENDANCE: 10,322; sold out
NOTES: This date is not present in SRO's records, and it is unconfirmed that Rush was on the bill.
FORT WAYNE NEWS-SENTINEL: "The concert built as two backup groups demonstrated their skills at working as separate units in keeping the crowd happy. Their total dependence on sounds with a heavy beat gave them a better reception than many backup bands receive, but it was Aerosmith that everyone came to see."

MAY 26, 1976
TERRE HAUTE, INDIANA
HULMAN CIVIC UNIVERSITY CENTER, Indiana State University, 200 North 8th Street. Venue opened on December 14, 1973.
OPENED FOR: Aerosmith
TICKETS: $6.00 (advance) / $7.00 (day of), general admission
CAPACITY: 10,243

MAY 27, 1976
GREEN BAY, WISCONSIN
BROWN COUNTY VETERANS MEMORIAL ARENA, 1901 South Oneida Street. Venue opened on November 11, 1957.
OPENED FOR: Blue Oyster Cult; Sunblind Lion opened the show.
TICKETS: $5.50 / $6.50
ATTENDANCE: 1,727
CAPACITY: 6,820
CONCERT GROSS: $9,305
GREEN BAY PRESS-GAZETTE: "It was Rush's drummer, Neil Peart, who provided the highlight of the night. With muscle and finesse, Peart roared through an act-closing solo. Rush is a concept band. It played side one from its latest album *2112*, and while vaguely interesting, it is definitely not the last word in futuristic predictions."

MAY 28, 1976
CHICAGO, ILLINOIS
RIVIERA THEATRE, 4746 North Racine Avenue. Venue opened on October 2, 1918.
WITH: Robin Steele
TICKETS: $7.50
ATTENDANCE: 1,500
CAPACITY: 2,500
NOTES: This was the band's first Chicago appearance as a headliner, with tickets going on sale a mere ten days before the show. The crowd was so responsive that Rush returned to the stage for three encores.
TORONTO SUN: "Outside pouring rain. Inside the Riviera Theatre, a damp impatience. A denim army of about 1,500 is growing militant towards a by-no-means incompetent local band called Robin Steele. Not to worry. As soon as the trio strode onstage, the crowd exploded. Rush didn't milk the encore. When it was obvious that Chicago was their kind of town, they came back. And when the following flare-up showed no signs of dying down, they came back again."

MAY 29, 1976
ST. PAUL, MINNESOTA
ST. PAUL CIVIC CENTER, 143 West Fourth Street. Venue opened on January 1, 1973.
OPENED FOR: Blue Oyster Cult, REO Speedwagon; the Boyzz opened the show.
TICKETS: $4.00
CAPACITY: 13,000
CONCERT GROSS: $40,457
NOTES: Billed as "4 bands for $4." Former Small Faces and Humble Pie leader Steve Marriott was slated to be on this show with an all-star lineup, but they disbanded less than a month into their first tour (less than two weeks before this St. Paul concert).

MAY 30, 1976
SPRINGFIELD, ILLINOIS
NELSON CENTER, Lincoln Park, 1601 North Fifth Street. Venue opened in 1974.
SUPPORT ACTS: Roller, Fat Tuesday, Smokehouse
TICKETS: $4.00 (with coupon) / $4.50 (advance)
CAPACITY: 4,000 (approximate)
NOTES: A festive set with the band in good spirits.

SET LIST: "Bastille Day," "Anthem," "Lakeside Park," "2112" (5 parts), "Fly by Night," "In the Mood," "By-Tor and the Snow Dog," "In the End," "Working Man," "Finding My Way" (with drum solo), "What You're Doing."
GEDDY (ONSTAGE): "This is called 'Tuning Man.' As soon as Alex is done, we'll begin."

JUNE 2, 1976
AUSTIN, TEXAS
ARMADILLO WORLD HEADQUARTERS, 525½ Barton Springs Road. Venue opened on August 7, 1970.
SUPPORT ACT: LA Jets
CAPACITY: 1,500

JUNE 3, 1976
AUSTIN, TEXAS
ARMADILLO WORLD HEADQUARTERS, 525½ Barton Springs Road
SUPPORT ACT: LA Jets (unconfirmed)
CAPACITY: 1,500
NOTES: Despite a May 27 concert listing in the *Seguin Gazette* stating New Riders of the Purple Sage playing this venue on June 3, this date is in SRO's records. The New Riders show was apparently rescheduled to June 1, and Rush was booked for a second night sometime after the May 27 ad went to print.

JUNE 4, 1976
AMARILLO, TEXAS
CIVIC CENTER AUDITORIUM, 401 South Buchanan Street. Venue opened on September 3, 1968.
SUPPORT ACT: Iron Butterfly
TICKETS: $5.00 (advance) / $6.00 (day of), general admission
CAPACITY: 2,848
NOTES: This gig was originally slated for the Civic Center Coliseum, with Styx billed as "special guest" but was moved to the Civic Center Auditorium when Styx canceled and was replaced by Iron Butterfly.

JUNE 5, 1976
EL PASO, TEXAS
UNIVERSITY OF TEXAS MEMORIAL GYM, 500 West University Avenue. Venue opened in December 1961.
SUPPORT ACTS: Iron Butterfly; Liberation opened the show.
TICKETS: $4.50 (students) / $5.50 (advance) / $6.00 (day of)

CAPACITY: 5,200
NOTES: Styx was originally on the bill as "special guest" but canceled and was replaced by Iron Butterfly.

JUNE 7, 1976
SAN ANTONIO, TEXAS
MUNICIPAL AUDITORIUM, 100 Auditorium Circle. Historic venue opened on April 19, 1926.
SUPPORT ACT: Thin Lizzy
TICKETS: $5.50 / $6.50
ATTENDANCE: 6,100
CAPACITY: 5,785; oversold
CONCERT GROSS: $38,000
NOTES: Despite early ads to the contrary, Styx did not perform. An ad from the week of the show confirms Thin Lizzy as opener.

JUNE 8, 1976
CORPUS CHRISTI, TEXAS
RITZ MUSIC HALL, 715 North Chaparral Street. Venue opened on December 25, 1929.
SUPPORT ACT: Too Smooth
CAPACITY: 1,348
JEFF CLARK (TOO SMOOTH GUITARIST): "The Ritz was an old converted movie theater, a great venue with theater seating. That was a great show and Rush were a very comfortable band to work with. As an opening act for many different touring acts in the '70s, there were a few that really had mutual respect and great communication with us. Usually, if they heard our sound check or opening set, these 'good guys' were very complimentary and gracious. Rush was one of those acts. They caught the tail end of our sound check, and after theirs, Neil Peart and Alex Lifeson asked Brian Wooten, our main lead guitarist extraordinaire, if he wanted to jam with them. They did for quite some time. Super nice guys, one of the best three-piece groups of all time."[22]

JUNE 11–13, 1976
TORONTO, ONTARIO
MASSEY HALL, 178 Victoria Street. Historic venue opened on June 14, 1894.
SUPPORT ACT: Max Webster
TICKETS: $4.50 / $5.50 / $6.50 CAD
ATTENDANCE: 2,550 per show; sold out
CONCERT GROSS: $13,854 CAD per show

NOTES: Recording for *All the World's a Stage*. Skip Gildersleeve introduced the band: "Oh . . . won't you please welcome home . . . *Rush*!" Neil's legendary drum solo for the album was taken from this gig. The first night's performance of "2112" is included as a bonus on the fortieth anniversary special edition of *2112*. Photographs from the Massey Hall stand reveal Neil's kit without the front bass drum heads, which were removed for recording purposes. Once replaced, the new heads sported their iconic blue color, as the background for "Rush" (in *Caress of Steel* font), as pictured on the *All the World's a Stage* cover. Most of the live album ends up being culled from the final night's performance, despite Neil having various equipment difficulties. Terry Brown spent most of the night freaking out in the Fedco mobile recording truck. At the time, this three-night stand marked the highest-grossing rock show in the history of the venue. "Something for Nothing" from this date is included as a bonus on the fortieth-anniversary special edition of *2112*.

IAN: "When you actually played there as a professional, you realized how small backstage was. The cases had to go back into the trucks because there was no room to stack them anywhere else, and the PA equipment was stacked as best we could at both sides of the stage. It's the kind of place that you can stand onstage, and speak at a normal volume, and someone sitting in the last row of the balcony can hear you perfectly. I know because I did just that as an experiment, to see for myself. At that time, the thought of playing and selling out Maple Leaf Gardens—as Rush would go on to do just six months later—was just too much to even consider."

TORONTO STAR: "Last night's effort by the band, complete with smoke bombs and a rather simple light show, was probably the best performance it has given here—although that's like saying you've just seen the best train wreck of your life."

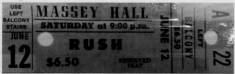

JUNE 15, 1976
CHATHAM, ONTARIO
MEMORIAL ARENA, 80 Tweedsmuir Avenue West. Venue opened in the fall of 1950.
CAPACITY: 3,600
NOTES: This date is not present in SRO's records but is corroborated by a tour advertisement and verified by a newspaper article from Welland, Ontario, though not present in the local *Chatham Daily News.*

JUNE 16, 1976
EVANSVILLE, INDIANA
ROBERTS MUNICIPAL STADIUM, University of Evansville campus, 2600 Division Street. Venue dedicated on December 1, 1956.
OPENED FOR: Aerosmith
TICKETS: $6.00 / $7.00
ATTENDANCE: 12,615; sold out
CONCERT GROSS: $79,736
NOTES: *Billboard* lists attendance as 12,165 (possibly a typo).

JUNE 17, 1976
WELLAND, ONTARIO
WELLAND ARENA, 501 King Street. Venue opened in 1946.
SUPPORT ACTS: Max Webster, John McLaughlin
TICKETS: $4.50 (advance) / $5.00 (at the door) CAD
ATTENDANCE: 1,800 (approximate)[24]
CAPACITY: 4,200
NOTES: The concert was part of Welland's annual Rose Festival. Fans lined up for hours before the show just to catch a glimpse of the band.
IVY RIDDELL (CHAIR OF THE 1976 ROSE FESTIVAL): "I've never seen so much audio equipment. I remember going out onto the walkway at the arena and thinking the music was so loud, but the young people loved them. My husband couldn't stand being inside the arena because the music was so loud for him. He went all the way to Burgar Street, and he could still hear them playing at the arena."[25]

JUNE 18, 1976
OSHAWA, ONTARIO
CIVIC AUDITORIUM, 99 Thornton Road South. Venue opened on December 11, 1964.
SUPPORT ACT: Max Webster
TICKETS: $5.00 (advance) / $6.00 (at the door) CAD

ATTENDANCE: 2,600
CAPACITY: 4,024
THIS WEEK: "A disappointing Oshawa crowd gets the Rush: Rush blasted its way into the hearts of 2,600 youthful rock fans. A large contingent of Toronto fans followed them to the auditorium to see them probably for the ninth time. According to record business reports, Rush's manager is planning an American tour where he will ask $20,000 a performance."

JULY 6, 1976
TULSA, OKLAHOMA
TULSA ASSEMBLY CENTER, 100 Civic Center. Venue opened on March 8, 1964.
OPENED FOR: Blue Oyster Cult; UFO opened the show.
TICKETS: $5.00 / $6.00
CAPACITY: 8,900
NOTES: Mott was on the bill as well and slated to play after Blue Oyster Cult (even though Mott was the opener). Time ran out and Mott didn't perform, resulting in a few fans throwing chairs to vent their displeasure.

JULY 8, 1976
SHREVEPORT, LOUISIANA
HIRSCH MEMORIAL COLISEUM, 3701 Hudson Avenue. Venue opened on April 10, 1954.
OPENED FOR: Blue Oyster Cult; Mott and Starz opened the show.
TICKETS: $5.00 (advance) / $6.00 (day of), general admission
CAPACITY: 10,300

JULY 10, 1976
DALLAS, TEXAS
SMU MOODY COLISEUM, 6024 Airline Road. Venue opened on December 3, 1956.
OPENED FOR: Blue Oyster Cult; Starz opened the show.
TICKETS: $6.00 / $7.00, general admission
CAPACITY: 8,900
NOTES: The first five thousand tickets sold were six dollars, general admission. UFO and Mott were originally slated for this bill, but were replaced by Starz at the eleventh hour.

JULY 11, 1976
HOUSTON, TEXAS
SAM HOUSTON COLISEUM, 801 Bagby Street. Venue dedicated on November 16, 1937.
OPENED FOR: Blue Oyster Cult; Starz opened the show.
TICKETS: $6.00 / $7.00, general admission
CAPACITY: 11,300
NOTES: During the encore someone threw a firecracker at Alex, temporarily halting the show.
MACLEAN'S: "Rush stormed on stage in Houston and received the kind of ear-splitting roar usually reserved for such legendary hard-rock bands as Led Zeppelin and Grand Funk Railroad."

JULY 14, 1976
ORLANDO, FLORIDA
ORLANDO SPORTS STADIUM, 2285 North Econlockhatchee Trail. Venue opened on November 13, 1967.
OPENED FOR: Blue Oyster Cult; Mott and Starz opened the show.
TICKETS: $5.00 (all seats)
CAPACITY: 7,200

JULY 16, 1976
WEST PALM BEACH, FLORIDA
WEST PALM BEACH AUDITORIUM, 1610 Palm Beach Lakes Boulevard. Venue dedicated on September 3, 1967.
OPENED FOR: Blue Oyster Cult and Mott; Starz was the fourth act on the bill and most likely performed last.
TICKETS: $6.50 (general admission show)
CAPACITY: 6,000
NOTES: "A Heavy Metal Mini-Feat." UFO was originally slated to perform but was replaced by Starz at the eleventh hour.

JULY 18, 1976
DOTHAN, ALABAMA
CIVIC CENTER, 126 North Saint Andrews Street. Venue dedicated on January 25, 1975.
OPENED FOR: Blue Oyster Cult
CAPACITY: 3,100
NOTES: General admission show.

JULY 20, 1976
CHATTANOOGA, TENNESSEE
SOLDIERS AND SAILORS MEMORIAL AUDITORIUM, 399 McCallie Avenue. Venue opened on February 22, 1924.
OPENED FOR: Blue Oyster Cult
TICKETS: $3.50 (advance) / $5.00 (day of)
CAPACITY: 3,866
NOTES: Equipment problems caused a short delay in Rush's set. During the delay, Geddy did a roll call of US states, asking if anyone attending the show was from the various locations.

JULY 23, 1976
GREENSBORO, NORTH CAROLINA
TRIAD ARENA, 825 Norwalk Street
OPENED FOR: Blue Oyster Cult; Mott opened the show.
TICKETS: $6.00 (advance) / $7.00 (day of), general admission
CAPACITY: 6,000 (approximate)
NOTES: Venue aka Piedmont Sports Arena.

JULY 24, 1976
FAYETTEVILLE, NORTH CAROLINA
CUMBERLAND COUNTY MEMORIAL ARENA, 1960 Coliseum Drive. Venue opened on January 23, 1968.
OPENED FOR: Blue Oyster Cult; Mott opened the show.
TICKETS: $5.50 (advance) / $6.50 (at the door)
CAPACITY: 7,000

JULY 25, 1976
WHEELING, WEST VIRGINIA
CAPITOL MUSIC HALL, 1015 Main Street. Venue opened on November 29, 1928.
OPENED FOR: Blue Oyster Cult
TICKETS: $5.50 / $6.50
ATTENDANCE: 2,500; sold out
CONCERT GROSS: $15,148

JULY 27, 1976
JACKSON, MISSISSIPPI
MISSISSIPPI COLISEUM, State Fairgrounds complex, 1207 Mississippi Street. Venue opened on June 7, 1962.
OPENED FOR: Black Oak Arkansas, Ruby Starr; Natural Gas opened the show.
CAPACITY: 10,000

JULY 28, 1976
MYRTLE BEACH, SOUTH CAROLINA
CONVENTION CENTER, 2101 North Oak Street. Venue opened in 1967.
OPENED FOR: Blue Oyster Cult
CAPACITY: 8,000
NOTES: This date is not present in SRO's records. Venue is also unconfirmed.

JULY 29, 1976
MONTGOMERY, ALABAMA
GARRETT COLISEUM, 1555 Federal Drive. Venue opened on July 15, 1951.
OPENED FOR: Blue Oyster Cult; Mott opened the show.
TICKETS: $5.50 (advance) / $6.50 (day of)
CAPACITY: 13,500
NOTES: This date is not present in SRO's records but is corroborated by an ad and a Bad Daddy's Productions backstage pass.

1. *The Hamilton Spectator*, June 22, 2013.
2. *BCI*.
3. Ian Grandy Facebook.com, April 8, 2017.
4. *The Daily Herald*, March 5, 1976.
5. Jim Bossier.
6. Ian Grandy. Facebook.com, December 5, 2014.
7. *Classic Rock*, October 4, 2004.
8. *Sacramento Union*.
9. *Sacramento Union*.
10. *Seattle Daily Times*.
11. Bill Banasiewicz. Interview with Steve Slater, January 9, 2018.
12. Bill Banasiewicz. Interview with Mike Konopka, July 2014.
13. Interview with Alex Lifeson. Teamrock.com, May 15, 2015.
14. *Q Classic: Pink Floyd and The Story Of Prog Rock*, July 2005.
15. *Q Classic: Pink Floyd and The Story Of Prog Rock*, July 2005.
16. Ian Grandy. Facebook.com, April 29, 2015.
17. *Waterloo Courier*.
18. *Waterloo Courier*.
19. Skip Daly. Interview with Ian Grandy, 2012.
20. *UMD Statesman*.
21. Interview with Neil Peart. *Sound*, May 23, 1976.
22. Bill Banasiewicz. Interview with Jeff Clark, June 2014.
23. *Billboard*.
24. *Welland Tribune*.
25. *Fort Erie Times*, December 13, 2012.

Chapter 6

THE ALL THE WORLD'S A STAGE TOUR

T he *All the World's a Stage* tour could reasonably be considered an extension of the *2112* trek. Rush took very little time off between the two jaunts, pausing only briefly in early-August 1976 to mix the live album. "A big advantage to doing a live album at this point is that it gives us a little breathing space creatively, because it's really hard to come up with something that is satisfying in that short length of time," Neil told *Circus.* "The release of *All the World's a Stage* gives us a full year between studio albums to get our brains cleaned up and get some new ideas generated."

Additionally, the success of *2112*, combined with the months of hard touring, had provided some much-needed momentum for the band, and everyone in the Rush organization was determined to make the most of this newfound success. Although there were still some opening-act performances on the *All the World's a Stage* tour, the trek would see Rush headlining and cobilling more frequently. By November 1976, the live record had broken into *Billboard*'s Top 200 Albums chart—a first for the band.

OPPOSITE: Toronto, Ontario; Alex, Geddy, and Neil onstage on New Year's Eve.

The set lists still varied quite a bit based on the amount of performance time. "Bastille Day" was the opening song, with "Anthem," "Lakeside Park," "2112," and the "Fly by Night" / "In the Mood" medley frequently featured. For headlining performances, the band would typically add "Something for Nothing," "By-Tor and the Snow Dog," "In the End," and the "Working Man" / "Finding My Way" medley (with drum solo). By the time they hit the stage for their New Year's Eve headlining show in Toronto, they had worked "The Twilight Zone" into the set and were performing the last two parts of "The Necromancer" in a medley with "By-Tor and the Snow Dog." Starting in May 1977, they began performing a prerelease version of "Xanadu."

The *All the World's a Stage* tour would also conclude with Rush's first live dates outside of North America, in June 1977. "We covered a lot of the United States and that's when we started to do really well as far as gigs were concerned," said Alex. "We were playing 2,500-to-5,000-seat halls, with a few exceptions here and there, and we were selling out in a lot of those halls. We were ready to make the next step up. We came home, then went to England for the first time."

Onstage at Irwin Mitchell Oval Hall in Sheffield, England, on June 1, 1977, Geddy made reference to the band's maiden voyage across the pond.

OPPOSITE: Alex onstage.
TOP: Youngstown, OH; Rush onstage.

TOP: Upper Darby, PA; Geddy, Alex, and Neil pose from their limo.

ABOVE LEFT: Geddy onstage with his modified teardrop P-bass during an encore.

ABOVE RIGHT: London, England; A photo of two awestruck fans taken by Geddy in front of the Hammersmith Odeon marquee.

OPPOSITE: Youngstown, OH; Alex, Geddy, and Neil onstage.

PAGE 108: Fall 1976 tour itinerary.

RUSH CANADIAN TOUR ITINERARY

(effective Sept. 16/76)

SEPTEMBER	28	MONCTON, NEW BRUNSWICK — LOUIS LEVEQUE ARENA
	29	CHARLOTTETOWN, P.E.I. — SIMMONS ARENA
OCTOBER	1	SYDNEY, NOVA SCOTIA — SYDNEY FORUM
	3	ST. JOHN, N.B. — LORD BEAVER BROOK RINK
	4	HALIFAX, NOVA SCOTIA — HALIFAX FORUM
	8	NORTHBAY, ONTARIO — ARENA
	9	SUDBURY, ONTARIO — ARENA
	10	OTTAWA, ONTARIO — CIVIC CENTRE
	11	KINGSTON, ONTARIO — MEMORIAL ARENA
	13	SAULT STE. MARIE, ONTARIO — MEMORIAL GARDENS
	15	THUNDERBAY, ONTARIO — FORT WILLIAM GARDENS
	18	WINNIPEG, MANITOBA — WINNIPEG PLAYHOUSE
	19	BRANDON, MANITOBA — KEYSTONE CENTRE
	20	REGINA, SASKATCHEWAN — ARENA
	21	SASKATOON, SASKATCHEWAN — ARENA
	23	EDMONTON, ALBERTA — KINSMEN FIELDHOUSE
	24	LETHBRIDGE, ALBERTA — SPORTS PLEX
	26	VANCOUVER, B.C. — VANCOUVER GARDENS
	27	VICTORIA, B.C. — VICTORIA ARENA

PRODUCTIONS (1975) INC. • SUITE 201/ 55 GLENCAMERON ROAD, THORNHILL, ONTARIO, CANADA   L3T 1P2

TOUR HISTORY
ALL THE WORLD'S A STAGE

SET LIST:
(Sample from December 31, 1976)
"Bastille Day"
"Anthem"
"Lakeside Park"
2112 (all parts except "Oracle: The Dream")

"The Twilight Zone"
"Something for Nothing"
"Best I Can"
"By-Tor and the Snow Dog" (abridged)
"The Necromancer" ("Under the Shadow" / "Return of the Prince")
"In the End"

"Working Man"
"Finding My Way"
"Drum Solo"
Encore:
"Fly by Night"
"In the Mood"

AUGUST 8, 1976
ERIE, PENNSYLVANIA
ERIE VETERANS MEMORIAL STADIUM, Academy High School campus, 148 West 21st Street. Venue built in 1924.
OPENED FOR: The Doobie Brothers (backed by the Memphis Horns); Heart was slated as opener.
TICKETS: $6.50 (advance) / $7.50 (day of), general admission
ATTENDANCE: 12,000
CONCERT GROSS: $80,000
NOTES: "The largest sound system and stage ever in Erie." Doors 12:30 p.m.; show time 2:00 p.m. (although the event didn't actually start until after 3:00 p.m.). Promoters, hoping for a throng of twenty thousand, ended up losing money as their target attendance didn't materialize. A young Jon Bon Jovi was in the crowd—his very first concert experience. Because of a threat of storms (though it never actually rained), the Doobies took the stage first, forcing the opening act, Heart, to close out the gig.
ERIE TIMES: "Doobie Concert Reversed: The Doobie Brothers simply walked onstage and with no introduction or explanation given, began playing, leaving the estimated crowd of 13,000 to guess what was going on. Rush [special guests] was next in line. Rush often played short explosive passages, which at times resembled the sound of heavy construction, and seemed more preoccupied with jolting the listener than anything else."

AUGUST 12, 1976
LAKE OKOBOJI, IOWA
NOTES: This date is not in SRO's records and is unconfirmed, though it is corroborated by several crew members.
IAN: "It (the gig) was just a fairly small beach house. Skip and I got to take a swim."

AUGUST 13, 1976
SIOUX CITY, IOWA
MUNICIPAL AUDITORIUM, 401 Gordan Drive. Historic venue dedicated on September 9, 1950.
OPENED FOR: Blue Oyster Cult
TICKETS: $5.00 (advance) / $6.00 (day of)
CAPACITY: 4,645
CONCERT GROSS: $13,865
NOTES: Point Blank is listed on many fans sites as the opener, but they are not included in any of the advertising. Documentation is still spotty this far back, but much of August would be spent supporting Blue Oyster Cult.

AUGUST 14, 1976
FARGO, NORTH DAKOTA
CIVIC MEMORIAL AUDITORIUM, 207 4th Street North. Venue opened on December 1, 1959.
OPENED FOR: Blue Oyster Cult
TICKETS: $5.00 (advance) / $6.00 (day of)
CAPACITY: 3,300
CONCERT GROSS: $16,305
NOTES: Aka Fargo Civic Center. Point Blank is listed on many fans sites as the opener, but they are not featured in any of the advertising (including the day of the show).

AUGUST 15, 1976
MINOT, NORTH DAKOTA
ALL SEASONS ARENA, North Dakota State Fairgrounds, 2005 Burdick Expressway West. Venue opened in fall 1975.
OPENED FOR: Blue Oyster Cult; Point Blank opened the show.
TICKETS: $5.00 (advance) / $6.00 (at the door)
CAPACITY: 3,900
CONCERT GROSS: $16,183

AUGUST 17, 1976
TOPEKA, KANSAS
TOPEKA MUNICIPAL AUDITORIUM, 214 Southeast Eighth Avenue. Venue dedicated on May 12, 1940.
OPENED FOR: Blue Oyster Cult; Point Blank opened the show.
TICKETS: $5.00 (advance) / $6.00 (day of)
CAPACITY: 4,246
NOTES: This date is not in SRO's records but is corroborated by an advertisement. However, based on fan accounts, Rush ended up not performing.
WILL KASTENS (BLUE OYSTER CULT FAN): "There were only a few hundred attending, no formal seating—just open floor. Most of the auditorium lights stayed on while Point Blank opened. The audience generally ignored them while playing frisbee or milling about. It was clear that the crowd was there for Blue Oyster Cult and Rush. Then it was announced that Rush had canceled and anyone could get a full refund if they left right then. I saw maybe a dozen people leave."[1]

AUGUST 20, 1976
WATERLOO, IOWA
MCELROY AUDITORIUM, 250
Ansborough Avenue. Venue opened on
September 28, 1936.
OPENED FOR: Blue Oyster Cult; Point
Blank opened the show.
TICKETS: $6.00 (advance) / $7.00
(day of)
CAPACITY: 8,735 (5,155 permanent
seats)

AUGUST 26, 1976
SCHAUMBURG, ILLINOIS
B'GINNINGS, 1227 East Golf Road.
Venue opened in September 1974.
TICKETS: $4.00, general admission
ATTENDANCE: 936; sold out

AUGUST 27, 1976
NORMAL, ILLINOIS
UNION AUDITORIUM, ILLINOIS STATE
UNIVERSITY (ISU), 100 North University
Street. Venue built in 1973.
WITH: Head East
CAPACITY: 3,457
TICKETS: Free show
THE VIDETTE (ISU): "Although Head East
and Rush are not full-fledged stars yet,
their names are on the lips of occultists
everywhere. Rush has just debuted their
fourth album, *2112*, and their presence
Friday says quite a bit for the continuity
of power trio rockers. On the movement
'2112,' a rock symphony which occupies
an entire side from the latest album,
Lifeson manages to coordinate the rock
rhythm and lead in such a way as to con-
vey well-placed feeling reminiscent of
more classical modes but adapted to the
electric guitars of hard rock. Head East,
on the other hand, have further rounded
out their sound to include more sophisticated rock movements striving for a
wider appeal than the rockers, Rush."

AUGUST 28, 1976
TRAVERSE CITY, MICHIGAN
GLACIER DOME, 1610 Barlow Street
TICKETS: $5.50 (advance) / $6.50
(day of)
CAPACITY: 4,154
NOTES: As of the date of the concert, an
opening act had not been announced.
"Plus very special guests" is all that was
listed. A proposed daylong outdoor festi-
val in Morgantown, North Carolina, on
this date that was canceled less than a

month beforehand. The lineup was
scheduled to include Blue Oyster Cult,
Ted Nugent, Rush, Angel, and Atlanta
Rhythm Section.

AUGUST 29, 1976
FRUITPORT CHARTER TOWNSHIP,
MICHIGAN
GREATER MUSKEGON ICE ARENA,
4470 Airline Road. Venue opened in
1975.
WITH: Styx (cobill)
TICKETS: $5.00 (advance) / $6.00
(day of)
CAPACITY: 6,316
NOTES: This date is not in SRO's records
but is confirmed by an ad two days
before the gig.

AUGUST 31, 1976
JACKSON, MISSISSIPPI
MISSISSIPPI COLISEUM, State
Fairgrounds complex, 1207 Mississippi
Street
OPENED FOR: Blue Oyster Cult, Bob
Seger
TICKETS: $5.00 (advance), general
admission
CAPACITY: 10,000
NOTES: Although canceled at the elev-
enth hour, this gig was still on as of the
August 29 edition of the *Clarion-Ledger*
(Jackson).

SEPTEMBER 3, 1976
DAYTON, OHIO
HARA ARENA, 1001 Shiloh Springs
Road. Venue opened on November 1,
1964.
OPENED FOR: Blue Oyster Cult, Styx
TICKETS: $5.50 / $6.50, general
admission
ATTENDANCE: 6,132
CONCERT GROSS: $35,840
NOTES: After this gig, band and crew
headed back to Toronto for a break.

SEPTEMBER 10, 1976
SAGINAW, MICHIGAN
WENDLER ARENA AT SAGINAW CIVIC
CENTER, 303 Johnson Street. Venue
opened on October 15, 1972.
OPENED FOR: Blue Oyster Cult
TICKETS: $5.50 (advance) / $6.50 (day
of)
CAPACITY: 7,000
SAGINAW NEWS: "Blue Oyster Cult and
Rush put on a dazzling display: A

memorable moment for the crowd was
the solo on drums and percussion by
Peart. His structured work was slightly
different than most drummers'. It was
interesting and refreshing to see and
hear a rock drummer play without relying
on electronic assistance."
SAGINAW NEWS, GEDDY: "It is good to
see the response from an audience primarily interested in seeing the headline
act. We have gotten to the point where we
are better able to select the kind of music
we play to the kind of audience that shows
up. I see a good future for the group."
IAN: "I was in a hotel room with Alex and
Buck Dharma, with the two of them both
playing the same doubleneck at the
same time switching back and forth.
Wish I'd had my camera."[2]

SEPTEMBER 13, 1976
MURRAY, KENTUCKY
MSU FIELDHOUSE, Murray State
University campus, 1399 Payne Street.
Venue opened on December 11, 1954.
OPENED FOR: Blue Oyster Cult, Angel
TICKETS: $5.50
ATTENDANCE: 4,500
CAPACITY: 5,500
NOTES: According to an ad from
September 10, this gig was originally
scheduled for Roy Stewart (football)
Stadium, but apparently moved to the
Fieldhouse at the last minute. During the
concert, ten people were arrested for
intoxication and rude behavior. Police
confiscated three pounds of bulk marijuana, twenty-five rolled joints, sixty
assorted pills, six syringes, and other
assorted smoking devices. It is security
director Joe Green's opinion that "MSU
should not be the promoter of such
undermining, sickening, and disgraceful
gatherings on this campus."

SEPTEMBER 15, 1976
MANCHESTER, NEW HAMPSHIRE
JFK MEMORIAL COLISEUM, 303 Beech
Street. Venue opened in February 1964.
OPENED FOR: Blue Oyster Cult; Angel
opened the show.
TICKETS: $5.50 (advance)
ATTENDANCE: 3,600; oversold
NOTES: General admission concert. Nine
people were arrested in a pre-gig melee
when the doors, scheduled to open at
7:00 p.m., weren't opened until about
7:45. Most of the arrests were for

disorderly conduct and public intoxication. Once concertgoers were permitted inside the venue, it was relatively "quiet for such a crowd. It could have been a lot worse," according to one police official.[3]

CEDRICK KUSHNER (PROMOTER): "Logistical problems materialized when a production technician became ill at the last minute."[4]

SEPTEMBER 17, 1976
BINGHAMTON, NEW YORK
BROOME COUNTY WAR MEMORIAL
ARENA, 1 Stuart Street. Venue opened on August 29, 1973.
OPENED FOR: Blue Oyster Cult; Angel opened the show.
TICKETS: $5.50 (advance) / $6.50 (day of), general admission
ATTENDANCE: 7,205
CONCERT GROSS: $39,493
NOTES: While Rush was firing on all cylinders, the band had not yet achieved the high level of consistency that would come in later years. Ian recorded the gig from the soundboard, with the band's performance on this night being somewhat lackluster.
IAN: "I called the tape 'Reeking in Binghamton.' We listened to it in our truck the next day, and Skip and Liam were laughing at the title I'd given it. I named the tape after the performance and would never have let the band hear it. I most definitely didn't copy it for anyone—you don't call it 'Reeking' for nothing. To be fair, it wasn't just the boys. It was also a shitty hall, a primitive tape deck, and an idiot sound guy [laughs]! They didn't always particularly like it, but I could say things to them that other people couldn't. Other roadies would be hanging around and would say to me, 'Holy shit, how can you talk to him like that?' I'd say, 'Because I've known him since he was fucking twelve!' Alex asked me once, 'How did I play tonight?' and I said, 'Possibly the worst I've ever seen you play.' He said, 'Geez, thanks a lot Ian!' and I said, 'Well, how do *you* think you played?' He said, 'Shitty,' so I just said, 'Well, what did you want me to say?' When we were first on the road, I was told, 'Every night, tell 'em it sounds great!' and I said, 'But it doesn't sound great every night—there's a different PA and different mics every night. It's not always going to sound great, and the

band know me well enough to know that I'm not going to blow smoke up their ass."[5]

SEPTEMBER 18, 1976
SYRACUSE, NEW YORK
ONONDAGA COUNTY WAR
MEMORIAL AUDITORIUM, 515
Montgomery Street. Venue opened on September 1, 1951.
OPENED FOR: Blue Oyster Cult; Angel opened the show.
TICKETS: $5.50 / $6.50
ATTENDANCE: 5,192
CAPACITY: 8,200
CONCERT GROSS: $29,585
THE RACQUETTE **(STATE UNIVERSITY OF NEW YORK):** "When they were announced, the crowd gave the virtually unknown band a polite reception. Little did they realize the high caliber of the group and the group's music. Alex Lifeson, possibly one of the best chord men in rock, punched out tons of power chords with plenty of tasteful solos. The crowd, previously polite in their welcome, was now on its feet and screaming for more."

SEPTEMBER 19, 1976
HARRISBURG, PENNSYLVANIA
ZEMBO MOSQUE ARENA, Zembo
Shrine Center, 2801 North 3rd Street. Venue dedicated on May 19, 1930.
SUPPORT ACT: Angel
TICKETS: $5.50
ATTENDANCE: 2,630; sold out
CONCERT GROSS: $15,000
ALEX: "Angel wore white, with big feathery things on their shoulders. Sound check would start at 4:30 for us. They'd show up at 3:30 and start working on their makeup and hair, and they wouldn't do a sound check because they were busy with the blow-dryers and doing their own thing. They were nice, fun guys. We taught them how to play Bop, one of these drinking games. I remember good times with them."

SEPTEMBER 20, 1976
ALLENTOWN, PENNSYLVANIA
AGRICULTURAL HALL, Great Allentown
Fairgrounds, 1725 Chew Street. Venue opened on September 16, 1957.
SUPPORT ACT: Angel
TICKETS: $5.00 (advance) / $5.50 (at the door), general admission
ATTENDANCE: 4,000; sold out
CONCERT GROSS: $20,000

NOTES: The venue (which is sweltering hot, with no AC) implemented a new entrance policy, whereby patrons entered in an orderly single file line, as opposed to the usual frenzied rush to gain access. The local newspaper lists a near-sellout crowd of one thousand, but the venue in fact holds four thousand. This was the largest concert attendance of 1976 in Allentown.
MORNING CALL: "Canadian Rush was greeted with a deafening roar and proceeded to lay down its trademark heavy metal. Aided by flash pods, smoke, and rows of lights dancing across the backdrop, Rush almost succeeded in making its fans forget about the heat."

SEPTEMBER 21, 1976
PLATTSBURGH, NEW YORK
CRETE MEMORIAL CIVIC CENTER, 41
City Hall Place. Venue built in 1974.
OPENED FOR: Blue Oyster Cult; Angel opened the show.
CAPACITY: 4,800
NOTES: Blue Oyster Cult's much-advertised laser show was malfunctioning and not used at this gig.
PLATTSBURGH STATE UNIVERSITY CARDINAL POINTS: "The powerhouse trio delivered a scorching set that obviously was very basic. They received their obligatory encore and were gone for the night."

SEPTEMBER 22, 1976
HENRIETTA, NEW YORK
DOME ARENA, Monroe County
Fairgrounds, 2695 East Henrietta Road. Venue built in 1973.
OPENED FOR: Blue Oyster Cult; Angel opened the show.
TICKETS: $5.50 / $6.50, general admission
ATTENDANCE: 5,699; sold out
CONCERT GROSS: $31,023
NOTES: Despite this gig sometimes being listed as "Rochester," the venue is in Henrietta, New York, thirteen miles from Rochester. Ads and other promotions frequently list the metro area for concerts. After Rush's set, a fight broke out, forcing the doors open, with many ticketless fans taking advantage and entering the venue for free.[6]
SET LIST: "Bastille Day," "Lakeside Park," "Fly by Night," "2112," "Finding My Way." "Working Man" (with drum solo; encore).

THE STYLUS (BROCKPORT STATE UNIVERSITY): "Rush is Canada's number-one band and Wednesday night they confirmed that fact. When they began with 'Bastille Day,' the audience went wild."[4]

SEPTEMBER 25, 1976

CHUM-FM World Radio Premiere of *All the World's a Stage*.

BILLBOARD (OCTOBER 16, 1976): "This indefatigable power fuzz trio, which has either been touring or in the studio for most of the past three years, recapitulates its first four albums and 1976 tour with a powerful two-disk live set recorded during a three-night June stand at Toronto's acoustically excellent Massey Hall. Rush has won many album fans with its constant touring and powerhouse music."

SEPTEMBER 28, 1976
MONCTON, NEW BRUNSWICK
JEAN-LOUIS LEVESQUE ARENA,

University of Moncton, 450 Universite Avenue. Venue built in 1966.

SUPPORT ACT: Wireless
TICKETS: $4.50 / $5.50 CAD
CAPACITY: 1,660
NOTES: Terry Brown was at the front-of-house mixing board, as Ian was away on his honeymoon. Government officials did a spot-check of the band's equipment as part of an intimidation campaign because of Rush's use of American firms for sound and lighting production, and the band was fined $15,000. Around this same time, Larry Allen officially joined the organization as drum technician, after a brief, initial stint driving the band's van. Larry, who would come to be known by the crew nickname "Shrav," had met Neil shortly before the recording of *Caress of Steel*. A friend of his had lived with Neil, and when the two eventually met, they hit it off. Larry had spent a lot of time in the studio during the recording of *Caress of Steel*, where he also got to know Alex and Geddy.

RECORD WEEK: "[Rush] had previously filed papers with the tax department in Ottawa and received the necessary approval to bring the gear in, but the governmental approval was revoked after a Canadian company applied pressure on the tax department, leading to a reversal on the decision. The grim news hit the band shortly before playing the first date in Moncton's Louis Levesque Arena, September 28. The same night, government officials swooped down on the arena to do a spot check on the group, continuing their case of blatant intimidation, but were unable to find any further points to quibble over and have since left the tour alone."

NEIL: "It is hard for us to justify a tour here; we have worked closely with promoters Donald K. Donald and CPI on doing this cross-country tour and it means a lot to us. You know, just being able to do it in our own country; but the fifteen thousand dollars is going to have to come out of our profits, and it brings our margin on the line. We obviously lost some money in the Maritimes, we knew we were going to because of the size of the population there, but we wanted to do it. Ontario will be good because of its size and the number of venues to play in, then it is pretty dry right through to the west. Last year we toured nationally with Nazareth; it was fun, but we wanted to do it on our own. This is our chance, and to look on the bright side—we will never have to pay that money again."[7]

SEPTEMBER 29, 1976
CHARLOTTETOWN, PRINCE EDWARD ISLAND
SIMMONS SPORTS CENTRE ARENA,

170 North River Road. Venue opened on August 10, 1973.

SUPPORT ACT: Wireless
TICKETS: $4.50 (advance) / $5.50 CAD, general admission
CAPACITY: 2,400
NOTES: The official venue capacity is three thousand, though the building manager of Simmons Arena claims that for past events, as many as four thousand were crammed into the venue. Terry Brown was at the front-of-house mixing board because Ian was away on his honeymoon. For this Canadian tour, Rush's guarantee per show was $2,000 CAD, with an additional $1,500 allocated to sound and lighting, and a $500 fee to the support act. [8]

OCTOBER 1, 1976
NORTH SYDNEY, NOVA SCOTIA
NORTH SYDNEY COMMUNITY FORUM,

124 Pierce Street. Venue opened in 1947.

SUPPORT ACT: Wireless
TICKETS: $4.50 / $5.50 CAD

CAPACITY: 2,200
NOTES: The venue is also know as the Sydney Forum, but the sign on the building reads "North Sydney Forum." Terry Brown was at the front-of-house mixing board because Ian was away on his honeymoon.

BRANDON SUN, GEDDY: "We're a Canadian band that never really has played Canada before. We played in most of the United States before we went east of Ottawa or west of Sudbury. The tour is to find out what the band means in Canada. The Maritimes were a disaster. The audiences were there, but there was a failure to communicate. We'll play Halifax and Moncton again, perhaps. But not Sydney, St. John, or Charlottetown. The audiences are primitive."

OCTOBER 2, 1976
ALL THE WORLD'S A STAGE DEBUTS AT #195 ON *BILLBOARD'S* TOP 200 ALBUMS CHART IN AMERICA.

OCTOBER 3, 1976
SAINT JOHN, NEW BRUNSWICK
LORD BEAVERBROOK RINK, 536 Main

Street. Venue built in 1960.

SUPPORT ACT: Wireless
TICKETS: $4.50 / $5.50 CAD
CAPACITY: 4,686
NOTES: Terry Brown was at the front-of-house mixing board because Ian was away on his honeymoon.

IAN: "Rush went down to the east coast of Canada and played three gigs in arenas with horrible acoustics. When I got back, the entire crew was shaking their heads at the difference in sound. I would have been a joke being an engineer in the studio, but Terry had zero clue live. The crew told me they had not heard a word Geddy sang in those barns. The band told me it had gone very well, but Terry took me aside and confessed that he'd never been so lost. There is a little bit of a difference between the studio and St. John, New Brunswick. In the studio, the opening act doesn't change all your settings—which totally threw him. To his credit, he had the class to admit it."

LETHBRIDGE HERALD: "Rush has succeeded where others have failed in taking hard rock music into a new area. Where many bands are content to churn out commercial tidbits, Rush sits back and works to create something. For that alone, they should be warmly congratulated. Rush may be one of Canada's greatest contributions to rock music, particularly for their work on *2112*."

OCTOBER 4, 1976
HALIFAX, NOVA SCOTIA
THE HALIFAX FORUM, 2901 Windsor Street. Venue opened on December 26, 1927.
SUPPORT ACT: Wireless
TICKETS: $4.50 / $5.50 CAD
ATTENDANCE: 6,200; sold out[9]
NOTES: A fire broke out when a sparkler landed on the scoreboard, and Rush's crew quickly extinguished the flames. Terry Brown was at the front-of-house mixing board because Ian was away on his honeymoon.
HALIFAX MAIL STAR: "Rush doesn't ignite listeners but sparklers flame in forum: Despite a high-energy presentation and some excellent lighting, the return concert of Rush at the Halifax Forum might best be described as disappointing. At the risk of eliciting red-faced rage from the cheering throng which pressed against the stage, the music was about as memorable as it was subtle— that is, not at all. The band could carve out their own niche in the strata of rock if they were willing to channel their talents more constructively. The performance was interrupted by a fire started by a wildly flung sparkler. Only the quick thinking of one young man, possibly a member of the band's crew, kept the fire from spreading as the flames were licking the wooden roof of the arena."
KEITH BROWN (PROMOTER STAFF): "To work with Rush is to love them. When we played Halifax, the crew was remarkable. The venue was the old Halifax Forum, which was filled to its 6,200 capacity. The rink was made entirely of wood and built on short piers so there was air beneath the floor. It could have burned to the ground in fifteen minutes, and it almost did. Just as the band took the stage, someone in the audience threw a burning sparkler up in the air which landed on top of the big score clock suspended over center ice. About three songs in, Geddy spotted the flames shooting up. He stopped the band and started yelling 'crew, crew, crew . . .' and pointed at the score clock. As if they had

practiced for that moment, the crew flew into action. Mike 'Lurch' Hirsch literally plowed a path through the crowd as four crew guys pushed the cherry picker (normally used for aiming par lights) toward the fire. As this was happening, another crew member was scrambling up the cherry picker armed with two fire extinguishers. In a minute the fire was out, a tragedy was averted, and a minute after that, Rush was back in business rocking the place. At the end of the show, the arena manager, Keith Lewis, entered the band's dressing room. Tears were rolling down his cheeks as he thanked Rush and their 'boys' for saving hundreds of lives. I never encountered a road crew that was more dedicated. And the band always ate with the crew to ensure that the promoters would provide good meals."[10]

OCTOBER 8, 1976
NORTH BAY, ONTARIO
MEMORIAL GARDENS, 100 Chippewa Street West. Venue opened on November 15, 1955.
SUPPORT ACT: Ian Thomas Band
TICKETS: $4.50 (advance); $5.50 (day of) CAD, general admission
CAPACITY: 6,500
NOTES: At this point, the Ian Thomas Band (which included Hugh Syme on keyboards) was touring in support of their third album, *Calabash*.
BARRIE EXAMINER: "Rush with special guests, The Ian Thomas Band. That match-up struck me as unthinkable. It's like asking Valdy to open for Kiss. Where is the common ground?"

OCTOBER 9, 1976
SUDBURY, ONTARIO
SUDBURY COMMUNITY ARENA, 240 Elgin Street. Venue opened on November 18, 1951.
SUPPORT ACT: Ian Thomas Band
TICKETS: $4.50 (limited advance) / $5.50 CAD, general admission
CAPACITY: 7,000

OCTOBER 10, 1976
OTTAWA, ONTARIO
OTTAWA CIVIC CENTRE, Lansdowne Park, 1015 Bank Street. Venue opened on December 29, 1967.
SUPPORT ACTS: Max Webster, Ian Thomas Band
TICKETS: $4.50 (advance) / $5.50 CAD

ATTENDANCE: "A few thousand."[11]
CAPACITY: 9,500
NOTES: After the performance, Polydor Records hosted the Canadian Music business's first joint press conference, attended by Rush and Ian Thomas Band.
RECORD WEEK, NEIL: "The Ottawa date on the 10th was really an amazing high. We had an excellent turnout, and of course Max Webster and Ian Thomas were also billed for that one show. I think that one concert made up for the hassles we went through in the Maritimes."
OTTAWA JOURNAL: "Rush: basically a shrieker: Rarely in the years of Civic Centre rock concerts has the sound been so unnecessarily loud and the music so sloppily presented. The worst offenders were Max Webster. Their sound—besides being excessive—was as unbalanced as professional music could be. Rush was better, but still not acceptable. Technically, the band is quite good, although the neat original touches used onstage are overworked to the point of boredom."

OCTOBER 11, 1976
KINGSTON, ONTARIO
KINGSTON MEMORIAL CENTRE ARENA, 303 York Street. Venue opened in November 1951.
SUPPORT ACT: Ian Thomas Band
TICKETS: $4.50 (limited advance) / $5.50 CAD, general admission
CAPACITY: 3,343

OCTOBER 13, 1976
SAULT STE. MARIE, ONTARIO
SAULT MEMORIAL GARDENS, 269 Queen Street East. Venue opened on February 20, 1949.
SUPPORT ACT: Ian Thomas Band
TICKETS: $4.50 / $5.50 CAD
ATTENDANCE: 2,100
CAPACITY: 5,000
THE STAR (SAULT STE. MARIE): "Rush fans filled Gardens: For almost one and a half hours, Rush took its audience on a journey through space. Moving pictures that weren't very elaborate accompanied the over-amplified music. The scenes resembled cell-like globs, lightning,

leafless trees, and Rush's album covers. Geddy Lee has a voice that's a cross between Donald Duck and the Wicked Witch from the Wizard of Oz. As unusual as it sounds, it's a voice that has found its place in rock music."

OCTOBER 15, 1976
THUNDER BAY, ONTARIO
FORT WILLIAM GARDENS, 901 Miles Street. Venue opened on March 6, 1951.
SUPPORT ACT: Max Webster
TICKETS: $4.50 (limited advance) / $5.50 CAD
CAPACITY: 5,209
NOTES: General admission show. Formed in Sarnia, Ontario, during 1973, Max Webster is a Zappa-esque, progressive, hard rock band. At this point in October 1976, they are touring in support of their self-titled debut with a lineup of Kim Mitchell on guitar and lead vocals, Terry Watkinson on keyboards, Mike Tilka on bass, and Gary McCracken (who recently joined the group) on drums. The majority of their lyrics were composed by Pye Dubois, who would later collaborate with Neil on several Rush songs including "Tom Sawyer," "Force Ten," "Between Sun and Moon," and "Test for Echo."

OCTOBER 17, 1976
WINNIPEG, MANITOBA
PANTAGES PLAYHOUSE THEATRE, 180 Market Avenue. Historic venue opened on February 19, 1914.
SUPPORT ACT: Max Webster
TICKETS: $4.50 / $5.50 CAD
ATTENDANCE: "Near capacity"
CAPACITY: 1,400
NOTES: As fans left the theatre the gentle strains of "Greensleeves" played over the PA.[12]
WINNIPEG FREE PRESS: "From the moment it burst on stage and exploded into 'Bastille Day' through the conclusion of encore number 'What You're Doing,' the band exhibited the sort of confidence and control lacking in so many Canadian hard-rock acts."
WINNIPEG FREE PRESS, GEDDY: "We're just too hard rock oriented for most radio stations. We've built up most of our following with our live show."

OCTOBER 19, 1976
BRANDON, MANITOBA
KEYSTONE CENTRE ARENA, 1175 18th Street. Venue opened on April 2, 1973.
SUPPORT ACT: Max Webster
TICKETS: $4.50 (advance) / $5.50 CAD, general admission
ATTENDANCE: 1,400
CAPACITY: 7,048
THE BRANDON SUN: "Rush couldn't ignite the crowd of teens at the Keystone Centre. The concert was lifeless. Three songs into the set, Rush lost momentum. The three-man band degenerated into the antics of rock and roll without substance. The band lacked tightness. Periods of time were frittered away while guitarist Alex Lifeson made adjustments. The crowd, already cooled by Wheat King ice, grew numb. When Rush went off the stage, both entertainers and the 1,400 entertained were relieved the show was over. The applause lasted all of fifteen seconds. There was no encore."
THE BRANDON SUN, GEDDY: "We've played hundreds of American towns, supporting whoever we could. We figured Canada would come naturally."

OCTOBER 20, 1976
REGINA, SASKATCHEWAN
AGRIBITION BUILDING, 1700 Elphinstone Street
SUPPORT ACT: Max Webster
TICKETS: $4.50 (limited advance) / $5.50 CAD, general admission
ATTENDANCE: 1,800[13]
NOTES: First-ever rock concert held at the Agribition Building. The gig was originally slated for Exhibition Stadium, however a scheduling conflict with Ice Capades prompted a change of venues.
THE LEADER-POST: "Slides of moon landings, paintings, magnified microbes, and logos from the group's albums made the show a visual, if not aural, delight."

OCTOBER 21, 1976
SASKATOON, SASKATCHEWAN
SASKATOON ARENA, 19th Street at First Avenue. Venue opened on October 30, 1937.
SUPPORT ACT: Max Webster
TICKETS: $4.50 (limited advance discount) / $5.50 (general admission) CAD
CAPACITY: 6,000
STAR PHOENIX: "Rush, Max Webster spark heavy metal rock package."

OCTOBER 23, 1976
EDMONTON, ALBERTA
KINSMEN FIELDHOUSE, 9100 Walter Dale Hill. Venue opened on January 3, 1968.
SUPPORT ACT: Max Webster
TICKETS: $4.50 / $5.50 CAD
ATTENDANCE: 3,500
CAPACITY: 6,000
EDMONTON JOURNAL: "Rush too serious: When somebody playfully tossed a beach ball onto the stage early in Rush's Fieldhouse concert, a stage hand quickly jumped out from behind the amplifiers to pounce on it. Whipping out a knife, he punctured the ball, which had been ignored by the musicians, and flung it behind the stage. And the mood of the evening was thereby established. Rush play loud and hard. But, when it comes right down to it, they are just not a whole bunch of fun. They take themselves and their music far too seriously. In fairness, it should be pointed out that Rush were called back for two encores by the crowd of 3,500."
EDMONTON JOURNAL (FAN'S RESPONSE): "If one wants to play with a beachball one goes to the beach—not around expensive sound equipment. Every person with whom I have discussed the concert can't say enough good about it."

OCTOBER 24, 1976
LETHBRIDGE, ALBERTA
LETHBRIDGE SPORTSPLEX, 2510 Scenic Drive South. Venue opened in September 1974.
SUPPORT ACT: Max Webster
TICKETS: $4.50 / $5.50 CAD
ATTENDANCE: 1,340
CAPACITY: 5,035
NOTES: Security was tight because of unruly behavior at some recent concerts in Lethbridge.
MARK CHERRY (ATLANTIC SYSTEMS): "We would be playing five cities a week, and in places I'd never even heard of, like Lethbridge. I remember playing in ice arenas where they wouldn't let the kids on the ice. They wouldn't cover it, so there would be open ice and the kids would be sitting like they would at a hockey game, but the band would be down there playing on the one end where the stage would be. They'd only cover the ice where the stage would be, so there was no floor area. And then all of our power cables would melt down into the ice during the course of the

show. You'd have to chip your way out at the end of the night before you could load the gear out!"[14]

OCTOBER 26, 1976
VANCOUVER, BRITISH COLUMBIA
PACIFIC NATIONAL EXHIBITION, GARDEN AUDITORIUM, Pacific National Exhibition Fairgrounds, 2901 East Hastings Street. Venue opened in 1940.
SUPPORT ACT: Max Webster
TICKETS: $4.50 / $5.50 CAD
ATTENDANCE: 2,300
CAPACITY: 2,600
VANCOUVER SUN: "Rush—it's either a band or an urge to use the exit: Rush made me feel as if I were a painted siding over which a blowtorch had made several concentrated passes. Lee had the same, ahem, qualities but his often-chilling falsetto was quite amazing, though often unintelligible because of excessive volume. He sometimes sounded as if the neighbor's cat had been attacked with a blowtorch."

OCTOBER 27, 1976
VICTORIA, BRITISH COLUMBIA
VICTORIA MEMORIAL ARENA, 1925 Blanshard Street. Venue opened on July 20, 1949.
SUPPORT ACT: Max Webster
TICKETS: $4.50 / $5.50 CAD
CAPACITY: 7,221
NOTES: "The Barn on Blanshard." The band is by now incorporating more visual elements into its concerts. The nascent use of film to provide a backdrop for certain songs was an early indicator of the direction that Rush would take in later years—their interest in combining film media into the live setting only grew over time. Howard was also working hard to take the light show to the next level, integrating specific effects to work in conjunction with the music, particularly during the performance of "2112."

OCTOBER 28, 1976
SEATTLE, WASHINGTON
PARAMOUNT NORTHWEST THEATRE, 901 Pine Street. Historic venue opened on March 1, 1928.
SUPPORT ACT: Tommy Bolin
CAPACITY: 3,054
NOTES: Venue aka Paramount Theatre. The whole first floor stood in appreciation throughout the entire gig.[15]

SEATTLE POST-INTELLIGENCER: "The band delivers the goods with skill and a great deal of flash. In a style where excess is the rule, those qualities are rare enough to be noteworthy. Not that the band is without its mega-rock eccentricities. The event featured two explosions, a light projection which without considerable knowledge of the band was simply incomprehensible, and generous billows of stage smoke. But what appears to link Rush and its fans (many of whom spent the entire concert on their feet) is the music."
THE SEATTLE TIMES: "You have to be young and love rock 'n' roll to understand that Geddy Lee's screaming is absolutely perfect, that Neil Peart's drumming is among the finest in rock, and Alex Lifeson's guitar work is frosting on the cake."

OCTOBER 29, 1976
TACOMA, WASHINGTON
BICENTENNIAL PAVILION, 1320 Broadway Plaza. Venue opened on June 22, 1976.
SUPPORT ACT: Tommy Bolin
CAPACITY: 1,800

OCTOBER 30, 1976
PORTLAND, OREGON
PARAMOUNT THEATRE, 1037 Southwest Broadway. Venue opened on March 8, 1928.
SUPPORT ACT: Tommy Bolin
TICKETS: $5.50 (advance) / $6.50 (day of)
ATTENDANCE: First show: 3,036 (sold out); second show: 2,095
CAPACITY: 3,036
NOTES: Two performances. Tommy Bolin opened the first gig but refused to do the second because he and his crew were tired and disputing the payment amount.[16]
BILLBOARD: "The night before Halloween is usually not the best time to schedule a concert; people frequently have already made plans for the evening. But this didn't appear to be a problem for Tommy Bolin and Rush, since their show sold out and they were even able to add a second one. Despite the intense volume, Rush was good. The show was just as bombastic visually as it was audibly. The lights combined with the music so that every time a song would take a new direction,

hues changed as well. The show lasted seventy-five minutes (with encore), leaving the audience powered out but very pleased."

NOVEMBER 1, 1976
YAKIMA, WASHINGTON
SHERAR GYMNASIUM, Yakima Valley Community College campus, 1000 South 12th Avenue. Venue opened in 1957.
SUPPORT ACT: Tommy Bolin
CAPACITY: 1,500 (seats)
NOTES: Venue unconfirmed.

NOVEMBER 3, 1976
ROSEBURG, OREGON
DOUGLAS HALL, Douglas County Fairgrounds Complex, 2110 SW Frear Street. Venue opened in 1970.
SUPPORT ACT: Tommy Bolin
TICKETS: $4.50 (advance) / $5.50 (day of)
CAPACITY: 2,500

NOVEMBER 4, 1976
MEDFORD, OREGON
MEDFORD ARMORY, 1701 South Pacific Avenue. Venue dedicated on May 25, 1957.
SUPPORT ACT: Tommy Bolin
TICKETS: $4.50 (advance) / $5.50 (day of)
CAPACITY: 3,000
NOTES: This date is not in SRO's records but is corroborated by a poster and was likely rescheduled from November 1.

NOVEMBER 13, 1976
ROCKFORD, ILLINOIS
NATIONAL GUARD ARMORY, 605 Main Street. Historic venue dedicated in 1937.
SUPPORT ACT: Cheap Trick; Paris opened the show.
TICKETS: $6.00 (advance) / $7.00 (at the door)
CAPACITY: 3,610
NOTES: The set list for this gig included "The Twilight Zone." The band was in a festive mood, with Alex and Geddy taking turns being wheeled around the stage on an ambulance gurney by the crew.

NOVEMBER 14, 1976
DAVENPORT, IOWA
RKO ORPHEUM THEATRE, 136 East Third Street. Historic venue opened on November 25, 1931.
OPENED FOR: Montrose; Ace opened this general admission show.
CAPACITY: 2,700

NOVEMBER 15, 1976
DES MOINES, IOWA
VETERANS MEMORIAL AUDITORIUM, 833 Fifth Avenue. Venue opened on February 1, 1955.
OPENED FOR: Kansas, Montrose
TICKETS: $6.00 (advance) / $7.00 (at the door)
CAPACITY: 15,411
NOTES: Mike Hirsch's first gig in the role of stage manager.
MIKE "LURCH" HIRSCH: "We had no stage manager, we had no production manager—Howard was theoretically doing it all, and it was kind of pandemonium. I had just been on the sound crew. I had no technical inclinations at all—I was really just there because I could stack sound. So I had a lot of time on my hands, and finally I just couldn't stand it anymore, so I said, 'All right folks, I'm going to start calling the shots—anybody got a fucking problem with that?' And everybody was like, 'Nope—go ahead.' So I continued on with them, now working for the band in an organizational role, as stage manager/production manager. So that's how I got away from being one of the lighting guys."[17]
IAN: "We called Mike 'Lurch' because the man is 6' 10". That was one of the big reasons we hired him. I was the

biggest of Skip, me, Larry, and Liam, and I was only 5'8", 155 lbs. at the time. Once in a while, we'd get bullied by other crews and stage managers. That never happened again once they had to deal with Mike. He actually wore a laminate the size of his security pass that said '6'10"' on one side and 'NO' on the other side. 'That saved him from having to always answer question #1—'How tall are you?' and question #2—'Do you play basketball?' fifty times a day. He'd just hold up the laminate and show side #1 and side #2 when these questions were asked. The first day he worked for us, Ronny Montrose's roadie (who was bigger than me) told me we'd have to wait to set up until he fucking said so. When you're first on a three-band show you don't get enough set-up time anyway. So this guy stands about four feet away from me and basically says, 'What the fuck are you gonna do about it?' I just said, 'Well, you should tell that to our stage manager.' I look over at Lurch, he looks back at me, and then I just look back at the guy and say, 'We're setting up right now.' He shrugged and said, 'Well, whatever.'"
MIKE "LURCH" HIRSCH: "I was a very hard-edged looking fellow at the time. In '76, I was two years out of hard-core bouncing at Good Guys in Georgetown, hanging out with hardcore bikers at the strip club."[18]

NOVEMBER 16, 1976
TOPEKA, KANSAS
TOPEKA MUNICIPAL AUDITORIUM, 214 SE Eighth Avenue. Venue dedicated on May 12, 1940.
TICKETS: $4.00 (advance)
CAPACITY: 4,246 (2,114 seats)
NOTES: This date is not in SRO's records.

NOVEMBER 19, 1976
YOUNGSTOWN, OHIO
TOMORROW CLUB, 213 Federal Plaza West. Venue built in 1927 (as the State Theater), the Tomorrow Club opened on October 20, 1974.
SUPPORT ACT: Great Lakes Band
TICKETS: $4.50 (advance) / $5.50 (day of)
CAPACITY: 2,142

NOVEMBER 20, 1976
PHILADELPHIA, PENNSYLVANIA
THE SPECTRUM, 3601 South Broad Street. Venue opened on October 1, 1967.
OPENED FOR: Robin Trower, Montrose
TICKETS: $6.00 / $7.00, general admission dance concert
ATTENDANCE: 19,500; sold out
CONCERT GROSS: $119,000
NEIL: "One of the first times we ever rode in a limo was in Philadelphia. I remember pulling up to the Spectrum while Emerson, Lake & Palmer were playing on the radio. It was a nice moment."
LIAM: "Opening for Robin Trower was an extremely big thrill to me. We did a couple of shows with him; not that many. I was quite heavily into Robin Trower, so working with people you almost idolized was quite a buzz unto itself."[19]
IAN: "The first time we played Philly was in '76, opening for Robin Trower, with Montrose in between us. The fans in Philly were saying to us that we'd been supposed to play there several times but had canceled. We got a good sound check in, and I knew the engineer, so he helped me with some settings. It was also the first time I'd mixed with cabinets flying and the panning was like it almost pulled you over. I was told the crowd was still chanting 'Rush' when Trower played and that they weren't real happy about that. Skip Gildersleeve and I then drove the truck 2,901 miles to San Francisco, and Liam and Larry drove the van. They should have been there at least twelve hours before us, but they were still checking into the Miyako Hotel when we got there because they had wandered around the west while we had actually planned what route to take. Man, you spent more than enough time driving without fucking around for half a day."[20]

NOVEMBER 24, 1976
SACRAMENTO, CALIFORNIA
SACRAMENTO MEMORIAL AUDITORIUM, 15th and J Street. Historic venue dedicated on February 22, 1927.
OPENED FOR: Ted Nugent, Be-Bop Deluxe
TICKETS: $4.65 / $5.65 / $6.65
ATTENDANCE: 4,500; sold out[21]

NOTES: Heading into the winter, it was obvious that the members of Rush were stretching their musical wings and aiming to expand the band's sound. With thoughts already turning toward the next studio project, both Geddy and Alex were now playing doublenecks onstage, and Geddy was incorporating Moog pedals in certain places, most notably during "Lakeside Park."

SACRAMENTO UNION: "Nugent dynamite? Loud, for sure! Canada's Rush opened the show with a forty-five-minute set featuring perfectly horrible vocals. Lee, who plays bass and tries to sing, just doesn't cut it. He screams. Only drummer Peart showed any overwhelming talent, but because their set was loud progressive-rock—spacey and very hard—the crowd got off enough to bring Rush back for one encore."

NOVEMBER 26, 1976
SAN FRANCISCO, CALIFORNIA
WINTERLAND BALLROOM, Post and Steiner Streets. Historic building opened on June 29, 1928.
OPENED FOR: Ted Nugent, Be-Bop Deluxe
TICKETS: $5.00 (advance) / $6.00 (at the door)
CAPACITY: 5,400

NOVEMBER 27, 1976
SAN FRANCISCO, CALIFORNIA
WINTERLAND BALLROOM, Post and Steiner Streets
OPENED FOR: Ted Nugent, Be-Bop Deluxe
TICKETS: $5.00 (advance) / $6.00 (at the door)
CAPACITY: 5,400
IAN: "While our intro tape is playing I get called over the headset. Some asshole is screaming at me that he has an emergency and needs to speak. I cut the tape and he smugly announces 'please welcome our good friends Mahogany Rush.' Ted's stage manager steps up and asks, 'Who the fuck was that?' and then announces the band."[22]

NOVEMBER 28, 1976
FRESNO, CALIFORNIA
SELLAND ARENA, 700 M Street, at Ventura. Venue opened on October 11, 1966.
OPENED FOR: Ted Nugent

CAPACITY: 7,158
SET LIST: "Bastille Day," "Anthem," "2112" (5 parts), "Lakeside Park," "Working Man," "Finding My Way" (with drum solo), "Fly by Night," "In the Mood."
GEDDY (ONSTAGE): "Thank You! How are you doing tonight? Everybody looks like they're getting pushed around pretty heavy. What is the reason for this?"

NOVEMBER 30, 1976
SAN DIEGO, CALIFORNIA
GOLDEN HALL, at San Diego Community Concourse, 202 C Street. Venue opened on November 13, 1964.
OPENED FOR: Ted Nugent; Rex opened the show.
TICKETS: $5.75 / $6.75
ATTENDANCE: 4,389; sold out
CONCERT GROSS: $28,528

DECEMBER 1, 1976
INGLEWOOD, CALIFORNIA
THE FORUM, 3900 West Manchester Boulevard. Venue opened on December 30, 1967.
OPENED FOR: Ted Nugent; Rex opened the show.
TICKETS: $5.50 / $6.50 / $7.50 (all seats reserved)
CAPACITY: 18,000
NOTES: "The Fabulous Forum."
HOLLYWOOD DAILY VARIETY: "This Canadian hard-rock trio played as if they were at double strength and displayed some adroitly paced ambitious tunes (notably '2112' a mini rock opera)."
CREEM: "Rush looked tiny up there, just the three of them. But the music was tight—'Working Man,' 'Anthem,' and 'Something for Nothing' were whipped up like William Buckley debate retorts. The Forum crowd, mostly assembled for mad-dog Nugent, went for Rush carnivorously."
THE LOS ANGELES TIMES: "Speaking of painful sound; the Canadian trio Rush provided precisely that throughout its supporting set of derivative, loud, empty rock."

DECEMBER 3, 1976
DENVER, COLORADO
AUDITORIUM ARENA, 1323 Champa Street. Venue opened on July 7, 1908.
OPENED FOR: Ted Nugent; Rex opened the show.

TICKETS: $5.00 / $6.00
ATTENDANCE: 5,777
CONCERT GROSS: $32,088

DECEMBER 8, 1976
WATERBURY, CONNECTICUT
PALACE THEATER, 100 East Main Street. Historic venue opened in January 1922.
OPENED FOR: Black Oak Arkansas; James Gang opened the show.
TICKETS: $6.50 (advance) / $7.50 (at the door), general admission
CAPACITY: 3,450

DECEMBER 9, 1976
SPRINGFIELD, MASSACHUSETTS
SPRINGFIELD CIVIC CENTER, 1277 Main Street. Venue opened on September 22, 1972.
OPENED FOR: Foghat; James Gang opened the show.
TICKETS: $6.50 / $7.50, general admission
ATTENDANCE: 5,517[23]
CONCERT GROSS: $36,500
NOTES: This was originally a hold date for Rush and the U.S. Radio Band at the Astor Theatre in Reading, which was moved to December 18 with Crack the Sky.
SPRINGFIELD UNION: "Through all that electronic gimmickry and showbiz body English, Rush's mediocrity emerged unscathed."

DECEMBER 10, 1976
PASSAIC, NEW JERSEY
CAPITOL THEATRE, 326 Monroe Street. Venue opened on October 8, 1926.
OPENED FOR: Foghat, Montrose
TICKETS: $6.00 / $7.00
ATTENDANCE: 3,355; sold out[24]
CONCERT GROSS: $22,375
NOTES: John Scher began promoting concerts at the Capitol in response to Bill Graham closing down his Fillmore East in June 1971. Scher incorporated closed-circuit video screens on each side of the stage, so even fans in the back could watch closeups of their favorite artists. This show was filmed by the venue, and the black and white footage eventually came to light in fan circles around 2004. The footage makes several notable appearances in the *Beyond The Lighted Stage* documentary and was released in 2014 as part of the *R40* box set.

SET LIST: "Bastille Day," "Anthem," "Lakeside Park," "2112" (5 parts), "Fly by Night," "In the Mood."

DECEMBER 11, 1976
NEW YORK, NEW YORK
THE PALLADIUM, 126 East 14th Street. Venue opened on October 11, 1926.
OPENED FOR: Foghat; Mother's Finest opened the show.
TICKETS: $6.50 / $7.50
ATTENDANCE: 3,387; sold out
CONCERT GROSS: $24,000
NOTES: Originally the Academy of Music, the (renamed) Palladium opened on September 18, 1976.
VARIETY: "The sound was ear shattering as Rush overpowered all. But for all their volume the trio was clean, sharp, and crowd pleasing."
BILLBOARD: "Second-billed group Rush did not rely on such pyrotechnics for its effects, but this band, too, looks good onstage."

DECEMBER 12, 1976
ALBANY, NEW YORK
PALACE THEATRE, 19 Clinton Avenue. Historic venue opened on October 23, 1931.
OPENED FOR: Black Oak Arkansas; the Mick Ronson Band opened the show.
CAPACITY: 2,997
NOTES: This date is not present in SRO's records.
KNICKERBOCKER NEWS: "Rush took away a good part of the audience's hearing by playing very loud, depressing/alienating music."

DECEMBER 13, 1976
MONTREAL, QUEBEC
MONTREAL FORUM, 2313 Saint Catherine Street West. Historic venue opened on November 29, 1924.
OPENED FOR: Aerosmith
TICKETS: $7.00 CAD
ATTENDANCE: 18,000; sold out[24]
NOTES: This date was originally scheduled for November 18, with Lynyrd Skynyrd as support, but was changed at the eleventh hour, with Rush added in place of Skynyrd on November 27. This is UK journalist Geoff Barton's first time seeing Rush. Barton would prove critical in helping break the band in the UK.
THE MONTREAL GAZETTE: "A double rock-bottom bill with volume if not value:

This was probably the loudest show at that venue this year. Rush, billing itself as 'America's premier road attraction' (mainly because it will open to anyone, anywhere, anytime), real dunderheads when it comes to volume, sounded almost like a group of angels compared to Aerosmith. But, then, Rush is outnumbered by two, so maybe it doesn't have the capacity for noise. It does put forth a buzz-saw, banshee-yelling approach to rock, with plenty of bleeding-fast guitar solos and general rhythmic bashing. Rush has had plenty of practice at it; at least the crudeness sounds rehearsed."

DECEMBER 16, 1976
CHICAGO, ILLINOIS
AUDITORIUM THEATRE, Roosevelt University, 50 East Congress Parkway. National Historic Landmark dedicated on December 9, 1889.
SUPPORT ACT: Cheap Trick
TICKETS: $5.50 / $6.50 / $7.50
ATTENDANCE: 3,982; sold out
CONCERT GROSS: $28,607
NOTES: According to fan Jim Bossier, "The Twilight Zone" was performed in the set. At the end of Neil's solo in "Working Man," Alex came out on Lurch's shoulders, and they chased Geddy around the stage for the song's finale.
IAN: "Mike (Lurch) is 6'10", so that's a long way up. I do recall looking up and thinking *WTF . . . don't fall!*"
CHICAGO SUN TIMES: "Rush is relentless. It is total body bombardment from the word go; it is punkish, it is physically painful, it is impossible to ignore. The brain is all but short-circuited by the driving urgency. Alex Lifeson's guitar work is frenetic and piercing, never soulful, always attacking. Geddy Lee's voice, plagued by a bad cold, was shrill and shaky, but even intact it knifes at the senses. The raised fists and stoned-out dances of sheer abandon in the aisles said it all. This is music to sacrifice one's mind and body to the God of Heavy Metal Rock."
WALRUS: "Rush could have played at a lower volume, but fans loved it."

DECEMBER 18, 1976
READING, PENNSYLVANIA
ASTOR THEATRE, 734 Penn Street. Historic venue opened on October 3, 1928.

SUPPORT ACT: Crack the Sky
TICKETS: $6.50 (advance) / $7.50 (day of)
ATTENDANCE: 1,250 (approximate)
JOE MACRE (CRACK THE SKY BASSIST): "I remember it well. When we finished our sound check—which, by the way, they gave us full power and lights—I was walking toward backstage and there was a bench up against the wall. Geddy and Alex were sitting there and had been listening. Geddy said, 'Sounds great, and we really love the record!' I was speechless. What class to see our situation and to be so encouraging. I always had a special place for them. Class act. Not many others like them except Supertramp and ARS [Atlanta Rhythm Section]."[25]
READING EAGLE: "Rush, in a music-related context, means an inspired high. The Canadian loud-rock trio of the same name provided that for the Astor Theatre audience with a heavy-metal performance that was powerful, but not overpowering. Rush was perhaps the best of the loud-rock entries for 1976. The trio, noted for its live performances, surprised a crowd of about 1,250 with crisp, illuminated space-rock."

DECEMBER 19, 1976
BUFFALO, NEW YORK
NEW CENTURY THEATRE, 511 Main Street. Venue opened on October 17, 1921.
SUPPORT ACTS: The James Gang; the Mick Ronson Band opened the show.
TICKETS: $6.50
CAPACITY: 3,076
NOTES: Venue aka Century Theatre.

DECEMBER 20, 1976
HENRIETTA, NEW YORK
DOME ARENA, Monroe County Fairgrounds, 2695 East Henrietta Road.
SUPPORT ACT: Rex
ATTENDANCE: 4,500
NOTES: The band returned to headline a venue where they opened for Blue Oyster Cult just two months before. An advance ad for this date has Rush performing with Lynyrd Skynyrd in Clarksville, Tennessee, which did not occur.
DEMOCRAT AND CHRONICLE (ROCHESTER): "4,500 fans receive 'Rush' enthusiastically: Rush's performance last night was an uneven one, but the enthusiastic crowd at the Dome

didn't seem to notice. By playing both guitar and bass through pedal synthesizers, they were able to greatly expand the number of sounds and textures produced by these two instruments."

DECEMBER 22, 1976
ALLENTOWN, PENNSYLVANIA
AGRICULTURAL HALL, GREAT ALLENTOWN FAIRGROUNDS, 1725 Chew Street
WITH: Styx
CAPACITY: 4,100, general admission
NOTES: Although the ad lists Mott on the bill, the band broke up after a November tour of England. Former Mott the Hoople guitarist Mick Ronson was touring in the area, and did perform a few shows with Rush, so perhaps it was The Mick Ronson Band that opened, and the promoter listed them as Mott in the advertising.

DECEMBER 27, 1976
INDIANAPOLIS, INDIANA
MARKET SQUARE ARENA, 300 East Market Street. Venue opened on September 15, 1974.
WITH: Bob Seger and the Silver Bullet Band (cobill); Atlanta Rhythm Section; Santa Claus; Roadmaster opened the show.
TICKETS: $6.00 (advance) / $7.00 (day of)
ATTENDANCE: 16,783
CONCERT GROSS: $104,967
NOTES: "WNAP and Sunshine Promotions presents the Fifth Annual Holiday Festival." During the concert nineteen people were arrested and two cars were stolen from the parking lot. Most of the arrests were for drunk and disorderly conduct.[26]

DECEMBER 29, 1976
ERIE, PENNSYLVANIA
ERIE COUNTY FIELDHOUSE, 5750 Wattsburg Road. Venue opened in early 1974.
SUPPORT ACT: Diamond Reo
TICKETS: $5.50 / $6.50
ATTENDANCE: 1,987
CAPACITY: 5,250
CONCERT GROSS: $11,900
FRANK CZURI (DIAMOND REO LEAD SINGER): "We had very different styles, but Rush pleased the local crowds. Lots of sound for three guys!"[27]

IAN: "There was a guy named John Powers, who fancied himself as a sound engineer. And at some point, the band came to me and said, 'Are you planning on quitting? Because this guy John says that you're leaving, and he's interested in applying for the position.' I said, 'Um, no, not unless I'm fired. He can wait until the body is dead before he applies for the job.' So they said, 'Oh, ok.' A little while later, we were playing a show with Diamond Reo. So, Rush was banging around onstage for like twenty minutes after sound check, just messing around, and finally I said, 'C'mon Diamond Reo, let's get something done!' So Geddy steps up to the mic and says, 'Well, thank you John Powers!' I was just like, 'OK, ha ha, touché, now can we get something done?' It's one thing if they were practicing something, but when they were just dicking around . . . I was one of the few people who could say, 'C'mon boys, let's get something done.'"[28]

DECEMBER 30, 1976
HAMILTON, ONTARIO
ARTHUR BURRIDGE GYMNASIUM, inside the Ivor Wynne Centre, Physical Education Complex, McMaster University campus, Steam Drive at Forsythe Avenue North. Venue built in 1966.
SUPPORT ACTS: Max Webster; Wireless opened the show.
TICKETS: $6.50 (advance) /$7.00 (at the door) CAD
ATTENDANCE: 3,500; sold out
NOTES: Approximately 2,000 people were turned away at the door when the concert sold out.
THE SPECTATOR: "RUSH excellent—but loud: With temperatures dipping below -10 degrees outside McMaster's Phys Ed complex, Rush faced 3,500 screaming, screeching, and half-drunk teenage fans and gave them what they wanted—ninety minutes and two encores of an ear-raping sonic attack of heavy-metal noise."
THE SPECTATOR, GEDDY: "We need volume to fill the void."

DECEMBER 31, 1976
TORONTO, ONTARIO
MAPLE LEAF GARDENS CONCERT BOWL, 60 Carlton Street. Historic venue opened on November 12, 1931.

SUPPORT ACTS: Chilliwack; Wireless opened the show.
TICKETS: $7.50 CAD
ATTENDANCE: 8,000 (approximate); sold out
NOTES: "A New Year's Treat For Toronto." Geddy was sporting his new doubleneck Rickenbacker bass/six-string guitar. At the stroke of midnight, following the traditional countdown, a recording of "Auld Lang Syne" was piped through the PA, and the band enjoyed an onstage toast. Maple Leaf Gardens Concert Bowl had a lower seating capacity than the full arena because the stage was moved forward, and curtains are up in an effort to make the cavernous venue more intimate. Advertising promotes the fact that the PA was flown from the ceiling, creating an unobstructed view—something that is ubiquitous these days.
SET LIST: "Bastille Day," "Anthem," "Lakeside Park," "2112" (5 parts), "The Twilight Zone," "Something For Nothing," "Best I Can," "Auld Lang Syne," "By-Tor and the Snow Dog," "The Necromancer" ("Under the Shadow"/"Return of the Prince"), "In the End," "Working Man," "Finding My Way" (with drum solo). Encore: "Fly by Night," "In the Mood."
THE VARSITY: "Toronto's New Year's Eve . . . The threesome seemed in complete control with polished stage antics, while transitions between songs like 'By-Tor and the Snowdog' and the 'Neck Romancer' [sic] were smooth. . . . New additions to the musical side included a new doubleneck sported by Alex and a 'first off the line' Ricki Bass six-string wielded by Geddy. And if this wasn't enough that Santa left under the tree, Geddy tried his hand, or rather feet, at a set of Moog bass peddles. The band has come a long way with sheer determination and hard work, experimenting at all steps of the way, but I think Neil Peart put it best when I asked who their major competitor was, and he replied 'Rush.'"

JANUARY 3, 1977
TORONTO, ONTARIO
MAPLE LEAF GARDENS CONCERT BOWL, 60 Carlton Street
SUPPORT ACTS: Chilliwack; Wireless opened the show.
TICKETS: $7.50 CAD
CAPACITY: 8,000, approximate

THE VARSITY: "Two years of steady touring has produced a tight, exciting stage show highlighting '2112,' their newest concept. The group has admitted that this is the theatrical showcase of their set, and it certainly stood as such. Unfortunately though, their slide show has not reached its full potential and could use some more work. Tattered film and 'Star Trek' slides detract little from the performance but steal some of the professional taste at times."

JANUARY 6, 1977
HOUSTON, TEXAS

MUSIC HALL, 801 Bagby Street. Venue opened in April 1938.
SUPPORT ACTS: Artful Dodger; Leslie West opened the show.
CAPACITY: 3,024
HOUSTON CHRONICLE: "Rush, a Canadian band that performed in the Music Hall, leaves not only your ears ringing, but also your body trembling, mind reeling, and eyes flashing from the band's taut, cohesive music and expertly synchronized lighting and retina-imprinting onstage explosions. Rush comes on like its name implies in an onslaught of decibels but pulls back before the volume of the amplifiers defeats its own purpose. Thus, the band doesn't have to continuously push its volume ever higher during a set to achieve the same aural and visceral effect it has at the start. Setting lyrical and technical virtuosity aside for a moment. I can only think of a handful of hard-rock bands with that much control over its music, which puts Rush in rare and esteemed company."

JANUARY 7, 1977
CORPUS CHRISTI, TEXAS

MEMORIAL COLISEUM, 402 South Shoreline Boulevard. Venue dedicated on September 26, 1954.
SUPPORT ACTS: Artful Dodger; Leslie West opened the show.
CAPACITY: 6,000 (2,615 permanent seats)

JANUARY 8, 1977
SAN ANTONIO, TEXAS

MUNICIPAL AUDITORIUM, 100 Auditorium Circle. Historic venue opened on April 19, 1926.
SUPPORT ACTS: Artful Dodger; Leslie West opened the show.
TICKETS: $6.00
ATTENDANCE: 6,500; sold out

JANUARY 9, 1977
SAN ANTONIO, TEXAS

MUNICIPAL AUDITORIUM, 100 Auditorium Circle
SUPPORT ACTS: Artful Dodger; Leslie West opened the show.
TICKETS: $6.00
CAPACITY: 5,800 (1,240 portable seats)

JANUARY 10, 1977
DALLAS, TEXAS

MUSIC HALL AT FAIR PARK, 909 First Avenue. Venue opened on October 10, 1925.
SUPPORT ACT: Artful Dodger
TICKETS: $6.75
ATTENDANCE: Less than 200
CAPACITY: 3,420
NOTES: A winter ice storm paralyzed the city, with only a few souls brave enough to venture out to the gig. Some sources indicate Leslie West on the bill, however a review states otherwise.
THE DALLAS MORNING NEWS: "A loud Rush to distortion: Performing before an extremely small crowd, it played with the energy of standing before a packed house at Madison Square Garden. I admit there is some market for this stuff. A handful of people shelled out $6.75 apiece of their own free will and subjected themselves to ninety minutes of this madness."

JANUARY 11, 1977
AUSTIN, TEXAS

PARAMOUNT THEATRE FOR THE PERFORMING ARTS, 713 Congress Avenue. Historic venue opened on October 11, 1915.
SUPPORT ACTS: Leslie West; Artful Dodger opened the show.
CAPACITY: 1,295
NOTES: According to the promoter, Leslie West went on second for this one gig, while Artful Dodger opened.

JANUARY 13, 1977
WICHITA, KANSAS

CENTURY II CONVENTION HALL, 225 West Douglas Avenue. Venue opened on January 11, 1969.
SUPPORT ACT: Artful Dodger
CAPACITY: 5,022

JANUARY 14, 1977
OKLAHOMA CITY, OKLAHOMA

STATE FAIR ARENA, Oklahoma State Fairgrounds, 333 Gordon Cooper Boulevard. Venue opened on September 25, 1965.
OPENED FOR: Ted Nugent; Artful Dodger opened the show.
TICKETS: $6.00 (advance) / $7.00 (day of)
ATTENDANCE: 9,604
CAPACITY: 10,944
CONCERT GROSS: $59,882

JANUARY 15, 1977
KANSAS CITY, MISSOURI

MUNICIPAL AUDITORIUM ARENA, 301 West 13th Street. Historic venue dedicated on October 13, 1936.
OPENED FOR: Ted Nugent; Artful Dodger opened the show.
TICKETS: $6.00 (advance) / $7.00 (day of)
ATTENDANCE: 10,360; sold out
CONCERT GROSS: $62,160

JANUARY 16, 1977
TULSA, OKLAHOMA

FAIRGROUNDS PAVILION, Tulsa State Fairgrounds, 4145 East 21st Street. Venue dedicated on March 28, 1932.
OPENED FOR: Ted Nugent; Artful Dodger opened the show.
TICKETS: $6.00 (advance) / $7.00 (day of)
ATTENDANCE: 7,902
CAPACITY: 10,000
CONCERT GROSS: $50,918

JANUARY 18, 1977
EL PASO, TEXAS

EL PASO COUNTY COLISEUM, 4100 East Paisano Drive. Venue opened on May 22, 1942.
OPENED FOR: Ted Nugent; Artful Dodger opened the show.
TICKETS: $5.50 (advance) / $6.50 (day of)
ATTENDANCE: 7,300
CAPACITY: 9,000
CONCERT GROSS: $39,000
NOTES: Rex was slated to open but were replaced at the last minute by Artful Dodger. Rush performed "Fly by Night" as their encore.
EL PASO TIMES: "'Overture' from 2112 brought a very positive response from the crowd."

JANUARY 19, 1977
LUBBOCK, TEXAS
LUBBOCK MUNICIPAL COLISEUM,
Texas Tech University campus. Fourth Street and University Avenue. Venue opened in March 1956.
OPENED FOR: Ted Nugent; Artful Dodger opened the show.
TICKETS: $5.50 (advance) / $6.50 (day of)
ATTENDANCE: 6,900
CAPACITY: 9,000
CONCERT GROSS: $38,700
LUBBOCK AVALANCHE-JOURNAL: "Many in the industry happen to feel this group (Rush) may be headlining concerts themselves in a very short time."

JANUARY 20, 1977
ODESSA, TEXAS
ECTOR COUNTY COLISEUM, 4201 Andrews Highway. Venue opened on January 19, 1955.
SUPPORT ACTS: Head East; Artful Dodger opened the show.
TICKETS: $5.00 (advance) / $6.00 (day of)
ATTENDANCE: 4,115
CAPACITY: 6,000
CONCERT GROSS: $22,600
KEVIN CAMPBELL (GUITARIST): "My first concert was Rush, January 20, 1977, Odessa, Texas. They inspired me to become a musician."
ABILENE REPORTER-NEWS: "Known to put on a good show, Rush uses lighting effectively. The drums Peart uses are made of chrome. The group often opens concerts rolling the drums on stage with lights focused on them, causing a blinding effect. Anyone going to see Rush can expect an extensive stage show and a lot of musical talent."

JANUARY 21, 1977
ABILENE, TEXAS
TAYLOR COUNTY COLISEUM, 1700 Highway 36. Venue opened on September 8, 1969.
SUPPORT ACTS: Head East; Artful Dodger opened the show.
TICKETS: $5.00 (advance) / $6.00 (day of)
ATTENDANCE: 3,551
CAPACITY: 7,000
CONCERT GROSS: $19,718
ABILENE REPORTER-NEWS: "Rush's effect is fuzzy, because they mix the images they try to get. They perform in hapi-coats, short, oriental-style robes with wide sleeves. Their sound, reinforced by projections on a black screen behind them, is based on outer-space themes. They even went as far as to have a film of a spaceship that looked exactly like the Enterprise from 'Star Trek.' Their name, on the other hand, has drug-use connotations. The triple imagery is confusing."

JANUARY 22, 1977
AMARILLO, TEXAS
AMARILLO CIVIC CENTER AUDITORIUM, 401 South Buchanan. Venue opened on September 3, 1968.
SUPPORT ACTS: Head East; Artful Dodger opened the show.
TICKETS: $5.00 (advance) / $6.00 (day of), general admission
ATTENDANCE: 2,424; sold out
CONCERT GROSS: $13,200

JANUARY 24, 1977
BEAUMONT, TEXAS
CITY HALL AUDITORIUM, 765 Pearl Street. Historic venue opened in 1928.
SUPPORT ACTS: Head East; Artful Dodger opened the show.
CAPACITY: 2,400

JANUARY 26, 1977
COLUMBUS, OHIO
VETERANS MEMORIAL AUDITORIUM, 300 West Broad Street. Venue dedicated on November 11, 1955.
SUPPORT ACTS: Starcastle; Max Webster opened the show.
TICKETS: $5.50 (advance) / $6.50 (day of)
ATTENDANCE: 3,825; sold out
CONCERT GROSS: $24,555
NOTES: The sound on this snowy night was questionable, with a buzz heard through the PA for a portion of the gig.[29]

JANUARY 27, 1977
COLUMBUS, OHIO
VETERANS MEMORIAL AUDITORIUM, 300 West Broad Street
SUPPORT ACTS: Starcastle; Max Webster opened the show.
TICKETS: $5.50 (advance) / $6.50 (day of)
CAPACITY: 3,893; sold out
CONCERT GROSS: $24,962

JANUARY 28, 1977
LOUISVILLE, KENTUCKY
LOUISVILLE GARDENS, 525 Walnut Street. Historic venue dedicated on December 31, 1905.
OPENED FOR: The Outlaws; Hydra opened the show.
TICKETS: $5.50 (advance) / $6.50 (day of), general admission
CAPACITY: 7,088
HENRY PAUL (SINGER/GUITARIST FOR THE OUTLAWS): "At the expense of appearing brain dead, I really don't recall working with Rush at any time. They very well could have been on some dates, but with the touring schedule we kept back then I was lucky to know anything other than the words to my songs."[30]

JANUARY 29, 1977
EVANSVILLE, INDIANA
SOLDIERS AND SAILORS MEMORIAL COLISEUM, 300 Court Street. Historic venue dedicated on April 18, 1917.
SUPPORT ACTS: Starcastle; Max Webster opened the show.
TICKETS: $5.50 (advance) / $6.50 (day of)
ATTENDANCE: 3,466
CAPACITY: 3,500
CONCERT GROSS: $20,200 (an alternate source lists $20,405)
NOTES: A snowy night in Evansville couldn't keep Rush or their fans away from the Coliseum.

JANUARY 30, 1977
SOUTH BEND, INDIANA
MORRIS CIVIC AUDITORIUM, 211 North Michigan Street. Venue opened on November 2, 1922.
SUPPORT ACTS: Starcastle; Max Webster opened the show.
TICKETS: $5.50 (advance) / $6.50 (day of)
ATTENDANCE: 2,228
CAPACITY: 2,400
CONCERT GROSS: $12,467.15
NOTES: One source lists Michael Henderson as the opener, though ads in the *South Bend Tribune* on January 16 and 28 list only Starcastle and Max Webster.
BILLBOARD (2/12/77): "Sunshine managed to get Rush from Evansville to South Bend on two consecutive snowy nights and missed only a few hundred seats from selling out both medium-hall dates."

JANUARY 31, 1977; FEBRUARY 1–8, 1977

It is likely that additional dates were performed during this period, as an in-depth interview with the band conducted on February 13 by the *St. Louis Post-Dispatch* states that Rush had "given concerts in different cities fourteen out of fifteen nights in a row prior to its show at Kiel."

FEBRUARY 9, 1977
SAGINAW, MICHIGAN
WENDLER ARENA AT SAGINAW CIVIC CENTER, 303 Johnson Street. Venue opened on October 15, 1972.
SUPPORT ACT: The Runaways
TICKETS: $5.50 (advance) / $6.50 (day of)
ATTENDANCE: 4,027
CAPACITY: 7,000
CONCERT GROSS: $25,123
IAN: "In Saginaw we had tech problems, but at Cobo our band did a quick sound check and the Runaways had the better part of an hour to get it together. Instead, they spent it arguing with each other. They bitched at each other like fourteen-year-olds."
JOAN JETT (THE RUNAWAYS): "[Rush] sat on the side of the stage and laughed at us. Initially, people would laugh at us and go, 'That's cute'. But then when they realized we were serious, they'd get nasty."[31]
GEDDY: "The Runaways had a ginormous chip on their shoulders. I remember we had trouble with our gear so our sound check got delayed and the Runaways never got one. But we were always good to whoever was opening for us. We had no bias against them because they were girls—none of that bullshit. I know they said that we were laughing at them when they played, but quite frankly they were too shitty to listen to. And forty years later they have a story to tell about it. Who knew?"[32]

FEBRUARY 10, 1977
DETROIT, MICHIGAN
COBO HALL ARENA, 1 Washington Boulevard. Venue opened on October 17, 1960.
SUPPORT ACTS: The Runaways; Max Webster opened the show.
TICKETS: $6.50 (advance) / $7.50 (day of)

ATTENDANCE: 8,154
CAPACITY: 11,400
CONCERT GROSS: $58,505
NOTES: *Billboard* lists attendance as 7,900 and gross as $58,500.
THE DETROIT NEWS: "They call themselves the Runaways but, being within earshot, we were instilled with a desire to run the other way. The Runaways accosted the audience with sloppy Led Zeppelin warm-overs and embarrassingly insincere punkiness."
WINDSOR STAR: "Rush is a diligent, utterly professional outfit whose proficiency on stage has increased steadily since three years ago when they were breaking into the market on lowly warm-up dates."

FEBRUARY 11, 1977
HAMMOND, INDIANA
HAMMOND CIVIC CENTER AUDITORIUM, 5852 Sohl Avenue. Venue opened on February 2, 1938.
SUPPORT ACT: Max Webster
TICKETS: $6.00 (advance) / $7.00 (day of)
ATTENDANCE: 4,686
CAPACITY: 5,000
CONCERT GROSS: $28,672

FEBRUARY 12, 1977
DAVENPORT, IOWA
RKO ORPHEUM THEATRE, 136 East Third Street. Historic venue opened on November 25, 1931.
SUPPORT ACT: Max Webster
TICKETS: $6.50
CAPACITY: 2,700

FEBRUARY 13, 1977
ST. LOUIS, MISSOURI
KIEL MUNICIPAL AUDITORIUM, 1401 Clark Street. Historic venue dedicated on April 14, 1934.
SUPPORT ACTS: Rex; Max Webster opened the show.
TICKETS: $4.50 / $5.50 / $6.50 (all seats reserved)
ATTENDANCE: 7,000
CAPACITY: 10,500
CONCERT GROSS: $40,000
NOTES: Venue named after Henry W. Kiel, longtime mayor and St. Louis native. "The Twilight Zone" was performed in the set.
ST. LOUIS POST-DISPATCH: "Rush, REX, Max Webster in Rock Music concert: Rush received a hero's welcome before

any member of the threesome had struck a note. Like the lighting and cryptic lyrics, a good measure of volume is an important part of this progressive rock band's art. It wouldn't sound right any other way."
ST. LOUIS POST-DISPATCH, GEDDY (BACKSTAGE BEFORE THE SHOW): "If there is something going on that we don't like, we just say we don't like it. That concerns everything we do from where we are playing to how we divide our money up."

FEBRUARY 15, 1977
CHATTANOOGA, TENNESSEE
SOLDIERS AND SAILORS MEMORIAL AUDITORIUM, 399 McCallie Avenue. Venue opened on February 22, 1924.
OPENED FOR: Kansas
TICKETS: $5.50 (advance) / $6.50 (day of)
CAPACITY: 3,866
NOTES: Rush was billed as "Special Guest." Kansas's *Leftoverture* was soaring up the *Billboard* Album Charts. This week it was #28 in America.

FEBRUARY 16, 1977
BIRMINGHAM, ALABAMA
BOUTWELL MEMORIAL AUDITORIUM, 1930 Eighth Avenue North. Venue dedicated on June 1, 1924.
OPENED FOR: Blue Oyster Cult; Piper opened the show.
TICKETS: $6.50 (advance) / $7.50 (day of), general admission
CAPACITY: 6,000

FEBRUARY 17, 1977
MOBILE, ALABAMA
MUNICIPAL AUDITORIUM, Exhibit Hall, 401 Civic Center Drive. Venue opened on July 9, 1964.
OPENED FOR: Blue Oyster Cult; Piper opened the show.
TICKETS: $6.00 (advance), general admission
CAPACITY: 4,000

FEBRUARY 18, 1977
LITTLE ROCK, ARKANSAS
T. H. BARTON COLISEUM, Arkansas State Fairgrounds, 2600 Howard Street. Venue dedicated on September 29, 1952.
OPENED FOR: Blue Oyster Cult; Piper opened the show.
TICKETS: $6.00 (advance) / $7.00 (at the door)

CAPACITY: 10,250, general admission
NOTES: This date is not in SRO's data but is confirmed by promoter records. Venue named after Colonel Thomas Harry Barton.

FEBRUARY 19, 1977
NEW ORLEANS, LOUISIANA
THE WAREHOUSE, 1820 Tchoupitoulas Street. Historic venue opened on January 30, 1970.
OPENED FOR: Blue Oyster Cult
TICKETS: $6.00, general admission
CAPACITY: 3,500
NOTES: Special Mardi Gras concert. The former cotton warehouse was host to hundreds of memorable concerts, including opening night when the Grateful Dead were busted down on Bourbon Street, and the final live performance by Jim Morrison with The Doors, among many others.

FEBRUARY 20, 1977
NEW ORLEANS, LOUISIANA
THE WAREHOUSE, 1820 Tchoupitoulas Street
OPENED FOR: Blue Oyster Cult
TICKETS: $6.00, general admission
CAPACITY: 3,500
NOTES: Special Mardi Gras concert.

FEBRUARY 22, 1977
COLUMBUS, GEORGIA
MUNICIPAL AUDITORIUM, 400 Fourth Street. Venue opened on September 6, 1957.
OPENED FOR: Blue Oyster Cult; Piper opened the show.
TICKETS: $6.00
ATTENDANCE: 3,916 (general admission); sold out
JIM TREMAYNE (BLUE OYSTER CULT FAN): "Piper was on the bill. I remember Billy Squier traipsing around, but not drawing much of a stir. Rush, on the other hand, blew doors. From the very beginning of their set, everyone looked around and said, 'Who are these guys?' It was one of those shows where half the audience ran out and bought *2112* the very next day—probably on eight-track."

FEBRUARY 25, 1977
CHARLOTTE, NORTH CAROLINA
COLISEUM, 2700 East Independence Boulevard
OPENED FOR: Blue Oyster Cult. REO Speedwagon was also on the bill.

TICKETS: $7.50 (limited advance), general admission show
CAPACITY: 12,900
NOTES: Some sources say that Rush opened, with R.E.O. second, but "RUSH!" was printed on the ticket stub in very large lettering, suggesting Rush might have played second instead.

FEBRUARY 26, 1977
FAYETTEVILLE, NORTH CAROLINA
CUMBERLAND COUNTY MEMORIAL ARENA, 1960 Coliseum Drive. Venue opened on January 23, 1968.
OPENED FOR: Blue Oyster Cult; REO Speedwagon opened the show.
TICKETS: $6.25 (advance) / $7.25 (day of concert)
CAPACITY: 7,000

FEBRUARY 27, 1977
ATLANTA, GEORGIA
THE OMNI, 100 Techwood Drive Northwest. Venue opened on October 14, 1972.
OPENED FOR: Blue Oyster Cult; REO Speedwagon opened the show.
TICKETS: $5.50 / $6.50 / $7.50
ATTENDANCE: 5,372
CONCERT GROSS: $38,259
NOTES: REO Speedwagon is a last-minute replacement for Starcastle. Here, R.E.O. is touring in support of the recently released *Live: You Get What You Play For* album.
STEVE PITTARD (BLUE OYSTER CULT FAN): "As for the openers—REO was mediocre, and I remember the house lights coming on during their set, which triggered a round of applause as we thought that meant their set was over. No such luck. Rush came on next and turned in a solid set which was dominated by songs from *2112*. It was clear they were on a path to success but, certainly in this case, they were no match for Blue Oyster Cult."[33]

MARCH 2, 1977
EAST LANSING, MICHIGAN
MSU CONCERT AUDITORIUM, Michigan State University campus, 149 Auditorium Road. Venue opened in 1940.
SUPPORT ACTS: Nils Lofgren; Max Webster opened the show.
TICKETS: $5.50 (advance) / $6.50 (day of)
CAPACITY: 3,600

MARCH 3, 1977
YOUNGSTOWN, OHIO
TOMORROW CLUB, 213 Federal Plaza West. Venue opened on October 20, 1974.
SUPPORT ACT: Max Webster
TICKETS: $5.00 (advance) / $6.00 (day of)
CAPACITY: 2,142

MARCH 4, 1977
CINCINNATI, OHIO
RIVERFRONT COLISEUM, 100 Broadway. Venue opened on September 9, 1975.
OPENED FOR: Boston; Starcastle opened the show.
TICKETS: $5.50 (advance) / $6.50 (day of), general admission
ATTENDANCE: 18,400; sold out
CONCERT GROSS: $113,637
NOTES: The *Beyond The Lighted Stage* documentary includes a few seconds of footage from this gig. According to Andrew Kowalchuk of Banger Films, the footage was for "a TV news report I found on a small roll of 16mm film at Anthem. The cameraperson only shot a few minutes of footage and started and stopped the camera during the song they covered. [Ed: "Finding My Way"]. The laboratory info in the film can indicated that it came from Cincinnati, but we could never confirm exactly what TV station shot it and when it went on the air."
THE JOURNAL NEWS: "Every teenybopper in Greater Cincinnati was at the concert, and they greeted Boston with more applause than I ever heard any band at the Coliseum get. At most concerts, it's pretty clear why the warm-up bands are warm-up bands and why the top-billed bands receive top billing. The line was harder to draw at Friday's concert. Both Starcastle and Rush have more albums under their belts than Boston, and they turned in performances which were almost equivalent to Boston's show. All three bands received standing ovations, and each did its best to please the sellout Coliseum crowd."

MARCH 5, 1977
MANSFIELD, PENNSYLVANIA
STRAUGHN AUDITORIUM, Mansfield State College campus, 35 Straughn Drive. Venue dedicated in September 1930.

SUPPORT ACT: Max Webster
TICKETS: $3.00 (with ID) / $4.00 / $5.00 (at the door)
ATTENDANCE: 1,500; sold out (over capacity)
NOTES: Poco was slated to perform, but was forced to cancel, with Rush a last-minute replacement.
FLASHLIGHT (MANSFIELD STATE COLLEGE): "Geddy and Alex would often play silhouetted by blue and yellow spotlights, presenting an eerie effect. This was done especially during selections from their *2112* album. Another effect they used is known as 'burning the audience.' During the performance of a song, especially during an intense climax, the group will shoot a huge ball of fire into the audience. Care is taken, of course, that no one or nothing is burned by this. Rush used this technique twice during their concert and had a very strong effect on the audience both times. Some people were so shocked by it that they felt seriously for a second that they had literally died. This was reinforced by the total darkness and silence the audience was engulfed in right after the fire was shot out. The music of Rush had the audience at such a high pitch during the concert that many fans came down front and crowded around the stage, clapping and cheering. One of the fans who was standing down in front of the speakers had a bottle which shattered due to the intensity of the music. The dynamic and progressive element in their music strongly suggests that they will go a long way further."

MARCH 8, 1977
NORFOLK, VIRGINIA
SCOPE ARENA, 201 East Brambleton Avenue. Venue opened on November 12, 1971.
OPENED FOR: Kansas, Derringer
TICKETS: $6.00 / $7.00
ATTENDANCE: 6,941
CONCERT GROSS: $44,659
NOTES: Rush's Tidewater debut was an opening set of about forty minutes. Backstage, the band was unhappy with the venue acoustics, with Neil and Alex citing a low-level hum throughout the performance.[34]

DAILY PRESS (NEWPORT NEWS): "Rush was loud, but their volume was in proportion to the size of the hall and they showed themselves to be a band with taste and restraint."[35]

MARCH 10, 1977
AUBURN, NEW YORK
CCCC GYMNASIUM, Cayuga County Community College campus, 197 Franklin Street. Founded in 1953.
SUPPORT ACT: Max Webster
TICKETS: $3.00 (advance students) / $4.00 (general admission advance) / $5.00 (day of)
ATTENDANCE: Sold out
NOTES: The concert is funded by the students' activity fees.

MARCH 11, 1977
UPPER DARBY, PENNSYLVANIA
TOWER THEATER, 69th and Ludlow. Venue opened on October 1, 1928.
SUPPORT ACTS: Max Webster; Cheap Trick opened the show.
TICKETS: $4.50 / $5.50 / $6.50
ATTENDANCE: 3,246; sold out
CONCERT GROSS: $17,668
NOTES: The band's first headline gig in the Philly area had them performing the entire *All The World's A Stage* album, plus "The Necromancer" ("Under the Shadow"/"Return of the Prince") and "The Twilight Zone." During the latter, Howard implemented a cool lighting effect: when Geddy sang "*You have entered The Twilight Zone,*" yellow beams of light shot out from each side of Neil's drum riser, silhouetting Alex and Geddy, á la "The Temples of Syrinx." The well-deserved encores featured Geddy sporting his blue Fender Precision teardrop bass. Due to the limitations of the Tower stage, the band was prevented from using their film projections.
AQUARIAN WEEKLY: "Rush has a penchant for long instrumental passages and bottom-heavy rhythm. They are loud, and proud of it."

MARCH 12, 1977
PASSAIC, NEW JERSEY
CAPITOL THEATRE, 326 Monroe Street
OPENED FOR: Kansas
TICKETS: $5.50 / $6.50
ATTENDANCE: 3,456; sold out
CONCERT GROSS: $22,988

MARCH 14, 1977
PITTSBURGH, PENNSYLVANIA
STANLEY THEATRE, 719 Liberty Avenue. Venue opened on February 27, 1928.
SUPPORT ACTS: Max Webster; Cheap Trick opened the show.
TICKETS: $7.50
CAPACITY: 3,400
NOTES: Rush's first headline date in Pittsburgh. Initially, Bob Seger and the Silver Bullet Band were slated to open, but they headlined on March 15 instead.
PITTSBURGH PRESS: "Rush Quick To Please Fans: It was their best outing here. Rush delivered, as always, ear-splitting vocals from Geddy Lee, powerful drumming from stick-twirling Neil Peart, and some of the best guitar work in the business from Alex Lifeson. Rush blasted from the beginning with 'Bastille Day,' 'Anthem,' and 'Lakeside Park,' and a lesser man than Lee would have super frogs in his throat for a week after those three. It's amazing how he maintains the pace throughout a show with minimal vocal help from Lifeson. Max Webster and Cheap Trick didn't do badly either, although neither could match Rush."

MARCH 17, 1977
NEW YORK, NEW YORK
THE PALLADIUM, 126 East 14th Street. Venue opened on October 11, 1926.
OPENED FOR: Bob Seger and the Silver Bullet Band; Starz opened the show.
TICKETS: $5.50 / $6.50 / $7.50
ATTENDANCE: 3,387; sold out
CONCERT GROSS: $24,200
NOTES: This concert was originally scheduled for March 6, but rescheduled because Silver Bullet Band drummer Charlie Allen Martin broke both legs after being struck from behind by a car with no lights on while he was walking down the road, after running out of gas. The incident left him unable to walk. Martin was replaced on drums by Dave Teegarden.
VARIETY: "Bob Seger capped a four-hour-plus concert at the Palladium, but most of the youthful crowd's cheers went to Rush and their ear-shattering turn."

MARCH 18, 1977
OSHAWA, ONTARIO
CIVIC AUDITORIUM, 99 Thornton Road South. Venue opened on December 11, 1964.
SUPPORT ACTS: Max Webster, Wireless
TICKETS: $6.00 (advance) / $7.00 (at door, after 5pm) CAD
CAPACITY: 4,024
NOTES: The band jammed around with "More Than A Feeling" by Boston at sound check.
BRAD HOPKINS (CHALK CIRCLE BASS-IST): "My very first concert was Rush in Oshawa, 1977. My Mom drove us to the show, and we walked in an open door and watched sound check. Geddy was a big influence on me, and our singer, especially in the early days. Rush was always at the top of the list. We liked how they grew with every record."[36]

MARCH 19, 1977
GUELPH, ONTARIO
W. F. MITCHELL ATHLETIC CENTRE GYMNASIUM, University of Guelph campus, Powerhouse Lane and Reynolds Walk. Venue opened in 1957.
SUPPORT ACT: Max Webster
TICKETS: $6.00 CAD
CAPACITY: 2,200
KIM MITCHELL (MAX WEBSTER FOUND-ING VOCALIST/GUITARIST): "Guelph I hold dear to my heart, because a long time ago Max Webster recorded a live album there (at U of G). There is a part in a Rush tune ['The Spirit of Radio'] where they go 'Concert Hall!' and there's a bunch of screaming and clapping. That is from part of the show we did."[37]

MARCH 20, 1977
LONDON, ONTARIO
LONDON GARDENS, 4380 Wellington Road South. Venue opened in September 1964.
SUPPORT ACT: Max Webster
ATTENDANCE: 2,500
CAPACITY: 5,075
THE FREE PRESS: "Peart is the group's showman. His twirling drumsticks and imaginative playing is a good background for the charisma of Lee's physical and vocal presence."

MARCH 23, 1977
KITCHENER, ONTARIO
KITCHENER MEMORIAL AUDITORIUM, 400 East Avenue. Venue opened on May 24, 1951.
SUPPORT ACT: Max Webster
TICKETS: $4.50 / $5.50 / $6.50 CAD
CAPACITY: 6,268
NOTES: The band thrills the youthful crowd by coming back for three encores.[38]
THE CORD (LAURIER UNIVERSITY): "Rush presentation talented and energetic."

APRIL 8, 1977
TOLEDO, OHIO
SPORTS ARENA, 1 North Main Street. Venue opened on November 13, 1947.
SUPPORT ACTS: Angel; Max Webster, opened the show.
TICKETS: $5.50 (advance) / $6.50 (day of)
ATTENDANCE: 5,040
CAPACITY: 7,000
CONCERT GROSS: $29,006

APRIL 9, 1977
DAYTON, OHIO
HARA ARENA, 1001 Shiloh Springs Road. Venue opened on November 1, 1964.
SUPPORT ACTS: Derringer; Max Webster opened the show.
TICKETS: $5.50 (advance) / $6.50 (day of), general admission
ATTENDANCE: 7,948; sold out
CONCERT GROSS: $45,214
NOTES: During the encore, members of the crew wheeled Alex out in a tennis judge's chair, while he continued playing atop the high perch.

APRIL 13, 1977
KALAMAZOO, MICHIGAN
WINGS STADIUM, 3600 Van Rick Drive. Venue opened on October 30, 1974.
OPENED FOR: ZZ Top
TICKETS: $6.50, general admission
ATTENDANCE: 7,200 (approximate); sold out
KALAMAZOO GAZETTE: "The last of close to 7,200 tickets were sold just min-utes before the show started so that out-side the stadium, as Rush was opening its act, disappointed concertgoers were waiting for an opening to rush the doors. Geddy Lee and crew of Rush probably had as many fans in the seats as ZZ Top

and got a strong reception. But the Rush set didn't seem to stand up as well as the 'little ol' band from Texas.' Stronger in amplification than variety, Rush's type of panic rock loses its interest after a while. Rush played sixty minutes as opening act, and came back to play the title cut, 'Fly by Night,' as its encore."

APRIL 14, 1977
FORT WAYNE, INDIANA
ALLEN COUNTY WAR MEMORIAL COLISEUM, 4000 Parnell Avenue. Venue dedicated on September 28, 1952.
SUPPORT ACTS: Starcastle; Roy Buchanan opened the show.
TICKETS: $5.50 (advance) / $6.50 (day of)
ATTENDANCE: 3,722
CAPACITY: 10,000, general admission
CONCERT GROSS: $21,536
NOTES: Neil took delivery of his new, "blackrome" Slingerland drum kit. The ebony set was played this night, with a few parts from the original silver kit still mixed in. The new drums were then taken back to the Percussion Center for modification.
NEAL GRAHAM (PERCUSSION CENTER OWNER): "We were involved in doing custom finishes and brass and gold plat-ing. The stands and the riser system Peart used, we were involved in all that. Ultimately, we started building drum sets for Peart, and we finished the first ten—I think it was ten—sets of his career."[39]

APRIL 15, 1977
CLEVELAND, OHIO
PUBLIC HALL, 500 Lakeside Avenue. Historic venue opened on April 15, 1922.
SUPPORT ACTS: Derringer; Max Webster opened the show.
TICKETS: $6.00 (advance) / $7.00 (day of)
ATTENDANCE: 7,200; sold out
CONCERT GROSS: $47,728
NOTES: Public Hall is located inside Public Auditorium, which contains two separate venues.

APRIL 16, 1977
GROVE CITY, PENNSYLVANIA
GROVE CITY COLLEGE ARENA, Grove City College campus, 100 Campus Drive. Venue opened on December 5, 1953.

SUPPORT ACT: Max Webster
TICKETS: Free to GCC Students with ID
CAPACITY: 1,800
THE COLLEGIAN (GROVE CITY COLLEGE): "Rush: Distinctly Unimpressive: Not only are they basically a bad band, they also have problems with any song that doesn't peak at 160 decibels. There is no way to compare 'Rush' with anyone else, because to mention them in the same sentence with a good band would be to drag down the name and reputation of the latter. Both 'Rush' and 'Max Webster' were too loud, both were basically untalented and neither group knew how to cut a song off cleanly, both dragging the endings out far too long."

APRIL 17, 1977
WASHINGTON, DC
LISNER AUDITORIUM, George Washington University campus, 730 21st Street, Northwest. Historic venue opened (for commercial use) on October 10, 1943.
SUPPORT ACT: Max Webster
TICKETS: $6.50
ATTENDANCE: 1,490; sold out
CONCERT GROSS: $9,763
NOTES: Geddy introduced Neil for his drum solo as "Farrah Fawcett Majors on the drum kit!"
SET LIST: "Bastille Day," "Anthem," "Lakeside Park," "2112" (5 parts), "The Twilight Zone," "Something For Nothing," "By-Tor and the Snow Dog," "The Necromancer" ("Under the Shadow"/"Return of the Prince"), "In the End," "Working Man," "Finding My Way," Drum Solo, "Fly by Night," "In the Mood," "What You're Doing," "Best I Can."
GEDDY (ONSTAGE): "Thank You! There's a lot of people on our road crew and on our sound and personal crew that live right here in DC and the surrounding area, so we'd like to dedicate this next tune to them. This is called 'By-Tor and the Snow Dog.'"
THE WASHINGTON POST: "Rush's music, amplified beyond the threshold of pain, is essentially characterless. Despite all this, Rush's ninety-minute set was extremely well-received. The highlight of the show—if one can use that word to describe a performance devoid of intelligence, feeling or anything else usually associated with music—was the

heavy-metal opera '2112,' performed in full with various special visual effects. Nevertheless, judging from the enthusiastic audience response, Rush may be bound next for the Capital Centre—where their stack of amplifiers will be less likely to drive dozens of unsuspecting fans out into the lobby, seeking relief from the juggernaut inside."

APRIL 18, 1977
WASHINGTON, DC
LISNER AUDITORIUM, George Washington University campus, 730 21st Street, Northwest.
SUPPORT ACT: Max Webster
TICKETS: $7.00
CAPACITY: 1,490
NOTES: Second date added due to popular demand.

APRIL 20, 1977
ALLENTOWN, PENNSYLVANIA
AGRICULTURAL HALL, Great Allentown Fairgrounds, 1725 Chew Street
SUPPORT ACTS: Angel; Max Webster opened the show.
TICKETS: $6.00 (advance) / $7.00 (at the door, if available)
ATTENDANCE: 4,181 (general admission); sold out
CONCERT GROSS: $22,975

APRIL 21, 1977
POUGHKEEPSIE, NEW YORK
MAIR HALL, MID-HUDSON CIVIC CENTER, 14 Civic Center Plaza. Venue opened on November 28, 1976.
SUPPORT ACTS: Angel; Max Webster opened the show.
TICKETS: $6.00 (advance) / $7.00 (day of) / $6.19 (average)
ATTENDANCE: 2,132
CAPACITY: 2,948
CONCERT GROSS: $13,044
NOTES: There are two venues located inside the Civic Center.

APRIL 22, 1977
BINGHAMTON, NEW YORK
BROOME COUNTY WAR MEMORIAL ARENA, 1 Stuart Street. Venue opened on August 29, 1973.
SUPPORT ACTS: Angel; Max Webster opened the show.
TICKETS: $5.50 (advance) / $6.50 (day of)
ATTENDANCE: 3,067

CAPACITY: 7,000
CONCERT GROSS: $16,868

APRIL 23, 1977
SYRACUSE, NEW YORK
ONONDAGA COUNTY WAR MEMORIAL AUDITORIUM, 515 Montgomery Street. Venue opened on September 1, 1951.
SUPPORT ACTS: Angel; Max Webster opened the show.
TICKETS: $5.50 (advance) / $6.50 (day of)
ATTENDANCE: 4,305
CAPACITY: 8,200
CONCERT GROSS: $24,376
SYRACUSE HERALD-JOURNAL: "The crowd was particularly enthusiastic in their response to such selections as 'Anthem,' 'Lakeside Park,' the title track from perhaps their best-known album, *2112,* 'Twilight Zone,' and 'Something For Nothing.' Banks of lights surrounded the stage, more were placed underneath the drums and, during '2112,' two flaming cans dazzled the senses of the concertgoers."[40]

APRIL 24, 1977
ALBANY, NEW YORK
PALACE THEATRE, 19 Clinton Avenue
SUPPORT ACTS: Angel; Max Webster opened the show.
TICKETS: $5.50 / $6.50 / $6.16 (average)
ATTENDANCE: 2,997; sold out
CONCERT GROSS: $18,471
NOTES: First confirmed performance of "Xanadu." An early ad lists both Styx and Starcastle as "Special Guests," however two reviews confirm the openers as Angel and Max Webster.
KNICKERBOCKER NEWS: "Theirs is plain old hard rock, with some fine guitar playing by Lifeson and clean vocal attacks by Lee. A song in which the two were exceptional was 'Xanadu,' scheduled for recording on their next album, they said."

APRIL 30, 1977
BILLINGS, MONTANA
YELLOWSTONE METRA, Billings MetraPark, 308 Sixth Avenue North. Venue opened on December 10, 1975.
SUPPORT ACT: Max Webster
CAPACITY: 10,903
NOTES: METRA stands for Montana Entertainment Trade and Recreation Arena.

MAY 1, 1977
MINOT, NORTH DAKOTA
MINOT MUNICIPAL AUDITORIUM, 420
Third Avenue SW. Venue opened on
November 15, 1954.
SUPPORT ACT: Max Webster
CAPACITY: 5,066

MAY 2, 1977
YANKTON, SOUTH DAKOTA
NASH GYM, Yankton College campus,
Pine Street, between East 10th Street
and East 12th Street. Venue dedicated
on October 27, 1948.
SUPPORT ACT: Max Webster
CAPACITY: 4,200
NOTES: Most likely the final concert with
Neil performing behind his chrome
Slingerland drum kit. The Yankton
College campus has since been trans-
formed into a minimum-security federal
prison camp.

MAY 4, 1977
OMAHA, NEBRASKA
**OMAHA CIVIC AUDITORIUM MUSIC
HALL**, North 17th Street at Davenport
Street. Venue opened on November 11,
1954.
SUPPORT ACTS: Angel; Max Webster
opened the show.
TICKETS: $5.00, general admission
ATTENDANCE: 2,500
CONCERT GROSS: $12,500

MAY 5, 1977
FARGO, NORTH DAKOTA
CIVIC MEMORIAL AUDITORIUM, 207
Fourth Street North. Venue opened on
December 1, 1959.
SUPPORT ACT: Max Webster
TICKETS: $5.50 (advance)
CAPACITY: 3,300

MAY 6, 1977
ST. PAUL, MINNESOTA
ST. PAUL CIVIC CENTER, 143 West
Fourth Street. Venue opened on January
1, 1973.
SUPPORT ACTS: Styx, Starcastle; Max
Webster opened the show.
TICKETS: $5.00 (advance) / $6.00 (day
of), general admission
ATTENDANCE: 9,293
CAPACITY: 13,000
CONCERT GROSS: $44,234
NOTES: "4 Bands for 5 Bucks!"

MAY 8, 1977
DULUTH, MINNESOTA
DULUTH ARENA, 350 Harbor Drive.
Venue opened on August 5, 1966.
SUPPORT ACTS: Styx; Max Webster
opened the show.
TICKETS: $6.00 (advance) / $7.00
(day of)
CAPACITY: 8,000, general admission
NOTES: This is the last time that Styx
shared a stage with Rush (though Tommy
Shaw would later open on the *Hold Your
Fire* tour).

MAY 9, 1977
WAUSAU, WISCONSIN
NEWMAN HIGH GYM, Newman Catholic
High School, 1130 West Bridge Street.
Founded in 1951. Venue opened in
September 1955.
SUPPORT ACT: Max Webster
TICKETS: $6.00 (advance) / $7.50 (day
of)
CAPACITY: 1,200

MAY 10, 1977
MILWAUKEE, WISCONSIN
RIVERSIDE THEATER, 116 West
Wisconsin. Historic venue opened on
April 29, 1928.
SUPPORT ACT: Max Webster
TICKETS: $5.00 / $6.00 / $7.00
ATTENDANCE: 2, 325; sold out
CONCERT GROSS: $15,103
NOTES: "A WZMF Musical Extravaganza!"
Originally scheduled for May 11, with
tickets already on sale, this date was
moved to the 10th during the final week
of April, with tickets for the 11th still
honored. This concert featured an early
performance of "Xanadu," with the boot-
leg representing the earliest known live
recording of the song. This prerelease
version contains some different lyrics.
"From an ancient book I took a clue" was
replaced by Geddy singing "Miracle of
ages coming true."
SET LIST:
"Bastille Day," "Anthem," "Lakeside
Park," "2112" (5 parts), "Xanadu,"
"Something for Nothing," "By-Tor and the
Snow Dog," "The Necromancer" ("Under
the Shadow"/"Return of the Prince"),
"Working Man," "Finding My Way," Drum
Solo, "Fly by Night," "In the Mood," "What
You're Doing," "Best I Can."
THE MILWAUKEE JOURNAL: "Sound of
Rush, Dynamic, Loud: Rush is far from

your basic hard-rock group. Its ideas are
fresh, its sound exciting. Some have
called Rush a young Led Zeppelin.
Others detect shades of Emerson, Lake
and Palmer or Yes in their music. But
Rush will soon be above these comparisons. It's creating a musical force of its
own. And judging by the ecstatic
response of Tuesday night's crowd, the
message is coming through loud and
clear."

MAY 12, 1977
GREEN BAY, WISCONSIN
BAY THEATRE, 117 South Washington
Street. Historic venue opened on
February 14, 1930.
SUPPORT ACT: Max Webster
TICKETS: $6.50 (advance) / $7.00 (day
of)
ATTENDANCE: 1,500 (approximate);
sold out
GREEN BAY PRESS-GAZETTE: "Blast of
Hot Rock Rushes In: Rush produced an
hour of tension in a relentless rush of
bug-eyed rock and was shouted back for
two encores. Urged on by the frenetic
crowd, the band was hot in nearly every-
thing it did, including 'Working Man,' 'Fly
by Night,' and 'Anthem.'"

MAY 13, 1977
WATERLOO, IOWA
MCELROY AUDITORIUM, 250
Ansborough Avenue
OPENED FOR: Ted Nugent; Michael
Stanley Band opened the show.
TICKETS: $6.50 (advance) / $7.50
(day of)
ATTENDANCE: 5,996[41]
CAPACITY: 8,735
CONCERT GROSS: $38,967
THE WATERLOO COURIER: "The middle
act on the Friday the thirteenth concert
was also giving a repeat performance.
Thirteen months after they graced the
stage for a scant twenty minutes, Rush
was back again, with more tunes, more
confidence, and more sound."

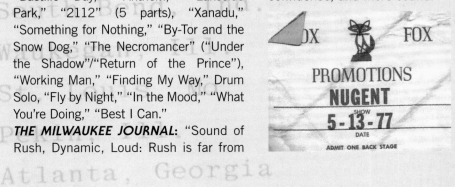

MAY 15, 1977
SPRINGFIELD, ILLINOIS
NELSON CENTER, Lincoln Park, 1601 North Fifth Street. Venue opened in 1974.
SUPPORT ACTS: Max Webster; Cheap Trick opened the show.
TICKETS: Only available at Co-op Tapes and Records outlets[42]
CAPACITY: 4,000 (approximate)
BUN E. CARLOS (CHEAP TRICK DRUMMER): "We didn't actually do a tour with Rush. We did a half-dozen dates with them in a period of about a year. The first one was in Rockford down at the Armory at the end of 1976, and they gave us about five feet of stage (laughs) and uhh . . . no sound check, and they wouldn't speak to us of course. Back then they were just a guitar, bass, and a double kick set of drums. They didn't have a lot of gear to start, but it seemed like each date we played they added stuff! One day Alex would add an acoustic guitar . . . the next date they would have two acoustic guitars on stands . . . the next they would have some synth stuff, and Neil would add bells or chimes and extra stands! So we didn't have much room! (Laughs.) After about the fourth show, they had begun to warm up to us a bit. One day before a show one of their roadies came down to our dressing room with a handful of joints and said 'Geddy sent these and wants you guys to come up and say hello!' They ended up being the nicest guys in the world after they realized that we weren't competing with them or anything."[43]

MAY 17, 1977
LA CROSSE, WISCONSIN
MARY E. SAWYER AUDITORIUM, Sixth Street North and Vine Street. Historic venue opened on August 27, 1955.
SUPPORT ACTS: Max Webster; Brownsville Station opened the show.
TICKETS: $5.50 (advance) / $6.50 (day of)
CAPACITY: 4,000
NOTES: General admission concert.

MAY 18, 1977
MARQUETTE, MICHIGAN
LAKEVIEW ARENA, 401 East Fair Avenue. Venue opened on February 23, 1974.
SUPPORT ACT: Max Webster
TICKETS: $5.50 (advance) / $6.50 (day of)
CAPACITY: 6,200

MAY 20–21, 1977
CHICAGO, ILLINOIS
ARAGON BALLROOM, 1106 West Lawrence Street. Venue dedicated in July 1926.
SUPPORT ACT: Max Webster
TICKETS: $6.50 (advance) / $7.50 (day of)
ATTENDANCE (MAY 20): 5,450
ATTENDANCE (MAY 21): 4,961
CAPACITY: 5,500
CONCERT GROSS (MAY 20): $35,522
CONCERT GROSS (MAY 21): $33,084
NOTES: As fans queued up for the show, Alex, Geddy, and Neil hung out on the balcony, throwing 2112 buttons down to the crowd, causing the street to be closed in both directions. The scene was photographed by Fin Costello, with one of the pictures appearing in the A Farewell To Kings tour book.

MAY 22, 1977
PORT HURON, MICHIGAN
MCMORRAN PLACE ARENA, 701 McMorran Boulevard. Venue opened on January 21, 1960.
SUPPORT ACT: Max Webster
TICKETS: $5.50 (advance), general admission
CAPACITY: 4,642
NOTES: Final North American date of the All The World's A Stage tour. Rush had worked relentlessly on the road since the previous summer, covering most of North America. By now, All The World's A Stage had sold over 400,000 copies, with 2112 poised to reach gold status.

JUNE 1, 1977
SHEFFIELD, ENGLAND
IRWIN MITCHELL OVAL HALL,
SHEFFIELD CITY HALL, Barkers Pool. Venue opened on September 22, 1932.
SUPPORT ACTS: Stray; Andy Dunkley opened the show.
TICKETS: £1.50 / £2.00 / £2.50
ATTENDANCE: 2,271; sold out
NOTES: Rush's first performance outside of North America. In the lead-up to the concert, fate seemed to conspire against them. Rush was unable to present their full show because of differences in British wattage and the fact that British customs held much of their specialized lighting at bay in a holding facility at Heathrow Airport. The crew grappled with all manner of technical difficulties.

When the band was introduced, instead of Alex's driving "Bastille Day" riff, the audience was initially treated to . . . silence. The crew scrambled to fix the problem, and then the band kicked into the song. From that point on, based on Geoff Barton's review in Sounds, the audience belonged to Rush. The band's first tour book is sold on these UK dates.
SET LIST: "Bastille Day," "Anthem," "Lakeside Park," "2112" (all except "Oracle: The Dream"), "Xanadu," "Something For Nothing," "By-Tor and the Snow Dog," "The Necromancer" ("Under the Shadow"/"Return of the Prince"), "Working Man," "Finding My Way," Drum Solo, "Fly by Night," "In the Mood."
GEDDY (ONSTAGE): "Thank you! How are you doing tonight? It's nice to be here in England! This is the very first gig on the tour for us. It's been a long time coming! You'll have to excuse a few technical difficulties tonight. We're just getting used to the English electricity."
SOUNDS: "Rush gain impetus and the kids lap it up—Lee and Lifeson sweep their guitar necks up and around in unison, good and posey without being pretentious, while music hits top gear and then smoothly slips into overdrive. 'Xanadu' follows, a brand-new number which has both Lee and Lifeson playing doublenecked guitars, an amazing sight. Multi-faceted, immaculately constructed, with an abundance of Moog swirlings, it's a potential classic. Rush is an experience, one that I look forward to repeating. As a heavy-rock group they're up there with the front runners."
JOE ELLIOTT (DEF LEPPARD LEAD SINGER): "I saw Rush play 'Xanadu' live at their first ever UK gig. This was at the Sheffield City Hall back in 1977. It was the solitary new song they played on that tour, and as I already had the live album All The World's A Stage, which is pretty much what they played, the only thing I wasn't familiar with. But it stood out as an epic piece. It's eleven minutes long and musically meandering from quiet to very loud all the way through . . . Amazing stuff."[44]

JUNE 2, 1977
MANCHESTER, ENGLAND
FREE TRADE HALL, Peter Street. Historic venue inaugurated on October 8, 1856.

SUPPORT ACTS: Stray; Andy Dunkley opened the show.

TICKETS: £1.50 / £2.00 / £2.50

ATTENDANCE: 2,500; sold out

NOTES: Fans standing in front of the stage before the concert were told that the show would not begin until they returned to their seats. "What You're Doing" closed out the set.

NEW MUSICAL EXPRESS: "The kids knew every note and lyric of each song. There were even odd attempts at lighting matches, á la American audiences. Rush played absolutely amazingly—no sloppiness, total control, all the flash licks, sharp riffs, jerk-off guitar solos brilliantly executed, carefully placed breaks, classy pinnacle vocals that the crowd was thirsting for. Their light show was maybe the best I've ever seen."

MELODY MAKER: "The place was packed, and the audience reaction was extraordinary. Rush delivered everything that was expected. It was a routine celebration of deafening, anglicized rock and I found it dull, depressing and dated. But they did ignite the two-and- a-half thousand denim-clad youngsters into fits of head-shaking frenzy and physical distortion.

JUNE 3, 1977
BIRMINGHAM, WEST MIDLANDS, ENGLAND

BIRMINGHAM ODEON, 139 New Street. Venue opened on September 4, 1937.

SUPPORT ACTS: Stray; Andy Dunkley opened the show.

TICKETS: £1.50 / £2.00 / £2.50

ATTENDANCE: 2,439; sold out

NOTES: After the gig, Alex, Geddy, and Neil signed autographs for the fans queued up outside the stage door.

JUNE 4, 1977
LONDON, ENGLAND

HAMMERSMITH ODEON, 45 Queen Caroline Street. Historic venue opened on March 28, 1932.

SUPPORT ACTS: Stray; Andy Dunkley opened the show.

TICKETS: £1.50 / £2.00 / £2.50

ATTENDANCE: 3,787 (3,485 seats, 302 standing room); sold out

GEDDY (ONSTAGE): "Thank You! How are you doing tonight? It's nice to finally be here in London. We'd like to do something for ya that goes back to our second album. I think we'll do this for the Queen tonight! This is called 'Anthem!'"

LIAM: "At London's Hammersmith Odeon, Alex switched from Marshalls (which he had been using in the States) to Hi-Watt cabinets and Marshall heads. I had set up a deal prior to us going to Britain to purchase them from Hi-Watt, and upon arriving in London I tried to go ahead and pick up the cabinets but ran into a couple of technical difficulties with the distributor. Actually, I had to rent Pete Townshend's Hi-Watt cabinets for the first stretch of the tour until ours were finally delivered. Alex has done a few switches where it's been Hi-Watt heads with Marshall cabinets and vice versa."[45]

SOUNDS, NEIL: "The London gig meant so much to me, having been involved in the city's music scene for so long, to do so well. As it was, I got the same buzz I get when we do a big show in Toronto. It was terrific!"

MELODY MAKER: "Rush of Blood to the Heads: The audience at London's Hammersmith Odeon on Sunday night, at the sound of the first chord being struck, turned into a pack of baying hounds, streaming down to the front on espying their quarry, and proceeded to twitch, strum imaginary guitars, shake clenched fists, flash peace signs, and generally display all the symptoms of a crowd of headbangers reaching nirvana."

JUNE 6, 1977
FRANKFURT, WEST GERMANY

NOTES: Canceled date.

JUNE 8, 1977
STOCKHOLM, SWEDEN

GOTA LEJON, Gotgatan 55. Venue opened on January 25, 1928.

CAPACITY: 1,307 (seats); sold out

JUNE 11, 1977
NEWCASTLE UPON TYNE, ENGLAND

NEWCASTLE CITY HALL, Northumberland Road and College Street. Historic venue dedicated on November 7, 1928.

SUPPORT ACTS: Stray; Andy Dunkley opened the show.

TICKETS: £1.50 / £2.00 / £2.50

ATTENDANCE: 2,133; sold out

JUNE 12, 1977
GLASGOW, SCOTLAND

THE APOLLO, 126 Renfield Street. Venue opened on September 5, 1973.

SUPPORT ACTS: Stray; Andy Dunkley opened the show.

TICKETS: £1.00 / £1.50 / £2.00 / £2.50

CAPACITY: 3,500

LIAM: "The United Kingdom has always been a great place for us to play, probably the heaviest cult-type following. One of the dates we did was in Glasgow, which is where I was born, and to play to an audience which for me held some family was quite an uplifting experience."[46]

JUNE 13, 1977
LIVERPOOL, ENGLAND

LIVERPOOL EMPIRE, Lime Street and London Road. Historic theater opened on March 9, 1925.

SUPPORT ACTS: Stray; Andy Dunkley opened the show.

TICKETS: £1.50 / £2.00 / £2.50

CAPACITY: 2,381

NOTES: Final live performance of "The Necromancer" ("Under the Shadow"/"Return of the Prince").

1. *Hot Rails.* hotrails.co.uk/history/1976.htm
2. Ian Grandy. Facebook.com, September 12, 2015.
3. *Manchester Union Leader.*
4. Interview with Cedrick Kushner. *New Hampshire Union Leader,* September 16, 1976.
5. Interview with Ian Grandy, 2012.
6. *The Stylus.*
7. *Record Week,* October 1976.
8. Music Shoppe itinerary document, September 3, 1976.
9. Promoter staff.
10. Bob Lefsetz. Interview with Keith Brown, 2011.
11. *Ottawa Citizen.*
12. *Winnipeg Tribune.*
13. *The Leader-Post.*
14. Skip Daley. Interview with Mark Cherry, December 17, 2012.
15. *The Seattle Times.*
16. *Walrus.*
17. Skip Daly. Interview with Mike Hirsch, July 17, 2012.
18. Skip Daly. Interview with Mike Hirsch, July 17, 2012.
19. Bill Banasiewicz. Interview with Liam Birt, January 20, 1984.
20. Skip Daly. Interview with Ian Grandy, 2012.
21. *Sacramento Union.*
22. Skip Daly. Interview with Ian Grandy, July 13, 2016.
23. *Springfield Union.*
24. *The Montreal Star.*
25. Skip Daly. Interview with Joe Macre, 2013.
26. *The Indianapolis News,* December 28, 1976.
27. Bill Banasiewicz. Interview with Frank Czuri, April 21, 2017.
28. Skip Daly. Interview with Ian Grandy, 2012.
29. *Columbus Dispatch.*
30. Bill Banasiewicz. Interview with Henry Paul, January 30, 2015.
31. *JamMusic,* January 29, 2010.
32. *PROG* no. 35, April 2013.
33. *Hot Rails.* hotrails.co.uk/history/1977.htm
34. *Daily Press.*
35. Mike Diana, March 11, 1977.
36. Bill Banasiewicz. Interview with Brad Hopkins, October 18, 2015.
37. Interview with Kim Mitchell, *570 News.*
38. *The Cord.*
39. *Fort Wayne Reader.*
40. Andrew Reschke. "Rush sounded great at Memorial concert," *Syracuse Herald-Journal,* April 25, 1977.
41. *Waterloo-Cedar Falls Courier.*
42. *State Journal-Register.*
43. Todd Huston. "Cheap Trick's Bun E. Carlos is alive and well and talks early Trick, touring and more," *Legendary Rock Interviews,* November 5, 2012.
44. Interview with Joe Elliott. *PROG,* January 2015.
45. Bill Banasiewicz. Interview with Liam Birt, January 20, 1984.
46. Bill Banasiewicz. Interview with Liam Birt, January 20, 1984.

Chapter 7
THE A FAREWELL TO KINGS TOUR

Dubbed the "Drive 'til You Die Tour" by band and crew, the *A Farewell to Kings* schedule was relentless, with relatively few nights off and long drives in between back-to-back shows. At one point, recalled Ian Grandy, the band "played twenty-three of twenty-four days and traveled on the one day 'off.' Tiring to even think about . . ."

OPPOSITE: Toronto, Ontario; Geddy onstage.

LEFT: Youngstown, OH; Alex and Geddy perform "Xanadu" with their doublenecks.

The tour kicked off on August 20, 1977, in Ontario—this opening date presumably featuring the live debuts of "A Farewell to Kings," "Closer to the Heart," and "Cygnus X-1." This was the last tour where Rush performed any shows as a supporting act, and nonheadlining shows in general had become rare. Bands that opened for them on this run included Cheap Trick, Tom Petty and the Heartbreakers, and AC/DC. Although concerts early in the tour featured a set list with "Cygnus X-1" preceding "Something for Nothing," those songs eventually traded places, and the set list was standardized for the rest of the tour, with the exception of "Anthem" being occasionally dropped (perhaps to give Geddy's vocal cords a much-needed rest). Thrifty's presented the Rush 1977 Canadian headlining tour, making the group one of the very first to have a corporate sponsorship.

A MODEST MAN FROM MANDRAKE.
TRAVELLED RICH TO THE CITY,
HE HAD A NEED TO DISCOVER
A USE FOR HIS WEALTH

BECAUSE HE WAS HUMAN,
BECAUSE HE HAD GOODNESS,
BECAUSE HE WAS MORAL,
THEY CALLED HIM INSANE,

DELUSIONS OF GRANDEUR
VISIONS OF SPLENDOUR
A MANIC DEPRESSIVE
HE WALKS IN THE RAIN

EYES WIDE OPEN
HEART UNDEFENDED
INNOCENCE UNTARNISHED

CINDERELLA MAN
DOING WHAT YOU CAN
THEY CAN'T UNDERSTAND
WHAT IT MEANS

CINDERELLA MAN
HANG ON TO YOUR PLANS
TRY AS THEY MIGHT THEY CANNOT STEAL
YOUR DREAMS.

THE DISCOVERY OF HIS LOVE'S
BETRAYAL
AND A LOOK IN THE EYES OF
THE HUNGRY

BROUGHT HIM TO A REALIZATION
OF WHAT HE COULD
DO.

HE HELD UP HIS RICHES
TO CHALLENGE THE HUNGRY
PURPOSEFUL MOTION
FOR ONE SO INSANE

THEY TRIED TO FIGHT HIM
JUST COULDN'T BEAT HIM
THIS MANIC DEPRESSIVE
WHO WALKS IN THE RAIN

CINDERELLA MAN
DOING WHAT YOU CAN
THEY CAN'T UNDERSTAND
WHAT IT MEANS

CINDERELLA MAN
HANG ON TO YOUR PLANS
TRY AS THEY MIGHT THE CANNOT
STEAL YOUR DREAMS.

"There are only two ways open to survival for a band in the music business," commented Neil in *RPM Weekly* in 1977. "[O]ne is by a quick capitalization on a manufactured or accidental hit single and the other is a slow, steady climb accomplished by long, hard touring. So, we toured."

The nearly yearlong jaunt wrapped on May 28, 1978, at the Alpine Valley Music Theatre in East Troy, Wisconsin, with a concert gross that set a house record. Over the course of the tour, Rush had performed for more than one million fans.

Following a show at the Santa Monica Civic Auditorium on October 2, 1977, *Performance* magazine noted Rush's rise: "Clearly Rush is one band on the brink of super heights. As to the rigors of the road, by the time their next tour winds up, Rush will have gone from headlining before several hundred thousand fans per tour to . . . who knows?"

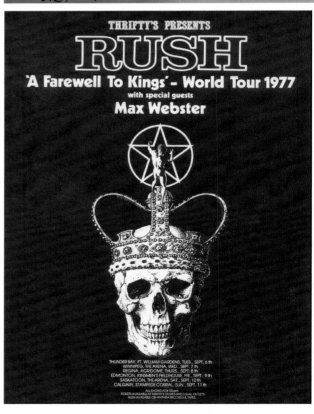

TOP: Geddy's original handwritten lyric sheets for "Cinderella Man."
ABOVE: "A Farewell To Kings" tour advertisement.
OPPOSITE: Youngstown, OH; Alex with his doubleneck.

TOP AND ABOVE: Alex and Geddy onstage.

OPPOSITE: Toronto, Ontario; Alex, Neil, and Geddy onstage.

TOUR HISTORY
A FAREWELL TO KINGS

SET LIST:
"Bastille Day"
"Lakeside Park"
"By-Tor and the Snow Dog" (abridged)
"Xanadu"
"A Farewell to Kings"

"Something for Nothing"
"Cygnus X-1"
"Anthem"
"Closer to the Heart"
2112 (all parts except "Oracle: The Dream")

"Working Man"
"Fly by Night"
"In the Mood"
Drum Solo
Encore: "Cinderella Man"

AUGUST 20, 1977
SUDBURY, ONTARIO
SUDBURY COMMUNITY ARENA, 240 Elgin Street. Venue opened on November 18, 1951.
SUPPORT ACT: A Foot in Coldwater
TICKETS: $5.00 CAD (limited advance) / $6.00 CAD, general admission
CAPACITY: 6,000 (4,760 seats)
NOTES: The opening date of the *A Farewell to Kings Tour* presumably featured the live debut of "A Farewell to Kings," "Closer to the Heart," and "Cygnus X-1." For the first time, Rush set out on the road definitively as a headline act. This was Tony Geranios's first gig as Geddy's keyboard technician; not long after, Tony would come to be known as "Jack Secret."

AUGUST 21, 1977
SAULT STE. MARIE, ONTARIO
SAULT MEMORIAL GARDENS, 269 Queen Street East. Venue opened on February 20, 1949.
SUPPORT ACT: A Foot in Coldwater
CAPACITY: 3,990

AUGUST 22, 1977
NORTH BAY, ONTARIO
MEMORIAL GARDENS, 100 Chippewa Street West. Venue opened on November 15, 1955.
SUPPORT ACT: A Foot in Coldwater
TICKETS: $5.00 (limited advance) / $6.00 CAD
CAPACITY: 4,025 (for general admission concerts)

AUGUST 23, 1977
TORONTO, ONTARIO
CNE GRANDSTAND, EXHIBITION STADIUM, Canadian National Exposition Grounds, Lake Shore Boulevard West. Venue opened on August 5, 1959.
SUPPORT ACT: Max Webster
TICKETS: $7.00 / $8.00 / $9.00 CAD

ATTENDANCE: 21,000; sold out; the *Globe and Mail* lists attendance at 20,800.
GRANDSTAND GROSS: $158,000 CAD; Rush's gross: $97,000 CAD
NOTES: As of this date, "Best I Can" was still the last song of the concert. This marks the band's largest headline show to date. Rush is the only artist to sell out the Grandstand in 1977, among major acts such as: Kansas, The Captain and Tennille, Paul Anka, and Neil Sedaka. During "By-Tor and the Snow Dog," Alex actually played the guitar echoes on two measures before the drum breaks, where they usually just echo. On "2112 The Temples of Syrinx," Neil doesn't play the first trademark fill on the high toms.
GEDDY (ONSTAGE): "This is a song that takes place up there. In the constellation of Cygnus."
THE GLOBE AND MAIL: "Cosmos cruising with Rush, at CNE Grandstand: How far can Peart and his cohorts go in a more artistic direction without overly disturbing the power-tripping sublimation of all that wattage, which is what the mob shows up for? It will be interesting to see how far Rush's fans are willing to travel with them."
THE GLOBE AND MAIL, NEIL: "Since Toronto is our home, we like to make the shows more of an event than a concert."

SEPTEMBER 5, 1977
COCHRANE, ONTARIO
TIM HORTON ARENA, 155 Third Avenue. Venue built in 1961.
SUPPORT ACT: Max Webster
CAPACITY: 800 (no seats)

SEPTEMBER 6, 1977
THUNDER BAY, ONTARIO
FORT WILLIAM GARDENS, 901 Miles Street. Venue opened on March 6, 1951.

SUPPORT ACT: Max Webster
TICKETS: $6.00 (advance) / $6.50 (at the door) CAD
CAPACITY: 5,204
THUNDER BAY CHRONICLE JOURNAL: "Rush making ear specialists rich: Rush hammered and slammered through almost two hours of brain damaging rock, which was comparable to the sound of a car radio amplified through a bullhorn."
THUNDER BAY CHRONICLE JOURNAL, GEDDY: "I don't think we appeal to a certain age group. We appeal to a certain mentality."

SEPTEMBER 7, 1977
WINNIPEG, MANITOBA
WINNIPEG ARENA, 1430 Maroons Road. Venue opened on October 18, 1955.
SUPPORT ACT: Max Webster
TICKETS: $6.00 (advance)/$6.50 (day of) CAD
ATTENDANCE: 4,000 (approximate)
CAPACITY: 11,000
WINNIPEG FREE PRESS: "4,000 fans respond to Rush show: This is one of the finest rock groups to perform here in some time. Though its members profess to prefer the term 'progressive rock' to the erstwhile tag 'heavy metal,' it comes out tight, together, and—wonder of wonders—imaginative. Geddy Lee has a high voice which I found initially disquieting but grew to accept. It fits the total texture of the trio and is employed accurately and musically. But my enthusiastic approbation must be reserved for the drummer, Neil Peart. Wild as it may seem, people, here is a rock drummer with both technique and taste. After a deserved ovation Rush encored with a wild romp featuring drummer Peart. This guy is only great. One could almost hear him in other eras propelling a Lunceford, Herman, or Basie band."

WINNIPEG TRIBUNE: "For any concert-goer of the late 60s and early 70s, watching Rush is like having time stand still."

SEPTEMBER 8, 1977
REGINA, SASKATCHEWAN
AGRIDOME, 1700 Elphinstone Street at Exhibition Park. Venue opened on August 1, 1977.
SUPPORT ACT: Max Webster
TICKETS: $6.00 (advance) / $6.50 (at the door) CAD
CAPACITY: 6,186

SEPTEMBER 9, 1977
EDMONTON, ALBERTA
KINSMEN FIELDHOUSE, 9100 Walter Dale Hill. Venue opened on January 3, 1968.
SUPPORT ACT: Max Webster
TICKETS: $6.00 (advance) / $7.00 (day of) CAD
ATTENDANCE: 4,000 [1]
CAPACITY: 7,500
EDMONTON JOURNAL: "Rush concert a boring affair."

SEPTEMBER 10, 1977
SASKATOON, SASKATCHEWAN
SASKATOON ARENA, 19th Street at First Avenue. Venue opened on October 30, 1937.
SUPPORT ACT: Max Webster
TICKETS: $6.00 (advance) / $6.50 (at the door) CAD
ATTENDANCE: 3,500 (approximate)[2]
CAPACITY: 5,000
SASKATOON STAR-PHOENIX: "The songs were repetitious and generally undistinguishable. Only the encore medley of 'Fly by Night' and 'In the Mood' had any impact. But even in these the vocals were thin and vacant compared to their recorded versions. 'Xanadu' managed to create an ethereal mood. Seductive guitar drifted across the smoke-filled stage and intertwined with tinkling tubular bells. It was a spellbinding interlude . . . "

SEPTEMBER 11, 1977
CALGARY, ALBERTA
STAMPEDE CORRAL, 10 Corral Trail SE. Venue opened on December 15, 1950.
SUPPORT ACT: Max Webster
TICKETS: $6.00 (advance) / $7.00 (day of) CAD
ATTENDANCE: 5,200[3]

CAPACITY: 7,475 (6,475 permanent seats)
NOTES: During Max Webster's encore, Geddy took to the stage dressed as Groucho Marx.
CALGARY HERALD: "The crowd was mesmerized as the trio jumped and pranced and went through a multitude of facial contortions while switching from obtuse space music to a hard-driving rock."
CALGARY HERALD, KIM MITCHEL: "Rush has expensive tastes, but all that stuff really makes me feel ill, sort of like living inside a vacuum cleaner."

SEPTEMBER 12, 1977
KAMLOOPS, BRITISH COLUMBIA
K. X. A. AUDITORIUM, K. X. A. Exhibition Grounds, 479 Chillcotin Street. Venue built in 1971.
SUPPORT ACT: Max Webster
CAPACITY: 1,048
NOTES: Venue unconfirmed.

SEPTEMBER 13, 1977
VANCOUVER, BRITISH COLUMBIA
PACIFIC COLISEUM CONCERT BOWL, Pacific National Exhibition Fairgrounds, 100 North Renfrew. Venue dedicated on January 8, 1968.
SUPPORT ACT: Max Webster
ATTENDANCE: 3,000 (approximate)
CAPACITY: 5,000, 1,208 floor seats
VANCOUVER SUN: "Slandering the sacred halls of truth: Smoke billows from the stage floor (the smoke from Columbia-grown hemp billows in the peanut gallery); somebody in the first tier aims, then fires a rocket flare onto the floor; a backdrop comes alive with mystical oranges and faraway blues as a kind of science fiction Tudor Rock begins whining its way out from the amplifiers. An audience of about 3,000 join in with a lights-out Bic flicking contest, unused toilet paper streamers are tossed into the air. In the mezzanine, appreciation is registered by stepping up to a booth and rescuing Rush from obscurity by purchasing a Rush World Tour '77 T-shirt ($5), or a Rush magazine ($2). An original Rush key chain is going for $1. But when the smoke drifted up to the rafters, and the underprivileged Rush were left alone onstage with only their guitar strings and those absurdly prophetic stage costumes, this is what we witnessed: Pomposity (one cut on the A Farewell to

Arms [sic] album is esoterically called Cygnus X-1, Book One, The Voyage)."

SEPTEMBER 14, 1977
VICTORIA, BRITISH COLUMBIA
VICTORIA MEMORIAL ARENA, 1925 Blanshard Street. Venue opened on July 20, 1949.
SUPPORT ACT: Max Webster
CAPACITY: 5,961 (4,461 permanent seats)

SEPTEMBER 16, 1977
SPOKANE, WASHINGTON
SPOKANE COLISEUM, 1101 North Howard Street. Venue opened on December 3, 1954.
SUPPORT ACTS: UFO; Max Webster opened the show.
TICKETS: $6.50 (advance) / $7.50 (day of)
ATTENDANCE: 5,112
CONCERT GROSS: $34,915
NOTES: Venue aka "The Boone Street Barn."
SPOKANE DAILY CHRONICLE: "Quantity, more than quality, was the emphasis of last night's rock show in the coliseum. On their first stop in the US during their current tour, Rush played old hits and new creations. Among the best were '2112,' 'Xanadu,' 'Working Man,' and 'Fly by Night.' For just three musicians, the band produced an immense wall of sound. And they were tight. But considering their numbers, it probably isn't difficult. The percussive set-up surrounding Neil Peart was elaborate. He handled it all like a wizard. The evening was long (over three-and-one-half hours), for the crowd of about 5,500. But if it's quantity rock and roll they wanted, they picked the right night."

SEPTEMBER 17, 1977
SEATTLE, WASHINGTON
SEATTLE CENTER COLISEUM, 305 Harrison Street. Venue opened on April 21, 1962.
SUPPORT ACTS: UFO; Max Webster opened the show.
TICKETS: $6.50 / $7.50, general admission
ATTENDANCE: 6,000
CONCERT GROSS: $39,000
THE SEATTLE TIMES: "Peart should get special mention for being an unusually intelligent and original drummer."

SUPPORT ACTS: UFO; Max Webster opened the show.

TICKETS: $5.50 (advance)

ATTENDANCE: 1,885 (approximate)[10]

CAPACITY: 2,880

CONCERT GROSS: $10,037[11]

NOTES: Not in SRO's records. One person was arrested for possession of marijuana. The Garden City police department was enraged by the unsupervised partying taking place.

RICHARD COLWELL (GARDEN CITY POLICE CHIEF): "Filthy—absolutely filthy! The building and surrounding area were strewn with trash, beer cans, and liquor bottles after the event. Crowd size and lack of manpower made it impossible for officers to make arrests for drinking and marijuana smoking."[12]

ALAN STOECKLEIN (GARDEN CITY POLICE OFFICER): "It is this officer's opinion that these concerts are not good for our community. There was a strong smell of marijuana in the audience all the time. The type of people these concerts bring in are resistant to authority. We were lucky nothing happened."[13]

OCTOBER 10, 1977
AMARILLO, TEXAS
CIVIC CENTER COLISEUM, 401 South Buchanan. Venue opened on September 3, 1968.

SUPPORT ACTS: UFO; Max Webster opened the show.

TICKETS: $5.00 (limited advance) / $6.00 (all remaining), general admission

CAPACITY: 7,200

NOTES: Onstage, Tony Geranios was not only working as Geddy's keyboard tech, but also assisting Liam with Alex's guitars. He ensures that the band is in tune with the keyboards and Taurus pedals. During the gig, he kept Alex's guitars in tune, and restrung them as needed while (in the days prior to wireless transmitters), Skip and Liam pulled the guitar cords out.

OCTOBER 11, 1977
EL PASO, TEXAS
EL PASO COUNTY COLISEUM, 4100 East Paisano Drive. Venue opened on May 22, 1942.

SUPPORT ACTS: UFO; Max Webster opened the show.

TICKETS: $5.00 (limited advance) / $6.00 (all remaining), general admission

ATTENDANCE: 6,000 (approximate)[14]

CAPACITY: 9,000

NOTES: Band and crew drove to the gig through raging thunderstorms, which caused the National Sound truck to arrive late.

EL PASO HERALD-POST: "Max Webster, UFO, Rush entertain: Rushing out on stage, the group went directly into their act, and the crowd went silent, trying to see if the singer on stage was male or female. Soon there was no question, as lead singer Geddy Lee stood on stage and greeted the crowd. They kept the crowd in a hand-clapping, foot-stomping mood."

THE EL PASO TIMES: "Rush entertained fans with an explosive light and smoke show, and a perfectly executed display of musical talent."

OCTOBER 12, 1977
ODESSA, TEXAS
ECTOR COUNTY COLISEUM, 4201 Andrews Highway. Venue opened on January 19, 1955.

SUPPORT ACTS: UFO; Max Webster opened the show.

TICKETS: $5.00 (limited advance) / $6.00 (all remaining)

CAPACITY: 6,000

NOTES: Venue aka "The Jack-Shack." A twenty-three-year-old man was arrested inside the venue for smoking a joint and possessing a large quantity of a substance believed to be heroin.[15]

OCTOBER 13, 1977
LUBBOCK, TEXAS
MUNICIPAL AUDITORIUM, Lubbock Memorial Civic Center, Texas Tech University campus, 2720 Drive of Champions. Venue opened on March 30, 1956.

SUPPORT ACTS: UFO; Max Webster opened the show.

TICKETS: $5.00 (limited advance) / $6.00 (all remaining), general admission

CAPACITY: 2,839 (1,432 lower and 1,407 balcony)

NOTES: During the afternoon, the band walked into the venue mimicking barnyard animals. Neil was heard emitting a hearty "Moo!" every so often. Howard was seen pacing the floors, concerned that his pyro wouldn't arrive in time from Dallas (the only place he can get it in Texas). The explosives enter the auditorium just before show time.[16]

LUBBOCK AVALANCHE-JOURNAL: "When the three-man band called Rush made their appearance, the front section of seats turned into a jungle, a battleground. Hundreds rushed the stage. The aisles filled. Everybody stood up. Those who had seats were now standing on them. Bodies jockeyed for position, many fans still trying to hold lighters aloft in tribute to music that had not even been played yet. They may earn chuckles with their loose barnyard imitations, but on stage they manage to draw screams of delight with their music."

OCTOBER 14, 1977
TULSA, OKLAHOMA
FAIRGROUNDS PAVILION, Tulsa State Fairgrounds, 4145 East 21st Street. Venue dedicated on March 28, 1932.

SUPPORT ACTS: UFO; Max Webster opened the show.

CAPACITY: 10,000 (4,500 permanent seats)

OCTOBER 15, 1977
OKLAHOMA CITY, OKLAHOMA
CIVIC CENTER MUSIC HALL, 201 North Walker Avenue. Venue opened on October 4, 1937.

SUPPORT ACTS: UFO; Max Webster opened the show.

TICKETS: $7.00 (orchestra)

CAPACITY: 2,477

OCTOBER 16, 1977
ABILENE, TEXAS
TAYLOR COUNTY COLISEUM, 1700 Highway 36. Venue opened on September 8, 1969.
SUPPORT ACTS: UFO; Max Webster opened the show.
TICKETS: $5.00 (limited advance) / $6.00 (all remaining)
ATTENDANCE: 2,703
CAPACITY: 7,000
ABILENE REPORTER-NEWS: "Rush mixes sci-fi, rock for unusual sound: Rush has come a long way since the early days when their chief claim to fame was a publicity campaign that had lead guitarist Alex Lifeson billed as the reincarnation of Jimi Hendrix." [Ed: He is confusing Alex with Frank Marino of Mahogany Rush.] "Sunday night, Rush sounded like a combination of Aerosmith and Pink Floyd. The interstellar music mixed with a mind-boggling (and blinding) stage show represents a merging of technology and music that wasn't possible five years ago. 'Working Man Blues' was their encore." [Ed: The review is mistaking "Working Man" with "Working Man Blues"—a song by Merle Haggard.]
ABILENE REPORTER-NEWS, **PHIL MOGG (UFO LEAD VOCALIST):** "I never even heard of Rush before this tour. We don't consider ourselves the warm-up band. We want to go out and take over."

OCTOBER 17, 1977
AUSTIN, TEXAS
MUNICIPAL AUDITORIUM, 400 South Street. Venue opened on January 5, 1959.
SUPPORT ACTS: UFO; Max Webster opened the show.
CAPACITY: 4,500 (3,000 floor and 1,500 mezzanine seats)
NOTES: In mid-October 1977, Alex, Geddy, and Neil stormed through Texas, which has by now become a strong region for the band. Two months into the tour, Rush was putting forth a powerful and energetic stage show. The expansive Kings material sits nicely with the trio's earlier, more direct music, but provides a broader scope to the overall set. As was stated by Neil in the *All the World's A Stage* liner notes, the live album had indeed marked the "close of chapter one," and the Kings tour now confirms that Rush is a band determined to continue growing and progressing.

OCTOBER 20, 1977
HOUSTON, TEXAS
MUSIC HALL, 801 Bagby Street. Venue opened in April 1938.
SUPPORT ACTS: UFO; Max Webster opened the show.
TICKETS: $7.50
ATTENDANCE: 3,024 (estimate); sold out
HOUSTON CHRONICLE: "Rush is embarrassing Destructo Rock show: Playing to a sellout crowd of youngsters, the band has pushed its music to such an extreme that only the near-deaf or dead could possibly appreciate it on any but the most stoned, adolescent, gut-wrenching level."

OCTOBER 21, 1977
FORT WORTH, TEXAS
WILL ROGERS AUDITORIUM, Will Rogers Memorial Center, 3401 West Lancaster. Historic venue opened on July 18, 1936.
SUPPORT ACTS: UFO; Max Webster opened the show.
CAPACITY: 2,856
NOTES: During "Fly by Night" and the encore of "Cinderella Man," Geddy spoofed on UFO bassist Pete Way, cracking up the opening band as they watch from the side of the stage.
PAIR **MAGAZINE, GEDDY:** "I call it progressive hard rock. It's heavy metal at times but it's not always heavy metal; yet it's always hard rock."
PAIR **MAGAZINE:** "Since the throngs who packed the Ft. Worth hall had probably seen their share of typical rock bands, they were much more appreciative of Rush's different approach to high energy music."

OCTOBER 22–23, 1977
SAN ANTONIO, TEXAS
MUNICIPAL AUDITORIUM, 100 Auditorium Circle. Historic venue opened on April 19, 1926.
SUPPORT ACTS: UFO; Max Webster opened the show.
TICKETS: $6.50 / $7.50
CAPACITY: 5,800 (1,240 portable seats)
NOTES: During this two-day San Antonio stand, Tony Geranios likely received his famous "Jack Secret" nickname.
IAN: "The promoter in San Antonio threw a party for us. I answered a knock on the door and there were four little honeys standing there. I was going to let them in anyway, when they said that Jack Secret had invited them. I said, 'Jack Secret?' Then they pointed to Tony and said 'him . . . that's Jack Secret.' He's been Jack Secret ever since. We used to paraphrase the Bowie song 'The Secret Lives of Arabia' as 'The secret life . . . of Jack Secret.'"[17]

OCTOBER 24, 1977
CORPUS CHRISTI, TEXAS
MEMORIAL COLISEUM, 402 South Shoreline Boulevard. Venue dedicated on September 26, 1954.
SUPPORT ACTS: UFO; Max Webster opened the show.
TICKETS: $6.25 (advance) / $7.25 (at the door)
ATTENDANCE: 6,000 (2,615 permanent seats); sold out
CORPUS CHRISTI CALLER-TIMES: "Rush was in typically fine form last night. The rejuvenation of heavy metal music is largely due to groups like this—groups that can take a basic heavy metal premise, add some clever innovations and shape its music into something truly extraordinary. As if it were written in a script, Rush bade 'Farewell to the Old Kings of Rock' as the older music was laid to rest. There is a new, progressive heavy metal-king and his name is Rush. Lee deserves credit for maintaining his concentration because there was a circus of craziness in full swing backstage all evening long. A running battle between Lee, UFO, and crew members kept things constantly appearing onstage, culminating in UFO's irrepressible bassist Pete Way's candy-striped pants being strung up on Lee's amps. As Rush prepared to return for its well-deserved encore, Lee and Way quickly exchanged clothes, and Way led Rush back out on stage. Running and jumping around and generally being crazy, Way clowned through most of Rush's three-song encore, which began with 'Working Man' and concluded with Lee laughing uncontrollably in Way's arms off the side of the stage following 'Cinderella Man.'"

OCTOBER 25, 1977
BEAUMONT, TEXAS
CITY HALL AUDITORIUM, 765 Pearl Street. Historic venue opened in 1928.
SUPPORT ACTS: UFO; Max Webster opened the show.
CAPACITY: 2,400

OCTOBER 27, 1977
LITTLE ROCK, ARKANSAS
ROBINSON CENTER MUSIC HALL, West Markham Street and Broadway. Historic venue opened on February 16, 1940.
SUPPORT ACTS: UFO; Max Webster opened the show.
TICKETS: $7.00 (all seats)
CAPACITY: 2,609 (1,061 orchestra, 678 mezzanine, 870 balcony)
NOTES: In 1977 the venue was also known as the Little Rock Convention Center.

OCTOBER 28, 1977
SHREVEPORT, LOUISIANA
SHREVEPORT MUNICIPAL AUDITORIUM, 705 Grand Avenue (Elvis Presley Avenue as of 2004). Historic venue dedicated on November 11, 1929.
SUPPORT ACTS: UFO; Max Webster opened the show.
TICKETS: $6.00 (advance), general admission
CAPACITY: 3,007 (572 floor, 545 orchestra, 556 mezzanine, 1334 balcony)

OCTOBER 29, 1977
NEW ORLEANS, LOUISIANA
THE WAREHOUSE, 1820 Tchoupitoulas Street. Historic venue opened on January 30, 1970.
SUPPORT ACTS: UFO; Max Webster opened the general admission concert.
CAPACITY: 3,500

OCTOBER 30, 1977
MEMPHIS, TENNESSEE
DIXON-MYERS HALL, ELLIS AUDITORIUM, 74 Poplar Avenue. Historic venue opened on October 17, 1924.
SUPPORT ACTS: UFO; Max Webster opened the show.
TICKETS: $6.00 (advance)
ATTENDANCE: 4,273; sold out
CONCERT GROSS: $25,638

OCTOBER 31, 1977
ATLANTA, GEORGIA
ALEX COOLEY'S ELECTRIC BALLROOM, corner of Peachtree Street NE and Ponce de Leon Avenue. Building opened in 1913.
ATTENDANCE: 1,100; sold out
NOTES: Special Halloween performance. An early tour ad lists a "tentative" show at the Fox Theatre, but the Alex Cooley appearance is corroborated by a fan account, and Kansas performed the first of two headline nights at the Fox Theatre on this date.

NOVEMBER 1, 1977
MOBILE, ALABAMA
EXPO HALL, Mobile Civic Center, 401 Civic Center Drive. Venue opened on July 9, 1964.
SUPPORT ACTS: UFO; Max Webster opened the show.
CAPACITY: 3,000, general admission

NOVEMBER 2, 1977
DOTHAN, ALABAMA
DOTHAN CIVIC CENTER, 126 North Saint Andrews Street. Venue dedicated on January 25, 1975.
SUPPORT ACT: UFO
CAPACITY: 3,100
NOTES: The actual date is unconfirmed, but most likely November 2, due to tour routing. As with most of the gigs, Max Webster was likely the opener, but that is also unconfirmed.

NOVEMBER 10, 1977
BUFFALO, NEW YORK
NEW CENTURY THEATRE, 511 Main Street. Venue opened on October 17, 1921.
SUPPORT ACTS: UFO; Max Webster opened the show.
TICKETS: $6.00 / $7.00
ATTENDANCE: 3,076; sold out
BUFFALO EVENING NEWS: "Crowd Warms to Rock Night: At the Century Theatre Thursday night a sellout crowd lusted for a night of hot and hard rock 'n' roll—glad to escape the outside's cold, winter-like weather to appreciate the music of Max Webster, UFO, and Rush."

NOVEMBER 11, 1977
BUFFALO, NEW YORK
NEW CENTURY THEATRE, 511 Main Street
SUPPORT ACTS: UFO; Max Webster opened the show.
TICKETS: $6.00 / $7.00
CAPACITY: 3,076
NOTES: Before the gig, Alex goofed around by playing bossa nova chords on his guitar. Geddy checked out the opening acts, while Neil shared some quiet time with Jackie.
THE CITY: "When the set ends, the audience goes wild, calling for encore after encore. Much to the disgust of many rock critics, they actually like this music. It may be a little pretentious, it may be completely humorless, it may be utterly overblown, but it's also magnificent in its way, great theatre, particularly for the very young audience Rush now attracts."

NOVEMBER 12, 1977
NEW YORK, NEW YORK
THE PALLADIUM, 126 East 14th Street. Venue opened on October 11, 1926.
SUPPORT ACTS: UFO; Cheap Trick opened the show.
TICKETS: $6.50 (balcony) / $7.50 (orchestra)
ATTENDANCE: 3,400; sold out
CONCERT GROSS: $24,000
NOTES: Backstage after the concert, the band was presented with their first gold records in America for *A Farewell to Kings*, *2112*, and *All the World's A Stage*, which were certified by the Recording Industry Association of America for sales in excess of 500,000 units. At the ceremony, Phonogram/Mercury president Irwin Steinberg also revealed that Rush had re-signed with Mercury Records.
VARIETY: "A full high-decibel concert at the Palladium featured a strong turn by Rush, solid Canadian trio. Geddy Lee was his screaming, effective self on lead vocals."

NOVEMBER 13, 1977
BALTIMORE, MARYLAND
BALTIMORE CIVIC CENTER, 201 West Baltimore Street. Venue opened on October 23, 1962.
SUPPORT ACTS: UFO; Cheap Trick opened the show.

TICKETS: $6.00 / $7.00 (average: $6.88)
ATTENDANCE: 4,665
CONCERT GROSS: $32,021

NOVEMBER 16, 1977
POUGHKEEPSIE, NEW YORK
MAIR HALL, MID-HUDSON CIVIC CENTER, 14 Civic Center Plaza. Venue opened on November 28, 1976.
SUPPORT ACT: AC/DC
TICKETS: $6.00 / $7.00
ATTENDANCE: 2,645
CAPACITY: 2,948
CONCERT GROSS: $16,225

NOVEMBER 17, 1977
ALBANY, NEW YORK
PALACE THEATRE, 19 Clinton Avenue. Historic venue opened on October 23, 1931.
SUPPORT ACT: AC/DC
TICKETS: $6.50 / $7.50 (average: $6.49)
ATTENDANCE: 2,906; sold out
CONCERT GROSS: $18,852
BON SCOTT (AC/DC LEAD SINGER): "We're going back to America to tour supporting Kiss and a band called Rush that you might not have heard of out there. And we're doing about twelve dates with those bands."[18]
ALEX: "We did a number of dates with AC/DC way back in the mid-1970s. It's funny because we never really got to know each other. We did these shows and we were on a three-act bill or a four-act bill, and I regret it because I think we could've become pretty good friends. We were the same sort of bands at that time, kind of on the fringe and cult following. It would've been an interesting time to create a relationship."[19]

NOVEMBER 18, 1977
SYRACUSE, NEW YORK
ONONDAGA COUNTY WAR MEMORIAL AUDITORIUM, 515 Montgomery Street. Venue opened on September 1, 1951.
SUPPORT ACTS: AC/DC; Crawler opened the show.
TICKETS: $6.00 / $7.00 (average: $6.12), general admission
ATTENDANCE: 5,632
CAPACITY: 8,200
CONCERT GROSS: $34,454

THE DAILY ORANGE (SYRACUSE UNIVERSITY): "The key component in Rush's sound is bassist Geddy Lee's vocals, which run the gamut between bloodcurdling screams and mating calls. Neil Peart's drum work is almost savage in its detonating power, and combined with Alex Lifeson's outstanding guitar work, theatrical prancing, and cascading hari, it proves hypnotizing to fans who nevertheless recount lyrics stanza for stanza."

NOVEMBER 19, 1977
ROCHESTER, NEW YORK
ROCHESTER COMMUNITY WAR MEMORIAL, 100 Exchange Boulevard. Venue opened on October 18, 1955.
SUPPORT ACT: Crawler
TICKETS: $6.50 / $7.50 (average: $6.68), general admission
ATTENDANCE: 10,250; sold out
CONCERT GROSS: $68,461
NOTES: AC/DC was scheduled to play but forced to cancel at the eleventh hour when lead singer Bon Scott was unable to perform after coming down with laryngitis. A few fans indicate that Walter Egan was added to the bill at the last minute. Others state UFO or Cheap Trick as the opener, but according to promoter documents, Crawler was the only support act.

NOVEMBER 20, 1977
ALLENTOWN, PENNSYLVANIA
AGRICULTURAL HALL, Great Allentown Fairgrounds, 1725 Chew Street. Venue opened on September 16, 1957.
SUPPORT ACT: Crawler
TICKETS: $6.50 (advance) / $7.50 (day of)
ATTENDANCE: 4,100 (approximate); sold out[20]
NOTES: AC/DC was slated to play but forced to cancel because Bon Scott was still unable to perform because of laryngitis. Rush makes it up to the audience by giving everyone in attendance a copy of *A Farewell to Kings*.
THE MORNING CALL: "Those with sensitive ears should stay away from Ag Hall Monday night."

NOVEMBER 22, 1977
PITTSBURGH, PENNSYLVANIA
STANLEY THEATRE, 719 Liberty Avenue. Venue opened on February 27, 1928.
SUPPORT ACT: Crawler

TICKETS: $7.00 (all seats)
ATTENDANCE: 2,525; sold out
CONCERT GROSS: $15,303.50

NOVEMBER 23, 1977
PITTSBURGH, PENNSYLVANIA
STANLEY THEATRE, 719 Liberty Avenue
SUPPORT ACT: Crawler
TICKETS: $7.00 (all seats)
ATTENDANCE: 2,525; sold out
CONCERT GROSS: $15,303.50

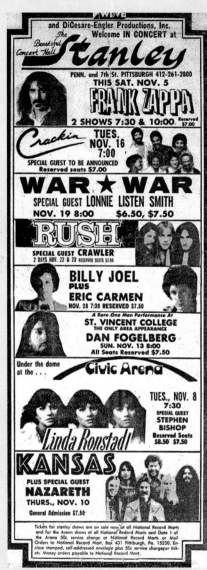

NOVEMBER 24, 1977
JOHNSTOWN, PENNSYLVANIA
CAMBRIA COUNTY WAR MEMORIAL ARENA, 326 Napoleon Street. Venue opened in October 16, 1950.
SUPPORT ACTS: Mark Farner, Cheap Trick opened the show.
TICKETS: $6.00 (advance) / $7.00 (day of)
CAPACITY: 5,500
NOTES: Second Annual WCRO Thanksgiving Jam.

JOHNSTOWN TRIBUNE-DEMOCRAT: "A rowdy crowd showed up Thursday night for a concert featuring Rush, and the crowd's energetic enthusiasm was met by an equally rowdy and rousing concert."

NOVEMBER 25, 1977
PASSAIC, NEW JERSEY
CAPITOL THEATRE, 326 Monroe Street. Venue opened on October 8, 1926.
SUPPORT ACT: Cheap Trick
TICKETS: $6.50 / $7.50 (average: $7.20)
ATTENDANCE: 3,235; sold out
CONCERT GROSS: $23,279

NOVEMBER 26, 1977
UPPER DARBY, PENNSYLVANIA
TOWER THEATER, 69th and Ludlow. Venue opened on October 1, 1928.
SUPPORT ACT: Tom Petty and The Heartbreakers
TICKETS: $4.50 / $5.50 / $6.50 (orchestra)
ATTENDANCE: 3,390; sold out
NOTES: Initially, two nights were scheduled at the Tower (November 26 and 27), as indicated by ads, though tickets never went on sale for the second gig. Although the twenty-sixth sold out in advance, the Erie date was changed to the twenty-seventh, and only one show was performed at the Tower.
TORONTO STAR: "'We're a working band,' says Geddy Lee, sitting backstage in Philadelphia before the opening act goes on. 'We were an opening act for three years before all of this.' He recalls pointing to the mountains of speakers and lights and dry-ice cauldrons. 'We played a lot of towns, a lot of times, for a lot of people, and although we didn't win over every audience, we made friends each night.'"
TORONTO STAR: "Tower Theater, Philadelphia. It's 10:35 p.m. Three-and-a-half thousand teenagers are on their feet at the end of a Rush concert. Their arms punch the air, marking time to a cry that is getting louder and louder: 'We want Rush. We want Rush.'"

NOVEMBER 27, 1977
ERIE, PENNSYLVANIA
ERIE COUNTY FIELDHOUSE, 5750 Wattsburg Road. Venue opened in early 1974.

SUPPORT ACT: UFO
TICKETS: $6.00 (advance) / $7.00 (day of), general admission
CAPACITY: 5,250 (3,750 permanent seats)
NOTES: This date was originally scheduled for November 28, but was moved to the twenty-seventh.

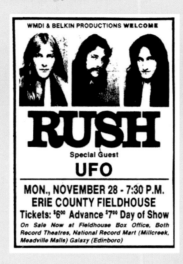

WMDI & BELKIN PRODUCTIONS WELCOME

RUSH
Special Guest
UFO
MON., NOVEMBER 28 - 7:30 P.M.
ERIE COUNTY FIELDHOUSE
Tickets: $6.00 Advance $7.00 Day of Show
On Sale Now at Fieldhouse Box Office, Both Record Theatres, National Record Mart (Millcreek, Meadville Malls) Galaxy (Edinboro)

DECEMBER 2, 1977
FITCHBURG, MASSACHUSETTS
FITCHBURG SHOWCASE CINEMA THEATER, 705 Main Street. Venue opened on February 7, 1929.
AN EVENING WITH RUSH!
TICKETS: $7.00, general admission
ATTENDANCE: 1,751; sold out

DECEMBER 3, 1977
WASHINGTON, DC
WARNER THEATRE, 513 13th Northwest. Venue opened on December 27, 1924.
SUPPORT ACT: City Boy
TICKETS: $7.00
CAPACITY: 1,847

DECEMBER 5, 1977
YOUNGSTOWN, OHIO
TOMORROW CLUB, 213 Federal Plaza West. Venue opened on October 20, 1974.
SUPPORT ACT: Rex
TICKETS: $5.50 (advance) / $6.50 (at the door)
CAPACITY: 2,142

DECEMBER 6, 1977
WHEELING, WEST VIRGINIA
CAPITOL MUSIC HALL, 1015 Main Street. Venue opened on November 29, 1928.

SUPPORT ACT: Lake
TICKETS: $6.00
CAPACITY: 2,501
NOTES: Likely rescheduled from December 14 (as listed in an early advertisement). Rush's Wheeling debut.

DECEMBER 8, 1977
COLUMBUS, GEORGIA
MUNICIPAL AUDITORIUM, 400 Fourth Street. Venue opened on September 6, 1957.
SUPPORT ACTS: Rare Earth, Southern Ash
TICKETS: $6.00
CAPACITY: 3,916, general admission
NOTES: "Four hours of rock and roll madness." Rare Earth is on the bill as late as a day of show article in the *Columbus Examiner*, although a fan account claims they did not perform.
GIL BRIDGES (FOUNDING MEMBER OF RARE EARTH; LEAD VOCALS, SAX, AND FLUTE): "I have absolutely no memory of the gigs we played with Rush. Getting old has taken most all of my memory from the old days."[21]

DECEMBER 9, 1977
LAKELAND, FLORIDA
LAKELAND CIVIC CENTER, 701 West Lime Street. Venue dedicated on November 14, 1974.
OPENED FOR: Bob Seger and the Silver Bullet Band; Nick Jameson opened the show.
TICKETS: $6.00, general admission
CAPACITY: 10,000

DECEMBER 10, 1977
PEMBROKE PINES, FLORIDA
HOLLYWOOD SPORTATORIUM, 17171 Pines Boulevard (Route 820). Venue opened in September 1970.
OPENED FOR: Bob Seger and The Silver Bullet Band; Nick Jameson opened the show.
TICKETS: $5.50 (limited advance) / $6.50 (all seats reserved)
ATTENDANCE: 15,533; sold out
NOTES: Sold-out two weeks prior to the gig. "Anthem" was not performed.

DECEMBER 11, 1977
JACKSONVILLE, FLORIDA
JACKSONVILLE VETERANS MEMORIAL COLISEUM, 1145 Adams Street. Venue dedicated on November 24, 1960.

OPENED FOR: Bob Seger and The Silver Bullet Band; Nick Jameson opened the show.
TICKETS: $6.00 / $7.00
ATTENDANCE: 8,474
CAPACITY: 12,000; 7,923 fixed seats
CONCERT GROSS: $57,988

DECEMBER 12, 1977
ATLANTA, GEORGIA
FOX THEATRE, 660 Peachtree Street, NE. Historic venue opened on December 25, 1929.
SUPPORT ACTS: Cheap Trick, The Motors
TICKETS: $6.75
CAPACITY: 4,678

DECEMBER 13, 1977
KNOXVILLE, TENNESSEE
KNOXVILLE CIVIC COLISEUM, 500 East Church Street. Venue opened on August 20, 1961.
OPENED FOR: Bob Seger and The Silver Bullet Band; Nick Jameson opened the show.
TICKETS: $6.00 / $7.00
CAPACITY: 6,673, general admission
NOTES: Bob Seger postponed this performance to December 30, due to illness. The Michael Stanley Band is special guest and Nick Jameson the opener.
IAN: "There was a Seger gig where we showed up and then were told it was canceled. We didn't even get out of the bus but drove to Detroit instead. I think Bob had hurt his back."[22]

DECEMBER 15, 1977
DETROIT, MICHIGAN
COBO HALL ARENA, 1 Washington Boulevard. Venue opened on October 17, 1960.
SUPPORT ACTS: UFO, The Motors
TICKETS: $8.50
CAPACITY: 11,400
NOTES: At the on-sale date, Detroit police forced the box office to open early, thus avoiding a possible riot. This was the infamous gig where UFO nailed slippers to the stage.
PETE WAY (UFO BASSIST): "We used to have a lot of fun together. Neil was always the quiet one, studying. And Alex and Geddy were always livewires, so we used to have a lot of fun. Actually, I used to travel with Alex and Geddy a lot. I don't know if I can repeat some of the

road stories, because I still go and see Alex and Geddy, and they'd go, 'Thanks Pete,' so I won't, no. We had a lot of fun. Things like Detroit during the *A Farewell to Kings Tour*. They bought those robes, and we put some bedroom slippers on the front of the stage, and a Mickey Mouse drum kit that we bought, and we put it in front of Neil's drums in between the changeover."[23]

DECEMBER 16, 1977
TOLEDO, OHIO
SPORTS ARENA, 1 North Main Street. Venue opened on November 13, 1947.
SUPPORT ACTS: UFO, The Motors
TICKETS: $6.50 (advance) / $7.50 (day of)
CAPACITY: 7,000

DECEMBER 17, 1977
CLEVELAND, OHIO
PUBLIC HALL, 500 Lakeside Avenue. Historic venue opened on April 15, 1922.
SUPPORT ACTS: Edgar Winter's White Trash, The Motors
TICKETS: $6.50 (advance) / $7.50 (day of)
ATTENDANCE: 7,200 (approximate); sold out
SCENE MAGAZINE: "The Canadian power trio rewarded the sellout crowd with a set that was fast and furious—and loud. Rush's music is strangely punctuated, and one wonders if the unexpected, sharp bursts they weave into their songs are artistically inspired or just a ploy to keep the listener's attention from wandering. With Rush's predictable, abrupt style, and their penchant for false endings, their songs have a tendency to sound the same. This tedious similarity was especially evident in overblown, futuristic pieces like '2112' and 'Cygnus X-1.'"

DECEMBER 18, 1977
DAYTON, OHIO
UNIVERSITY OF DAYTON ARENA, 1801 Edwin C. Moses Boulevard. Venue opened on December 6, 1969.
SUPPORT ACT: Grinderswitch
TICKETS: $6.00 (advance) / $7.00 (day of), general admission
ATTENDANCE: 7,544
CAPACITY: 11,078
CONCERT GROSS: $46,943
NOTES: Ram Jam was originally scheduled to open (and was still listed on the

day-of-show ad), but was replaced at the last minute by Grinderswitch, a southern rock band from Warner Robbins, Georgia. In Dayton, Grinderswitch was performing in support of their fourth album, *Redwing*, and was booed off the stage in less than thirty minutes.[24]
THE JOURNAL HERALD: "Rush is essentially technocratic flash, cool and unencumbered. Last night, it didn't even work up a sweat."

DECEMBER 19, 1977
KALAMAZOO, MICHIGAN
WINGS STADIUM, 3600 Van Rick Drive. Venue opened on October 30, 1974.
SUPPORT ACT: Legs Diamond
TICKETS: $6.50 (advance), general admission
CAPACITY: 8,596
KALAMAZOO GAZETTE: "Rush Offers Its Fans A Long, Satisfying Concert."
MICHAEL PRINCE (LEGS DIAMOND KEYBOARDIST/GUITARIST): "I definitely remember that show in Michigan, because as soon as we were done with our set, I rushed (really) out to see Rush and was in amazement the entire show. Musically, we were all pushing boundaries at that time, but what I remember most was that they had the best lights and lighting director I had ever seen—up to that time. He had a perfect sense of rhythm and the lights were so in sync with the music, it was surreal."[25]

DECEMBER 27, 1977
LONDON, ONTARIO
LONDON GARDENS, 4380 Wellington Road South. Venue opened in September 1964.
SUPPORT ACT: Max Webster
ATTENDANCE: 5,000[26]
CAPACITY: 5,075
THE FREE PRESS: "Rush doubled its audience for this second appearance of 1977 at London Gardens. With Rush, everything is on the beat—lights, flash pots; the whole metal rock shot comes off the end of Peart's sticks."

DECEMBER 28, 1977
KITCHENER, ONTARIO
KITCHENER MEMORIAL AUDITORIUM, 400 East Avenue. Venue opened on May 24, 1951.
SUPPORT ACT: Max Webster
TICKETS: $7.00 CAD, all seats reserved

Chapter 8
THE TOUR OF THE HEMISPHERES

T he ten-month Tour of the Hemispheres, so named by the band, was another marathon outing that brought Rush to almost every corner of North America. It included a return to the UK and a first-ever tour of mainland Europe. And of course, as was now standard operating procedure, the tour kicked off with a run of Canadian dates. "Our time is planned from now until next June," Geddy said in October 1978.

Everything about Rush's live show continued to grow. The live production now included over 200 lights (including 159 spotlights at 1,000 watts each), a Nick Prince–directed film highlighting the "Cygnus X-1" epic, over $150,000 worth of sound equipment, and over $80,000 of band gear—including two amp-lined walls, Neil's black Slingerland kit with twenty-three microphones, an Oberheim synthesizer, two sets of Moog pedals, and nine prerecorded tapes.

"Rush makes rock and roll look so magnificent," read a review of the October 27, 1978, show at Northlands Coliseum in Edmonton, Alberta. "With a barrage of speakers, an array of instruments, and visual effects second to none, percussionist Neil Peart, bass-guitarist-singer Geddy Lee, and Alex Lifeson are putting on a two-hour show of magnificent proportions."

The music performed on the Tour of the Hemispheres was a reflection of the band at their progressive rock pinnacle, featuring many of the longer concept pieces. "In a long piece you've got a lot more freedom to feel around with dynamics and change things around a bit," Alex told *Sounds* in 1979. The set list, which featured the *Hemispheres* album in its entirety, side one of *2112* (except for "Oracle: The Dream"), and both parts of the "Cygnus" suite, remained the same throughout the tour until "Circumstances" was dropped during the UK dates. In addition, "Something for Nothing" and "Cygnus X-1" were dropped from the set list for the remaining dates of the continental European tour.

On December 14, 1978, *Hemispheres* was certified gold by the Recording Industry Association of America (RIAA). On March 21 of the next year, Rush won their second consecutive Juno Award for Group of the Year. Additionally, *Hemispheres* was nominated for Best Selling Album and Terry Brown was nominated for Best Producer. *Billboard* proclaimed, "Rush presently [are] Canada's biggest tour-grossing band internationally and the hard-edged trio has sold hundreds of thousands of albums in Canada in the past few years."

Rush were now a full-fledged success, having earned their stripes largely through relentless touring and word of mouth. Commented Alex, "It's nice for a band like

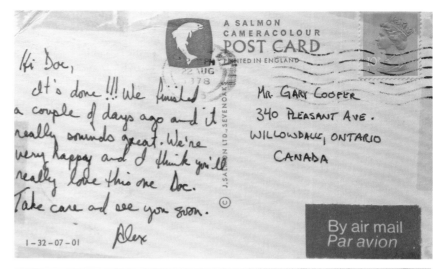

Boston to come out with a big hit album or any of those type of bands and become successful like that, but it's not nearly as satisfying as knowing that the people are there and they've been with you for four or five years."

Reasoned Geddy: "We're unfashionable, we're not trendy, and we do things people think are pretentious. But if a critic pans your album, what does it really mean? If an album is good, people will find out about it on their own."

OPPOSITE TOP: Toronto, Ontario; Alex onstage.

OPPOSITE BOTTOM: Toronto, Ontario; Alex, Neil, and Geddy onstage.

TOP: Postcard from Alex to his band friend Doc Cooper expressing excitement about the completion of the *Hemispheres* recording sessions.

ABOVE: Alex in the studio.

OPPOSITE: Geddy on the road.
ABOVE: Geleen, Holland; Rush onstage at the Pinkpop Festival.

TOUR HISTORY
HEMISPHERES

OCTOBER 14, 1978
KINGSTON, ONTARIO
KINGSTON MEMORIAL CENTRE ARENA,
303 York Street. Venue opened in
November 1951.
SUPPORT ACT: Aerial
ATTENDANCE: 2,825
CAPACITY: 3,300
NOTES: The opening date of the Tour of
the Hemispheres featured the live debut
of "Hemispheres," "Circumstances,"
"The Trees," "La Villa Strangiato," and
"A Passage to Bangkok," the latter an
older song that could now be performed
live, thanks to technological advances. In
what had become the band's standard
approach, the Hemispheres Tour kicked
off with a run of Canadian dates.

OCTOBER 15, 1978
GUELPH, ONTARIO
GUELPH MEMORIAL GARDENS, 33
Carden Street. Venue opened on
November 11, 1948.
SUPPORT ACT: Aerial
TICKETS: $7.00 CAD, all seats
ATTENDANCE: 1,427
CAPACITY: 4,248

OCTOBER 17, 1978
NORTH BAY, ONTARIO
MEMORIAL GARDENS, 100 Chippewa
Street West. Venue opened on
November 15, 1955.
SUPPORT ACT: Aerial
TICKETS: $6.00 (limited advance) /
$7.00 CAD, general admission
ATTENDANCE: 994
CAPACITY: 4,025 for general admission
concerts

OCTOBER 18, 1978
SUDBURY, ONTARIO
SUDBURY COMMUNITY ARENA, 240
Elgin Street. Venue opened on
November 18, 1951.

SUPPORT ACT: Aerial
TICKETS: $6.00 (limited advance) /
$7.00 CAD, general admission
ATTENDANCE: 1,537
CAPACITY: 6,000
NOTES: The stage right crew was kept
busy by Alex, who kept getting his guitar
cord tangled up.
LAMBDA **(LAURENTIAN UNIVERSITY):**
"Rush Controls: No matter what song,
they played with a surging energy that
radiated fourth and was felt by every
member of the audience."
LAMBDA, **GEDDY:** "It's like growing up.
You just keep getting better every year."

OCTOBER 20, 1978
THUNDER BAY, ONTARIO
FORT WILLIAM GARDENS, 901 Miles
Street. Venue opened on March 6,
1951.
SUPPORT ACT: Streetheart
TICKETS: $6.00 CAD, limited advance
ATTENDANCE: 1,685
CAPACITY: 5,024

OCTOBER 21, 1978
WINNIPEG, MANITOBA
WINNIPEG ARENA, 1430 Maroons
Road. Venue opened on October 18,
1955.
SUPPORT ACT: Streetheart
TICKETS: $7.00 CAD
ATTENDANCE: 5,549
NOTES: Ten audience members were
arrested on various drug charges.[1]
THE TRIBUNE: "Rush serves fans extra-
loud drivel: The band's sound is defi-
nitely dated, circa the turn of the current
decade, and does not justify the fans'
enthusiastic response. The two hours of
incoherent drivel could and should be
shortened to an hour."
WINNIPEG FREE PRESS: "About 6,000
rock fans turned out for Rush at the
Winnipeg Arena. They eagerly savored

two hours of frantic hard rock, played
almost nonstop. But two straight hours
of driving, screaming rock, even though
it was presented with all possible finesse,
began to dull the senses. While there is
no doubt that Rush is a fine hard rock
band with a good grasp on the style they
have chosen, I think they need to try a
few new directions. It would add greater
depth and dimension to their work without hurting their image or their sound."

OCTOBER 22, 1978
BRANDON, MANITOBA
KEYSTONE CENTRE ARENA, 1175 18th
Street. Venue opened on April 2, 1973.
SUPPORT ACT: Streetheart
TICKETS: $7.50 CAD
ATTENDANCE: 1,442
CAPACITY: 5,022

OCTOBER 24, 1978
REGINA, SASKATCHEWAN
AGRIDOME, 1700 Elphinstone Street at
Exhibition Park. Venue opened on
August 1, 1977.
SUPPORT ACT: Streetheart
TICKETS: $6.75 (limited advance) /
$7.75 (general admission)
ATTENDANCE: 3,183
CAPACITY: 6,186
NOTES: *Hemispheres* was released in
North America on this date. (SRM-1-
3743, ANR-1-1014). In Canada, the first
10,000 albums contained a special Rush
T-shirt offer.

OCTOBER 25, 1978
SASKATOON, SASKATCHEWAN
SASKATOON ARENA, 19th Street at
First Avenue. Venue opened on October
30, 1937.
SUPPORT ACT: Streetheart
TICKETS: $7.00 CAD (day of)
ATTENDANCE: 2,140
CAPACITY: 5,000

SASKATOON STAR-PHOENIX: "The special effects Rush trundled out for the occasion held the audience spellbound. Young people wandered about at the bases of the monolithic banks of speakers, grogged on sound. Music rattled the arena's superstructure. Sensory overdose. It was an ecstatic, if slightly benumbed audience that left the arena."

OCTOBER 27, 1978
EDMONTON, ALBERTA
NORTHLANDS COLISEUM, 7424 118th Avenue Northwest. Venue opened on November 10, 1974.
SUPPORT ACT: Streetheart
TICKETS: $6.50 / $7.50 CAD
CAPACITY: 13,049

OCTOBER 28, 1978
CALGARY, ALBERTA
STAMPEDE CORRAL, 10 Corral Trail SE. Venue opened on December 15, 1950.
SUPPORT ACT: Streetheart
TICKETS: $7.50 (advance) CAD
CAPACITY: 7,475 (6,475 permanent seats)

OCTOBER 29, 1978
LETHBRIDGE, ALBERTA
LETHBRIDGE SPORTSPLEX, 2510 Scenic Drive South. Venue opened in September 1974.
SUPPORT ACT: Streetheart
TICKETS: $6.50 (advance) / $7.50 (day of) CAD
CAPACITY: 7,100, general admission
LETHBRIDGE HERALD: "On stage, their role as epic storytellers is helped along by a gigantic screen in the background displaying star voyages and multitudes of flashing colors as the space opera 'Cygnus X-1' unfolded. They move quickly into 'Hemispheres' to complete the saga of the pilot who disappears in space."

OCTOBER 31, 1978
KAMLOOPS, BRITISH COLUMBIA
K. X. A. AUDITORIUM, K. X. A. Exhibition Grounds, 479 Chillcotin Street. Venue built in 1971.
SUPPORT ACT: Streetheart
CAPACITY: 1,048
NOTES: Canceled date. In the middle of three days off in Vancouver, the crew celebrated Halloween by getting costumes from a local shop and hitting the bar. Ian made a memorable appearance as a Canadian Mountie, playing a prank for the ages.
IAN: "On Halloween, I heard that some of the crew had gone to a costume place and were hitting a bar later. When I finally got to the costume place, all that was left was a Mountie hat, jacket, pants, black duct-taped boots, and shades. In one of the rooms, people were getting 'tuned up.' So, in costume, I knock hard and announce 'R.C.M.P. OPEN THE DOOR NOW!! The room goes silent, the door opens, and I stride in and bark 'Everybody in this room is under arrest!' Five long seconds pass and then someone says, 'It's Ian.' One of the guys later said 'Man . . . in a foreign country, with lines on the mirror and a cop telling me I'm busted . . .' Anyway, that was my best prank ever."

NOVEMBER 2, 1978
VICTORIA, BRITISH COLUMBIA
VICTORIA MEMORIAL ARENA, 1925 Blanshard Street. Venue opened on July 20, 1949.
SUPPORT ACT: Streetheart
TICKETS: $6.50 / $7.50 CAD
ATTENDANCE: "Nearly 4,000"[2]
CAPACITY: 5,961 (4,461 permanent seats)
NOTES: During the show, a sixteen-year-old male detonated an explosive device in the men's bathroom at the south-end mezzanine, causing an estimated $500 in damages, according to the *Victoria Times*. The teen was detained for police and promptly arrested.

NOVEMBER 3, 1978
NANAIMO, BRITISH COLUMBIA
FRANK CRANE ARENA, Beban Park Complex, 2300 Bowen Road. Venue opened on January 2, 1976.
SUPPORT ACT: Streetheart
CAPACITY: 2,906
NOTES: Venue aka Beban Park Arena.

NOVEMBER 4, 1978
VANCOUVER, BRITISH COLUMBIA
PACIFIC COLISEUM CONCERT BOWL, Pacific National Exhibition Fairgrounds, 100 North Renfrew. Venue dedicated on January 8, 1968.
SUPPORT ACT: Streetheart
CAPACITY: 8,000 (1,208 floor seats)
NOTES: Alex's guitar went out during the early section of "By-Tor and the Snow Dog." Concert Bowl capacities varied between 5,000 and 8,000 total seats.

NOVEMBER 6, 1978
PORTLAND, OREGON
MEMORIAL COLISEUM, 1401 North Wheeler. Venue opened on November 3, 1960.
SUPPORT ACT: Pat Travers Band
TICKETS: $7.50 (advance) / $8.50 (general admission)
ATTENDANCE: 11,000
CONCERT GROSS: $83,268
NOTES: *Billboard* lists gross as $83,298. Robert "Fuzzy" Frazer's first date working for Rush as part of the National Sound crew.

NOVEMBER 7, 1978
SEATTLE, WASHINGTON
SEATTLE CENTER COLISEUM, 305 Harrison Street. Venue opened on April 21, 1962.
SUPPORT ACT: Pat Travers Band
TICKETS: $7.50 / $8.50
ATTENDANCE: 13,100; sold out
CONCERT GROSS: $98,930
NOTES: Geddy was battling a case of laryngitis and the show was almost canceled, but he reluctantly took the stage. Ironically, later in the year, KZOK-FM held their annual Puget Sound Music Awards, where this gig was chosen as the Best Seattle Concert of 1978. Rush won by a wide margin over Styx and Van Halen. One thousand tickets, which were slated for distribution in the Tacoma area, were stolen on October 3.[3]
SEATTLE DAILY TIMES: "Lee's voice is an acquired taste, but within the context of Rush's extremely intense music it works perfectly. You can hear what he's singing above the din of heavy metal and often he has interesting things to say."

NOVEMBER 8, 1978
SPOKANE, WASHINGTON
SPOKANE COLISEUM, 1101 North Howard Street. Venue opened on December 3, 1954.
SUPPORT ACT: Pat Travers Band
TICKETS: $8.00
ATTENDANCE: 6,000 (approximate)
CAPACITY: 8,500
SPOKANE DAILY CHRONICLE: "Peart is one of the best drummers ever to set up on the Coliseum stage. It's hard to believe that human hands can move that fast. His drum solo made others seem like children with pots and pans. As always, acoustics were poor, and words

Hemispheres album, the band has stretched its ideas, allowing for an exploration that few trios have the instrumentation to muster. But while Rush has come to demonstrate a talent for pacing, chord changes, dynamics and showmanship, their repetitive music is too contrived for spontaneity."

DECEMBER 8, 1978
GREEN BAY, WISCONSIN
BROWN COUNTY VETERANS MEMORIAL ARENA, 1901 South Oneida Street. Venue opened on November 11, 1957.
SUPPORT ACT: Golden Earring
TICKETS: $6.50 (advance) / $7.50 (day of), general admission
ATTENDANCE: 4,500 (approximate)
CAPACITY: 7,000
NOTES: Just ten minutes into the band's performance, a shirtless climber was discovered eighty feet above the crowd. A spotlight operator shined a beam on him, and the man waved to the crowd. He climbed the rafters above the audience for an hour, while an unaware Rush ran through their set. Eventually, the seventeen-year-old came down and was taken to a local hospital suffering from cuts, bruises, and alcohol intoxication.
GREEN BAY PRESS-GAZETTE: "Rush Plays at Peak Intensity: Its songs run forever, deal with deep thoughts and are giant in scope for a three-man outfit. Of course, it is amplified to the hilt. Rush socks you in the eye with visual effects. Rolling fog, flash pots, and excited colored lights are part of the show. Rush's production company has an added dimension as it plays motion picture shots of interstellar travel on a screen behind the band. At the end of the show, big and blinding lights flashed at the crowd. The intended impression was a glaring landing by invaders from space. An ominous voice told the audience, 'We have assumed control.' If your tastes run to things loud, long, and spectacular, Rush provides the licks. Audience report: There was staggering and lurching among some of the concertgoers due to surreptitious drinking and inhaling of controlled substances which were secreted under heavy winter clothes. The town-and-gown crowd was elsewhere Friday evening."

DECEMBER 9, 1978
ST. PAUL, MINNESOTA
ST. PAUL CIVIC CENTER, 143 West Fourth Street. Venue opened on January 1, 1973.
SUPPORT ACT: Golden Earring
TICKETS: $6.50 (advance) / $7.50 (day of), general admission
CAPACITY: 13,000
CONCERT GROSS: $76,807

DECEMBER 10, 1978
DES MOINES, IOWA
VETERANS MEMORIAL AUDITORIUM, 833 Fifth Avenue. Venue opened on February 1, 1955.
SUPPORT ACT: Golden Earring
TICKETS: $7.00 (advance) / $8.00 (day of)
CAPACITY: 14,000

DECEMBER 11, 1978
KANSAS CITY, MISSOURI
MUNICIPAL AUDITORIUM ARENA, 301 West 13th Street. Historic venue dedicated on October 13, 1936.
SUPPORT ACT: Golden Earring
TICKETS: $7.50 (advance) / $8.50 (day of) (average: $7.79), general admission
ATTENDANCE: 9,250
CAPACITY: 10,360
CONCERT GROSS: $72,029

DECEMBER 13, 1978
ST. LOUIS, MISSOURI
THE CHECKERDOME, 5700 Oakland Avenue. Venue opened on September 23, 1929.
SUPPORT ACT: Golden Earring
TICKETS: $8.00
ATTENDANCE: 13,300 (approximate)
CAPACITY: 18,940
NOTES: On the previous evening, the band and crew went to see the Montreal Canadians play the Blues as guests of the Canadians who scored a 6–0 victory. "It was a really good time," according to Neil. "Geddy [had] some pals on the team."[13]
ST. LOUIS TIMES: "Rush, a three-man rock orchestra from Toronto, walked onstage at the Checkerdome into a sea of warm light. More than 13,000 persons were on hand to salute their arrival with blazing cigarette lighters and small torches. A few were even launching bottle rockets and firecrackers from the balconies. Rush responded with a

brilliant two-hour concert. Rush has progressed into one of the foremost musical forces and performing ensembles in the world. Like all great musical forces, it has assimilated and synthesized the best elements from a wide range of sources and forged those elements into its own powerful and distinctive musical identity."

DECEMBER 14, 1978
CHICAGO, ILLINOIS
INTERNATIONAL AMPHITHEATRE, 4220 South Halsted Street. Venue opened on December 1, 1934.
SUPPORT ACT: Starz
TICKETS: $9.50
ATTENDANCE: 10,700; sold out

DECEMBER 15, 1978
CHICAGO, ILLINOIS
INTERNATIONAL AMPHITHEATRE, 4220 South Halsted Street
SUPPORT ACT: Starz
TICKETS: $9.50
ATTENDANCE: 10,700; sold out
NOTES: Mercury Executives presented Alex, Geddy, and Neil with their fourth gold record in America for *Hemispheres*.

DECEMBER 16, 1978
CHICAGO, ILLINOIS
INTERNATIONAL AMPHITHEATRE, 4220 South Halsted Street
SUPPORT ACT: Starz
TICKETS: $9.50
ATTENDANCE: 10,700; sold out
WALRUS: "The lighting was superb!"

DECEMBER 17, 1978
MADISON, WISCONSIN
DANE COUNTY VETERANS MEMORIAL COLISEUM, Dane County Expo Center Fairgrounds, 2200 Rimrock Road. Venue opened on March 16, 1967.
SUPPORT ACT: Missouri
TICKETS: $7.50 (advance) / $8.50 (day of), general admission
ATTENDANCE: 7,500
CAPACITY: 12,000[14]
VARIETY: "Canadian heavy metal sci-fi rock trio Rush fell far short of selling out the Dane Coliseum, but nonetheless pleased its fans with its technical proficiency and special effects-filled show."
WALRUS: "Excellent musicianship."

DECEMBER 19, 1978
LONDON, ONTARIO
LONDON GARDENS, 4380 Wellington Road South. Venue opened in September 1964.
SUPPORT ACT: Wireless
CAPACITY: 5,300
NOTES: Venue aka Treasure Island Gardens. This date is not in SRO's official records but is listed in an Anthem Records press release. CHUM-FM in Toronto held a contest that had aspiring artists design a Rush Christmas card. Winning entries, along with twenty-five runners-up, had their ideas displayed in downtown Toronto. Kevin Jutzi, of Kitchener, was the winner. Jutzi received an entire Rush catalog, and his design was used as the group's official Christmas card in 1979. He also attended the December 31, 1978, show as a guest of the band.[15]

DECEMBER 20, 1978
KITCHENER, ONTARIO
KITCHENER MEMORIAL AUDITORIUM, 400 East Avenue. Venue opened on May 24, 1951.
SUPPORT ACT: Wireless
TICKETS: $7.50 CAD
CAPACITY: 6,733
NOTES: Ian surprised the band by playing the "Death to the Peasants" intro tape from 1975. Wireless was now a quartet, touring in support of their second Anthem release, *Positively Human, Relatively Sane*. Ray Danniels had signed the band and become their manager earlier in the year.
IAN: "I had found the old 'Peasants' intro tape in a drawer and tested it and decided to use it one more time as a joke. Lurch told the band to be ready, and when they were coming to the stage they all laughed when they heard it. The boys took it in stride."[16]

DECEMBER 21, 1978
OTTAWA, ONTARIO
OTTAWA CIVIC CENTRE, Lansdowne Park, 1015 Bank Street. Venue opened on December 29, 1967.
SUPPORT ACT: Wireless
TICKETS: $7.50 CAD
ATTENDANCE: 6,000 (approximate)
CAPACITY: 10,000
NOTES: The stage was moved forward to accommodate the rear-projection screen. Toward the end of the set, the band threw in a little holiday cheer by performing a short version of "The First Noel."
THE OTTAWA CITIZEN: "The Civic Centre was the scene of frenzied hand-clapping, foot-stomping, building-shaking mayhem as Rush returned with its dazzling array of musical and lighting wizardry. Rush's performance proved the band has come a long way since 1974. With five albums out, it has gained a loyal following who have come to expect perfection from the band. And the heavy metal threesome delivered. In answer to the crowd's chants for more, Rush relied on cuts from its earlier albums. 'In the Mood' featured a drum solo by Peart. It was one of the most memorable solos a percussionist has made in concert in Ottawa in a long while."

DECEMBER 27, 1978
MONTREAL, QUEBEC
MONTREAL FORUM CONCERT BOWL, 2313 Saint Catherine Street West. Historic venue opened on November 29, 1924.
SUPPORT ACT: Wireless
TICKETS: $7.00 CAD
ATTENDANCE: 6,500[17]
CAPACITY: 7,500
MONTREAL GAZETTE: "Lee and Lifeson lurched and darted about the stage as if on hot coals. The crazed act mesmerized its young fans."
YOUTH MAGAZINE **(MONTREAL):** "Little new in Rush show."

DECEMBER 28–29, 1978
TORONTO, ONTARIO
MAPLE LEAF GARDENS, 60 Carlton Street. Historic venue opened on November 12, 1931.
SUPPORT ACT: Wireless
TICKETS: $9.50 CAD
ATTENDANCE: 12,000 per show (approximate); sold out
TORONTO STAR: "Imagine the cheer that would result if Daryl Sitler scored the Stanley Cup-winning goal in the seventh game, in overtime, before a packed Maple Leaf Gardens against the dreaded Montreal Canadians. Loud? Perhaps. But it would be a mere whisper compared to the roar produced by the 11,000 fans who turned up for the first of Rush's three homecoming concerts at the Gardens last night. This was the titanic of hellos, the ultimate ho-ha complete with a standing ovation, hundreds of lit matches and a bevy of nervous ushers."
MAPLE LEAF GARDENS MEMORIES AND DREAMS 1931-1999: "The band might have become a big deal internationally, selling two million albums worldwide and grossing an estimated $18 million in 1978, but in Toronto it's just three guys from Willowdale returning as your basic, paranormal superstars."
GEDDY: "We got word that 'the powers that be' would not permit a billboard of our *Hemispheres* album cover to promote an upcoming performance at Maple Leaf Gardens. They said, 'No way. We're not allowing this naked man on Yonge Street,' which is the main street in Toronto. So we said, 'Okay, we'll compromise, we'll paint leotards on him.' We felt that wouldn't really interfere with the idea that we were trying to get across. And they said 'No.' And then what really came out was the fact that it was the brains that offended them. They said, 'No brains on Yonge Street. You can't put these gigantic brains on Yonge Street. It will offend people.' They said no brains, so we ended up using our pictures instead."[18]

DECEMBER 30, 1978
PETERBOROUGH, ONTARIO
PETERBOROUGH MEMORIAL CENTRE, 121 Lansdowne Street West. Venue opened on November 8, 1956.
SUPPORT ACT: Wireless
TICKETS: $8.50 CAD
CAPACITY: 5,000
NOTES: This date was canceled with tickets already on sale.
MICHAEL LANTZ (RUSH FAN): "I had tickets but turned them in for the refund. The only reason they gave us for the cancellation was that Rush played three times in four nights at Maple Leaf Gardens with Peterborough happening on the off night. Someone decided it was too much to tear down, set up in Peterborough, then get back to Toronto for the New Years' Eve show. Maybe the boys just wanted time off to spend with their families."[19]

DECEMBER 31, 1978
TORONTO, ONTARIO
MAPLE LEAF GARDENS, 60 Carlton Street
SUPPORT ACT: Max Webster
TICKETS: $11.50 CAD

ATTENDANCE: 12,000 (approximate); sold out

NOTES: Following "La Villa Strangiato," Geddy led the crowd in a countdown to the new year, before the band dove into "2112." The trio of sellout dates set a new Indoor Canadian Attendance Record.

BILLBOARD: "The most significant change in Rush's sound is vocalist Geddy Lee's switch from the shrill voice of old to the almost melodic instrument he uses today. Where a year ago he had intentionally screamed out the lyrics to 'Closer to the Heart,' he has now dropped an octave and has gained control in his delivery. While no fault is to be found in the performance, the trio appears to have lost its stage presence—while Lifeson and Lee once charged around the stage, they now stand practically motionless. And the aristocratic image the group presents on its album covers lost all impact seeing it onstage dressed in what looked like ordinary street clothes."

NEIL: "We did the same thing (for New Year's Eve) last year. We had champagne on the stage at midnight, streamers and everything. It was a special kind of party and that's why we're doing it again. That, coupled with the fact that we're playing not far from home."[20]

JANUARY 11, 1979
BOSTON, MASSACHUSETTS
MUSIC HALL, 252–272 Tremont Street. Historic venue opened on October 17, 1925.
SUPPORT ACT: Starz
TICKETS: $7.50 / $8.50 (average: $8.36)
ATTENDANCE: 3,780 (Anthem/SRO)
CONCERT GROSS: $31,750
NOTES: An abrupt power outage near the end of "Xanadu" brought the concert to a halt for several minutes. When the power returned, the band checked out their instruments, with Geddy playing what will become the keyboard run to "Tom Sawyer" on his Minimoog. During "Anthem," Geddy added a little vocal improv by singing "power isn't all that money buys, is it Neil?" Venue opened as the Metropolitan Theatre in 1925 and was renamed the Music Hall in 1962.
THE BOSTON GLOBE: "The Rush: All flash no fire."

JANUARY 12, 1979
SPRINGFIELD, MASSACHUSETTS
SPRINGFIELD CIVIC CENTER, 1277 Main Street. Venue opened on September 22, 1972.
SUPPORT ACT: Starz
TICKETS: $7.50
ATTENDANCE: 3,200

JANUARY 13–14, 1979
NEW YORK, NEW YORK
PALLADIUM, 126 East 14th Street. Venue opened on October 11, 1926.
SUPPORT ACT: Starz
TICKETS: $7.50 / $8.50
ATTENDANCE (JAN. 13): 3,387 (Anthem/SRO); sold out
ATTENDANCE (JAN. 14): 3,000 (Anthem/SRO)
CAPACITY: 3,387
CONCERT GROSS: $26,000 per show
NOTES: Second show added by popular demand.
THE NEW YORK TIMES: "Even if Rush feels a bit miffed about the way it's ignored by the supposed tastemakers of rock, it can take consolation in its audience's enthusiasm. A big, demonstrative crowd was on hand Saturday. What Rush does is play tight, energetic progressive rock with a strong science-fantasy overlay. Rush's distinction is that, by confining itself to three players, it keeps its music free of the clutter and fuss that afflict too many science-fantasy bands. There can be no denying that Rush answers some sort of need, and answers it with crisp, professional dispatch."

JANUARY 16, 1979
ALBANY, NEW YORK
PALACE THEATRE, 19 Clinton Avenue. Historic venue opened on October 23, 1931.
SUPPORT ACT: Starz
ATTENDANCE: 2,807; sold out
NOTES: This date was initially scheduled for Agricultural Hall in Allentown, PA, with tickets already on sale, but was rescheduled to September 12 at Allentown Fairgrounds. Tickets in Albany are SRO within minutes of going on sale. An out-of-control audience at a J. Geils Band concert the week before (which ended in seventeen arrests) put this gig in jeopardy, but only for a moment.

Palace manger Evelyn Knoll telephoned Mayor Erasius Corning, asking "if we should cancel Rush" (at the city-owned facility). But the mayor replied, "Don't you dare let a few people ruin something for everybody else."[21] And, while there weren't any problems with the Rush crowd, the same could not be said for the sound system, which had "a total malfunction about two-thirds of the way through the show."[22] During an hour-long intermission (used to work on the PA), a second Rush concert was announced for the following Tuesday January 23).
KNICKERBOCKER NEWS: "Lifeson's guitar work was worthwhile, relying on quick chord-change work as much as thousand-note leads."

JANUARY 17, 1979
PASSAIC, NEW JERSEY
CAPITOL THEATRE, 326 Monroe Street. Venue opened on October 8, 1926.
SUPPORT ACT: Starz
TICKETS: $7.50 / $8.50 (average: $8.15)
ATTENDANCE: 3,456 (3,386—Anthem/SRO); sold out
CONCERT GROSS: $28,172
NOTES: Journalist David Fricke joined up with the entourage to gather material for a *Circus* magazine feature.[23] The resulting piece provided fascinating insight into life on the road. Fricke immediately took note of one of the seemingly mundane challenges that cause real angst for Rush's production efforts: the stage was too small for the band's rear-projection visuals, but the venue compensated with two close-up video screens hanging from above each side of the stage. Of the fifteen tons of equipment Rush carries from city to city, seven of them stayed in the trucks tonight. After the show, the crew dismantled their afternoon's work in twenty-eight minutes ("a crew record."). Mike Hirsch's comments in the *Circus* article are a telling indicator of the current geographical footprint of Rush's fan base.
CIRCUS: "Lurch is not happy with the situation, and not just because of the inconvenience. Elsewhere in the States, the Canadian power trio can play stadium stages to SRO crowds. But album sales are lagging on the East Coast, forcing the band into smaller theatres for economy's sake. To Lurch, crew, and band, that's a matter of pride. 'In the Midwest,' Lurch

complains to a Capitol stagehand, 'we're a coliseum act. In the West and the South, we're a coliseum act. But in the Northeast, we're shit.'"

CIRCUS, LARRY ALLEN: "Being a roadie is like a factory job. You have a certain schedule you adhere to so that everything's ready on time and a certain procedure of working so it gets done right. But instead of being nine-to-five, it's more like ten-to-two in the morning.'"

CIRCUS, GREG CONNOLLY (MONITOR ENGINEER): "I was working in this sound store in Toronto when Geddy comes in and says to me 'I hear you mix monitors real well. We're having some troubles with ours.' They haven't had any trouble since. But I'd never even seen the band before that."

JANUARY 19, 1979
PITTSBURGH, PENNSYLVANIA
CIVIC ARENA, 300 Auditorium Place. Venue opened on September 17, 1961.
SUPPORT ACT: Starz
TICKETS: $7.75, general admission
ATTENDANCE: 14,240 (Anthem/SRO); 14,032 (*Billboard*); sold out
CONCERT GROSS: $110,421
NOTES: Journalist David Fricke continued his research for a *Circus* magazine feature.

CIRCUS, DAVID FRICKE: "My job is to help Skip Gildersleeve with Geddy's guitar changes. 'Now all you have to do,' Skip instructs me, 'is when Geddy comes offstage after the first song ['Anthem'], take the bass from him while I give him the other one [a doubleneck Rickenbacker]. Then hold the flashlight down so I can plug the cord in.' It sounds easy enough, but when Geddy rushes to stage left and thrusts his guitar into my waiting mitts, it's barely a split second before he's strapped on the Rickenbacker and is back at center stage for Alex's introductory riff to 'A Passage to Bangkok.' It all happens so fast I feel energized just standing there."

CIRCUS: "Regardless of their individual backgrounds, duties, and salaries (a Rush average of $300 a week depending on the job), the Rush roadies work as one and are well-known for their proficiency. 'Promoters say our crew is one of the most professional around,' Geddy Lee says later with pride. 'But they are also very demanding. If our crew is going to do the job right, they

feel they deserve everything that's coming to them. If there is no milk at the crew breakfast, or there aren't as many stagehands as stipulated in the contract rider, they'll complain about it. Because complaining is the only way they have to let out their frustrations on the road.'"

JANUARY 20, 1979
BALTIMORE, MARYLAND
BALTIMORE CIVIC CENTER, 201 West Baltimore Street. Venue opened on October 23, 1962.
SUPPORT ACT: Stillwater
TICKETS: $6.50 (advance) / $7.50 (day of) (average: $6.98)
ATTENDANCE: 9,794 (Anthem/SRO); 8,676 (*Billboard*)
CAPACITY: 13,641
CONCERT GROSS: $60,578

JANUARY 21, 1979
PHILADELPHIA, PENNSYLVANIA
THE SPECTRUM, 3601 South Broad Street. Venue opened on October 1, 1967.
SUPPORT ACT: Blondie
TICKETS: $6.50 (advance) / $7.50 (day of) (average: $7.23); mostly general admission with limited $7.50 reserved seats
ATTENDANCE: 14,028 (Anthem/SRO); 13,064 (*Billboard*)
CONCERT GROSS: $94,467
NOTES: A fanatical throng of fans started chanting "Rush!" before Blondie ever set foot on the stage. After a song or two, trash and various objects begin taking flight toward Debbie Harry and company. They were booed off the stage in less than twenty minutes. Upon departing, Blondie guitarist Chris Stein gave the rabid audience his middle finger and, right at that very moment, someone in the general admission crowd threw a bottle that hit him square in the head. Drummer Clem Burke kicked over his drums as he walked off in a fit of frustration. Though their set was short, they did perform the single "One Way or Another" to the unappreciative Spectrum crowd. In May, Blondie appeared on American Bandstand with host Dick Clark stating, "The band has played some large venues like the Spectrum in Philadelphia." This was the first concert ever attended by Stone Temple Pilots bassist Robert DeLeo. "For my first gig," says Robert, "I had to learn

thirty songs in two weeks, including 'Red Barchetta' by Rush."[24]
IAN: "Blondie showed up with rented equipment and rented roadies. Their road manager asked if Rush's sound guy (i.e., me) would mix their sound. Our band put the kibosh on that, so Dave Hoover from National Sound agreed to mix. He did a good job, but the crowd was having none of it. Cascades of boos after even the first song. Within twenty minutes they walked off stage to thunderous booing. I was looking forward to seeing them and was embarrassed for them. It was a lot like Rush opening for Sha Na Na. Gonna play in front of 19,000, ya gotta have your gig together. Sadly, they did not."[25]
JEWISH EXPONENT: "The Spectrum concert featuring Rush confirmed what radio programmers have known for five years: This band is hard to listen to over extended periods of time."
TOM KEIFER (FOUNDING GUITARIST AND VOCALIST FOR CINDERELLA): "The first time that I really wanted to be in a band, was after seeing Rush play at The Spectrum in 1979. They put on an incredible show, and from that point on, all that I ever thought about was forming my own band and playing at the Spectrum."[26]

JANUARY 22, 1979
SYRACUSE, NEW YORK
ONONDAGA COUNTY WAR MEMORIAL AUDITORIUM, 515 Montgomery Street. Venue opened on September 1, 1951.
CAPACITY: 9,000
NOTES: Concert postponed due to sluggish ticket sales.[27] Date unconfirmed.

JANUARY 23, 1979
ALBANY, NEW YORK
PALACE THEATRE, 19 Clinton Avenue
SUPPORT ACT: Starz
ATTENDANCE: 2,463
CAPACITY: 2,997
NOTES: Second show added by popular demand: This date was announced just a week before the concert.

JANUARY 24, 1979
BUFFALO, NEW YORK
BUFFALO MEMORIAL AUDITORIUM, 140 Main Street. Venue opened on October 14, 1940.

SUPPORT ACT: Starz
TICKETS: $7.00 / $8.00
ATTENDANCE: 11,624
CAPACITY: 14,605
NOTES: Venue aka The Aud.
BUFFALO EVENING NEWS: "Rush's Rock Is High-Decibel, Highly Stylized: In spite of a sometimes rambling, often mega-loud performance, the band exhibited remarkable tightness and straight-ahead vision in its delivery."

JANUARY 26, 1979
CINCINNATI, OHIO
RIVERFRONT COLISEUM, 100 Broadway Street. Venue opened on September 9, 1975.
SUPPORT ACT: Starz
TICKETS: $6.50 / $7.50
ATTENDANCE: 8,236
CAPACITY: 10,687

JANUARY 27, 1979
HUNTSVILLE, ALABAMA
VON BRAUN CIVIC CENTER, 700 Monroe Street. Venue opened on March 14, 1975.
SUPPORT ACT: Starz
TICKETS: $6.50 / $7.50 (average: $6.85)
ATTENDANCE: 6,619 (Anthem/SRO); 6,850 (*Venue/Billboard*)
CONCERT GROSS: $46,891
NOTES: The first 3,000 tickets were $6.50, with the remainder selling for $7.50.

JANUARY 28, 1979
MEMPHIS, TENNESSEE
MID-SOUTH COLISEUM, Memphis Fairgrounds Park, 996 Early Maxwell Boulevard Venue opened on December 2, 1964.
SUPPORT ACT: Starz
TICKETS: $6.00 (advance) / $7.00 (day of)
ATTENDANCE: 7,380 (Anthem/SRO); 7,263 (*Billboard*)
CAPACITY: 9,263
CONCERT GROSS: $50,833

JANUARY 30, 1979
LOUISVILLE, KENTUCKY
LOUISVILLE GARDENS, 525 Muhammad Ali Boulevard. Historic venue dedicated on December 31, 1905.
SUPPORT ACT: Toto

TICKETS: $6.50 (advance) / $7.50 (day of) (average: $6.75), general admission
ATTENDANCE: 7,088 (Anthem/SRO); 7,201 (promoter); sold out
CONCERT GROSS: $48,612
NOTES: In 1978, Walnut Street (previous address of this venue) was renamed Muhammad Ali Boulevard.
THE COURIER-JOURNAL: "Rush concert gives feeling you've heard it all before: The band played with the precision and energy the likes of which Greg Lake or Yes's Steve Howe were never able to master in concert. But as impressive as the precision constantly was, the end product, the music itself, slowly became repetitive and sluggish. If one of Toto's members had been really smart, he would have pulled the plug on Rush."

JANUARY 31, 1979
BLOOMINGTON, INDIANA
I. U. AUDITORIUM, Indiana University campus, 1211 East 17th Street. Venue opened on March 22, 1941.
SUPPORT ACT: The Boyzz
TICKETS: $6.50 / $7.00 / $7.50 (all seats reserved)
ATTENDANCE: 1,968 (Anthem/SRO)
CAPACITY: 3,200
CONCERT GROSS: $14,498

FEBRUARY 1, 1979
COLUMBUS, OHIO
ST. JOHN ARENA, The Ohio State University campus, 410 Woody Hayes Drive. Venue completed on November 1, 1956.
SUPPORT ACT: April Wine
TICKETS: $7.00 / $8.00 (all seats reserved) (average: $7.88)
ATTENDANCE: 7,355
CONCERT GROSS: $57,950
NOTES: As soon as the band took the stage, the entire (seated) floor "stampeded" into the first ten rows for a closer glimpse.[28]
COLUMBUS DISPATCH: "Lee is getting older, yet his voice has remained as powerful and clear as a siren in the night."
OSU LANTERN: "Rush's performance well-balanced, precise."
OSU LANTERN, **ALEX:** "We've been to Columbus five or six times now . . . it's always been a good place to play."

FEBRUARY 2, 1979
SAGINAW, MICHIGAN
WENDLER ARENA AT SAGINAW CIVIC CENTER, 303 Johnson Street. Venue opened on October 15, 1972.
SUPPORT ACT: April Wine
TICKETS: $8.50
ATTENDANCE: 7,104; sold out
CONCERT GROSS: $60,384

FEBRUARY 3, 1979
RICHFIELD, OHIO
RICHFIELD COLISEUM, 2923 Streetsboro Road. Venue opened on October 26, 1974.
SUPPORT ACT: April Wine
TICKETS: $7.50 (advance) / $8.50 (day of)
ATTENDANCE: 16,336
NOTES: Venue aka the Coliseum at Richfield. "The Palace on the Prairie." At the time of this gig, the Cleveland area was in the midst of twenty-two straight days with temperatures below freezing.
THE AKRON BEACON JOURNAL: "If you aren't really into it, Rush makes for a long night: Their extra heavy music is supposed to weave majestic epics of extra heavy happenings. And if you like it, you love it. If you don't like it, however, you can hate it. It all sounds the same—loud and tedious."

FEBRUARY 15, 1979
COLUMBIA, SOUTH CAROLINA
TOWNSHIP AUDITORIUM, 1703 Taylor Street. Venue opened in November 1930.
SUPPORT ACT: Head East
TICKETS: $6.50 (advance); $7.50 (day of), general admission
ATTENDANCE: 2,695
CAPACITY: 3,200

FEBRUARY 16, 1979
ASHEVILLE, NORTH CAROLINA
CIVIC CENTER, 87 Haywood Street. Venue opened on June 23, 1974.
SUPPORT ACT: Head East
TICKETS: $6.50 (limited advance) / $7.50 (remaining), general admission
ATTENDANCE: 3,978
CAPACITY: 7,000
NOTES: SRO lists Nantucket as support, likely prior to Head East assuming the role.

FEBRUARY 17, 1979
FAYETTEVILLE, NORTH CAROLINA
CUMBERLAND COUNTY MEMORIAL ARENA, 1960 Coliseum Drive. Venue opened on January 23, 1968.
SUPPORT ACT: Head East
TICKETS: $6.25 (advance); $7.25 (at the door), general admission
ATTENDANCE: 6,780
CAPACITY: 7,000

FEBRUARY 18, 1979
CHARLOTTE, NC
CHARLOTTE PARK CENTER, Central Piedmont Community College, 310 North Kings Highway Drive. Venue dedicated on July 16, 1956.
CAPACITY: 3,102
NOTES: Rescheduled to April 12, 1979 because of snow.
IAN: "Six inches of snow, and the city totally shut down! Thank god there was a diner down the street that was open, or we'd have gone hungry. The police came to the gig and told Lurch the show was canceled. He started to argue and was told the show was canceled whether he was in jail or not. 'Ok, the show's canceled.'"[29]
HOWARD: "We were stuck in the hotel and we weren't going anywhere because of the storm, and we got so hammered that, after the lounge act finished, Alex got up onstage on the piano and started making up crazy songs, with crazy lyrics. He entertained people for about an hour in that bar, just doing this crazy impromptu comedy act. It was a riot."[30]

FEBRUARY 20, 1979
KNOXVILLE, TENNESSEE
KNOXVILLE CIVIC COLISEUM, 500 East Church Street. Venue opened on August 20, 1961.
SUPPORT ACT: Head East
TICKETS: $7.00 (advance) / $8.00 (day of) (average: $7.25), general admission
ATTENDANCE: 3,792 (Anthem/SRO); 3,901 (*Billboard*)
CAPACITY: 6,673
CONCERT GROSS: $28,265

FEBRUARY 22, 1979
LITTLE ROCK, ARKANSAS
T. H. BARTON COLISEUM, Arkansas State Fairgrounds, 2600 Howard Street. Venue dedicated on September 29, 1952.

SUPPORT ACT: April Wine
TICKETS: $7.50
ATTENDANCE: 3,978
CAPACITY: 10,250, general admission

FEBRUARY 23, 1979
SHREVEPORT, LOUISIANA
HIRSCH MEMORIAL COLISEUM, 3701 Hudson Avenue. Venue opened on April 10, 1954.
SUPPORT ACT: April Wine
TICKETS: $7.50, general admission
ATTENDANCE: 4,465
CAPACITY: 5,000
SHREVEPORT TIMES: "Rush, April Wine was quite a surprise—a Rush actually."

FEBRUARY 24, 1979
OKLAHOMA CITY, OKLAHOMA
STATE FAIR ARENA, Oklahoma State Fairgrounds, 333 Gordon Cooper Boulevard. Venue opened on September 25, 1965.
SUPPORT ACT: April Wine
TICKETS: $7.50
ATTENDANCE: 6,247
THE OKLAHOMAN: "Solid Rock Reputation Being Erected by Rush: While the Canadian trio gets little radio exposure and hasn't taken the record world by storm, they are an exciting, distinctive, often compelling stage attraction. In fact, the stage is where Rush is determined to build its audience, as guitarist Alex Lifeson acknowledged after Saturday night's concert at the State Fairgrounds Arena. The stage is where Rush blossoms. There's an eerie, other-worldly aura about the band's performance that gives Rush an unsettling magnetism."

FEBRUARY 25, 1979
AUSTIN, TEXAS
MUNICIPAL AUDITORIUM, 400 South Street. Venue opened on January 5, 1959.
SUPPORT ACT: April Wine
TICKETS: $8.00
ATTENDANCE: 4,845; sold out

FEBRUARY 27, 1979
CORPUS CHRISTI, TEXAS
MEMORIAL COLISEUM, 402 South Shoreline Boulevard. Venue dedicated on September 26, 1954.
SUPPORT ACT: April Wine
TICKETS: $7.75 (all seats), general admission

ATTENDANCE: 4,784
CAPACITY: 6,000 with 2,615 permanent seats
NEIL: "Rush is not supposed to be anything, it's just a concentrated creative flux."

MARCH 1, 1979
HOUSTON, TEXAS
SAM HOUSTON COLISEUM, 801 Bagby Street. Venue dedicated on November 16, 1937.
SUPPORT ACT: April Wine
TICKETS: $7.50
ATTENDANCE: 11,273
CAPACITY: 11,300

MARCH 2, 1979
DALLAS, TEXAS
DALLAS CONVENTION CENTER ARENA, 650 South Griffin Street. Venue opened on September 8, 1957.
SUPPORT ACT: April Wine
TICKETS: $7.50 (advance) / $8.00 (day of)
ATTENDANCE: 9,286; sold out
NOTES: Venue aka Dallas Memorial Auditorium.
IAN: "We stayed at the old Baker Hotel in Dallas before they imploded it. We checked in late one night and I was rooming with Larry. We walk into our room, he slams the door, and a three-foot square piece of plaster falls from the ceiling onto one of the beds. I look at him and say, 'That's your bed.' We laughed for half an hour."[31]
MIKE "LURCH" HIRSCH: "Mr. Grandy can be one of the most amusing, funny friggin guys on the planet when he's in the mood. When he was in a funny mood, he would have everyone in complete stitches."[32]

MARCH 3, 1979
SAN ANTONIO, TEXAS
CONVENTION CENTER ARENA, HemisFair Park Complex, 601 Hemisfair Way. Venue opened on April 6, 1968.
SUPPORT ACT: April Wine
TICKETS: $7.50 / $8.00 / $8.50
ATTENDANCE: 12,869; sold out
NOTES: Upon entrance, fans were greeted by a huge inflatable pink brain (à la the *Hemispheres* cover), which hovered above the crowd.[33]

MARCH 4, 1979
BEAUMONT, TEXAS
FAIR PARK COLISEUM, Beaumont Fairgrounds Complex, 2600 Block of Gulf Street. Venue opened on April 17, 1978.
SUPPORT ACT: April Wine
TICKETS: $7.00 (all seats), general admission
ATTENDANCE: 2,946
CAPACITY: 7,100
NOTES: While the Coliseum has a roof, the sides were open on a frigid (thirty-seven degrees) Texas night, causing Geddy to wear a jacket for the entire performance.
LAMAR UNIVERSITY PRESS: "While Rush does have the material, the talent, and the desire to be a starkly original rock ensemble, their Beaumont performance was more the flavor of a local band rehearsing in a makeshift garage studio."

MARCH 6, 1979
NEW ORLEANS, LOUISIANA
MUNICIPAL AUDITORIUM, 1201 Saint Peter Street. Venue opened on January 30, 1930.
SUPPORT ACT: April Wine
ATTENDANCE: 4,835
CAPACITY: 6,000
NOTES: General admission concert.

MARCH 8, 1979
MOBILE, ALABAMA
EXPO HALL, Mobile Civic Center, 401 Civic Center Drive. Venue opened on July 9, 1964.
SUPPORT ACT: April Wine
TICKETS: $7.50 (all seats)
ATTENDANCE: 2,228
CAPACITY: 3,000, general admission

MARCH 9, 1979
JACKSONVILLE, FLORIDA
CIVIC AUDITORIUM, 300 West Waters Street. Venue dedicated on September 16, 1962.
SUPPORT ACT: UFO
TICKETS: $6.00 (advance) / $7.00 (day of)
ATTENDANCE: 3,125 (Anthem/SRO)
CAPACITY: 3,338
CONCERT GROSS: $20,875

MARCH 10, 1979
PEMBROKE PINES, FLORIDA
HOLLYWOOD SPORTATORIUM, 17171 Pines Boulevard (Route 820). Venue opened in September 1970.
SUPPORT ACT: UFO
TICKETS: $5.50 (limited advance) / $6.50 (remaining) (average: $6.11), general admission
ATTENDANCE: 10,069 (Anthem/SRO); 9,937 (*Billboard*)
CAPACITY: 12,837
CONCERT GROSS: $60,757

MARCH 11, 1979
TAMPA, FLORIDA
CURTIS HIXON CONVENTION HALL, 600 North Ashley Drive. Venue opened on January 23, 1965.
SUPPORT ACT: UFO
TICKETS: $5.98, general admission
ATTENDANCE: 7,600 (Anthem/SRO); sold out
CONCERT GROSS: $45,077

MARCH 13, 1979
BIRMINGHAM, ALABAMA
BOUTWELL MEMORIAL AUDITORIUM, 1930 Eighth Avenue North. Venue dedicated on June 1, 1924.
SUPPORT ACT: UFO
TICKETS: $7.50, general admission
ATTENDANCE: 3,461
CAPACITY: 6,000

MARCH 15, 1979
CHATTANOOGA, TENNESSEE
SOLDIERS AND SAILORS MEMORIAL AUDITORIUM, 399 McCallie Avenue. Venue opened on February 22, 1924.
SUPPORT ACT: Molly Hatchet
TICKETS: $6.50 / $7.50 (average: $6.99), general admission
ATTENDANCE: 3,130 (Anthem/SRO); sold out
CONCERT GROSS: $21,868

MARCH 16, 1979
NASHVILLE, TENNESSEE
NASHVILLE MUNICIPAL AUDITORIUM, 417 Fourth Avenue North. Venue opened on October 7, 1962.
SUPPORT ACT: Molly Hatchet
TICKETS: $6.50 (first 3,000) / $7.50 (remaining), general admission
ATTENDANCE: 8,468 (Anthem/SRO)
CAPACITY: 9,990
CONCERT GROSS: $43,844

THE TENNESSEAN: "Rush won fans here in its double-bill concert with Uriah Heep last year."
THE DAILY NEWS-JOURNAL **(MURFREESBORO):** "Rush can put out more sound than most rock bands with five or more members."

MARCH 17, 1979
JOHNSON CITY, TENNESSEE
FREEDOM HALL CIVIC CENTER, 1320 Pactolas Road. Venue opened on July 5, 1974.
SUPPORT ACTS: Angel, Raggedy Anne
TICKETS: $7.00
ATTENDANCE: 4,103

MARCH 18, 1979
WHEELING, WEST VIRGINIA
WHEELING CIVIC CENTER, 2 14th Street. Venue opened on April 19, 1977.
SUPPORT ACT: Sad Café
TICKETS: $7.00 / $8.00, general admission
ATTENDANCE: 6,233 (Anthem/SRO)
CAPACITY: 9,000
CONCERT GROSS: $46,812

MARCH 26, 1979
The crew travels to Salt Lake City via Chicago's O'Hare International Airport.
Ian: "We all reassembled in Chicago O'Hare airport and spent some time in the bar . . . 'refreshing' ourselves. Halfway through the flight, the head stewardess asks who's in charge of our group and they tell her it was me. She sits next to me and says 'ok, you guys are smoking pot in the washroom, one of your guys and his lady friend have been back together in the washroom having sex for the last twenty minutes, and your guys are snorting coke openly.' Just as she says that, the guy in front of me sticks a little loaded spoon back through the space by the window. She says 'hey, we can have the police waiting if you want to push it any further.' I went around and told everyone to fucking settle down. We walked through the Salt Lake airport as twelve individuals. I kept as far away from everyone else as I could."[34]

MARCH 27, 1979
SALT LAKE CITY, UTAH
SALT PALACE, 100 S West Temple.
Venue dedicated on July 11, 1969.
SUPPORT ACT: April Wine
TICKETS: $7.00 / $8.00
ATTENDANCE: 10,251
CAPACITY: 13,000
NOTES: Geddy performed using a rented
Oberheim.
TONY GERANIOS: There are a lot of
parts that Geddy played that we had to
set up. I had to call up some charts to
get the programming right, for some of
the sounds. They worked around it for
that show. I don't remember it being
disastrous. It wasn't that bad. Anyway,
I'm running around getting things set up,
and they might have had to cut a couple
songs out of the set. So, the show is
going on, and I hadn't met the guy who
owned the keyboard yet. He showed up
after his keyboard, because he was still
working. At some point during the show,
he came up on Geddy's side of the stage,
and just walked up the stairs to the
stage. One of the sound guys said, 'Who
are you, what are you doing, where's your
pass?' The kid must have said something
like, 'I don't need a pass', and kept walking up the stairs onto the stage. Well, the
sound guy just flattened him. He just
punched him in the face. You don't just
come wandering up onto the stage. As
security was carrying him off, people
overheard him saying, 'But wait . . .
that's my keyboard on stage . . .' He
busted his lip wide open. I think we got
sued over that one."[35]

MARCH 28, 1979
DENVER, COLORADO
AUDITORIUM ARENA, 1323 Champa
Street. Historic venue opened on July 7,
1908.
SUPPORT ACT: Wireless
TICKETS: $8.80
ATTENDANCE: 4,119
CAPACITY: 6,841

MARCH 29, 1979
LINCOLN, NEBRASKA
PERSHING MEMORIAL AUDITORIUM,
226 Centennial Mall South. Venue
dedicated on March 10, 1957.
SUPPORT ACT: Kickin' (last-minute
replacement for Angel)

TICKETS: $6.50 (advance) / $7.50 (day
of) (average: $7.20), general admission
ATTENDANCE: 4,597 (Anthem/SRO);
4,275 (*Billboard*)
CAPACITY: 7,500
CONCERT GROSS: $30,800
NOTES: Twenty-two people were arrested
for alleged marijuana possession.
Although Angel is listed as the opener on
advance ads, Kickin' was the sole
support.
LINCOLN JOURNAL: "Rush music
sounds powerful, but it sometimes lacks
a bite: Although only a trio, Rush multi-
plies its effect by using a number of
electronic effects. The result is often a
lack of bite in the band's attack."

MARCH 30, 1979
TOPEKA, KANSAS
TOPEKA MUNICIPAL AUDITORIUM, 214
SE Eighth Avenue. Venue dedicated on
May 12, 1940.
SUPPORT ACT: Granmax
TICKETS: $7.00 (advance)
ATTENDANCE: 4,200 (Anthem/SRO);
4,246 (*Variety*); sold out
CONCERT GROSS: $28,400
NOTES: Some concert-goers got out of
hand, breaking glass panes and door
handles in two of the south doors of the
auditorium, with damages estimated at
$3,000.

APRIL 2, 1979
SYRACUSE, NEW YORK
ONONDAGA COUNTY WAR
MEMORIAL AUDITORIUM, 515
Montgomery Street. Venue opened on
September 1, 1951.
SUPPORT ACT: Horslips
ATTENDANCE: 2,862
CAPACITY: 9,000
NOTES: One concertgoer was the first
person arrested in violation of the coun-
ty's new ban on smoking and drinking
alcohol at Memorial Auditorium.

APRIL 3, 1979
POUGHKEEPSIE, NEW YORK
MAIR HALL, MID-HUDSON CIVIC
CENTER, 14 Civic Center Plaza. Venue
opened on November 28, 1976.
SUPPORT ACT: Falcon Eddy
TICKETS: $8.50
ATTENDANCE: 3,325 (Anthem/SRO);
3,372 (*Billboard*); oversold
CONCERT GROSS: $28,263

APRIL 4, 1979
ROCHESTER, NEW YORK
ROCHESTER COMMUNITY WAR
MEMORIAL, 100 Exchange Boulevard.
Venue opened on October 18, 1955.
SUPPORT ACT: Madcats
TICKETS: $8.50, general admission
ATTENDANCE: 10,442 (Anthem/SRO);
10,500 (*Billboard*); sold out
CONCERT GROSS: $89,253

APRIL 6, 1979
UNIONDALE, NEW YORK
NASSAU COUNTY VETERANS
MEMORIAL COLISEUM, 1255
Hempstead Turnpike. Venue dedicated
on May 29, 1972.
SUPPORT ACT: The Good Rats
TICKETS: $7.50 / $8.50 (average:
$8.19)
ATTENDANCE: 10,428 (Anthem/SRO);
10,400 (*Billboard*)
CAPACITY: 15,546
CONCERT GROSS: $85,160

APRIL 7, 1979
NEW HAVEN, CONNECTICUT
NEW HAVEN VETERAN'S MEMORIAL
COLISEUM, 275 South Orange Street.
Venue opened on September 27, 1972.
SUPPORT ACT: The Good Rats
TICKETS: $6.50 / $8.50 (average:
$8.21)
ATTENDANCE: 5,793 (Anthem/SRO);
5,800 (*Billboard*)
CAPACITY: 9,500
CONCERT GROSS: $47,597
NOTES: Alex was pissed off because his
classical guitar was not working properly
and he was forced to play the intro to
"The Trees" on electric guitar.

APRIL 8, 1979
PROVIDENCE, RHODE ISLAND
PROVIDENCE CIVIC CENTER, 1 La Salle
Square. Venue opened on November 3,
1972.
SUPPORT ACT: The Good Rats
TICKETS: $7.00 / $7.50 (average: $7.24)
ATTENDANCE: 6,528 (Anthem/SRO);
6,684 (*Billboard*)
CAPACITY: 9,200
CONCERT GROSS: $48,370

Chapter 9
THE SUMMER TOUR '79

Nicknamed the "Semi Tour of the Some of the Hemispheres" by the band, and consisting of only nineteen dates, this short trek was designed primarily as a warm-up for the band before they entered the studio. Alex, Geddy, and Neil had taken a break at the end of the *Tour of the Hemispheres* and then reconvened over the summer to compose what would become *Permanent Waves*. Thus, the summer of 1979 marked a subtle yet important turning point in how Rush went about touring and recording. If the band had continued the pattern of the previous two years, the end of the *Tour of the Hemispheres* would have been followed by several months of writing and recording in Wales, a very short break at home, and then another grueling ten-month tour. At this point, however, even though the finances could only marginally permit it, the band pulled back. After the *Tour of the Hemispheres* finale at the Pinkpop Festival in the Netherlands, Alex, Geddy, and Neil returned home for a much-needed, well-earned six-week break with their families. It was the longest they'd been home since Neil joined the band five years earlier.

The Semi Tour of the Some of the Hemispheres featured the debut of two songs from the upcoming *Permanent Waves*—"The Spirit of Radio" and "Freewill"—in rough prerelease form. Other new compositions ("Jacob's Ladder," "Entre Nous") were rehearsed at sound checks.

The new material, in particular "The Spirit of Radio" and "Freewill," signaled a change in direction for the band. "With *Permanent Waves*, we found that it was very challenging to write shorter songs, trying to pack as much into four or five minutes as we would into a ten-minute song," said Alex. "It wasn't really an easy thing for us to do, but it was very enjoyable. Very satisfying, challenging; we enjoyed it."

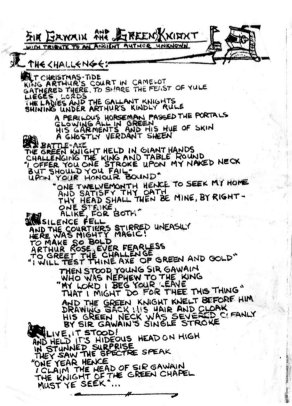

OPPOSITE TOP:
Lexington, KY; Alex shredding on his white Gibson ES-335.

OPPOSITE BOTTOM:
Lexington, KY; Neil behind his new Tama kit.

LEFT: Neil's handwritten lyric sheet for "Sir Gawain and the Green Knight," which was originally intended to be part of the *Permanent Waves* album before being scrapped. Its intended slot on the album was later replaced with the hastily written "Natural Science."

TOUR HISTORY

SUMMER TOUR '79

<table>
<tr><td colspan="3">SET LIST:</td></tr>
<tr><td>"2112: Overture"</td><td>"The Trees"</td><td>"Finding My Way"</td></tr>
<tr><td>"2112: The Temples of Syrinx"</td><td>"Cygnus X-1"</td><td>"Anthem"</td></tr>
<tr><td>"2112: Presentation"</td><td>"Hemispheres: Prelude"</td><td>"Bastille Day"</td></tr>
<tr><td>"2112: Soliloquy"</td><td>"Hemispheres: Apollo"</td><td>"In the Mood"</td></tr>
<tr><td>"2112: Grand Finale"</td><td>"Hemispheres: Armageddon"</td><td>"Drum Solo"</td></tr>
<tr><td>"A Passage to Bangkok"</td><td>"Hemispheres: Cygnus"</td><td>Encore:</td></tr>
<tr><td>"By-Tor and the Snow Dog" (abridged)</td><td>"Hemispheres: The Sphere"</td><td>"La Villa Strangiato"</td></tr>
<tr><td>"Xanadu"</td><td>"Closer to the Heart"</td><td></td></tr>
<tr><td>"The Spirit of Radio" (prerelease version)</td><td>"Freewill" (prerelease version)</td><td></td></tr>
<tr><td></td><td>"Working Man" (reggae intro)</td><td></td></tr>
</table>

AUGUST 17, 1979
DAVENPORT, IOWA
RKO ORPHEUM THEATRE, 136 East Third Street. Historic venue opened on November 25, 1931.
SUPPORT ACT: Hot Mama Silver
TICKETS: $7.50 (advance) / $8.50 (day of), general admission
ATTENDANCE: 2,891; sold out
NOTES: The opening date of the "Summer Tour '79" featured the live debut of "The Spirit of Radio" and "Freewill," and introduced the reggae intro to "Working Man." This date also marked an important event in Rush's overall live sound: the debut of Geddy's Moog Taurus pedal interface, which allowed him to play full chords with his feet through his Oberheim polyphonic synthesizer. From this point forward, Geddy's goal of becoming the world's "smallest symphony orchestra" began to come to fruition. Neil worked on that dream behind a brand-new kit of Tama drums with rosewood finish. For the first week or so, the front heads were black, before the *2112* starman logo was added.
QUAD CITY TIMES, GEDDY (BACKSTAGE AFTER THE SHOW): "We seemed to have worked ourselves into a small place with dedicated fans. As long as we hold up our end, they won't let us down."
NEIL: "The RKO Theatre is a lovely sounding hall. Onstage, the sound is just perfect. All of the characteristics are very nice, and the sound is powerful. It sounds very full and very pleasant. It's nice to play here, for sure."
BOB KNIFFEN: "We reconvened in Davenport, Iowa. We were setting everything up, and the band came in for sound check. Geddy came over and said, 'Hey, Mo, we've got this new tune, and it's in

15/18 time' or something like that, and Nick Kotos replied 'Well, you motherfuckers better learn how to swing 4/4 before you start going off into that other shit,' and then everybody would laugh. They would come to me and Nick because they knew we liked jazz, which is often in odd meter, odd time signatures."[1]
HERB EIMERMAN (HOT MAMA SILVER BASSIST): "It was a very exciting time for us—Rush was huge, and we were fans. I had just gotten a Rickenbacker bass, black and chrome with pinstripe binding, and Geddy loved it. We were backstage after sound check. I also had a '62 Fender jazz bass, and he loved that as well. We played great and got a standing ovation. To be honest, they saw us wheel amps with no cases and [we only had] a couple roadies and I don't think they expected us to be good. We saw their set from backstage . . . it was very powerful. Geddy's bass playing was great, as always. They had a lot of bombs going off—a big, loud, rock show. It was a great night."[2]

AUGUST 18, 1979
DUBUQUE, IOWA
FIVE FLAGS ARENA, Five Flags Civic Center, 405 Main Street. Venue opened on March 24, 1979.
AN EVENING WITH RUSH
TICKETS: $7.00 (advance) / $8.00 (day of), general admission
ATTENDANCE: 2,851 (Anthem/SRO); 2,950 (*Billboard*)
CONCERT GROSS: $20,000
NOTES: A mellow crowd made for a mellow mood—at one point, Alex sat down on Neil's drum riser (while playing guitar), so he could concentrate on the new songs.

AUGUST 19, 1979
CHICAGO, ILLINOIS
COMISKEY PARK ("CHICAGO JAM II"), 324 West 35th Street. Historic baseball stadium opened on July 1, 1910.
WITH: Foghat (co-bill); Southside Johnny and the Asbury Jukes; Roadmaster; the Tubes opened the show at 10:00 a.m.
TICKETS: $15.00 (advance) / $20.00 (at the gate), general admission
ATTENDANCE: 31,000
CAPACITY: 65,000 (approximate)
NOTES: Fifty-nine people were arrested for selling/possessing drugs at this outdoor gig. One Chicago police officer estimated that 70 percent of the concertgoers were using some sort of illegal drug. Chicago Jam I, which was held the day before, featured Sha Na Na, Blondie, and the Beach Boys.
CHICAGO TRIBUNE: "Sunday's show fared better in turnout, drawing about four times as many folks as Saturday's disaster, though still leaving the park at least half empty. Few had come for the Jukes' brand of rock with horns; the day belonged to headliner Rush and blues-rock band Foghat, both of whom performed with a great deal of energy if little subtlety and, in the case of the alternately droning and shrill Rush, even less discernible talent."
IAN: "We were late on the second day, stage deep in center field. The infield was roped off, but the fans sat in the rain-soaked, gelatinous black-mud outfield."

AUGUST 21, 1979
CHARLESTON, WEST VIRGINIA
CHARLESTON CIVIC CENTER ARENA, Reynolds Street. Venue dedicated on January 25, 1959.

SUPPORT ACT: Blackfoot
TICKETS: $8.00, general admission
ATTENDANCE: 4,473

AUGUST 22, 1979
LARGO, MARYLAND
CAPITAL CENTRE, 1 Harry S. Truman Drive. Venue opened on December 2, 1973.
SUPPORT ACT: Nantucket
TICKETS: $4.50 / $5.50
ATTENDANCE: 13,215

AUGUST 24, 1979
HAMILTON, ONTARIO
IVOR WYNNE STADIUM, 75 Balsam Avenue North. Venue opened on August 16, 1930.
SUPPORT ACT: Streetheart
TICKETS: $8.00 / $10.00 / $12.00 CAD
ATTENDANCE: 8,057
NOTES: Supersession '79. Brief sound check and preconcert interview footage from this date would be included many years later as a bonus feature on the *R30* DVD set, released in 2005. This was the first show at Ivor Wynne Stadium after a ban on concerts was put in place by the Hamilton city council following a June 28, 1975, Pink Floyd gig that drew more than 55,000 people and caused public outcry due to massive crowds, lewd behavior, and rampant drug use. That show was Pink Floyd's final North American date of their *Wish You Were Here* tour, so the Floyd had extra pyro- technics stockpiled that needed to be used, and they ended up burning down the stadium's scoreboard. Rush's set went on "largely without incident."[3] Although more than 100 people were arrested, mostly on narcotics charges, that was not a large number for events of this nature. "This was a pretty well- behaved crowd," police inspector Norm Thompson told the *Hamilton Spectator*. "We could see a few doing things they shouldn't, but it was not a problem."
IAN: "We were kicking a soccer ball around in the afternoon, and I got what they call 'turf toe' by catching my big toe and breaking it badly. I could barely walk, and the soundboard was halfway up the stands. Tommy Linthicum had to help me get up there."
SPECTATOR: "Crowd's Gold-Star Behavior Subdues Rush's Thunder: While the calm and restrained atmosphere made for

easy breathing by promoters and security staff, it didn't do much for the music. Rush performed for almost two hours, but they never really seemed to break through the subdued atmosphere."

AUGUST 26, 1979
DALLAS, TEXAS
THE COTTON BOWL, Texas State Fairgrounds, Fair Park, 1300 Robert B. Cullum Boulevard. Historic football stadium opened on October 11, 1930.
WITH: Co-bill with Foghat (8:45 to 10:15); Rush (10:40 to midnight) closed the show. Little River Band (7:15 to 8:15); Billy Thorpe (5:45 to 6:45); Pat Travers Band (4:15 to 5:15); Point Blank (3:00 to 3:45)
TICKETS: $12.50 (advance) / $15.00 (gate), general admission
ATTENDANCE: 40,000 (promoter estimate)[4]
CAPACITY: 80,000
NOTES: This gig is also referred to as "Farewell to Texas Summer," aka "The Last Concert of the Last Weekend of the Last Summer of the '70s." Because of ticket fraud, the first 10,000 tickets were made invalid, with replacements offered to those who bought them from an authorized source.
DALLAS HERALD: "Solid rock music rolls away summer: The crowd was vocal and ready to hear some solid rock music. And solid rock music was what they got—an abundance of it."
IAN: "Seriously, the first time you mix in front of a lot of people, like the Cotton Bowl in Dallas with 60,000 people lis- tening to every note, it's literally hard not to shake with nerves. I am not technical, but I had good teachers with Tommy Linthicum, Hot Sam (Jay Barth) with Kiss, and George Geranios with BOC, and will acknowledge that forever."[5]
NICK KOTOS: "When we did the show at the Cotton Bowl, it got really, really windy—to the point where the projection screen started to flop around in the air, and it almost hit Neil a couple times. It was putting a lot of stress on the roof. I went to the band, I went to Ged, and I said, 'We have to take the projection screen down—it's too dangerous,' and he said, 'No, it has to stay up.' I said, 'It's too dangerous,' and he said, 'No, it has to stay up.' And I just went 'Fuck it,' and I went up in the air with my knife,

and I cut it down. So when the show ended, they came back, and we kind of got into it. And I just said, 'Did you want the whole roof to land on your fucking heads?' And they went, 'No, okay.'"[6]

AUGUST 28, 1979
CLARKSTON, MICHIGAN
PINE KNOB MUSIC THEATRE, 7774 Sashabaw Road. Venue opened on June 25, 1972.
TICKETS: $10.50
RESCHEDULED TO SEPTEMBER 10, 1979.

AUGUST 29, 1979
LANSING, MICHIGAN
LANSING CIVIC CENTER, 525 West Allegan. Venue opened on October 30, 1955.
SUPPORT ACT: New England
TICKETS: $7.50 / $8.50 (average: $8.35)
ATTENDANCE: 5,070 (Anthem/SRO); sold out
CONCERT GROSS: $42,324
HIRSH GARDNER (NEW ENGLAND DRUMMER): "It seemed every day another one of our musical dreams were coming true. 'Don't Ever Wanna Lose Ya' was quickly becoming the #1 most played song on rock radio, and we had just finished a slew of dates with Kiss. What good fortune was next? The honor of hitting the stage with Rush. Now, talk about being nervous! Can you imagine being a drummer and having to open for Rush, knowing that the great Neil Peart was taking the stage? We arrived in Lansing that afternoon, did some radio interviews and press, then headed over to the Civic Center. I walked in, and there he was, already in sound check and just wailing on his massive kit. I immediately went to my dressing room, set up my practice pads, and got to work. By the time we went on, I was ready to go. You know, I had a great time playing that night, and just know- ing that I had an opportunity to play on the same stage as Neil was extremely gratifying. I think all the guys in the band consider it one of our most mem- orable shows. Watching Rush and what they brought musically to the show in terms of power but still leaving pockets for each other to fill should be a lesson to all bands."[7]

AUGUST 30, 1979
SAGINAW, MICHIGAN
WENDLER ARENA AT SAGINAW CIVIC CENTER, 303 Johnson Street. Venue opened on October 15, 1972.
SUPPORT ACT: The Rockets
TICKETS: $8.50, general admission
ATTENDANCE: 3,673
CAPACITY: 7,000
JOHNNY "BEE" BADANJEK (THE ROCKETS DRUMMER): "They were good guys and treated us well. On the road I would talk with Geddy and Alex. But it's not like we'd get to hang out that much—it was always set up, sound check (if there was time), eat dinner, get on stage and play, change your clothes, watch a few songs from the stage of Rush, get onto the bus, and drive to the next show. I did talk to Neil a few times. He's a fantastic drummer, and he's an amazing technician. It's always great to watch Neil during his drum solo!"[8]
SAGINAW NEWS: "Rush not limited: On stage, Lee, Lifeson, and Peart multiply their efforts as individual musicians and as a collective unit. The result is a show blending a wide range of music, effective lighting, near flawless sound, and a series of films projected on a screen behind the stage."

AUGUST 31, 1979
DAYTON, OHIO
HARA ARENA, 1001 Shiloh Springs Road. Venue opened on November 1, 1964.
SUPPORT ACT: Roadmaster
TICKETS: $7.50 / $8.50 (average: $7.72), general admission
ATTENDANCE: 5,628 (Anthem/SRO); 5,064 (promoter)
CAPACITY: 7,900
CONCERT GROSS: $39,102
NOTES: The band worked on the new material during sound check, performing "The Spirit of Radio," "Freewill," and "Entre Nous."

SEPTEMBER 2, 1979
TORONTO, ONTARIO
VARSITY STADIUM, University of Toronto campus, 299 Bloor Street West. Venue opened on September 30, 1911.
SUPPORT ACT: FM
TICKETS: $12.50 CAD, general admission
ATTENDANCE: 8,134

NOTES: The stage at the end of the soggy football field was about eight feet high. Early fans secured spots, sitting down about five yards from the front of the stage, thinking that everyone would sit down for the show. Once Rush took the stage, enthusiastic fans flooded the front, obstructing the view of the mellow people who wanted to sit. People in the middle of the field began ripping up the grass and throwing hunks of sod at the fans down front. Howard's dry ice cauldrons had nothing on all the dirt flying through the air. This scenario continued for about an hour, while the band wailed away. Today, Varsity Stadium is home to the Toronto Rush, the city's professional ultimate frisbee team, who chose their name as a tribute to Alex, Geddy, and Neil.

TORONTO GLOBE AND MAIL: "Rush fans are an intensely loyal lot, primed for their heroes and having little regard for anyone else. Personally, I find the idea of a power trio with a singer who sounds like Lucy Ricardo rather trying after an hour or so. But the Rush fans who hung in through the seemingly endless (often as long as twenty minutes) songs seemed to be satisfied. For their perseverance, the fans were treated to some brand-new material from the band, including a song called 'The Spirit of Radio.' The new material sounded much like the old material: pretentious and bombastic."

TORONTO STAR: "Rush tries to bludgeon audience: Most of what the band does—such as 'The Spirit of Radio,' a new song they introduced to their fans last night—is wildly exciting. But the other material is pointless electronic overkill of the highest order."

IAN: "I turned around and there were about six Toronto soundmen standing behind me while I mixed. And they were all rubbing their chins at various points, and I could hear them mumbling, 'Aw, no . . .' I was like, 'OK, guys . . . I'm still standing right here, OK?'"

SEPTEMBER 5, 1979
LEXINGTON, KENTUCKY
RUPP ARENA THEATER, Lexington Center, 430 West Vine Street. Venue opened on October 7, 1976.
SUPPORT ACT: Pat Travers Band
TICKETS: $7.25 / $8.25

ATTENDANCE: 4,511 (Anthem/SRO); 5,500 (*Billboard*); sold out
CONCERT GROSS: $36,894 ($38,000—*Billboard*)

SEPTEMBER 7, 1979
CEDAR RAPIDS, IOWA
FIVE SEASONS CENTER, 370 First Avenue Northeast. Venue opened on January 25, 1979.
SUPPORT ACT: Pat Travers Band
TICKETS: $8.00 (advance) / $9.00 (day of), general admission
ATTENDANCE: 3,500 (approximate)
CAPACITY: 8,600
NOTES: Unbeknownst to the crowd, the venue's fire alarm went off toward the end of Rush's set. Everyone was unfazed, because it sounded like part of the concert. The alarm was due to sensors being ignited in the adjacent Stouffer's Five Seasons Hotel. Police and fire units searched the hotel and determined that it was a false alarm.[9]

CEDAR RAPIDS GAZETTE: "The sound itself reverberated as in an echo chamber—it came at the audience from the front of the hall and again, a half-second later from the rear of the hall. The effect was unnerving. But whether it's the fault of the hall's acoustics or the fault of sound crews and musicians who insist on turning up the amps just one more notch, Friday's concert was an assault on the senses that didn't have to be. Lee's vocals were frequently drowned out by Lifeson's guitar and Peart's drumming. That's a shame in the case of 'The Trees,' a message song in a decade that seems to have turned its back on 'messages.' A change of pace would have been welcome had Rush toned down 'The Trees' and allowed the audience to hear what the song had to say. Rush is a group that tends to produce thinking man's rock. But the sound system wouldn't allow a man to hear himself think."

SEPTEMBER 8, 1979
EAST TROY, WISCONSIN
ALPINE VALLEY MUSIC THEATRE, 2699 Highway D. Venue opened on June 30, 1977.
SUPPORT ACT: Pat Travers Band
TICKETS: $9.00 / $10.00 (includes a fifty cent parking fee)
ATTENDANCE: 18,730; sold out

SEPTEMBER 9, 1979
MOUNT PLEASANT, MICHIGAN
DANIEL P. ROSE CENTER ("ROSE ARENA"), Central Michigan University campus, 360 West Bloomfield Street. Venue opened on August 27, 1973.
SUPPORT ACT: Pat Travers Band
TICKETS: $7.50 (general admission) / $8.50 (reserved) / $8.22 (average)
ATTENDANCE: 4,170
CAPACITY: 5,200
CONCERT GROSS: $34,281
NOTES: The gig was delayed an hour, with Rush not taking the stage until 10:00 p.m.
CENTRAL MICHIGAN LIFE: "The intensity of the members while playing justified the quality of the concert and helped display them as exceptionally good live artists. The band seemed up for the performance and not disappointed by the less than overwhelming crowd size. 'Spirit of Radio,' off of the upcoming Rush album, seemed to portray a different sound for the band. The steady rhythm, compared to the band's earlier works, marks a notable difference."

SEPTEMBER 10, 1979
CLARKSTON, MICHIGAN
PINE KNOB MUSIC THEATRE, 7774 Sashabaw Road. Venue opened on June 25, 1972.
SUPPORT ACT: Pat Travers Band
TICKETS: $8.00 / $10.50
ATTENDANCE: 10,900
CAPACITY: 12,500

SEPTEMBER 12, 1979
ALLENTOWN, PENNSYLVANIA
FAIRGROUNDS GRANDSTAND, Great Allentown Fairgrounds, 302 North 17th Street. Venue opened on September 19, 1911. Original grandstand built in 1902, rebuilt in 1911.
SUPPORT ACT: Pat Travers Band
ATTENDANCE: 9,000 (approximate)[10]
CAPACITY: 10,500 (7,070 seats)
NOTES: Rush's final North American appearance of the '70s, and Neil's twenty-seventh birthday. Outdoor, general admission gig. The venue took the entire ticket upon entry, leaving fans without a stub. During sound check on this hot, sunny afternoon, the band blazed through the new songs, including "Entre Nous." A jovial mood permeated the set, with Pat Travers joining Rush onstage for a unique version of "Working Man."

GEDDY (ONSTAGE): "We would like to thank you for making the last gig of the tour very enjoyable!"
BETHLEHEM-GLOBE TIMES: "With science-fiction-like music and the high voice of lead singer Geddy Lee, the rock group Rush seems to be a cross between Yes and Alvin and the Chipmunks . . . with the volume turned up. The searingly loud music would be incomprehensible in an enclosed space. Rush is a rock group with a little more finesse than the Pat Travers Band. The music was not as loud or maybe my ears had just been sufficiently numbed, and the group had somewhat more coherence."

SEPTEMBER 21, 1979
STAFFORD, ENGLAND
NEW BINGLEY HALL, Staffordshire County Showground, Weston Road. Venue opened in 1975.
SUPPORT ACT: Wild Horses
TICKETS: £4.50
ATTENDANCE: 10,000 (approximate); oversold
NEIL WARNOCK (INTERNATIONAL AGENT): "Bingley Hall is an agricultural hall, and the promoter at that time was John Curd. This was one of those 'rubber-walled' venues, back in the day when these things were totally unsupervised. That venue would probably be licensed for about 7,000 people these days, but at that time, John would have offered about 10,000 or 11,000 people, and he would have offered a very good commercial fee to just do the two shows. It got very dangerous in there . . . I don't even want to think about what we got away with and what could have happened. It was animal. Health and safety would never allow it now. You wouldn't even begin to think about it. Back in those days, you took the fire marshal out for a drink. It was a different world."[11]
MIKE HIRSCH: "Bingley Hall . . . They oversold the shit out of that place. It was a small little ice hockey rink. You could really only fit about 4,000 people, and there must have been at least twice that. There were only two doors onto the floor, both off of stage right, halfway out. That's where they had the merch stand, and it was just nuts. We had a guy named Lofty on our traveling stage crew, and he was about 6'4", and he was literally holding the wall up by the merch booth. The foundation of the concrete wall was starting to crack and

break away from the wall. I'm just watching the crack move down the wall. So, I went over and shut the merch booth down. People were not happy, but I was not going to see my picture in the paper the next day standing by a bunch of dead people just to sell some more merch . . . that was not going to happen on my watch."[12]

SEPTEMBER 22, 1979
STAFFORD, ENGLAND
NEW BINGLEY HALL, Staffordshire County Showground, Weston Road
SUPPORT ACT: Wild Horses
TICKETS: £4.50
ATTENDANCE: 10,000 (approximate); oversold
NOTES: Rush's final live performance of the '70s. The band learned that a young fan had died in a car crash en route to the gig, so they dedicated "La Villa Strangiato" to him.
SOUNDS: "Rush's second New Bingley Hall gig is launched at 5.30 on a dismal Saturday afternoon. Geddy Lee (Neil and Alex are still at the hotel) is ushered unsuspectingly to a window and sees a hot air balloon hovering low over the hall. Its appearance coincides with an eruption of noisy cheering from the fans milling around the hall. Writ large across the balloon is the word 'Rush' . . . A starfield is expanding on the back-projection screen behind the band, and the crowd is going apeshit. Gothic sci-fi atmo electronics introduce 'Cygnus' as a star nova's onscreen. A rocket swims out through the cluster of planets, and Geddy is spotlit, stage-center, powering out a stormy riff and pushing the trio into maximum thrust. You wouldn't believe the hysteria going on down in that throng as a collapsar seethes on screen, and the band goes thundering into it. Clouds of mist part to reveal two cerebral hemispheres. They bowl through the epic, aflourish with energy, drama and contrast."
NICK KOTOS: "'Bingley Bash,' as the two shows at Bingley were promoted, was in an awful place. The rest was a six-week cloud of debauchery stuffed in between two other tours."[13]

1. Eric Hansen. Interview with Bob Kniffen, January 13, 2013.
2. Bill Banasiewicz. Interview with Herb Eimerman, October 15, 2014.
3. *CBC News Hamilton*, October 6, 2012. Joey Coleman.ca
4. *Dallas Herald.*
5. Skip Daly. Interview with Ian Grandy, 2012–2013.
6. Skip Daly. Interview with Nick Kotos, June 7, 2012.
7. Bill Banasiewicz. Interview with Hirsh Gardner, October 13, 2014.
8. Bill Banasiewicz. Interview with Johnny "Bee" Badanjek, June 11, 2016.
9. *The Cedar Rapids Gazette.*
10. *The Morning Call.*
11. Skip Daly. Interview with Neil Warnock, September 20, 2012.
12. Skip Daly. Interview with Mike Hirsch, July 17, 2012.
13. Skip Daly. Interview with Nick Kotos, June 7, 2012.

Chapter 10

THE PERMANENT WAVES TOUR

The *Permanent Waves* tour saw Rush perform to more than 650,000 fans over the course of ninety-six shows. The tour included several "evening with" engagements—a special treat that, some sixteen years later, would become a Rush norm. The set list, particularly beloved by longtime fans, was culled primarily from the band's more epic compositions, including "2112," "By-Tor and the Snow Dog," "Xanadu," "Natural Science," "Cygnus X-1 Book I: The Voyage," "Cygnus X-1 Book II: Hemispheres," "Jacob's Ladder," and "La Villa Strangiato."

While the band was seeking better work-life balance in their touring schedule, they were also making breakthroughs in the accessibility of their recorded music. *Permanent Waves* turned out to be a truly landmark release, with the success of "The Spirit of Radio" on the singles charts bringing Rush's music to a much broader audience. Within two months of its release, the record peaked at number four on the *Billboard* Top 200 Albums chart.

The band's growing popularity was reflected in the size of the new show. The full production was transported by three sixty-foot Kenworth tractor-trailers and included sixty tons of equipment. The front-of-house mixing console manned nightly by Ian was valued at $50,000 and was responsible for sending out the 120 decibels of sound that comprised the aural elements of a Rush performance at this time. The band also expanded their visual offerings, as Geddy's interest in film media began to influence the Rush concert experience. A slide display accompanied the live performance of "Natural Science," featuring a series of paintings by a Cleveland-based fan.

Furthermore, Rush was now headlining arenas. "We were starting to get so big that we were doing three or four nights in most places, five nights in some of those theaters, and it just wasn't practical," Neil said. "We couldn't say [playing arenas] was a compromise. It was a limitation that we faced, that too many people wanted to see us. It's not something that we're able to control. So we were pushed into the arenas basically by the laws of supply and demand."

Overall, the *Permanent Waves* tour lasted six months—a long run by most measures but a short one by Rush's historical standards. Quite astonishingly, this was the first Rush tour that actually turned a profit—a just reward after spending six nonstop years on the road. But the financial benefits, as Neil was quick to point out, were hardly the main reason for being out on the road.

"I'm not working toward some goal of success," he said. "What I'm doing now is what I've always wanted to do. We've been at it for six years now, and I still like the work part. I get fed up with being on the road, but it has nothing to do with the performing. It has to do with the unnecessary garbage that happens in the other twenty-two hours of the day. When it comes down to those two hours that we stand onstage and play, I still enjoy them a lot."

OPPOSITE TOP: South Yarmouth, MA; The Rush road crew.

OPPOSITE BOTTOM: Alex and Geddy at the mic.

Rush Crew
Sept. 1980 So. Yarmouth, Mass.

TOP: Binghamton, NY; Alex sporting his white doubleneck at the Broome County Arena.

ABOVE: Binghamton, NY; In a lighter moment at the Broome County Arena, Alex strumming the guitar of Geddy's doubleneck during "Xanadu."

TOUR HISTORY
PERMANENT WAVES

SET LIST:		
"2112: Overture"	"Natural Science"	"Jacob's Ladder"
"2112: The Temples of Syrinx"	"A Passage to Bangkok"	"Working Man" (reggae intro)
"2112: Presentation"	"The Trees"	"Finding My Way"
"2112: Soliloquy"	"Cygnus X-1" (abridged)	"Anthem"
"2112: Grand Finale"	"Hemispheres: Prelude"	"Bastille Day"
"Freewill"	"Hemispheres: Armageddon"	"In the Mood"
"By-Tor and the Snow Dog" (abridged)	"Hemispheres: Cygnus"	"Drum Solo"
"Xanadu"	"Hemispheres: The Sphere"	**Encore:**
"The Spirit of Radio"	"Closer to the Heart"	"La Villa Strangiato"(with electric
	"Beneath, Between, and Behind" (abridged)	guitar intro)

JANUARY 17, 1980
FREDERICTON, NEW BRUNSWICK
AITKEN UNIVERSITY CENTRE, University of New Brunswick campus, 20 MacKay Drive. Venue opened on May 16, 1976.
SUPPORT ACT: Max Webster
TICKETS: $7.50 CAD
ATTENDANCE: 2,320
CAPACITY: 4,258
NOTES: The opening date of the 1980 *Permanent Waves* Tour featured the live debut of "Natural Science" and "Jacob's Ladder."

JANUARY 18, 1980
MONCTON, NEW BRUNSWICK
MONCTON COLISEUM, 377 Killam Drive. Venue opened on April 19, 1973.
SUPPORT ACT: Max Webster
TICKETS: $7.50 CAD (all seats reserved)
ATTENDANCE: 4,221

JANUARY 19, 1980
HALIFAX, NOVA SCOTIA
METRO CENTRE, 1800 Argyle Street. Venue opened on February 17, 1978.
SUPPORT ACT: Max Webster
TICKETS: $7.50 CAD
ATTENDANCE: 5,896
CAPACITY: 5,000 to 7,000 (depending upon setup)

JANUARY 21, 1980
MONTREAL, QUEBEC
MONTREAL FORUM, 2313 Saint Catherine Street West. Historic venue opened on November 29, 1924.
SUPPORT ACT: Garfield
TICKETS: $8.50 CAD
ATTENDANCE: 8,405
CAPACITY: 16,500 for ice hockey / 19,000 with standing room

GARFIELD FRENCH (GARFIELD LEAD SINGER): "I think it was the last show we gave. I didn't hear much of Rush that night because I left very shortly after finishing, but what I heard sounded great."[1]
GREG LUKENS (NATIONAL SOUND): "Michael Hirsch's mother is Belgian, and Mike happens to speak very good French. So, we were at a show in Montreal, and Mike is an intimidating guy. Well, he was—how shall we say—'forthright' with his instructions to the union crew. The union crew assumed that these idiot Americans wouldn't speak French, so they were seething oaths about Michael in French. Michael finally turned around and pointed his finger at them, and in perfect Belgian French described exactly how he was going to carve them up and choke them with their knotted entrails. That was the end of that."[2]

JANUARY 22–23, 1980
ALBANY, NEW YORK
PALACE THEATRE, 19 Clinton Avenue. Historic venue opened on October 23, 1931.
SUPPORT ACT: Max Webster
TICKETS: $9.50
ATTENDANCE: 2,251 per show; sold out
NOTES: Second show added by popular demand.
KNICKERBOCKER NEWS: "Rush opens two-night stand with force: Its audience has an intensity, standing, filling the aisles, and waving its arms in the air during various emotional portions of the music. The lights have as much emotional purpose as some of the music."

JANUARY 24, 1980
ROCHESTER, NEW YORK
ROCHESTER COMMUNITY WAR MEMORIAL, 100 Exchange Boulevard. Venue opened on October 18, 1955.
SUPPORT ACT: Max Webster
TICKETS: $8.50 / $9.50 (all seats reserved)
ATTENDANCE: 7,214
CAPACITY: 10,250
NOTES: The band demanded that the concert be entirely reserved seating.[3] A Big Gulp was spilled on the lighting board, creating a frustrating situation for Howard.
DEMOCRAT AND CHRONICLE: "Rush gives you your money's worth. They performed for more than two hours and framed their set with stunning lighting effects."
PIONEER (ST. JOHN FISHER COLLEGE): "The band's new album and Rochester show proved to its followers that everything must change—even what was a proven, if limited success."
HOWARD: "Rochester was my worst horror story. The show was about to start, and as I called the house lights and the place went dark, a huge Big Gulp came over in the air, flipped upside down and doused the complete lighting board. We had to do the whole show that night with just spotlights because all of my consoles, including the backup, were flooded with ignorance and a Big Gulp. I had my new Electrosonic board that I loved so much. I had two of them and they were useless after that. I had to get two new ones. I was less busy for that show and very upset. I was young, and I had a very bad temper when I was young."[4]

JANUARY 26, 1980
POUGHKEEPSIE, NEW YORK
MAIR HALL, MID-HUDSON CIVIC CENTER, 14 Civic Center Plaza. Venue opened on November 28, 1976.
SUPPORT ACT: Max Webster
TICKETS: $9.00 (all tickets, reserved show)
ATTENDANCE: 3,226; oversold
NOTES: Geddy introduced "Working Man" with an Italian accent during the reggae intro. This date was a last-minute addition, and was put on sale just two weeks before the gig. The addition to the itinerary wasn't in time to be listed on the tour shirts, which had already been printed.

JANUARY 27, 1980
BINGHAMTON, NEW YORK
BROOME COUNTY WAR MEMORIAL ARENA, 1 Stuart Street. Venue opened on August 29, 1973.
SUPPORT ACT: Max Webster
TICKETS: $7.50 / $8.50
ATTENDANCE: 3,054
CAPACITY: 7,000
NOTES: Fans filed out of the show to the gentle strains of "We'll Meet Again" by Vera Lynn.

JANUARY 29, 1980
BIRMINGHAM, ALABAMA
BOUTWELL MEMORIAL AUDITORIUM, 1930 Eighth Avenue North. Venue dedicated on June 1, 1924.
SUPPORT ACT: Max Webster
TICKETS: $7.50
ATTENDANCE: 2,721
CAPACITY: 6,000
THE BIRMINGHAM NEWS: "How Can 'Rush' Threesome Be So Loud?"

JANUARY 30, 1980
ATLANTA, GEORGIA
THE OMNI, 100 Techwood Drive Northwest. Venue opened on October 14, 1972.
SUPPORT ACT: Max Webster
TICKETS: $7.50 / $8.50
ATTENDANCE: 5,200

FEBRUARY 1, 1980
OKLAHOMA CITY, OKLAHOMA
MYRIAD ARENA, One Myriad Gardens. Venue opened on November 5, 1972.
SUPPORT ACT: Max Webster
ATTENDANCE: 6,699

FEBRUARY 2, 1980
FORT WORTH, TEXAS
TARRANT COUNTY CONVENTION CENTER, 1111 Houston Street. Venue dedicated on November 21, 1968.
SUPPORT ACT: Max Webster
TICKETS: $8.00
ATTENDANCE: 11,905
THE DALLAS NEWS, LISA ALSTON (LONGTIME FAN IN RESPONSE TO A NEGATIVE REVIEW): "The Convention Center was packed with enthusiastic rockers who witnessed one of the best-performed rock concerts ever."

FEBRUARY 3, 1980
SAN ANTONIO, TEXAS
CONVENTION CENTER ARENA, HemisFair Park Complex, 601 Hemisfair Way. Venue opened on April 6, 1968.
SUPPORT ACT: Max Webster
TICKETS: $8.00 / $8.50
ATTENDANCE: 14,150 (Anthem/SRO); sold out
CONCERT GROSS: $117,818
HOWARD: "There was a murder in San Antonio on one tour. Somebody got murdered in the audience. It was general admission, and when the show was over and house lights were up, everybody had left and there was a dead body lying there. That wasn't a great night."[5]

FEBRUARY 5, 1980
HOUSTON, TEXAS
SAM HOUSTON COLISEUM, 801 Bagby Street. Venue dedicated on November 16, 1937.
SUPPORT ACT: Max Webster
TICKETS: $8.50
ATTENDANCE: 10,341 (Anthem/SRO)
CAPACITY: 12,000
CONCERT GROSS: $87,543
NOTES: Someone dropped a cherry bomb down a toilet, and the backstage area flooded. As a result, the encore ("La Villa Strangiato") was not performed.
ROBERT FRAZER (SEE FACTOR): "We were doing the show, and the house disconnect for power was on the back wall of the venue. Well, the restroom was upstairs on the second floor, and the kids upstairs had destroyed this restroom, and the water was just flowing down—right over this disconnect. There was a puddle of water about twenty feet wide, and the water was just flowing right over this switch. Somebody threw down a pallet so that you could stand on the pallet, and then some brave soul went out there and threw the disconnect breaker so that they could get the water shut off upstairs and so that no one would get electrocuted. I think it was Mike Hirsch that threw the breaker."[6]

FEBRUARY 6, 1980
CORPUS CHRISTI, TEXAS
MEMORIAL COLISEUM, 402 South Shoreline Boulevard. Venue dedicated on September 26, 1954.
SUPPORT ACT: Max Webster
TICKETS: $8.00 (all seats), general admission floor
ATTENDANCE: 4,503
CAPACITY: 6,000, with 2,615 permanent seats
NOTES: This was the first major rock concert in Corpus Christi after eleven people died at a general admission show by the Who in Cincinnati, so there was a police crackdown (complete with drug-sniffing dogs) at the Coliseum. Twenty-one arrests were made for marijuana possession and public intoxication, "which is not unusual for a crowd of almost 5,000," according to police chief Bill Banner.[7]

FEBRUARY 7, 1980
AUSTIN, TEXAS
MUNICIPAL AUDITORIUM, 400 South Street. Venue opened on January 5, 1959.
SUPPORT ACT: Max Webster
TICKETS: $8.50
ATTENDANCE: 5,124; sold out

FEBRUARY 8, 1980
DALLAS, TEXAS
DALLAS CONVENTION CENTER ARENA, 650 South Griffin Street. Venue opened on September 8, 1957.
SUPPORT ACT: Max Webster
TICKETS: $8.00
ATTENDANCE: 7,759
CAPACITY: 9,286
FORT WORTH (2/2/80) AND DALLAS (2/8/80) COMBINED GROSS: $155,954

FEBRUARY 10, 1980
VALLEY CENTER, KANSAS
BRITT BROWN ARENA, Kansas Coliseum complex, 1229 East 85th Street North. Venue opened on September 28, 1978.
SUPPORT ACT: Roadmaster
TICKETS: $8.75 (including parking)
NOTES: Rescheduled to February 28, most likely a result of NBC Radio recording the shows in St. Louis.

FEBRUARY 11–13, 1980
ST. LOUIS, MISSOURI
HENRY W. KIEL MUNICIPAL AUDITORIUM, 1401 Clark Street. Historic venue dedicated on April 14, 1934.
SUPPORT ACT: Max Webster
TICKETS: $5.95 / $6.95
ATTENDANCE: 9,845 per show; sold out
CONCERT GROSS: $67,291 per show
NOTES: KSHE-FM's Third Annual Valentine's Day Massacre Concert. Recorded by NBC's Source Radio Network for future broadcast. The edited recording culled from the three St. Louis concerts aired March 28 to 30, 1980, and featured about half of the full tour set list, with particular highlights being "2112," "Natural Science," and the set-ending medley. The band's three sold-out concerts in St. Louis set an in-house attendance record for Kiel Auditorium and were the week's top-grossing dates.[8]
***ST. LOUIS POST-DISPATCH*:** "The pace set by Rush was furious. They played super loud amidst a diamond bright light show. The effect was totally impressive although occasionally the melody in some of the new songs was nowhere to be found. This was not the case with one of the group's best-known new songs, 'The Spirit of Radio.' Lifeson's guitar part conjured up visions of crazed radio waves beaming through the night. The presence of spurts of reggae in the song was hard to explain, though. Another new song called 'Natural Science' had the potential to become another 'Fly by Night,' a Rush anthem. It was trio music at its finest."

FEBRUARY 15, 1980
EVANSVILLE, INDIANA
ROBERTS MUNICIPAL STADIUM, University of Evansville campus, 2600 Division Street. Venue dedicated on December 1, 1956.
SUPPORT ACT: Max Webster
TICKETS: $7.00 / $8.00
ATTENDANCE: 7,681 (Anthem/SRO)
CONCERT GROSS: $56,055

FEBRUARY 16, 1980
DAYTON, OHIO
UNIVERSITY OF DAYTON ARENA, 1801 Edwin C. Moses Boulevard. Venue opened on December 6, 1969.
SUPPORT ACT: Max Webster
TICKETS: $7.50 / $8.50
ATTENDANCE: 7,761 (Anthem/SRO)
CAPACITY: 11,078
CONCERT GROSS: $65,761
NOTES: Members of the Cincinnati City Task Force on Crowd Control and Public Safety were in attendance and met with the band after the show to gain their input for ways to avoid a recurrence of the Who concert tragedy, where eleven people were killed trying to enter the venue, which had festival seating.[9]

FEBRUARY 17, 1980
DETROIT, MICHIGAN
JOE LOUIS ARENA, 600 Civic Center Drive. Venue opened on December 12, 1979.
SUPPORT ACT: Max Webster
TICKETS: $9.00 / $10.00 / $11.00
ATTENDANCE: 14,399; sold out
NOTES: The first rock concert ever held at this new venue. When tickets went on sale for this gig back in January, about 2,000 fans who had queued in subfreezing temperatures got riled up after a rumor spread about a lack of tickets for everyone. The result was six glass doors smashed and another broken. Detroit police responded with fifty officers, who arrested one overanxious fan for disorderly conduct. There were no injuries reported.
***THE DETROIT NEWS*:** "A feeling of breaking new ground permeated the air. 'You know something?' bellowed the show's emcee, WABX disc jockey Steve Kostan. 'You, me, everybody in this whole . . . place, we're making history tonight!' Rush is obviously in its natural element when it comes to the concert

environment, and the band is composed of three consummately talented musicians. But Rush imprisons its music in such wearisome heavy metal conventions that its skills rarely have the opportunity to come forth. The whole affair ultimately became as predictable and grating as Geddy Lee's high-pitched 'Thank YEW' at the end of each song. Nevertheless, Rush undeniably fills a need: The throngs roared their unbridled delight at every change of key or tempo, and the rafters held more banners than you're ever likely to see for McCourt or Nedomansky. Still, Joe Louis coulda had a real contendah for its musical debut. The pushover that served as main event was game but couldn't go the distance."

FEBRUARY 18, 1980
RICHFIELD, OHIO
RICHFIELD COLISEUM, 2923 Streetsboro Road. Venue opened on October 26, 1974.
SUPPORT ACT: Max Webster
TICKETS: $7.50 (advance) / $8.50 (day of)
ATTENDANCE: 17,349 (Anthem/SRO); sold out
CONCERT GROSS: $131,100
***SCENE MAGAZINE*:** "It was the kind of show that nobody there wanted to end; Rush—the Money's Worth Band of Rock—enthralled, delighted, mesmerized, and totally controlled nearly 18,000 Rush fanatics with a near-perfect display of rock mastery. Tonight, Rush—masters of metallic moods—gave three of the finest individual performances ever presented at the Coliseum. No excuse for missing this one. Rush lives up to, and also sets, standards that all touring bands of the '80s must follow."

FEBRUARY 19, 1980
DETROIT, MICHIGAN
JOE LOUIS ARENA, 600 Civic Center Drive
SUPPORT ACT: Max Webster
TICKETS: $9.00 / $10.00 / $11.00
ATTENDANCE: 8,627 (Anthem/SRO)
TWO-DAY DETROIT GROSS: $260,495
***SOUNDS*:** "Five minutes into the opener, '2112', and the front rows were a mass of writhing bodies. Alex, having a bird's-eye view from the stage, said afterwards security men were punching out kids,

dragging them out of the melee. A trickle of limp bodies, victims of fights or pharmaceutical cocktails, was carried from the stage-front area to backstage before the bouncers finally quelled the crowd. This threw the band who, although steaming full-tilt through the set, afterwards complained of distraction and loss of energy. A contributory factor might have been that their close friends Max Webster were leaving the tour after Detroit. Also, Max Webster's keyboard player was leaving the band that night. Things didn't improve backstage, where dozens of people, friends, and freeloaders, milled around the band. Neil sat in one corner, hoping no one would notice him there, while Alex and Geddy sloped off to Max Webster's dressing room."

FEBRUARY 27, 1980
KANSAS CITY, MISSOURI
KEMPER ARENA, 1800 Genessee Street at 17th Street. Venue dedicated on October 18, 1974.
SUPPORT ACT: Roadmaster
TICKETS: $8.00 / $9.00
ATTENDANCE: 13,047 (Anthem/SRO); sold out
CONCERT GROSS: $112,939
NOTES: First concert since the venue reopened on February 20, 1980, following a June 4, 1979, roof collapse caused by flooding rains and 70 mph winds.
UNIVERSITY NEWS: "Rush Concert Boring, Offensive to Ears: If only Rush had some songs to play, rather than discordant progressions, the concert might have been bearable. Instead it was so dull that I found myself wandering to the rebuilt ceiling, wondering how many decibels it could stand."

FEBRUARY 28, 1980
VALLEY CENTER, KANSAS
BRITT BROWN ARENA, Kansas Coliseum complex, 1229 East 85th Street North. Venue opened on September 28, 1978.
SUPPORT ACT: Roadmaster
TICKETS: $8.75 (including parking)
ATTENDANCE: 7,305
NOTES: Rescheduled from February 10. Originally, this date was slated for Pershing Auditorium in Lincoln, Nebraska, but that gig was canceled on February 12 to make room for the Valley Center show. Venue aka "the big brown barn."

Thirty-one people were arrested on various drug charges, including about fifteen juveniles. Most of the arrests stem from minor marijuana possession, according to Sedgwick County sheriff Johnnie Darr, who also stated that "drug use at the Rush concert was heavy and the twenty undercover officers assigned to the Coliseum weren't able to arrest everyone using dope."[10]

MARCH 1, 1980
DENVER, COLORADO
MCNICHOLS SPORTS ARENA, 1635 Clay Street. Venue opened on August 22, 1975.
SUPPORT ACT: Roadmaster
TICKETS: $7.00 / $9.00
ATTENDANCE: 13,363 (Anthem/SRO)
CONCERT GROSS: $126,125
NOTES: *Amusement Business* lists a gross of $126,121. Top-grossing concert of the week.[11] Rush was chosen "Band of the Year" by the readers of *Sounds* magazine.

MARCH 2, 1980
ALBUQUERQUE, NEW MEXICO
TINGLEY COLISEUM, New Mexico State Fairgrounds, 300 San Pedro Drive Northeast. Venue dedicated on September 28, 1957.
SUPPORT ACT: Roadmaster
TICKETS: $8.50 (general admission show)
ATTENDANCE: 6,018 (Anthem/SRO)
CONCERT GROSS: $72,000
CANADIAN PRESS: "Canada's biggest rock 'n' roll stars are sitting in a shabby dressing room in Albuquerque, New Mexico. Back here it's almost peaceful. These three guys don't look like rock stars. Apart from a case of beer, some half-eaten sandwiches and a warm bottle of Dom Perignon, there are no signs of a bacchanalian feast."[12]

MARCH 3, 1980
TUCSON, ARIZONA
TUCSON COMMUNITY CENTER ARENA, 260 South Church Street. Venue opened on November 8, 1971.
SUPPORT ACT: Roadmaster
TICKETS: $9.00
ATTENDANCE: 4,773
CAPACITY: 8,600
ARIZONA DAILY STAR: "Rush is still feeding the need: By the time Rush hit the

stage, the audience were rarin' to go, greeting the band with a sea of upraised fists."

MARCH 4, 1980
PHOENIX, ARIZONA
ARIZONA VETERANS MEMORIAL COLISEUM, Arizona State Fairgrounds, 1826 West McDowell Road. Venue opened on November 3, 1965.
SUPPORT ACT: Roadmaster
TICKETS: $8.50, general admission
ATTENDANCE: 13,971 (Anthem/SRO); sold out
CONCERT GROSS: $118,754
ARIZONA REPUBLIC: "In place of their new-wave contemporaries, Peart, Lifeson, and Lee bring to the present scene a sense of artistic discipline that alone is enough to give them distinction."

MARCH 6, 1980
SAN DIEGO, CALIFORNIA
SAN DIEGO SPORTS ARENA, 3500 Sports Arena Boulevard. Venue opened on November 17, 1966.
SUPPORT ACT: 38 Special
TICKETS: $8.50
ATTENDANCE: 7,969 (Anthem/SRO)
CAPACITY: 9,364
CONCERT GROSS: $74,353
NOTES: Rush's California run was so successful that promoters asked them to headline the massive Anaheim Stadium next October,[13] but that date never came to fruition.

MARCH 7, 1980
SAN BERNARDINO, CALIFORNIA
SWING AUDITORIUM, National Orange Show Grounds, 689 E Street. Historic venue dedicated on March 10, 1949.
SUPPORT ACT: 38 Special
TICKETS: $8.00 / $9.00
ATTENDANCE: 7,200; sold out
CONCERT GROSS: $57,600
NOTES: In Southern California, the band reunited with their families, who flew down from Ontario to visit.
LOS ANGELES TIMES: "38 Special was a godsend next to headliner Rush. Alex Lifeson did get almost every possible sound from his battery of guitars, but they were mostly recycled. Neil Peart is a vigorous drummer and contributes most of the band's 'what's-life-all-about' lyrics. Geddy Lee, who sings in a squeaky Robert Plant voice, doubled on bass and keyboards. It was all very workmanlike."

MARCH 9, 1980
LONG BEACH, CALIFORNIA
LONG BEACH ARENA, 300 East Ocean Boulevard. Venue opened on October 6, 1962.
SUPPORT ACT: 38 Special
TICKETS: $8.50 / $9.50
ATTENDANCE: 9,423 (Anthem/SRO)
CAPACITY: 13,500
CONCERT GROSS: $87,674

MARCH 10, 1980
INGLEWOOD, CALIFORNIA
THE FORUM, 3900 West Manchester Boulevard. Venue opened on December 30, 1967.
SUPPORT ACT: 38 Special
TICKETS: $8.75 / $9.75
ATTENDANCE: 10,304 (Anthem/SRO)
CAPACITY: 18,000
CONCERT GROSS: $96,290
NOTES: Geddy was irked that the band was forced to attend a music business function.
GEDDY (BACKSTAGE AFTER THE GIG): "Who are these people? I don't care if this is LA. These people in radio, in the record industry, they never supported us getting here. The kids did. We were pressured into being here and smiling. We shouldn't be here."[14]
LOS ANGELES TIMES: "One fan's T-shirt Friday read: 'Rush—God's Gift to Me.' After the group's two-hour set, I leaned more toward 'Lord, Have Mercy.' Like a hapless but successful TV situation comedy, Rush employs enough familiar rock elements to be diverting: Led Zeppelin assault, Moody Blues' cosmic musings, and Emerson, Lake and Palmer technology. Friday's highly responsive audience didn't seem to mind that most of those ingredients have long been exhausted in rock and that Rush does little to revitalize them."[15]

MARCH 11, 1980
FRESNO, CALIFORNIA
SELLAND ARENA, 700 M Street, at Ventura. Venue opened on October 11, 1966.
SUPPORT ACT: 38 Special
TICKETS: $8.75 / $9.75
ATTENDANCE: 5,116
CAPACITY: 7,158

MARCH 13, 1980
SACRAMENTO, CALIFORNIA
SUPPORT ACT: 38 Special
NOTES: This date is not in SRO's records and may have been canceled.

MARCH 14–15, 1980
DALY CITY, CALIFORNIA
COW PALACE, 2600 Geneva Avenue. Venue opened on April 20, 1941.
SUPPORT ACT: 38 Special
TICKETS: $8.00 / $9.00 / $10.00 (very limited reserved)
ATTENDANCE: 7,250; sold out[16]
CONCERT GROSS: $50,493
NOTES: Mostly a general admission concert.

MARCH 16, 1980
EUGENE, OREGON
MCARTHUR COURT ARENA, University of Oregon campus, 1801 University Street. Venue opened on January 14, 1927.
SUPPORT ACT: 38 Special
ATTENDANCE: 3,100.
JEFF CARLISI (38 SPECIAL GUITARIST): "Rush were great to tour with, and we also had a lot of fun offstage with them."[17]

MARCH 18–19, 1980
SEATTLE, WASHINGTON
SEATTLE CENTER COLISEUM, 305 Harrison Street. Venue opened on April 21, 1962.
SUPPORT ACT: 38 Special
TICKETS: $9.50 / $10.50
ATTENDANCE: 13,190 per show; sold out; *Billboard* lists the two-day attendance as 26,627
CONCERT GROSS: $127,291 per show
NOTES: After these two Seattle dates, trash and broken bottles littered the grounds outside the Coliseum, causing community concerns. The cleanup expense was $500 per night, which was included in the venue rental of $14,807 each day (12 percent of ticket sale gross).[18] The two Seattle dates were the week's top-grossing concerts.[19]

MARCH 20, 1980
PORTLAND, OREGON
MEMORIAL COLISEUM, 1401 North Wheeler. Venue opened on November 3, 1960.
SUPPORT ACT: 38 Special
TICKETS: $8.50 / $9.00 / $9.50 (all seats reserved)

ATTENDANCE: 10,047 (Anthem/SRO); sold out
CONCERT GROSS: $92,649
PORTLAND OREGON JOURNAL: "Rush galvanized a capacity crowd with a wall of sound. For its massive following of teen-age fans, Rush creates a musical suit of armor. Loud, technically exact guitars mixed with science-fiction fantasy shield the audience against the dull, gray world. For this, Rush shows they do care about their fans. For all their cosmic doodling, the main point of Rush is to open the audience to different kinds of music. Unfortunately, the band is dry, cumbersome, and mechanized. Next time, the trio should show more feeling."

MARCH 21, 1980
SPOKANE, WASHINGTON
SPOKANE COLISEUM, 1101 North Howard Street. Venue opened on December 3, 1954.
SUPPORT ACT: 38 Special
TICKETS: $9.00 (day of)
ATTENDANCE: 6,972
CAPACITY: 8,500
NOTES: Due to venue constraints, the band was unable to use their film projector.
SPOKANE DAILY CHRONICLE: "Rush may be only a three-man rock-and-roll band, but it performs better than many groups twice its size. A large crowd warmly applauded the good show-opening band, 38 Special, from Florida. But the warmest response was saved for Rush, which treated the audience to a light and sound extravaganza."

MARCH 23, 1980
EDMONTON, ALBERTA
NORTHLANDS COLISEUM, 7424 118th Avenue NW. Venue opened on November 10, 1974.
SUPPORT ACT: Saga
TICKETS: $9.50 CAD
ATTENDANCE: 10,025; sold out
EDMONTON SUN: "Rush smashing sci-fi rockers: On the way to super-stardom, Rush has relaxed and returned to earth. The three enjoyed each other's performing talents and were loose and comfortable on stage. Throughout the show, the 10,000-strong audience listened rhapsodically, with almost worship respect."

MICHAEL SADLER (SAGA LEAD VOCALIST): "We always had a lot of fun doing shows with Rush. I think it made for a great double bill. They're a great bunch of guys, and I really respect their music."[20]

MARCH 24, 1980
CALGARY, ALBERTA
MAX BELL MEMORIAL ARENA, 1001 Barlow Trail SE. Venue opened on November 7, 1978.
SUPPORT ACT: Saga
ATTENDANCE: 2,223; sold out
NOTES: *Calgary Herald* lists attendance at 3,000.
CALGARY HERALD: "Decibels decimate Rush's imagination: Where the argument that Rush's lyric abilities are an important facet of their music might hold up on recorded material, it loses credibility in the cellar-like acoustics of Max Bell Arena. The attempt to challenge the audience's intellect, regardless of how meaningful the lyrics might be, degenerates into a more basic mood created by a bass line pulsing in the pit of your stomach while the guitarist strikes chord after pulsing chord."

MARCH 25, 1980
CALGARY, ALBERTA
MAX BELL MEMORIAL ARENA, 1001 Barlow Trail SE
SUPPORT ACT: Saga
ATTENDANCE: 2,223; sold out
NOTES: *Calgary Herald* lists attendance at 3,000.

MARCH 27, 1980
VICTORIA, BRITISH COLUMBIA
VICTORIA MEMORIAL ARENA, 1925 Blanshard Street. Venue opened on July 20, 1949.
SUPPORT ACT: Saga
ATTENDANCE: 3,086
CAPACITY: 5,961

MARCH 28, 1980
NANAIMO, BRITISH COLUMBIA
FRANK CRANE ARENA, Beban Park Complex, 2300 Bowen Road. Venue opened on January 2, 1976.
SUPPORT ACT: Saga
CAPACITY: 2,906
NOTES: Concert canceled at the eleventh hour due to technical requirements.[21] NBC Radio aired the previously recorded St. Louis concert throughout America.

MARCH 29, 1980
VANCOUVER, BRITISH COLUMBIA
PACIFIC COLISEUM, Pacific National Exhibition Fairgrounds, 100 North Renfrew. Venue dedicated on January 8, 1968.
SUPPORT ACT: Saga
TICKETS: $9.00 CAD
ATTENDANCE: 7,012
CAPACITY: 16,123
VANCOUVER SUN: "Rush: not just another hard rock band."

MARCH 31, 1980
REGINA, SASKATCHEWAN
AGRIDOME, 1700 Elphinstone Street at Exhibition Park. Venue opened on August 1, 1977.
SUPPORT ACT: Saga
CAPACITY: 6,186
NOTES: This date is not in SRO's records. No ads or reviews could be found in the *Regina Leader-Post*, though a full-page record store advertisement, with the band's entire catalog on sale, appeared the day after the show, which indicates the possibility that it took place.
STEVE NEGUS (SAGA DRUMMER): "The thing that made Saga different from other progressive bands was my R&B background. The grooves are totally different from say, what King Crimson, Yes, Genesis, or Rush were playing. I was actually compared to Neil Peart back then, but apart from the fact that we both play drums and grew up five miles from each other, there is no other comparison. Neil plays from a prog rock angle with a lot more time signatures. But back in the day, the big three were Rush, Max Webster, and Saga, so we did shows at Maple Leaf Gardens and Saga and Rush toured together. All coming up at the same time, of course there were comparisons. This was our peer group."[22]

APRIL 1, 1980
WINNIPEG, MANITOBA
WINNIPEG ARENA, 1430 Maroons Road. Venue opened on October 18, 1955.
SUPPORT ACT: Saga
TICKETS: $8.50 CAD
ATTENDANCE: 3,490
CAPACITY: 15,393
WINNIPEG TRIBUNE: "Rush electrifying at Arena concert: From the moment they appeared on stage, the audience entered

a musical trance which carried them through an entire evening of some of the best rock Winnipeg has heard in a long time. Their music is hard and deliberate, holding nothing back; they are masters at their profession."

APRIL 3–6, 1980
CHICAGO, ILLINOIS
INTERNATIONAL AMPHITHEATRE, 4220 South Halsted Street. Venue opened on December 1, 1934.
AN EVENING WITH RUSH
TICKETS: $10.50
ATTENDANCE: 14,103 per show; sold out
CONCERT GROSS: $110,432
NOTES: Rush became the first act to sell out the International Amphitheatre four nights. April 6 was Bob "Mo" Kniffen's last date working with the band.
DAILY INTELLIGENCER: "Five golds and four nights in Chicago add up to success: The banner hanging from the balcony at stage left in International Amphitheatre reads 'Chicago Freaks Love Rush.' Rush fans roar their approval as the first crashing, sustained chords of '2112' open the show. For over two hours, the group blasts out crowd pleasers from their eight albums using background visuals for several numbers, most spectacularly for the long space opera 'Cygnus,' a science-fiction tale that took two albums to work out. However, the audience cheers loudest when Rush plays several numbers from *Permanent Waves*."
BOB KNIFFEN (SEE FACTOR): "That was the end of it with them for me. I was going to quit being a roadie altogether, but Nick Kotos called me to do a Billy Joel tour in the summer, and then I quit after that. 1980 was the end of my roadie career. I was just sick of it because I was a musician, and I was sick of setting other people's shit up. I wasn't working a lot as a musician. I was some poor yobbo from upstate New York, and I took this gig to get out of the area and make some money and travel and have a good time. And I sure did that. With Rush, they would put everybody's name in their record jackets and tour programs. Every crew member, everybody was on there. Even the guy who did their laundry! They were just wonderful about that. While I didn't necessary gravitate towards their music as a listener, in my opinion it

is totally honest. They don't do anything that they don't really believe in. They don't do anything with an idea towards *Hey, this is going to sell because so and so is doing that and we can capture that market.* They are very honest people and musicians. Rush usually gave people bonuses and well-thought-out items like coats that would be warm in the winter, bathrobes that you could keep, really nice stuff. Sandy Pearlman from Blue Oyster Cult said about roadies, 'Just give them a T-shirt and some sandwich meat and fuck 'em.' To be treated that way and then come onto the Rush tour, you're like, *When is the bubble going to bust and these guys turn out to be assholes?* It never busted; they were always what they were."

APRIL 17–19, 1980
MILWAUKEE, WISCONSIN
MECCA AUDITORIUM, 500 West Kilbourn Avenue. Venue dedicated on September 21, 1909.
SUPPORT ACT: 38 Special
TICKETS: $8.50 / $9.50
ATTENDANCE: 5,528 per show; sold out
CONCERT GROSS: $50,686 per show
NOTES: *Billboard* lists total (three-day) attendance at 16,943, or 5,647 per show.
MILWAUKEE JOURNAL SENTINEL: "Band Rush blasts off with heavy-metal thunder: The ride threw the young audience into uncontrolled outbursts or plunged them deeply into what seemed like almost a comatose state. Although spacey instrumental rock has few places to go, Rush strides near its top."

APRIL 20, 1980
MADISON, WISCONSIN
DANE COUNTY VETERANS MEMORIAL COLISEUM, Dane County Expo Center Fairgrounds, 2200 Rimrock Road. Venue opened on March 16, 1967.
SUPPORT ACT: 38 Special
TICKETS: $7.50 (advance) / $8.50 (day of), general admission
ATTENDANCE: 10,100 (Anthem/SRO); sold out
CONCERT GROSS: $75,113
VARIETY: "Always a top draw here, Rush again sold-out Dane Coliseum and thrilled a youthful house in a program that was excellent on all counts. Lee and

Lifeson stood up front and expertly manipulated a wide assortment of electronic sound modifiers in sonically depicting the material's expansive futuristic and prehistoric cosmologies. This unusually strong Coliseum show was also largely due to Howard Ungerleider, whose dazzling light show was music in itself and merits equal note."

APRIL 22, 1980
GREEN BAY, WISCONSIN
BROWN COUNTY VETERANS MEMORIAL ARENA, 1901 South Oneida Street. Venue opened on November 11, 1957.
SUPPORT ACT: 38 Special
TICKETS: $7.50 (advance) / $8.50 (day of), general admission
ATTENDANCE: 3,383
CAPACITY: 7,000
NOTES: *Green Bay Press-Gazette* lists attendance at 5,500.
GREEN BAY PRESS-GAZETTE: "Rush concert loud, wild and appreciated: Rush is a formidable band. What it does is long, winding, intricate, fantasy-oriented rock. It is high on drama and abstract images. It takes you to such exotic places as Xanadu, outer space, Bangkok, Olympus. Lee's voice is riveting in its uniqueness. Its upper reaches seem unreal. Lifeson is a total rock guitarist. He plays his electrics with scorching intensity. Peart is a fireball. Arms and legs flailing away at his elaborate percussion set, it's a wonder he can walk away after two hours of attack."

APRIL 23, 1980
KALAMAZOO, MICHIGAN
WINGS STADIUM, 3600 Van Rick Drive. Venue opened on October 30, 1974.
SUPPORT ACT: 38 Special
TICKETS: $8.75 (advance)
ATTENDANCE: 6,777
CAPACITY: 8,596
KALAMAZOO GAZETTE: "*Permanent Waves* showed such an improvement over previous studio efforts that last night's performance had plenty of potential to be a worthwhile night of rock and roll. Instead, Rush provided one of the worst concerts in memory. In retrospect, it was a bit much to expect a few good tunes to cover up for a fist full of overblown anthems to indulgence. Rush attempts to make music complicated to

impress audiences, without ever realizing that the most complicated aspect of a good rock and roll song is its simplicity."

APRIL 24, 1980
TOLEDO, OHIO
SPORTS ARENA, 1 North Main Street. Venue opened on November 13, 1947.
SUPPORT ACT: 38 Special
ATTENDANCE: 6,001
CAPACITY: 7,000

APRIL 26, 1980
LOUISVILLE, KENTUCKY
LOUISVILLE GARDENS, 525 Muhammad Ali Boulevard. Historic venue dedicated on December 31, 1905.
SUPPORT ACT: 38 Special
TICKETS: $8.50 (advance) / $9.50 (day of), general admission
ATTENDANCE: 5,205 (Anthem/SRO); 5,081 (promoter)
CAPACITY: 7,088
CONCERT GROSS: $45,138

APRIL 27, 1980
INDIANAPOLIS, INDIANA
MARKET SQUARE ARENA, 300 East Market Street. Venue opened on September 15, 1974.
SUPPORT ACT: 38 Special
TICKETS: $7.50 / $8.50
ATTENDANCE: 10,061 (Anthem/SRO); 9,859 (promoter)
CAPACITY: 16,510
CONCERT GROSS: $82,647
THE INDIANAPOLIS NEWS: "The light syncopation with the onstage instrumentation was precise and especially good on 'Jacob's Ladder,' with its cross-firing spots."

APRIL 28, 1980
FORT WAYNE, INDIANA
ALLEN COUNTY WAR MEMORIAL COLISEUM, 4000 Parnell Avenue. Venue dedicated on September 28, 1952.
SUPPORT ACT: 38 Special
TICKETS: $7.50 (advance) /$8.50 (day of)
ATTENDANCE: 4,860 (Anthem/SRO); 4,801 (promoter)
CAPACITY: 10,000, general admission
CONCERT GROSS: $37,482

APRIL 29, 1980
COLUMBUS, OHIO
ST. JOHN ARENA, The Ohio State University campus, 410 Woody Hayes Drive. Venue completed on November 1, 1956.
SUPPORT ACT: 38 Special
TICKETS: $7.50 / $8.50 (all seats reserved)
ATTENDANCE: 7,252 (Anthem/SRO); 7,230 (promoter)
CONCERT GROSS: $60,565
NOTES: The venue roof was unable to support the weight of the band's lighting rig, so front and back trusses, each weighing three to four tons, were raised from the stage.
THE LANTERN, MICHAEL HIRSCH (PRODUCTION MANAGER): "Each person has specific responsibilities that have to be completed by a certain time. That's why everyone is always asking what time it is."

MAY 8–11, 1980
NEW YORK CITY, NEW YORK
PALLADIUM, 126 East 14th Street. Venue opened on October 11, 1926.
AN EVENING WITH RUSH
TICKETS: $9.50 / $10.50
ATTENDANCE: 3,427 per show; sold out
CONCERT GROSS: $34,467 per show
NOTES: A wildly enthusiastic crowd greeted the band. Alex's double-neck went out for a moment during "Xanadu," before his solo. At the urging of Cliff Burnstein, and encouraged by their recent experiments during sound checks, the band decided to temporarily shelve their previously planned live album and instead record a new studio record after the *Permanent Waves* tour is finished.
NEIL: "In the midst of a crowded and chaotic backstage scene, a few quiet words of agreement became the unlikely conception for *Moving Pictures*. Prior to this, it had been our announced intention to record and release a second live album, but an unlooked-for charge of ambition and enthusiasm caused a last-minute resolution to throw caution out of the window (onto 52nd Street!), and dive headlong into the making of a studio LP instead."
PHILADELPHIA JOURNAL: "We certainly didn't want to wait until a Spectrum date is announced, so we headed up to New York to catch the first of four nights at

the Palladium. The bottom line on the band is the fact that they are the perfect blending of two distinct types of rock and roll. On the one hand, they were as bombastic as Led Zeppelin or Van Halen—complete with punchy, rock bottom drumming and screaming power chords. But at the same time, they were as tasty in their playing and intricate in their arrangements as Yes or Genesis. It is this strange mixture that makes Rush one of the most interesting bands around. In all, Rush proved itself to be one of the best bands performing these days— talented, different and exciting."

MAY 13, 1980
HERSHEY, PENNSYLVANIA
HERSHEY PARK ARENA, Hershey Amusement Park, 100 West Hershey Park Drive at Route 39. Venue opened on December 19, 1936.
SUPPORT ACT: Laurie and the Sighs
TICKETS: $7.75 / $8.75
ATTENDANCE: 6,167 (Anthem/SRO); sold out
CONCERT GROSS: $55,642
NOTES: *Billboard* lists attendance at 6,546. This was a reserved seat show, until the lights went out and a few hundred fans stormed the stage, turning the front into a general admission frenzy for the entire evening. During one of the breaks in "2112: Overture," Neil threw his drumstick so high that it spun out of sight. Looking up only once, he caught it right on cue without missing a beat. During "By-Tor and the Snow Dog," Geddy didn't sing the line "square for battle." WYSP-FM Philadelphia sent a busload of fans to Hershey after the band was unable to secure a date at the Spectrum because of NHL and NBA playoff games. Laurie and the Sighs was a hard rock band from New York. In Hershey, they were touring in support of their self-titled Atlantic debut.
DEREK FOX (LAURIE AND THE SIGHS KEYBOARDIST): "I have always been amazed by Geddy's voice. Truly one of a kind with an amazing range."[23]

MAY 14, 1980
PITTSBURGH, PENNSYLVANIA
CIVIC ARENA, 300 Auditorium Place. Venue opened on September 17, 1961.
SUPPORT ACT: Sue Saad and the Next
TICKETS: $8.75

ATTENDANCE: 11,741 (Anthem/SRO)
CONCERT GROSS: $101,923
NOTES: *Billboard* lists attendance at 12,247. Despite some reports of Laurie and the Sighs opening, they did not. Sue Saad and the Next was a new-wave rock band from Los Angeles (in the vein of Blondie). In Pittsburgh, they were touring in support of their self-titled debut album.

MAY 16, 1980
PROVIDENCE, RHODE ISLAND
PROVIDENCE CIVIC CENTER, 1 La Salle Square. Venue opened on November 3, 1972.
SUPPORT ACT: The Fools
TICKETS: $7.50 / $8.50
ATTENDANCE: 9,810 (Anthem/SRO)
CAPACITY: 12,641
CONCERT GROSS: $81,803
NOTES: *Billboard* lists attendance at 10,183. A girl in the front row of the Civic Center was removed by security, police, and firefighters for having a nine-foot boa constrictor wrapped around her neck, until they realized the snake wasn't real.[24]
THE DAY, NEW LONDON, CT: "Every 17-year-old boy in Providence must have been in the sell-out crowd of at least 15,000, and since Rush has a reputation of attracting a rowdy bunch, every policeman in Providence was there, too. The Civic Center was a sea of screaming, beer-drinking Rush fans."

MAY 17, 1980
SOUTH YARMOUTH, MASSACHUSETTS
CAPE COD COLISEUM, White's Path off of Route 6. Venue opened on October 13, 1972.
SUPPORT ACT: The Fools
TICKETS: $8.50 / $9.50
CAPACITY: 5,000
NOTES: Concert postponed at the last minute, due to Geddy injuring his finger.[25] It was promptly rescheduled for September 27.
IAN: "Larry and I had just finished setting up the kit (and the twenty-four mics) in South Yarmouth. And I was sitting outside having a smoke when Lurch came out and told me the gig was canned and to tear down. I'll give the boys their due: they played various times with buckets on standby in case they had to puke. But if you're just too ill, you can't play."

MAY 18, 1980
PORTLAND, MAINE
CUMBERLAND COUNTY CIVIC CENTER,
Spring Street at Center Street. Venue opened on March 3, 1977.
SUPPORT ACT: The Fools
TICKETS: $8.50, general admission
CAPACITY: 9,500
NOTES: Concert postponed at the eleventh hour, due to Geddy's injured finger, delaying the band's Maine debut. It was promptly rescheduled for October 1.

MAY 20, 1980
NEW HAVEN, CONNECTICUT
NEW HAVEN VETERAN'S MEMORIAL COLISEUM, 275 South Orange Street. Venue opened on September 27, 1972.
SUPPORT ACT: The Fools
TICKETS: $7.50 / $8.50
ATTENDANCE: 6,396
RICH BARTLETT (THE FOOLS GUITARIST): "Rush couldn't have been any nicer!"[26]

MAY 21, 1980
BUFFALO, NEW YORK
BUFFALO MEMORIAL AUDITORIUM,
140 Main Street. Venue opened on October 14, 1940.
SUPPORT ACT: Max Webster
TICKETS: $8.00 / $9.00
ATTENDANCE: 12,431 (Anthem/SRO); sold out
CONCERT GROSS: $109,082
NOTES: Some portion of the gig was filmed (at least a short clip from "2112"), perhaps by a local television station. Since a Toronto date was never added to the itinerary, several busloads of Rush fans traveled from the band's hometown to the auditorium in Buffalo.[27]
BUFFALO EVENING NEWS: "Predictable Style No Sin to Fans of Spectacular Rush: This triumvirate of musicians exhibits extreme dexterity toward its respective instruments, especially drummer Peart."

MAY 22, 1980
UTICA, NEW YORK
MEMORIAL AUDITORIUM, 400 Oriskany Street West. Historic venue opened on March 9, 1960.
SUPPORT ACT: Sue Saad and the Next
TICKETS: $8.50 / $9.50, general admission
ATTENDANCE: 3,158

NOTES: To date, *Permanent Waves* had sold over 800,000 copies in America, 160,000 in Canada and 80,000 in the UK.[28]

MAY 23, 1980
UNIONDALE, NEW YORK
NASSAU COUNTY VETERANS MEMORIAL COLISEUM, 1255 Hempstead Turnpike. Venue dedicated on May 29, 1972.
SUPPORT ACT: The Fools
TICKETS: $9.50 / $10.50
ATTENDANCE: 9,225 (Anthem/SRO)
CONCERT GROSS: $96,317
NOTES: *Billboard* lists attendance at 9,215. Final date of the North American tour. For the encore, the band took to the stage wearing Islanders jerseys and dedicated "La Villa Strangiato" "to the Islanders, who are going to win the Stanley Cup tomorrow." Geddy played through the gig with precision, despite a broken pinky. Backstage, he responded to the news of a petition asking for the band to perform in Philadelphia by stating: "Don't worry Philly, we'll be coming in September!" Upon departure, Alex (who was close to getting his pilot's license), flew his co-workers back home to Toronto.
GEDDY (BACKSTAGE AFTER THE SHOW): "We're going to record this upcoming European tour and a couple of dates on the next US and Canadian tour and combine that for a total live thing. So the next album is going to be a studio album. We were gonna do a live album next, but we felt like writing some more songs, which we'll do this summer, then go back into the studio."[29]

JUNE 1–2, 1980
SOUTHAMPTON, HAMPSHIRE, ENGLAND
GAUMONT THEATRE, 22–26 Commercial Road. Venue opened on December 22, 1928.
SUPPORT ACT: Quartz
TICKETS: £2.50 / £3.50 / £4.50
ATTENDANCE: 2,419 per show (2,289 seats plus 130 standing room); sold out
NOTES: Significantly, Rush recorded much of this European tour for use on a future live album, despite having already decided to postpone the live release. Tickets were originally sold for a June 2 Portsmouth Guildhall date, due to a

promoter mix-up, with a rep for Straight Music Promotions later saying that they would "try and work something out for the Southampton gigs."
MICK HOPKINS (QUARTZ GUITARIST): "While we were in the wings waiting to take to the stage in Southampton for our sound check following Rush, Geddy Lee approaches me and says, 'I know you.' I laughed and replied, 'Yeah, I know you too.' Geddy then went on to explain that he watched Fludd play at the Abbey Road Pub in Toronto about nine years ago, when I was playing guitar, and that he is a big fan of my guitar playing and music. Both bands and crew members quickly struck up an instant friendship and mutual camaraderie and respect for each other."[30]
NME: "Rush stand on the threshold with a forceful but contained style, playing movements rather than numbers which are as atmospheric as they are idiosyncratic to their colorful nature. The light show is spectacular, the sounds are extraordinary, ranging from the painful scream to a mundane drone; correct chemistry for the audience—playing imaginary guitars, they shake their skulls until their leather-denim collars are worn thin, and thump the air with every pounding strum of the bass, concluding the opening dose of this decibel fury with an explosion that rocks you in your seat."

JUNE 4–8, 1980
LONDON, ENGLAND
HAMMERSMITH ODEON, 45 Queen Caroline Street. Historic venue opened on March 28, 1932.
AN EVENING WITH RUSH
TICKETS: £2.50 / £3.50 / £4.50
ATTENDANCE: 3,787 per show (3,485 seats, 302 standing room); sold out
NOTES: Recorded to multitrack for possible future release. The London shows were "an evening with" because Rush was taking extra time to focus on the live recordings.
SOUNDS: "The Odeon foundations creaked audibly when the roadies tore the cloth from Neil's drum cage and Alex and Geddy rocketed on from the wings. The crowd was on its feet and baying before the first note of '2112' gunned from the speakers. Rush seemed to be having trouble reaching their usual peak of precision bombardment, but the crowd was too far

gone to care, roaring in unison to every concussive note or rhythm. Smoke bombs and searing white lights aimed at the crowd gave it that class *sturm und drang* feel, but there was a certain excitement and finesse missing. The apocalyptic finale, with Neil's message to the Solar Federation, usually turns me to jelly, but this time it left me bemused. It took an angry, punchy version of 'By-Tor' and a slick, teasing run through of 'Xanadu' before the band began to lift. Fast. 'Xanadooooo-hoo-hoo!' hooted 3,700 informal backing vocalists. After two-and-a-quarter hours of non-stop fiery performance, they still manage to infuse it with freshness, style, complexity, and adrenalin. And that's an aspect of Rush which, as an explanation for why they're where they are and why this was an 'HM event of events,' needs no further elaboration."

NEIL: "It is never too late to change plans—not so with arrangements. Thus, we went ahead with the live tapings we had planned, recording our five shows at the Hammersmith Odeon, as well as dates from Glasgow, Manchester, and Newcastle."[31]

JUNE 10–11, 1980
GLASGOW, SCOTLAND
THE APOLLO, 126 Renfield Street. Venue opened on September 5, 1973.
AN EVENING WITH RUSH
TICKETS: £2.50 / £3.50 / £4.50
ATTENDANCE: 3,500 per show; sold out
NOTES: Recorded to multitrack for possible future release. As with the London dates, the band took some extra time to focus on capturing a solid mix for the live recordings. Two thousand tickets were available via mail only, in response to a petition by Edinburgh fans. It was at one of these two Glasgow shows that the magical *Exit . . . Stage Left* recording of "Closer to the Heart" was captured, with the crowd (credited as the "Glaswegian chorus") singing the first couple verses of the song. Three additional tracks from this European run of dates—"A Passage to Bangkok," "Beneath, Between, and Behind," and "Jacob's Ladder"—would join "Closer to the Heart" in comprising side two of the *Exit . . . Stage Left* album.
ALEX: "The live version we recorded in Scotland was really powerful. It's an amazing feeling, not being able to hear the monitors, or yourself playing, because

the audience is singing so loud. It was just one of those magical things. They were a really fired up crowd in Glasgow. It was great, and actually that happens throughout the world wherever we play. 'Closer to the Heart' seems to get a lot of people singing and the arena becomes filled with matches and lighters. I guess the song sort of drops down a bit; it goes into acoustic and it's easy to sing along."[32]

TERRY: "We just put up the mikes, and the audience was fired up. They sang so loud that when we mixed it, we pushed up the audience mikes. I had about five or six audience mikes. Fortunately, it's not overbearingly loud musically, so when you push up the audience mikes it still retains some quality. That's the audience in Scotland untouched by human hands [*laughs*]."[33]

JUNE 12–13, 1980
NEWCASTLE UPON TYNE, ENGLAND
NEWCASTLE CITY HALL, Northumberland Road and College Street. Historic venue dedicated on November 7, 1928.
SUPPORT ACT: Quartz
TICKETS: £2.50 / £3.50 / £4.50
ATTENDANCE: 2,133 per show; sold out
NOTES: Recorded to multitrack for possible future release. Alex, Geddy, and Neil were made aware that the members of Quartz were staying in only B&B accommodations for the tour, so they invited them to use their catering facilities and chefs for the rest of the tour. "It was a nice touch," according to the guys in Quartz.

JUNE 15, 1980
LEEDS, WEST YORKSHIRE, ENGLAND
QUEENS HALL, Sovereign Street off Swinegate. Venue opened on May 5, 1961.
SUPPORT ACT: Quartz
TICKETS: £4.00
CAPACITY: 4,500
NOTES: Geddy forgot the words to "Closer to the Heart," so the audience lent a hand, singing the tune and helping him back on track. Queens Hall was originally built as Swinegate Depot, the city's main tram shed and headquarters, in July 1914 (one reason the hall suffered from poor acoustics). Upon reopening in 1961 as Queens Hall, it was the largest exhibition space outside of London.

GEDDY: "One time in Leeds, England, I went onstage to sing 'Closer to the Heart,' and, for the life of me, the lyrics would not come into my mind. I just stood there silently waiting for them to come back. It was just like when sometimes you're having a conversation and you blank on what you were going to say. I just looked to the audience and the kids are singing it, and they're trying to prod me on. Eventually, it came back."[34]

JUNE 16, 1980
QUEENSFERRY, FLINTSHIRE, WALES
DEESIDE LEISURE CENTRE, Chester Road West, Route B5129. Venue opened on July 23, 1971.
SUPPORT ACT: Quartz
TICKETS: £4.00
CAPACITY: 4,500
NOTES: A huge wall inside the venue collapsed during Quartz's set. Thankfully, no one was injured, and the concert continued pretty much without incident.
BIG TIM PERRY (QUARTZ MANAGEMENT TEAM): "The guys remember the tour well, as it was a highlight of their career. They were blown away by how friendly Geddy, Alex, and Neil were and the interest they had in the band Quartz and their members."[35]

JUNE 17–18, 1980
MANCHESTER, ENGLAND
MANCHESTER APOLLO, Stockport Road, Ardwick Green. Venue opened on August 29, 1938.
SUPPORT ACT: Quartz
TICKETS: £2.50 / £3.50 / £4.50
ATTENDANCE: 3,500 per show (2,514 standing, 986 seats); sold out
NOTES: Recorded to multitrack for possible future release. On September 1, 2009, a live version of "The Spirit of Radio" from this date was released via the Guitar Hero 5 video game. On December 18, 2012, "A Passage to Bangkok" was released as part of the Super Deluxe edition of *2112*.
MIKE "TAFFY" TAYLOR AND MICK HOPKINS (QUARTZ): "The guys in Rush were so friendly and down-to-earth. Everyone got on really well and it was mentioned that our band and crew had been one of the best that Rush had worked with over the years. We were very impressed by the immense wall of sound that the three of them in Rush created

each night onstage and by their musicianship as well."[36]

JUNE 20, 1980
BIRMINGHAM, WEST MIDLANDS, ENGLAND
BIRMINGHAM ODEON, 139 New Street. Venue opened on September 4, 1937.
SUPPORT ACT: Quartz
TICKETS: £2.50 / £3.50 / £4.50
ATTENDANCE: 2,441; sold out
NOTES: Immediately after load-out, band and crew drove on to Leicester and checked in to their hotel. Van Halen and crew were at the same hotel, and the two groups mingled in the bar.

IAN: "I was amazed to have played, packed, traveled (albeit maybe forty miles) to Leicester, and been in my room going to bed before midnight. Never did that before. I didn't realize anything was on, so I took the opportunity to actually sleep. Usually, parties with other bands were a blast . . . but the next day, Skip is telling me how Van Halen showed up and were offered hospitality. Skip had his cassette deck there with his tape on. Eddie Van Halen starts fucking with it. Skip tells him to back off, and two heavies tell him to leave Eddie alone. Then it was them with the 'We got more equipment than you' shit. Skip was told by their bass tech that he was a fool because he didn't change strings every gig. He also told me it was good that I wasn't there or for sure there would have been a fight. We knew how to party with other bands. Not sure if they ever learned that."[37]

GEDDY: "The guys in Van Halen were a little inebriated, and we were on our way to getting inebriated. So I think some beer was spilt, yes."[38]

JUNE 21, 1980
LEICESTER, EAST MIDLANDS, ENGLAND
DE MONTFORT HALL, Granville Road, Victoria Park. Historic venue opened on June 23, 1913.
SUPPORT ACT: Quartz
TICKETS: £2.50 / £3.50 / £4.50
ATTENDANCE: 2,200; sold out
MIKE "TAFFY" TAYLOR (QUARTZ LEAD VOCALIST): "There was one gig where the lighting guy from Rush was working up in the rigging and he suddenly abseiled down onto the stage during our set. I'm not sure if he had fallen or not, but he then winds up onstage and ends up singing some of the song 'Wildfire' with me before exiting stage left, no doubt."[39]

JUNE 22, 1980
BRIGHTON, EAST SUSSEX, ENGLAND
BRIGHTON CENTRE, Kings Road, Route A259 at Brighton Beach. Venue opened on September 19, 1977.
SUPPORT ACT: Quartz
TICKETS: £2.50 / £3.50 / £4.50
CAPACITY: 5,100 (2,100 permanent seats)
NOTES: The final date of the *Permanent Waves* tour broke upon the seaside town of Brighton. This concert featured the final live performance of "Cygnus X-1" into "Hemispheres."

***MELODY MAKER*, COUNCILLOR RICHARD BATES:** "It took a group of the caliber of Rush to induce me to go and see a concert at the Brighton Centre. Their live performance was excellent, highlighted by 'Xanadu.' As a politician, I find close to the heart 'A Farewell to Kings' an inspiring theme. The two-hour set was a pleasure to sit through."

1. Skip Daly. Interview with Garfield French, July 16, 2018.
2. Skip Daly. Interview with Greg Lukens, March 4, 2013.
3. *Democrat and Chronicle*.
4. Eric Hansen. Interview with Howard Ungerleider, July 11, 2012.
5. Brad Parmerter. Interview with Howard Ungerleider. Livejournal.com, July 22, 2013.
6. Skip Daly. Interview with Robert Frazer, November 2012.
7. *Corpus Christi Caller Times*, February 8, 1980.
8. *Billboard*.
9. *Cincinnati Post*.
10. *Wichita Beacon*.
11. *Billboard*.
12. *Canadian Press*, May 3, 1980.
13. *The Toronto Star*, March 15, 1980.
14. Interview with Geddy Lee. *The Toronto Star*, March 15, 1980.
15. Robert Hilburn. *The Los Angeles Times*.
16. *Amusement Business*.
17. Swampland.com.
18. *Seattle Daily Times*.
19. *Billboard*.
20. Bill Banasiewicz. Interview with Michael Sadler, September 21, 1982.
21. *Nanaimo Times*.
22. Live Music Head. "NEGUS: from Saga to the Collective – an interview with Steve Negus and George Roche," November 15, 2009. livemusichead.blogspot.com
23. Bill Banasiewicz. Interview with Derek Fox, September 28, 2014.
24. *The Day*.
25. *Maine Sunday Telegram*, May 18, 1980.
26. Mike Girard. "The Fools Story." thefools-band.com
27. *The Toronto Star*, May 18, 1980.
28. *The Toronto Star*, May 18, 1980.
29. Bill Banasiewicz. Interview with Geddy Lee, May 23, 1980.
30. Bill Banasiewicz. Interview with Mick Hopkins, November 18, 2014.
31. Neil Peart. "A Rush Newsreel," *Moving Pictures Tour Book*, 1981.
32. Bill Banasiewicz. Interview with Alex Lifeson, December 20, 1981.
33. Bill Banasiewicz. Interview with Terry Brown, February 1982.
34. Interview with Geddy Lee. *Onstage Magazine*, 2002.
35. Bill Banasiewicz. Interview with Big Tim Perry, October 31, 2014.
36. Bill Banasiewicz. Interview with Quartz members, November 18, 2014.
37. Skip Daly. Interview with Ian Grandy, November 14, 2014.
38. "Rush's Geddy Lee Answers Your Twitter Questions," RollingStone.com, November 14, 2014.
39. Bill Banasiewicz. Interview with Mike "Taffy" Taylor, November 18, 2014.

Chapter 11
THE FALL 1980 TOUR

A limited trek by Rush standards, the fall 1980 tour saw Alex, Geddy, and Neil perform to more than 95,000 fans over the course of only sixteen shows. The dates, which featured New Wave of British Heavy Metal act Saxon as support, also enabled the band to perform as promised in Philadelphia—where 16,101 fans had signed a petition asking for a Rush show.

The set list for these shows revealed a band in transition, with its "epic" songs scaled down—"2112" was reduced, for the first time ever, to just the two opening segments, "Overture" and "The Temples of Syrinx," while only "Prelude" remained from the "Hemispheres" suite. Functioning as a warm-up for the forthcoming *Moving Pictures* studio sessions, prerelease versions of "Limelight" (or "Living in the Limelight," as it was initially called) and "Tom Sawyer" were performed. "When we entered Le Studio [in Quebec], I had a really good idea of what we were going for, because they played two tunes live on the road, and several during sound check," said *Moving Pictures* producer Terry Brown. Onstage, "Limelight" featured a slightly different arrangement, while "Tom Sawyer" was played at an amphetamine-like tempo with alternate lyrics in one section. The distinctive guitar solos for these songs were not yet in place, and Alex's ongoing experiments with these new tracks can be heard in unofficial recordings from the tour.

The short jaunt wrapped on October 1, 1980, at the Cumberland County Civic Center in Portland, Maine; this show, along with one a few nights earlier in South Yarmouth, Massachusetts, were makeup dates for *Permanent Waves* gigs that had been canceled after Geddy injured his finger.

"It was here we concluded a short tour," said Neil, "mainly the Eastern Seaboard of the United States, in which we rehearsed the five completed songs whenever possible. We introduced 'Tom Sawyer' and 'Limelight' into our shows, although both would undergo some changes before being committed to tape."

OPPOSITE TOP: Alex and Neil performing the intro to "Xanadu."

OPPOSITE BOTTOM: Rush onstage.

LEFT: Philadelphia, PA; After the show at the Spectrum, Neil and Geddy looking over the fan petitions to bring the band back to Philly.

TOP: Morin-Heights, Québec; Alex and Terry Brown at Le Studio.
ABOVE: Morin-Heights, Québec; Neil at Le Studio.

TOUR HISTORY

FALL 1980

SET LIST:

"2112: Overture"
"2112: The Temples of Syrinx"
"Freewill"
"By-Tor and the Snow Dog" (abridged)
"Xanadu"
"Limelight" (prerelease version)
"The Trees"
"Hemispheres: Prelude"

"The Spirit of Radio"
"Closer to the Heart"
"Beneath, Between, and Behind" (abridged)
"Tom Sawyer" (prerelease version)
"Jacob's Ladder"
"A Passage to Bangkok"
"Natural Science"
"Working Man" (reggae intro)

"Finding My Way"
"Anthem"
"Bastille Day"
"In the Mood"
Drum Solo
Encore:
"La Villa Strangiato" (with electric guitar intro)

SEPTEMBER 11, 1980
HAMPTON, VIRGINIA
HAMPTON COLISEUM, 1000 Coliseum Drive
SUPPORT ACT: Saxon
TICKETS: $7.50 / $8.50 (average: $8.12)
ATTENDANCE: 4,283 (Anthem/SRO)
CONCERT GROSS: $34,820
NOTES: The opening date of the fall 1980 tour featured the live debuts of "Limelight" and "Tom Sawyer." Tight security didn't allow fans to stand during the concert. Two guys in the front row were hassled several times, then five security guards stood in the front of the low stage, obstructing the view of everyone forced to sit. Alex saw what was going down and stopped his intro to "The Trees," came to the front of the stage, and yelled, "You guards get the hell out of there! If they want to stand, then let them stand!" The security force left, and all tensions were eased for the remainder of the gig.
PAUL QUINN (SAXON GUITARIST): "Of course, Rush had been breaking Europe in a large way, so we were fans before meeting them, but the extreme bravery of premiering unreleased songs was an eye- and ear-opener. One could tell they had another hit album, and a groundbreaking way of introducing the audience to their new stuff, as well as 'working it in' (as the bishop said to the reverend). We could hear most of their influences, but their quirky fusion of progressive-rock-reggae spoke to us and the world."[1]

SEPTEMBER 12, 1980
CHARLOTTE, NORTH CAROLINA
CHARLOTTE COLISEUM, 2700 East Independence Boulevard. Venue dedicated on September 11, 1955.
SUPPORT ACT: Saxon
TICKETS: $7.50 (limited advance) / $8.50 (remaining)
ATTENDANCE: 5,047

SEPTEMBER 13, 1980
CHARLESTON, WEST VIRGINIA
CHARLESTON CIVIC CENTER COLISEUM, 200 Civic Center Drive. Venue dedicated on August 3, 1980.
SUPPORT ACT: Saxon
TICKETS: $7.50 / $8.50 (average: $8.10)
ATTENDANCE: 3,068 (Anthem/SRO); 3,198 (Billboard)
CONCERT GROSS: $25,894

SEPTEMBER 14, 1980
NASHVILLE, TENNESSEE
NASHVILLE MUNICIPAL AUDITORIUM, 417 Fourth Avenue North. Venue opened on October 7, 1962.
SUPPORT ACT: Saxon
TICKETS: $7.50 (limited advance) / $8.50 (remaining)
ATTENDANCE: 7,251
BIFF BYFORD (SAXON VOCALIST): "It's a lot different for us playing in America, because in England we headline our own shows and play for a couple of hours, as opposed to opening for Rush, where we only get to play for fifty minutes."[2]

SEPTEMBER 16, 1980
BATON ROUGE, LOUISIANA
RIVERSIDE CENTROPLEX, 275 South River Road. Venue opened on November 10, 1977.
SUPPORT ACT: Saxon
TICKETS: $9.50, general admission
ATTENDANCE: 8,500
NOTES: Inside the venue was a rowdy scene, with bottles being thrown into the glass doors and one person arrested.[3]
STATE TIMES ADVOCATE: "This band offers proof that there might be something to think about after the ringing in your ears stops."

SEPTEMBER 18, 1980
NORTH FORT MYERS, FLORIDA
LEE COUNTY CIVIC CENTER, 11831 Bayshore Road, Route 78. Venue opened in October 1978.
SUPPORT ACT: Saxon
TICKETS: $7.50 (advance) / $8.00 (at the door); face value minus fees
ATTENDANCE: 3,149
NEWS-PRESS: "Rush rides Permanent Waves to Fort Myers."

SEPTEMBER 19, 1980
PEMBROKE PINES, FLORIDA
HOLLYWOOD SPORTATORIUM, 17171 Pines Boulevard (Route 820). Venue opened in September 1970.
SUPPORT ACT: Saxon
TICKETS: $7.75 / $8.75 (fifty-cent parking fee included)
ATTENDANCE: 5,722
CAPACITY: 15,533

SEPTEMBER 20, 1980
LAKELAND, FLORIDA
LAKELAND CIVIC CENTER, 701 West Lime Street. Venue dedicated on November 14, 1974.
SUPPORT ACT: Saxon
TICKETS: $8.50 / $9.00 (average: $8.46), general admission
ATTENDANCE: 10,000 (Anthem/SRO); sold out
CONCERT GROSS: $84,600

SEPTEMBER 21, 1980
JACKSONVILLE, FLORIDA
JACKSONVILLE VETERANS MEMORIAL COLISEUM, 1145 Adams Street. Venue dedicated on November 24, 1960.
SUPPORT ACT: Saxon
TICKETS: $7.50 (advance) / $8.50 (at the door)
ATTENDANCE: 3,509
CAPACITY: 12,000
NOTES: The infamous "The Bus Won't Fall Out of the Sky" T-shirts were distributed to the crew, inadvertently shocking local venue personnel. Lynyrd Skynyrd had of course suffered their horrific plane crash on October 20, 1977, and they hailed from Jacksonville.

BIFF BYFORD (SAXON VOCALIST): "I do remember the tour well. It was our first tour of the US. We were quite big in the UK and Europe by then, on the *Wheels of Steel* album, but to walk onstage in front of thousands of people was a fantastic and daunting experience. It was the first time we saw lighters in the air as we walked onstage. We were traveling in a day van, which was purgatory. I remember on the second show, Geddy invited me onto their tour bus and, like a fool, I said 'No thanks,' not wanting to upset my band. It was a great tour, and we were treated very well by Rush and their crew. I did have a bit of an affair with their wardrobe girl for a while. I think Alex was learning to fly and was making a model plane every day. For the tour, they had some T-shirts with a picture of the tour bus with wings with the slogan 'The Bus Won't Fall Out of the Sky' on the front. (I think they were afraid to fly with Alex.) She gave me one of these shirts, which I still have. I think only a few were made for the band and close crew. Oh and don't forget the room they had on every show with a video game console—I think it was Galactica. The room had to be pitch-black!"[4]

PAUL QUINN (SAXON GUITARIST): "As a long-serving Saxon guitarist, that tour holds a special place in my memory. Alex, Geddy, and Neil are the epitome of fair treatment for employees and opening acts, as well as great players and writers. I am not ass kissing, either, as not all bands are magnanimous. The crew were very well treated, as an amusement arcade was set up daily for their and Rush's use. We came from a headline tour of Europe and were surprised that the whole entourage not only knew our music but applauded us offstage nightly. I still own a prized 'Philadelphia Spectrum—Sold Out' T-shirt from that tour. Alex had started his love of flying by taking flying lessons and building model airplanes, so the merchandiser had made jokey band/crew shirts of an Eagle Bus with wings, and the words, 'The Bus Won't Fall Out of the Sky.' Even big stars like a giggle (at someone else's expense.)"[5]

MIKE "LURCH" HIRSCH: "Neil had gone out and gotten T-shirts made up that said, 'The Bus Won't Fall Out of the Sky,' and then handed them out to the crew. On the day he handed them out, we just happened to be in Jacksonville—not knowing at all that Lynyrd Skynyrd was a local Jacksonville band. So, the local promoter was coming up to us going, 'Dude . . . you guys can't wear that here!' and we were just like, 'Why?' Then they explained, and we were like, 'Oh, oops . . . sorry!'"[6]

FLORIDA TIMES-UNION: "Rush lacks the true spirit of rock 'n' roll: Plenty of illusions were shattered last night: the illusions of fans who came to hear rock 'n' roll, and instead were served up long, boring solos and pseudo 'art rock,' all of it as sterile as an operating room."

SEPTEMBER 23, 1980
CINCINNATI, OHIO
RIVERFRONT COLISEUM, 100 Broadway Street. Venue opened on September 9, 1975.
SUPPORT ACT: Saxon
TICKETS: $6.75 / $7.75 / $8.75
ATTENDANCE: 4,616
NOTES: There was no pyro, per the Cincinnati Fire Department. Eighteen people were arrested, with about a hundred cited for various violations, mostly drug and alcohol offenses.[7] Riverfront Coliseum is the site of the notorious Who concert tragedy. On December 3, 1979, eleven people were killed and twenty-six were injured in a rush to gain access to a sold-out concert by the Who. The show was festival (general admission) seating. When the waiting fans outside the venue heard the band performing a late sound check, they thought the concert had started and tried to push into the still-closed doors. Some at the front of the crowd were trampled, as those pushing from behind were unaware that the doors were still closed. At the time of the tragedy, Rush had already been lobbying promoters for a long time to disallow festival seating at their shows whenever possible. Shortly after the Who concert melee, the Cincinnati City Council passed strict new ordinances at rock concerts, including a smoking ban and tougher enforcement of drug and liquor violations, which resulted in the ejection of 450 fans from this Rush gig.[8]
CINCINNATI POST: "Crowd small but loyal as Rush rocks Coliseum."
NEIL: "I have wanted to get rid of festival seating for several years now. But before the Cincinnati incident, no one would take that request seriously. Our audiences (like the Who's) have the tendency to get very fired up. I like an enthusiastic audience, but I do not like to watch people in physical pain."[9]

SEPTEMBER 25, 1980
PHILADELPHIA, PENNSYLVANIA
THE SPECTRUM, 3601 South Broad Street. Venue opened on October 1, 1967.
SUPPORT ACT: Saxon
TICKETS: $7.50 / $9.00 (average: $8.31)
ATTENDANCE: 14,324 (Anthem/SRO); sold out
CONCERT GROSS: $120,483
NOTES: *Billboard* lists attendance at 14,500. The band's tour bus was broken into, and personal items were stolen. Rush was presented with a petition (that included 16,101 names) from fans asking that they play in Philly. Earlier in the day, Led Zeppelin drummer John Bonham had passed away.
LEVITTOWN COURIER TIMES: "Rush rocks, rolls the Spectrum: The rafters at the Spectrum had the right to shake and rattle last night. It was clearly a Rush crowd and Rush showed its appreciation

by putting on an extremely tight, well-mixed presentation of heavy-metal rock at its best. The amazing factor is the fullness the group can obtain from within its three-member ranks."

PAUL QUINN (SAXON GUITARIST): "Saxon had an invitation to Rush's dressing room after one show, and the banter was definitely as cutting as our own. You always hurt the one you love, as the song goes. We could tell the band had the wacky Marx Brothers/Monty Python humor, so we felt right at home, even learning the Canadian pronunciation ('two' sounds like 'toy'). They seemed shocked that we showed up in a Dodge camper van, and I can say that the only comfortable places were the front seat or the floor . . . Both bands became 'down in the mouth' during that tour, when Led Zeppelin's John Bonham died. It was a tragic end to his glorious grooving. Fortunately, like Zeppelin, Rush lock together and listen to each other to maximum effect. That makes their music fly, and the fans' hearts with it."[10]

SEPTEMBER 26, 1980
LARGO, MARYLAND
CAPITAL CENTRE, 1 Harry S. Truman Drive. Venue opened on December 2, 1973.
SUPPORT ACT: Saxon
TICKETS: $7.70 / $8.80 (includes taxes and fees)
ATTENDANCE: 15,895

SEPTEMBER 27, 1980
SOUTH YARMOUTH, MASSACHUSETTS
CAPE COD COLISEUM, White's Path off of Route 6. Venue opened on October 13, 1972.
SUPPORT ACT: Saxon
TICKETS: $8.50 / $9.50 (average: $8.56)
ATTENDANCE: 7,181 (Anthem/SRO); 7,200 (*Billboard*); sold out
CONCERT GROSS: $61,637
NOTES: Rescheduled from May 17, 1980.

SEPTEMBER 28, 1980
SPRINGFIELD, MASSACHUSETTS
SPRINGFIELD CIVIC CENTER, 1277 Main Street. Venue opened on September 22, 1972.
SUPPORT ACT: Saxon
TICKETS: $9.50
ATTENDANCE: 2,200
NOTES: During sound check, the band worked on recently written material.
SPRINGFIELD MORNING UNION: "The multitalented trio played a unique arrangement of heavy metal, space and classical music that often mixes symphonic passages with hard-hitting guitar rock. Rather than working from a single riff, Rush constructs progressive music that reads like a searing symphony with twilight-zone lyrical themes. Traces of Yes, U.K., the Who, and others pop up in their music. By playing so much new material, Rush had to leave behind many of the better songs from the early days."

SEPTEMBER 30, 1980
ALLENTOWN, PENNSYLVANIA
FAIRGROUNDS GRANDSTAND, Great Allentown Fairgrounds, 302 North 17th Street. Venue opened in September 1911. Original grandstand built in 1902, rebuilt in 1911.
SUPPORT ACT: Saxon
TICKETS: $9.50 (advance)
CAPACITY: 10,500 (7,070 seats), general admission
NOTES: Outdoor gig. Geddy played a few lines of "Dueling Banjos" on bass with his black Rickenbacker double-neck during the extended intro to "Xanadu."
GEDDY (ONSTAGE): "We'd like to do a very old quiz show theme song for you. It was written by Orson Bean. This is 'Jacob's Thing.'"
JOHN BOYD (RUSH FAN): "That was the night that Geddy came to our rescue. We were a band from Baltimore (all about eighteen years old) at our fourth Rush show in a week. We just walked backstage after the show, and there was Alex and Geddy watching [the crew] destroy the equipment setup in a mock battle royale. I'll never forget when the gong came crashing over and hit the stage floor. Our van was out of gas, so naturally, when my bass player was fortunate enough to have a few private words with

Ged, he told him of our dilemma. Geddy, grasping at his pockets, said, 'Well, I don't have any gas on me, but here's ten bucks, if it'll help you guys get home.' Priceless memories!"[11]

OCTOBER 1, 1980
PORTLAND, MAINE
CUMBERLAND COUNTY CIVIC CENTER, Spring Street at Center Street. Venue opened on March 3, 1977.
SUPPORT ACT: Saxon
TICKETS: $8.50, general admission
CAPACITY: 9,500
NOTES: Rescheduled from May 16, 1980. Ian's final date as front-of-house sound engineer. After this gig, "Jacob's Ladder" would not be performed again until May 8, 2015, almost thirty-five years later.
PAUL QUINN (SAXON GUITARIST): "Rush fans were welcoming to a basically unknown (but cooking) UK band. Another first for us (and a lesson in our treatment of our own crew) was the mainly gourmet food served by the backstage catering, which goes a long way in making road warriors feel 'at home.' A good example would be the Maine lobster in Portland. That was my first lobster, and the whole rigmarole of wearing a bib/apron to stop splashback was like a weird ceremonial bonding of everyone in silly plastic bibs."[12]

1. Bill Banasiewicz. Interview with Paul Quinn, November 5, 2014.
2. Bill Banasiewicz. Interview with Biff Byford, September 1980.
3. *State Times Advocate.*
4. Bill Banasiewicz. Interview with Biff Byford, November 3, 2014.
5. Bill Banasiewicz. Interview with Paul Quinn, November 5, 2014.
6. Skip Daly. Interview with Mike Hirsch, July 17, 2012.
7. *Cincinnati Post.*
8. *Dayton Daily News.*
9. Bill Banasiewicz. Interview with Neil Peart.
10. Bill Banasiewicz. Interview with Paul Quinn, November 5, 2014.
11. John Boyd. Facebook.com, December 5, 2015.
12. Bill Banasiewicz. Interview with Paul Quinn, November 5, 2014.

Chapter 12

THE MOVING PICTURES TOUR

The *Moving Pictures* trek saw Rush perform to more than 900,000 fans over the course of seventy-nine shows. The opening date, in Kalamazoo, Michigan, on February 20, 1981, contained the live debut of "Red Barchetta," "YYZ," "The Camera Eye," and "Vital Signs." It was this album and tour where the band truly broke through and found large-scale mainstream success—with all of the associated rewards and trappings of fame.

Remarked Neil, "For that one year, our audience suddenly doubled (if temporarily), and on that *Moving Pictures* tour, as we played two nights in cities where we had always played one, we noticed a lot of people in the audience who had no idea about our music or our songs; we just happened to be the concert to be at that year. ('Are you going to Rush?' 'Oh yeah man, for sure.') Briefly, and uncomfortably (for us and our real fans), we were 'in.'"

Said Geddy at the time, "I really don't see what all the fuss is about. We're not exactly newcomers to this business, but all of a sudden it seems like the music world has discovered that we exist."

Following a show in San Antonio, the band boarded a hired jet to Cape Canaveral, Florida, to witness the launch of the first space shuttle, the *Columbia*, which would eventually serve as the inspiration for the song "Countdown." The next day, April, 13, 1980, *Moving Pictures* was certified gold by the RIAA for five hundred thousand units sold in the US; two weeks later, the album was certified platinum for one million units sold.

Neil began keeping a running diary on the *Moving Pictures* tour. His first two weeks of entries were later published via Rush's fan club under the title "For Whom the Bus Rolls."

Neil (excerpted from "For Whom the Bus Rolls"): *The three of us, with towels and drinks, stand huddled together in the darkness, before the encore. The only light is from the audience; the mystic ritual of matches and lighters held aloft. We catch our breath, wipe away the sweat, and prepare ourselves for the final stretch: 'La Villa Strangiato.' 'Good one tonight!' remarked Geddy, his breathless voice almost lost in the clamoring crowd. I nodded in agreement silently, as I realized that yes, it had been a good one!*

OPPOSITE: Alex onstage.
LEFT: Geddy performing "Xanadu" with his doubleneck.

TOP: The dueling doublenecks.
ABOVE: Neil at center stage.

TOUR HISTORY
MOVING PICTURES

SET LIST:
"2112: Overture"
"2112: The Temples of Syrinx"
"Freewill"
"Limelight"
"Hemispheres: Prelude"
"Beneath, Between, and Behind" (abridged)
"The Camera Eye"
"YYZ" (with drum solo)

"Broon's Bane"
"The Trees"
"Xanadu"
"The Spirit of Radio"
"Red Barchetta"
"Closer to the Heart"
"Tom Sawyer"
"Vital Signs"
"Natural Science"
"Working Man" (with reggae intro)

"Hemispheres: Armageddon"
"By-Tor and the Snow Dog"
"In the End"
"In the Mood"
"2112: Grand Finale"
Encore:
"La Villa Strangiato" (with electric guitar intro)

FEBRUARY 20, 1981
KALAMAZOO, MICHIGAN
WINGS STADIUM, 3600 Van Rick Drive
SUPPORT ACT: Max Webster
TICKETS: $10.00 (includes twenty-five-cent parking fee)
ATTENDANCE: 7,888
CAPACITY: 8,596
NOTES: The opening date of the 1981 *Moving Pictures* tour featured the live debut of "Red Barchetta," "YYZ," "The Camera Eye," and "Vital Signs." It was also the first gig with Jon Erickson running front-of-house sound, replacing Ian Grandy, who was now the head of security.
"FOR WHOM THE BUS ROLLS," NEIL: "Around nine, I slip unnoticed between the cases back of the stage, and up under the 'tent' which covers my drums before the show. It's nice to get settled in a bit early and avoid the panic of running on when the house lights go down. The lights are down, the intro tape starts, and there is an incredible roar from the audience. Larry and Dave pull the cloth back, as Alex and Geddy come running on, plugging in their guitars as they move over to center stage, standing in front of me to count in the beginning of '2112.' We share a 'here goes!' look, 2, 3, 4, and we're away! The pace of this set is furious; it's a good thing I'm in good shape this year! We're about five songs into it, and I'm soaking, before I even have a second to grab a quick gulp of Canada Dry, let alone wiping my dripping face and hands with a towel. I can feel that we are playing well, and the audience roars its warm approval. Alex has a colorful new wardrobe in the best of bad taste and is dancing magnificently. Perception becomes snail-like when I'm playing; peeking out for a moment when the going is smooth, then instantly retreating back inside to concentrate in difficult areas. Images are fragmentary and diverse; a face, the roof, a weird hat, stage right crew, Geddy's tapping foot, someone singing along, Alex dancing, et cetera. These are all punctuated by the oblivious, inner space of drums, cymbals, hands, feet, tempo; and is this drumstick going to break in the middle of this roll? (They always do.) Back in the dressing room there's a beautiful array of seafood; oysters, crabmeat, and smoked salmon. It looks delicious, but I never develop an appetite until an hour or two after the show, when there will only be sandwiches and peanuts on the bus. More fool me! There is nothing so fine as champagne after a show, and tonight we really have something to celebrate. The first show is behind us, and it went very well."

FEBRUARY 21, 1981
DUBUQUE, IOWA
FIVE FLAGS ARENA, Five Flags Civic Center, 405 Main Street. Venue opened on March 24, 1979.
SUPPORT ACT: Max Webster
TICKETS: $8.00 / $9.00
ATTENDANCE: 3,945
"FOR WHOM THE BUS ROLLS," NEIL: "Unfortunately, Alex suffered string trouble, breaking three in the course of the show, and Geddy also has a few spots of trouble, but generally it's a good one. The audience is enthusiastic and enjoyable; excepting a few firecracker morons. Back on the bus, we're driving to Davenport tonight, a relatively short drive. The video golf game is the latest rage, and Howard, Kevin, Geddy, and Broon are engrossed in that. Alex and I listen to some music and drift in and out of conversation. Sitting back, tired and relaxed, I recognize that at this moment I am truly content. Life is actually good! These moments are rare for any of us, and I savor it."

FEBRUARY 22, 1981
DAVENPORT, IOWA
PALMER ALUMNI AUDITORIUM, Palmer College of Chiropractic campus, 169 West 11th Street. Venue opened in 1970.
SUPPORT ACT: Max Webster
ATTENDANCE: 4,500; sold out
NOTES: General admission concert. According to fan accounts, the gig was completely oversold.
THE DISPATCH (MOLINE, IL): "Rush's appearance was a long-awaited triumphant return."

FEBRUARY 24, 1981
LA CROSSE, WISCONSIN
LA CROSSE CENTER ARENA, 300 Harbor View Plaza. Venue opened on October 11, 1980.
SUPPORT ACT: Max Webster
TICKETS: $7.50 (advance)
ATTENDANCE: 4,608
NOTES: Terry Brown filmed the band's performance with a handheld camera.
"FOR WHOM THE BUS ROLLS," NEIL: "Tonight it's my turn for equipment trouble; bass drum pedal, snare head, tom-tom head, cymbal stands, and warped sticks all joining in an inanimate conspiracy against me. This is very frustrating, and the constant distractions are very upsetting to the concentration. Alex

is particularly entertaining tonight, and a wordless exchange soon has me smiling again. Sometimes one can rise above a night, although rarely, I find. An interesting telepathy has grown among the three of us over the years. Between Geddy and myself, it's more of a musical thing; we'll suddenly play some new little accent together, without ever having spoken of it, while Alex can have me weak with laughter over a mutually understood private joke. Broon took our portable video camera out to the mixing board tonight, and taped the show, which we looked at on the way to Chicago. Since we have never seen our own show, it's interesting in a 'home-movie' kind of way, to see the projections and lighting effects that go on around us every night."

FEBRUARY 26–28; MARCH 1, 1981
CHICAGO, ILLINOIS
INTERNATIONAL AMPHITHEATRE, 4220 South Halsted Street. Venue opened on December 1, 1934.
SUPPORT ACT: Max Webster
TICKETS: $9.50 / $11.50
ATTENDANCE: 9,854 per show; sold out
CONCERT GROSS: $112,724 per show
NOTES: Band and crew celebrated after the second show with an all-night party at the Italian Village. As a special treat for Chicago fans, Alex and Geddy performed an untitled acoustic instrumental about a minute in length during the last show.
"FOR WHOM THE BUS ROLLS," NEIL: "Tonight is our second annual blowout at the Italian Village; last year was so much fun we wanted to repeat it. And we did. Everyone is there: ourselves, our crew, Max and their crew, some of the wives, all of the drivers, personal friends, friends from our office and the record company, and our hosts: the promoter and his people. So, we have about fifty people; eating, drinking, laughing, and talking. The level rises, and the pace accelerates; the room becomes a living thing. It vibrates, and boils, and roars and bubbles in a whirling storm of images. It gathers force; the air is kinetic, charged with an electric joy and a magnetic camaraderie. There is no world outside this room, only THE PARTY! The party lives!"

MARCH 2, 1981
MILWAUKEE, WISCONSIN
MECCA ARENA, 400 West Kilbourn Avenue. Venue opened on April 9, 1950.
SUPPORT ACT: Max Webster
TICKETS: $9.50 / $10.50
ATTENDANCE: 9,741 (Anthem/SRO); sold out
CONCERT GROSS: $98,990
NOTES: *Billboard* lists attendance as 9,700.
MILWAUKEE SENTINEL: "Rush gains fans in hard times."

MARCH 4–5, 1981
ST. LOUIS, MISSOURI
THE CHECKERDOME, 5700 Oakland Avenue. Venue opened on September 23, 1929.
SUPPORT ACT: Max Webster
TICKETS: $8.50 / $9.50
ATTENDANCE: 11,394 per show; sold out
CONCERT GROSS: $106,412 per show
NOTES: *Billboard* also had both St. Louis shows as sellouts, with two-day attendance at 22,758 (11,379 per show).
ST. LOUIS POST-DISPATCH: "No one would ever walk away from one of the trio's concerts humming one of its tunes. Still, one cannot help but have a deep appreciation of what they are able to achieve with what they have. Being just a trio on a large stage makes them look pretty small from much of the Checkerdome. They have taken pains to reduce those visual shortcomings by using large rear-screen projections to illustrate some of their songs. When they opened, the crowd rushed the stage. The security people did their best to keep people seated throughout the show, but never quite got the crowd settled down."[1]

MARCH 7, 1981
LOUISVILLE, KENTUCKY
FREEDOM HALL, Commonwealth Convention Center grounds, 927 Phillips Lane. Venue dedicated on December 20, 1956.
SUPPORT ACT: Max Webster
TICKETS: $8.00 (advance) / $9.00 (day of)
ATTENDANCE: 8,145 (Anthem/SRO); 8,250 (promoter); sold out
CONCERT GROSS: $66,671

NOTES: Geddy joined Max Webster onstage to sing his parts during "Battlescar."[2]

MARCH 8, 1981
DAYTON, OHIO
HARA ARENA, 1001 Shiloh Springs Road. Venue opened on November 1, 1964.
SUPPORT ACT: Max Webster
TICKETS: $8.00 (advance) / $9.00 (day of), general admission
ATTENDANCE: 8,000; sold out
CONCERT GROSS: $44,000
NOTES: Backstage, the band was in a relaxed mood. After sound check, Geddy chatted for a while with Kim Mitchell directly behind the stage. A loud and rowdy general admission crowd had the arena foundation shaking. The audience went wild as yellow lights silhouetted Alex and Geddy from behind during "2112: The Temples of Syrinx." Alex's guitar went out during "Closer to the Heart," right as the bass and drums kicked in. The lighthearted mood before the show carried over to the gig as Alex and Neil jammed during Geddy's introduction to "Tom Sawyer." During the opening solo guitar intro to "La Villa Strangiato," Alex added lines from the classic Greek song "Never on Sunday," something which would continue for most of this leg of the tour.
KIM MITCHELL (MAX WEBSTER GUITARIST/VOLCALIST, BACKSTAGE, AFTER SOUND CHECK): "'Battle Scar' has been going over really well for us, thus far on this tour."[3]

MARCH 10, 1981
EVANSVILLE, INDIANA
ROBERTS MUNICIPAL STADIUM, University of Evansville campus, 2600 Division Street. Venue dedicated on December 1, 1956.
SUPPORT ACT: Max Webster
TICKETS: $7.75 (includes twenty-five-cent transaction fee)
ATTENDANCE: 5,054 (Anthem/SRO); 4,979 (promoter)
CONCERT GROSS: $39,585

MARCH 11, 1981
INDIANAPOLIS, INDIANA
MARKET SQUARE ARENA, 300 East Market Street. Venue opened on September 15, 1974.
SUPPORT ACT: Max Webster

TICKETS: $7.50 (advance) / $8.50 (day of)
ATTENDANCE: 16,000 (Anthem/SRO)
CAPACITY: 16,510
CONCERT GROSS: $121,363
NOTES: Geddy (in Nixon mask) joined Max Webster on stage to provide vocals on "Battle Scar." At the gig, 153 fans were arrested by various state and local authorities. The majority of offenses were for marijuana possession, disorderly conduct, and public intoxication.[4] The arrest tally is the largest ever at a rock concert by the Indianapolis Police Department.[5]
INDIANAPOLIS STAR: "16,000 See Rush Roar Through Powerful Concert: Whether Rush is ready to assume the role as hard rock's kingpin now that Led Zeppelin has stepped down remains to be seen, but one thing's for certain: the Canadian rock group is getting closer. The band is improving with each tour and album. The PA has improved and the lights, which already were very good, are even better. Whether the Indianapolis crowd realized it or not, they witnessed an American tour first last night as Lee joined Max Webster on stage to sing part of 'Battle Scar.' During a phone conversation earlier this week, Mitchell stated that Lee, who sings the entire second verse on the recorded version, was not doing the same in concert. 'But before the show he asked if he could do it,' Mitchell explained last night backstage. 'What could I say?' When the second verse arrived, Lee appeared at a microphone wearing a Richard Nixon mask and glasses. When he began singing, the crowd went bananas. 'I didn't know there were so many Republicans in Indianapolis,' Lee joked backstage."[6]

MARCH 13–15, 1981
DETROIT, MICHIGAN
COBO HALL ARENA, 1 Washington Boulevard. Venue opened on October 17, 1960.
SUPPORT ACT: Max Webster
TICKETS: $10.00 / $11.00
ATTENDANCE: 11,603 per show; sold out
CONCERT GROSS: $117,699.67 per show
NOTES: *Billboard* lists attendance as 10,983 per show (sold out). As the Rush entourage arrived in Detroit, longtime crew member Skip Gildersleeve was

treated to a surprise. Knowing that Detroit is Skip's hometown, the band arranged for an addendum on the venue marquee that night—instead of just saying "Rush—March 14 & 15—8:00 p.m." it bore the extra line "Skip Gildersleeve nite!"
DETROIT FREE PRESS: "Rush fills house, a need: From the onset, Rush worked out its scientific, artistic and classical fantasies through Alex Lifeson's complicated guitar lines and Neil Peart's adept, if not busy, drumming."

MARCH 21, 1981
LONDON, ONTARIO
LONDON GARDENS, 4380 Wellington Road South. Venue opened in September 1964.
SUPPORT ACT: FM
TICKETS: $9.50 CAD
ATTENDANCE: 6,000; sold out

MARCH 23–25, 1981
TORONTO, ONTARIO
MAPLE LEAF GARDENS, 60 Carlton Street. Historic venue opened on November 12, 1931.
SUPPORT ACT: FM
TICKETS: $10.50 CAD
ATTENDANCE: 13,060 per show; sold out
NOTES: Recorded to multitrack by Le Mobile.
TORONTO STAR: "Rush may be the most serious band around these days. Perhaps too serious? What you saw on stage—just bassist Geddy Lee, Neil Peart, astronaut-like, folded away in his percussion kit, and guitarist Alex Lifeson—was in no way representative of what you heard. Visually, this was a power trio on stage; musically, the sound had the texture of an orchestra."[7]
THE GLOBE AND MAIL: "The show was also filled out by a boggling array of colored spotlights, (very impressive, but ultimately gave the group the aura of Niagara Falls on an August night) back-projected slides and cartoons, fire pots, and dry ice. Nice touches all, but not exactly crucial to the overall effect. Rush played with enough flashy power to hold the stage all by itself."

MARCH 27, 1981
MONTREAL, QUEBEC
MONTREAL FORUM, 2313 Saint Catherine Street West. Historic venue opened on November 29, 1924.

SUPPORT ACT: Max Webster
TICKETS: $9.50 CAD
ATTENDANCE: 14,055; sold out
NOTES: Filmed and recorded for the *Exit . . . Stage Left* video by Le Mobile with Terry Brown and Guy Charbonneau at the controls. A mini riot ensued when some fans were unable to obtain tickets to the SRO gig.
ROLLING STONE: "When Lee announces that the band is recording the show for an upcoming live album, the cheering and applause seem to shake the Forum to its foundation. And by the end of the lengthy encore, 'La Villa Strangiato,' the audience looks almost as exhausted as the musicians."
MONTREAL GAZETTE, GEDDY: "We don't feel further away from our audience and from what we were doing ten years ago. We just see more clearly now, that's all."
IAN: "I've seen dumb things on the web that give me a 'movie credit' for *Exit . . . Stage Left*. Yes, I can be seen taking the band to the stage in Montreal. I would bring Neil up the back of stage and he'd be snuck into his kit and be ready before Ged and Alex were escorted to the stage. I would get near the dressing room and shout out, 'Elwood!' and he knew to go."[8]

MARCH 28, 1981
OTTAWA, ONTARIO
OTTAWA CIVIC CENTRE, Lansdowne Park, 1015 Bank Street. Venue opened on December 29, 1967.
SUPPORT ACT: FM
TICKETS: $9.50 CAD
ATTENDANCE: 9,349; sold out
NOTES: Recorded to multitrack by Le Mobile, though Geddy had to fight through the performance with a bad chest infection (contracted in Montreal). Journalist David Fricke rode along to the gig with Neil and Geddy, interviewing them en route for a piece in *Rolling Stone*.
OTTAWA CITIZEN: "The crowd listened intently, enjoying the nuances of the music rather than merely treating the show as a social event. And always, the band was in command, bringing the audience up and down, but never letting things get out of control."

APRIL 3, 1981
TUCSON, ARIZONA
TUCSON COMMUNITY CENTER ARENA, 260 South Church Street. Venue opened on November 8, 1971.
SUPPORT ACT: Max Webster
TICKETS: $9.50
ATTENDANCE: 8,407; sold out
ARIZONA DAILY STAR: "Rush deserved one—to the exit: Canadian trio loud, distracting."

APRIL 4, 1981
PHOENIX, ARIZONA
ARIZONA VETERANS MEMORIAL COLISEUM, Arizona State Fairgrounds, 1826 West McDowell Road. Venue opened on November 3, 1965.
SUPPORT ACT: Max Webster
ATTENDANCE: 14,137; sold out

APRIL 5, 1981
ALBUQUERQUE, NEW MEXICO
TINGLEY COLISEUM, New Mexico State Fairgrounds, 300 San Pedro Drive Northeast. Venue dedicated on September 28, 1957.
SUPPORT ACT: Max Webster
TICKETS: $8.50, general admission show
ATTENDANCE: 10,153; sold out
NOTES: General admission concert. Fans in the front were crushed against the stage barrier.
GEDDY (ONSTAGE): "Hey, look, you guys have got to calm down a bit in the front because there's people getting crushed, and this barricade could fall down, and that would be game over. So everybody has got to move back a little bit. You gotta have a little bit of consideration for some guys in the front that are getting too close. So everybody move back just a bit, okay, and we'll continue the show."

APRIL 7–8, 1981
HOUSTON, TEXAS
SAM HOUSTON COLISEUM, 801 Bagby Street. Venue dedicated on November 16, 1937.
SUPPORT ACT: Max Webster
TICKETS: $10.00
ATTENDANCE: 9,463 per show; sold out

APRIL 10, 1981
DALLAS, TEXAS
REUNION ARENA, 777 Sports Street. Venue dedicated on April 28, 1980.

SUPPORT ACT: Max Webster
TICKETS: $10.00
ATTENDANCE: 15,439; sold out
NOTES: Alex, Geddy, and Neil began the day at Cape Canaveral and flew to Dallas after the planned shuttle launch was canceled. The sound of Geddy's vocals was adjusted during the first three songs, then was "very good" afterward.[9]
DALLAS MORNING NEWS: "Rock trio gives a monotonous performance. The drawbacks detract way too much from what, instrumentally, is a solid rock trio."[10]
NEIL: "We flew into Orlando on a day off [April 9], checked into a hotel, and slept until about 4:00 a.m. [on April 10], when we had to leave for our rendezvous at the air force base near the Cape. There we were met by our liaison man, who conducted us safely into the VIP zone (red sector A) in the predawn hours. We stood around listening to the announcements, as the sun rose higher and hotter in the sky. We were due to play that night in Dallas, so we couldn't wait much longer. Finally, they announced that the launch would be scrubbed for that day. The computers weren't speaking! Well, we ran for the car, and our daring driver sped off, around traffic jams, down the median of the highway, and got us to the airport barely in time."
ALEX: "We had waited until the last possible minute to leave the Cape and make our plane to Dallas. We were so late that our limo driver had to actually drive the car onto the runway in order to get us there in time. We made it to Dallas all right, but we hired a private plane to take us back to the Cape the next day—we weren't gonna take any chances."

APRIL 11, 1981
SAN ANTONIO, TEXAS
CONVENTION CENTER ARENA, HemisFair Park Complex, 601 Hemisfair Way. Venue opened on April 6, 1968.
SUPPORT ACT: Max Webster
TICKETS: $9.50 / $10.00
ATTENDANCE: 14,118; sold out
NOTES: The band headed for the airport immediately after the gig to fly back to Orlando.
NEIL: "The next night, we had a show in San Antonio, after which we drove off immediately, clambered into a hired jet, and flew straight back to Florida."[11]

APRIL 12, 1981
FORT WORTH, TEXAS
TARRANT COUNTY CONVENTION CENTER, 111 Houston Street. Venue dedicated on November 21, 1968.
SUPPORT ACT: Max Webster
TICKETS: $10.00
ATTENDANCE: 13,766; sold out
NOTES: The band was in Cape Canaveral, Florida, to witness the early morning launch of the first space shuttle, *Columbia.* The experience eventually served as inspiration for the song "Countdown."
NEIL: "This time, the launch of *Columbia* took place on schedule, and it was SOMETHING!! Again, we raced back to the plane and flew off once more, back to Fort Worth, where we had a show that night. Fortunately, the day after that was a day off, so we had a chance to catch up on all of that sleep! I remember thinking to myself as we flew back to Fort Worth after a couple of days without sleep: 'We've got to write a song about this!' It was an incredible thing to witness . . . truly a once-in-a-lifetime experience."[12]

APRIL 14, 1981
LITTLE ROCK, ARKANSAS
T. H. BARTON COLISEUM, Arkansas State Fairgrounds, 2600 Howard Street. Venue dedicated on September 29, 1952.
SUPPORT ACT: Max Webster
TICKETS: $8.50 / $9.50
ATTENDANCE: 5,251
CAPACITY: 10,250, general admission

APRIL 15, 1981
JACKSON, MISSISSIPPI
MISSISSIPPI COLISEUM, State Fairgrounds complex, 1207 Mississippi Street. Venue opened on June 7, 1962.
SUPPORT ACT: Max Webster
TICKETS: $9.50, general admission
ATTENDANCE: 6,676 (Anthem/SRO)
CONCERT GROSS: $62,339
NOTES: *Billboard* lists attendance as 6,562.

APRIL 16, 1981
MEMPHIS, TENNESSEE
MID-SOUTH COLISEUM, Memphis Fairgrounds Park, 996 Early Maxwell Blvd. Venue opened on December 2, 1964.

SUPPORT ACT: Max Webster
TICKETS: $8.00 / $9.00
ATTENDANCE: 9,537 (Anthem/SRO); sold out
CONCERT GROSS: $83,523
NOTES: *Billboard* lists attendance as 9,931.

APRIL 18, 1981
MOBILE, ALABAMA
MUNICIPAL AUDITORIUM, 401 Civic Center Drive. Venue opened on July 9, 1964.
AN EVENING WITH RUSH
TICKETS: $9.50, general admission
ATTENDANCE: 9,772; sold out
NOTES: Upon arriving at the venue, members of the Rush and Max Webster entourages were shocked by the news of Kim Mitchell's departure.
ALEX: "I remember pulling into that gig and all the guys were sitting on the grass and they looked so despondent. 'Kim's had enough. He can't take it anymore. He was on a flight this morning and went home.'"[13]
IAN: "Stixy told me about Max Webster's breakup right after they walked in. An hour later I mentioned to their roadies what a drag it was, and they hadn't been told. I went and asked Rob Gunn to maybe let their crew know. Felt so sorry for the other members and the crew. They were playing sellouts and couldn't ever get on a better tour. The crowd was loving them. Stixy had just bought a Walkman and sold it to someone on the tour because he needed the $100."

APRIL 19, 1981
NEW ORLEANS, LOUISIANA
MUNICIPAL AUDITORIUM, 1201 Saint Peter Street. Venue opened on January 30, 1930.
AN EVENING WITH RUSH
TICKETS: $11.00, general admission
ATTENDANCE: 8,100; sold out

APRIL 21, 1981
SHREVEPORT, LOUISIANA
HIRSCH MEMORIAL COLISEUM, 3701 Hudson Avenue. Venue opened on April 10, 1954.
AN EVENING WITH RUSH
TICKETS: $9.50, all seats
ATTENDANCE: 8,182; sold out

APRIL 23–24, 1981
KANSAS CITY, MISSOURI
KEMPER ARENA, 1800 Genessee Street at 17th Street. Venue dedicated on October 18, 1974.
AN EVENING WITH RUSH
TICKETS: $9.50 / $11.50
ATTENDANCE: 12,219 per show; sold out
CONCERT GROSS: $115,140 per show
THE KANSAS CITY STAR: "Heavy metal made it big Thursday night when 13,000 fans welcomed Rush to Kemper Arena. Rush, noted for its futuristic themes and populist politics, plugged in the first segment of a two-night stand here. The group demonstrated its refined style of heavy metal, which made it a favorite of rock lovers if not of most critics."

APRIL 25, 1981
OKLAHOMA CITY, OKLAHOMA
MYRIAD ARENA, One Myriad Gardens. Venue opened on November 5, 1972.
AN EVENING WITH RUSH
TICKETS: $10.00
ATTENDANCE: 13,552; sold out
THE OKLAHOMAN, NEIL: "The road improves your skills as a writer and your understanding as a person. There's nothing like playing every day for two hours to keep you improving."

APRIL 26, 1981
TULSA, OKLAHOMA
TULSA ASSEMBLY CENTER, 100 Civic Center. Venue opened on March 8, 1964.
AN EVENING WITH RUSH
TICKETS: $9.50
ATTENDANCE: 5,287
NOTES: According to Tulsa police, about twenty people were arrested on various drug charges, which was "fewer than usual." Venue aka Tulsa Convention Center.
TULSA WORLD: "Rush Loud but OK: First its show is carefully produced and packaged, with intriguing light and visual displays, and lush songs, nicely constructed and performed. Second, it's loud—maybe the loudest band to play here since Grand Funk Railroad nearly a decade ago. Their instruments are electronically embellished, so the sound is much fuller and more complex than you would expect from a three-piece group. There even is some subtlety, if that's possible at about two million decibels."

MAY 6, 1981
PITTSBURGH, PENNSYLVANIA
CIVIC ARENA, 300 Auditorium Place. Venue opened on September 17, 1961.
SUPPORT ACT: FM
TICKETS: $9.75
ATTENDANCE: 13,265 (Anthem/SRO); sold out
CONCERT GROSS: $140,020
NOTES: *Billboard* lists attendance as 14,361.
PITTSBURGH PRESS: "A big show, a symphony of lights and screen effects: a receding, vertigo-creating spiral; blue 'fountains'; Star Wars-style 'spaceships'; 'swords'; a 'Cosmos'-style journey through the stars."

MAY 7–8, 1981
RICHFIELD, OHIO
RICHFIELD COLISEUM, 2923 Streetsboro Road. Venue opened on October 26, 1974.
SUPPORT ACT: FM
TICKETS: $9.00 / $10.00
ATTENDANCE: 15,300 per show (Anthem/SRO); sold out
CONCERT GROSS: $137,945 per show
NOTES: *Billboard* lists attendance as 15,196 per show.

MAY 9, 1981
BUFFALO, NEW YORK
BUFFALO MEMORIAL AUDITORIUM, 140 Main Street. Venue opened on October 14, 1940.
SUPPORT ACT: FM
TICKETS: $8.50 / $9.50
ATTENDANCE: 15,020; sold out
NOTES: A bottom-end fuzz through the PA distracted from Alex's acoustic solo.[14]
BUFFALO EVENING NEWS: "One waited for Rush to get into a song, a rhythm, but when they did it was gone in a flash."

MAY 11, 1981
BINGHAMTON, NEW YORK
BROOME COUNTY WAR MEMORIAL ARENA, 1 Stuart Street. Venue opened on August 29, 1973.
SUPPORT ACT: FM
TICKETS: $10.50
ATTENDANCE: 5,558
CAPACITY: 7,000
NOTES: Alex, Geddy, and Neil had some fun performing an extended version of "Wipe Out" to an enthusiastic Binghamton audience.

MAY 12, 1981
ROCHESTER, NEW YORK
ROCHESTER COMMUNITY WAR MEMORIAL, 100 Exchange Boulevard. Venue opened on October 18, 1955.
SUPPORT ACT: FM
TICKETS: $10.50
ATTENDANCE: 10,130 (Anthem/SRO); sold out
CONCERT GROSS: $107,100
NOTES: *Billboard* lists attendance as 10,200. Although some advance ads list Saga as the opener, promoter records indicate FM was sole support.

MAY 13, 1981
SYRACUSE, NEW YORK
ONONDAGA COUNTY WAR MEMORIAL AUDITORIUM, 515 Montgomery Street. Venue opened on September 1, 1951.
SUPPORT ACT: FM
TICKETS: $9.00
ATTENDANCE: 7,072
CAPACITY: 8,200

MAY 15, 1981
GLENS FALLS, NEW YORK
GLENS FALLS CIVIC CENTER, 1 Civic Center Plaza. Venue opened on May 18, 1979.
TICKETS: $10.00
ATTENDANCE: 6,759 (Anthem/SRO)
CONCERT GROSS: $66,000

MAY 16–17, 1981
LARGO, MARYLAND
CAPITAL CENTRE, 1 Harry S. Truman Drive. Venue opened on December 2, 1973.
SUPPORT ACT: FM
TICKETS: $8.80 / $9.90
ATTENDANCE: 18,626 per show; sold out
NOTES: Alex spent time in the afternoon before the second show flying his remote-control airplane in the Cap Centre parking lot. The fun abruptly ended when it crashed, getting stuck atop a tree. Sound check featured a drum duet by Neil and FM's Marty Deller. After the show, Geddy hung out in FM's dressing room, where he and Ben Mink proceeded to crack each other up doing Yiddish impressions. Ben, who grew up in Toronto, is also from a family of Polish Jews who had survived the Holocaust. With so much in common, it's no wonder

that he and Geddy soon become good friends. A very wasted young fan stumbled up to Geddy and asked him if he wanted to do some drugs. Geddy responded by telling him that drugs are bad for him, and that he should not be doing them.
GREG LUKENS (NATIONAL SOUND): "As an illustration of how closely integrated National Sound was with Rush, Dave Berman acted as the backup tech for their backline roadies. So, if one of their guys was sick or something, Dave would step in and cover. Skip Gildersleeve, Geddy's tech, dropped a kidney stone here at the Capital Centre, so Dave Berman doubled for Skip while he was off in the hospital. A sound company guy doubling as backline guy? That wasn't typical, but it did happen in our relationship, and nobody thought twice about it."[15]

MAY 18, 1981
NEW YORK, NEW YORK
MADISON SQUARE GARDEN, 4 Pennsylvania Plaza (8th Avenue between 31st & 33rd Streets). Historic venue opened on February 11, 1968.
SUPPORT ACT: FM
TICKETS: $10.50 / $11.50
ATTENDANCE: 17,292; sold out
CONCERT GROSS: $195,000
NOTES: Rush's Madison Square Garden debut was the week's top-grossing concert.[16] *Billboard* lists attendance as 17,500. During sound check, Rush and FM shared some Canadian improvisation, with both bands jamming together. The fruits of these experiments would later surface in the form of "Losing It." After sound check, Uncle Cliff Burnstein and David Fricke dined with a younger Rush-fanatic journalist, sharing past stories with a longtime sense of pride that Rush was able to not only headline MSG, but also sell it out in the process.
CAMERON HAWKINS (FM VOCALIST/ KEYBOARDIST/BASSIST): "Talk about rock 'n' roll zoo! At Madison Square Garden, the Ringling Brothers Circus pulled out of the main arena and then Rush came in. You're walking in and there's dwarves and elephants and white tigers—we were in Fairyland. Then you walk out and play for 17,000 people who immediately react 100 percent positively, and I suddenly thought:

'I have long hair and a Rickenbacker bass and I'm playing keyboards— maybe they think we're Rush?' Something amazing happened throughout the whole tour—our crew and their crew, our band and their band, and their audience . . . it was magical. We'd do our sound check and then the cover would come off Neil's drums, Geddy would come over and pick up a bass, Alex would plug into his amp behind Ben, and we'd just start playing together. It was a wonderful thing."[17]
IAN: "We had to load everything in at 8:00 a.m. They assured us the animals would be fine. I was standing at the entrance when I realized there was a giraffe above me, checking me out. Lurch was allowed to get up on the back of an elephant—the elephant didn't like it, so it dropped a shoulder and flicked him off."
CIRCUS: "Each identical performance on this five-month extravaganza holds all the excitement of a Howard Johnson's omelet. Though you wouldn't know it from the crowd's reaction."

MAY 20, 1981
UNIONDALE, NEW YORK
NASSAU COUNTY VETERANS MEMORIAL COLISEUM, 1255 Hempstead Turnpike. Venue dedicated on May 29, 1972.
SUPPORT ACT: FM
TICKETS: $10.50 / $11.50
ATTENDANCE: 10,567
NOTES: Loud, disturbing feedback disrupted the end of "Tom Sawyer," while Alex created an otherworldly feedback to close out "2112: Grand Finale." For the encore, Alex continued to add "Never on Sunday" to the intro of "La Villa Strangiato."
GEDDY (ONSTAGE): "I think this is the second year in a row that we've played for you on the eve of the Stanley Cup."

MAY 22, 1981
PHILADELPHIA, PENNSYLVANIA
THE SPECTRUM, 3601 South Broad Street. Venue opened on October 1, 1967.
SUPPORT ACT: FM
TICKETS: $8.00 / $9.50
ATTENDANCE: 15,423 (Anthem/SRO); sold out
CONCERT GROSS: $137,703

NOTES: Rush performed four of the week's five top-grossing concerts. Before the gig, Neil passed the time in FM's dressing room jamming on keyboard and electronic percussion with Marty. For the show's encore, Alex continued to add "Never on Sunday" to the intro of "La Villa Strangiato."

MAY 23, 1981
BOSTON, MASSACHUSETTS
BOSTON GARDEN, 150 Causeway Street. Venue opened on November 17, 1928.
SUPPORT ACT: FM
TICKETS: $9.50 / $10.50
ATTENDANCE: 11,406; sold out
CONCERT GROSS: $120,391
NOTES: *Billboard* lists attendance at 11,500.
THE BOSTON GLOBE: "It Wasn't Easy Standing Up to the Rush: Around me were The Noises of Arena War—a combination of Rush's guitar thunder and its constant companion, a fusillade of firecrackers tossed by the denizens of the upper deck."

MAY 24, 1981
PROVIDENCE, RHODE ISLAND
PROVIDENCE CIVIC CENTER, 1 La Salle Square. Venue opened on November 3, 1972.
SUPPORT ACT: FM
TICKETS: $8.50 / $9.50
ATTENDANCE: 10,408; sold out
CONCERT GROSS: $93,251
NOTES: *Billboard* lists attendance at 10,558.
GEDDY (ONSTAGE): "Well, all right, Providence! I'd like you to do me a favor. All those people around who are throwing those green things, I'd wish they would stop throwing them around, or somebody's gonna get hurt pretty badly tonight."

JUNE 1, 1981
DENVER, COLORADO
MCNICHOLS SPORTS ARENA, 1635 Clay Street. Venue opened on August 22, 1975.
SUPPORT ACT: FM
ATTENDANCE: 14,572; sold out

JUNE 3, 1981
SALT LAKE CITY, UTAH
SALT PALACE, 100 S West Temple. Venue dedicated on July 11, 1969.
SUPPORT ACT: FM
ATTENDANCE: 12,228; sold out

JUNE 5–6, 1981
OAKLAND, CALIFORNIA
OAKLAND-ALAMEDA COUNTY COLISEUM ARENA, 7000 Coliseum Way. Venue opened on November 9, 1966.
SUPPORT ACT: FM
TICKETS: $7.50 / $8.50 / $9.50
ATTENDANCE: 11,876 per show (Anthem/SRO); sold out
CONCERT GROSS: $106,334 per show
NOTES: These two Oakland dates were the top-grossing concerts of the week, according to *Billboard*, which lists attendance at 11,726 per show.

JUNE 7, 1981
FRESNO, CALIFORNIA
SELLAND ARENA, 700 M Street, at Ventura. Venue opened on October 11, 1966.
SUPPORT ACT: FM
TICKETS: $9.50 (advance) / $11.00 (at the door), general admission
ATTENDANCE: 6,995 (Anthem/SRO); sold out
CONCERT GROSS: $66,291
NOTES: *Billboard* lists attendance at 6,982.

JUNE 9, 1981
SAN DIEGO, CALIFORNIA
SAN DIEGO SPORTS ARENA, 3500 Sports Arena Boulevard. Venue opened on November 17, 1966.
SUPPORT ACT: FM
TICKETS: $8.75 / $9.75
ATTENDANCE: 12,339 (Anthem/SRO); sold out
CONCERT GROSS: $114,670
NOTES: *Billboard* lists attendance at 12,145.
RECORD REVIEW: "Geddy Lee's vocals are as strong and as accessible as they have ever been. A little magic from Lifeson and Peart adds up to a worthy reason why Rush is now one of the world's most successful progressive bands."

JUNE 10–11, 1981
INGLEWOOD, CALIFORNIA
THE FORUM, 3900 West Manchester Boulevard. Venue opened on December 30, 1967.
SUPPORT ACT: FM
TICKETS: $8.75 / $10.75
ATTENDANCE: 14,672 per show (Anthem/SRO); sold out
CONCERT GROSS: $137,620 per show
NOTES: *Billboard* lists attendance at 13,623 per show.
LOS ANGELES TIMES: "Rush's opening night at the Forum started quite literally with a bang—several of them. Understandably elated that their band had finally overcome critical barbs and radio apathy to perch comfortably in the Top 10, the band's fans unleashed a loud, foolhardy barrage of firepower: a string of firecrackers, a smoke bomb, two skyrockets and three huge explosions. All that before the band had been on stage for fifteen minutes. Such a welcome has been a long time coming for Rush, a trio that struggled for six years and seven albums before last year's *Permanent Waves* album made it one of rock's biggest draws. Rush's audience has always been remarkably dedicated; the size of that audience didn't significantly increase, though, until the group released *2112*."[18]

JUNE 12, 1981
ANAHEIM, CALIFORNIA
CONVENTION CENTER, 800 West Katella Avenue. Venue dedicated on July 12, 1967.
SUPPORT ACT: FM
TICKETS: $8.75 / $10.75
ATTENDANCE: 7,321 (Anthem/SRO); sold out
CONCERT GROSS: $74,884
NOTES: *Billboard* lists attendance at 7,163.
CREEM: "I think it's safe to say that Paul McCartney can not only play bass better than Geddy Lee, but he can probably play guitar better than Lifeson, play drums better than Peart, and write 80,000 times better than Rush and the NHL put together. If you think 'Mary had a little lamb' is outright drivel, I invite you to listen to 'The Temples of Syrinx' or 'Cygnus X-1 Book II' by Peart and Company."

JUNE 14, 1981
LONG BEACH, CALIFORNIA
LONG BEACH ARENA, 300 East Ocean Boulevard. Venue opened on October 6, 1962.
SUPPORT ACT: FM
TICKETS: $8.75 / $10.75
ATTENDANCE: 12,796 (Anthem/SRO); sold out
CONCERT GROSS: $131,438

JUNE 15, 1981
LAS VEGAS, NEVADA
ALADDIN THEATRE FOR THE PERFORMING ARTS, Aladdin Hotel Casino, 3667 Las Vegas Boulevard South. Venue opened on July 2, 1976.
AN EVENING WITH RUSH
TICKETS: $12.00
ATTENDANCE: 7,450; sold out
CONCERT GROSS: $89,400

JUNE 16, 1981
RENO, NEVADA
CENTENNIAL COLISEUM, 4590 South Virginia Street. Venue opened on March 3, 1965.
AN EVENING WITH RUSH
TICKETS: $9.50, general admission
ATTENDANCE: 6,500; sold out

JUNE 18–19, 1981
SEATTLE, WASHINGTON
SEATTLE CENTER COLISEUM, 305 Harrison Street. Venue opened on April 21, 1962.
SUPPORT ACT: FM
TICKETS: $9.00 / $10.00
ATTENDANCE: 12,320 per show; sold out
CONCERT GROSS: $118,662 per show
NOTES: Geddy's double-neck Rickenbacker was worked on by renowned Seattle bass builder Mike Lull. In the hope of having it signed by Geddy, Lull brought along his 1959 Fender bass, which Geddy loved and offered to buy, but Lull declined, later selling it to Jeff Ament of Pearl Jam.
THE SEATTLE TIMES, MIKE LULL: "When I returned the bass to the Edgewater Hotel, Lee walked in with a briefcase handcuffed to his wrist. He opens it, and it's cash—lots of it," adding that before credit cards had no limits, touring band members had to carry their own money. "They don't take your check in Japan."

JUNE 20, 1981
PORTLAND, OREGON
MEMORIAL COLISEUM, 1401 North Wheeler. Venue opened on November 3, 1960.
SUPPORT ACT: FM
TICKETS: $9.00 / $10.50 (average: $10.12)
ATTENDANCE: 9,780 (Anthem/SRO); sold out
CONCERT GROSS: $98,944
PORTLAND JOURNAL: "In terms of zeal and number of followers, Rush could qualify as one of North America's major religions. There is some good music there to be appreciated, but not worshipped."

JUNE 21, 1981
SPOKANE, WASHINGTON
SPOKANE COLISEUM, 1101 North Howard Street. Venue opened on December 3, 1954.
SUPPORT ACT: FM
TICKETS: $8.50 / $9.50 (average: $8.74), general admission
ATTENDANCE: 6,172 (Anthem/SRO); sold out
CONCERT GROSS: $53,930
NOTES: The Robert Klein Radio Show (with Alex and Geddy as special guests) aired throughout America.
ROBERT KLEIN: "Rush recently filled Madison Square Garden."
ALEX: "They were all Geddy's cousins [laughs]."
GEDDY: "I've got a very large family here in New York."
THE SPOKESMAN REVIEW: "No one accused Rush of subtlety: Awash in Technicolor splashes of purple and green, Rush gave a nearly full Coliseum its money's worth."

JUNE 23, 1981
VANCOUVER, BRITISH COLUMBIA
PACIFIC COLISEUM, Pacific National Exhibition Fairgrounds, 100 North Renfrew. Venue dedicated on January 8, 1968.
SUPPORT ACT: Goddo
TICKETS: $10.50 / $11.50 CAD (average: $10.67)
ATTENDANCE: 11,645 (Anthem/SRO); sold out
CONCERT GROSS: $121,668 CAD
NOTES: Billboard lists attendance at 11,408. Recorded to multitrack by Le Mobile for possible future release.
VANCOUVER SUN: "A Rush concert is

not so much a musical event as a very large philosophy lecture, and a more serious, solemn trio of professors would be harder to find."
GREG GODOVITZ (FOUNDING BASSIST FOR GODDO): "We opened for Rush at the Pacific Coliseum with no sound check. I was pissed off enough to give a great show, and we earned an encore, with Geddy watching our entire set from the side of the stage."[19]

JUNE 25, 1981
EDMONTON, ALBERTA
NORTHLANDS COLISEUM, 7424 118th Avenue NW. Venue opened on November 10, 1974.
SUPPORT ACT: Goddo
TICKETS: $10.50 (advance) / $11.50 (day of) CAD
ATTENDANCE: 11,363 (Anthem/SRO); sold out
CONCERT GROSS: $129,661 CAD
NOTES: Billboard lists attendance at 11,285. Recorded to multitrack by Le Mobile. "2112: Overture" and "2112: The Temples of Syrinx" from this show were eventually released on December 18, 2012, as part of the Super Deluxe edition of 2112.
EDMONTON JOURNAL: "Sandwiching arty pretense with heavy metal drive is nothing new, but judging by the wild response, it works just fine in 1981."

JULY 2–3, 1981
BLOOMINGTON, MINNESOTA
METROPOLITAN SPORTS CENTER, 7901 Cedar Avenue South. Venue opened on October 21, 1967.
SUPPORT ACT: The Joe Perry Project
TICKETS: $9.75 / $10.75
ATTENDANCE: 11,845 per show; sold out
CONCERT GROSS: $124,695 per show
CHARLIE FARREN (JOE PERRY PROJECT GUITARIST/VOCALIST): "It was a lot of fun touring with Joe because he had all of these great stories from his years on the road with Aerosmith. And we got the dates with Rush and Joe became nervous, because Rush used to open for Aerosmith back in the early days, and for whatever reason, Steven Tyler didn't like them and treated them poorly. He made sure they didn't get a sound check, and messed with them, so there was definitely some animosity there, and Joe told

us all to 'get ready for some rough treatment,' because being an opening act, you never know how you're going to get treated by the headliner. So we arrive in Minnesota, and Geddy and Neil went out of their way to make sure that we were treated well. And I mean really well. The dressing room was stocked by the caterer. They made sure that we got a sound check every day, and that we were happy with the monitors and the monitor mix. And Joe knew something was up, that this was their way of handling how poorly Aerosmith had treated them as an opener. They handled the situation with class."[20]

GEDDY: "It's not about how Aerosmith's crew screwed over our crew or any of that. It's just the fact that we were out there too. We were a band out there trying to make it, just like they were. We learned a lot on that tour."[21]

NEIL: "Joe Perry's solo band opened for us . . . and we had to decide what to do. Geddy's and my memories agree that published reports of the dialogue at that time are more fanciful than factual, but, yes, we did take the high road."[22]

JOE PERRY: "I want to thank them for treating the Project so good and actually taking the time to ask if everything was OK. I hope I had the presence of mind back then to apologize. I want to congratulate Rush on their longevity, because like us, they are still around to tell the tales."[23]

JULY 4–5, 1981
EAST TROY, WISCONSIN
ALPINE VALLEY MUSIC THEATRE, 2699 Highway D. Venue opened on June 30, 1977.
SUPPORT ACT: The Joe Perry Project
TICKETS: $9.00 / $12.50 (two-day average: $9.87)
TWO-DAY EAST TROY ATTENDANCE (ANTHEM/SRO): 28,211
TWO-DAY EAST TROY CONCERT GROSS: $394,900
NOTES: On July 4, Rush jammed part of "Cygnus X-1" during sound check, which ended as laughing crew members covered Neil's kit with a sun-resistant silver tarp, while the band was still playing. The festive evening was capped off with an explosive fireworks display. After the show, band and crew celebrated with an end-of-tour party at the nearby Alpine Valley Resort. Though Rush had handled matters with their former Aerosmith tour mate with class, a point was still made when the Joe Perry Project was not invited to the end-of-tour party. The following day, Joe was visibly shaken up by it, asking one journalist, 'What's their problem?' July 5 was the final performance on the *Moving Pictures* tour. *Billboard* lists two-day East Troy attendance as 40,000.

CANADIAN MUSICIAN: "[There] was enough to clear not only their mammoth lighting, sound, staging, and transportation expenses, but additionally to pay crew wages and retainers for a full year until August 1982, when Rush's rigid schedule prescribes their next major North American tour. Considering most bands of megabuck dimensions expect to lose money on national tours that are considered necessary for the promotion of monster album sales, the real source of income, according to traditional values, Alex, Geddy, and drummer Neil Peart are way ahead of the game."

1. Neil Peart. *Roadshow: Landscape with Drums: A Concert Tour by Motorcycle*. Rounder Books, 2006.
2. MaxWebsterLive.ca
3. Bill Banasiewicz. Interview with Kim Mitchell, March 8, 1981.
4. *The Indianapolis News.*
5. *The Courier-Journal.*
6. *Indianapolis Star*, March 12, 1981.
7. *The Toronto Star*, March 24, 1981.
8. Skip Daly. Interview with Ian Grandy, 2011–2012.
9. *Dallas Morning News.*
10. Pete Oppel, April 13, 1981.
11. Neil Peart. "Stories from *Signals*," *Sounds*, October 16, 1982.
12. Neil Peart. "Stories from *Signals*," *Sounds*, October 16, 1982.
13. Max Webster live.ca
14. *Buffalo Evening News.*
15. Skip Daly. Interview with Greg Lukens, March 4, 2013.
16. *Billboard.*
17. Phil Ashcroft. "FM discuss the turbulent past, touring with Rush and their big return," *PROG*, February 26, 2016. loudersound.com
18. *The Los Angeles Times*, June 12, 1981.
19. Greg Godovitz. *Travels With My Amp*. Annyfield Pub, February 1, 2002.
20. Bill Banasiewicz. Interview with Charlie Farren, December 2, 2014.
21. Bill Banasiewicz. Interview with Geddy Lee, July 4, 1981.
22. Neil Peart. *Far And Wide: Bring That Horizon to Me!*. ECW Press, September 13, 2016.
23. Interview with Joe Perry. *Rolling Stone*, July 2, 2015.

Chapter 13

THE EXIT . . . STAGE LEFT TOUR

The *Exit . . . Stage Left* tour, which coincided with the release of the band's second live album, could be seen as an extension of the *Moving Pictures* outing. Rush was riding a continued wave of mainstream success and performed to more than 180,000 fans over the course of thirty-four shows. The first half of the trek consisted of European dates ("I was a little nervous, 'cause of the fact that we were playing to a non-English-speaking audience, and we don't do that very often," remarked Geddy following a gig in Hamburg, West Germany), after which they wrapped up 1981 with a short run through the eastern US. The set list for these shows was similar to that of the *Moving Pictures* tour, save for the addition of the newly written "Subdivisions," which would appear on the following year's *Signals* and was performed live here for the first time. Another *Signals* track, "Digital Man," was worked on at sound checks.

The short tour finished on December 22, 1981, in East Rutherford, New Jersey, with Geddy telling the more than eighteen thousand fans in attendance, "On behalf of the band, we'd like to wish you a very Merry Christmas and a Happy New Year!" In the previous twelve months, Rush had achieved an undreamed-of level of popularity, with two hugely successful tours and three platinum albums, but the members were beginning to pay a price in terms of reduced privacy and other celebrity-associated stresses. They were also feeling the effects of the many years of focused attention on the band, often to the exclusion of almost anything else in their lives. Paradoxically, the year of incredible success led the band members to speak about the future in a more contemplative manner.

"There are other interests I have that I'd like to get into a little more—and I think I'm missing out on them sometimes," said Alex. "I guess, no matter who you are or what you do, there are always things you'd love to get around to that somehow you know you never will. It may sound

strange, but I have this urge to go work with my brother-in-law sometime, putting up fences for a couple of weeks—or just take some time to get in some decent flying hours. I don't know—I don't spend much time worrying about it, but it's there, way off in the distance. As far as the band goes, I don't think our relationship will ever change, even if we didn't see each other for ten years. In fact, if it wasn't for this particular band, I wouldn't do all this. I wouldn't do it all over again."

RIGHT AND TOP: East Rutherford, NJ; Ticket stub.

RIGHT AND BOTTOM LEFT: East Rutherford, NJ; Invitation to a band party at the Barge Club.

RIGHT AND BOTTOM RIGHT: London, England; Backstage pass for Wembley Arena.

OPPOSITE: Munich, Germany; Alex at sound check at Circus Krone.

ABOVE: Munich, Germany; A smiling Neil at sound check at Circus Krone.

OPPOSITE TOP: Alex, Neil, and Geddy onstage.

OPPOSITE BOTTOM: Alex performing "Xanadu."

TOUR HISTORY
EXIT . . . STAGE LEFT

SET LIST:
"2112: Overture"
"2112: The Temples of Syrinx"
"Freewill"
"Limelight"
"Hemispheres: Prelude"
"Beneath, Between, and Behind" (abridged)
"Subdivisions" (prerelease version)
"The Camera Eye"

"YYZ" (with drum solo)
"Broon's Bane"
"The Trees"
"Xanadu"
"The Spirit of Radio"
"Red Barchetta"
"Closer to the Heart"
"Tom Sawyer"
"Vital Signs"

"Working Man" (with reggae intro)
"Hemispheres: Armageddon"
"By-Tor and the Snow Dog"
"In the End"
"In the Mood"
"2112: Grand Finale"
Encore:
"La Villa Strangiato"
(with electric guitar intro)

OCTOBER 29–30, 1981
STAFFORD, ENGLAND
NEW BINGLEY HALL, Staffordshire
County Showground, Weston Road.
Venue opened in 1975.
AN EVENING WITH RUSH
TICKETS: £5.00, general admission
ATTENDANCE: 8,000 per show; sold out
NOTES: The opening date of the 1981
Exit . . . Stage Left tour featured the live
debut of "Subdivisions."
MELODY MAKER: "The audience lis-
tened with rapt attention, breaking their
almost religious silence with great roars
of appreciation at the end of numbers."

OCTOBER 31, 1981
QUEENSFERRY, FLINTSHIRE, WALES
DEESIDE LEISURE CENTRE, Chester
Road West, Route B5129. Venue
opened on July 23, 1971.
AN EVENING WITH RUSH
TICKETS: £5.00, general admission
CAPACITY: 4,500

NOVEMBER 2, 1981
BRIGHTON, EAST SUSSEX, ENGLAND
BRIGHTON CENTRE, Kings Road, Route
A259 at Brighton Beach. Venue opened
on September 19, 1977.
AN EVENING WITH RUSH
TICKETS: £5.00, general admission
CAPACITY: 5,100 (2,100 permanent
seats)
NOTES: Alex broke a string near the end
of the solo in "Freewill." He continued
playing until the vocal break, when he
got a new axe, so there was no guitar as
Geddy sang: "Each of us, a cell of aware-
ness, imperfect."
SOUNDS: "A mammoth two-hour set—a
feast of hard-hitting hyper-complexity

delivered with considerable poise, ele-
gance and (thankfully) nary a trace of
po-faced seriousness. Peart paradiddles,
jangly Lifeson licks, and squeaky-clean
vocals . . . characteristics that will
undoubtedly shine through any musical
form the outfit choose to involve themselves with in the future."

NOVEMBER 4–6, 1981
LONDON, ENGLAND
WEMBLEY ARENA, Arena Square at
Engineers Way. Venue opened on
August 4, 1934.
AN EVENING WITH RUSH
TICKETS: £5.00 / £5.50
ATTENDANCE: 10,000 per show
(approximate); sold out
NOTES: Venue was originally called
Empire Pool at Wembley. An enthusiastic crowd sang and clapped throughout
the performance. The sound check jam
before the second show featured scraps
of information that would eventually be
incorporated into the *Signals* album.
Alex and Neil concentrated on rhythm,
while Geddy focused on keyboard
leads. After sound check, Geddy shared
a recording of Bob and Doug McKenzie's
"Take Off" with the band, the crew,
and a few friends. The song blasted
through the PA, and everyone was
cracking up after hearing it for the very
first time. At the show, the band was
welcomed by a fired-up crowd. During
the opening to "The Trees," the punters sang louder than Geddy. Afterward,
the band signed autographs, then
headed to Monksberry Tonight for a
private party, which lasted into the wee
hours. After each of the British shows,
fans lined up outside the venues and

Alex, Geddy, and Neil spend ninety
minutes or so signing autographs for
each and every one of them.
NEIL: "Yeah, whenever the circumstances
permit, we try and sign autographs over
here. It's peculiar to England. There are a
lot of reasons for it that are sociological
and very difficult to go into. Things are
different for people over here; life is
smaller here than for American kids, so
consequently, I think the level of fanati-
cism towards any band, not exclusively
ourselves . . . but whenever people like a
band here, they *really* like them!

NOVEMBER 8, 1981
INGLISTON, NEAR EDINBURGH,
SCOTLAND
ROYAL HIGHLAND AGRICULTURAL
EXHIBITION HALL, Royal Highland
Exhibition Centre, Glasgow Road (A8).
Venue opened on June 21, 1960.
AN EVENING WITH RUSH
TICKETS: £5.00, general admission
ATTENDANCE: 11,000 (approximate);
sold out
NOTES: Fans mobbed the nearby airport
to greet the band. Onstage, Alex and
Geddy performed an extended country
jam before "Closer to the Heart," while
the crowd's clapping kept time.
THE ROCK REPORT: "The venue is a
large arena floor with no seats, and
inside it's cold! So cold, in fact, that one
can see one's breath during sound check.
Outside, 13,000 or so Scottish fans
(many of whom can be heard on the *Exit
. . . Stage Left* album) await entry on a
damp, dreary day. One problem, the
venue only holds about 11,000. The
cold, empty arena floor soon becomes
jam packed with punters vying for

218

position. The temperature of the venue begins to rise to a swelter. In the stair-wells, which connect the venue with the dressing rooms, the conflict of extreme warmth and cold colliding produces an intense fog. It was like walking onstage during 'Xanadu.' Rush opens with 'Overture' and the place erupts into a frenzy. After every break in the song the entire arena floor raises their hands above their heads and yells "Rush!" in perfect time, not missing a beat. The chill in the air was replaced by a chill of amazement running down one's spine. Everyone claps in unison during 'Freewill,' 'Prelude,' and Neil's solo creating a loud, thunderous metronome for him to bounce off of. Those once freezing fans are now drenched in sweat, as many of them take off their shirts to ring out all of the mois-ture. The crowd sings the opening verse to 'The Trees' so loudly that Geddy adds a thank you. 'And the oaks ignore their pleas, thank you.' During 'Red Barchetta,' Neil tosses his stick up out of sight, then catches it like clockwork to a roaring applause that literally shakes the venue. Next up is 'Closer to the Heart,' and the audience is singing so loudly that it's sometimes hard to hear Geddy. The per-fect interaction between the band and their fanatical audience made this show a truly 'holy grail' Rush concert for fans and band alike. Their efforts did not go unnoticed by Geddy, who walked off the stage saying: 'Thank you Edinburgh. You guys are one fired-up crowd!'"

NOVEMBER 9, 1981
STAFFORD, ENGLAND

NEW BINGLEY HALL, Staffordshire County Showground, Weston Road. Venue opened in 1975.
AN EVENING WITH RUSH
TICKETS: £5.00, general admission
ATTENDANCE: 8,000; sold out

NOVEMBER 11, 1981
HAMBURG, WEST GERMANY

GROBER SAAL (GRAND HALL), MUSIKHALLE HAMBURG, Johannes-Brahms-Platz. Historic venue inaugu-rated on June 4, 1908.
SUPPORT ACT: Girlschool
TICKETS: 20 DEM / 24 DEM
CAPACITY: 2,025 seats
GEDDY: "The European tour was great. The first gig we did in Hamburg was a

pretty small theater, and that was kind of neat from one aspect because you could actually hear everything very clearly. From the performance point of view, it was kind of interesting to play under those conditions once again, and Neil made an interesting observation at the end of the show. He commented . . . how many Rush fans in the United States would probably give their right arm to see us in that kind of circumstance, where it was an intimate theater, and everybody was real close to everybody else. So, even though it's an adjustment to go from playing to the adulation of twenty thousand fans to two thousand, four thousand, five thousand fans, it's really not that big of an adjustment to make. I think we made the transition pretty well, and we still got to really present a fair representation of the show, and a lot of the places weren't as small as we'd thought they'd be."[1]

NOVEMBER 12, 1981
NEUNKIRCHEN AM BRAND, NEAR NUREMBURG, BAVARIA, WEST GERMANY

HEMMERLEINHALLE, In der Selau, near Schwabachstrabe. Venue originally built in 1973, opened as a concert hall on January 31, 1977.
SUPPORT ACT: Girlschool
TICKETS: 20 DEM / 24 DEM
CAPACITY: 4,000

NOVEMBER 14, 1981
ROTTERDAM, SOUTH HOLLAND, THE NETHERLANDS

AHOY SPORTPALEIS, Ahoy-weg 10. Venue opened on January 15, 1971.
SUPPORT ACT: Girlschool
TICKETS: 20 NLG / 24 NLG
ATTENDANCE: 11,500 (approximate); sold out

NOVEMBER 16, 1981
MUNICH, BAVARIA, WEST GERMANY

CIRCUS KRONE, Marsstrabe 43. Venue opened on December 12, 1962.
SUPPORT ACT: Girlschool
TICKETS: 20 DEM / 24 DEM
CAPACITY: 3,000

NOVEMBER 17, 1981
RUSSELSHEIM, HESSE, WEST GERMANY
WALTER KOBEL HALLE, Evreuxring 31. Venue opened in 1972.

SUPPORT ACT: Girlschool
TICKETS: 20 DEM / 24 DEM
CAPACITY: 4,500

NOVEMBER 18–19, 1981
BOBLINGEN, NR. STUTTGART, BADEN-WURTTEMBERG, WEST GERMANY

SPORTHALLE, Schonbuchstrabe 20. Venue opened on September 24, 1966.
SUPPORT ACT: Girlschool
TICKETS: 20 DEM / 24 DEM
CAPACITY: 6,000
NOTES: The November 18 date is not in SRO's records. It may have been added to satisfy demand after strong sales for the November 19 show.
STUTTGART RADIO, ALEX: "We spend about eight months of the year touring America, and we do a short tour of Canada. We cover Canada in two or three weeks' time. And we try to get to England once a year, and now, to Europe, and possibly the Far East."

NOVEMBER 20, 1981
KARLSRUHE, BADEN-WURTTEMBERG, WEST GERMANY

SCHWARZWALDHALLE (BLACK FOREST HALL), Festplatz 3–9. Venue opened on August 29, 1953.
SUPPORT ACT: Girlschool
TICKETS: 20 DEM / 24 DEM
CAPACITY: 5,000

NOVEMBER 21, 1981
ESSEN, NORTH RHINE-WESTPHALIA, WEST GERMANY

GRUGAHALLE, Gruga Complex, Ruettenscheid, NorbertstraBe. Venue opened on October 25, 1958.
SUPPORT ACT: Girlschool
TICKETS: 20 DEM / 24 DEM
CAPACITY: 10,000
NOTES: Michael Hirsch's last date with the band.
NICK KOTOS (SEE FACTOR): "Mike came up to me and said, 'Tonight's my last show.' And I said, 'Tonight's every-one's last show—the tour is over.' And he said, 'No, this is my last show working for Rush. I got hired to be the stage manager for the Jackson reunion tour.' I said, 'Who was hired to take your place?' and he said, 'Probably you.' I said, 'Yeah, right.' Then Howard came up, since he was the tour manager at the time, and said, 'The band wants to talk to you.' So, I walked up to them, in my semi-inebriated state, and

they asked me if I wanted to be production manager. I said, 'Yeah—I just have a couple questions. Do I have to move to Canada?' and they said, 'No.' At that time, they gave their crew a retainer during the time off the road, but it was partial pay. So I said that I'd probably still do other tours, and they said, 'Oh, we expect you to do other tours. We encourage you to do other tours.' So, I thought, *great*. Then I took the plunge, because at that point we'd known each other for three years, and I said, 'You probably already know this . . . but I'm not exactly a big fan of your music.' And they said, 'Oh, yeah, we know that, but we're not hiring you to be a fan. We're hiring you to manage the production of the show. We've got enough fans already.' So, I said, 'Great! I'd love to do it.' Honestly, I think they are all brilliant players, brilliant musicians . . . and really, nice—and intelligent—guys. I'm just not a fan of their music."[2]

MIKE "LURCH" HIRSCH: "I will always cherish those guys because they gave me the opportunity to learn and prove myself at their expense, and to find myself. But because of their touring schedule . . . they liked to go out and just crush it for five or six months, and then bag it up and wait for spring training to go back out for six weeks—after a point, it was like . . . it's great, I love everybody . . . but six months of sitting around on low wages in between tours, when nobody else would hire me because I'm 'Rush's guy' . . . and after seven years, when I was up to about seventh in seniority, I just thought *It's time for me to make the change and become my own guy.* I wanted to leave everything on good terms and not burn any bridges, and I still talk to the guys regularly, and we're on great terms. I just needed to go on and do my thing."[3]

NOVEMBER 28, 1981
PEMBROKE PINES, FLORIDA
HOLLYWOOD SPORTATORIUM, 17171 Pines Boulevard (Route 820). Venue opened in September 1970.
SUPPORT ACT: Riot
TICKETS: $10.50, all seats reserved, includes fifty-cent parking fee
ATTENDANCE: 12,837; sold out
CONCERT GROSS: $122,480
NOTES: Neil was delayed en route, so the doors opened late. This created some crowd-control problems, which led to local police using tear gas. Twenty-two people, including eleven police officers, were injured, and two fans were arrested. The overreaction by Florida police foreshadowed Alex's experience some twenty-two years later.

NEIL: "I missed my flight from St. Thomas to Miami. A later flight would get me in before the show, so I found a Western Union office and sent a telegram to the venue (no cell phones, e-mails, or even production-office telephones in those days), booked a seat on the next flight, and waited it out. However, if I was dealing calmly with the situation, the notorious Dade County [actually, Broward County—ed.] police were not (the same guardians of the peace who had arrested Elvis Presley, Jim Morrison, Janis Joplin, David Lee Roth, and Tommy Lee at concerts for 'public indecency'). My telegram didn't arrive, and in those pre–Homeland Security days, the airline I was flying on wouldn't release their passenger manifest. Fearing a riot inside the building, the promoter didn't want to open the doors until they were sure I was going to show up, but their failure to communicate that situation to the restless crowd waiting outside, and the overreaction of the police, very nearly caused a riot outside the arena. Helicopters circled, and tear gas grenades were lobbed into the crowd, who doubtless already had reason to distrust their local police. When I walked off the plane, our assistant, Kevin, was waiting at the gate, standing at the pay phone with the receiver in his hand, ready to tell them if I was there or not. We raced to the venue, I went straight to the stage—tear gas wafting through the arena—and feigned nonchalance to my bandmates as we kicked off the first song."

MIAMI HERALD: "As a veteran concert-goer at the Hollywood Sportatorium, Chris Harris has seen his share of wild musical events. But nothing shocked him more than the bloody, tear gas choked scene that rocked a sold-out Sportatorium. 'It was nothing but blood and gore,' Harris said of the preconcert melee that injured 11 police officers, damaged 8 police cars and shook up nearly 15,000 rock fans. 'There were kids running around with their heads busted open,' Harris said. 'It was like a war zone.'"

NOVEMBER 29, 1981
JACKSONVILLE, FLORIDA
JACKSONVILLE VETERANS MEMORIAL COLISEUM, 1145 Adams Street. Venue dedicated on November 24, 1960.
SUPPORT ACT: Riot
TICKETS: $9.50, general admission
ATTENDANCE: 9,467 (Anthem/SRO); 9,334 (*Pollstar*)
CAPACITY: 11,628
CONCERT GROSS: $88,673

DECEMBER 1, 1981
BIRMINGHAM, ALABAMA
BIRMINGHAM-JEFFERSON CIVIC CENTER COLISEUM, 1 Civic Center Plaza at 19th Street North. Venue opened in September 1976.
SUPPORT ACT: Riot
TICKETS: $9.50, general admission
ATTENDANCE: 7,398 (Anthem/SRO)
CAPACITY: 9,000
CONCERT GROSS: $70,281
THE BIRMINGHAM NEWS: "The muddled, confused acoustics of the hollow coliseum chewed up most of the band's music and spat out blurred, faded songs. The punching power chords, lightning-quick bass and guitar runs, and syncopated swing of 'La Villa Strangiato' and a few other songs showed that Rush's sound deserved a better setting. The brilliant blues, greens, yellows, reds, whites, and velvets of the stage lighting, psychedelic movies in the background, and jumping around by Lee and Lifeson gave eyes quite a sight at the concert. But ears would have been better served listening to Rush's new live album, *Exit . . . Stage Left*."

DECEMBER 2, 1981
NASHVILLE, TENNESSEE
NASHVILLE MUNICIPAL AUDITORIUM, 417 Fourth Avenue North. Venue opened on October 7, 1962.
SUPPORT ACT: Riot
TICKETS: $8.50 (advance) / $9.50 (at the door), general admission
ATTENDANCE: 9,900 (Anthem/SRO); sold out
CONCERT GROSS: $83,742

DECEMBER 4, 1981
CHARLOTTE, NORTH CAROLINA
CHARLOTTE COLISEUM, 2700 East Independence Boulevard. Venue dedicated on September 11, 1955.
SUPPORT ACT: Riot
TICKETS: $8.50 / $9.50 (average: $8.89), general admission
ATTENDANCE: 12,900 (Anthem/SRO); sold out
CONCERT GROSS: $111,616

DECEMBER 5, 1981
FAYETTEVILLE, NORTH CAROLINA
CUMBERLAND COUNTY MEMORIAL ARENA, 1960 Coliseum Drive. Venue opened on January 23, 1968.
SUPPORT ACT: Riot
TICKETS: $9.75
ATTENDANCE: 6,500
CAPACITY: 7,000, general admission

DECEMBER 6, 1981
GREENSBORO, NORTH CAROLINA
GREENSBORO COLISEUM, 1921 West Lee Street. Venue opened on October 29, 1959.
SUPPORT ACT: Riot
TICKETS: $8.50 / $9.50 (average: $9.38)
ATTENDANCE: 8,534 (Anthem/SRO); 8,532 (*Pollstar*)
CAPACITY: 11,176
CONCERT GROSS: $76,826

DECEMBER 8, 1981
KNOXVILLE, TENNESSEE
KNOXVILLE CIVIC COLISEUM, 500 East Church Street. Venue opened on August 20, 1961.
SUPPORT ACT: Riot
TICKETS: $8.50 / $9.50, general admission
ATTENDANCE: 8,959 (Anthem/SRO); 8,583 (promoter)
CAPACITY: 10,000
CONCERT GROSS: $76,610

DECEMBER 9, 1981
ATLANTA, GEORGIA
THE OMNI, 100 Techwood Drive. Venue opened on October 14, 1972.
SUPPORT ACT: Riot
TICKETS: $11.00
ATTENDANCE: 13,558; sold out

DECEMBER 11, 1981
GREENVILLE, SOUTH CAROLINA
GREENVILLE MEMORIAL AUDITORIUM, 401 East North Street. Venue opened on December 1, 1958.
SUPPORT ACT: Riot
TICKETS: $8.50 / $9.50 (average: $8.68)
ATTENDANCE: 7,000 (Anthem/SRO); sold out
CONCERT GROSS: $60,735

DECEMBER 12, 1981
JOHNSON CITY, TENNESSEE
FREEDOM HALL CIVIC CENTER, 1320 Pactolas Road. Venue opened on July 5, 1974.
SUPPORT ACT: Riot
TICKETS: $8.50 / $9.50, general admission
ATTENDANCE: 6,802 (Anthem/SRO); 6,877 (*Pollstar*); 6,811 (promoter)
CAPACITY: 8,500
CONCERT GROSS: $60,750

DECEMBER 13, 1981
ROANOKE, VIRGINIA
ROANOKE CIVIC CENTER COLISEUM, 710 Williamson Road. Venue opened on March 27, 1971.
SUPPORT ACT: Riot
TICKETS: $8.50 (limited advance) / $9.50
ATTENDANCE: 7,406 (Anthem/SRO)
CAPACITY: 11,000
CONCERT GROSS: $63,568
ROANOKE TIMES AND WORLD-NEWS: "Wide spectrum of rock aficionados appreciate Rush: 7,400 came out on a chilly December night for Rush, probably the most lyrically ambitious and musically adept rock band around, and it was a night those in the crowd won't soon forget."

DECEMBER 15, 1981
NORFOLK, VIRGINIA
SCOPE ARENA, 201 East Brambleton Avenue. Venue opened on November 12, 1971.
SUPPORT ACT: Riot
TICKETS: $8.00, general admission
ATTENDANCE: 13,140; sold out

DECEMBER 20, 1981
HARTFORD, CONNECTICUT
CIVIC CENTER, 1 Civic Center Plaza. Venue opened January 9, 1975.
SUPPORT ACT: Riot
TICKETS: $9.50 / $10.50
ATTENDANCE: 12,385 (*Billboard*); sold out
CONCERT GROSS: $128,825
NOTES: Alex experienced problems with his guitar throughout the show. At the start of "2112: Overture," no guitar was heard, while Geddy and Neil continued playing. Once resolved, the guitar was just straight, with no phasing effects added. On the "Subdivisions" chorus, Alex sang, "Subdivisions" in his straight voice—it wasn't electronically altered at this point. During "The Camera Eye," Alex and Neil traded off syncopated licks on the intro. In "Closer to the Heart," the guitar went out during the second chorus. This fired Neil up even more, as he launched his stick, higher than usual, into the air and caught it on the final measure without missing a beat, causing the capacity crowd to go wild.

DECEMBER 21–22, 1981
EAST RUTHERFORD, NEW JERSEY
BRENDEN BYRNE MEADOWLANDS ARENA, Meadowlands Sports Complex, 50 State Route 120. Venue opened on July 2, 1981.
SUPPORT ACT: Riot
TICKETS: $10.50 / $12.50
ATTENDANCE (DEC. 21): 19,135; sold out
ATTENDANCE (DEC. 22): 18,112
CAPACITY: 19,135
CONCERT GROSS (DEC. 21): $224,212
CONCERT GROSS (DEC. 22): $213,531
NOTES: The band experimented with new musical ideas during sound check, with Alex and Neil working on rhythmic foundations while Geddy focused more on keyboards. A fired-up crowd roared during "The Camera Eye" when Geddy sang, "An angular mass of New Yorkers," and "the streets of Manhattan." After a stunning, energetic show, the band and crew celebrated with an end-of-tour party at the Barge Club. Crew members, along with Uncle Cliff Burnstein, were presented platinum discs for *Moving Pictures*. Second show added due to popular demand.

1. Skip Daly. Interview with Nick Kotos, June 7, 2012.
2. Skip Daly. Interview with Mike Hirsch, July 17, 2012.
3. Neil Peart. *Roadshow: Landscape With Drums, A Concert Tour By Motorcycle.* Rounder Books, 2006.

Chapter 14

THE DEEP SOUTH SPRING TRAINING TOUR

A ten-date, two-week jaunt, the "Deep South Spring Training Tour," as the band called its spring pre–*New World Tour*, opened on April 1, 1982, in Little Rock, Arkansas, and continued through Mississippi, Louisiana, and Florida. Road manager and lighting director Howard Ungerleider jokingly referred to the short southeastern trek as the "Tour of the Nadars" because all the gigs were scheduled in Tornado Alley during peak tornado season. The band liked the phrase so much that they had Tour of the Nadars shirts printed up for themselves and the crew. The primary purpose of this run of dates was to get Rush into peak shape for the upcoming *Signals* recording sessions. "We've been off for three months over the winter, and you get a little lazy," Geddy said. "So rather than going in to do an album after sitting around for three months, it's better to go out and play as a band, and get everything happening once again."

Over the course of the short outing, Alex, Geddy, and Neil performed to more than seventy-five thousand fans. The set list was identical to that of the *Exit . . . Stage Left* shows, with the exception of a new *Signals* song, "The Analog Kid," replacing "Xanadu" (an abridged version of "Xanadu" would later return for the *New World Tour* in support of *Signals*).

The Deep South Spring Training jaunt wrapped on April 12 at the Bayfront Center Arena in St. Petersburg, Florida. Backstage after sound check, Geddy looked ahead to the next album and tour: "We have nine days off, and then we go to Le Studio to record with Terry Brown producing once again. It's hard to say how long it will take to do. We've done albums in recent history, take *Permanent Waves* for example, which took us five weeks to do—a ridiculously short period of time. We actually had to cancel studio time, but we had problems with equipment for *Moving Pictures* and various things, and we ended up running over, so that was about two-and-a-half months. So we're planning on two months.

"Hopefully we are going to see a lot of changes for the next tour," he continued. "What those changes are going to be, I don't know yet. The tour is going to start around September 1 and is probably going to go right through the remaining few months of '82, and probably the first few months of '83. So, it's going to be a long tour."

ABOVE: Toronto, Ontario; Rush onstage.

OPPOSITE: Toronto, Ontario; Alex onstage.

TOUR HISTORY
DEEP SOUTH SPRING TRAINING TOUR, 1982

SET LIST:
"2112: Overture"
"2112: The Temples of Syrinx"
"Freewill"
"Limelight"
"Hemispheres: Prelude"
"Beneath, Between, and Behind" (abridged)
"Subdivisions" (prerelease version)
"The Camera Eye"

"YYZ" (with drum solo)
"Broon's Bane"
"The Trees"
"The Analog Kid" (prerelease version)
"The Spirit of Radio"
"Red Barchetta"
"Closer to the Heart"
"Tom Sawyer"
"Vital Signs"

"Working Man" (with reggae intro)
"Hemispheres: "Armageddon""
"By-Tor and the Snow Dog"
"In the End"
"In the Mood"
2112: "Grand Finale"
Encore:
"La Villa Strangiato"
(with electric guitar intro)

APRIL 1, 1982
LITTLE ROCK, ARKANSAS
T. H. BARTON COLISEUM, Arkansas State Fairgrounds, 2600 Howard Street
SUPPORT ACT: Riggs
TICKETS: $10.50, general admission
ATTENDANCE: 10,250 (Anthem/SRO); 10,000 (*Pollstar*); sold out
CONCERT GROSS: $105,000
NOTES: The opening date of the 1982 "Deep South Spring Training Tour" featured the live debut of "The Analog Kid."

APRIL 2, 1982
JACKSON, MISSISSIPPI
MISSISSIPPI COLISEUM, State Fairgrounds complex, 1207 Mississippi Street. Venue opened on June 7, 1962.
SUPPORT ACT: Riggs
TICKETS: $9.50, general admission
ATTENDANCE: 9,638 (Anthem/SRO); 9,500 (*Pollstar*); sold out
CONCERT GROSS: $90,250

BE-BOP PRODUCTIONS AND MID-SOUTH CONCERTS
PRESENT

RUSH

FRIDAY, APRIL 2
7:30 p.m. - Coliseum
Jackson, MS
Tickets $9.50

APRIL 3, 1982
MONROE, LOUISIANA
CIVIC CENTER ARENA, 401 Lea Joyner Memorial Expressway. Venue opened on September 2, 1967.
SUPPORT ACT: Riggs
TICKETS: $10.00, general admission
ATTENDANCE: 10,000 (Anthem/SRO); sold out
CONCERT GROSS: $100,000
NOTES: After staking out the Holiday Inn, a fifteen-year-old Kevin Griffin (Better Than Ezra) drove Alex and Geddy around in his Honda after their limo didn't show up. The band's jaunt through Louisiana saw a police crackdown resulting in a plethora of fan arrests. Here in Monroe, twenty-four people (including six juveniles) were arrested, mostly for possession of "small amounts" of marijuana.[1]
KEVIN GRIFFIN (BETTER THAN EZRA GUITARIST/VOCALIST): "I just got my driver's license, and I'm driving around Geddy and Alex, who are scrunched up in my back seat. We took them to the Four Seasons tennis store, then a health food store, and then back to the hotel. They offered us passes to sound check. Can you imagine your idol doing this? I got to play Alex's guitar onstage. We even got our photos with them in the newspaper. This cemented my being in a band."[2]

APRIL 5, 1982
LAKE CHARLES, LOUISIANA
CIVIC CENTER COLISEUM, 900 Lakeshore Drive. Venue dedicated on September 22, 1972.
SUPPORT ACT: Riggs
TICKETS: $10.50
ATTENDANCE: 8,000, general admission

NOTES: Fifty-four people were arrested, as plainclothes deputies from the Calcasieu Parish Sheriff's Department cracked down on illegal drug use at public gatherings.[3]
THE *LAMAR UNIVERSITY PRESS* (BEAUMONT): "Rush brings tremendous concert to rock lovers in Civic Center: With each song, hundreds of cigarette lighter flames filled the arena."

APRIL 6, 1982
BATON ROUGE, LOUISIANA
RIVERSIDE CENTROPLEX, 275 South River Road. Venue opened on November 10, 1977.
SUPPORT ACT: Riggs
TICKETS: $12.00
ATTENDANCE: 9,078
NOTES: Not to be outdone by authorities in Lake Charles, Baton Rouge police arrested fifty-four fans. "We had a little of everything," spokesperson Bob Love told the *Daily World* (Opelousas). "Battery on a police officer, ticket scalping, but most of them were drug charges."

APRIL 7, 1982
BILOXI, MISSISSIPPI
MISSISSIPPI COAST COLISEUM, 2350 Beach Boulevard. Venue opened on November 1, 1977.
SUPPORT ACT: Riggs
TICKETS: $9.50 / $10.50 (average: $9.91), general admission
ATTENDANCE: 10,082 (Anthem/SRO); 10,092 (*Pollstar*)
CAPACITY: 11,000
CONCERT GROSS: $99,984

APRIL 9, 1982
TALLAHASSEE, FLORIDA
TALLAHASSEE-LEON COUNTY CIVIC
CENTER ARENA, Florida State
University campus, 505 West Pensacola
Street. Venue opened on September 14,
1981.
SUPPORT ACT: Krokus
TICKETS: $10.00
ATTENDANCE: 10,000 (Anthem/SRO);
7,459 (*Pollstar*)
CAPACITY: 10,035
CONCERT GROSS: $72,670
NOTES: Nine people were arrested in
and around the venue, mostly for
marijuana possession and disorderly
intoxication.[4]
THE *TALLAHASSEE DEMOCRAT*: "The
technology gives Rush's sound a texture
and variety most trios—and many larger
bands—would envy, breathing life into
compositions like the instrumental 'YYZ.'
In a battle of the bands, Rush was the
clear winner. Krokus gave heavy metal
fans just what they asked for; the
Canadian band delivered a bit more than
they expected."

APRIL 10–11, 1982
LAKELAND, FLORIDA
LAKELAND CIVIC CENTER, 701 West
Lime Street. Venue dedicated on
November 14, 1974.
SUPPORT ACT: Krokus
TICKETS: $10.50 / $11.00, general
admission
ATTENDANCE: 10,000 per show; sold
out
CONCERT GROSS: $104,333 per show
NOTES: Rush jammed on "The Analog
Kid," "Subdivisions," "Digital Man," and
an instrumental version of "The Weapon"
during sound checks. Following the first
show, the band and crew celebrated the
end of the tour with an all-night bowling
party. Onstage the second night, Alex
spaced out on the electric guitar prior to
the "La Villa Strangiato" encore. Then, in
the middle of his long solo introduction,
Alex stopped playing and looked at the

crowd, who roared in approval. He then
hit a high sustained note before continuing on with the opening solo of
"Strangiato."
TIM WENDT (RIGGER): "They seemed to
like to rent bowling alleys for some reason,
and we would take over the women's bathroom, and that would be the point of . . .
well, those were the days of cocaine and
pot and all the stuff that went on in the
industry. The band wasn't that interested
in that shit, but the road crew was. We
stayed up late a lot—let's put it that way.
Anywhere we sold out more than a couple
days, there would always seem to be a
party that the promoter put on. In those
years, Rush would sell out three or four
days in a place, and they were the largest-
grossing band at that time too, so they sold
out a lot of dates and we threw a party just
about everywhere we went."[5]
***ST. PETERSBURG TIMES*:** "Rush now seems
to rock with a little more respect: The
band members, while playing very well,
exhibited an engaging self-effacement.
The band simply concentrated on
musicianship rather than poses. A
well-coordinated light show gave the
concert all the flash it needed. Rush's
songs are long, but they're not plodding
extensions of one theme. The music was
lively and interesting—it moves. It's not
the most danceable material you'll hear,
but it kept most of us away from the concession stands."

APRIL 12, 1982
ST. PETERSBURG, FLORIDA
BAYFRONT CENTER ARENA, 400 First
Street South. Venue dedicated on May
1, 1965.
SUPPORT ACT: Krokus
TICKETS: $10.50, general admission
ATTENDANCE: 8,600; sold out
CONCERT GROSS: $90,121
NOTES: Final performances of "Beneath,
Between, and Behind" and "In the End."

1. *The Town Talk*.
2. Interview with Kevin Griffin. *Now Magazine*, November 1996.
3. *American Press*, April 7, 1982.
4. *The Tallahassee Democrat*.
5. Skip Daly. Interview with Tim Wendt, December 7, 2012.

Chapter 15

THE NEW WORLD TOUR

On tour in support of the *Signals* album, Rush performed to more than 825,000 fans over the course of 107 shows—a sizable jaunt, to be sure, but the band approached touring differently this time. Said Neil, "We're calling it the *New World Tour*, because that's as far as the future projects right now. We're going to tour as long as we have in the past, but not all in a row. We're going out for three months, then taking a break, and then we go out for another three months. So, we'll spend our allotted six months on the road, but we'll try to do it a little more humanely."

The band thoroughly enjoyed themselves on the trek, and this sense of fun often found its way into the show. They began taking the stage each night to the Three Stooges theme—which, Geddy pointed out, was "not the original theme, because they won't let you use that. So I hired my friend, violinist Ben Mink, who's a musician extraordinaire and a very big Three Stooges fan, and we had him re-create the original version. The three 'Hello's you hear at the beginning are the three of us talking to him on the phone." Furthermore, Geddy would often play around with the lyrics to some of the older songs, singing "the spirit of baseball" in "The

ABOVE: Alex sporting a bow tie.
OPPOSITE: Geddy onstage.

Spirit of Radio," and "we are the plumbers, who fix your sinks" in "The Temples of Syrinx."

"On our last tour, we really played too many shows," Geddy said. "We were becoming too tight, too mechanical. A lot of the spontaneity had gone out of us. I found myself going out onstage thinking about baseball rather than the night's show! So, for this tour, we hardly rehearsed at all. We wanted to become less slick, more unpredictable. We figured people would prefer to see a human display with errors than something cool, calculated, and mechanical."

For the *New World Tour*, "The Camera Eye" was abbreviated such that only the New York or London section was performed on a given night. Otherwise, the set list remained consistent throughout most of the outing, with the exception of "Chemistry" and "The Camera Eye" being omitted from the German gigs. Although "The Camera Eye" returned for later dates, "Chemistry" did not. Song choices leaned heavily in favor of the new material, with every track on *Signals* (save for "Losing It") performed on a regular basis.

"This tour, we made a conscious effort to break away from a pattern in our live performances," Neil said. "This time, we started with a clean sheet, and changed everything from top to bottom in terms of the musical content of our show."

He continued, "We had so much from *Signals* to play, and we still didn't want to drop anything from *Moving Pictures*, so consequently, some of the really early albums aren't being represented this tour. It's unfortunate in one way, but on the other hand, of course, the weight has to go toward the newer material."

OPPOSITE: The Professor in full flight.
ABOVE: Geddy with his Rickenbacker 4001.

TOP: Toronto, Ontario; Alex and Neil with their fathers, and Geddy with his stepfather at Maple Leaf Gardens
ABOVE: Toronto, Ontario; The band with their mothers at Maple Leaf Gardens.

TOUR HISTORY
SIGNALS

SET LIST:
Intro (Three Stooges theme)
"The Spirit of Radio"
"Tom Sawyer"
"Freewill"
"Digital Man"
"Subdivisions"
"Vital Signs"
"The Camera Eye" (abridged)

"Closer to the Heart"
"Chemistry"
"The Analog Kid"
"Broon's Bane"
"The Trees"
"Red Barchetta"
"The Weapon" (with Count Floyd intro)
"New World Man"
"Limelight"

"Countdown"
"2112: Overture"
"2112: The Temples of Syrinx"
"Xanadu"
"La Villa Strangiato"
"In the Mood"
Encore:
"YYZ" (with drum solo)

SEPTEMBER 3, 1982
GREEN BAY, WISCONSIN
BROWN COUNTY VETERANS MEMORIAL ARENA, 1901 South Oneida Street. Venue opened on November 11, 1957.
SUPPORT ACT: Rory Gallagher
TICKETS: $10.50, general admission
ATTENDANCE: 6,800 (Anthem/SRO)
CAPACITY: 7,000
CONCERT GROSS: $70,980
NOTES: The opening date of the 1982 to 1983 *New World Tour* featured the live debut of "Chemistry," "Digital Man," "The Weapon," "New World Man," and "Countdown." Alex, Geddy, and Neil watched Rory Gallagher from the side of the stage as the Irish guitar legend ripped blues riffs on his Fender Strat.
RORY GALLAGHER: "It's nice to be working with Rush again. We haven't worked together since about 1974, and they seem to be the same human beings that they were back then, and it's a pleasure to see that, because so many rock bands start becoming Frankenstein monsters. It's hard not to become a little spooky in this rat race, but it's great to meet people who still have their feet on the ground a little bit."[1]
GREEN BAY PRESS-GAZETTE: "[The tour includes a] travelling crew of 31, four 40-foot semitrailer trucks and one 28-foot truck to carry all the show's gear, three custom-built buses to carry everyone, at least 22 hotel rooms a night to house the travelers. In each town, the band will hire another 20 persons to help pack and unpack the gear, plus at least eight more to run spotlights."[2]

SEPTEMBER 4, 1982
LA CROSSE, WISCONSIN
LA CROSSE CENTER ARENA, 300 Harbor View Plaza. Venue opened on October 11, 1980.
SUPPORT ACT: Rory Gallagher
TICKETS: $10.00, general admission
ATTENDANCE: 6,035 (Anthem/SRO)
CAPACITY: 8,000
CONCERT GROSS: $58,890
GEDDY (ONSTAGE): "Tonight is a little unusual. We have this album coming out, and none of you have heard it yet. You'll be one of the first to hear the album."
THE *LA CROSSE TRIBUNE*: "There are so many elements that go into a Rush concert that it is difficult to pin down a predominant one. Only in a live performance does the full force of Rush make its full impact. It is then you realize all that music is coming out of just three sources—four, actually, if you count the audience. And surely the cheers and screaming was music to the ears of Rush."

SEPTEMBER 5, 1982
DUBUQUE, IOWA
FIVE FLAGS ARENA, Five Flags Civic Center, 405 Main Street. Venue opened on March 24, 1979.
SUPPORT ACT: Rory Gallagher
TICKETS: $10.00, general admission
ATTENDANCE: 4,709

SEPTEMBER 7, 1982
SIOUX FALLS, SOUTH DAKOTA
SIOUX FALLS ARENA, 1201 N. West Avenue. Venue dedicated on December 10, 1961.
SUPPORT ACT: Rory Gallagher
TICKETS: $9.50 / $10.50, general admission

ATTENDANCE: 5,168 (Anthem/SRO); 5,258 (*Pollstar*); sold out
CONCERT GROSS: $49,805

SEPTEMBER 8, 1982
DES MOINES, IOWA
VETERANS MEMORIAL AUDITORIUM, 833 Fifth Avenue. Venue opened on February 1, 1955.
SUPPORT ACT: Rory Gallagher
TICKETS: $9.50 (advance) / $10.50 (day of), general admission
ATTENDANCE: 9,148 (Anthem/SRO); sold out
CONCERT GROSS: $86,871
NOTES: The concert was a rowdy affair, with fans "pushing and shoving" in order to secure the closest spot on the general admission floor.[3]

SEPTEMBER 9, 1982
OMAHA, NEBRASKA
CIVIC AUDITORIUM ARENA, 1804 Capitol Avenue. Venue dedicated on January 2, 1955.
SUPPORT ACT: Rory Gallagher
TICKETS: $10.00 / $11.00 (average: $10.05), general admission
ATTENDANCE: 12,022 (Anthem/SRO); 11,000 (*Pollstar*); sold out
CONCERT GROSS: $120,049
NOTES: *Billboard* listed attendance at 11,942.

SEPTEMBER 11, 1982
RAPID CITY, SOUTH DAKOTA
RUSHMORE PLAZA CIVIC CENTER ARENA, 444 North Mt. Rushmore Road. Venue opened on June 21, 1977.
SUPPORT ACT: Rory Gallagher
TICKETS: $9.50 (advance) / $10.50 (day of), general admission
ATTENDANCE: 4,726

SEPTEMBER 12, 1982
BISMARCK, NORTH DAKOTA
BISMARCK CIVIC CENTER, 315 South
Fifth Street. Venue opened on
September 5, 1969.
SUPPORT ACT: Rory Gallagher
TICKETS: $9.50 (advance) / $10.50 (day
of), general admission
ATTENDANCE: 4,722
CAPACITY: 10,100
NOTES: The gig was a bit late in starting.
For the tour, fans were treated to a
preshow music mix, personally compiled
by Neil.

SEPTEMBER 14, 1982
BILLINGS, MONTANA
YELLOWSTONE METRA, Billings
MetraPark, 308 Sixth Avenue North.
Venue opened on December 10, 1975.
SUPPORT ACT: Rory Gallagher
TICKETS: $10.00 (advance)
ATTENDANCE: 4,613 (*Billings Gazette*
lists attendance at 3,622.)
CAPACITY: 10,903
NOTES: On the night off before this show
(September 13), members of the crew
headed out to a club and jammed with
one of the local bands. Alex, Tim Wendt,
and cohorts flooded the hotel.
TIM WENDT (RIGGER): "It sounded like
everyone was a little drunk, so I said I
would come up and see what was happening. I got up there to the room, and
Billy Collins and Alex were playing tennis
with the fire sprinkler. They had tennis
rackets up there, and Alex hit it one time,
then Billy hit it one time, and then Alex
hit it really hard and it bent. Then Billy
went over and gave it a little tap just to
straighten it, and it broke off! It was
20,000 gallons a minute coming out of
this sprinkler, and we were on the seventh floor, and water flooded the whole
hotel [*laughs*]! Of course, we had to get
rid of the rock star right away, and he
was in his underwear and all fucked up!
So we ran him out of there and down the
elevator and pretended like nothing happened. We came back up and the fire
department opened the door and the
water came rushing out of the hotel
room, and Billy's Halliburton suitcase
floated out the door [*laughs*]. We acted
really surprised, but Montana people
don't really take to rock-and-roll guys.
We all had long hair, and there were
women in their curlers and their pajamas

standing downstairs, as they had to evac-
uate the hotel. We hid on the bus for the
next forty-eight hours."[4]

SEPTEMBER 15, 1982
CASPER, WYOMING
CASPER EVENTS CENTER, One Events
Drive. Venue opened on April 17, 1982.
SUPPORT ACT: Rory Gallagher
TICKETS: $10.00 (advance), general
admission
ATTENDANCE: 4,000
NOTES: Neil took time to pen a piece for
Modern Drummer announcing the results
of his first drum giveaway, via the publi-
cation. 4,625 letters from every corner
of the globe had been submitted for the
essay contest, and the winner, Adam
Roderick, was awarded Neil's set of red
Tama drums (used on *Permanent Waves*,
Moving Pictures, and *Exit . . . Stage Left*).
NEIL: "The reason why I gave them away
in the first place is that I figured they were
too good to keep at home as a practice set.
I already have my old black Slingerlands at
home, which serve me very well as a practice set, so it seemed kind of wasteful and
indulgent to have all these drum sets sitting around. It bothered my Anglo-Saxon
soul. Out of almost 5,000 entries that I
had to read over my summer holiday, I did
finally select a winner. The person who
won my drums gave his drums to a second
runner-up, which was a pretty good thing.
There were about 50 entries that I chose
as being worthy of special consideration,
and I sent all of them a little conciliatory
note saying, 'Well you didn't win, but I
liked your entry.' Between all of those
things I had my whole family working for
me, opening envelopes, then sealing and
addressing envelopes at the end. It was
quite an undertaking."[5]

SEPTEMBER 17, 1982
DENVER, COLORADO
MCNICHOLS SPORTS ARENA, 1635
Clay Street. Venue opened on August
22, 1975.
SUPPORT ACT: Rory Gallagher
TICKETS: $9.00 / $10.00 / $11.00
ATTENDANCE: 15,500 (Anthem/SRO);
15,145 (*Pollstar*)
CAPACITY: 18,000
CONCERT GROSS: $174,848
NOTES: The concert was delayed approx-
imately forty-five minutes because of
technical issues after lightning hit the

venue, causing problems with the synthesizers, which forced Jack Secret to do
some serious scrambling. Ian ran back
and forth between Jack and Geddy, with
Geddy relaying troubleshooting suggestions. (Since the doors had already been
opened, Geddy couldn't go up on stage.)
The difficulties delayed the show enough
that it ended up costing the band
$14,000 in extra union expenses, and
one or two songs had to be either dropped
or modified.
TONY GERANIOS (AKA JACK SECRET):
"There was a storm going on outside.
Lightning had hit the building and taken
out some of the computer circuitry that
had to do with the scoreboard. It threw a
spike through the whole system—a
'power-related incident.' I lost programs
out of the synths onstage, and I whisked
these keyboards off into the dressing
room right before the show and used the
tape backup to reinstall everything. But
then, when I'd bring them back to the
stage and turned them back on, it was all
gone again . . . so it was almost acting
like there was no RAM. There were power
fluctuations that were interfering with
the synths' ability to retain their memory.
That was disastrous. I was running
around, and nothing was working. It held
up the show for about forty-five minutes.
It was very silly. The thing is, I hadn't
known about the electrical problems, so
I just thought the system was having a
meltdown, and it was very disturbing. I
finally got the keys up and working."[6]
ROCKY MOUNTAIN NEWS: "Rush is not
a band for the genteel. This isn't sledgehammer music. It's wrecking ball stuff—
music to destroy your ears by. Friday
night, Rush lit up the place with a colorful light show that caught the eye a
thousand ways."

SEPTEMBER 19, 1982
POCATELLO, IDAHO
ASISU MINIDOME, Idaho State
University campus, 550 Memorial Drive.
Venue opened on September 26, 1970.
SUPPORT ACT: Rory Gallagher
ATTENDANCE: 5,222
CAPACITY: 13,895

SEPTEMBER 20, 1982
BOISE, IDAHO
BSU PAVILION, Boise State University
campus, 1401 Bronco Lane. Venue

opened on May 16, 1982.
SUPPORT ACT: Rory Gallagher
TICKETS: $10.00
ATTENDANCE: 5,847
NOTES: BSU 50th Anniversary Founders Week concert.

SEPTEMBER 21, 1982
SALT LAKE CITY, UTAH
SALT PALACE, 100 S. West Temple. Venue dedicated on July 11, 1969.
SUPPORT ACT: Rory Gallagher
TICKETS: $10.00
ATTENDANCE: 12,354; sold out
SALT LAKE TRIBUNE: "Rush rocks and rolls for sellout crowd: The mostly teen-age audience went wild, enthusiastically applauding Rush's every note."
THE *DESERET NEWS:* "The light show was magnificent, music incomparable, and the performance refreshing."

SEPTEMBER 30, 1982
VANCOUVER, BRITISH COLUMBIA
PACIFIC COLISEUM, Pacific National Exhibition Fairgrounds, 100 North Renfrew. Venue dedicated on January 8, 1968.
SUPPORT ACT: Wrabit
TICKETS: $12.50 / $13.50 (average: $12.66) CAD
ATTENDANCE: 6,851 (Anthem/SRO); 10,536 (*Pollstar*)
CAPACITY: 11,977
CONCERT GROSS: $133,348 CAD

OCTOBER 2, 1982
CALGARY, ALBERTA
STAMPEDE CORRAL, 10 Corral Trail SE. Venue opened on December 15, 1950.
SUPPORT ACT: Wrabit
TICKETS: $12.50 CAD
ATTENDANCE: 7,500 (Anthem/SRO); 7,403 (*Pollstar*); sold out
CONCERT GROSS: $92,562 CAD

OCTOBER 3, 1982
EDMONTON, ALBERTA
NORTHLANDS COLISEUM, 7424 118th

Avenue NW. Venue opened on November 10, 1974.
SUPPORT ACT: Wrabit
TICKETS: $12.50 / $13.50 (average: $12.72) CAD
ATTENDANCE: 11,584 (Anthem/SRO); 11,194 (*Pollstar*)
CAPACITY: 11,640
CONCERT GROSS: $142,398 CAD
THE *EDMONTON JOURNAL:* "Rush and crowd work up a sweat: The show was structured but appeared seamless, paced but spontaneous."

OCTOBER 5, 1982
WINNIPEG, MANITOBA
WINNIPEG ARENA, 1430 Maroons Road. Venue opened on October 18, 1955.
SUPPORT ACT: Wrabit
TICKETS: $12.00 CAD
ATTENDANCE: 7,423 (Anthem/SRO); 7,136 (*Pollstar*)
CAPACITY: 8,584
CONCERT GROSS: $85,632 CAD
THE *WINNIPEG FREE PRESS:* "Rush, Wrabit split in approach to heavy metal: With the looming presence of this technological armament, the show threatened to run away with itself. It was rock 'n' roll on such a vast scale that it could have dwarfed the three players. But Rush, unlike most bands on the arena circuit, uses—rather than gets used by—its mammoth support systems."

OCTOBER 7, 1982
DULUTH, MINNESOTA
DULUTH ARENA, 350 Harbor Drive. Venue opened on August 5, 1966.
SUPPORT ACT: Rory Gallagher
TICKETS: $10.00 / $11.00
ATTENDANCE: 5,000 (Anthem/SRO); 6,615 (*Pollstar*)
CAPACITY: 7,755
CONCERT GROSS: $67,474
NOTES: SRO records indicate this date as being on October 8, but a review corroborates it as being on October 7.
DULUTH NEWS TRIBUNE: "7,000 roar to crash of Rush heavy metal: It's a showbiz maxim that the second song is the most important in a concert. Rush used 'Tom Sawyer,' one of its more popular numbers, and from then on never lost its audience for a second in the 100 minutes of professionally executed music that followed."

OCTOBER 9, 1982
MILWAUKEE, WISCONSIN
MECCA ARENA, 400 West Kilbourn Avenue. Venue opened on April 9, 1950.
SUPPORT ACT: Rory Gallagher
TICKETS: $10.50 / $12.50 (average: $11.94)
ATTENDANCE: 9,636 (Anthem/SRO); 9,750 (*Pollstar*); sold out
CONCERT GROSS: $116,434
NOTES: Geddy attended a Brewers/Angels playoff game in the afternoon, with Milwaukee winning 9–5. Onstage, the band received a fanatical response throughout the show, with fans stomping their feet in unison, literally shaking the venue. Ged introduced "The Weapon" in a thick, Yiddish accent, as the crowd clapped in time with Neil. On "2112: Overture," the echo on Alex's guitar came in a measure late. Neil played through the first break in "2112: The Temples of Syrinx," with Alex and Geddy both singing the chorus. Geddy saluted the hometown Brewers with a few lyrical rewrites, as he sang, "One likes to believe in the freedom of baseball" in "The Spirit of Radio" and "Hey, Angels, the hour is late" during "In the Mood." After a fantastic gig, the band left the stage to an endless cacophony of *"We want Rush!"*
GEDDY (ONSTAGE): "How about those wall-bangers out there? It's gonna be pretty hard to compete with the Brewers tonight."

OCTOBER 10, 1982
MADISON, WISCONSIN
DANE COUNTY VETERANS MEMORIAL COLISEUM, Dane County Expo Center Fairgrounds, 2200 Rimrock Road. Venue opened on March 16, 1967.
SUPPORT ACT: Rory Gallagher
TICKETS: $10.50
ATTENDANCE: 10,100 (Anthem/SRO); sold out
CONCERT GROSS: $105,346
NOTES: Geddy had a television set up in the dressing room so that he could watch the National League Championship Series before the gig. He was rooting for the Cardinals, who ended up winning in three straight.
THE *WISCONSIN STATE JOURNAL:*
"Gallagher teaches, Rush entertains: More significant, however, was the hearty reception [Rory] Gallagher received for his introduction to Rush fans, obviously dominant in the capacity crowd. Apparently,

these youngsters do know the good stuff when they hear it . . . While accurately negotiating intricate changes in meter and dynamics remains a Rush trademark, something vital was lost in the mushy vocal mix. In short, few can do it better than Rush, but Rush has done it better, even at the Coliseum."

OCTOBER 12, 1982
ST. LOUIS, MISSOURI
THE CHECKERDOME, 5700 Oakland Avenue. Venue opened on September 23, 1929.
SUPPORT ACT: Rory Gallagher
TICKETS: $10.00 / $11.00
ATTENDANCE: 9,649; sold out
CONCERT GROSS: $104,088
NOTES: Geddy appeared onstage sporting a Cardinals hat in honor of the team opening game one of the 1982 World Series (at the same time, just down the road). The Cardinals, however, lost 10–0 to the Brewers.
THE *ST. LOUIS POST-DISPATCH*: "Ever since Geddy Lee discovered synthesizers, it seems they've bought the farm on high-tech and given up on Rand. Listen, that's 'Freewill.' They haven't forgotten Rand. All this new stuff, though—'Digital Man,' 'Subdivisions' with visuals to match the lyrics yet. This is some well-considered show. Modern, fresh, their new stuff is almost New Wavy it's so brash. They're still a great group. Their new songs are so tight, they're not so loose and meandering."

OCTOBER 13, 1982
CHAMPAIGN, ILLINOIS
UNIVERSITY OF ILLINOIS ASSEMBLY HALL, 1800 South 1st Street. Venue opened on March 2, 1963.
SUPPORT ACT: Rory Gallagher
TICKETS: $5.99 (sale price week of show) / $8.00
ATTENDANCE: 9,578

OCTOBER 15, 1982
ST. LOUIS, MISSOURI
THE CHECKERDOME, 5700 Oakland Avenue
SUPPORT ACT: Rory Gallagher
TICKETS: $10.00 / $11.00
ATTENDANCE: 9,649; sold out
CONCERT GROSS: $104,088
NOTES: Second show added by popular demand.

OCTOBER 16, 1982
KANSAS CITY, MISSOURI
KEMPER ARENA, 1800 Genessee Street at 17th Street. Venue dedicated on October 18, 1974.
SUPPORT ACT: Rory Gallagher
TICKETS: $11.50
ATTENDANCE: 14,232 (Anthem/SRO); sold out
CONCERT GROSS: $161,886
NOTES: This date was originally scheduled for October 15. Tickets were already printed and sold when it was moved to the 16th in order to accommodate a second performance in St. Louis on the 15th.

OCTOBER 17, 1982
VALLEY CENTER, KANSAS
BRITT BROWN ARENA, Kansas Coliseum complex, 1229 East 85th Street North. Venue opened on September 28, 1978.
SUPPORT ACT: Rory Gallagher
TICKETS: $11.75 (includes twenty-five-cent parking fee), general admission
ATTENDANCE: 10,666; sold out

OCTOBER 19, 1982
MEMPHIS, TENNESSEE
MID-SOUTH COLISEUM, Memphis Fairgrounds Park, 996 Early Maxwell Blvd. Venue opened on December 2, 1964.
SUPPORT ACT: Rory Gallagher
TICKETS: $8.50 / $10.50 (average: $10.21)
ATTENDANCE: 9,263 (Anthem/SRO); sold out
CAPACITY: 9,931
CONCERT GROSS: $95,536

OCTOBER 20, 1982
NASHVILLE, TENNESSEE
NASHVILLE MUNICIPAL AUDITORIUM, 417 Fourth Avenue North. Venue opened on October 7, 1962.
SUPPORT ACT: Rory Gallagher
TICKETS: $8.50 (limited advance) / $9.50 (average: $9.36), general admission
ATTENDANCE: 9,900 (Anthem/SRO); sold out
CONCERT GROSS: $92,660
THE *NASHVILLE BANNER*: "Rush blasts sellout crowd at auditorium: For three musicians, Rush can put out a lot of sound. When the band was in its finest

form, playing its more popular numbers, thousands were dancing and clapping in unison. At a couple of stages, the same driving sound got a bit loud and monotonous, but overall, it was a well-played and appreciated concert."

OCTOBER 30, 1982
LEXINGTON, KENTUCKY
RUPP ARENA, 430 West Vine Street. Venue opened on October 7, 1976.
SUPPORT ACT: Rory Gallagher
TICKETS: $9.50 / $10.50 (average: $10.21)
ATTENDANCE: 9,336 (Anthem/SRO)
CAPACITY: 10,000
CONCERT GROSS: $95,297

OCTOBER 31, 1982
EVANSVILLE, INDIANA
ROBERTS MUNICIPAL STADIUM, University of Evansville campus, 2600 Division Street. Venue dedicated on December 1, 1956.
SUPPORT ACT: Rory Gallagher
TICKETS: $9.00 (advance), general admission
ATTENDANCE: 6,025
CONCERT GROSS: $57,525

NOVEMBER 1, 1982
INDIANAPOLIS, INDIANA
MARKET SQUARE ARENA, 300 East Market Street. Venue opened on September 15, 1974.
SUPPORT ACT: Rory Gallagher
TICKETS: $10.00 (advance) / $11.00 (day of) (average: $9.88), general admission
ATTENDANCE: 16,510 (Anthem/SRO); sold out
CONCERT GROSS: $163,110
INDIANAPOLIS STAR: "Rush pleases fans."

NOVEMBER 3–4, 1982
RICHFIELD, OHIO
RICHFIELD COLISEUM, 2923 Streetsboro Road. Venue opened on October 26, 1974.
SUPPORT ACT: Rory Gallagher
TICKETS: $11.00
ATTENDANCE: 13,966 per show; sold out

NOVEMBER 5, 1982
SOUTH BEND, INDIANA
NOTRE DAME ATHLETIC AND CONVOCATION CENTER ARENA,
University of Notre Dame campus, Moose Krause Circle at Leahy Drive. Dedicated on December 1, 1968.
SUPPORT ACT: Rory Gallagher
TICKETS: $10.00 / $11.00
ATTENDANCE: 7,692 (Anthem/SRO); 7,582 (*Pollstar*)
CAPACITY: 7,927
CONCERT GROSS: $78,347

NOVEMBER 7–8, 1982
DETROIT, MICHIGAN
JOE LOUIS ARENA, 600 Civic Center Drive. Venue opened on December 12, 1979.
SUPPORT ACT: Rory Gallagher
TICKETS: $11.50 / $12.50
ATTENDANCE: 14,511 (Anthem/SRO); 15,004 per show (*Pollstar*); sold out
CONCERT GROSS: $182,367
NOTES: The first night, Alex's guitar went out during "The Trees." The two Detroit dates were the week's top-grossing concerts, with *Billboard* indicating just the first show as SRO.
THE *DETROIT PRESS*: "Rush wasn't at its greatest, but it was better than most: Rush punted the musical balance, performing only six songs recorded before 1979. Three of those—'Xanadu,' 'La Villa Strangiato,' and '2112'—were dismissed in severely abbreviated forms during a show-closing medley."

NOVEMBER 9, 1982
DAYTON, OHIO
UNIVERSITY OF DAYTON ARENA, 1801 Edwin C. Moses Boulevard. Venue opened on December 6, 1969.
SUPPORT ACT: Rory Gallagher
TICKETS: $10.00 / $11.50 (average: $11.31)
ATTENDANCE: 9,815 (Anthem/SRO)
CAPACITY: 11,078
CONCERT GROSS: $111,035
RORY GALLAGHER: "Rush are very nice people, and we toured with them in the past. It's not like working with some groups who shall remain contaminated! These guys have the decency to give you the facilities to work with. I'm really glad to see Rush doing so well."[7]

NOVEMBER 11, 1982
KALAMAZOO, MICHIGAN
WINGS STADIUM, 3600 Van Rick Drive. Venue opened on October 30, 1974.
SUPPORT ACT: Rory Gallagher
TICKETS: $10.75, plus twenty-five-cent parking fee
ATTENDANCE: 8,079
CAPACITY: 8,596
THE *GRAND RAPIDS PRESS*: "For Rush, the concept of 'selling out' remains a foreign proposition. The band has never responded to commercial pressures to homogenize its sound. As a result, Rush has built a very loyal following."

NOVEMBER 12, 1982
TOLEDO, OHIO
SPORTS ARENA, 1 North Main Street. Venue opened on November 13, 1947.
SUPPORT ACT: Rory Gallagher
TICKETS: $11.00, general admission
ATTENDANCE: 7,097 (Anthem/SRO); sold out
CONCERT GROSS: $77,748
***TOLEDO BLADE*:** "Anticipation of Rush's elaborate stage show has already assured a virtual sell-out."

NOVEMBER 15–17, 1982
TORONTO, ONTARIO
MAPLE LEAF GARDENS, 60 Carlton Street. Historic venue opened on November 12, 1931.
SUPPORT ACT: The Payolas
TICKETS: $11.50 / $12.50 CAD
ATTENDANCE: 13,752 (Anthem/SRO); 13,837 per show (*Pollstar*); sold out
CONCERT GROSS: $163,458 CAD per show
NOTES: On November 15, Boys Brigade performed for Rush and friends at an after-show party in a local Toronto club. Geddy entertained thoughts of producing the techno-pop band, who were managed by Howard. The next night, Rush threw a postshow party inside Maple Leaf Gardens for family and friends. The November 17 date was a charity benefit, with the band donating $161,560.53 CAD to the United Way.
GEDDY (ONSTAGE): "We'd like to thank you very much for a great three days down here at the old Garden. We'd also like to thank everybody for giving and coming out in support of the United Way. You're all okay!"

HARMONIX, ALEX: "We played in Toronto, and that was really crazy. It's always crazy when we play at home. The backstage area is packed, and there are ten thousand people backstage that you haven't seen in a while. It's a tough thing to deal with. I don't feel relaxed at all."[8]
***TORONTO STAR*:** "Rush master of Gardens: What last night really represented was that point where the old concept of rock was stretched into the future."
ANDY CREEGAN (BARENAKED LADIES): "When I was 15, I saw my very first concert at Maple Leaf Gardens: Rush on the *Signals Tour*. I was blown away like the other 15,000 people. And most importantly, I was inspired."[9]

NOVEMBER 19–21, 1982
ROSEMONT, ILLINOIS
ROSEMONT HORIZON, 6920 N. Mannheim Road. Venue opened on July 2, 1980.
SUPPORT ACT: Rory Gallagher
TICKETS: $11.50 / $12.50
ATTENDANCE: 13,092 (Anthem/SRO); 13,895 per show (*Pollstar*); sold out
CONCERT GROSS: $162,392

NOVEMBER 29, 1982
LANDOVER, MARYLAND
CAPITAL CENTRE, 1 Harry S. Truman Drive. Venue opened on December 2, 1973.
SUPPORT ACT: Rory Gallagher
TICKETS: $12.50
ATTENDANCE: 18,698 (Anthem/SRO); 18,394 (*Pollstar*); sold out
CONCERT GROSS: $229,925
NOTES: "Digital Man" was a sound check staple for the tour, and that day, Geddy cracked everyone up by changing the lyrics from "Love to spend the night in Babylon" to "Mr. Herns loves to babble on," referring to Howard.

NOVEMBER 30, 1982
HAMPTON, VIRGINIA
HAMPTON COLISEUM, 1000 Coliseum Drive. Venue opened on January 31, 1970.
SUPPORT ACT: Rory Gallagher
TICKETS: $9.50 (advance) / $10.50 (day of), general admission
ATTENDANCE: 13,800; sold out

DECEMBER 2–3, 1982
NEW YORK, NEW YORK
MADISON SQUARE GARDEN, 4 Pennsylvania Plaza (8th Avenue between 31st and 33rd Streets). Historic venue opened on February 11, 1968.
SUPPORT ACT: Rory Gallagher
TICKETS: $10.50 / $12.50
ATTENDANCE: 16,515 (Anthem/SRO); 18,000 per show (*Pollstar*); sold out
CONCERT GROSS: $198,000 per show
NOTES: On the first night, most of the crowd stood on their seats for the entire show, loudly shouting every lyric to every song. The rear-projection films for "Subdivisions," "Countdown," and "Red Barchetta" whipped them into a frenzy.
IAN: "The security position is basically 'no win' . . . it's a thankless job. I remember once at Madison Square Garden, this kid jumped out of the stands right as the band was coming off the stage, and I just gave him a little shov—just enough, no violence, just enough to deposit him in the corner, out of the way. A couple of the other guys were like, 'That was perfect! You just moved him out of the way!' but Geddy asked me why I pushed the guy. I said, 'What could I do? You were coming offstage and he was right there in the way—he can't stay.' Alex backed me up on that one. I had no choice but to get the guy out of the way."[10]
VARIETY: "The wild crowd response for this SRO Madison Square Garden gig indicates that the group's audience is fully sympathetic to Rush's relatively adventurous direction. Songs like 'Subdivisions' and 'The Analog Kid' elicited a wildly passionate response of cultural identification from the teenage crowd. Rush articulates the seething emotional restlessness of its suburban constituency with penetrating accuracy."[7]

DECEMBER 5, 1982
PROVIDENCE, RHODE ISLAND
PROVIDENCE CIVIC CENTER, 1 La Salle Square. Venue opened on November 3, 1972.
SUPPORT ACT: Rory Gallagher
TICKETS: $10.50 / $11.50 (average: $11.11)
ATTENDANCE: 12,322 (Anthem/SRO); 12,300 (*Pollstar*); 12,159 (*Billboard*); sold out
CONCERT GROSS: $135,060

DECEMBER 6, 1982
BOSTON, MASSACHUSETTS
BOSTON GARDEN, 150 Causeway Street. Venue opened on November 17, 1928.
SUPPORT ACT: Rory Gallagher
TICKETS: $10.50 / $11.50 (average: $11.41)
ATTENDANCE: 12,396 (Anthem/SRO); 12,332 (*Pollstar*); 12,300 (*Billboard*); sold out
CONCERT GROSS: $140,346
NOTES: Throughout the tour, Geddy added in his own lyrical interpretations. On this night he changed "We are the Priests of the Temples of Syrinx" to "We are the plumbers who fix your sinks."
GEDDY (ONSTAGE): "I'd like you to do me a favor, though. Please don't throw anything around in the air, or at the stage. Somebody's gonna get hit with one and it could be a real bad scene."

DECEMBER 8–9, 1982
UNIONDALE, NEW YORK
NASSAU COUNTY VETERANS MEMORIAL COLISEUM, 1255 Hempstead Turnpike. Venue dedicated on May 29, 1972.
SUPPORT ACT: Rory Gallagher
TICKETS: $10.50 / $12.50
ATTENDANCE (DEC. 8): 16,000 (Anthem/SRO, *Pollstar*); sold out
ATTENDANCE (DEC. 9): 5,533 (Anthem/SRO); 8,000 (*Pollstar*)
CAPACITY: 16,000
TWO-DAY UNIONDALE GROSS: $264,000 (*Pollstar*); $262,177 (*Billboard*)
NOTES: On December 8, Neil dazzled the crowd during "The Weapon," as his drumstick was tossed into the air throughout the main verses of the song, in perfect time, with machine-like precision.
JOHN PETRUCCI (DREAM THEATER GUITARIST): "Seeing Rush the first time was huge for me. It was during the *Signals Tour* at the Nassau Coliseum. That was my favorite band, and I couldn't believe they were actually in the same building as me. I was totally freaking out when the show started, and when they started to play, it was almost like cartoon characters coming to life. I couldn't get my head around the fact that it was really them. When they played 'La Villa Strangiato,' the solo that Alex played

really had a huge influence on me. I think I remember every note to this day. They just seemed bigger than life to me in that untouchable way before social media and MTV and all those other things that brought rock stars down to earth."[11]

DECEMBER 11, 1982
NEW HAVEN, CONNECTICUT
NEW HAVEN VETERAN'S MEMORIAL COLISEUM, 275 South Orange Street. Venue opened on September 27, 1972.
SUPPORT ACT: Rory Gallagher
TICKETS: $10.50 / $11.50 (average: $11.38)
ATTENDANCE: 10,075 (Anthem/SRO); 10,145 (*Pollstar*); sold out
CONCERT GROSS: $115,422

DECEMBER 13–14, 1982
PHILADELPHIA, PENNSYLVANIA
THE SPECTRUM, 3601 South Broad Street. Venue opened on October 1, 1967.
SUPPORT ACT: Rory Gallagher
TICKETS: $9.00 / $11.00
ATTENDANCE: 15,296 (Anthem/SRO); 15,072 per show (*Pollstar*); sold out
CONCERT GROSS: $157,852 per show
NOTES: On the December 13 show, Alex's mic was turned down, so even though he sang "Subdivisions," it couldn't be heard on either chorus. During the second chorus of "2112: The Temples of Syrinx," Geddy sang, "We are the Priests of the Temples of Syrinx" while Alex sang "We are the plumbers who fix your sinks" at the same time. Geddy walked onstage for the encore sporting his new Steinberger bass (one of its earliest appearances), which he only played during "YYZ." After the show, the band hosted its annual holiday party at the East Side Club in downtown Philly.
THE *PHILADELPHIA INQUIRER*: "This would make Rush obnoxious enough, but its screeds are sung by Geddy Lee, whose piercing, high voice only makes the band's paeans to aggressive individualism all the more painful."

DECEMBER 15, 1982
WORCESTER, MASSACHUSETTS
THE CENTRUM, 50 Foster Street. Venue opened on September 2, 1982.
SUPPORT ACT: Rory Gallagher
TICKETS: $11.50 / $12.50

ATTENDANCE: 11,301 (Anthem/SRO); 11,562 (*Pollstar*); sold out
CONCERT GROSS: $138,538
NOTES: In the venue parking lot a fight broke out involving some forty people, three of whom were stabbed, resulting in multiple arrests.[12] Since Frank Sinatra christened the Centrum in September, Rush became the first artist to sell out all three regional arenas: Boston Garden, Providence Civic Center, and the Centrum.[13]

FEBRUARY 11–12, 1983
ALBUQUERQUE, NEW MEXICO
TINGLEY COLISEUM, New Mexico State Fairgrounds, 300 San Pedro Drive Northeast. Venue dedicated on September 28, 1957.
SUPPORT ACT: Golden Earring
TICKETS: $10.50 / $11.50, general admission
ATTENDANCE (FEB. 11): 10,000 (SRO/Anthem); (*Pollstar/Billboard*); sold out
ATTENDANCE (FEB. 12): 6,234 (Anthem/SRO); 6,107 (*Pollstar*)
TWO-DAY ALBUQUERQUE GROSS: $171,078
TIM WENDT (RIGGER): "Golden Earring was a really good band. Both of them, Golden Earring and Rush, would watch each other's set. And that was really cool; you could tell that they had a respect for them. Usually, bands . . . when you're over with your set, you get out of there, but they had respect for the musicianship."[14]

FEBRUARY 14–15, 1983
LONG BEACH, CALIFORNIA
LONG BEACH ARENA, 300 East Ocean Boulevard. Venue opened on October 6, 1962.
SUPPORT ACT: Golden Earring
TICKETS: $10.75 / $11.75
ATTENDANCE: 12,691 (Anthem/SRO); 13,555 per show (*Pollstar*); sold out
CONCERT GROSS: $146,312 per show
LOS ANGELES TIMES: "Loftiness, Showiness and Noise from Rush: About 13,000 teenagers screamed and hollered and stood on their chairs and played along on imaginary instruments. And the rock critics in the audience—this one, anyway—thought the whole thing was silly and empty and pompous. The set Rush performed in Long Beach was clearly the most succinct, appealing show it's turned in in recent years."

FEBRUARY 17–18, 1983
INGLEWOOD, CALIFORNIA
THE FORUM, 3900 West Manchester Boulevard. Venue opened on December 30, 1967.
SUPPORT ACT: Golden Earring
TICKETS: $10.00 / $12.50
ATTENDANCE: 14,964 (Anthem/SRO); 14,995 per show (*Pollstar*); sold out
CONCERT GROSS: $176,034 per show
NOTES: Rush and Golden Earring hung out during the day of the February 17 show at the Sunset Marquis pool. Sound check was running late, so crew members enjoyed a few moments in the warm California sun. Onstage, during "The Weapon," Ged added some extra emphasis to the lyric "He's a lot more afraid of your lying." Geddy's family was in town for a visit, and after the concert there was a small record company party inside the Forum Club. Rush's two Forum performances were the week's top-grossing concerts, according to *Billboard*.

FEBRUARY 21, 1983
SAN DIEGO, CALIFORNIA
SAN DIEGO SPORTS ARENA, 3500 Sports Arena Boulevard. Venue opened on November 17, 1966.
SUPPORT ACT: Golden Earring
TICKETS: $10.50 / $12.50
ATTENDANCE: 12,768 (Anthem/SRO); 12,573 (*Pollstar/Billboard*); sold out
CONCERT GROSS: $154,024
NOTES: After dinner, Geddy went outside to throw the baseball around, but within minutes there were too many fans hanging about for it to be relaxing, so the mound was moved indoors. A Geddy fastball almost hit the building manager, which resulted in the end of the toss. Onstage, the show was marred with various technical problems, and would be remembered as one of the looser Rush performances.

FEBRUARY 23, 1983
TUCSON, ARIZONA
TUCSON COMMUNITY CENTER ARENA, 260 South Church Street. Venue opened on November 8, 1971.
SUPPORT ACT: Golden Earring
TICKETS: $11.50
ATTENDANCE: 8,106 (Anthem/SRO) 7,908 (*Pollstar*)
CAPACITY: 8,000
CONCERT GROSS: $90,942

FEBRUARY 24, 1983
PHOENIX, ARIZONA
ARIZONA VETERANS MEMORIAL COLISEUM, Arizona State Fairgrounds, 1826 West McDowell Road. Venue opened on November 3, 1965.
SUPPORT ACT: Golden Earring
TICKETS: $12.50, general admission
ATTENDANCE: 17,000 (Anthem/SRO); 16,868 (*Pollstar*); sold out
CONCERT GROSS: $210,850
NOTES: Venue capacity was increased from 12,660 to 17,000 in 1981.

FEBRUARY 26, 1983
LAS CRUCES, NEW MEXICO
PAN AMERICAN CENTER, New Mexico State University campus, 1810 East University Avenue. Venue opened on November 30, 1968.
SUPPORT ACT: Golden Earring
TICKETS: $10.00 / $12.00 (average: $11.33)
ATTENDANCE: 8,925 (Anthem/SRO); 10,744 (*Pollstar*); sold out
CONCERT GROSS: $121,770
NOTES: *Billboard* initially listed attendance at 8,925 on March 19, but stated 10,744 the following week (March 26), which is believed to be the correct figure. Geddy did a phone interview for CHOM-FM (Montreal).

FEBRUARY 28; MARCH 1, 1983
DALLAS, TEXAS
REUNION ARENA, 777 Sports Street. Venue dedicated on April 28, 1980.
SUPPORT ACT: Golden Earring
TICKETS: $11.00 / $12.50
ATTENDANCE: 15,457 (Anthem/SRO); 15,357 per show (*Pollstar*); sold out
CONCERT GROSS: $190,404 per show
IAN (FEB. 28): "The last episode of *M.A.S.H.* airs for the first time. A lot of crew (not me) watched backstage. There's a cement wall that ends up maybe 20 feet high by the time it's by the load-out. A guy and a girl fell and were in distress. I tried to help until police and then ambulance arrived and took care of them. I still see them fall and hear their screams in my sleep sometimes."[15]

MARCH 2, 1983
SAN ANTONIO, TEXAS
CONVENTION CENTER ARENA, HemisFair Park Complex, 601 Hemisfair Way. Venue opened on April 6, 1968.

SUPPORT ACT: Golden Earring
TICKETS: $10.00 / $12.50
ATTENDANCE: 14,508 (Anthem/SRO); 13,281 (*Billboard*); sold out
CONCERT GROSS: $167,647

MARCH 4, 1983
OKLAHOMA CITY, OKLAHOMA
MYRIAD ARENA, One Myriad Gardens. Venue opened on November 5, 1972.
SUPPORT ACT: Golden Earring
TICKETS: $12.50
ATTENDANCE: 13,671 (Anthem/SRO); 13,000 (*Pollstar*); 13,761 (*Billboard*); sold out
CONCERT GROSS: $172,013
NOTES: Rush reconnected with their original bassist from 1968, Jeff Jones, over a postshow dinner.
JEFF JONES (RUSH ALUMNUS AND RED RIDER BASSIST): "I was on tour in Red Rider (opening for Pat Benatar), and we got to Oklahoma City on a night off and Rush was playing (with Golden Earring opening) at the same venue we were playing the next night. We all got together after their show and had a bite to eat and talked for quite some time. Out of that evening came the idea that Red Rider should open for Rush on a few shows. We did Toronto, Montreal, Quebec City, and Buffalo [on the 1984 *Grace Under Pressure* tour]. It was good all around. I occasionally see Alex and/or Geddy—great guys. Neil as well. We all know and respect that he's a more private person."[16]
THE OKLAHOMAN, GEDDY: "Everyone wants to pigeonhole a band because it's convenient. But from the beginning it's been a fusion of different kinds of music . . . a little bit of reggae, a little bit of jazz, a little bit of classical, a little hard rock, heavy metal. It's a very eclectic kind of music."

MARCH 6–7, 1983
HOUSTON, TEXAS
THE SUMMIT, 3700 Southwest Freeway. Venue opened on November 1, 1975.
SUPPORT ACT: Golden Earring
TICKETS: $10.00 / $12.00 (two-day average: $11.62)
ATTENDANCE: 14,295 per show (Anthem/SRO); sold out
CONCERT GROSS: $166,177 per show
NOTES: After the first show, a party went into the early morning hours, with the members of Golden Earring and Vandenberg sharing in the festivities. Rush's two Summit performances were the week's top-grossing concerts.[17]

MARCH 16, 1983
JACKSONVILLE, FLORIDA
JACKSONVILLE VETERANS MEMORIAL
COLISEUM, 1145 Adams Street. Venue dedicated on November 24, 1960.
SUPPORT ACT: Jon Butcher Axis
TICKETS: $10.75
ATTENDANCE: 9,906 (Anthem/SRO)
CAPACITY: 11,000
CONCERT GROSS: $105,662
NOTES: Geddy commented after sound check: "Nothing like these round coliseums for sound!" The crowd was particularly rowdy, with many arrests for public intoxication. A knife-wielding man "starts slashing everyone"[18] toward the end of Jon Butcher Axis's set (resulting in five people stabbed, with three victims hospitalized). A group of fans detained the twenty-one-year-old man, taking away his knife, until police were able to make their way through the crowd and arrest the suspect on five counts of aggravated battery and one count of aggravated assault. The Coliseum was known for rowdy crowds, with a police station adjacent to the venue. The band was unaware of the incident until after the show.
CHARLES KRAMER (JACKSONVILLE POLICE): "They all gathered around the stage to get a better look at the warm-up group. The guy, who had pulled out a knife ahead of time, came through the crowd with it, someone saw it, and a scuffle broke out."[19]
DEREK BLEVINS (JON BUTCHER AXIS DRUMMER): "The first show that we did in Jacksonville was a bit of a struggle for us, just to get through it. We had filmed a music video into the wee hours of the morning, then jumped on the bus to travel to Florida. We were all really exhausted, and not feeling so well. During the show, it was a pretty rowdy crowd, with people throwing stuff all over. Someone in the upper level threw a glass that shattered on my bass drum, but we finished our set, and from then on it went well."[20]

MARCH 17–18, 1983
PEMBROKE PINES, FLORIDA
HOLLYWOOD SPORTATORIUM, 17171
Pines Boulevard (Route 820). Venue opened in September 1970.
SUPPORT ACT: Jon Butcher Axis
TICKETS: $10.75, includes fifty-cent parking fee
TWO-DAY HOLLYWOOD ATTENDANCE: 19,697 (Anthem/SRO); 19,498 (*Pollstar*)
CAPACITY: 12,000 (*Pollstar*)
TWO-DAY HOLLYWOOD CONCERT GROSS: $198,686
NOTES: Ben Mink was in town visiting and sat in with the band for a jam during sound check on the first night. Terry Brown was also down for the Florida dates to discuss Rush's production future. Eventually, Neil ended up breaking the news to him that they would be using a different producer for the next album. During the show, the band and crowd were fired up, with an unending stream of fireworks being tossed down from the upper levels. Sound check ran late the second day, as Geddy, Alex, Ben Mink, Larry Allen, and Alex's son Justin attended an afternoon Expos game in West Palm Beach. Members of the team presented the band with several gifts, including a pro glove that was given to Justin. Several of the Expos, including Geddy's friends Warren Cromartie and Bryn Smith, spent the show rocking out at the lighting board.
TERRY BROWN: "They were going in a more techno direction, and it just didn't excite me. We parted on good terms, though."[21]

MARCH 20–21, 1983
LAKELAND, FLORIDA
LAKELAND CIVIC CENTER, 701 West Lime Street. Venue dedicated on November 14, 1974.
SUPPORT ACT: Jon Butcher Axis
TICKETS: $11.50, general admission
ATTENDANCE: 10,077; (Anthem/SRO); 10,000 per show (*Pollstar*); sold out
CONCERT GROSS: $115,782 per show
NOTES: Howard sat in for sound check on the first night, playing bass while Geddy focused on keyboards. Though the gig was sold out and the crowd enthusiastic, the audience was more civilized than the rowdy crowds in Hollywood and Jacksonville. Following the show,

band and crew enjoyed a late-night bowling party into the wee hours. Geddy arrived back at the hotel to find that his room had been broken into and was a mess (though nothing was stolen). The March 20 concert sold out in a matter of hours, so the second date was quickly added.[22] Alex, Geddy and Neil spent much of sound check jamming and improvising.

THE *TAMPA BAY TIMES*: "Rush dazzled a packed house with old favorites and new hits."

IAN: "I bowled a 235 and a 258—that's damn good bowling. Meanwhile, thieves removed the door to Geddy's room—he was not happy."

MARCH 23, 1983
ATLANTA, GEORGIA
THE OMNI, 100 Techwood Drive Northwest. Venue opened on October 14, 1972.
SUPPORT ACT: Jon Butcher Axis
TICKETS: $12.50
ATTENDANCE: 12,751 (Anthem/SRO); 12,319 (*Pollstar*)
CAPACITY: 14,000
CONCERT GROSS: $153,988

MARCH 25, 1983
CHARLOTTE, NORTH CAROLINA
CHARLOTTE COLISEUM, 2700 East Independence Boulevard. Venue dedicated on September 11, 1955.
SUPPORT ACT: Jon Butcher Axis
TICKETS: $10.50 (limited advance) / $12.50, general admission
ATTENDANCE: 12,325

MARCH 26, 1983
COLUMBIA, SOUTH CAROLINA
CAROLINA COLISEUM, University of South Carolina campus, 701 Assembly Street. Venue opened on November 30, 1968.
SUPPORT ACT: Jon Butcher Axis
TICKETS: $12.50
ATTENDANCE: 6,445

MARCH 27, 1983
GREENSBORO, NORTH CAROLINA
GREENSBORO COLISEUM, 1921 West Lee Street. Venue opened on October 29, 1959.
SUPPORT ACT: Jon Butcher Axis
TICKETS: $12.50
ATTENDANCE: 8,205

MARCH 29, 1983
CHARLESTON, WEST VIRGINIA
CHARLESTON CIVIC CENTER COLISEUM, 200 Civic Center Drive. Venue dedicated on August 3, 1980.
SUPPORT ACT: Jon Butcher Axis
TICKETS: $10.50 / $11.50
ATTENDANCE: 6,644 (Anthem/SRO); 6,475 (*Pollstar*)
CAPACITY: 8,000
CONCERT GROSS: $72,067
NOTES: Alex broke a string during the solo to "Closer to the Heart," so Geddy quickly improvised on his bass pedals in an attempt to compensate.

MARCH 30, 1983
CINCINNATI, OHIO
RIVERFRONT COLISEUM, 100 Broadway Street. Venue opened on September 9, 1975.
SUPPORT ACT: Jon Butcher Axis
TICKETS: $9.00 / $11.00
ATTENDANCE: 10,777 (Anthem/SRO); 10,569 (*Pollstar*)
CAPACITY: 12,650
CONCERT GROSS: $113,815
CINCINNATI POST: "Alex Lifeson employed a wide assortment of techniques. From delicate classical finger style to raunchy power chords, he kept the guitar sounds rich and varied."

APRIL 1, 1983
HARTFORD, CONNECTICUT
CIVIC CENTER, 1 Civic Center Plaza. Venue opened on January 9, 1975.
SUPPORT ACT: Jon Butcher Axis
TICKETS: $9.50 / $11.50
ATTENDANCE: 13,582 (Anthem/SRO); 13,588 (*Pollstar*); sold out
CONCERT GROSS: $151,602
NOTES: In the afternoon, members of the crew threw a baseball around inside the venue. Geddy was not feeling well but took to the stage without issue. After the gig, he was very low key, thankful that he was able to perform despite being under the weather. Neil spent time chatting with drum reps, and Alex was his usual lively self, cracking up friends and members of the crew.

APRIL 2, 1983
SYRACUSE, NEW YORK
CARRIER DOME, Syracuse University campus, 900 Irving Avenue. Venue opened on September 20, 1980.

SUPPORT ACT: Jon Butcher Axis
TICKETS: $12.00
ATTENDANCE: 19,470
NOTES: Everyone seemed a little on edge because of the massive dome they found themselves in. Sound check began with Neil pounding out the opening fill to "Digital Man." Eventually, a funny scene evolved, as Alex and Geddy stood in front of Neil, trying to make him laugh while he was playing. After sound check, Geddy threw the baseball around with Larry Allen and a few friends. "I feel a lot better than yesterday," Geddy said. During Jon Butcher Axis's set, sound engineer Jon Erickson climbed to the top of the massive dome, checking out the sound from every angle. "It's something that I like to do for every show," said Jon. "Just so I can get a feel for the venue." During intermission, Howard rocked out at the lighting board to "Eminence Front" by the Who, which was a tour favorite. After an okay performance in Hartford, Rush bounced back and presented a strong show in Syracuse.

GEDDY (ONSTAGE): "There's a lot of people in here. Maybe we can try to warm this big balloon up tonight!"

SYRACUSE HERALD-JOURNAL: "Rush audience roused to its feet for two hours: Lifeson displayed his tremendous talent on the acoustic guitar in 'Closer to the Heart.' Not to be out-done, Peart dazzled the crowd with a drum solo lasting about five and one-half minutes in their encore, 'YYZ.'"[23]

APRIL 4, 1983
PITTSBURGH, PENNSYLVANIA
CIVIC ARENA, 300 Auditorium Place. Venue opened on September 17, 1961.
SUPPORT ACT: Jon Butcher Axis
TICKETS: $11.75
ATTENDANCE: 14,200 (Anthem/SRO); 14,270 (*Pollstar*); sold out
CONCERT GROSS: $165,410
THE *PITTSBURGH POST-GAZETTE*: "Rush's balancing act: The three musicians all know how to make themselves anonymous, to subordinate themselves

to the total sound of the ensemble and to their ideological message. And the result last night was a solid, at times an inspiring, performance that had the crowd screaming its approval from beginning to end."

APRIL 5, 1983
BUFFALO, NEW YORK
BUFFALO MEMORIAL AUDITORIUM, 140 Main Street. Venue opened on October 14, 1940.
SUPPORT ACT: Jon Butcher Axis
TICKETS: $12.00
ATTENDANCE: 12,690; sold out
BUFFALO NEWS: "Rush in concert is the perfect marriage of MTV, video arcades, and heavy metal rock: laser light beams, smoky explosions, anonymously played synthesizers, rear-screen projections, and power chords. This is not to say Rush is talentless—you don't sell out Memorial Auditorium in 1983 Buffalo with pure frills—but their merits are so watered down as to preclude appreciation. Nobody else seemed to notice. They were on their feet from the start through 'Tom Sawyer.' Through all the futuristic sounds, Rush seems to speak directly to its fans."

APRIL 7, 1983
QUEBEC CITY, QUEBEC
COLISEE DE QUEBEC, 250 Boulevard Wilfrid-Hamel. Venue opened on December 8, 1949.
SUPPORT ACT: The Tenants
TICKETS: $12.50 CAD
ATTENDANCE: 12,388 (Anthem/SRO); 12,200 (*Pollstar*); sold out
CONCERT GROSS: $152,500 CAD
LE SOLEIL: "A good Rush: The Colisee filled once again. A happy crowd of 12,500 Rush maniacs were visibly delighted with the set served by the Canadian trio."

APRIL 8–9, 1983
MONTREAL, QUEBEC
MONTREAL FORUM, 2313 Saint Catherine Street West. Historic venue opened on November 29, 1924.
SUPPORT ACT: The Tenants
TICKETS: $12.50 CAD
ATTENDANCE: 13,972 per show (Anthem/SRO); sold out
CONCERT GROSS: $177,931 CAD per show

NOTES: April 9 was the final North American performance on the *New World Tour* and was also Ian Grandy's last date with the band.
IAN: "It was time for me to go on and do something else. I thought Rush had a chance to make it, I really did, but anybody working for a band that they really like wants to see them succeed. It's what everybody dreams of, and it all pretty much came true!"[24]
JOHN WETTON (KING CRIMSON, UK, ASIA BASSIST/VOCALIST): "I was recording Asia's *Alpha* album in Canada at Le Studio, about sixty miles north of Montreal. I decided to take a night off to drive into the city to see Rush at the Forum. The entry in my diary reads simply: 'Friday, April 8th—Rush absolutely devastating.'"[25]

MAY 3, 1983
ROTTERDAM, SOUTH HOLLAND, THE NETHERLANDS
AHOY SPORTPALEIS, Ahoy-weg 10. Venue opened on January 15, 1971.
SUPPORT ACT: Vandenberg
TICKETS: 25 NLG / 30 NLG
CAPACITY: 11,500 (approximate)
NOTES: Final live performance of "Chemistry."
SOUNDS: "The venue's in Rotterdam and boy, it's a big one. It's a massive domelike affair with a steeply-banked cycle track running around inside. My impression is that Rush seem hell bent on abandoning their past heritage and leaping headlong into a twitching, synthing, modernistic wild blue yonder. On one hand it's good 'n' light-hearted to hear Alex croaking a few 'Oooh-aaahs' during the brief '2112' segment, and naturally the well-documented 'lyrical alterations' cause a degree of amusement, but I wonder if Rush may be treating their 'formative' beginnings too flippantly?"
SOUNDS, **NICK KOTOS:** "We brought this lighting rig over from America. A lot of bands come over here to do a show, and because the venues are smaller, they bring a smaller rig. We bring the whole show, so the public see the same show everywhere we play."

MAY 4, 1983
PARIS, FRANCE
LE ZENITH DE PARIS, Parc de La Villette, 211 Avenue Jean-Jaures. Venue inaugurated on January 12, 1984.

CAPACITY: 9,000
NOTES: Canceled show. The band's bad luck with venues in Paris continued, as Le Zenith wasn't quite ready to open in time for this gig.

MAY 6, 1983
BOBLINGEN, NR. STUTTGART, BADEN-WURTTEMBERG, WEST GERMANY
SPORTHALLE, Schonbuchstrabe 20. Venue opened on September 24, 1966.
SUPPORT ACT: Nazareth
TICKETS: 24 DEM / 28 DEM
CAPACITY: 6,000
NOTES: As had been the case on earlier European tours, the mainland dates saw the band performing a slightly abbreviated set, with "Chemistry" and "The Camera Eye" shelved for the German dates.

MAY 7, 1983
FRANKFURT, HESSE, WEST GERMANY
FESTHALLE, Ludwig Erhard Anlage, 8000. Venue opened on May 19, 1909.
SUPPORT ACT: Nazareth
TICKETS: 24 DEM / 28 DEM.
ATTENDANCE: 12,000; sold out
MUZIK SCENE (GERMANY): "With the skillful blend of hard-rocking rhythms, complex compositions, and epic texts, Rush have long since jumped to the top in the US, Canada, and Great Britain."

MAY 8, 1983
HAMBURG, WEST GERMANY
CONGRESS CENTER HAMBURG, Am Dammtor / Marseiller Strasse Venue opened on April 14, 1973.
SUPPORT ACT: Nazareth
CAPACITY: 12,500

MAY 10, 1983
DUSSELDORF, NORTH RHINE-WESTPHALIA, WEST GERMANY
PHILIPSHALLE, Siegbuger Strasse 15. Venue opened on May 31, 1971.
SUPPORT ACT: Nazareth
CAPACITY: 7,500

MAY 11, 1983
EPPELHEIM, NEAR HEIDELBERG, BADEN-WURTTEMBERG, WEST GERMANY
RHEIN-NECKAR-HALLE, Pestalozzi Strasse 10. Venue built in 1970.
SUPPORT ACT: Nazareth
TICKETS: 24 DEM / 28 DEM
CAPACITY: 5,500, general admission

NOTES: A spirited crowd (largely consisting of US servicemen) clapped enthusiastically throughout, most notably on "Tom Sawyer," "Digital Man," "Broon's Bane," "The Weapon," and "In the Mood." Alex sang the high part during "2112: Overture," with Geddy stating, "What a singer. Is that guy a singer, or what?"

MAY 12, 1983
BRUSSELS, BELGIUM
FOREST NATIONAL, Avenue Victor Rousseau 208. Venue opened on October 8, 1970.
SUPPORT ACT: Vandenberg
TICKETS: 450 BEF / 480 BEF
CAPACITY: 5,500
DICK KEMPER (VANDENBERG BASSIST/ KEYBOARDIST): "I can still remember those performances. They were great shows for both bands, and everything was sold out. We hung out with Rush on the tour, and we were also at a party of theirs in Houston, Texas, during 1983. Just like Geddy, I play bass along with Moog Taurus pedals and synthesizers. I find their music fantastic, especially since it's played by only three people."[26]

MAY 14–15, 1983
BIRMINGHAM, WEST MIDLANDS, ENGLAND
NATIONAL EXHIBITION CENTRE ARENA, Pendigo Way and Perimeter Road, Marston Green. Venue opened on December 5, 1980.
AN EVENING WITH RUSH
TICKETS: £5.00 / £6.00
ATTENDANCE: 10,939 per show; sold out
NOTES: Venue aka Birmingham NEC Arena.
KERRANG!: "How can a gig like this be summed up in mere words? An avalanche of superlatives will only seem sycophantic so just believe THIS WAS SOMETHING VERY SPECIAL. Band, plus light and picture show, came together in a way quite unique, whilst ten-and-a-half thousand people magically combined to create real atmosphere even in this vast arena. The air was charged with appreciation."

MAY 17–18 AND 20–21, 1983
LONDON, ENGLAND
WEMBLEY ARENA, Arena Square at Engineers Way. Venue opened on August 4, 1934.
AN EVENING WITH RUSH

TICKETS: £5.00 / £6.00
ATTENDANCE: 10,211 per show; sold out
NOTES: The fourth date was added by public demand. That night, during the beginning of "The Camera Eye," Alex scratched on his electric guitar as a rhythmic counterpoint to Neil. At the instrumental break in "The Trees," Geddy sang "la, la, la, la" three times for a unique intro into Alex's solo. In "2112: Overture," Alex sang Geddy's high part in a very low voice, with Ged stating, "Wow! What a guy." During the latter segment of Neil's drum solo, electronic enhancements—phasing and echo—were added to the low toms, vibrating through the arena. For the conclusion of the "YYZ" encore, Neil and Geddy punctuated some pauses as Alex soloed over the top.
GEDDY (ONSTAGE ON MAY 21): "We don't play football, but we'll try to do what we do."
MUSIC EXPRESS **(CANADA):** "A four-night engagement at Wembley Arena, London's largest regular music venue, is eloquent testimony to the continued hold Rush has on the thin wallets of Britain's heavy metal fanatics. Old classics received rapturous applause, with the crowd uniting in a sing-along, but the strength of the new numbers is such that they will surely be regarded as classics a few years hence."
TORONTO STAR: "Rush at Wembley Arena for an unprecedented four evenings. It's probably the greatest coup here by any Canadian act ever."

MAY 22, 1983
BIRMINGHAM, WEST MIDLANDS, ENGLAND
NATIONAL EXHIBITION CENTRE ARENA, Pendigo Way and Perimeter Road, Marston Green
AN EVENING WITH RUSH
TICKETS: £5.50 / £6.00
ATTENDANCE: 10,939; sold out
NOTES: Show moved from Deeside due to a fire.

MAY 23, 1983
QUEENSFERRY, FLINTSHIRE, WALES
DEESIDE LEISURE CENTRE, Chester Road West, Route B5129. Venue opened on July 23, 1971.
TICKETS: £5.50
CAPACITY: 4,500
NOTES: This gig was moved to Birmingham National Exhibition Centre Arena on May 22 because of a fire in March.

MAY 24, 1983
INGLISTON, NEAR EDINBURGH, SCOTLAND
ROYAL HIGHLAND AGRICULTURAL EXHIBITION HALL, Royal Highland Exhibition Centre, Glasgow Road (A8). Venue opened on June 21, 1960.
AN EVENING WITH RUSH
TICKETS: £5.00, general admission
CAPACITY: 11,000 (approximate)
RADIO CLYDE, **NEIL:** "There were a lot of people being pulled out tonight. It's one of the things that makes us despise a building like this. It wasn't because the building was too full. Sometimes we quarrel because it is just greed, and we've had that over here before, when they just try to fill a building up too full. It wasn't that tonight. This building could have held twice as many people, but that mob mentality thing made half the building in the first twenty feet of the audience. A lot of people were being hurt, fainting and having to be pulled out of the audience. It's a terrible thing to watch. It really destroys the fun of being onstage if you're watching people in such an inhuman attitude. They're coming out of there unconscious and being dragged out by their feet. It's such an indignity that I take it as an affront too. I hate to watch that."

MAY 25, 1983
INGLISTON, NR. EDINBURGH, SCOTLAND
ROYAL HIGHLAND AGRICULTURAL EXHIBITION HALL, Royal Highland Exhibition Centre, Glasgow Road (A8)
AN EVENING WITH RUSH
TICKETS: £5.00, general admission
CAPACITY: 11,000 (approximate)
NOTES: Final date of the *New World Tour*. Mark Cherry's last gig working with Rush.

1. Bill Banasiewicz. Interview with Rory Gallagher, September 3, 1982.
2. *Green Bay Press-Gazette*, September 3, 1982.
3. *Des Moines Tribune*.
4. Skip Daly. Interview with Tim Wendt, December 7, 2012.
5. Bill Banasiewicz. Interview with Neil Peart, September 3, 1982.
6. Skip Daly. Interview with Tony Geranios, August 7, 2012.
7. Bill Banasiewicz. Interview with Rory Gallagher, September 3, 1982.
8. *Harmonix*, January 1983.
9. Interview with Andy Creegan. Juno Awards, 1994.
10. Skip Daly. Interview with Ian Grandy, 2011–2012.
11. Interview with John Petrucci. *Loudwire*, October 8, 2013.
12. *Hartford Courant*.
13. *The Boston Globe*.
14. Skip Daly. Interview with Tim Wendt, December 7, 2012.
15. Ian Grandy. Facebook.com, November 13, 2015.
16. Skip Daly. Interview with Jeff Jones, March 3, 2011.
17. *Billboard*.
18. *The Palm Beach Post*, March 18, 1983.
19. Interview with Charles Kramer. *News-Press*, March 18, 1983.
20. Bill Banasiewicz. Interview with Derek Blevins, December 8, 2014.
21. *Classic Rock Presents Prog*, February 2010.
22. *Tampa Bay Times*.
23. *Syracuse Herald-Journal*, April 4, 1983.
24. Bill Banasiewicz. Interview with Ian Grandy, March 21, 1983.
25. Bill Banasiewicz. Interview with John Wetton, February 20, 1987.
26. Bill Banasiewicz. Interview with Dick Kemper, December 7, 2014.

Chapter 16

RADIO CITY MUSIC HALL, 1983

The run of five shows at Radio City Music Hall offered North American Rush devotees the unique opportunity to see the band in an intimate setting, while also giving Neil, Alex, and Geddy a space to hone their chops and work on new material prior to recording *Grace Under Pressure*. "Our usual habit after writing new songs was to go out and play a few small shows, a few big shows, and then go right into the studio," Neil said. "This time we felt it would be suitably dangerous to come right out of hibernation and onto one of the most prestigious stages in the world."

Over the course of five sold-out shows, Rush performed to 29,370 fans (as well as members of Blue Öyster Cult, Utopia, and U2), setting an in-house gross record for a rock group. From an aesthetic standpoint, Geddy was sporting a brand-new, much shorter haircut for these gigs. Also, Neil debuted his 360-degree drum set, with a new electronic kit in the back. The rotating riser had not been developed yet, so he played some of the newer material with his back to the audience.

The set list was similar to that of the *New World Tour*, but with early versions of "Kid Gloves," "Red Sector A," and "The Body Electric" replacing "The Camera Eye" and "Chemistry." The new songs were played both live and at sound check over the course of the week.

Onstage, Geddy joked about the band's Radio City residency. "Nice to be here again for our whatever row in a night, night in a row, here at Radio City Music Hall," he said. "We've been here so long now."

ABOVE: New York, NY; The sellout crowd filing out of Radio City Music Hall.

OPPOSITE: New York, NY; Marquee at Radio City Music Hall.

TOUR HISTORY
RADIO CITY MUSIC HALL, 1983

SET LIST:
Intro (Three Stooges theme)
"The Spirit of Radio"
"Tom Sawyer"
"Digital Man"
"Kid Gloves" (prerelease version)
"Subdivisions"
"Vital Signs"
"Red Sector A" (prerelease version)

"Closer to the Heart"
"The Analog Kid"
"The Body Electric" (prerelease version)
"Broon's Bane"
"The Trees"
"Red Barchetta"
"The Weapon" (with Count Floyd intro)
"New World Man"
"Limelight"

"Countdown"
"2112: Overture"
"2112: The Temples of Syrinx"
"Xanadu"
"La Villa Strangiato"
"In the Mood"
Encore:
"YYZ" (with drum solo)

SEPTEMBER 18, 1983
NEW YORK, NEW YORK
RADIO CITY MUSIC HALL, 1260
Avenue of the Americas (Sixth Avenue).
Venue opened on December 27, 1932.
SUPPORT ACT: Marillion
TICKETS: $17.50
ATTENDANCE: 5,874; sold out
CONCERT GROSS: $100,772
NOTES: For the entire week in New York, the band was warmly greeted by wildly enthusiastic crowds, who yelled, screamed, whistled, and clapped throughout every show. During sound check, the band performed the three new songs twice, although Howard was still concerned because of his lack of familiarity with the new material. At dinner, the members of Marillion were excited to be playing at Radio City with Rush. Unfortunately, the Rush audience did not share the same enthusiasm for their brand of prog, which was cut from the same cloth as Peter Gabriel-era Genesis.
GEDDY (ONSTAGE): "Alex Lifeson on the plastic guitar."
NICK KOTOS (PRODUCTION MANAGER): "Radio City is on a Broadway contract, which means the show stops at eleven. If it goes one second past eleven, you just paid for a whole eight-hour call. So, we sat down together ahead of time and worked out the set, and we arranged it so there would be a ten-minute buffer at the end. We get to the first night, and the band's playing. They get to the end, and they're playing 'YYZ,' with Neil's solo in it. And they're playing . . . and they're playing . . . and I come down from my office, and I look at the clock, and I go, 'What the fuck?' It's five minutes to eleven, and they're still playing. I go to the stage wing and get Alex's attention,

and I point to my watch, and he points me over to Geddy. I run over to the other side, and I get Geddy's attention, and I point to my watch, and he points me over to Neil. I go over to Neil and I point to my watch, and he looks back at me like, 'And?' So I had to mouth the words 'Get the fuck off the stage!' All of a sudden, he finishes up the solo, they finish the song in like, quadruple time, and everyone rushes off the stage, and they call house lights at one second before 11. We stopped at the elevator on the way up to the dressing room, and I go, 'What the fuck happened?!' and Neil said, 'I got lost! I couldn't figure out how to get out of that.' After that, they decided to cut 'Freewill' out for the rest of the five-night stand. So, for the other nights we finished ten minutes early. Ray and Pegi weren't too happy that they cut a song, but they knew that if they went over they would have to pay . . . and they didn't want to pay."[1]

SEPTEMBER 19, 1983
NEW YORK, NEW YORK
RADIO CITY MUSIC HALL, 1260
Avenue of the Americas (Sixth Avenue)
SUPPORT ACT: Marillion
TICKETS: $17.50
ATTENDANCE: 5,874; sold out
CONCERT GROSS: $100,772
NOTES: Neil was scheduled to do an afternoon session with photographer Dimo Safari, and he was a little nervous about it. He didn't mind having his picture taken by a friend, but this was a big, onstage shoot, behind his new kit at Radio City. The previous night, Dimo, like many others, had had his share of celebration, and he lost track of the time.

Neil managed to find him and was none too happy about it. In the limo ride over to the gig, Neil's displeasure was evident, though he did his best to break up any tension by telling funny stories. En route, Alex was seen casually walking down 52nd Street. Neil's photo shoot took place before sound check, and it was a success, with many of the photos appearing in a future issue of *Modern Drummer*. For the gig, "Freewill" was subtracted from the set, and in the dressing room afterward the band was much happier with the shorter performance, citing a better pacing to the concert.
AQUARIAN WEEKLY: "Rushing Dressing Wows Radio City Crowd: For two full hours Rush gave them what they'd come for: a mixed bag of hit after hit from their various platinum albums and an extravagant multimedia show complete with Jedi-like lights and video clips."

SEPTEMBER 21, 1983
NEW YORK, NEW YORK
RADIO CITY MUSIC HALL, 1260
Avenue of the Americas (Sixth Avenue)
SUPPORT ACT: Marillion
TICKETS: $17.50
ATTENDANCE: 5,874; sold out
CONCERT GROSS: $100,772
NOTES: In the afternoon, Howard was excited to hear Boys Brigade on WNEW-FM. Later, he got a call from someone claiming to be Mick Jagger's

manager, who wanted tickets left in Jagger's name at the door. Howard, being very skeptical, told the gentleman that if Mick Jagger showed up at the stage door, "I will personally let him in." The so-called manager kept insisting that tickets be left at the box office, but Howard didn't bite, and Jagger never appeared (that anyone knows of).

SEPTEMBER 22, 1983
NEW YORK, NEW YORK
RADIO CITY MUSIC HALL, 1260 Avenue of the Americas (Sixth Avenue)
SUPPORT ACT: Marillion
TICKETS: $17.50
ATTENDANCE: 5,874; sold out
CONCERT GROSS: $100,772
NOTES: After sound check, Geddy did an interview for MTV with a VJ who had professed a profound hatred of the band just a few years before. Geddy was so excited that the Montreal Expos had a chance to make the playoffs that he had a small television set up on his keyboard bank so he could monitor the score onstage. Unfortunately, the Phillies swept the doubleheader. During the gig, "Kid Gloves" was performed later in the set, between "New World Man" and "Limelight." Despite a less-than-favorable audience response at Radio City, the guys in Marillion continued to maintain a positive, professional attitude.

SEPTEMBER 23, 1983
NEW YORK, NEW YORK
RADIO CITY MUSIC HALL, 1260 Avenue of the Americas (Sixth Avenue)
SUPPORT ACT: Marillion
TICKETS: $17.50
ATTENDANCE: 5,874; sold out
CONCERT GROSS: $100,772
NOTES: Rush's five-day gross of $503,860 set an in-house record for a rock band. During Marillion's performance, their lead singer, Fish, yelled, "If you don't want to listen, then leave!" The support act had a tough time finding their footing with Rush's single-minded, rabid fan base during the entire five-night run. In Rush's set, Geddy sang "the spirit of baseball" to a fired-up crowd during "The Spirit of Radio." He accidentally introduced "The Body Electric" as "Red Sector A." In "Red Barchetta," Geddy changed the line "suddenly ahead of me" to "suddenly in front of me." Alex

played a blistering solo on "La Villa Strangiato," after which Neil came in too early with his tom rhythm, but caught himself and made a fill out of it, which worked quite nicely. The week at Radio City ended with the sounds of "Take Me Out to the Ballgame." This was Robert "Fuzzy" Frazer's last date working for Rush.

NBC SOURCE RADIO, *ROCK REPORT*: "The three new songs reflected a refined musical progression, each featuring Alex Lifeson with some outstanding guitar textures. To see an incredible production like Rush live in a great atmosphere like Radio City was a thrill for all in attendance."

NEIL: "[I brought my parents to] the last show of that run, putting them up at the same hotel where we were staying, and bringing them with me to the venue in a limousine in the afternoon. Mom and Dad sat in the stage-left wings during the show, and the next night I arranged for them to attend another concert in the same theater—Linda Ronstadt singing standards with an orchestra."[2]

1. Skip Daly. Interview with Nick Kotos, June 7, 2012.
2. Neil Peart. *Roadshow: Landscape With Drums, A Concert Tour By Motorcycle.* Rounder Books, 2006.

Chapter 17

THE GRACE UNDER PRESSURE TOUR

The *Grace Under Pressure* trek began somewhat inauspiciously: On the second date, May 9, 1984, at the Tucson Community Center Arena in Arizona, an audience member threw a disposable lighter from the upper reaches of the arena during "Distant Early Warning," hitting Geddy in the head. After a brief break, the performance continued. Meanwhile, fans who witnessed the incident grabbed the perpetrator and held him for security. After the set was completed, Geddy received several stitches in the dressing room.

"I have a hole in my head, and besides that, I got hit by something and I have a hole in my head," Geddy remarked backstage after the show. "It's ignorant to throw things at the stage. It's the most ignorant thing a person can do. It's mindless; it's senseless. You can do some serious damage. It's too stupid for words. Don't do it!"

According to Neil, in addition to being injured by the lighter, Geddy was frustrated about what had happened. "In the end, Geddy just told the security people to let the guy go. He would have liked to confront him and perhaps share a few choice words, but therein lay another dilemma—it would have given the guy the satisfaction of actually meeting Geddy, a twisted reward for his idiocy."

Lighter incident aside, the *Grace Under Pressure* tour was another massive success, with Rush performing seventy-six shows in North America (including Hawaii) and Japan. Highlights of the set included the then-complete "Fear" trilogy, performed in sequence, featuring the debut of "Witch Hunt." For the first leg of the tour, "Afterimage" followed "Closer to the Heart," and the drum solo was aligned with "Red Lenses." After the summer break, "Kid Gloves" replaced "Afterimage," and an extended jam section was added to "Closer to the Heart." Beginning on October 18, Neil's solo found its way back to "YYZ," as on previous tours, and a new bass intro and full bass solo were added to

"Red Lenses." For the Japanese leg, "Kid Gloves" was dropped from the lineup. This tour also marked the first time since *Hemispheres* that Rush featured every song from its new album in the set (albeit not all in a single show).

"Every year, it's another difficult decision to decide what songs stay in the show, and what don't," Geddy remarked on radio station WLS-FM in Chicago. "The ones that are just too boring to play anymore have to go regardless of their popularity. Sometimes you just can't bear to play a song anymore—you played it so many times!"

RIGHT: Alex making Neil laugh at center stage.

OPPOSITE: Two heads are better than one—Alex and Geddy onstage.

Among the many highlights of the *Grace Under Pressure* trek were the Japan dates, which included a sold-out show at the legendary Nippon Budokan in Tokyo, and the Texxas Jam shows in Houston and Dallas, where Rush played to close to one hundred thousand fans over the course of two nights—its largest headline audiences to date. "There were a gazillion people at the gig," recalled Alex of the second date, at the Cotton Bowl in Dallas, "and it was outdoors in the afternoon, and I did this cool running-backwards thing, and there was a little lip on the stage, and I caught the lip and landed smack on my ass. And

I sat there on the stage playing, thinking, How am I going to get up out of this position without looking horribly awkward? So, I looked horribly awkward."

In an effort to make life on the road more tolerable, this was also the tour where Neil discovered the freedom of traveling solo—for some of the time, at least—by bicycle. His wife, Jackie, bought him a bike prior to the tour, but he didn't bring it along. In Salt Lake City, after attempting unsuccessfully to find a rental, he purchased a bike, stashing it in the bus luggage bay when he wasn't using it.

OPPOSITE AND TOP: Alex and Geddy onstage.
ABOVE LEFT: Toronto, Ontario; Geddy at a video shoot rehearsal.
ABOVE RIGHT: Valley Forge, PA; Neil and his bike.

TOUR HISTORY
GRACE UNDER PRESSURE TOUR

SET LIST:
Intro (Three Stooges theme)
"The Spirit of Radio"
"Subdivisions"
"The Body Electric"
"The Enemy Within"
"The Weapon"
"Witch Hunt"

"New World Man"
"Between the Wheels"
"Red Barchetta"
"Distant Early Warning"
"Red Sector A"
"Closer to the Heart"
"Afterimage"
"YYZ"

"2112: The Temples of Syrinx"
"Tom Sawyer"
Encore:
"Red Lenses"
"Vital Signs"
"Finding My Way"
"In the Mood"

MAY 7, 1984
ALBUQUERQUE, NEW MEXICO
TINGLEY COLISEUM, New Mexico State Fairgrounds, 300 San Pedro Drive Northeast. Venue dedicated on September 28, 1957.
SUPPORT ACT: Gary Moore
TICKETS: $12.50
CAPACITY: 10,656 (Anthem/SRO)
NOTES: The opening date of the 1984 *Grace Under Pressure* tour featured the live debut of "Distant Early Warning," "Afterimage," "The Enemy Within," "Red Lenses," "Between the Wheels," and "Witch Hunt." The tour encore featured "Vital Signs," emphasizing how strongly the band felt about the song. Alex, Geddy, and Neil's instrumentation marked a departure from the past, as Alex now favored Fenders over Gibsons, and Neil incorporated electronic drums into the new songs and his solo. Beginning on the *New World Tour*, Geddy had started using a new Steinberger L2 bass. The Steinberger was now his main axe, which added a distinctive look to stage left. Two of the new songs include no bass at all, with Geddy playing keyboards exclusively on "Afterimage" and "Red Sector A."
GEDDY (ONSTAGE): "It all starts right here tonight. So you might hear a few unexpected things."

MAY 8, 1984
TUCSON, ARIZONA
On this day off, band members enjoyed the sunshine in between interviews, while the crew relaxed at the pool with a few frozen drinks. In the late afternoon, Geddy wanted to watch the Braves baseball game, but the hotel didn't have TBS, so he took a cab to the nearest location that did—a redneck bar some fifteen

miles away—only to find the game had a rain delay. During the evening, the entourage played a game of softball, complete with lighted field, fans, photographers, hot dogs, and beer.
ALEX: "We had a big softball game with Gary Moore's band and crew, and us, our crew, and the 'lighties' and the 'soundies.' We all went out to a baseball diamond, got it late at night, we got the lights up there, and we had a small following of people out there and we played softball. It was a fantastic way for everyone to get to know each other. Have fun, get back to the hotel, have a swim and talk baseball all night, eat Mexican food, and go to bed at 11:30. It was great! It was a real cold winter and it's sweltering, up in the hundreds here. It's a great place to start the tour."[1]
GEDDY (DURING THE AFTERNOON, IN THE HOTEL): "I think Detroit is going to win the World Series. That's a pretty bold statement, I know, and I said it before the season started. My prediction is on record in the *Toronto Daily Star*. It's in print."[2]

MAY 9, 1984
TUCSON, ARIZONA
TUCSON COMMUNITY CENTER ARENA, 260 South Church Street. Venue opened on November 8, 1971.
SUPPORT ACT: Gary Moore
TICKETS: $13.50 (all seats)
ATTENDANCE: 7,500 (approximate)
CAPACITY: 7,900 (Anthem/SRO)
NOTES: In the early morning, Alex drove out to Marana, Arizona and rented a Cessna to do some flying while being interviewed midflight. At sound check, the band stretched out on their improvisation, taking them into musically uncharted waters. Afterward, Geddy did

an onstage interview for NBC Radio, demonstrating his new keyboard setup. During the show, someone in the audience threw a disposable lighter from the upper reaches of the arena during "Distant Early Warning," which hit Geddy in the head.
ALEX (LATE MORNING, IN-FLIGHT OVER ARIZONA): "I've always thought there's something beautiful about airplanes. Just the fact that a large piece of machinery can fly in the air is really an incredible thing. So that sparked an interest, and also the challenge of getting a pilot's license while being on the road. It's very difficult to find the time to do it."[3]
GEDDY'S PHYSICIAN (BACKSTAGE AFTER THE SHOW): "At this time, Mr. Lee has had a head injury. His prognosis is fair. The stitches will be removed in about a week. He tolerated the surgery very well."[4]
LARRY ALLEN (BACKSTAGE AFTER THE SHOW): "Ged gets hit in the head, and it only makes him meaner!"[5]

MAY 10, 1984
LAS VEGAS, NEVADA
THOMAS AND MACK CENTER, University of Nevada–Las Vegas campus, 4505 South Maryland Parkway. Venue opened on September 16, 1983.
SUPPORT ACT: Gary Moore
TICKETS: $15.00
CAPACITY: 15,000 (Anthem/SRO)

MAY 12, 1984
RENO, NEVADA
LAWLOR EVENTS CENTER, University of Nevada–Reno campus, 1500 North Virginia Street. Venue opened on November 4, 1983.

SUPPORT ACT: Gary Moore
TICKETS: $14.00
CAPACITY: 10,500 (Anthem/SRO)
RENO GAZETTE-JOURNAL: "The Lawlor management's decision to fill the floor area with reserved seats helped keep the audience subdued. It's not that Rush wasn't appreciated. Many audience members expressed great admiration for the band's depth and musical virtuosity."

MAY 14, 1984
SALT LAKE CITY, UTAH
SALT PALACE, 100 S West Temple. Venue dedicated on July 11, 1969.
SUPPORT ACT: Gary Moore
TICKETS: $12.50
ATTENDANCE: "Near capacity"[6]
CAPACITY: 11,500
SALT LAKE TRIBUNE: "Powerhouse performance from Rush in Salt Palace: The new cuts showed Rush to be creatively expanding their sound, blending the talents of the group with some imaginative compositions."

MAY 15, 1984
BOISE, IDAHO
BSU PAVILION, Boise State University campus, 1401 Bronco Lane. Venue opened on May 16, 1982.
SUPPORT ACT: Gary Moore
TICKETS: $11.50
CAPACITY: 8,500 (Anthem/SRO)

MAY 17, 1984
PORTLAND, OREGON
MEMORIAL COLISEUM, 1401 North Wheeler. Venue opened on November 3, 1960.
SUPPORT ACT: Gary Moore
TICKETS: $13.50
ATTENDANCE: 8,033
CAPACITY: 9,042
CONCERT GROSS: $108,446

MAY 18, 1984
TACOMA, WASHINGTON
TACOMA DOME, 2727 East D Street. Venue opened on April 21, 1983.
SUPPORT ACT: Gary Moore
TICKETS: $13.50, general admission
ATTENDANCE: "More than 19,000"[7]
CAPACITY: 26,500
NOTES: The large, rowdy crowd was slow getting into the Dome, as security checked every patron with handheld metal detectors. Once inside, they tossed glow sticks and light fireworks, with Geddy asking that they please refrain from throwing things.
THE NEWS TRIBUNE: "Rush concert was like a homecoming: For a trio, the band produced a fully dynamic show—visually as well as aurally. The overpowering impact was the music. Not really heavy metal, the band plays in a techno-rock format with a lean towards hard rock."

MAY 19, 1984
VANCOUVER, BRITISH COLUMBIA
PACIFIC COLISEUM, Pacific National Exhibition Fairgrounds, 100 North Renfrew. Venue dedicated on January 8, 1968.
SUPPORT ACT: Gary Moore
TICKETS: $13.50 / $14.50 CAD
ATTENDANCE: 6,390
CAPACITY: 8,500
CONCERT GROSS: $87,173 CAD

MAY 21, 1984
San Francisco, California
KRQR Studios, 865 Battery Street
Geddy appeared on the syndicated radio call-in show *Rockline*.
ROCKLINE, GEDDY: "A lot of what *Grace Under Pressure* is, is Alex reasserting his role as a guitarist. With *Signals,* he felt a little frustrated because of the dominance of the keyboards, and with this album we tried to sort of correct that, and sort of give him his fair share. He really worked hard on this one to win the job back [*laughs*]."

MAY 24–26, 1984
DALY CITY, CALIFORNIA
COW PALACE, 2600 Geneva Avenue. Venue opened on April 20, 1941.
SUPPORT ACT: Gary Moore
TICKETS: $15.00
ATTENDANCE: (MAY 24–25): 10,000 per show; sold out
ATTENDANCE (MAY 26): 7,449; 7,440 (*Amusement Business*)
CAPACITY: 10,000
THREE-DAY DALY CITY CONCERT GROSS: $407,910
NOTES: Third show added by popular demand. During the run of shows at San Francisco's Cow Palace, Neil played host to a special guest, as young drummer Adam Roderick visited. Adam had won Neil's red Tama drum kit in the fall of 1982 in the *Modern Drummer* essay contest, and Neil now gave Adam the chance to play his current drums during sound check.
SACRAMENTO BEE: "The tremendously popular trio Rush in a three-night stand at the Cow Palace proved they're a breed apart. One might think that Rush's choice to focus on the music and avoid the head-banging clichés and shameless grandstanding of heavy metal would elevate it to a grander status. But it does essentially the same thing with its pretentious lyrics and pompous music, letting effect dominate communication, and the result—tedium—remains the same."

MAY 28, 1984
SAN DIEGO, CALIFORNIA
SAN DIEGO SPORTS ARENA, 3500 Sports Arena Boulevard. Venue opened on November 17, 1966.
SUPPORT ACT: Gary Moore
TICKETS: $11.00 / $13.00
ATTENDANCE: 10,517
CAPACITY: 14,217
CONCERT GROSS: $131,863

MAY 29–30, 1984
INGLEWOOD, CALIFORNIA
THE FORUM, 3900 West Manchester Boulevard. Venue opened on December 30, 1967.
SUPPORT ACT: Gary Moore
TICKETS: $12.00 / $14.00
ATTENDANCE: 13,238 per show; sold out
CONCERT GROSS: $179,118 per show
LOS ANGELES TIMES: "Rush Slows Down the Pace at Forum: At times, the trio locked into pulsing, Police-like instrumental passages. Just as often, Rush produced some orchestral maneuvers that recalled 70s progressive rock. Very skillful, very boring."

JUNE 2, 1984
IRVINE, CALIFORNIA
IRVINE MEADOWS AMPHITHEATER, 8808 Irvine Center Drive. Venue opened on August 21, 1981.
SUPPORT ACT: Gary Moore
TICKETS: $9.50 (lawn) / $14.00 (upper reserved) / $16.00 (lower reserved)
ATTENDANCE: 14,933; sold out
CONCERT GROSS: $195,835

JUNE 4, 1984
PHOENIX, ARIZONA
ARIZONA VETERANS MEMORIAL COLISEUM, Arizona State Fairgrounds, 1826 West McDowell Road. Venue opened on November 3, 1965.
SUPPORT ACT: Gary Moore
TICKETS: $13.50
ATTENDANCE: 13,839; sold out
CONCERT GROSS: $186,827
ARIZONA REPUBLIC: "Rush appears to be in no hurry to achieve originality: *Grace Under Pressure* inspired some to believe Rush was on a comeback, however, the same old concert tricks prove the band is still the same old rock 'n' roll mutt."
ARIZONA REPUBLIC, GEDDY: "I feel the band is very solid at this point."

JUNE 5, 1984
LAS CRUCES, NEW MEXICO
PAN AMERICAN CENTER, New Mexico State University campus, 1810 East University Avenue. Venue opened on November 30, 1968.
SUPPORT ACT: Gary Moore
TICKETS: $12.00 / $13.50
ATTENDANCE: 6,867
CAPACITY: 8,800
CONCERT GROSS: $87,049
NOTES: Crew member Tim Wendt suffered injuries after falling from the venue rafters while rigging the stage. The band took time out to visit him in the hospital.

JUNE 6, 1984
ODESSA, TEXAS
ECTOR COUNTY COLISEUM, 4201 Andrews Highway. Venue opened on January 19, 1955.
SUPPORT ACT: Gary Moore
TICKETS: $11.00 / $12.00 / $13.00, general admission floor
ATTENDANCE: 5,827
CAPACITY: 8,500

JUNE 8, 1984
HOUSTON, TEXAS
ASTRODOME (THE TEXXAS JAM), 8400 Kirby Drive. Historic venue opened on April 9, 1965.
SUPPORT ACTS: Ozzy Osbourne, Bryan Adams, 38 Special, Gary Moore
TICKETS: $18.50, general admission
ATTENDANCE: 35,000 (estimate)
CAPACITY: 60,000
NOTES: Texxas World Music Festival '84,

aka Texxas Jam. The band's dressing room looked down from mid-level into the massive dome, and Neil was a bit uneasy about playing such a large stadium, stating: "We're a hockey team. We're not a football team." Alex and Geddy were calm and cool, and Geddy walked around backstage laughing and joking while checking out the sights and the sounds of the afternoon. En route to Dallas, a funny scene unfolded when Geddy wanted a hamburger, so the band's tour bus pulled up to a McDonald's drive-through and twelve Quarter Pounders were ordered. The cashier was quite surprised.
HOWARD: "This is a team effort. All of the bands have very professional road crews and were coming on and off the stage very smooth. In the Astrodome, for a five-act show of this nature, times were actually running early, and looking real good. I have a lot of respect for those bands and their crews for doing such a great job in coming on and off the stage, as well as our stage management of Liam Birt and Nick Kotos."[8]
BOB DAISLEY (OZZY OSBOURNE BASSIST): "Unfortunately, we didn't see Rush on those shows, so I can't really comment on them. In general, though, I think Rush were then, and still are, an original, innovative band, led by a great singer/bass player. Funnily enough, he bought my Zemaitis bass from me in late 2013, and he loves it."[9]

JUNE 10, 1984
DALLAS, TEXAS
COTTON BOWL (THE TEXXAS JAM), Texas State Fairgrounds, Fair Park, 1300 Robert B. Cullum Boulevard. Historic football stadium opened on October 11, 1930.
SUPPORT ACTS: Ozzy Osbourne, Bryan Adams, 38 Special, Gary Moore
TICKETS: $18.50
ATTENDANCE: 60,000 (approximate)
CAPACITY: 80,000
NOTES: Texxas World Music Festival '84, aka Texxas Jam. Rush's largest headline show to date. A laser generator was broken, forcing Howard to fly one in from LA just in time for the gig.
HOWARD: "When you play outdoors, you have the elements of weather to contend with. Normally, indoors, there's no wind, and the building retains smoke

effects, so you can see all of the special effects and lights. As it looks tonight, the winds are about 30 mph and we probably won't be able to put up our rear-projection screen, so what we'll do is put up two video screens and use our backup video to show the exact same movies. You have problems like this that you have to compensate for. It's a lot of fun, when you're out there with 60,000 people. The energy levels are so high, and that energy coming off of the crowd makes you just as fired up as they are, if not more, to put on a great show. In a big outdoor show in this sweltering heat, there are always a few people consuming alcoholic refreshments, and some of them can't take it. The heat gets to them, and you have people passing out. We have medical tents set up just for that reason, and we have some fire hoses out there. We want to make sure that the crowd is happy at all times, without anyone getting hurt."[10]

JUNE 12, 1984
LITTLE ROCK, ARKANSAS
T. H. BARTON COLISEUM, Arkansas State Fairgrounds, 2600 Howard Street. Venue dedicated on September 29, 1952.
SUPPORT ACT: Gary Moore
TICKETS: $13.50, general admission
CAPACITY: 10,250
NOTES: In the afternoon, Geddy enjoyed a baseball toss alongside the Arkansas River. During sound check, the band let loose with some inspired improvisation.

JUNE 13, 1984
TULSA, OKLAHOMA
TULSA CONVENTION CENTER, 100 Civic Center. Venue opened on March 8, 1964.
SUPPORT ACT: Gary Moore
TICKETS: $13.50
ATTENDANCE: 5,203
CAPACITY: 8,000
CONCERT GROSS: $70,240
NOTES: Venue aka Tulsa Assembly Center. Alex and Geddy did some phone interviews after playing two sets of tennis.

JUNE 15, 1984
VALLEY CENTER, KANSAS
BRITT BROWN ARENA, Kansas Coliseum complex, 1229 East 85th

Street North. Venue opened on September 28, 1978.

SUPPORT ACT: Gary Moore
TICKETS: $13.75 (price includes twenty-five-cent parking fee), general admission
CAPACITY: 12,200 (Anthem/SRO)

JUNE 16, 1984
KANSAS CITY, MISSOURI
KEMPER ARENA, 1800 Genessee Street at 17th Street. Venue dedicated on October 18, 1974.

SUPPORT ACT: Gary Moore
TICKETS: $13.50
ATTENDANCE: 9,000 (approximate)
CAPACITY: 12,300 (Anthem/SRO)
KANSAS CITY TIMES: "Rush proves to be still much alive: More outstanding than the music was the superb light show, which was synchronized down to the last power chord."

JUNE 25, 1984
MILWAUKEE, WISCONSIN
MECCA ARENA, 400 West Kilbourn Avenue. Venue opened on April 9, 1950.

SUPPORT ACT: Gary Moore
TICKETS: $12.00 / $13.50
ATTENDANCE: 9,200[11]
CAPACITY: 11,649
THE MILWAUKEE SENTINEL: "Rush attracts new fans with leaner sounds: "Vocalist Geddy Lee's singing used to sound more like a small animal in pain. But Monday night he showed the restraint and control necessary for the band's demanding newer material, including 'The Body Electric' and 'The Enemy Within.'"

JUNE 26–27 1984
BLOOMINGTON, MINNESOTA
MET CENTER, 7901 Cedar Avenue South. Venue opened on October 21, 1967.

SUPPORT ACT: Gary Moore
TICKETS: $11.50 / $13.50
ATTENDANCE (JUNE 26): 10,993; 11,000 (*Amusement Business*); sold out[12]
ATTENDANCE (JUNE 27): 8,095; 8,888 (*Amusement Business*)
TWO-DAY BLOOMINGTON CONCERT GROSS: $249,389
NOTES: Venue aka Metropolitan Sports Center.
MINNEAPOLIS STAR AND TRIBUNE: "Rush performance fails to project

concert dimension: Concerts should offer fans a dimension not experienced on an artist's records. Rush did little more than try to re-create its records; seeing the players in the flesh was simply not enough. Without a show, the trio's redundant sound was not enough to elevate Rush to the top of the hard-rock concert heap."

JUNE 29–30, 1984
ROSEMONT, ILLINOIS
ROSEMONT HORIZON, 6920 N. Mannheim Road. Venue opened on July 2, 1980.

SUPPORT ACT: Gary Moore
TICKETS: $15.00
CAPACITY: 13,895 (Anthem/SRO)

JULY 2, 1984
ST. LOUIS, MISSOURI
ST. LOUIS ARENA, 5700 Oakland. Venue opened on September 23, 1929.

SUPPORT ACT: Gary Moore
TICKETS: $12.50 / $13.50
CAPACITY: 13,072 (Anthem/SRO)
NOTES: Venue aka the Checkerdome.
ST. LOUIS POST-DISPATCH: "Rush Power Undimmed at Arena: Rush proved once again, in an exciting show Monday night at the Arena, why it is Canada's premier rock band. The trio performed with style, flawless musicianship, and enough energy to live up to its name even after ten years of recording."

JULY 3, 1984
INDIANAPOLIS, INDIANA
MARKET SQUARE ARENA, 300 East Market Street. Venue opened on September 15, 1974.

SUPPORT ACT: Pat Travers
TICKETS: $12.50 (all seats)
ATTENDANCE: 9,694
CAPACITY: 10,500
CONCERT GROSS: $121,175
NEIL: "The building is dark. The darkness is charged. A fury of sound and light plays out in the smoky inferno. Sound reverberates around the walls, while the stage is alternately washed in color, picked out by powerful spotlights, or slashed by intense laser beams. Ten thousand youthful faces reflect back the shifting glare. Their upraised arms and roaring exuberance reflect back the electric energy to the three musicians who work upon the lighted stage. I sit behind

the drum kit, center stage, drum sticks dancing from drum to drum, cymbal to cymbal. My body is centered, my concentration is focused, while my arms and legs, hands and feet, are flailing away like blades. Executing a difficult passage with care, or pounding out a climax with abandon, I am driving at ten-tenths. Sweat streams and shines in the hot summer night."[13]

JULY 5–6, 1984
RICHFIELD, OHIO
RICHFIELD COLISEUM, 2923 Streetsboro Road. Venue opened on October 26, 1974.

SUPPORT ACT: Gary Moore
TICKETS: $13.00 (advance) / $14.00 (day of)
ATTENDANCE: 12,000 per show (approximate)[14]
CAPACITY: 14,000 (Anthem/SRO)
NOTES: Before the show on July 4, Neil spent the day off on his bike, completing his first "century," bicycling over 100 miles. July 6 was Gary Moore's final date with Rush.
THE AKRON BEACON JOURNAL: "Rush fans cheer steady pummeling."
ALEX: "We worked a lot with Thin Lizzy in the early days, but Gary had already left the band at that time, but we were well aware of Gary's playing and his influence on the scene, particularly in Britain. My recollection of him is that he was a very sweet, gentle guy—quick to smile and really a lot of fun to be with, but so absolutely passionate about the instrument and about playing."[15]

JULY 7, 1984
BUFFALO, NEW YORK
BUFFALO MEMORIAL AUDITORIUM, 140 Main Street. Venue opened on October 14, 1940.

CAPACITY: 12,195 (Anthem/SRO)
NOTES: Rescheduled to July 12. On this day off, Neil spent time bicycling around Pittsburgh's labyrinth network of streets, while Geddy took in the local fireworks display (which had been rescheduled from July 4), in between watching televised baseball games. In the crowd of thousands, he was only moderately hassled by fans, with one aggressive girl grabbing his arm. Later in the evening, Howard held a mini laser light display in his room, showing some friends exactly

what his new mini-laser could do. The room was fully engulfed in pot smoke, which allowed Howard to create dazzling cones and vectors of light. Eventually, the attention shifted out the window of the fifteenth-floor hotel room and onto the high-rise across the street. In one apartment, people were gathered in their dining room, and Howard placed the beam right in the middle of their meal, and watched them freak out. A phone call from the hotel concierge alerted him that the police on their way. The weed and paraphernalia were removed as Howard instructed one person to turn a hot shower all way up and put an entire pizza in the tub to take away the pungent smell, which it did. The cops interviewed him, and he was able to convince them that he was repairing the laser, and had no idea about the beam out the window. In the report, the woman told police that "when she moved, the beam followed."

JULY 8, 1984
PITTSBURGH, PENNSYLVANIA
CIVIC ARENA, 300 Auditorium Place. Venue opened on September 17, 1961.
SUPPORT ACT: Pat Travers
TICKETS: $13.75
ATTENDANCE: 10,695
CAPACITY: 15,000
CONCERT GROSS: $144,542
NOTES: Onstage, Geddy checked his keyboards during the Three Stooges intro tape. The opening synthesizer sequence for "Vital Signs" had taken on an otherworldly tone for the entire tour and sounded very different from the album.
PITTSBURGH POST-GAZETTE:
"'Rush' show a musical and visual circus: Suffice to say that last night, Rush was distinguished by a clarity and conviction that made you want to salute all those Maple Leaf flags around the arena."

JULY 9, 1984
DETROIT, MICHIGAN
JOE LOUIS ARENA, 600 Civic Center Drive. Venue opened on December 12, 1979.
SUPPORT ACT: Pat Travers
TICKETS: $15.00
ATTENDANCE: 13,754; sold out
CONCERT GROSS: $206,310
NOTES: Rush's final show with Pat Travers.

JULY 10, 1984
DAYTON, OHIO
HARA ARENA, 1001 Shiloh Springs Road. Venue opened on November 1, 1964.
NOTES: Rescheduled to October 6.

JULY 12, 1984
BUFFALO, NEW YORK
BUFFALO MEMORIAL AUDITORIUM, 140 Main Street. Venue opened on October 14, 1940.
SUPPORT ACT: Red Rider
TICKETS: $12.50
ATTENDANCE: 12,000 (approximate)
CAPACITY: 12,195
CONCERT GROSS: $149,876
NOTES: Original date was slotted for July 7, but later rescheduled.
BUFFALO NEWS: "Nearly all in the audience seemed delighted and thrilled by the performance of Rush and Red Rider. The shouting and applause were nearly as thunderous as the bands themselves, and the crowd was more energetic and enthusiastic than the acts onstage. Regardless of the tiredness of an act built around a minimum of talent, Rush remains a crowd pleaser."[16]
STREETBEAT BUFFALO: "The music Rush delivered was entertaining and exciting. However, their stage presence leaves a bit to be desired."

JULY 14–15, 1984
MONTREAL, QUEBEC
MONTREAL FORUM, 2313 Saint Catherine Street West. Historic venue opened on November 29, 1924.
SUPPORT ACT: Red Rider
TICKETS: $13.50 CAD
CAPACITY (VENUE): 16,500 for ice hockey / 19,000 with standing room
NOTES: After being reminded that July 14 is Bastille Day, Alex tried to resurrect the song of that title from the band's 1975 *Caress of Steel* album in the tuning room before the gig but had trouble remembering some of the parts. Members of the Expos were in attendance, with a postconcert party at Douze Twelve 34 raging away into the wee hours of the morning.
MONTREAL GAZETTE: "Lasers cut deep in Rush spectacle: Lifeson, looking more and more as if he's about to defect to Duran Duran, eschews the easy guitar solo, concentrating instead on weaving

his edgy riffs through classics such as 'Red Sector A' and 'Closer to the Heart.'"

JULY 16, 1984
QUEBEC CITY, QUEBEC
COLISEE DE QUEBEC, 250 Boulevard Wilfrid-Hamel. Venue opened on December 8, 1949.
SUPPORT ACT: Red Rider
TICKETS: $13.50 CAD
ATTENDANCE: 11,000[17]
CAPACITY: 11,500 (Anthem/SRO)
NOTES: Final live performance of "Afterimage."
LE SOLEIL: "Rush: breathtaking spectacle."

SEPTEMBER 14, 1984
PORTLAND, MAINE
CUMBERLAND COUNTY CIVIC CENTER, Spring Street at Center Street. Venue opened on March 3, 1977.
SUPPORT ACT: Fastway
TICKETS: $12.50, general admission
CAPACITY: 9,200 (Anthem/SRO)
NOTES: "Afterimage" was replaced by "Kid Gloves," which was last heard live in its early form at Radio City Music Hall.
"FAST" EDDIE CLARKE (FOUNDING FASTWAY GUITARIST): "I remember at the first show, Rush was using a very compact PA, I think it was a Meyer system, and when I saw the monitors I said, 'Well, they will not be loud enough.' I was told to wait and see, and sure enough, I came offstage with an almighty ringing in my ears, which I had not had since Motörhead. They were loud enough!"[18]

SEPTEMBER 15, 1984
GLENS FALLS, NEW YORK
GLENS FALLS CIVIC CENTER, 1 Civic Center Plaza. Venue opened on May 18, 1979.
SUPPORT ACT: Fastway
TICKETS: $12.50 / $13.50
CAPACITY: 6,062 (Anthem/SRO)

SEPTEMBER 17, 1984
NEW YORK, NEW YORK
MADISON SQUARE GARDEN, 4 Pennsylvania Plaza (8th Avenue between 31st and 33rd Streets). Historic venue opened on February 11, 1968.
SUPPORT ACT: Fastway
TICKETS: $13.50 / $15.00
CAPACITY: 15,977 (Anthem/SRO)

NOTES: Dubbed the "French flu," a nasty bug was making the rounds through the band and crew, taking people down one by one, with Geddy being the latest casualty. Before the gig, he was sick as a dog and looked awful but still took to the stage and delivered a top-notch performance, though his voice cracked on the chorus to "The Enemy Within." Neil was a rhythm machine on a brilliant version of "The Weapon" that also featured a memorable solo by Alex. Laser vectors on "The Body Electric" whipped the MSG audience into a frenzy. The near-capacity crowd was wildly enthusiastic, unaware of Geddy's plight. Backstage after the show, he looked completely wiped out, and rightly so.

GEDDY (ONSTAGE): "You guys are happening out there tonight."

VARIETY: "Good musicianship alone doesn't pull in arena-sized crowds, and Rush anticipated the full range of their audience's taste with blistering volume, banks of lasers, and blinding floodlights to assure complete sensory overload. The high decibel level, combined with an emphasis on riffs, rather than melodies in the songwriting, made for long stretches of monotony."

SEPTEMBER 18, 1984
LAKE PLACID, NEW YORK
OLYMPIC CENTER ARENA, 2634 Main Street. Historic venue opened on September 25, 1979.
SUPPORT ACT: Fastway
TICKETS: $12.50 (all seats reserved)
CAPACITY: 7,450 (Anthem/SRO)
NOTES: In the morning, Neil attempted a steep bike ride up the side of Whiteface Mountain before deciding (after two murderous miles) that it would be wiser to conserve some of his energy for the gig.

SEPTEMBER 21–22, 1984
TORONTO, ONTARIO
MAPLE LEAF GARDENS, 60 Carlton Street. Historic venue opened on November 12, 1931.
SUPPORT ACT: Red Rider
TICKETS: $15.50 / $16.50 CAD
TWO-DAY TORONTO ATTENDANCE: 23,162
TWO-DAY CAPACITY: 24,000
TWO-DAY TORONTO CONCERT GROSS: $357,052 CAD
NOTES: Recorded and filmed for the

Grace Under Pressure tour video, with David Mallet directing and Terry Brown and Jon Erikson in charge of audio production. After sound check, Mallet talked with members of the band's entourage, asking questions and taking suggestions for the shoot. The entire audience was given 3-D glasses, which they wore during "The Weapon." For these two homecoming gigs, Geddy was in great performance form, despite his ongoing battle with the French flu.

GLOBE AND MAIL: "Rush looks very impressive but sounds very much the same: The audience was bathed in pink and yellow lights, giving a soft checkerboard effect to the whole stadium. This drew the audience into the performance, uniting fans and performer."

STEVE HOWARD (CONCERT PRODUCTIONS INTERNATIONAL): "The production, which included the use of 12 cameras, 40 Vari-Lites and 300 PAR audience lights, was on par with our coproduction of Bowie's *Serious Moonlight* show, and the same director, David Mallett, was used."[19]

SEPTEMBER 24, 1984
NEW HAVEN, CONNECTICUT
NEW HAVEN VETERAN'S MEMORIAL COLISEUM, 275 South Orange Street
NOTES: Rescheduled to September 28 because of Geddy's continuing bout with the flu.

SEPTEMBER 25, 1984
PROVIDENCE, RHODE ISLAND
PROVIDENCE CIVIC CENTER, 1 La Salle Square
NOTES: Rescheduled to November 7 because of Geddy's continuing bout with the flu.

SEPTEMBER 27, 1984
LARGO, MARYLAND
CAPITAL CENTRE, 1 Harry S. Truman Drive. Venue opened on December 2, 1973.
SUPPORT ACT: Helix
TICKETS: $13.50
ATTENDANCE: 16,575
CAPACITY: 19,110
CONCERT GROSS: $223,762
NOTES: Alex sang the choruses with Geddy on "Subdivisions." During the second chorus, Ged extended the lyric to "*Be-e cast out*." The intro to "The Body

Electric" featured Geddy popping the strings of his Steinberger. The bass's carbon graphite fingerboard accentuated the popping with treble attack. At the end of the song, his voice cracked a bit on some of the high notes. On the intro to "Witch Hunt," Alex created a loud, otherworldly sound on his guitar. During "Red Barchetta," Alex broke a string just after the vocal "As another joins the chase." Neil and Geddy drove on until Alex was given a new guitar. During "Red Sector A," Alex added echo on his guitar in the verses, creating a unique version of the song. Geddy was finally feeling better, and the band was firing on all cylinders, delivering a hot performance. Unfortunately, the French flu continued to spread through the crew like wildfire, with Larry Allen its latest victim.

SEPTEMBER 28, 1984
NEW HAVEN, CONNECTICUT
NEW HAVEN VETERAN'S MEMORIAL COLISEUM, 275 South Orange Street. Venue opened on September 27, 1972.
SUPPORT ACT: Mama's Boys
TICKETS: $10.50 / $12.50 (average: $12.30)
ATTENDANCE: 9,830; sold out
CONCERT GROSS: $120,932
NOTES: Rescheduled from September 24 due to illness.

PAT MCMANUS (FOUNDING MAMA'S BOYS GUITARIST): "I am still very proud to have played that gig with Rush, as they are a band we looked up to, and I still love them today. In fact, I often talk of how kind the guys in Rush were to me and my brothers that day. My strongest memory from New Haven is that Rush were doing their sound check, and after a little while, Geddy told Alex and Neil that it was time to leave the stage so that the Mama's Boys could do their sound check. This totally amazed me and my brothers, not only that Rush would give us, a support act, a good sound check time, but that Geddy even knew who we were! In my eyes Rush are the classiest three-piece band in the world still to this day!"[20]

SEPTEMBER 29, 1984
EAST RUTHERFORD, NEW JERSEY
MEADOWLANDS ARENA, Meadowlands Sports Complex, 50 State Route 120. Venue opened on July 2, 1981.
SUPPORT ACT: Helix
TICKETS: $13.50 / $14.50
ATTENDANCE: 18,340; sold out
CONCERT GROSS: $247,837
NOTES: The afternoon sound check was inspired, featuring a lot of improvisation. Alex was informed that the Philadelphia date, which went on sale the same day, had sold out in less than two hours. Much to Ray's dismay, Alex said, "We'll just have to add another show in Philly." Ray preferred the band cover as much ground as possible by doing one-off shows instead of two nights in the same city. "We still have to make up the date in Providence," he reminded Alex. Onstage, during "New World Man," Geddy screamed "Oh, man!" after the lyric "Trying to pave the way for the third world man," to the crowd's delight. Meanwhile, Alex plays some well-placed harmonics at the conclusion of "Between the Wheels."

SEPTEMBER 30, 1984
UNIONDALE, NEW YORK
NASSAU COUNTY VETERANS MEMORIAL COLISEUM, 1255 Hempstead Turnpike. Venue dedicated on May 29, 1972.
SUPPORT ACT: Helix
TICKETS: $12.50 / $14.50 (average: $13.95)
ATTENDANCE: 11,947
CAPACITY: 12,500
CONCERT GROSS: $166,708
NOTES: After the concert, Howard continued an annual tradition of having the dressing room transformed into a Japanese sushi bar. Alex opened up several bottles of Dom Perignon and led everyone in a toast.
BRIAN VOLLMER (HELIX LEAD VOCALIST): "It was at Nassau Coliseum, playing with Rush, that we heard *Walking the Razor's Edge* had gone gold in Canada. Two weeks later it went platinum, and everything started to go crazy. Years later, Alex and I would be in the same

scenes in *Countdown to Liquor Day*, the second *Trailer Park Boys* movie. I spent a crazy night with Alex the day before shooting. Can't get into that one—might be a libel suit. LOL."[21]

OCTOBER 2–3, 1984
WORCESTER, MASSACHUSETTS
THE CENTRUM, 50 Foster Street. Venue opened on September 2, 1982.
SUPPORT ACT: Fastway
TICKETS: $12.50 / $13.50
TWO-DAY WORCESTER ATTENDANCE: 21,319
TWO-DAY CAPACITY: 22,862
TWO-DAY WORCESTER CONCERT GROSS: $284,382
NOTES: The Three Stooges intro theme started early, forcing the band to race for the stage. Once onstage, they all laughed as they caught their breath. After the gig, Alex and Geddy unwound by watching a baseball game on TV, while Neil did an interview for *Circus* magazine.
CIRCUS: "At the Worcester Centrum, Rush pulled off a triumph themselves, proving that lingering rumors and the band's worst fears were groundless: rumors that the Canadian trio was fragmenting after years of almost non-stop touring."

OCTOBER 4, 1984
ROCHESTER, NEW YORK
ROCHESTER COMMUNITY WAR MEMORIAL, 100 Exchange Boulevard. Venue opened on October 18, 1955.
SUPPORT ACT: Fastway
TICKETS: $12.50 / $13.50, general admission
ATTENDANCE: 10,200; sold out
CONCERT GROSS: $126,539

OCTOBER 6, 1984
DAYTON, OHIO
UNIVERSITY OF DAYTON ARENA, 1801 Edwin C. Moses Blvd. Venue opened on December 6, 1969.
SUPPORT ACT: Fastway
TICKETS: $12.50
ATTENDANCE: 7,282

CAPACITY: 10,500
CONCERT GROSS: $91,025
NOTES: Rescheduled from July 10. Alex broke a string during "YYZ."

OCTOBER 7, 1984
COLUMBUS, OHIO
OHIO EXPO CENTER COLISEUM, Ohio State Fairgrounds, 717 East 17th Street. Venue opened on October 18, 1917.
SUPPORT ACT: Fastway
TICKETS: $13.50
ATTENDANCE: 6,534; sold out
CONCERT GROSS: $87,668 (promoter data: $84,669)
NOTES: Venue nicknamed "the Barn."

OCTOBER 18, 1984
TOLEDO, OHIO
SPORTS ARENA, 1 North Main Street. Venue opened on November 13, 1947.
SUPPORT ACT: Fastway
TICKETS: $12.00, general admission
CAPACITY: 7,000
TOLEDO BLADE: "Rush Proves it Outreaches its Heavy-Metal-Band Tag: While many people in the music industry slap a heavy metal tag on Rush, this Canadian trio proved last night that it defies categorization. The crowd proved to be quite lively, bursting into one of the more crazed greetings a band has received in the Sports Arena in the recent past. Few groups can reproduce their studio sound on stage as faithfully and precisely as Rush did last night."[22]

OCTOBER 19, 1984
SAGINAW, MICHIGAN
WENDLER ARENA AT SAGINAW CIVIC CENTER, 303 Johnson Street. Venue opened on October 15, 1972.
SUPPORT ACT: Fastway
TICKETS: $13.50
ATTENDANCE: 6,582; sold out
CONCERT GROSS: $88,857

OCTOBER 21, 1984
LEXINGTON, KENTUCKY
RUPP ARENA, 430 West Vine Street. Venue opened on October 7, 1976.
SUPPORT ACT: Fastway
TICKETS: $11.75 / $12.75
ATTENDANCE: 5,771
CAPACITY: 13,346
CONCERT GROSS: $73,476
HERALD-LEADER: "New Material aids

Rush show: A much-improved Rush returned to Rupp Arena last night and put on their best show yet. All in all, it was a big improvement for Rush. If the group can keep the momentum of *Grace Under Pressure* on its next album, sharpen its lyrical approach, and tone down Neil Peart a bit, the next Rupp show may be quite an event."

OCTOBER 23, 1984
MEMPHIS, TENNESSEE
MID-SOUTH COLISEUM, Memphis Fairgrounds Park, 996 Early Maxwell Blvd. Venue opened on December 2, 1964.
TICKETS: $12.50 (all seats reserved)
SUPPORT ACT: Fastway
ATTENDANCE: 5,124
CAPACITY: 9,800
CONCERT GROSS: $64,050

OCTOBER 24, 1984
JACKSON, MISSISSIPPI
MISSISSIPPI COLISEUM, State Fairgrounds complex, 1207 Mississippi Street. Venue opened on June 7, 1962.
SUPPORT ACT: Fastway
TICKETS: $12.50 (all seats), general admission
ATTENDANCE: 2,945
CAPACITY: 8,000
CONCERT GROSS: $36,812

OCTOBER 26, 1984
BILOXI, MISSISSIPPI
MISSISSIPPI COAST COLISEUM, 2350 Beach Boulevard. Venue opened on November 1, 1977.
SUPPORT ACT: Fastway
TICKETS: $12.50, general admission
CAPACITY: 15,000 (Anthem/SRO)
NOTES: According to fan accounts, this gig was "packed."

94 QID Welcomes
RUSH
IN CONCERT
MISSISSIPPI COAST COLISEUM
26
OCT
1984
BILOXI, MS
FRIDAY
8:00 P.M.
A BRASS RING PRODUCTION
$12.50
GEN. ADM.
10300

OCTOBER 27, 1984
NEW ORLEANS, LOUISIANA
UNO LAKEFRONT ARENA, University of New Orleans East Campus, 6801 Franklin Street. Venue opened on November 1, 1983.

SUPPORT ACT: Fastway
TICKETS: $13.50, general admission
ATTENDANCE: 7,000; sold out
CONCERT GROSS: $94,500

OCTOBER 29, 1984
NASHVILLE, TENNESSEE
NASHVILLE MUNICIPAL AUDITORIUM, 417 Fourth Avenue North. Venue opened on October 7, 1962.
SUPPORT ACT: Fastway
TICKETS: $11.50 (limited advance) / $12.50 (all remaining tickets); average: $12.21
ATTENDANCE: 8,393
CAPACITY: 9,900
CONCERT GROSS: $102,514

OCTOBER 30, 1984
ATLANTA, GEORGIA
THE OMNI, 100 Techwood Drive Northwest. Venue opened on October 14, 1972.
SUPPORT ACT: Fastway
TICKETS: $13.50
ATTENDANCE: 13,364; sold out
CONCERT GROSS: $180,414

NOVEMBER 1, 1984
CHARLESTON, WEST VIRGINIA
CHARLESTON CIVIC CENTER COLISEUM, 200 Civic Center Drive. Venue dedicated on August 3, 1980.
SUPPORT ACT: Y&T
TICKETS: $12.50 (all seats)
ATTENDANCE: 4,166
CAPACITY: 10,000
CONCERT GROSS: $52,075

NOVEMBER 2, 1984
JOHNSON CITY, TENNESSEE
FREEDOM HALL CIVIC CENTER, 1320 Pactolas Road. Venue opened on July 5, 1974.
SUPPORT ACT: Y&T
TICKETS: $12.50, general admission
ATTENDANCE: 3,626
CONCERT GROSS: $45,325
GEDDY (BACKSTAGE AFTER DINNER): "We're just getting ourselves psyched up for making another record. Originally, our tour was supposed to go a couple of weeks longer, but we're starting to have a lot of good ideas, and we're talking about what we want to do next and getting itchy to get into the studio. So we cut our tour short a little bit so that we can start working on some new material."[23]

NOVEMBER 3, 1984
HAMPTON, VIRGINIA
HAMPTON COLISEUM, 1000 Coliseum Drive. Venue opened on January 31, 1970.
SUPPORT ACT: Y&T
TICKETS: $12.50 (advance) / $13.50 (day of), general admission
ATTENDANCE: 13,800 (approximate); sold out[24]
DAILY PRESS (NEWPORT NEWS): "Lifeson thrilled the crowd with his exceptional guitar playing, whether he was gently stroking chords or hitting harsh notes."

NOVEMBER 5-6, 1984
PHILADELPHIA, PENNSYLVANIA
THE SPECTRUM, 3601 South Broad Street. Venue opened on October 1, 1967.
SUPPORT ACT: Y&T
TICKETS: $9.50 / $11.50 / $13.50
ATTENDANCE: 15,435 per show; sold out
CONCERT GROSS: $188,231.50 per show
NOTES: On the November 5 date, Howard implemented some new lighting changes during "Red Lenses." As Geddy sang: "You see black and white. I see red—not blue," the lights follow the same pattern, in perfect time. The result was quite stunning. Following a brilliant show, band and crew enjoyed the end-of-tour party on the historic tall ship *Moshulu* (1904), which is docked at Penn's Landing along the Delaware River. The festive affair, which included a live band, lasted well into the early morning. Second show, added due to popular demand, also sold out.
LEONARD HAZE (Y&T DRUMMER): "An hour before each show, we were asked to be quiet backstage [while Alex, Geddy, and Neil took French lessons]. Not easy for us, considering that we had just finished touring with Mötley Crüe. So it was a major effort to settle down, but we accomplished it. The end-of-tour party in Philly was a great time. It was on a tall ship in the river with so much food and booze on it. At the party I thanked Neil for the dates, and he said something like, 'We liked your ability, that's why we picked you.' That was a very cool thing for him to say."[25]
GEDDY: "After Philly, we have a date in Providence, and then we have a few days

off before we go to Japan. We're going to play there, and then the last date of the tour is going to be in Hawaii. So, we'll go down there for about two weeks. It's going to be fun. We tried to go to Bangkok, but we couldn't get a show that worked in the right time frame. If we played there, we were definitely going to play 'A Passage to Bangkok.' Not sure I'd bring out the doubleneck—we could do a different version."[26]

NOVEMBER 7, 1984
PROVIDENCE, RHODE ISLAND
PROVIDENCE CIVIC CENTER, 1 La Salle Square. Venue opened on November 3, 1972.
SUPPORT ACT: Y&T
TICKETS: $11.50 / $12.50 (average: $12.32)
ATTENDANCE: 11,357
CAPACITY: 12,159
CONCERT GROSS: $139,875
NOTES: Originally slated for September 25, but rescheduled because of illness. At the gig, Alex, Geddy, and Neil were introduced to their future producer, Peter Collins.

NOVEMBER 16, 1984
SETO-SHI, AICHI PREFECTURE, JAPAN
SITO-SHI BUNKA HALL (CULTURE HALL), Seto City Cultural Center, 113-3 Nishiibara-cho
AN EVENING WITH RUSH
TICKETS: 4,500 JPY
ATTENDANCE: 1,871
CAPACITY: 2,000
NOTES: The crowds were subdued compared to what Rush was accustomed to, but the band was well received, and the concert well attended. In an effort to minimize shipping costs, Rush used mainly rented gear in Japan, though Alex and Geddy played their own guitars. Alex was unhappy with the amp line, stating, "Next time, I'd bring my own gear."[27] Tama drums, headquartered in Seto-shi, made a special replica kit just for Neil. (As with the previous year's Radio City dates, the riser didn't spin, so Neil played with his back to the audience for the arrangements that involved the electronic drums.)

NOVEMBER 18, 1984
FUKUOKA-SHI, FUKUOKA PREFECTURE, JAPAN
FUKUOKA SUN PALACE GREAT HALL, Fukuoka Sun Palace Hotel, 2-1 Chikkohon-machi, Hakata Ward
AN EVENING WITH RUSH
TICKETS: 4,500 JPY
ATTENDANCE: 2,316; sold out
NOTES: At the Japanese shows, no pyro or lasers were used, and all of the concerts started at the early time of 6:30. A half hour before each gig, the concert regulations were read in both English and Japanese: "Please do not leave your seats and go into the aisles, or stand on your seats, or rush the stage. No smoking is allowed, and please do not light matches during or prior to the encore. If those cautions cannot be followed, we may be forced to cancel the concert."

NOVEMBER 19, 1984
OSAKA, JAPAN
On a day off, the Japanese promoter took the band and crew out to a posh restaurant for a huge Japanese feast. Back at the hotel bar, everyone met up around midnight for an impromptu party. After the bar closed, in the wee hours of November 20, Neil and two crew members walked into the lobby, where they witnessed a man beating a woman in the middle of one of the most elegant hotels in Osaka. The only other people around, the hotel clerks, ignored the whole affair, leaving Neil stunned. After a moment, Neil shouted, "Knock it the fuck off!" The man then began to kick even harder. Alex, Geddy, Liam, and the promoter's liaison, Yoshi, walked over to see what was going on. A plea for help from the front desk yielded no response as the man caught up with the fleeing woman and began striking her yet again. Eventually, she stopped moving altogether. As Yoshi attempted to close an unbridgeable cultural gap, saying, "It's okay, it happens all the time . . . it's not your affair . . . just go to the elevator," he unsuccessfully tried to push Rush and their entourage onto the elevator. Meanwhile, the man then began venting his anger at the band. Hurrying over to the other side of the lobby, he picked up a steel crowd controller and headed toward the group. Alex, Geddy, and Neil now faced a big

man waving a large weapon, poised to attack the entire entourage, repeating, "My wife! My wife!" in English. With a truly classic display of "grace under pressure," Alex walked right up to the man with a smile on his face and said, "I wish you come to my country of Canada," which caused the man to relax for a moment and lower the steel stand. Then Alex added, "so I could kick the living shit out of you." As the man picked the stand back up, security guards finally arrived and pushed everyone into the elevator. In the confusion, Neil spat on the man. During the ensuing angry elevator ride, Liam repeatedly shouted, "I can't believe this!" and suddenly punched the compartment wall with all of his might, which resulted in a broken hand. "Many Western bands have seen similar sights and closed their eyes," Yoshi later commented. "This is the first time that I have ever seen such a reaction by a band."[28]

NOVEMBER 20, 1984
OSAKA-SHI, OSAKA PREFECTURE, JAPAN
OSAKA FURITSU TAIIKUKAIN (OSAKA PREFECTURAL GYMNASIUM), 3-4-36 Nanbanaka, Naniwa Ward. Venue opened in December 1952.
AN EVENING WITH RUSH
TICKETS: 3,000 / 4,000 JPY
ATTENDANCE: 4,652; sold out (3,131 fixed seats)
NOTES: Rush gave a strong performance. Although fans clapped in time with much of the music, between songs, it was so quiet that you could hear a pin drop. An American fan was heard yelling for "Caress of Steel" during one break. During Neil's solo, the capacity crowd clapped in time with the infamous cowbell section. During the "Red Lenses" encore, fans clapped throughout, with Geddy wailing away on the bass where the drum solo had been. In the car back to the hotel, Neil expressed concern over the band's future writing sessions and the fact that he would soon have to write an album's worth of lyrics, which was foremost in his mind.
GEDDY (ONSTAGE): "*Domo arigato*! It's nice to be here in Osaka."
JAPANESE FAN: "It was a great show from beginning to end! I have all of their albums. The ones they don't sell in Japan, I got from America."[29]

AMERICAN FAN: "I'm in Japan to see Rush! We're with the Marines here recruiting, and we're big Rush fans from way back. The audiences here in Japan are a lot more subdued. We try to get them rockin', but sometimes it doesn't work."[30]

JAPANESE FAN: "It was a great show tonight. They have good technique. The highlights were: 'YYZ,' 'Tom Sawyer,' 'The Body Electric,' and the drum solo. Neil Peart is so great! He is the best drummer I have ever seen."[31]

NOVEMBER 21, 1984
TOKYO, JAPAN

NIPPON BUDOKAN, Kitanomaru Park, 2-3 Kitanomaruken. Historic venue opened on October 3, 1964.

AN EVENING WITH RUSH
TICKETS: 3,000 / 3,900 JPY
ATTENDANCE: 11,431; sold out
NOTES: The band took the famous bullet train to Tokyo. En route, they passed Mount Fuji and several Japanese baseball stadiums. Fans waited at the station to see the band, but were very polite, and if they were told no photos or autographs, they just smiled and left the band alone. Alex and Geddy signed a few autographs, but their primary focus was getting to the hotel. At the show, a 30 percent American presence in the crowd really energized the proceedings, giving the atmosphere a much rowdier feel than the previous three gigs. After the performance, the president of CBS/Sony Records took the band out for dinner. Later, the entourage headed to the Tokyo Bar for a night of partying. The band had an early morning flight the next day, so Geddy, Alex, and Neil made a pact to stay up all night. "Whomever falls asleep, we'll stick with a pin until they wake up," declared a laughing Alex.

TOSHIO OZAWA (PRESIDENT CBS/SONY GROUP OF JAPAN): "That is the best audience response to a concert that I have ever seen. I loved the lights."[32]

NEIL: "It was interesting to finally play in Japan. We have been trying to get there for years now. The best part of the trip was a brief trip to Hong Kong, Macao, and a daylong bus trip into China. Amazing! Of course what we saw was such a small part of such an enormous country, so many images and

ideas to try to absorb and evaluate—it's not really possible. Geddy and I were discussing on the plane to Hawaii whether or not our trip to China was a 'setup,' but decided that it wasn't really nice enough to be a special 'tourist trap.' It's no wonder they have no unemployment there. There is no mechanical aid except for these ancient little garden tractors, people were quarrying stone with hammers and chisels, and I counted nine people down on their hands and knees in the middle of a road painting white lines on it—by hand. One with a little brush would outline it, then the medium and larger brushes would fill it in, one by one. Wild!"

NOVEMBER 24–25, 1984
HONOLULU, HAWAII

NBC ARENA, Neal Blaisdell Center, 777 Ward Avenue. Venue dedicated on September 12, 1964.
SUPPORT ACT: Strict-Neine
TICKETS: $15.00
TWO-DAY HONOLULU ATTENDANCE: 11,450
TWO-DAY CAPACITY: 15,600
TWO-DAY HONOLULU CONCERT GROSS: $168,750
NOTES: During these two Honolulu

dates, lasers and pyro were added back into the set. On both nights, the venue was engulfed in a massive cloud of pungent marijuana, with a large contingent of female fans in attendance. Onstage during "Subdivisions" on November 24, Geddy added some extra emphasis to the lyrics: "Backs of cars!" and a second scream "Of youth!" During the "Red Lenses" encore, the band was in a festive mood, with Ged adding the line "I said I'm talking about big Ed. Big Ed's all red." During sound check on November 25, Geddy played keyboards and sang a few lines of "Losing It." Appropriately, fans left the venue to the sounds of "Take Me Out to the Ballgame," the band's exit music for the entire outing. Geddy's wife, Nancy, flew in, and the couple spent a weeklong second honeymoon in Hawaii.

GEDDY (ONSTAGE ON NOVEMBER 25): "Thank you, aloha, good evening. I don't know if you know that this is the very last gig on the *Grace Under Pressure* tour. So, we'd like to thank you."

1. Bill Banasiewicz. Interview with Alex Lifeson, May 9, 1984.
2. Bill Banasiewicz. Interview with Geddy Lee, May 8, 1984.
3. Bill Banasiewicz. Interview with Alex Lifeson, May 9, 1984.
4. Bill Banasiewicz. Interview with Geddy's physician, May 9, 1984.
5. Bill Banasiewicz. Interview with Larry Allen, May 9, 1984.
6. *Salt Lake Tribune.*
7. *News Tribune.*
8. Bill Banasiewicz. Interview with Howard Ungerleider, June 10, 1984.
9. Bill Banasiewicz. Interview with Bob Daisley, February 20, 2015.
10. Bill Banasiewicz. Interview with Howard Ungerleider, June 10, 1984.
11. *Milwaukee Sentinel.*
12. *Star and Tribune.*
13. Neil Peart. "Turn of The Century," unpublished magazine article, 1984.
14. *Akron Beacon Journal.*
15. Interview with Alex Lifeson. Gibson.com, February 18, 2011.
16. *Buffalo News*, July 13, 1984.
17. *Le Soleil.*
18. Bill Banasiewicz. Interview with Eddie Clarke, February 14, 2015.
19. *Canadian Musician*, May 1985.
20. Bill Banasiewicz. Interview with Pat McManus, October 2, 2015.
21. Bill Banasiewicz. Interview with Brian Vollmer, February 16, 2015.
22. *The Blade*, October 19, 1984.
23. Bill Banasiewicz. Interview with Geddy Lee, November 2, 1984.
24. *Daily Press.*
25. Bill Banasiewicz. Interview with Leonard Haze, February 17, 2015.
26. Bill Banasiewicz. Interview with Geddy Lee, November 2, 1984.
27. Bill Banasiewicz. Interview with Alex Lifeson, November 21, 1984.
28. Bill Banasiewicz. Interview with Yoshi, November 19, 1984.
29. Bill Banasiewicz. Fan interviews, November 20, 1984.
30. Bill Banasiewicz. Fan interviews, November 20, 1984.
31. Bill Banasiewicz. Fan interviews, November 20, 1984.
32. Bill Banasiewicz. Interview with Toshio Ozawa, November 21, 1984.

Chapter 18
SPRING TRAINING 1985

The 1985 "Spring Training Tour," as the band called it, allowed Rush to dust off some cobwebs prior to recording *Power Windows*. Over the course of four Florida shows in a five-day period, Rush performed to 32,461 fans. The outing also allowed Geddy to indulge in one of his favorite pastimes: attending baseball games. The set list was similar to that of the original *Grace Under Pressure* show, but with early versions of "The Big Money" and "Middletown Dreams" replacing "Kid Gloves," which had been dropped in Japan.

"I remember 'The Big Money' really improved after that," Geddy recalled. "We got the right kind of rock-out attitude in certain parts of the song; when we played it, certain parts of the song got an instant cheer. And that kind of thing is a great confidence builder."

Two additional *Power Windows* tracks, "Marathon" and "Mystic Rhythms," were performed at sound checks.

"Looking down from a hotel room window in Miami, you see hundreds of shiny bodies baking in the Florida sun," remarked Neil about being ensconced in the Sunshine State. "The heat feels good after the long Canadian winter, but with another show tonight, you're not really relaxed. Putting your coffee cup down, you put on your headphones and have a listen to the five new songs. The pool looks inviting down there, and white sails drift across the blue sea. As ever, we are out doing a few shows before going into the studio, to sharpen up our playing skills and give us a chance to play some of the new songs live and at sound checks."

OPPOSITE TOP: Lakeland, FL; Alex chatting with engineer Jimbo "J.J." Barton while J.J. works on his guitar at the Civic Center.

OPPOSITE BOTTOM: Lakeland, FL; Alex and Neil discussing one of their new songs while rehearsing at the Civic Center.

LEFT: Dunedin, FL; Geddy taking in a Blue Jays game at Grant Field with John Candy in the background.

TOP: Lakeland, FL; Howard's lighting console at the Civic Center.
ABOVE: Lakeland, FL; Geddy in rehearsal at the Civic Center.

TOUR HISTORY
"SPRING TRAINING" '85 TOUR

SET LIST:
Intro (Three Stooges theme)
"The Spirit of Radio"
"Subdivisions"
"The Body Electric"
"The Enemy Within"
"The Weapon"
"Witch Hunt"
"The Big Money" (prerelease version)
"New World Man"

"Between the Wheels"
"Red Barchetta"
"Distant Early Warning"
"Red Sector A"
"Closer to the Heart"
"Middletown Dreams" (prerelease version)
"YYZ"
"2112: The Temples of Syrinx"
"Tom Sawyer"

Encore:
"Red Lenses" (with drum solo)
"Vital Signs"
"Finding My Way"
"In the Mood"

MARCH 11–12, 1985
LAKELAND, FLORIDA
LAKELAND CIVIC CENTER, 701 West Lime Street. Venue dedicated on November 14, 1974.
AN EVENING WITH RUSH
TICKETS: $14.00, general admission
TWO-DAY ATTENDANCE: 16,875
TWO-DAY CAPACITY: 20,000
TWO-DAY CONCERT GROSS:
$232,890
NOTES: The opening date of the 1985 Spring Training Tour featured the live debut of "The Big Money" and "Middletown Dreams." All four of the completed new songs, including, "Mystic Rhythms" and "Marathon," were performed at sound check. In the afternoon, Geddy went to a Phillies–Mets game in Clearwater, where he was excited to see pitching legend Steve Carlton for the first time. In later years, it was revealed that Carlton's two sons were big Rush fans, and they presented the band with jerseys from their father. The game went extra innings, so Geddy, recalling what happened last tour in Dallas, left early, but still encountered stopped traffic on I-4. His driver traveled for miles on the shoulder, delivering him to Lakeland just in time for the start of sound check.

GEDDY (ONSTAGE): "You look marvelous! Absolutely marvelous! We'd like to do a marvelous new song for you. This is going to be on our next record, probably. This is called 'The Big Money.'"

NEIL: "At Lakeland, we met up with 'Jimbo' Barton for the first time, the irrepressible Australian who will be our engineer on this album. He has been recommended by our new producer, Peter Collins, and is full of high spirits and confidence. He's sure he can make my drums sound 'a hundred percent bettah!' We'll see. He's a nice dresser, though."[1]

MARCH 14, 1985
NORTH FORT MYERS, FLORIDA
LEE COUNTY CIVIC CENTER, 11831 Bayshore Road, Route 78. Venue opened in October 1978.
TICKETS: $14.00, general admission (including parking and fees)
ATTENDANCE: 4,375
CAPACITY: 4,500
CONCERT GROSS: $56,875
NOTES: In the morning, Neil was poolside, playing air drums to "Marabi" and "Champion (of the World)," the two songs he'd soon be recording with former Bill Bruford bassist Jeff Berlin. After a Royals game in the blistering heat, it was off to sound check, where Geddy recognized a Detroit fan outside the venue from the two Lakeland gigs. He got him a pass and invited him in to sound check. During the show, Geddy welcomed the crowd to "his" civic center.

GEDDY (ONSTAGE): "Well, hello, and welcome to my civic center!"

MARCH 15, 1985
PEMBROKE PINES, FLORIDA
HOLLYWOOD SPORTATORIUM, 17171 Pines Boulevard (Route 820). Venue opened in September 1970.
TICKETS: $14.00 (including one-dollar parking fee)
ATTENDANCE: 11,211
CAPACITY: 11,500
CONCERT GROSS: $144,885
NOTES: Final live performance of "The Enemy Within." During the afternoon, Geddy took in an Expos game in Pompano. Montreal pitcher Bryn Smith gave him a tour of the locker room and introduced him to some of the players, who followed him back to the gig. After sound check, the Expos pitchers shared some trade secrets while tossing the baseball around outside the venue. During the show, Geddy had an equipment issue after "Witch Hunt," so Alex and Neil improvised and got the whole venue clapping along. As "Tom Sawyer" started, a rowdy mob overran security down front, creating a general admission floor, with chairs left in a tangled mess.

THE PALM BEACH POST: "Rock Group Delivers 'Rush' of Excitement: Rush whipped their audience to a frenzy. 'Big Money,' a brand-new song, sounded incredibly strong."

VANCE LAW (EXPOS THIRD BASEMAN): "You're the guys who play 'The Trees.' I love that song."[2]

BRYN SMITH (EXPOS PITCHER): "I have been a fan of Rush since I was a teenager. I love how they still manage to let their music grow from album to album."[3]

1. Neil Peart. "Looking Through Power Windows," *Power Windows Tour Book,* 1985.
2. Bill Banasiewicz. Interview with Vance Law, March 15, 1985.
3. Bill Banasiewicz. Interview with Bryn Smith.

Chapter 19

THE POWER WINDOWS TOUR

T he *Power Windows* tour saw Rush perform to 710,613 fans over the course of sixty-nine shows. The set list was fine-tuned during the first week: "The Weapon" was only played the first two nights, and "Witch Hunt" was added beginning with the second show (following "The Weapon," which was permanently dropped as of the third gig). Starting on the sixth date of the tour, "Witch Hunt" was moved up in the set list to follow "Middletown Dreams." Additionally, "New World Man" was dropped for the last month of the jaunt, sometime after April 22, 1986. It would not be performed again until 2002's *Vapor Trails* tour.

For these shows, the band also began using more electronic elements. Said Alex, "When we started preparing for concert rehearsals, Geddy went in with Jim Burgess, a programmer in Toronto that we use for a lot of stuff, and he set it up so that we got a lot of the sequenced parts down on an Emulator [a digital sampling keyboard]. They're constantly being programmed throughout the evening for the different songs. We put all the old synth sounds from the Oberheims and the Minimoogs onto the Emulator. We condensed the whole keyboard setup and made it a little more sophisticated."

Additionally, Rush's stage show featured plenty of lasers, lights, smoke, video screen

projections, and other visual stimuli, which one magazine reviewer praised as "guaranteed to satisfy the *Star Wars* generation." But with the added effects came added risk. At the San Diego Sports Arena on February 3, the sound went out twice. The first occurred halfway into "Marathon"; following a brief pause, Geddy, Alex, and Neil started the song over from the beginning. The second outage hit toward the end of "Distant Early Warning." It was determined that the lasers were draining too much of the venue power supply, so they were cut from the rest of the set.

The band members were becoming increasingly aware of the hazards posed by the more elaborate stage production. "When I'm playing a show," said Neil, "it's so concentrated and there is so much to worry about and there are many things that can go wrong, and with the number of electronics we've grown into, the level of possibility for breakdown increases."

Taking a more lighthearted approach to the mishaps at the San Diego Sports Arena, Geddy remarked from the stage, "Guess what? We blew this place up! We got everything going now. I think it's just going to take us a couple of minutes to make sure all of these fancy electronic gizmos are plugged back in. That was pretty weird, wasn't it? It seems like the gods of electricity are conspiring against us this evening."

OPPOSITE: Philadelphia, PA; Geddy performing with his black Steinberger at the Spectrum.

LEFT: Alex and Geddy onstage.

ABOVE: Philadelphia, PA; Geddy onstage.

TOUR HISTORY
POWER WINDOWS

Columbus, Ohio
Baltimore, Md.
Toronto, Ontario
London, Ontario
Hamilton, Ont.
Waterloo, Ont.
Kingston, Ont.
Brantford, Ont.
Ottawa, Ont.
Mt. Prospect, Ill.
Sioux City, Iowa
Long Beach, Calif.
Sacramento, Calif.
Fresno, Calif.
Medford, Oregon
Seattle, Wash.
Spokane, Wash.
Portland, Oregon
Yakima, Wash.
Pittsburgh, Penn.
Indianapolis, Ind.
South Bend, Ind.
Waukegan, Ill.
St. Louis, Mo.
Peoria, Ill.
Atlanta, Georgia
Akron, Ohio

SET LIST:
Intro (Three Stooges theme)
"The Spirit of Radio"
"Limelight"
"The Big Money"
"New World Man"
"Subdivisions"
"Manhattan Project"
"Middletown Dreams"
"Witch Hunt"
"Red Sector A"
"Closer to the Heart"
"Marathon"
"The Trees"
"Mystic Rhythms"
"Distant Early Warning"
"Territories"
"The Weapon"
"YYZ" (with drum solo)
"Red Lenses"
"Tom Sawyer"
Encore:
"2112: Overture"
"2112: The Temples of Syrinx"
"Grand Designs"
"In the Mood"

DECEMBER 4, 1985
PORTLAND, MAINE
CUMBERLAND COUNTY CIVIC CENTER, Spring Street at Center Street. Venue opened on March 3, 1977.
SUPPORT ACT: Steve Morse Band
TICKETS: $13.50, general admission
ATTENDANCE: 6,114
CAPACITY: 9,500
NOTES: The opening date of the 1985 *Power Windows* tour featured the live debut of "Grand Designs," "Manhattan Project," "Marathon," "Territories," and "Mystic Rhythms." Onstage, no pyro was used at this gig. This year's edition of "The Trees" highlighted a space-jam ending, complete with electronic barking dogs.
GEDDY (ONSTAGE): "As you may or may not know, this is the very first show on the *Power Windows* tour for us. We haven't been playing in a little while, so we hope that we don't make too many mistakes for ya tonight."
SWEET POTATO: "Say what you will about Rush; there's no group playing music more adventurous in rock and roll today. The band proved this to be true at the Civic Center. Together for eleven years, they don't need to exhort or browbeat their audience to excite them. Their skillful, ingenious music does all the work."

DECEMBER 5, 1985
PROVIDENCE, RHODE ISLAND
PROVIDENCE CIVIC CENTER, 1 La Salle Square. Venue opened on November 3, 1972.
SUPPORT ACT: Steve Morse Band
TICKETS: $13.50 / $14.50 (average: $14.05).
ATTENDANCE: 10,792 (Anthem/SRO); 11,330 (*Pollstar*); 11,033 (*Amusement Business*); sold out
CONCERT GROSS: $155,020
NOTES: Final live performance of "The Weapon." "Witch Hunt" was added to the set. For the 1985 version, Geddy popped the strings of his bass to replace the prominent keyboard accent after the line: "They say there is strangeness too dangerous."
GEDDY: "The show's not as tight as I'd like it to be. It's only the second show, and I've been battling a sore throat."[1]
THE PROVIDENCE JOURNAL: "Rush has the skill, but not the soul: Spark and imagination were absent from Rush's show, along with any glimmer of humor and warmth. This was one of those shows where, after the first hour or so, I hoped that each song would be the last. To my regret, and to the delight of a full house of thundering, mostly teenage fans, Rush kept on for a full two hours."

DECEMBER 7, 1985
NEW HAVEN, CONNECTICUT
NEW HAVEN VETERAN'S MEMORIAL COLISEUM, 275 South Orange Street. Venue opened on September 27, 1972.
SUPPORT ACT: Steve Morse Band
TICKETS: $12.50 / $14.50
ATTENDANCE: 7,099
NOTES: Before Rush's set, a local DJ came out and started screaming, "Are you ready for some rock 'n' roll? Rush! Rush! Rush!" causing Uncle Cliff Burnstein to sarcastically comment, "Just what this band needs." Onstage, Geddy's vocals were rough in spots, and the band seemed to be struggling with some of the new material. The timing of "New World Man" was off, with Alex breaking a string near the end of the song. Despite the occasional moments of brilliance, it was a somewhat tentative set, with no pyro. The uncharacteristically rocky performance led Uncle Cliff to ask the band (in his typical direct fashion) how long they had rehearsed for the tour. Regardless of the evening's challenges, Alex, Geddy, and Neil seemed to be in good spirits backstage.
HARTFORD COURANT: "Rush's Power Performance Is Big, Bold Even Literate: Rush's concert at New Haven Coliseum was an exercise in power. The emphasis was on the *Power Windows* tunes. Fortunately, songs such as 'The Big Money,' 'Marathon,' 'Territories,' 'Manhattan Project' and 'Middletown Dreams' are some of the band's best work—clean, crisp, and streamlined, but bigger than life, sort of high-tech heavy metal with a social conscience."

DECEMBER 8, 1985
HARTFORD, CONNECTICUT
CIVIC CENTER, 1 Civic Center Plaza. Venue opened on January 9, 1975.
SUPPORT ACT: Steve Morse Band
TICKETS: $12.50 / $14.50
ATTENDANCE: 10,595
NOTES: Afternoon sound check was very long, with a ticked-off band working very hard to smooth over any rough edges in the set. After dinner, Neil had a French lesson, while Alex read a paperback, and Geddy threw a baseball around inside the venue. Steve Morse's drummer, Rod Morgenstein soon came over, and Geddy gave him a Canadian history lesson in between hard tosses. As the discussion about Canada went on, Rod kept saying, "I didn't know that." For the show, the band instructed

their sound engineer, Jon Erickson, to record the gig, so they could play it back on the bus. For a Sunday night with no pyro, the crowd was fired up, and the band fed off the energy. Alex broke a string during "The Spirit of Radio" and again in "Grand Designs." For some reason, this would become a common occurrence during the *Power Windows* tour. It was a much better performance than the previous night's gig, though the band still wasn't satisfied. Backstage, they had a meeting with the Steve Morse Band to discuss problems with the onstage sound.

GEDDY (ONSTAGE): "I believe there's one [a town called Middletown] not too far from here. This is called 'Middletown Dreams.'"

DECEMBER 10, 1985
ROCHESTER, NEW YORK
ROCHESTER COMMUNITY WAR MEMORIAL, 100 Exchange Boulevard. Venue opened on October 18, 1955.
SUPPORT ACT: Steve Morse Band
TICKETS: $13.50 / $14.50, general admission
ATTENDANCE: 10,048 (Anthem/SRO); 10,200 (*Pollstar*); sold out
CONCERT GROSS: $135,716

DECEMBER 12–13, 1985
WORCESTER, MASSACHUSETTS
THE CENTRUM, 50 Foster Street. Venue opened on September 2, 1982.
SUPPORT ACT: Steve Morse Band
TICKETS: $13.50 / $14.50
ATTENDANCE (DEC. 12): 10,681 (Anthem/SRO); 10,625 (*Pollstar*); sold out
ATTENDANCE (DEC. 13): 10,282 (Anthem/SRO); 10,625 (*Pollstar*); sold out
CONCERT GROSS: $150,408 per show
NOTES: Early in the *Power Windows* tour, all of the film clips were not yet present. "The Big Money" had some video segments, while the "Overture" encore featured the *2112* star logo in laser form. As the tour progressed, video elements were added.
THE BOSTON GLOBE: "Rush comes through with drama, smarts: Rush has always longed to be taken seriously, writing complex songs with philosophical lyrics. At times, they've failed, carrying art-rock to excess. Happily, they've become stronger through the years. Most

of the show proved that Rush's present is far better than their past."

DECEMBER 15, 1985
RICHMOND, VIRGINIA
RICHMOND COLISEUM, 601 East Leigh Street. Venue dedicated on August 21, 1971.
SUPPORT ACT: Steve Morse Band
TICKETS: $13.50, general admission
ATTENDANCE: 7,829
RICHMOND TIMES-DISPATCH: "Non-Traditional Band Continues to Draw Crowds: Despite getting bogged down in a couple of overwrought compositions, Rush's performance last night sparkled. It's nice to hear a band that has followed its own musical instincts rather than commercial trends."

DECEMBER 16, 1985
LARGO, MARYLAND
CAPITAL CENTRE, 1 Harry S. Truman Drive. Venue opened on December 2, 1973.
SUPPORT ACT: Steve Morse Band
TICKETS: $14.50
ATTENDANCE: 16,040; 16,140 (*Amusement Business*)
CAPACITY: 16,500
CONCERT GROSS: $232,580
NOTES: During the encore ending of "In the Mood," Alex and Geddy hooked arms and swung each other around in circles.

DECEMBER 18, 1985
PITTSBURGH, PENNSYLVANIA
CIVIC ARENA, 300 Auditorium Place. Venue opened on September 17, 1961.

102.5FM WDVE Rocks
RUSH
WED. DEC. 18 CIVIC ARENA PGH

SUPPORT ACT: Steve Morse Band
TICKETS: $13.75 (all seats)
ATTENDANCE: 10,782 (Anthem/SRO); 11,053 (*Pollstar*)
CAPACITY: 17,500
CONCERT GROSS: $148,353
PITTSBURGH PRESS: "Rush keeps proving that they're no 'Fly by Night' rock band: Rush has survived for eleven years, no mean feat in the mercurial world of rock 'n' roll."

DECEMBER 19, 1985
RICHFIELD, OHIO
RICHFIELD COLISEUM, 2923 Streetsboro Road. Venue opened on October 26, 1974.
SUPPORT ACT: Steve Morse Band
TICKETS: $15.00 (all seats)
ATTENDANCE: 14,880
NOTES: Geddy's vocals went out during the second verse of "Red Sector A." Alex broke a guitar string during the encore of "The Temples of Syrinx," but he was quickly given another axe.
THE AKRON BEACON JOURNAL: "Though Fans Gush, Rush Should Hush: The films were more interesting than the music. Of course, that's not saying much. But then, neither was Rush."

JANUARY 9, 1986
PENSACOLA, FLORIDA
PENSACOLA CIVIC CENTER, 201 East Gregory Street. Venue opened on January 21, 1985.
SUPPORT ACT: Steve Morse Band
TICKETS: $14.50
ATTENDANCE: 5,426 (Anthem/SRO); 5,813 (*Pollstar*)
CAPACITY: 7,000
CONCERT GROSS: $78,677
NOTES: Geddy had some keyboard issues at the start of "Grand Designs." Alex broke a string during the solo to "The Trees," threw that guitar to the crew, grabbed a second guitar out of the air, hit a chord, and got nothing. He was quickly given a third guitar just in time for the final verse, making for a unique version of the song, including a bass solo.

JANUARY 10, 1986
LAFAYETTE, LOUISIANA
CAJUNDOME, 444 Cajundome Boulevard. Venue dedicated on November 10, 1985.
SUPPORT ACT: Steve Morse Band
TICKETS: $14.50
ATTENDANCE: 8,151

JANUARY 12–13, 1986
DALLAS, TEXAS
REUNION ARENA, 777 Sports Street. Venue dedicated on April 28, 1980.
SUPPORT ACT: Steve Morse Band
TICKETS: $15.95
ATTENDANCE (JAN. 12): 13,353 (Anthem/SRO); sold out
ATTENDANCE (JAN. 13): 11,344 (Anthem/SRO)
CAPACITY: 13,225
TWO-DAY DALLAS CONCERT GROSS: $371,182

JANUARY 15–16, 1986
HOUSTON, TEXAS
THE SUMMIT, 3700 Southwest Freeway. Venue opened on November 1, 1975.
SUPPORT ACT: Steve Morse Band
TICKETS: $13.65 / $15.65
ATTENDANCE (JAN. 15): 10,918 (Anthem/SRO); sold out
ATTENDANCE (JAN. 16): 7,257 (Anthem/SRO)
CAPACITY: 10,918
TWO-DAY HOUSTON CONCERT GROSS: $284,382; $272,569 (*Amusement Business*)
NOTES: The two Houston dates were the week's top-grossing concerts.[2]
HOUSTON CHRONICLE: "Almost a night of serious music with Rush: They've managed to retain their original heavy-metal following while attracting newcomers (hence, two shows during their Houston stopover), and a crowd of 14,000—mostly young, mostly male—howled and stomped their approval Wednesday."

JANUARY 18, 1986
AUSTIN, TEXAS
FRANK ERWIN SPECIAL EVENTS CENTER, University of Texas at Austin campus, 1701 Red River Street. Venue opened on November 29, 1977.
SUPPORT ACT: Steve Morse Band
TICKETS: $13.00 / $14.00 / $15.00 (average: $14.17)
ATTENDANCE: 13,671 (Anthem/SRO); 14,055 (*Pollstar*); sold out
CONCERT GROSS: $199,154

JANUARY 19, 1986
SAN ANTONIO, TEXAS
CONVENTION CENTER ARENA, HemisFair Park Complex, 601 Hemisfair Way. Venue opened on April 6, 1968.
SUPPORT ACT: Steve Morse Band
TICKETS: $14.00 / $14.50
ATTENDANCE: 9,397 (Anthem/SRO); 9,331 (*Pollstar*)
CAPACITY: 10,500
CONCERT GROSS: $135,486

JANUARY 30, 1986
DALY CITY, CALIFORNIA
COW PALACE, 2600 Geneva Avenue. Venue opened on April 20, 1941.
SUPPORT ACT: Steve Morse Band
TICKETS: $15.00
ATTENDANCE: 11,034 (Anthem/SRO); sold out
CONCERT GROSS: $165,510
NOTES: Expos pitcher Bryn Smith was in attendance, as were some members of Metallica. Howard was Metallica's road manager for a tour, and he was happy to reunite with guitarist Kirk Hammett in the afternoon. Sound check was an extended affair, as the band shook off the dust from their recent break, playing full songs with no jamming. Geddy concluded sound check with a solo version of "Subdivisions." The capacity crowd gave both bands a warm reception on this chilly evening. During Rush's performance, tunnels of laser light were created amid suspended clouds of smoke during "Mystic Rhythms." After the show, members of Metallica discussed their forthcoming album, *Master of Puppets*, with Geddy and Alex. Neil was suffering from the flu and was drained following his performance. Geddy and Bryn Smith headed out on the town. Inside a wharf-area club, a couple of Rush fans were freaked that Geddy was there, but they were polite and courteous.
GEDDY: "We just started getting our pace in the shows, then we take a ten-day break."[3]
BRYN SMITH (EXPOS PITCHER): "Without him knowing it, Ged helped me to be able to go out in front of 40,000 people and produce at a high level, and really kind of close everything out."[4]
KIRK HAMMETT (METALLICA GUITARIST): "[Rush] are one of the most consistent yet overlooked bands around. The amount of power and noise that they create out of just three musicians is really amazing. There's no one like them. Rush is like a combination of a Philip K. Dick novel and Cream. When they came out, they were in between Led Zeppelin, Black Sabbath, and us. They are so influential in the rock world."[5]

JANUARY 31, 1986
OAKLAND, CALIFORNIA
OAKLAND-ALAMEDA COUNTY COLISEUM ARENA, 7000 Coliseum Way. Venue opened on November 9, 1966.
SUPPORT ACT: Steve Morse Band
TICKETS: $16.00
ATTENDANCE: 13,711 (Anthem/SRO); sold out
CONCERT GROSS: $219,376
NOTES: Despite his bout with the flu, Neil was the first to arrive for afternoon sound check. He usually swam in the afternoon, then rode his bike to the gigs, but for these Bay Area concerts, it was quite enough for him to play the drums. The band put on an excellent show, and backstage, Neil, Alex, and Geddy were all pleased with the performance.

FEBRUARY 2, 1986
LAS VEGAS, NEVADA
THOMAS AND MACK CENTER, UNLV campus, 4505 South Maryland Parkway. Venue opened on September 16, 1983.
SUPPORT ACT: Steve Morse Band
TICKETS: $15.00
ATTENDANCE: 4,340 (Anthem/SRO); 4,530 (*Amusement Business*)
CAPACITY: 6,650
CONCERT GROSS: $65,100
NOTES: Geddy's keyboards faded in and out about halfway into "Manhattan Project." Video clips were added throughout the set, including an additional backdrop to "The Big Money," explosions and Hiroshima segments during "Manhattan Project," violins at the end of "Marathon," and visual stimuli for "Mystic Rhythms." The *2112* star logo during the "Overture" encore was now a video instead of a laser image.

GEDDY (ONSTAGE): "Nice to be here in Lost Wages, Nevada, to play for you."

FEBRUARY 3, 1986
SAN DIEGO, CALIFORNIA
SAN DIEGO SPORTS ARENA, 3500 Sports Arena Boulevard. Venue opened on November 17, 1966.
SUPPORT ACT: Steve Morse Band
TICKETS: $12.50 / $14.50 (average: $13.88)
ATTENDANCE: 10,817 (Anthem/SRO); 11,121 (*Pollstar*); sold out
CONCERT GROSS: $154,344
NOTES: During sound check, the band performed most of *Power Windows*, and it sounded quite good. After dinner, Geddy tossed the baseball around in a lit hallway until Steve Morse went on and the area went pitch-black, mid-toss. Neil was feeling much better, excited about the next day's bike ride to Los Angeles. Despite an otherwise great show, there were two sound outages during the set, but the lights remained on. After the show, the band was in good spirits despite the lapses in power. At the concert, thirty-six minors were arrested for underage drinking, causing the Sports Arena to introduce a stricter policy on alcohol sales.[6]

SAN DIEGO UNION: "Intellectual music gets lost in Rush: Despite all the care Rush put into the music, the group's excessive number of shifts and changes—designed to show off the impressive instrumental prowess of the Canadian trio—left precious little space for actual songs. Worse, when Rush did fall into a concise melody, singer Geddy Lee invariably had to open his mouth."

FEBRUARY 4, 1986
Neil bicycles from San Diego to Los Angeles
NEIL: "I spent my days off cycling around the countryside in the US, looking at these little towns and getting a new appreciation of them. When you pass through them at fifteen miles per hour, you see them a little differently. So I was looking at these places and kind of looking at the people in them—fantasizing, perhaps romanticizing, a little about their lives. I guess I was even getting a little literary in imagining the present, past, and future of these men, women, and children. There was that romantic way of looking at each small town."[7]

FEBRUARY 5–6, 1986
INGLEWOOD, CALIFORNIA
THE FORUM, 3900 West Manchester Boulevard. Venue opened on December 30, 1967.
SUPPORT ACT: Steve Morse Band
TICKETS: $15.00 / $16.50
ATTENDANCE: 12,225 per show (Anthem/SRO); 15,003 per show (*Pollstar*); sold out
CONCERT GROSS: $212,654.50 per show
NOTES: Members of Metallica, Van Halen, and Armored Saint were in attendance. During the afternoon, Geddy was excited because Jeff Berlin gave him a lesson on how to "pop" the bass strings. He walked around the dressing room popping the strings of Jeff Berlin's bass. Neil chimed in, "Great, now do it in 'Closer to the Heart.'" Sound check included "The Big Money," "Mystic Rhythms," and "Middletown Dreams," with little jamming. During the extended ending to "New World Man," Geddy had his bass strings popping. After the show, Ray talked Geddy into making an appearance at a party at the Forum Club. Meanwhile, Neil talked drumming with Rod Morgenstein into the night. On February 6, Neil hosted his first-ever drum clinic onstage during the early afternoon. Fifty students from the Percussion Institute of Technology gathered at center stage and Neil mesmerized them for some ninety minutes. Rush's two Forum dates were the week's top-grossing concerts.[8]

BILLBOARD: "The Mercury act offers neither sturm nor drang, yet excites the fans every bit as much as all David Lee Roth's acrobatics. Rush's worst vice is that the band can be, well, just plain boring. But it's also refreshing to see an act in the heavy metal genre that can satisfy its fans without pandering to them. There were more than 30,000 people who considered that they were given their money's worth and then some. Which, at today's ticket prices, is a feat."

ALEX VAN HALEN (VAN HALEN DRUMMER, BACKSTAGE AFTER THE SHOW): "Rush was all right. They reminded me of seeing the Who."[9]

JAMES HETFIELD (METALLICA GUITARIST / SINGER): "I also like Rush's Alex Lifeson—people wouldn't think of him as a rhythm player, but he comes up with some pretty amazing, offbeat things."[10]

NEIL (BACKSTAGE PRIOR TO DRUM CLINIC): "I thought it would be easier to hold the drum clinic onstage, with my drums already set up. This way, Larry wouldn't have to move them."[11]

FEBRUARY 8, 1986
PHOENIX, ARIZONA
ARIZONA VETERANS MEMORIAL COLISEUM, Arizona State Fairgrounds, 1826 West McDowell Road. Venue opened on November 3, 1965.
SUPPORT ACT: Steve Morse Band
TICKETS: $15.00, general admission
ATTENDANCE: 13,755 (Anthem/SRO); 12,755 (*Pollstar*); sold out
CONCERT GROSS: $191,325
NOTES: SRO data lists this date as February 9, but promoter documents and newspaper accounts indicate it was February 8.

JOHN KULON (BASSIST): "I was working at the Point at Squaw Peak in the cantina. I think it was 1985 and Rush had played in Phoenix, and they came in our little place for breakfast. Alex and Geddy had plates in hand, coming through the line. And I said, 'Hello, fellow bass player.'" This led to Kulon jamming with Rush and a bass lesson with Geddy.[12]

FEBRUARY 10, 1986
TUCSON, ARIZONA
TUCSON COMMUNITY CENTER ARENA, 260 South Church Street. Venue opened on November 8, 1971.
SUPPORT ACT: Steve Morse Band
TICKETS: $14.50 (all seats)
ATTENDANCE: 5,002
CAPACITY: 8,600
TUCSON CITIZEN: "Rush pushes to galactic dimensions: Rush had evolved from its original mythic pretensions to a band that favored more condensed artistic statements."

ARIZONA DAILY STAR: "Rush rocks on an intellectual plane."

FEBRUARY 12, 1986
ALBUQUERQUE, NEW MEXICO
TINGLEY COLISEUM, New Mexico State Fairgrounds, 300 San Pedro Drive Northeast. Venue dedicated on September 28, 1957.
SUPPORT ACT: Steve Morse Band
TICKETS: $13.75 (advance), general admission
ATTENDANCE: 3,345
NOTES: General admission show.
ALBUQUERQUE JOURNAL: "Rush Takes Audience Into 'Space Metal': Well-timed lighting, laser and explosive effects succinctly accented the numerous rhythm and chord changes and breaks in Rush's songs. Lee's high-pitched voice was clean and clear throughout the show. The sound in the coliseum was well-mixed but much too loud."

FEBRUARY 14, 1986
DENVER, COLORADO
MCNICHOLS SPORTS ARENA, 1635 Clay Street. Venue opened on August 22, 1975.
SUPPORT ACT: Steve Morse Band
TICKETS: $13.20 / $15.40 (average: $15.13)
ATTENDANCE: 11,474 (Anthem/SRO)
CAPACITY: 18,590
CONCERT GROSS: $173,562
NOTES: Steve Morse Band's final date with Rush.

FEBRUARY 27, 1986
BUFFALO, NEW YORK
BUFFALO MEMORIAL AUDITORIUM, 140 Main Street. Venue opened on October 14, 1940.
SUPPORT ACT: Marillion
TICKETS: $13.50 / $14.50
ATTENDANCE: 11,258
CAPACITY: 14,605
NOTES: Despite some initial tickets sold indicating the Steve Morse Band on the bill, Marillion opened the show.
GEDDY (ONSTAGE): "You look like a bunch of Buffalonians!"
MARK KELLY (MARILLION KEYBOARD-IST): "They came back and said, 'Please do it.' On the opening night, there was a bottle of champagne in our dressing room, saying, 'Welcome to the tour, hope you enjoy it!'"[13]
BUFFALO STATE RECORD: "The intensity of the entire two-hour performance was phenomenal. With hard, honest work and

an innovative use of their effects, Rush didn't have to hide behind their stage visuals. Three talented musicians have now come up with a show that is truly impressive."

FEBRUARY 28, 1986
HAMILTON, ONTARIO
COPPS COLISEUM, 101 York Boulevard. Venue opened in November 1985.
SUPPORT ACT: FM
TICKETS: $18.50 CAD
ATTENDANCE: 6,797
HAMILTON SPECTATOR: "New Rush Show Like a Breath of Fresh Air: This time out, the pacing was better organized. There were other playful moments—with either Geddy chasing Alex around the stage, or Alex chasing Geddy around the stage. It was refreshing to watch the guys fool around and have some fun. For fans of the band, they witnessed a superlative show. Rush isn't getting any older, just better."

MARCH 1, 1986
OTTAWA, ONTARIO
OTTAWA CIVIC CENTRE, Lansdowne Park, 1015 Bank Street. Venue opened on December 29, 1967.
SUPPORT ACT: FM
TICKETS: $17.50 CAD
ATTENDANCE: 7,421
CAPACITY: 8,000
CONCERT GROSS: $129,868 CAD

MARCH 3, 1986
QUEBEC CITY, QUEBEC
COLISÉE DE QUEBEC, 250 Boulevard Wilfrid-Hamel. Venue opened on December 8, 1949.
SUPPORT ACT: Marillion
TICKETS: $17.50 CAD
ATTENDANCE: 13,059; sold out
CONCERT GROSS: $228,532 CAD
LE SOLEIL: "13,000 Fans Du Rock Au Colisée: Rush presented an efficient, flawless, impeccable show in the good tradition of this Toronto group. Could we expect anything else from these perfectionists?"

MARK KELLY (MARILLION KEYBOARD-IST): "There were the Rush dates in '86, followed by our own, and [us] being absolutely amazed that we'd gone up a level because of the Rush dates—the support act doesn't normally get so much out of [opening], but we came back probably less than a year later, and in Quebec City we played the same venue that we opened for Rush at, which was 7,000 people."[14]

MARCH 4, 1986
MONTREAL, QUEBEC
MONTREAL FORUM, 2313 Saint Catherine Street West. Historic venue opened on November 29, 1924.
SUPPORT ACT: Marillion
TICKETS: $14.50 / $19.50 CAD
ATTENDANCE: 14,618; sold out
CONCERT GROSS: $283,481 CAD
NOTES: The band performed a lengthy sound check. Prior to the gig, Alex warmed up in the tuning room by playing "Stormy Monday Blues."
CIRCUS: "Fourteen thousand Montrealers have turned out to welcome Rush and its multimedia stage extravaganza. And with good reason. The one weakness Rush displays live is in the vocals; but Geddy Lee's voice is strong, melodic too, as it cuts through on 'Grand Designs,' his tour-de-force from *Power Windows.* Lifeson spins out some lovely lead acoustic guitar (suitably amplified for the Forum) on 'Mystic Rhythms.'"

MARCH 6–7, 1986
TORONTO, ONTARIO
MAPLE LEAF GARDENS, 60 Carlton Street. Historic venue opened on November 12, 1931.
SUPPORT ACT: FM
TICKETS: $19.50 CAD
ATTENDANCE (MAR. 6): 11,751
ATTENDANCE (MAR. 7): 10,394
CAPACITY: 12,000
TWO-DAY TORONTO CONCERT
GROSS: $431,827 CAD
NOTES: On March 6, the ending of "Subdivisions," with the CN Tower on the screen, brought the Toronto house down. During the "Grand Designs" encore, a fan jumped onto the stage near Alex but was quickly escorted off. On the second night, spotlights scanned the crowd during "Manhattan Project." During the drum solo, someone threw a glow stick that just missed Neil and his kit.

TORONTO STAR: "Prophets may not be loved in their hometowns, but you can bet your last power chord that rock bands are. The band looked young and fit despite its years on the road. The guys seemed to be having as much fun as the crowd."

MARCH 20, 1986
INDIANAPOLIS, INDIANA
MARKET SQUARE ARENA, 300 East Market Street. Venue opened on September 15, 1974.
SUPPORT ACT: Marillion
TICKETS: $13.50 / $14.50
ATTENDANCE: 10,100 (Anthem/SRO)
CAPACITY: 11,500
CONCERT GROSS: $146,450
GEDDY (ONSTAGE): "Looks like a bunch of Hoosiers out there! Yea, okay Hoosiers!"

MARCH 21–22, 1986
ROSEMONT, ILLINOIS
ROSEMONT HORIZON, 6920 N. Mannheim Road. Venue opened on July 2, 1980.
SUPPORT ACT: Marillion
TICKETS: $15.50 (all seats)
ATTENDANCE (MAR. 21): 13,491; sold out
ATTENDANCE (MAR. 22): 12,956

MARCH 24, 1986
MILWAUKEE, WISCONSIN
MECCA ARENA, 400 West Kilbourn Avenue. Venue opened on April 9, 1950.
SUPPORT ACT: Marillion
TICKETS: $14.50
ATTENDANCE: 8,883
CAPACITY: 11,000
CONCERT GROSS: $127,615
NOTES: No pyro at this gig. Alex broke a string during the bass and drum fill section of "YYZ" but was handed a new guitar just in time for his solo.

MARCH 25, 1986
ST. PAUL, MINNESOTA
ST. PAUL CIVIC CENTER, 143 West Fourth Street. Venue opened on January 1, 1973.
SUPPORT ACT: Marillion
TICKETS: $15.00
ATTENDANCE: 8,917 (Anthem/SRO)
CAPACITY: 15,406
CONCERT GROSS: $133,755
NOTES: Alex broke a string during "The Spirit of Radio" but was promptly given another guitar.

MARCH 28, 1986
DETROIT, MICHIGAN
JOE LOUIS ARENA, 600 Civic Center Drive. Venue opened on December 12, 1979.
SUPPORT ACT: Marillion
TICKETS: $15.00
ATTENDANCE: 15,036 (Anthem/SRO); 15,482 (*Amusement Business*); sold out
CONCERT GROSS: $232,230
MICHAEL ZACK (DETROIT FAN): "Aside from the crowd gathered up front during Marillion's set, few in the crowd dug their Genesis-inspired set. Some misdirected folks threw coins and miscellaneous items at the band, prompting lead singer Fish to walk to the edge of the stage and say something to the effect of 'For those of you not enjoying the show and throwing things up at the stage, these people up front have two words for you: FUCK OFF!'"

MARCH 29, 1986
CINCINNATI, OHIO
RIVERFRONT COLISEUM, 100 Broadway Street. Venue opened on September 9, 1975.
SUPPORT ACT: Marillion
TICKETS: $15.00
ATTENDANCE: 11,378

MARCH 31, 1986; APRIL 1, 1986
EAST RUTHERFORD, NEW JERSEY
MEADOWLANDS ARENA, Meadowlands Sports Complex, 50 State Route 120. Venue opened on July 2, 1981.
SUPPORT ACT: Marillion
TICKETS: $13.50 / $15.50
ATTENDANCE (MAR. 31): 17,160 (Anthem/SRO)
ATTENDANCE (APRIL 1): 13,849 (Anthem/SRO)

CAPACITY: 21,000
TWO-DAY EAST RUTHERFORD
CONCERT GROSS: $438,016
NOTES: Recorded to multitrack by Le Mobile, with "Mystic Rhythms" and "Witch Hunt" from these two Meadowlands dates later included on *A Show of Hands*. Before the gig, a certain tension was felt by the entire entourage, as everyone was focused on the evening's live recording. After sound check, Geddy altered some of his focus by tossing the baseball around, but he seemed to have a lot on his mind.
CREEM: "Rush—amazingly—manage to get a very full sound for a trio, and any audio problems Marillion experienced were not evident for the headliners. Even the huge stage seemed to be filled by the presence of Geddy Lee, Alex Lifeson, and Neil Peart. The visuals seem well thought-out, so as not to talk down to their fans. Judging by the drunken and stoned stupor many in the audience seemed to be in, it looks like Rush's music can be enjoyed on a number of levels."

APRIL 3, 1986
SPRINGFIELD, MASSACHUSETTS
SPRINGFIELD CIVIC CENTER, 1277 Main Street. Venue opened on September 22, 1972.
SUPPORT ACT: Marillion
TICKETS: $14.50, general admission
ATTENDANCE: 8,460
NOTES: Recorded to multitrack for possible future release. Guy Charbonneau engineered the taping in the Le Mobile recording truck, which was parked just outside of the venue. A video camera and television were set up so he could monitor the show in real time.

APRIL 4, 1986
UNIONDALE, NEW YORK
NASSAU COUNTY VETERANS MEMORIAL COLISEUM, 1255 Hempstead Turnpike. Venue dedicated on May 29, 1972.
SUPPORT ACT: Marillion
TICKETS: $14.50 / $16.50 (average: $15.96)
ATTENDANCE: 15,531 (Anthem/SRO); 15,931 (*Amusement Business*); sold out
CONCERT GROSS: $254,211
NOTES: Recorded to multitrack by Le Mobile for possible future release. Afternoon sound check included lots of

improvisation. Before the show, Geddy and Uncle Cliff reviewed picks for their rotisserie baseball team. After the gig, the dressing room was transformed into the annual Nassau sushi bar, where a good time was had by all, as fish and sake were consumed.

APRIL 13, 1986
BINGHAMTON, NEW YORK
BROOME COUNTY WAR MEMORIAL ARENA, 1 Stuart Street. Venue opened on August 29, 1973.
SUPPORT ACT: Blue Oyster Cult
TICKETS: $14.50 (advance) / $15.50 (day of)
ATTENDANCE: 7,061 (Anthem/SRO)
CONCERT GROSS: $102,754
NOTES: Recorded to multitrack by Le Mobile for possible future release.
PRESS AND SUN-BULLETIN: "Rush was in first class form as they pummeled and soared their way through the tight, exotic show. Most immediately noticeable was how well they worked together as a team."
GEDDY: "You'd be surprised. Sometimes when recording shows, the smaller secondary markets turn out to be the best ones, and the ones you'd use."[15]

APRIL 14, 1986; APRIL 16, 1986
PHILADELPHIA, PENNSYLVANIA
THE SPECTRUM, 3601 South Broad Street. Venue opened on October 1, 1967.
SUPPORT ACT: Blue Oyster Cult
TICKETS: $12.50 / $15.50; (two-day Philadelphia average: $14.89)
ATTENDANCE (APRIL 14): 14,549 (Anthem/SRO); 15,193 (*Pollstar*); sold out
ATTENDANCE (APRIL 16): 15,279 (Anthem/SRO); 15,193 (*Pollstar*); sold out
CONCERT GROSS: $226,191 per show
NOTES: Recorded to multitrack for possible future release. On April 14, Neil spent the day cycling in Philadelphia, pedaling to the venue, riding down the ramp and right into the dressing room. Though difficult to tell from the audience's perspective, the band was unhappy with their performance, and felt as though it would be magnified on the recording. After the show, the crew packed the gear back into the trucks for the night in order to accommodate the

next day's Flyers playoff game. On April 16, the rainy day moved Alex and Geddy to sing songs about the rain en route to the Spectrum. Jimi Hendrix and the Beatles were featured. Neil cycled to the gig through pouring rain and played along to James Brown for forty-five minutes as a warm-up before sound check. Backstage after the show, Neil did an interview with Q104-FM out of Halifax and discussed the ongoing petition to bring the band back to the Maritime provinces. Ray blamed the Maritime non-appearance on "logistical problems."

APRIL 17, 1986
BALTIMORE, MARYLAND
BALTIMORE CIVIC CENTER, 201 West Baltimore Street. Venue opened on October 23, 1962.
AN EVENING WITH RUSH
TICKETS: $14.50
ATTENDANCE: 10,036
CAPACITY: 13,641
CONCERT GROSS: $145,522
NOTES: Marillion was slated to open for Blue Oyster Cult (who played the venue with Kiss just a week before), but canceled. The band and crew were in an easygoing mood. After sound check, Geddy tossed the baseball around inside a venue hallway. Perhaps this date provided the genesis for the next album title, as Neil gave a friend a lighter after the show and told him to "hold your fire." Later in 1986, the venue name was changed to Baltimore Arena.

APRIL 19, 1986
HAMPTON, VIRGINIA
HAMPTON COLISEUM, 1000 Coliseum Drive. Venue opened on January 31, 1970.
SUPPORT ACT: Blue Oyster Cult
TICKETS: $13.50 (advance) / $14.50 (day of), general admission
ATTENDANCE: 11,466

APRIL 20, 1986
CHARLOTTE, NORTH CAROLINA
CHARLOTTE COLISEUM, 2700 East Independence Boulevard. Venue dedicated on September 11, 1955.
SUPPORT ACT: Blue Oyster Cult
TICKETS: $15.00, general admission
ATTENDANCE: 6,998
NOTES: Geddy was selected Best Rock Bassist by the readers of *Guitar Player*

magazine for the fifth consecutive year, thus earning his place in the magazine's Gallery of the Greats.
CHARLOTTE OBSERVER: "Rush, Blue Oyster Cult at Coliseum: Rush stated a convincing case for progressive rock before a crowd of 7,000. Only the muddy sound system and singer Lee`s eternally screechy tenor got in the way of a clear victory for the band."

APRIL 22, 1986
GREENSBORO, NORTH CAROLINA
GREENSBORO COLISEUM, 1921 West Lee Street. Venue opened on October 29, 1959.
SUPPORT ACT: Blue Oyster Cult
TICKETS: $15.00
ATTENDANCE: 6,918
NOTES: As the tour rolled on, Geddy began calling out different colors during "Red Lenses" after the line "not blue," in order to trip Howard up, who would bathe the stage in the color requested: "Not green, not yellow, not magenta," etc.
DAILY TAR HEEL: "Rush concert shows band a step ahead of the rest in talent: Overall, Rush showed that although they've been together for seventeen years, they have no intentions of slowing down just yet."

APRIL 23, 1986
AUGUSTA, GEORGIA
AUGUSTA-RICHMOND COUNTY CIVIC CENTER ARENA, 601 7th Street. Venue opened on December 14, 1979.
SUPPORT ACT: Blue Oyster Cult
TICKETS: $15.00, general admission
ATTENDANCE: 3,364
AUGUSTA CHRONICLE: "King Lerxst has his day as Rush rules musical kingdom."

APRIL 25, 1986
ATLANTA, GEORGIA
THE OMNI, 100 Techwood Drive Northwest. Venue opened on October 14, 1972.
SUPPORT ACT: Blue Oyster Cult
TICKETS: $15.00
ATTENDANCE: 12,806 (Anthem/SRO); sold out
CONCERT GROSS: $192,090

APRIL 26, 1986
BIRMINGHAM, ALABAMA
BIRMINGHAM-JEFFERSON CIVIC
CENTER COLISEUM, 1 Civic Center
Plaza at 19th Street North. Venue
opened in September 1976.
SUPPORT ACT: Blue Oyster Cult
TICKETS: $14.50
ATTENDANCE: 5,454

APRIL 28, 1986
ST. LOUIS, MISSOURI
ST. LOUIS ARENA, 5700 Oakland.
Venue opened on September 23, 1929.
AN EVENING WITH RUSH
TICKETS: $15.00
ATTENDANCE: 11,369 (Anthem/SRO);
sold out
CONCERT GROSS: $170,535
NOTES: According to fan accounts, the
opener canceled, with promoter docu-
ments confirming that only Rush
performed. The band's current touring
partner (Blue Oyster Cult) played St.
Louis on May 16. Tickets were listed as
$15.00 by both *Pollstar* and *Amusement
Business*. A stub shows $16.50 but may
include $1.50 in charges.
ST. LOUIS POST-DISPATCH: "Rush's
Power Windows a Triumph at the Arena:
Although many of the epic-length compositions that characterized Rush's earlier
efforts no longer fill its live concerts, the
group still can string together a half dozen
current songs and several 'classics' with
inventive video clips and laser effects for
a thoroughly entertaining show."

APRIL 29, 1986
KANSAS CITY, MISSOURI
KEMPER ARENA, 1800 Genessee Street
at 17th Street. Venue dedicated on
October 18, 1974.
SUPPORT ACT: Blue Oyster Cult
TICKETS: $13.00 / $14.00
ATTENDANCE: 11,236 (Anthem/SRO);
11,436 (*Pollstar*)
CAPACITY: 12,200
CONCERT GROSS: $162,922
NOTES: *Amusement Business* lists a
concert gross of: $162,972.
THE KANSAS CITY STAR: "Rock progres-
sives rush for onstage perfection."

MAY 1, 1986
OKLAHOMA CITY
MYRIAD ARENA, One Myriad Gardens.
Venue opened on November 5, 1972.

SUPPORT ACT: Blue Oyster Cult
TICKETS: $14.50
ATTENDANCE: 7,719
NOTES: Geddy missed the lyrical verse,
"More than just a spark. More than just
the bottom line. Or a lucky shot in the
dark" in "Marathon." During Blue Oyster
Cult's set, a bit of crew hijinks took place
in the beginning of "Godzilla." The Cult
had a prerecorded opening with the
sound of giant footsteps, and Eric Bloom
asked the crowd, "Who is it? Is it Rodan?"
Out of the PA came the voice of TV's
talking horse, "Hello, I'm Mr. Ed."[16]

MAY 2, 1986
VALLEY CENTER, KANSAS
BRITT BROWN ARENA, Kansas
Coliseum complex, 1229 East 85th
Street North. Venue opened on
September 28, 1978.
SUPPORT ACT: Blue Oyster Cult
TICKETS: $14.75 (twenty-five-cent
parking fee included), general admission
ATTENDANCE: 6,357

MAY 11, 1986
WINNIPEG, MANITOBA
WINNIPEG ARENA, 1430 Maroons
Road. Venue opened on October 18,
1955.
NOTES: Tour shirts initially listed this
date, but the show was canceled (or
never actually confirmed), possibly as
part of a tour restructuring to allow for
the May 12 concert in Salt Lake City and
the May 15 date in Calgary.

MAY 12, 1986
SALT LAKE CITY, UTAH
SALT PALACE, 100 S West Temple.
Venue dedicated on July 11, 1969.
SUPPORT ACT: The Fabulous
Thunderbirds
TICKETS: $15.00
ATTENDANCE: 7,495
CAPACITY: 13,000
SALT LAKE TRIBUNE: "Canadian rock
group lives up to its name: Two years
since their last Palace appearance have
given the group even more dimension
due in part to the extensive effects
involving lasers, computer-generated
screen art, and brilliant lighting. The
visual bombast could have been overwhelming, but Rush worked the music
skillfully into the presentation to deliver a
multifaceted performance. An orchestral

effect was created by these three musicians, a sound so big that the cavernous
hall took on an unusual intimacy. With
the intelligent lyrics and dynamic
arrangements, Rush's music is as complex and riveting as a symphony
performance."

MAY 14, 1986
EDMONTON, ALBERTA
NORTHLANDS COLISEUM, 7424 118th
Avenue NW. Venue opened on
November 10, 1974.
NOTES: Tour shirts initially list this date
as May 15, preceded by Calgary on the
14th. The show order was later switched,
and the Edmonton performance ended up
being canceled due to a freak May blizzard, which stranded the trucks in Calgary.
The blinding snow reached a depth of
thirty centimeters, a Calgary record for
spring. No makeup date was scheduled
for Edmonton's 7,500 ticket holders.

MAY 15, 1986
CALGARY, ALBERTA
OLYMPIC SADDLEDOME, 555
Saddledome Rise SE. Venue opened on
October 15, 1983.
SUPPORT ACT: Kick Axe
TICKETS: $18.00 / $19.00 CAD
ATTENDANCE: 7,770 (SRO/Anthem);
8,036 (*Amusement Business*)
CAPACITY: 10,000 (SRO/Anthem);
14,000 (*Amusement Business*)
CONCERT GROSS: $134,914 CAD
NOTES: Tour shirts initially list this date
as being in Edmonton, with Calgary
slated for May 14. Edmonton was can-
celed (because of a blizzard), and Calgary
was played on May 15. Kick Axe was a
Canadian heavy metal band from Regina.
CALGARY HERALD: "Rush showed class:
The band performed its older songs,
such as 'Closer to the Heart,' and new
tunes from *Power Windows* with intelligence, intensity, and integrity. The trio is
at the peak of heavy-rock evolution."

MAY 17, 1986
VANCOUVER, BRITISH COLUMBIA
PACIFIC COLISEUM, 100 North Renfrew
Street. Venue opened in 1967.
SUPPORT ACT: Kick Axe
TICKETS: $18.00 / $19.00 CAD
ATTENDANCE: 8,354
CAPACITY: 9,000
CONCERT GROSS: $151,617 CAD

NOTES: An enthusiastic crowd displayed their approval by screaming and holding lighters as Rush commenced their encore. Ben Mink and k.d. lang visited with the band backstage, and lang discussed the logistics of touring with Geddy. (She was preparing to embark on her first tour.)

MAY 19, 1986
PORTLAND, OREGON
MEMORIAL COLISEUM, 1401 North Wheeler. Venue opened on November 3, 1960.
SUPPORT ACT: The Fabulous Thunderbirds
TICKETS: $16.50
ATTENDANCE: 6,882
NOTES: The band boarded their bus an hour and a half after the show. A crowd of stoned fans waited for autographs in the pouring rain. Geddy stopped to sign and commented to the crowd, "Are all of you people tripping on acid?"
THE OREGONIAN: "The world that Rush inhabits contains all of the good—and bad—that can be found in rock 'n' roll. And as an enthusiastic crowd found out at Memorial Coliseum, the good comes in a slick and polished light show, master musicianship, and high energy; the bad comes in repetition and reliance on formulas. Still, even with all the pyrotechnics from Lifeson and Lee, it wasn't hard to pick out the real star of the evening: Neil Peart."

MAY 21, 1986
SEATTLE, WASHINGTON
SEATTLE CENTER COLISEUM, 305 Harrison Street. Venue opened on April 21, 1962.
SUPPORT ACT: The Fabulous Thunderbirds
TICKETS: $16.50, general admission
ATTENDANCE: 10,640
NOTES: Sound check featured lots of cohesive improvisation, with Geddy popping the strings on his Steinberger bass. At dinner, members of the Fabulous Thunderbirds discussed their gig the day before at the maximum-security Oregon State Penitentiary in Salem before 1,750 inmates: "It was great fun. They really dug us."
THE SEATTLE TIMES: "Rush brings literacy to rock stage."

MAY 24, 1986
SACRAMENTO, CALIFORNIA
CAL EXPO AMPHITHEATRE, California State Fairgrounds, 1600 Exposition Boulevard. Venue opened on July 26, 1983.
SUPPORT ACT: The Fabulous Thunderbirds
TICKETS: $16.50, general admission
ATTENDANCE: 12,200 (Anthem/SRO); sold out
CONCERT GROSS: $201,300
SACRAMENTO BEE: "Instead of a Rush, We Get a Crashing Letdown: Worst of all, Lee has one of the most irritating voices in rock—not an easy distinction to earn. He manages little variation in tone, usually favoring a shrill, high-pitched whine that resembles a bug in one's ear."

MAY 25–26, 1986
COSTA MESA, CALIFORNIA
PACIFIC AMPHITHEATRE, Orange County Fairgrounds, 100 Fair Drive. Venue opened on July 29, 1983.
SUPPORT ACT: The Fabulous Thunderbirds
TICKETS: $17.50 (reserved) / $12.50 (lawn)
ATTENDANCE (MAY 25): 12,155
ATTENDANCE (MAY 26): 9,378
NOTES: After the first show, an end-of-tour party was held in a trailer backstage, eventually continuing back at the hotel. May 26 was the final date of the *Power Windows* tour. Before Alex and Geddy arrived, Neil took a seat in the amphitheater and proceeded to play air drums to early Genesis, which was blasting from the PA on this sunny Southern California day. At sound check, Rush broke into an instrumental version of "Lakeside Park." Neil remembered the band's early days when they were a struggling opening act, so he made up a nice, encouraging card for the Fabulous Thunderbirds (whose brand of popish blues had not gone over well with Rush's audience), had Geddy and Alex sign it, and gave it to the opener. During Neil's drum solo on this night, he included some of the *Flintstones* theme. With the tour complete, Geddy and Nancy enjoyed a West Coast vacation, Alex flew back to Ontario and the chaos of constructing his new house—Lerxst's Graceland North—and Neil spent the summer with his family.

He also found the time to bike through Switzerland and write the percussion composition "Pieces of Eight."
GEDDY (ONSTAGE): "Thank you for making this a great last night of the tour."

1. Bill Banasiewicz. Interview with Geddy Lee, December 6, 1985.
2. *Amusement Business.*
3. Bill Banasiewicz. Interview with Geddy Lee, January 30, 1986.
4. Bill Banasiewicz. Interview with Bryn Smith, January 1986.
5. *Noisecreep,* April 3, 2009.
6. *The Los Angeles Times.*
7. *Canadian Composer,* April 1986.
8. *Amusement Business.*
9. Bill Banasiewicz. Interview with Alex Van Halen, February 5, 1986.
10. Interview with James Hetfield, *Guitar World Magazine.*
11. Bill Banasiewicz. Interview with Neil Peart, February 6, 1986.
12. *The Bulletin.*
13. Jon Collins. *Chemistry.* Helter Skelter Books, 2006.
14. Interview with Mark Kelly. *Montreal Gazette,* March 12, 2013.
15. Bill Banasiewicz. Interview with Geddy Lee, April 4, 1986.
16. *Hot Rails.* hotrails.co.uk/history/1986.htm

Chapter 20

THE HOLD YOUR FIRE TOUR

Rush performed seventy-eight shows throughout North America and Europe on the *Hold Your Fire* tour. Continuing the trend that began on *Power Windows,* the band operated at the pinnacle of onstage automation, with elaborate use of synthesizers and sequencers, all pumped through a fully quadraphonic PA system. "The change in the music is very much the important thing," said Neil. "We worked hard this year, and because we extended ourselves in the studio more, it's that much harder to produce live. I started [rehearsing] by myself and Geddy started by himself two weeks before we rehearsed together. We needed the time to develop the hardware and software. And the stamina."

TOP LEFT: Birmingham, UK; Neil at the NEC.

TOP RIGHT: Troy, NY; Alex and Geddy onstage at the RPI Fieldhouse.

RIGHT: Birmingham, UK; The band onstage at the NEC.

OPPOSITE: New York, NY; Marquee at Madison Square Garden.

While the band members chose to use the electronics and effects employed in their shows, the group began to feel dissatisfied with, as well as enslaved to, all the technology.

"As much as I love the challenge of trying to reproduce everything onstage, I do love to play bass," said Geddy. "And I like to be left alone to play bass sometimes. Sometimes I find that frustrating. And sometimes I feel like [with all of the keyboard responsibilities] I am sacrificing a bit of audience interaction as well, because I like to move around, and I like to get in front of the people, and try to sort of edge them on and loosen them up a bit. Especially in Canada—I find that Canadians need a little loosening up at times!"

The set list incorporated the new *Hold Your Fire* songs, including the single "Time Stand Still," which featured 'Til Tuesday singer Aimee Mann on the studio version. (Neil: "In concert, we have a film of her singing so that we have her presence. It was the most honest way we could think of to do it live.") The band also brought "La Villa Strangiato" into the encore for the first time since 1983. Primary support on the US dates came from the McAuley Schenker Group, led by former Scorpions and UFO guitarist Michael Schenker, and later from Tommy Shaw, who was embarking on a solo career following his time in Styx.

Tommy Shaw's drummer Michael Cartellone joked about the imbalance between the number of males and females that made up a typical Rush audience at the time: "Styx and Tommy have a lot of female fans, and some of them would come out to see Tommy," he said. "They were very easy to spot from the stage, as the Rush audience is a sea of dudes. The fact that girls were now in a Rush audience was not lost on anybody!"

Following the North American trek, Rush headed to Europe for ten shows. The first three

dates, at the National Exhibition Centre in Birmingham, were recorded for the *A Show of Hands* live album and video. Guy Charbonneau engineered the audio inside the Advision Mobile truck, and fourteen cameras were employed to film the entire show. Alex's babbling during "La Villa Strangiato" received a humorous treatment by Geddy during the video's postproduction when he had a "Warning—radiation!" symbol added to the screen.

Explained Alex, "It's more spontaneous babbling! You get kinda goofy at the end of a show, especially near the end of a lengthy tour. That was just crazy rambling, verbal farting. It was Geddy's idea to put it on the video."

The three-night stand in Birmingham was followed by a gig in Glasgow and three shows at London's Wembley Arena. The band then performed in Holland and ended the *Hold Your Fire* tour with two dates in Germany. On the final night, at Schleyer-Halle in Frankfurt, Neil entered the venue and asked, in a thick German accent, "Vich vay to verk?"

RIGHT TOP: Geddy and Alex jamming during "Closer to the Heart."

RIGHT BOTTOM: Birmingham UK; Geddy saying "good night" to the crowd at the NEC.

280

TOUR HISTORY
HOLD YOUR FIRE

SET LIST:
Intro (Three Stooges theme)
"The Big Money"
"Subdivisions"
"Limelight"
"Marathon"
"Turn the Page"
"Prime Mover"
"Manhattan Project"
"Closer to the Heart"

"Red Sector A"
"Force Ten"
"Time Stand Still"
"Distant Early Warning"
"Lock and Key"
"Mission"
"Territories"
"YYZ"
"The Rhythm Method" (drum solo)
"Red Lenses" (abridged)

"The Spirit of Radio"
"Tom Sawyer"
Encore:
"2112: Overture"
"2112: The Temples of Syrinx"
"La Villa Strangiato"
"In the Mood"

OCTOBER 29–30, 1987
ST. JOHN'S, NEWFOUNDLAND
MEMORIAL STADIUM, Kings Bridge Road. Venue opened in January 1955.
SUPPORT ACT: Chalk Circle
TICKETS: $19.50 CAD, general admission
ATTENDANCE (OCT. 29): 3,756
ATTENDANCE (OCT. 30): 4,851
CAPACITY: 5,500
NOTES: October 29 was the opening date of the 1987 to 1988 *Hold Your Fire* tour. It featured the live debut of "Force Ten," "Time Stand Still," "Prime Mover," "Lock and Key," "Mission," and "Turn the Page." Maritime fans had petitioned the band, so Alex, Geddy, and Neil thought it would be nice to open the tour in Newfoundland, the first time Rush had ever performed there. Onstage the second night, "The Big Money" included a longer ending, Alex's vocals were silent during "Subdivisions," the quadrophonic enhancement during "Prime Mover" made the crowd go wild, flash pots exploded during "Red Sector A," Neil's solo featured the "Pieces of Eight" electronic marimba section, and the keyboard solo in "Tom Sawyer" wasn't played on a Minimoog, which offered a different flavor. Neil decided to embrace the start of the tour in a unique fashion by hitching an overnight ride with one of the band's longtime truck drivers, Art (Mac) Maclear.
MUSE **(MEMORIAL UNIVERSITY OF NEWFOUNDLAND):** "The visual effects perfectly complemented the music, and swept the onlookers away into a world far, far from the inside of Memorial Stadium. Something about the flow of the pictures on the screen, in combination with the lighting, did more than entertain—these were the images of prophecy; these were intelligent analyses of human existence. . . ., Rush's stage presence and the emotion at the show were more than enough to make it one of the, if not the, best concerts seen in Memorial Stadium in quite some time."
NEIL: "I had ridden with Mac in his truck myself a few times in the early days, and other truck drivers too, just for the adventure of it. I rode all night across Newfoundland with Mac, heading for the ferry to Nova Scotia at Port-aux-Basques. The band had started our *Hold Your Fire Tour* in St. John's . . . with a week of production rehearsals and the first show at the Memorial Arena. In the afternoons, before going to work, I rode my bicycle all around St. John's, and down to Cape Spear, the easternmost point of North America. That had been our first visit to Newfoundland, and all of us were especially charmed by the people, so friendly and open-hearted. After the [second] show in St. John's, we had a day off to travel to the show in Sydney, Nova Scotia. My bandmates would be flying from St. John's to Sydney, but I wanted to avoid that dreaded short flight, and see more of Newfoundland, so I hitched a ride with Mac. I don't know why I thought I would see more of Newfoundland driving all night in a truck, but I will always associate that long drive with the music of Percy Sledge playing on Mac's tape deck while I tried to sleep in the bouncing sleeper."[1]

NOVEMBER 1, 1987
SYDNEY, NOVA SCOTIA
CENTRE 200, 481 George Street. Venue opened in February 1987.
SUPPORT ACT: Chalk Circle
TICKETS: $19.50 CAD (unconfirmed)
CAPACITY: 6,225
BRAD HOPKINS (CHALK CIRCLE BASSIST): "For us, just getting the opportunity to play with Rush was something special. It was fulfilling a dream. Rush took the time and treated us really well. They greeted us with a bottle of champagne and a card welcoming us to the tour. We got to hang out with them, and you could tell right away that they were nice people. Everything had a positive vibe to it, and we got a really good response at the shows as well."[2]

NOVEMBER 2, 1987
HALIFAX, NOVA SCOTIA
METRO CENTRE, 1800 Argyle Street. Venue opened on February 17, 1978.
SUPPORT ACT: Chalk Circle
TICKETS: $19.50 CAD
ATTENDANCE: 8,000+[3]
CAPACITY: 5,000 to 7,000 (depending upon setup)
Q104-FM, HALIFAX, GEDDY (BACKSTAGE AFTER THE SHOW): "It's always tough to get everything in sync at the beginning of a tour, but tonight everything happened. It was a really good feeling out there. This was a gig that we really wanted to be ready for."[4]

NOVEMBER 4, 1987
MONCTON, NEW BRUNSWICK
MONCTON COLISEUM, 377 Killam Drive. Venue opened on April 19, 1973.
SUPPORT ACT: Chalk Circle
TICKETS: $19.50 CAD, general admission

NOVEMBER 6–7, 1987
PROVIDENCE, RHODE ISLAND
PROVIDENCE CIVIC CENTER, 1 La Salle Square. Venue opened on November 3, 1972.
SUPPORT ACT: McAuley Schenker Group
TICKETS: $16.50
ATTENDANCE (NOV. 6): 10,100; sold out[5]
ATTENDANCE (NOV. 7): 4,982
CAPACITY: 10,100
THE PROVIDENCE JOURNAL: "Canadian trio Rush needs to develop a strong front man to anchor show: Rush could do itself and its fans a favor by setting aside do-it-yourself macho and hiring a sideman to play the synths."

NOVEMBER 9, 1987
SPRINGFIELD, MASSACHUSETTS
SPRINGFIELD CIVIC CENTER, 1277 Main Street. Venue opened on September 22, 1972.
SUPPORT ACT: McAuley Schenker Group
TICKETS: $15.50 (advance) / $16.50 (day of), general admission
CAPACITY: 10,000

NOVEMBER 10, 1987
UTICA, NEW YORK
MEMORIAL AUDITORIUM, 400 Oriskany Street West. Historic venue opened on March 9, 1960.
SUPPORT ACT: McAuley Schenker Group
TICKETS: $16.50, general admission
ATTENDANCE: 3,698
CAPACITY: 6,000
NOTES: MSG had technical difficulties, with their mics cutting out.
GUITAR WORLD: "The set is an intense high-tech demonstration of the band's evolving arrangement strategy. The emphasis has moved gradually away from the power-trio format that characterized early Rush toward densely arranged melodic slabs of sound played with surgical precision. Guitarist Alex Lifeson plays with discipline and concentration despite the fact that his guitar sound is fluctuating wildly in the mix. Lifeson manages to slice through his technical problems with spirited playing."
***GUITAR WORLD*, ALEX (BACKSTAGE AFTER THE SHOW):** "Last night it sounded 98 percent right, so I thought another few minor changes might make it perfect. Instead, everything fell apart. After struggling through most of the set, I gave up and went back to the old setup."

NOVEMBER 12, 1987
TROY, NEW YORK
RPI FIELDHOUSE, Rensselaer Polytechnic Institute campus, 1900 Peoples Avenue. Venue dedicated on October 13, 1949.
SUPPORT ACT: McAuley Schenker Group
TICKETS: $16.50
ATTENDANCE: 8,420; sold out
NOTES: The individual instrumentation, using the very latest in musical technology, dazzled the audience. The quadrophonic PA surrounded the building with various sounds. During "Force Ten," the jackhammer spun around in complete quad. This, combined with visuals of hurricanes and other natural forces, heightened the musical experience. On "Time Stand Still," Aimee Mann made a rear-projected appearance to sing her part during the choruses. New arrangements of older songs also benefited from the new production elements employed. The surround sound debuted during the crescendo choir that closes out "Marathon." By the final line, the impact from the speakers shook the venue's foundation. Quadrophonic versions of "2112: Overture," "Distant Early Warning," "YYZ" (including drum solo), "Manhattan Project," and "Lock and Key" were particular highlights. During the "In the Mood" section of the encore, hundreds of red *Hold Your Fire* balloons descended upon the fired-up crowd of exuberant fans.

NOVEMBER 13, 1987
BINGHAMTON, NEW YORK
BROOME COUNTY WAR MEMORIAL ARENA, 1 Stuart Street. Venue opened on August 29, 1973.
SUPPORT ACT: McAuley Schenker Group
TICKETS: $16.50, general admission
ATTENDANCE: 8,000 (approximate), general admission[6]
BINGHAMTON PRESS AND SUN-BULLETIN: "Band's musicianship, restraint gives Arena a Rush: What makes Rush a great band—instead of just a good one—is that they transcend every aspect of rock they embrace."

NOVEMBER 14, 1987
BUFFALO, NEW YORK
BUFFALO MEMORIAL AUDITORIUM, 140 Main Street. Venue opened on October 14, 1940.

SUPPORT ACT: McAuley Schenker Group
TICKETS: $16.50
ATTENDANCE: 11,000 (approximate)
CAPACITY: 14,605
BUFFALO NEWS: "Rush's New Sound Scores as Solid Hit: Saturday night's performance wisely concentrated on the newer, more substantial songs, which drop shallow pretense for deeper meaning. Thankfully, Rush never has stood still, and if Saturday's show is any indication, then the band will continue to stretch its art to limitless boundaries."

NOVEMBER 24, 1987
JOHNSON CITY, TENNESSEE
FREEDOM HALL CIVIC CENTER, 1320 Pactolas Road. Venue opened on July 5, 1974.
SUPPORT ACT: McAuley Schenker Group
NOTES: Canceled date.

NOVEMBER 25, 1987
ATLANTA, GEORGIA
THE OMNI, 100 Techwood Drive Northwest. Venue opened on October 14, 1972.
SUPPORT ACT: McAuley Schenker Group
TICKETS: $17.50
ATTENDANCE: 10,353[7]
CAPACITY: 13,700
CONCERT GROSS: $169,208
NOTES: Coming off the eleven-day break, Geddy forgot a few lyrics during the gig.
GEDDY: "It was really strange. Here we were onstage playing songs that we've played for years, and I totally blanked on some lines. I just kind of hummed along to the melody, or repeated lines to get through. It was a very uneasy feeling."[8]

NOVEMBER 27, 1987
CHARLOTTE, NORTH CAROLINA
CHARLOTTE COLISEUM, 2700 East Independence Boulevard. Venue dedicated on September 11, 1955.
SUPPORT ACT: McAuley Schenker Group
TICKETS: $16.50, general admission
ATTENDANCE: 9,186
CAPACITY: 11,009
CONCERT GROSS: $143,121
NOTES: Outside the venue, scalpers were selling tickets for three times the face value. In the dressing room, Geddy studied the song lyrics, some of which he'd forgotten in Atlanta. The homework paid off, as the band was in top form in Charlotte. Part of the tour staging included

red balloons suspended from atop the venue—the balloons were dropped on the crowd during the encore. After the concert, more than seventy people were arrested, mostly on drug-related charges, according to Charlotte police.[9]

NEIL (BACKSTAGE BEFORE THE SHOW): "It's a really difficult thing to remember all of the words. There are so many songs that we've done over the years. I know that I have to refer back to the albums for the lyrics, and I wrote the lyrics!"[10]

NOVEMBER 28, 1987
HAMPTON, VIRGINIA

HAMPTON COLISEUM, 1000 Coliseum Drive. Venue opened on January 31, 1970.

SUPPORT ACT: McAuley Schenker Group

TICKETS: $14.50, general admission

CAPACITY: 13,900

NOTES: Rescheduled to January 14, 1988, because Geddy had laryngitis. As the crew broke down the set in the afternoon, stage manager Nick Kotos had some fun by telling a few friends when they arrived, "It was moved to a noon show. It was a great gig, and you missed it."

LIAM: "The band bus went on to Washington, so hopefully Ged will be okay. In all our years of touring, I can't ever remember him having laryngitis. It's a very weird thing."[11]

GEDDY: "It was the weirdest thing that's ever happened to me. I woke up and I couldn't talk."[12]

NOVEMBER 30, 1987
LARGO, MARYLAND

CAPITAL CENTRE, 1 Harry S. Truman Drive. Venue opened on December 2, 1973.

SUPPORT ACT: McAuley Schenker Group

TICKETS: $16.50

CAPACITY: 15,770

NOTES: Sound check was a bit tentative. Before the gig, Neil demonstrated his new portable computer to friends and was very excited to discuss his latest writing project about the recent trip he had taken through Africa. The concert was energetic, with Geddy's voice in fine form, and he didn't miss a beat with the lyrics.

DECEMBER 2–3, 1987
WORCESTER, MASSACHUSETTS

THE CENTRUM, 50 Foster Street. Venue opened on September 2, 1982.

SUPPORT ACT: McAuley Schenker Group

TICKETS: $15.00 / $17.50

TWO-DAY WORCESTER ATTENDANCE: 17,173

TWO-DAY CONCERT CAPACITY: 20,286

TWO-DAY WORCESTER CONCERT GROSS: $288,672

THE BOSTON GLOBE: "Rush veterans just keep on getting better: Rush's recent songs have been so complicated that they have to work extra-hard to play them live, which can result in a certain coldness. But that wasn't the case Wednesday night, when they played tricky songs with the energy of three-chord rock. The more difficult the tune, the easier they made it sound."

DECEMBER 5, 1987
NEW HAVEN, CONNECTICUT
NEW HAVEN VETERAN'S MEMORIAL

COLISEUM, 275 South Orange Street. Venue opened on September 27, 1972.

SUPPORT ACT: McAuley Schenker Group

TICKETS: $15.99 / $19.99

CAPACITY: 9,900

NOTES: The performance footage featured in the "Lock and Key" promotional video was filmed. The song was shot a few times in sound check, and the band seemed a bit on edge because of it all. The filming of just one song had created a tension in the air. During the gig, "Lock and Key" was videotaped again, and things went well, with three giant red *Hold Your Fire* balloons released into the crowd, but then for some reason, the film crew entered the stage and began shooting again on "Territories," with an angry band yelling at them to get off the stage. For the encore, a lighting change had been implemented, where Howard utilized his full arsenal of lights and lasers for the extended finale to "In the Mood." Backstage, the band was still upset about the video crew's unscheduled appearance onstage.

NEIL: "We're trying to put on a show, and then those idiots come back onstage after they already finished filming the song that they were supposed to."[13]

GEDDY: "These kinds of incidents are very frustrating."[14]

DECEMBER 7, 1987
EAST RUTHERFORD, NEW JERSEY
MEADOWLANDS ARENA, Meadowlands

Sports Complex, 50 State Route 120. Venue opened on July 2, 1981.

SUPPORT ACT: Tommy Shaw

TICKETS: $16.50 / $17.50

ATTENDANCE: 14,483

CAPACITY: 17,963

CONCERT GROSS: $272,503

NOTES: Originally slated for December 6 but rescheduled to December 7 to accommodate Frank Sinatra's agenda. A sold-out Sinatra/Liza Minnelli concert at this venue was called off ten minutes before showtime because the orchestra's sheet music never arrived, and the date was rescheduled for December 6, which bumped Rush to December 7.

NEIL: "No problem—I like Sinatra."[15]

GEDDY (BACKSTAGE): "Where were you last night? Frank and I did a duet on 'My Way.'"[16]

GEDDY (ONSTAGE): "We forgot the sheet music tonight, but that's okay!"

ROCK EXPRESS: "There are a million reasons why a particular concert doesn't work: band fatigue, hectic touring schedule, bad vibes, poor audience reaction, chilly weather, whatever. But those excuses seem moot when you're subjected to two hours of drivel."

DECEMBER 9, 1987
UNIONDALE, NEW YORK
NASSAU COUNTY VETERANS
MEMORIAL COLISEUM, 1255

Hempstead Turnpike. Venue dedicated on May 29, 1972.

SUPPORT ACT: Tommy Shaw

TICKETS: $16.50 / $17.50

ATTENDANCE: 11,754

CAPACITY: 16,375

CONCERT GROSS: $198,079

DECEMBER 11, 1987
NEW YORK, NEW YORK
MADISON SQUARE GARDEN, 4

Pennsylvania Plaza (8th Avenue between 31st and 33rd Streets). Historic venue opened on February 11, 1968.

SUPPORT ACT: Tommy Shaw

TICKETS: $17.50 / $19.50

CAPACITY: 16,489

NOTES: Atlantic Records president Ahmet Ertegun visited the band's dressing room with Ray. Rush's contractual obligations with Polygram were close to wrapping up, so the band's management was exploring options.

AHMET ERTEGUN: "I'm here to see Tommy [Shaw] play, and I just thought I'd say hello. I'm going to stay and watch your set. I'm looking forward to it."[17]

DECEMBER 13–14, 1987
PHILADELPHIA, PENNSYLVANIA
THE SPECTRUM, 3601 South Broad Street. Venue opened on October 1, 1967.
SUPPORT ACT: Tommy Shaw
TICKETS: $14.50 / $16.50
ATTENDANCE (DEC. 13): 14,206; sold out
ATTENDANCE (DEC. 14): 7,823
TWO-DAY PHILADELPHIA CONCERT GROSS: $331,413
NOTES: After the December 13 show, Geddy worked on the editing for the "Lock and Key" video in the Spectrum's film facility, while the Rush Christmas party took place at the venue inside Ovations.
THE PHILADELPHIA INQUIRER: "Loudly, Rush Plays Spectrum: Despite the aid of a dazzling light and video presentation, the group delivered a monotonous performance that was both deafening and tiring. The audience responded wildly to guitarist Alex Lifeson's bombastic power chords on the surging classic 'Fly by Night.'" [Ed: "Fly by Night" was not performed.]

DECEMBER 16, 1987
PITTSBURGH, PENNSYLVANIA
CIVIC ARENA, 300 Auditorium Place. Venue opened on September 17, 1961.
SUPPORT ACT: Tommy Shaw
TICKETS: $16.75 (all seats)
ATTENDANCE: 6,945
CAPACITY: 13,539
PITTSBURGH POST-GAZETTE: "Rush resists lure of pop music: While their cosmic art rock contemporaries—particularly Genesis and Yes—are falling over themselves for pop acceptance, Rush is still fighting off the temptation to compromise. Rolling into Pittsburgh again, Rush put on an aural and visual barrage."

DECEMBER 17, 1987
RICHFIELD, OHIO
RICHFIELD COLISEUM, 2923 Streetsboro Road. Venue opened on October 26, 1974.

SUPPORT ACT: Tommy Shaw
TICKETS: $16.50 (all seats)
CAPACITY: 18,500
CLEVELAND PLAIN DEALER, NEIL: "We do what seems good and right to us and hope people will like it. You hope that conviction communicates itself, and that's why you reach people."
MICHAEL CARTELLONE (TOMMY SHAW DRUMMER): "Being on the *Hold Your Fire* tour was a wonderful experience. I have many vivid memories of those four months. Without question, my fondest memory was performing at Richfield Coliseum in my hometown. That was where I saw my first concert (Kiss). It was a dream come true to play there with my family in attendance."[18]

JANUARY 14, 1988
HAMPTON, VIRGINIA
HAMPTON COLISEUM, 1000 Coliseum Drive. Venue opened on January 31, 1970.
SUPPORT ACT: Tommy Shaw
TICKETS: $14.50 (advance) / $15.50 (day of), general admission
CAPACITY: 13,900
NOTES: Rescheduled from November 28, 1987.
DAILY NEWS (NEWPORT NEWS): "Rush makeup date worth the wait."
TOMMY SHAW (BACKSTAGE AFTER SOUND CHECK): "It's great being an opening act. Rush are great people, and I don't have to worry about the sound, the lights, or anything. All I have to do is go out and play my best."[19]

JANUARY 15, 1988
RALEIGH, NORTH CAROLINA
REYNOLDS COLISEUM, NC State University campus, 2411 Dunn Avenue. Venue opened on December 2, 1949.
SUPPORT ACT: Tommy Shaw
TICKETS: $17.50
CAPACITY: 11,267
NOTES: A strong sound check warmed up the chilly venue with lots of improvised jamming. Geddy and Neil laid down a syncopated rhythm, which was in sync with Alex, who wove the guitar in, around, and through the arrangement until the next section, where Geddy took the lead role and Alex and Neil became the foundation. After dinner, Geddy went looking (unsuccessfully) for the indoor batting cages that

are part of the facility, while Neil worked on writing *The African Drum*. A friend gave the band a copy of the new Metallica album, *Garage Days Revisited*, which they blasted before going onstage.

JANUARY 16, 1988
BIRMINGHAM, ALABAMA
BIRMINGHAM-JEFFERSON CIVIC CENTER COLISEUM, 1 Civic Center Plaza at 19th Street North. Venue opened in September 1976.
SUPPORT ACT: Tommy Shaw
TICKETS: $16.50, general admission
ATTENDANCE: 5,892
CAPACITY: 12,500
THE BIRMINGHAM NEWS: "The show was entertaining, the music was interesting, the light show was spectacular, the audience got their money's worth."

JANUARY 18, 1988
JACKSON, MISSISSIPPI
MISSISSIPPI COLISEUM, State Fairgrounds complex, 1207 Mississippi Street. Venue opened on June 7, 1962.
SUPPORT ACT: Tommy Shaw
TICKETS $15.00 (all seats), general admission
CAPACITY: 10,000
NOTES: Based on fan accounts, the arena was half full, with a sedate crowd.

JANUARY 20, 1988
DALLAS, TEXAS
REUNION ARENA, 777 Sports Street
SUPPORT ACT: Tommy Shaw
TICKETS: $17.50
CAPACITY: 13,476
NOTES: Rescheduled from January 19, as confirmed by the promoter.

JANUARY 21, 1988
SAN ANTONIO, TEXAS
CONVENTION CENTER ARENA, HemisFair Park Complex, 601 Hemisfair Way. Venue opened on April 6, 1968.
SUPPORT ACT: Tommy Shaw
TICKETS: $16.50 / $18.50
CAPACITY: 12,474

JANUARY 23, 1988
OKLAHOMA CITY
MYRIAD ARENA, One Myriad Gardens. Venue opened on November 5, 1972.
SUPPORT ACT: Tommy Shaw
ATTENDANCE: 8,000 (approximate)[20]
CAPACITY: 13,000

THE OKLAHOMAN: "Rush a Convincing Success: Peart, Lee, and Lifeson played a flawless two-hour set punctuated by a great working of most of the songs from *Hold Your Fire*. At times, bright flood-lights flashed into the crowd. Often, a series of bright green beams bounced all over the Myriad, creating a seemingly endless, dazzling light show."

JANUARY 24, 1988
SHREVEPORT, LOUISIANA
HIRSCH MEMORIAL COLISEUM, 3701 Hudson Avenue. Venue opened on April 10, 1954.
SUPPORT ACT: Tommy Shaw
TICKETS: $16.00, general admission
ATTENDANCE: 5,289
CAPACITY: 10,000
NOTES: Fifteen people were arrested for drug-related offenses.
THE *TIMES*: "The major stimulant at this concert was a combination of loud but wonderfully clear contemporary music and a light show that was the best to invade Hirsch Coliseum in over a decade."

JANUARY 26, 1988
LITTLE ROCK, ARKANSAS
T. H. BARTON COLISEUM, Arkansas State Fairgrounds, 2600 Howard Street. Venue dedicated on September 29, 1952.
SUPPORT ACT: Tommy Shaw
TICKETS: $16.00, general admission
CAPACITY: 10,250
NOTES: Recorded to multitrack by Le Mobile for possible future release.

JANUARY 27, 1988
NEW ORLEANS, LOUISIANA
UNO LAKEFRONT ARENA, University of New Orleans east campus, 6801 Franklin Street. Venue opened on November 1, 1983.
SUPPORT ACT: Tommy Shaw
TICKETS: $16.50 / $17.50, general admission
ATTENDANCE: 7,000 (approximate)
CAPACITY: 8,500
NOTES: Recorded to multitrack by Le Mobile, with "Turn the Page" appearing on the *A Show of Hands* album. "Lock and Key" was added as an MTV Breakout video.
MARQUEE: "Rush delivers with perks at UNO: Rush offered a two-hour set

backed by a video/laser light show that perfectly enhanced the performance."

JANUARY 29, 1988
HOUSTON, TEXAS
THE SUMMIT, 3700 Southwest Freeway. Venue opened on November 1, 1975.
SUPPORT ACT: Tommy Shaw
TICKETS: $17.00
ATTENDANCE: 12,765
CAPACITY: 17,064
CONCERT GROSS: $206,907
NOTES: Recorded to multitrack by Le Mobile for possible future release.

JANUARY 30, 1988
AUSTIN, TEXAS
FRANK ERWIN SPECIAL EVENTS CENTER, University of Texas at Austin campus, 1701 Red River Street. Venue opened on November 29, 1977.
SUPPORT ACT: Tommy Shaw
TICKETS: $14.00 / $16.00
ATTENDANCE: 10,567[21]
CAPACITY: 12,494
CONCERT GROSS: $160,848
NOTES: Recorded to multitrack by Le Mobile for possible future release. Geddy and Alex checked out Bob "Mo" Kniffen's band at a local club after the show.
BOB "MO" KNIFFEN (EX-SEE FACTOR CREW): "I had eventually settled in Austin, Texas, and when they were play-ing at the Erwin Center, I had gone to see them just to say 'hello.' They asked if I was going to stay and see the show, and I said 'No, I've got a gig down at Touche's on 6th Street—when you guys are done, why don't you come down?' I was just kidding, but after the Rush show, Alex and Geddy actually came down to where I was playing in a band in this little hole in the wall. They sat there and listened to my gig, and I didn't see them at first. The place was packed, and eventually people noticed them, because their lim-ousine was outside, and my wife said, 'Hey, Alex and Geddy came!' And I looked and, son of a bitch, they're sitting at a table."[22]

FEBRUARY 1, 1988
PHOENIX, ARIZONA
ARIZONA VETERANS MEMORIAL COLISEUM, Arizona State Fairgrounds, 1826 West McDowell Road. Venue opened on November 3, 1965.
SUPPORT ACT: Tommy Shaw

TICKETS: $16.50 (all seats), general admission
ATTENDANCE: 12,346
CAPACITY: 12,660 (12,500 according to *Amusement Business*)
CONCERT GROSS: $203,709
NOTES: Recorded to multitrack by Le Mobile, with "Manhattan Project" and "Force Ten" appearing on the *A Show of Hands* album.

FEBRUARY 3, 1988
SAN DIEGO, CALIFORNIA
SAN DIEGO SPORTS ARENA, 3500 Sports Arena Boulevard. Venue opened on November 17, 1966.
SUPPORT ACT: Tommy Shaw
TICKETS: $17.50
ATTENDANCE: 11,182; sold out
CONCERT GROSS: $187,793
NOTES: Recorded to multitrack by Le Mobile, with "Mission" appearing on the *A Show of Hands* album.

FEBRUARY 4–5, 1988
INGLEWOOD, CALIFORNIA
THE FORUM, 3900 West Manchester Boulevard. Venue opened on December 30, 1967.
SUPPORT ACT: Tommy Shaw
TICKETS: $18.50
ATTENDANCE: 13,793 per show; sold out
CONCERT GROSS: $241,628.50 per show
NOTES: Both shows recorded to multi-track by Le Mobile for possible future release.
NEIL: "Our concerts have always been better seen than explained."[23]
***LOS ANGELES TIMES*:** "Rush Delivery: They Could Have Mailed It In: The show was unquestionably high-tech—and high-technique—but emotionally parched."

FEBRUARY 15, 1988
LAKELAND, FLORIDA
LAKELAND CIVIC CENTER, 701 West Lime Street. Venue dedicated on November 14, 1974.
SUPPORT ACT: Tommy Shaw
TICKETS: $18.00 (includes fifty-cent facility fee and $1.50 service charge), general admission
ATTENDANCE: 10,000; sold out
CONCERT GROSS: $172,725
NOTES: Geddy introduced "Force Ten"

with a country accent. Neil played a marimba solo during the opening to "Overture."

GEDDY (ONSTAGE): "Catch the spirit, catch the fish!"

FEBRUARY 16, 1988
ST. PETERSBURG, FLORIDA
BAYFRONT CENTER ARENA, 400 First Street South. Venue dedicated on May 1, 1965.
SUPPORT ACT: Tommy Shaw
TICKETS: $17.50
NOTES: Show canceled. Although tickets were already on sale, this gig was nixed because the production was too large for the venue. The Pembroke Pines concert was rescheduled to this date, with purchased tickets either refunded or exchanged for the Lakeland gig on February 15.[24]

FEBRUARY 16, 1988
PEMBROKE PINES, FLORIDA
HOLLYWOOD SPORTATORIUM, 17171 Pines Boulevard (Route 820). Venue opened in September 1970.
SUPPORT ACT: Tommy Shaw
TICKETS: $16.50 / $17.50
ATTENDANCE: 12,352; sold out
CONCERT GROSS: $201,333
NOTES: Rescheduled from February 13.

FEBRUARY 18, 1988
JACKSONVILLE, FLORIDA
JACKSONVILLE VETERANS MEMORIAL COLISEUM, 1145 Adams Street. Venue dedicated on November 24, 1960.
SUPPORT ACT: Tommy Shaw
TICKETS: $16.50, general admission
ATTENDANCE: 5,809
CAPACITY: 7,500
CONCERT GROSS: $90,833

FEBRUARY 19, 1988
PENSACOLA, FLORIDA
CIVIC CENTER, 201 East Gregory Street. Venue opened on January 21, 1985.
SUPPORT ACT: Tommy Shaw
TICKETS: $15.00, general admission
ATTENDANCE: 7,020
CAPACITY: 7,500
CONCERT GROSS: $99,405
PENSACOLA NEWS JOURNAL: "Rush: Reliable, not inspired: Rush is a band whose concept is built on contradiction and irony, and this concept keeps the

band evolving. Sometimes the songs stumbled on contradiction and confusion, but it was always confusion laced with honesty."

FEBRUARY 21, 1988
MEMPHIS, TENNESSEE
MID-SOUTH COLISEUM, Memphis Fairgrounds Park, 996 Early Maxwell Blvd. Venue opened on December 2, 1964.
SUPPORT ACT: Tommy Shaw
TICKETS: $16.00
ATTENDANCE: 5,691
CAPACITY: 12,065
CONCERT GROSS: $91,056
CONRAD CORIZ (SEE FACTOR): "My favorite memory is when we all went to Graceland. It was my first time there, and we got the VIP treatment. At the gift shop, I found an awesome little pink Elvis pin—one like I never saw before. I was wearing it, and Geddy saw it and commented, 'Wow, that's a cool pin.' The way he looked at it awhile, I knew he really did like it, so after sound check, Skip and I pinned it on his guitar strap. During the show, while they were playing, he walked across the stage (I was on stage right in the dimmer pit), and he had this awesome smile on his face, pointing at the pin, and gestured *Thank you!* Years later, I saw it on his guitar strap in one of the videos."[25]

FEBRUARY 22, 1988
NASHVILLE, TENNESSEE
NASHVILLE MUNICIPAL AUDITORIUM, 417 Fourth Avenue North. Venue opened on October 7, 1962.
SUPPORT ACT: Tommy Shaw
TICKETS: $16.00 (all seats)
CAPACITY: 7,277

FEBRUARY 23, 1988
CINCINNATI, OHIO
RIVERFRONT COLISEUM, 100 Broadway Street. Venue opened on September 9, 1975.
SUPPORT ACT: Tommy Shaw
TICKETS: $16.50
CAPACITY: 12,500

FEBRUARY 25–26, 1988
ROSEMONT, ILLINOIS
ROSEMONT HORIZON, 6920 N. Mannheim Road. Venue opened on July 2, 1980.

SUPPORT ACT: Tommy Shaw
TICKETS: $16.50 / $17.50
ATTENDANCE (FEB. 25): 12,981; sold out
ATTENDANCE (FEB. 26): 10,003
TWO-DAY ROSEMONT CONCERT GROSS: $391,772
NOTES: A few of Tommy Shaw's former bandmates in Styx (James Young, John Panozzo, and Chuck Panozzo) checked out the second show.
CHICAGO TRIBUNE: "Rush is one of those bands that has managed to triumph on the concert circuit despite lack of radio airplay. The trio has been going strong for nearly fifteen years and shows no signs of slackening."

FEBRUARY 28, 1988
PEORIA, ILLINOIS
CIVIC CENTER ARENA, 201 SW Jefferson Street. Venue opened on June 7, 1982.
SUPPORT ACT: Tommy Shaw
TICKETS: $16.50
CAPACITY: 12,000

MARCH 1, 1988
ST. LOUIS, MISSOURI
ST. LOUIS ARENA, 5700 Oakland. Venue opened on September 23, 1929.
SUPPORT ACT: Tommy Shaw
TICKETS: $16.50 / $18.50
ATTENDANCE: 10,971
CAPACITY: 11,500
CONCERT GROSS: $175,032
ST. LOUIS POST-DISPATCH:
"Rush Captivates Crowd with Sight-Sound Collage: Rush transcended the basic power-trio format with a collage of lyrical and sonic textures and the use of fast-moving film images that delighted spellbound fans."

MARCH 2, 1988
INDIANAPOLIS, INDIANA
MARKET SQUARE ARENA, 300 East Market Street. Venue opened on September 15, 1974.
SUPPORT ACT: Tommy Shaw
TICKETS: $15.50
ATTENDANCE: 7,456
CAPACITY: 13,500
CONCERT GROSS: $115,568

MARCH 4–5, 1988
DETROIT, MICHIGAN
JOE LOUIS ARENA, 600 Civic Center Drive. Venue opened on December 12, 1979.
SUPPORT ACT: Tommy Shaw
TICKETS: $17.50
ATTENDANCE: 15,904 per show (approximate); sold out[26]
DETROIT FREE PRESS: "Rush show proves to be musical, visual event."

MARCH 7–8, 1988
TORONTO, ONTARIO
MAPLE LEAF GARDENS, 60 Carlton Street. Historic venue opened on November 12, 1931.
SUPPORT ACT: Chalk Circle
TICKETS: $19.50 / $22.50 CAD
ATTENDANCE (MAR. 7): 11,480
ATTENDANCE (MAR. 8): 9,010
TWO-DAY TORONTO CONCERT
GROSS: $458,181 CAD
TORONTO STAR: "Rush Happily Dwarfed by Its Own Technology: The three Torontonians have merely used available technology to subtly retool what remains a wildly bombastic machine."
BRAD HOPKINS (CHALK CIRCLE BASSIST): "To have the opportunity to play such an iconic building as Maple Leaf Gardens was a dream come true. Growing up as a hockey fan, it was such a thrill. actually, I saw Rush there on the *Hemispheres* tour. I grew up in Newcastle, Ontario, which is where Alex was filmed living on a farm in the *Come on Children* movie. It was crazy to see that, because I lived right near there. During 1975, I was working in a gas station on the 401, and was shocked at 4 a.m. when one by one, Alex, Geddy, and Neil came in to fill up their cars. They must have been driving home from a gig in Quebec. It was a very brief, very nice encounter. I got them to sign two credit card slips, instead of just one."[27]

MARCH 10, 1988
MONTREAL, QUEBEC
MONTREAL FORUM, 2313 Saint Catherine Street West. Historic venue opened on November 29, 1924.
SUPPORT ACT: Chalk Circle
TICKETS: $19.50 CAD
ATTENDANCE: 11,379
CAPACITY: 12,500
CONCERT GROSS: $221,891 CAD[28]

NOTES: A rowdy heavy metal crowd presented a challenge to Chalk Circle, with beer bottles thrown (one just missing drummer Derrick Murphy) and middle fingers raised, despite them playing a set of their heavier tunes.
MONTREAL GAZETTE: "Last night's show was endlessly inventive, and even tasteful. Most impressive of all was the reaction of the crowd. Despite a dearth of older hits from the Days of Olde, the full house at the Forum was rabidly enthusiastic."

MARCH 11, 1988
QUEBEC CITY, QUEBEC
COLISÉE DE QUEBEC, 250 boulevard Wilfrid-Hamel. Venue opened on December 8, 1949.
SUPPORT ACT: Chalk Circle
TICKETS: $19.50 CAD
ATTENDANCE: 9,580
CAPACITY: 11,800
CONCERT GROSS: $186,810 CAD[29]
ROCK EXPRESS: "Rush's glory days are admittedly behind them. Album sales and fan reaction prove that . . . the new material is horrendous."
LE SOLEIL: "The trio really surpassed last night for the pleasure of our ears and our eyes."

MARCH 12, 1988
OTTAWA, ONTARIO
OTTAWA CIVIC CENTRE, Lansdowne Park, 1015 Bank Street. Venue opened on December 29, 1967.
SUPPORT ACT: Chalk Circle
TICKETS: $19.50 CAD (unconfirmed)
CAPACITY: 9,349

APRIL 2, 1988
OMAHA, NEBRASKA
CIVIC AUDITORIUM ARENA, 1804 Capitol Avenue. Venue dedicated on January 2, 1955.
SUPPORT ACT: The Rainmakers
TICKETS: $16.50, general admission
ATTENDANCE: 7,609[30]
CAPACITY: 12,000
NOTES: Feedback during "Prime Mover" forced Geddy to make a brief pause.
OMAHA WORLD-HERALD: "Fans of Enduring Rush Hear Power—Rock Sampler: Rush's music is not always the most melodic, but Peart's lyrics are intelligent, and Saturday night's concert offered plenty of spectacle."

BOB WALKENHORST (THE RAINMAKERS GUITARIST / VOCALIST): "Oh, I clearly remember those gigs with Rush. We were on the same label in 1988, so our managers got us on the bill. What I didn't know was that we got the gig because Tommy Shaw couldn't take the abuse every night, and he was bailing from the tour. Our booking agent, Chip Hooper, called me up and said, 'I want to go on record right now as saying that you should *not* take this gig opening for Rush. Rush fans are extremely dedicated and make a nightly ritual of slaughtering the opening act, sort of as a sacrifice. I know—I was one of those guys in a Rush T-shirt in the front row, standing there with my middle finger/arm in the air during the opening act's entire set. I don't even know who it was—could have been the Beatles and it wouldn't have mattered.' I said, 'Hey, Chip, these are Midwestern dates—cities where we have strong followings—I think we will be OK.' Chip said, 'All right, I warned you.' First night was in Omaha, where we had been playing for years with a good local following. We ran onstage, and before we played a note, we were pelted with Skoal cans, rolls of toilet paper, and other crap. We started playing, gave it our best, and got booed continuously. When we left the stage, the stage manager pointed out that we were supposed to play forty minutes, and we had only played twenty-three. We kept on walking."[31]

APRIL 4, 1988
BLOOMINGTON, MINNESOTA
MET CENTER, 7901 Cedar Avenue South. Venue opened on October 21, 1967.
SUPPORT ACT: The Rainmakers
TICKETS: $17.50
ATTENDANCE: 8,664
CAPACITY: 10,500
CONCERT GROSS: $151,620

APRIL 5, 1988
MILWAUKEE, WISCONSIN
MECCA ARENA, 400 West Kilbourn Avenue. Venue opened on April 9, 1950.
SUPPORT ACT: The Rainmakers
TICKETS: $17.50
ATTENDANCE: 9,605; sold out
CONCERT GROSS: $164,133

APRIL 7, 1988
KANSAS CITY, MISSOURI
KEMPER ARENA, 1800 Genessee Street at 17th Street. Venue dedicated on October 18, 1974.
SUPPORT ACT: The Rainmakers
TICKETS: $16.75
ATTENDANCE: 9,524
CAPACITY: 11,200
CONCERT GROSS: $152,609
BOB WALKENHORST (THE RAINMAKERS GUITARIST / VOCALIST): "The next three shows went much better, ending in our hometown of Kansas City. I still have people to this day say that they had never heard of the Rainmakers until we opened for Rush, and they became fans of ours. So I guess it was worth it. But it was brutal. We were treated well, paid well, and everything was very professional. Plenty of space onstage, thorough sound check. Met the guys in Rush very briefly on a couple dates. They were friendly and polite, like they clearly knew what we were in for."[32]

APRIL 9, 1988
LOUISVILLE, KENTUCKY
LOUISVILLE GARDENS, 525 Muhammad Ali Boulevard. Historic venue dedicated on December 31, 1905.
AN EVENING WITH RUSH
TICKETS: $15.50 (advance) / $16.50 (day of)
ATTENDANCE: 3,965
CAPACITY: 5,000
CONCERT GROSS: $62,668
NOTES: Sound check featured an extended jam. Tommy Shaw was announced as the opener, but he ended up canceling the final six dates of the tour. All blurbs in the Louisville *Courier-Journal* through April 9 continued to list him as support.
COURIER-JOURNAL **(LOUISVILLE):** "High-tech gadgetry has been a big part of the Rush sound in the 1980s, but the group has reached the point now where it isn't in control of its music during live performances—and that has caused the band to lose a lot of the spontaneity it had onstage in the 1970s . . ."

APRIL 10, 1988
DAYTON, OHIO
HARA ARENA, 1001 Shiloh Springs Road. Venue opened on November 1, 1964.

AN EVENING WITH RUSH
TICKETS: $15.50 / $16.50, general admission
ATTENDANCE: 5,430
CAPACITY: 7,500
CONCERT GROSS: $85,069
NOTES: Final North American date of the *Hold Your Fire* tour. Neil pedaled his Fuji into the gig and was the first one onstage, where he was soon joined by Alex and Geddy for a spirited sound check. During the show, Alex played some prominent harmonics before the break in "Force Ten." In "Lock and Key," Geddy sang the line "On that we all agree" in rhythm to Alex's guitar part, which added a refreshing take. For the encore, Alex was in good voice, as he "la la la'd" his way through the intro to "La Villa Strangiato."
GEDDY (ONSTAGE): "You might be interested to know that this is the last date of our American tour this year, so thank you, USA!"

APRIL 21, 23–24, 1988
BIRMINGHAM, WEST MIDLANDS, ENGLAND
NATIONAL EXHIBITION CENTRE ARENA, Pendigo Way and Perimeter Road, Marston Green. Venue opened on December 5, 1980.
AN EVENING WITH RUSH
TICKETS: £9.00 / £10.00
ATTENDANCE: 11,000 per show (approximate); sold out
NOTES: On April 21, *A Show of Hands* was recorded, and test filming was done in preparation for the April 23 video shoot. Rush broke the NEC's in-house record for merchandise sold. The crew drove on to Glasgow (289 miles) after the gig, while the band spent the night in Birmingham.
GEDDY: "A lot of tracks on *A Show of Hands* were recorded from the last show we recorded, in Birmingham, UK. The second-to-last night, we also did a video shoot and there were a large number of cameras onstage. What I think happened was, the next night the cameras were all gone, so it almost felt like nothing was happening. Everybody relaxed. Everybody gave a very loose performance in relief that there was no camera pointed at us."[33]

APRIL 26, 1988
GLASGOW, SCOTLAND
SCOTTISH EXHIBITION AND CONFERENCE CENTRE, Hall 4, Exhibition Way. Venue opened on September 7, 1985.
AN EVENING WITH RUSH
ATTENDANCE: 9,000 (approximate), general admission; sold out
TICKETS: £9.50
NOTES: Venue aka Glasgow SECC. After the show, the entourage made its way to London. Alex and Geddy took a late flight, while the crew drove the 401 miles.
PETER BROCKBANK: "I really enjoyed the long night drives between gigs. Having quickly changed into fresh clothes, Neil would start to relax by drinking a small single malt whiskey and smoking a cigarette. One of my jobs to make sure there were always some of both in the BMW for this purpose. Neil never slept for a second during any of these long drives, often acting as navigator when required. After the SECC show in Glasgow, Neil had to run down an adjacent hall, around 200 yards, to reach the car. This hall was covered in carpet tiles, and no matter how hard I tried or what financial inducement I offered, the supervisor wouldn't allow me to drive the car over them. I even made the suggestion of removing one tile each side of the car, all the way to the back, so I could reverse without doing any damage. I told the guy I would take up the tiles myself, and pay to have them replaced, after we left, with no joy. Having just finished a two-hour set and that sprint, Neil arrived at the car and was hardly out of breath. I guess you have to be super fit to be a rock drummer!"[34]

APRIL 28–30, 1988
LONDON, ENGLAND
WEMBLEY ARENA, Arena Square at Engineers Way. Venue opened on August 4, 1934.
AN EVENING WITH RUSH
TICKETS: £10.00
ATTENDANCE: 8,700 per show (approximate); sold out
NOTES: After the second show at Wembley, Alex was in the dressing room cracking up because an intoxicated Yngwie Malmsteen thought that one of Alex's friends was Neil. "I just loved the way you played," he says, while Alex was just rolling with laughter.

MAY 2, 1988
ROTTERDAM, SOUTH HOLLAND, THE NETHERLANDS
AHOY SPORTPALEIS, Ahoy-weg 10. Venue opened on January 15, 1971.
AN EVENING WITH RUSH
TICKETS: 32.50 / 37.50 NLG
ATTENDANCE: 11,540; sold out
NOTES: The venue is a large bicycle velodrome, so there is a big space where the track is, between the floor and the stands, making for an interesting setting. Before the show, Alex was in a festive mood as he sat playing his guitar in the tuning room. While Neil read a book, Geddy greeted his old friend Kees Baars, manager of the Dutch rock band Vandenburg, who opened for Rush on the *Signals* tour. A fired-up crowd was rewarded with an impressive set, complete with rear-projected laser writing in Dutch. After the gig, back in Amsterdam, Geddy, Kees, and Howard headed out for a drink and a meal, with Kees reminiscing about seeing Rush for the first time in 1979: "Remember when Tony fell off the stage and broke his legs at the Pink Pop Festival?"

MAY 3, 1988
The crew flew to Frankfurt on KLM Flight 243 and arrives at 2:05 pm. Geddy toured Amsterdam with Nancy and Kees, while Neil drove through the Black Forest in Germany.

PETER BROCKBANK: "After the show, we traveled over night to Frankfurt, and as the next day was a day off, Neil wanted to have an afternoon in the Black Forest. . . . He put the BMW into sports mode, which dropped the suspension and enabled it to be driven manually. Then he drove it like a rally car round the narrow winding roads. As with everything Neil does, his driving was excellent. He had taken racing car lessons in Canada, and it showed."

MAY 4, 1988
FRANKFURT, HESSE, WEST GERMANY
FESTHALLE, Ludwig Erhard Anlage, 8000. Venue opened on May 19, 1909.
SUPPORT ACT: Wishbone Ash
TICKETS: 33 DEM / 38 DEM (advance); 35 DEM / 40 DEM (day of)
CAPACITY: 12,400
NOTES: Geddy and Alex arrived in Frankfurt on KLM Flight 243 at 2:05 p.m. The band's dressing room was situated right over the crowd as they entered the hall. The band

observed all the different types of people walking in, while they told funny stories.

PETER BROCKBANK: "After dropping Neil off at the rear of the Festhalle, I parked the car outside, as I wasn't allowed to leave it in the hall (as I normally would at most venues). At the end of the show, I wandered backstage. There was no hurry, as I knew Neil was having a couple of drinks before we left. As I passed the place where I had parked the car, I realized it wasn't there. Total panic immediately set in. I found a security guard and managed to explain the problem. I showed him the empty space, and he explained I had parked over a sign written on the ground which said, in German, 'Parking for emergency vehicles only.' It had been towed to a compound. Not only was it over a mile away, there was a hundred-marks fine to pay. As we were staying that night in Frankfurt, I had left most of my money in the hotel. I quickly found Liam Birt and borrowed the necessary marks without telling him what it was for. As the concert had just finished, the road was full of people, and I couldn't find a taxi anywhere. I ran to the compound, and after a lengthy argument (was it my car? etc.), I paid the fine and drove it back to the hall, being very careful where I parked! I was still out of breath and no doubt totally disheveled as I tried to casually walk into the inner sanctum. I entered, everyone looked at me, and then Neil came over and asked if I had found the car. The whole room burst out clapping and laughing. I thought I had got away with it, but one of the security guards had asked for the driver and, when I couldn't be found, told Liam Birt it had to be removed because it was illegally parked. Everyone from the band to all of the crew knew about it, and they were highly amused. That wasn't the only time I would 'lose' a car on a Rush tour. No need to say there were car jokes aimed in my direction for the rest of the tour. The whole episode did keep a lot of people amused for a while, so I guess some good came out of it."

MAY 5, 1988
STUTTGART, GERMANY
SCHLEYER-HALLE, Mercedes Strabe 69. Venue inaugurated on September 14, 1983.
SUPPORT ACT: Wishbone Ash
TICKETS: 33 DEM / 38 DEM (advance); 35 DEM / 40 DEM (day of)

NOTES: Final date of the *Hold Your Fire* tour. This was front-of-house engineer Jon Erickson's final date with Rush. Alex was in a vocal mood and did most of the singing during sound check. The band rocked out on some '60s classics, including a couple of blues jams. Outside the gig, members of the Rush Italian Fan Club waited in anticipation of their first Rush concert. Two entire busloads made the trek from Milan. During the gig, a great version of "Force Ten" was performed, with Alex wailing on his tremolo bar along with Ged's vocals. For the encore, the crew rigged the balloons to rain down on the stage as a surprised band continued playing through the hilarity of the moment. After the show, and several interviews, Geddy pondered, "Why do people always ask the same questions in interviews?"

PETER BROCKBANK: "Throughout the tour, during the last number of every show, dozens of red balloons were released from their netting to fall down on the audience. One of the crew told me to watch the final song but wouldn't tell me why. I did find out that something was always arranged as a surprise for the band on the last night of a tour. As all those balloons were released, they fell onto the stage rather than the audience, much to the huge amusement of Alex, Geddy, and Neil. Apparently, the riggers had spent hours moving the netting back to achieve this goal. In no time, the stage was covered in balloons, with the guys all laughing. Alex threw himself on top of a load of them. It was almost a bouncy-castle situation. Insanely grinning, he continued playing as he bounced horizontally across the stage—an amazing and hilarious sight."

1. Neil Peart. *Roadshow: Landscape With Drums, A Concert Tour By Motorcycle*. Rounder Books, 2006.
2. Bill Banasiewicz. Interview with Brad Hopkins, October 18, 2015.
3. *The Chronicle Herald*.
4. Halifax Q104 FM, November 2, 1987.
5. *Billboard*.
6. *Binghamton Press and Sun Bulletin*.
7. *Amusement Business and Pollstar*.
8. Bill Banasiewicz. Interview with Geddy Lee, November 27, 1987.
9. *Charlotte Observer*.
10. Bill Banasiewicz. Interview with Neil Peart, November 27, 1987.
11. Bill Banasiewicz. Interview with Liam Birt, November 28, 1987.
12. Bill Banasiewicz. Interview with Geddy Lee, November 30, 1987.
13. Bill Banasiewicz. Interview with Neil Peart, December 5, 1987.
14. Bill Banasiewicz. Interview with Geddy Lee, December 5, 1987.
15. Interview with Neil Peart. *Scene Magazine*, December 12, 1987.
16. Bill Banasiewicz. Interview with Geddy Lee, December 7, 1987.
17. Bill Banasiewicz. Interview with Ahmet Ertegun, December 11, 1987.
18. Bill Banasiewicz. Interview with Michael Cartellone, November 13, 2015.
19. Bill Banasiewicz. Interview with Tommy Shaw, January 14, 1988.
20. *The Oklahoman*.
21. *Amusement Business and Pollstar*.
22. Eric Hansen. Interview with Bob Kniffen, January 13, 2013.
23. Interview with Neil Peart. *The Oklahoman*, January 22, 1988.
24. *Tampa Bay Times*.
25. Skip Daly. Interview with Conrad Cortiz, 2013.
26. *Detroit Free Press*.
27. Bill Banasiewicz. Interview with Brad Hopkins, October 18, 2015.
28. *Amusement Business*.
29. *Amusement Business*.
30. *Omaha World-Herald*.
31. Bill Banasiewicz. Interview with Bob Walkenhorst, September 29, 2015.
32. Bill Banasiewicz. Interview with Bob Walkenhorst, September 29, 2015.
33. Interview with Geddy Lee. *Greenville News*, February 16, 1990.
34. Peter Brockbank. *Legends of Brocklehurst*. brocklehusrtsroadiestories.blogspot.com/2012/10/legends-of-brocklehurst.html

Chapter 21

THE PRESTO TOUR

The *Presto* tour saw Rush perform to more than 650,000 fans over the course of sixty-three concerts. The set list was refined as the outing progressed: Initially, "Superconductor" followed "Show Don't Tell," and "The Big Money" began the encore. Five days into the run, "Superconductor" was slotted before "Show Don't Tell." Beginning on March 31, "The Spirit of Radio" replaced "The Big Money." Older songs like "Xanadu," "Freewill," and "Red Barchetta" returned to the set for the first time in years (with Geddy remarking at the time that he had to relearn parts of "Red Barchetta"). Curiously, the title track from *Presto* was omitted from the set list; it would not be performed live until the 2010 *Time Machine* trek.

"As always, there was a lot of work involved in preparing for a new tour, but especially this one," Neil remarked during *Presto* tour rehearsals in February 1990. "[We] were determined not to make it a continuation of previous tours, but a whole new thing: the first Rush tour of the '90s. So we had a lot to think about, in the music and presentation of the show."

The new production elements for the tour expanded on the *Presto* cover art theme and included lasers, multicolored Vari-Lites that dropped from the trusses on accordion-like extensions, rear PA speakers (two sets, flown at the back end of the floor) for quadrophonic-like sound, surreal films on the rear-projection screen (including the opening video sequence with cartoon people waiting in line to see *Attack of the Killer Rabbits*), and two giant rabbits that emerged from similarly oversized magicians' hats on each side of the stage during "War Paint." In "Scars," a transparent screen was lowered in front of the stage, obscuring the band while various light patterns and shapes were projected from behind for a particularly cool effect.

A review in the *Washington Post* following the band's May 5 show at the Capital Centre in Largo, Maryland, reported, "No one ever accused Rush, the veteran Canadian arena rock trio, of being unbridled showmen. In fact, compared with most heavy rock-cum-metal bands, the group could pass for a still life on stage. But that's not to say the show wasn't colorfully animated. What with cartoons and vintage films flickering on a screen behind them, multihued laser beams crisscrossing the arena and giant inflatable bunnies popping out of huge hats on stage, there were diversions galore."

Occasionally, audience members supplied their own diversions. At the UNO Lakefront Arena in New Orleans on February 25, 1990, fans threw Mardi Gras beads onstage throughout the show, much to Geddy's dismay. He joked from the stage that night, "I guess a happy Mardi Gras is in order. All right, I've got my beads now. Careful! I want to get out of here alive! Whoa! Okay, I got some beads now—you can stop throwing them."

OPPOSITE: St. Petersburg, FL; Geddy at spring training.

ABOVE: The team photo of Rush and Mr. Big with their crews.

TOUR HISTORY
PRESTO

SET LIST:
Intro ("A Show of Hands" video)
"Force Ten"
"Freewill" (abridged)
"Distant Early Warning"
"Time Stand Still"
"Subdivisions"
"Marathon"
"Red Barchetta"

"Superconductor"
"Show Don't Tell"
"The Pass"
"Closer to the Heart"
"Manhattan Project"
"Xanadu"
"YYZ"
"The Rhythm Method" (drum solo)
"Scars"

"War Paint"
"Mission"
"Tom Sawyer"
Encore:
"The Big Money"
"2112: Overture"
"La Villa Strangiato"
"In the Mood"
"Wipe Out"

FEBRUARY 17, 1990
GREENVILLE, SOUTH CAROLINA
GREENVILLE MEMORIAL AUDITORIUM, 401 East North Street. Venue opened on December 1, 1958.
SUPPORT ACT: Mr. Big
TICKETS: $19.00, general admission
ATTENDANCE: 7,230; sold out
NOTES: The opening date of the 1990 *Presto* tour featured the live debut of "Show Don't Tell," "The Pass," "Superconductor," "War Paint," and "Scars." This was Robert Scovill's first concert with Rush as their front-of-house sound engineer, and Andrew MacNaughtan joined the entourage as personal assistant. By late afternoon, a line of several thousand stretched around the venue on a sunny, springlike day. The first chords of sound check added to the air of excitement. Overall, except for a few minor technical problems, the band was in great form for an opening show, with Geddy donning glasses onstage for the very first time and Neil debuting his new (black-purple) Ludwig Super Classic kit. During "Time Stand Still," Geddy had some vocal trouble and missed the lyric "Let my defenses down." Throughout the night, he talked through certain lines, giving the songs a unique feel. After the guitar solo in "Tom Sawyer," he sang a different melody on the chorus, while "Superconductor" featured a big, lengthy drum-flurry ending. Geddy triggered Alex's voice echoing "That's nice!" from the end of "Chain Lightning" (during the finale of "The Big Money"), and fans started going nuts in anticipation of the song being performed, only to be disappointed when it was not played. The encore began with "The Big Money" for the first six weeks of the trek,

while "The Spirit of Radio" was not performed at this point—marking the first time this song had been "benched" since its 1979 debut.
GEDDY (ONSTAGE): "It's a great pleasure for us to be back in America and opening our tour here tonight."
ANDREW MACNAUGHTAN (PERSONAL ASSISTANT): "It was the chance of a lifetime to go on the road with a rock and roll band. I can unequivocally state that they are the most boring band on the road. We would leave the concert, get on the bus, eat hot dogs, watch a movie, and go to bed. They're three boring guys. There aren't chicks, there aren't parties—it's not them."[1]
PAUL GILBERT (MR. BIG GUITARIST): "The very first day of the tour, I walked into the catering room where everybody was eating and I saw Geddy, who was just sitting there eatin' some dinner, minding his own business. And before we had gotten there that day, I thought to myself, 'I've gotta be cool; I don't want to bug these guys. They're big and famous, and I'm sure people are buggin' them all the time.' But as soon as I saw Geddy, I had to, like, run over and go, 'Geddy, it's so great to meet you! You're so great!' I mean, I completely alienated him for a month there."[2]

FEBRUARY 19, 1990
JACKSONVILLE, FLORIDA
JACKSONVILLE VETERANS MEMORIAL COLISEUM, 1145 Adams Street. Venue dedicated on November 24, 1960.
SUPPORT ACT: Mr. Big
TICKETS: $18.50
ATTENDANCE: 7,254 (*Florida Times-Union*: 7,038)

CAPACITY: 7,500
CONCERT GROSS: $128,279
NOTES: A late addition to the itinerary, this date was originally scheduled for St. Petersburg.
***FLORIDA TIMES-UNION*(JACKSONVILLE):** "Rush gets old quickly, until instrumental encore: For thirty minutes, Rush is a pretty good band. Too bad the trio played for more than two hours before a packed Coliseum crowd. Like Pink Floyd, Rush makes rock a visual experience. Unfortunately, this band is more pleasing to the eye than to the ear."

FEBRUARY 20, 1990
ST. PETERSBURG, FLORIDA
BAYFRONT CENTER ARENA, 400 First Street South. Venue dedicated on May 1, 1965.
SUPPORT ACT: Mr. Big
TICKETS: $18.50
ATTENDANCE: 7,094
CAPACITY: 8,400
CONCERT GROSS: $124,838
NOTES: Originally slated for February 19, but rescheduled after the on-sale date, with tickets for the February 19 honored on the 20th.

FEBRUARY 22, 1990
MIAMI, FLORIDA
MIAMI ARENA, 701 Arena Boulevard. Venue opened on July 13, 1988.
SUPPORT ACT: Mr. Big
TICKETS: $18.50 (all seats)
ATTENDANCE: 13,541; sold out
CONCERT GROSS: $245,662
NOTES: "Superconductor" and "Show Don't Tell" swap places in the set.

293

FEBRUARY 23, 1990
ORLANDO, FLORIDA
ORLANDO ARENA, 600 West Amelia Street. Venue opened on January 29, 1989.
SUPPORT ACT: Mr. Big
TICKETS: $18.50
ATTENDANCE: 12,156; sold out
CONCERT GROSS: $220,650
NOTES: This gig was much more cohesive than the Greenville opener. The band seemed a lot more comfortable and in control of the proceedings. During the first verse of "War Paint," Geddy missed the lyric "It has to be today." Typical of the *Hold Your Fire* and *Presto* tours, the "In the Mood" finale concluded with some jazz bass and hi-hat improv. In the dressing room after the show, Geddy and Alex were quite pleased with their performance. Alex joked around, while Geddy spent some time with Nancy and Julian, who were down for the Florida portion of the tour.

FEBRUARY 25, 1990
NEW ORLEANS, LOUISIANA
UNO LAKEFRONT ARENA, University of New Orleans East campus, 6801 Franklin Street. Venue opened on November 1, 1983.
SUPPORT ACT: Mr. Big
TICKETS: $17.50 / $18.50, general admission
ATTENDANCE: 9,204; sold out
CONCERT GROSS: $165,113
NOTES: Rush played a festive set to a fired-up crowd. Much to Geddy's dismay, fans threw Mardi Gras beads onstage throughout the show. During "Tom Sawyer," Geddy yelled, "The river!" with inspired emphasis.

FEBRUARY 26, 1990
HOUSTON, TEXAS
THE SUMMIT, 3700 Southwest Freeway. Venue opened on November 1, 1975.
SUPPORT ACT: Mr. Big
TICKETS: $18.65
ATTENDANCE: 13,153; sold out
CONCERT GROSS: $240,119
NOTES: A few obstructed-view seats remained on the day of the show.
HOUSTON CHRONICLE: "Rush hour at the Summit more style than substance: The longstanding trio spent the night convincing a sellout crowd of some 15,000 that their tedious, bloated arrangements actually housed rock 'n' roll of such complexity, such keening import, daring, and imagination that the music could never go back to its three-chord simplicity and remain interesting."

FEBRUARY 28, 1990
SAN ANTONIO, TEXAS
CONVENTION CENTER ARENA, HemisFair Park Complex, 601 Hemisfair Way. Venue opened on April 6, 1968.
SUPPORT ACT: Mr. Big
TICKETS: $16.50 / $17.50
ATTENDANCE: 9,656
CAPACITY: 11,468
CONCERT GROSS: $158,698
NOTES: The band spent sound check focusing on the newer material, with "Superconductor," "The Pass," and "Scars" all performed. Later, Alex and Neil left the stage, while Geddy concluded with a solo rendition of "Subdivisions," something that would become ubiquitous at future sound checks.
KERRANG!: "There are a lot of Rush fans in South Texas, and it looks like every one of them got a seat for this show. How else can you explain the tremendous roar that goes that goes up when the lights go black, the vibration that rolls up your spine as thirteen thousand people rise to their feet, the applause that crackles like prairie fire from balcony to stage-edge? Let me tell ya, I'm not going over the top here; these are easily the most exciting concert moments I've experienced in years. How can the music be so hot, while the band is so cool?"

MARCH 1, 1990
DALLAS, TEXAS
REUNION ARENA, 777 Sports Street. Venue dedicated on April 28, 1980.
SUPPORT ACT: Mr. Big
TICKETS: $17.50 / $18.50
ATTENDANCE: 15,666; sold out
CONCERT GROSS: $239,509
NOTES: During an energetic show, two Playboy bunnies appeared onstage to bring Geddy a beverage. Backstage after the concert, Geddy, Alex, and Ray spent a solid hour meeting and greeting the various media and record-industry people gathered at the gig.
DALLAS MORNING NEWS: "A real Rush of power rock—Trio delivers message to conscientious crowd: March came in like a lion Thursday night as Rush roared into Reunion. The Canadian trio delivered just what the adoring fans in the packed arena came for—two hours of tight rock with something to say—and had a great time doing it."
METAL HAMMER: "Rush played each song with a meticulous perfection; I'm not sure if I'm okay with that or not."

MARCH 3, 1990
KANSAS CITY, MISSOURI
KEMPER ARENA, 1800 Genessee Street at 17th Street. Venue dedicated on October 18, 1974.
SUPPORT ACT: Mr. Big
TICKETS: $18.50 (upper level)
ATTENDANCE: 12,145[3]
CAPACITY: 16,000

MARCH 5, 1990
ST. LOUIS, MISSOURI
ST. LOUIS ARENA, 5700 Oakland. Venue opened on September 23, 1929.
SUPPORT ACT: Mr. Big
TICKETS: $18.50 (all seats)
ATTENDANCE: 12,750; sold out
CONCERT GROSS: $228,309
ST. LOUIS POST-DISPATCH: "Rush Brings Plenty of Power to Stage: Not since Pink Floyd has a group redefined the experience like Rush did at the Arena. The flawlessly executed show, complete with brilliant sound and lighting systems, as well as an array of lasers and other special effects, was worth the price of admission. The three handled their chores with great dexterity and panache. The interplay between drums and bass, most evident in 'Show Don't Tell,' was classic Rush."

MARCH 6, 1990
CINCINNATI, OHIO
RIVERFRONT COLISEUM, 100 Broadway Street. Venue opened on September 9, 1975.
SUPPORT ACT: Mr. Big
TICKETS: $18.50
ATTENDANCE: 13,032; sold out
CONCERT GROSS: $235,968

MARCH 8–9, 1990
AUBURN HILLS, MICHIGAN
THE PALACE OF AUBURN HILLS, 6 Championship Drive. Venue opened on August 13, 1988.

SUPPORT ACT: Mr. Big
TICKETS: $20.00
ATTENDANCE (MAR. 8): 14,000; sold out
ATTENDANCE (MAR. 9): 13,622
CAPACITY: 14,000
TWO-DAY AUBURN HILLS CONCERT GROSS: $572,440 (This differs from *Pollstar*; *Amusement Business* lists two sellouts with total attendance as 38,633.)
NOTES: As with most of the shows at the Palace, the concert on March 8 was filmed and broadcast via closed-circuit television, with much of the footage eventually landing in the 2016 *Time Stand Still* documentary as part of the "Live from the Rabbit Hole" bonus feature.
DETROIT FREE PRESS: "Canadian power trio makes successful rush on Palace: A full house of fans standing and waving their fists throughout the twenty-two-song show. The group was giving its faithful what it's grown to expect of a Rush concert."

MARCH 20, 1990
EDMONTON, ALBERTA
NORTHLANDS COLISEUM, 7424 118th Avenue NW. Venue opened on November 10, 1974.
SUPPORT ACT: Mr. Big
TICKETS: $24.25 CAD
ATTENDANCE: 7,500
CAPACITY: 13,049
EDMONTON JOURNAL: "Rush breaks the rules to reign supreme: Twenty-year veterans of the stage, these musicians have a respect for the audience and an inner dignity that's quite remarkable. Musically the band strives to be challenging, unpredictable and unique—and succeeds on all counts."

MARCH 21, 1990
CALGARY, ALBERTA
OLYMPIC SADDLEDOME, 555 Saddledome Rise SE. Venue opened on October 15, 1983.
SUPPORT ACT: Mr. Big
TICKETS: $22.50 CAD
ATTENDANCE: 8,107
CAPACITY: 11,754
CONCERT GROSS: $150,124 CAD

MARCH 23, 1990
VANCOUVER, BRITISH COLUMBIA
PACIFIC COLISEUM, Pacific National Exhibition Fairgrounds, 100 North Renfrew. Venue dedicated on January 8, 1968.
SUPPORT ACT: Mr. Big
TICKETS: $22.50 / $25.00 CAD
ATTENDANCE: 12,701; sold out
CONCERT GROSS: $254,485 CAD
THE PROVINCE: "Rush pulls in most Vancouver fans ever: This was the most fully realized of the band's Vancouver productions. Where there used to be three ordinary-looking but dedicated musicians furiously and earnestly whacking and thrashing in the name of progressive rock, now there is an environment in which they truly belong."

MARCH 24, 1990
PORTLAND, OREGON
MEMORIAL COLISEUM, 1401 North Wheeler. Venue opened on November 3, 1960.
SUPPORT ACT: Mr. Big
TICKETS: $19.00
ATTENDANCE: 8,931[4]
CAPACITY: 9,300
THE OREGONIAN: "Rush Dishes Up Feast for Eyes, Ears: The band has cultivated its art-rock sound to the point that even Lee's high tenor vocals have become likable. Somehow his dramatic tone fits. Lifeson's growling, powerful guitar was another high point. His windmilling solos and crashing runs carried what might have been standard pop fare to sonic heights."

MARCH 26, 1990
SEATTLE, WASHINGTON
SEATTLE CENTER COLISEUM, 305 Harrison Street. Venue opened on April 21, 1962.
SUPPORT ACT: Mr. Big
TICKETS: $18.50 (plus fees)
ATTENDANCE: 12,299; sold out
CONCERT GROSS: $219,410
SEATTLE POST-INTELLIGENCER, GEDDY: "Stylistically and technically we have spanned an ideal period of time. We're very much responsive to the changes in popular music. We don't feel threatened by them."
METAL HAMMER: "I think it's safe to say that in the massive realm of rock drummers, Neil Peart is about the best there is. The guy just makes it look so easy."

MARCH 28, 1990
SACRAMENTO, CALIFORNIA
ARCO ARENA, One Sports Parkway. Venue opened on November 8, 1988.
SUPPORT ACT: Mr. Big
TICKETS: $19.50 / $21.00 / $22.00
ATTENDANCE: 12,236; sold out
CONCERT GROSS: $232,602

MARCH 30–31, 1990
OAKLAND, CALIFORNIA
OAKLAND-ALAMEDA COUNTY COLISEUM ARENA, 7000 Coliseum Way. Venue opened on November 9, 1966.
SUPPORT ACT: Mr. Big
TICKETS: $19.50 / $21.00 / $22.00
ATTENDANCE: 13,062 per show; sold out
CONCERT GROSS: $254,718 per show
NOTES: "The Spirit of Radio" replaced "The Big Money" as the encore opener on March 31.

APRIL 2–3, 1990
INGLEWOOD, CALIFORNIA
GREAT WESTERN FORUM, 3900 West Manchester Boulevard. Venue opened on December 30, 1967.
SUPPORT ACT: Mr. Big
TICKETS: $20.00
ATTENDANCE: 14,000 per show; sold out
CONCERT GROSS: $267,650 per show
NOTES: Venue aka the Forum.
LOS ANGELES TIMES: "To the unconverted, the Rush show at the Forum still sounded like a Rush show from the '70s, the kind of screeched melodies (ever-evocative, rarely memorable) you're more likely to hear on Broadway these days than in rock arenas, floating on a stale wash of guitar drone. Rush might be the Andrew Lloyd Webber of stadium-rock cliché."
LOS ANGELES DAILY NEWS: "Effusive Mastery Rush's Tragic Flaw: Most of the songs performed Monday weren't really songs at all. Rather, they were complex suites bustling with disorienting tempo changes. But therein lies Rush's appeal. The typical Rush fan is a young music student impressed by the band's overwhelming virtuosity."

APRIL 5, 1990
SAN DIEGO, CALIFORNIA
SAN DIEGO SPORTS ARENA, 3500
Sports Arena Boulevard. Venue opened
on November 17, 1966.
SUPPORT ACT: Mr. Big
TICKETS: $18.50
ATTENDANCE: 12,000; sold out
CONCERT GROSS: $218,300
NOTES: Alex and Neil jammed with Billy
Sheehan at sound check because Geddy
was running late. An extended improvi-
sation of bass, guitar, and drums ensued.
"The Spirit of the Radio" once again
replaced "The Big Money" as the encore
opener—a position it would hold for the
remainder of the tour.
SAN DIEGO UNION: "Rush beats Mr.
Big in a Sports Arena battle of the bands:
Happily, Rush didn't need the diversions
all that often. The smart, sharp playing
of bassist Lee, guitarist Lifeson, and
drummer Peart generated a good deal of
internal instrumental tension."
**NICK KOTOS (PRODUCTION MAN-
AGER):** "Geddy forgot the words to
'Spirit of Radio.' Liam, myself, the head
sound company guy, and the head electrician were back in the band dressing
room during the show, and all of a
sudden, we hear . . . nothing. We all
panicked. The electrician sprints out to
make sure the power hadn't gone out to
something, the head sound guy sprints
out to make sure the PA hadn't blown
up. . . . . Liam was the stage manager at
that point, so he runs out to make sure
something hadn't happened to the
stage, and I ran out to make sure there
wasn't some other issue. Then all of a
sudden, the band starts playing again
and he starts singing. I walk over to the
side of the stage, and he comes over
and I say, 'What the fuck happened?'
and he says 'I forgot where I was . . . I
forgot the lyrics—I forgot the song! It
wasn't until Neil hit me with a drum
stick that I remembered where I was!' It
happens."[5]

APRIL 7, 1990
COSTA MESA, CALIFORNIA
PACIFIC AMPHITHEATRE, 100 Fair Drive
SUPPORT ACT: Mr. Big
TICKETS: $19.25 / $24.75
ATTENDANCE: 13,856
CAPACITY: 18,861
CONCERT GROSS: $298,250

APRIL 8, 1990
PHOENIX, ARIZONA
**ARIZONA VETERANS MEMORIAL
COLISEUM**, Arizona State Fairgrounds,
1826 West McDowell Road. Venue
opened on November 3, 1965.
SUPPORT ACT: Mr. Big
TICKETS: $18.50 (all seats)
ATTENDANCE: 13,669; sold out
CONCERT GROSS: $243,040

APRIL 19, 1990
ROCHESTER, NEW YORK
**ROCHESTER COMMUNITY WAR
MEMORIAL**, 100 Exchange Boulevard.
Venue opened on October 18, 1955.
SUPPORT ACT: Mr. Big
TICKETS: $19.50
NOTES: Rescheduled to April 28 due to
illness (Geddy had the flu). The
postponement came after the ice was
removed from the arena floor and a play-
off hockey game by the AHL Rochester
Americans delayed one day. The addi-
tional expenditure of removing and
resurfacing the ice cost the promoter
roughly $5,000, according to the
Democrat and Chronicle.

APRIL 20, 1990
EAST RUTHERFORD, NEW JERSEY
MEADOWLANDS ARENA, Meadowlands
Sports Complex, 50 State Route 120.
Venue opened on July 2, 1981.
SUPPORT ACT: Mr. Big
TICKETS: $18.50 / $20.00
ATTENDANCE: 18,717; sold out
CONCERT GROSS: $350,944
NOTES: Geddy was still sick, and the
sound was a little substandard. It was as
if the band hadn't played in a couple of
weeks. Someone threw something
onstage, causing some technical issues
with the keyboards, and knocking out
critical sounds to several songs, including "Subdivisions." Geddy broke a string
on his Wal bass during "Time Stand
Still," so Skip quickly produced his
backup bass—marking a rare appearance of the white Steinberger. During a
break, Nick Kotos made an onstage
appearance, giving Neil a drink in a large
bunny suit, while smoking a cigar, as two
Playboy bunnies brought refreshments to
Alex and Geddy. "In the Mood" featured
Mr. Big's Eric Martin screaming in a high
falsetto on the chorus. It was followed by
Rush's take on the 1963 Surfaris classic

"Wipe Out," which helped close out the
encore.
THE RECORD (HACKENSACK): "Rush
Lets Its Standards Carry the Show: As
long as there are teenage males (the
chief component of Rush's audience)
who like loud, flashy, and sometimes
pompous music, the trio's approach fills
the bill."

APRIL 22, 1990
UNIONDALE, NEW YORK
**NASSAU COUNTY VETERANS
MEMORIAL COLISEUM**, 1255
Hempstead Turnpike. Venue dedicated
on May 29, 1972.
SUPPORT ACT: Mr. Big
TICKETS: $18.50 / $20.00
ATTENDANCE: 15,546; sold out
CONCERT GROSS: $302,391
NOTES: At the end of "Subdivisions,"
Geddy scat-sang after the vocal line "Of
youth." During "Show Don't Tell," he
flubbed a chorus, but quickly recovered,
singing "I've heard it all short," instead
of "Let's try to keep this short." In
"Mission," Neil added a nice triplet fill
out of the marimba section.

APRIL 24, 1990
PHILADELPHIA, PENNSYLVANIA
THE SPECTRUM, 3601 South Broad
Street. Venue opened on October 1,
1967.
SUPPORT ACT: Mr. Big
TICKETS: $18.50
ATTENDANCE: 14,130; sold out
CONCERT GROSS: $256,937
(*Amusement Business*)
NOTES: A vocal crowd sang throughout a
great show. Alex sang "M-m-m-m" on
the chorus to "In the Mood."
THE PHILADELPHIA INQUIRER: "At least
the light show and special effects were
innovative at last night's sold-out Rush
concert. The music sure wasn't. One of
the premier power trios of the progressive movement, once staples of the FM
airwaves, sounded as dated as the worst
Mersey beat sounds or '70s disco
music."

APRIL 25, 1990
EAST RUTHERFORD, NEW JERSEY
MEADOWLANDS ARENA, Meadowlands
Sports Complex, 50 State Route 120
SUPPORT ACT: Mr. Big
TICKETS: $18.50 / $20.00

ATTENDANCE: 13,138
CAPACITY: 14,953
CONCERT GROSS: $241,334
NOTES: This Meadowlands performance was much tighter and more together than the one just five days before, though Alex did break a string after the instrumental section of "Force Ten" and it took him almost until the end of the song to get a new guitar.

APRIL 27, 1990
PHILADELPHIA, PENNSYLVANIA
THE SPECTRUM, 3601 South Broad Street
SUPPORT ACT: Mr. Big
TICKETS: $18.50
ATTENDANCE: 14,130; sold out
CONCERT GROSS: $256,937
(*Amusement Business*)
NOTES: The band's bus was late to arrive from New York, so sound check didn't happen until after 5 p.m. Backstage, Geddy pondered the upcoming baseball season and which games he could attend, while Neil was excited about Roger Waters's upcoming performance of *The Wall* in Berlin. After the show, as the band bus pulled up the Spectrum ramp, Geddy was in the front of the coach, blessing the crowd.
GEDDY (ONSTAGE): "You all sound in very good voice out there tonight!"
NEIL: "It sounds like the *Wall* show will be amazing. A production of that scale could only be performed once."[6]

APRIL 28, 1990
ROCHESTER, NEW YORK
ROCHESTER COMMUNITY WAR MEMORIAL, 100 Exchange Boulevard
SUPPORT ACT: Mr. Big
TICKETS: $19.50
ATTENDANCE: 8,418; sold out
CONCERT GROSS: $158,866
NOTES: Originally slated for April 19, but rescheduled because of Geddy's bout with the flu.
GEDDY (ONSTAGE): "It's nice to finally get here! Sorry we couldn't play the last time. It was kind of unfortunate, but we're here now."

MAY 1, 1990
ATLANTA, GEORGIA
THE OMNI, 100 Techwood Drive Northwest. Venue opened on October 14, 1972.

SUPPORT ACT: Mr. Big
TICKETS: $19.50
ATTENDANCE: 12,186; sold out
CONCERT GROSS: $221,384
NOTES: Part of Mr. Big's set includes Paul Gilbert playing his guitar with a Makita power drill. In a *Spinal Tap* moment, he accidentally got the drill seriously tangled in his hair in front of a sellout crowd.
PAUL GILBERT (MR. BIG GUITARIST): "I was alone, onstage, playing my solo in front of 15,000 people. I had long, permed heavy-metal hair. The drill was spinning. Suddenly, they met! And a tangle ensued. Like Excalibur could not be pulled from the stone, the drill could not be untangled from my hair. My roadie got the scissors, but I protested. 'Hair is too important!' I screamed. Suddenly, I was surrounded by the entire Rush and Mr. Big crew, all with various plans to remove the drill and pointing flashlights at my head. Luckily, I had put leave-in conditioner in my hair before the show, and, combined with slowly unwinding the drill by hand, the heroic crew was able to pull the power tool from my precious locks. Billy provided an impromptu bass solo while all this was going on."[7]

MAY 2, 1990
CHARLOTTE, NORTH CAROLINA
CHARLOTTE COLISEUM, 100 Paul Buck Boulevard. Venue opened on August 11, 1988.
SUPPORT ACT: Mr. Big
TICKETS: $19.50
ATTENDANCE: 7,985
CAPACITY: 16,003
CONCERT GROSS: $155,708
NOTES: In reference to Paul Gilbert's onstage accident the previous night, Alex made a sign of a man holding a power drill to his head that reads, "A Power Tool Is Not a Toy. Beware!" He placed it next to the drill onstage, while the crew joined in on the joke by placing an array of new power tools on the side fill monitor.
TED LEAMY (ELECTROTEC): "The drill used to sit on a side fill where Paul could reach for it, and the next day in Charlotte, every fucking power utensil that you could possibly find in the building was piled up on top of the side fills next to the drill. There was a toaster, an air hammer, the vacuum cleaner . . . we put

hammers up there. There was every kind of dangerous utensil that Paul could kill himself or electrocute himself with—and of course the drill was sitting in the middle of them all."[8]

MAY 4, 1990
RICHMOND, VIRGINIA
RICHMOND COLISEUM, 601 East Leigh Street. Venue dedicated on August 21, 1971.
SUPPORT ACT: Mr. Big
TICKETS: $18.50
ATTENDANCE: 6,819
CAPACITY: 9,543
CONCERT GROSS: $126,152
NOTES: A brilliant performance, complete with Playboy bunnies serving refreshments.
GEDDY (ONSTAGE): "These are our dough bunnies. Just checking the freshness!"
RICHMOND TIMES-DISPATCH: "Backed by an overwhelming array of technology and assisted by rabbits, Canadian rock superheroes Rush descended on a delighted audience at the Coliseum. Fists pumped, and lighters flared as Rush powered their way through 'Closer to the Heart,' 'Tom Sawyer' and other radio staples."

MAY 5, 1990
LARGO, MARYLAND
CAPITAL CENTRE, 1 Harry S. Truman Drive. Venue opened on December 2, 1973.
SUPPORT ACT: Mr. Big
TICKETS: $19.50
CAPACITY: 18,100
NOTES: This date was originally scheduled for Hampton, Virginia, but that gig was moved to June 5. A fan from Chester County, Pennsylvania, attended this show instead of taking his girlfriend to their junior prom. Unfortunately, she sued him and was awarded $79.50 to cover the costs.[9]

MAY 7, 1990
PROVIDENCE, RHODE ISLAND
PROVIDENCE CIVIC CENTER, 1 La Salle Square. Venue opened on November 3, 1972.
SUPPORT ACT: Mr. Big
TICKETS: $19.50
ATTENDANCE: 11,888
CAPACITY: 12,100

a program on satellite imaging, and they were literally making a road map of Jupiter, and they were talking about rivers that they'd been able to map under the Sahara, which used to be a tropical rain forest. Just the imagery of that captured me."

JUNE 13, 1990
COLUMBUS, OHIO
COOPER STADIUM, 1125 W. Mound Street. Venue dedicated on June 3, 1932.
SUPPORT ACT: Mr. Big
TICKETS: $20.00 (general admission stadium) / $22.50 (reserved infield)
ATTENDANCE: 9,654
CONCERT GROSS: $207,515
NOTES: The venue is a AAA baseball stadium—a great setting for a strong performance. 6,000 portable (reserved) seats were set up on the infield. Howard lit up the trees behind the stage during "Xanadu" for a nice effect.
COLUMBUS DISPATCH: "Rush delivers without gimmicks: The band's spirited and efficient set certainly overcame any lyrical indulgences."

JUNE 14, 1990
NOBLESVILLE, INDIANA
DEER CREEK MUSIC CENTER, 12880 East 146th Street. Venue opened on May 20, 1989.
SUPPORT ACT: Mr. Big
TICKETS: $16.50 (lawn) / $19.50 (reserved pavilion)
ATTENDANCE: 7,904 (8,267— *Indianapolis Star*)
CAPACITY: 18,062
CONCERT GROSS: $135,198
INDIANAPOLIS STAR: "Rush's concert gives the fans what they want: This show generated a lot of musical heat and more than a little light."

JUNE 16–17, 1990
EAST TROY, WISCONSIN
ALPINE VALLEY MUSIC THEATRE, 2699 Highway D. Venue opened on June 30, 1977.
SUPPORT ACT: Mr. Big
TICKETS: $18.50 (lawn) $24.50 (upper reserved) / $29.50 (lower reserved)
TWO-DAY EAST TROY ATTENDANCE: 40,269
TWO-DAY CAPACITY: 60,000
TWO-DAY EAST TROY CONCERT

GROSS: $886,384
NOTES: On the second night, Mr. Big's Paul Gilbert and Eric Martin joined Rush onstage for "In the Mood."
PAUL GILBERT (MR. BIG GUITARIST): "I always try to catch at least a portion of Rush's set, after the business of Mr. Big is over for the night, and I can unwind a bit. This time usually finds me at the side of the stage for the end of their set. Eric began singing backup on 'In the Mood' early on in the tour, so while I'm sitting on the side of the stage the second night at Alpine Valley during the song, Skip hands me my guitar and tells me to go out and jam, so I did, and it was great fun! Alex kind of came over and told me the chords, but I said, 'It's cool. I already know them.' We had a great time, and we've been doing it ever since."[14]

JUNE 19, 1990
BLOOMINGTON, MINNESOTA
MET CENTER, 7901 Cedar Avenue South. Venue opened on October 21, 1967.
SUPPORT ACT: Mr. Big
TICKETS: $19.50
ATTENDANCE: 10,725; sold out
CONCERT GROSS: $201,864

JUNE 20, 1990
OMAHA, NEBRASKA
CIVIC AUDITORIUM ARENA, 1804 Capitol Avenue. Venue dedicated on January 2, 1955.
SUPPORT ACT: Mr. Big
TICKETS: $19.75
ATTENDANCE: 5,349[15]
CAPACITY: 8,000
NOTES: Just before the show, undercover police witnessed four individuals snorting a substance (believed to be cocaine) in a Chevy Cavalier near the venue. The four were arrested and the vehicle impounded.[16]
OMAHA WORLD-HERALD: "Slick Show Ushers Rush Into the '90s: The group's immediacy has slowed to the point that Rush could be called Reasonable Haste. But even though Rush has a lower profile, the group still has a following."

JUNE 22, 1990
ENGLEWOOD, COLORADO
FIDDLER'S GREEN AMPHITHEATRE, 6350 Greenwood Plaza Blvd. Venue opened on June 11, 1988.
SUPPORT ACT: Mr. Big
TICKETS: $16.00 (lawn) / $20.00 (orchestra)
CAPACITY: 16,416
NOTES: The band was a little surprised that it was still light as they took to the stage. After "The Rhythm Method" ended and "Scars" began, the overwhelmed crowd chanted, "Neil! Neil! Neil!"
ROCKY MOUNTAIN NEWS: "Canadian Power Band Gives Fans Radical Rush at Fiddler's Green: It was hardcore Rush-land, with the fans on their feet, stabbing the air with their fists and mouthing the lyrics nonstop from the minute the band stepped onstage."

JUNE 24, 1990
SALT LAKE CITY, UTAH
SALT PALACE, ACCORD ARENA, 100 S. West Temple. Venue dedicated on July 11, 1969.
SUPPORT ACT: Mr. Big
TICKETS: $18.00
CAPACITY: 13,000
NOTES: Part of Neil's agenda on the *Presto* tour involved a quest for America's cheapest motel. On his way to this show, however, things didn't quite go as planned, as he found himself having to bike over a mountain, at night, in the middle of a snowstorm. It was the price that had to be paid in order to escape from the relentless monotony of the tour. After their sound check, Paul Gilbert sat in Mr. Big's dressing room with his colorful Ibanez guitar, taking requests and talking Rush with another big fan. He performed sections of *Caress of Steel*, note perfect, off the top of his head. This was the last indoor gig of the tour, and Howard took full advantage, using the smoke-filled venue as his canvas to paint a dazzling display of light. During the encore, fans from the back of the hall stormed the stage and rocked out all through the finale.
THE DESERET NEWS: "Rhythms, Visuals Rush to Cast Spell: With lasers slicing through billowing smoke and abstract

cartoon characters flitting about a massive movie screen, Rush took the stage for another installment in a long history of visually and musically impeccable performances."

JUNE 26, 1990
SACRAMENTO, CALIFORNIA

CAL EXPO AMPHITHEATRE, California State Fairgrounds, 1600 Exposition Boulevard. Venue opened on July 26, 1983.

SUPPORT ACT: Mr. Big

TICKETS: $22.50 (general admission, field) / $25.00 (reserved) / $26.50 (orchestra)

ATTENDANCE: 14,355; sold out

CONCERT GROSS: $327,218

NOTES: A festive sound check was performed in shorts and sunglasses under a hot California sun. Fans stood atop a giant water slide, adjacent to the gig, to try and catch a glimpse of the band. The gig was a rowdy affair, with items thrown onstage throughout, and Alex and Geddy ducking the flying debris. During "Marathon," Alex added some high-sustained echo to the end of the first chorus. In "Show Don't Tell," Geddy literally shouted, "I the jury!"

GEDDY (BACKSTAGE AFTER SOUND CHECK): "I like doing these outdoor gigs. They make for a great environment on a nice day, although I think they are a bit harder on the sound man. They seem more difficult to mix. I don't know why, but that seems to be the case."[17]

JUNE 27, 1990
MOUNTAIN VIEW, CALIFORNIA

SHORELINE AMPHITHEATRE, One Amphitheatre Parkway. Venue opened on July 5, 1986.

SUPPORT ACT: Mr. Big

TICKETS: $19.50 (lawn) / $22.50 (reserved)

ATTENDANCE: 15,400

CAPACITY: 20,000

CONCERT GROSS: $287,931

NOTES: A professionally shot video was filmed. It was a scorching-hot day, and Neil (as always) was the first to arrive onstage. Within minutes, he was drenched in sweat, yet continued playing the drums very hard for a good half hour before Alex and Geddy joined him in a jam-filled sound check. Afterward, the crew covered up all of the gear with special heat-resistant material. The shiny silver covering gave the empty stage a unique look. During "Marathon," Geddy started off on the wrong note on his keyboards. For the encore, all four members of Mr. Big joined the band onstage for a spirited version of "In the Mood." Alex cracked up while doing his solo using a power drill (à la Paul Gilbert and Eddie Van Halen).

JUNE 28, 1990
LOS ANGELES, CALIFORNIA, AT THE PRESTO END-OF-TOUR PARTY

NEIL: "The first time we played the Shoreline Amphitheatre, on the *Presto* tour in 1990, I arrived there by bicycle with my brother Danny, who had flown down from Vancouver (with his bicycle) to spend a few days traveling the West Coast with me by bus and bicycle . . . We had a big party in a private section of a local nightclub. The theme of our party was the movie *Moon Over Parador* (another bus classic we could recite from memory), with the movie playing on television screens and the DJ dressed like the puppet dictator. On the fictional Caribbean island of Parador, the national cocktail was called a *puna*, and when the military dictator of Parador died, the evil power behind the throne, played by Raul Julia, scowled and said, 'Too many damn punas.' So, naturally, the official drink of our end-of-tour party was the puna, whipped up with cases of strong drink and tropical fruits by our irrepressible lighting director, Howard. Danny learned that night what too many damn punas meant, and the next day, when he was supposed to fly home, I had to go to his room and box up his bicycle for him while he lay in bed paralyzed and groaning."[18]

JUNE 29, 1990
IRVINE, CALIFORNIA

IRVINE MEADOWS AMPHITHEATER, 8808 Irvine Center Drive. Venue opened on August 21, 1981.

SUPPORT ACT: Mr. Big

TICKETS: $20.00 (general admission, lawn) / $26.50 (reserved)

ATTENDANCE: 15,000; sold out

CONCERT GROSS: $337,203

NOTES: Final date of the *Presto* tour. After sound check, Andrew MacNaughtan took the "team photo," with both bands and crews huddled onstage. Before Mr. Big's set, Rush joined them for a few more photos. The capacity crowd led Ray to joke that "it looks like they can fit five more people up on the lawn." Alex's younger son, Adrian, took in all of the excitement at the lighting board. All of Mr. Big joined Rush onstage for "In the Mood" (its final live performance). After the show, Geddy flew to New York for a few days, Neil flew home to Ontario, and Alex hung out telling jokes in the dressing room. (He flew home the next day.)

GEDDY (ONSTAGE): "I guess you may know this is the last date on our American tour this year. This is a nice place to come back and end it."

1. Jon Collins. *Chemistry*. Helter Skelter Books, 2006.
2. "Mr. Big Guitarist Paul Gilbert Can Deal With A Number-One Single At 25," *The Georgia Straight*, March 19, 1992. earofnewt.com
3. *Kansas City Star*.
4. *The Oregonian*.
5. Skip Daly. Interview with Nick Kotos, June 7, 2012.
6. Bill Banasiewicz. Interview with Neil Peart, April 27, 1990.
7. "20 Questions with Paul Gilbert," *Metal Sludge*, April 27, 2004.
8. Skip Daly. Interview with Ted Leamy, May 17, 2013.
9. *Associated Press*, July 1990.
10. Unpublished interview with Geddy Lee, May 7, 1990.
11. Bill Banasiewicz. Interview with Geddy Lee, May 8, 1990.
12. Bill Banasiewicz. Interview with Michel Langevin, October 15, 2015.
13. Bill Banasiewicz. Interview with Geddy Lee, June 2, 1990.
14. Bill Banasiewicz. Interview with Paul Gilbert, June 24, 1990.
15. *Omaha World-Herald*.
16. *Omaha World-Herald*.
17. Bill Banasiewicz. Interview with Geddy Lee, June 26, 1990.
18. Neil Peart. *Roadshow: Landscape With Drums, A Concert Tour By Motorcycle*. Rounder Books, 2006.

Chapter 22

THE ROLL THE BONES TOUR

More than 960,000 fans attended the *Roll the Bones* tour's 101 shows. The opening date of the trek featured the live debut of four new songs, "Dreamline," "Bravado," "Roll the Bones," and the funk instrumental "Where's My Thing?" ("I like the fact that we're getting a little funkier in our middling years," Geddy told *Bass Player* in 1992. "Considering that we're white and Canadian, we've got a lot going against us in terms of playing any sort of vaguely funky music, but it's definitely fun to play around with.") The most noteworthy element of the new songs' live presentation was the band's newfound willingness to improvise in certain sections. "Dreamline" and "Bravado" featured new, off-the-cuff guitar solos, while "Where's My Thing" began with a jazzy, atmospheric introduction.

"When we were putting this tour together, we started immediately playing with the arrangements of the new songs and putting some spontaneous bits in them," Neil explained to the *Orlando Sentinel*. "At this point, we feel that we can really perform a song as well live as it is on the record, so we have to push ourselves beyond that. It's just an ongoing learning process and refinement of what you're really supposed to be doing."

While no one would ever mistake Rush for a band much interested in improvisation, on March 3, 1992, Neil and tour manager Liam

Birt took advantage of a night off to attend a Grateful Dead gig at the Omni in Atlanta, with Neil remarking that "seeing the Grateful Dead was impressive, realizing just how much improvisation goes on at their shows." Rush played the same venue the following evening, and Grateful Dead drummer Mickey Hart attended as Neil's guest.

For this tour, "In the Mood" and "YYZ" were not included in the set list, while "Anthem" returned for the first time since 1980. "Ghost of a Chance" made its live debut on December 4, 1991, in Maryland. Beginning on the European leg, a short "Cygnus X-1" teaser was added to close the show. In Denver, with less than a month left in the tour, "Subdivisions" and "The Pass" were dropped and replaced by "The Trees," and at the next gig, in Salt Lake City, "Vital Signs" and "The Analog Kid" were added. These three songs remained in the set list for the duration of the tour. Updated keyboard technology gave many of the older songs, most notably "Distant Early Warning," "Tom Sawyer," and "La Villa Strangiato," a different flavor. Additionally, the encore

ABOVE: Mansfield, MA; Performing "2112" at Great Woods.

OPPOSITE: Mansfield, MA; Circling the drum kit at Great Woods.

featured a medley of older songs such as "The Spirit of Radio," "Finding My Way," and "Anthem," among others.

"We're closing with a monster medley of old songs," Neil told the *Hartford Courant*. "Some of them we had not played for fifteen years. Most of them we wouldn't feel like playing a whole song, but we put in a minute of it. It's great for us to do and a constant surprise for the audience."

Among the many opening acts on the tour were Primus, with whom Rush sparked a musical and personal friendship, engaging in regular jam sessions prior to shows. "Everyone would kind of just gravitate around the Primus dressing room about an hour or two before they went on," Geddy said. "Les [Claypool, Primus singer and bassist] would sometimes have a stand-up bass or a guitar, drums, whatever was around. I remember one jam just playing drumsticks on gym lockers. In Berlin, I was playing a garbage can. Neil was playing guitar, and he can't play guitar. It was fantastic. I love Primus, I love Les."

In an unusual move, the massive jaunt also saw Rush insert a full European leg of dates

into the middle of the tour, after which they returned for another month of shows in the US. It would be Rush's only European trek in the '90s.

In all, the *Roll the Bones* tour was one of Rush's longest outings. As such, the band tried to build in personal time whenever they could. "Being on the road can be very difficult, very boring, a procession of buses, hotel rooms, bars, with a constant craving to change your head space. And unless you get out and do something else, it's easy to fall into very bad habits," Alex told *Guitarist* magazine. "After all these years, I think we've finally found the balance. So Neil cycles, Geddy plays tennis, I play golf, and these are positive lifestyle diversions for us. The two hours on stage is still the absolute highlight, though, and I enjoy my playing more than ever."

According to Neil, the band was keeping busy during their hours offstage. "Our manager is complaining that when we're on tour he has to book a bicycling tour, a golf tour, and an art museum tour," he said. "You adopt other agendas on the road. This time, we're taking French lessons."

ABOVE: Mansfield, MA; Dirk and Lerxst switching places at Great Woods.

OPPOSITE: Mansfield, MA; Alex and Geddy locking in the groove at Great Woods.

TOUR HISTORY

ROLL THE BONES

SET LIST:
Intro (modified "A Show of Hands" video: "Skulls On Ice")
"Force Ten"
"Limelight"
"Freewill" (abridged)
"Distant Early Warning"
"Time Stand Still"
"Dreamline"
"Bravado"
"Roll the Bones"
"Show Don't Tell"
"The Big Money"
"Ghost of a Chance"
"Subdivisions" (abridged)
"The Pass"
"The Trees"
"Where's My Thing?"
"The Rhythm Method" (drum solo)
"Closer to the Heart"
"Xanadu"
"Superconductor"
"Tom Sawyer"
Encore:
"The Spirit of Radio"
"2112: Overture"
"Finding My Way"
"La Villa Strangiato"
"Anthem"
"Red Barchetta"
"The Spirit of Radio" (reprise)
"Cygnus X-1" (teaser)

OCTOBER 25, 1991
HAMILTON, ONTARIO
COPPS COLISEUM, 101 York Boulevard. Venue opened on November 30, 1985.
SUPPORT ACT: Andy Curran and Soho 69
TICKETS: $24.50 (CAD)
ATTENDANCE: 12,315; sold out
CONCERT GROSS: $268,529 ($301,718 CAD)
NOTES: The opening date of the *Roll the Bones* tour featured the live debut of "Dreamline," "Bravado," "Roll the Bones," and "Where's My Thing?" The most noteworthy element of the new songs' live presentation was the band's newfound willingness to improvise in certain sections. "Dreamline" and "Bravado" featured new, off-the-cuff guitar solos, while "Where's My Thing" began with a jazzy, atmospheric introduction. Updated keyboard technology gave many of the older songs a different flavor, most notably "Distant Early Warning," "Tom Sawyer," and "La Villa Strangiato." Onstage, Alex was late playing into the vocal verse of "Time Stand Still." During "Roll the Bones," Geddy didn't sing on the second chorus, so Alex was faintly heard picking up the vocals. For the encore, Geddy sang "The spirit of music" instead of "The freedom of music" during "The Spirit of Radio." Alex was playing so hard on "Finding My Way" that he broke a string in the middle of the song but was quickly given a new guitar.
HAMILTON SPECTATOR: "No Bones about it, Rush is great: The newest offering was Peart's drum solo, which surpasses his previous exhibitions and for the first time incorporated a melody.

The African-flavored polyrhythms, which included an impressive cross-wrist sticking technique, lauded him a two-minute standing ovation."
GEDDY (ONSTAGE): "It's a great pleasure for us to be here tonight to kick off our *Roll the Bones* tour. And because it's our first night, anything can happen, so keep your eyes open."
ANDY CURRAN: "Opening up for Rush, they had a bottle of champagne in our dressing room with a note wishing us luck . . . very classy. That's how they are today, even after all these years."[1]

OCTOBER 26, 1991
ROCHESTER, NEW YORK
ROCHESTER COMMUNITY WAR MEMORIAL, 100 Exchange Boulevard. Venue opened on October 18, 1955.
SUPPORT ACT: Eric Johnson
TICKETS: $20.00
ATTENDANCE: 8,404; sold out
CONCERT GROSS: $168,080
NOTES: A fired-up crowd welcomed the band on their first American date. During "Limelight," Alex broke a string in the first chorus. His solo in the extended section of "Bravado" brought down the house. The opening to "Subdivisions" changed, with Neil pounding out the rhythm on his low toms along with Geddy's F# F# F# keyboard line. The professor also added a counterrhythm with his bass drum. During the extended

introduction to "Xanadu," Neil created a musical aura using bells and chimes. He added high toms on the temple block parts and low tom and cymbal accents to the echo chimes passage. Both of these unique intros were performed for the duration of the tour. In "Superconductor," Geddy missed the first vocal line "Packaged like a rebel or a hero," and he spoke the lyrics "Hit you in a soft place with sentimental ease. She knows the fantasies that you romance to."
GEDDY (ONSTAGE): "This being only our second show on the tour, I hope you'll forgive us if something screws up."

OCTOBER 28, 1991
PITTSBURGH, PENNSYLVANIA
CIVIC ARENA, 300 Auditorium Place. Venue opened on September 17, 1961.
SUPPORT ACT: Eric Johnson
TICKETS: $19.75 / $25.00
ATTENDANCE: 11,956 (14,581— *Pittsburgh Press*)
CAPACITY: 12,479
CONCERT GROSS: $239,597
PITTSBURGH PRESS: "Rush delivers first-rate sound, visuals."

OCTOBER 29, 1991
CINCINNATI, OHIO
RIVERFRONT COLISEUM, 100 Broadway Street. Venue opened on September 9, 1975.
SUPPORT ACT: Eric Johnson
TICKETS: $19.50 (all seats)
ATTENDANCE: 10,601
CAPACITY: 12,904
CONCERT GROSS: $206,720
DAYTON DAILY NEWS: "Rush Stands Still with Show of Leftovers: Geddy Lee's

adenoidal vocals carried quite well through the arena. Lee focused more on his bass playing and less on his synthesizers compared to last year's tour, which allowed for more interplay with guitarist Alex Lifeson, especially on 'Bravado' and the instrumental 'Where's My Thing?'"

OCTOBER 31, 1991
INDIANAPOLIS, INDIANA
MARKET SQUARE ARENA, 300 East Market Street. Venue opened on September 15, 1974.
SUPPORT ACT: Eric Johnson
TICKETS: $19.50 (all seats)
ATTENDANCE: 9,243
CAPACITY: 12,000
CONCERT GROSS: $180,238

NOVEMBER 1, 1991
ROSEMONT, ILLINOIS
ROSEMONT HORIZON, 6920 N. Mannheim Road. Venue opened on July 2, 1980.
SUPPORT ACT: Eric Johnson
TICKETS: $22.50 / $32.50
ATTENDANCE: 14,815; sold out
CONCERT GROSS: $343,478

NOVEMBER 3, 1991
MINNEAPOLIS, MINNESOTA
TARGET CENTER, 600 First Avenue North. Venue opened on October 13, 1990.
SUPPORT ACT: Eric Johnson
TICKETS: $21.50 (all seats)
ATTENDANCE: 10,435
CAPACITY: 12,500
CONCERT GROSS: $219,135
NOTES: The show took place the day after the Halloween Blizzard of '91, when the Twin Cities received twenty-eight inches of snow over the course of three days, a single-storm record for the area.

NOVEMBER 4, 1991
OMAHA, NEBRASKA
CIVIC AUDITORIUM ARENA, 1804 Capitol Avenue. Venue dedicated on January 2, 1955.
SUPPORT ACT: Eric Johnson
TICKETS: $19.50
ATTENDANCE: 5,995
CONCERT CAPACITY: 6,700
VENUE CAPACITY: 10,960
CONCERT GROSS: $116,903
NOTES: The *Omaha World-Herald* lists attendance at 10,387, with an auditorium spokeswoman as their source.

OMAHA WORLD-HERALD: "Unusual Imagery Accompanies Rush: Even though Lee, Lifeson, and Peart have now been together seventeen years, the group seems to have as big a following as ever. The group's lighting effects are slightly more elaborate than the typical concert lighting. The most dazzling laser display made it seem as though clouds were drifting along the auditorium ceiling."

NOVEMBER 6, 1991
TOPEKA, KANSAS
LANDON ARENA, KANSAS EXPOCENTRE, 1 Expocentre Drive. Venue opened on April 17, 1987.
SUPPORT ACT: Eric Johnson
TICKETS: $19.50
ATTENDANCE: 6,436
CAPACITY: 7,000
CONCERT GROSS: $125,502

NOVEMBER 7, 1991
ST. LOUIS, MISSOURI
ST. LOUIS ARENA, 5700 Oakland. Venue opened on September 23, 1929.
SUPPORT ACT: Eric Johnson
TICKETS: $19.50 / $22.50
ATTENDANCE: 11,492
CAPACITY: 13,000
CONCERT GROSS: $224,094
NOTES: During "Limelight," Geddy sang "Living in the limelight universal dream." Not "the universal dream," thus creating a different phrasing, which he continued for most of the tour. On "Subdivisions," he screamed "Out!" on the lyric "Be cool or be cast out." At the finale to "Where's My Thing?" a voice intoned the Monty Python reference "Nobody expects the Spanish Inquisition." During "2112: Overture," Neil's left foot hit an electronic trigger, which accented the moment fans yelled, "Rush!" At the conclusion of "The Spirit of Radio," Neil did one last flurry on the drums after Alex and Geddy had stopped playing. Fans exited the venue to the gentle strains of Frank Sinatra's "Come Fly with Me."
ST. LOUIS POST-DISPATCH: "Rush Melds Showmanship, Great Music: "Based on the band's performance at the Arena Thursday night, it appears Rush has been able to maintain the spectacular nature of its stage show through the years without taking anything away from its thoughtful, intelligent, highly developed musical compositions."

NOVEMBER 9, 1991
NORMAL, ILLINOIS
REDBIRD ARENA, Illinois State University campus, 702 West College Avenue. Venue opened on January 13, 1989.
SUPPORT ACT: Eric Johnson
TICKETS: $19.50 (all seats)
ATTENDANCE: 8,666; sold out
CONCERT GROSS: $168,987
NOTES: Alex broke a string after the instrumental section of "Force Ten." He ran to stage right and was quickly given a new guitar.

NOVEMBER 10, 1991
MILWAUKEE, WISCONSIN
BRADLEY CENTER, 1001 North Fourth Street. Venue opened on October 1, 1988.
SUPPORT ACT: Eric Johnson
TICKETS: $19.00 / $25.00
ATTENDANCE: 12,813
CAPACITY: 15,500
CONCERT GROSS: $247,248

NOVEMBER 13–14, 1991
AUBURN HILLS, MICHIGAN
THE PALACE OF AUBURN HILLS, 6 Championship Drive. Venue opened on August 13, 1988.
SUPPORT ACT: Eric Johnson
TICKETS: $22.50 / $32.50
TWO-DAY AUBURN HILLS ATTENDANCE: 22,454
TWO-DAY CAPACITY: 26,000
TWO-DAY AUBURN HILLS CONCERT GROSS: $521,955
PAT MADDEN (RUSH FAN): "During 'The Big Money,' at the end, Alex and Geddy were talking and motioning to each other, and then to Neil. Suddenly, Neil breaks into a Chinese-sounding thing on the xylophone, while Alex and Geddy perform mock karate, just like in the picture in the tour book. Very funny."[2]

NOVEMBER 16, 1991
TOLEDO, OHIO
JOHN F. SAVAGE HALL, UNIVERSITY OF TOLEDO, 2801 W Bancroft Street. Venue opened on December 1, 1976.

SUPPORT ACT: Eric Johnson
TICKETS: $20.00 / $30.00
ATTENDANCE: 5,647
CAPACITY: 7,000
CONCERT GROSS: $119,510
TOLEDO BLADE: "Veteran rockers Rush still have imagination: Although Rush is a trio, Lee really acts as the band's third and fourth musician, displaying his versatility by frequently switching between bass and synthesizer during the same song."

NOVEMBER 17–18, 1991
RICHFIELD, OHIO
RICHFIELD COLISEUM, 2923 Streetsboro Road. Venue opened on October 26, 1974.
SUPPORT ACT: Eric Johnson
TICKETS: $20.00 / $30.00 (gold circle)
ATTENDANCE: 12,500; sold out
ATTENDANCE (NOVEMBER 18): 8,867
CAPACITY: 12,500
TWO-DAY RICHFIELD CONCERT GROSS: $430,443
NOTES: On the first night, during "2112: Overture," Alex's infamous guitar echo sounded different in quarter notes, instead of the usual eighth notes, creating slower, more pronounced echoes. He would keep this sound for a good portion of the tour. Though the early part of the tour featured good performances by the band, the lighting wasn't quite up to Rush's usual high standards. As the tour progressed, this changed as Howard came in for a few days to help smooth over the rough edges created by his absence.
THE PLAIN DEALER: "Trio Pleases Fans, Sticks to Business: Lee, who also plays guitar and keyboards, enunciates clearly so you can actually understand the words—a rarity in hard-rock groups today. He has such conviction in his voice you would naturally suppose he wrote the lyrics."

NOVEMBER 26, 1991
OTTAWA, ONTARIO
OTTAWA CIVIC CENTRE, Lansdowne Park, 1015 Bank Street. Venue opened on December 29, 1967.
SUPPORT ACT: Andy Curran and Soho 69
TICKETS: $29.50 CAD
CAPACITY: 9,349

NOVEMBER 28, 1991
MONTREAL, QUEBEC
MONTREAL FORUM, 2313 Saint Catherine Street. Historic venue opened on November 29, 1924.
SUPPORT ACT: Andy Curran and Soho 69
TICKETS: $19.50 / $26.50 CAD
ATTENDANCE: 9,000[3]
CAPACITY: 16,500 for ice hockey, 19,000 with standing room
MONTREAL GAZETTE: "With every chop, time change, film clip and laser in place, Rush did everything right."

NOVEMBER 29, 1991
QUEBEC CITY, QUEBEC
COLISÉE DE QUEBEC, 250 Boulevard Wilfrid-Hamel. Venue opened on December 8, 1949.
SUPPORT ACT: Andy Curran and Soho 69
TICKETS: $26.50 CAD
ATTENDANCE: 8,000 (approximate)[4]
CAPACITY: 14,981 (SRO)
LE SOLEIL: "Last night at the Colisée, Lee, Lifeson, and Peart once again gave their fans a flawless performance."

DECEMBER 1, 1991; DECEMBER 3, 1991
PHILADELPHIA, PENNSYLVANIA
THE SPECTRUM, 3601 South Broad Street. Venue opened on October 1, 1967.
SUPPORT ACT: Vinnie Moore
TICKETS: $19.50 / $29.50
TWO-DAY PHILADELPHIA ATTEN-DANCE: 24,397
TWO-DAY CAPACITY: 28,058
TWO-DAY PHILADELPHIA CONCERT GROSS: $491,422 (estimate)
NOTES: The gig on December 1 was booked on the very same date as one scheduled for Hartford Civic Center, with tickets for Hartford already on sale. That concert was rescheduled to Friday December 13, with refunds available for any of the 8,000 tickets already sold up to 6:00 p.m. on the 13th.
VINNIE MOORE: "One of the highlights of the *Meltdown* tour was opening up for Rush on their *Roll the Bones* tour, which included playing at my hometown arena, the Spectrum, in Philadelphia. That was a dream come true."[5]
BRIAN TICHY (VINNIE MOORE DRUM-MER): "We were on a club tour in a van,

playing six nights a week, having a great time. One day backstage, Vinnie's manager, Pete Morticelli, says, 'Guys, Eric Johnson just had to cancel his last two weeks opening for Rush, and you guys are going to take his place . . . starting in three days . . . ten shows; two nights at the Philly Spectrum followed by two nights at Madison Square Garden.' We tripped out with excitement! We were all diehard Rush fans, so to get the opportunity to share their stage was nothing short of awesome! Not to mention, this was my first time playing in an arena, the coolest type of venue to play in. I was still using my Tama Swingstars I got as a Christmas present back in ninth grade! I chose that brand mainly because of Neil Peart! So, those drums made it on Neil's stage. We met the guys after the first show. They were all very kind and gracious. I recorded all their sound checks onto my cassette recorder and used to listen to them for months after the tour."[6]

DECEMBER 4, 1991
LARGO, MARYLAND
CAPITAL CENTRE, 1 Harry S. Truman Drive. Venue opened on December 2, 1973.
SUPPORT ACT: Vinnie Moore
TICKETS: $22.50 / $28.50
ATTENDANCE: 14,070
CAPACITY: 15,565
CONCERT GROSS: $321,543 (estimate)
NOTES: During the afternoon, Neil did a telephone interview with the *Buffalo News*. "Ghost of a Chance" was performed live for the first time. During the set, Alex

encountered a few technical issues early on, but they were quickly resolved. He went on to play a hip, scat guitar line during the rap section of "Roll the Bones." During "The Pass," Geddy broke a bass string and he was given a new bass—marking a rare appearance (on this tour) of the black Wal. A festive night was brought home on the "Finding My Way" encore, where Neil did a few guitar windmills à la Pete Townshend. Venue aka US Air Arena.

BALTIMORE SUN: "It's the same old Rush tour, and that's good news: From tour to tour—and they seem to come like clockwork every two years—the band changes its show minimally, but there's still so much to see and hear."

DECEMBER 6–7, 1991
NEW YORK, NEW YORK
MADISON SQUARE GARDEN, 4 Pennsylvania Plaza (8th Avenue between 31st and 33rd Streets). Historic venue opened on February 11, 1968.
SUPPORT ACT: Vinnie Moore
TICKETS: $20.00 / $25.00 / $35.00
ATTENDANCE: 15,500; sold out
CONCERT GROSS: $388,095
NOTES: The second show was added by popular demand. *Amusement Business* lists the first night's attendance at 15,000, SRO. Alex was in a festive mood, even playing keyboards with his nose during "Time Stand Still." A sample was triggered early in "Show Don't Tell." Neil (who was nursing a head cold) threw a stick up so high that it was almost out of sight. When it came down in front of his kit, fans thought there was no way he could grab it, but he did, making a great catch. *Amusement Business* listed the second night's attendance at 15,000, SRO. During the two-night stand, the band received Madison Square Garden's prestigious Golden Ticket Award to commemorate more than 100,000 tickets sold between 1981 and 1991. John McEnroe and Tatum O'Neal visited with Neil after the second concert.

THE NEW YORK TIMES: "More Technological than Human: Rush's concert at Madison Square Garden was so overwhelming that it was easy to forget there were actually three men onstage. The thousands of teenagers in the audience, most of them male, screamed every lyric and punched their fists in the air."

DECEMBER 9, 1991
PROVIDENCE, RHODE ISLAND
PROVIDENCE CIVIC CENTER, 1 La Salle Square. Venue opened on November 3, 1972.
SUPPORT ACT: Vinnie Moore
TICKETS: $19.50
ATTENDANCE: 9,431
CAPACITY: 11,500
CONCERT GROSS: $183,904
THE PROVIDENCE JOURNAL: "A Rush of great talent but little charisma: The drum solo, usually little more than a pounding indulgence for rock bands, was nicely done, with Neil Peart making intriguing use of speakers placed near the back of the arena plus various electronic effects."

DECEMBER 10, 1991
WORCESTER, MASSACHUSETTS
THE CENTRUM, 50 Foster Street. Venue opened on September 2, 1982.
SUPPORT ACT: Vinnie Moore
TICKETS: $19.50 / $27.50
ATTENDANCE: 12,266; sold out
CONCERT GROSS: $249,347
NOTES: For the "Finding My Way" encore, Neil continued his Pete Townshend windmill imitation, this time joined by Geddy.
WORCESTER TELEGRAM AND GAZETTE: "Rush Plays with Enthusiasm: After almost two decades of touring and recording, these guys still look like they are having a good time up there. Better yet, they still sound great."

DECEMBER 12, 1991
ALBANY, NEW YORK
KNICKERBOCKER ARENA, 51 S Pearl Street. Venue opened on January 30, 1990.
SUPPORT ACT: Vinnie Moore
TICKETS: $17.50 / $27.50
ATTENDANCE: 10,614
CAPACITY: 13,690
CONCERT GROSS: $210,794
ALBANY TIMES UNION, NEIL: "When we walk onstage, we're professionals, but offstage, we're just as goofy as any other bunch of guys in a band."

DECEMBER 13, 1991
HARTFORD, CONNECTICUT
CIVIC CENTER, 1 Civic Center Plaza. Venue opened on January 9, 1975.
SUPPORT ACT: Vinnie Moore
TICKETS: $17.50 / $21.50 / $27.50

ATTENDANCE: 12,263
CAPACITY: 13,805
CONCERT GROSS: $256,934
NOTES: Rescheduled from December 1. A great show, despite a few technical mishaps. During "Force Ten," a loud, weird, electronic sound was heard during the instrumental section. In "Roll the Bones," triggers were set off early during the lines "Losers seldom take that blame" and "On the heads of the innocent children." During "The Big Money," "That's nice!" was triggered early, before the guitar break, and was not heard at the end. Alex hit a few bad notes in "The Pass" during the lyric "The act of a noble warrior."

HARTFORD COURANT: "Rush Appeals to Eyes, Ears with Animation, Drum Solo: The trio drew one of the largest crowds for a rock show at the Civic Center in months with a show so rewarding, scarcely a soul left his or her seat for the entire two-hour performance."

DECEMBER 15, 1991
BUFFALO, NEW YORK
BUFFALO MEMORIAL AUDITORIUM, 140 Main Street. Venue opened on October 14, 1940.
SUPPORT ACT: Vinnie Moore
TICKETS: $19.50 / $22.50 / $27.50
ATTENDANCE: 12,703
CAPACITY: 14,605
CONCERT GROSS: $278,905
NOTES: During the extended ending to "Closer to the Heart," Alex wandered over to the side of stage left, pulled out some money, and handed it to one of the crew. He was given a golf ball and putter and took a shot on a small green and cup that was set up behind Geddy. He missed the shot and continued the song.

VINNIE MOORE: "Opening for Rush was definitely a highlight for me. I watched their show almost every night. I really liked Alex's playing, and I especially dug his rhythm parts. He has some very catchy riffs and cool, half-distorted sounds. I like the chord voicings he uses and the way he orchestrates his parts—I think that's his signature. I will tell you one thing, though—Alex can't play very well when you put pictures from girlie magazines on his pedal board and monitors. I tried this on the last show of the tour, and he made more mistakes in five minutes than he has probably ever made.

He had to get his tech to take them away so he could get through the second song!"[7]

DECEMBER 16, 1991
TORONTO, ONTARIO
MAPLE LEAF GARDENS, 60 Carlton Street. Historic venue opened on November 12, 1931.
SUPPORT ACT: The Tragically Hip
TICKETS: $22.50 / $28.50 CAD; face value minus fees
ATTENDANCE: 11,906; sold out
CONCERT GROSS: $337,767 CAD
NOTES: Benefit concert for the United Way, with 15,000 pounds of crowd-donated food going to the Daily Bread food bank. John Rutsey visited backstage.
TORONTO STAR: "That was some Rush! The band just keeps getting better."
NEIL: "For our *Roll the Bones* tour in '91, I lobbied our manager, Ray, to book the Hip as our opening act on a major tour of the US and Canada, a tour that would have put them in front of more than a million potential fans. However, their manager turned the offer down, saying there was a buzz starting for the band in Europe, and the record company wanted them to go there. I don't know, but that may have been a missed opportunity for them."[8]

JANUARY 18, 1992
LAS CRUCES, NEW MEXICO
PAN AMERICAN CENTER, New Mexico State University campus, 1810 East University Avenue
SUPPORT ACT: Primus
TICKETS: $20.00
ATTENDANCE: 9,803; sold out
CONCERT GROSS: $196,060
TIM "HERB" ALEXANDER (PRIMUS DRUMMER): "At the venue, I got to meet Neil and Geddy, and they also welcomed us onto the tour with open arms. The crew was also awesome to us as well. The whole team they put together was top notch."[9]
ROBERT SCOVILL: "I'll never forget the first night Primus opened for us. I had never heard Primus prior to that. I don't know how they got chosen for the tour or anything. I was standing off of stage right when they came out and started playing. It was the typical thing with Les, where he had the hip waders on and had

the fish on the microphone so it looked like he was kissing the fish whenever he started singing, and I can remember standing next to Alex when they started, and we kind of looked at each other like, 'What the hell is going on out there? What the hell is this?' And then, by the end of their set, we were just like, 'Oh my God, this is the greatest thing that is ever going to happen for us opening act–wise here.' Musically, it was just so left field and so cool. The crowds started picking up on it and really started digging them. As a collection of people, they were just as hilarious and fun-loving as the Rush guys, so it really was a marriage made in heaven for a couple of tours."[10]

JANUARY 20, 1992
SAN DIEGO, CALIFORNIA
SAN DIEGO SPORTS ARENA, 3500 Sports Arena Boulevard. Venue opened on November 17, 1966.
SUPPORT ACT: Primus
TICKETS: $20.50 / $28.50
ATTENDANCE: 11,607
CAPACITY: 12,068
CONCERT GROSS: $241,317
SAN DIEGO UNION: "Whatever its style, Rush satisfies fans: Despite the catchy hooks of Rush's older material, a new song proved to be the musical highlight of the evening. 'Roll the Bones,' the title track off last year's album, percolated with energy and vitality."

JANUARY 22–23, 1992
INGLEWOOD, CALIFORNIA
GREAT WESTERN FORUM, 3900 West Manchester Boulevard. Venue opened on December 30, 1967.
SUPPORT ACT: Primus
TICKETS: $19.50 / $22.00 / $27.50
ATTENDANCE: 14,658 per show; sold out
CONCERT GROSS: $326,832 per show
LOS ANGELES TIMES: "Critics generally trash the Canadian hard-rock trio, but hordes of fans continue to ignore the reviews and pack their concerts."

JANUARY 25, 1992
FRESNO, CALIFORNIA
SELLAND ARENA, 700 M Street, at Ventura. Venue opened on October 11, 1966.
SUPPORT ACT: Primus
TICKETS: $18.50 / $20.00

ATTENDANCE: 9,011; sold out
CONCERT GROSS: $156,640
NOTES: Alex did a phone interview with the *Georgia Straight*. From an aesthetic point of view, Geddy was wearing his hair down for the gigs on the second leg.
THE FRESNO BEE: "Maybe This Canadian Trio Shouldn't Be in Such a Rush: Rush's performance wasn't a total wash. The trio appeared to be having fun, and it isn't often you get to see a band entirely eclipsed by its laser lights, video screen, and a pair of giant inflated rabbits."

JANUARY 27, 1992
SACRAMENTO, CALIFORNIA
ARCO ARENA, One Sports Parkway. Venue opened on November 8, 1988.
SUPPORT ACT: Primus
TICKETS: $22.50 / $25.00
ATTENDANCE: 11,067
CAPACITY: 12,000
CONCERT GROSS: $250,710
NOTES: Geddy was hit in the face by a shoe, which triggered a sample on his synth when it landed on a pedal.
SACRAMENTO BEE: "Rush Offers Dramatics but No True Drama: Rush fans expect spectacle from the group, and they get it. They also seem to think they're getting musical artistry, but Monday the group's performance was mostly show despite its brawny sound."

JANUARY 28, 1992
SAN FRANCISCO BAY, OFF RED ROCK ISLAND, NEAR THE RICHMOND–SAN RAFAEL BRIDGE. LES CLAYPOOL TAKES GEDDY FISHING ON HIS BOAT, THE *EL BASTARDO*. THE FAN BELT BREAKS, LEAVING THE PAIR STRANDED FOR SIX HOURS.
GEDDY: "[Les said,] 'Come on out—we'll go fishing. We'll have a nice, chill day. It will be fun.' So, I said, 'Sure.' We had the day off. I was meeting some friends for dinner later that night, so they picked me up and we set sail out. And the engine died when we were out in the middle of the bay! Poor Les was mortified."[11]

JANUARY 29–30, 1992
OAKLAND, CALIFORNIA
OAKLAND-ALAMEDA COUNTY COLISEUM ARENA, 7000 Coliseum Way. Venue opened on November 9, 1966.
SUPPORT ACT: Primus
TICKETS: $22.50 / $25.00

ATTENDANCE: 12,627; sold out
CONCERT GROSS: $285,970
NOTES: The hilarity of the ill-fated fishing trip even made its way to the stage, as Primus played "Fish On" and "John the Fisherman" in their Oakland set. The entire proceeds of the January 30 show were donated to the American Foundation for AIDS Research, a nonprofit group founded in 1985.
NEIL: "[AIDS is] something we feel very strongly about. We normally do these things privately—for example, our Christmas presents to one another tend to be donations to charitable organizations—but we thought there was a message here. We thought that being in a rock band, which is a world of homophobia and misogyny, it might be good that this is publicized, that we're very moved by the AIDS tragedy and want to contribute."[12]
SAN FRANCISCO CHRONICLE: "Rush Sticks to Polished Routine—Canadian trio hasn't swayed from its '70s arena-rock sound: In the first of two sold-out shows, Rush displayed flawless production, admirable musicianship, and just enough of a singular vision to make the band's artistic statement stand out without straining the imagination of the enthusiastic, largely male following."

FEBRUARY 2, 1992
VANCOUVER, BRITISH COLUMBIA
PACIFIC COLISEUM, Pacific National Exhibition Fairgrounds, 100 North Renfrew. Venue dedicated on January 8, 1968.
SUPPORT ACT: Primus
TICKETS: $38.00 CAD
ATTENDANCE: 9,000[13]
CAPACITY: 16,123
NOTES: Backstage, Alex was interviewed live on the radio during Primus' sound check, which drowned him out half of the time. Onstage, the lyrics to "Dreamline" presented a challenge to Geddy, but he managed to regain his composure.
VANCOUVER SUN: "In a show dominated by lengthy suites punctuated by complex time, chord, and key changes, Rush dazzled even nonbelievers by being able to hold it all together."

FEBRUARY 4, 1992
SEATTLE, WASHINGTON
SEATTLE CENTER COLISEUM, 305 Harrison Street. Venue opened on April 21, 1962.
SUPPORT ACT: Primus
TICKETS: $21.50 / $35.00
ATTENDANCE: 12,453; sold out
CONCERT GROSS: $274,610
THE SEATTLE TIMES: "Rush brought in as big a crowd as the Coliseum has seen in quite a while. Just shy of capacity, it was a house that roared louder than the thundering trio itself, which was a considerable accomplishment."

FEBRUARY 5, 1992
PORTLAND, OREGON
MEMORIAL COLISEUM, 1401 North Wheeler. Venue opened on November 3, 1960.
SUPPORT ACT: Primus
TICKETS: $22.50 / $36.50
ATTENDANCE: 8,826
CAPACITY: 9,500
CONCERT GROSS: $203,429

FEBRUARY 15, 1992
SAN ANTONIO, TEXAS
CONVENTION CENTER ARENA, HemisFair Park Complex, 601 Hemisfair Way. Venue opened on April 6, 1968.
SUPPORT ACT: Primus
TICKETS: $18.00 / $22.00
ATTENDANCE: 11,491
CAPACITY: 14,518
CONCERT GROSS: $212,438
SAN ANTONIO EXPRESS-NEWS: "Rush concerts have always been high-tech marriages of sight and sound, and Saturday's nearly sold-out show was no exception. But despite the sights—streams of emerald-green lasers; a multitude of video images projected on a screen behind the band—the sound was still the star. Demonstrating why it is a perennial favorite with San Antonio audiences, the Canadian trio pumped out a two-hour show that touched on every facet of its career."

FEBRUARY 16, 1992
DALLAS, TEXAS
REUNION ARENA, 777 Sports Street. Venue dedicated on April 28, 1980.
SUPPORT ACT: Primus
TICKETS: $22.00 / $25.00
ATTENDANCE: 14,690; sold out

CONCERT GROSS: $317,466
FORT WORTH STAR-TELEGRAM: "Rock 'n' Rush—Evolution shows improved touch: It's to Rush's credit that it isn't simply bashing out the same old sludge. And to the audience's credit, many of the new songs—including 'Roll the Bones' and 'Ghost of a Chance'—sailed right through."

FEBRUARY 18, 1992
HOUSTON, TEXAS
THE SUMMIT, 3700 Southwest Freeway. Venue opened on November 1, 1975.
SUPPORT ACT: Primus
TICKETS: $22.65 / $25.65
ATTENDANCE: 11,784
CAPACITY: 13,608
CONCERT GROSS: $274,431
DAILY COUGAR (UNIVERSITY OF HOUSTON): "Integrity of Music Remains Intact Tuesday: From the onset, it was apparent the band was honed, loose, and in fine form. Every dead spot in the Summit seemed enveloped with surprising clarity of bombast, and even Lee's voice, which doesn't hit the high notes as it once did, was bold and piercing, sounding better than ever. The only disappointments were the encore numbers, in which the band teased the audience with a jumbled medley of some of its older, classic tunes, leaving one with a feeling of dissatisfaction."

FEBRUARY 20, 1992
AUSTIN, TEXAS
FRANK ERWIN SPECIAL EVENTS CENTER, University of Texas at Austin campus, 1701 Red River Street. Venue opened on November 29, 1977.
SUPPORT ACT: Primus
TICKETS: $19.50 / $24.00
ATTENDANCE: 9,222
CAPACITY: 12,589
CONCERT GROSS: $190,314
NOTES: During his stay in Austin, Alex had dinner with Eric Johnson and gave him his red Gibson EDS 1275 double-neck guitar.

FEBRUARY 22, 1992
SHREVEPORT, LOUISIANA
HIRSCH MEMORIAL COLISEUM, 3701 Hudson Avenue. Venue opened on April 10, 1954.
SUPPORT ACT: Primus
TICKETS: $19.50

CAPACITY: 10,300

NOTES: Canceled at the eleventh hour because Geddy had contracted laryngitis. The band was in Shreveport all day on the 21st, where Geddy saw a doctor. His throat was in such bad shape that they were forced to nix the concert, which was never rescheduled.

FEBRUARY 23, 1992
NEW ORLEANS, LOUISIANA
UNO LAKEFRONT ARENA, University of New Orleans East campus, 6801 Franklin Street. Venue opened on November 1, 1983.
SUPPORT ACT: Primus
TICKETS: $20.00 / $27.50
ATTENDANCE: 7,495; sold out
CONCERT GROSS: $160,904

FEBRUARY 25, 1992
PENSACOLA, FLORIDA
PENSACOLA CIVIC CENTER, 201 East Gregory Street. Venue opened on January 21, 1985.
SUPPORT ACT: Primus
TICKETS: $21.00
ATTENDANCE: 6,190
CAPACITY: 7,500
CONCERT GROSS: $129,990
NOTES: Primus paid homage to Rush by performing an excerpt of "Cygnus X-1" in their set. After the show, a twenty-one-year-old man was injured outside the venue after falling thirty feet and hitting his head on the pavement.[14]

FEBRUARY 26, 1992
JACKSONVILLE, FLORIDA
JACKSONVILLE VETERANS MEMORIAL COLISEUM, 1145 Adams Street. Venue dedicated on November 24, 1960.
SUPPORT ACT: Primus
TICKETS: $22.50
ATTENDANCE: 5,166
CAPACITY: 6,000
CONCERT GROSS: $116,235
NOTES: Alex performed the opening to "Finding My Way" while standing on one leg.

FEBRUARY 28, 1992
MIAMI, FLORIDA
MIAMI ARENA, 701 Arena Boulevard. Venue opened on July 13, 1988.
SUPPORT ACT: Primus
TICKETS: $22.50 / $35.00
ATTENDANCE: 12,364; sold out

CONCERT GROSS: $295,428
***SUN-SENTINEL* (FORT LAUDERDALE):** "Rush Rolls the Arena: A large screen to the rear of the stage portrayed cartoonlike visions of skeletons and of the *Roll the Bones* album cover during the concert."

FEBRUARY 29, 1992
ST. PETERSBURG, FLORIDA
FLORIDA SUNCOAST DOME, One Tropicana Drive. Venue opened on March 3, 1990.
SUPPORT ACT: Primus
TICKETS: $22.50
ATTENDANCE: 12,075
CAPACITY: 12,500
CONCERT GROSS: $271,688
NOTES: Venue aka Thunderdome. Geddy spent the afternoon working out with the St. Louis Cardinals in full uniform, shagging flies and taking batting practice. He invited several players to the gig, creating quite a festive backstage scene.
GEDDY: "They taught me how to miss fly balls, and how to get jammed in the batting cage. I have a new appreciation for what it feels like to get jammed."[15]
BRYN SMITH (CARDINALS PITCHER): "I taught him everything about pitching. The hitting we still need to work out."[16]
JOE TORRE (CARDINALS MANAGER): "That makes us even. I haven't played too many of those rock concerts, either."[17]
JIM RHODES (STAGE LEFT TECHNICIAN): "We were in Florida and, like any avid baseball fan, you want to be close to the baseball action. It was at the Suncoast Dome, where the Rays now play. We were within a short drive of about five grapefruit-league ballparks, so Geddy could take in all the spring training baseball he could find. Anyway, Geddy told me to work with the caterers and prepare a large room for some ballplayers that he had invited to the show, and to have plenty of shrimp and beer on hand. So I arranged for an old cast iron bathtub and filled it with shrimp and arranged for a skid of beer. In any case, the ballplayers showed up . . . about forty or fifty of them! From the Mets, Expos, Royals, and Dave Stieb, Kelly Gruber, and Candy Maldonado from the Blue Jays. I asked Dave Stieb, 'Did you rent a car to get here?' and he said, 'No, I just picked up a used Porsche 911 to get around so I could come see Rush!!!' Now, that's a fan! Anyway, after what seemed like fifteen

minutes, all of the beer and shrimp were running out, and Geddy said, 'Just make sure the players have lots of beer!' We needed to order lots more beer. Don't know how much we went through, but it was more than the crew would drink, for sure. Gotta love ballplayers, just a bunch of rock fans! Good on Ged for bringing all those guys to the show—it was awesome!"[18]

MARCH 2, 1992
ORLANDO, FLORIDA
ORLANDO ARENA, 600 West Amelia Street. Venue opened on January 29, 1989.
SUPPORT ACT: Primus
TICKETS: $22.50
ATTENDANCE: 10,859; sold out
CONCERT GROSS: $244,328
***ORLANDO SENTINEL*:** "High-Tech Engineering Doesn't Keep Rush from Rocking Out: Fortunately, Rush still knows how to stretch out on stage. In its sold-out show at the Orlando Arena, there were plenty of long, interesting instrumental passages."

MARCH 4, 1992
ATLANTA, GEORGIA
THE OMNI, 100 Techwood Drive Northwest. Venue opened on October 14, 1972.
SUPPORT ACT: Primus
TICKETS: $21.50 / $29.00; face value, minus fees
ATTENDANCE: 13,966; sold out
CONCERT GROSS: $309,569
NOTES: The Grateful Dead drummer Mickey Hart was in attendance as Neil's guest. Neil and Liam had attended the Grateful Dead concert at the Omni the night before.

MARCH 5, 1992
COLUMBIA, SOUTH CAROLINA
CAROLINA COLISEUM, University of South Carolina campus, 701 Assembly Street. Venue opened on November 30, 1968.
SUPPORT ACT: Primus
TICKETS: $20.50
ATTENDANCE: 5,616
CAPACITY: 8,712
CONCERT GROSS: $115,128

MARCH 7, 1992
CHAPEL HILL, NORTH CAROLINA
DEAN E. SMITH CENTER, 300 Skipper

Bowles Drive. Venue opened on January 17, 1986.
SUPPORT ACT: Primus
TICKETS: $20.50; face value, minus $3.30 in fees
ATTENDANCE: 11,039
CAPACITY: 13,114
CONCERT GROSS: $226,300
NOTES: Venue aka the Dean Dome.
DURHAM HERALD SUN: "Thinking fans' band plays Chapel Hill."

MARCH 8, 1992
HAMPTON, VIRGINIA
HAMPTON COLISEUM, 1000 Coliseum Drive. Venue opened on January 31, 1970.
SUPPORT ACT: Primus
TICKETS: $19.50
ATTENDANCE: 7,653
CAPACITY: 9,880
CONCERT GROSS: $149,234
M.E.A.T., **ALEX:** "When you're on the road, you are so separated from the really important things in your life, like family and friends, and, to some degree, you're in a prison—sitting in a hotel, then sitting in a dressing room, then sitting on a bus—while working for two hours where you have to pack in everything, then repeating the same ritual over and over again. Your whole life is just that for months on months, and the price you pay for that, over a long period of time, is quite great."

MARCH 10, 1992
RICHMOND, VIRGINIA
RICHMOND COLISEUM, 601 East Leigh Street. Venue dedicated on August 21, 1971.
SUPPORT ACT: Primus
TICKETS: $19.50
ATTENDANCE: 5,152
CAPACITY: 9,692
CONCERT GROSS: $100,464
NOTES: Neil spent the afternoon bicycling around Richmond, eventually ending up at the venue for sound check.

MARCH 12, 1992
BINGHAMTON, NEW YORK
BROOME COUNTY WAR MEMORIAL ARENA, 1 Stuart Street. Venue opened on August 29, 1973.
SUPPORT ACT: Primus
TICKETS: $23.50 / $35.00
ATTENDANCE: 5,627

CAPACITY: 5,800
CONCERT GROSS: $139,112
NOTES: After sound check, Alex, Geddy, and Neil gathered in Primus's dressing room for their daily jam session. Stagehands and building personnel hung outside the door to listen to the bizarre sounds. Onstage, the band was in a loose, celebratory mood. During "The Big Money," the prominent sound after the lyric "Big money make no sound" was not triggered. At the end of "Subdivisions," a fired-up Geddy sang "Of youth!" three times. During "The Pass," for the lyric "It's not as if this barricade blocks the only road," a barricade of lights was created at the front of the stage to nice effect. On the introduction to "Where's My Thing?" Alex used harmonics to maximize impact. He was joined by Geddy who played some impromptu bass runs, which was followed by a stellar improvised guitar solo from Alex. The trigger for "Nobody expects the Spanish Inquisition" inadvertently went off during the middle of the song. During "Tom Sawyer," Geddy added some delightful pauses on bass during the guitar solo. In "La Villa Strangiato," Alex got a bit tied up right before the bass solo.
GEDDY (ONSTAGE): "We'd like to thank you all for braving the cold and the snow and coming out tonight. We hope to make it worth your while."

MARCH 14, 1992
NEW HAVEN, CONNECTICUT
NEW HAVEN VETERAN'S MEMORIAL COLISEUM, 275 South Orange Street. Venue opened on September 27, 1972.
SUPPORT ACT: Primus
TICKETS: $21.50 / $27.50
ATTENDANCE: 8,881
CAPACITY: 9,500
CONCERT GROSS: $197,850
NOTES: A brilliant sound check was performed, where instead of jamming, the band played a lengthy, coherent piece of music, which sounded like a new instrumental, ready to record. The venue was unable to handle the weight of Rush's complete production, so it was scaled back for this gig, with no rear PA speakers at the back of the hall, no lights over the audience, and no curtain hanging between bands. Onstage, a festive night was topped off by some crew hijinks.

During "Closer to the Heart," one of the crew shot a foam arrow at Alex, who threw it back at him.
GEDDY (ONSTAGE): "I remember this town being a lot louder. You guys sound a little quiet out there."

MARCH 15, 1992
UNIONDALE, NEW YORK
NASSAU COUNTY VETERANS MEMORIAL COLISEUM, 1255 Hempstead Turnpike. Venue dedicated on May 29, 1972.
SUPPORT ACT: Primus
TICKETS: $20.00 / $22.50 / $30.00
ATTENDANCE: 15,290
CAPACITY: 15,503
CONCERT GROSS: $347,855
NOTES: During sound check, the band jammed on the same new instrumental piece that they had played the day before in New Haven. Chuck D from Public Enemy paid Primus a surprise visit backstage, then watched Rush's set. In 2013, the Public Enemy leader would perform with Alex, Geddy, and Neil at the Rock and Roll Hall of Fame induction ceremony in Los Angeles. Amid their set, Les Claypool talked about seeing his first concert, Rush on the *Hemispheres* tour, before Primus performed their unique take on "La Villa Strangiato." A rockin' concert incited one person to run up on Geddy's side of the stage and dive into the seats. During "Closer to the Heart," Alex used the foam bow and arrow to shoot Neil.
LARRY "LER" LALONDE (PRIMUS GUITARIST): "Chuck D and Hank Shocklee [producer] showed up. They walked in and everyone was silent—no one knows what to say. And I'm sure he's like, 'Do these guys even remember being on tour with us?' And we're freaking out! I remember going out and watching Rush with Chuck. I don't think he'd ever seen anything quite like that."[19]

APRIL 10, 1992
SHEFFIELD, ENGLAND
SHEFFIELD ARENA, Broughton Lane
SUPPORT ACT: Primus
TICKETS: £12.00 / £14.00
CAPACITY: 11,477 (reserved seating)
NOTES: Venue aka Hallam FM Arena and Motorpoint Arena.

APRIL 12–13, 1992
BIRMINGHAM, WEST MIDLANDS, ENGLAND
NATIONAL EXHIBITION CENTRE ARENA, Pendigo Way and Perimeter Road, Marston Green. Venue opened on December 5, 1980.
SUPPORT ACT: Primus
TICKETS: £12.00 / £14.00
CAPACITY: 11,000

APRIL 14, 1992
ALEX AND ROBERT ENJOY A ROUND OF GOLF AT TURNBERRY ISLE. THE CREW DRIVES ON TO GLASGOW, WHILE GEDDY, LIAM BIRT, AND ANDREW MACNAUGHTAN FLY TO GLASGOW.
ROBERT SCOVILL: "One of the great memories I have is going to play Turnberry in Scotland with Alex. We had a couple of really great days together, just bonding and hanging out. I think Alex is the most underrated guitar player in the history of rock music. I cannot believe that guy does not get the respect that he deserves. Obviously, Neil gets a lot of the attention because he was the focal point of the band both lyrically and rhythmically. But if you look at the body of work that Alex has produced in this band, and the diversity—not only in the sounds, but also in the styles of playing—I defy you to put anybody up against that and say that they've done an equal task. It's mind-blowing. He's also one of the most underrated soloists in rock. The measuring stick that I use is that I can go through the songs in my head and I can sing those solos. It's kind of like a Peter Frampton thing—you just know every note of those solos in your head, and there are no wasted or superfluous notes. You talk about that over the course of twenty or thirty albums, and that is an incredible thing to say about somebody's playing."[20]

APRIL 15, 1992
GLASGOW, SCOTLAND
SCOTTISH EXHIBITION AND CONFERENCE CENTRE, Hall 4, Exhibition Way. Venue opened September 7, 1985.
SUPPORT ACT: Primus
TICKETS: £11.50 / £13.50
CAPACITY: 9,000

APRIL 17–18, 1992
LONDON, ENGLAND
WEMBLEY ARENA, Arena Square at Engineers Way. Venue opened on August 4, 1934.
SUPPORT ACT: Primus
TICKETS: £12.00 / £14.00
CAPACITY: 8,800
NOTES: The first night was recorded for radio broadcast. Onstage, Geddy laid down some impactful, improvised bass runs during the end of "Time Stand Still." The band was staying at the Mayfair Hotel, as were a whole host of rock royalty, in town for the Freddie Mercury Concert for AIDS Awareness on April 20 at Wembley Stadium. On the second night, members of Black Sabbath, Def Leppard, and Anthrax, and Liza Minnelli, are all seen hanging out. Producer Rupert Hine drove Geddy to the gig in his Range Rover.
LIFE AND TIMES: "The thinking man's headbangers: The first of two Wembley shows was such a tight-scripted affair that any passion or personality which the band might have possessed was squeezed out like juice from a lemon, leaving a dry husk with a distinctive tang. The show's appeal rested on flawless production values and a display of monumentally efficient musicianship."
ROCK WORLD: "Rush's recent two nights at Wembley Arena, stunned even their die-hard fans. For they brought with them their full US arena show, including the combination of back-projected cartoons, laser beams, quadraphonic stereo PA sound, and the two giant inflatable rabbits (or were they hares?) popping out of conjurors' top hats on either side of the stage."

APRIL 21, 1992
HANOVER, GERMANY
MUSIC HALL, Gottinger Strasse 14, 3000. Venue built in 1943.
SUPPORT ACT: Primus
TICKETS: 40 DEM / 45 DEM
CAPACITY: 5,000
ROBERT SCOVILL: "There was no more extreme version of the backstage jam sessions than in Hanover. We were playing this gig, and it wasn't a huge show—not a typical arena gig. We didn't have indoor dressing rooms. They had set up trailers . . . like RVs, for the band dressing room outside the building, kind

of in a horseshoe semicircle. So there was no place to set up the '60s jam room,' so we decided to just set up outside the RV, and do it outside. I remember actually playing in the jam that day. Neil, Ged, and Alex were all there, and the guys from Primus were all there, and we started this noisy jam . . . we were playing on bleachers, and anything we could find, we were banging on. So, we're about twenty minutes into this crazy, insane jam, and then we noticed that there was this five- or six-story parking garage right behind where we were . . . and we looked up, and there were probably two thousand people standing there on this parking garage just watching us play and going absolutely nuts. I don't know if any of them knew that the actual band members were involved in this . . . it didn't look like a band at all—there were probably twenty of us making all this noise."

APRIL 23, 1992
COLOGNE, GERMANY
SPORTHALLE, Sporthallenweg, 5000. Venue opened on December 13, 1958.
SUPPORT ACT: Primus
TICKETS: 40 DEM / 45 DEM
CAPACITY: 8,000
NOTES: Like most dates on this European tour, the crew drove on to the next city after the show, as did Neil and Peter Brockbank. Geddy and Alex stayed the night and flew out the next morning.

APRIL 24, 1992
FRANKFURT, HESSE, WEST GERMANY
FESTHALLE, Ludwig Erhard Anlage, 8000. Venue opened on May 19, 1909.
SUPPORT ACT: Primus
TICKETS: 40 DEM / 45 DEM
CAPACITY: 12,000
NOTES: During the show, the band had several technical issues, with both Alex and Geddy swapping out guitars at various points, while Neil was a bit off during "2112: Overture."

APRIL 27, 1992
BERLIN, GERMANY
EISSPORTHALLE, Charlottenburg, Jaffestrasse, 1000. Venue opened on October 28, 1973.
SUPPORT ACT: Primus
TICKETS: 40 DEM / 47 DEM
CAPACITY: 12,000

NOTES: The venue was unable to accommodate the entire lighting rig, so the crew was forced to improvise. Primus played a few verses of "A Passage to Bangkok" during their set and teased some of "Cygnus X-1" during "Harold of the Rocks" (providing Rush with inspiration to add the "Cygnus X-1" teaser to the end of their own set starting on this European leg). The crew drove on to Nuremberg (275 miles) after the show, as did Neil and Peter Brockbank. Geddy and Alex stayed the night in Berlin.

GEDDY: "We had a great time in Berlin. At the gig, we had one of our unusual jam sessions, but this time, we were playing this arena that didn't really have suitable dressing rooms—so we were in a couple of trailers outside. We did our jam session outside, between the two trailers. It was a great time, and we had fun on that whole European leg. [Primus] were really a lot of fun."[21]

APRIL 28, 1992
NUREMBERG, GERMANY
FRANKENHALLE, NUREMBERG
CONVENTION CENTRE, Messezentrum, 90471. Venue opened on December 14, 1984.
SUPPORT ACT: Primus
TICKETS: 40 DEM / 45 DEM
CAPACITY: 8,000 (5,000 seats)
NOTES: During Rush's set, an enthusiastic crowd (with many American GIs in attendance) propelled a fired-up band.

APRIL 29, 1992
STUTTGART, GERMANY
SCHLEYER-HALLE, Mercedes Strabe 69. Venue inaugurated on September 14, 1983.
SUPPORT ACT: Primus
TICKETS: 40 DEM / 45 DEM
CAPACITY: 12,400
NOTES: During the middle section of "Closer to the Heart," Alex went nuts, talking and going on and on and on, to which Geddy replied, "Did you get all that?"

MAY 1, 1992
PARIS, FRANCE
LE ZENITH DE PARIS, Parc de La Villette, 211 Avenue Jean-Jaures. Venue inaugurated on January 12, 1984.
SUPPORT ACT: Primus
TICKETS: 145 FRF

ATTENDANCE: 5,000
CAPACITY: 6,293
NOTES: Rush's French debut, originally scheduled for April 30. Neil was late for sound check, so Geddy and Alex got the members of Primus to join in for a jam. Outside the gig, scalpers were everywhere, with tickets in high demand. During Primus's set, they played a verse of "A Passage to Bangkok" within "Those Damn Blue-Collar Tweekers."

JIM RHODES (STAGE LEFT TECHNICIAN): "It was a strange day, as Neil was late for sound check, whereas most times you could set your watch to the big guy. Usually, he would arrive every day, come up onstage, summon stage manager Skip Gildersleeve on guitar and me on bass, and Skip and I would get to play with Neil for ten to fifteen minutes as a warm-up before Geddy and Alex came in. It was always fun to play with him. However, on this day Neil's usual arrival time of 2:30 p.m. passed, Ged and Al arrived, and there was still no Neil. So, as a bit more time slipped by, everyone was getting concerned for Neil, and the Primus guys gathered around the stage with all of us, and since Neil wasn't there yet, Geddy and Alex thought to invite the Primus guys up for a jam. So Geddy jumped on keys, Les on bass, Alex and Larry on guitars, and Tim slowly walked toward the Holy Grail drum riser, where no man had ever gone before. So Tim got up onto the drums, reluctantly . . . and the five of them began an amazing jam that was, by all accounts for everyone that was there, some spinal, crazy shit!"[22]

TIM "HERB" ALEXANDER: "I entered Neil's monster drum set that has drums all the way around. I was frozen. Geddy asked me what I wanted to play and, as I look around at a sea of drums, all I could think of was . . . nothing. Of all the times for me to not know a single Rush song, this is not the time. I began to slowly hit a couple of drums to pretend to get comfortable while I was searching my head, desperately, for some sliver of a memory of a song. I hit an electronic pad that triggers a sound for 'Roll the Bones'—a song I was only really familiar with from watching shows. Well, we started playing it. Wow. Here I am. I have mentally created this moment from years of visualization, practice, and dedication to the art of drumming . . . and I'm playing a

song I don't know. What the fuck? I blew it. Suddenly, off to the right, Neil walks onstage and is watching. Fun's over for me now. I fucked up my only chance to really live that vision of us playing '2112,' or 'By-Tor and the Snow Dog,' or 'Subdivisions,' or 'Natural Science,' or 'Cygnus X-1.'"[23]

MAY 3, 1992
ROTTERDAM, SOUTH HOLLAND, THE NETHERLANDS
AHOY SPORTPALEIS, Ahoy-weg 10. Venue opened on January 15, 1971.
SUPPORT ACT: Primus
TICKETS: 42.50 NLG
CAPACITY: 12,000 (approximate)
NOTES: Final date of the 1992 European Tour—Rush's only European trek of the '90s.

MAY 21, 1992
MEMPHIS, TENNESSEE
MID-SOUTH COLISEUM, Memphis Fairgrounds Park, 996 Early Maxwell Blvd. Venue opened on December 2, 1964.
SUPPORT ACT: Mr. Big
TICKETS: $18.50
ATTENDANCE: 6,503
CAPACITY: 8,500
CONCERT GROSS: $120,306
NOTES: The final six weeks of dates saw a change at front-of-house, as Brad Madix stepped in to temporarily cover for Robert Scovill.

MAY 23, 1992
KANSAS CITY, MISSOURI
KEMPER ARENA, 1800 Genessee Street at 17th Street. Venue dedicated on October 18, 1974.
SUPPORT ACT: Mr. Big
TICKETS: $18.50 / $21.50
ATTENDANCE: 9,544
CAPACITY: 16,871
CONCERT GROSS: $194,682

MAY 24, 1992
VALLEY CENTER, KANSAS
BRITT BROWN ARENA, Kansas Coliseum complex, 1229 East 85th Street North. Venue opened on September 28, 1978.
SUPPORT ACT: Mr. Big
TICKETS: $20.00 (includes twenty-five-cent parking fee)
ATTENDANCE: 5,541

CAPACITY: 9,237
CONCERT GROSS: $110,820

MAY 25, 1992
OKLAHOMA CITY
MYRIAD ARENA, One Myriad Gardens. Venue opened on November 5, 1972.
SUPPORT ACT: Mr. Big
TICKETS: $19.50 / $25.00
ATTENDANCE: 6,796
CAPACITY: 10,500
CONCERT GROSS: $140,843
NOTES: Expanding on a previously established Toronto tradition, the band began holding food drives at their concerts during the third leg of the tour. At Myriad Arena, the collected items benefited the Oklahoma City Food Bank. Attendees who brought at least three nonperishable food items had their names entered in a drawing, where eleven winners got a pair of front-row tickets to the show and tour books. One lucky winner also got to meet both Rush and Mr. Big after the performance and was given copies of their latest CDs.
THE OKLAHOMAN: "High-Tech Rush Show Wows Fans: Lee, Lifeson, and Peart produce a seamless sound which was enhanced by the visual effects projected on the giant screen behind them, a state-of-the-art light show, and their version of 'surround sound.'"
THE OKLAHOMAN, ALEX: "We've held food drives in Toronto for the past twelve or thirteen years. It's a great way to do something for the community. The benefits are great, it makes you feel good. It's a small thing and we do it in as many cities as we can . . . We haven't really stopped touring, we just pace it differently. After eighteen years we're a little worn out. We just returned from a month in Europe. It's a nice break in the middle of touring to go to England, Germany, Paris, Amsterdam, and Scotland, then come back here."[24]

MAY 27, 1992
ENGLEWOOD, COLORADO
FIDDLER'S GREEN AMPHITHEATRE, 6350 Greenwood Plaza Blvd. Venue opened on June 11, 1988.
SUPPORT ACT: Mr. Big
TICKETS: $15.50 (general admission, lawn) / $17.50 / $19.50
ATTENDANCE: 16,212
CAPACITY: 17,990

CONCERT GROSS: $277,806
NOTES: Rush held a food drive, which gathered three tons of food for the Food Bank of the Rockies. A cold and rainy night (with temps in the low 40s) didn't dampen the spirits of the golf enthusiast on stage right, as Alex took some putts during the gig. Onstage, it was a shortened set as the band replaced "Subdivisions" and "The Pass" with "The Trees."
THE GAZETTE (COLORADO SPRINGS): "Rush is still a spirited, surprisingly strong band: Like a bottle of fine wine, Rush keeps getting better with age. An instrumental song from the new album, 'Where's My Thing?' provided nonstop excitement as the band rolled through the song's funky progressions. Rush was at its best when the music gave the band a chance to let loose and jam."

MAY 29, 1992
SALT LAKE CITY, UTAH
DELTA CENTER, 301 W South Temple. Venue opened on October 4, 1991.
SUPPORT ACT: Mr. Big
TICKETS: $20.00 / $22.00
ATTENDANCE: 11,046
CAPACITY: 14,000
CONCERT GROSS: $221,998
NOTES: "Vital Signs" and "The Analog Kid" were added to the set. Neil would later recount that he'd been inspired to bring "The Analog Kid" back after hearing it being blasted out by some fans in a preconcert tailgate gathering earlier in the tour, which left him thinking, "That sounds pretty good!"
SALT LAKE TRIBUNE: "Rush Outrocks Mr. Big in Delta Center Show: Rush combined light and video with the music to create an interesting stage show. However, for anyone unfamiliar with Rush's music, it could have been a lost night. At times, the sound mix drowned out Mr. Lee's quirky high-pitched vocals, and in the process losing drummer's Neil Peart's lyrics."

MAY 31, 1992
MOUNTAIN VIEW, CALIFORNIA
SHORELINE AMPHITHEATRE, One Amphitheatre Parkway. Venue opened on July 5, 1986.
SUPPORT ACT: Mr. Big
TICKETS: $19.50 (lawn) / $25.00 (reserved)

ATTENDANCE: 15,691
CAPACITY: 20,000
CONCERT GROSS: $306,356

JUNE 1, 1992
RENO, NEVADA
LAWLOR EVENTS CENTER, University of Nevada-Reno campus, 1500 North Virginia Street. Venue opened on November 4, 1983.
SUPPORT ACT: Mr. Big
TICKETS: $22.50
ATTENDANCE: 4,236
CAPACITY: 8,500
CONCERT GROSS: $95,310
NOTES: The band held a food drive to benefit Reno-area food banks.

JUNE 2, 1992
ANAHEIM, CALIFORNIA; ANAHEIM STADIUM. ALEX AND GEDDY WORKED OUT WITH THE CALIFORNIA ANGELS IN FULL UNIFORM, FURTHER REALIZING GEDDY'S DREAM OF WORKING OUT WITH EVERY MLB TEAM.
JOHN WATHAN (ANGELS MANAGER): "I'd never heard of them, but my kid wanted an autograph. That's the way to do it—millionaire musicians. Less stress than managing."[25]
ALEX: "[Angels hitting coach Rod Carew] told me three things: First, it was 'Keep your hands out in front,' then 'That's enough,' and third was, 'Don't give up the day job.'"[26]

JUNE 3–4, 1992
IRVINE, CALIFORNIA
IRVINE MEADOWS AMPHITHEATER, 8808 Irvine Center Drive. Venue opened on August 21, 1981.
SUPPORT ACT: Mr. Big
TICKETS: $17.50 (general admission, lawn) / $29.00 (reserved) / $34.00 (orchestra)
TWO-DAY ATTENDANCE: 28,492
TWO-DAY CAPACITY: 30,000
TWO-DAY IRVINE CONCERT GROSS: $724,294 (*Amusement Business* lists $724,295)
NOTES: The second night was filmed by Atlantic Records, though the footage has yet to see the light of day. Venue aka Verizon Wireless Amphitheater.

JUNE 6, 1992
LAS VEGAS, NEVADA
THOMAS AND MACK CENTER, UNLV

campus, 4505 South Maryland Parkway. Venue opened on September 16, 1983.
SUPPORT ACT: Mr. Big
TICKETS: $20.00 / $22.50 / $29.50
ATTENDANCE: 8,993
CAPACITY: 10,500
CONCERT GROSS: $206,198
NOTES: During "Closer to the Heart," a crew member donning a red cape and devil's hood entered the stage, so Alex took out the foam bow and arrow and shot him, and he played dead.
JIMMY LANG (RUSH FAN): "One guy on the floor was air drumming with glow sticks and decides to hurl one onstage during Neil's solo. It hits his bass drum and bounces off. I'm sure Neil must have been pissed. He grabbed another pair of glow sticks and continued to air drum, which was great because security saw him and dragged him away."[27]

JUNE 7, 1992
PHOENIX, ARIZONA
DESERT SKY PAVILION, 2121 North 83rd Avenue. Venue opened on November 11, 1990.
SUPPORT ACT: Mr. Big
TICKETS: $20.00 (lawn) / $22.50 (reserved) / $27.50 (orchestra); prices include $1.50 service charge
ATTENDANCE: 14,523
CAPACITY: 19,945
CONCERT GROSS: $294,957
ARIZONA REPUBLIC: "Rush shows that it has aged well: As befits a band that has always been known for its love of the high-tech, the stage lights and audiovisual work that accompanied its playing was flashy and surreal."

JUNE 9, 1992
ALBUQUERQUE, NEW MEXICO
TINGLEY COLISEUM, New Mexico State Fairgrounds, 300 San Pedro Drive Northeast. Venue dedicated on September 28, 1957.
SUPPORT ACT: Mr. Big
TICKETS: $19.50 / $20.50
ATTENDANCE: 5,916
CAPACITY: 7,500
CONCERT GROSS: $115,974

JUNE 10, 1992
LUBBOCK, TEXAS
LUBBOCK MUNICIPAL COLISEUM, Texas Tech University campus. Fourth

Street and University Avenue. Venue opened in March 1956.
SUPPORT ACT: Mr. Big
TICKETS: $19.50 / $20.50
ATTENDANCE: 7,199; sold out
CONCERT GROSS: $140,746
NOTES: The very first reserved-seat concert at Lubbock Coliseum. 8,000 Lubbock fans had signed a petition for the band to perform in their city. Once on sale, 3,000 tickets were sold the first day, with 2,000 sold the second day of sale.
LUBBOCK AVALANCHE-JOURNAL: "Venerable Rush acclaimed for diverse rock program: What the audience received was a full aural and visual entertainment package, but it was the intricately played music which kept bodies swaying. This Canadian trio has maintained its winning combination of class and talent. The result was another winning performance."

JUNE 12, 1992
MARYLAND HEIGHTS, MISSOURI
RIVERPORT AMPHITHEATRE, 14141 Riverport Drive. Venue opened on June 14, 1991.
SUPPORT ACT: Mr. Big
TICKETS: $20.00 (general admission, lawn) / $24.00 (reserved)
ATTENDANCE: 13,955
CAPACITY: 19,861
CONCERT GROSS: $254,910
TED LEAMY (ELECTROTEC): "During the *Roll the Bones* tour, we used to always make fun of George Steinart. George has been with the band for a hundred million years, and George is the carpenter, and there is a lot of locker room humor that goes on . . . it's like a fraternity—guys are always making fun of one another. So, we would always laugh and say, 'Really, the only thing George does is vacuum the carpet.' And he would say, 'Oh, you guys don't know how hard my job is,' and we're like, 'Oh, all you do is vacuum the carpet.' It became a running gag. We used to tease George and say, 'Aw, you're getting a new vacuum cleaner—the technology has improved!' And this kind of fraternity humor would often come to include the band. I don't know how this started, but Scovill and I suggested to Alex that during one of his solos he grab the vacuum cleaner, and I got the guy on the PA crew to mic the

vacuum cleaner and slowly turn it up. And the first night we did it, George was so pissed off, he almost quit the tour. It wasn't just a crew joke anymore—now it was part of the frickin' show!"[28]

JUNE 13, 1992
ANTIOCH, TENNESSEE
STARWOOD AMPHITHEATRE, 3839 Murfreesboro Pike. Venue opened on June 21, 1986.
SUPPORT ACT: Mr. Big
TICKETS: $12.50 (general admission, lawn) / $17.50 (reserved)
ATTENDANCE: 8,426
CAPACITY: 17,128
CONCERT GROSS: $122,247
THE TENNESSEAN: "Rush packs 'em in, sets 'em thinking: Saturday night's jam-packed show at Starwood was exceptional."

JUNE 14, 1992
CHARLOTTE (HARRIS-HOUSTON), NORTH CAROLINA
BLOCKBUSTER PAVILION, 707 Pavilion Boulevard. Venue opened on July 4, 1991.
SUPPORT ACT: Mr. Big
TICKETS: $18.50 (general admission, lawn) / $22.25 (upper pavilion) / $25.00 (orchestra)
ATTENDANCE: 6,440
CAPACITY: 18,728
CONCERT GROSS: $129,839
NOTES: Venue aka Verizon Wireless Amphitheatre. This day's "Food Rush" benefited Metrolina Food Bank. Onstage, Alex hit a bad note near the end of "Limelight." Geddy added, "Oh, oh" to the first verse of "Freewill." Alex broke a string near the end of "The Big Money," so Neil's cowbell section was extended while Alex got a new guitar. During the recently added "Vital Signs," Alex found himself lost midway through the song. A guitar solo was incorporated into the finale, after the vocal "Everybody got to elevate from the norm." The newly added version of "The Trees" contains all kinds of cow and dog sounds during the middle section, before the guitar solo. Near the end, Alex played a few verses of the Beach Boys 1966 classic "Sloop John B," which he continued to do for the entire run.

JUNE 16, 1992
COLUMBIA, MARYLAND
MERRIWEATHER POST PAVILION,
10475 Little Patuxent Parkway. Venue opened on July 15, 1967.
SUPPORT ACT: Mr. Big
TICKETS: $18.50 (general admission, lawn) / $23.50 (reserved)
ATTENDANCE: 11,600
CAPACITY: 15,772
CONCERT GROSS: $239,770
NOTES: Late-tour hijinks were in full effect at Merriweather Post. A female fan arrived late and sat in the second row just as Alex was about to solo in "Limelight." He walked over to her, tapped his watch, and mimed *You're late*. During "Roll the Bones," Alex snuck behind one of his amps when the lights were down and placed his head on the top cabinet, so when the stage was relit, all you see is Lerxst's head bobbing along with the music. Neil briefly missed a transition during "The Spirit of Radio." Alex had a foam-bow-and-arrow fight with members of the lighting crew, who were up in the truss. On stage left, the putting green was set up, and Alex practiced his golf skills.[29]

JUNE 17, 1992
MANSFIELD, MASSACHUSETTS
GREAT WOODS CENTER FOR THE PERFORMING ARTS, 885 South Main Street. Venue opened on June 13, 1986.
SUPPORT ACT: Mr. Big
TICKETS: $12.50 (general admission, lawn) / $24.50 (reserved) / $30.00 (orchestra)
ATTENDANCE: 14,978; sold out
CONCERT GROSS: $299,997
THE BOSTON GLOBE: "Rush drops the stone-faced act and has fun: The power trio's crew had trouble sharpening the sound mix in the Great Woods shed for a rare outdoor local show by Rush, they're used to arenas. But Rush often tends toward busy, methodical execution that works its way into a blur anyway. Lifeson was especially frisky, playing to fans near the stage with hand motions to mimic his whammy bar sustains."

JUNE 19, 1992
EAST RUTHERFORD, NEW JERSEY
MEADOWLANDS ARENA, Meadowlands Sports Complex, 50 State Route 120.

Venue opened on July 2, 1981.
SUPPORT ACT: Mr. Big
TICKETS: $20.00 / $30.00
ATTENDANCE: 15,634
CAPACITY: 18,650
CONCERT GROSS: $335,081
NOTES: The band held a food drive to benefit local food banks.

JUNE 20, 1992
WANTAGH, NEW YORK
JONES BEACH MARINE THEATER, Jones Beach State Park, 1000 Ocean Parkway. Venue dedicated on June 26, 1952.
SUPPORT ACT: Mr. Big
TICKETS: $25.00 / $35.00
ATTENDANCE: 10,700; sold out
CONCERT GROSS: $279,365
NOTES: The band held a food drive to benefit local food banks. Venue aka Jones Beach Amphitheater.
GEDDY (ONSTAGE): "Nice to be out here playing so close to the water for a change. I'd like to thank those of you that brought food for the food drive. The food banks really appreciate it. It's a good thing."

JUNE 21, 1992
BURGETTSTOWN, PENNSYLVANIA
STAR LAKE AMPHITHEATER, 665 SR 18. Venue opened on June 17, 1990.
SUPPORT ACT: Mr. Big
TICKETS: $15.00 (lawn) / $19.00 (reserved) / $25.00 (orchestra)
ATTENDANCE: 13,129
CAPACITY: 20,131
CONCERT GROSS: $184,752
NOTES: Venue aka Post-Gazette Pavilion. The concert was performed on a cold, drizzly night, with temperatures in the 40s. The day's "Food Rush" benefited Community Action Southwest, a Washington County food bank.

JUNE 22, 1992
SARATOGA, NEW YORK
SARATOGA PERFORMING ARTS CENTER, 108 Avenue of Pines. Venue opened on July 9, 1966.
SUPPORT ACT: Mr. Big
TICKETS: $16.00 / $25.00
NOTES: With tickets about to go on sale, this gig was canceled and the itinerary rerouted.

JUNE 23, 1992
FAIRBORN, OHIO
NUTTER CENTER, Wright State University campus, 3640 Colonel Glenn Highway. Venue opened on December 1, 1990.
SUPPORT ACT: Mr. Big
TICKETS: $20.00 (all seats); face value, minus fees
ATTENDANCE: 9,026; 9,314 (promoter); 9,734 (*Dayton Daily News*)
CAPACITY: 9,324
CONCERT GROSS: $180,520
NOTES: The day's "Food Rush" benefited the American Red Cross Emergency Food Bank.
DAYTON DAILY NEWS: "High-tech Rush lacks spontaneity: Was it Rush, or Memorex? But before the 9,734 devoted fans in attendance start firing off their usual bunch of angry letters, let it be said that Rush's intricately arranged and impressively played material was fine. It's just that the band's overreliance on technology robbed the first half of the show of any signs of life."

JUNE 24, 1992
NOBLESVILLE, INDIANA
DEER CREEK MUSIC CENTER, 12880 East 146th Street. Venue opened on May 20, 1989.
SUPPORT ACT: Mr. Big
TICKETS: $19.50 (lawn) / $23.50 (reserved pavilion)
ATTENDANCE: 9,120; 9,180 (promoter)
CAPACITY: 12,000
CONCERT GROSS: $168,230

JUNE 26, 1992
CLARKSTON, MICHIGAN
PINE KNOB MUSIC THEATRE, 7774 Sashabaw Road. Venue opened on June 25, 1972.
SUPPORT ACT: Mr. Big
TICKETS: $20.00 (lawn) / $22.50 (pavilion) / $40.00 (orchestra)
ATTENDANCE: 14,977; sold out
CONCERT GROSS: $325,965

JUNE 27, 1992
EAST TROY, WISCONSIN
ALPINE VALLEY MUSIC THEATRE, 2699 Highway D. Venue opened on June 30 1977.
SUPPORT ACT: Mr. Big
TICKETS: $17.50 (general admission, lawn) / $25.00 (reserved) / $35.00 (orchestra)

ATTENDANCE: 21,474 (reserved and orchestra tickets sold out)
CAPACITY: 35,000
CONCERT GROSS: $359,932
NOTES: The day's "Food Rush" benefited the Milwaukee Hunger Task Force. During the afternoon sound check, the band ran through "Roll the Bones," "The Analog Kid," "Red Barchetta," and "Force Ten." Onstage, Alex hit some sour notes toward the conclusion of "The Big Money." In "Where's My Thing?" Geddy sang along with the melody. Always one to joke around, Alex sang, "Stupid conductor" on the chorus. During "Tom Sawyer," Geddy changed up a lyric and sang, "Don't put him down is all you get."

JUNE 28, 1992
TINLEY PARK, ILLINOIS
WORLD MUSIC THEATRE, 19100 Ridgeland Avenue. Venue opened on June 2, 1990.
SUPPORT ACT: Mr. Big
TICKETS: $15.00 / $32.50; face value, minus $2.25 parking fee
ATTENDANCE: 11,944
CAPACITY: 15,000
CONCERT GROSS: $288,410
NOTES: Venue aka New World Music Theatre. Final date of the *Roll the Bones* world tour. The band held a food drive to benefit local Chicago food banks. Neil had Andrew MacNaughtan secretly shave his head into a Mohawk before the show, and then pull off his bandanna in the encore (during his Pete Townshend windmill in "Finding My Way"), to the great amusement of band, crew, and crowd. During "Closer to the Heart," Alex shot a foam arrow at Neil, who promptly put it in his mouth for the rest of the song. This was production manager Nick Kotos's final date with the band. This tour would also be the final time that Mr. Big opened for Rush, and in 1996, Eric Martin covered "Mission" for the *Working Man* tribute disc.
GEDDY (ONSTAGE): "I'd like to say, because it's the last show of our tour, and seeing as we do have the best crew, I think, in the world, we'd like to thank them tonight in front of all of you. Appreciate all of their hard work. Oh gosh, we're gonna cry now."
NEIL: "I was wearing bandannas on my head on that tour, to keep the sweat out of my eyes, and before the show, I got Andrew to shave my head into a Mohawk, which I kept hidden until the encore. Then I pulled off the bandanna and got a big laugh out of Alex and Geddy and the crew."[30]

1. Interview with Andy Curran. *One Louder Magazine*, June 3, 2011.
2. *The National Midnight Star*, 1991.
3. *Montreal Gazette*.
4. *Le Soleil*.
5. www.vinniemoore.com/2010/
6. Bill Banasiewicz. Interview with Brian Tichy, April 17, 2016.
7. *Guitar Player*, September 2007.
8. Neil Peart. *Traveling Music: Playing Back the Soundtrack to My Life and Times*. ECW Press, June 2004.
9. Interview with Tim "Herb" Alexander. *Primus, Over the Electric Grapevine*. Akashic Books, September 16, 2014.
10. Skip Daly. Interview with Robert Scovill, November 29, 2012.
11. Interview with Geddy Lee. *Primus, Over the Electric Grapevine*. Akashic Books, September 16, 2014.
12. Interview with Neil Peart. *Houston Chronicle*, February 16, 1992.
13. *The Vancouver Sun*.
14. *Pensacola News Journal*.
15. *St. Louis Post-Dispatch*, March 1, 1992.
16. *St. Louis Post-Dispatch*, March 1, 1992.
17. *St. Louis Post-Dispatch*, March 1, 1992.
18. Skip Daly. Interview with Jim Rhodes, December 2012.
19. Interview with Tim "Herb" Alexander. *Primus, Over the Electric Grapevine*. Akashic Books, September 16, 2014.
20. Skip Daly. Interview with Robert Scovill, November 29, 2012.
21. Interview with Geddy Lee. *Primus, Over the Electric Grapevine*. Akashic Books, September 16, 2014.
22. Skip Daly. Interview with Jim Rhodes, December 2012.
23. Interview with Tim "Herb" Alexander. *Primus, Over the Electric Grapevine*. Akashic Books, September 16, 2014.
24. *Daily Oklahoman*, May 22, 1992.
25. *The San Diego Union-Tribune*, June 1992.
26. Interview with Alex Lifeson. *The Denver Post*, June 7, 1992.
27. Interview with Jimmy Lang. *The National Midnight Star*, 1992.
28. Interview with Ted Leamy, May 17, 2013.
29. *The National Midnight Star*, 1992.
30. Neil Peart. *Roadshow: Landscape with Rums, A Concert Tour by Motorcycle*. Rounder Books, 2006.

Chapter 23

THE COUNTERPARTS TOUR

The *Counterparts* tour was short but successful: Over the course of just fifty-four shows, Rush played to 589,137 fans. On opening night, the band sauntered onstage to the strains of "Also Sprach Zarathustra," the symphonic slab of bombast immortalized in Stanley Kubrick's *2001: A Space Odyssey*—the perfect scoring for when the *Counterparts* album cover's nut-and-bolt image came together on the rear screen. The set included the live debuts of "Animate," "Stick It Out," "Nobody's Hero," "Double Agent," "Leave That Thing Alone," and "Cold Fire." Neil sported a new Ludwig Super Classic drum set with black cherry finish, Alex played his white Gibson EDS-1275 double-neck guitar during "Xanadu," and Geddy's main bass was his black Fender Jazz.

The dates kicked off in early 1994—Alex, Geddy, and Neil's twentieth year as a band. "Our rhinestone anniversary, I believe it's called," said Neil. "But really, can you imagine—the same three guys staying together through a score of years, and finding an audience to keep buying all that racket? We can't think of another group which has survived for so long with the same individuals, and since those individuals are us, we think the occasion deserves some tribute. We haven't decided exactly what tribute yet, but we are thinking about the possibility of retrospective shows, live recordings, and videos. Later in the year we will have a clearer idea of what, exactly, we're going to do. But we're going to do something—at least have cake!"

Counterparts marked the first tour that featured nothing from Rush's first four albums—and the only tour ever to skip *2112* completely. The run did, however, mark the return of *Hemispheres*, with the "Prelude" performed for the first time in twelve years.

Explained Alex, "It was Primus that got us to bring back parts from *Hemispheres*. They would jam at sound check [on the *Roll the Bones* tour] with all this stuff, and we'd stand at the side of the stage and laugh. We got very close with them and hung out a lot and they said, 'You know, you should bring some of that stuff back, it was so cool, it's what we grew up with.' So we figured, 'Yeah, okay!'"

The shows also included a few moments of planned humor. Geddy would introduce "Cold Fire" as a country and western song, usually with Alex playing Johnny Cash's classic "I Walk the Line" in the background. And for the band introductions that accompanied the "Closer to the Heart" jams, Alex would make up amusing names off the top of his head, usually introducing each member as a celebrity. At the final US date, in Rochester, New York, he used this part of the show to pay homage to Rush's early history.

"On the funky bass guitar, wearing all black, Mr. Doc Cooper," Alex said from the stage. "Back there on the drums, after a long, long time away, Mr. John Rutsey. Me? You probably recognize me from earlier tour programs and

album covers. I've been away too. I feel better now. I only spent a little time in the hospital. I feel much better now. My name is Ian Grandy."

The set list for the tour remained consistent until the addition of "Bravado" for only the final two weeks of the proceedings. Although not included in the final set, "Distant Early Warning" was performed between "Force Ten" and "YYZ" in rehearsals. Late in the outing, "Force Ten" was omitted from the set for some gigs, when Geddy was sick, in order to give his voice a much-needed break.

Additionally, the entire *Counterparts* trek was scaled when Geddy and his wife Nancy learned they were expecting a baby. Originally slated to run until the end of June, the tour instead concluded on May 7, 1994, with a sold-out show at Toronto's Maple Leaf Gardens. Geddy and Nancy's daughter, Kyla, was born the following week.

"Over the last ten years, my private life and my family life has become increasingly more important," Geddy explained. "So when I found out that another child was coming, I was adamant that I would be around more for that whole experience, for the sake of my child, for the sake of myself."

BELOW: Alex, Geddy, and Neil with their crew and the Candlebox entourage.
OPPOSITE: Worcester, MA; Geddy hamming it up for the camera at the Centrum.

TOUR HISTORY
COUNTERPARTS

SET LIST:
Intro (Also Sprach Zarathustra)
"Dreamline"
"The Spirit of Radio"
"The Analog Kid"
"Cold Fire" (with country music intro)
"Time Stand Still"
"Nobody's Hero"
"Roll the Bones"
"Animate"

"Stick It Out" (with introduction by Alex)
"Double Agent"
"Limelight"
"Bravado"
"Mystic Rhythms"
"Closer to the Heart" (with band introductions by Alex)
"Show Don't Tell"
"Leave That Thing Alone"
"The Rhythm Method" (drum solo)

"The Trees"
"Xanadu"
"Hemispheres: Prelude"
"Tom Sawyer"
Encore:
"Force Ten"
"YYZ"
"Cygnus X-1" (teaser)

JANUARY 22, 1994
PENSACOLA, FLORIDA
PENSACOLA CIVIC CENTER, 201 East Gregory Street
SUPPORT ACT: Candlebox
TICKETS: $20.00 / $25.00
ATTENDANCE: 8,422; sold out
CONCERT GROSS: $176,550
NOTES: The opening date of the 1994 *Counterparts* tour. Rush sauntered onto the stage to the strains of "Also Sprach Zarathustra," the symphonic slab of bombast immortalized in Stanley Kubrick's *2001: A Space Odyssey*, which is the perfect scoring for when the nut and bolt unite on the screen. The set included the live debut of "Animate," "Stick it Out," "Nobody's Hero," "Double Agent," "Leave That Thing Alone," and "Cold Fire." Onstage, the band was met by cheering fans, many of whom had traveled from far and wide to be at the opening show. Neil was sporting a new Ludwig Super Classic drum set with black cherry finish, Alex played his white Gibson EDS-1275 doubleneck guitar during "Xanadu," and Geddy's main bass is his black Fender Jazz.
GEDDY (ONSTAGE): "It's nice to be here in Pensacola. Thank you all for your hospitality all week while we've been here. It's a great place to start a tour."

JANUARY 23, 1994
NEW ORLEANS, LOUISIANA
UNO LAKEFRONT ARENA, University of New Orleans, East Campus, 6801 Franklin Street. Venue opened on November 1, 1983.
SUPPORT ACT: Candlebox
TICKETS: $22.25 / $27.25

ATTENDANCE: 7,432; sold out
CONCERT GROSS: $180,302
NOTES: Pyro was not permitted at this venue.
ALEX: "Jimmy (Johnson) had probably the worst night ever. One thing after another with the guitars. I mean, he's just always on the ball—he forgot a guitar change. He gave me a guitar that was out of tune. It was . . . just constant. That was a nightmare gig, and I wore these shoes. It was the only night I wore these shoes . . . they're like huge, giant shoes. I couldn't hit the pedals [*laughs*]."[1]

JANUARY 25, 1994
AUSTIN, TEXAS
FRANK ERWIN SPECIAL EVENTS CENTER, University of Texas at Austin campus, 1701 Red River Street. Venue opened on November 29, 1977.
SUPPORT ACT: Candlebox
TICKETS: $22.50 / $25.00 / $28.50
ATTENDANCE: 8,338
CAPACITY: 11,781
CONCERT GROSS: $208,414

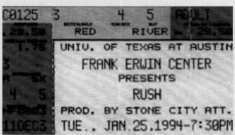

JANUARY 26, 1994
HOUSTON, TEXAS
THE SUMMIT, 3700 Southwest Freeway. Venue opened on November 1, 1975.
SUPPORT ACT: Candlebox

TICKETS: $24.25 / $28.25 / $35.25
ATTENDANCE: 12,529
CAPACITY: 17,055
CONCERT GROSS: $321,661

JANUARY 28, 1994
DALLAS, TEXAS
REUNION ARENA, 777 Sports Street. Venue dedicated on April 28, 1980.
SUPPORT ACT: Candlebox
TICKETS: $25.00 / $28.00 / $35.00
ATTENDANCE: 14,619; sold out
CONCERT GROSS: $400,920
DALLAS MORNING NEWS: "Band insists on Rush to bombast: Each band member was too busy showing off his chops to create any kind of union with the others. Lee's nearly operatic voice sounded beautiful and was echoed by prerecorded harmonies that came from the opposite end of the arena."

JANUARY 29, 1994
SAN ANTONIO, TEXAS
CONVENTION CENTER ARENA, HemisFair Park Complex, 601 Hemisfair Way. Venue opened on April 6, 1968.
SUPPORT ACT: Candlebox
TICKETS: $22.00 / $28.00
ATTENDANCE: 11,210
CAPACITY: 12,273
CONCERT GROSS: $256,822

JANUARY 31, 1994
LAS CRUCES, NEW MEXICO
PAN AMERICAN CENTER, New Mexico State University campus, 1810 East University Avenue. Venue opened on November 30, 1968.
SUPPORT ACT: Candlebox
TICKETS: $20.00 / $25.00

ATTENDANCE: 8,387
CAPACITY: 9,500
CONCERT GROSS: $176,800
EL PASO TIMES: "Lasers light up concert: Songs such as 'Cold Fire' and 'Stick It Out,' with Alex Lifeson's unusually raw guitar, brought more life to Monday's performance compared with the show two years ago. As usual, the trio's performance was energetic but mature, with little rock-star pretense."

FEBRUARY 1, 1994
PHOENIX, ARIZONA
ARIZONA VETERANS MEMORIAL COLISEUM, Arizona State Fairgrounds, 1826 West McDowell Road. Venue opened on November 3, 1965.
SUPPORT ACT: Candlebox
TICKETS: $22.50 / $27.50
ATTENDANCE: 13,970; sold out
CONCERT GROSS: $328,026
NEIL: "Phoenix was the last show we played, and I remember being onstage and thinking, *why?* All these people still come back to see us. I guess it's a holistic thing, where the sum is greater than the parts. It must be this larger thing that surrounds us like an aura—the sounds we create together and the integrity and dedication we bring to it."[2]

FEBRUARY 3, 1994
INGLEWOOD, CALIFORNIA
GREAT WESTERN FORUM, 3900 West Manchester Boulevard. Venue opened on December 30, 1967.
SUPPORT ACT: Candlebox
TICKETS: $23.50 / $37.50
ATTENDANCE: 13,755; sold out
CONCERT GROSS: $313,826
LOS ANGELES DAILY NEWS: "Rush Not Nearly as Colorful As Rush-Hour Traffic, Limbaugh: In the two-hour appearance, Rush gave three generations of stoners a smattering of hits, lots of meandering solos and some new material."

FEBRUARY 5, 1994
ANAHEIM, CALIFORNIA
ARROWHEAD POND, 2695 E. Katella Avenue. Venue opened (as Anaheim Arena) on June 19, 1993.
SUPPORT ACT: Candlebox
TICKETS: $23.50 / $37.50
ATTENDANCE: 13,460; sold out
CONCERT GROSS: $333,646
NOTES: Venue aka Honda Center. First hard rock show at Arrowhead Pond. Entrance security was tight, with patrons required to empty out their pockets while being yelled at by the guards.[3]
LOS ANGELES TIMES: "Fans—If Not Critics—Get Rush at Arena Concert: Most members of the capacity audience were on their feet throughout, singing along, clapping, toking, and acting as if they were having a tremendous time. Good thing we critics know better!"

FEBRUARY 7, 1994
SAN DIEGO, CALIFORNIA
SAN DIEGO SPORTS ARENA, 3500 Sports Arena Boulevard. Venue opened on November 17, 1966.
SUPPORT ACT: Candlebox
TICKETS: $20.00 / $22.50 / $27.50
ATTENDANCE: 11,242
CAPACITY: 11,668
CONCERT GROSS: $226,598

FEBRUARY 8, 1994
FRESNO, CALIFORNIA
SELLAND ARENA, 700 M Street at Ventura. Venue opened on October 11, 1966.
SUPPORT ACT: Melvins
TICKETS: $21.50 (advance) / $23.50 (day of)
ATTENDANCE: 6,249
CAPACITY: 9,011
CONCERT GROSS: $127,674
NOTES: Rush welcomed the Melvins to the tour with a bottle of champagne and a postcard that read, "To the Mervins . . . Murphtones . . . Melons . . . Melvins . . . Welcome to the tour. We hope it's not too long and tiring for you. Please accept this bottle of champagne in lieu of any cash payment. Thank you for your cooperation, and we hope you don't suck like Primus. —Alex, Geddy, Neil."
THE FRESNO BEE: "Rush's Routine All Too Familiar: They rarely played with self-indulgence. Many songs made sudden twists and turns. They are musicianly musicians, playing precisely in odd time signatures. They play in an easily studied but not necessarily easily mastered style."
MARK DEUTROM (MELVINS BASSIST): "I think the Melvins ended up with Rush for those shows since our manager at the time, David Lefkowitz, also managed Primus, and they had done some touring with them . . . When your manager calls you up and asks if you would like to do some gigs with Rush, it's really a formality, like when actors would get asked if they were available for Stanley Kubrick! . . . I remember seeing a photo of Geddy wearing a Melvins shirt at a Rush show and thinking how cool that was. I think that was even before the gigs, so someone must have put the band in their ear by that point. Melvins have plenty of progressive tendencies, so it's not as weird of a mix as some people might think. The first day, Rush left a bottle of champagne in our dressing room with a welcome note. A classic move that put everyone at ease, and a great example of the humor and grace that they have managed to retain into their huge success."[4]

FEBRUARY 10, 1994
SACRAMENTO, CALIFORNIA
ARCO ARENA, One Sports Parkway. Venue opened on November 8, 1988.
SUPPORT ACT: Melvins
TICKETS: $25.00 (all seats)
ATTENDANCE: 9,799
CAPACITY: 12,000
CONCERT GROSS: $244,975 (estimate)
SACRAMENTO BEE: "Sound Problems Plague Rush: The sound began dense and muddy, obscuring much of singer Lee's work, and grew only marginally clearer as the show went on. That was a pity, for, from what could be heard, the band's playing was crisp and tight."

FEBRUARY 11, 1994
DALY CITY, CALIFORNIA
COW PALACE, 2600 Geneva Avenue.
Venue opened on April 20, 1941.
SUPPORT ACT: Melvins
TICKETS: $25.00 (all seats)
ATTENDANCE: 9,214
CAPACITY: 12,000
CONCERT GROSS: $230,350 (estimate)
MARK DEUTROM (MELVINS BASSIST): "I didn't get to see Rush as a teenager, but I was more than making up for it at that point. One thing that is utterly unique that happens at a Rush show is watching 8,000 middle-aged men and women playing air drums. Didn't matter which city, and I suspect it happens in every city they play in—without fail, 'Tom Sawyer' brings the air drums. Such a great communal celebratory and joyous moment! Watching Geddy made you aware of just what a polymath he is. The bass playing is just huge, the keyboards are perfect, and the voice is unmistakable and iconic. I feel Geddy might be somewhat underrated as a bass player, but that's probably just because Rush itself has such iconic status that it is greater than the sum of its parts. Everything about them is unique: Their arrangements, sound, and subject matter are continually evolving, and you could just tell there are thinking individuals behind what is coming from them. It's impossible to predict what they will do next, and always a pleasure to discover the next phase they're moving into."[5]

FEBRUARY 12, 1994
SAN JOSE, CALIFORNIA
SAN JOSE ARENA, 525 West Santa Clara Street. Venue opened on September 7, 1993.
SUPPORT ACT: Melvins
TICKETS: $25.00 (all seats)
ATTENDANCE: 13,274
CAPACITY: 15,000
CONCERT GROSS: $331,850 (estimate)
MARK DEUTROM (MELVINS BASSIST): "We didn't have much contact with the band, since their traveling schedules were quite different than ours. Neil would ride his bicycle to the venues from whatever hotel they were at, and I would see him riding in sometimes and he would always wave . . . I managed to catch their sound check a couple of times, and that

can be a definite no-go area for a lot of bands. When they started playing, someone saw me looking in the doorway and waved me in. 'Go sit in the front row,' he said, 'wherever you want.' So I just walked over and sat in the front row, and I'm the only person sitting in the seats in San Jose Arena and Rush is just killing it with all the house lights on. They stop playing the song, and Geddy looks at me and asks, 'Sound okay?' I said, 'Yeah . . . sounds pretty good.' He just laughed and said, 'Okay, good.' I'm really grateful I got to have that experience with an absolutely legendary band. May their road go ever on."[6]

FEBRUARY 23, 1994
MURFREESBORO, TENNESSEE
MURPHY ATHLETIC CENTER, Middle Tennessee State University campus, 2650 Middle Tennessee Boulevard. Venue opened on December 11, 1972.
SUPPORT ACT: Candlebox
TICKETS: $20.00 / $25.00
ATTENDANCE: 6,632
CAPACITY: 8,500
CONCERT GROSS: $149,442

FEBRUARY 24, 1994
ATLANTA, GEORGIA
THE OMNI, 100 Techwood Drive Northwest. Venue opened on October 14, 1972.
SUPPORT ACT: Candlebox
TICKETS: $23.50 / $30.50
ATTENDANCE: 11,495
CAPACITY: 12,500
CONCERT GROSS: $281,906

FEBRUARY 25, 1994
CHARLOTTE, NORTH CAROLINA
CHARLOTTE COLISEUM, 100 Paul Buck Boulevard. Venue opened on August 11, 1988.
SUPPORT ACT: Candlebox
TICKETS: $22.50 (all seats)
ATTENDANCE: 9,675
CAPACITY: 14,000
CONCERT GROSS: $217,688 (estimate)

FEBRUARY 27, 1994
MIAMI, FLORIDA
MIAMI ARENA, 701 Arena Boulevard. Venue opened on July 13, 1988.
SUPPORT ACT: Candlebox
TICKETS: $23.50 / $32.50
ATTENDANCE: 10,696
CAPACITY: 13,000
CONCERT GROSS: $275,242 (estimate)
NOTES: Recorded to multitrack, with "Show Don't Tell" being culled for the *Different Stages* live album.

MARCH 1, 1994
ORLANDO, FLORIDA
ORLANDO ARENA, 600 West Amelia Street. Venue opened on January 29, 1989.
SUPPORT ACT: Candlebox
TICKETS: $22.50 / $29.50
ATTENDANCE: 9,644
CAPACITY: 10,000
CONCERT GROSS: $237,542
NOTES: After sound check, Geddy did a phone interview with the *Worcester Phoenix*.

MARCH 2, 1994
JACKSONVILLE, FLORIDA
JACKSONVILLE VETERANS MEMORIAL COLISEUM, 1145 Adams Street. Venue dedicated on November 24, 1960.
SUPPORT ACT: Candlebox
TICKETS: $22.50 / $27.50
ATTENDANCE: 4,752
CAPACITY: 9,000
CONCERT GROSS: $114,252 (estimate)

MARCH 4, 1994
ST. PETERSBURG, FLORIDA
THUNDERDOME, One Tropicana Drive. Venue opened on March 3, 1990.
SUPPORT ACT: Candlebox
TICKETS: $22.50 / $29.50
ATTENDANCE: 8,377
CAPACITY: 15,000
CONCERT GROSS: $210,910 (estimate)
NOTES: Venue aka Tropicana Field.

TAMPA TRIBUNE: "Loyal rockers rush to hear old-time trio: The nostalgia buzz was almost reassuring, as lasers twirled, fists pounded the air in time with the often-syncopated rhythm, the floor became slick with beer, marijuana made its presence known, and air drummers sprouted up everywhere."

MARCH 6, 1994
CHAPEL HILL, NORTH CAROLINA
DEAN E. SMITH CENTER, 300 Skipper Bowles Drive. Venue opened on January 18, 1986.
SUPPORT ACT: Candlebox
TICKETS: $22.50
ATTENDANCE: 7,318
CAPACITY: 8,000
CONCERT GROSS: $164,665
GREENSBORO NEWS AND RECORD: "Rush Less Enthralling Onstage, Better in Theory: Truly a people's band, despite the increasing intellectual pretensions of their records, Rush works hard to strike a balance between the cerebral and the visceral onstage. Unfortunately, a soupy, distorted sound mix and the bomb-shelter acoustics of the Smith Center conspired to rob the songs of their lyrical coherence and musical nuance. Alex Lifeson's guitar sounded like the din inside a sheet-metal factory, while Lee's vocals were indecipherable, only occasionally penetrating the wall of mud."

MARCH 8–9, 1994
NEW YORK, NEW YORK
MADISON SQUARE GARDEN, 4 Pennsylvania Plaza (8th Avenue between 31st and 33rd Streets). Historic venue opened on February 11, 1968.
SUPPORT ACT: Candlebox
TICKETS: $22.50 / $27.50 / 35.00
ATTENDANCE: 14,416 per show; sold out
CONCERT GROSS: $419,747 per show
NOTES: The band held a food drive at both MSG concerts in support of New York–area food banks.
THE NEW YORK TIMES: "Unfortunately, Rush lacks even a rudimentary sense of dynamics. Except in those songs where Mr. Lifeson switched from acoustic to electric guitar, the music all proceeded at one unvarying volume, without any breathing space. Like the walls of a

musical fortress, the band's unyielding performance keeps insiders protected and outsiders away."
GEDDY (ONSTAGE): "Nice to be back here at Madison Square for our second night. Home of the great Rangers." [Boo!] "Ah, mixed crowd out there. Some of you are from the Island, it seems." [Boo!] "I can't win."
ALEX (ONSTAGE): "I was thinking about inviting everyone back to my room for a drink, but you're way too noisy . . . This was written by a friend of ours, Doc Cooper. It was called 'Doc's Lament,' but we changed it. Now it's called 'Stick It Out.'"
KEVIN MARTIN (CANDLEBOX VOCALIST): "[The most memorable show would] be Madison Square Garden with Rush, just because . . . That's the garden! You've basically gone to heaven at that point."[7]

MARCH 11–12, 1994
WORCESTER, MASSACHUSETTS
THE CENTRUM, 50 Foster Street. Venue opened on September 2, 1982.
SUPPORT ACT: Candlebox
TICKETS: $22.50 / $35.00
ATTENDANCE (MAR. 11): 12,504; sold out
ATTENDANCE (MAR. 12): 9,623
TWO-DAY CONCERT CAPACITY: 25,008
TWO-DAY WORCESTER CONCERT GROSS: $535,570
NOTES: On the first night, Alex did a lyrical rewrite during the chorus of "Closer to the Heart," singing "Closer to your house. A closet in your house. A mouse in your house."

WORCESTER TELEGRAM AND GAZETTE: "Rush generates heat, light: They sold out the Centrum. No one was over twenty. Everyone knew the words. Girls thought Geddy Lee was cute. Is this 1994? Surprisingly, Lee strayed from his stratospheric falsetto to actually give a somewhat homey treatment of the lyrics. It was personal and focused—terms that don't usually spring to mind when describing Rush."

MARCH 22, 1994
AUBURN HILLS, MICHIGAN
THE PALACE OF AUBURN HILLS, 6 Championship Drive. Venue opened on August 13, 1988.
SUPPORT ACT: Primus
TICKETS: $22.50 / $35.00
ATTENDANCE: 14,848; sold out
CONCERT GROSS: $367,117

NOTES: Recorded to multitrack, with "The Analog Kid" being culled for the *Different Stages* live album.

MARCH 23, 1994
RICHFIELD, OHIO
RICHFIELD COLISEUM, 2923 Streetsboro Road. Venue opened on October 26, 1974.
SUPPORT ACT: Primus
TICKETS: $22.50 (reserved) / $35.00 (gold circle)
ATTENDANCE: 14,717; sold out
CONCERT GROSS: $360,270
THE PLAIN DEALER (CLEVELAND): "Opening Primus Outshines Pretentious Rush: I have never experienced anything quite as excruciating as the Rush concert at the Coliseum. The lyrics that seem

profound to the drunk sitting next to you strike your sober mind as sophomoric and stupid."

MARCH 25, 1994
CINCINNATI, OHIO
RIVERFRONT COLISEUM, 100 Broadway Street. Venue opened on September 9, 1975.
SUPPORT ACT: Primus
TICKETS: $22.50 / $29.50
ATTENDANCE: 10,687; sold out
CONCERT GROSS: $256,375
NOTES: The *Cincinnati Enquirer* lists attendance as 10,746 (sold out). A trigger was inadvertently set off before the middle bass section of "Stick it Out."
CINCINNATI ENQUIRER: "Rush has not lost its edge in twenty years and will probably still have it next time around."

MARCH 26, 1994
INDIANAPOLIS, INDIANA
MARKET SQUARE ARENA, 300 East Market Street. Venue opened on September 15, 1974.
SUPPORT ACT: Primus
TICKETS: $22.50 (reserved) / $29.50 (gold circle)
ATTENDANCE: 12,035
CAPACITY: 14,000
CONCERT GROSS: $286,282
NOTES: Primus is limited to a thirty-minute set because of Indiana's law that the stage must be dark by 11:00 p.m.
INDIANAPOLIS STAR: "Rush is in no hurry to leave the '70s: When you look at this show—and the reaction of the crowd, who cheered every lighting pattern, firework, flame and image on the stage-wide video screen—you have to think they're on to something. Playing at monumental volume, the group pumped out fearsome versions of old hits and acquitted itself nicely on five songs from its latest disc, *Counterparts*."

MARCH 27, 1994
AUBURN HILLS, MICHIGAN
THE PALACE OF AUBURN HILLS, 6 Championship Drive
SUPPORT ACT: Primus
TICKETS: $22.50 / $35.00
ATTENDANCE: 14,848; sold out
CONCERT GROSS: $367,117
NOTES: Neil's drum solo from this show appeared as a bonus feature on his 2005 instructional DVD release *Anatomy of a Drum Solo*.

MARCH 29–30, 1994
ROSEMONT, ILLINOIS
ROSEMONT HORIZON, 6920 N. Mannheim Road. Venue opened on July 2, 1980.
SUPPORT ACT: Primus
TICKETS: $22.50 / $32.50
ATTENDANCE: 10,832 per show; sold out
CONCERT GROSS: $264,181 per show
NOTES: Alex had a technical issue with his acoustic guitar, so he played the opening to "Closer to the Heart" on his Paul Reed Smith electric.
CHICAGO SUN-TIMES: "Rush Concert is Half Gimmicks, Half Good Stuff: The Horizon show offered plenty to laugh at, but fans came to hear the music, and those who predate the mid-1980s left a bit disappointed."
CHICAGO TRIBUNE: "Bombs Away—Rush trapped in '70s time warp, but new generation of fans falls for old concert tricks."

MARCH 31, 1994
PEORIA, ILLINOIS
NEWMAN GOLF COURSE
Members of the Rush crew and all three member of Primus hit the links on a day off.
JIM RHODES (STAGE LEFT TECHNICIAN): "My favorite memory of Neil, whom we affectionately call Bubba, was from a crew golf tournament on the *Counterparts* tour. It was at an air force base golf course on one of our days off. Respectfully, Bubba is great at many things, but golf was not really one of them. He didn't have much interest in golf, nor was he gifted at it . . . I was fortunate to share a golf cart that day with the big guy and was happy to be playing on his team. Well, with video crew on hand, and everyone standing around the first tee box watching everyone tee off, Bubba's turn came to tee off. We all went silent, as he was showing a golf form that was—well, let's say, 'not pretty,' . . . similar to that of oh, say, Charles Barkley. The kicker was that we had a few beverage carts well stocked and ready for duty, and one of them was positioned off to the left and slightly ahead of the tee box, but not by much. The cart had a big Gatorade bucket strapped into the back of the golf cart full of ice and beers, and, as we all watched with anticipation, Bubba took a few practice swings, then stepped up to hit it. The ball went straight up into the air about 100 feet, and came down directly into the ice bucket on the back of the beverage cart! It scared the shit out of a bunch of people, because none of us knew where the ball went. Nothing but net—the ball went straight into the ice bucket! I don't know who shouted it, but someone said, 'Gotta play it where it lies, Neil!' The entire bunch of us cracked up . . . just pissing our pants, it was so funny. Bubba probably will never hit another golf ball, period, especially not one like that. Love ya, Bubba!"[8]

APRIL 1, 1994
PEORIA, ILLINOIS
PEORIA CIVIC CENTER ARENA, 201 SW Jefferson Street. Venue opened on June 7, 1982.
SUPPORT ACT: Primus
TICKETS: $22.50
ATTENDANCE: 8,345; sold out
CONCERT GROSS: $187,762
NOTES: The *Peoria Journal Star* lists attendance at 8,689. The night's "Food Rush" benefited Peoria-area food banks.
PEORIA JOURNAL STAR: "As Rock Concerts Go, This One Was a Rush to Greatness—Nuts and Bolts Show Exudes Excellence, Even After All These Years: For more than two hours, few of the 8,700 fans took time to sit in their seats, preferring to stand while bobbing heads and thrusting fists to the relentless hard rock. Lee's inimitable caterwaul sounds as sweet live as on recordings, easily piercing through the deafening musical roar—a feat impossible for lesser vocalists."

APRIL 2, 1994
MADISON, WISCONSIN
DANE COUNTY VETERANS MEMORIAL COLISEUM, Dane County Expo Center Fairgrounds, 2200 Rimrock Road. Venue opened on March 16, 1967.
SUPPORT ACT: Primus
TICKETS: $22.50 / $29.50
ATTENDANCE: 8,013
CAPACITY: 9,000
CONCERT GROSS: $197,680
NOTES: During Primus's set, Les Claypool advised fans to shout for "By-Tor and the Snow Dog" when Rush took the stage. He then proceeded to play a verse of "A Passage to Bangkok."

APRIL 4, 1994
ST. LOUIS, MISSOURI
ST. LOUIS ARENA, 5700 Oakland.
Venue opened on September 23, 1929.
SUPPORT ACT: Primus
TICKETS: $22.50 / $27.50
ATTENDANCE: 13,570; sold out
CONCERT GROSS: $322,505
ST. LOUIS POST-DISPATCH: "Still Getting
a Rush From (the Group) Rush: What was
striking is how naturally the threesome
has matured musically, with synthesizer
and sequencer embellishments combin-
ing with its power trio roots seamlessly."

APRIL 5, 1994
KANSAS CITY, MISSOURI
KEMPER ARENA, 1800 Genessee Street
at 17th Street. Venue dedicated on
October 18, 1974.
SUPPORT ACT: Primus
TICKETS: $23.00 / $28.00
ATTENDANCE: 11,561; sold out
CONCERT GROSS: $277,330
THE KANSAS CITY STAR: "Rush is
impressive in big rock pageant: Band
sounds good, and it looks good, too.
Visuals are smashing: The Canadian trio,
which wowed an audience in the nearly
packed Kemper Arena, played with spirit,
ease, and apparent enjoyment."

APRIL 7, 1994
MILWAUKEE, WISCONSIN
BRADLEY CENTER, 1001 North Fourth
Street. Venue opened on October 1,
1988.
SUPPORT ACT: Primus
TICKETS: $22.50 / $29.50; face value
minus fees
ATTENDANCE: 9,809
CAPACITY: 15,000
CONCERT GROSS: $245,490 (estimate)
MILWAUKEE JOURNAL SENTINEL: "Arena
master Rush gives fist-pumping performance: Not only does Rush seem to be
stronger than ever, but in Milwaukee anyway, it's probably a stronger concert draw
than Nirvana or Metallica. This show, like
the group's others, is state-of-the-art rock
circus: bursts of flame, explosions, lavish
lights, giant puppets, and animation. All of
that stuff is used sparingly enough that it
serves the show, rather than vice versa."

APRIL 8, 1994
MINNEAPOLIS, MINNESOTA
TARGET CENTER, 600 First Avenue
North. Venue opened on October 13,
1990.
SUPPORT ACT: Primus
TICKETS: $22.50 / $29.50; face value
minus fees
ATTENDANCE: 12,772; sold out
CONCERT GROSS: $307,600

APRIL 9, 1994
MOLINE, ILLINOIS
THE MARK OF THE QUAD CITIES, 1201
River Drive. Venue opened on May 29,
1993.
SUPPORT ACT: Primus
TICKETS: $18.75 / $29.50
ATTENDANCE: 7,053; sold out
CONCERT GROSS: $177,350
NOTES: Venue aka iWireless Center.

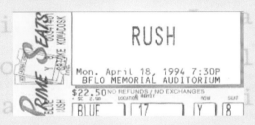

APRIL 18, 1994
BUFFALO, NEW YORK
BUFFALO MEMORIAL AUDITORIUM,
140 Main Street. Venue opened on
October 14, 1940.
SUPPORT ACT: Candlebox
TICKETS: $22.50 / $29.50
ATTENDANCE: 10,608
CAPACITY: 13,700
CONCERT GROSS: $263,334
BUFFALO NEWS: "For fans in the Aud, a
Rush of good music and visual tricks:
The near sell-out crowd witnessed a rock
show that reached grand proportions
without becoming an overdone specta-
cle. Lee, who turned forty last year,
looked about a decade younger and
acted like he was having the time of his
life. Sweeping colored lights bedazzled
the Aud, which probably hasn't sounded
that good since the last time Rush played
there."

APRIL 20, 1994
PITTSBURGH, PENNSYLVANIA
CIVIC ARENA, 300 Auditorium Place.
Venue opened on September 17, 1961.
SUPPORT ACT: Candlebox
TICKETS: $22.50 / $29.50

ATTENDANCE: 11,062
CAPACITY: 12,000
CONCERT GROSS: $267,991
PITTSBURGH POST-GAZETTE: "After Two
Decades, Rush Still Doesn't Know Rock:
There is something to be said for bring-
ing a degree of musical sophistication to
your rock 'n' roll. More often than not,
however, it only gets in the way of the
music itself."

APRIL 22, 1994
EAST RUTHERFORD, NEW JERSEY
MEADOWLANDS ARENA, Meadowlands
Sports Complex, 50 State Route 120.
Venue opened on July 2, 1981.
SUPPORT ACT: Candlebox
TICKETS: $20.00 / $24.50 / $35.00
ATTENDANCE: 14,083
CAPACITY: 14,679
CONCERT GROSS: $365,829;
(*Billboard:* $387,803)
NOTES: Alex was under the weather but
still managed to perform a spirited show.
During "Double Agent," Geddy sang,
"Anywhere," then paused and added
extra emphasis to "But here!" An enthusi-
astic crowd clapped along to the marimba
section of "The Rhythm Method."
ALEX (ONSTAGE): "I'd like to get straight
to the point. I feel like shit! . . . But I'll
be okay. It's just the twenty-four-hour
lung-cancer bug. I shouldn't complain.
I'm sure the Buffalo Sabres feel a lot
worse."

APRIL 23, 1994
UNIONDALE, NEW YORK
**NASSAU COUNTY VETERANS
MEMORIAL COLISEUM**, 1255
Hempstead Turnpike. Venue dedicated
on May 29, 1972.
SUPPORT ACT: Candlebox
TICKETS: $20.00 / $24.50 / $35.00
ATTENDANCE: 11,585
CAPACITY: 15,600
CONCERT GROSS: $313,286
NOTES: The band held a "Food Rush" to
benefit Long Island food banks.
GOOD TIMES (LONG ISLAND): "One of
the truly amazing success stories in
modern music, the trio continues to chal-
lenge rock's frontiers and deliver
thought-provoking words to accompany
their highly praised musicianship. The
faithful followers filled the coliseum just
as they have tour in and tour out, loudly
expressing their affection after every

song. Any Rush show is a good show, and this visit was good in many ways. Up against their own enormous standards, though, this wasn't anywhere near their capabilities."

APRIL 24, 1994
HARTFORD, CONNECTICUT
CIVIC CENTER, 1 Civic Center Plaza. Venue opened on January 9, 1975.
SUPPORT ACT: Candlebox
TICKETS: $22.50 / $30.00 / $35.00
ATTENDANCE: 9,747
CAPACITY: 13,000
CONCERT GROSS: $240,758
NOTES: The band and crew continued to battle a nasty flu bug that had been circulating. Being professionals, they made sure the show went on.
HARTFORD COURANT: "Rush Endures with Virtuosity: Seeing the band in concert offers several clues to their longevity. Bikers, heavy metal fans, teeny-boppers and even parents with their kids attended the concert at the Civic Center."

APRIL 26, 1994
LARGO, MARYLAND
USAIR ARENA, 1 Harry S. Truman Drive. Venue opened on December 2, 1973.
SUPPORT ACT: Candlebox
TICKETS: $22.50 / $35.00
ATTENDANCE: 14,746; sold out
CONCERT GROSS: $357,485
NOTES: Venue aka Capital Centre. Geddy and Alex were both sick, with Geddy having noticeable problems delivering the vocals. "Force Ten" was omitted from the encore.
ALEX: "We were playing in Washington to 15,000 people and Geddy's voice was cracking up after the third song, and that's pretty tough for him—it's frustrating, it's embarrassing."[9]

APRIL 27, 1994
HAMPTON, VIRGINIA
HAMPTON COLISEUM, 1000 Coliseum Drive. Venue opened on January 31, 1970.
SUPPORT ACT: Candlebox
TICKETS: $22.50 / $29.50.
NOTES: Canceled due to illness (Geddy).

APRIL 29–30, 1994
PHILADELPHIA, PENNSYLVANIA
THE SPECTRUM, 3601 South Broad Street. Venue opened on October 1, 1967.
SUPPORT ACT: Candlebox
TICKETS: $19.50 / $22.50 / $35.00
ATTENDANCE (APRIL 29): 13,545; sold out
ATTENDANCE (APRIL 30): 10,434
CAPACITY: 13,545
TWO-DAY PHILADELPHIA CONCERT GROSS: $586,134
NOTES: Both nights were recorded to multitrack for possible future release. The first date was initially announced with Primus as support, which was changed to Candlebox the day before the on-sale. Geddy was feeling better, and it was demonstrated in a strong performance, with his voice only giving out on "Limelight" and "Xanadu." During the end of the latter, he literally yelled, "Xanadu!" On the chorus of "Time Stand Still" and in the "Prelude" finale, Geddy performed improvised riffs on his Fender Jazz. Alex started humming the *Rocky* theme, stating, "A little thing I was working on in my spare time." On the second night, "Bravado" was culled for the *Different Stages* live album. He stated, "This song is evidence of dementia" before "Double Agent."
THE PHILADELPHIA INQUIRER: "Rush still makes rock that is progressive, not regressive. Scoffed at by so-called alternative-rock fans, overlooked by classic-rock radio, Rush often finds itself teetering precariously in the middle of an expanding musical generation gap. But its influence is still felt in the music of new bands such as Primus and instrumental rockers Don Caballero."

MAY 1, 1994
PROVIDENCE, RHODE ISLAND
PROVIDENCE CIVIC CENTER, 1 La Salle Square. Venue opened on November 3, 1972.
SUPPORT ACT: Candlebox
TICKETS: $22.50 / $35.00
ATTENDANCE: 7,234
CAPACITY: 9,200
CONCERT GROSS: $184,415
THE PROVIDENCE JOURNAL: "Rush has everything—except charisma: Never a critics' favorite, the band has a loyal core of fans who were immensely satisfied by a show that lasted more than two hours."

MAY 3, 1994
ALBANY, NEW YORK
KNICKERBOCKER ARENA, 51 S. Pearl Street. Venue opened on January 30, 1990.
SUPPORT ACT: Candlebox
TICKETS: $22.50 / $29.50
ATTENDANCE: 10,001
CAPACITY: 12,250
CONCERT GROSS: $245,728
NOTES: The band performed "Double Agent" and "Bravado" during sound check. Onstage, there was some loud feedback in the early part of "Cold Fire."
DAILY GAZETTE: "Special effects lift Rush's music from familiar to classic-looking: Bursting with vivid, livid lighting effects and the swelling flash and boom of fireworks, it looked more interesting than it sounded—which describes the whole show."

MAY 4, 1994
ROCHESTER, NEW YORK
ROCHESTER COMMUNITY WAR MEMORIAL, 100 Exchange Boulevard. Venue opened on October 18, 1955.
SUPPORT ACT: Candlebox
TICKETS: $22.50 / $29.50
ATTENDANCE: 8,138; sold out
CONCERT GROSS: $198,848
NOTES: The final US date of the *Counterparts* tour was also the last show with Candlebox, and both bands were in a festive mood, despite pyro not being permitted. During Candlebox's set, they played the opening to "Working Man," with Geddy singing the first verse from offstage. During Rush's set, Alex played the opening riff to "Working Man," with Ged saying, "That's enough for one night." During "Time Stand Still," Geddy sang the lyric "Make each sensation a little bit longer" instead of "stronger."
GEDDY (ONSTAGE): "It's nice to be back here in your town on this, our special *Counterparts* Country and Western Tour. Yes, it's a new direction the band has taken. We decided that all we do is country and western music now. We know you love it. So right now we'd like to do one of the old country and western favorites. I think Johnny Cash recorded this one. This is called 'Cold Fire.'"
ALEX (ONSTAGE): "Here we are in Rochester, the last American show of the tour. It's a pretty good place to end it. You've always been great here. It's an

opportunity to also say thanks and good-bye to the guys in Candlebox. They've been with us the whole tour. They're a bunch of really nice guys who care a lot about their music. Let's hope that they have a very long, successful, happy future and they can 'Stick it Out.'"

MAY 6, 1994
MONTREAL, QUEBEC
MONTREAL FORUM, 2313 Saint Catherine Street West. Historic venue opened on November 29, 1924.

SUPPORT ACT: The Doughboys

TICKETS: $24.50 / $29.50 / $35.50 CAD

ATTENDANCE: 12,913; sold out

CONCERT GROSS: $289,945 ($402,701 CAD)

NOTES: During Rush's set, the video to "Force Ten" was not shown, and Alex played a couple of bad notes during "YYZ." Despite these minor hiccups, the band's sound engineer recalls this as a legendary gig.

ROBERT SCOVILL: "I've never witnessed anything like it before or since. Rush had finished its standard encore, and the Montreal crowd was simply going nuts. At nearly all shows, there is that predictable moment of appreciation the audience gives the band at the end of the show while the band is onstage, waving good-bye, maybe taking a bow or two, and then they go running offstage into the fading lights. The production manager calls for the house lights to come up, and the roar of applause and cheering typically dies down just as quickly as the carefully selected walkout music fades up, signaling that it's time for everyone to start heading for the door. As a point of reference for a building of this capacity, the building is usually clear of all fans before the end of the first walkout song. But on this night, the crowd is simply not responding to the cues to take their leave of the building. A good fifteen to twenty minutes after the house lights have been up, at least 60 to 70 percent of the Montreal audience is still on their feet cheering and applauding what they have just experienced. At some point, I remember looking around and checking out my fellow crew members, and many were staring out to the crowd as well, kind of taking it all in. I remember turning around to see Herns

and kind of mouthing the word 'Wow!' to him. As the chanting and cheering continued, I started navigating my way through the deluge of empty cups and spilled drinks to make my way back to the dressing room because I wanted to make sure the band was hearing what was happening. I walked in and ran into Ged and Alex, and frankly, I don't remember much of the conversation, but I remember saying, 'Do you hear what's going on out there?' We all kind of just soaked it in for a few minutes. Not much said, but big smiles all around. It seemed to go on forever, and I simply drank it in as affirmation of the effort and execution that we put on display that night. Montreal's willingness to show appreciation on that night, for whatever the reason, was breathtaking, and I, for one, will never ever forget it."[10]

MAY 7, 1994
TORONTO, ONTARIO
MAPLE LEAF GARDENS, 60 Carlton Street. Venue opened in 1931.

SUPPORT ACT: I Mother Earth

TICKETS: $20.50 / $33.25 CAD

ATTENDANCE: 13,671; sold out

CONCERT GROSS: $300,227 ($416,982 CAD)

NOTES: The grand finale. Final date of the 1994 *Counterparts* tour. The outing was originally slated to go until the end of June but was scaled back with Geddy and Nancy expecting a child. Their daughter, Kyla, was born the following week. Before the gig, the band held a food drive to benefit local Toronto food banks. During the show opening, one of the rear-screen projectors wasn't working, so that the bolt was seen, but much of the nut was not. As he had done for most of the tour, Geddy added some impressive bass improvisation during the chorus to "Time Stand Still."

GEDDY (ONSTAGE): "Toronto! Hometown of ours. Nice to be back here to play downtown. Always nice to come back home, see faces we know. I think I know you."

ALEX (ONSTAGE): "I'm not a religious man, but please, dear God, let there be hockey here next week. If only they can 'Stick it Out.'"

TORONTO STAR: "Rush puts it out for hometown crowd: Rush draws capacity crowd with slick show."

1. Stewart Gilray. "FACE 2 FACE with Alex Lifeson," *The Spirit of Rush* no. 27, July 1994.
2. Interview with Neil Peart. *San Francisco Chronicle*, February 9, 1994.
3. *The Los Angeles Times.*
4. Bill Banasiewicz. Interview with Mark Deutrom, December 3, 2015.
5. Bill Banasiewicz. Interview with Mark Deutrom, December 3, 2015.
6. Bill Banasiewicz. Interview with Mark Deutrom, December 3, 2015.
7. Interview with Kevin Martin. *Live High Five*, May 11, 2012.
8. Skip Daly. Interview with Jim Rhodes, December 2012.
9. Stewart Gilray. "FACE 2 FACE with Alex Lifeson," *The Spirit of Rush* no. 27, July 1994.
10. Skip Daly. Interview with Robert Scovill, November 29, 2012.

Chapter 24

THE TEST FOR ECHO TOUR

Comprised of two distinct legs, the *Test for Echo* tour drew 660,000 fans over sixty-eight shows. For the first time, the band exclusively employed the "evening with" format: With no opening acts, they could perform an extended set and thus explore some long-neglected areas of their back catalog. The *2112* suite was featured in its entirety for the very first time, including "Oracle: The Dream," which had never been performed live. (Alex: "We were still opening a lot of shows back then [circa 1976 to 1977]; we were playing forty minutes a night, and we couldn't really give twenty minutes of that to one piece.") Furthermore, Neil suggested as a joke that they play all nine minutes and eighteen seconds of "Natural Science"; much to his surprise, Alex and Geddy agreed.

The "evening with" approach, said Neil at the time, was "something we've always stayed away from, because we came up as an opening act, and we hated to close that door. Without having radio or particular media support, as we didn't in the beginning, we were still able to go out and tour as an opening act and build an audience that way. In the short of it, we've always resisted that idea up until this point, based on that, and we finally decided that at this point in the program, we owe ourselves that sort of latitude."

The set list remained fairly consistent throughout the trek, but with some alterations. Only the first two shows included both "Resist" and "Time and Motion"; following the second date in Buffalo, the band alternated the two songs from one night to the next, with Geddy often introducing one or the other with a Scottish reference. Beginning on November 9 in Boston, "Time and Motion" was permanently dropped in favor of "Resist," with the set list then remaining consistent throughout the rest of the first leg. The Surfaris' 1963 drumming hit "Wipe Out" was brought back as the climactic ending of "The Big Money," but for the second leg of the tour, "The Big Money" was removed and replaced with "Limelight" and "Stick It Out." "Subdivisions" was also dropped, with "Red Sector A" moved up in the set to follow "Freewill."

Another aspect of the show that underwent some modification was Geddy's backline, which now featured a large working refrigerator stocked with drinks (a practice that would continue, with adjustments, on all future outings). In his tour book "kwipment list," Geddy's complete list of effects included "Commodore Deluxe Shake Maker Trio, Osterizer Deluxe 2-Speed Blender, Proctor-Silex Deluxe Juicit Oscillating Strainer, Frigidaire Deluxe Refrigerator, Beatrice Deluxe

RIGHT: A driven Rush.
OPPOSITE: Darien Center, NY; Geddy playing his "Driven" bass solo.

332

#2 Manual Meat Grinder, Morphy-Richards Deluxe Automatic Toaster."

"The museum-quality refrigerator and appliances on stage left are just a lighthearted response to Alex filling up stage right with giant amps and every electronic effect known to megalomaniacal guitar players," Neil explained.

Overall, the *Test for Echo* outing proved a massive success, the band reinvigorated by playing the longer sets. Said Alex, "The tour was great; doing an 'evening with' was really a lot of fun for us. The tour went really, really well. We were healthy through the whole thing, and we got to the end of it fine. I think we were really planning on taking a relatively short break and then back in for the next record."

But, he added, "no one could know that what happened would happen."

On August 10, 1997, just over a month after the conclusion of the *Test for Echo* tour, tragedy struck when Neil's daughter, Selena, was killed in a single-car accident outside of Brighton, Ontario. Rush went on indefinite sabbatical, and it looked like the band was over; the drummer told his bandmates to "consider me retired." Less than a year later, on June 20, 1998, Neil's wife Jackie succumbed to cancer and passed away. On August 20, 1998, Peart embarked on his "Ghost Rider" travels, and as Geddy explained it, "Rush was all just very quietly 'put away.'"

It would be almost five years before the band took to the stage again.

OPPOSITE TOP: Darien Center, NY; Geddy and Alex share a look during "Dreamline."

OPPOSITE BOTTOM: Darien Center, NY; Rush playing "Stick It Out."

ABOVE: Albany, NY; Neil during "The Big Money."

TOUR HISTORY
TEST FOR ECHO

SET LIST:
Intro (Also Sprach Zarathustra)
"Dreamline"
"Limelight"
"Stick It Out"
"The Big Money" (with "Wipe Out" ending)
"Driven"
"Half the World"
"Red Barchetta"
"Animate"
"Limbo"

"The Trees"
"Red Sector A"
"Virtuality"
"Nobody's Hero"
"Closer to the Heart"
2112 (complete)
(Intermission)
"Test for Echo"
"Subdivisions"
"Freewill"
"Roll the Bones"

"Resist"
"Leave That Thing Alone"
"The Rhythm Method" (drum solo)
"Natural Science"
"Force Ten"
"Time and Motion"
"The Spirit of Radio"
"Tom Sawyer"
Encore:
"YYZ"
"Cygnus X-1" (teaser)

OCTOBER 19, 1996
ALBANY, NEW YORK
KNICKERBOCKER ARENA, 51 South Pearl Street. Venue opened on January 30, 1990.
AN EVENING WITH RUSH
TICKETS: $24.50 / $35.00
ATTENDANCE: 9,727; sold out
CONCERT GROSS: $297,458
NOTES: The opening date of the 1996 to 1997 *Test for Echo* tour reintroduced the "Evening with Rush" format, something that would become ubiquitous from this point forward. The set list featured the live debut of "Test for Echo," "Driven," "Half the World," "Time and Motion," "Virtuality," "Resist," and "Limbo." It also marked the live debut of the complete "2112" side-long suite. Neil added a nice improvised fill on "Dreamline," just before the vocal "Lonely as an eagle's cry." A triggered sample intoned "Whatever happened to my Transylvania twist?" (from Bobby "Boris" Pickett and the Crypt-Kickers's 1962 hit "Monster Mash") during "Limbo," as on the album version, and it was also heard during the finale of "The Big Money" as it led into "Wipe Out." On "Driven," Alex played a searing guitar after the bass solo. Fans sang along to "Red Barchetta," with Geddy popping bass strings in a counterpoint rhythm at the conclusion. During "Nobody's Hero," Neil missed the fill after the lyric "Solves great mysteries." He added a quarter-note cymbal ride to the chorus of "2112: Overture/The Temples of Syrinx." During "Freewill," Alex lost his place after the first chorus, and "Roll the Bones" featured a lyrical rewrite, with Geddy singing "We draw our own designs. Losers seldom take that blame," instead of "But fortune has to make that frame."

GEDDY (ONSTAGE): "Welcome to the opening of our *Test for Echo* tour. It's the first show, so you're going to be hearing some strange things, probably. See some strange things. But remember, there are no mistakes tonight, just new parts. It's been a while since we've been to America—over two years."

THE TIMES UNION: "Rush is greeted with open arms: In concert, these days, the band has still got the stuff to dazzle an audience—their bedazzling light show is still second to none—but this time around, they toned down the gimmicky end of the show in favor of the music. Rush was coming back from a three-year break (their longest ever), and the time off clearly did them good. They were considerably more animated and looser onstage than they've been in the past, yet they've sacrificed none of their precision."

OCTOBER 20, 1996
BUFFALO, NEW YORK
MARINE MIDLAND ARENA, One Seymour Knox III Plaza. Venue opened on September 21, 1996.
AN EVENING WITH RUSH
TICKETS: $24.50 / $35.00
ATTENDANCE: 8,898
CAPACITY: 9,876
CONCERT GROSS: $259,886
NOTES: Venue aka First Niagara Center. On "Roll the Bones," when Geddy switched to his keyboard mic, it was turned down, so the line "We come into this world" wasn't heard, though he sang it. In "Leave That Thing Alone," Alex was late on the first lead melody, while Neil performed a very strong solo.

BUFFALO NEWS: "Rush in no hurry with memorable three-hour concert: It's the longest show the trio has ever put together. This extended play provided its dedicated legion of Buffalo fans some of the most memorable treats of their concert-going lives. Lifeson, trim and dressed in black, refrained from his usual comic banter, delivering his guitar parts with intensity. Lee's bass lines were blistering and dominant and his vocals were right on target, at times soaring with melodic emotion, and shifting from higher to lower registers with ease. The air drummers in the crowd rested their arms and paid close attention as Peart offered the latest version of his masterful solo 'The Rhythm Method.'"

OCTOBER 22, 1996
FAIRBORN, OHIO
NUTTER CENTER, Wright State University campus, 3640 Colonel Glenn Highway. Venue opened on December 1, 1990.
AN EVENING WITH RUSH
TICKETS: $27.50 / $35.00
ATTENDANCE: 7,835; 7,401 (promoter)
CAPACITY: 9,000
CONCERT GROSS: $237,802
NOTES: Beginning with the *Test for Echo* tour, "2112: Overture" featured the entire band joining in on the infamous eighth note echoes, just like on the studio album. Before that, only Alex's guitar would echo, à la "All the World's a Stage."

OCTOBER 23, 1996
GRAND RAPIDS, MICHIGAN
VAN ANDEL ARENA, 130 West Fulton Street. Venue opened on October 8, 1996.
AN EVENING WITH RUSH

TICKETS: $25.00 / $37.50
ATTENDANCE: 6,537
CAPACITY: 10,000
CONCERT GROSS: $213,138
NOTES: This was the first concert held at the new venue.

OCTOBER 25, 1996
AUBURN HILLS, MICHIGAN
THE PALACE OF AUBURN HILLS, 6 Championship Drive. Venue opened on August 13, 1988.
AN EVENING WITH RUSH
TICKETS: $27.50 / $40.00
ATTENDANCE: 14,673 (*Billboard*: 15,197); sold out
CONCERT GROSS: $467,308
FLINT JOURNAL: "Band: What's the Rush Anymore? The show's first half was a bit more sluggish, but once they got with it, the cobwebs acquired after a two-year layoff were blown away. It's nice to see a band secure enough to play serious music and have fun doing it."

OCTOBER 26, 1996
ROCKFORD, ILLINOIS
ROCKFORD METROCENTRE, 300 Elm Street. Venue opened on January 31, 1981.
AN EVENING WITH RUSH
TICKETS: $27.50
ATTENDANCE: 4,933
CAPACITY: 8,614
CONCERT GROSS: $135,675
NOTES: Following a fan petition, Rush returned to Rockford for the first time in twenty years. This date was originally scheduled for Savage Arena in Toledo, Ohio, with tickets ($25.00 / $29.50) already on sale (as of September 28), but the venue was unable to accommodate Rush's large production, so the concert

was rescheduled to Rockford at the eleventh hour. Onstage, Halloween lights were placed around the refrigerator behind Geddy.
ROCKFORD REGISTER STAR: "Rush sticks with tradition for Rockford concert: Except for a few acoustic introductions, the volume was loud enough to make me wonder how many in this mostly Gen-X/late-Baby Boomer crowd will begin losing their hearing now."

OCTOBER 28, 1996
CHICAGO, ILLINOIS
UNITED CENTER, 1901 West Madison Street. Venue opened on August 18, 1994.
AN EVENING WITH RUSH
TICKETS: $27.50 / $35.00 / $40.00
ATTENDANCE: 13,400
CAPACITY: 16,595
CONCERT GROSS: $466,705
CHICAGO SUN-TIMES: "Rush shows it still can rock after twenty-two years: Monday night at United Center, Rush proved again why it has endured despite the lack of endorsement from snobbish, pretty-boy critics: they simply rock like hell."

OCTOBER 29, 1996
MINNEAPOLIS, MINNESOTA
TARGET CENTER, 600 First Avenue North. Venue opened on October 13, 1990.
AN EVENING WITH RUSH
TICKETS: $25.00 / $35.00; face value minus fees
ATTENDANCE: 7,753
CAPACITY: 11,000
CONCERT GROSS: $256,315

OCTOBER 31, 1996
ST. LOUIS, MISSOURI
KIEL CENTER, 1401 Clark Avenue. Venue opened on October 8, 1994.
AN EVENING WITH RUSH
TICKETS: $25.00 / $35.00
ATTENDANCE: 10,157
CAPACITY: 13,500
CONCERT GROSS: $313,705
NOTES: Halloween, complete with orange lights adorning Geddy's refrigerator.
GEDDY: "These days, getting everybody to agree to tour is a monumental feat."[1]
ST. LOUIS POST-DISPATCH: "Rush Lets Music Roar: On Halloween night, the band pumped out big, virtuosic anthems like there was no tomorrow. And also like it was still yesterday. Instead of coming on like sad, rumbling dinosaurs, the members of

Rush let their music roar. The genre could be dismissed as dated, but what can't be dismissed is that Lee, Lifeson, and Peart are virtuosos. These three guys have their chops down and know how to slam it up to the nosebleed section."

NOVEMBER 1, 1996
MILWAUKEE, WISCONSIN
BRADLEY CENTER, 1001 North Fourth Street. Venue opened on October 1, 1988.
AN EVENING WITH RUSH
TICKETS: $23.50 / $36.50
ATTENDANCE: 9,730
CAPACITY: 12,777
CONCERT GROSS: $298,266
MILWAUKEE JOURNAL SENTINEL: "Performance by 70s band brings a Rush of memories: If you were a believer, you were among those who could be spotted at the basement weekend beer bash, splayed out in a bean bag chair and musing over the band's pseudospiritual lyrics while passing around a bong and gazing at black light posters (of bands such as Rush)."

NOVEMBER 3, 1996
PITTSBURGH, PENNSYLVANIA
CIVIC ARENA, 300 Auditorium Place. Venue opened on September 17, 1961.
AN EVENING WITH RUSH
TICKETS: $27.50 / $35.00
ATTENDANCE: 9,255
CAPACITY: 12,000
CONCERT GROSS: $284,692
GEDDY (ONSTAGE): "It was right here, on August 14, 1974, that we played our first American date. The only difference between then and now is that tonight we're going to play a lot longer."
PITTSBURGH POST-GAZETTE: "Fans Here Get the Same Rush That They Got Twenty-two Years Ago: Rush's music—a complex mix of rhythms that sometimes take their time interlocking into a foot-stomping melody—has always been arena-friendly in part because seeing Lee, Peart, and Lifeson at work makes you appreciate the music's intricacy all the more. Lee, in particular, was dazzling all night on bass. Peart again proved himself a master of the drum cage. He launched into an eight-minute solo that produced many pretenders in the crowd—and many cheers of appreciation."

NOVEMBER 4, 1996
CLEVELAND, OHIO
GUND ARENA, 1 Center Court. Venue opened on October 17, 1994.

AN EVENING WITH RUSH

TICKETS: $25.00 / $40.00

ATTENDANCE: 10,743

CAPACITY: 12,000

CONCERT GROSS: $339,855

NOTES: The film intro to "Half the World" was added, along with a collection of trailers for old biker movies, which were projected on the video screen during intermission.

GEDDY (ONSTAGE): "I think I've seen all you guys before somewhere."

THE PLAIN DEALER (CLEVELAND): "Canadian Trio Proves It Was Built to Last: While fans pumped their fists in the air or played air guitar along with Lifeson's bristling lick, Lee sang what could have been the concert's epitaph: 'All this machinery making modern music can still be open-hearted.' Rush proved as much, putting on a state-of-the-art show, but playing with a lot of heart, too."

NOVEMBER 6, 1996
PHILADELPHIA, PENNSYLVANIA
CORESTATES CENTER, 3601 S. Broad Street. Venue opened on August 12, 1996.

AN EVENING WITH RUSH

TICKETS: $24.50 / $35.00

ATTENDANCE: 14,759

CAPACITY: 15,147

CONCERT GROSS: $444,804

NOTES: The $35.00 tickets sold out. During the guitar break in "Red Sector A," Neil added a flurry of improvised fills, as he would do throughout the tour. In "Subdivisions," there was feedback during the opening verse, with Geddy's Minimoog lead really low in the mix until the end, while the lyric "Subdivisions" wasn't heard on the second chorus. On "Roll the Bones," Alex augmented the rap section with some funk guitar. In "The Spirit of Radio," a trigger was inadvertently hit prior to the break before the guitar solo, which added a distinct swirling keyboard sound.

GEDDY (ONSTAGE): "Philly, you are animated as always. We appreciate it!"

THE PHILADELPHIA INQUIRER: "Arena rock's Rush shows staying power: In the 70s, Rush defined metal. In the 80s, its classic rock effectively absorbed new wave and post-punk. In the 90s, Lee, Peart, and Lifeson are a better grunge band than their younger counterparts. At the sold-out CoreStates Center, Rush displayed equal parts musicianship and showmanship for three hours."

NOVEMBER 7, 1996
LARGO, MARYLAND
USAIR ARENA, 1 Harry S. Truman Drive. Venue opened on December 2, 1973.

AN EVENING WITH RUSH

TICKETS: $25.00 / $38.50

ATTENDANCE: 11,077

CAPACITY: 13,000

CONCERT GROSS: $326,366

NOTES: Final performance of "Time and Motion." In that song, Geddy sang "The silent forest echoes" but omitted the line "with the loon" two times. His mic was also turned down during the last verse. Geddy began introducing songs in a Scottish accent. During "Subdivisions," the vocal "Subdivisons" was late on the first and second choruses.

GEDDY (ONSTAGE): "Contrary to popular belief, this is not a song about dance. This is a song about our state of mind. This is called 'Limbo.'"

NOVEMBER 9, 1996
BOSTON, MASSACHUSETTS
FLEETCENTER, 100 Legends Way. Venue opened on September 30, 1995.

AN EVENING WITH RUSH

TICKETS: $25.00 / $35.00

ATTENDANCE: 14,003

CAPACITY: 19,580

CONCERT GROSS: $403,255 (estimate)

NOTES: The band performed to an exceptionally enthusiastic crowd. Neil's new book, *The Masked Rider*, was now available at the gigs.

THE BOSTON GLOBE: "Rush bridges the decades with ease: The emphasis remains on the trio's precise musicianship, which married hard-rock flourishes with tricky, fusion-like shifts."

NOVEMBER 10, 1996
HARTFORD, CONNECTICUT
CIVIC CENTER, 1 Civic Center Plaza. Venue opened on January 9, 1975.

AN EVENING WITH RUSH

TICKETS: $26.00 / $36.00

ATTENDANCE: 9,642

CAPACITY: 10,500

CONCERT GROSS: $276,260

HARTFORD COURANT: "Rush spectacular though predictable: Although Rush draws a relatively sedate crowd, the band has a distinct effect on its audience. The band's instrumental wizardry compels many fans to become professional air-musicians. The less outgoing fans wore an expression of

mesmerization probably due to Rush's elaborate visual production."

NOVEMBER 20, 1996
SAN JOSE, CALIFORNIA
SAN JOSE ARENA, 525 West Santa Clara Street. Venue opened on September 7, 1993.

AN EVENING WITH RUSH

TICKETS: $25.00 / $35.00

ATTENDANCE: 10,581

CAPACITY: 12,500

CONCERT GROSS: $340,720

CONTRA COSTA TIMES: "Rush Mired in Performing Rut: The crowd at San Jose Arena may have preferred to sit for most of the show, but when the air drumming started during Neil Peart's signature 'Rhythm Method' solo, it was like a high school reunion."

NOVEMBER 21, 1996
SACRAMENTO, CALIFORNIA
ARCO ARENA, One Sports Parkway. Venue opened on November 8, 1988.

AN EVENING WITH RUSH

TICKETS: $25.00 / $35.00

ATTENDANCE: 6,984

CAPACITY: 12,550

CONCERT GROSS: $235,455

NOVEMBER 23, 1996
SAN DIEGO, CALIFORNIA
SAN DIEGO SPORTS ARENA, 3500 Sports Arena Boulevard. Venue opened on November 17, 1966.

AN EVENING WITH RUSH

TICKETS: $22.50 / $30.00

ATTENDANCE: 8,532

CAPACITY: 11,084

CONCERT GROSS: $211,215

NOTES: Geddy popped his bass strings on the verses to "The Big Money" along with his vocals. During "Half the World," Neil did an engrossing double bass drum roll into the break. On "2112," the opening sounds of "Overture" reappear prior to "Oracle: The Dream."

DAVE BURNETTE (NEIL'S BUS DRIVER): "There was an incident in San Diego during *Test for Echo.* About ten minutes before the end of the show, I was in front of the bus talking with about five or six police officers. I had the door open on the bus, and this five-foot-tall, probably 90-pound, forty-year-old blonde goes walking right between all of us and steps right up on the bus. We're all standing there with our jaws open, and then I went in after her. She wasn't a fan—just somebody who happened to be drunk and walking through. She had gotten to about the galley, headed toward the back room, when I just walked up behind her and got her into a bear hug. I picked her up and carried her to the front of the bus. We got to the steps, and there was a female police sergeant who reached in and got her by the hair, pulled her out the door, and threw her on the ground and then handcuffed her. I was standing there with my jaw open, like, 'I just wanted her off the bus—you don't have to kill her [*laughs*]!'"[2]

NOVEMBER 24, 1996
LAS VEGAS, NEVADA
THOMAS AND MACK CENTER, UNLV campus, 4505 South Maryland Parkway. Venue opened on September 16, 1983.
AN EVENING WITH RUSH
TICKETS: $23.50 / $29.50; face value minus fees
ATTENDANCE: 7,373
CAPACITY: 9,000
CONCERT GROSS: $199,618
NOTES: Geddy was a little under the weather, so "Resist" was cut from the set.

NOVEMBER 26–27, 1996
INGLEWOOD, CALIFORNIA
GREAT WESTERN FORUM, 3900 West Manchester Boulevard. Venue opened on December 30, 1967.
AN EVENING WITH RUSH
TICKETS: $25.00 / $40.00
TWO-DAY INGLEWOOD ATTENDANCE: 19,319
TWO-DAY CAPACITY: 25,000
(*Billboard*)
TWO-DAY INGLEWOOD CONCERT GROSS: $596,855
NOTES: The band performed selections from *Test for Echo* during the first date's sound check.
LOS ANGELES TIMES: "Fans Get a Power Rush: Rush's energetic, three-hour concert was an old-fashioned rock show, strictly for adoring fans. There was no stage-diving, no crowd-surfing—just an elated, near-capacity crowd flicking its Bics and cheering on its heroes. The

veteran Canadian power trio provided everything a Rush aficionado could want: hits, favorites and songs from *Test for Echo*."
NEIL: "Brutus and I rode our motorcycles west over the San Gabriels on our way to the Los Angeles Forum for a pair of concerts. I came around a corner behind Brutus to experience the novel sight of my friend sliding down the road on his back at 50 miles per hour. Beside him, his fallen motorcycle was spinning slowly on its side, trailing sparks, the bright headlight rotating toward me and then away. The bike came to rest on one side of the road, Brutus on the other. He seemed to be all right, though well shaken up, and we picked up his bike, which also seemed to be all right, scraped but undamaged, and carried on. Later, backstage at the Forum, Brutus was limping around and telling people how he'd 'sacrificed' himself to save me, all for the sake of the show—addressing a crew member with a slowly wagging finger, 'To save YOUR job, my friend!' Brutus' foot was sore for the next couple of days."[3]

NOVEMBER 29, 1996
PHOENIX, ARIZONA
AMERICA WEST ARENA, 201 East Jefferson. Venue opened on June 6, 1992.
AN EVENING WITH RUSH
TICKETS: $25.00 / $35.00
ATTENDANCE: 10,858
CAPACITY: 12,000
CONCERT GROSS: $320,540
NOTES: Venue aka US Airways Center. On the chorus of "Animate," Neil and Geddy injected some syncopated drum and bass pauses.
GEDDY (ONSTAGE): "This is a song that's not about dancing, although you can dance to it. It's not about dancing with a big stick, although you can have a big stick if you wish. And it's not a song about a radio talk show host. This is a song called 'Limbo.'"

NOVEMBER 30, 1996
EL PASO, TEXAS
UTEP SPECIAL EVENTS CENTER, University of Texas at El Paso campus, 500 West University Avenue. Venue opened in early January 1977.
AN EVENING WITH RUSH
TICKETS: $25.00 / $32.50

ATTENDANCE: 5,295
CAPACITY: 8,000
CONCERT GROSS: $155,835
NOTES: Venue aka Don Haskins Center.

DECEMBER 2, 1996
SAN ANTONIO, TEXAS
THE ALAMODOME, 100 Montana Street. Venue opened on May 15, 1993.
AN EVENING WITH RUSH
TICKETS: $23.50 / $37.50
ATTENDANCE: 10,104
CAPACITY: 15,000
CONCERT GROSS: $302,548 (estimate)
SAN ANTONIO EXPRESS-NEWS: "Rush delivers precisely what fans want: Lee's high, nasal vocal still cuts distinctively through the three-piece bombast. The singer roamed the stage freely with his Fender Jazz bass, often joking with Lifeson, who lorded over a barrage of guitar pedals. Peart's drums sounded like cannon fire. The numerous high-pitched tom-toms were mercilessly whacked in inimitable trademark fashion by the gifted drummer, so fond of odd time signatures."

DECEMBER 3, 1996
DALLAS, TEXAS
REUNION ARENA, 777 Sports Street. Venue dedicated on April 28, 1980.
AN EVENING WITH RUSH
TICKETS: $25.00 / $35.00
ATTENDANCE: 12,500[4]
CAPACITY: 15,450
NEIL: "The show had gone well, and the audience clapped, sang, whistled, and roared their appreciation. They were a happy bunch, and it was a nice feeling to look out and see people enjoying themselves like that—especially when I was sweating and straining so hard for them. A guy in the middle, back a few rows, was holding up a cellular phone, its keypad lit up green when the arena was dark between songs. The green light jerked up and down as he talked into the phone. Then as we started another song, he held it out toward the stage again, perhaps for a friend who couldn't make it to the show, listening in from work, or from his bedroom. I could feel I was playing well that night, but it was never easy; I could never relax and take it for granted or let down my professional intensity. And, as always, I was aiming higher. In the end, it was a solid nine-out-of-ten show, but I wanted eleven. Journal note: 'Tried hard to make it great, but just wouldn't happen!'"[5]

DECEMBER 5, 1996
HOUSTON, TEXAS
THE SUMMIT, 3700 Southwest Freeway. Venue opened on November 1, 1975.
AN EVENING WITH RUSH
TICKETS: $26.25 / $30.25 / $38.25
ATTENDANCE: 10,413
CAPACITY: 17,050
CONCERT GROSS: $318,349 (estimate)
NOTES: During "The Trees," Geddy was a tad late on the vocals out of the break.
GEDDY (ONSTAGE): "How about an instrumental? This gives me a break. I like that. This is a weird song from our new weird album. This is called 'Limbo.'"

DECEMBER 6, 1996
NEW ORLEANS, LOUISIANA
UNO LAKEFRONT ARENA, University of New Orleans East campus, 6801 Franklin Street. Venue opened on November 1, 1983.
AN EVENING WITH RUSH
TICKETS: $27.50 / $35.00
ATTENDANCE: 7,019; sold out
CONCERT GROSS: $216,070
THE TIMES-PICAYUNE:
"Marathon Concert a Real Rush: This was one of the most energized sets that I've experienced, deftly showcasing the trademark mix of brains and brawn that Rush acolytes revel in."

DECEMBER 8, 1996
WEST PALM BEACH, FLORIDA
CORAL SKY AMPHITHEATRE, South Florida Fairgrounds, 601–607

Sansburys Way. Venue opened on April 26, 1996.
AN EVENING WITH RUSH
TICKETS: $15.75 / $35.75
ATTENDANCE: 13,297
CAPACITY: 18,840
CONCERT GROSS: $266,803
NOTES: Venue aka Mars Music Amphitheatre. This night's food drive benefited needy families in Palm Beach County.
THE PALM BEACH POST: "Rush Covers 20-Year Career in 3-Hour Show: The band's playing was tight, and Geddy Lee's voice was strong throughout, even during some of the older, more vocally demanding songs. Neil Peart's drumming was accurate and stunning as always. Rush always brings something special to a concert. Sunday was no exception; they proved again that rock can be musical, mature, and exciting."

DECEMBER 9, 1996
TAMPA, FLORIDA
ICE PALACE, 401 Channelside Drive. Venue opened on October 12, 1996.
AN EVENING WITH RUSH
TICKETS: $25.75 / $35.75
ATTENDANCE: 7,961
CAPACITY: 9,500
CONCERT GROSS: $237,190
NOTES: Venue aka St. Pete Times Forum.

DECEMBER 11, 1996
ATLANTA, GEORGIA
THE OMNI, 100 Techwood Drive Northwest. Venue opened on October 14, 1972.
AN EVENING WITH RUSH
TICKETS: $25.00 / $35.00
ATTENDANCE: 10,143
CAPACITY: 11,000
CONCERT GROSS: $301,475
NEIL: "Of the many oil changes I had performed in backstage loading areas and parking lots, I always remembered one at the Omni arena in Atlanta, during the *Test for Echo* tour. Lying on the floor under the bike, I was installing a new filter and the drain plug, when a formidable black woman in an Omni uniform loomed up beside and above me. I looked up and said, 'Hello.' She pointed to another security guard across the backstage area and said, 'He says you are the best drummer in the world.' I laughed, 'Well, I don't know about that—maybe the best drummer, um, under this motorcycle right now!' 'Hmm,' she

said. Then she put her hands on her ample hips and shook her head: 'You the only rich man I ever saw change his own oil!'"[6]

DECEMBER 12, 1996
CHARLOTTE, NORTH CAROLINA
CHARLOTTE COLISEUM, 100 Paul Buck Boulevard. Venue opened on August 11, 1988.
AN EVENING WITH RUSH
TICKETS: $19.50 / $35.00
ATTENDANCE: 7,258
CAPACITY: 10,000
CONCERT GROSS: $194,163 (estimate)

DECEMBER 14, 1996
UNIONDALE, NEW YORK
NASSAU COUNTY VETERANS MEMORIAL COLISEUM, 1255 Hempstead Turnpike. Venue dedicated on May 29, 1972.
AN EVENING WITH RUSH
TICKETS: $19.50 / $24.50 / $40.00
ATTENDANCE: 12,222
CAPACITY: 12,500
CONCERT GROSS: $371,712
THE ISLAND EAR: "The moment the house lights dimmed and the band took the stage, there was no doubt that this was going to be an evening to remember. From Lee's growling basslines and vocal acrobatics and Lifeson's fanciful fretwork, to Peart's solid, explosive drumming, the trio was in top condition. Physically, they were extremely energetic on stage, playing each song with the vim and vigor of a band half their age."

DECEMBER 15, 1996
EAST RUTHERFORD, NEW JERSEY
CONTINENTAL AIRLINES ARENA, Meadowlands Sports Complex, 50 State Route 120. Venue opened on July 2, 1981.
AN EVENING WITH RUSH
TICKETS: $19.50 / $24.50 / $40.00
ATTENDANCE: 15,621; sold out
CONCERT GROSS: $453,538
NOTES: Venue aka Meadowlands Arena.
THE NEW YORK TIMES: "Rush settles in as 1980s specialty act: The presentation was so hard and shiny that it was nearly impossible to discern whether the players were having a good or bad night."

DECEMBER 18, 1996
TORONTO, ONTARIO
PHOENIX CONCERT THEATRE, 410 Sherbourne Street. Venue opened in 1991.

AN EVENING WITH RUSH
ATTENDANCE: 900; sold out
NOTES: Special "Blind Date" performance, sponsored by Molson Golden. Contest-winner attendees did not know what band they are going to see, though hardcore fans caught wind of the gig in advance. This was the smallest venue Rush had performed in since circa 1975. The show featured an abridged version of the full tour set list, performed as a single set.
SET LIST: "Dreamline," "The Big Money" (with "Wipe Out" ending), "Driven," "Half the World," "Red Barchetta," "Animate," "Virtuality," "Nobody's Hero," "Closer to the Heart," "Test for Echo," "Subdivisions," "Freewill," "Roll the Bones," "Resist," "Leave That Thing Alone," "The Spirit of Radio," "Tom Sawyer." Encore: "YYZ"
GEDDY (ONSTAGE): "Hello, Canadians! It's nice to be in such intimate surroundings for a change. I can see each and every one of you."
ROBERT SCOVILL: "It was certainly a weird thing for them to do. It was a big Molson promotion. It felt like trying to put ten pounds of stuff into a Dixie cup; we were trying to cram as much as we could in there . . . Luckily, Rush hadn't been a band that had a huge amount of gear onstage. The guitar rig and bass rig both had pretty small footprints . . . the drum kit was always really the big thing. But it's a three-piece, so stage size isn't a huge issue . . . And the front-of-house gear—I probably had the biggest footprint of anybody in the band, with all the effects racks and everything. For the lighting, Howard just supplemented what was there. You're not going to go into a space like that and start hanging trusses or anything like that. But for the band, it must have been a pretty wild, weird gig. From my point of view, though, it was purely the technical challenge of taking this big monstrosity into such a tight space. We could barely get it into an arena!"[7]

MAY 7, 1997
SAN DIEGO, CALIFORNIA
HOSPITALITY POINT, San Diego Symphony Embarcadero, Mission Bay Park, 2510 Qulvira Way. Summer Pops concert series began in 1985.
AN EVENING WITH RUSH
TICKETS: $25.00 / $36.00 / $50.00
ATTENDANCE: 5,119; sold out
CONCERT GROSS: $190,810

NOTES: This date was originally slated for May 8. Russ Ryan's first show as Geddy's bass tech. Howard dubbed the concert "the Wedding Gig" because of the folding chairs and intimate setting.

MAY 8, 1997
PHOENIX, ARIZONA
DESERT SKY PAVILION, 2121 North 83rd Avenue. Venue opened on November 11, 1990.
AN EVENING WITH RUSH
TICKETS: $20.00 (lawn) / $28.00 (upper reserved) / $38.00 (lower reserved) / $45.50 (gold circle)
ATTENDANCE: 9,856
CAPACITY: 20,144
CONCERT GROSS: $267,785
NOTES: Venue aka Cricket Pavilion. Alex experienced some technical issues during "Limelight." For the evening's finale, Howard lit up the desert sky with a dazzling laser display.

MAY 10, 1997
DEVORE, CALIFORNIA
GLEN HELEN BLOCKBUSTER PAVILION, 2575 Glen Helen Parkway. Venue opened on July 9, 1993.
AN EVENING WITH RUSH
TICKETS: $20.50 (lawn) / $28.00 (pavilion) / $43.00 (orchestra)
ATTENDANCE: 18,040; sold out
CONCERT GROSS: $379,270 (estimate)
NOTES: KLOS-FM offered special $9.50 lawn seats. During the band's stay in Southern California, they were presented the Outstanding Contribution to Music Award by the Foundations Forum in a ceremony at the Burbank Hilton.

MAY 11, 1997
MOUNTAIN VIEW, CALIFORNIA
SHORELINE AMPHITHEATRE, One Amphitheatre Parkway. Venue opened on July 5, 1986.
AN EVENING WITH RUSH
TICKETS: $19.50 (lawn) / $35.00 (reserved)
ATTENDANCE: 10,099
CAPACITY: 20,000
CONCERT GROSS: $294,449

MAY 14, 1997
PORTLAND, OREGON
ROSE GARDEN, 1 Center Court. Venue opened on October 13, 1995.
AN EVENING WITH RUSH
TICKETS: $27.50 / $32.50

ATTENDANCE: 8,243
CAPACITY: 10,412
CONCERT GROSS: $232,778 (estimate)
NOTES: In "2112: Overture," a keyboard was inadvertently triggered, and the first echoes were of a high-pitched, tinny quality. The band played right through the end of "Overture" without the usual pauses, where fans yell, "Rush!" At the beginning of "Oracle: The Dream," a trigger was inadvertently employed, causing a loud keyboard noise. Alex's guitar went out at the end of the "Permanent Waves" section of "Natural Science," leaving the vocal passage "Tide after tide will flow and recede, leaving life to go on as it was" with just bass and drums. The guitar problems were rectified just in time for the final two chords.
GEDDY (ONSTAGE): "Welcome to Part Two: The Torture Continues!"

MAY 15, 1997
COQUITLAM, BRITISH COLUMBIA
WESTWOOD PLATEAU GOLF AND COUNTRY CLUB. ON A DAY OFF, ALEX AND SOME FRIENDS TAKE TO THE LINKS.
JIM RHODES (FORMER-CREW MEMBER): "My funniest memory of Alex was a golf outing in Coquitlam. I hired a driver to get Lerxst and Larry Allen there and back. Coming down the eighteenth fairway, there's this guy leaning out over the upper patio railing of the clubhouse bar, trying to get Lerxst's attention. It was Bruce Thrasher, the course superintendent, and an ex-schoolmate of Lerxst. We ended up in the bar afterwards, sampling numerous quality beverages with Thrasher, talking old days, etc, and after quite a few samplings, Lerxst and Thrasher challenged Larry and I to more golf at $3,000 per hole. Larry was about a six handicap, and the drinks had been flowing enough to put a bit more fade on the ball for Lerxst and Thrasher, so our odds were promising. On the first tee, Bruce takes a divot the size of Iowa out of the tee box, missing the ball entirely . . . We all laughed, and, with a smile, he proceeds to attempt to get it out onto the fairway, which didn't happen. It got messy. Anyway, three holes later (and numerous lost balls by all of us), we realized that not one of us had kept score, and all bets were sadly off, so we packed it in. Al turned to me and said, 'Oh no, I have to be Tojo's Sushi in Vancouver at

7:30 p.m.' It was already close to 8:00 p.m., so Lerxst slipped Chris the driver $100 and said, 'Get me there as quick as you can.' Our man Chris got us downtown in less than 20 minutes at about 80 miles per hour. Chris had a bandana in the van, which Lerxst took an interest in right away. So, with bandana on head, golf cleats still on, and golf bag in hand, Lerxst jumps out of the van, walks briskly toward the double glass doors at Tojo's, and, mis-judging the two doors completely, elects to try and enter the restaurant through the double-paned glass windows on the right side of the doors—which fortunately didn't budge—and oops, down go the clubs, and Lerxst hits the sidewalk on his ass. The bandana stayed on. Lerxst was quick to his feet, and with a smile he waved a nice ol' 'good night' before head-ing into the restaurant, where he and guests proceeded to chip balls until well after closing—until very, very late into the morning! I still think we took the three holes, so God love ya, Lerxst: where's that $9,000 you owe Larry and I?"[8]

MAY 16, 1997
VANCOUVER, BRITISH COLUMBIA
GENERAL MOTORS PLACE, 800 Griffiths Way. Venue opened on September 17, 1995.
AN EVENING WITH RUSH
TICKETS: $29.50 / $40.00 CAD; face value minus $4.00 finance charge
ATTENDANCE: 5,497
CAPACITY: 13,340
CONCERT GROSS: $154,162 ($214,114 CAD)
NOTES: In "Virtuality," Alex had a prob-lem with his electric guitar during the first chorus. On "Roll the Bones," Alex said "Roll them bones, gently" during the first chorus. In "Force Ten," Ged lit-erally yelled the lyric "And the lights!"
GEORGIA STRAIGHT (VANCOUVER): "The band's technical prowess was prom-inently displayed here, and a camera set directly above Peart's massive drum kit offered an eye-opening angle on his intri-cate art-rock percussion style. During one particularly busy segment of '2112,' the Buddy Rich of rock actually knocked one of his larger cymbals clear off its stand."

MAY 17, 1997
GEORGE, WASHINGTON
THE GORGE AMPHITHEATRE, 754 Silica Road Northwest. Venue opened

for major concerts on August 20, 1988.
AN EVENING WITH RUSH
TICKETS: $29.95 (lawn) / $34.15 (reserved) / $44.65 (orchestra)
ATTENDANCE: 19,968
CAPACITY: 20,000
CONCERT GROSS: $519,100
GEDDY (ONSTAGE): "Good evening, Washington State! Gorgeous George out there. It's a great pleasure for us to be here in such a beautiful spot to play for you guys as the sun sets behind us."
SEATTLE POST-INTELLIGENCER: "Geddy-up and Rush over to the Gorge: In the coming year, Rush will likely, surpass the 30 million mark in [US] album sales."

MAY 19, 1997
BOISE, IDAHO
BSU PAVILION, Boise State University campus, 1401 Bronco Lane. Venue opened on May 16, 1982.
AN EVENING WITH RUSH
TICKETS: $24.00
ATTENDANCE: 5,535
CAPACITY: 8,500
CONCERT GROSS: $121,206 (estimate)
NOTES: The first part of "Limbo" was performed with uncertainty.
IDAHO STATESMAN: "The chance to check out the one-man percussion orchestra that is Neil Peart alone is worth the $24 ticket."

MAY 20, 1997
SALT LAKE CITY, UTAH
DELTA CENTER, 301 W. South Temple. Venue opened on October 4, 1991.
AN EVENING WITH RUSH
TICKETS: $25.00 / $35.00; face value minus $3.50 finance charge or $4.50 phone charge
ATTENDANCE: 10,837
CAPACITY: 11,512
CONCERT GROSS: $330,750 (estimate)
NOTES: Geddy has some technical issues with his keyboards during "Roll the Bones."
THE DESERET NEWS: "Band holds audi-ence in its palm and gives it a Rush: Instead of a band whose members try to outdo each other, Rush worked collec-tively to bring out a terrific live show."

MAY 22, 1997
ENGLEWOOD, COLORADO
FIDDLER'S GREEN AMPHITHEATRE, 6350 Greenwood Plaza Blvd. Venue opened on June 11, 1988.

AN EVENING WITH RUSH
TICKETS: $18.50 (lawn) / $25.00 (reserved) / $27.50 (orchestra)
ATTENDANCE: 11,156
CAPACITY: 17,416
CONCERT GROSS: $257,616

MAY 24, 1997
DALLAS, TEXAS
COCA-COLA STARPLEX
AMPHITHEATRE, Fair Park, 1818 First Avenue. Venue opened on July 23, 1988.
AN EVENING WITH RUSH
TICKETS: $15.00 (lawn) / $32.50 (reserved)
ATTENDANCE: 9,414
CAPACITY: 20,111
CONCERT GROSS: $234,936
NOTES: Recorded to multitrack, with "The Trees" being culled for the *Different Stages* live set. Venue aka Smirnoff Music Centre.
DALLAS MORNING NEWS: "Rush has momentum to spare—Band builds on technique, tunes, and turns of phrase: For a band supposedly trapped in the hoary 70s, Rush sounded surprisingly fresh at Starplex. Guitarist Lifeson opted for short, brooding outbursts instead of long solos. His riffing in new songs such as 'Driven' and 'Virtuality' was closer to death-metal than prog-rock."

MAY 25, 1997
THE WOODLANDS, TEXAS
C. W. MITCHELL PAVILION, 2005 Lake Robbins Drive. Venue opened on April 27, 1990.
AN EVENING WITH RUSH
TICKETS: $26.00 (lawn) / $35.00 (reserved) / $45.00 (orchestra)
ATTENDANCE: 13,024; sold out
CONCERT GROSS: $382,245
NOTES: Venue aka the Woodlands Pavilion.
RAY: "They still do sound checks for every show. They play forty-five minutes together every day and then do a three-hour show at night. Not many guys would do that after all this time—well, the Grateful Dead did it, but they were on drugs—they didn't know."[9]

JUNE 4, 1997
CINCINNATI, OHIO
RIVERBEND MUSIC CENTER, 6295 Kellogg Avenue. Venue opened on July 4, 1984.
AN EVENING WITH RUSH

Chapter 25

THE VAPOR TRAILS TOUR

In May 2002, Rush commenced rehearsals for their first tour in almost five years, starting in Ontario before moving to Glens Falls, New York, in June. "The first week of rehearsal we sounded like a very bad Rush cover band, and then after that we slid into it and got our sea legs back," Alex said. "But there was definitely that period of having to get back on the horse."

When they finally returned to the road for the *Vapor Trails* tour, it was with a vengeance, performing to more than 720,000 fans over sixty-six shows. The opening night in Hartford, Connecticut, was an emotional event for the band members and their audience, with fans traveling from around the globe to welcome Alex, Geddy, and especially Neil back to the stage.

"There have been many amazing things that happened to this band, but probably the one outstanding moment was after Neil's double tragedy," Alex said. "The first show on the *Vapor Trails* tour was in Hartford. Ged and I walked over to the drum kit and leaned in, past Neil's hardware, looked at Neil and we smiled at each other and we all shared this moment when we couldn't believe that we were here again after that long, dark journey. It connected us in such a powerful way. We were all teary at that point. That was a pretty momentous moment. I can still picture it to this day."

Neil said, "It was so emotional for the three of us, because they had been so strong for me and so supportive through my troubles. We hadn't played in front of an audience for so long. I said to Ray, our manager, at the end of that show, that it would have been a shame if

this had never happened again. Because of course a few years previously I was convinced that it was never going to happen again."

On the tour, Rush broke from the tradition of keeping set lists rigidly consistent. Instead, they performed two primary set lists which, with few exceptions, were alternated each night: A first set included "Between Sun and Moon" (performed live for the first time), "Vital Signs," and "Ceiling Unlimited"; a second replaced these songs with "The Trees," "Freewill," and

OPPOSITE: Scranton, PA; Alex rocking out playing "Tom Sawyer."

LEFT: Tour ad: "First tour in 5 years . . ."

"Ghost Rider." "We try to make both sets quite different, and we try to ease into the show and have it develop," Geddy told the *Chicago Sun-Times*. "At the present moment, it's really working well. We are able to visit the past with the same enthusiasm that we're playing the new material."

Additionally, "Closer to the Heart" and "Force Ten" were dropped from the live show for the first time since their inceptions, although the former was brought back for the final US date, as well as for performances in Mexico and Brazil. Said Neil, "We had a surprise just before we went to Mexico City. Apparently our most popular song there was 'Closer to the Heart,' and we weren't playing it [on the] tour. The three of us talked about it, decided we didn't want to disappoint the audience by not playing our most popular song for them, and agreed we could relearn it pretty quickly."

The South America outing was Rush's first trip to the continent, and the Sao Paulo, Brazil, concert set a record for the largest attendance in the band's history as a headlining act: sixty thousand people. Additionally, the last date in Rio de Janeiro was filmed for the *Rush in Rio* concert DVD, which topped the charts upon its release. In all, the *Vapor Trails* tour proved an incredible welcoming back for the band. The trek clocked in at number twenty-one on a list of the highest-grossing tours of 2002, netting Rush $13.4 million. Additionally, it reaffirmed the band's commitment to the stage and to their fans.

"When you've been away for a while, a lot of things change and you don't know what your level of enthusiasm will be and what the crowd enthusiasm will be," Geddy said in an interview with the *Star Tribune*: "On both those fronts, it's been excellent. When you've gone on a long break—and a difficult break—I think you come in with a real appreciation for the opportunity to play."

OPPOSITE TOP: Mansfield, MA; Neil drumming "Distant Early Warning."

OPPOSITE BOTTOM: Scranton, PA; Neil and his kit during "Distant Early Warning."

TOP: Scranton, PA; Geddy playing "New World Man."

ABOVE: New York, NY; RIAA sales award presentation; From left to right: Val Azzoli (Atlantic Records), Ray Danniels, Alex, Neil, Geddy, Steve Marks (RIAA), and John Henkel (RIAA).

PAGE 350, TOP: Manchester, NH; Rush performing "Natural Science."

PAGE 350, BOTTOM: Saratoga Springs; NY; Rush onstage during "One Little Victory."

TOUR HISTORY
VAPOR TRAILS

SET LIST:
"Tom Sawyer" (with Three Stooges intro)
"Distant Early Warning"
"New World Man"
"Roll the Bones"
"Earthshine"
"YYZ"
"The Pass"
"Bravado"
"The Big Money"
"Between Sun & Moon" / "The Trees"

"Vital Signs / Freewill"
"Closer to the Heart"
"Natural Science"
(Intermission)
"One Little Victory" (with dragon intro)
"Driven"
"Ceiling Unlimited" / "Ghost Rider"
"Secret Touch"
"Dreamline"
"Red Sector A"
"Leave That Thing Alone"

"The Rhythm Method" (drum solo)
"Resist" (Geddy and Alex acoustic)
"2112: Overture" / "The Temples of Syrinx"
"Limelight"
"La Villa Strangiato" (with Lerxst rant)
"The Spirit of Radio"
Encore:
"By-Tor and the Snow Dog" (abridged)
"Cygnus X-1: Prologue"
"Working Man"

JUNE 28, 2002
HARTFORD, CONNECTICUT
MEADOWS MUSIC CENTRE, 61 Savitt Way. Venue opened on July 10, 1995.
AN EVENING WITH RUSH
TICKETS: $30.00 (lawn) / $45.00 (upper reserved) / $65.00 (lower reserved) / $85.00 (orchestra)
ATTENDANCE: 9,985
CAPACITY: 24,140
CONCERT GROSS: $446,275
NOTES: The opening date of the *Vapor Trails* tour featured the live debut of "One Little Victory," "Ceiling Unlimited," "Secret Touch," "Earthshine" and "Between Sun and Moon." Rush's first show in almost five years is an emotional comeback for both the band and its fans, with a spirited audience singing loudly throughout. John Entwistle, the Who's bassist extraordinaire passed away the day before, so Geddy dedicated "Between Sun and Moon" to him by stating "We'd like to do this for a fallen brother, comrade John Entwistle. He will rock on!" Prior to the intermission (after "Natural Science"), Alex walked off in front of the stage, where he gave his pick to a security guard and has him give it to a girl in a wheelchair in the front row. Andrew MacNaughtan shot some footage that was later made available on Rush.com. After their performance, the band shared a group hug and Neil stuck around to celebrate with Geddy and Alex.
NEIL: "It was so emotional for the three of us, because they had been so strong for me and so supportive through my troubles. We hadn't played in front of an audience for so long. I said to Ray at the end of that show that it would have been

a shame if this had never happened again. Because of course a few years previously I was convinced that it was never going to happen again. And in that show we just looked at each other and it was just so very powerful and emotional."[1]
GEDDY (ONSTAGE): "Thank you, just checking my drying. We appreciate it. It's been a long time since we've done a concert, and you guys made us very welcome tonight and that means a lot to us."
HARTFORD COURANT: "Rush Returns with Few Changes: The band seemed relaxed and almost giddy at times. While past Rush shows have had all the spontaneity of open-heart surgery, Lifeson stretched out on guitar and Lee demonstrated his bass chops a few times with mini solos, including one on 'Driven.'"

JUNE 29, 2002
SCRANTON, PENNSYLVANIA
MONTAGE MOUNTAIN PERFORMING ARTS CENTER, 1000 Montage Mountain Road. Venue opened on June 24, 2000.
AN EVENING WITH RUSH
TICKETS: $32.50 (lawn) / $47.50 (pavilion) / $67.50 (orchestra)
ATTENDANCE: 9,307
CAPACITY: 17,714
CONCERT GROSS: $421,893
NOTES: "Ghost Rider" made its stage debut. The afternoon tailgate took place in a pseudo-police state, with officers stationed in each aisle of the parking lot on horseback, bicycle, and on foot, rooting through vehicles and arresting fans by the dozens for various minor infractions, most notably open containers and underage drinking.

THE TIMES LEADER: "Rush's long-running act hits all the right notes: Rush showed 12,000 fans at Montage Mountain what much of the rock world has known for decades: The Canadian progressive hard-rock trio is simply one of the premier acts to ever grace a concert stage."

JULY 1, 2002
CHARLOTTE (HARRIS-HOUSTON), NORTH CAROLINA
VERIZON WIRELESS AMPHITHEATRE, 707 Pavilion Boulevard. Venue opened on July 4, 1991.
AN EVENING WITH RUSH
TICKETS: $24.50 (lawn) / $47.00 (pavilion) / $72.00 (orchestra)
ATTENDANCE: 8,335
CAPACITY: 18,776
CONCERT GROSS: $302,007
NOTES: Venue aka Blockbuster Pavilion. Alex did a phone interview with the *Boston Herald*, while Geddy conversed with the *Buffalo News*.

JULY 3, 2002
VIRGINIA BEACH, VIRGINIA
VERIZON WIRELESS VIRGINIA BEACH AMPHITHEATER, 3550 Cellar Door Way. Venue opened on May 15, 1996.
AN EVENING WITH RUSH
TICKETS: $16.00 (lawn) / $32.50 (pavilion) / $47.25 (orchestra)
ATTENDANCE: 8,226
CAPACITY: 20,000
CONCERT GROSS: $239,305
NOTES: For the tour, while Neil traveled by bus and BMW motorcycle, Alex and Geddy had a series of regional base hotels, central to the dates on the

itinerary. After the show, they took a short flight to their stable hotel location, which was in Charlotte for the opening dates.

JULY 4, 2002
RALEIGH, NORTH CAROLINA
ALLTEL PAVILION AT WALNUT CREEK, near the I-40/US 64/I-440 (Beltline) interchange. Venue opened in 1991.
AN EVENING WITH RUSH
TICKETS: $24.50 (lawn) / $47.50 (pavilion) / $72.00 (orchestra); face value minus $3.00 finance charge and parking
ATTENDANCE: 8,297
CAPACITY: 20,000
CONCERT GROSS: $246,023
NOTES: The band wished everyone a happy Fourth of July via the rear-screen. Venue aka Walnut Creek Amphitheatre.

JULY 6, 2002
SARATOGA SPRINGS, NEW YORK
SARATOGA PERFORMING ARTS CENTER, 108 Avenue of Pines. Venue opened on July 9, 1966.
AN EVENING WITH RUSH
TICKETS: $30.00 (lawn) / $45.00 (upper pavilion) / $65.00 (lower pavilion) / $85.00 (orchestra); prices increased $2.00 day of show
ATTENDANCE: 8,884
CAPACITY: 25,120
CONCERT GROSS: $424,169
NOTES: At the end of Neil's "The Rhythm Method" solo Geddy said, "That guy is pretty good. I think we'll keep him."
GEDDY (ONSTAGE): "We've been away from this life for a few years, and we appreciate the warm welcome back."
THE SUNDAY GAZETTE: "Rush entertains with old, new hits: The loud crowd, delighted to be seeing Rush again, erupted into cheers when Lee, Lifeson, and Peart nonchalantly stepped onstage and kicked into 'Tom Sawyer' to open the show."

JULY 7, 2002
DARIEN CENTER, NEW YORK
SIX FLAGS DARIEN LAKE PERFORMING ARTS CENTER, Fun Country Amusement Park, 9993 Allegheny Road. Venue opened on June 15, 1993.
AN EVENING WITH RUSH
TICKETS: $35.00 (lawn) / $60.00 (reserved)
ATTENDANCE: 9,300
CAPACITY: 12,500
CONCERT GROSS: $461,150
NOTES: The band's base hotel was now in Manhattan, where Geddy enjoyed some time in Central Park with Nancy and Kyla.
NOW MAGAZINE, GEDDY: "Today in sound check we started jamming, and it felt good and fresh. There are two directions we can go in. We'll have this tour and we might decide we don't have the fortitude to carry on and we'll go our separate ways, or we'll continue this rebirth that we're experiencing. Today it felt a lot like that would be the likely road we'd go down."
BUFFALO NEWS: "The amazing show that Rush gave to Buffalo was proof enough that its music has withstood the test of time."

JULY 9, 2002
BRISTOW, VIRGINIA
NISSAN PAVILION, 7800 Cellar Door Drive. Venue opened on June 3, 1995.
AN EVENING WITH RUSH
TICKETS: $26.00 / $75.00
ATTENDANCE: 12,141
CAPACITY: 22,556
CONCERT GROSS: $541,958
WASHINGTON POST: "Rush at Nissan Pavilion, Still Living in the Limelight: Air drummers of all ages and sizes packed Nissan Pavilion to welcome the roadworthy trio. Not surprisingly, most of the new material unveiled blended seamlessly with the old."

JULY 11, 2002
HOLMDEL, NEW JERSEY
PNC BANK ARTS CENTER, Exit 116, Garden State Parkway. Venue opened on June 15, 1968.
AN EVENING WITH RUSH
TICKETS: $27.75 (lawn) / $72.75 (orchestra)
ATTENDANCE: 12,477
CAPACITY: 16,462

CONCERT GROSS: $564,820
NOTES: Sound check featured half versions of "Distant Early Warning," "New World Man," "Red Sector A," and "Tom Sawyer" with no solos, as well as lots of improvisation from Neil.
THE COURIER-NEWS: "Rush drove the near-capacity crowd into a frenzy."

JULY 12, 2002
MANSFIELD, MASSACHUSETTS
TWEETER CENTER FOR THE PERFORMING ARTS, 885 South Main Street. Venue opened on June 13, 1986.
AN EVENING WITH RUSH
TICKETS: $30.00 (lawn) / $45.00 (pavilion) / $65.00 (orchestra)
ATTENDANCE: 15,222
CAPACITY: 19,800
CONCERT GROSS: $723,355
NOTES: Venue aka Great Woods Center for the Performing Arts. Sully Erna and members of Godsmack enjoyed the show from the lighting board.
BOSTON HERALD: "Rush revels in its return: Hitting town for the first time in five years, the band simply picked up where it left off. That meant another epic show that ran three hours. It meant lots of tricky instrumentals and metaphorical film clips. For those who love this band's odd mix of heavy metal, art-rock, and the occasional pop hook, it was as technically dazzling and musically inventive as ever."

JULY 14, 2002
CAMDEN, NEW JERSEY
TWEETER CENTER, 1 Harbour Boulevard. Venue opened on June 2, 1995.
AN EVENING WITH RUSH
TICKETS: $29.50 (lawn) / $75.00 (orchestra)
ATTENDANCE: 12,916
CAPACITY: 16,880
CONCERT GROSS: $589,409
NOTES: Venue aka E-Centre. At the end of "2112 Overture," Alex sang in a funny, high-pitched voice.
GEDDY (ONSTAGE): "By the way, happy Bastille Day!"

JULY 15, 2002
WANTAGH, NEW YORK
JONES BEACH THEATER, Jones Beach State Park, 1000 Ocean Parkway. Venue dedicated on June 26, 1952.

AN EVENING WITH RUSH
TICKETS: $30.00 / $75.00
ATTENDANCE: 14,113
CAPACITY: 14,229
CONCERT GROSS: $747,604
NOTES: Venue aka Jones Beach Amphitheater. Alex experienced some technical problems during "Tom Sawyer" and "Ghost Rider."
MTV NEWS: "Rush Descend Into Hades, Get Laundry Done At New York Show: Imbued with a renewed sense of purpose after surviving more than their share of turmoil in recent years, Rush looked especially alive as they performed in front of a projection screen that switched between shots from the concert and computer-generated imagery."

JULY 17, 2002
TORONTO, ONTARIO
THE MOLSON AMPHITHEATRE, Ontario Place, 909 Lake Shore Boulevard West. Venue opened on May 18, 1995.
AN EVENING WITH RUSH
TICKETS: $35.00 / $85.00 CAD
ATTENDANCE: 14,210; sold out
CONCERT GROSS: $532,212 ($813,220 CAD)
NOTES: Venue aka the Molson Canadian Amphitheatre.
TORONTO SUN: "A Rush back: Rush definitely possess a dry sense of humor. What else could explain the appearance of three dryers on stage with them—respectively containing red, white, and black clothes—that would be fed coins by a roadie whenever one finished its cycle? A Spinal Tap moment if there ever was one."

JULY 19, 2002
MILWAUKEE, WISCONSIN
MARCUS AMPHITHEATER, Henry Maier Festival Park, Summerfest grounds, 200 North Harbor Drive. Venue opened on June 25, 1987.
AN EVENING WITH RUSH
TICKETS: $30.00 (lawn) / $45.00 (reserved) / $65.00 (orchestra)
ATTENDANCE: 11,042
CAPACITY: 17,314
CONCERT GROSS: $426,611
MILWAUKEE JOURNAL SENTINEL: "Rush has changed with the times, but fans are as fervent as ever: Rarely have I seen a crowd so enthralled."

JULY 20, 2002
TINLEY PARK, ILLINOIS
TWEETER CENTER, 19100 S Ridgeland. Venue opened on June 2, 1990.
AN EVENING WITH RUSH
TICKETS: $30.00 (lawn) / $40.00 (upper pavilion) / $52.00 (lower pavilion) / $75.00 (orchestra); price included $3.00 parking fee
ATTENDANCE: 13,951
CAPACITY: 29,519
CONCERT GROSS: $677,914
CHICAGO SUN-TIMES: "Powered by Peart, Rush hasn't slowed a bit: The group proved that it is still a vibrant and vital force, a band that is 'driven' to continue to break new ground. Long may they revel in the limelight."

AUGUST 1, 2002
BONNER SPRINGS, KANSAS
SANDSTONE AMPHITHEATRE, 633 North 130th Street. Venue opened on June 5, 1984.
AN EVENING WITH RUSH
TICKETS: $30.00 (lawn) / $47.50 (reserved) / $60.00 (orchestra)
ATTENDANCE: 8,436
CAPACITY: 18,000
CONCERT GROSS: $383,958
NOTES: Venue aka Verizon Wireless Amphitheatre.
ALEX: "Geddy and I were sitting in the dressing room after the show in Kansas City. We like to have a little meal and share a glass of wine for twenty minutes before it gets all crazy in the dressing room, it's just nice and quiet. And we were talking about how we have these moments of intense clarity on stage where you look at the audience going 'What the hell is going on here; 16,000 people freaking out because I'm playing guitar or I'm singing a song?' We're still freaked out by it after all these years. But a Rush audience can do that to you. I don't think there's any other rock band whose fans are anywhere close to being what our fans are like."[2]

AUGUST 2, 2002
MARYLAND HEIGHTS, MISSOURI
UMB BANK PAVILION, 14141 Riverport Drive. Venue opened on June 14, 1991.
AN EVENING WITH RUSH
TICKETS: $30.00 (lawn) / $50.00 (reserved) / $65.00 (orchestra)
ATTENDANCE: 11,158

CAPACITY: 20,993
CONCERT GROSS: $471,025
NOTES: Venue aka Riverport Amphitheatre. Alex does a phone interview with the *Pittsburgh Post-Gazette*. During the middle of "La Villa Strangiato" Lerxst sings "Happy Birthday" to KSHE-FM.
GEDDY (ONSTAGE): "Nice to be here on this hot, sultry evening to celebrate KSHE's thirty-fifth Birthday with you guys."

AUGUST 4, 2002
CINCINNATI, OHIO
RIVERBEND MUSIC CENTER, 6295 Kellogg Avenue. Venue opened on July 4, 1984.
AN EVENING WITH RUSH
TICKETS: $29.50 / $50.00 / $65.00
ATTENDANCE: 7,034
CAPACITY: 20,500
CONCERT GROSS: $309,467
CINCINNATI ENQUIRER: "Rush gives fans same rush: Their return, especially the return of Lee's cartoonish whine, is welcome in an era when the rock-rap hybrid has overtaken good old hard rock."

AUGUST 6, 2002
BURGETTSTOWN, PENNSYLVANIA
POST-GAZETTE PAVILION, 665 SR 18. Venue opened on June 17, 1990.
AN EVENING WITH RUSH
TICKETS: $25.00 / $65.00
ATTENDANCE: 10,414
CAPACITY: 23,144
CONCERT GROSS: $354,596
NOTES: Venue aka Star Lake Amphitheater.
PITTSBURGH POST-GAZETTE: "Rush worth five-year wait: After five years off the road, they still put on a show that's best enjoyed by people who subscribe to *Modern Drummer* and at least two other magazines they sell at music stores. But few bands give those people more of what they're after."

AUGUST 8, 2002
COLUMBUS, OHIO
POLARIS AMPHITHEATER, 2200 Polaris Parkway. Venue opened on June 18, 1994.
AN EVENING WITH RUSH
TICKETS: $29.50 (lawn) / $50.00 (upper pavilion) / $65.00 (lower pavilion)

ATTENDANCE: 9,072
CAPACITY: 20,000
CONCERT GROSS: $390,274
NOTES: Venue aka Germain Amphitheater. WLVQ-FM's Twenty-fifth Anniversary Concert.
COLUMBUS DISPATCH: "Group rocks with expansive set: The group switched among obscure album tracks (with help from fan polling on rushpetition.com), new tunes and some old favorites. What sometimes has sounded sterile on disc rocked furiously in concert."

AUGUST 9, 2002
NOBLESVILLE, INDIANA
VERIZON WIRELESS MUSIC CENTER, 12880 East 146th Street. Venue opened on May 20, 1989.
AN EVENING WITH RUSH
TICKETS: $30.00 (lawn) / $50.00 (upper pavilion) / $65.00 (lower pavilion)
ATTENDANCE: 8,642; 7,553 (promoter)
CAPACITY: 24,188
CONCERT GROSS: $356,410; $310,441 (promoter)
NOTES: Venue aka Deer Creek Music Center.
INDIANAPOLIS STAR: "Rush rocks crowd with unfailing unity: As human proof of a triangle's strength, the members of Rush thrilled an audience of 8,200 Friday night."

AUGUST 11–12, 2002
CLARKSTON, MICHIGAN
DTE ENERGY MUSIC THEATRE, 7774 Sashabaw Road. Venue opened on June 25, 1972.
AN EVENING WITH RUSH
TICKETS: $29.50 (lawn) / $59.50 (pavilion); face value minus $3.00 finance charge
TWO-DAY CLARKSTON ATTENDANCE: 18,505
TWO-DAY CAPACITY: 30,404
TWO-DAY CLARKSTON CONCERT GROSS: $823,692
NOTES: Venue aka Pine Knob Music Theatre.
THE OAKLAND PRESS (PONTIAC, MI): "Rush satisfies fans in first show since '96: It was the sound, more than the sights, that dazzled the fans and showed that Rush hadn't lost a step during its time apart."

AUGUST 14, 2002
ANTIOCH, TENNESSEE
AMSOUTH AMPHITHEATRE, 3839 Murfreesboro Pike. Venue opened on June 21, 1986.
AN EVENING WITH RUSH
TICKETS: $25.00 / $45.00
ATTENDANCE: 11,890
CAPACITY: 17,241
CONCERT GROSS: $242,970
NOTES: Venue aka Starwood Amphitheatre.

AUGUST 16, 2002
THE WOODLANDS, TEXAS
C. W. MITCHELL PAVILION, 2005 Lake Robbins Drive. Venue opened on April 27, 1990.
AN EVENING WITH RUSH
TICKETS: $39.50 / $79.50
ATTENDANCE: 11,598
CAPACITY: 15,802
CONCERT GROSS: $561,999
THE HOUSTON CHRONICLE: "Rush returns with a treat for the fans: Rush's attention to live arrangements is what propels it above most choreography and video-driven shows today. Lifeson's guitar shots on 'YYZ' sound as vital today as they did in the 80s while Lee quietly added modern touches with funky bass flicks. One of the best shows of the summer."

AUGUST 17, 2002
SELMA, TEXAS
VERIZON WIRELESS AMPHITHEATER, 16765 Lookout Road. Venue opened on May 19, 2001.
AN EVENING WITH RUSH
TICKETS: $22.50 / $72.50
ATTENDANCE: 14,267
CAPACITY: 20,000
CONCERT GROSS: $554,983
SAN ANTONIO EXPRESS-NEWS: "Magical Rush keeps its spell alive: Here were three rock heroes playing nose down and focused on bringing out the core melodic juices of their music, amazing onlookers with their passionate focus."

AUGUST 19, 2002
DALLAS, TEXAS
SMIRNOFF MUSIC CENTRE, Fair Park, 1818 First Avenue. Venue opened on July 23, 1988.
AN EVENING WITH RUSH
TICKETS: $35.50 / $75.00
ATTENDANCE: 9,686
CAPACITY: 12,000
CONCERT GROSS: $455,497
NOTES: Venue aka Coca-Cola Starplex Amphitheatre.
FORT WORTH STAR-TELEGRAM: "Rush's solid performance rewards devoted fans: Bolstered by excellent, crisp sound, the band sounded sure from the beginning."

AUGUST 21, 2002
ALBUQUERQUE, NEW MEXICO
ABQ JOURNAL PAVILION, 5601 University Blvd SE. Venue opened on June 11, 2000.
AN EVENING WITH RUSH
TICKETS: $28.50 / $46.50 / $66.50 (with $3.75 fee)
ATTENDANCE: 12,157
CAPACITY: 16,453
CONCERT GROSS: $281,275
NOTES: "Red Sector A" and "Tom Sawyer" were performed at sound check. Geddy did an Egyptian dance during the guitar solo to "Secret Touch."
ALBUQUERQUE JOURNAL: "Rush Don't Rest on Laurels: The crowd went berserk, the music whipping the fans into a frenzy. Lee and Lifeson, beaming, looked like two kids in a candy store, obviously enjoying themselves immensely and working the crowd like the seasoned professionals they are."

AUGUST 22, 2002
NEIL WAS INTERVIEWED BY CYCLE WORLD'S EXECUTIVE EDITOR, BRIAN CATTERSON, WHO IS ALSO A LIFE-LONG RUSH FAN. CATTERSON JOINED NEIL AND MICHAEL EARLY IN THE MORNING AND THE TRIO RODE TOGETHER TO MOAB, UTAH.
BRIAN CATTERSON (CYCLE WORLD): "We'd rendezvoused at a truck stop off I-40 in Gallup. By this point, I'd been in touch with Peart's publisher, publicist, and security manager, but I'd not actually spoken to the man himself. And as I approached the tour bus door, there was only one Rush lyric on my mind. It was from 'Limelight,' about the harsh reality of fame: 'Living in a fisheye lens / Caught in the camera eye / I have no heart to lie / I can't pretend a stranger is a long-awaited friend.' And so it was with apprehension that I knocked. An anxious few moments

passed, and then Neil himself threw open the door and greeted me with a warm handshake and a smile . . . Not surprisingly, the TV in the bus was tuned to the Weather Channel. Looking at the forecast, I noted that it read 'Ceiling Unlimited'—title to one of the songs on *Vapor Trails*. 'Yes, that's where that came from,' Neil said, smiling. 'You're the first person to make that connection.' . . . We had dinner at a restaurant that Neil had discovered during a previous visit, predictably talking about music and motorcycles . . . And maybe it was the wine, but as we talked about past albums and concerts I could feel myself regressing—the inquisitive journalist replaced by the teenage Rush fan I used to be. A teenage Rush fan sitting across the dinner table from Neil friggin' Peart . . . "[3]

AUGUST 23, 2002
SALT LAKE CITY, UTAH
DELTA CENTER, 301 West South Temple. Venue opened on October 4, 1991.
AN EVENING WITH RUSH
TICKETS: $29.00 / $45.00 / $57.00
ATTENDANCE: 7,406
CAPACITY: 10,979
CONCERT GROSS: $325,627
BRIAN CATTERSON (*CYCLE WORLD*): "In Price, bus-driver Dave joined us on Neil's old R1100GS and led us on the final leg of our journey into Salt Lake City. We arrived at the Delta Center early that afternoon, and Neil and Michael got straight to work—changing their oil! 'Ah, the life of a rock star,' I remarked as I watched. 'If ever there were a term that I despise, that's it,' Neil shot back. He prefers the unadorned title, 'musician.'
SALT LAKE TRIBUNE: "After 30 Years on the Road, Rush Still Thrills SLC Fans: New songs from Vapor Trails were greeted almost as enthusiastically as the older songs."

AUGUST 24, 2002
ENGLEWOOD, COLORADO
FIDDLER'S GREEN AMPHITHEATRE, 6350 Greenwood Plaza Boulevard. Venue opened on June 11, 1988.
AN EVENING WITH RUSH
TICKETS: $27.00 / $75.00 / $86.50 (with $4.00 parking and $4.00 facility fees)
ATTENDANCE: 8,747

CAPACITY: 16,823
CONCERT GROSS: $450,039
THE DAILY CAMERA (BOULDER): "Rush hasn't lost its touch—Canadian rockers return from five-year break as good as ever: Canada's elder statesmen of transcendent prog and occasionally synth-heavy power trio rock 'n' roll, has emerged from its recent half-decade respite from touring and its members are as tight and strong as ever."

SEPTEMBER 8, 2002
VANCOUVER, BRITISH COLUMBIA
GENERAL MOTORS PLACE, 800 Griffiths Way. Venue opened on September 17, 1995.
AN EVENING WITH RUSH
TICKETS: $39.00 / $59.00 / $79.00 CAD
ATTENDANCE: 6,145
CAPACITY: 7,498
CONCERT GROSS: $192,330 ($298,918 CAD)
NOTES: Neil breaks his snare drum head during the end of "Roll the Bones."
ALEX (ONSTAGE): "Man it smells funny in BC. I like the way it smells in BC. Got a good smell. Maybe the best smell. I'm from BC. I was born in Fernie, way over on the other side, where there's no water. But there are mountains and trees and rocks."
JIMMY JOE RHODES (EX-CREW MEMBER): "Years after I had been on the crew, I'd retired from touring to stay home in Vancouver and spend time with my family. When Rush came to town I brought my wife Renee and daughter Ashley to see the show. We went in to say hi to the guys, which was great because I hadn't seen them in some time, with a bit of a reluctant wife and daughter in tow. My daughter Ashley was nine, and didn't really know bands other than 'N Sync. She wasn't exactly up on the Rush catalogue, let alone who the guys were. Alex, being the great guy he is, looked down at Ashley, chatted her up, gave her some picks and a few of Neil's sticks, and after making her feel really at home, sent her on her way, like 'Cindy Lou Who,' with a pat on the head and a glass of water! The band went on for the show and jumped into 'Tom Sawyer,' and with all the people in the audience to look at, Alex looks over and sees Ashley stage right with me, cruises over to the edge of

the stage in front of Ashley, and rocks out a verse of 'Tom Sawyer' five feet from her . . . and at that moment I swear she forgot about 'N Sync from that day on!"[4]

SEPTEMBER 10, 2002
EDMONTON, ALBERTA
SKYREACH CENTRE, 7424 118th Avenue NW. Venue opened on November 10, 1974.
AN EVENING WITH RUSH
TICKETS: $39.00 / $59.00 / $79.00 CAD
ATTENDANCE: 7,629
CAPACITY: 8,788
CONCERT GROSS: $178,098 ($276,799 CAD)
NOTES: Venue aka Northlands Coliseum. This was the first show at this venue where tickets were not ripped upon entry. Instead the ticket's bar code was scanned by handheld "access managers."[5]
THE EDMONTON SUN: "Oh, what a Rush!: Canadian icons rock. Thanks to a video and a bright-green laser show that was both anachronistic and beautiful, even the hardest of hearing had something to talk about while spilling out of Skyreach along with 8,000 others."

SEPTEMBER 12, 2002
CALGARY, ALBERTA
PENGROWTH SADDLEDOME, 555 Saddledome Rise SE. Venue opened on October 15, 1983.
AN EVENING WITH RUSH
TICKETS: $39.00 / $59.00 / $79.00 CAD
ATTENDANCE: 7,989
CAPACITY: 10,677
CONCERT GROSS: $212,123 ($329,680 CAD)
NOTES: Neil's fiftieth Birthday. Venue aka Olympic Saddledome. While in Calgary, the band took part in the Great Bordeaux-Napa Wine Challenge tasting and auction. The charity event raises money for the White Ribbon Campaign (which fights violence against women) and the Calgary Firefighters Burn Treatment Society.[6]
THE CALGARY SUN: "What a rush!: Too cerebral and arty and progressive to be metal; too metal to be mainstream—there is no other band that does what Rush does. It was a long, memorable and classic arena rock show."

SEPTEMBER 14, 2002
GEORGE, WASHINGTON
THE GORGE AMPHITHEATRE, 754
Silica Road Northwest. Venue opened
for major concerts on August 20, 1988.
AN EVENING WITH RUSH
TICKETS: $48.30 / $74.55
ATTENDANCE: 12,556
CAPACITY: 13,500
CONCERT GROSS: $767,026
THE SEATTLE TIMES, GEDDY: "[The
Gorge] has gotta be one of the best ven-
ues in the world. I loved it there. Beautiful
place. I'm really, really proud of the tour
we're bringing around."
**JOHN ARROWSMITH (PYRO TECHNI-
CIAN):** "Neil would always have his
motorcycle trailer with him. One afternoon at the Gorge in Washington State,
Chris Blair and I had parked our scooters
in the trailer where Neil and Michael
would park their bikes, and we were anxiously waiting for them to arrive at the
gig. Like two school children we hid
behind one of the touring trucks when we
saw them arrive and peeked around from
the truck tires to see Neil pull up and
start laughing. We couldn't see his face
but his helmet was bobbing up and
down. He parked his bike, got his camera
and took a photo of it."[7]

SEPTEMBER 15, 2002
PORTLAND, OREGON
ROSE GARDEN, 1 North Center Court.
Venue opened on October 13, 1995.
AN EVENING WITH RUSH
TICKETS: $25.50 / $69.50
ATTENDANCE: 6,014
CAPACITY: 12,951
CONCERT GROSS: $286,974
NOTES: Venue aka Moda Center.

SEPTEMBER 17, 2002
CONCORD, CALIFORNIA
CHRONICLE PAVILION, 2000 Kirker
Pass Road. Venue opened on May 16,
1975.
AN EVENING WITH RUSH
TICKETS: $27.50 / $75.50
ATTENDANCE: 7,391
CAPACITY: 12,503

CONCERT GROSS: $398,769
CONTRA COSTA TIMES: "Rush plays
powerful but lengthy show at Concord:
Rush never sells anyone short in terms of
lights and effects, indulging their collective technical interests into creating a
vivid ambience matching the sonic mood
onstage."

SEPTEMBER 18, 2002
WHEATLAND, CALIFORNIA
AUTOWEST AMPHITHEATRE, 2677
Forty Mile Road. Venue opened on June
10, 2000.
AN EVENING WITH RUSH
TICKETS: $29.50 (lawn) / $45.50
(pavilion) / $75.50 (orchestra)
ATTENDANCE: 6,367
CAPACITY: 18,500
CONCERT GROSS: $303,088
NOTES: Afternoon thunderstorms pro-
duced power outages in the area, which
delayed the show some twenty minutes.
CHICO ENTERPRISE-RECORD: "Classic
rock trio delivers the goods at AutoWest
Amphitheatre: The players looked like
they weren't teenagers anymore, but they
played with the vitality of young men."

SEPTEMBER 20, 2002
MOUNTAIN VIEW, CALIFORNIA
SHORELINE AMPHITHEATRE, One
Amphitheatre Parkway. Venue opened
on July 5, 1986.
AN EVENING WITH RUSH
TICKETS: $32.50 / $55.50 / $75.50
ATTENDANCE: 10,437
CAPACITY: 22,000
CONCERT GROSS: $562,946

SEPTEMBER 21, 2002
LAS VEGAS, NEVADA
MGM GRAND GARDEN ARENA, 3799
Las Vegas Boulevard South. Venue
opened on December 31, 1993.
AN EVENING WITH RUSH
TICKETS: $35.00 / $82.50; face value
minus $4.00 finance charge
ATTENDANCE: 8,264
CAPACITY: 12,595
CONCERT GROSS: $524,526
NOTES: Fans the world over ventured to
Sin City. During "Dreamline," Geddy
emphasized the word "Vegas" in the line
"She's got a sister out in Vegas," which
received added applause from the crowd.
Alex played with energy and enthusiasm
despite nursing a head cold.

DAVE BURNETTE (NEIL'S BUS DRIVER):
"We were heading from Shoreline to Las
Vegas when I pulled over in the Mojave
Desert and went to sleep for the night.
Neil and Michael took off the next morning, and I was in my bunk asleep when
Neil came back on the bus and woke me
up. He said 'Dave, I need you to come
and pick up Michael, he's had a problem
with his bike.' So I got up and followed
Neil, and we found Michael sitting on the
side of the road. There was an oil line
that came up through the forks of the
bike, and because of the way we tied it
down, the oil line had weakened from the
tie-down straps. When he took off down
the road, the oil line broke and started
shooting oil right into his helmet. When I
got there, he looked like something from
The Blob. Of course I was laughing at
him, and he gave me the 'you know
where you can go' look. When I think
back I have to laugh about it because he
did look pitiful standing there, dripping
motor oil from his bike. Because Michael
was so covered with oil, his gear was covered, and he had to have that cleaned, so
he stripped off, got on the bus, and rode
the bus that day while Neil went off by
himself."[8]
THE LAS VEGAS SUN: "On Saturday
night, Las Vegas was Rush, Nevada:
Back from the longest hiatus in its thirty-
four-year career, Rush showed no signs
of rust in its Las Vegas return, playing to
a venue packed near capacity."

SEPTEMBER 23, 2002
LOS ANGELES, CALIFORNIA
STAPLES CENTER, 1111 South Figueroa
Street. Venue opened on October 17,
1999.
AN EVENING WITH RUSH
TICKETS: $45.00 / $65.00 / $95.00
ATTENDANCE: 11,637
CAPACITY: 13,769
CONCERT GROSS: $770,545
LOS ANGELES TIMES: "Always Reliable
Rush Unseals the Time Capsule: An out-
sider might have chafed at the redundancy
and sheer silliness of it all, but Rush is a
band that exists for initiates."
DAVE BURNETTE (NEIL'S BUS DRIVER):
"We were at the Staples Center and I had
noticed this guy out in the first or second
row: a great big tall guy with long red hair
and a straw cowboy hat on, that looked as
goofy as can be. After the show, I'm

standing outside the band dressing room, and here comes this guy . . . and I didn't have a clue who he was until he opened his mouth: it was Nicolas Cage. He just goes walking into the band dressing room like it was his dressing room. He didn't want to be bothered at the show, which is perfectly understandable, so he was in disguise."[9]

SEPTEMBER 25, 2002
CHULA VISTA, CALIFORNIA
COORS AMPHITHEATRE, 2050 Entertainment Circle. Venue opened on July 21, 1998.
AN EVENING WITH RUSH
TICKETS: $35.00 / $40.00 / $75.00
ATTENDANCE: 6,970
CAPACITY: 18,842
CONCERT GROSS: $427,115

SEPTEMBER 27, 2002
PHOENIX, ARIZONA
CRICKET PAVILION, 2121 North 83rd Avenue. Venue opened on November 11, 1990.
AN EVENING WITH RUSH
TICKETS: $30.00 / $65.00
ATTENDANCE: 9,265
CAPACITY: 19,337
CONCERT GROSS: $391,116
NOTES: Venue aka Desert Sky Pavilion. The soundboard recording of "Between Sun and Moon" on the *Rush in Rio* live CD release is sourced from this show.
ARIZONA REPUBLIC: "Rush's joy evident to fans: As usual, Rush brought along an enormous stage show, including dozens of lights, lasers and an enormous video screen, which alternated showing close-ups of the band, psychedelic computer graphics and silly cartoons. Only Pink Floyd can top Rush's presentation. But unlike the wooden band members of Floyd, Rush band members are animated and exciting onstage."

SEPTEMBER 28, 2002
IRVINE, CALIFORNIA
VERIZON WIRELESS AMPHITHEATER, 8808 Irvine Center Drive. Venue opened on August 21, 1981.
AN EVENING WITH RUSH
TICKETS: $31.75 / $91.75
ATTENDANCE: 12,911
CAPACITY: 16,192
CONCERT GROSS: $733,352
NOTES: Venue aka Irvine Meadows Amphitheater.

OCTOBER 5, 2002
MEXICO CITY, MEXICO
FORO SOL, Av. Viaducto Río Piedad y Río Churubusco s/n. Venue opened on November 10, 1993.
AN EVENING WITH RUSH
TICKETS: $150.00 / $1,300.00 (pesos)
ATTENDANCE: 20,116
CAPACITY: 24,848
CONCERT GROSS: $834,327 (7,827,443 pesos)
NOTES: Rush's Latin American debut. Following "Freewill," Geddy announced "a special gift for the fans of Mexico," as the band broke into "Closer to the Heart" for the first time this tour.
NEIL: "We had a surprise just before we went to Mexico City. Apparently our most popular song there was 'Closer to the Heart,' and we weren't playing it that tour (the periodic rest some older songs require). The three of us talked about it, decided we didn't want to disappoint the audience by not playing our most popular song for them, and agreed we could relearn it pretty quickly. After playing it through a few times during our sound checks leading up to Mexico City, we added it to the show for that one night."[10]
GEDDY (ONSTAGE): "Hola, buenas noches, no hablo español! [Hello, good evening, I can't speak Spanish!]"

OCTOBER 10, 2002
TAMPA, FLORIDA
ST. PETE TIMES FORUM, 401 Channelside Drive. Venue opened on October 12, 1996.
AN EVENING WITH RUSH
TICKETS: $35.00 / $65.00
ATTENDANCE: 7,784
CAPACITY: 13,616
CONCERT GROSS: $406,975
NOTES: Venue aka the Ice Palace.
ST. PETERSBURG TIMES: "Overcoming tragedy, Rush returns to form: fans relish—and critics often malign—Rush's sprawling compositions, quirky time signatures and those oh-so-lengthy solos. Thursday night found both Peart and Lifeson indulging in several of them."

OCTOBER 11, 2002
WEST PALM BEACH, FLORIDA
CORAL SKY AMPHITHEATRE, South Florida Fairgrounds, 601–607 Sansburys Way. Venue opened on April 26, 1996.

AN EVENING WITH RUSH
TICKETS: $29.50 / $65.00
ATTENDANCE: 10,649
CAPACITY: 19,271
CONCERT GROSS: $436,813
NOTES: Venue aka Sound Advice Amphitheatre.
THE PALM BEACH POST: "Rush stronger than ever after hiatus: Rush came out of a five-year hiatus with an enthusiastic dose of pile-driving rock. They played for three hours, and their adoring audience never once sat down."

OCTOBER 13, 2002
ATLANTA, GEORGIA
PHILLIPS ARENA, 1 Philips Drive Northwest. Venue opened on September 24, 1999.
AN EVENING WITH RUSH
TICKETS: $35.50 / $69.50
ATTENDANCE: 8,580
CAPACITY: 10,185
CONCERT GROSS: $406,792

OCTOBER 15, 2002
BALTIMORE, MARYLAND
BALTIMORE ARENA, 201 West Baltimore Street. Venue opened on October 23, 1962.
AN EVENING WITH RUSH
TICKETS: $32.50 / $62.50
ATTENDANCE: 5,714
CONCERT GROSS: $296,170
GEDDY (ONSTAGE): "HELLO! Good evening, Baltimore. Home of the Orioles . . . [The crowd booed]. You don't like them anymore?"

OCTOBER 16, 2002
ROCHESTER, NEW YORK
BLUE CROSS ARENA AT THE WAR MEMORIAL, 100 Exchange Boulevard. Venue opened on October 18, 1955.
AN EVENING WITH RUSH
TICKETS: $36.50 / $47.50 / $59.50
ATTENDANCE: 4,444
CAPACITY: 9,795
CONCERT GROSS: $196,410
NOTES: The *Democrat and Chronicle* lists attendance as 5,500. Venue aka Rochester Community War Memorial. The concert industry in 2002 was a struggling business, and Rush, although doing better than most acts, was no exception. When the band passed through the same markets they had played just a few months before

management asked if they'd like to cancel some of the lesser-performing dates on the second leg. But the band decided to play them anyway, performing every show with the energy and conviction of an SRO gig.

DEMOCRAT AND CHRONICLE: "70s relic Rush still crashing into future: Alex Lifeson, perhaps the most overlooked of the arena-rock guitar gods, could play with any band that needs a guy who knows how to really tear at the strings."

OCTOBER 18, 2002
MONTREAL, QUEBEC
CENTRE BELL, 1909 Avenue des Canadiens-de-Montréal. Venue opened on March 16, 1996.
AN EVENING WITH RUSH
TICKETS: $39.50 / $79.50 CAD
ATTENDANCE: 9,343
CAPACITY: 12,920
CONCERT GROSS: $445,111 ($691,789 CAD)
NOTES: Venue aka Molson Centre. Alex did a phone interview with *Harrisburg Patriot News*.
MONTREAL GAZETTE: "Fans get their expected Rush: There was a calm, centered resolve to play the music, and play it well. As a result, the music seems barely to have changed. Now that could be a bad thing. But to the faithful in attendance last night, it was probably just about perfect."

OCTOBER 19, 2002
QUEBEC CITY, QUEBEC
COLISÉE PEPSI, 250 Boulevard Wilfrid-Hamel. Venue opened on December 8, 1949.
AN EVENING WITH RUSH
TICKETS: $39.50 / $59.50 CAD
ATTENDANCE: 6,960
CAPACITY: 10,000
CONCERT GROSS: $263,474 ($409,490 CAD)
NOTES: Venue aka Colisée de Quebec. The soundboard recording of "Vital Signs" on the *Rush in Rio* live CD release is sourced from this concert.

OCTOBER 22, 2002
TORONTO, ONTARIO
AIR CANADA CENTRE, 40 Bay Street. Venue dedicated on February 19, 1999.
AN EVENING WITH RUSH
TICKETS: $38.50 / $85.50 CAD

ATTENDANCE: 10,917
CAPACITY: 13,750
CONCERT GROSS: $404,034 ($627,947 CAD)
TORONTO SUN: "A Full-On Rush! Unlike their summer performance, when they had only been on the road for two weeks after a lengthy break, the three musicians were a well-oiled and muscled machine."

OCTOBER 24, 2002
NEW YORK, NEW YORK
MADISON SQUARE GARDEN, 4 Pennsylvania Plaza (8th Avenue between 31st and 33rd Streets). Historic venue opened on February 11, 1968.
AN EVENING WITH RUSH
TICKETS: $35.00 / $69.50 / $90.00; face value minus $4.50 finance charge
ATTENDANCE: 11,967
CAPACITY: 12,677
CONCERT GROSS: $688,205.
NEW YORK POST: "Fans' Engines Rev Through Tiresome Rush Hours: Rush's music is tiresome in small doses. In supersize quantities like Thursday's concert, the tedium was monumental."

OCTOBER 25, 2002
HERSHEY, PENNSYLVANIA
GIANT CENTER, 550 West Hersheypark Drive. Venue opened on October 15, 2002.
AN EVENING WITH RUSH
TICKETS: $35.00 / $47.50 / $57.50; face value not including $2.50 finance charge
ATTENDANCE: 6,674
CAPACITY: 9,406
CONCERT GROSS: $285,035
NOTES: Neil improvised a new drum fill out of the guitar solo in "Driven."
THE PATRIOT NEWS: "Veteran Rush band delivers energy, ferocity to fans: Rush instrumentals are anything but mindless noodling; every note has a place and a reason. It's truly the sign of a great band when even nonvocal tracks are compelling and listenable."

OCTOBER 27, 2002
PHILADELPHIA, PENNSYLVANIA
FIRST UNION CENTER, 3601 South Broad Street. Venue opened on August 12, 1996.
AN EVENING WITH RUSH

TICKETS: $35.00 / $45.00 / $65.00 (sold out)
ATTENDANCE: 7,840
CAPACITY: 15,000
CONCERT GROSS: $416,285
NOTES: Pitcher Randy Johnson was at the gig, alternating his time between watching the show from stage left and watching game 7 of the World Series in the band's production office.

OCTOBER 28, 2002
BOSTON, MASSACHUSETTS
FLEETCENTER, 100 Legends Way. Venue opened on September 30, 1995.
AN EVENING WITH RUSH
TICKETS: $35.00 / $65.00
ATTENDANCE: 8,807
CAPACITY: 14,600
CONCERT GROSS: $414,215
NOTES: Venue aka TD Garden. Before the gig, Neil was presented the Zildjian Cymbal Plaque Award in recognition of his contributions to drumming. The plaque features a vintage cymbal from Armond Zildjian's personal collection.
RUSS RYAN (STAGE LEFT TECHNICIAN): "We used to send special guests to start the dryers. Randy Johnson, the pitcher, is a friend of Geddy's. Randy was at the show and happened to be standing there when it was time for the dryers to be started. We had the dryers timed and they would always stop during a certain song of each set. A crew guy was getting ready to go up and do it, and I turned around and said 'Randy, you want to deal with those dryers? There are quarters up on the stage, those dryers are going to stop, we need someone to put quarters in each of those slots, push it in and it'll automatically start.' He said, 'Yeah I'll do it!' So we had 6'10" Randy Johnson going up on stage."[11]

OCTOBER 30, 2002
CHICAGO, ILLINOIS
UNITED CENTER, 1901 West Madison Street. Venue opened on August 18, 1994.
AN EVENING WITH RUSH
TICKETS: $35.00 / $75.00
ATTENDANCE: 8,539
CAPACITY: 10,012
CONCERT GROSS: $486,465

NOVEMBER 1, 2002
AMES, IOWA
HILTON COLISEUM, Iowa State University campus, 1700 Center Drive. Venue opened on December 2, 1971.
AN EVENING WITH RUSH
TICKETS: $37.50 / $47.50; price included $1.50 finance charge
ATTENDANCE: 4,261
CAPACITY: 11,670
CONCERT GROSS: $192,069
NOTES: The *Des Moines Register* lists the attendance at 4,909. "Ceiling Unlimited" was performed for the final time. During "La Villa Strangiato," Alex ranted on and on about football and Iowa, doing his own take on the I.S.U. fight song "Go, Cyclones, Go!" and causing the big football player security force in the front of the stage to laugh hysterically.
THE DES MOINES REGISTER: "New songs give lift to Rush: The concert proved that Rush's newest material is arguably its finest, rawest stuff in twenty years."

NOVEMBER 2, 2002
MINNEAPOLIS, MINNESOTA
TARGET CENTER, 600 First Avenue North. Venue opened on October 13, 1990.
AN EVENING WITH RUSH
TICKETS: $32.50 / $62.50 (plus fees)
ATTENDANCE: 7,074
CAPACITY: 12,808
CONCERT GROSS: $326,742
NOTES: The band contemplated adding some European dates to the itinerary, but after sixty-seven shows, ending in Brazil, they (or at least Neil) had "had enough."[12]

NOVEMBER 4, 2002
CLEVELAND, OHIO
GUND ARENA, 1 Center Court. Venue opened on October 17, 1994.
AN EVENING WITH RUSH
TICKETS: $35.00 / $47.50 / $60.00
ATTENDANCE: 6,962
CAPACITY: 10,809
CONCERT GROSS: $333,300
NOTES: The gig was exactly six years to the day that Rush last performed in Cleveland at the very same venue.
THE PLAIN DEALER: "Art rockers in no hurry to get serious: Three hours of jaw-dropping, fleet-fingered workouts, tricky time signatures and science

fiction-leaning lyrics that make Rush the thinking man's music throughout the Midwest and Canada."

NOVEMBER 6, 2002
EAST RUTHERFORD, NEW JERSEY
CONTINENTAL AIRLINES ARENA, Meadowlands Sports Complex, 50 State Route 120. Venue opened on July 2, 1981.
AN EVENING WITH RUSH
TICKETS: $39.50 / $50.00 / $75.00 / $94.50
ATTENDANCE: 9,777
CAPACITY: 14,827
CONCERT GROSS: $443,295
NOTES: A month before the show, only 6,000 tickets had been sold, and several times it was in danger of being canceled outright, but the band insisted upon playing it anyway, with almost 10,000 fans showing up on a cold Wednesday evening.
HERALD NEWS (WEST PATTERSON): "The Rush machine keeps rolling along: Peart's long absence from the music scene did not slow his abilities a bit. Throughout the concert he was his usual amazing self, executing daring crossovers while his hands and feet worked independently to create snappy polyrhythms."

NOVEMBER 8, 2002
UNCASVILLE, CONNECTICUT
MOHEGAN SUN ARENA, Mohegan Sun Casino, 1 Mohegan Sun Boulevard. Venue opened on September 25, 2001.
AN EVENING WITH RUSH
TICKETS: $25.00 / $80.00
ATTENDANCE: 5,554
CONCERT GROSS: $341,175
NOTES: A DVD filming was planned, but Rush could not come to terms with Mohegan Sun. The casino wanted Geddy to plug the venue during the concert, and the band refused to do this, so they moved the shoot to Brazil.
THE DAY (NEW LONDON, CT): "Rush

delved into past and future at Mohegan Sun: Rush at once proved they'd musically grown over the years and, yet, had no reason to be anything but proud of their past."

NOVEMBER 10, 2002
MANCHESTER, NEW HAMPSHIRE
VERIZON WIRELESS ARENA, 555 Elm Street. Venue opened on November 15, 2001.
AN EVENING WITH RUSH
TICKETS: $30.50 / $46.50 / $66.50 (plus fees)
ATTENDANCE: 6,143
CAPACITY: 8,602
CONCERT GROSS: $300,631
NOTES: Final North American date of the *Vapor Trails* tour. "Closer to the Heart" was performed. In a nice gesture, the band closed the furthest sections of the arena and upgraded those fans to the lower level (which they'd been doing in the less-than-full halls). The move backfired here, however, when a long line to gain admittance was then followed by another long line to exchange tickets. More than 100 fans become irate when they heard "Tom Sawyer" while they were still standing in line. The venue management told them they could use their original tickets or wait for an upgrade. All but about thirty people ran into the concert.[13]
GEDDY (ONSTAGE): "We're happy to have you all here tonight to celebrate with us the completion of our *Vapor Trails* tour here in North America. We did about a million shows, I think. We're happy to have you here for the finale. Nice to see a few familiar faces out there, gluttons for punishment you are."
THE UNION LEADER: "Rush rocks Manchester, quells near-riot of stuck fans: Wherever one stood in the arena, one could never be assured of being safe from the flying fists of impromptu air drumming."

NOVEMBER 20, 2002
PORTO ALEGRE, BRAZIL
EASTADIO OLIMPICO MONUMENTAL, Largo Patrono Fernando Kroeff n 1. Venue opened on September 19, 1954.
AN EVENING WITH RUSH
TICKETS: R$50.00 (general admission) / R$250.00 (VIP reserved)
ATTENDANCE: 32,000 (approximate)

Chapter 26

THE R30 TOUR

In 2004, Rush celebrated its thirtieth anniversary with the *R30* tour, performing fifty-seven shows in eight countries. The jaunt included the band's first return to Europe in twelve years, with inaugural visits to the Czech Republic and Italy. (Geddy, onstage in Milan: "*Gratzie!* I'm sorry, I don't speak Italian. I'm sorry it took us so long to come here to Italy, but we're here now.") The tour also featured Rush's first concerts at Radio City Music Hall since 1983, as well as debut appearances at the Hollywood Bowl, as well as Red Rocks in Morrison, Colorado. One of the final shows, in Frankfurt, Germany, was filmed and later released on DVD as *R30: 30th Anniversary World Tour*.

The shows opened with the "R30 Overture," a six-song medley of instrumental themes from various classic Rush songs, accompanied by an all-new CG presentation combining images from many of the studio albums, comingled with photos of the band throughout the years and culminating in a clip of actor Jerry Stiller waking up from a dream to urge the band to take the stage. The visuals were created by Geddy's brother, Allan Weinrib.

"*R30* kind of started the whole thing with the animated opening," Allan explained. "Geddy liked it but thought it was too serious and he came up with this idea to have someone wake up out of a dream. The first concept was actually to have a stoner wake up and say, 'Hey man what was that!' We started kicking around all of these names and in the end we got Jerry Stiller! We had to fly to New York to film Stiller in the Trump Hotel, waking up from this bad dream with a tight Rush T-shirt: We got him jumping up and down with power poses, and then he goes to the bed and pretends to fall asleep as Dale Heslip whistled 'Closer to the Heart' for the ending."

Also included in the set list were live debuts of "The Seeker," "Heart Full of Soul," "Summertime Blues" and "Crossroads," all of which were featured on *Feedback*, a collection of cover tunes—Rush's first since their 1973 debut single, "Not Fade Away."

"When we put this thirtieth-anniversary tour together, we realized that we didn't have

RIGHT TOP: Prague, Czech Republic; The Polish Fan Cub from Warsaw at the T-Mobile Arena.

RIGHT BOTTOM: Virginia Beach, VA; A busload of fans welcoming the band at the Amphitheatre.

OPPOSITE: Holmdel, NJ; Geddy rocking out on the thirtieth anniversary of Rush's first show with Neil.

TOUR HISTORY
R30

SET LIST:
Jerry Stiller intro film
"R30 Overture": "Finding My Way,"
"Anthem," "Bastille Day," "A Passage to
Bangkok," "Cygnus X-1: Prologue," and
"Hemispheres: Prelude"
"The Spirit of Radio"
"Force Ten"
"Animate" (abridged)
"Subdivisions"
"Earthshine"
"Red Barchetta"
"Roll the Bones"
"Bravado"

"YYZ"
"The Trees"
"The Seeker"
"One Little Victory" (with dragon intro)
**(Intermission: "Darn That Dragon"
intro film)**
"Tom Sawyer"
"Dreamline"
"Secret Touch"
"Between the Wheels"
"Mystic Rhythms"
"Red Sector A"
Drum Solo ("Der Trommler")
"Resist" (acoustic)

"Heart Full of Soul" (acoustic)
"2112: Overture"
"2112: The Temples of Syrinx"
"2112: Grand Finale"
"La Villa Strangiato" (with Lerxst rant)
"By-Tor and the Snow Dog" (abridged)
"Xanadu" (abridged)
"Working Man" (reggae ending)
Encore:
"Summertime Blues"
"Crossroads"
"Limelight" (with Jerry Stiller outro film)

MAY 26, 2004
ANTIOCH, TENNESSEE
STARWOOD AMPHITHEATRE, 3839 Murfreesboro Pike. Venue opened on June 21, 1986.
AN EVENING WITH RUSH
TICKETS: $6.50 (lawn, limited advance Clear Channel promotion) / $19.00 (lawn) / $49.50 (reserved)
ATTENDANCE: 5,580
CAPACITY: 17,279
CONCERT GROSS: $231,553 (estimate)
NOTES: Opening date of the *R30* tour. The day's sound check is a long one, with "Resist," "Heart Full of Soul," "Summertime Blues," "The Seeker," parts of "Red Sector A," and the "R30 Overture" all performed. Producer Peter Collins visited with the band. In the afternoon, he and Alex fly model airplanes together (true to form, Lerxst crashes two of them). Geddy played the wrong keyboard melody in "Subdivisions," and there was a minor train wreck during "Earthshine."
GEDDY (ONSTAGE): "If you hear any mistakes, please ignore them."
NEIL: "The hardest show of the tour is always the first one, with all the preparation it takes to bring everything to that point of readiness, and the pressure of actually doing it, just once, in front of an audience. The first stage, in many ways, was the final stage. After that, no matter how difficult it was to perform at that level every night, it could never be as uncertain, or as exciting as the first show

. . . First show went very well, everything seemed to work, including me."[1]
NASHVILLE SCENE: "Rush light up the shed: Surrounded by sensory-overloading lasers, lights and graphics, Rush performed as freshly and intensely as they do on record."

MAY 28, 2004
CHARLOTTE (HARRIS-HOUSTON), NORTH CAROLINA
VERIZON WIRELESS AMPHITHEATRE, 707 Pavilion Boulevard. Venue opened on July 4, 1991.
AN EVENING WITH RUSH
TICKETS: $25.00 (lawn) / $35.00 (upper reserved) / $50.00 (lower reserved) / $75.00 (gold circle)
ATTENDANCE: 8,573
CAPACITY: 18,812
CONCERT GROSS: $299,578
GEDDY (ONSTAGE): "We appreciate all of your support these last thirty years here, touring around the United States, making us Canadians feel very welcome."

MAY 29, 2004
VIRGINIA BEACH, VIRGINIA
VERIZON WIRELESS VIRGINIA BEACH AMPHITHEATER, 3550 Cellar Door Way. Venue opened on May 15, 1996.
AN EVENING WITH RUSH
TICKETS: $24.75 / $49.50 (plus $2.00 day of show)
ATTENDANCE: 6,557
CAPACITY: 6,962

CONCERT GROSS: $256,574
NOTES: Neil played a near-perfect drum solo, only to hit the final trigger with no sound heard. Continuing the tradition begun on the *Vapor Trails* tour, each night Alex performed a unique "rant" during "La Villa Strangiato." In addition, at the end of "The Trees" he played a bit of the Beatles' "I Feel Fine" followed by "Day Tripper"—not coincidentally, two songs he once singled out as inspiring him to first play the guitar as a teenager.
GEDDY (ONSTAGE): "For those of you who've been around us a while, it means that you're getting older too. We're not alone."

MAY 31, 2004
BURGETTSTOWN, PENNSYLVANIA
POST-GAZETTE PAVILION, 665 SR 18. Venue opened on June 17, 1990.
AN EVENING WITH RUSH
TICKETS: $28.00 (lawn) / $33.00 (upper pavilion) / $55.50 (lower pavilion) / $75.50 (pit and orchestra) (plus $2.00 day of show)
ATTENDANCE: 8,828
CAPACITY: 23,079
CONCERT GROSS: $276,435
NOTES: During the afternoon, the crew passed the downtime by driving golf balls across a small lake from the backstage area. For the encore, Geddy donned a Pirates 1979 World Champion T-shirt.
GEDDY (ONSTAGE): "We were talking in the dressing room, how we think we've played Pittsburgh more than any other

city in America. It was the first one for us, so it's a special place for us."

PITTSBURGH POST-GAZETTE: "Rock-steady Rush shows why it has lasted for thirty years: Rush may still be around simply because, well, it's still around. But the band's thirtieth anniversary show re-emphasized what a multifaceted, surprising and, yes, fun group this can be."

JUNE 2, 2004
COLUMBUS, OHIO
GERMAIN AMPHITHEATER, 2200 Polaris Parkway. Venue opened on June 18, 1994.
AN EVENING WITH RUSH
TICKETS: $35.50 (lawn) / $53.00 (pavilion) / $71.50 (orchestra)
ATTENDANCE: 8,143
CAPACITY: 12,500
CONCERT GROSS: $357,677
NOTES: Venue aka Polaris Amphitheater.
COLUMBUS DISPATCH: "Power Trio Takes Plunge into the Mystic: Getting into the proper Rush mood requires darkness, a green laser-light show, reefer madness among the audience, and the song 'Tom Sawyer.' Sunshine is for Rush's fellow Canadians the Barenaked Ladies."

JUNE 4, 2004
NOBLESVILLE, INDIANA
VERIZON WIRELESS MUSIC CENTER, 12880 East 146th Street. Venue opened on May 20, 1989.
AN EVENING WITH RUSH
TICKETS: $10.00 (lawn, limited advance

Clear Channel promo, sold only in pairs) / $35.50 (lawn) / $58.00 (reserved) / $72.50 (orchestra)
ATTENDANCE: 8,647
CAPACITY: 11,868
CONCERT GROSS: $368,860
NOTES: Alex was a little frustrated with his stage sound, delivering gestures to the sound crew to correct it.
NEIL: "The Indy show had been a good one. In general, the tempos were well locked. I noticed certain areas that could be improved—transitions that felt pushed, that kind of thing—but I knew the next night I would remember those parts and adjust them."[2]
JOURNAL REVIEW (CRAWFORDSVILLE, IN): "Rush plays it safe on thirtieth birthday: The absence of many Rush originals made the decision to perform songs by the Who and Cream that much more frustrating. While consummately played, Rush has too much of its own good material to be displaying the best of other legends."

JUNE 5, 2004
TINLEY PARK, ILLINOIS
TWEETER CENTER, 19100 Ridgeland Avenue. Venue opened on June 2, 1990.
AN EVENING WITH RUSH
TICKETS: $10.00 (lawn, limited advance Clear Channel promo, sold only in pairs) / $85.50 (orchestra)
ATTENDANCE: 13,346
CAPACITY: 20,330
CONCERT GROSS: $707,022
NOTES: Venue aka Midwest Bank Amphitheatre. While in Chicago, Alex spent much of his time doing phone interviews. The band played host to Chicago Cubs radio announcer Chip Carrey and Cubs pitcher Matt Clement. Alex broke a string during "Secret Touch," while Neil's solo featured some spirited improvisation.
CHICAGO TRIBUNE: "Rush treats fans with classics, recent hits: If many of Rush's erstwhile peers were weighed down by classical and jazz aspirations, Rush has remained at heart a rock band, and no matter how busy its music gets, the songs still stay relatively economical."
CHICAGO RED STREAK: "Still a Rush after thirty years: It appeared that more than a few fans have actually tried to play these songs at some point in their lives.

People do not naturally bob their heads in perfect 7/4 time. Clearly, they've put some serious time into figuring out how to groove to the band's unique sense of time. Thirty years of practice has left Lee, Lifeson, and Peart alone atop rock's pantheon of virtuosos who remain relevant."

JUNE 7, 2004
MILWAUKEE, WISCONSIN
MARCUS AMPHITHEATER, Henry Maier Festival Park, Summerfest grounds, 200 North Harbor Drive. Venue opened on June 25, 1987.
AN EVENING WITH RUSH
TICKETS: $22.75 (lawn) / $27.50 (reserved bleacher) / $45.00 (reserved) / $60.25 (orchestra)
ATTENDANCE: 8,750
CAPACITY: 11,791
CONCERT GROSS: $349,690
NOTES: Neil's book *The Masked Rider* is put on sale at this gig, but Neil soon discovers the print run is riddled with errors.
MILWAUKEE JOURNAL SENTINEL: "Rush delivers fine-tuned show of the classics: In the night's first mass sing-along, Lee led the crowd through 'The Spirit of Radio,' wailing away with his trademark granny-specs arched across his nose and wearing a vintage Milwaukee Brewers T-shirt."

JUNE 8, 2004
CLARKSTON, MICHIGAN
DTE ENERGY MUSIC THEATRE, 7774 Sashabaw Road. Venue opened on June 25, 1972.
AN EVENING WITH RUSH
TICKETS: $35.50 (lawn) / $72.50 (pavilion), price included parking
ATTENDANCE: 10,835
CAPACITY: 15,074
CONCERT GROSS: $539,932
NOTES: Geddy played the entire show with strep throat, though it didn't hinder his performance. Continuing a tradition started on the *Vapor Trails Tour*, celebrities are again invited to step on stage for the ritual of restarting the clothes dryers. Tonight, actor Mike Smith appears in character, as "Bubbles" from the *Trailer Park Boys* during "2112" to restart the dryers. He gestures to the audience a couple of times and performs an air drum roll before sauntering back off stage. Neil sends Michael out with a pair of sticks for

a fan in the audience wearing a Zildjian T-shirt—but also gives the fan a Sabian shirt and, with tongue firmly in cheek, Michael says he has to put it on "now."

NEIL: "Note how loud the background vocals (crowd) were for 'Heart Full of Soul.' Seems to be an audience-participation act that's catching on more and more and night by night. It's a cool one!"[3]

JUNE 10, 2004
CUYAHOGA FALLS, OHIO
BLOSSOM MUSIC CENTER, 1145 West Steels Corners Road. Venue opened on July 19, 1968.
AN EVENING WITH RUSH
TICKETS: $25.00 (lawn) / $50.00 (rear pavilion) / $62.50 (reserved pavilion) / $75.00 (orchestra)
ATTENDANCE: 7,836
CAPACITY: 18,500
CONCERT GROSS: $373,145
THE PLAIN DEALER: "Rush stands the test of time: Fortunately, as the ultimate Rush tribute act, they're still good for a rush."

JUNE 12, 2004
MARYLAND HEIGHTS, MISSOURI
UMB BANK PAVILION, 14141 Riverport Drive. Venue opened on June 14, 1991.
AN EVENING WITH RUSH
TICKETS: $10.00 (lawn, limited advance Clear Channel promo, sold only in pairs) / $30.00 (lawn) / $50.00 (upper level) / $75.00 (lower level)
ATTENDANCE: 10,177
CAPACITY: 15,784
CONCERT GROSS: $433,036
NOTES: Venue aka Verizon Wireless Amphitheater. KSHE-FM Thirty-seventh Birthday Concert.
ST. LOUIS POST-DISPATCH: "Rush puts career highs on display: Lee proved early on that his high-pitched voice—a Rush trademark—is still intact. The group's tight ensemble playing and adventurous solos served them well."

JUNE 13, 2004
BONNER SPRINGS, KANSAS
VERIZON WIRELESS AMPHITHEATRE, 633 North 130th Street. Venue opened on June 5, 1984.
AN EVENING WITH RUSH
TICKETS: $10.00 (lawn, limited advance Clear Channel promo, sold only in pairs) / $30.00 (lawn) $49.50 (reserved) / $65.00 (orchestra)

ATTENDANCE: 7,176
CAPACITY: 13,910
CONCERT GROSS: $330,229
NOTES: Venue aka Sandstone Amphitheatre.
THE KANSAS CITY STAR: "Radio-free Rush rocks on: Mostly modern-day warriors still have that mean, mean stride: The three-man prog-rock army brought its thirtieth anniversary party to Bonner Springs Sunday, putting on a show for a big crowd that largely worshipped the band's every move."

JUNE 23, 2004
DALLAS, TEXAS
SMIRNOFF MUSIC CENTRE, Fair Park, 1818 First Avenue. Venue opened on July 23, 1988.
AN EVENING WITH RUSH
TICKETS: $18.00 (lawn, limited advance promo) / $39.50 (lawn) / $59.50 (pavilion) / $79.50 (orchestra), included parking
ATTENDANCE: 9,485
CAPACITY: 14,871
CONCERT GROSS: $513,160
NEIL: "'Bravado' gave us breathing space, as it began with a mid-tempo instrumental groove, more textural and gentle than what had gone before. While we played that introduction, I had a good chance to let my gaze wander around the audience, and I couldn't help noticing a scattered few-dozen silhouettes rising and walking away, choosing that song as a good opportunity to get up and wander around—head off to get some more beer, or to 'offload' some. That bothered me more than it should have."[4]
FORT WORTH STAR-TELEGRAM: "What a Rush—even after thirty long years: The show put Rush's accomplishments into sharp focus: excellent ensemble playing, intelligent lyrics and a way of blending progressive rock and pop. And you can add that they're an excellent cover band."

JUNE 25, 2004
SELMA, TEXAS
VERIZON WIRELESS AMPHITHEATRE, 16765 Lookout Road. Venue opened on May 19, 2001.
AN EVENING WITH RUSH
TICKETS: $10.00 (lawn, limited advance Clear Channel promo, sold only in pairs) / $28.75 (lawn) / $55.75 (reserved) / $78.25 (orchestra); price included parking

ATTENDANCE: 11,288
CAPACITY: 16,762
CONCERT GROSS: $457,305
NEIL: "Best show yet for me. Strong, solid, smooth and effortless. The show poured out of us like a force of nature, sweeping out in waves from the stage and the lights and the speaker cabinets, ebbing and flowing over a cheering, smiling delighted crowd. We were all locked together in a long, tireless moment of sublime pleasure, and as song after song played out into the ether, I felt energized to make this the one."[5]
THE AUSTIN CHRONICLE: "Like an atomic clock, Rush performed seamlessly. Instead of using the big birthday to pull proverbial rabbits out of the catalog hat, Rush played it too safe. And still, it was the best three hours around."

JUNE 26, 2004
THE WOODLANDS, TEXAS
C. W. MITCHELL PAVILION, 2005 Lake Robbins Drive. Venue opened on April 27, 1990.
AN EVENING WITH RUSH
TICKETS: $40.50 (lawn) / $86.00 (orchestra)
ATTENDANCE: 10,392
CAPACITY: 15,821
CONCERT GROSS: $541,229
NOTES: During "2112," Geddy sang in a "pirate" voice "We are the pirates of the Temple of Syrinx, Arrrgh!" And thus began a pirate theme that would continue throughout the tour. *Motor Cyclist's* Brian Catterson joined Neil and Michael as the trio rode for the next three days from Texas to Colorado.

JUNE 29, 2004
MORRISON, COLORADO
RED ROCKS AMPHITHEATRE, 18300 West Alameda Parkway. Historic venue dedicated on June 15, 1941.
AN EVENING WITH RUSH
TICKETS: $40.00 / $68.50 / $85.00
ATTENDANCE: 8,561; sold out
CONCERT GROSS: $580,225
NOTES: Rush's inaugural performance at Red Rocks.
NEIL: "It was simply a magical show and would remain in my memory as one of the best nights of the tour."[6]
GEDDY: "One of those questions we always ask our managers is, 'How come we never play Red Rocks? It's supposed

to be so beautiful.' So we accommodated. I don't think we can get our full show in there, but we'll get most of it in there. I've never been to the venue itself. But I saw the U2 video and it just looks beautiful . . ."[7]

GEDDY: "It's an amazing location. One of the most beautiful concert venues in America . . . or anywhere. I would hazard a guess that it's one of the most beautiful anywhere. It was great, I was happy to do it."[8]

ROCKY MOUNTAIN NEWS: "Camaraderie shines as trio celebrates thirty-year anniversary: The fans are about the most rabid around; the sight of thousands of people simultaneously playing air bass on the intro to 'Red Barchetta' was worth the price of admission alone."

JUNE 30, 2004
WEST VALLEY CITY, UTAH
USANA AMPHITHEATRE, 5150 South 6055 West. Venue opened on July 3, 2003.
AN EVENING WITH RUSH
TICKETS: $26.00 (lawn) / $56.00 (upper reserved) / $81.00 (lower reserved); parking included
ATTENDANCE: 8,754
CAPACITY: 14,661
CONCERT GROSS: $401,684 (estimate)
NOTES: Ironically, the venue is located just off of Bacchus Plateau. Alex, Geddy, and Neil walked onstage into bright sunshine, with Alex donning sunglasses. Alex picked up on the pirate theme, using his "La Villa" rant to speak in a pirate voice about being a pirate captain.
THE DESERET MORNING NEWS: "Rush is nothing short of excellent: The studio-quality mix was crisp. Lee's bass lines and Lifeson's leads, even backed by Peart's relentless, syncopated drumming, were clear and clean."

JULY 2, 2004
AUBURN, WASHINGTON
WHITE RIVER AMPHITHEATRE,
Muckleshoot Indian Reservation, 40601 Auburn Enumclaw Road. Venue opened on June 14, 2003.
AN EVENING WITH RUSH
TICKETS: $10.00 (lawn, limited advance Clear Channel promo, sold only in pairs) / $85.00 (orchestra)
ATTENDANCE: 11,854

CAPACITY: 20,000
CONCERT GROSS: $590,810
NOTES: Long-time crew member Liam Birt suffered a heart attack in the morning and was taken to a Seattle hospital. During the gig, the crew donned pirate hats and eye patches.
THE NEWS TRIBUNE (TACOMA): "Rush shows it still has it after thirty years: Lifeson's spidery fingers raced back and forth across his fret board, projected on the video screen during scorching solos."

JULY 3, 2004
RIDGEFIELD, WASHINGTON
CLARK COUNTY AMPHITHEATER,
17200 NE Delfel Road. Venue opened on July 10, 2003.
AN EVENING WITH RUSH
TICKETS: $6.50 (lawn, limited advance Clear Channel promo) / $28.50 (lawn) / $68.50 / $128.50; price included fees
ATTENDANCE: 6,844
CAPACITY: 17,780
CONCERT GROSS: $359,249 (estimate)
BRAD MADIX (FRONT-OF-HOUSE SOUND ENGINEER): "Geddy had two dryers and a vending machine. He filled that thing with bobbleheads and little balls and stuff that he picked up. He had this logic to it where everything was in the vending machine as it went around. It was some kind of hierarchy to it—he moved stuff around in there. I remember in Seattle, he found a knick-knack store and bought *bags* of dolls and bobbleheads and things, and up to that point we had been stuffing random stuff in it. But in Seattle we held the doors while he rearranged the vending machine. He was *so* into it, he was so excited, it was more important than sound check to get stuff arranged in the vending machine just so. Something got into his head about how these things had to be arranged in this thing, and he was not going to stop until it was done!"[9]

JULY 6, 2004
HOLLYWOOD, CALIFORNIA
HOLLYWOOD BOWL, 2301 North Highland Avenue. Historic venue officially opened on July 11, 1922.
AN EVENING WITH RUSH
TICKETS: $43.50 (upper promenade) / $53.50 (promenade 2) / $99.50 (box)
ATTENDANCE: 14,100
CAPACITY: 17,602
CONCERT GROSS: $903,275

NOTES: Rush's debut performance at Hollywood Bowl. Neil attended a post-show party at the Legion Hall, with Carrie and about a hundred friends, including fellow musicians: Doane Perry (Jethro Tull), Matt Scannell (Vertical Horizon), Taylor Hawkins (Foo Fighters) and Rupert Hine (producer). Actor Nicolas Cage was also in attendance.
VARIETY: "Surely neither the band's fans nor many dismissive critics nor the band members themselves could have imagined in 1974 that Rush would be playing large arenas thirty years down the road. But the group has charted a uniquely successful course over the years, marked by complete artistic control and an ever-evolving sound that's produced one of the all-time great live rock bands."

JULY 7, 2004
CHULA VISTA, CALIFORNIA
COORS AMPHITHEATRE, 2050 Entertainment Circle. Venue opened on July 21, 1998.
AN EVENING WITH RUSH
Tickets: $23.00 (lawn, limited advance Clear Channel promo) / $31.50 (lawn) / $75.50 (orchestra)
ATTENDANCE: 7,408
CAPACITY: 19,492
CONCERT GROSS: $344,690

JULY 9, 2004
MOUNTAIN VIEW, CALIFORNIA
SHORELINE AMPHITHEATRE, One Amphitheatre Parkway. Venue opened on July 5, 1986.
AN EVENING WITH RUSH
TICKETS: $20.00 (lawn) / $36.50 (reserved) / $83.50 (orchestra)
ATTENDANCE: 9,178
CAPACITY: 17,000
CONCERT GROSS: $485,111
NOTES: This show was selected as one of the Year's Best Concerts by the *San Jose Mercury News*.
SAN JOSE MERCURY NEWS: "After thirty years on the road, they know how to play their instruments with more skill than almost anyone else out there."

JULY 10, 2004
CONCORD, CALIFORNIA
CHRONICLE PAVILION, 2000 Kirker Pass Road. Venue opened on May 16, 1975.
AN EVENING WITH RUSH

TICKETS: $20.00 (lawn, limited advance Clear Channel promo) $35.00 (lawn) / $52.25 (upper level) / $79.50 (lower level)
ATTENDANCE: 9,877
CAPACITY: 12,500
CONCERT GROSS: $453,514
NOTES: Venue aka Sleep Train Pavilion.

JULY 12, 2004
WHEATLAND, CALIFORNIA
SLEEP TRAIN AMPHITHEATRE, 2677 Forty Mile Road. Venue opened on June 10, 2000.
AN EVENING WITH RUSH
TICKETS: $29.50 (lawn) / $33.50 (upper reserved) / $56.00 (lower reserved) / $79.00 (orchestra); prices included $4.00 finance charge
ATTENDANCE: 7,346
CAPACITY: 8,011
CONCERT GROSS: $306,058
NOTES: Venue aka AutoWest Amphitheater.
SACRAMENTO BEE: "Rush at 30: Oldies but goodies: Peart could have been Keith Moon's straight-faced older brother, the one who took his drum lessons seriously instead of passing the time with horse tranquilizers."

JULY 14, 2004
IRVINE, CALIFORNIA
VERIZON WIRELESS AMPHITHEATER, 8808 Irvine Center Drive. Venue opened on August 21, 1981.
AN EVENING WITH RUSH
TICKETS: $32.50 (lawn) / $65.00 (lodge) / $95.00 (orchestra)
ATTENDANCE: 11,720
CAPACITY: 16,258
CONCERT GROSS: $685,304
NOTES: Jack Black appeared on stage to feed the dryers. The pirate theme reached an inevitable point, as Geddy appeared on stage with a stuffed parrot on his shoulder. These types of antics continued throughout the remainder of the tour, and were even adopted by fans, as the pirate theme expanded out into the audience.
NEIL: "Shaking his hand, I told Jack Black how pleased I had been by the reference in 'School of Rock.' Jack said, 'That was my idea!' I also mentioned how we had originally wanted him to play the part of the 'awakening dreamer' in our opening film, the part Jerry Stiller had ended up doing . . . He spread his

arms and said, with obvious sincerity, 'I am at your service.' Michael and I told him about the dryer ritual, how we sometimes had guests come out onstage to put quarters in the dryers and asked if he would like to do it. He said, 'Well, yeah!' and Michael said he would tell him when. At the beginning of '2112', I saw Jack come bounding out from stage left in an improvised pirate costume—skull-and-crossbones hat, eye-patch, and some kind of multicolored skirt thing—do a somersault, and strike some 'rock poses' as the crowd roared its delight. He fell to his knees in front of Geddy at the front of the stage, acting out more rock poses, then came back to the dryers and started to take his clothes off. 'Oh-oh,' I thought, 'Is this where somebody gets arrested?' Fortunately he stopped at his boxers, then climbed on top of the dryers, just as the 'star-man' logo appeared on the screen. Standing on the dryers, his pudgy body framed in the lights, and his boxers displaying the classic plumber's crack, he struck the same pose as the naked man on the screen, arms up and hands splayed in resistance to oppression. While I played on, I looked over at him in profile, and saw his face intent against the lights, immersed in the role, then he jumped down again, gathered up his clothes, and did a somersault offstage. The audience loved it, of course, laughing and cheering, and Geddy and I exchanged headshaking smiles of disbelief. Before the encore, when we stood backstage for a quick swallow of water and a towel-off, Geddy said to me, 'That wasn't just an appearance—that was some kind of performance art!'"[10]

JULY 16, 2004
PHOENIX, ARIZONA
CRICKET PAVILION, 2121 North 83rd Avenue. Venue opened on November 11, 1990.
AN EVENING WITH RUSH
TICKETS: $14.25 (lawn, limited advance Clear Channel promo) / $36.00 (lawn) / $49.50 (pavilion) / $73.00 (orchestra); price included $3.50 parking fee
ATTENDANCE: 10,247
CAPACITY: 19,312
CONCERT GROSS: $435,145
NOTES: Neil broke a bass drum pedal, necessitating a midsong repair by Gump.

LORNE "GUMP" WHEATON: "There are times when equipment fails, and you have to be out there far too long on the stage trying to fix something. For other people, that can be funny, but at the time you aren't exactly laughing your ass off. I've changed bass drum pedals in the middle of a song. On the *R30* kit, they gold-plated anything that was metal in 14k gold. Once you plate something . . . it goes into such a heat for the plating process that it breaks down the energy in the metal. So, little things . . . like bass drum pedal springs and stuff like that . . . they just plated the whole thing. It all looked beautiful. But a few nights into the tour things started failing. One night in Phoenix, the main spring on his right foot pedal snapped and that pedal went dead. So all he had was the slave pedal. He really is a very talented drummer, but something like that can really throw you off. All of a sudden, he had to start playing the bass drum with his left foot . . . and close the hi-hats so they weren't sloshing around, so that he could keep some kind of pattern going. So I crawled up in there, disconnected the slave pedal from the main pedal, ripped the main pedal out, put the new one in, connected it to the slave . . . and all of this was in the middle of a song. I think they might have been playing 'Bravado' or something like that. We managed to do it, but then I got stuck in between all of the hardware. One of the audio guys had to run out there and pull me out by my feet! That was a little embarrassing."[11]

JULY 17, 2004
LAS VEGAS, NEVADA
MGM GRAND GARDEN ARENA, 3799 Las Vegas Boulevard South. Venue opened on December 31, 1993.
AN EVENING WITH RUSH
TICKETS: $40.00 / $95.00 (face value, minus $5.00 finance charge)
ATTENDANCE: 9,613
CAPACITY: 10,165
CONCERT GROSS: $684,745
NOTES: First indoor show of the tour. Cathy and Nick Rich visited Neil before the sound check. The crowd sang the melody during "YYZ," to which Geddy said, "Thanks." Two crew members donned a horse costume and went onstage to feed the dryers. While introducing "Subdivisions," Geddy said, "This

next song comes from our *Subdivisions* album." He then corrected himself.

NEIL: "All considered, it was another really good show, in front of a roaring crowd. A fitting end to what had been a tough but successful West Coast leg."[12]

LAS VEGAS SUN: "Rush makes birthday No. 30 something: The hulking Lifeson scrunched up his eyebrows as he shredded and performed a hilarious 'Pirate Blues' rant midway through his signature tune, 'La Villa Strangiato.' Most importantly, the three lived up to their reputation for sounding as super-tight in concert as they do on album, no easy task given the intricacies of many Rush compositions."

JULY 29, 2004
WEST PALM BEACH, FLORIDA
SOUND ADVICE AMPHITHEATRE, South Florida Fairgrounds, 601–607 Sansburys Way. Venue opened on April 26, 1996.
AN EVENING WITH RUSH
TICKETS: $10.00 (lawn, limited advance Clear Channel promo, sold only in pairs) $32.50 (lawn) / $52.50 (pavilion) / $69.50 (orchestra); face value, minus $4.00 in fees
ATTENDANCE: 12,203
CAPACITY: 19,247
CONCERT GROSS: $486,563
NOTES: Venue aka Coral Sky Amphitheatre. A warm summer rain shower passes through on the band's true "thirtieth birthday" (with Neil on drums), and also Geddy's fifty-first birthday. Two women dressed in revealing pirate outfits walked onstage carrying a cake with candles burning, which they set on the dryers. Fans cheered as it was shown on the screen with the caption "Happy Birthday Geddy." As the first set ended, the flames at the finale to "One Little Victory" shoot so high that they incinerated the bugs and spiders residing in the venue roof. Neil came out for the second set, only to find dead bugs and a few live spiders falling onto his kit. During the beginning of his drum solo, he felt the sharp burning stab of a spider bite on his shoulder. Always the true professional, he didn't miss a beat. "Birthday Blues" was added to the set during "La Villa Strangiato," with Alex lamenting the fact that it wasn't his

birthday, while the band played a slow blues pattern. During intermission, a fan slipped past security and into Neil's dressing room, much to his dismay.

SUN-SENTINEL **(FORT LAUDERDALE):** "Still in the Limelight: The air guitarists went nuts on Thursday night. And their gearless counterparts on drums and bass? Their eyes were rolling up into their heads as they, too, flailed in time to the music: The band that had taught them all how to play was back for a refresher course, and prog-rock pantomime was breaking out everywhere."

JULY 30, 2004
TAMPA, FLORIDA
FORD AMPHITHEATRE, Florida State Fairgrounds, 4802 US Highway 301 North. Venue opened July 25, 2004.
AN EVENING WITH RUSH
TICKETS: $10.00 (lawn, limited advance Clear Channel promo, limit 4) / $25.00 (lawn) / $39.00 (upper pavilion) / $49.00 (pavilion) / $75.00 (orchestra)
ATTENDANCE: 12,486
CAPACITY: 13,107
CONCERT GROSS: $538,760
NOTES: Though not the inaugural concert, Rush was the first band booked at the new venue, and they drew the second largest attendance in its very short history. When tickets were initially put on sale, a naming rights agreement had yet to be finalized, so initial tickets state "Tampa Bay Amphitheatre." By the time of the show, it had become Ford Amphitheatre.

THE LEDGER **(LAKELAND):** "Rush Concert in Tampa Light, Satisfying; 12,000 Fans Attend: Despite Lifeson's misfortunes (and those of Peart), the group continues to perform with a kind of uplifting buoyancy. And it seemed to enjoy key highlights of the show as much as the audience."

AUGUST 1, 2004
ATLANTA, GEORGIA
HI-FI BUYS AMPHITHEATRE, 2002 Lakewood Way. Venue opened on July 11, 1989.
AN EVENING WITH RUSH
TICKETS: $36.00 (lawn) / $75.50 (orchestra)
ATTENDANCE: 8,657
CAPACITY: 15,000
CONCERT GROSS: $505,866

AUGUST 3, 2004
BRISTOW, VIRGINIA
NISSAN PAVILION, 7800 Cellar Door Drive. Venue opened on June 3, 1995.
AN EVENING WITH RUSH
TICKETS: $6.50 (lawn, limited advance Clear Channel promo, sold only in pairs) / $37.50 (lawn) / $50.00 (pavilion) / $85.00 (orchestra); face value, minus $3.50 for parking
ATTENDANCE: 12,571
CAPACITY: 22,575
CONCERT GROSS: $539,221
NOTES: The concert was delayed, allowing fans more time to navigate the DC-area traffic and the long walk from parking lot to the venue. In the morning, Geddy and Alex taped a session at XM radio's Washington, DC studio for XM's "Artist Confidential." After taking part in a Q&A session with fans in the studio, the pair performed acoustic renditions of "Heart Full of Soul" and "Resist." The performance was broadcast on XM Radio the following week.

WASHINGTON POST: "Rush revisited its musical beginnings with covers of songs that influenced the musicians. While the band's interpretations were more straightforward than Rushified (in fact, Lee's vocals dropped from the stratosphere to a more human register), it was clear, here and throughout the rest of this stellar show, that Rush was just having fun with songs it loves to play."

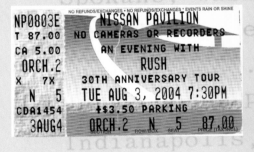

AUGUST 4, 2004
CAMDEN, NEW JERSEY
TWEETER CENTER, 1 Harbour Boulevard. Venue opened on June 2, 1995.
AN EVENING WITH RUSH
TICKETS: $10.00 (lawn, limited advance Clear Channel GetAccess promo, sold only in pairs) $15.00 (lawn, limited advance promo) / $33.00 (lawn) / $58.00 (pavilion) / $82.00 (orchestra)
ATTENDANCE: 10,332
CAPACITY: 24,867

and thousands of ceramic garden gnomes. There was everything from elves to Santa Claus, to parrots, to sheep, to movie characters, there was E.T. . . . all these bizarre gnomes, and you can imagine being that drunk and stepping off the bus to all these gnomes."

HOWARD: "It was just really bizarre, and we finally said, 'we've got to get one of these gnomes.' So we get off the bus, and no one could walk . . . especially Brad. He was just out of his mind. He's not a happy drunk. They wouldn't even serve him at the gnome shop . . . I picked up two gnomes—a sheep and one that looked just like the 'Travelocity' gnome . . . We ended up putting one of the gnomes up on stage for the rest of the tour, in a spot that it would show up on the screen whenever Alex went to do a guitar solo."[20]

BRAD MADIX: "I would emphasize that all of this was happening after the show! I tried to buy a six-foot tall ceramic parrot. The guy refused to deal with me. In fact, every time I made an offer his price went up! To be fair, I was drunk and probably pretty obnoxious. But who else shows up at a roadside gnome stand at that hour? At any rate, when I woke up the next morning . . . I was greeted by a foot-and-a-half tall ceramic sheep . . . As he mentioned, we put it on the stage for the rest of the tour and it frequently featured prominently in the live video portion of the show. Howard dubbed it 'Fleece-or,' as a play on 'By-Tor.'"

SEPTEMBER 27, 2004
HAMBURG, GERMANY
ALSTERDORFER SPORTHALLE, Krochmannstraße 55. Venue opened on November 16, 1968.

AN EVENING WITH RUSH
TICKETS: €40.00, general admission show
ATTENDANCE: 2,824
NOTES: The crew placed a garden gnome next to Alex's pedal board, which made the band laugh as they took the stage. Howard had been worried all week about this gig, because he was only allowed to hang two of his three lighting trusses due to weight restrictions, which dramatically limited his vector capability. Despite the sparse attendance (lowest of the tour), and a third fewer lights, the concert turned

out to be one of the best of the entire *R30* run. During intermission, a friend was overheard saying to Howard: "The show looks great. Let's face it, you could make twenty Christmas floodlights look amazing." The small crowd was really into the show, clapping along and enjoying themselves, most notably on "Resist," where spontaneous audience participation broke out. The performance was so good that Neil used the drum solo in his *Anatomy of a Drum Solo* DVD.

NEIL: "We did play really well that night, and for me, the solo was particularly strong, confident, and inventive—one of the best of the tour. After I ended it with the big gong sample (the only possible conclusion to all that bombast), I climbed down and sat behind the dryers during the acoustic interlude. Gump gave me his rare praise, 'Nice one, man,' and I said, 'Why wasn't that one caught on film?' Gump must have talked to the video crew about that, because at the next show, Bob from the video crew gave me a DVD of the Hamburg show. It was only an arbitrary view from a couple of their cameras, and a rough mix off the board, but still—at least it was captured. (And would appear on *Anatomy of a Drum Solo*, as a 'sidebar.')"[21]

SEPTEMBER 29, 2004
STOCKHOLM, SWEDEN
GLOBE ARENA, Globentorget 2. Venue opened on February 19, 1989.

AN EVENING WITH RUSH
TICKETS: 350.00 / 450.00 / 525.00 kr
ATTENDANCE: 11,265
CAPACITY: 12,800
NOTES: The uniquely shaped venue is the largest spherical building in the world. As the tour neared its finale, crew hijinks were in full effect. During the beginning of "One Little Victory," Alex was pelted with empty plastic bottles thrown from the side of stage right. In "2112: The Temples of Syrinx," an onslaught of pirate balloons was unleashed from stage left.

OCTOBER 1, 2004
ROTTERDAM, SOUTH HOLLAND, THE NETHERLANDS
AHOY SPORTPALEIS, Ahoy-weg 10. Venue opened on January 15, 1971.

AN EVENING WITH RUSH
TICKETS: €39.00 / €43.00
ATTENDANCE: 10,076; sold out.
CONCERT GROSS: €392,119
NOTES: Final date of the *R30* tour.
GEDDY (ONSTAGE): "It's our last night, so some thank yous are in order. First, I'd like to thank the greatest crew in the world. They are just awesome. They're really funny guys too. And all you great fans who've been supportive all these years that we haven't been here. We appreciate you hanging in with us."
THE TELEGRAPH: "Rush phenomenal unfashionable: We can safely label Rush as the most successful cult band of all time. The trio gave a packed Ahoy a memorable exercise that lasted more than three hours. Since Rotterdam was the last stop of a huge world tour, the grand finale was extra emotional and impressive."

MEN
arena

WARNING!
STROBE LIGHTING & PYROTECHNIC EFFECTS ARE IN USE DURING THIS SHOW

1. Neil Peart. *Roadshow: Landscape with Drums.* Rounder Books, 2006.
2. Neil Peart. *Roadshow: Landscape with Drums.* Rounder Books, 2006.
3. Neil Peart. *Roadshow: Landscape with Drums.* Rounder Books, 2006.
4. Neil Peart. *Roadshow: Landscape with Drums.* Rounder Books, 2006.
5. Neil Peart. *Roadshow: Landscape with Drums.* Rounder Books, 2006.
6. Neil Peart. *Roadshow: Landscape with Drums.* Rounder Books, 2006.
7. *Rocky Mountain News,* June 28, 2004.
8. FYE.com, July 9, 2004.
9. Skip Daly. Interview with Brad Madix, June 21, 2012.
10. Neil Peart. *Roadshow: Landscape with Drums.* Rounder Books, 2006.
11. Skip Daly. Interview with Lorne Wheaton, June 22, 2012.
12. Neil Peart. *Roadshow: Landscape with Drums.* Rounder Books, 2006.
13. Neil Peart. *Roadshow: Landscape with Drums.* Rounder Books, 2006.
14. Neil Peart. *Roadshow: Landscape with Drums.* Rounder Books, 2006.
15. Neil Peart. *Roadshow: Landscape with Drums.* Rounder Books, 2006.
16. Bill Banasiewicz. Interview with Howard Ungerleider, September 27, 2004.
17. Douglas Maher. "Producer Sheds Light On Working With Rock Band Rush," *All Headline News,* October 12, 2005.
18. MTV.com, December 28, 2005.
19. Neil Peart. *Roadshow: Landscape with Drums.* Rounder Books, 2006.
20. Eric Hansen. Interview with Howard Ungerleider, July 11, 2012.
21. Neil Peart. *Roadshow: Landscape with Drums.* Rounder Books, 2006.

Chapter 27

THE SNAKES & ARROWS TOUR

Rush returned to the stage for the first time in three years for the *Snakes & Arrows* tour. The trek, consisting of sixty-four shows, took the band across the US and Canada before ending with a run through Europe, including the UK and Scandinavia. The outing was the twenty-fifth-highest-grossing North American tour of 2007 according to *Billboard* magazine, netting $29.6 million in ticket sales (attendance was 517,211 out of a 720,497 capacity over forty-eight shows).

In contrast to the band's typical inclusion of four or five new songs in a set list, the shows featured nine tracks from the *Snakes & Arrows* album: "Far Cry," "Armor and Sword," "Workin' Them Angels," "Spindrift," "The Way the Wind Blows," "Malignant Narcissism," "Hope," "The Larger Bowl," and "The Main Monkey Business." The performances also included the live premiere of "Entre Nous"—a full twenty-seven years after its release on *Permanent Waves*. Other older songs resurrected for the tour included "A Passage to Bangkok," "Digital Man," "Circumstances," and "Mission."

RIGHT: Geddy and Alex at Red Rocks.

OPPOSITE: Alex rocks out onstage.

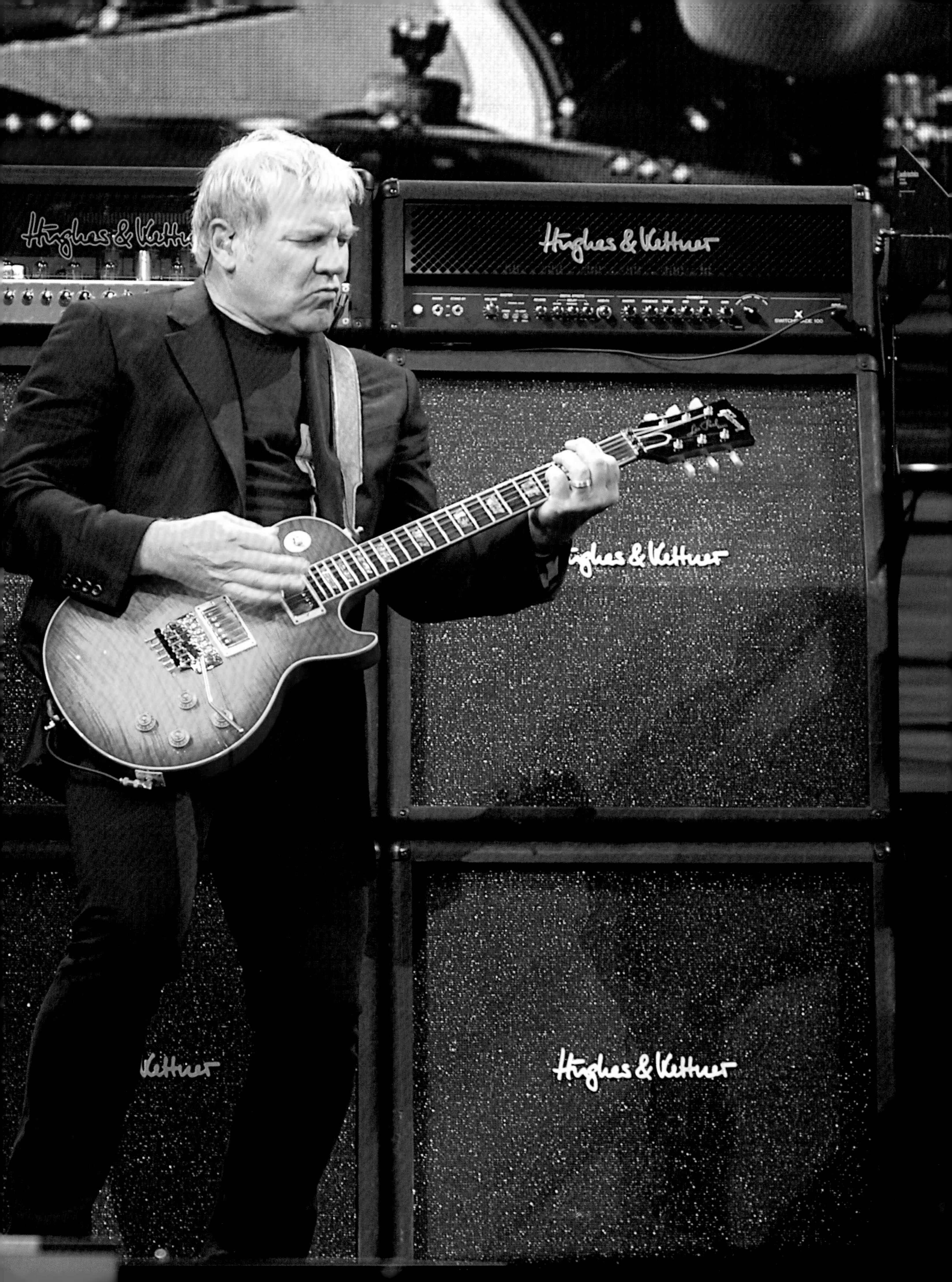
Hughes & Kettner
Hughes & Kettner
Hughes & Kettner

ABOVE: Cincinnati, OH; Geddy singing onstage.

OPPOSITE TOP: Holmdel, NJ; "Big Al's Babes."

OPPOSITE BOTTOM: Holmdel, NJ; The load in.

"After doing the thirtieth-anniversary tour, which was very much a nod to the past, we needed to go back and refresh the whole show," Geddy said. "We felt pretty happy with the new material so we ingested a lot of it, and then went looking for songs we hadn't played in a while. You can play it safe, but I think our fans like to be surprised. They look deeper into the albums than just the radio hits."

The *Snakes & Arrows* staging boasted several newly created pieces of humorous video, including one from fictional Canadian brothers Bob and Doug McKenzie, who, on Geddy's request, filmed an intro to "The Larger Bowl."

"I sent them some titles of our songs and that's the one they chose," Geddy said. Additional humor was provided by *South Park* creators Trey Parker and Matt Stone, via a "Tom Sawyer" intro clip that featured *South Park* characters Cartman, Stan, Kyle, and Kenny playing the song as a garage band named Lil' Rush. (After confusing Tom Sawyer with Huckleberry Finn, an angry Cartman yells, "I am Geddy Lee! And I will sing whatever lyrics I want!")

Furthermore, for the first time ever the band members themselves appeared in the rear screen concert videos—as actors. Similar to the *R30* opening film, the *Snakes & Arrows* intro video began with a dream sequence—this time a dream within a dream that featured Geddy, Alex, Neil, and Geddy again as "Harry Satchel," a kilt-wearing Scot complete with accent and bagpipes (for the first leg of the tour, the video intro for the second set was "The Plane of Dharma," which featured Alex in rare comical form, playing several characters on the *Snakes & Arrows* Leela board). Continuing the Scottish theme, a bagpipe arrangement of "Limelight" was used as the exit music at each show.

Toward the end of the tour, a two-night stand at the Ahoy Sportpaleis in Rotterdam was filmed, and later released as the *Snakes & Arrows Live* CD and DVD. "It was a very relaxed night," Alex said after the second show, "which is unusual, for that kind of 'pressure' night. Whenever we're recording, there's always a sense of tension onstage. But we were really relaxed that night, and I think it was because we had the two nights. We were in the European portion—halfway through it—and we really enjoy traveling through Europe, so we were all in a pretty good headspace and relaxed. And I think it shows—there are moments throughout the DVD where there is interplay between the three of us and the audience—and you sense that we're having fun."

1 LIMELIGHT
2 DIGITAL MAN
3 GHOST OF A CHANCE
4 MISSION
5 FREEWILL
6 MONKEY BUSINESS
7 LARGER BOWL
8 RED BARCHETTA
9 TREES

10 BETWEEN THE WHEELS
11 DREAMLINE

12 FAR CRY
13 WORKING THEM ANGELS
14 ARMOR AND SWORD
15 SPINDRIFT
16 WIND BLOWS
17 SUBDIVISIONS
18 NATURAL SCIENCE
19 WITCH HUNT
20 MALNAR
HOPE

21 THE SPIRIT OF RADIO
22 2112
23 TOM SAWYER

ENCORE
24 ONE LITTLE VICTORY
25 A PASSAGE TO BANGKOK
26 YYZ

ABOVE: Alex using his Omega guitar stand, an invention of his own design.

OPPOSITE TOP: Neil's drumhead graphics for the *Snakes & Arrows* tour.

OPPOSITE BOTTOM: Geddy onstage.

TOUR HISTORY
SNAKES & ARROWS

SET LIST:
"Limelight" (with dream sequence intro video)
"Digital Man"
"Entre Nous"
"Mission"
"Freewill"
"The Main Monkey Business"
"The Larger Bowl" (with McKenzie Brothers intro video)
"Secret Touch"
"Circumstances"
"Between the Wheels"
"Dreamline"
(Intermission: "The Plane of Dharma" intro video)
"Far Cry"
"Workin' Them Angels"
"Armor and Sword"
"Spindrift"
"The Way the Wind Blows"
"Subdivisions"
"Natural Science"
"Witch Hunt"
"Malignant Narcissism"
"De Slagwerker" (drum solo)
"Hope"
"Summertime Blues" / "Distant Early Warning"
"The Spirit of Radio"
"Tom Sawyer" (with *South Park* intro video)
Encore:
"One Little Victory"
"A Passage to Bangkok"
"YYZ"

JUNE 13, 2007
ATLANTA, GEORGIA
HI-FI BUYS AMPHITHEATRE, 2002 Lakewood Way. Venue opened on July 11, 1989.
AN EVENING WITH RUSH
TICKETS: $28.50 (lawn) / $52.00 (reserved) / $77.00 (covered reserved) / $92.00 (orchestra)
ATTENDANCE: 8,998
CAPACITY: 15,949
CONCERT GROSS: $505,255
NOTES: The band was in great form, with only a couple minor flubs. Alex had some issues with his guitar at the beginning of "Between the Wheels." The Guitar Center had a replica R30 drum kit on display, which could be purchased for a mere $30,000. This was Robert "Bucky" Huck's first show as guitar technician.

JUNE 15, 2007
WEST PALM BEACH, FLORIDA
SOUND ADVICE AMPHITHEATRE, South Florida Fairgrounds, 601–607 Sansburys Way. Venue opened on April 26, 1996.
AN EVENING WITH RUSH
TICKETS: $31.00 (lawn) / $52.00 (pavilion) / $72.00 (orchestra); face value, minus fees
ATTENDANCE: 9,432
CAPACITY: 19,238
CONCERT GROSS: $492,908
NOTES: Venue aka Mars Cruzan Amphitheatre. The *Snakes and Arrows* tour offered something new for fans: VIP ticket packages. Though the tickets were priced at a premium, fanatics now had the option of paying more in exchange for a guaranteed seat in the first fifteen rows. The VIP bundles came with a collection of swag, including T-shirt, tour program, and more. Alex, Geddy, and Neil resisted the temptation to follow the practice of other artists and did not sell "meet-and-greets" directly to devotees, though contests and drawings still gave fans a chance at meeting the band.
THE PALM BEACH POST: "Rush Delivers Energetic Music Along With Technical Twists: The show was a loud, energetic collision of impressively colorful computer graphics, the expected but still surprising pyrotechnics, and a nonstop collection of Rush songs, classic and new."

JUNE 16, 2007
TAMPA, FLORIDA
FORD AMPHITHEATRE, Florida State Fairgrounds, 4802 US Highway 301 North. Venue opened July 25, 2004.
AN EVENING WITH RUSH
TICKETS: $26.50 (lawn) / $46.00 (300 level) / $76.00 (100 level, orchestra); face value, minus fees
ATTENDANCE: 13,434
CAPACITY: 19,508
CONCERT GROSS: $605,896
NOTES: Venue aka 1-800-ASK-GARY Amphitheatre. The band performed "Distant Early Warning" in sound check, raising speculation that it would soon be added to the set. Alex, Geddy, and Neil took the stage at 7:45 p.m. in complete daylight, with the sun still blazing. The intro to "One Little Victory" was a bit of a train wreck, with Alex's guitar out of tune. The band stopped playing, with Geddy stating, "A brief pause." Then they continued on. During the tour, just before "Natural Science," Geddy took out a video camera and filmed each audience saying, "Hi Canada!" In a bout of Canadian humor, he sometimes stated that a fictitious prime minister, Jean Poutine, has asked him to do so.
GEDDY (ONSTAGE): "Geez, it's hot here for us Canadians, eh."
TAMPA TRIBUNE: "Audience Gets Quite A Rush from The Past: Lifeson's guitar has plenty of flash but a goodly portion of soul as well. Lee's voice has mellowed over the years to become a versatile and expressive instrument."

JUNE 18, 2007
CHARLOTTE (HARRIS-HOUSTON), NORTH CAROLINA
VERIZON WIRELESS AMPHITHEATRE, 707 Pavilion Boulevard. Venue opened on July 4, 1991.
AN EVENING WITH RUSH
TICKETS: $20.00 (lawn) / $67.00 (pavilion) / $87.00 (orchestra)
ATTENDANCE: 8,287
CAPACITY: 18,700
CONCERT GROSS: $408,908
NOTES: "Distant Early Warning" was performed in sound check on a blazing afternoon. Geddy's new backline used three rotisserie chicken roasters; he jokingly explained that "those are part of the secret to my bass sound. Those roasters give me a hotter and tastier sound."[1]

GEDDY (ONSTAGE): "It's been a few years since we've been down south, and as Canadians you know that we're not used to this weather you guys have. So we're gonna sweat along with you tonight."

JUNE 20, 2007
RALEIGH, NORTH CAROLINA
WALNUT CREEK AMPHITHEATRE, near the I-40/US 64/I-440 (Beltline) interchange. Venue opened on July 4, 1991.
AN EVENING WITH RUSH
TICKETS: $20.00 (lawn) / $56.00 (upper reserved) / $88.00 (lower reserved)
ATTENDANCE: 8,085
CAPACITY: 20,036
CONCERT GROSS: $348,592
NOTES: Venue aka Alltel Pavilion at Walnut Creek. Not to be outdone in the humor department, Alex brought a new set of groupies out on the road—several Barbie dolls (dubbed "Big Al's Babes") who were arranged on stage near Alex's pedals holding Post-it notes with various sayings, courtesy of Bucky.

JUNE 22, 2007
VIRGINIA BEACH, VIRGINIA
VERIZON WIRELESS VIRGINIA BEACH AMPHITHEATER, 3550 Cellar Door Way. Venue opened on May 15, 1996.
AN EVENING WITH RUSH
TICKETS: $20.00 (lawn, limited advance promo) / $36.00 (lawn) / $71.00 (orchestra)
ATTENDANCE: 8,567
CAPACITY: 20,055
CONCERT GROSS: $378,512
NOTES: Venue aka Farm Bureau Live at Virginia Beach. Before the show, Alex hung out with guitarist Stephen Bennett. He had met the "finger-style" player after he performed in Toronto. During the gig, someone in the front of stage right thought it was funny to throw marshmallows at Alex. He was promptly removed from the venue.
THE VIRGINIAN-PILOT: "Rush concert offered quite a range: The classic Rush material was an enjoyable flashback, but the songs performed from *Snakes* were evidence these aging rock stars are exploring new and interesting hemispheres."

JUNE 23, 2007
BRISTOW, VIRGINIA
NISSAN PAVILION, 7800 Cellar Door

Drive. Venue opened on June 3, 1995.
AN EVENING WITH RUSH
TICKETS: $25.50 (lawn) / $40.50 (upper pavilion) / $120.50 (orchestra) / $58.05 (average ticket price); face value, minus $6.00 finance charge
ATTENDANCE: 12,203
CAPACITY: 22,661
CONCERT GROSS: $708,378
NOTES: Fans tailgating heard the echoes of "Distant Early Warning" during sound check. In "Entre Nous," Alex attempted to play the scat guitar line after the lyric, "Drifting in our orbits to a brief eclipse" (thus far on the tour, he had been playing it straight). During "Mission," Geddy stopped twice on the keyboard intro and said "Whoops." Alex closed out the tune with a brilliant solo. On "One Little Victory," Neil started playing the opening drum pattern, then stopped. There was a brief pause, with Geddy saying: "Now we're gonna take a short break," then they restarted the song.
WASHINGTON POST: "While Peart attacked his well-stocked drum kit, Lee and Lifeson commanded the stage with the energy unleashed less often by their peers than the newly signed. The nearly fifty-four-year-old Lee was in incredible voice too, not needing to trade in his high, shrill, loved-or-hated register for lower keys as many aging rock stars must."

JUNE 25, 2007
BURGETTSTOWN, PENNSYLVANIA
POST-GAZETTE PAVILION, 665 Route 18. Venue opened on June 17, 1990.
AN EVENING WITH RUSH
TICKETS: $26.00 (lawn) / $81.00 (orchestra)
ATTENDANCE: 9,257
CAPACITY: 23,070
CONCERT GROSS: $380,157
NOTES: Onstage, Geddy donned a 1979 Pittsburgh Pirates World Champions T-shirt, as he did in Burgettstown three years earlier.
PITTSBURGH POST-GAZETTE: "Rush Quick to Show Love for Local Fans: The band had to be especially heartened by the crowd's reaction to material from the new album. Many fans already knew enough of the lyrics to sing along, and the instrumental 'The Main Monkey Business' drew a roar of recognition during its opening notes."

BEAVER COUNTY TIMES: "More impressive was how strong the new material sounded, particularly 'Working Them Angels' and 'Armor and Sword,' which both received rapturous applause from the pavilion faithful."

JUNE 27, 2007
MANSFIELD, MASSACHUSETTS
TWEETER CENTER FOR THE PERFORMING ARTS, 885 South Main Street. Venue opened on June 13, 1986.
AN EVENING WITH RUSH
TICKETS: $25.50 (lawn) / $40.50 (open-air reserved) / $58.00 (upper pavilion) / $78.00 (lower pavilion) / $55.83 (average ticket price)
ATTENDANCE: 12,358
CAPACITY: 14,245
CONCERT GROSS: $689,995
NOTES: Venue aka Comcast Center. Richard S. Foster, author of "A Nice Morning Drive," attended his first Rush concert.
GEDDY (ONSTAGE): "Boston Red Sox nation! How are you guys out there?"
BOSTON HERALD: "Rush Mines Rarities in Energetic Outing: It was a gold-Rush of goodies new, old, and obscure for longtime fans of Canada's premier progressive trio."

JUNE 29, 2007
SCRANTON, PENNSYLVANIA
TOYOTA PAVILION AT MONTAGE MOUNTAIN, 1000 Montage Mountain Road. Venue opened on June 24, 2000.
AN EVENING WITH RUSH
TICKETS: $30.00 (lawn) / $50.00 (pavilion) / $70.00 (orchestra)
ATTENDANCE: 8,482
CAPACITY: 17,161
CONCERT GROSS: $405,990
THE TIMES-TRIBUNE: "Rush Rocks the Mountain: Despite maddening traffic and a distinct chill in the mountain air, more than 8,500 music fans seemed ecstatic with the performance given by Canadian rock legends Rush on Friday night."

JUNE 30, 2007
SARATOGA SPRINGS, NEW YORK
SARATOGA PERFORMING ARTS CENTER, 108 Avenue of Pines. Venue opened on July 9, 1966.
AN EVENING WITH RUSH

TICKETS: $33.00 (lawn) / $55.00 (pavilion) $90.00 (orchestra)
ATTENDANCE: 10,847
CAPACITY: 25,240
CONCERT GROSS: $525,626
NOTES: This was a special "Kids in Free" concert, with children under twelve gaining free admission with every adult lawn ticket purchased.
ALBANY TIMES UNION: "Timeless Rush Rocks Out At SPAC: Fans were on their feet and playing air guitar from the moment Rush took the stage."

JULY 2, 2007
WANTAGH, NEW YORK
JONES BEACH THEATER, Jones Beach State Park, 1000 Ocean Parkway. Venue dedicated on June 26, 1952.
AN EVENING WITH RUSH
TICKETS: $29.50 (mezzanine) / $60.50 (stadium) / $125.50 (orchestra) / $69.97 (average ticket price)
ATTENDANCE: 12,300
CAPACITY: 13,851
CONCERT GROSS: $860,672
NEWSDAY: "Geddy Lee Takes Rush Album to Jones Beach: Rush's set became one big guys' night, with all the fist-pumping music, goofy humor and stoned philosophizing that have made the band an enduring favorite."

JULY 4, 2007
DARIEN CENTER, NEW YORK
DARIEN LAKE PERFORMING ARTS CENTER, Darien Lake Theme Park, 9993 Allegheny Road. Venue opened on June 15, 1993.
AN EVENING WITH RUSH
TICKETS: $24.12 (limited advance promo, lawn) / $37.50 (lawn) / $59.50 (pavilion) / $79.50 (orchestra)
ATTENDANCE: 7,624
CAPACITY: 21,800
CONCERT GROSS: $429,109
NOTES: After being rehearsed many times during sound checks, "Distant Early Warning" was performed for the first time this tour.
BUFFALO NEWS: "Rush's Power Rock Still Soars: Getting into Rush is a rite of passage for any budding rock musician, so it was not surprising to see plenty of teens and twenty-somethings in attendance. The music they heard should have captured their imaginations. It is redolent of a time when musical

ambition, passion, and a commitment to excellence were not anomalous in rock."

JULY 6, 2007
CAMDEN, NEW JERSEY
TWEETER CENTER, 1 Harbour Boulevard. Venue opened on June 2, 1995.
AN EVENING WITH RUSH
TICKETS: $35.00 (lawn) / $45.00 (upper pavilion) / $65.00 (lower pavilion) / $90.00 (orchestra) / $54.37 (average ticket price)
ATTENDANCE: 12,180
CAPACITY: 24,956
CONCERT GROSS: $662,267
NOTES: Venue aka Susquehanna Bank Center.

JULY 8, 2007
HOLMDEL, NEW JERSEY
PNC BANK ARTS CENTER, Exit 116, Garden State Parkway. Venue opened on June 15, 1968.
AN EVENING WITH RUSH
TICKETS: $31.00 (lawn) / $61.00 (pavilion) / $81.00 (loge and orchestra) / $52.34 (average ticket price)
ATTENDANCE: 12,014
CAPACITY: 16,996
CONCERT GROSS: $628,792

JULY 9, 2007
UNCASVILLE, CONNECTICUT
MOHEGAN SUN ARENA, Mohegan Sun Casino, 1 Mohegan Sun Boulevard. Venue opened on September 25, 2001.
AN EVENING WITH RUSH
TICKETS: $65.00 / $85.00
ATTENDANCE: 7,793; sold out
CONCERT GROSS: $452,900
NOTES: During the first leg of sixteen shows, Neil logged 7,257 miles of motorcycling.
HARTFORD COURANT: "Mixing Old and New, Rush Enraptures Rabid Fans: The silliness of a Rush show is an almost necessary counterbalance to the seriousness of the music, both in theme and complexity."

JULY 18, 2007
CALGARY, ALBERTA
PENGROWTH SADDLEDOME, 555 Saddledome Rise SE. Venue opened October 15, 1983.
AN EVENING WITH RUSH
TICKETS: $65.50 / $85.50 CAD
ATTENDANCE: 11,006
CAPACITY: 12,026
CONCERT GROSS: $792.316 ($843,203 CAD)
THE CALGARY SUN: "Convincing Rush of Tunes: While I did not gain a new love of Rush, the thousands of fans chanting the band's name at the end of the night assured me, or rather convinced me, they rocked."

JULY 20, 2007
AUBURN, WASHINGTON
WHITE RIVER AMPHITHEATRE, Muckleshoot Indian Reservation, 40601 Auburn Enumclaw Road. Venue opened on June 14, 2003.
AN EVENING WITH RUSH
TICKETS: $19.50 (lawn) / $39.50 (upper pavilion) / $49.40 (lower pavilion) / $69.50 (box) / $92.00 (orchestra) / $46.64 (average ticket price)
ATTENDANCE: 13,689
CAPACITY: 15,552
CONCERT GROSS: $638,462
NOTES: Torrential afternoon rains left the grounds flooded in spots.
SEATTLE POST-INTELLIGENCER: "A Disappointingly Delightful Evening with Rush: Delighting because the musicianship, something that is never of poor quality with Rush, was spectacular. Disappointing because too much material from the band's latest album, *Snakes and Arrows*, made its way into a set list that should have included more rarities and fan favorites."

JULY 21, 2007
RIDGEFIELD, WASHINGTON
THE AMPHITHEATER AT CLARK COUNTY, 17200 NE Delfel Road. Venue opened on July 10, 2003.
AN EVENING WITH RUSH
TICKETS: $35.00 (lawn) / $57.50 (pavilion) / $79.50 (orchestra) / $52.97 (average ticket price)
ATTENDANCE: 10,986
CAPACITY: 13,188
CONCERT GROSS: $581,898
NOTES: *The Columbian* states attendance

as being 11,376, the venue's largest crowd of the year, thus far. Porcupine Tree guitarist John Wesley walked onstage and basted the chickens in the rotisserie, and also the one hanging from Neil's kit.

THE COLUMBIAN (VANCOUVER, WA): "Local Concert Showed Why Rush Remains Relevant: When you have some of the finest artists in rock on the stage, it can be fascinating to view them in their medium. For Rush, that medium has remained largely unchanged, the result of an uncompromising dedication to who they are and what they do."

JULY 23, 2007
HOLLYWOOD, CALIFORNIA
HOLLYWOOD BOWL, 2301 North Highland Avenue. Historic Venue opened on July 11, 1922.
AN EVENING WITH RUSH
TICKETS: $45.00 / $177.00 (average ticket price: $73.12)
ATTENDANCE: 14,696
CAPACITY: 17,563
CONCERT GROSS: $1,074,586
NOTES: John Wesley accompanied Neil and Michael for the motorcycle ride to the gig. *Extra*'s Adam Weissler interviewed Alex and Geddy backstage. As had been the case for most of the run, the gig began in complete daylight. Tool guitarist Adam Jones and Foo Fighters drummer Taylor Hawkins were in attendance.
GEDDY: "You walk around these hallways, and you see these great pictures of shows from the 20s and shows from the 40s, and that's very cool. That's probably the coolest thing about playing this venue . . . that it's got this historic aspect to it that many venues we play don't have."[2]
VARIETY: "The band does take a significant risk by starting the second set with five new songs that dealt largely with faith and spirituality; galvanizing numbers like the closers 'Spirit of Radio' and 'Tom Sawyer,' if spread throughout the set, would have made the show more of a crowd-pleaser."

JULY 25, 2007
IRVINE, CALIFORNIA
VERIZON WIRELESS AMPHITHEATER, 8808 Irvine Center Drive. Venue opened on August 21, 1981.
AN EVENING WITH RUSH
TICKETS: $28.50 (lawn) / $86.00

(pavilion) / $121.50 (orchestra) / $65.00 (average ticket price); orchestra seats sold out
ATTENDANCE: 10,347
CAPACITY: 11,563
CONCERT GROSS: $682,819
NOTES: Several retired baseball players from the Angels were in attendance including: Mike Witt, Mark Langston, and Tim Salmon.
THE ORANGE COUNTY REGISTER: "Rush Lives Up to The Hype: The Canadian hard-rock trio blends virtuosity and humor in an immensely satisfying show."

JULY 27, 2007
PHOENIX, ARIZONA
CRICKET WIRELESS PAVILION, 2121 North 83rd Avenue. Venue opened on November 11, 1990.
AN EVENING WITH RUSH
TICKETS: $30.50.00 (lawn) / $55.50 (pavilion) / $75.50 (orchestra); price included parking and fees
ATTENDANCE: 12,276
CAPACITY: 16,066
CONCERT GROSS: $485,795
NOTES: Venue aka Desert Sky Pavilion. A police officer was shot and killed at a nearby check-cashing store just prior to the start of the concert. Afterward, all exits were closed except one, as police searched cars for the shooting suspect, whom they did eventually capture. Many fans waited several hours to exit but were understanding of the situation.
DAVE BURNETTE: "While we were in Phoenix, I took off on my bike during the show and ran down the street about a half a mile to a convenience store to get some cigarettes. As I came out, I noticed a police car pulling into the parking lot. I got on my bike and went back to the venue. Within five minutes after getting back, four or five policemen in jumpsuits were in the backstage area, the venue went into lockdown, and there were helicopters overhead. What had happened was the police officer that I saw pull into the parking lot was shot and killed there. The whole venue went into lockdown. The audience didn't know anything, but backstage we were well aware of it because they had the whole area cordoned off to find this guy. It took some time to get out of there while they were trying to find him, which they did. The next time we were in Phoenix, the

band presented a memorial plaque to his family. Michael Mosbach had a lot to do with that. It let the police department know that as an organization that we did care; that we were touched by it and we were aware of what was going on."[3]
ARIZONA REPUBLIC: "Rush Rocks the West Valley Amidst Tragedy: During the concert, the only indication of any trouble was the police copters circling overhead. The band gave a passionate three-hour performance, surprisingly, the high points were the songs from *Snakes and Arrows* like the bluesy 'The Way the Wind Blows' and the instrumental 'The Main Monkey Business.'"

JULY 28, 2007
LAS VEGAS, NEVADA
MGM GRAND GARDEN ARENA, 3799 Las Vegas Boulevard South. Venue opened on December 31, 1993.
AN EVENING WITH RUSH
TICKETS: $50.00 / $75.00 / $125.00; face value, minus $6.00 finance charge
ATTENDANCE: 10,002
CAPACITY: 11,034
CONCERT GROSS: $922,675
NOTES: According to the *Las Vegas Review-Journal*, "About 100 stagehands are assigned to tonight's show. They work various eight-hour shifts on a freelance basis, earning $20 to $26 an hour. Provided today by the MGM Grand Garden and an independent valley contractor called Rhino Staging, they're the schleppers. A roadie's job is basically to bark orders at them."
THE LAS VEGAS REVIEW-JOURNAL: "Trio's Virtuosity Delivers It Hard, Easy: During a teeth-rattling 'Freewill,' Lifeson's solos ricocheted around the arena like gunfire bouncing off of metal sheeting, while Lee plucked out acrobatic bass lines that practically swung from the rafters."

JULY 30, 2007
CHULA VISTA, CALIFORNIA
COORS AMPHITHEATRE, 2050 Entertainment Circle. Venue opened on July 21, 1998.
AN EVENING WITH RUSH
TICKETS: $28.50 / $71.00 / $96.00
ATTENDANCE: 8,959
CAPACITY: 9,831
CONCERT GROSS: $412,235

AUGUST 1, 2007
MOUNTAIN VIEW, CALIFORNIA
SHORELINE AMPHITHEATRE, One Amphitheatre Parkway. Venue opened on July 5, 1986.
AN EVENING WITH RUSH
TICKETS: $32.50 (lawn) / $42.50 (pavilion) / $79.50 (orchestra); orchestra seats sold out
ATTENDANCE: 9,101
CAPACITY: 11,000
CONCERT GROSS: $507,546
NOTES: Geddy took the stage donning a T-shirt with a motorcyclist on it, which read "Don't ever stop doing wheelies."
CONTRA COSTA TIMES: "Rush Classics, Big Drum Solos, And Peart-Fu At Shoreline: Most of Rush's contemporaries have long since joined the 'greatest hits' trail, [with] fans only interested in hearing the old stuff. Rush listeners, however, are a different breed. These folks are maniacal in their enthusiasm for the band, boasting the kind of passion that one normally sees from costumed Trekkies at a sci-fi convention. They have yet to come to grips with the fact that Rush ranks as a 'classic' rock act, instead choosing to see the band as utterly contemporary."

AUGUST 3, 2007
CONCORD, CALIFORNIA
SLEEP TRAIN PAVILION, 2000 Kirker Pass Road. Venue opened on May 16, 1975.
AN EVENING WITH RUSH
TICKETS: $25.00 (lawn) / $41.00 (upper pavilion) / $86.00 (orchestra)
ATTENDANCE: 9,775
CAPACITY: 10,916
CONCERT GROSS: $529,150
NOTES: Venue aka Chronicle Pavilion.

AUGUST 4, 2007
WHEATLAND, CALIFORNIA
SLEEP TRAIN AMPHITHEATRE, 2677 Forty Mile Road. Venue opened on June 10, 2000.
AN EVENING WITH RUSH
TICKETS: $29.00 (lawn) / $73.50 (orchestra)
ATTENDANCE: 8,428
CAPACITY: 9,000
CONCERT GROSS: $409,880
CHICO ENTERPRISE-RECORD: "Progressive rock dinosaurs Rush not dead yet: To their credit, the threesome has remained just

that. Never have they resorted to bringing in an additional musician to fill out the sound for a tour. Lee energetically bounced around stage and his high alto voice sounded good and unstrained. Lifeson showed that he still has quick and nimble fingers."

AUGUST 6, 2007
WEST VALLEY CITY, UTAH
USANA AMPHITHEATRE, 5150 South 6055 West. Venue opened on July 3, 2003.
AN EVENING WITH RUSH
TICKETS: $32.50 (lawn) / $50.00 (pavilion) / $75.00 (orchestra)
ATTENDANCE: 10,971
CAPACITY: 14,500
CONCERT GROSS: $492,950
NOTES: Much to Howard's dismay, the concert started in bright sunlight, washing out the lighting, with Alex donning sunglasses. The band delivered one of the best gigs of the tour. During "Digital Man," the crowd cheered as Geddy sang the line "Love to spend the night in Zion," probably because many fans visited the nearby Zion National Park, which has nothing to do with the lyric.
SALT LAKE TRIBUNE: "Rush gives fans their money's worth: The classic-rock trio overwhelmed a near-packed USANA with its musical dexterity and more than three hours of memorable hard-rock."
THE DESERET MORNING NEWS: "Old guys' deliver a real Rush: As is the standard with Rush shows, the lighting, lasers, pyrotechnics and large digital screens in the rear of the stage complemented the music, making for a full assault on both the ears and eyes. Unfortunately, the west-facing USANA stage doesn't get dark until after 9 p.m."
THE DAILY HERALD (PROVO): "Rush gets its concert moxie aura on: For those scoring at home, only nine of twenty-seven songs Monday were repeats from the show three years ago. Rush showed that an old dog is capable of learning new tricks. I only wish others in the rock and roll kennel would follow suit."

AUGUST 8, 2007
MORRISON, COLORADO
RED ROCKS AMPHITHEATRE, 18300 West Alameda Parkway. Historic venue dedicated on June 15, 1941.
AN EVENING WITH RUSH

TICKETS: $48.00 / $75.50 / $95.50
ATTENDANCE: 8,753; sold out
CONCERT GROSS: $674,504
NOTES: Ticket sales went SRO well in advance. Neil received a threat from a deranged "fan," so security was on red alert. In "Mission," Neil had some technical issues with the MalletKAT during the marimba solo.

AUGUST 11, 2007
DALLAS, TEXAS
SMIRNOFF MUSIC CENTRE, Fair Park, 1818 First Avenue. Venue opened on July 23, 1988.
AN EVENING WITH RUSH
TICKETS: $35.50 (lawn) / $75.00 (orchestra)
ATTENDANCE: 13,366
CAPACITY: 16,500
CONCERT GROSS: $690,086
NOTES: The outdoor gig was performed in sweltering, record heat. The high of 104 degrees was the hottest day of the entire year in Dallas. Alex changed his shirt three times during the show, attempting to keep his strings dry.
GEDDY (ONSTAGE): "I'm not gonna complain about the heat, I know we're all hot here."
DALLAS MORNING NEWS: "Rush's Signature Humor, Talent Pack Smirnoff: Smirnoff's large quota (15K for one band—impressive) of disciples was treated to a set list with surprises and a dialed-in, transcendental sense of musicianship."

AUGUST 12, 2007
SELMA, TEXAS
VERIZON WIRELESS AMPHITHEATRE, 16765 Lookout Road. Venue opened on May 19, 2001.
AN EVENING WITH RUSH
TICKETS: $26.00 (lawn) / $55.00 (pavilion) / $76.00 (orchestra)
ATTENDANCE: 11,469
CAPACITY: 15,155
CONCERT GROSS: $527,568
NOTES: A steady drizzle didn't dampen the spirits of the fans on the lawn. On the way to the gig, Neil hit a deer with his motorcycle. He miraculously escaped injury, though the deer was not so lucky.
NEIL: "Thankfully I was only going about forty miles per hour when a blur of brown dashed right in front of me, so sudden that my first sight of the deer was when

my front wheel hit it squarely. The handle-bar wobbled between my hands and the adrenaline began to surge, as time seemed to hang suspended. The small deer was shunted aside, and I rode on for a few seconds, still taking in what had just happened—and already marveling that I was still upright. I looked in my mirrors and saw Michael turn around. Riding behind me, he had seen me hit the deer, felt the start of fear you always get for your riding partner, then saw that I was still riding. He passed the deer where it lay twisted on the road, flailing its legs, its back obviously broken. He knew what he had to do. I pulled up behind where he'd parked his bike, right on the road (we hadn't seen a car for many miles). I'll never forget the sight of Michael standing in the middle of the road in his riding suit, helmet flipped up, taking out his 40 caliber Glock 23, holding it in both hands, and taking careful aim. I heard the sharp report even through my earplugs, and saw the poor mangled deer give one final jerk. Michael took hold of its legs and dragged it into the bushes beside the road. Everything was quiet for an awful moment. Michael walked back to his bike and said, 'That's what I was always taught to do—stop its suffering.' I nodded agreement."[4]

SAN ANTONIO EXPRESS-NEWS: "Feel the Rush: the trio delivered what the fans came looking for—intense music, maximum volume and solid, melodic guitar hooks—for almost three hours."

AUGUST 14, 2007
THE WOODLANDS, TEXAS
C. W. MITCHELL PAVILION, 2005 Lake Robbins Drive. Venue opened on April 27, 1990.
AN EVENING WITH RUSH
TICKETS: $42.50 / $90.00
ATTENDANCE: 11,904
CAPACITY: 14,490
CONCERT GROSS: $646,748
NOTES: After thirty-two shows, Neil had logged 13,211 motorcycle miles.
NEIL: "The tour continues to go pretty well. The audiences have been wonderfully large and unbelievably appreciative, and the shows themselves have been going smoothly for us and our crew. But . . . just now counting up what we've done, and what we still have to do, I must admit to feeling a little apprehension at the realization that we are only now at the

halfway point of the tour. We've done 32 shows and have exactly that many to go. It seems a lot—in both directions."[5]

AUGUST 23, 2007
BONNER SPRINGS, KANSAS
VERIZON WIRELESS AMPHITHEATRE, 633 North 130th Street. Venue opened on June 5, 1984.
AN EVENING WITH RUSH
TICKETS: $22.25 (limited advance promotion, lawn) / $34.50 (lawn) / $52.00 (pavilion) / $77.00 (orchestra)
ATTENDANCE: 8,104
CAPACITY: 12,500
CONCERT GROSS: $406,416
NOTES: While in the Kansas City area, Geddy visited the Negro Leagues Baseball Museum and was thrilled by the experience. The venue stage was not very high, causing the lighting trusses to hang low. While this created an intense lighting effect for the fans in the front, it partially obstructed the video screens for the audience further back.
THE KANSAS CITY STAR: "Rush at Amphitheater: A string of songs from the new album created a lull in the middle of the show. People in the front section mostly stayed standing but with less rocking, and a lot of people in the second tier were sitting. The show felt a little leisurely during that stretch."

AUGUST 24, 2007
MARYLAND HEIGHTS, MISSOURI
VERIZON WIRELESS AMPHITHEATER, 14141 Riverport Drive. Venue opened on June 14, 1991.
AN EVENING WITH RUSH
TICKETS: $26.00 (lawn) / $81.00 (orchestra); face value minus $6.00 finance charge
ATTENDANCE: 12,135
CAPACITY: 16,500
CONCERT GROSS: $490,721
NOTES: Venue aka Riverport Amphitheatre, UMB Bank Pavilion. A rainy day cleared up just in time for the gig, but the grounds were saturated. For a second straight night, the stage was low, and so were the lighting trusses.

AUGUST 26, 2007
NOBLESVILLE, INDIANA
VERIZON WIRELESS MUSIC CENTER, 12880 East 146th Street. Venue opened on May 20, 1989.

AN EVENING WITH RUSH
TICKETS: $35.00 (lawn) / $51.50 / (upper pavilion) / $83.00 (lower pavilion); price included fees
ATTENDANCE: 9,599
CAPACITY: 12,500
CONCERT GROSS: $424,449
INDIANAPOLIS STAR: "Rush Raises Questions About Human Condition: It wasn't a concert designed to pacify casual fans, as soul-searching lyrics from drummer Neil Peart guided the program while several hit singles didn't make the twenty-eight-song set."

AUGUST 28, 2007
CLARKSTON, MICHIGAN
DTE ENERGY MUSIC THEATRE, 7774 Sashabaw Road. Venue opened on June 25, 1972.
AN EVENING WITH RUSH
TICKETS: $32.00 (lawn) / $66.50 (pavilion) / $97.00 (orchestra)
ATTENDANCE: 11,384
CAPACITY: 13,213
CONCERT GROSS: $602,300
THE OAKLAND PRESS (PONTIAC, MI): "Skill, Humor Mix at Rush Concert: All combined for an exhaustive but invigorating night, one on which it proved possible to smile at the same time your jaw is dropping in respectful awe of a rare display of exceptional musicality."

AUGUST 30, 2007
CUYAHOGA FALLS, OHIO
BLOSSOM MUSIC CENTER, 1145 West Steels Corners Road. Venue opened on July 19, 1968.
AN EVENING WITH RUSH
TICKETS: $30.00 (lawn) / $75.00 (orchestra); price included $6.00 in fees
ATTENDANCE: 10,527
CAPACITY: 13,491
CONCERT GROSS: $449,578
NOTES: Geddy, wearing an Ohio State University T-shirt, had some keyboard issues during "Subdivisions." The first lead run in the song was not heard, replaced by some feedback. The problem was quickly fixed by the crew in time for the second lead.
THE PLAIN DEALER: "Rush Digs Deep to Deliver Ultimate Geek Jam At Blossom: This wasn't a show for the casual Rush admirer. Lee, Lifeson, and Peart eschewed some of their most popular standbys in

favor of lesser-known selections. The more obscure the song, the louder hard-core fans cheered."

SEPTEMBER 1, 2007
CINCINNATI, OHIO
RIVERBEND MUSIC CENTER, 6295 Kellogg Avenue. Venue opened on July 4, 1984.
AN EVENING WITH RUSH
TICKETS: $32.50 (lawn) / $58.25 (pavilion) / $78.25 (orchestra); price included $3.25 parking fee
ATTENDANCE: 10,776
CAPACITY: 16,435
CONCERT GROSS: $479,040
NOTES: A fired-up crowd greeted the band and serenaded them throughout. The vocal accompaniment does not go unnoticed by Geddy, who said, "You guys were awesome tonight!"

SEPTEMBER 2, 2007
COLUMBUS, OHIO
GERMAIN AMPHITHEATER, 2200 Polaris Parkway. Venue opened on June 18, 1994.
AN EVENING WITH RUSH
TICKETS: $30.50 (lawn) / $51.00 / $81.00 (orchestra); face value, minus $6.00 finance charge
ATTENDANCE: 10,241
CAPACITY: 12,891
CONCERT GROSS: $463,661
NOTES: QFM-96 Birthday Bash! Fifteen days after this gig, the venue closed its doors for the final time, with Rush being the second-to-last band to ever play there. Upon leaving the concert, a fifty-five-year-old woman was killed by a hit-and-run driver while crossing Polaris Parkway.
COLUMBUS DISPATCH: "Rush's Engine Still Running Strong: The most consistent moments last night came during the instrumentals, when power and improvisation were sometimes balanced with sensitivity and soul."

SEPTEMBER 6, 2007
MILWAUKEE, WISCONSIN
MARCUS AMPHITHEATER, Henry Maier Festival Park, Summerfest grounds, 200 North Harbor Drive. Venue opened on June 25, 1987.
AN EVENING WITH RUSH
TICKETS: $27.20 (lawn) / $41.20 (rear reserved) / $67.20 (front reserved)

ATTENDANCE: 12,100
CAPACITY: 13,299
CONCERT GROSS: $516,155
MILWAUKEE JOURNAL SENTINEL: "Rush Still Roars with Rugged Appeal: One of the downsides of the music is that it's fairly humorless. Wisely, the band side-stepped that problem by using video to inject some levity."
ONMILWAUKEE.COM: "Rush delivers a knockout show: Rush doesn't just endure; they thrive, wow, amaze and time after time show why the term 'power trio' should have been coined just for them."

SEPTEMBER 8, 2007
TINLEY PARK, ILLINOIS
FIRST MIDWEST BANK AMPHITHEATRE, 19100 Ridgeland Avenue. Venue opened on June 2, 1990.
AN EVENING WITH RUSH
TICKETS: $24.00 (lawn) / $53.75 (lower pavilion) / $83.75 (orchestra); price included $6.00 parking fee
ATTENDANCE: 16,613
CAPACITY: 18,174
CONCERT GROSS: $847,695
NOTES: Venue aka Tweeter Center.
CHICAGO SUN-TIMES: "Oldies, Goodies, and More: Rush Doesn't Disappoint: Lifeson's delicate acoustic 'Hope' proved as intoxicating as his angular riffs during 'YYZ' were invigorating. Peart's drum solo mixed dizzying technique and industrial crunch."

SEPTEMBER 9, 2007
ST. PAUL, MINNESOTA
XCEL ENERGY CENTER, 199 Kellogg Boulevard West. Venue opened on September 29, 2000.
AN EVENING WITH RUSH
TICKETS: $42.50 / $60.00 / $85.00
ATTENDANCE: 11,402
CAPACITY: 14,956
CONCERT GROSS: $752,618
NOTES: During "Circumstances," Neil went out on a limb, adding an extended, improvised fill going into the break. Unfortunately, he and Alex got a bit lost exiting that same section.

ST. PAUL PIONEER PRESS: "A Very Back-to-the-Future Rush Delivery: Split into two sections, the show boasted a whopping nine of the thirteen songs found on the new *Snakes and Arrows* album. Just try to find any arena-level performer who, more than three decades into a career, could pull off such a move—and have the fans following every last moment."

SEPTEMBER 12, 2007
LONDON, ONTARIO
JOHN LABATT CENTRE, 99 Dundas Street. Venue opened on October 11, 2002.
AN EVENING WITH RUSH
TICKETS: $57.25 / $81.25 CAD
ATTENDANCE: 8,608
CAPACITY: 8,936
CONCERT GROSS: $627,749 CAD
NOTES: Neil's fifty-fifth birthday. He began his "De Slagwerker" drum solo with "Wipe Out," as a nod to the first song he ever learned to play on the drums.
THE LONDON FREE PRESS: "The great Canadian band entertained 8,700 fans at the John Labatt Centre: Having bitched about lousy drum solos, I bow to Peart who showed magnificent command of dynamics and rhythms over his enormous set, including its electronic percussion tools."

SEPTEMBER 14, 2007
QUEBEC CITY, QUEBEC
COLISEE PEPSI, 250 Boulevard Wilfrid-Hamel. Venue opened on December 8, 1949.
AN EVENING WITH RUSH
TICKETS: $44.50 / $88.50 CAD
ATTENDANCE: 6,604
CAPACITY: 7,000
CONCERT GROSS: $510,918 CAD
NOTES: Due to new fire codes in Quebec, the pyro was extremely limited, with just small amounts of fire present during "One Little Victory" only. A fired-up crowd yelled and cheered throughout the entire gig. Alex got a bit lost during the intro to "Freewill," but quickly recovered. At the beginning of "Armor and Sword," Lerxst came in a measure late. Segments were filmed for the *Backstage Secrets* documentary.

SEPTEMBER 15, 2007
MONTREAL, QUEBEC
CENTRE BELL, 1909 Avenue des

Canadiens-de-Montréal. Venue opened on March 16, 1996.

AN EVENING WITH RUSH
TICKETS: $59.50 / $89.50 CAD
ATTENDANCE: 11,662
CAPACITY: 12,000
CONCERT GROSS: $1,007,423 CAD
NOTES: No pyro during "Witch Hunt," and only minimal fire on "One Little Victory."
GEDDY (ONSTAGE): "Merci. I'm making a movie of you, Montréal. But I need your help. On the count of three, would you say, 'Vive les habitants.'"
MONTREAL GAZETTE: "Rush Takes Crowd for a Ride: The recent songs fit comfortably alongside the old, and fans seemed to delight in hearing them all, cheering for the second-set opener 'Far Cry' like it was an old favorite."

SEPTEMBER 17, 2007
NEW YORK, NEW YORK
MADISON SQUARE GARDEN, 4 Pennsylvania Plaza (8th Avenue between 31st and 33rd Streets). Historic venue opened on February 11, 1968.
AN EVENING WITH RUSH
TICKETS: $45.00 / $75.00 / $125.00; face value, minus $4.50 finance charge
ATTENDANCE: 11,786
CAPACITY: 12,125
CONCERT GROSS: $1,022,675
THE NEW YORK TIMES: "Arena Rock with A Worldview and All the Flash Trimmings: Mr. Lee uses his high, cutting voice to sing philosophical lyrics, calling for heroic honesty in a corrupt and shallow world: cultish conviction to defy scoffers."
NEIL: "As our traveling circus of band and crew has continued to mount and perform our roadshow almost fifty times now, earning that gas money has continued to be a difficult, physically demanding job. As always seems to happen in the middle of every tour, when the routine grinds on into the third and fourth months, the mood at work among band and crew can sometimes sink to a tense, dark state of mind that combines homesickness, fatigue, edginess, frustration, friction, physical pain, and a feeling that threatens to approach 'fed up.' Still, most of us 'keep the sunny side up.' Daily smiles and nightly jokes leave the potential for tedium and—most

important—the band has continued to play at a high standard, supported by a first-rate and highly entertaining crew."[6]

SEPTEMBER 19, 2007
TORONTO, ONTARIO
AIR CANADA CENTRE, 40 Bay Street. Venue dedicated on February 19, 1999.
AN EVENING WITH RUSH
TICKETS: $55.50 / $121.25 CAD
ATTENDANCE: 11,950; sold out
CONCERT GROSS: $605.304 USD
NOTES: One fan brings his seventy-nine-year-old mother to the show. Afterward, she commented: "I liked their old stuff better."
TORONTO STAR: "Rush Saves the Best for Last: Against other so-called progressive rock survivors, Rush remains a curiosity—well-informed and convincingly concerned about the state of the world, philosophical, humanistic, and seriously studious about their art. They constantly challenge themselves with an array of difficult puzzles, absurd chord progressions, melodic non sequiturs and ever-shifting time signatures, while working in a milieu that more often than not offers little more than smoke and mirrors."

SEPTEMBER 21, 2007
KANATA, ONTARIO
SCOTIABANK PLACE, 1000 Palladium Drive. Venue opened on January 15, 1996.
AN EVENING WITH RUSH
TICKETS: $39.50 / $49.50 / $75.50 CAD
ATTENDANCE: 8,558
CAPACITY: 9,438
CONCERT GROSS: $570,113 CAD
NOTES: Both the *Ottawa Sun* and the *Ottawa Citizen* state attendance as a 10,200 sell-out. Venue aka Corel Centre. Geddy had a couple of senior moments early in the show. He introduced the new album as *Snakes and Ladders*, but quickly recovered, saying: "*Snakes and Arrows*, whatever the hell it's called. I can't remember, I'm getting so old." He then proceeded to announce "Mission" as "Hold Your Fire." Segments were filmed for the *Backstage Secrets* documentary.
GEDDY (ONSTAGE): "This is my camera. I'm making a special documentary of you. I've been doing this for the whole

tour. Down in the United States, the crowd has been kind enough to send us a message saying, 'Hi Canada!' So, I wonder if you could help me out tonight and send out a message, and I think it appropriately should be 'Take Off, Eh!' Beauty!"
THE OTTAWA CITIZEN: "Old Masters Rush Present a Quality Show: You have to respect an act that has such high standards for performance and production."

SEPTEMBER 22, 2007
TORONTO, ONTARIO
AIR CANADA CENTRE, 40 Bay Street
AN EVENING WITH RUSH
TICKETS: $55.50 / $121.25 CAD
ATTENDANCE: 10,304
CAPACITY: 11,950
CONCERT GROSS: $592,306 USD
NOTES: Final North American date on the *Snakes and Arrows* tour. Alex attempted the scat guitar part in "Entre Nous" after the lyric "Drifting in our orbits to a brief eclipse."
GEDDY (ONSTAGE): "Hello hometown! Nice to be back here for our second night this week. It's like a big club for us."

OCTOBER 3, 2007
GLASGOW, SCOTLAND
SCOTTISH EXHIBITION AND CONFERENCE CENTRE, Hall 4, Exhibition Way
AN EVENING WITH RUSH
TICKETS: £39.00 / £45.00
THE HERALD: "Rush, SECC: The almost-epic 'Natural Science' was given a rare outing and they finished with the instrumental 'YYZ,' backed by a bouncing, delirious, throng. The hall cleared to the strains of Harry Satchel playing 'Limelight' on the bagpipes. Mission accomplished."

OCTOBER 5, 2007
NEWCASTLE UPON TYNE, ENGLAND
METRO RADIO ARENA, Arena Way. Venue opened on November 18, 1995.
AN EVENING WITH RUSH
TICKETS: £39.00 / £45.00
NOTES: Rush's first Newcastle appearance since June 13, 1980.

NEIL: "At two of those British venues we looked out all night at a scowling female, front-row center, each with her fingers in her ears for the whole show. Hardly inspiring for them or us!"[7]

OCTOBER 6, 2007
SHEFFIELD, ENGLAND
HALLAM FM ARENA, Broughton Lane. Venue opened on May 30, 1991.
AN EVENING WITH RUSH
TICKETS: £39.00 / £45.00
NOTES: Venue aka Motorpoint Arena.
SOUTH YORKSHIRE STAR: "Rush, Hallam FM Arena: Through it all Rush remains a one-off, a rare example of ability and inimitable style over fashion with a peerless loyalty to match."

OCTOBER 9–10, 2007
LONDON, ENGLAND
WEMBLEY ARENA, Arena Square at Engineers Way. Venue opened on August 4, 1934.
AN EVENING WITH RUSH
TICKETS: £39.00 / £45.00
NOTES: Alex and Geddy were interviewed backstage by James Dean Bradfield and Nicky Wire (both huge Rush fans) of *Manic Street Preachers* for *Classic Rock* magazine on October 9.
THE GUARDIAN: "Rush, Wembley Arena: Rush play for a very, very long time. This is due in no small part to the fact that the aging Canadian trio is essentially their own support act."

OCTOBER 12, 2007
BIRMINGHAM, WEST MIDLANDS, ENGLAND
NATIONAL EXHIBITION CENTRE ARENA, Pendigo Way and Perimeter Road, Marston Green. Venue opened on December 5, 1980.
AN EVENING WITH RUSH
TICKETS: £39.00 / £45.00
ATTENDANCE: 11,077
CAPACITY: 11,932
CONCERT GROSS: £445,989

OCTOBER 14, 2007
MANCHESTER, ENGLAND
MANCHESTER EVENING NEWS ARENA, corner of Trinity Way, Hunts Bank and Great Ducie Street. Venue opened on July 15, 1995.
AN EVENING WITH RUSH
TICKETS: £39.00 / £45.00
ATTENDANCE: 10,417
CAPACITY: 11,454
CONCERT GROSS: £429,981 ($886,961 USD)
THE MANCHESTER EVENING NEWS: "Rush @ MEN Arena: It's a happy irony that, in this era obsessed with youth, celebrity and fame, it is a trio of unfashionable veterans who can still show the young 'uns how to put on a rock show."

OCTOBER 16–17, 2007
ROTTERDAM, SOUTH HOLLAND, THE NETHERLANDS
AHOY SPORTPALEIS, Ahoy-weg 10. Venue opened on January 15, 1971.
AN EVENING WITH RUSH
TICKETS: €49.00
TWO-DAY ROTTERDAM ATTENDANCE: 10,944
TWO-DAY ROTTERDAM CAPACITY: 17,200
TWO-DAY ROTTERDAM CONCERT GROSS: €505,902
NOTES: Both nights filmed with twenty-one high-definition cameras for the *Snakes and Arrows Live* DVD. Additional lighting rigs were flown to cast light over the audience. Neil unwound before the show by changing his oil.
GEDDY: "With this one we wanted to focus on the playing. So a lot of the camerawork features the interaction between Neil, Alex, and myself—a lot of the details that you don't normally cover in a DVD performance. So, for fans of the music who love to see what everybody's fingers are doing and how we interact back and forth with each other, that became the overriding focus on this one."[8]

NEIL: "The arenas in North America and Europe are usually in the middle of a busy city, and the buses and trucks are often parked on the street or in a public area. There is no privacy for me outdoors, so if I want to, say, change the oil in my bike, it takes some . . . logistical strategy—like at the Ahoy in Rotterdam. Before Brutus and I arrived, Michael had

Mark park the bus close along a wall near the backstage entrance, then arranged to have some free-standing curtains from the building placed at each end of the bus, between it and the wall. When we rolled up, Kevin pointed me behind the bus and trailer, and pulled back the curtain at one end for me to ride through. Thus I had a private area to work on the bike, hidden from gawkers, rockers, talkers, and stalkers. (An audience is very good to have when you're performing, but not so much when you're lying on the ground changing your oil.)"[9]

OCTOBER 19, 2007
OBERHAUSEN, GERMANY
KONIG-PILSENER ARENA, Arenastrabe 1. Venue opened on September 8, 1996.
AN EVENING WITH RUSH
TICKETS: €49.45
NOTES: The band seemed relieved that the pressures of the DVD filming were behind them. They play loose, festive sets in front of an enthusiastic crowd. During the concert, Alex started reading all of the Post-it notes stuck to his Barbie collection and began laughing so hard during "Entre Nous" that he drops his pick, and was forced to strum the acoustic and electric with a short finger nail before retrieving another pick from his amps. The hilarity of the evening continues when a member of the Blue Man Group appeared onstage to baste the chickens.
BRAD MADIX: "In Oberhausen, we went and saw the Blue Man Group the night before our show. Somebody managed to talk one of the Blue Men into coming to our show and going up on stage to baste the chickens. He went onstage in full-on Blue Men Group mode, and did the whole thing looking out at the audience like 'oh my god there's an audience' with the big buggy eyes. It was hysterical. I wasn't sure if the band could make it through it—Neil was looking the other way laughing!"[10]

OCTOBER 21, 2007
MANNHEIM, GERMANY
SAP-ARENA
AN EVENING WITH RUSH
TICKETS: €40.00 / €50.00
ATTENDANCE: 6,000
CAPACITY: 9,000

CONCERT GROSS: €255,000

NOTES: Venue opened on September 2, 2005. The rigors of touring had taken their toll on center stage, with Neil battling an agonizing bone bruise to his left index finger. He adjusted by turning the grip on his stick just slightly, but that little adjustment caused his shoulder to hurt as well. He was also plagued by an ear infection that just wouldn't go away. Like the two previous tours, before the encore, the band threw T-shirts out to fans. The shirt for the *Snakes and Arrows* tour was black and didn't have "Rush" printed anywhere; the front had an image of a waitress holding up a roast chicken, stating, "Feel like chicken?" while the back had the same phrase in Dutch, German, Italian, Norwegian, Swedish, and Finnish—listed in the same order as the itinerary.

OCTOBER 23, 2007
ASSAGO (MILAN), ITALY
DATCH FORUM DI ASSAGO, Parco Agricolo Sud Milano, Via Giuseppe di Vittorio, 6. Venue opened on October 26, 1990.

AN EVENING WITH RUSH
TICKETS: €52.00 / €65.00
ATTENDANCE: 3,752
CAPACITY: 6,000
CONCERT GROSS: €188,982
NOTES: According to an account by Ross Halfin, the photographer who shot the band during the European leg, the band has some fun running through "Cinderella Man," "The Analog Kid," and "Here Again" during sound check.[11] At the gig, Geddy had to stop himself from laughing during his introduction to "Mission," as fans loudly cheered: "Geddy, Geddy, Geddy . . ." The fired-up crowd also added a soccer chant to the beginning of "YYZ" à la Rio.

OCTOBER 26, 2007
OSLO, NORWAY
OSLO SPEKTRUM ARENA, Sonja Henies Plass 2. Venue opened on December 9, 1990.

AN EVENING WITH RUSH
TICKETS: 510.62 / 575.00 kr
ATTENDANCE: 5,498
CAPACITY: 5,828
CONCERT GROSS: 2,807,365 kr
NOTES: Rush's first appearance in

Norway since May 22, 1979. Alex played the scat guitar part in "Entre Nous."
GEDDY (ONSTAGE): "Hello Oslo! It's nice to be here in your country. In your city. It's been a really long time since we've been here. The late 70s we played a small club here. Sorry it's taken us so long to get back."

OCTOBER 27, 2007
STOCKHOLM, SWEDEN
GLOBE ARENA, Globentorget 2. Venue opened on February 19, 1989.

AN EVENING WITH RUSH
TICKETS: 595.00 / 558.55 kr
ATTENDANCE: 7,414
CAPACITY: 10,850
CONCERT GROSS: 4,141,060 kr
NOTES: Alex, Geddy, and Neil sound check "Beneath, Between, and Behind" and an edited version of "La Villa Strangiato" accoding to Ross Halfin.[12]
AFTONBLADET: "Geddy Lee and his Rush impresses in the Globe: Brilliance, balance, distance. The reason Rush succeeds where most of the genre fails . . . it consists of brilliance not haughty display. It is only in every riff and melody. In three extra-galactic musicians, who know they have nothing to prove. All built on a technical, challenging IQ rock lasting more than three hours."

OCTOBER 29, 2007
HELSINKI, FINLAND
HARTWALL ARENA, Areenankuja 1. Venue opened on April 19, 1997.

AN EVENING WITH RUSH
TICKETS: €59.00.
ATTENDANCE: 10,621; sold out
CONCERT GROSS: €605,219 ($874,360 USD)
NOTES: Final date on the *Snakes and Arrows* tour. Alex experienced technical difficulties during "Far Cry." Neil began the improvised start of his "De Slagwerker" drum solo with "Wipe Out," for just the second time this tour. He logged 4,543 motorcycle miles during the European leg for a total of 24,412 miles during the entire tour.
ROBERT "BUCKY" HUCK: "I just didn't feel comfortable enough when I was first starting out to say to Alex Lifeson 'hey man, your rig sucks!' I kept making little remarks along the way, just to start putting it into his head. Then, on the final gig of 2007, in Helsinki, right when we

started the second set . . . they went into 'Far Cry' and all of a sudden . . . no guitar. Nothing. I was like 'shit!' The way the guy had the rig set up, there were three separate racks of gear, plus all the heads on top of that. So, there are 360 cables in the damn thing . . . how am I supposed to figure out which cable is bad? And I have to do it before the end of the song. So I have to go around and jiggle cables and figure out which cable was bad and go from there. And I did. We missed the first song, but the rest of the set was fine. After that, that's when I finally said 'Dude, your rig is terrible. Let me use the upcoming break to rebuild your rig.' He said 'OK,' so I worked with a buddy of mine in New York named Mark Snyder, a guitar tech who worked with Billy Joel . . . When I came back for rehearsals in 2008, I brought the new rig in. Alex was flying in from Florida and called me to say, 'I'm not gonna get in until around 8 tonight, but I want to hear the rig . . . can we just meet for ten minutes?' He got there at 8:30, and he was so happy with the new sound that we left there at about 3:30 in the morning. He told me that he'd never had a better guitar tone, even in the studio, ever in his life. So, that was a big honor for me to hear that."[13]

1. *National Post*, April 15, 2008.
2. Adam Weissler. Interview with Geddy Lee and Alex Lifeson. *Extra*, 2007.
3. Skip Daly. Interview with Dave Burnette, August 12, 2012.
4. NeilPeart.net, August 2007.
5. Neil Peart. *Far and Away A Prize Every Time*. ECW Press, 2011.
6. Neil Peart. *Far and Away A Prize Every Time*. ECW Press, 2011.
7. Neil Peart. *Far and Away A Prize Every Time*. ECW Press, 2011.
8. Billboard.com, November 18, 2008.
9. NeilPeart.net, December 2007.
10. Skip Daly. Interview with Brad Madix, June 21, 2012.
11. http://www.rosshalfin.com/diary/october-2007/diary-october-2007.php
12. http://www.rosshalfin.com/diary/october-2007/diary-october-2007.php
13. Skip Daly. Interview with Robert Huck, August 2, 2012.

Chapter 28

THE SNAKES & ARROWS LIVE TOUR

rguably simply an extension of the *Snakes & Arrows* tour, the 2008 outing in support of the newly released live album consisted of forty-nine shows; according to *Rolling Stone*, the trek came in at number eight among the year's top-grossing rock and pop tours, with $18.3 million in earnings.

There were a few tweaks from the previous year's tour: "Ghost of a Chance" replaced "Entre Nous," "Red Barchetta" replaced "Secret Touch," and "The Trees" replaced "Circumstances." Said Alex, "[W]e wanted to mix up the second half of the tour a little bit, and because we had 'Entre Nous' and 'Circumstances' in there, we wanted to come up with something that was a little more obscure, and 'Ghost of a Chance' seemed to be a pretty good candidate. I think Geddy brought it up. And we all went, 'Oh! Well, I hadn't thought of that. Let's try that.' We all spent our own individual time relearning it and getting comfortable with it, and then we went in to rehearse, and the very first time we played it we went, 'Yeah! This is fun!'"

RIGHT: Lerxst and his trusty Gibson ES-355.

FAR RIGHT: Geddy Lee.

OPPOSITE TOP: Bending those notes.

OPPOSITE BOTTOM: Dirk and Lerxst.

Additionally, a new video intro called "What's that Smell?" which included Geddy and Alex as well as Barbie dolls, fried chicken, and the return of both Harry Satchel and Jerry Stiller, was used for the second set. Finally, a sitar arrangement of "Limelight" (rather than the first leg's bagpipes rendition) was featured as the show's exit music each night.

The tour span was notable for several significant nonshow events. Sadly, on May 11, the band's original drummer John Rutsey passed away at the age of fifty-five. That same week, Alex, Geddy, and Neil filmed a cameo scene for the comedy film *I Love You, Man*, in which they performed a mock concert. Director and cowriter John Hamburg, a longtime Rush fan, employed the band as a bonding device for the lead characters, played by costars Paul Rudd and Jason Segel, both Rush fans in real life as well.

"When I met the band and I was explaining the scene to them, I was so hypersensitive that they would enjoy themselves and not feel as if we were making fun of them because we were not at all," Rudd recalled. "So I was explaining it to them, like, 'Jason and I are dancing around and we're really, really excited, and Rashida Jones, her character is weirded out by us but she's kind of bored because we're totally ignoring her. So that's what's going on in the scene. We're way into it and she's kind of bored.' And Geddy Lee said, 'So it's just like any one of our concerts.'"

Toward the end of the tour, Geddy, Alex, and Neil used a day off in New York to film an appearance on Comedy Central's *The Colbert Report*. The taping marked Rush's first live television appearance in over thirty years, and Stephen Colbert's production team made the most of it, with abundant Rush references peppered throughout the show. Backstage beforehand, Rush answered a challenge and

took a stab at playing the *Rock Band* video game version of "Tom Sawyer." After failing with an admirable 31 percent completion on expert difficulty, Geddy quipped, "I'm going to go join another band!" as Alex cried out, "I'm just starting to get a feel for it!" Onstage, Colbert praised the band, asking, "You are yet to be inducted into the Rock and Roll Hall of Fame. Is there any chance that your next album will be titled *That's Bullshit?*"

Following the interview, the band performed "Tom Sawyer" out to a commercial break. At the return, the performance was still underway, and Colbert could be seen taking a nap, complete with blanket, pillow, and sleeping cap.

"Some fans loved it, and some were upset that Stephen interrupted our performance with comedy," Geddy said. "We were putting on this joke where we're playing this song that's so long it really can't fit on a thirty-minute show. It was us who suggested, 'Why don't you just interrupt us and do some shtick?' A lot of fans got the joke and thought it was great, and some were upset that he dared to besmirch the song with his interruption. It was blasphemous behavior, let's face it!"

OPPOSITE: The *Rotisserie* tour.

TOUR HISTORY

SNAKES & ARROWS LIVE

SET LIST:
"Limelight" (with dream sequence intro video)
"Digital Man"
"Ghost of a Chance"
"Mission"
"Freewill"
"The Main Monkey Business"
"The Larger Bowl" (with McKenzie Brothers intro video)
"Red Barchetta"
"The Trees"
"Between the Wheels"
"Dreamline"
(Intermission: "The Plane of Dharma" intro video)
"Far Cry"
"Workin' Them Angels"
"Armor and Sword"
"Spindrift"
"The Way the Wind Blows"
"Subdivisions"
"Natural Science"
"Witch Hunt"
"Malignant Narcissism"
"De Slagwerker" (drum solo)
"Hope"
"Distant Early Warning"
"The Spirit of Radio"
"2112: Overture"
"2112: The Temples of Syrinx"
"Tom Sawyer" (with *South Park* intro video)
Encore:
"One Little Victory"
"A Passage to Bangkok"
"YYZ"

APRIL 11, 2008
SAN JUAN, PUERTO RICO
COLISEO DE PUERTO RICO, 500 Arterial B Street. Venue opened on September 4, 2004.
AN EVENING WITH RUSH
TICKETS: $95.00 / $150.00
ATTENDANCE: 6,855
CAPACITY: 9,598
CONCERT GROSS: $740,155
NOTES: The opening date of the *Snakes and Arrows Live* tour was Rush's Puerto Rican debut. This was the first gig with Alex using his new amp rig, and the difference in sound was dramatic. For example, during the opening power chords of "Limelight," it was totally clean, with no sustain, as heard on the live album.
EL NUEVO DÍA: "A Memorable Night."

APRIL 13, 2008
SUNRISE, FLORIDA
BANKATLANTIC CENTER, 2555 NW 136th Avenue. Venue opened on October 3, 1998.
AN EVENING WITH RUSH
TICKETS: $50.75 / $75.75 / $95.75
ATTENDANCE: 8,432; sold out
CONCERT GROSS: $568,067
NOTES: The upper deck of the venue was curtained-off, with any ticket holders reissued tickets for the lower level.

APRIL 15, 2008
ORLANDO, FLORIDA
AMWAY ARENA, 600 West Amelia Street. Venue opened on January 29, 1989.

AN EVENING WITH RUSH
TICKETS: $45.00 / $75.00 / $95.00
ATTENDANCE: 7,612
CAPACITY: 8,517
CONCERT GROSS: $513,348
ORLANDO SENTINEL: "Rush Does It Big at Amway Arena: There was music that was complex, intense and still utterly grand. A band that never met an excessive musical gesture that it didn't love, Rush is easy to parody. It's also highly influential, which was obvious from the demographic mix of a crowd that ranged from baby-boomers to pre-teens."

APRIL 17, 2008
JACKSONVILLE, FLORIDA
JACKSONVILLE VETERAN'S MEMORIAL ARENA, 300 A Philip Randolph Boulevard. Venue opened on November 28, 2003.
AN EVENING WITH RUSH
TICKETS: $46.00 / $76.00
ATTENDANCE: 6,271
CAPACITY: 12,234
CONCERT GROSS: $341,025
FLORIDA TIMES-UNION: "Rush still rocks hard, has fun. Thursday's concert shows why band has such devoted fans: They showed they're still doing it without looking or sounding pretentious. There was no posturing, no pandering, no forced scowling, or lame attempts to appear sexy. Just three guys in their fifties playing hard rock really well and having fun doing it."

APRIL 19, 2008
THE WOODLANDS, TEXAS
C. W. MITCHELL PAVILION, 2005 Lake Robbins Drive. Venue opened on April 27, 1990.
AN EVENING WITH RUSH
TICKETS: $45.00 (lawn) / $113.00 (orchestra)
ATTENDANCE: 7,653
CAPACITY: 11,033
CONCERT GROSS: $507,265
NOTES: This concert was originally slated for April 20, but was swapped out with a New Orleans date (on April 17) due to NBA scheduling conflicts, with existing tickets being honored. Fans attending the new date were given a free tour book while entering the venue; a note on the bins says something to the effect of: "Geddy, Alex, and Neil would like to apologize for any inconvenience caused by the rescheduling." During the gig, a woman in the front row was crying, so Alex brought her over a tissue and asked her if she was okay.

APRIL 20, 2008
NEW ORLEANS, LOUISIANA
NEW ORLEANS ARENA, 1501 Girod Street. Venue opened on October 19, 1999.
AN EVENING WITH RUSH
TICKETS: $43.00 / $73.00 / $93.00; face value, minus fees
ATTENDANCE: 10,529
CAPACITY: 12,987
CONCERT GROSS: $663,000
NOTES: This gig was originally scheduled

for April 19, but switched at the eleventh hour when the New Orleans Hornets clinched their first NBA playoff berth in four years, with the series opening on April 19 in the Big Easy. April 20 was the only possible date to save the concert, otherwise it would have been canceled outright. Tickets for Saturday's show were honored on Sunday. Onstage, Geddy's keyboards malfunctioned during "Subdivisions," though the problem was rectified midway through the song. He went on to apologize for flip-flopping the two concerts and joked that it was to accommodate "some kind of hockey game." Rush contributed $100,000 of the show's proceeds to Brad Pitt's Make it Right Foundation (which helped with the revitalization of the city post hurricane Katrina), to sponsor construction of a house in the Lower Ninth Ward dubbed "The House that Rush Built."

RAY DANNIELS: "You always know that there is a slight possibility that this could happen, but no one was expecting it to. We have to congratulate the New Orleans Hornets on capturing their first division title in their twenty-year franchise history. Concerts are often booked on potential playoff dates using an educated guess at the time, in all our years of touring this is a first time a date has been forced to change. We apologize to any Rush fan who is inconvenienced by this. It's disappointing—we have forty crew members who are logging a lot of extra miles and additional expense as a result of this shift."

BILL CURL (ARENA SPOKESMAN): "We were in hopes that the Hornets might get the Sunday game. It was 50–50 going into last week. There was no way to make this announcement ahead of time. You have to hold your breath and see what happens and do the best you can."[1]

APRIL 23, 2008
AUSTIN, TEXAS
FRANK ERWIN SPECIAL EVENTS CENTER, University of Texas at Austin campus, 1701 Red River Street. Venue opened on November 29, 1977.
AN EVENING WITH RUSH
TICKETS: $45.00 / $65.00 / $95.00
ATTENDANCE: 7,049
CAPACITY: 7,836
CONCERT GROSS: $417,260
NOTES: Rush's first appearance in Austin since January 25, 1994.

GEDDY (ONSTAGE): "How are you Texans? I've been told it's been fourteen years since we've played here. How'd that happen? We're sorry."
THE AUSTIN AMERICAN-STATESMAN: "Rush Rocks the Erwin Center: This is a band that never fails to give their army of fans what they want while keeping it real for themselves, and in today's musical climate, that's no mean feat. Possibly one of the best shows Austin will see this year."

APRIL 25, 2008
DALLAS, TEXAS
SUPERPAGES.COM CENTER, Fair Park, 1818 First Avenue. Venue opened on July 23, 1988.
AN EVENING WITH RUSH
TICKETS: $36.50 (lawn; four-pack advance promotion available) / $104.00 (lower reserved)
ATTENDANCE: 8,496
CAPACITY: 11,500
CONCERT GROSS: $546,048
NOTES: Venue aka Smirnoff Music Centre.
NEIL: "At the very end of the show in Dallas, when I stood up to bow and wave and the lights were bright on the audience, I saw a sign way back on the stage-left side: 'Let Neil Sing.' I laughed out loud at that. As the old saying goes, 'Be careful what you wish for.'"[2]
DALLAS OBSERVER: "When the pot smoke clears and the air-drumming ceases, there is one truth that remains: Rush rocks!"

APRIL 26, 2008
OKLAHOMA CITY, OKLAHOMA
FORD CENTER, 100 West Reno Avenue. Venue opened on June 8, 2002.
AN EVENING WITH RUSH
TICKETS: $49.50 / $65.00 / $85.00; price included $1.00 finance charge
ATTENDANCE: 7,953
CAPACITY: 8,497
CONCERT GROSS: $477,831
NOTES: Rush's first Oklahoma City appearance since May 25, 1992.
THE OKLAHOMAN: "Backed by Spinning Fowl, Rush Takes Fans On A Ride: The show was a full-sensory experience topped with fireworks, fire balls shooting up and a fairly lengthy encore. It was an amazing concert."
THE OKLAHOMAN, ALEX: "I don't think we've been in Oklahoma City since the

early 90s, but judging by ticket sales, it's gonna be a great show. We can't wait. I remember playing there. We were there with Hawkwind in the early days. We opened for them. That was like '75."

APRIL 29, 2008
ALBUQUERQUE, NEW MEXICO
ABQ JOURNAL PAVILION, 5601 University Blvd SE. Venue opened on June 11, 2000.
AN EVENING WITH RUSH
TICKETS: $23.25 (limited advance, four-pack lawn promotion) / $31.00 (lawn) / $80.00 (orchestra); price included parking
ATTENDANCE: 7,653
CAPACITY: 11,496
CONCERT GROSS: $345,952
NOTES: Venue aka The Pavilion.
GEDDY (ONSTAGE): "Welcome to the second half of the show . . . and it looks like this is definitely the drunker half!"

MAY 1, 2008
PHOENIX, ARIZONA
CRICKET PAVILION, 2121 North 83rd Avenue. Venue opened on November 11, 1990.
AN EVENING WITH RUSH
TICKETS: $23.25 (limited advance, four-pack lawn promotion) / $32.00 (lawn) / $39.50 (upper pavilion) / $65.50 (lower pavilion) / $85.50 (orchestra); prices included parking
ATTENDANCE: 8,531
CAPACITY: 12,000
CONCERT GROSS: $420,818
NOTES: Two lucky women won a radio station contest and watched the show from the side of stage left, complete with their own monitor.

MAY 3, 2008
RENO, NEVADA
RENO EVENTS CENTER, 400 North Center Street. Venue opened on January 1, 2005.
AN EVENING WITH RUSH
TICKETS: $58.25 / $78.25 / $98.25
ATTENDANCE: 6,114; sold out
CONCERT GROSS: $468,486
RENO GAZETTE-JOURNAL: "Rush Still Relavant."

MAY 4, 2008
CONCORD, CALIFORNIA
SLEEP TRAIN PAVILION, 2000 Kirker

Pass Road. Venue opened on May 16, 1975.

AN EVENING WITH RUSH

TICKETS: $29.00 (lawn) / $53.50 (upper pavilion) / $73.50 (lower pavilion) / $93.50 (orchestra)

ATTENDANCE: 9,451

CAPACITY: 11,500

CONCERT GROSS: $469,767

NOTES: It was a chilly evening, with temps in the low 50s, to which Geddy commented: "Great weather for hockey!" There' was a technical glitch at the beginning of "YYZ."

MAY 6, 8, 2008

LOS ANGELES, CALIFORNIA

NOKIA THEATRE, 777 Chick Hearn Court. Venue opened on October 18, 2007.

AN EVENING WITH RUSH

TICKETS: $69.50 / $94.50 / $154.50

ATTENDANCE (MAY 6): 6,308; sold out

ATTENDANCE (MAY 8): 4,930

CAPACITY: 6,308

TWO-DAY LOS ANGELES CONCERT

GROSS: $1,185,575

NOTES: Second show added due to popular demand. Drummers Chad Smith (Red Hot Chili Peppers) and Taylor Hawkins (Foo Fighters) were in attendance along with producer Rupert Hine.

VARIETY: "Concert Review: Rush: At a sold-out Nokia, the trio deftly playing their instruments with a casual air, flawlessly re-creating and never reinventing their recordings, the devoted fan base reacting with air drums, air guitars, and air batons. Unlike their peers, Rush can step forward from the past and venture beyond prog-rock confines."

MAY 10, 2008

LAS VEGAS, NEVADA

MANDALAY BAY EVENTS CENTER, Mandalay Bay Resort and Casino, 3950 Las Vegas Boulevard South. Venue opened on April 10, 1999.

AN EVENING WITH RUSH

TICKETS: $57.00 / $87.00 /$127.00

ATTENDANCE: 7,762

CAPACITY: 8,449

CONCERT GROSS: $680,901

NOTES: At the show, there was a large contingent of fans with a Chilean flag. During the first leg of the tour, Neil had logged over 7,000 motorcycle miles.

LAS VEGAS SUN: "Rush makes time stand still at Mandalay Bay: It seems Rush is becoming the next Grateful Dead, with a loyal collection of fans hooking onto large segments of each world tour. Rush is the rare band that can actually tour in support of a live album."

MAY 11, 2008

IRVINE, CALIFORNIA

VERIZON WIRELESS AMPHITHEATER, 8808 Irvine Center Drive. Venue opened on August 21, 1981.

AN EVENING WITH RUSH

TICKETS: $29.00 (lawn) / $80.00 (pavilion) / $125.00 (orchestra)

ATTENDANCE: 9,488

CAPACITY: 12,298

CONCERT GROSS: $615,582

NOTES: Founding Rush drummer John Rutsey passed away on this date, at the age of fifty-five.

ALEX AND GEDDY (VIA RUSH.COM): "Our memories of the early years of Rush when John was in the band are very fond to us. Those years spent in our teens dreaming of one day doing what we continue to do decades later are special. Although our paths diverged many years ago, we smile today, thinking back on those exciting times and remembering John's wonderful sense of humor and impeccable timing. He will be deeply missed by all he touched."

BILL RUTSEY: "To this day, both Alex and Geddy are very nice, very genuine people. They both have a great deal of respect for my brother. Whenever I see them, to the extent that we talk about John, they only have very nice things to say. It was a long time ago, and it was almost a different life from the life that they're living now, but they both look back on those times very fondly and they're both very respectful of John. Both Alex and Geddy came to John's funeral, and Alex spoke very tenderly about their time together. It was really quite moving. I'll always be really thankful for what he did say and I have a great degree of respect for him."

MAY 20, 2008

MOLINE, ILLINOIS

IWIRELESS CENTER, 1201 River Drive. Venue opened on May 29, 1993.

AN EVENING WITH RUSH

TICKETS: $45.00 / $55.00 / $75.00; price included $2.50 finance charge

CONCERT CAPACITY: 5,789

VENUE CAPACITY: 6,526

CONCERT GROSS: $298,153

NOTES: Venue aka the MARK of the Quad Cities. Sabian's Chris Stankee was in attendance to ride with Neil to the next show in St. Paul. This was lucky for the band, as Gump is out with appendicitis, eventually rejoining the tour four days later in Winnipeg. Stankee was called on to fill in as Neil's drum tech, while Jim Burgess handled Neil's electronics. With little preparation, a comedy of errors ensued, but they put forth a valiant effort in getting the job done. Longtime fans noticed that something was amiss right from the very start, but they couldn't quite put their finger on exactly what.

CHRIS STANKEE: "The band launches into 'Ghost of a Chance.' Anson walks in front of the kit in the middle of the song to move a mic. 'Everything OK?' I ask. 'The snare drum sounds funny.' I couldn't even tell in my headphone mix. Neil hits so hard that unless he breaks the drum in half I probably wouldn't notice. The song finishes and he comes leaping off the riser looking right at me. 'The snare drum head broke! Tell Dirk to stretch it out between songs!' I dive into the riser and my radio tangles up in something. I remove the snare and pass it to Anson, then lock down the spare that was already prepared. Back to business in no time, but what are the chances of that happening to us tonight? It happens maybe once every 100 shows, Neil would tell me later. The head simply pulled out of the metal collar that holds it. What next? When the band starts into 'The Main Monkey Business,' I lean over to Jim. 'Do you hear a pigeon?' He gives me the 'are you nuts?' look. Great. I can't hear a broken snare head and now I'm hearing pigeons. It turned out that Neil was trying to get the snare back into the correct place after I swapped it, and it made its way up against the DAUZ trigger activating a pigeon 'coo' sound every time he hit the drum. It was comical, but Neil wasn't laughing . . ."[3]

ROCK ISLAND ARGUS: "Rush crafts top-notch show at i-wi: Those guys are probably the most talented rock musicians to grace a Quad Cities stage. Because of deadline constraints, for all I know Rush may still be playing."

MAY 22, 2008
ST. PAUL, MINNESOTA
XCEL ENERGY CENTER, 199 Kellogg Boulevard West. Venue opened on September 29, 2000.
AN EVENING WITH RUSH
TICKETS: $47.75 / $89.75; price included $2.00 finance charge
ATTENDANCE: 7,901
CAPACITY: 12,440
CONCERT GROSS: $494,340
CHRIS STANKEE: "We get to the venue in St. Paul with plenty of time to get things right. Neil changes the oil on both motorcycles while I work on the kit with the rest of the crew . . . Neil comes up early for sound check and we make sure to get him comfortable. Geddy stops by the drum riser for a bit of the old 'bassist vs. drummer.' 'Will our pigeon be back tonight?' he asks. Hardy har har . . ."[4]

MAY 24, 2008
WINNIPEG, MANITOBA
MTS CENTER, 300 Portage Avenue. Venue opened on November 16, 2004.
AN EVENING WITH RUSH
TICKETS: $45.00 / $65.00 / $85.00 CAD
ATTENDANCE: 7,802
CAPACITY: 10,333
CONCERT GROSS: $419,459 CAD
NOTES: Rush's first concert in Winnipeg since October 5, 1982. The band donated $100,000 of the show's proceeds to the Canadian Museum for Human Rights. They also sold specially designed T-shirts (which state: "My pals Rush and I support the Canadian Museum for Human Rights") at all remaining Canadian dates to benefit the museum.
GEDDY: "My bandmates and I are proud to be associated with the creation of a Canadian Museum for Human Rights in Winnipeg. Canadians are uniquely positioned to be leaders in championing such causes and we applaud the efforts of the Asper family in making this museum a reality. We hope that Canadians across the country will join us in lending their support."

WINNIPEG SUN: "Can't Rush Perfection: Canadian prog-rock trio's return to Winnipeg worth the quarter-of-a-century wait. Rush concerts aren't about mayhem and untethered passion. They're about the sort of drill-team precision and consistent perfection on display last night."

MAY 25, 2008
REGINA, SASKATCHEWAN
BRANDT CENTRE, 1700 Elphinstone Street at Exhibition Park. Venue opened on August 1, 1977.
AN EVENING WITH RUSH
TICKETS: $65.00 / $85.00 CAD
ATTENDANCE: 5,548
CAPACITY: 6,186
CONCERT GROSS: $375,778 CAD
NOTES: Venue aka Agridome. Rush's first Regina appearance since March 3, 1980 was on a chilly spring day (complete with snow flurries). An odd moment occurred during "The Larger Bowl," when the PA cut out just before the lyric "some are cursed." Alex's solo piece, "Hope," was recorded from this gig and donated to *Songs for Tibet—The Art of Peace* benefit album, which was released in August of 2008; the performance would eventually be nominated for a Grammy.
REGINA LEADER POST: "Rush Returns to Rock Regina: It was the complete experience—you heard it, you saw it, you felt it. The sound was crisp and loud and the theatrics included everything that makes a rock show great, from flashpots to lasers to pyrotechnics. Lee's distinctive voice was in fine form. The fifty-four-year-old was a multitasking machine. In addition to singing, he pounded out the bass lines, played keyboards and synthesizer, and manipulated numerous trigger foot pedals. He still, however, was quick to slip away from his mic stand whenever the opportunity presented itself, rocking out only as Geddy Lee can."

MAY 27, 2008
EDMONTON, ALBERTA
REXALL PLACE, 7424 118th Avenue NW. Venue opened on November 10, 1974.
AN EVENING WITH RUSH
TICKETS: $45.00 / $65.00 / $85.00 CAD
ATTENDANCE: 8,779

CAPACITY: 11,250
CONCERT GROSS: $496,569 CAD
NOTES: Venue aka Skyreach Centre.
EDMONTON SUN: "Masters of Their Domain: Rush proves rock-ability only improves with age. Also of interest was 'The Larger Bowl,' which seemed to have something to do with various inequities and injustices in the world, to judge by the images on the video screens. The song was as intricate, powerful and interesting as any of Rush's best work, plus it had a worthy message."

MAY 29, 2008
VANCOUVER, BRITISH COLUMBIA
GENERAL MOTORS PLACE, 800 Griffiths Way. Venue opened on September 17, 1995.
AN EVENING WITH RUSH
TICKETS: $45.00 / $65.00 / $85.00 CAD
ATTENDANCE: 10,150
CAPACITY: 14,000
CONCERT GROSS: $589,540 CAD
NOTES: Venue aka Rogers Arena.
THE PROVINCE: "Rush Still Close to The Heart: Rush did seem to be playing with more conviction Thursday night. The last studio album, *Snakes and Arrows*, shows a band that has reinvigorated itself. The subsequent live album, *Snakes and Arrows Live*, shows how Rush has carried that enthusiasm onto the stage."

MAY 31, 2008
GEORGE, WASHINGTON
THE GORGE AMPHITHEATRE, 754 Silica Road Northwest. Venue opened for major concerts on August 20, 1988.
AN EVENING WITH RUSH
TICKETS: $44.10 (lawn) / $70.35 (reserved) / $91.35 (orchestra); face value, minus fees
ATTENDANCE: 10,450
CAPACITY: 14,482
CONCERT GROSS: $638,211
NOTES: A howling wind caused difficulties for the crew, with many lights and lasers remaining dormant. During the gig, the fierce breezes had the sound going in and out from a distance, with the PA swinging back and forth above the stage. Geddy (with hair tied-up) made several references to the wind, including the possibility of "being blown off the stage."
CENTRAL KITSAP REPORTER: "The concert almost took a second stage for me

because I was having such a great time watching the crowd. It was great to see a crowd of about 90 percent men be so caught up in the moment that they forgot they were supposed to play it cool."

JUNE 1, 2008
RIDGEFIELD, WASHINGTON
THE AMPHITHEATER AT CLARK COUNTY, 17200 NE Delfel Road. Venue opened on July 10, 2003.
AN EVENING WITH RUSH
TICKETS: $30.00 (lawn) $40.00 (upper pavilion) / $57.50 (lower pavilion) / $87.50 (orchestra)
ATTENDANCE: 8,157
CAPACITY: 10,790
CONCERT GROSS: $449,155
NOTES: Venue aka Sleep Country Amphitheater. The first amphitheater show of the 2008 season was on a cold, blustery night, with temps in the low fifties, so Geddy took to the stage with a long coat and scarf. At the start of "Witch Hunt," he warmed his hands in the direction of the massive flames behind his non-amp line. During "YYZ," Alex flubbed the chorus, then looked back at a laughing Neil. He went on to make self-deprecating gestures to the crowd—like holding his nose—in response to his mistake.

JUNE 3, 2008
NAMPA, IDAHO
IDAHO CENTER, 16200 Idaho Center Boulevard. Venue opened on February 20, 1997.
AN EVENING WITH RUSH
TICKETS: $51.50 / $67.00 / $87.00; face value, minus fees
ATTENDANCE: 5,568
CAPACITY: 6,160
CONCERT GROSS: $330,479
IDAHO STATESMAN: "Rush, Idaho Center: The rich sound created by three men was awesome to experience. Not only was Rush's immensity near-breathtaking, but the band executed its ambitious music with CD perfection. These were true musicians. Sadly, arena rock is becoming an extinct art form. As long as Rush exists, it will not die."

JUNE 5, 2008
MORRISON, COLORADO
RED ROCKS AMPHITHEATRE, 18300 West Alameda Parkway. Historic venue

dedicated on June 15, 1941.
AN EVENING WITH RUSH
TICKETS: $49.50 / $99.50
NOTES: On the twenty-fifth Anniversary of U2's legendary performance at Red Rocks, Rush's show was postponed in the morning due to severe weather conditions (rain, wind, and fog), prohibiting the stage setup. Ironically, the weather that evening wasn't too bad, just chilly. The concert was promptly rescheduled for June 25, 2008.
CRAIG "C. B." BLAZIER (PRODUCTION MANAGER): "One of the toughest gigs that we've done has been Red Rocks because it is such a difficult load-in. You bring your trucks down to a certain point at the bottom of the hill, but then you have to offload them into smaller state trucks, straight-beds, and take those up. So, it takes quite a lot more time to do that. In 2008 we got rained out. There were storms coming in, so we called the show. It rained heavily, there was an inch of water on the stage itself, and it was still raining at 8:00 in the morning, and we knew that if we didn't start loading in there was no way we could get the show up in time. So, we postponed it. We took off . . . and of course two hours later the storm had passed through . . . but it was too late at that point. We were barreling our way east to Kansas City, outrunning tornadoes—you could actually see them off to the north of us. We're driving through all this wind, rain and hail, whipping the bus. It was quite an exciting time, to say the least."[5]

JUNE 7, 2008
KANSAS CITY, MISSOURI
STARLIGHT THEATRE, Swope Park, 4600 Starlight Road. Venue opened on June 4, 1950.
AN EVENING WITH RUSH
TICKETS: $50.00 (terrace) / $78.50 (plaza) / $97.50 (orchestra)
ATTENDANCE: 6,339
CAPACITY: 7,733
CONCERT GROSS: $373,564
NOTES: Starlight Theatre is a castle-shaped venue. A strong performance on a very hot night. Geddy donned a champion Kansas Jayhawks T-shirt after Neil's drum solo, much to the delight of the crowd.
THE PITCH **(KANSAS CITY):** "Rush at Starlight: After about three hours, it

appeared that the crowd had gotten about everything out of the apparently exhausted Rushsters on a sweltering night."

JUNE 9, 2008
CHICAGO, ILLINOIS
UNITED CENTER, 1901 West Madison Street. Venue opened on August 18, 1994.
AN EVENING WITH RUSH
TICKETS: $47.50 / $85.00 / $125.00
ATTENDANCE: 10,600
CAPACITY: 10,863
CONCERT GROSS: $802,843
THE SOUTHTOWN STAR **(TINLEY PARK, IL):** "Rush Rocks Out at The United Center: The hard-rockin' trio delivered the goods in a big way. The West Side has not rocked this hard in a long time."

JUNE 10, 2008
DETROIT, MICHIGAN
JOE LOUIS ARENA, 19 Steve Yzerman Drive. Venue opened on December 12, 1979.
AN EVENING WITH RUSH
TICKETS: $42.50 / $75.50 / $99.50
ATTENDANCE: 8,744
CAPACITY: 13,835
CONCERT GROSS: $571,309
NOTES: Backstage, the band was presented with Red Wings championship jerseys. The team had adopted "One Little Victory" as their theme song en route to winning the Stanley Cup.
GEDDY (ONSTAGE): "This is Hockeytown, right? Somebody told me that."
GO AND DO MICHIGAN: "Rush Rocks In Repeat Visit To Metro Area: As the group left the stage, Lee saluted the Joe Louis crowd as 'awesome'—which it certainly was. But the same adjective could absolutely be applied to Rush, too."

JUNE 12, 2008
MONTREAL, QUEBEC
CENTRE BELL, 1909 Avenue des Canadiens-de-Montréal. Venue opened on March 16, 1996.
AN EVENING WITH RUSH
TICKETS: $59.50 / $77.00 / $89.50 CAD; price did not include fees
ATTENDANCE: 7,575
CAPACITY: 9,468
CONCERT GROSS: $655,450 CAD
MONTREAL GAZETTE: "Rush Gives

Encore Worth Celebrating: One of the most daring moves Rush has ever made in concert: a solid block of five songs from *Snakes and Arrows* after intermission. The flatly produced album may not be a highlight of their catalogue, but 'Armor and Sword,' 'Spindrift,' and especially a vital 'Far Cry' were edgier and more alive on stage and merited the pride of place they received."

JUNE 14, 2008
PHILADELPHIA, PENNSYLVANIA
WACHOVIA CENTER, 3601 South Broad Street. Venue opened on August 12, 1996.
AN EVENING WITH RUSH
TICKETS: $65.00 / $85.00 / $123.00
ATTENDANCE: 9,801
CAPACITY: 12,017
CONCERT GROSS: $662,621
NOTES: Jimmy Buffett was playing a stadium show across the street, so a party atmosphere permeated the tailgate as fans of both bands intermingled in a pre-show ritual. Geddy took to the stage during the second set, wearing a 1980 Phillies championship T-shirt.
BILLBOARD: "Rush / Philadelphia, June 14: Rush fans are a diehard, Grateful Dead-like community of people from all walks of life. Rush shows might be some of the only places in America where a staunch conservative Bushie and a radical Ron Paul fan can hang back and put away their political differences to wax nostalgic about their first Rush concerts, as did happen in the parking lot of the Wachovia Center."

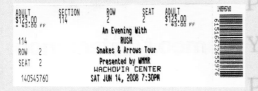

JUNE 15, 2008
MANSFIELD, MASSACHUSETTS
COMCAST CENTER FOR THE PERFORMING ARTS, 885 South Main Street. Venue opened on June 13, 1986.
AN EVENING WITH RUSH
TICKETS: $28.00 (lawn) / $48.00 (upper pavilion) / $75.00 (middle pavilion) / $95.00 (lower pavilion); face value, minus $7.00 finance charge and other fees

ATTENDANCE: 8,263
CAPACITY: 10,734
CONCERT GROSS: $617,859
NOTES: Venue aka Tweeter Center. Tickets went on sale when the venue was still called Tweeter Center, with the name being changed to Comcast Center before the gig. Sports and concerts really seemed to be intermingled on this tour, and this night was no exception. The Celtics were playing game five against the Lakers in the NBA finals. Geddy made reference to the fact several times to a fired-up crowd. In fact, the audience chanted "Beat LA!" periodically during the sets. Geddy wore a "Beat LA!" T-shirt during the encore, and the place erupted. After thirty-two concerts, Neil has logged almost 14,000 motorcycle miles.
THE BOSTON GLOBE: "Rush Delivers, But We've Seen It Before: Its admirers remain staunchly loyal. Thousands of them descended upon the Comcast Center, despite the fact that the concert competed with Game 5 of the Celtics-Lakers series. And they loved every minute of it."

JUNE 25, 2008
MORRISON, COLORADO
RED ROCKS AMPHITHEATRE, 18300 West Alameda Parkway. Historic venue dedicated on June 15, 1941.
AN EVENING WITH RUSH
TICKETS: $49.50 / $99.50
ATTENDANCE: 8,412; sold out
CONCERT GROSS: $672,514
NOTES: Originally slated for June 5, this concert was rescheduled due to inclement weather. To allow room in the itinerary, a previously booked date in Noblesville, Indiana on June 25 was moved to the end of the run on July 24. During the gig, an ominous-looking thunderstorm stayed to the south, giving fans a lightning show in the distance.
THE DENVER POST: "Rush at Red Rocks Amphitheatre: Rush surely won over any younger fans last night, and the die-hard older ones were more than satisfied."

JUNE 27, 2008
MILWAUKEE, WISCONSIN
MARCUS AMPHITHEATER, Summerfest grounds, Henry Maier Festival Park, 200 North Harbor Drive. Venue opened on June 25, 1987.
AN EVENING WITH RUSH
TICKETS: $40.00 (lawn) / $60.00 (rear

reserved) / $75.00 (front reserved); price excluded fees
ATTENDANCE: 11,272
CAPACITY: 25,000
CONCERT GROSS: $787,005
NOTES: 2008 Milwaukee Summerfest. Other acts performing on various different stages include Sevendust, Rusted Root, and the Rush tribute band, Animation-A.
MILWAUKEE JOURNAL SENTINEL: "Rush Proves Everything People Say about It: One, it is not nearly so bad a band as its detractors would swear in affidavits. Two, it is not nearly so awe-inspiring a band as its fanatics would claim in heated tavern conversations."

JUNE 28, 2008
MARYLAND HEIGHTS, MISSOURI
VERIZON WIRELESS AMPHITHEATER, 14141 Riverport Drive. Venue opened on June 14, 1991.
AN EVENING WITH RUSH
TICKETS: $30.00 (lawn) $59.00 / $95.00 (orchestra); price included $6.00 finance charge
ATTENDANCE: 9,744
CAPACITY: 12,000
CONCERT GROSS: $443,455
NOTES: This is Russ Ryan's last show as Geddy's bass tech.
ST. LOUIS POST-DISPATCH: "Rush adds gags, but few new songs to this gig: Lifeson showed he can still shred with the best of them, stretching out on the instrumental 'The Main Monkey Business,' accenting the metallic reggae of 'Digital Man' and playing with grace and economy on one of the set's new additions, 'Ghost of a Chance.'"

JUNE 30, 2008
CINCINNATI, OHIO
RIVERBEND MUSIC CENTER, 6295 Kellogg Avenue. Venue opened on July 4, 1984.
AN EVENING WITH RUSH
TICKETS: $25.00 (lawn, limited advance promotion) / $34.00 (lawn) / $66.00 (pavilion) / $86.00 (orchestra)
ATTENDANCE: 7,894
CAPACITY: 10,000
CONCERT GROSS: $419,600

JULY 2, 2008
BURGETTSTOWN, PENNSYLVANIA
POST-GAZETTE PAVILION, 665 Route 18. Venue opened on June 17, 1990.

go

MAGAZINE

8.19.10 - 8.25.10

'THE WORLD'S MOST POPULAR CULT BAND'

THE FEVER FOR RUSH HASN'T BROKEN.

BY KEVIN COFFEY >> 10

Chapter 29

THE TIME MACHINE TOUR

The *Time Machine* tour was split into two distinct legs. The 2010 jaunt, with a total of forty-four shows, kicked off on June 29 in Albuquerque, New Mexico, and concluded on October 17 in Santiago, Chile. It ranked number twenty-nine on *Pollstar's* top fifty North American tours, grossing $26.4 million with 372,407 tickets sold over thirty-six shows. The 2011 leg began on March 30 in Ft. Lauderdale, Florida, and logged another thirty-eight dates. In the tour announcement, Rush stated, "To benefit the relief efforts in Haiti, one dollar of each ticket sold will be donated through several charities including Doctors Without Borders. Rush will also contribute a portion of their proceeds at the culmination of the tour."

The set list was notable for the inclusion of two songs from the yet-to-be-released *Clockwork Angels* record—"BU2B" and "Caravan"—as well as a full-album performance of 1981's *Moving Pictures*, played in sequence.

"We thought it would be fun to put together a tour that was sort of 'future/past,' because those are some of the themes that are floating around the lyrical content and visual content that we're using for these new songs," Geddy said about the set list. "So we thought, 'Let's go out and do this *Time Machine* tour, where we can go mine our past, and at the same time, point to the future, try some new songs, and get us in shape.'"

Along with the two new *Clockwork Angels* songs, "Faithless" and "Presto" received their live debuts on the tour, while "Stick It Out" was played for the first time in thirteen years, "Marathon" for the first time in twenty years, and "The Camera Eye" for the first time in twenty-seven years.

"'The Camera Eye' was the last really epic song we wrote," Geddy said. "It's eleven minutes long. At the time, we really didn't appreciate it. Back then we thought it was too long and repetitive. We didn't understand the mood it generated . . . it was a song we never thought worked. But the way we revamped it made this come alive. One thing the tour did for us was to make us aware of how good 'The Camera Eye' always was. I'm so glad we've become friends with it again."

As with the previous tour, Alex, Geddy, and Neil served as actors during the videos shown before and after the show and during the intermission. The opening video, titled "Rash, the 'Real' History of Rush," featured the "Gershons Haus of Sausage" diner with Geddy working the counter, Alex (in a fat suit and eating sausage) as "Slobovich," and Neil as an Irish cop named O'Malley, and a live polka band named Rash playing "The Spirit of Radio" on accordion, tuba, and drums. The intro video for the second set was part two of "The 'Real' History of Rush," from an alternate timeline. A third video, "I Still Love You, Man," with Paul Rudd and Jason Segel reprising their roles from *I Love You, Man,* closed out the show. A polka

OPPOSITE: The Grateful Dead? Hold my beer.

rendition of "Closer to the Heart" was played as exit music.

In terms of visual aesthetics, the staging was a steampunk representation of "the future as envisioned from the past," with Neil's new, fantastically ornate DW kit as the centerpiece. The steampunk theme carried over to the set design, with heavy use of copper accents as well as both video and amplifier tubes. When not displaying production videos, the primary screen appeared as a steampunk tube-style television complete with spinning gears. Designed by Dale Heslip, Alex's Hughes & Kettner amps were housed in steampunk cabinets and Geddy's backline was replaced with a time machine combined with a sausage maker, both of which were rigged to release steam throughout the show. Twice during the evening, crewmembers would come out onstage pushing a shopping cart containing rubber chickens, which they would drop into the sausage machine.

The first leg of the *Time Machine* tour included stops in Argentina and Chile—Rush's first-ever concerts in those countries. During the second leg, they gave their debut performance in Ireland, and the April 15, 2011, date at Quicken Loans Arena in Cleveland was filmed and recorded for the *Time Machine 2011: Live in Cleveland* CD/DVD release. This would be the first full-length DVD produced from a US show (not counting the "Oh, Atlanta!" bonus tracks from the previous tour).

"We realized after all these years that we've shot films in all these different locations," Geddy said. "But we've never really shot an entire film in America. We thought, 'Well, that's just wrong.' So where do we want to shoot? And it dawned on me that it was appropriate to shoot in Cleveland, where our entire American adventure began. I don't think we would've had a record deal if it hadn't been for Donna Halper

at WMMS playing 'Working Man' and some other songs from our first album."

After just over a year of dates, the *Time Machine* tour wrapped on July 2, 2011, at the Gorge, near Seattle, Washington.

When it was over, Neil looked back on the extensive run: "Added to the forty-four shows and more than 23,000 miles of motorcycling from summer 2010, my bandmates and I had now performed a total of eighty-one shows, before almost one million people. With riding partners Michael and Brutus, I had ridden 36,729 motorcycle miles, covering North America, South America, and Europe. . . . An audience of more than 13,000 people attended the final show of our *Time Machine* tour, on July 2, 2011. Most of them had traveled a considerable distance—the Gorge is a long way from anywhere (the nearest town, humorously, is George, Washington). But we too had traveled a long way to get to that stage. And despite how many shows we had played, our weariness, and our sheer age, we managed to pull off a magic show that night."

OPPOSITE: Sharp-dressed Lerxst.
BELOW: "2112: Overture."

TOP: Outside George, WA; Sunset at the Gorge.

ABOVE: Outside George, WA; Geddy at the Gorge.

OPPOSITE: Outside George, WA; Alex can't believe the tour is almost over.

TOP: Louisville, KY; Alex on keys during "Time Stand Still" at the Yum! Center.

ABOVE: Neil on the *Time Machine* kit.

OPPOSITE TOP: Alex and Geddy.

OPPOSITE BOTTOM: The Holy Triumvirate jamming.

TOUR HISTORY
TIME MACHINE 2010–2011

SET LIST:
SET 1:
"The 'Real' History of Rush, Part 1" intro video
"The Spirit of Radio"
"Time Stand Still"
"Presto"
"Stick It Out"
"Workin' Them Angels"
"Leave That Thing Alone"
"Faithless"
"BU2B"
"Freewill"
"Marathon"
"Subdivisions"
SET 2:
"The 'Real' History of Rush, Part 2" intro video
"Tom Sawyer"
"Red Barchetta"
"YYZ"
"Limelight"
"The Camera Eye"
"Witch Hunt"
"Vital Signs"
"Caravan"
"Moto Perpetuo" / "Love for Sale" (drum solo)
"O'Malley's Break" (guitar solo)
"Closer to the Heart" (with acoustic intro)
"2112: Overture"
"2112: The Temples of Syrinx"
"Far Cry"
Encore:
"La Villa Strangiato" (with polka intro)
"Working Man" (with new reggae intro)
"I Still Love You, Man" outro video
"Closer to the Heart" (polka; exit music)

JUNE 29, 2010
ALBUQUERQUE, NEW MEXICO
THE PAVILION, 5601 University Blvd SE. Venue opened on June 11, 2000.
AN EVENING WITH RUSH
TICKETS: $25.00 (lawn) / $49.50 (upper bowl) / $65.00 (lower bowl) / $90.00 (orchestra) / $186.88 (average price of tickets sold including VIP); face value, $6.00 parking and fees additional
ATTENDANCE: 6,624
CAPACITY: 8,516
CONCERT GROSS: $384,086
NOTES: The opening date of the *Time Machine* tour featured the live debut of "Caravan," "BU2B," "Faithless," and—after a twenty-year wait—"Presto." Alex played a new piece on his Martin 12-string, titled "O'Malley's Break," which he jokingly referred to as "Hopeless." This was Scott Appleton's first gig as guitar technician.

JULY 1, 2010
KANSAS CITY, MISSOURI
STARLIGHT THEATRE, Swope Park, 4600 Starlight Road. Venue opened on June 4, 1950.
AN EVENING WITH RUSH
TICKETS: $29.50 (upper terrace) / $49.50 (terrace) / $78.50 (plaza) / $97.50 (box and orchestra) / $300.00 (VIP) / $197.54 (average price of tickets sold including VIP)
ATTENDANCE: 6,042
CAPACITY: 7,733
CONCERT GROSS: $428,754

NOTES: Due to venue weight constraints, the spider lighting rig remained stationary.
THE KANSAS CITY STAR: "Rush's Starlight show sounds too much like the tired old records: Everyone who was miming Peart's fills and singing along with Geddy Lee surely owns the records. Why, then, their evident delight in paying $50 essentially to witness the records being played back while the creators nod approvingly?"

JULY 3, 2010
MILWAUKEE, WISCONSIN
MARCUS AMPHITHEATER, Henry Maier Festival Park, Summerfest grounds, 200 North Harbor Drive. Venue opened on June 25, 1987.
AN EVENING WITH RUSH
TICKETS: $20.00 (lawn, advance promo) / $32.00 (lawn) / $47.00 (rear reserved) / $67.00 (front reserved) / $77.00 (orchestra) / $158.36 (average price of tickets sold including VIP); face value (excluding fees). Prices included admission to Summerfest.
ATTENDANCE: 14,521
CAPACITY: 22,895
CONCERT GROSS: $669,185
NOTES: 2010 Milwaukee Summerfest. Also performing this day on various stages were Peter Frampton, Levon Helm Band, Modest Mouse, Counting Crows, John Hiatt, and the Rush cover band Animation. Onstage, Geddy added some vocal improv to "Vital Signs," singing "Everybody got to evaporate from the norm" on the outro.

During "La Villa Strangiato," Alex had some technical issues, so the first stanza was just bass and drums.
GEDDY (ONSTAGE): "Hello, Milwaukee; hello Brew Crew! This is not beer in my cup."
MILWAUKEE JOURNAL SENTINEL: "Proven formula just fine with the fans: Rush didn't really offer the fans much more than they got the last time the band came through Milwaukee. And the fans didn't really care."

JULY 5, 2010
CHICAGO, ILLINOIS
CHARTER ONE PAVILION, Northerly Island, 1300 South Linn White Drive. Venue opened on June 24, 2005.
AN EVENING WITH RUSH
TICKETS: $40.00 (lawn) / $80.00 (reserved grandstand) / $125.00 (reserved floor) / $217.98 (average price of tickets sold including VIP); price included $9.50 parking fee. Ticketmaster was offering a summer waiver program, where tickets were devoid of fees.
ATTENDANCE: 6,247
CAPACITY: 7,068
CONCERT GROSS: $568,858
NOTES: Geddy took to the stage with his hair tied up on a windy night in the Windy City. No pyro was used, and the spider lighting rig remained stationary.
CHICAGO TRIBUNE: "Three-hour set shows Rush not in any hurry: Best of all, the band—while still mostly improv-averse—had fun messing with the

arrangements of such warhorses as 'Closer to the Heart' and 'Working Man.' Indeed, Lifeson, Peart, and Lee (in strong voice) somehow found space for new flourishes in their formidable arrangements."

NEIL: "At dinner before the fourth or fifth show, Geddy, Alex, and I were talking about how the shows were going, and Geddy said, 'I don't think we've peaked yet.'"[1]

JULY 7, 2010
CHICAGO, ILLINOIS
CHARTER ONE PAVILION, Northerly Island, 1300 South Linn White Drive
AN EVENING WITH RUSH
TICKETS: $40.00 (lawn) / $80.00 (reserved grandstand) / $125.00 (reserved floor) / $172.33 (average price of tickets sold including VIP); price included $9.50 parking fee
NOTES: Postponed due to rainout. Rescheduled to August 23. Venue staff distributed free rain ponchos to the crowd. After waiting forty-five minutes inside the rain-soaked pavilion, fans were informed that the show had been postponed and their tickets would be honored at the new date. The unhappy groan of 7,500 people in unison can be heard by fans in the parking garage, almost a mile away. The difficult decision to cancel the performance was made by Live Nation, Rush's production team and Ray Danniels, though their hands were tied by puddles on the stage and little in the way of protection to the stage area.
MARK CAMPANA (PRESIDENT OF LIVE NATION MIDWEST MUSIC): "The key was the amount of water that had fallen. The wind caused the water to blow onstage. We all decided not to test the electrical system. We could have cranked up the electricity, but we felt a test could cause harm to people since they were already in the theater. Equipment was set up. We are always going to err on the conservative side when it comes to safety."[2]

JULY 9, 2010
SARNIA, ONTARIO
SARNIA BAYFEST, Centennial Park, Front Street at Exmouth. Venue opened on July 15, 1999.
AN EVENING WITH RUSH
TICKETS: $45.99 (unlicensed general admission) / $49.99 (licensed general admission) / $119.99 (unlicensed VIP) /

$149.99 (licensed VIP) CAD; licensed tickets are located within areas serving alcohol
ATTENDANCE: 19,546
CAPACITY: 20,000
CONCERT GROSS: $1,220,000 CAD
NOTES: Incredibly, the steampunk spider lighting truss weighed around 80,000 pounds. Before their performance on July 9 at Bayfest, the show's organizers authorize $30,000 in upgrades to the festival's stage to allow for the lighting unit. A concert usually requires a maximum of 1,200 amps. Rush required 1,200 amps just for lighting, along with 200 for movement, 400 for sound, and 200 for video. Due to venue weight constraints, the spider lighting rig remained stationary. Since there was no opener, an assortment of local bands were scattered throughout the grounds, performing between the opening gates and Rush.
MICHELE STOKLEY (BAYFEST): "What they have is really built for an arena, not a stage like ours. They don't do a lot of festivals like this, but they wanted to do the full show and we wanted to give everyone else the full show. Our capacity for the roof is 60,000 pounds and they went over by 20,000 pounds because of their moving lighting unit that looks like a giant spider. We have to build special trussing for it. We basically had to go back to the power company and say, how are we going to do this? We generally bring in three generators for sound, lights and video. So we've had to bring in a fourth generator, and another for backup."[3]
SARNIA OBSERVER: "Two Rush sets get two thumbs up: On a beautiful night in Sarnia, the crowd showed up, but Rush showed up too. After thirty-six years playing together, they're still one of the best live acts around, and they'll keep loyal throngs of fans coming back again and again, even if they play for another thirty-six."

JULY 11, 2010
OTTAWA, ONTARIO
OTTAWA BLUESFEST, Canadian War Museum, LeBreton Flats Park, 1 Vimy Place. Festival first held in 1994, at this location since 2007.
AN EVENING WITH RUSH
TICKETS: $50.00 (general admission) / $150.00 / $62.40 CAD (average price)

ATTENDANCE: 31,298
CAPACITY: 35,000
CONCERT GROSS: $1,970,000 CAD
NOTES: Also performing today at Bluesfest on various different stages were Ozomatli, Levon Helm Band, and John Hiatt. Due to venue weight constraints, the spider lighting rig remained stationary.

JULY 13, 2010
TORONTO, ONTARIO
THE MOLSON AMPHITHEATRE, Ontario Place, 909 Lake Shore Boulevard West. Venue opened on May 18, 1995.
AN EVENING WITH RUSH
TICKETS: $144.75 (orchestra) / $344.75 (VIP) / $177.67 CAD (average price of tickets sold including VIP)
ATTENDANCE: 12,453
CAPACITY: 14,528
CONCERT GROSS: $813,868 CAD
NOTES: A hot, humid night, with Alex changing shirts three times in an effort to keep the sweat off of his strings. Due to venue weight constraints, the spider lighting rig remained stationary.
TORONTO SUN: "Rush perform classic album live: Given the quality of the performance, considering the quantity of material played and all three being forty-something-challenged, maybe they actually have a time machine."

JULY 15, 2010
QUEBEC CITY, QUEBEC
FESTIVAL D'ETE DE QUEBEC, Plains of Abraham, Avenue Wilifrid-Laurier. Festival originated in 1968.
TICKETS: $54.00 (CAD) for festival pass
ATTENDANCE: 88,550
CAPACITY: 100,000
CONCERT GROSS: $3,860,000 CAD
NOTES: Rush's largest headline show to date. Onstage, Alex, Geddy, and Neil were flawless on a beautiful evening, feeding off the energy of the massive crowd.
GEDDY (ONSTAGE, IN FRENCH): "Good evening Québec! We are happy to be here, to see your beautiful faces in the crowd."
LE JOURNAL DE QUEBEC: "Rush wall to wall!: Our three virtuosos have lost none of their agility through individual and group performance that raised the crowd to the seventh heaven, from beginning to end!"

JULY 17, 2010
TORONTO, ONTARIO

AIR CANADA CENTRE, 40 Bay Street. Venue dedicated on February 19, 1999.

AN EVENING WITH RUSH

TICKETS: $55.00 / $75.00 / $119.00 / $139.00 / $221.35 CAD (average price of tickets sold including VIP); face value, minus fees

ATTENDANCE: 12,191; sold out

CONCERT GROSS: $1,258,740 CAD

NOTES: Stage-right tech Scott Appleton was out of sorts, and Lerxst was none too happy about it. His mandolin was left onstage during "Workin' Them Angels," with Alex kicking it to get the tech's attention. The problems continued, with technical glitches during "YYZ" and "Limelight." On the latter, Alex was given a new guitar and the sound cut out on the iconic opening riff. Being a consummate professional, Lerxst took out his frustration on blistering versions of "La Villa Strangiato" and "Working Man."

NATIONAL POST: "Some 15,000 fans at Air Canada Centre, predominately males wearing black T-shirts and jeans, explode out of their seats at the opening riff of 'The Spirit of Radio.' The atmosphere bristles with the energy of air instruments: air drums, air guitars and, because this is Rush, even air basses."

JULY 19, 2010
UNCASVILLE, CONNECTICUT

MOHEGAN SUN ARENA, Mohegan Sun Casino, 1 Mohegan Sun Boulevard. Venue opened on September 25, 2001.

AN EVENING WITH RUSH

TICKETS: $70.00 / $90.00 / $188.27 (average price of tickets sold including VIP); face value, minus fees

ATTENDANCE: 5,291

CAPACITY: 7,626

CONCERT GROSS: $452,430

HARTFORD COURANT: "Rush Still Summons Fire, Virtuosity in Sun Concert: It's paradoxical that the trio seemed the most spontaneous as it played through the seven songs on *Moving Pictures*—everyone knew what was coming next, after all."

JULY 21, 2010
CAMDEN, NEW JERSEY

SUSQUEHANNA BANK CENTER, 1 Harbour Boulevard. Venue opened on June 2, 1995.

AN EVENING WITH RUSH

TICKETS: $35.00 (lawn) / $65.00 (pavilion) / $90.00 (lodge) / $110.00 (orchestra) / $150.00 (gold circle) / $350.00 (VIP)

ATTENDANCE: 9,760

CAPACITY: 14,880

CONCERT GROSS: $696,214

NOTES: Venue aka Tweeter Center.

GEDDY (ONSTAGE): "It's pretty hot and sticky tonight, which makes the music sound better—hot and sticky!"

JULY 23, 2010
SARATOGA SPRINGS, NEW YORK

SARATOGA PERFORMING ARTS CENTER, 108 Avenue of Pines. Venue opened on July 9, 1966.

AN EVENING WITH RUSH

TICKETS: $35.00 (lawn) / $65.00 (pavilion) / $125.00 (orchestra) / $148.93 (average price of tickets sold including VIP); face value, minus fees

ATTENDANCE: 8,297

CAPACITY: 13,977

CONCERT GROSS: $575,493

NOTES: Downpours during the day became a drizzle by showtime, with a sea of ponchos covering the lawn. No pyro was used. Neil's entire performance (including preshow warm-up and sound check) was filmed, with the footage used in the *Taking Center Stage* DVD release (October 11, 2011). The Professor was also combating an inner-ear infection, to the point where one of his ears was almost completely blocked. A doctor arrived backstage to evaluate his condition, and despite the fact that he could barely hear, Neil played well.

JOE BERGAMINI (CO-PRODUCER): "The footage we captured there is a dream come true for fans of Neil who want to observe and understand his playing: four separate cameras look at him from various angles, showing Neil only, playing every song in the set list. We also created a special audio mix for the concert performances, with the drums turned up slightly louder than normal. This aspect of the DVD is unprecedented; not only do you get to see and hear Neil talk about and demonstrate the drum parts, but you also get to see the entire concert documented especially for drummers."[4]

NEIL: "The Saratoga one was specifically focused on getting the drums on camera, and then the mixes are quite enhanced. I think it's a normal sort of balance—that's about where I hear the drums! We always laugh about that in the studio, because I really do like loud drums. I think they're exciting, and not just because it's me. Yeah, I like that mix. I'll just say it."[5]

JULY 24, 2010
WANTAGH, NEW YORK

NIKON AT JONES BEACH, 1000 Ocean Parkway. Venue dedicated on June 26, 1952.

AN EVENING WITH RUSH

TICKETS: $36.50 (mezzanine) / $61.50 (stadium 2) / $91.50 (stadium 1) / $151.50 (orchestra) / $165.21 (average price of tickets sold including VIP)

ATTENDANCE: 13,586

CAPACITY: 14,090

CONCERT GROSS: $1,022,344

NOTES: The full moon and cool ocean breezes couldn't break the swelter of the day's record ninety-seven-degree heat. Before the gig, many fans took advantage of the beach, which is just across the parking lot from the venue. During the show, two healthy-looking barmaids took the stage, with Geddy looking agitated when one of them couldn't remove herself from the spotlight. During the first leg of the tour, Neil logged 8,500 motorcycle miles.

GEDDY (ONSTAGE): "Thanks for coming out and enduring the heat. We're gonna sweat tonight."

NICK KOTOS (EX-PRODUCTION MANAGER): "I didn't see them perform during the 2007 tour . . . I saw them on the *Time Machine* tour though. I stopped in and said 'hello.' It was just like seeing a buddy that you hadn't seen for a few years . . . we chit-chatted and caught up. They are still friendly guys. You really have to do something horrendous to fall out of favor. They all have great memories. Guys who were on the lighting crew or the sound crew for two legs of a tour . . . and we'd have these guys show up, and these guys would just completely remember them and were still friendly with them."[6]

THE AQUARIAN WEEKLY: "Rush: Nikon Beach: It was a chance to hear 'The Camera Eye' a rarely played fan favorite about the cultural differences between Manhattan and London. Montages of New York City flashed on the screen, sending the crowd into that frenzy that occurs when a song about their home city is played."

NEIL: "Before starting this tour, I had spent nearly every early morning with baby Olivia. After a month away, I returned home to an eleven-month-old baby who didn't know me."[7]

AUGUST 5, 2010
WEST VALLEY CITY, UTAH
USANA AMPHITHEATRE, 5150 South 6055 West. Venue opened on July 3, 2003.
AN EVENING WITH RUSH
TICKETS: $32.50 (lawn) / $65.00 / $100.00 / $125.00 / $199.35 (average price of tickets sold including VIP)
ATTENDANCE: 8,660
CAPACITY: 14,500
CONCERT GROSS: $558,868
NOTES: Forecasted rain held off until the encore, when it began to drizzle during "Working Man."
NEIL: "A good show at the amphitheatre. After a break of even eight or nine days, my bandmates and I often feel as though we have probably forgotten all the songs, but of course they come right out again—plus we're all rested and refreshed, and don't hurt anywhere, so the first show back is always a pleasure for us."[8]

AUGUST 7, 2010
AUBURN, WASHINGTON
WHITE RIVER AMPHITHEATRE, Muckleshoot Indian Reservation, 40601 Auburn Enumclaw Road. Venue opened on June 14, 2003.
AN EVENING WITH RUSH
TICKETS: $44.50 (lawn) / $74.50 (pavilion) / $109.50 (orchestra) / $300.00 (VIP; face value) / $239.12 (average price of tickets sold including VIP)
ATTENDANCE: 11,742
CAPACITY: 15,865
CONCERT GROSS: $855,997
NOTES: Sound check on a rainy afternoon included "Faithless," "Presto," "The Spirit of Radio," and "Subdivisions." Onstage, Neil's sticks went higher and higher with each toss and catch. During "2112: The Temples of Syrinx," after Geddy sang: "And the meek shall inherit the earth," Alex didn't play the guitar part, with Geddy saying "Where is that guy?" Lerxst then snuck off behind his amps to hide in shame, with Geddy laughing at him.

GEDDY (ONSTAGE, AFTER PERFORMING "MOVING PICTURES"): "It's hard to believe that was thirty years ago. I was six years old when we wrote that."
***THE NEWS TRIBUNE* (TACOMA):** "Reigning kings of prog-rock turn back time in Auburn."

AUGUST 9, 2010
MOUNTAIN VIEW, CALIFORNIA
SHORELINE AMPHITHEATRE, One Amphitheatre Parkway. Venue opened on July 5, 1986.
AN EVENING WITH RUSH
TICKETS: $23.50 (lawn, limited advance promotion) $39.50 (lawn) / $53.50 (upper pavilion) / $73.50 (lower pavilion) / $119.50 (orchestra) / $204.17 (average price of tickets sold including VIP)
ATTENDANCE: 13,994
CAPACITY: 14,852
CONCERT GROSS: $695,844
NOTES: Metallica bassist Robert Trujillo rocks out in the pit. During the polka intro to "La Villa Strangiato," Alex tuned his white Gibson ES-335 with Geddy wondering what he's doing. For "Working Man" he switched over to his Les Paul.
KTVU: "Canadian Power Trio Rocks Mountain View."

AUGUST 11, 2010
UNIVERSAL CITY, CALIFORNIA
GIBSON AMPHITHEATRE, 100 University City Plaza. Venue opened for music on June 28, 1972.
AN EVENING WITH RUSH
TICKETS: $63.25 / $93.25 / $148.25 / $353.00 (VIP) / $299.71 (average price of tickets sold including VIP)
ATTENDANCE: 5,455
CAPACITY: 5,954
CONCERT GROSS: $705,455
NOTES: Musicians in attendance include guitarist Tom Morello, drummer Chad Smith, and Alice In Chains bassist Mike Inez.
TOM MORELLO (RAGE AGAINST THE MACHINE GUITARIST): "Saw Rush last night. And, at the risk of sounding like one of those bromance dudes in *I Love You, Man* . . . they totally rule."
***SOUND SPIKE*:** "Rush at Gibson Amphitheatre was masterful musicianship energetically performed."

AUGUST 13, 2010
IRVINE, CALIFORNIA
VERIZON WIRELESS AMPHITHEATER, 8808 Irvine Center Drive. Venue opened on August 21, 1981.
AN EVENING WITH RUSH
TICKETS: $25.50 (lawn) / $39.50 (upper pavilion) / $69.50 (lower pavilion) / $149.50 (orchestra) / $349.50 (VIP) / $183.71 (average price of tickets sold including VIP)
ATTENDANCE: 12,403
CAPACITY: 14,956
CONCERT GROSS: $870,119
NOTES: "Presto" and "Subdivisions" were performed in sound check. Musicians in attendance include Danny Carey, Taylor Hawkins, and No Doubt guitarist Tom Dumont. Onstage, Alex was upset with someone upfront who continued to video the entire show, despite being asked to stop, so during "Closer to the Heart," he conveyed his feelings directly to the perpetrator.
***HOLLYWOOD REPORTER*:** "Rush concert a workout for air drummers: Geddy Lee delivered a reined-in yet expressive vocal, adding expertly placed and paced bass line and runs; Alex Lifeson added sharp, purposeful guitar licks; and master drummer Neil Peart—perfectly re-created some of his most satisfying timekeeping and fills. Stunning. For nearly three hours, Rush proved why it remains among rock's top live acts."

AUGUST 14, 2010
LAS VEGAS, NEVADA
MGM GRAND GARDEN ARENA, 3799 Las Vegas Boulevard South. Venue opened on December 31, 1993.
AN EVENING WITH RUSH
TICKETS: $55.00 / $85.00 / $150.00 / $350.00 (VIP; face value) / $259.60 (average price of tickets sold including VIP)
ATTENDANCE: 9,591
CAPACITY: 10,258
CONCERT GROSS: $993,351
NOTES: It was a progressive rock weekend in Vegas, with Porcupine Tree playing the night before and Primus taking the stage at midnight after Rush's gig. On the way to Las Vegas, Neil's bus broke down, leaving him and Michael bus-less for days.
NEIL: "Riding my own motorcycle out of

the MGM Grand Arena after the show was certainly a novel experience (unique even, as I have never actually left a show by motorcycle), and I confess that I was mildly thrilled at having our two motorcycles led by two police bikes, with flashing lights and everything. (Nice to have them in front of me, for once, instead of behind)."[9]

LAS VEGAS REVIEW-JOURNAL: "This is the duality of a Rush gig: They're simultaneously brainy and goofy, self-assured and self-effacing, a bunch of smart kids reveling in the joys of dumb fun. Rush's music is like a secret handshake between friends: Not everyone gets it, but those that do share a bond. The highlight of the suite—and perhaps the entire show—was a hard-nosed, wide-eyed take on 'The Camera Eye,' an epic eleven-minute jam that somehow managed to be simultaneously funky, dissonant and melodic. This is perhaps Rush's greatest skill: to be several things all at once, immediate and textured, overblown and nuanced, unorthodox and mainstream."

AUGUST 16, 18, 2010
MORRISON, COLORADO
RED ROCKS AMPHITHEATRE, 18300 West Alameda Parkway. Historic venue dedicated on June 15, 1941.
AN EVENING WITH RUSH
TICKETS: $55.50 / $85.50 / $110.50 / $154.24 (average price of tickets sold including VIP)
TWO-DAY RED ROCKS ATTENDANCE: 16,376
TWO-DAY CAPACITY: 17,320
TWO-DAY RED ROCKS CONCERT GROSS: $1,501,369
NOTES: The crew were kept on their toes right from the start, when the opening film stopped early (during Rash's country and western version), before the band was even onstage. Alex casually sauntered on, looking for Geddy and Neil. During "Time Stand Still," Alex broke a string, but continued playing his foot pedals until the tech brought his Telecaster onstage as replacement. In "Working Man," Neil didn't miss a beat, as Gump was practically in his lap, tightening a stand. Despite the technical issues, Alex, Geddy, and Neil turned in a strong performance at an amazing venue. Due to weight constraints at Red Rocks, the spider lighting rig remained stationary. On the second night, Neil's ear

infection was really bothering him, so he consulted with an ENT specialist in Denver who advised him to use headphones in place of inner-ear monitors, which he did beginning with this show (held on with duct tape, à la Keith Moon). Onstage, "Marathon" featured a great extended guitar solo from Alex.
GEDDY (ONSTAGE, AFTER VIDEO MALFUNCTIONS): "Hello Denver! Sometimes magic doesn't happen."
THE DENVER POST: "Rush was clearly performing in top form, perhaps to make up for some of the technical glitches that plagued them at their Monday night show. Though Rush and their fans spent the evening moving through time, it seemed the perfect evening where everyone truly wished time did stand still."
NEIL: "Both ears were badly infected, aggravated by wearing the in-ear monitors onstage, and perhaps by wearing earplugs on the motorcycle, too—heat and moisture create a rainforest environment for bacteria, fungus, eczema, and psoriasis. The doctors prescribed a heavy regimen of three different antibiotics and recommended that I switch to headphones (and no earplugs on the bike, but its Cee Bailey windscreen is pretty quiet). Within a few days, they had given me back two reasonably healthy ears. Never again will I take for granted simply hearing what I'm playing, what the other guys are playing, and—in everyday life—what people are saying to me."[10]

AUGUST 20, 2010
WICHITA, KANSAS
INTRUST BANK ARENA, 500 East Waterman Street. Venue opened on January 2, 2010.
AN EVENING WITH RUSH
TICKETS: $45.00 / $65.00 / $90.00 / $156.08 (average price of tickets sold including VIP)
ATTENDANCE: 5,119
CAPACITY: 6,676
CONCERT GROSS: $382,710
NOTES: First Wichita-area performance since the May 24, 1992. Onstage, Neil continued wearing headphones. During "Vital Signs," Geddy took vocal liberties by adding "everybody got to emancipate from the norm" on the outro.
THE WICHITA EAGLE: "Rush pleases Wichita crowd with 3-hour show: Lee wasted little time with banter. Instead,

the music, played to near perfection, and a spectacular light display—something the band has always been known for—went on almost nonstop."

AUGUST 22, 2010
MARYLAND HEIGHTS, MISSOURI
VERIZON WIRELESS AMPHITHEATER, 14141 Riverport Drive. Venue opened on June 14, 1991.
AN EVENING WITH RUSH
TICKETS: $30.00 (lawn) / $37.50 / $65.00 / $82.50 / $125.00 (orchestra) / $325.00 (VIP) / $165.19 (average price of tickets sold including VIP); prices included $6.00 finance charge
ATTENDANCE: 11,008
CAPACITY: 13,000
CONCERT GROSS: $614,821
NOTES: On July 23, Kings of Leon left the stage after playing only three songs at the same venue, due to pigeon poop falling down from the stage roof. Geddy can't resist making a comment.
GEDDY (ONSTAGE): "So this is where they had that pigeon thing, huh? Well I don't care how much those pigeons shit, he's not leaving (pointing to Alex)!"
ST. LOUIS POST-DISPATCH: "Rush rocks hard during encore: One of the most memorable moments of Rush's concert began with one of several bits of self-deprecating humor."

AUGUST 23, 2010
CHICAGO, ILLINOIS
CHARTER ONE PAVILION, Northerly Island. Venue built in 2005.
AN EVENING WITH RUSH
TICKETS: $40.00 / $80.00 / $125.00 (face value)
ATTENDANCE: 6,247
CAPACITY: 7,068
CONCERT GROSS: $568,858
NOTES: Rescheduled from July 7, 2012, because of a rainout. As a thank you for any inconvenience, Rush gave attending fans an exclusive baseball hat, which featured the stitching "The Rain Date Chicago-2010." Onstage, the band was very apologetic about the July postponement, with Geddy referring to "that horrible rain thing." A crew bus broke down at the venue, but was quickly replaced.

AUGUST 25, 2010
OMAHA, NEBRASKA
QWEST CENTER OMAHA, 455 North 10th Street. Venue opened on September 12, 2003.
AN EVENING WITH RUSH
TICKETS: $50.00 / $75.00 / $95.00 / $123.58 (average price of tickets sold including VIP); face value, minus $2.00 finance charge
ATTENDANCE: 6,236
CAPACITY: 7,461
CONCERT GROSS: $479,519
NOTES: Rush's first Omaha appearance since November 4, 1991.
OMAHA WORLD-HERALD: "Rush's superfans don't miss a beat: All three played with absolute precision, close enough to their albums that their fans knew every note. It was a fun show, and the band displayed a mastery that shows why they have such devoted fans."

AUGUST 27, 2010
NORTH ST. PAUL, MINNESOTA
MINNESOTA STATE FAIR GRANDSTAND, 1265 Snelling Avenue North
AN EVENING WITH RUSH
TICKETS: $38.00 / $58.00 / $68.00 / $176.70 (average price of tickets sold including VIP); face value, minus $2.00 finance charge
ATTENDANCE: 12,882
CAPACITY: 13,248
CONCERT GROSS: $779,606
NOTES: "Presto" "The Spirit of Radio" (short, jam version), and "Subdivisions" (with jam-ending) were performed in sound check. Exactly thirty-six years prior, Rush played the Minnesota State Fair on Alex's 21st birthday. Now, in celebration of Alex's fifty-seventh birthday, the crew distributed "Big Al'z 57th" T-shirts, with Neil sporting one onstage. After "Presto," Geddy wished Lerxst happy birthday while a crew member gave him his "special" gifts, a foot-long pronto pup and a pork-chop on a stick (two Minnesota State Fair staples which, when put together, offer sexual connotations). Due to venue weight constraints,

the spider lighting rig remained stationary. A fireworks display closed out the night, right after the outro video.
GEDDY (ONSTAGE): "The whole band and crew chipped in and bought him a very, very special gift, which we'd like to bring out . . . we spare no expense for this guy. Happy birthday, Lerxst!"
NEIL: "The special T-shirt was made up by the crew for everyone to wear that day, and just after dinner more than thirty of us gathered in front of the 'dressing trailer' to sing 'Happy Birthday.' I decided to wear it onstage for the first set. John Arrowsmith was able to capture this shot of me while walking across the stage in the hotdog costume (you have to have seen our show to get that reference, I guess), with his Nikon and fisheye lens around his neck. Of course I had to smile at that. More than one friend has already remarked that this photo captures the 'real me' they know, and that's nice. My mother has always complained that I don't smile enough onstage. But it's a grim, arduous, sometimes painful job, and I never trust a drummer who smiles too much while he's playing."[11]

AUGUST 29, 2010
COLUMBUS, OHIO
NATIONWIDE ARENA, 200 West Nationwide Boulevard. Venue opened on September 9, 2000.
AN EVENING WITH RUSH
TICKETS: $50.00 / $70.00 / $95.00 / $300.00 (VIP) / $184.41 (average price of tickets sold including VIP); face value, minus $2.00 finance charge
ATTENDANCE: 11,402
CAPACITY: 12,354
CONCERT GROSS: $831,186
NOTES: With the show almost SRO, the promoter decided to move the stage back one section to accommodate demand.
COLUMBUS DISPATCH: "Rockers use time to their advantage: Rush used a time machine to stage a superb three-hour, two-part concert Sunday night in Nationwide Arena."

AUGUST 31, 2010
ALLENTOWN, PENNSYLVANIA
FAIRGROUNDS GRANDSTAND, Great Allentown Fairgrounds, 302 North 17th Street. Venue opened in September 1911. Original grandstand built in 1902, rebuilt in 1911.

AN EVENING WITH RUSH
TICKETS: $49.00 / $69.00 / $85.00 / $185.60 (average price of tickets sold including VIP)
ATTENDANCE: 9,622
CAPACITY: 9,694
CONCERT GROSS: $706,830
NOTES: *The Morning Call* states attendance as 10,011. The band's first Allentown appearance since September 30, 1980. Rush's gross of $706,830 broke the box office record of $700,000 set by the Jonas Brothers in 2008.[12] Fans purchased all of the $85.00 tickets (the fair's most expensive ever) within the first thirty minutes of sale. Due to venue weight constraints, the spider lighting rig remained stationary.
THE MORNING CALL: "Rush at Allentown Fair is one for the ages—well, almost: So virtuoso was the playing of Rush's members that for more of the show, the crowd was staid, as if listening to a symphony. It erupted occasionally—and hardily—to reward a particularly good solo or to cheer a favorite song."

SEPTEMBER 2, 2010
GEDDES, NEW YORK
NEW YORK STATE FAIR GRANDSTAND, EMPIRE EXPO CENTER, 581 State Fair Boulevard. Venue opened on August 27, 1978.
AN EVENING WITH RUSH
TICKETS: $45.00 / $65.00 / $145.29 (average price of tickets sold including VIP)
ATTENDANCE: 12,364
CAPACITY: 17,367
CONCERT GROSS: $710,980
NOTES: Rush's first Syracuse-area appearance since April 2, 1983. Rush's impressive attendance figure outpaces that of Aerosmith, Tim McGraw, and Rascal Flatts by a wide margin. Onstage, a woman performs sign language for the hearing impaired, and Alex can't resist trying to flirt with her.
THE POST STANDARD: "Rush treats Syracuse fans to rousing *Moving Pictures* and more at New York State Fair Grandstand: Singer and bass player Lee took the stage wearing a Rash T-shirt. Priceless. As soon as he opened his mouth to the strains of 'Spirit of Radio,' the fans—many men, many forty or up, knew it was good. For a man who's been putting his voice way up there with this

band for forty years, Lee can still hit those oh-so-high notes."

SEPTEMBER 3, 2010
HOLMDEL, NEW JERSEY
PNC BANK ARTS CENTER, Exit 116, Garden State Parkway. Venue opened on June 15, 1968.
AN EVENING WITH RUSH
TICKETS: $29.75 (lawn) / $50.25 (pavilion) / $90.25 (loge) / $150.25 (orchestra) / $350.00 (VIP) / $219.89 (average price of tickets sold including VIP); face value, minus $6.00 finance charge
ATTENDANCE: 10,974
CAPACITY: 14,000
CONCERT GROSS: $784,117
NOTES: A potential bad situation was averted when Hurricane Earl moved further offshore, leaving only rain and wind in its wake. Due to venue restrictions and the forecast high winds, the spider lighting rig remained stationary.
THE STAR LEDGER: "Rockers take new spin on old format: They came to Holmdel to be startled and amazed by three outstanding musicians who have never been hip, but have always shot for the stratosphere."

SEPTEMBER 14, 2010
BOSTON, MASSACHUSETTS
TD GARDEN, 100 Legends Way. Venue opened on September 30, 1995.
AN EVENING WITH RUSH
TICKETS: $50.00 / $85.00 / $125.00 / $300.00 (VIP) / $169.16 (average price of tickets sold including VIP); price includes $2.50 finance charge
ATTENDANCE: 11,331
CAPACITY: 11,903
CONCERT GROSS: $948,004
NOTES: Venue aka Fleet Center. It was a tough night on stage right, as Alex was forced to deal with guitar outages. The first one occurred just after the "circuits blowing" explosion in "Far Cry." Alex stayed onstage, playing guitar and pedals, with only bass and drums heard for the duration. He then returned to the stage for the encore, and with his guitar still not working, Neil started into "La Villa Strangiato." Lerxst turned the entire polka intro into a hilarious ad-lib jam: "I have no guitar. Still no guitar. I hate my guitar, I hate my amps, etc, etc," which goes on for quite a while (much to the delight of the crowd, though

Lerxst is clearly far from amused), until the matter is resolved. No pyro used during "Witch Hunt" or "2112."
BOSTON HERALD: "Rush Deserves The 'Limelight': The Canadian power trio never takes things easy. That's one reason they're still selling out large halls after thirty-five years. Whether you came to concentrate intensely or just play air drums along with Neil Peart, the show offered plenty for the faithful."

SEPTEMBER 16, 2010
PITTSBURGH, PENNSYLVANIA
CONSOL ENERGY CENTER, 1001 Fifth Avenue. Venue opened on August 15, 2010.
AN EVENING WITH RUSH
TICKETS: $40.50 / $62.00 / $90.50 / $300.00 (VIP) / $150.91 (average price of tickets sold including VIP)
ATTENDANCE: 11,053
CAPACITY: 11,487
CONCERT GROSS: $687,691
NOTES: During "Marathon," the explosion after the vocal "lucky shot in the dark" kicked out Neil's bass drum mic. Members of the crew took to the stage dressed as a hot dog, a gorilla, and a shopping cart guy with an apron. For the "La Villa Strangiato" encore, Alex added some vocal accompaniment to the polka intro, stating: "I have guitar . . . I have guitar" in response to "not" having one in Boston.
PITTSBURGH POST-GAZETTE: "Rush makes time stand still: It was so generous that at the end it was hard to imagine any of the thirteen shows the band played at the old arena topping this one. Thirty years from now people will wish they had a time machine to go back to Thursday night."

SEPTEMBER 18, 2010
BRISTOW, VIRGINIA
NISSAN PAVILION, 7800 Cellar Door Drive. Venue opened on June 3, 1995.
AN EVENING WITH RUSH
TICKETS: $25.00 (advance lawn promo) / $49.00 (lawn) / $80.00 (pavilion) / $120.00 (orchestra) / $346.00 (VIP) / $188.70 (average price of tickets sold including VIP); face value, minus $6.00 parking fee
ATTENDANCE: 13,999
CAPACITY: 16,639
CONCERT GROSS: $866,704

NOTES: Venue aka Jiffy Lube Live. During sound check, the band ran through "Faithless," "Presto," "The Spirit of Radio," and "Subdivisions."
THE MYCENAEAN: "1970s Rock Trio Proves Its Lasting Relevance: The impressive comeback of a long-unpopular group in the new decade is a legitimate possibility; many now see the genius behind the music that for so long has sat in obscurity."

SEPTEMBER 21, 2010
TULSA, OKLAHOMA
BOK CENTER, 200 South Denver Avenue West. Venue opened on August 30, 2008.
AN EVENING WITH RUSH
TICKETS: $47.50 / $75.00 / $95.00 / $179.88 (average price of tickets sold including VIP); face value, minus $2.00 finance charge
ATTENDANCE: 7,110
CAPACITY: 10,027
CONCERT GROSS: $577,753
NOTES: The band's first Tulsa appearance since June 13, 1984. Neil (still wearing headphones) hit the drums so hard that he broke his snare drum head during the middle of "Subdivisions," right before the lyric "drawn like moths we drift into the city." The song continued, as he improvised, keeping the beat, and banging home a solid rendition to close out the first set.
NEIL: "When there is an equipment failure during the show—a broken head, loose snare mount—we choreograph the change almost automatically. I pick the break between songs when it's possible, step down off the riser and out of the way, while Gump and Anson make the trade. Usually nobody else will even know what happened."[13]

SEPTEMBER 23, 2010
SAN ANTONIO, TEXAS
AT&T CENTER, 1 AT&T Center Parkway. Venue opened on October 18, 2002.
AN EVENING WITH RUSH
TICKETS: $50.00 / $75.00 / $95.00 / $125.00 / $327.00 (VIP) / $190.16 (average price of tickets sold including VIP); face value, minus $2.00 finance charge
ATTENDANCE: 9,289
CAPACITY: 11,326
CONCERT GROSS: $731,550

NOTES: The venue's "luxurious" Terrace Restaurant dished out a special "Rush Dinner" for $32.95 per person.
GEDDY (ONSTAGE): "Does anyone remember 'Randy's Rodeo?'"
SAN ANTONIO EXPRESS-NEWS: "Rush rocks AT&T Center: The pace was relentless, the audience's enthusiasm seemingly endless as Lee, Peart, and Lifeson opened with riff-laden classics 'The Spirit of Radio,' 'Time Stand Still,' and 'Presto.' The tight trio played precisely, with Lee's high vocals leading the assault. Fans were on their feet the whole time at this virtuosic concert, one of the best of the year."

SEPTEMBER 25, 2010
THE WOODLANDS, TEXAS
C. W. MITCHELL PAVILION, 2005 Lake Robbins Drive. Venue opened on April 27, 1990.
AN EVENING WITH RUSH
TICKETS: $35.00 (lawn) / $60.00 (upper reserved) / $85.00 (lower reserved) / $110.00 (orchestra) / $310.00 (VIP) / $221.56 (average price of tickets sold including VIP); face value, minus fees
ATTENDANCE: 15,225
CAPACITY: 15,858
CONCERT GROSS: $897,778
NOTES: The venue was packed on a sweltering day. Neil came in too early during "Time Stand Still," but the band was quick to find their groove, and put on a great show. The sweat poured off of Alex, who changed his shirt four times in an effort to keep his strings dry.
HOUSTON PRESS: "Rush At The Woodlands: Ladies, if you want your pick of occasionally attractive, probably employed, mostly shy and retiring males, get thee to a Rush concert."

SEPTEMBER 26, 2010
DALLAS, TEXAS
SUPERPAGES.COM CENTER, Fair Park, 1818 First Avenue. Venue opened on July 23, 1988.
AN EVENING WITH RUSH
TICKETS: $29.00 (lawn) / $54.00 (pavilion) / $83.00 (upper reserved) / $104.00 (lower reserved) / $195.78 (average price of tickets sold including VIP)
ATTENDANCE: 11,420
CAPACITY: 13,715

CONCERT GROSS: $723,024
NOTES: The *Dallas Morning News* reports an attendance figure of 11,445, and chose this gig as one of the Best Concerts of 2010.
DALLAS MORNING NEWS: "These Canadians remain relevant with an engulfing, musically precise brand of progressive rock that draws the diehards and the curious. The crowd adored every minute. Lee's muscular bass thumps, Peart's thunderous drumming and Lifeson's piercing electric guitar licks brought 'Tom Sawyer,' 'Limelight,' 'YYZ' and the other four 'Pictures' tunes to expansive life. 'Pictures' is Rush's finest collection of songs. Live is the best way to appreciate them."

SEPTEMBER 29, 2010
ALPHARETTA, GEORGIA
VERIZON WIRELESS AMPHITHEATRE, 2200 Encore Parkway. Venue opened in May, 2008.
AN EVENING WITH RUSH
TICKETS: $40.00 (lawn) / $59.00 (upper pavilion) / $75.00 (lower pavilion) / $89.00 (orchestra) / $284.00 (VIP) / $238.01 (average price of tickets sold including VIP)
ATTENDANCE: 11,437
CAPACITY: 12,086
CONCERT GROSS: $745,988
NOTES: CNN's John Roberts interviewed the band before the show, and then jammed with them on "Limelight" at sound check. During "2112: Overture," members of the crew entertained the band by dressing as a gorilla and a hot dog, taking to the stage on bicycles.
GEDDY (ONSTAGE): "Pardon me. I almost swallowed my own tongue, and that's not easy to do."

OCTOBER 1, 2010
TAMPA, FLORIDA
1-800-ASK-GARY AMPHITHEATRE, Florida State Fairgrounds, 4802 US Highway 301 North. Venue opened July 25, 2004.
AN EVENING WITH RUSH

TICKETS: $41.00 (lawn) / $58.50 (300 level) / $85.50 (200 level) / $101.00 (100 level) $117.80 (orchestra) / $190.99 (average price of tickets sold including VIP)
ATTENDANCE: 11,418
CAPACITY: 13,415
CONCERT GROSS: $728,923
NOTES: Venue aka Ford Amphitheatre.
TAMPA BAY TIMES (ADVANCE): "Rush brings sense of humor, decades of hits to Tampa: Ready for a revelation? Rush might be the funniest rock band in the world. Yes, Canada, the same country that gave us Dan Aykroyd, John Candy, and Rich Little also can boast of Geddy Lee, Alex Lifeson, and Neil Peart."

OCTOBER 2, 2010
WEST PALM BEACH, FLORIDA
CRUZAN AMPHITHEATRE, South Florida Fairgrounds, 601–607 Sansburys Way. Venue opened on April 26, 1996.
AN EVENING WITH RUSH
TICKETS: $35.00 (lawn) / $55.00 (upper pavilion) / $75.00 (lower pavilion) / $125.00 (orchestra) / $221.14 (average price of tickets sold including VIP)
ATTENDANCE: 10,647
CAPACITY: 15,116
CONCERT GROSS: $611,647
NOTES: Venue aka Sound Advice Amphitheatre. During "Marathon," the explosion, which accompanies the lyric "or a lucky shot in the dark" shorts out Geddy's vocal mic. The crew changed it out in record time, so the band didn't miss a stride. Tour hijinks were in full effect, as members of the crew dressed as a hot dog and a gorilla and performed ballet during "Closer to the Heart," then re-entered the stage during "2112."
BROWARD PALM BEACH NEW TIMES: "Rush completed the North American leg of its *Time Machine* tour on a stage that seemed to unite the past, present, and future. The creative antique stage design—complete with copper hardware, drums, amplifiers, and other mechanical gadgets—served as the perfect metaphor for this time-travel journey. Occasionally, steam blew out of pipes, creating a magical, clockwork atmosphere. The lighting included retro colors of amber, orange, and green. This colorful stage synched nicely with the dynamic musical patterns of Lee, Lifeson, and Peart."

OCTOBER 8, 2010
SAO PAULO, BRAZIL
ESTADIO DO MORUMBI, Praça Roberto Gomes Pedroza 1, Morumbi. Venue opened on October 2, 1960.

AN EVENING WITH RUSH

TICKETS: R$160.00 (orange bleachers) / R$180.00 (blue and red stands) / R$200.00 (special red bleachers) / R$250.00 (lower chair and track) / R$300.00 (top chair) / R$500.00 (premium track)

ATTENDANCE: 26,015

CAPACITY: 50,600

CONCERT GROSS: R$3,337,130

NOTES: Brazilian publications list attendance as 38,000. Premium, as well as blue and orange seats sold out in advance. The promoter placed 6,000 tickets on sale at a 30 percent discount for ten days beginning September 13. Age Rating: Children under twelve not permitted; twelve years to fifteen years allowed entry when accompanied by parent or legal guardian. In preparation for the massive show, the military police implemented a special security plan, which included 164 officers, 24 vehicles, and 48 motorcycles placed strategically around the area of the stadium. Fans were advised to bring only the money they needed and not to flash cellphones or cameras while walking to or from the concert.

IG, ALEX: "São Paulo is a very vibrant city, has almost the entire population of Canada. Brazil is very modern, and Sao Paulo seems to be the financial and technological center of the country and South America, a major international city. They always treat us very well here."

NEIL: "Oct. 8, 2010, São Paulo, Brazil—Here and now is the perfect time and place to reflect upon Rush's history as a touring band. Tonight, after more than 36 years together, we will be performing at a soccer stadium here, in front of more than 30,000 people. Live performance is the ultimate test of a musician, and of a band. The price, of course, is the nomadic, exhausting, potentially alienating alternate reality of touring life—and it can take a heavy toll (witness so many lost individuals and wrecked relationships, romantic and musical). As long ago as 1989, I decided that such a life was just too much for

me—the grind of traveling, the tedium, the repetition, the separation from home and loved ones, and the constant whirl of strangers around my nucleus of self-contained, reflective peace. Yet twenty-one years later, here I am, doing it all over again. Again and again. And no end in sight."[14]

O ESTADÃO: "Rush in São Paulo: In their return to Brazil after eight years, the Canadian trio brought their conceptual *Time Machine* tour which is a gift for the fans who have followed the band from the beginning. In a full (but not crowded) stadium, it was easy to see how Rush bridged generations without trepidation. The crowd was mainly middle-aged, but one could see many adolescents and even pre-adolescents. The gigantic stage had the habitual pyrotechnics, with high definition big screens and acrobatic cameras. Yet the scenery created a counterpoint to the all the equipment, decorated with jukeboxes and flares hidden behind metal scraps. At the end of the show, another comedy sketch jokes about the idolatry of the fans. The result, however, is ambiguous. When trying to show that they are 'just regular people' and don't take themselves so seriously, Rush end up being even more idolized."

OCTOBER 10, 2010
RIO DE JANEIRO, BRAZIL
PRACA DA APOTEOSE, Av. Marquês de Sapucaí, center Rio. Venue opened in 1983.

AN EVENING WITH RUSH

TICKETS: R$110.00 / R$250.00 (track and bleachers) / R$500 (premium track)

ATTENDANCE: 10,308

CAPACITY: 32,400

CONCERT GROSS: R$1,049,950

NOTES: In March of this year, heavy rains and a tornado caused the stage to collapse prior to a Guns N' Roses concert at Praca da Apoteose. The promoter placed 6,000 tickets on sale at a 30 percent discount for ten days beginning September 13. Age Rating: Children under twelve not permitted; twelve years to fifteen years allowed entry when accompanied by parent or legal guardian.

GEDDY (ONSTAGE): "Hello, good evening Rio! Welcome Brazil! It's a pleasure to be back. I wish I could speak your language better."

WHIPLASH: "Rush: twenty-four songs and almost three-hour show in Rio de Janeiro: The implementation in full of the *Moving Pictures* was perfect. It's amazing the sounds that these three musicians can perform on stage. The instrumental 'YYZ' is sung in chorus by the audience. The hit 'Limelight' comes next, keeping the excitement of both the band and the crowd, which also happens in 'The Camera Eye,' 'Witch Hunt,' and 'Vital Signs.' After nearly three hours of show, twenty-four songs plus a drum solo from one of the best rock drummers in history, the happy Brazilian crowd walked out of Apotheosis Square sure to have seen one of the best rock shows of today."

OCTOBER 15, 2010
BUENOS AIRES, ARGENTINA
ESTADIO GEBA, 3600 Dorrego Avenue, Av. Cnel Jorge Newbery, Marcelino Freire 3381, Bosques de Palermo. Venue opened in 1910.

AN EVENING WITH RUSH

TICKETS: $250.00 (campo) / $405.00 (VIP) ARS; face value, does not include fees of $45.00 and $80.00 ARS respectively

ATTENDANCE: 8,528

CAPACITY: 18,392

CONCERT GROSS: $655,162

NOTES: Rush's Argentina debut. Initially, the show was slated for the Desarrollo al Rio, but was moved to the larger Estadio GEBA. Alex was suffering with the flu, but powered through the performance. The stage setup was moved to the middle of the stadium (closer to the railroad tracks), instead of lengthwise (as noted on the initial ticket sale), which caused some confusion for fans.

ALEX: "I had the flu. I was ill for three days, I was so sick, and I was so worried about it. My wife and I came a few days early to Buenos Aires, and I was so looking forward to seeing the city. And then we spent two days in bed just coughing and sneezing, and we were quite ill. So, that put a little bit of a damper on the gig for me, but the fans were amazing, the audience was terrific, even though the train was going by every five minutes at the stadium."[15]

ROLLING STONE **(ARGENTINA):** "Rush: the powerful time machine: Another debt paid off for a devoted public: for Rush in

Argentina is an old dream. Last night's show at GEBA improved the perception of even the most enthusiastic fan. The band of three showed a surprising technique to recreate imaginatively classic and master the mix of progressive rock and heavy-metal. Rush humorously dodged the pitfalls of virtuosity and excessive pomposity. During the encores, the audience was screaming like Vikings in heat. Tremendous show."

OCTOBER 17, 2010
SANTIAGO, CHILE
ESTADIO NACIONAL, Avenue Grecia 2001, Nunoa. Venue initially opened on December 3, 1938. After renovations, it was re-inaugurated on September 12, 2010.
AN EVENING WITH RUSH
TICKETS: $24,000.00 (gallery) / $35,000.00 (court) / $65.000.00 (lateral and andes) / $100,000.00 (VIP court) / $110.000.00 (silver and golden pacific) / $150,000.00 (VIP pacific) CLP
ATTENDANCE: 36,840
CAPACITY: 51,000
CONCERT GROSS: $3,720,293.00 CLP
NOTES: Rush's Chilean debut. 10,000 tickets were sold first day of sale. Leading up to the concert, the entire world was closely following the fate of "the 33" Chilean miners trapped underground after a shaft collapsed on August 5. The miners were rescued on October 13, just days before the gig. At the stadium the celebration continued. With a Chilean flag onstage and photos of the rescue on rear-screen, Geddy dedicated "Stick It Out" to the miners, as Alex played the song with number 33 painted on his Les Paul. Before the break, Geddy stated that because of their age, they need to go the bathroom (in Spanish), and the entire stadium laughed.
GEDDY (ONSTAGE): "Hola Chile, que son una maravilla. Disculpen mi español Debido a nuestra edad tenemos que tener un intermedio de 20 minutos para que podamos ir al baño."
LA TERCERA, **GEDDY:** "In some countries, we are a cult band and in others we are a mainstream band. Who knows? Who cares? While we're on tour, we see flags from around the world and it is difficult to count how many fans we have in each country. As we've been getting older, we decided to experience new

places. This time we will go to Chile and we are very excited."
ROCKAXIS: "The trio made history debuting in Chile. Sure, it was a show essentially highlighting the glories of the past, but with a band looking and thinking about the future with the certainty that they are one of the most powerful acts in rock music of all time. And many may die in peace. That is sure."

MARCH 30, 2011
SUNRISE, FLORIDA
BANKATLANTIC CENTER, 2555 NW 136th Avenue. Venue opened on October 3, 1998.
AN EVENING WITH RUSH
TICKETS: $49.75 / $79.75 / $129.75 / $311.00 (VIP) / $165.24 (average price of tickets sold including VIP)
ATTENDANCE: 7,671; sold out
CONCERT GROSS: $599,150
NOTES: For the 2011 run, a short segment of "Cygnus X-1" was added to the finale of "Working Man." Onstage, Alex was playing a new red Gibson Axcess guitar. Bicycle legend Lance Armstrong was in attendance this evening.
GEDDY (ONSTAGE): "United States of America. Thanks for having us back for the first date in part two of our *Time Machine* tour. You know how cold it is in Canada? It's really cold there. So we're really happy."
BROWARD PALM BEACH NEW TIMES: "It goes without saying that there wasn't a note out of place the entire night, and the interplay between these three legendary musicians is really quite inspiring, making for a really great show."

APRIL 2, 2011
GREENSBORO, NORTH CAROLINA
GREENSBORO COLISEUM, 1921 West Lee Street. Venue opened on October 29, 1959.
AN EVENING WITH RUSH
TICKETS: $50.50 / $76.00 / $111.00 / $300.00 (VIP) / $210.30 (average price of tickets sold including VIP)
ATTENDANCE: 10,183
CAPACITY: 11,304
CONCERT GROSS: $704,352
NOTES: Rush's first Greensboro appearance since April 22, 1986 was rescheduled from April 1, due to "unforeseen circumstances." The change also delayed a Toledo gig slated for April 6 (which

would have been the fourth show in five days), with a new Toledo date set for April 13.
YES WEEKLY: "Rush delivers in return to Greensboro: These guys can absolutely shred. You hear stories about the prodigious sound created by these three guys in a live setting, but you don't realize how effortless they make it seem until seeing it up close. There's a cold pragmatism to how Lee and Peart approach their hyper-methodical and hopelessly complex rhythms, but Lifeson's pyrotechnics are reproduced in his body language."

APRIL 3, 2011
NASHVILLE, TENNESSEE
BRIDGESTONE ARENA, 501 Broadway. Venue opened on December 18, 1996.
AN EVENING WITH RUSH
TICKETS: $46.00 / $66.00 / $91.00 / $205.28 (average price of tickets sold including VIP)
ATTENDANCE: 10,093
CAPACITY: 11,122
CONCERT GROSS: $651,738
NOTES: Rush producer (and Nashville-area resident) Nick Raskulinecz rocked out in the tenth row. For the 2011 leg, Alex began running his guitar straight through the PA, instead of his onstage amp cabinets, making for a quieter stage and a cleaner sound throughout the gig, though the backline remained on stage.
GEDDY (ONSTAGE): "The next song we'd like to do has a Nashville connection. Isn't that weird for Rush? It just sounds so weird. One of our new songs, from our forthcoming album, this was recorded here in Nashville, this is called 'Brought Up To Believe.'"
NASHVILLE EXAMINER: "Rush, *Time Machine* tour, Nashville: Sunday evening's performance was very well-paced and allowed the band members to do what they do best, which is play very difficult music extremely well."

APRIL 5, 2011
LOUISVILLE, KENTUCKY
KFINANCE CHARGE YUM! CENTER, 1 Arena Plaza. Venue opened on October 10, 2010.
AN EVENING WITH RUSH
TICKETS: $46.00 / $76.00 / $97.00 / $293.00 (VIP) / $224.47 (average price of tickets sold including VIP)
ATTENDANCE: 8,139

CAPACITY: 8,358

CONCERT GROSS: $545,149

NOTES: Rush's first Louisville appearance since April 9, 1988. The mellow crowd sat during any song that wasn't a "hit."

THE COURIER-JOURNAL: "A big musical Rush: All three are virtuosos who have rarely fallen in love with their technical abilities at the expense of musicality."

APRIL 8, 2011
HERSHEY, PENNSYLVANIA

GIANT CENTER, 950 West Hersheypark Drive. Venue opened on October 15, 2002.

AN EVENING WITH RUSH

TICKETS: $46.00 / $66.00 / $91.00 / $126.00 / $224.47 (average price of tickets sold including VIP)

ATTENDANCE: 9,158; sold out

CONCERT GROSS: $744,298

NOTES: During "Marathon," Geddy mimicked shooting a gun at the exact moment the explosion went off on the lyric: "lucky shot in the dark."

THE BIG TAKEOVER: "Rush—Hershey, Pa: Still retaining his castrato vocal range and powering his Fender bass into jaw-dropping interludes, Geddy is the focal point. Fifty-seven years old, the man moves around stage, can play synth, bass and sing all at the same time; and has the comic sense of a Borscht Belt comedian."

APRIL 10, 2011
NEW YORK, NEW YORK

MADISON SQUARE GARDEN, 4 Pennsylvania Plaza (8th Avenue between 31st and 33rd Streets). Historic venue opened on February 11, 1968.

AN EVENING WITH RUSH

TICKETS: $46.00 / $70.50 / $171.50 / $220.25 (average price of tickets sold including VIP); face value, without fees

ATTENDANCE: 13,207; sold out

CONCERT GROSS: $1,276,798

NOTES: Scalpers and brokers were commanding top dollar for this concert, which sold out well in advance. Despite several production flaws, and no pyro,

the band delivered a very strong performance. The crowd roared during the New York section of "The Camera Eye," bringing a big smile to Alex's face. There were many problems with videos and live feeds freezing and being out of sync with the audio. The opening film froze almost halfway through, then started over from the beginning.

EXAMINER: "Rush amaze the crowd at Madison Square Garden."

APRIL 12, 2011
CHICAGO, ILLINOIS

UNITED CENTER, 1901 West Madison Street. Venue opened on August 18, 1994.

AN EVENING WITH RUSH

TICKETS: $46.00 / $66.00 / $86.00 / $126.00 (face value) / $199.72 (average price of tickets sold including VIP)

ATTENDANCE: 11,670

CAPACITY: 12,178

CONCERT GROSS: $1,009,885

NOTES: No flash pots used, but some fire. Geddy dedicated several songs to former Blackhawks players, including: "Stick It Out" to Stan Mikita and "BU2B" to Pierre Pilote.

GEDDY (ONSTAGE): "This is where the Stanley Cup champs live, right? I had a dream, I thought it was Toronto. That was such a dream. You guys are probably gonna win it again. Well, good luck with that."

CHICAGO EXAMINER: "Rush at The United Center: Rush really got the crowd going on their instrumental piece 'YYZ,' the audience was playing air drums, guitar, bass, and keyboards."

APRIL 13, 2011
TOLEDO, OHIO

HUNTINGTON CENTER, 500 Jefferson Avenue. Venue opened on October 3, 2009.

AN EVENING WITH RUSH

TICKETS: $40.50 / $60.50 / $86.00 / $137.66 (average price of tickets sold including VIP)

ATTENDANCE: 5,736

CAPACITY: 5,969

CONCERT GROSS: $370,004

NOTES: Rescheduled from April 6, 2011. Geddy was a bit under the weather, but carried on a spirited performance nonetheless. Onstage, he dedicated "Far Cry" to former Toledo Mud Hen, Gabe Kapler

(aka: the Hebrew Hammer).

TOLEDO BLADE: "Rush in 'Limelight' at Huntington Center: Rush returned to Toledo and proved to be one of the few remaining groups of the classic-rock era that can claim to be musically relevant. The hallmark of any Rush concert has always been the band's skilled musicianship. Throughout the concert the band exceeded that reputation as Lifeson and Lee traded virtuoso licks while Peart crashed away in perfect rhythm."

APRIL 15, 2011
CLEVELAND, OHIO

QUICKEN LOANS ARENA, 1 Center Court. Venue opened on October 17, 1994.

AN EVENING WITH RUSH

TICKETS: $46.50 / $69.00 / $93.50 / $300.00 (VIP) / $212.43 (average price of tickets sold including VIP)

ATTENDANCE: 14,970; sold out

CONCERT GROSS: $958,727

NOTES: Filmed and recorded for the *Time Machine* tour DVD/CD release. Producers Scot McFadyen and Sam Dunn (Banger Films, makers of *Rush Beyond The Lighted Stage*) addressed the crowd just before the show. Since the recording was announced well in advance, diehard fans from the world over converged on Cleveland, uniting as one incredible Friday night audience. Neil took the stage using in-ear monitors, instead of the doctor-ordered headphones he'd been using since Red Rocks last August. During the afternoon, a group of fans converged on the Rock 'n' Roll Hall of Fame to protest Rush's exclusion.

ALEX: "Cleveland was hugely important for us, because up until we were embraced there, we were just basically a bar band in Toronto. We were on the Southern Ontario high school dance circuit and doing clubs. To come to America was such a huge deal, and to come to Cleveland—with its rich connections and rock music heritage and be embraced by the city and crowd there—it was a really great experience for us. It all started for us in Cleveland and the city has a giant place in our hearts. It couldn't be more appropriate to be doing the DVD in Cleveland. I can't tell you the number of gigs we played at the Agora when we were starting out. I definitely remember those gigs! The genuine interest in the band was amazing, the place was always packed and we were on that little stage playing our hearts out. When I close my eyes as a guy who calls himself 'forty-seventeen' (fifty-seven years old) now, I can still see myself up there playing and miss the skinny, sweaty long-haired guitar guy who was up on stage!"[16]

SAM DUNN: "We were worried. It was the day of the show, just a few hours before, when we got word that Geddy wasn't feeling well and his voice was suffering. A lot of those songs, as you know, the register is really high; it's his trademark voice, and I think it takes its toll. There'd been a weekend before that, back in Toronto, when he had to go and see these crazy witch doctors. There was a lot of voodoo involved! The show really was in jeopardy, but Geddy's been through it before, and he's a trouper."[17]

CLEVELAND SCENE: "Rush at Quicken Loans Arena: Visually and musically arresting, live shows don't get better than this."

APRIL 17, 2011
AUBURN HILLS, MICHIGAN
THE PALACE OF AUBURN HILLS, 6 Championship Drive. Venue opened on August 13, 1988.
AN EVENING WITH RUSH
TICKETS: $50.50 / $126.00 / $186.04 (average price of tickets sold including VIP)
ATTENDANCE: 9,987; sold out
CONCERT GROSS: $826,549
NOTES: Geddy was still under the weather, but continued to perform with intensity.
OAKLAND PRESS: "Rush took fans on a *Time Machine* trip at the Palace: It was an exhaustive display that threw bones to both casual fans and hardcore devotees."

APRIL 19, 2011
HAMILTON, ONTARIO
COPPS COLISEUM, 101 York Boulevard. Venue opened on November 30, 1985.
AN EVENING WITH RUSH
TICKETS: $86.50 / $239.53 CAD (average price of tickets sold including VIP)
ATTENDANCE: 12,000; sold out[18]
NOTES: First Hamilton performance since October 25, 1991. Geddy was now suffering from full-blown strep throat, but soldiered on through the gig despite being very ill. Onstage, he jokingly stated that

Neil was born in Hamilton, thirty years ago, when *Moving Pictures* was released.
GEDDY: "I've been lucky. I've never gotten a voice polyp. I've never gotten nodes. But I do get sick, usually every tour, and to varying degrees. Sometimes it's a sinusitis. In the [*Time Machine*] tour, I had a really bad strep throat. And I had to do a gig that night in Hamilton, Ontario. I did it and I woke up the next day and my ear was so infected, the whole thing had gone into my ear. I had to fly to Montreal. This is kind of gross, but I had to go to a doctor and he had to puncture my ear. This was on the day of a show. I did the show, and I spent the next three days in absolute hell. I got through the show, but it was a nightmare. My worst memory ever on tour."[19]

APRIL 20, 2011
MONTREAL, QUEBEC
CENTRE BELL, 1909 Avenue des Canadiens-de-Montreal. Venue opened on March 16, 1996.
AN EVENING WITH RUSH
TICKETS: $46.80 / $67.60 / $93.07 / $134.67 / $185.08 (average price of tickets sold including VIP)
ATTENDANCE: 11,590; sold out
CONCERT GROSS: $1,008,250 CAD
NOTES: Pyro not permitted in the Province of Quebec. Geddy's sickness had now evolved into a full-blown ear infection, requiring a doctor's visit to have his ear punctured. Game 4 of a Canadiens vs. Bruins playoff game was pushed back one day to accommodate Rush. After Alex's "O'Malley's Break" solo, Geddy took the stage wearing a red Canadiens shirt, much to the delight of the Montreal faithful.
GEDDY (ONSTAGE): "Merci! Merci beaucoup. Thank you so much. That was "Moving Pictures," from 1980. An album which we wrote about sixty miles north of here in Morin Heights, Quebec. So, bringing it home."

APRIL 22, 2011
BALTIMORE, MARYLAND
1ST MARINER ARENA, 201 West Baltimore Street. Venue opened on October 23, 1962.
AN EVENING WITH RUSH
TICKETS: $46.00 / $111.00 (price included $2.00 finance charge) / $217.32 (average price of tickets sold including VIP)

ATTENDANCE: 11,006; sold out
CONCERT GROSS: $821,493
NOTES: Venue aka Baltimore Civic Center. Geddy continues to take the stage while battling health issues. He's noticeably struggling, with his voice cracking in spots. Nonetheless, it's an enjoyable performance for fans. After the first 2011 leg of 13 concerts, Neil logs 3,800 motorcycle miles.
DCIST: "Rush at 1st Mariner Arena: Though highlights were many, even a performance with experienced musicians and great songs will have its faults. The bass sound, in particular, was a bit muddy and failed to cut through the amplification. Lee also appeared to struggle with his vocals at times. While the characteristic wail from Rush's early years has been subdued over time, Lee still tests his voice's upper limits and, on this night, fell short on a few occasions. Those shortcomings were minor in the context of what was overall a very good show."

MAY 4, 2011
HELSINKI, FINLAND
HARTWALL ARENA, Areenankuja 1. Venue opened on April 19, 1997.
AN EVENING WITH RUSH
TICKETS: €67.00
ATTENDANCE: 11,000 (approximate); sold out
NOTES: After a much-needed break, Alex, Geddy, and Neil put on a great show in front of a packed house.

MAY 6, 2011
STOCKHOLM, SWEDEN
GLOBE ARENA, Globentorget 2. Venue opened on February 19, 1989.
AN EVENING WITH RUSH
TICKETS: 750 kr
ATTENDANCE: 5,637
CAPACITY: 10,764
CONCERT GROSS: $456,028
SVENSKA DAGBLADET: "Technical Perfect Rush: Proto heavy metal in symbiosis with an obvious love for The Police-pop to create something that's easy to like. The entire 1981 classic *Moving Pictures* is rendered with joy."

MAY 8, 2011
MALMO, SWEDEN
MALMO ARENA, Hyllie Stationstorg 2, Arenagatan 15. Venue inaugurated on November 6, 2008.

AN EVENING WITH RUSH

TICKETS: 650 kr

ATTENDANCE: 6,800 (approximate)

NOTES: The gig was only twenty-eight miles from Copenhagen, with many Danes making the trek, so Geddy sent them a shout-out during the show. Alex and Geddy set up residence in Copenhagen for a few days.

GEDDY: "We're musicians first, always were. And so for us, it's important that we're in shape to do the best possible show we can do. Our music is a little on the complex side. And you just cannot do that for three hours a night if you're not in good shape mentally and physically. Yes, we like wine and scotch. And yes, I'm looking forward to coming to Dublin and drinking some Guinness, and that whole bit, but that comes after the show, and that comes on your day off. And you have to make sure that you're still in shape to do the show."[20]

SKÅNSKAN DAGBLADET: "One obvious playfulness: The trio's interaction during the almost three-hour concert was razor sharp with a joy of playing. This was a stylish and musically brilliant event with often suggestive moves. The band enthralled, quite simply."

MAY 12, 2011
DUBLIN, IRELAND
THE O2, East Link Bridge, North Wall Quay. Venue opened on December 16, 2008.

AN EVENING WITH RUSH

TICKETS: €57.80 / €79.25

ATTENDANCE: 6,278

CAPACITY: 7,000

CONCERT GROSS: $602,861[21]

NOTES: Rush's Irish debut. The band and crew enjoyed a few days off in Dublin, where they visited the famed Guinness Brewery and the Phil Lynott memorial statue.

RADIO NOVA, GEDDY: "No word a lie. Every UK tour we've ever done I've requested that we play an Irish show. It's something I've always asked my manager. And every time I get the itinerary back I see there's no Irish show included. And I'm always disappointed. I've always wanted to come to play here. I really don't understand, to this day, why it's taken so long. The only thing I can think of is the promoters were waiting for us to mature and be good enough. It's my first visit. I'm very excited about it."

NEIL: "We played that first-ever show in Ireland, in Dublin, and that was a thrill. In the comic movie that opens our Time Machine shows, I have a minor role as an Irish cop named O'Malley, and I was delighted when the audience cheered when O'Malley said, 'Jesus, Mary, and Joseph—sounds like the damned howling in Hades,' and they cheered again when Alex's 'Slobovich' mentioned the name 'O'Malley.'"[22]

NEIL WARNOCK: "They only did Ireland for the first time in 2011, and that was because Ged was insistent they get there at some point. Now he wants to get to Poland, and I have to explain that 'Well, you can go there, but here's what's available,' and with their huge production it's always extremely expensive."[23]

STATE.IE: "Rush—O2, Dublin: Finally making their first visit to Ireland, Rush treated their patient fans to a spectacle of giant screens, retractable rigs, resplendent lighting, revolving drum kits and indoor fireworks. Oh, and then there was the music which wasn't bad either."

MAY 14, 2011
GLASGOW, SCOTLAND
SCOTTISH EXHIBITION AND CONFERENCE CENTRE, Hall 4, Exhibition Way. Venue opened September 7, 1985.

AN EVENING WITH RUSH

TICKETS: £45.00/ £55.00 / £65.00 / £75.00

ATTENDANCE: 8,900 (approximate); sold out

THE SCOTSMAN: "Gig review: Rush: Despite the tour's title, and unlike so many relentless, lumbering progressive behemoths, the trio aren't relying on their exceptional musicianship to simply revisit past glories—new tracks like the multilayered, style-shifting 'Caravan' and the monstrously heavy 'BU2B' reflect an act not resting on its laurels."

MAY 16, 2011
SHEFFIELD, ENGLAND
MOTORPOINT ARENA, Broughton Lane. Venue opened on May 30, 1991.

AN EVENING WITH RUSH

TICKETS: £45.00/ £55.00 / £65.00 / £75.00

CAPACITY: 11,477 (reserved seating)

NOTES: Steven Wilson from Porcupine Tree was on the show's guest list.

SELBY TIMES: "Rush Excel in Epic Sheffield show."

THE STAR: "Rush, Motorpoint Arena: Rush have always courted formidable loyalty and while numbers were down on this third visit to Sheffield's arena, reaction was anything but muted for a band who have always created sound greater than the sum of their parts—and show little sign of slowing."

MAY 19, 2011
MANCHESTER, ENGLAND
MANCHESTER EVENING NEWS ARENA, corner of Trinity Way, Hunts Bank and Great Ducie Street. Venue opened on July 15, 1995.

AN EVENING WITH RUSH

TICKETS: £45.00/ £55.00 / £65.00 / £75.00

ATTENDANCE: 9,115

CAPACITY: 10,285

CONCERT GROSS: $861,850

NOTES: Venue aka Manchester Arena. A punter walked around the venue dressed as a Dalmatian.

MAY 21, 2011
NEWCASTLE UPON TYNE, ENGLAND
METRO RADIO ARENA, Arena Way. Venue opened on November 18, 1995.

AN EVENING WITH RUSH

TICKETS: £45.00/ £55.00 / £65.00 / £75.00

ATTENDANCE: 5,151

CAPACITY: 6,508

CONCERT GROSS: $505,613

THE SHIELDS GAZETTE: "Rush, Metro Radio Arena: ALL the world has been their stage for almost forty years. Yet from the vitality of this performance Rush could easily pass for the new kids on the block. It seems the Canadian rock trio's will to excel leaves them with no scope to slow down or burn out, as evidenced in this spellbinding three-hour set."

MAY 22, 2011
BIRMINGHAM, WEST MIDLANDS, ENGLAND
BIRMINGHAM LG ARENA, National Exhibition Centre, Pendigo Way and Perimeter Road, Marston Green. Venue opened on December 5, 1980.

AN EVENING WITH RUSH

TICKETS: £45.00/ £55.00 / £65.00 / £75.00

ATTENDANCE: 11,287
CAPACITY: 12,628
CONCERT GROSS: $1,092,646
NOTES: Venue aka National Exhibition Centre Arena. Note on ticket: "People around you may stand!"
CLASSIC ROCK: "Rush LG Arena: The real star of the show is the vast screen behind them. As entertaining as it might be watching Lee hopping across the stage like an arthritic chicken, or his and Lifeson's vain attempts to make Peart crack up while attempting a tricky para-diddle, the band know that they're hardly the most visually engaging proposition."

MAY 25, 2011
LONDON, ENGLAND
THE O2, Drawdock Road, North Greenwich. Venue opened on June 24, 2007.
AN EVENING WITH RUSH
TICKETS: £45.00/ £55.00 / £65.00 / £75.00 / £360.08 (average price of tickets sold including VIP)
ATTENDANCE: 12,984
CAPACITY: 13,517
CONCERT GROSS: $1,221,530
NOTES: At sound check, Alex, Geddy, and Neil jammed around on "Day Tripper" (The Beatles), "Satisfaction" (The Rolling Stones), "Tom Sawyer," "Subdivisions," and an abbreviated take on "The Spirit of Radio." The band was late arriving onstage in order to give fans more time to gain entry.
NEIL: "Every show is important to a dedicated professional, but somehow London, like Toronto, is always 'a big one' for me—a kind of hometown show."24
KERRANG!: "Canadian Legends Confirm Their Status As The World's Biggest, And Best, Cult Band."

MAY 27, 2011
ROTTERDAM, SOUTH HOLLAND, THE NETHERLANDS
AHOY SPORTPALEIS, Ahoy-weg 10. Venue opened on January 15, 1971.
AN EVENING WITH RUSH
TICKETS: €59.00
CAPACITY: 15,000
NOTES: During "The Camera Eye," Neil was without his main thirteen-inch tom for the opening three minutes and twenty seconds (and forced to improvise), as Gump scrambled to repair and replace it.

MAXAZINE.NL: "It should be obvious that the band after all these years still at the top, in fact, they have only become better."

MAY 29, 2011
FRANKFURT, HESSE, WEST GERMANY
FESTHALLE, Ludwig Erhard Anlage, 8000. Venue opened on May 19, 1909.
AN EVENING WITH RUSH
TICKETS: €55.75 / €73.00
ATTENDANCE: 13,000 (approximate); sold out (in advance)
NOTES: After using headphones for the entire European leg, Neil went back to in-ear monitors just in time for this ecstatic general-admission crowd. The soccer chant was in full effect during "YYZ," as the SRO audience clapped, yelled, and punted in-time throughout the show.

JUNE 8, 2011
GREENVILLE, SOUTH CAROLINA
BI-LO CENTER, 650 North Academy Street. Venue opened on September 3, 1998.
AN EVENING WITH RUSH
TICKETS: $40.50 / $50.50 / $58.50 / $88.00 (face value) / $159.66 (average price of tickets sold including VIP)
ATTENDANCE: 8,027
CAPACITY: 10,422
CONCERT GROSS: $503,228
NOTES: Rush's first Greenville appearance since February 17, 1990. Pyro was used, but there were no explosions during "Marathon" and "Far Cry." Onstage, the band appeared to be in great spirits, smiling and goofing around as if it were the end of the tour. During "Closer to the Heart," a smiling Neil counted out 1-2-3-4 prior to the improv jam finale.
THE GREENVILLE NEWS: "Rush delivers powerful rock: The band played furiously for more than three hours to the joy of a near-capacity, fist-pumping crowd at the Bi-Lo Center. Lee and Lifeson were downright peppy at times as they filled several numbers with frenzied, lightning-fast riffs. These two clearly enjoy each other's company after all these years, and it's fun to watch."

JUNE 10, 2011
NEW ORLEANS, LOUISIANA
NEW ORLEANS ARENA, 1501 Girod

Street. Venue opened on October 19, 1999.
AN EVENING WITH RUSH
TICKETS: $48.50 / $96.00 / $298.00 (VIP) / $239.15 (average price of tickets sold including VIP); face value, minus fees
ATTENDANCE: 9,804; sold out
CONCERT GROSS: $671,618
NOTES: The crowd threw Mardi Gras beads onstage throughout the gig. Neil closed out a great jam ending on "Closer to the Heart" with one final splash cymbal accent and a smile. During "2112: Overture," the crew chicken and gorilla took the stage, throwing beads to the crowd and hanging them on Neil's cymbal stands. At the finale to "2112: The Temples of Syrinx," Geddy handed beads to Neil, which he promptly wore.
THE TIMES-PICAYUNE: "Rush explored its past, present and future at the New Orleans Arena: Once again, they made something new out of something old, and were better off for it."

JUNE 12, 2011
AUSTIN, TEXAS
FRANK ERWIN SPECIAL EVENTS CENTER, University of Texas at Austin campus, 1701 Red River Street. Venue opened on November 29, 1977.
AN EVENING WITH RUSH
TICKETS: $54.00 / $96.00 / $296.00 (VIP) / $227.27 (average price of tickets sold including VIP)
ATTENDANCE: 10,525; sold out
CONCERT GROSS: $693,912
NOTES: For the second set, Geddy ran onstage just in time to sing "Tom Sawyer," to which Alex came over, wiping his brow ("Whew!") and laughing at Geddy. During the encore, a Band-Aid (covering a blister) on his thumb, was bothering Lerxst, so he ripped it off with his mouth during "La Villa Strangiato."25
THE AUSTIN CHRONICLE: "Vital Signs: True rarity 'The Camera Eye' again proved perhaps the ultimate highlight, its New Wave flounce and progressive lurch raw and fast, and, at ten minutes, as expertly edited as its video backdrop images of Manhattan. Lifeson's sleek solo rose like a steel and glass skyline, while closing sleeper 'Vital Signs,' DOA last year, blipped the guitarist's lo-fi Telecaster chank."

JUNE 14, 2011
EL PASO, TEXAS
DON HASKINS CENTER, University of Texas at El Paso campus, 500 West University Avenue. Venue opened in early January 1977.
AN EVENING WITH RUSH
TICKETS: $56.00 / $76.00 / $96.00 (face value, minus fees) / $128.94 (average price of tickets sold including VIP)
ATTENDANCE: 6,338; sold out
CONCERT GROSS: $428,500
NOTES: Venue aka UTEP Special Events Center. First El Paso appearance since November 30, 1996.
EL PASO TIMES: "'Nothing but Rush:' Rockers celebrate decades of success with *Time Machine* tour."

JUNE 16, 2011
PHOENIX, ARIZONA
US AIRWAYS CENTER, 201 East Jefferson. Venue opened on June 6, 1992.
AN EVENING WITH RUSH
TICKETS: $51.00 / $76.00 / $96.00. Average price: $167.32 (tickets sold, including VIP).
ATTENDANCE: 10,777
CAPACITY: 12,472
CONCERT GROSS: $713,851.
NOTES: Venue aka America West Arena. The venue AC was broken and the building was hot as a sauna. During "BU2B," Neil tossed a stick high, and nonchalantly grabs it, without even looking. The crew chicken and gorilla casually walked onstage during "2112: Overture" and drank a glass of wine in front of Neil's kit. Several other musicians attended the gig, including Megadeth bassist Dave Ellefson and the four members of Poison (Bret Michaels, C.C. DeVille, Rikki Rocket, and Bobby Dall).
DAVE ELLEFSON (MEGADETH BASSIST): "I think growing up, the one lyricist to my age group that probably rocked all of our worlds was Neil Peart. Rush suddenly became this band that was not only musically progressive and really spoke to our musical sensibilities, but his lyrics added a whole other dimension and also a whole other intellectual dimension to Rush's music."[26]

JUNE 18, 2011
CHULA VISTA, CALIFORNIA
CRICKET WIRELESS AMPHITHEATRE, 2050 Entertainment Circle. Venue opened on July 21, 1998.
AN EVENING WITH RUSH
TICKETS: $36.50 (lawn) / $106.50 (orchestra) / $306.50 (VIP) / $192.11 (average price of tickets sold including VIP); prices included $6.00 finance charge
ATTENDANCE: 9,912
CAPACITY: 11,183
CONCERT GROSS: $606,918
NOTES: Sound check included "Presto" and "Subdivisions." The crew chicken and gorilla took the stage during "2112: Overture," carrying a set of golf clubs. The gorilla proceeded to putt in front on Neil's kit, as the band laughed.
THE CHRISTIAN SCIENCE MONITOR: "'Rush' in concert, pleasing three generations of fans: Grey-haired grandparents to kids being led around by mom or dad, this is truly a family affair. One that parents can be comfortable with because Rush is and always has been a class act, leaving the foul language for more appropriate times and places. This was a magical evening spent with the greatest rock band in the world putting on the greatest show on earth . . . period."

JUNE 20; JUNE 22, 2011
UNIVERSAL CITY, CALIFORNIA
GIBSON AMPHITHEATRE, 100 University City Plaza. Venue opened on June 28, 1972.
AN EVENING WITH RUSH
TICKETS (JUNE 20): $69.00 / $154.00 / $354.00 (VIP) / $282.36 (average price of tickets sold including VIP)
TICKETS (JUNE 22): $69.00 / $154.00 / $354.00 (VIP) / $287.44 (average price of tickets sold including VIP)
TWO-DAY UNIVERSAL CITY ATTENDANCE: 11,393[27]
TWO-DAY CAPACITY: 11,602
TWO-DAY UNIVERSAL CITY CONCERT GROSS: $1,289,447[28]
NOTES: On June 20 Jack Black was in attendance, rocking out down front, taking photos, and playing air-drums on his stomach. Kiss guitarist Tommy Thayer met with Alex backstage. The pair are the only two guitarists with their own signature-model Hughes and Kettner amps. On June 22 the crew chicken and gorilla

took center stage during "2112: Overture," and laid down to nap. Alex led the band through a blistering version of "La Villa Strangiato," playing a pinch harmonic to sustain a high note during one of his solos as the crowd erupted. As is usually the case in LA, a plethora of other musicians attend the show, including Danny Carey, Taylor Hawkins, Tom Morello, Matt Scannell, Chad Smith, John Wesly, Stephen Perkins (Jane's Addiction), Tim Commerford and Brad Wilk (Rage Against the Machine), Eric Kretz (Stone Temple Pilots), and Dirk Lance (former Incubus bassist), along with actor Adam Baldwin.
NEIL: "During a series of shows in Southern California, I was able to 'commute' from home, which was nice. Though I was only 'half-home'—still mentally in mid-tour, in mid-flight—half was better than none."[29]
LOS ANGELES DAILY NEWS (JUNE 20): "Rush fans pack Gibson Amphitheatre for the real rock 'n' roll deal: Of course, the band played great, as Rush always does. And though Rush's long series of concerts that began last year is called the *Time Machine* tour, it's obvious Lee, Lifeson, and Peart are vital forces in today's world. The band sounded exactly as they did the last time I saw them at the Forum back when tickets were $12.50 with no extra fees."

JUNE 24, 2011
LAS VEGAS, NEVADA
MGM GRAND GARDEN ARENA, 3799 Las Vegas Boulevard South. Venue opened on December 31, 1993.
AN EVENING WITH RUSH
TICKETS: $63.00 / $86.00 / $158.00 / $355.00 (VIP) / $241.98 (average price of tickets sold including VIP)
GEDDY (ONSTAGE): "A couple of songs we're gonna play tonight are gonna be on our next album, which we will finish one of these days, hopefully before Christmas."
THE LAS VEGAS SUN: "A big Rush of nostalgia: It's satisfying to watch these masters of their instruments, who have played together for decades, wring an astounding amount of sound from their equipment. Geddy Lee sang and played his Fender Jazz and keyboards. At points, he quickly pulled his hand from his bass to add a keyboard flourish. When both

hands were occupied, his feet added synth notes on foot pedals. It was an impressive choreography."

JUNE 26, 2011
CONCORD, CALIFORNIA
SLEEP TRAIN PAVILION, 2000 Kirker Pass Road. Venue opened on May 16, 1975.
AN EVENING WITH RUSH
TICKETS: $39.50 (lawn) / $68.50 / $126.00 / $156.00 / $223.15 (average price of tickets sold including VIP)
SFGATE: "The Rush show rocked. The band sounded tight—impressive because this was the third-to-last show on a marathon tour."

JUNE 28, 2011
RIDGEFIELD, WASHINGTON
SLEEP COUNTRY AMPHITHEATRE, 17200 NE Delfel Road. Venue opened on July 10, 2003.
AN EVENING WITH RUSH
TICKETS: $39.30 (lawn) / $56.65 (upper pavilion) / $80.00 (lower pavilion) / $100.75 (orchestra) / $152.24 (average price of tickets sold including VIP)
ATTENDANCE: 9,356; sold out
CONCERT GROSS: $417,903
NOTES: Venue aka The Amphitheater at Clark County.
THE OREGONIAN: "Band knows its place as object of worship among hardcore fans: This was a stadium show with triple-digit ticket prices and an elaborate stage setup that involved multiple video screens and pyrotechnics. Near perfection was darn near a requirement."

JUNE 30, 2011
VANCOUVER, BRITISH COLUMBIA
ROGERS ARENA, 800 Griffiths Way. Venue opened on September 17, 1995.
AN EVENING WITH RUSH
TICKETS: $40.00 / $61.50 / $90.50 / $116.00 / $300.00 (VIP) / $210.25 CAN (average price of tickets sold including VIP)
ATTENDANCE: 13,000 (approximate)[30]
CAPACITY: 14,000 (approximate)
NOTES: Venue aka General Motors Place. Rock 101-FM's Big 4-0 Anniversary Concert. The station aired a recent pre-recorded interview with Geddy before the show. In the afternoon, Neil talked with the *Los Angeles Times* about fitness.

Neil (wearing headphones for the first time since Rotterdam) delivered a strong improvisational section during his solo. Out of the break in "Red Barchetta," Geddy triggered a pedal which voices: "No more for me now, because I'm driving," as he mouths the words. In a parody of the recent riot that ensued after Boston beat Vancouver in game 7 of the Stanley Cup Finals, the gorilla took the stage (during "2112: Overture") wearing a Canucks jersey and beat up the chicken (who was wearing a Bruins jersey) with a baseball bat, much to the delight of the crowd. Brian Catterson joined Neil and Michael as the trio rode to the final date at the Gorge.

CTV: "Rush move pictures, crowd at Rogers Arena: Rush have kept going this long by proving themselves smarter, funnier and tougher than their competition. Above all, they still rock. That's the coolest thing about them."

JULY 2, 2011
GEORGE, WASHINGTON
THE GORGE AMPHITHEATRE, 754 Silica Road Northwest. Venue opened for major concerts on August 20, 1988.
AN EVENING WITH RUSH
TICKETS: $52.00 (lawn) / $82.00 (reserved) / $117.00 (orchestra) / $189.19 (average price of tickets sold including VIP)
ATTENDANCE: 11,911
CAPACITY: 12,206
CONCERT GROSS: $748,934
GEDDY (ONSTAGE): "This is the last date of this tour. The very last show. We've had a blast playing around the world, and we're ending it here tonight. Just for a short while . . . Thank you guys. Thank you USA. We've had an awesome tour. A fucking awesome tour! We so appreciate your support. We hope we'll see you again sometime. Bye Bye!"

1. Neil Peart. *Far and Away: A Prize Every Time*. ECW Press, May 1, 2011.
2. *Chicago Sun Times*, July 15, 2010.
3. *London Free Press*, July 6, 2010.
4. Joe Bergamini. "The Making of Taking Center Stage," TakingCenterStage.net, September 1, 2011.
5. *Modern Drummer*, December, 2011.
6. Skip Daly. Interview with Nick Kotos, June 7, 2012.
7. Neil Peart. *Far and Away: A Prize Every Time*. ECW Press, May 1, 2011.
8. Neil Peart. *Far and Away: A Prize Every Time*. ECW Press, May 1, 2011.
9. Neil Peart. *Far and Away: A Prize Every Time*. ECW Press, May 1, 2011.
10. NeilPeart.net, September 2010.
11. NeilPeart.net, September 2010.

Chapter 30
THE CLOCKWORK ANGELS TOUR

For the *Clockwork Angels* tour, Rush threw out the playbook and offered up a completely fresh set list with multiple variations. The first set was heavy on '80s-era tracks, beginning with the three album openers from *Signals*, *Power Windows*, and *Hold Your Fire* performed sequentially to kick off the show, followed by three ultrarare '80s live tracks and more featured later in the show. As with previous Rush tours, various minor set list changes were made over the first few performances, including refining the nightly alternates in the second set's *Clockwork Angels* suite and finalizing the encore. From the start of the tour, slightly differing set lists were planned to allow for the nightly rotation of four songs and their alternates. These eventually included "The Body Electric," "Bravado," "Seven Cities of Gold," and "Manhattan Project"; those songs were replaced the following night by "Middletown Dreams," "The Pass," "Wish Them Well," and "Dreamline," respectively. The eight songs remained alternates throughout the tour with a few exceptions, such as the occasional inclusion of "Limelight." Additionally, the second set included ten of the twelve tracks from *Clockwork Angels*, the most songs ever performed in support of a new album.

OPPOSITE: Sunrise, FL; Neil on the steampunk kit at the BB&T Center.

BELOW: Universal City, CA; Geddy, Alex, Neil, and the *Clockwork Angels* String Ensemble at the Gibson Amphitheatre.

"What happened is the thing that always happens—the set was much longer than what we had to limit ourselves to," Alex said. "We didn't want to get rid of those songs, so we picked a Set A and a Set B, and since then we've been tweaking it a bit, playing a couple and moving them around. I mentioned to Ged the other day: It's kind of nice to arrive at a gig in the afternoon and decide which songs to switch out that night and keep it mysterious, especially now that everything is blogged and tweeted and emailed. And it's been a whole set list controversy. Having a deep catalog like this makes it difficult to play enough songs that everybody wants to hear. Everybody has their favored and less favored songs. Rush fans are great at debating the merits of songs, and good at expressing their disappointment and elation."

Visually, the band members once again served as actors for the *Clockwork Angels* rear-screen videos. As with previous tours, Geddy's backline was all-new, featuring a giant brain in a jar, a similarly giant popcorn machine and various steampunk devices. Alex's backline also

saw a major change, with no speaker cabinets present anywhere on the stage.

Most notably, for the first time in the band's history, Rush performed with extra musicians onstage, with an eight-piece string section dubbed the *Clockwork Angels* String Ensemble joining them for the second set.

"I kept talking about it with the other guys and Neil was more ready for that than Alex initially," Geddy said about adding the ensemble. "Alex is a little reticent—he likes to have the three-piece, no strangers on the stage. I think by day two in the rehearsals, that all changed. We were just loving it, and loving the fact that we had these new guys to hang around

OPPOSITE TOP LEFT: Alex warming up.

OPPOSITE TOP RIGHT: Sound check.

OPPOSITE BOTTOM: Geddy, Neil, and Alex backstage.

TOP: The *Clockwork Angels* String Ensemble travel in crates.

ABOVE: Hollywood, CA; Hand pressings on the Rock Walk of Fame at the Guitar Center.

with on tour. They were contributing so much visually by being so into it and being such great players. It brought a new life to the tour, and we crossed our fingers our fans would see it the way we saw it and I think they certainly did."

The *Clockwork Angels* tour itself was divided into two legs. The first kicked off on September 7 in Manchester, New Hampshire, and consisted of thirty-five shows, coming to a close on December 2 in Houston, Texas. The November 25 and November 28 dates were filmed for the *Clockwork Angels Tour* DVD release. The 2013 leg began on April 23 in Austin, Texas, and consisted of thirty-seven shows, concluding on August 4 in Kansas City, Missouri. The June 8 headlining date at the Sweden Rock Festival marked Rush's first European festival performance in thirty-four years.

In between the two legs, Rush was welcomed, after fourteen years of eligibility, into the Rock and Roll Hall of Fame. The Foo

Fighters' Dave Grohl and Taylor Hawkins inducted the band at the ceremony, and Alex's two-minute acceptance speech consisted entirely of the words "blah blah blah." Afterward, Grohl and Hawkins, along with coproducer Nick Raskulinecz, performed "2112: Overture" while dressed up as Rush circa 1976, complete with kimonos. The band members joined in for the end of the song, then performed "Tom Sawyer" and "The Spirit of Radio." Other inductees and presenters, including Ann and Nancy Wilson of Heart, Tom Morello, Chuck D, Gary Clark Jr., John Fogerty, Chris Cornell, Darryl McDaniels, Grohl, and Hawkins joined Alex, Geddy, and Neil for an all-star jam on "Crossroads."

Dave Grohl (onstage): "When the fuck did Rush become cool?!"

OPPOSITE: Virginia Beach, VA; Lerxst nailing a solo, while Neil stoically holds down the tempo. **ABOVE:** Edmonton, Alberta; Geddy hitting a high note.

TOP: Universal City, CA; "Far Cry."
ABOVE: Universal City, CA; "The Garden."

SET LIST A:

"Gearing Up" intro video
"Subdivisions"
"The Big Money"
"Force Ten"
"Grand Designs"
"The Body Electric" / "Middletown Dreams"
/ "Limelight"
"Territories"
"The Analog Kid"
"Bravado" / "The Pass"
"Where's My Thing?"
"Here It Is!" (drum solo)

"Far Cry"
(Intermission)
"The Appointment" intro video
"Caravan"*
"Clockwork Angels"*
"The Anarchist"*
"Carnies"*
"The Wreckers"*
"Headlong Flight"*
"Drumbastica" (drum solo)
"Peke's Repose" (acoustic guitar intro)
"Halo Effect"*
"Seven Cities of Gold"* / "Wish Them

Well"*
"The Garden"*
"Manhattan Project"* / "Dreamline"*
"The Percussor" (drum solo)
"Red Sector A"*
"YYZ"*
"The Spirit of Radio"
Encore:
"Tom Sawyer"
"2112: Overture"
"2112: The Temples of Syrinx"
"2112: Grand Finale"
"Office Of The Watchmaker" outro video
*Performed with *Clockwork Angels* String Ensemble

SEPTEMBER 7, 2012
MANCHESTER, NEW HAMPSHIRE
VERIZON WIRELESS ARENA, 555 Elm Street. Venue opened on November 15, 2001.
AN EVENING WITH RUSH
TICKETS: $48.50 / $74.00 / $94.00 / $325.00 / $350.00 (Tickmaster platinum); face value, minus $2.00 finance charge.
ATTENDANCE: 8,137; sold out
CONCERT GROSS: $608,383
NOTES: The opening date of the *Clockwork Angels* tour featured Set list A, and the live debut of "Clockwork Angels," "The Anarchist," "Carnies," "The Wreckers," "Headlong Flight," "Halo Effect," "Wish Them Well," and "The Garden." For the first time in their history, Rush performed with an eight-piece string section onstage during the second set. Dubbed "The Clockwork Angels String Ensemble," performers included violinists Gerry Hilera, Mario De Leon, Audrey Solomon, Jonathan Dinklage, Joel Derouin, Entcho Tudorov, and cellists Adele Stein and Jacob Szekely. During "Wish Them Well," the band played a thirty-second instrumental break of "Dance to the Music" by Sly and the Family Stone. A technical glitch after "The Garden" temporarily brought the show to a halt. Jack Secret attended to the keyboard issues while Alex stepped up and told a joke.
NEIL: "All my earliest bands were R&B, and we played all that kind of stuff. So I expect that it's a direct influence."[1]

SEPTEMBER 9, 2012
BRISTOW, VIRGINIA
JIFFY LUBE LIVE, 7800 Cellar Door Drive. Venue opened on June 3, 1995.
AN EVENING WITH RUSH
TICKETS: $26.00 (lawn) / $81.00 (pavilion) / $126.00 (orchestra) / $325.00 / $350.00 (Ticketmaster platinum); face value, minus $6.00 parking fee
ATTENDANCE: 10,345
CAPACITY: 12,822
CONCERT GROSS: $757,162
NOTES: Set list B, which swaps out "The Body Electric" for "Middletown Dreams" (first performance since 1986), "Bravado" for "The Pass," "Carnies" for "Seven Cities of Gold" (live debut), "Manhattan Project" for "Dreamline," and "The Spirit of Radio" was replaced by "2112: Overture," "The Temples of Syrinx" and "Grand Finale." Venue aka Nissan Pavilion.
ROLLING STONE: "This was not a gig for the casual Rush fan. The band eschewed signature songs like 'The Spirit Of Radio' and 'Limelight' in favor of nine tracks from its new album and a bevy of 1980s synth-era superdeep cuts like 'Middletown Dreams.' Geddy Lee's voice shows shockingly little wear for its 59 years, and the band is ridiculously tight."[2]

SEPTEMBER 11, 2012
PITTSBURGH, PENNSYLVANIA
CONSOL ENERGY CENTER, 1001 Fifth Avenue. Venue opened on August 18, 2010.
AN EVENING WITH RUSH
TICKETS: $48.25 / $70.50 / $96.00 / $350.00 (VIP); face value minus fees

ATTENDANCE: 8,655
CAPACITY: 10,268
CONCERT GROSS: $507,952
NOTES: Set list A (2.0), with "Seven Cities of Gold" performed in place of "Carnies" and "2112: Overture," "The Temples of Syrinx" and "Grand Finale" replacing "The Spirit of Radio." Geddy dedicated "Bravado" to the victims of 9/11. The *Pittsburgh Post-Gazette* and *Beaver County Times* both vote this one of the best concerts of the year. A few days before, on September 6, a federal judge ordered federal marshals and local police to seize any unlicensed Rush T-shirts, recordings, or other memorabilia that sprang up in Pittsburgh and also authorized similar actions in other cities. Showtech Merchandising Inc. requested the order in anticipation of bootleggers arriving in Pittsburgh before, during, and after this performance. US District Judge David Cercone said the company, which holds the exclusive license for Rush tour merchandise, had to post a $5,000 bond and agree to pay for the marshals' time in seizing the merchandise.[3]
GEDDY (ONSTAGE): "This place is like home to us. I think we've played Pittsburgh more than any other American city. Our first gig was at the Civic Arena. Let's see if we can outlast this one here, too."
PITTSBURGH POST-GAZETTE: "Rush Burns Up the Stage On *Clockwork Angels* tour: If the first set was a little on the mechanical side, the second one was full of fire, literally and sonically. It was like the stage suddenly came alive for the nine *Clockwork Angels* songs."

SEPTEMBER 13, 2012
INDIANAPOLIS, INDIANA
BANKERS LIFE FIELDHOUSE, 125 South Pennsylvania Street. Venue opened on November 6, 1999.
AN EVENING WITH RUSH
TICKETS: $36.00 / $56.00 / $76.00 / $111.00
ATTENDANCE: 7,303
CAPACITY: 10,899
CONCERT GROSS: $489,034
NOTES: Set list B (2.0), with "Carnies" replacing "Seven Cities of Gold."

SEPTEMBER 15, 2012
CHICAGO, ILLINOIS
UNITED CENTER, 1901 West Madison Street. Venue opened on August 18, 1994.
AN EVENING WITH RUSH
TICKETS: $50.50 (300 level) / $70.50 (300 level) / $96.00 (100, 200 level) / $151.00 (floor, 100 level) / $325.00 / $350.00 (Ticketmaster platinum); face value, minus fees
ATTENDANCE: 11,307
CAPACITY: 12,130
CONCERT GROSS: $1,113,292
NOTES: Set list A (3.0), "Seven Cities of Gold" replaced "Wish Them Well," "The Spirit of Radio" replaces "Working Man" in the set, and "2112: Overture," "The Temples of Syrinx," and "Grand Finale" replaced "The Spirit of Radio" in the encore. A strong show with a fired-up Saturday night crowd. Geddy's energy was relentless, and his voice near flawless. A new film was introduced during "2112: Overture," with Stewie (from *Family Guy*) beating up and replacing the Starman. Later in the song, the crew chicken and gorilla took the stage wearing Blackhawks jerseys, only to have five Blackhawks players come out and beat them up. The team rocked out all night in seats just off of stage left. In the afternoon, Neil's "Chromey" drum set was on display at Vic's Drum Shop, where fans could play the kit and have their photo taken for charity.
JAMBANDS.COM: "Rush, United Center: One constant through all phases has been the masterful drumming and deep lyrics of Neil Peart. 'Subdivisions' built to a climax with Geddy Lee stepping away from his keyboards to let loose on his bass and dance across the stage as Alex Lifeson tore into his first solo of the evening. The groove of 'Force Ten' slowly

built to a thunderous finale as Peart tore apart the end with a flourish."

SEPTEMBER 16, 2012
KEVIN J. ANDERSON AND NEIL PEART'S *CLOCKWORK ANGELS* **NOVELIZATION DEBUTS AT #18 ON** *THE NEW YORK TIMES* **HARDCOVER FICTION BEST SELLERS LIST.**
NOTES: The *Clockwork Angels* novelization by Kevin J. Anderson and Neil Peart (ECW Press) would later be adapted into a graphic novel (BOOM! Studios). In 2015, Anderson and Peart would work together again to write a sequel to the novel, *Clockwork Lives* (ECW Press), which would also be adapted into a graphic novel (Insight Comics).
KEVIN J. ANDERSON: "While I approach these ideas as a novelist, Neil was looking at it as a lyricist to fit the songs. As a result, I think the story is really wonderful and the characters are great, along with all the little Rush references throughout the book. In a way, I feel like I've been preparing my whole life to write this book."[4]

SEPTEMBER 18, 2012
AUBURN HILLS, MICHIGAN
THE PALACE OF AUBURN HILLS, 6 Championship Drive. Venue opened on August 13, 1988.
AN EVENING WITH RUSH
TICKETS: $49.50 / $72.50 / $100.00 / $126.00 / $300.00 (VIP) / $325.00 / $350.00 (Ticketmaster platinum)
ATTENDANCE: 8,238
CAPACITY: 13,485
CONCERT GROSS: $616,595
NOTES: Set list B (2.0), with "Working Man" performed for the final time this tour. Fans on the upper level were upgraded to the lower bowl.
GEDDY (ONSTAGE): "We come bringing greetings from your neighbors from the north."
DETROIT FREE PRESS: "Rush Brings New Set, Ageless Rock Sizzle to Palace."

SEPTEMBER 20, 2012
COLUMBUS, OHIO
NATIONWIDE ARENA, 200 West Nationwide Boulevard. Venue opened on September 9, 2000.
AN EVENING WITH RUSH
TICKETS: $45.00 / $73.00 / $93.00; face value, minus $3.00 finance charge
ATTENDANCE: 8,611
CAPACITY: 10,204

CONCERT GROSS: $587,173
NOTES: Set list A (3.0).
COLUMBUS DISPATCH: "Rush—Stellar trio thrills with old and new: Lee, Lifeson, and Peart immediately showed that their chops are intact. Not only did the band sound good, but Lee's vocals were spot-on."

SEPTEMBER 22, 2012
ST. LOUIS, MISSOURI
SCOTTRADE CENTER, 1401 Clark Avenue. Venue opened on October 8, 1994.
AN EVENING WITH RUSH
TICKETS: $39.95 / $125.95; price included $2.50 finance charge
ATTENDANCE: 10,772
CAPACITY: 10,942
CONCERT GROSS: $790,134
NOTES: Set list B (3.0), with "The Spirit of Radio" replacing "Working Man" before one fired-up crowd. Geddy congratulated KSHE-FM on their forty-fifth anniversary. The station had long supported Rush, going all the way back to 1974. Alex and Neil played a brief jam (complete with cowbell and hi-hat solo) while Geddy had his in-ear monitor fixed at the start of "Dreamline," with Geddy stating: "Sorry about that, I lost one ear."
GEDDY (ONSTAGE): "The boy pulls down his Cardinals cap."
ST. LOUIS EXAMINER: "Rush delivers a wide array of songs in St Louis: Rush delivered a performance that leaned forward while nodding at their past."

SEPTEMBER 24, 2012
MINNEAPOLIS, MINNESOTA
TARGET CENTER, 600 First Avenue North. Venue opened on October 13, 1990.
AN EVENING WITH RUSH
TICKETS: $46.00 / $66.00 / $96.00 / $300.00 (VIP); price included $2.00 finance charge
ATTENDANCE: 8,013
CAPACITY: 10,652
CONCERT GROSS: $561,972
NOTES: Set list A (3.0).
ST. PAUL PIONEER PRESS: "Four decades later, Rush is still proving it matters: The standout among the new tunes was 'The Garden,' a song that had the feel of an anthem, swirling with a kind of wistful melancholy seldom found in this band's music. Yes, Rush can still rock, but age

and experience are evidently inspiring them to bring more beauty into their music. So, rather than a fond look back, Monday's concert felt like the beginning of a fascinating new chapter in this band's admirably lengthy history."

SEPTEMBER 26, 2012
WINNIPEG, MANITOBA

MTS CENTRE, 300 Portage Avenue. Venue opened on November 16, 2004.

AN EVENING WITH RUSH

TICKETS: $42.25 / $116.00 / $131.00 CAD; face value, minus $1.50 finance charge

ATTENDANCE: 9,000[5]

NOTES: Set list B (3.0). There were some technical issues during "Grand Designs" and "Middletown Dreams." Long & McQuade Music held a contest to win the Ultimate Rush Experience, with tickets and meet 'n' greet passes up for grabs for all Canadian dates on the tour.

WINNIPEG METRO: "Rush blazes to a loud, rockin' set at the MTS Centre: Rush took to the stage Wednesday night to a hugely enthusiastic crowd and treated them to a litany of hits over their forty-year multi-Juno-winning and Grammy-nominated career."

SEPTEMBER 28, 2012
SASKATOON, SASKATCHEWAN

CREDIT UNION CENTER, 3515 Thatcher Avenue. Venue opened on February 9, 1988.

AN EVENING WITH RUSH

TICKETS: $40.25 / $100.50 / $117.00 CAD

ATTENDANCE: 8,000 (approximate)

NOTES: Set list A (3.0). Rush's first Saskatoon appearance since October 25, 1978. The band was welcomed by a spirited crowd, but venue security was extremely vigilant about not letting fans take photographs.

GEDDY (ONSTAGE): "It's time to say 'A Farewell to Strings.'"

SEPTEMBER 30, 2012
EDMONTON, ALBERTA

REXALL PLACE, 7424 118th Avenue NW. Venue opened on November 10, 1974.

AN EVENING WITH RUSH

TICKETS: $39.76 / $116.00 / $325.00 (VIP) / $375.00 (platinum) CAD; face value, minus fees

ATTENDANCE: 11,000 (approximate)[6]

CAPACITY: 13,049

NOTES: Set list B (3.0). A virtuoso gig closes out the first leg, with Alex, Geddy, and Neil in peak form.

EDMONTON SUN: "Canadian rock icons Rush impressive in Edmonton show: Rush is as much a rite of passage as a concert experience—judging by all the fathers and sons who turned up at the concert Sunday night. Rush appears to have lost little of the magic that made it such a big deal to begin with."

OCTOBER 10, 2012
BRIDGEPORT, CONNECTICUT

WEBSTER BANK ARENA, 600 Main Street. Venue opened on October 10, 2001.

AN EVENING WITH RUSH

TICKETS: $46.75 / $66.75 / $91.75 / $126.75

ATTENDANCE: 7,339; sold out

CONCERT GROSS: $650,355

NOTES: Set list A (3.0). Alex is his usual animated self, joining the string ensemble, walking down the stairs, as if one of them, as they depart the stage after "YYZ."

SOUND SPIKE: "Rush in Bridgeport: Perhaps the biggest surprise of all on this balmy night, was that Rush's newest music—from *Clockwork Angels*—represented some of the best and most memorable material played during their nearly three-hour show. Lifeson covered the guitar sections with brilliance, coaxing jangling acoustic guitar effects at one moment, and pitching off into spacey or sharply articulated leads the next. His intense power chords on 'Headlong Flight' and screaming leads on 'Seven Cities of Gold' repeatedly propelled the audience to its feet."

OCTOBER 12, 2012
PHILADELPHIA, PENNSYLVANIA

WELLS FARGO CENTER, 3601 South Broad Street. Venue opened on August 12, 1996.

AN EVENING WITH RUSH

TICKETS: $43.00 / $75.00 / $123.00 / $300.00 (VIP)

ATTENDANCE: 11,885

CAPACITY: 12,810

CONCERT GROSS: $943,272

NOTES: Set list B (3.0). During "YYZ" crew members took the stage as a garden gnome and Father Time.

GEDDY (ONSTAGE): "The boy pulls down his Phillies cap."

BURLINGTON COUNTY TIMES: "The band delivered a balanced show in Philadelphia. It featured fresh material that was complemented by a number of deep album cuts, as well as familiar favorites."

NEIL: "After a show in Philadelphia, I had awakened on the bus lying on my left arm, and feeling a sharp pain. It didn't bother me on the motorcycle that day, riding through the Catskills and Adirondacks of upstate New York to Cape Vincent for the night. Next morning my elbow felt tender, but tolerable, crossing into Canada on a cold, rainy morning via a pair of ferries through Wolfe Island to Kingston, and a long wet slog along Highway 401 to Toronto . . . Unfortunately, while I was struggling up the mountain that night [on stage in Toronto] (every night a mountain, and me always Sisyphus), I had a painful attack of tendinitis in my left elbow."[7]

OCTOBER 14, 16, 2012
TORONTO, ONTARIO

AIR CANADA CENTRE, 40 Bay Street. Venue dedicated on February 19, 1999.

AN EVENING WITH RUSH

TICKETS: $56.50 / $76.50 / $120.50 / $140.50 (CAD) / $325.00 (USD) VIP; face value, minus $2.50 finance charge

ATTENDANCE (OCT. 14): 11,000 (approximate); sold out

NOTES: October 14 featured Set list A (3.0). October 16 featured Set list B (3.0). The second show was added due to overwhelming demand. The Twelfth Annual RushCon fan convention was held in conjunction with the ACC shows.

GEDDY (ONSTAGE ON OCTOBER 14): "Good evening Toronto—my hometown! It's great to be back at home playing for you guys for the next couple of nights . . ." "The boy pulls down his Blue Jays cap."

NEIL: "Before the first hometown show in Toronto, I planned to host my mother and father for dinner in the Bubba Gump room, and to meet with my first drum teacher, Don George—for the first time in over forty-five years. In 1965, at the age of thirteen, I started drum lessons with Don. When he stopped teaching a year or so later, I didn't see him again until the day of that first show in Toronto. For his part, when talking about this long-ago student, Don was once quoted, 'Neil didn't have another teacher for thirty years, so I must have done something right.' Essentially, Don kept me climbing that mountain for three decades, until I needed Freddie Gruber and Peter Erskine to guide me to higher elevations."[8]

***TORONTO SUN* (OCTOBER 14):** "Rush highlights new album at ACC show: A staggering drum solo by Peart dominated the first set which also featured material stretching from the '80s to the twenty-first century like 'Force Ten,' 'Grand Designs,' 'Territories,' 'The Analog Kid,' 'Bravado,' and 'Far Cry,' the latter complete with firebursts."

NEIL: "During [the first show in Toronto] the pain in my elbow grew steadily worse. Toward the end it hurt so badly that I simply couldn't hit as hard as I usually do with my left hand. Before the second Toronto show, I consulted a local doctor, who prescribed some anti-inflammatories and an elbow brace, and that helped me enough that at least I could play properly. It still hurt quite a lot, but as I had learned during a similar attack on my other arm, back on the *Test for Echo* tour in 1997, I didn't mind the pain as long as it didn't interfere with 'the job.'"[9]

OCTOBER 18, 2012
MONTREAL, QUEBEC
CENTRE BELL, 1909 Avenue des Canadiens-de-Montréal. Venue opened on March 16, 1996.
AN EVENING WITH RUSH
TICKETS: $59.25 / $90.50 / $130.50 CAD; minus $6.00 in fees
ATTENDANCE: 12,400[10]
NOTES: Set list A (3.0).
***MONTREAL GAZETTE*:** "Rush at the Centre Bell: Rush has never sought easy applause. Instead of skimming the surface of their back catalogue and *Clockwork Angels*, Lee, Lifeson, and Peart took pride in the richness of their past and present. All hall-of-famers should have as much to celebrate."

OCTOBER 20, 2012
NEWARK, NEW JERSEY
PRUDENTIAL CENTER, 165 Mulberry Street. Venue officially opened on October 25, 2007.
AN EVENING WITH RUSH
TICKETS: $37.50 / $71.00 / $96.00 / $148.00 / $300.00 (VIP); face value, minus fees
ATTENDANCE: 12,139; sold out
CONCERT GROSS: $1,022,913
NOTES: Set list B (3.0). Technical issues

made for a loose, tentative first set. The "Gearing Up" intro film had no audio. Neil's bass drum pedal broke during "The Big Money." Gump tried to replace it during the song but was unable. Geddy stalled for a bit on the introduction to "Force Ten" while the situation at center stage was rectified. In "Grand Designs," Alex's guitar dropped out for a moment, but was quickly fixed. The band regrouped and performed a fantastic second set (complete with David Campbell conducting the orchestra onstage).

GEDDY (ONSTAGE): "We got the show tonight off to a bit of a funny start, but it's great to be back in New Jersey."

LORNE "GUMP" WHEATON: "Neil is surrounded by the kit. It's not a case of where I can slip in there like I can with other drummers who play smaller kits. So when we break a head, he plays something else till we get to the end of the song, then he darts out of the kit, I jump in, switch the head, and then he jumps back on. That's the only way we can do it."[11]

NJ.COM: "Rush (plus string section) plays gutsy show at Prudential Center: At forty-plus years old and running, Rush is as loose, smart, skilled, and funny as it has ever been."

OCTOBER 22, 2012
BROOKLYN, NEW YORK
BARCLAYS CENTER, 620 Atlantic Avenue. Venue opened on September 28, 2012.
AN EVENING WITH RUSH
TICKETS: $46.00 / $67.00 / $166.00. Average ticket price (includes VIP): $233.92;[12] face value, minus fees
ATTENDANCE: 9,904
CAPACITY: 10,815
CONCERT GROSS: $870,736
NOTES: Set list A (3.0). Rush was the first rock band to perform at the brand-new venue and the sound was a bit dicey, with fans on the upper levels stating that "it's bouncing all over the place." Onstage, the *Clockwork Angels* String Ensemble was conducted by David Campbell. Violinist Audrey Solomon donned a blonde wig for the performance. During "2112: The Temples of Syrinx," Alex's guitar went out, but his tech was packing the guitars for the night, and didn't have a new one ready, so Al does an impromptu jig at the side of the stage, not once, but twice to

stall. Eventually, after thirty-five seconds, he was given a new axe to close out the show. After sound check, Alex and Geddy did a video interview with the *Wall Street Journal*.

OCTOBER 24, 2012
BOSTON, MASSACHUSETTS
TD GARDEN, 100 Legends Way. Venue opened on September 30, 1995.
AN EVENING WITH RUSH
TICKETS: $48.50 / $86.00 / $126.00; face value, minus $2.50 finance charge
ATTENDANCE: 9,861
CAPACITY: 10,031
CONCERT GROSS: $841,953
NOTES: Set list B (4.0), with "Seven Cities of Gold" replacing "Wish Them Well." No pyro at this show. During "The Wreckers," Geddy's teleprompter wasn't working, but he didn't miss a vocal, while trying to get the crew's attention with his head. More than three minutes into the song, Skully replaced the unit onstage, however it was still malfunctioning, so he again took to the stage toward the song's conclusion, but Geddy wasn't having it and told him to remove himself until it was finished.

GEDDY (ONSTAGE): "The boy pulls down his Red Sox cap."

***THE BOSTON PHOENIX*:** "Rush distance themselves from prog during marathon set at the Garden: The spirit of Rush can, in a sense, be read on the stoic face of drummer Neil Peart. Throughout last night's marathon set, his visage was unchanging, a chiseled topographic map of sheer concentration and determination, neither smiling nor grimacing even while his arms and body accomplished unimaginable feats of drum action. The quiet Canadian doesn't blow out his momentum in bursts of explosive crashing, but rather methodically crushes each drumming hurdle like a long-distance runner, eyes constantly aimed at the distant horizon."

OCTOBER 26, 2012
BUFFALO, NEW YORK
FIRST NIAGARA CENTER, One Seymour Knox III Plaza. Venue opened on September 21, 1996.
AN EVENING WITH RUSH
TICKETS: $46.50 / $66.00 / $91.00; price included $2.50 finance charge
ATTENDANCE: 13,215; sold out
CONCERT GROSS: $831,239

NOTES: Set list A (4.0), with "Limelight" replacing "The Body Electric." Rush's first indoor gig in western New York since October 16, 2002 in Rochester. Out of the break in "Far Cry," Geddy hit two pedals, which triggered a different vocal part that seemed to fit right into the song. Venue aka Marine Midland Arena.

BUFFALO NEWS: "Rush strikes inspirational gold: It was an epic event on every level. The crowd greeted the *Clockwork Angels* material with rabid enthusiasm, and as it concluded, the assembled reaped its reward? A smoldering 'Manhattan Project' into Peart's final drum improvisation, and then 'Red Sector A' and the ebullient instrumental 'YYZ.' The addition of the string ensemble to this material elevated the proceedings as it emphasized color and texture and added harmony."

OCTOBER 28, 2012
CLEVELAND, OHIO
QUICKEN LOANS ARENA, 1 Center Court. Venue opened on October 17, 1994.
AN EVENING WITH RUSH
TICKETS: $48.50 / $76.00 / $96.00; face value, minus fees
ATTENDANCE: 8,025
CAPACITY: 10,383
CONCERT GROSS: $594,890
NOTES: Set list B (3.0). Earlier in 2012, Alex, Geddy, and Neil had learned of Karl Sloman from London, Ontario, who was being highlighted in an upcoming Global Network documentary, *Walk the Walk*. A six-part series spotlighting everyday "heroes" in communities that do things for others without expectation of recognition for their efforts, Karl was featured for his achievements working with disabled children. In January, while filming and interviewing Karl, one of the producers realized he was a huge Rush fan, and hatched a plan: The producers flew Karl to Cleveland supposedly for a production meeting for the upcoming documentary. He didn't realize it, but Rush just "happened" to be performing in Cleveland that very same night. Before he knew it, he was inside Quicken Loans Arena, where he recognized Rush's tour bus, and Neil's motorcycle. The adrenaline starts pumping, and minutes later, Karl was face-to-face with Neil, the man who had inspired him in so many different ways over the years. He later met Alex and

Geddy, who presented him with front-row tickets to the show. Karl told Neil, "This has probably been the single most remarkable day of my life." Neil replied "Well, you've earned it . . . The main purpose of art is to inspire, and if you can inspire someone, what else can you do?"

THE PLAIN DEALER: "Sounding as good as ever, band Rush gives fans a ride in a time machine: The sound probably was the best ever produced in the acoustically challenging Quicken Loans Arena. In a venue that turns crowd noise into sonic mud during sporting events, notes remained remarkably pure and unadulterated."

OCTOBER 30, 2012
CHARLOTTE, NORTH CAROLINA
TIME WARNER CABLE ARENA, 333 East Trade Street. Venue opened on October 21, 2005.
AN EVENING WITH RUSH
TICKETS: $41.00 / $72.00 / $111.00; face value, minus fees
ATTENDANCE: 7,523
CAPACITY: 10,095
CONCERT GROSS: $541,143
NOTES: Set list A (3.0). Neil's planned motorcycle route to Charlotte (through the Smokey Mountains) was abandoned due to forecast snow. Instead, Dave picked him up in Knoxville and he was driven to the gig on a snowy interstate.
NEIL: "Charlotte was the night before Halloween, and lately we had been seeing plenty of decorations around the Midwest . . . Our two female string players, cellist Adele and violinist Audrey, appeared onstage in wildly elaborate face makeup that night, from David Bowie's Aladdin Sane to rhinestone arabesques. The Guys at Work and I always appreciate it when those around us go out of their way to entertain not just the audience, but us."[13]

NOVEMBER 1, 2012
ALPHARETTA, GEORGIA
VERIZON WIRELESS AMPHITHEATRE AT ENCORE PARK, 2200 Encore Parkway. Venue opened on May 10, 2008.
AN EVENING WITH RUSH
TICKETS: $40.00 (lawn) / $59.00 (reserved) / $79.00 (upper pavilion) / $89.00 (pavilion) / $99.00 (lower pavilion) / $129.00 (orchestra); face value, minus fees
NOTES: Set list B (5.0), with "Limelight" replacing "Middletown Dreams." Before

the show, the band learned of the passing of Ray Danniels' son Shane. Co-producers Peter Collins and Nick Raskulinecz visited with Alex, Geddy, and Neil. It was a very cold night (temps in the low forties), with Geddy wearing a leather jacket and scarf throughout the entire performance. During "Grand Designs," Neil dropped a stick right after the lyric "some are merely spaced," but didn't miss a beat. The stick fell in front of the kit, so Alex picked it up and started playing his guitar with it, eventually tossing it out into the crowd. For "Clockwork Angels," Nick Raskulinecz went into the pit and conducted the band "miming along with every note, beat and word."[14]

GEDDY (ONSTAGE): "Thank you so much for coming out and braving this unusual weather for you guys. Of course it's normal for us Canadians."

NEIL: "We have been visited by another family tragedy—manager Ray's twenty-three-year-old son Shane was struck down by a brain tumor, succumbing on November 1, only nine weeks after the terrible diagnosis. It was the day of our show in Atlanta, and that night Geddy gave a subtle reference to Shane in his introduction to 'The Garden,' which had been one of Shane's favorite songs ["This is one of our favs, especially tonight"]. Two nights later, after the final show in that leg, in Tampa, I flew to Toronto with the other Guys at Work in their 'bus' (Challenger C-605), and spent some time with Ray. I knew how it felt to lose a child. After fifteen years, I think of Selena every single day, and from time to time (birthdays, black anniversaries), I am still rendered helpless with grief at that unbearable loss. Before heading for the airport to get back to my own (second) family in Los Angeles, I attended the memorial gathering, and it was achingly sad and hard for me to bear. My sorrow must have been obvious, because it seemed like Ray was comforting and supporting me. And in the following days I received messages from several friends asking if I was okay."[15]

NOVEMBER 3, 2012
TAMPA, FLORIDA
1-800-ASK-GARY AMPHITHEATRE, Florida State Fairgrounds, 4802 US Highway 301 North. Venue opened on July 25, 2004.
AN EVENING WITH RUSH
TICKETS: $27.50 (lawn) / $50.50 /

$100.00 / $250.00 (Ticketmaster premium) / $325.00 (VIP); face value, minus fees.
ATTENDANCE: 10,567
CAPACITY: 11,542
CONCERT GROSS: $720,653
NOTES: Set list A (3.0). The band wrapped up the second leg of the tour with a strong performance. A fired-up energy was emitted from both the stage and the crowd, as band and audience fed off of one another. After "YYZ," the string ensemble entered the pit and rocked out for the rest of the set.
TAMPA BAY TIMES: "Rush deftly mixes new songs, old favorites in Tampa: Not unexpectedly, the strings added layers of warmth to melodic tunes such as 'Halo Effect' and 'The Garden.' Equally impressive, though, was the tension they brought to riff-oriented numbers such as album and second-set opener 'Caravan.'"

NOVEMBER 13, 2012
SEATTLE, WASHINGTON
KEY ARENA, 205 Harrison Street. Venue opened on April 21, 1962.
AN EVENING WITH RUSH
TICKETS: $56.00 / $86.00 / $126.00 / $300.00 (VIP) / $350.00 (VIP); face value, minus $3.00 finance charge
ATTENDANCE: 9,793
CAPACITY: 10,199
CONCERT GROSS: $823,060
NOTES: Set list B (3.0). Before sound check, Neil did a radio interview with veteran drummer Michael Shrieve, of Santana fame. Alex had some technical issues early in the first set. In "Wish Them Well," Lerxst commented on Washington's new law legalizing marijuana by stating "I love you, Washington State. Light it up!" During the ending of "Tom Sawyer," Alex was a full measure behind, as Geddy and Neil laughed at him through the song's conclusion.

NOVEMBER 15, 2012
SAN JOSE, CALIFORNIA
HP PAVILION, 525 West Santa Clara Street. Venue opened on September 7, 1993.
AN EVENING WITH RUSH
TICKETS: $43.00 / $87.50 / $123.00; face value, minus $3.00 finance charge
ATTENDANCE: 10,719; sold out
CONCERT GROSS: $846,843
NOTES: Set list A (3.0). Despite a few technical glitches, the band delivered a good, solid performance. Geddy's keyboards went out in "Subdivisions" during the lyric "Drawn like moths we drift into the city" but were back just in time for the next chorus. In the second set, two of the upper right video screens were only half visible.

NOVEMBER 17, 2012
ANAHEIM, CALIFORNIA
HONDA CENTER, 2695 East Katella Avenue. Venue opened on June 19, 1993.
AN EVENING WITH RUSH
TICKETS: $56.50 / $91.00 / $108.00 / $160.50 / $325.00 (VIP); face value, minus $4.00 finance charge
ATTENDANCE: 9,065
CAPACITY: 10,102
CONCERT GROSS: $761,265
NOTES: Set list B (4.0). Venue aka Arrowhead Pond.
NEIL: "By now the sound check routine was well established. Together we played the first half of *Clockwork Angels* and the first half of 'Red Sector A,' which checked out everybody's various 'systems.' Then the three of us gave sound engineer Brad the beginning of the opening song, 'Subdivisions,' so he was set for the start of the show. When Brad had heard enough, he would shoot up his hand for us to stop, and that became a game among us—watching for that upraised hand, and stopping immediately, laughing as we all froze on the same beat."[16]

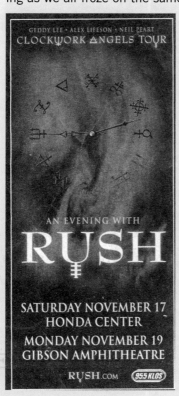

NOVEMBER 19, 2012
UNIVERSAL CITY, CALIFORNIA
GIBSON AMPHITHEATRE, 100, University City Plaza. Venue opened in 1973, converted to indoor venue in 1982.
AN EVENING WITH RUSH
TICKETS: $70.00 / $100.50 / $158.50
ATTENDANCE: 5,981; sold out
CONCERT GROSS: $706,342
NOTES: Set list A (3.0). Spectacular lights, sound, and performance make for a stand-out show. Onstage the *Clockwork Angels* String Ensemble was conducted by David Campbell. Guests in attendance included musicians Danny Carey, Matt Scannell and Robert Trujillo, Playboy centerfold Carrie Stevens, and actors Adam Baldwin and Eric McCormack.
LOS ANGELES TIMES: "Rush knows how to put on a show. Decades of touring have provided it with expert knowledge, and as it has built its fan base, it has continually reimagined the concert experience. Monday's show was well paced, and the presentation was at times stunningly beautiful, a multimedia feast anchored in steampunk aesthetics and featuring an array of visual thematics to tie it all together."

NOVEMBER 21, 2012
SAN DIEGO, CALIFORNIA
VALLEY VIEW CASINO CENTER, 3500 Sports Arena Boulevard. Venue opened on November 17, 1966.
AN EVENING WITH RUSH
TICKETS: $15.50 / $36.50 / $42.50 / $146.50; face value, minus $4.00 finance charge
ATTENDANCE: 7,065
CAPACITY: 10,101
CONCERT GROSS: $359,321
NOTES: Set list B (3.0). This gig was a late addition to the itinerary, with an on-sale date of September 14. Venue aka San Diego Sports Arena.

NOVEMBER 23, 2012
LAS VEGAS, NEVADA
MGM GRAND GARDEN ARENA, 3799 Las Vegas Boulevard South. Venue opened on December 31, 1993.
AN EVENING WITH RUSH
TICKETS: $59.00 / $94.00 / $154.00; price includes $4.00 finance charge
ATTENDANCE: 7,847
CAPACITY: 10,006
CONCERT GROSS: $839,405

NOTES: Set list A (4.0).

LAS VEGAS SUN: "Rush keeps in time with *Clockwork Angels* show at MGM Grand: Alex Lifeson still is flawless on guitar and even performed some keyboard work of his own while engaging those standing near the stage in a running, mimed commentary of the songs being played."

NOVEMBER 25, 2012
PHOENIX, ARIZONA
US AIRWAYS CENTER, 201 East Jefferson. Venue opened on June 6, 1992.
AN EVENING WITH RUSH
TICKETS: $45.75 / $59.00 / $91.25 / $300.00 (VIP); face value, minus fees
ATTENDANCE: 8,858
CAPACITY: 10,121
CONCERT GROSS: $604,667
NOTES: Set list B (6.0), with "Manhattan Project" replacing "Dreamline." The alternate songs were filmed for the *Clockwork Angels* tour DVD release. A much quieter than usual Sunday crowd lead Geddy to ask "Is anyone out there?" after "Grand Designs."

PHOENIX EXAMINER: "*Clockwork Angels*, Rush and there's one in every crowd: Alex, Geddy, and Neil played on as if driven by supernatural forces."

NOVEMBER 28, 2012
DALLAS, TEXAS
AMERICAN AIRLINES CENTER, 2500 Victory Avenue. Venue opened on July 17, 2001.
AN EVENING WITH RUSH
TICKETS: $43.00 / $123.00; face value, minus $3.50 finance charge
ATTENDANCE: 10,509; sold out
CONCERT GROSS: $764,483
NOTES: Set list A (5.0), with "Seven Cities of Gold" and "Wish the Well" both performed. The entire show was filmed for the *Clockwork Angels* tour DVD release. The *Dallas Morning News* selected this concert as one of the year's best.
GEDDY: "This tour, we didn't make any plans originally to record it, but then after we saw that our work was paying off and we were so proud of the show, we thought, 'Okay, we have to record this.' We had a second leg planned in the new year, and at the time we didn't know whether we would change songs or not. The feeling was, 'Life is too unpredictable. Let's not record it next year. Let's record it now because at least we know what the show is.' So we quickly found a venue that was appropriate, or really a couple of venues, and that's how we did it."[17]

DALLAS MORNING NEWS:
"Rush remains an epic force: What continues to be paramount is this group's inspired longevity. *Clockwork Angels* is one of the best Rush albums, period. Lee kept it all cohesive with his still strong, wailing voice and double duty on the bass and keyboards."

NOVEMBER 30, 2012
SAN ANTONIO, TEXAS
AT&T CENTER, 1 AT&T Center Parkway. Venue opened on October 18, 2002.
AN EVENING WITH RUSH
TICKETS: $49.00 / $94.00 / $124.00 / $225.00 (Ticketmaster platinum); face value, minus $2.00 finance charge
ATTENDANCE: 9,396
CAPACITY: 10,150
CONCERT GROSS: $742,544
NOTES: Set list B (6.0). With the less than enthusiastic response in Phoenix, the band scrambled to film Friday audience shots in San Antonio. The day of the week makes a big difference when it comes to audience enthusiasm. Due to the filming, a strict "no cameras" policy was implemented and enforced for this gig. A female fan in the upper level of stage right got the attention of many patrons by dancing strip-club style to Rush. Blue Jays manager John Gibbons (a San Antonio native) met with Geddy and Alex backstage.
GEDDY (ONSTAGE): "You look like Texans. Well, most of you do."
JOHN GIBBONS (BLUE JAYS MANAGER): "The thrill of a lifetime. They were big down here when I was in high school, I always liked them. Geddy Lee is pretty sharp when it comes to baseball. He told me that the last time he came out to shag flies during batting practice, [the Blue Jays] won the World Series."[18]

DECEMBER 2, 2012
HOUSTON, TEXAS
TOYOTA CENTER, 1510 Polk Street. Venue opened on October 6, 2003.
AN EVENING WITH RUSH
TICKETS: $46.00 / $66.00 / $91.00 / $126.00; face value, minus fees
ATTENDANCE: 11,091; sold out
CONCERT GROSS: $904,931
NOTES: Set list A (6.0) with "Limelight" replacing "The Body Electric" and "Dreamline" replacing "Manhattan Project." The audio cut out during the "Office of the Watchmaker" intro film. "Dreamline" was dedicated to Neil Armstrong, which took on special significance, with NASA mission control located nearby. During the opening to "2112: Overture," Alex's guitar was down, but was quickly back on, with Al ranting into the mic: "You're fired! After this gig, I don't want to see you anymore," while pointing at his tech. Alex, Geddy, and Neil seemed relieved that the filming was complete, and despite a few technical issues, they let loose with a wonderful, spirited performance to close out 2012.
HOUSTON PRESS: "Rush Toyota Center: Like jazz musicians, the members of Rush have improved as they have aged, yet still manage to maintain a very high energy level."
NEIL: "Before sound check at the final show in Houston, the three of us gathered in front of the string players, which had become a daily custom. After they had tested their instruments and monitors, and before we all played together, I would sit cross-legged on the subwoofer behind my drums, while Alex and Geddy came in from their sides of the stage and we talked and joked for a few minutes with the 'stringers' . . . After thirty-five shows, and 13,632 motorcycle miles, we finished the Houston show on a very high note, so to speak. The performance itself felt triumphant, and after, we gathered with the stringers for a champagne celebration. It was the first time I stayed after a show on the whole tour, and a couple of the stringers joked that they were used to seeing me as a blur on my sprint to the bus."[19]

APRIL 18, 2013
LOS ANGELES, CALIFORNIA
NOKIA THEATRE, 777 Chick Hearn Court
ROCK & ROLL HALL OF FAME INDUCTION CEREMONY.
WITH: Albert King, Public Enemy, Randy Newman, Heart, Donna Summer, Quincy Jones, and Lou Adler
TICKETS: $35.00 (limited) / $75.00 / $350.00 / $750.00; face value, minus fees)
ATTENDANCE: 7,100; sold out
NOTES: Dave Grohl and Taylor Hawkins officially inducted Rush to the Rock & Roll Hall of Fame.

up on their stage left riser to close out the song.

THE SHEFFIELD TELEGRAPH: "Rush at Sheffield Motorpoint Arena: With a brilliant light show and stage set that was a mix of *Close Encounters* and a hint of steampunked Terry Pratchett, the band were in dazzling form."

THE STAR (SHEFFIELD), ALEX: "The Arena at Sheffield is a really good arena. We've played there a few times now and it has a pretty good sound for that type of venue. It's important for us to play outside London too so we try to play as many places that we possibly can when we're here."

MAY 30, 2013
GLASGOW, SCOTLAND
SCOTTISH EXHIBITION AND CONFERENCE CENTRE, Hall 4, Exhibition Way. Venue opened September 7, 1985.
AN EVENING WITH RUSH
TICKETS: £35.00 / £60.00 / £75.00
NOTES: Set list B (5.0). The height of the venue is low, which obscured some of the visuals from a distance, but gave the lights additional saturation. At the end of the first set, Geddy did his best Harry Satchel (Scottish) accent, "ack in a wee minute," much to the audience's delight. Alex was in fine form, clowning around with the stringers during "YYZ," and going up on their stage right platform. He scratched up and down his guitar neck during the keyboard break, creating a unique accompaniment.
THE HERALD (SCOTLAND): "Rush SECC, Glasgow: As known for their mind-bending live performances as much as their polarizing musical tendencies and goofball humour, the three-hour display by Rush was perhaps their most ambitious outing to date."

JUNE 2, 2013
AMSTERDAM, HOLLAND
ZIGGO DOME, De Passage 100. Venue opened on June 24, 2012.
AN EVENING WITH RUSH
TICKETS: €62.00; face value, minus fees
ATTENDANCE: 8,500 (approximate)
CAPACITY: 17,000
NOTES: Set list A (4.0). The show was general admission floor, with punters lining up for hours to secure their positioning at the front of the stage.

GEDDY (ONSTAGE): "So great to be back in such a beautiful city. A city that we love to come to, and we're happy to be back."

JUNE 4, 2013
COLOGNE, GERMANY
LANXESS ARENA, Willy-Brandt-Platz 3. Venue opened on September 11, 1998.
AN EVENING WITH RUSH
TICKETS: €50.00 / €60.00 / €70.00 / €85.00; face value, minus fees
ATTENDANCE: 6,000 (approximate)
CAPACITY: 20,000
NOTES: Set list B (3.0).
GENERAL ANZEIGER: "Cannon in the Wunderkammer: the great Peart . . . The man is not a musician, the man is a giant, one of the last, if not the very last of his league. From him and his two bandmates, the young can learn a lot."

JUNE 6, 2013
BERLIN, GERMANY
O2 WORLD BERLIN, Mühlenstraße 12. Venue opened on September 10, 2008.
AN EVENING WITH RUSH
TICKETS: €38.00 / €63.50 / €75.00 / €102.25
ATTENDANCE: 5,589
CAPACITY: 8,934
CONCERT GROSS: $401,180
NOTES: Set list A (3.0). A "magical" show. Fans down front swayed their hands in time with the chorus of "The Analog Kid."
BERLINER ZEITUNG: "Rush Concert Berlin people learn drums! Peart is the clock and ideas of the band, the organizing center. His heart rate, his pulse makes Rush alive."
NEIL: "The arena concerts in the UK, Amsterdam, and Germany had gone very well, the audiences enthusiastic, and we thought we were playing okay. The string section continued to be an uplifting presence, musically and socially."[25]

JUNE 8, 2013
SOLVESBORG, SWEDEN
SWEDEN ROCK FESTIVAL, Village of Norje, Nygatan 27 294 34. Festival site opened on June 5, 1998.
TICKETS: 1290 SEK (single day), 2290 SEK (3-days), 2490 SEK (4-days, sold out)
ATTENDANCE: 33,000; sold out
SET LIST: Video Intro ("Gearing Up"), "Subdivisions," "The Big Money," "Grand

Designs," "Limelight," "The Analog Kid," "Where's My Thing" (with drum solo), "Far Cry", (*Clockwork Angels* String Ensemble enters), Video Intro ("The Appointment"), "Caravan," "Clockwork Angels," "The Anarchist," "Carnies," "Headlong Flight" (with drum solo), "The Garden," "Red Sector A," "YYZ," (*Clockwork Angels* String Ensemble exits), "The Spirit of Radio," Encore: "Tom Sawyer," "2112: Overture"/"The Temples Of Syrinx"/"Grand Finale," Video Outro ("Office Of The Watchmaker").

NOTES: Rush's first European festival performance since June 4, 1979 at Pink Pop. Headlining the final day of this four-day festival, the band performed an abbreviated set, omitting eight songs from their usual show. Upon arriving, Alex and Geddy ran into Kiss guitarist Paul Stanley, who performed at Sweden Rock on June 6. The band took the stage in daylight, with the sun setting behind them. The height of the stage was very low, giving the lights extra intensity, upon darkness. Other acts appearing on five different stages included Accept, Skid Row, Kreator, and Nine Below Zero.

PAUL STANLEY (KISS GUITARIST): "When we were on the tarmac getting ready to take off from headlining our night at Sweden Rock Festival, another private jet landed, and I had to get off to greet and spend a few minutes catching up with the next night's headliners—my long lost friends Alex and Geddy. Time flies and thankfully we're all still having fun!"

NEIL: "This was something far outside our usual performance routine—headlining one night of a huge festival called Sweden Rocks. Bands were playing all day on three or four different stages, more-or-less continuously, so there would be no sound check. Our show would start a couple of hours later than usual, and instead of our two sets with intermission, we would play one long set, about two hours—and we would play to 35,000 people. That was a little overwhelming to contemplate, but I didn't really have a sense of that crowd from the stage—with all the barricades and photo pits, even the closest people were farther away than usual. I really like to see people's faces-to see them smiling, singing along, getting excited—but still, it was an impressive sea of humanity."[26]

HOWARD: "When you play a festival, a

lot of times you don't have your rig. We had our rig in Sweden, but that's unusual. Most festivals you just go on and . . . it's a generic rig for everybody to use, so you're not going to get anything spectacular . . . You don't have much programming time. It's tough."[27]

JUNE 10, 2013
HELSINKI, FINLAND
HARTWALL ARENA, Areenankuja 1. Venue opened on April 19, 1997.
AN EVENING WITH RUSH
TICKETS: €75.00 / €85.00
ATTENDANCE: 10,200 (approximate)
NOTES: Set list B (5.0). During the European leg of the tour, Neil logged 3,321 motorcycle miles.
GEDDY (ONSTAGE): "Finland Hello, nice to be in your beautiful country again."
HELSINGIN UUTISET: "Rush played amongst the finest works: Canada's gift to the world of music, Rush performed yesterday at a nearly full Hartwall Arena. Multipath compositions contain many infectious elements and a finishing virtuosic playing. Perfect, once again a fabulous show and a great band."

JUNE 21, 2013
HERSHEY, PENNSYLVANIA
GIANT CENTER, 950 West Hersheypark Drive. Venue opened on October 15, 2002.
AN EVENING WITH RUSH
TICKETS: $46.00 / $66.00 / $91.00 / $126.00 / $195.00 (Ticketmaster platinum) / $300.00 (VIP); face value, minus $2.85 finance charge
ATTENDANCE: 7,972
CAPACITY: 8,564
CONCERT GROSS: $699,975
NOTES: Set list A (4.0). A fired-up crowd welcomed the band back to the States for an epic show. Neil took delivery of a new motorcycle and the band presented all of their crew with a gift of commemorative watches. Backstage, the town of Hershey presented Alex and Geddy with a giant chocolate bar.
PENN LIVE: "Rush in 2013: Peerless instrumental virtuosity. Truly Rush are among the greatest instrumentalists in rock history. All three members deserve a place near the top of the list of the best who ever played. And, after decades together, Rush play not as soloists but as a single unit."

JUNE 23, 2013
WANTAGH, NEW YORK
JONES BEACH THEATER, 1000 Ocean Parkway. Venue dedicated on June 26, 1952.
AN EVENING WITH RUSH
TICKETS: $37.50 / $92.50 / $152.50 / $300.00 (VIP)
ATTENDANCE: 9,692
CAPACITY: 10,647
CONCERT GROSS: 748,560
NOTES: Set list B (3.0). This was just the fourth Jones Beach concert since reopening after Superstorm Sandy flooded the venue, causing major damage. Geddy took to the stage with his hair tied back on a windy evening. It began to rain during "The Garden," and continued through the finale.
GEDDY (ONSTAGE): "Glad to see this place is still standing."

JUNE 25, 2013
SARATOGA, NEW YORK
SARATOGA PERFORMING ARTS CENTER, 108 Avenue of Pines. Venue opened on July 9, 1966.
AN EVENING WITH RUSH
TICKETS: $36.00 (lawn) / $66.00 (upper orchestra) /$126.00 (lower orchestra) / $300.00 (VIP)
ATTENDANCE: 7,557
CAPACITY: 8,129
CONCERT GROSS: $491,853
NOTES: Set list A (3.0).
THE SARATOGIAN: "Rush thrills fans with three-hour-long set: Many—not just Rush fans—believe Peart holds the unofficial title of 'World's Best Drummer' and his performance Tuesday did nothing to refute that. Like a heartbeat with an arrhythmia, Peart leads the band's seemingly irregular transitions from a dead stop to full sprint."

JUNE 28, 2013
TINLEY PARK, ILLINOIS
FIRST MIDWEST BANK AMPHITHEATRE, 19100 Ridgeland Avenue. Venue opened on June 2, 1990.
AN EVENING WITH RUSH
TICKETS: $36.50 / $56.00 / $86.00 / $129.00 / $300.00 (VIP); face value, minus $21.00 finance charge
ATTENDANCE: 7,626
CAPACITY: 8,382 (no lawn)
CONCERT GROSS: $657,505
NOTES: Set list B (5.0). A celebratory night in Chi-town. For the second set,

Neil donned his special "hockey theme" hat, which included the logos of the six original NHL teams, with the Blackhawks emblem prominently displayed in front. Prior to "YYZ," Geddy announced a special guest: Lord Stanley. The G'nomes brought out a roadcase and produced a tiny Stanley Cup (à la Spinal Tap), in celebration of the Blackhawks recent win (their victory parade was earlier in the day). Then some players brought out the real cup, with left-winger Daniel Carcillo holding it up, so Alex and Geddy could touch it, and Neil could tap on it with his sticks, while the crowd goes nuts.
CHICAGO TRIBUNE: "Watching the group live emphasized their uncanny (and sometimes overlooked) knack for contributing just the right flourish at the right time to the right song, whether a wash of atmospheric guitar or a furious 'round-the-kit fill."

JUNE 30, 2013
GRAND RAPIDS, MICHIGAN
VAN ANDEL ARENA, 130 West Fulton Street. Venue opened on October 8, 1996.
AN EVENING WITH RUSH
TICKETS: $36.00 / $56.00 / $76.00 / $111.00 / $300.00 (VIP); face value, minus $2.50 finance charge
ATTENDANCE: 8,786
CAPACITY: 9,726
CONCERT GROSS: $612,081
NOTES: Set list A (4.0). First Grand Rapids appearance since October 23, 1996. As in Chicago, it was hockey night on Canada Day. The Grand Rapids Griffins recently won the AHL championship, so during "YYZ," a G'nome took to the stage with a small trophy. Then, a Griffins player brought out the Calder Cup, with the string ensemble donning moustaches for the celebration.
THE GRAND RAPIDS PRESS: "Rush still rocks—band showcases past, present in Van Andel show: Lee shifted seamlessly between keyboards and bass, and his finger-playing technique on the stringed instrument is rivaled by few. His voice, a shrieky, acquired taste, was capably strong for the upper-register rock screams of 'Headlong [Flight]" but cracked and strained for 'Limelight."

JULY 2, 2013
CINCINNATI, OHIO
RIVERBEND MUSIC CENTER, 6295 Kellogg Avenue. Venue opened on July 4, 1984 (expanded May 24, 2008).
AN EVENING WITH RUSH
TICKETS: $31.00 (lawn) / $76.00 (upper pavilion) / $96.00 (lower pavilion) / $300.00 (VIP) / $325.00 (VIP); prices included $3.50 parking fee
ATTENDANCE: 9,965
CAPACITY: 10,445
CONCERT GROSS: $487,860
NOTES: Set list B (3.0). A hot show on a hot night. Just nine miles away, as Homer Bailey threw a no-hitter for the Reds, Rush delivered a flawless performance in front of a throng of fanatical fans, who sing, clap, and cheer as if there is no tomorrow.

JULY 4, 2013
MILWAUKEE, WISCONSIN
MARCUS AMPHITHEATER, Summerfest grounds, Henry Maier Festival Park, 200 North Harbor Drive. Venue opened on June 25, 1987.
AN EVENING WITH RUSH
TICKETS: $20.00 (lawn) / $35.00 / $60.00 (pavilion) / $75.00 (orchestra) / $300.00 (VIP). Face value, minus $14.50 finance charge. Price included Summerfest admission.
ATTENDANCE: 14,423
CAPACITY: 22,861
CONCERT GROSS: $714,020
NOTES: Set list A (3.0). 2013 Milwaukee Summerfest. Other bands performing this day on various different stages included Animation (Rush tribute), Barenaked Ladies (who attend the Rush gig), Guster, Skillet, and Dark Star Orchestra, who paid homage to Alex, Geddy, and Neil with an impromptu jam of "YYZ" and "Tom Sawyer" shortly after fans filed out of Marcus Amphitheater.
MILWAUKEE JOURNAL SENTINEL: "Rush deftly mixes new and old music at Marcus Amphitheater: Songs like 'The Anarchist' and 'Headlong Flight' showcased each member's skills: Peart's relentless, rarely fussy drumming; Lifeson's mixture of crunchy riffs and shining melodies and Lee's deep-pocket bass and instantly recognizable high-pitched vocals."

JULY 6, 2013
HAMILTON, ONTARIO
COPPS COLISEUM, 101 York Boulevard. Venue opened on November 30, 1985.
AN EVENING WITH RUSH
TICKETS: $42.50 / $59.50 / $87.50 / $118.50 CAD
ATTENDANCE: 12,000; sold out[28]
CAPACITY: 19,000 (approximate)
NOTES: Set list B (5.0). Long known for their philanthropic support, with little fanfare Rush donated $1 for every ticket sold at five of their seven Canadian dates to the Unison Benevolent Fund; only the two Canadian festivals were excluded from this effort.[29] The nonprofit fund provides counseling, emergency relief, and benefits for Canadian musicians faced with unemployment, personal difficulties, or illness.
HAMILTON SPECTATOR: "How will Rush top this one?: The Canadian rock icons performed a magnificent three-hour concert at Copps Coliseum before a sellout crowd of 12,000 exuberant fans, framing the show with timeless classics like 'Subdivisions,' 'Limelight', 'Tom Sawyer,' 'Spirit of Radio,' and 'YYZ'. The meat of the concert, however, was the band's performance of its latest work, *Clockwork Angels*, a record that stands up well even when played alongside the classics. Everyone seems to agree that they are playing as good [sic], if not better, than they ever have before. The creative spark remains and this band still has at least another great album to record."

JULY 8, 2013
OTTAWA, ONTARIO
RBC ROYAL BANK OTTAWA BLUESFEST, Canadian War Museum, LeBreton Flats Park, 1 Vimy Place. Festival first held in 1994, at this location since 2007.
AN EVENING WITH RUSH
TICKETS: $65.00 CAD (general admission daily festival pass) / $150.00 (gold seating). Complete Festival passes were $99.00 (youth) / $195.00 (advance presale) and $199.00 (youth) / $249.00 CAD
NOTES: Due to stage constraints, the video screen behind Neil was much smaller than normal. Also performing in the day's sweltering heat on different stages were the Specials, Grace Potter and the Nocturnals, and Baauer.
SET LIST: Video Intro ("Gearing Up"), "Subdivisions," "The Big Money," "Grand

Designs," "Limelight," "The Analog Kid," "Where's My Thing?" (with drum solo), "Far Cry", (*Clockwork Angels* String Ensemble enters): Video Intro ("The Appointment"), "Caravan," "Clockwork Angels," "The Anarchist," "Carnies," "The Wreckers," "Headlong Flight" (with drum solo), "The Garden," "Red Sector A," "YYZ", (*Clockwork Angels* String Ensemble exits), "The Spirit of Radio," Encore: "Tom Sawyer," "2112: Overture"/"The Temples Of Syrinx"/"Grand Finale," Video Outro ("Office Of The Watchmaker").
OTTAWA SUN: "Rush rolls through decades of hits at Bluesfest: Rush transported the fans 'back in time thirty years with 'The Analog Kid,' with Lee finding strange frequencies on the Moog, casting out a blanket of space-age synth tones, or bounding across the stage pounding out the bass for Lifeson's blistering solos."

JULY 10, 2013
QUEBEC CITY, QUEBEC
FESTIVAL D'ETE DE QUEBEC, Plains of Abraham, Avenue Wilifrid-Laurier. Initial festival was held in 1968.
AN EVENING WITH RUSH
TICKETS: $30.00 day pass / $76.00 full festival pass (limited to 75,000) / $535.00 VIP Pass for entire festival (limited to 3,000) CAD
ATTENDANCE: 40,000 (approximate)
NOTES: Set list A (7.0). 150,000 total passes were sold, 60,000 of which were presold before a lineup was even announced. The massive stage was 86 feet tall and 224 feet long, with a performance area of 5,310 square feet. Even though the venue is a wide expanse of real estate, the sound was clear in all directions, thanks to a series of time-aligned speakers throughout the property. The film sequences for this gig included French subtitles. Unfortunately, the show was cut short due to thunderstorms. As a result, "Tom Sawyer" was not performed for the first time during a show in over thirty-three years (since June 22, 1980). To help make up for the abbreviated gig, the band later posted a free soundboard recording of "Manhattan Project," "Red Sector A," "YYZ," "The Spirit of Radio," "Tom Sawyer," "2112: Overture," "The Temples of Syrinx," and "Grand Finale" from the Halifax show at the festival website.

SET LIST: Set 1: Video Intro ("Gearing Up"), "Subdivisions," "The Big Money," "Force Ten," "Grand Designs," "Limelight," "Territories," "The Analog Kid," "Bravado," "Where's My Thing?" (with drum solo), "Far Cry." Set 2 (*Clockwork Angels* String Ensemble enters): Video Intro ("The Appointment"), "Caravan," "Clockwork Angels," "The Anarchist," "Carnies," "The Wreckers," "Headlong Flight" (with drum solo), "Halo Effect" (with guitar solo intro), "Seven Cities Of Gold," "The Garden." Show canceled at this point due to inclement weather.

GEDDY (ONSTAGE): "We would like to travel back in time thirty years to our *Signals* album which was actually recorded in Quebec."

NEIL: "With something like 40,000 people in front of us—making more of a landscape than an audience—the first set went very well. During intermission, Geddy remarked how much he enjoyed playing these festival-style shows. (We had recently played similar events in Ottawa and Sweden. He liked how the younger fans were able to make their way up front, instead of the older (and wealthier) people buying up the front rows, and the overall energy and excitement in such a setting. I agreed, but said, 'The weather always makes me nervous.' During the second set, just before we began 'The Garden,' I started to see flurries of raindrops in the spotlight beams over the crowd. As we launched into the song, the wind gusted up, swirling rain all through the colored light beams flashing around the stage . . . Of greatest concern were the exposed electronics—keyboards and foot pedals—and the delicate violins and cellos. Later cellist Jacob told us, 'If it had been anyone but you guys, I would have been off that stage'. Just as we finished the song, Brent's voice came over our ear monitors, 'The show is over. A storm is right on us. Make an announcement, and get off the stage.' Hard to believe that in almost forty years, we had never had to stop a show in the middle like that . . . although it was extremely strange for us, and we regretted the coitus interruptus, we didn't feel we had cheated anyone . . . But unfortunately, there was some unpleasant fallout the next day. Geddy had made a quick announcement before we ran, but it must be remembered that Quebec in general is 90 percent francophone, and

Quebec City closer to 100 percent—and no one came out to explain the situation in French. It turned out that the storm veered away, and the rain stopped after fifteen or twenty minutes . . . The Quebec City press spread the impression that it had been Geddy personally who had stopped the show, which was wrong and misleading. So . . . the next day we issued a public apology, and even went so far as to record the six songs we had missed playing that night at the next show in Halifax, and gave them free to a Quebec City rock station. Nothing more we could do."[30]

GEDDY: "My bandmates and I are extremely disappointed and apologetic over the sudden and unexpected ending of our show last night at the Festival D'ete de Quebec. The lightning storm that was approaching made it extremely dangerous for all the technicians working the sound and lights, and there was a high risk to the audience members as well as the musicians on stage. We were enjoying the show tremendously at the time, and we were hoping we could get the whole show finished before the storm returned but unfortunately we were unlucky and were forced to end the show for the safety of all concerned. Thanks to all of our amazing fans for braving the weather and once again our sincere apologies for what had transpired. Hope to see you all again soon!!!"

LE SOLEIL: "Rush muzzled by rain: Lee, Lifeson, and Peart were in control of their complex repertoire. Festival goers were treated to a show that was solid and spectacular . . . but ended prematurely."

JULY 12, 14, 2013
HALIFAX, NOVA SCOTIA
METRO CENTRE, 1800 Argyle Street. Venue opened on February 17, 1978.
AN EVENING WITH RUSH
TICKETS: $60.50 / $90.50 / $125.50 CAD; face value, minus fees
ATTENDANCE (JULY 12): 6,946; sold out
ATTENDANCE (JULY 14): 6,527
CAPACITY: 6,946
CONCERT GROSS: $599,940 CAD per show
NOTES: July 12: Set list A (4.0). Rush's first Maritime performance since November 1987. Local celebrities the Trailer Park Boys welcomed Rush to Nova Scotia. The band recorded the six

songs it didn't play in Quebec City and uploaded them to the festival's website. July 14: Set list B (5.0). Second show added by popular demand.

GEDDY (ONSTAGE): "A funny thing happened on the way to Nova Scotia, we were so stupid we forgot to come back for twenty-five years! We're going to make up for it though, we've brought along about 1,000 songs."

THE CHRONICLE HERALD: "My first live Rush experience rocks: The assault on the eyes was secondary to the delights for our ears, and songs like 'The Anarchist' showed why Rush is a band still playing in peak form, looking fit and meshing like the gears assembled by the 'watchmaker on carnies,' Lee and Lifeson grinned like kids as the latter played spaghetti western twangs and crunchy rock chords over the former's rumbling bass runs."

GEDDY: "I feel bad when we're not able to get to a place. We had the same thing with Winnipeg. We didn't get there in forever. And people were making up crazy stories about why we wouldn't come to Winnipeg."[31]

JULY 24, 2013
RED DEER, ALBERTA
ENMAX CENTRIUM, 4847-A 19th Street. Venue opened on November 29, 1991.
AN EVENING WITH RUSH
TICKETS: $60.00 / $86.00 / $116.00 CAD; face value, minus fees.
ATTENDANCE: 5,400[32]
CAPACITY: 7,210
NOTES: Set list A (4.0). This date was originally slated for the Saddledome in Calgary, but severe flooding prompted a rescheduling, some 90 miles away in Red Deer. Calgary fans were given the opportunity to exchange their seats, with 3,500 of them doing so. The remaining public on-sale was just nine days before the gig (September 15). At Neil's suggestion, all the show's proceeds, and Rush's fee were donated to help flood victims, with Enmax Centrium donating the venue, Live Nation Canada and Ticketmaster Canada donating time and service fees. The combined efforts raised $575,000 (CAD) for flood relief.[33] Of the proceeds, $400,000 went to the Canadian Red Cross, while $125,000 was destined for the flood-ravaged town of High River. The remaining $50,000

went to local charities. The concert itself was delayed an hour because of monitor board issues, which required the band to play the first set with the house mix in their monitor feeds. Hiroko Taguchi replaced Gerry Hilera for this gig. On sale at the venue were special Rush in Red Deer T-shirts, which benefited Red Cross flood relief efforts.

GEDDY: "After seeing the devastation from the recent floods, we felt compelled to do what we could. While we had hoped to avoid canceling the Calgary show, safety concerns have closed the venue. Our apologies to all of the fans that bought tickets for any inconvenience. We're hoping they—along with the great people of Red Deer—can come to the Enmax Centrium for what has now become a benefit concert. We'd like to thank everyone helping to put on this show for joining us in donating their time and services so we can raise as much money as possible to help those in need."[34]

NEIL: "However noble our motives, even what should have been our golden karma could not prevent that show from throwing up a unique challenge just before showtime . . . this would be the first time in 39 years we ever played without monitors! Just before showtime we were informed that the monitor board was down, and being worked on feverishly. There would certainly be a delay. The possibility of having to cancel this show, out of any of them—a benefit for many worthy causes that would eventually raise over half a million dollars to help them— seemed a particularly cruel twist of fate. I tried to think how we might possibly work around it. Half-joking, I said, 'Oh never mind—we'll just play to the house mix.' A little later, Geddy said, 'It looks like you might get your wish.' Not exactly my wish! Yikes! Talk about a juggling act! To explain what that actually meant, each of our pairs of in-ear monitors receives a unique mix of 'information.' For myself, I have an ever-changing blend that always includes drums and vocals, and usually bass and guitar, but sometimes eliminates those so I can concentrate on a sequence of keyboard patterns or vocal effects that I need to play in sync with and set up the tempo for in advance, perhaps the biggest challenge of all . . . In the 'house mix,' these elements are all blended, with lead vocals and guitars to

the fore. The things I need to be in sync with are just background textures, barely audible. But . . . we did it! For the first set, anyway, because the audio crew was able to get the mixing board fixed in time for the second set. (Much relief there, on my part—and others' too, I'm sure) . . . As I said to the Guys at Work during intermission, 'My poor brain! I think we got through it okay—but I wouldn't want to hear a recording of it!'"[35]

RED DEER ADVOCATE: "Rush brings a big-city show to Red Deer: Some 7,000 fans from across Alberta packed the local arena to the rafters to hear the band's complex, hard-driving, progressive rock. The appreciative roar from fans was deafening. Fists were pumped in the air, rock fingers were raised. The bro-heavy audience of mostly fathers and sons would have gathered in Calgary for the Rush experience, had the Saddledome not been flooded. Out of Calgary's misfortune, Red Deer inadvertently got what many band fanatics will consider the concert of a lifetime."

JULY 26, 2013
VANCOUVER, BRITISH COLUMBIA
ROGERS ARENA, 800 Griffiths Way. Venue opened on September 17, 1995.
AN EVENING WITH RUSH
TICKETS: $40.00 / $60.00 / $86.00 / $116.00 CAD; face value, minus fees
ATTENDANCE: 12,500 (approximate)
NOTES: Set list B (3.0). Hiroko Taguchi replaced Gerry Hilera for this show.
VANCOUVER SUN: "Rush turns out a performance like clockwork: They remain infinitely less annoying than their '70s contemporaries like Yes or Genesis and markedly more concerned about writing good songs than modern colleagues such as Dream Theater or Mastodon. It's what has kept the fans around and brought in generation after generation of new ones."
JACOB SZEKELY (CELLIST): "I met the original violinist on 'Losing It' . . . Ben Mink. He came, and we actually saw the violin that he built himself that he used to play the electric violin solo. Very cool guy. Johnny Dinklage does a lot of electric violin and I think he said 'Losing It' was one of the first solos he transcribed and learned . . . so he was begging Alex and Geddy to do that song, and they thought it was kind of a cool idea. There was some discussion about the next tour, which was going to be smaller . . . maybe smaller venues and

more intimate. There was some talk of having him come out and maybe play that with them. So who knows."[36]

JULY 28, 2013
RIDGEFIELD, WASHINGTON
SLEEP COUNTRY AMPHITHEATER, 17200 NE Delfel Road. Venue opened on July 10, 2003.
AN EVENING WITH RUSH
TICKETS: $35.00 (lawn) / $52.50 (upper pavilion) / $65.00 (lower pavilion) / $95.00 (orchestra) / $300.00 (VIP); face value, minus fees
ATTENDANCE: 8,552
CAPACITY: 9,214
CONCERT GROSS: $482,640
NOTES: Set list A (3.0). During "YYZ" a couple of crew G'nomes take to the stage, acting sloppy drunk and holding a "Happy Birthday" sign upside down in honor of Ged's sixtieth birthday.
THE PORTLAND MERCURY: "The Fine Art of Air Instrumentation: Rush and their devoted fan base have a deep respect for each other. These fans keep up with their discography; they catch them every time they tour through town. Rush knows this, so they don't play all the tired, old radio songs or acknowledged classics. They don't have to reach deep into their past to pluck out gems to appease their fans, because they know the fans actually want to hear the new stuff. Seeing a band that's been playing together just shy of forty years do that was a heartwarming change of pace."

JULY 31, 2013
WEST VALLEY CITY, UTAH
USANA AMPHITHEATRE, 5150 South 6055 West. Venue opened on July 3, 2003.
AN EVENING WITH RUSH
TICKETS: $36.50 (lawn) / $69.00 (300 level) / $104.00 (200 level) / $129.00 (100 level, orchestra) / $300.00 (VIP)
ATTENDANCE: 11,216
CAPACITY: 11,637
CONCERT GROSS: $626,706
NOTES: Set list B (5.0). The first set is played in daylight, with the sun setting during intermission.
SALT LAKE TRIBUNE: "Rush takes concert in three directions: While Rush is nothing if not polarizing, the show proved that sometimes rock is at its best when it's at its biggest and most spectacular. The performance was baroque in spirit

and Victorian in style. It was also a welcome throwback to an era in rock that valued spectacle and bombast."

AUGUST 2, 2013
DENVER, COLORADO
PEPSI CENTER, 1000 Chopper Circle. Venue opened on October 1, 1999.
AN EVENING WITH RUSH
TICKETS: $36.00 / $51.00 / $81.50 / $106.50 / $300.00 (VIP); face value, minus $4.00 finance charge
ATTENDANCE: 10,409
CAPACITY: 11,266
CONCERT GROSS: $816,641
NOTES: Set list A (4.0).
NEIL: "These days some historic stages like Red Rocks and the legendary Hollywood Bowl can no longer fit our show. (A touching sign I saw held up in the arena audience in Denver, 'I'm Pretending I'm at Red Rocks'). Maybe sometime we'll bring a smaller one. Doubt it—'Can't stop thinking big' and all that."[37]
THE DENVER POST: "Rush at the Pepsi Center: Rock band continues to impress."

AUGUST 3, 2013
KANSAS CITY, MISSOURI
Z STRIKE, 1370 Grand Boulevard
END OF TOUR BOWLING PARTY.
NEIL: "Actor Paul Rudd spent much of his youth around Kansas City, and was visiting at the time of our show—so he joined us for the bowling party. We had kept in touch since our scene together in *I Love You, Man*, and Paul's appearance with Jason Segel in the show-ending movie for our *Time Machine* tour. The bowling alley kicked us out at nine o'clock, because it was time for the all-important, perhaps even sacred 'Leagues' to have their turn, and Paul took us to a private room in a friend's bar—with Kansas City truly rocking in the streets all around us. What a party town on an uptown Saturday night!"[38]

AUGUST 4, 2013
KANSAS CITY, MISSOURI
SPRINT CENTER, 1407 Grand Boulevard. Venue opened on October 10, 2007.
AN EVENING WITH RUSH
TICKETS: $51.00 / $76.00 / $126.00 / $300.00 (VIP); face value, minus $2.00 finance charge
ATTENDANCE: 8,450
CAPACITY: 8,789

CONCERT GROSS: $654,900
NOTES: Set list B (5.0). Final date of the Clockwork Angels Tour. During sound check, Alex began playing "Garden Road," with Geddy and Neil joining in for an instrumental rendition of this archaic Rush original. Before the show, the Stringers presented Alex, Geddy, and Neil with a CD entitled "Closer to our Hearts" (a complex string arrangement of their song). An emotional and exhilarating gig closed out the tour. During the "Dance to the Music" section of "Wish Them Well," the crew G'nome, chicken, gorilla, and professor all danced on stage. On the introduction to "The Garden," fans held up their cell phones, lighting up the venue "like fireflies."[39] In the middle break of "YYZ," Paul Rudd appeared, conducting the *Clockwork Angels* String Ensemble to the delight of the crowd.
GEDDY (ONSTAGE): "Thank you Kansas City. Thank you USA. Thank you, all the amazing people that work for us. We have the best crew you could ever want in your life. It's been an amazing tour. And we do hope to see you all sometime, somewhere down the road. Thank you. Bye Bye!"
THE KANSAS CITY STAR: "Rush delivers a three-hour rock odyssey: Lee turned sixty in late July, but he can still deliver vocals that resemble the way he recorded them. And he can do it for three hours a night, which is even more impressive."
NEIL: "The emotional resonance of the final show, in Kansas City, inside us and around us, could only compare to the first show of our *Vapor Trails* tour, in Hartford, on June 28, 2002. Eleven years later, that August night was the ultimate tour-ending show in all our thirty-nine years of 'roadwork.' It affected us in ways we could never have expected, and most of that emotion was centered on the *Clockwork Angels* String Ensemble. Usually the Guys at Work, band and crew, finish a tour believing it's just a break—that it will all start up again at some point and we'll all see each other again. All seven of the 'stringers' knew that this time it truly was, like the lovely title of a Hemingway story, 'The End of Something.'. . ."[40]

1. *Drum!*, October 2012.
2. *Rolling Stone*, October 11, 2012.
3. *Pittsburgh Tribune-Review*, September 6, 2012.
4. Interview with Kevin J. Anderson. *Rock Cellar*, November 2012.
5. *The Winnipeg Sun*.
6. *Edmonton Sun*.
7. NeilPeart.net, November 2012.
8. NeilPeart.net, November 2012.
9. NeilPeart.net, November 2012.
10. *Montreal Gazette*.
11. *DW's Edge*, Issue 10.
12. *Forbes*.
13. NeilPeart.net, November 2012.
14. Neil Peart. *Far and Near: On Days Like These*. ECW Press, 2014.
15. NeilPeart.net, November 2012.
16. NeilPeart.net, December 2012.
17. Rollingstone.com, September 23, 2013.
18. Interview with John Gibbons, *Toronto Sun*.
19. NeilPeart.net, December 2012.
20. RollingStone.com, September 23, 2013.
21. Interview with Alex Lifeson. *The Globe and Mail*, December 11, 2012.
22. Interview with Ray Danniels. *Celebrity Access*, March 11, 2015.
23. "Limited Edition Rush Special," *PROG*, Issue 35, April 2013.
24. Interview with Alex Lifeson. *The Star*, May 23, 2013.
25. NeilPeart.net, June 2013.
26. NeilPeart.net, June 2013.
27. Brad Parmerter. "Howard Ungerleider Interview—Rush's Clockwork Angels Tour 2013 & Lighting Rush for almost 40 years," *Live Journal*, June 22, 2013.
28. *The Hamilton Spectator*.
29. *Broadcaster Magazine*, June 24, 2013.
30. Neil Peart. *News Weather and Sports*, July 2013.
31. Interview with Geddy Lee. *Canadian Press*, July 4, 2013.
32. *Calgary Sun*.
33. *Calgary Herald*.
34. Rush.com, July 11, 2013.
35. NeilPeart.net, August 2013.
36. *Rushcast* interview, March 7, 2015.
37. NeilPeart.net, August 2013.
38. NeilPeart.net, August, 2013.
39. Neil Peart. *Far and Near: On Days Like These*. ECW Press, 2014.
40. Neil Peart. "News Weather and Sports," neilpeart.net, August 2013.

Chapter 31

THE R40 LIVE TOUR

Rush celebrated their fortieth Anniversary with the *R40 Live* tour. The set list and staging theme reflected a march backward through time, beginning with *Clockwork Angels* material and proceeding backward chronologically throughout the show. The backlines, meanwhile, progressed from steampunk-themed to dryers to, finally, walls of amplifiers. For the second set, Neil switched to a replica of his old chrome drum kit from the '70s, while Geddy played numerous basses from his personal collection. Alex and Geddy's dueling double necks also reappeared for a full rendition of "Xanadu."

"The concept for this tour began with an idea I had about devolution," Geddy explained. "And I thought it would be kind of neat to do a retrospective at some point, where we began in the present day and went back in time. I shared this concept during a creative meeting with [art director] Dale Heslip, and he started expanding upon it, and suggested the idea if we were going to go back musically in time, why don't we go back physically in a more theatrical sense."

RIGHT: Aerial view of the Professor's kit.

OPPOSITE: Lerxst and his Marshalls.

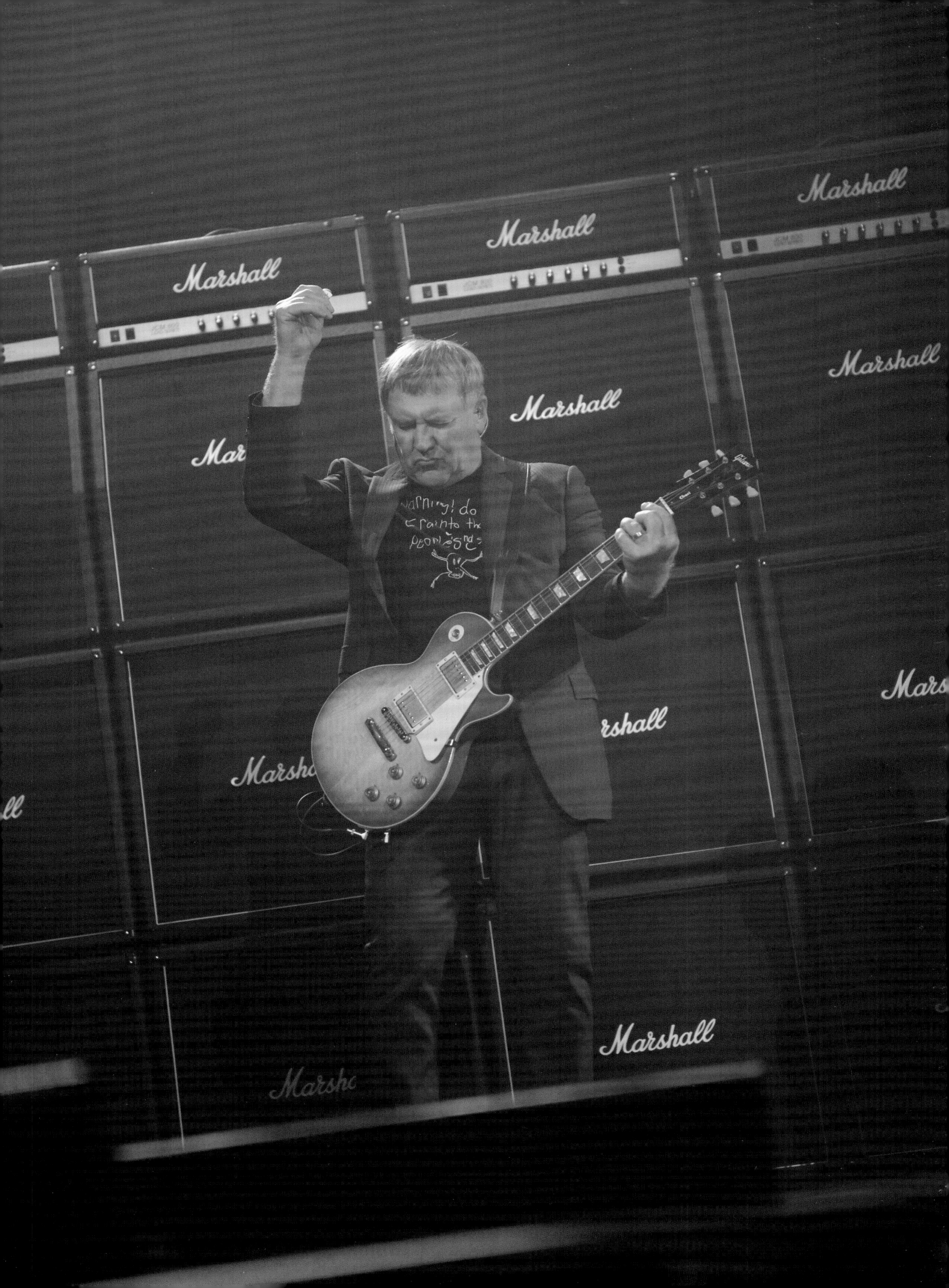
Marshall
Marshall
Marshall
Marshall
Marshall
Marshall

Three sets (A, B, and C) alternated songs from four albums. Set A included "Red Barchetta" (*Moving Pictures*), "Distant Early Warning" (*Grace Under Pressure*), "One Little Victory" (*Vapor Trails*), and "Clockwork Angels" (*Clockwork Angels*); those songs were replaced in Set B with their respective album companions "The Camera Eye," "Between the Wheels," "How It Is," and "The Wreckers." Set C was nearly the same as A, except "YYZ" replaced "Red Barchetta," and "Natural Science" was added as a bonus track. During five shows of the tour, the *Clockwork Angels* alternating song was dropped to make room for the *Signals* track "Losing It," performed on tour for the first time ever.

"My attitude was this is an anniversary tour, so we should really celebrate our most popular songs," Geddy reasoned. "And in order to do that, you have to have the discussion: Well, popular by whose metric? . . . If you look at some of the hardcore fans and their requests, they want the more obscure, deeper tracks. So we tried to strike a balance."

Added Alex, "We've dug deep. We've pulled out some songs that we haven't played in a very long time . . . some real fan favorites. And we're enjoying playing them. We've revisited every era except maybe the mid-'80s era, which we covered in a good portion of the set on the last tour. We've got three sets—A, B, C—which we'll be rotating throughout the tour. Ged and I have gone crazy on bringing out all of our old instruments and buying up vintage gear all over the place. His goal is to play a different bass for every song in the show."

While not exactly billed as a farewell tour, the press release announcing the *R40 Live* trek included a statement indicating that the band's touring days would most likely be coming to an end: "After forty years together and twenty gold and platinum studio albums—Rush is ready to celebrate with the most loyal fans in the world by embarking on their twenty-first tour, one which will most likely be their last major tour of this magnitude."

Geddy explained, "It's clear that we are at a point in our career that we have to slow down—and slow down dramatically. So, I'm not a guy who's in love with the 'farewell tour' idea, but it's clear that this is going to be the last big tour that we're going to do for a while, anyway. In terms of 'are we still a band?' Yeah, of course we're still a band. Do we talk about writing? Yes, we talk about writing. Will we do gigs in the future? I don't see why not. But, when you are talking about a tour that's thirty-five shows, forty shows, fifty shows . . . at our age at this point in our lives, I don't know how many of those are still left in us."

Indeed, prior to the tour, Neil had met with Alex, Geddy, and manager Ray Danniels to let them know that he was "done." But, he noted, "Not in any bitter or jaded way—quite the contrary. I simply felt that fifty years of playing drums, forty of them with Rush, might be enough for these old bones . . ."

OPPOSITE: Neil on the "El Darko" drum kit.

TOP: Rush performing the *R40* tour encore.

ABOVE: Rush in full flight beneath Howard's vectoring lights.

TOP: The Professor on the "El Darko" drum kit.
ABOVE: "Xanadu," complete with Ged on doubleneck.

As for what changed his mind, "In my secret heart of hearts, the one tiny door I left open was that if one of the guys said he really wanted to do it one more time, and wasn't sure he'd be able to in another year, I would have to . . . surrender. Well. Of course Alex didn't know about that little door, or that my decision hinged on it, but he said exactly that—explaining that his creeping arthritis was affecting his hands, that he really wanted to play live again, and didn't know if he would be able to do it in another year."

In the end, Neil agreed to three months of touring, and the *R40 Live* trek saw the band perform thirty-five shows in thirty-four cities across North America, beginning on May 8, 2015, in Tulsa, Oklahoma, and wrapping on August 1 at the Forum in Inglewood, California. Celebrities in attendance at the final show included the likes of Jack Black, as well as famous drummers Stewart Copeland, Chad Smith, and Taylor Hawkins. Jonathan Dinklage joined the band for the fifth live performance of "Losing It," and at the end of "Working Man," Neil took photos of Geddy, Alex, and the crowd.

Following "Garden Road," Neil broke with tradition to joined Alex and Geddy at the front of the stage for a group hug and bow.

Geddy (onstage at the Forum): "Thank you so much, Los Angeles! On behalf of the greatest crew and organization in the world . . . on behalf of our whole organization—thank you United States of America for forty awesome years. And I do hope we'll meet again sometime. Bye-bye!"

TOUR HISTORY

R40 LIVE

SET LIST A:

"The World Is . . . The World Is . . ." intro video

"The Anarchist"

"Clockwork Angels" / "The Wreckers"

"Headlong Flight"

"Drumbastica" (drum solo)

"Far Cry"

"The Main Monkey Business"

"One Little Victory" / "How It Is"

"Animate"

"Roll the Bones"

"Distant Early Warning" / "Between the Wheels"

"Losing It"

"Subdivisions"

(Intermission: "No Country for Old Hens" video)

"Tom Sawyer"

"Red Barchetta" / "The Camera Eye" / "YYZ"

"The Spirit of Radio"

"Natural Science"

"Jacob's Ladder"

"Hemispheres: Prelude"

"Cygnus X-1: Prologue"

"Cygnus X-1: The Story So Far" (drum solo)

"Cygnus X-1: Part 3"

"Closer to the Heart"

"Xanadu"

"2112: Overture"

"2112: The Temples of Syrinx"

"2112: Presentation"

"2112: Grand Finale"

Encore ("Mel's Rockpile" video):

"Lakeside Park" (abridged)

"Anthem" (abridged)

"What You're Doing"

"Working Man"

"Garden Road" (teaser)

"Exit Stage Left" outro video

MAY 8, 2015
TULSA, OKLAHOMA
BOK CENTER, 200 South Denver Avenue West. Venue opened on August 30, 2008.

AN EVENING WITH RUSH
TICKETS: $48.00 / $68.00 (upper level) / $93.00 / $128.00 (floor, lower level, club level) / $302.00 (VIP silver) / $402.00 (VIP gold); face value, includes $2.00 finance charge
ATTENDANCE: 9,830
CAPACITY: 10,355
CONCERT GROSS: $817,400
INTRO VIDEO CITY SLOGAN: "A Great Place For Drag."
NOTES: Opening date of the *R40 Live* tour. Set list A, which includes "Red Barchetta," "Distant Early Warning," "One Little Victory," and "Clockwork Angels." This tour opener revealed the R40 theme as a steady march backward in time, reflected in both set list and stage presentation. As the concert progressed, the backline changes from steampunk to dryers to stacks of amplifiers. For the second set, Neil switched to a replica of his double-bass black chrome kit from the '70s, while Geddy played an astonishing number of vintage basses from his personal collection. "Jacob's Ladder" returned to the stage for the first time since 1980 (with Geddy erroneously introducing it as a "song we've never played [live] before"). "Xanadu" re-appeared in unedited form for the first time since 1981, complete

with dueling doubleneck guitars. The encore knocked old school fans out of their seats, featuring "Lakeside Park" (for the first time since May, 1978), "Anthem," and "What You're Doing." The band closed out the show with the main riff from "Garden Road" at the conclusion of "Working Man."
GEDDY (ONSTAGE): "As you know, this is the very first show on this tour, this R40 celebration of way too many years of music."
GEDDY: "There was a guy in the second row during 'Xanadu,' I thought his head was gonna pop off and roll away. He couldn't fucking contain himself! I thought he was gonna have a heart attack."[1]
NEIL: "My journal note from the first show in Tulsa: 'Show report—after all that preparing. Pretty good overall, except for two hardest bits, in 'Headlong' and 'Monkey Biz.' Made it through, anyway, in every sense. Feeling pretty good about EVERYTHING right now. It cannot last . . .'"[2]
TULSA WORLD: "Rush brings forty years of iconic rock to the BOK Center: Peart sets the bar, able to play engaging drum solos that tell a story, have a beginning, middle and end. It's remarkable to watch. Lifeson on guitar played effortlessly, solos that sung and showed his control of the instrument that was total. But probably Rush's most iconic quality is the vocal work from Lee. His remarkably high and clear voice was impressive when the

band was taking off, but he hasn't lost a single note after more than forty years. It's still as high and strong as ever, with a few exceptions on the highest range. But Lee was able to sustain notes for a long time through several songs."

MAY 10, 2015
LINCOLN, NEBRASKA
PINNACLE BANK ARENA, 400 Pinnacle Arena Drive. Venue opened on August 16, 2013.

AN EVENING WITH RUSH
TICKETS: $49.00 / $69.00 / $89.00 / $129.00 / $300.00 (VIP silver) / $400.00 (VIP gold)
ATTENDANCE: 9,357
CAPACITY: 10,280
CONCERT GROSS: $654,434
INTRO VIDEO CITY SLOGAN: "Home Of The Real Red Sea."
NOTES: Set list B, with "The Camera Eye" replacing "Red Barchetta," "Between The Wheels" in place of "Distant Early Warning," "How It Is" (performed for the very first time) replacing "One Little Victory," and "The Wreckers" in place of "Clockwork Angels." Afternoon sound check featured "Jacob's Ladder," "The Anarchist," "The Main Monkey Business," and "How It Is." Onstage,

Geddy corrected his statement in Tulsa that "Jacob's Ladder" had never been performed live, by saying "apparently we have. It's completely fallen out of my mind," as he does a "V8" head slap.

LINCOLN JOURNAL STAR: "Rush rocks Pinnacle Bank Arena: Lee had no trouble hitting the high notes. Lifeson zipped up and down his guitar fret with ease, and Peart, well, he's still the best percussionist in rock 'n' roll. He wowed the audience with drum solos on 'Headlong Flight' and 'Cygnus X-1,' working up a sweat each time."

NEIL: "The Lincoln show was a little better than the one in Tulsa, but still marred by a few rough spots—it would not be until the third show, in St. Paul, that I thought we hit our groove."[3]

MAY 12, 2015
ST. PAUL, MINNESOTA
XCEL ENERGY CENTER, 199 Kellogg Boulevard West. Venue opened on September 29, 2000.
AN EVENING WITH RUSH
TICKETS: $48.50 / $68.50 / $98.50 / $128.50 / $300.00 (VIP silver) / $400.00 (VIP gold)
ATTENDANCE: 11,835; sold out
CONCERT GROSS: $973,166
INTRO VIDEO CITY SLOGAN: "Two Is Better Than One."
NOTES: Set list C, with "YYZ" replacing "Red Barchetta" and "Natural Science" added. Afternoon sound check was a shocker for fans, as "Losing It" (the only song from *Signals* never performed live) was played, as well as "Jacob's Ladder," "How It Is," and "Clockwork Angels."
STAR TRIBUNE: "Rush presses on at Xcel Center—Perhaps not long for the road, the Canadian rock vets at least went long: Tuesday's concert was ultimately a Rush show even non-diehards could appreciate. The sheer velocity and virtuosity were impressive, as was the obvious deep-mining of the catalog. Perhaps no other band can go that far into its discography that effectively. Neither Peart nor his bandmates showed any signs of slipping or slowing down."

MAY 14, 2015
ST. LOUIS, MISSOURI
SCOTTRADE CENTER, 1401 Clark Avenue. Venue opened on October 8, 1994.

AN EVENING WITH RUSH
TICKETS: $49.00 / $99.00 / $154.00 / $303.00 (VIP silver) / $403.00 (VIP gold); face value, price includes $3.00 finance charge.
ATTENDANCE: 13,096; sold out
CONCERT GROSS: $1,092,824
INTRO VIDEO CITY SLOGAN: "Go Cards Go."
NOTES: Set list A. During the intro video, which is customized for each concert, a roadsign appears displaying the name of the city where Rush is performing, the city's population (which is accurate), and a humorous city slogan created for each show. To the right of the roadsign a physical landmark, person, or mascot that is unique to that city is pictured.
GEDDY (ONSTAGE): "We've played here almost as much, if not more than any other American city. We're always comfortable here."
NEIL: "Friend Matt Scannell attended the St. Louis show with some friends, and reported that on the way out 'strangers were high-fiving each other.' Nice."[4]
ST. LOUIS POST-DISPATCH: "Rush hints at last hurrah in concert—Band shows what it does best: the big spectacle: The crowd roared its approval for favorites 'Roll the Bones' and 'Subdivisions.' But the highlight was 'Headlong Flight,' which gave each of the band members chances to shine; especially Lee, who was in full roar with his still strong, impossibly high-pitched vocals, and Peart, who turned in the first of the show's two drum solos."

MAY 16, 2015
DEL VALLE, TEXAS
AUSTIN360 AMPHITHEATER, 9201 Circuit of the Americas Boulevard. Venue opened on April 5, 2013.
AN EVENING WITH RUSH
TICKETS: $39.50 (lawn) / $75.00 / $90.00 / $130.00 / $300.00 (VIP silver) / $400.00 (VIP gold)
ATTENDANCE: 12,898; sold out
CONCERT GROSS: $791,645
INTRO VIDEO CITY SLOGAN: "Keeping It Weird!"
NOTES: Set list B, with this tour's version of "The Camera Eye" dedicated to Andrew MacNaughtan. Afternoon sound check featured "Subdivisions" (partial), "Jacob's Ladder," "Losing It," "How It Is," and "The Anarchist" (partial).
TEXAS ROCK REPORT: "Rush Celebrates

Fortieth Anniversary Tour at Austin360: As fans exited the arena, some wondered if they would ever get to see a band with this much history play a concert of this caliber again."

MAY 18, 2015
DALLAS, TEXAS
AMERICAN AIRLINES CENTER, 2500 Victory Avenue. Venue opened on July 17, 2001.
AN EVENING WITH RUSH
TICKETS: $50.00 / $100.00 / $155.00 / $300.00 (VIP silver) / $400.00 (VIP gold); prices included $4.00 finance charge
ATTENDANCE: 13,320; sold out
CONCERT GROSS: $1,032,215.
INTRO VIDEO CITY SLOGAN: "Our Cheerleaders Are Better."
NOTES: Set list C. In a Spinal Tap moment, Geddy mistakenly greeted the crowd with "Hello, Houston!"
FORT WORTH STAR-TELEGRAM: "Rush at American Airlines Center: Judging from the near-capacity crowd's rapturous response to tracks like 'Subdivisions,' 'YYZ,' or 'Xanadu,' Rush's absence from the landscape would be keenly felt. Spectacle in lockstep with skill, a deeply intellectual pursuit but also one inspiring tremendous emotion—even now, in the twenty-first century, there isn't another act doing what Rush does so well. Simply put, Rush is a singular creation, and seeing them live is, fittingly, a singular experience."

MAY 20, 2015
HOUSTON, TEXAS
TOYOTA CENTER, 1510 Polk Street. Venue opened on October 6, 2003.
AN EVENING WITH RUSH
TICKETS: $46.00 / $66.00 / $96.00 / $151.00 / $300.00 (VIP silver) / $400.00 (VIP gold)
ATTENDANCE: 11,202; sold out
CONCERT GROSS: $1,046,297
INTRO VIDEO CITY SLOGAN: "The Capital Of Air Conditioning."
NOTES: Set list A.
HOUSTON CHRONICLE: "Rush rumbles for rabid fans at Toyota Center: Rush remains one of those rare musical acts that can bridge the generations without anything getting lost in translation. On Wednesday night devotees got one heck of a last look, with ringing eardrums to

match, if this is in fact the end of the touring line."

MAY 22, 2015
NEW ORLEANS, LOUISIANA
SMOOTHIE KING CENTER, 1501 Girod Street. Venue opened on October 19, 1999.

AN EVENING WITH RUSH

TICKETS: $46.00 / $66.00 / $98.00 / $126.00 / $300.00 (VIP silver) / $400.00 (VIP gold); face value, minus fees
ATTENDANCE: 10,786
CAPACITY: 11,547
CONCERT GROSS: $884,926
INTRO VIDEO CITY SLOGAN: "Jambalaya Anyone?"
NOTES: Set list B. Venue aka New Orleans Arena. One of the looser performances of the tour. During "Between the Wheels," Alex's guitar was out, so Geddy and Neil add a few more measures to the intro, but Alex's replacement axe was also down, with the problem not being rectified until a third guitar was heard during the first chorus, which drew a big cheer from the crowd.
NEIL: "New Orleans was a welcome 'intermission' in the run, in every way. Michael and I took three days off the bikes while I had a visit from Carrie and Olivia. We all enjoyed our time in that great city, eating well and wandering around the enduringly unique French Quarter. It was also Olivia's first Rush concert, and she loved it. I had thought she might last a song or two, but she danced and air-drummed right to the end. Manager Ray arranged a 'box' for them, high up over everything, and Olivia couldn't get over all the people. 'There must be two-thousand-and-eighteen people,' she said. Ray laughed and told her, 'Actually there are about eleven thousand!' Olivia looked puzzled, 'Are they all here to see my dad and Uncle Alex and Uncle Geddy?' When Ray assured her they were, she said, 'That's too silly.' Then she wondered, 'Do they know he's my dad?' Ray laughed and said, 'They probably do.' During intermission she came backstage and ran up to me, arms raised for me to pick her up. Still wearing her big red 'ear defenders,' she was so excited that she bounced in my arms . . . 'Daddy! It was great!'"[5]

MAY 24, 2015
TAMPA, FLORIDA
AMALIE ARENA, 401 Channelside Drive. Venue opened on October 12, 1996.

AN EVENING WITH RUSH

TICKETS: $46.00 / $66.00 / $96.00 / $151.00 / $300.00 (VIP silver) / $400.00 (VIP gold); face value, minus fees
ATTENDANCE: 13,914; sold out
CONCERT GROSS: $1,176,535
INTRO VIDEO CITY SLOGAN: "Love It Or Leave It."
NOTES: Set list C. Venue aka St. Pete Times Forum. The *Tampa Bay Times* lists attendance as 14,827. Longtime fans hoped that the band would extend "Lakeside Park" to include the lyric: "Everyone would gather on the twenty-fourth of May," but it was not meant to be.
TAMPA BAY TIMES: "Rush powers through four decades of music in a three-hour show, giving fans a performance to remember: One thing that hasn't changed over forty years is the band's jaw-dropping musicianship. Lee, Lifeson, and Peart twisted and tumbled their way through every knotty number with stoic precision. Peart gave the crowd's air-drumming die-hards what they came for during Cygnus X-1, twirling his sticks and walloping every skin at his disposal during a prism-lit solo of epic proportions. His legendary pounding even sparked a fist-pump out of Lifeson at the end of 'Roll the Bones.'"

MAY 26, 2015
ALPHARETTA, GEORGIA
VERIZON WIRELESS AMPHITHEATRE AT ENCORE PARK, 2200 Encore Parkway. Venue opened on May 10, 2008.

AN EVENING WITH RUSH

TICKETS: $40.50 (lawn) / $129.50 / $149.50 / $300.00 (VIP) / $400.00 (VIP gold); face value, included parking and finance charge
ATTENDANCE: 11,500 (approximate)
CAPACITY: 12,000
INTRO VIDEO CITY SLOGAN: "Land Of Fried Wonder."

NOTES: Set list A. Torrential rains with heavy traffic delayed the start of the show. Those in attendance included Rush co-producer Peter Collins, John Wesley, and Blackberry Smoke keyboardist Brandon Still.
GWINNETT CITIZEN: "Rush *R40* Tour . . . for the generations: Fans were frenetically overjoyed to witness one of the most intricate displays of musicianship in the history of rock. The quality and power generated by three guys from Ontario brought a cool breeze to a sultry and stormy southern night where fans wanted nothing more than for time to stand still . . ."

MAY 28, 2015
GREENSBORO, NORTH CAROLINA
GREENSBORO COLISEUM, 1921 West Lee Street. Venue opened on October 29, 1959.

AN EVENING WITH RUSH

TICKETS: $46.00 / $66.00 / $86.00 / $126.00 / $300.00 (VIP silver) / $400.00 (VIP gold)
ATTENDANCE: 10,861
CAPACITY: 11,135
CONCERT GROSS: $895,380
INTRO VIDEO CITY SLOGAN: "Our BBQ Is Better."
NOTES: Set list B.
THE PROG REPORT: "A Headlong Flight Down the Garden Road: The entire presentation had to be the most authentic feeling of time travel anyone in the room had ever experienced prior to this evening."

MAY 30, 2015
BRISTOW, VIRGINIA
JIFFY LUBE LIVE, 7800 Cellar Door Drive. Venue opened on June 3, 1995.

AN EVENING WITH RUSH

TICKETS: $37.00 (lawn) / $87.00 / $127.00 / $302.00 (silver) / $402.00 (gold)
ATTENDANCE: 16,579; sold out
CONCERT GROSS: $1,094,711
INTRO VIDEO CITY SLOGAN: "We Were Here First!"
NOTES: Set list C. Sound check featured a unique jam, "Jacob's Ladder," and "Losing It." During the show, "Distant Early Warning" became a bit of a train wreck, and equipment problems haunted Alex throughout "2112," as he was forced to change guitars twice, midsong.

Neil missed the major drum fill before the guitar solo in "Natural Science" and ended up just keeping time with a straight beat to get through the section.

BALTIMORE POST EXAMINER: "Fans arrived decked out in every variation of past Rush tour shirt imaginable, and while wearing a shirt from the band you're seeing that night may be a 'true breach of cool' in some circles, in this case it highlights the devotion of the band's fans. What's the difference between a Rush fan and a terrorist? Sometimes, you can reason with a terrorist."

NEIL: "Michael and I made it through almost 7,000 miles of motorcycling, and the Guys at Work and me through twelve shows. Though for that last one at the Bristow amphitheater I was under attack from a bug that gave me stomach cramps, general malaise, and light-headedness—but everyone else seemed to have a good time. Then a long, early flight the next morning for a painfully brief few days at home . . . before a long flight back east, toward the next show in Columbus."[6]

JUNE 8, 2015
COLUMBUS, OHIO
NATIONWIDE ARENA, 200 West Nationwide Boulevard. Venue opened on September 9, 2000.
AN EVENING WITH RUSH
TICKETS: $49.00 / $89.00 / $129.00 / $300.00 (VIP silver) / $400.00 (VIP gold)
ATTENDANCE: 14,079; sold out
CONCERT GROSS: $1,076,164
INTRO VIDEO CITY SLOGAN: "Don't Step In The Doo Dah."
NOTES: Set list A. During "The World Is . . . The World Is . . ." intro video there's a radio station in the film with the call letters WMMS, a special shout out to the city of Cleveland. During "2112: Overture," two crew members took the stage wearing Lifeson and Peart robes. En route to the gig, Neil and Michael were caught in a speed trap with the Ohio State Highway Patrol writing them up "to the full extent of the law."
GEDDY (ONSTAGE): "Of course, if we do anything, we do it backwards."
COLUMBUS DISPATCH: "Rush—Band explores forty years of music: The Canadian power trio rocked out in grand style, going through parts of their catalog

in a completely logical format over the course of three hours."

JUNE 9, 2015
DURING A LONG, WET RIDE FROM BATH, NEW YORK TO LAKE PLACID, NEIL'S BOOTS GET COMPLETELY SOAKED, SOWING THE SEEDS OF AN INFECTION WHICH WOULD HAUNT HIM THROUGHOUT THE REMAINDER OF THE TOUR.
NEIL: "I hope it goes without saying that I put everything I have into every performance . . . But as that output every second night exceeded the available supply of mental and physical energy, it wormed deeper and deeper into my reserves. Thus I had no resistance to any kind of physical attack. This time the weak link was apparently my *skin*, and the chain reaction apparently began on the long, wet ride from our drop-off point in Bath, New York to Lake Placid. Hours of riding under a steady downpour had overwhelmed our normally waterproof riding gear. One of my boots stayed dry inside, but the other was flooded—leaving my right foot wet and cold, and the boot would not dry by morning. So I would ride another day with a wet foot—the perfect breeding ground for . . . a fungus among us. The inevitable casual exchange of socks carried it to the other foot, and at first it was just a little 'hotspot' in the arch of each sole. But day by day it was growing and mutating into a fungus-eczema-psoriasis-bacterial-infection monster that would be attacking me for the rest of the tour—and long after."[7]

JUNE 10, 2015
BUFFALO, NEW YORK
FIRST NIAGARA CENTER, One Seymour Knox III Plaza. Venue opened on September 21, 1996.
AN EVENING WITH RUSH
TICKETS: $48.50 / $68.50 / $88.50 / $128.50 / $303.50 (VIP silver) / $403.50 (VIP gold); price included $2.50 finance charge

ATTENDANCE: 13,913; sold out
CONCERT GROSS: $1,132,154
INTRO VIDEO CITY SLOGAN: "Our Wings Are Better!"
NOTES: Set list B.
GEDDY (ONSTAGE): "Welcome, we have a birthday celebration of over forty years."
BUFFALO NEWS: "Rush delivers forty years of hits in thrilling *R40 Live* show: Watching virtuosos in throes of impassioned performance is always electrifying; beholding power-rock trio Rush perform before a sold-out First Niagara Center crowd was just that."

JUNE 12, 2015
CHICAGO, ILLINOIS
UNITED CENTER, 1901 West Madison Street. Venue opened on August 18, 1994.
AN EVENING WITH RUSH
TICKETS: $45.00 / $69.50 (300 level) / $69.50 / $95.00 (200 level) / $95.00 / $175.00 (100 level and floor) / $300.00 (VIP silver) / $400.00 (VIP gold); face value, minus fees
ATTENDANCE: 14,256; sold out
CONCERT GROSS: $1,450,746
INTRO VIDEO CITY SLOGAN: "Vienna Dogs Rule."
NOTES: Set list C. In the "retro" spirit of the tour, Neil donned a fake mustache (gifted by a fan) midshow.

JUNE 14, 2015
DETROIT, MICHIGAN
THE PALACE OF AUBURN HILLS, 6 Championship Drive. Venue opened on August 13, 1988.
AN EVENING WITH RUSH
TICKETS: $49.50 / $73.50 / $99.00 / $129.00 / $300.00 (VIP silver) / $400.00 (VIP gold)
ATTENDANCE: 13,083; sold out
CONCERT GROSS: $1,092,767
INTRO VIDEO CITY SLOGAN: "Heal With Our Steel."
NOTES: Set list A. One fan's Frenchtown home was burglarized, with six Rush tickets (two for Chicago and four to Auburn Hills) stolen in the process.[8]

MACOMB DAILY: "Rush rocks the Palace with forty-plus years of music: Rush thrilled the sold-out Palace crowd by digging deep into its catalog for favorites that haven't been played in many years."

JUNE 17, 19, 2015
TORONTO, ONTARIO

AIR CANADA CENTRE, 40 Bay Street. Venue dedicated on February 19, 1999.

AN EVENING WITH RUSH

TICKETS: $95.50 / $175.00 / $375.00 CAD; face value, minus $3.00 finance charge

ATTENDANCE: 14,182 per show; sold out

CONCERT GROSS: $1,270,992 per show

INTRO VIDEO CITY SLOGAN (JUNE 17): "Go Jays Go."

INTRO VIDEO CITY SLOGAN (JUNE 19): "Now With More Pandas."

NOTES: June 17: Set list A. Filmed with fourteen HD cameras for future DVD release. Despite rampant rumors in the days leading up to this gig, "Losing It" did not get its live debut. During a lackluster concert, Geddy had bass difficulties at the beginning of "Headlong Flight." June 19: Set list D, with the first half being Set list B, minus "The Wreckers" with "Losing It" (live debut with Ben Mink on electric violin) added before "Subdivisions. The second set continued the course of Set list C. After a spotty performance on the first night, Alex, Geddy, and Neil bounced back and delivered a once-in-a-lifetime show that had fanatics pinching themselves. Prior to the four Canadian gigs, Neil's hockey-themed kit was on display at the venue, with fans able to have their picture taken behind it, to benefit the Princess Margaret Cancer Foundation of Toronto. All totaled, more than $20,000 was raised. Alex, Geddy, and Neil graced the iconic cover of *Rolling Stone* magazine.

GEDDY (ONSTAGE ON JUNE 17): "Hey, Toronto, Canada, how are you doing tonight? So great to be home. Thank you for coming out tonight and over the last forty-plus years."

NEIL (ON JUNE 17 SHOW): "When we reached the intro reprise to 'The Anarchist,' I was suddenly way ahead of it. I immediately blamed myself, as I do, and guessed that I must be so anxious that I was pushing the tempo. Not a problem I usually had, at least in recent years, but . . . I pulled back on the tempo until it was in sync again. Then everything would be fine until the next such entry, when again, I would be early, ahead of everything. I kept thinking, 'What is wrong with me?' I was like that all the way through the second song, 'Clockwork Angels,' too—and by then I was going crazy. At least I thought I was—and that amounts to the same thing. Before the third song, one of the backstage 'geniuses' finally switched over to the backup keyboard system. Suddenly everything was fine—but of course we were not fine. Geddy had a problem starting 'Headlong Flight' and stopped playing to switch bass guitars, leaving Alex and me unsure whether to stop or carry on. We kept playing, Geddy joined in again, and we continued on—but it was pretty much all over for us right there. We played on through the show—because what else?—but I couldn't say we 'recovered.' We merely survived. Before the second Toronto show, Geddy described that first one as 'the worst experience I've ever had onstage.'"[9]

TORONTO STAR: "Hometown superstars Rush put on a show for the ages: Glancing around the ACC, you could see and feel the sense of hometown pride flowing from the fans, as well as the forty-plus years of blood, toil, sweat and laughter emanating from the stage."

NEIL: "We went into the second show feeling anything but relaxed and confident. Glad to say we pulled it off, and the DVD turned out really well—but it didn't feel good at the time."[10]

JUNE 21, 2015
MONTREAL, QUEBEC

CENTRE BELL, 1909 Avenue des Canadiens-de-Montréal. Venue opened on March 16, 1996.

AN EVENING WITH RUSH

TICKETS: $58.50 / $78.50 / $96.50 / $136.50 / $155.00 (CAD); price included $6.00 finance charge

ATTENDANCE: 13,024; sold out

CONCERT GROSS: $939,304

INTRO VIDEO CITY SLOGAN: "Bring Back The Expos!"

NOTES: Set list A.

NEIL: "After the nightmare of the Toronto shows, we were determined both to play well 'and' have a good time. And we did."[11]

MONTREAL GAZETTE: "Rush turns the Bell Centre into a time machine: The trio's enduring camaraderie was visible from the start, the players trading grins and swinging the spotlight back and forth with the mutual admiration inherent in a 41-year partnership that clearly hasn't been taken for granted."

MONTREAL GAZETTE, GEDDY (WHEN ASKED IF ANY THOUGHT WAS GIVEN TO CALLING IT THE 41ST-ANNIVERSARY TOUR?): "[*Laughs*] Yes there was. But forty had a nicer ring to it."

JUNE 23, 2015
BOSTON, MASSACHUSETTS

TD GARDEN, 100 Legends Way. Venue opened on September 30, 1995.

AN EVENING WITH RUSH

TICKETS: $49.50 / $114.50 / $154.50 / $304.50 (VIP silver) / $404.50 (VIP gold)

ATTENDANCE: 12,953; sold out

CONCERT GROSS: $1,232,122

INTRO VIDEO CITY SLOGAN: "A Place For Great Feelings."

NOTES: Set list B. Mike Portnoy watched sound check and rocked out during the gig.

THE BOSTON GLOBE: "Rush plays its history in reverse at TD Garden: Peart played as though he was doing equations in his head (which he was, in a way), and he forged a genuine rhythm section with Lee's muscular bass, rather than two independent virtuosos nodding at one another."

JUNE 25, 2015
PHILADELPHIA, PENNSYLVANIA

WELLS FARGO CENTER, 3601 South Broad Street. Venue opened on August 12, 1996.

AN EVENING WITH RUSH

TICKETS: $46.00 / $86.00 / $118.00 / $151.00 / $285.00 (venue deluxe suite) / $300.00 (VIP silver) / $400.00 (VIP gold)

ATTENDANCE: 13,476; sold out

CONCERT GROSS: $1,340,006

INTRO VIDEO CITY SLOGAN: "Home Of A Large Bell."

NOTES: Set list C.

THE MERCURY (POTTSTOWN): "Rush Rocks the Wells Fargo Center in Philly: Exhibiting the energy and intensity that remains the staple of a Rush concert, the crowd hung on every note, often singing in unison with Lee."

JUNE 27, 2015
NEWARK, NEW JERSEY
PRUDENTIAL CENTER, 165 Mulberry Street. Venue opened on October 25, 2007.
AN EVENING WITH RUSH
TICKETS: $50.75 / $100.75 / $195.25 / $304.75 (VIP silver) / $404.75 (VIP gold); price included $4.75 finance charge
ATTENDANCE: 12,483; sold out
CONCERT GROSS: $1,289,222
INTRO VIDEO CITY SLOGAN: "We Don't Pump Our Own Gas."
NOTES: Set list E (which is set list B, with "The Wreckers" not performed and "Losing It" added). Jonathan Dinklage joined Alex, Geddy, and Neil for the second live performance of "Losing It." Backstage, Neil as interviewed by *Modern Drummer* magazine.
NEIL: "At this point in the tour, you have no reserves. So a thing like this [bacterial-infection] attacks, and it wears down your resistance in every other way too. And there's no getting better. I got tendinitis in one elbow on the '96/'97 *Test for Echo* tour, and then I didn't have it again for fifteen years—and it was the other elbow. For the rest of the tour I have to wear a brace to play, and I wear a brace at night. People say, 'Oh, you just need to rest it.' Ok, I'll do that. We'll just send these 10,000 people home tonight while I have a rest."[12]
BILLBOARD: "Rush Rocks Harder Than Ever at Fortieth Anniversary Tour Stop in New Jersey: The band's energy never diminished throughout the night, which contributed to its share of transcendent moments."

JUNE 29, 2015
NEW YORK, NEW YORK
MADISON SQUARE GARDEN, 4 Pennsylvania Plaza (8th Avenue between 31st and 33rd Streets). Historic venue opened on February 11, 1968.
AN EVENING WITH RUSH
TICKETS: $71.00 / $101.00 / $195.50 / $300.00 (VIP silver) / $400.00 (VIP gold); face value, minus $5.00 finance charge

ATTENDANCE: 13,554; sold out
CONCERT GROSS: $1,507,393
INTRO VIDEO CITY SLOGAN: "Our Pizza Is Better!"
NOTES: Set list F (which is set list A with "Clockwork Angels" not performed and "Losing It" added). Jonathan Dinklage joined the band for the third live performance of "Losing It." The finale to a strong run of shows which began the second night in Toronto and carried right through Montreal, Boston, Philly, Newark, and MSG.

JULY 9, 2015
KANSAS CITY, MISSOURI
SPRINT CENTER, 1407 Grand Boulevard. Venue opened on October 10, 2007.
AN EVENING WITH RUSH
TICKETS: $48.00 / $68.00 / $98.00 / $153.00 / $300.00 (VIP silver) / $400.00 (VIP gold)
ATTENDANCE: 10,629
CAPACITY: 10,736
CONCERT GROSS: $914,828
INTRO VIDEO CITY SLOGAN: "Our BBQ Is Better!"
NOTES: Set list B. Rush is demonstrated against by the Westboro Baptist Church. Back in Toronto, Foo Fighters paid homage to Rush by performing a medley which included "The Spirit of Radio," "2112 Discovery," "2112 Overture," and "Tom Sawyer" at Molson Amphitheatre. Dave Grohl stopped a train wreck version of "The Spirit of Radio" abruptly, by saying "It's too hard! If we start playing Rush songs, you're all gonna be here all fucking night, because we don't fucking know them dude. Too hard!"
NEIL: "This time in Kansas City we were particularly honored to be picketed by the local maniacs—I mean people of faith—from the Westboro Baptist Church."[13]
WESTBORO BAPTIST CHURCH PRESS RELEASE: "Neil Peart, Geddy Lee, and Alex Lifeson should be known only for their protestations against the sins of their neighbors. So far from fulfilling that duty—they have been the chief proponent in the world of rock n' roll of the lying, antichristic doctrine of free will (and specifically against the Bible doctrine of predestination)."
THE KANSAS CITY STAR: "Rush takes Sprint Center crowd on a long, nostalgic trip: If this is their final tour, Rush's

concert was a hell of a farewell. Health concerns may push the band off the road, but all three appeared in fine form. Guitarist Alex Lifeson acted out the lyrics during 'Tom Sawyer' and made his bandmates laugh with a corny dance near the end of 'Working Man.'"

JULY 11, 2015
DENVER, COLORADO
PEPSI CENTER, 1000 Chopper Circle. Venue opened on October 1, 1999.
AN EVENING WITH RUSH
TICKETS: $46.00 / $86.00 / $126.00 / $300.00 (VIP silver) / $400.00 (VIP gold); face value, minus $4.00 finance charge
ATTENDANCE: 12,681; sold out
CONCERT GROSS: $1,119,150
INTRO VIDEO CITY SLOGAN: "A Higher State Of Mind."
NOTES: Set list C. Eddie Trunk attended the gig and interviewed Alex. Before the show, Neil's driver, Dave Burnette, was badly burned, causing him to have to leave the tour. Neil would have a replacement driver for the remainder of the *R40 Live* dates, with Dave not returning until the end-of-tour party.
EDDIE TRUNK (THAT METAL SHOW): "I had the very special opportunity to watch the band sound check and also hung with Geddy and Alex after the show. Geddy told me changes to his diet have really helped his voice as well as thirty-six hours of rest (as in not talking at all) before show days. It shows big time!"[14]
NEIL: "The day had grown hot in Denver, and as we sat around the front lounge of the bus that afternoon in a parking lot outside the venue, the generator suddenly shuddered and died. Dave got out and went to check on it, and after a few minutes he came back in—soaking wet, and with a fraught look on his face. At first I thought he must be dripping with sweat from the hot generator bay, but then he quietly asked Michael to call a medic. He had tried to remove the radiator cap—knowing and even thinking at the time, 'This is a bad idea.' Steam and boiling water had exploded out on his hand and face, scalding him badly."[15]
HEY REVERB: "Rush at the Pepsi Center: Judging by Saturday's show, it certainly seemed as if the band could tour as much as it wants."

JULY 13, 2015
WEST VALLEY CITY, UTAH
MAVERIK CENTER, 3200 South Decker Lane. Venue opened on September 22, 1997.
AN EVENING WITH RUSH
TICKETS: $46.00 / $89.00 / $126.00 / $300.00 (VIP silver) / $400.00 (VIP gold); face value, minus fees
ATTENDANCE: 9,564
CAPACITY: 10,156
CONCERT GROSS: $805,899
INTRO VIDEO CITY SLOGAN: "We Can Hug It Out."
NOTES: Set list A.
SALT LAKE TRIBUNE: "Rush in West Valley City: The night spanned decades of the legendary trio's catalog, rolling through their patented progressive rock laced with drum solos, precision bass and driving guitar."

JULY 15, 2015
CALGARY, ALBERTA
SCOTIABANK SADDLEDOME, 555 Saddledome Rise SE. Venue opened on October 15, 1983.
AN EVENING WITH RUSH
TICKETS: $30.50 / $60.50 / $90.50 / $140.50 CAD; face value, minus fees
CAPACITY: 10,677
INTRO VIDEO CITY SLOGAN: "Our Air Is Superb."
NOTES: Set list B. First Calgary appearance since July 18, 2007 after a July 2013 concert was moved to Red Deer because of flooding in Calgary. Venue aka Pengrowth Saddledome.
GEDDY (ONSTAGE): "Good evening, Calgary. Nice to be back in our home and native land."
MUSIC EXPRESS: "Reconstructing History—Rush: Performing a synopsis of their catalog as a reverse retrospective while allowing their staging to be constructed into smaller and smaller pieces, a deconstruction of sorts, played with the imagination and offered touch points to the older fans who witnessed these changes in real time throughout the years."

JULY 17, 2015
VANCOUVER, BRITISH COLUMBIA
ROGERS ARENA, 800 Griffiths Way. Venue opened on September 17, 1995.
AN EVENING WITH RUSH
TICKETS: $30.50 / $60.50 / $90.50 /

$140.50 CAD; face value, minus $2.75 finance charge.
CAPACITY: 14,000 (approximate).
INTRO VIDEO CITY SLOGAN: "No Man Is An Island."
NOTES: Set list G. (A variation of Set list C, with "Clockwork Angels" dropped and "Losing It" added). Ben Mink once again joined the band onstage for the fourth live rendition of "Losing It."
GEDDY (ONSTAGE): "We'd like to do something a little special tonight. And because our very special guest for this song lives in Vancouver, he's very generously agreed to appear with us here tonight. Our very good friend and orchestra member Mr. Ben Mink."
VANCOUVER SUN: "Rush delivers a riff-ready farewell in Vancouver: No one will ever cast any doubts on the musical skills of Lee, Lifeson, or Peart. Well-rehearsed doesn't begin to describe how tight the concert was."

JULY 19, 2015
SEATTLE, WASHINGTON
KEY ARENA, 205 Harrison Street. Venue opened on April 21, 1962.
AN EVENING WITH RUSH
TICKETS: $50.00 / $90.00 / $115.00 / $155.00 / $305.00 (VIP silver) / $405.00 (VIP gold); price included $4.00 finance charge
ATTENDANCE: 11,933; sold out
CONCERT GROSS: $1,055,071
INTRO VIDEO CITY SLOGAN: "Don't Forget Your Raincoat!"
NOTES: Set list B. During sound check, Geddy (who had a newly acquired flu bug) was concerned about his voice, prompting a change from the "A" to "B" set list. "Losing It" was performed in sound check. For the "Lakeside Park" encore, crew members held up a large cardboard cutout of Kiss on stage left.
GEEK WIRE: "The geeky Canadian rockers are still at the top of their game: Lifeson brought the precision and intensity that has influenced countless other rock guitarists."

JULY 21, 2015
PORTLAND, OREGON
MODA CENTER, 1 Center Court. Venue opened on October 13, 1995.
AN EVENING WITH RUSH
TICKETS: $46.00 / $66.00 / $96.00 / $126.00 / $305.00 (VIP silver) /

$405.00 (VIP gold)
ATTENDANCE: 12,684; sold out
CONCERT GROSS: $971,350
INTRO VIDEO CITY SLOGAN: "Unlimited Bridges!"
NOTES: Set list A. Due to Geddy's flu bug, a chair with tissues and a beverage were placed on stage left for him. During "2112: Overture," two roadies take the stage wearing a horse costume. For the "Lakeside Park" encore, the Kiss cardboard cutout made a return appearance, this time on stage right. Venue aka Rose Garden.
THE OREGONIAN: "Rush blasts through forty glorious years in epic Portland show: Lee was an indefatigable frontman, yelping through 'Tom Sawyer,' 'The Anarchist,' and more with eyebrow-raising glee."

JULY 23, 2015
SAN JOSE, CALIFORNIA
SAP CENTER AT SAN JOSE, 525 West Santa Clara Street. Venue opened on September 7, 1993.
AN EVENING WITH RUSH
TICKETS: $49.00 / $69.00 / $99.00 / $154.00 / $303.00 (VIP silver) / $403.00 (VIP gold); price included $3.00 finance charge
ATTENDANCE: 12,534; sold out
CONCERT GROSS: $1,210,279
INTRO VIDEO CITY SLOGAN: "Upbeat and Effervescent."
NOTES: Set list C. Geddy (and now Alex) continued to battle a nasty flu. The Kiss cardboard cutout appeared during "Lakeside Park," on stage left. Venue aka HP Pavilion.

JULY 25, 2015
LAS VEGAS, NEVADA
MGM GRAND GARDEN ARENA, 3799 Las Vegas Boulevard South. Venue opened on December 31, 1993.
AN EVENING WITH RUSH
TICKETS: $59.00 / $89.00 / $114.00 / $179.00 / $304.00 (VIP silver) / $404.00 (VIP gold); face value, minus fees
ATTENDANCE: 13,434; sold out
CONCERT GROSS: $1,401,719
INTRO VIDEO CITY SLOGAN: "Three Is Better Than One!"
NOTES: Set list A. Alex and Geddy both deliver an energetic performance despite still being under the weather.
LAS VEGAS SUN: "If this is it for Rush, they leave on a high note: The crowd

stood throughout punching the air with requisite air-drum solos. Gray- and thin-haired devotees slapped one another's backs and exuberantly grabbed their buddies' shoulders (and, in some cases, the shoulders of strangers)."

JULY 27, 2015
PHOENIX, ARIZONA
US AIRWAYS CENTER, 201 East Jefferson. Venue opened on June 6, 1992.

AN EVENING WITH RUSH
TICKETS: $50.75 / $70.75 / $100.75 / $130.75 / $304.75 (VIP silver) / $404.75 (VIP); price included $4.75 finance charge
ATTENDANCE: 12,282
CAPACITY: 12,551
CONCERT GROSS: $944,212
INTRO VIDEO CITY SLOGAN: "Vitamin D Capital Of The Universe."
NOTES: Set list B. The venue was extremely hot because of an overextended air-conditioning system. During "2112: Overture," the crew horse took the stage holding a "Neigh" sign up for the audience participation segment.
NEIL: "Everybody knew we were 'counting down' now, and everything felt just a little more urgent and heartfelt that night—for the band and the audience, I know, and probably for the rest of the Guys at Work, too."[16]
ARIZONA REPUBLIC: "Rush *R40* tour crackles with life in Phoenix: If this is their final major tour, they're exiting . . . stage left at the top of their game."

JULY 29, 2015
MANHATTAN BEACH, CALIFORNIA.
END OF TOUR PARTY.
LOS ANGELES, CALIFORNIA
CANADIAN CONSULATE, 550 South Hope Street.
The Consulate General of Canada in Los Angeles, James Villeneuve, holds a special reception for Rush (on Geddy's 62nd birthday), where the band is honored with the inaugural award for Canadian Excellence in Los Angeles in recognition of the many times Rush has played there over the years (complete with certificate from Los Angeles Mayor Eric Garcetti). At the party, Neil tells Jack Black that touring is *over for him*."
NEIL: "A beautiful setting with plenty of food, plenty of drinks, and plenty of laughs."[17]

RAY: "I don't think they should end. They're playing as well as they ever have. Shorter tours, longer breaks, more days between shows, shorter sets, opening acts or just one last hurrah would be my vote. I would explore ways to make it work for a little while longer while it's this good. It matters to a lot of people."[18]

JULY 30, 2015
IRVINE, CALIFORNIA
VERIZON WIRELESS AMPHITHEATER, 8808 Irvine Center Drive. Venue opened on August 21, 1981.

AN EVENING WITH RUSH
TICKETS: $30.00 (lawn) / $87.00 / $145.00 / $300.00 (VIP silver) / $400.00 (VIP gold); face value, minus fees
ATTENDANCE: 14,933; sold out
CONCERT GROSS: $1,042,380
INTRO VIDEO CITY SLOGAN: "Orange Rhymes With Blorenge."
NOTES: Set list C. For this gig, the band auctioned off two VIP tickets, meet-and-greet passes, a tour of the stage and backstage area, and a chance to watch sound check, all to benefit the John Varvatos 13th Annual Stuart House Benefit for sexually abused children. "Polite manners and respect for the generous donor and adherence to any rules or parameters are a must." Afternoon sound check featured "Subdivisions," "Jacob's Ladder," and "Losing It."
OC WEEKLY: "Rush Entrances Audience at Irvine Meadows: They still perform like the incredibly gifted youths that have since inspired many other musicians and pop cultural icons."
RAY: "I've always said that I was at Rush's first shows and I plan on being at the last. That hasn't changed."[19]
GEDDY: "How am I feeling? Sad. The tour's gone so well. I'm really proud of it—we're playing really well. I love the way the show has lived up to my expectations and I'd just like to keep going."[20]

AUGUST 1, 2015
INGLEWOOD, CALIFORNIA
THE FORUM, 3900 West Manchester Boulevard. Venue opened on December 30, 1967.

AN EVENING WITH RUSH
TICKETS: $51.00 / $65.00 / $101.00 /

$185.50; price included $5.00 charge
ATTENDANCE: 12,894; sold out
CONCERT GROSS: $1,406,214
INTRO VIDEO CITY SLOGAN: "It Rarely Rains Here!"
NOTES: Final Date of the *R40 Live* tour. Set list F. Geddy's wife Nancy took in this special sound check, with "Subdivisions," "Jacob's Ladder," and "Losing It" all performed. Initially, the band had thought of ending the tour in Toronto, Cleveland, or Pittsburgh, but logistics prohibited that, so Los Angeles became the tour finale. Musicians in attendance included Jack Black, Danny Carey, Stewart Copeland, Taylor Hawkins, Robby Krieger, Doane Perry, Chad Smith, Matt Stone, and Jon Theodore. Jonathan Dinklage joined the band for the fifth live performance of "Losing It." At the end of "What You're Doing," Neil played Alex's guitar with his sticks. After "Working Man" wound down, Neil took photos of Geddy, Alex, and the crowd. At the conclusion of "Garden Road," he then broke with tradition and joined Alex and Geddy at the front of the stage for a group hug and bow.
CHAD SMITH (RED HOT CHILI PEPPERS): "I spent my sophomore year of high school in the parking lot, smoking weed and listening to 2112. That's when my Rush education began. I do believe it's a prerequisite for all rock drummers to go through a Neil Peart phase."[21]
MATT STONE (SOUTH PARK CREATOR): "Totally amazing show! I invited a couple of friends of mine that I grew up with in Denver. We saw Rush in 1985 at McNichols Arena, and it was really cool to bring it full circle here in 2015."[22]
JON THEODORE (QUEENS OF THE STONE AGE DRUMMER): "The solo was so impressionistic. Stripped down to just Neil and the drums. No vids or sequences. I never saw that much flow and color and instinct set free in him before. Just fucking beautiful."[23]
THE HOLLYWOOD REPORTER: "Star-Studded Crowd Toasts Rush at the Forum for Last (Ever?) Show: The beloved band wraps fortieth anniversary tour in Los Angeles with a powerful and memorable career-spanning set for the ages."
NANCY YOUNG (GEDDY'S WIFE): "You go out to sound check when you're young and in love. It's been so long since I've been to one of these, people are asking

me what I'm doing here today. What do they think I'm doing here? It's just hit me—this might be it and for forty years this has, for the most part, been our life."[24]

NEIL: "When Alex, Geddy, Jonny, and I played 'Losing It' . . . the song carried just a little more meaning for me, and perhaps for many others. As Jonny walked offstage beside my drum riser, I stood and gave him a 'bow . . .' One major reality is that my style of drumming is largely an athletic undertaking, and it does not pain me to realize that, like all athletes, there comes a time to . . . take yourself out of the game. I would much rather set it aside than face the fate described in 'Losing It.' Because I am keeping it, baby! No regrets here; I feel proud, grateful, and satisfied with what I have accomplished with two lumps of wood . . . That I could feel good about this occasion—well, I can only compare it to the way I feel at the end of a long motorcycle journey. I don't regret that the ride has to be over, but rather feel grateful for the miles I have traveled, for the sights along the way, and to be exactly where I am."[25]

ALEX: "Eventually, one day, we're not going to be able to do it anymore. That's a reality, and I don't think we should get too caught up in it. When it happens it happens, and that's it. We've had a great run, we've left a great legacy that we're proud of, and who knows what'll come after that? I mean, I think my fingers will still work for a little while longer [laughs]. I like to do stuff at home, to work with other people and continue to be musical, but there are other things in life, too—especially when you've dedicated so much of your life to touring. There's no doubt that we absolutely love what we do, and we know that we're very, very fortunate to have been able to do this. But eventually it does come to an end. I don't want to be seventy years old jumping around onstage. Maybe if we're still making great music, sure. But I kind of doubt it by that point. Most seventy-year-old rock musicians I see now are not really that enjoyable to watch."[26]

NEIL: "As the three of us discussed the songs we would play, it was all about how we and the fans might be able to live it all again—just this once. Because it was quite a ride, wasn't it?"[27]

Columbus, Ohio
Baltimore, Md.
Toronto, Ontario
London, Ontario
Hamilton, Ont.
Waterloo, Ont.
Kingston, Ont.
Brantford, Ont.
Ottawa, Ont.
Mt. Prospect, Ill.
Sioux City, Iowa
Los Angeles, Calif.
Sacramento, Calif.
Fresno, Calif.
Medford, Oregon
Seattle, Wash.
Spokane, Wash.
Portland, Oregon
Yakima, Wash.
Pittsburgh, Penn.
Indianapolis, Ind.
South Bend, Ind.
Waukegan, Ill.
St. Louis, Mo.
Pekin, Ill.
Atlanta, Georgia
Akron, Ohio

1. Interview with Geddy Lee. *Rolling Stone*, July 2, 2015.
2. NeilPeart.net, June 14, 2015.
3. NeilPeart.net, June 14, 2015.
4. NeilPeart.net, June 2015.
5. NeilPeart.net, June 14, 2015.
6. NeilPeart.net, June 14, 2015.
7. Neil Peart. *Far and Wide: Bring That Horizon To Me!*. ECW Press, 2016.
8. *The Monroe Evening News*, April 29, 2015.
9. Neil Peart. *Far and Wide: Bring That Horizon To Me!*. ECW Press, 2016.
10. Neil Peart. *Far and Wide: Bring That Horizon To Me!*. ECW Press, 2016.
11. Neil Peart. *Far and Wide: Bring That Horizon To Me!*. ECW Press, 2016.
12. Interview with Neil Peart. *Modern Drummer*, January 2016.
13. Neil Peart. *Far and Wide: Bring That Horizon To Me!*. ECW Press, 2016.
14. EddieTrunk.com, July 15, 2015.
15. Neil Peart. *Far and Wide: Bring That Horizon To Me!*. ECW Press, 2016.
16. Neil Peart. *Far and Wide: Bring That Horizon to Me!*. ECW Press, 2016.
17. Neil Peart. *Far And Wide: Bring That Horizon to Me!*. ECW Press, 2016.
18. *Classic Rock*, October 2015.
19. Interview with Ray Danniels. *Hamilton Spectator*, March 16, 2015.
20. *Classic Rock Magazine*, October 2015.
21. Interview with Chad Smith. *Classic Rock*, October 2015.
22. Interview with Matt Stone. *Classic Rock*, October 2015.
23. Interview with Jon Theodore. *Classic Rock*, October 2015.
24. Interview with Nancy Young. *Classic Rock*, October 2015.
25. Neil Peart. *Far and Wide: Bring That Horizon To Me!*. ECW Press, 2016.
26. Interview with Alex Lifeson. *Premier Guitar*, November 2012.
27. *R40 Live* tour book.

STEWART COPELAND

Somewhere in deep West Los Angeles is an industrial park that provides sanctuary for a curious man from a curious band. It's where Neil keeps his cars. A silver row of exotic period machines takes up most of the space, leaving a small, comfy seating zone and another corner where the brand-new, state-of-the-art motorcycles hang from hooks.

It's all so very Rush. For toys that are fun to mess with and examine with great curiosity, those Rush guys are old-school. Let it be the storied artifacts that get pride of place, more beautiful than practical.

But when the band saddles up, they go for the latest technology. Neil's motorcycles are not vintage Harleys. For hurling himself across continents, out in the elements at high speed, he entrusts his life to only the most precisely engineered models on the cutting-edge of locomotive design.

Rush's albums and tours have all started with a nostalgic idea and then hit the stage with the very latest technology. The band members themselves are dreamers and believers, but they hit their instruments with merciless precision.

This tally of works showcases the functionality of this hugely important band, but life in RushWorld has been more soulful than all of this efficiency suggests. Sure it's an impressive inventory, and it probably looks like a lot of grueling hard work, toiling day after day in the salt mines of prog rock! But really, the touring machine with all of its industry was just a structure that provided an excellent place for three guys to screw around and do cool stuff. Why go home?

Visiting backstage with the band has a very human, dedicated vibe. They *really* enjoy the mission. They're not fully casual until after the show, but at intermission, you can see them glowing with the blessing of a full immersion in music. Whatever dues they paid in the starvation years, *this* is what it was all for.

And the dues that they paid were substantial. They pretty much starved for half a decade before starting to stoke the flames. After coming together on Hendrix, Cream, and Zep, they spent years supporting Kiss and Ted Nugent. But the spirit lived! That's how strong their love is.

It's hard to pick a moment when the band "hit" because they didn't. There was no sudden addition to radio playlists that yanked them from obscurity to the big league. They got no free ride; they ran the whole way on foot. Well, at least until Neil got into the bikes.

But with true Canadian grit and persevering moral fiber, the band got its bounty. They got to lay into lit-up multitudes with every musical toy a kid could dream of. Double-necked guitar *and* double-necked bass!

Strangely, the only fly in their ointment was that they didn't feel "cool" and often joked ruefully about it. This has always been a head-scratcher for their peers. Whaaat? Not cool? What part of godhead is not cool? The Rush fan

base may not be wide—as you get with flavors of the month—but it runs way, way deep. Their loyal fans know what the *Rolling Stone* guy doesn't understand. Rush music is not for quick appraisal and fashion assignment. Some of those hairdos did set them back somewhat with the cognoscenti, but every day, over years, one by one, people tuned in to "By-Tor" and "Tom Sawyer," and the cult grew. One devoted fanatic at a time. Just when everyone else was cutting their hair, dropping proficiency, and going for shock rather than depth, Rush were following their own instincts and digging ever deeper into wherever their instrumental virtuosity led them.

Well praise be to Mozart, there are folks out there who love that! In another era, such folks might have been jazz fans. Blessed be the fans who want you to play as many notes as you like! It's fun to torch your instrument and light it up. It took a lot of passion to get that good so let's rock! And I guess Neil, Geddy, and Alex just never had time for a haircut.

In fact, my own first perception of them was that long hair. Right when I was making my escape from the hippy generation, there was this band that was cheerfully going the other way.

At the Pinkpop Festival in Holland in 1979, Rush was coheadliner, and my band, the Police, was almost at the bottom of the bill—which had us onstage in the blistering heat of early afternoon. Rush not only got to play in the cool night air (with light show) but also had their gear assembled onstage all day. Us support acts had to set up in front of their rig. We were done and long gone when they played, so we missed their set, but some things stuck in the mind.

First of all, I envied the cool band name because I had started thinking our band name sucked about twenty minutes after we were committed to it. But it was the drum set that got me pining, just a little bit, for my own prog rock days with Curved Air. Backstage, the set was the talk of the crew, under a drape but hulking

ABOVE: Geleen, Netherlands; Geddy and Alex performing "Xanadu" at the Pinkpop Festival.

massively. Peering under the hood, you could see that you needed to crawl through a hatch to get *into* the mighty chariot.

Forty years have gone by since that summer in Holland. During that time, my band came and went, but those three Canucks are still so deeply bonded that they hang out when *not touring*!

Neil brought Alex over to my jam hut one night, and you could feel among them that they still inspire each other. Still chuckle buddies after half a century! Other bands look on and wonder how it's possible. U2 are like that, villagers who bust out of the hinterland together. They met and made their clan when they were young and unformed. They never yearned for artistic independence. Their homeboys had all the tricks they needed to stay inspired for life.

At the last Rush concert at the Forum, they made it *darned* clear that it would be the *final* show, but I'm writing this in present tense because it's harder to kill a band like Rush than the Rush guys think.

Best,
Stewart

ABOVE: Geleen, Netherlands; The dueling doublenecks at the Pinkpop Festival.

RIGHT: Geleen, Netherlands; Rush at the Pinkpop Festival.

OPPOSITE: Toronto, Ontario; Geddy at Maple Leaf Gardens.

ACKNOWLEDGMENTS

"The Future Disappears into Memory . . ."

We'd like to acknowledge all of those who so generously spent time helping us capture and document all of the "memories in flight" from the fifty-year history of this incredible band. This project—all the data, photographs, and stories—could not have come to fruition without the participation of many, many people.

First, we'd like to thank the band—for their timeless, magical music and for the inspiration they have given to so many. It's not just about what they produced but also how they went about it: with unwavering integrity, dogged determination, good humor, and loyalty, both to each other and to the fans. We are ever grateful to them for giving their blessing to this project.

Many Rush crew and associates past and present selflessly donated their time to speak with us, often being kind enough to provide ongoing fact-checking along the way. This group includes the following folks: Larry Allen, John Arrowsmith, William Birt, Craig (C. B.) Blazier, Michael Bossi, Peter Brockbank, Terry Brown, Jim Burgess, David Burnette, Uncle Cliff Burnstein, Brent Carpenter, Mark Cherry, Steve Cohen, Bruce Cole, Gary "Doc" Cooper, Conrad Coriz, Ray Danniels, Ed Duda, Gerry Fielding, Kevin Flewitt, Robert "Fuzzy" Frazer, Jack Funk, Tony "Jack Secret" Geranios, Skip "Slider" Gildersleeve, Ian Grandy, Hal Greenson, Lynton Guest, Michael "Lurch" Hirsch, Bobby Huck, JJ Johnson, Jeff Jones, Robert Kniffen, Adam Kornfeld, Nick Kotos, Ted Leamy, Greg Lukens, Wayne King, Arthur MacLear, Brad Madix, Patrick McLoughlin, Anson Moore, Gerald O'Brien, Jimmy Joe Rhodes, Bill Rutsey, Mike Rutsey, Russ Ryan, Frank Scilingo, Robert Scovill, Joe Szilagy, John Trojan, Howard "Herns" Ungerleider, Neil Warnock, Allan Weinrib, Michael Weiss, Tim Wendt, Lorne "Gump" Wheaton, Tom "Whitey" Whittaker, and Lindy Young (sincere apologies if we're missing anyone!).

"Major" Ian Grandy deserves an extra-special tip of the hat for enduring countless follow-up questions over the course of a *decade*. As one who was there from the very early beginnings, he had unique and invaluable insights. Thankfully, he bore this cross well, always made us laugh, and steadfastly supported the project. We'd like to thank him for his friendship and support.

The project would never have left the ground if not for the blessing and support from Rush's excellent, dedicated management team. Our deepest thanks to everyone at Anthem/SRO, but especially those we had the pleasure of interacting with directly: Pegi Cecconi, Sheila Posner, Andy Curran, and Emma Sundstrom. Pegi gets the MVP award for shepherding this project through delicate waters on more than one occasion and managing to keep the ship afloat—as only she could have done (QOFE indeed!). Thanks to Patrick McLoughlin and the Showtech Merchandise team for recognizing the potential, connecting us with Insight Editions, and partnering with us to get it done.

This whole exercise would have been purely academic if not for our publisher, Insight Editions. Executive editor Mark Irwin's boundless enthusiasm, support, and attention to detail were invaluable, as was the thoroughness of his team, Holly Fisher and Jeric Llanes. Richard Bienstock took our massive, but rudimentary manuscript and patiently reworked it into the coherent work you now hold. We are grateful to him and in awe of the job he did.

We thank Hugh Syme for his friendship, support, collaboration, and artistic vision. Likewise, we are humbled by the contributions from our introduction, foreword, and afterword authors: Howard Ungerleider, Les Claypool, and Stewart Copeland. It's an honor to have such rock dignitaries providing the frame for our "little" book.

Additional thanks are owed to all of the photographers who contributed "the pictures that give pleasure to your eyes"—the beautiful photographs (some never before seen) that grace these pages. These photographers not only allowed use of their work but also took the time to dig out old negatives, gather high-resolution scans, etc. Andrew MacNaughtan, John Arrowsmith, Donald Gadziola, Bob Wegner, David Martin, Nick Bayus, David Arnold, Anna Livojevich, Peter Buster, Jeffrey Holmes, Robert Frazer, Dimo Safari, Jeff Topping, Joe Morisseau, Steve Marks, Bert Van Dijk, Pete Koza, Andy Yarrish, Bruce Cole, Philip Kamen, Fin Costello, Bill Banasiewicz, Ray Wawrzyniak, Bill O'Leary, Monica Zimmerman, Paul Toz, Brad Parmerter, Scott Weiner, Janet Balmer, Scott Burgan, Sean Doran, and Martin Urionaguena. Thank you!

And then there are all of the people—many of them fans, and too numerous to name—who contributed information, memorabilia, and various tidbits that really flesh out the story. Greg Shery; Kevin Stone; Ray Wawrzyniak; Dean Nicholas; Jeff Promish; Linda Salvatore; Linda Cara and Jim Biros at the Toronto Musicians' Association; Pirkko Vega at the Canadian Musicians' Pension Fund; Martin Popoff; Paul Miil; Sam Dunn, Scot McFadyen, Andrew Kowalchuk, and the kind folks at Banger Films; Ed Stenger at rushisaband.com; John Patuto at cygnus-x1.net; the contributors to Eric's Power Windows site (2112.net/powerwindows); Jeff Erwin; Joe Pesch and the members of the Rush Historical Society Facebook group; Heiko Klages; Chris Irwin; Bill Banasiewicz; and all of those in the Rush fan community who have supported the project.

Last but most certainly not least, our thanks to our families for allowing us time away from "nurturing our gardens" to indulge in this project. We didn't think it would take a decade, but as they say, "Life is what happens when you're busy making plans."

Eric would like to thank his family, especially his dear wife Kelly, for indulging him in his Rush addiction for the past thirty years, nine of them from this book's inception to publication. Eric would also like to thank Skip Daly for never giving up and always staying the course. Thank-yous also go out to everyone else who contributed to the book—you know who you are, and we couldn't have done it without you. Thank you to Pegi Cecconi for going to bat for us, and to Mark Irwin for helping us put it to paper. Lastly, to Neil, Geddy, Alex, and John, thank you for the music, and to the road crew who made the shows happen night after night, thank you very kindly—good night!

This book was brought to you by the letters A-Z.

INSIGHT
EDITIONS

PO Box 3088
San Rafael, CA 94912
www.insighteditions.com

Find us on Facebook: www.facebook.com/InsightEditions
Follow us on Twitter: @insighteditions

Library of Congress Cataloging-in-Publication Data available.

ISBN: 978-1-68383-450-2

Publisher: Raoul Goff
President: Kate Jerome
Associate Publisher: Vanessa Lopez
Designer: Leah Lauer
Executive Editor: Mark Irwin
Associate Editor: Holly Fisher
Editorial Assistant: Jeric Llanes
Senior Production Manager: Greg Steffen

Insight Editions, in association with Roots of Peace, will plant two trees for
each tree used in the manufacturing of this book. Roots of Peace is an
internationally renowned humanitarian organization dedicated to eradicating
land mines worldwide and converting war-torn lands into productive farms
and wildlife habitats. Roots of Peace will plant two million fruit and nut
trees in Afghanistan and provide farmers there with the skills and support
necessary for sustainable land use.

Manufactured in China by Insight Editions

10 9 8 7 6 5 4 3 2 1